NICHOLSON

LONDON STREET ATLAS

CONTENTS

Key to Map Pages 2-3

Key to Map Symbols 4-5

Central London Maps 6-21

Main London Maps 22-104

Theatres and Cinemas Map 105

Shopping Map 105

Index to Places of Interest 106-107

Index to Place Names 108-109

Index to Street Names 110-268

Underground Map 269

Nicholson
An *Imprint* of HarperCollins *Publishers*

First published 1994 © Nicholson 1996

Generated from the Bartholomew London Digital Database.

The Ordnance Survey is not responsible for the accuracy of the National Grid in this publication.

London Underground Map by permission of London Regional Transport LRT Registered User Number 96/1496

Printed in Italy by Printer Trento Srl

ISBN 0 7028 3385 1   Spiral Version
ISBN 0 7028 3540 4   Vinyl Version

Nicholson
HarperCollins*Publishers*
77-85 Fulham Palace Road
London W6 8JB

Great care has been taken throughout this atlas to be accurate but the publishers cannot accept responsibility for any errors which appear or their consequences. Queries or information regarding the London Street Atlas should be addressed to the Publishing Director at the above address.

JE8763/JE8837   LNR

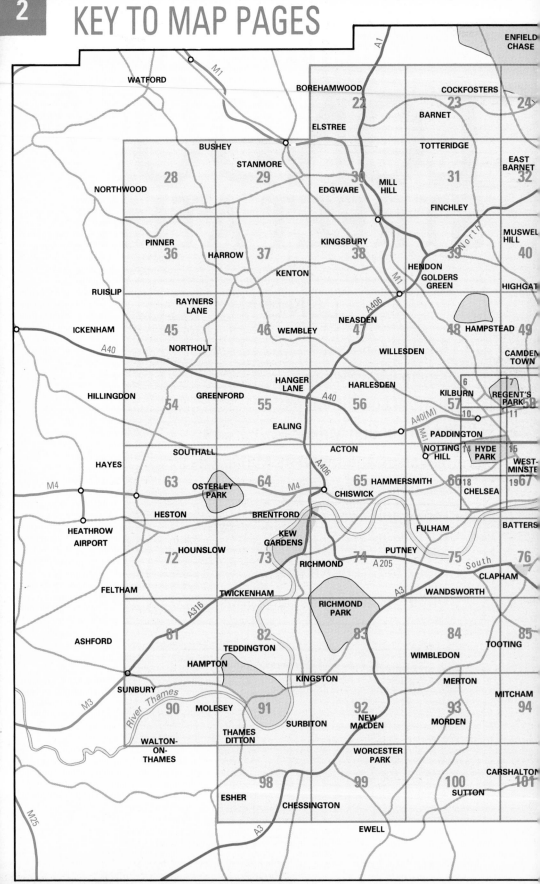

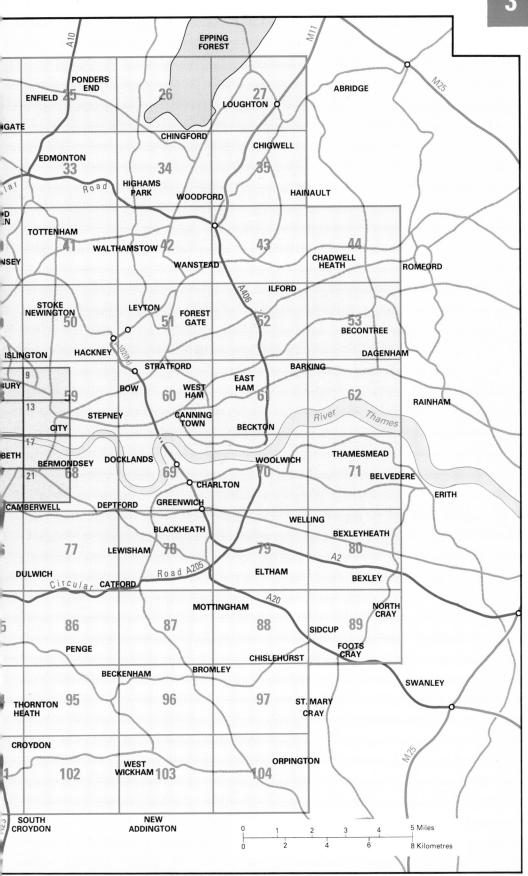

EPPING FOREST

A10

M11

M25

PONDERS END
ENFIELD **25**

26

27
LOUGHTON
CHINGFORD

ABRIDGE

GATE

EDMONTON

33

34

CHIGWELL

35

HIGHAMS PARK

WOODFORD

HAINAULT

Road

ROMFORD

TOTTENHAM

41
WALTHAMSTOW **42**

WANSTEAD

43

CHADWELL HEATH

44

ROMFORD

NSEY

A406

ILFORD

STOKE NEWINGTON
50

LEYTON

51
FOREST GATE

52

53
BECONTREE

ISLINGTON
HACKNEY

A102(M)

DAGENHAM

BURY

9

STRATFORD

BARKING

59

13

BOW

60
WEST HAM

EAST HAM

61

62

RAINHAM

STEPNEY

CANNING TOWN

BECKTON

River   Thames

17

CITY

BETH

BERMONDSEY
68

DOCKLANDS

69

WOOLWICH

70

THAMESMEAD

71
BELVEDERE

21

CHARLTON

ERITH

CAMBERWELL

DEPTFORD

GREENWICH

BLACKHEATH

WELLING

BEXLEYHEATH

DULWICH

77

LEWISHAM

78

79

A2

80

Circular

CATFORD

Road A205

ELTHAM

BEXLEY

MOTTINGHAM

A20

NORTH CRAY

86

87

88

SIDCUP

89

PENGE

FOOTS CRAY

CHISLEHURST

SWANLEY

BECKENHAM

BROMLEY

THORNTON HEATH

95

96

97

ST. MARY CRAY

CROYDON

M25

102

WEST WICKHAM **103**

ORPINGTON

104

SOUTH CROYDON

NEW ADDINGTON

| 0 | 1 | 2 | 3 | 4 | 5 Miles |
| 0 | 2 | 4 | 6 | 8 Kilometres |

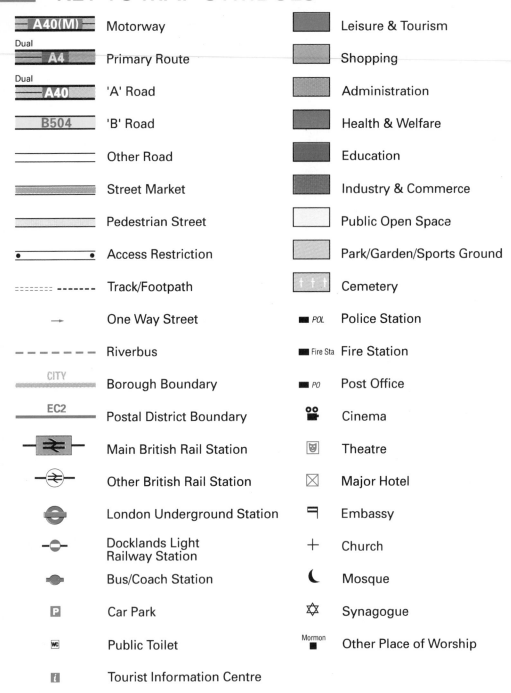

A40(M)	Motorway			Leisure & Tourism
Dual **A4**	Primary Route			Shopping
Dual **A40**	'A' Road			Administration
B504	'B' Road			Health & Welfare
	Other Road			Education
	Street Market			Industry & Commerce
	Pedestrian Street			Public Open Space
	Access Restriction			Park/Garden/Sports Ground
	Track/Footpath			Cemetery
→	One Way Street		POL	Police Station
	Riverbus		Fire Sta	Fire Station
CITY	Borough Boundary		PO	Post Office
EC2	Postal District Boundary			Cinema
	Main British Rail Station			Theatre
	Other British Rail Station			Major Hotel
	London Underground Station			Embassy
	Docklands Light Railway Station		+	Church
	Bus/Coach Station			Mosque
P	Car Park			Synagogue
WC	Public Toilet		Mormon	Other Place of Worship
i	Tourist Information Centre			

The reference grid on this atlas coincides with the Ordnance Survey National Grid System. The grid interval is 250 metres.

A	Grid Reference			Page Continuation Number

0	0.25	0.50	0.75	1 kilometre
0	¼		½ mile	

M41	Motorway		Leisure & Tourism
Dual A4	Primary Route	USA	Administration & Law Embassy
Dual A40	'A' Road		Health & Welfare
B504	'B' Road		Education
	Other Road		Industry & Commerce
	Toll		Cemetery
	Street Market		Golf Course
	Pedestrian Street		Public Open Space/ Allotments
	Cycle Path		Park/Garden/Sports Ground
	Track/Footpath		Wood/Forest
→	One Way Street	Pol	Police Station
P	Pedestrian Ferry	Fire Sta	Fire Station
V	Vehicle Ferry	PO	Post Office
	County/Borough Boundary	Lib	Library
	Postal District Boundary	▲	Youth Hostel
	Main British Rail Station	□	Tower Block
	Other British Rail Station	ℹ	Tourist Information Centre
	London Underground Station	Ⓗ	Heliport
	Docklands Light Railway Station	✗	Windmill
	Bus/Coach Station	+	Church
P	Car Park	☾	Mosque
WC	Public Toilet	✡	Synagogue

The reference grid on this atlas coincides with the Ordnance Survey National Grid System. The grid interval is 500 metres.

A	Grid Reference	24	Page Continuation Number
25	OS National Grid Kilometre Square		

0	0.25	0.50	0.75	1 kilometre
0	¼		½ mile	

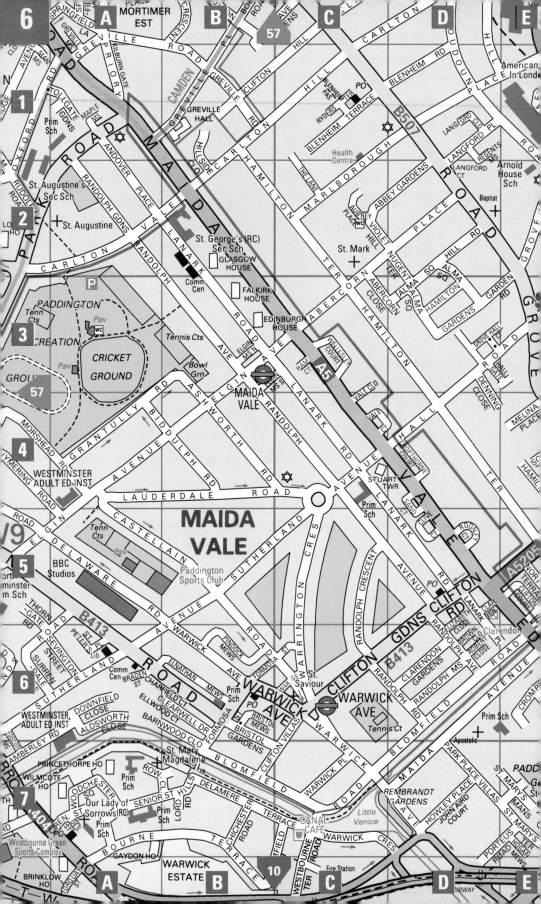

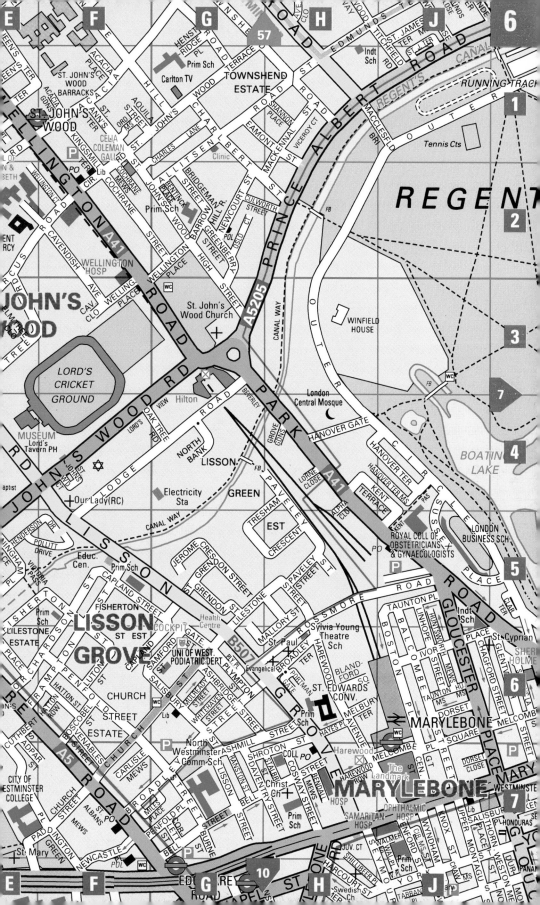

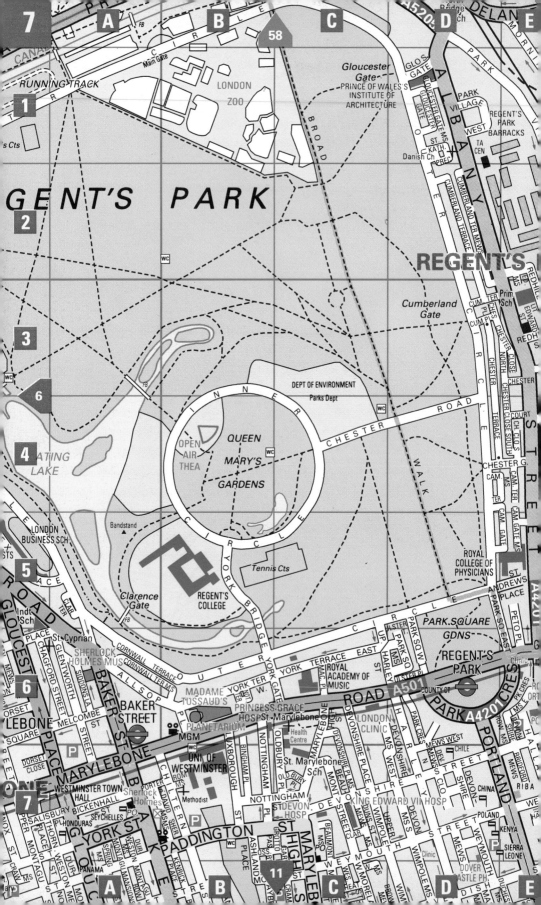

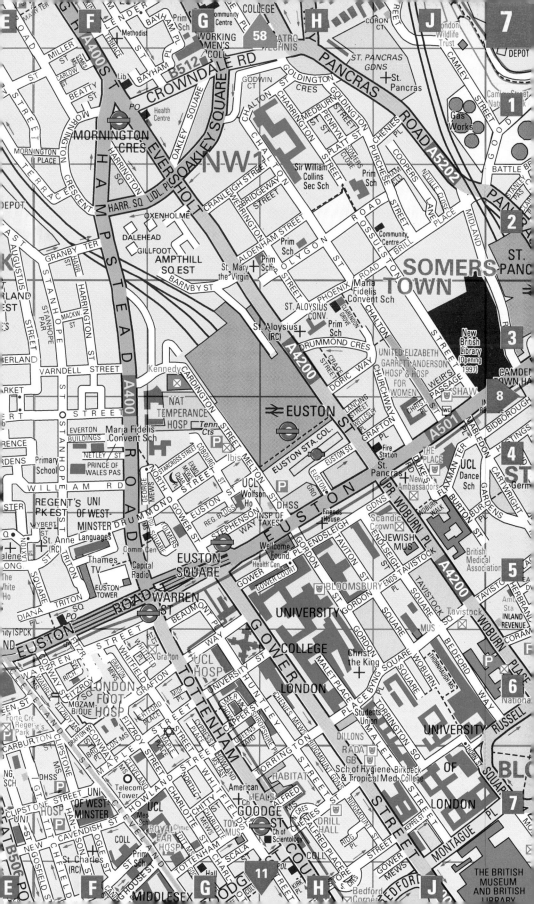

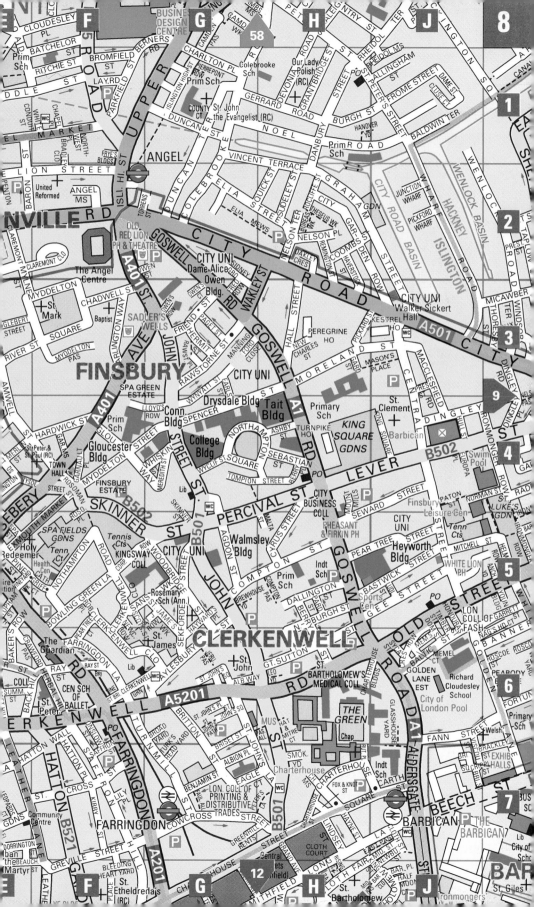

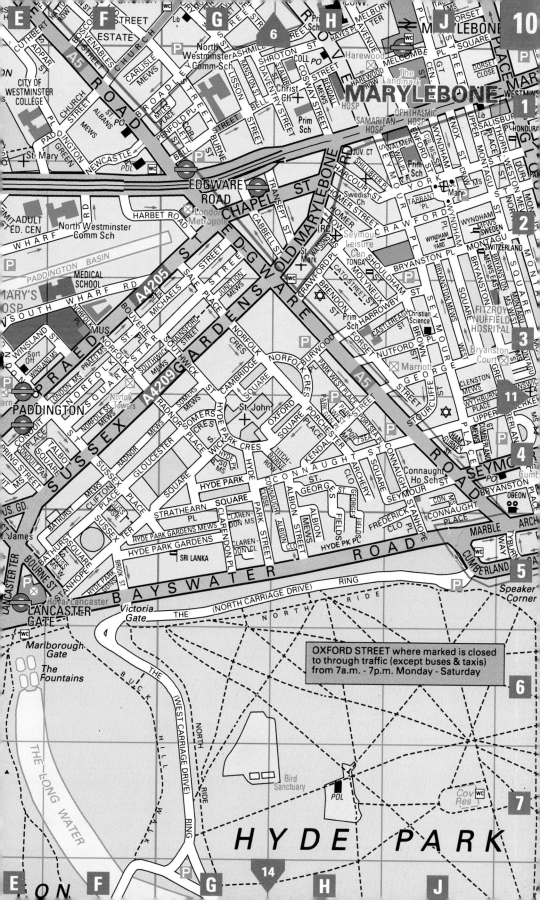

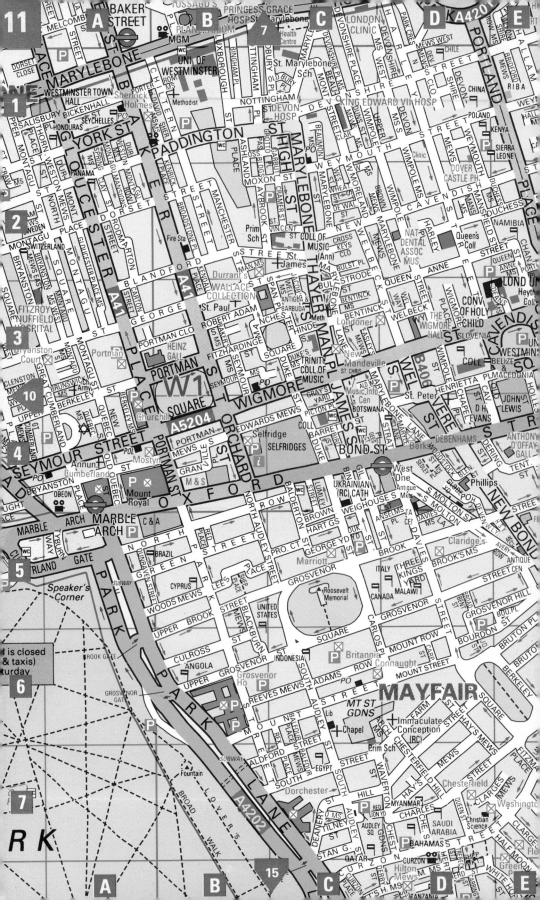

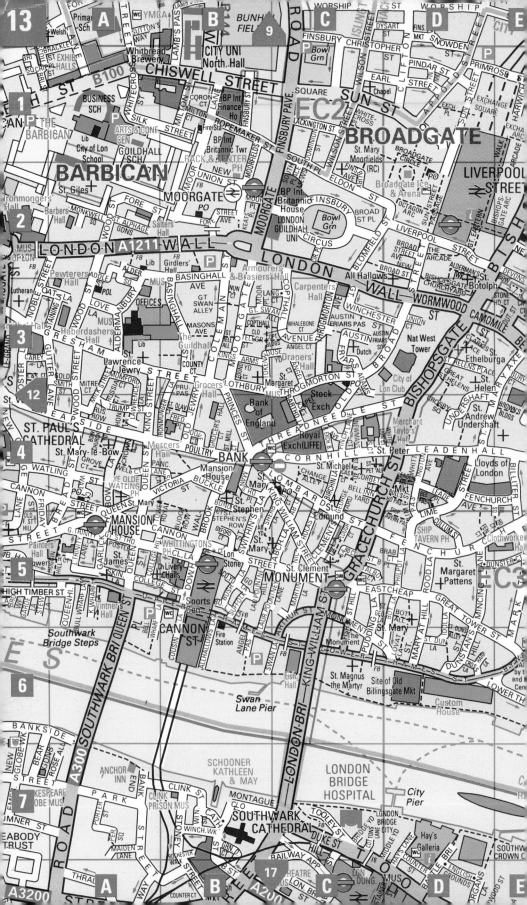

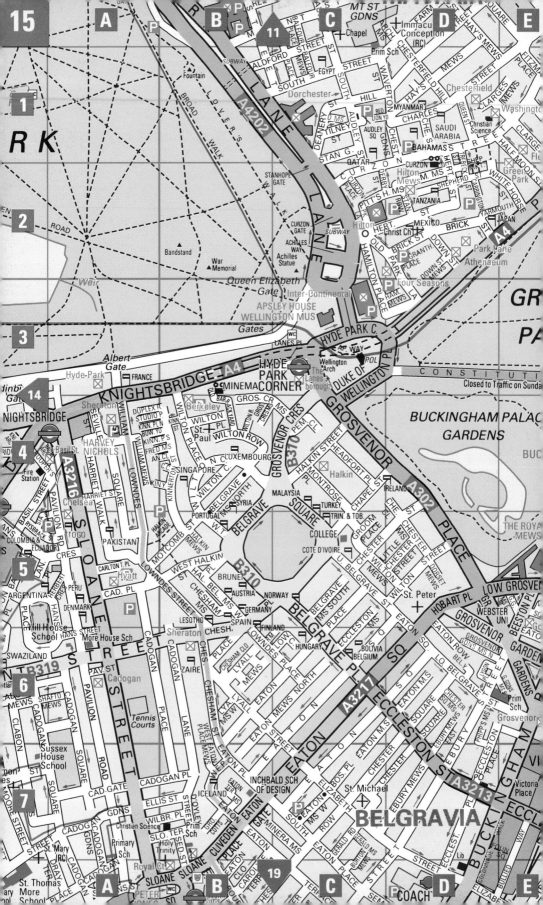

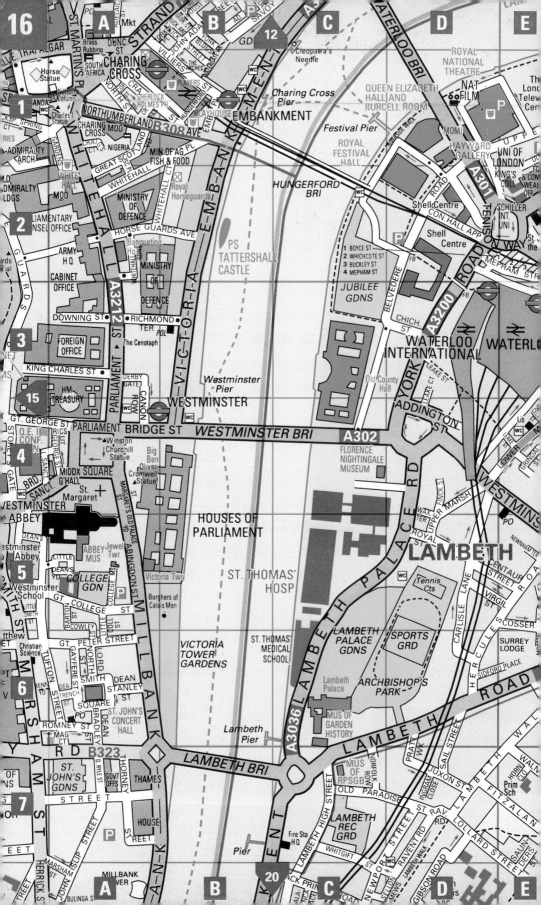

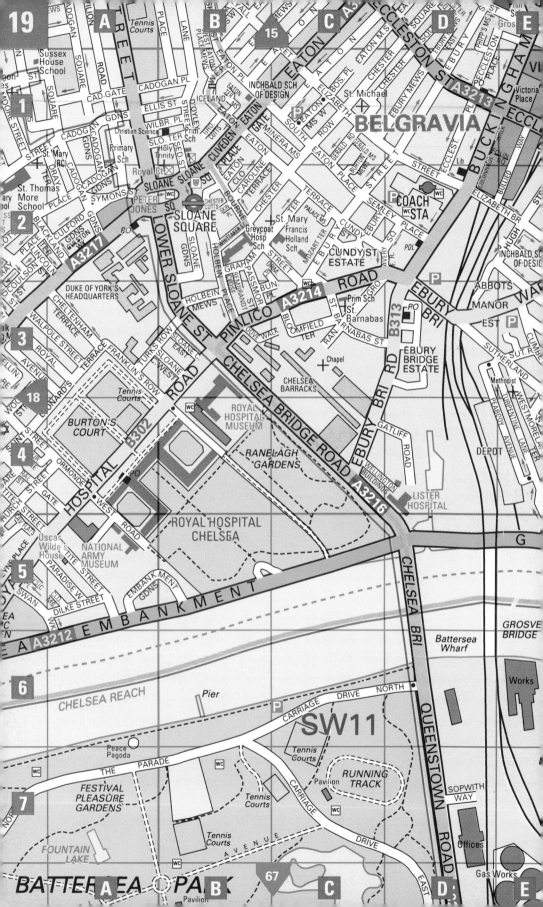

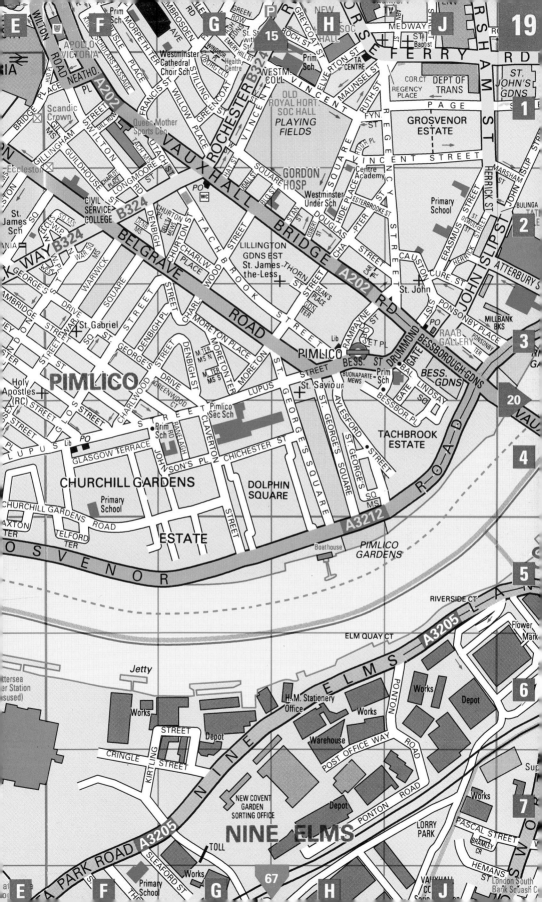

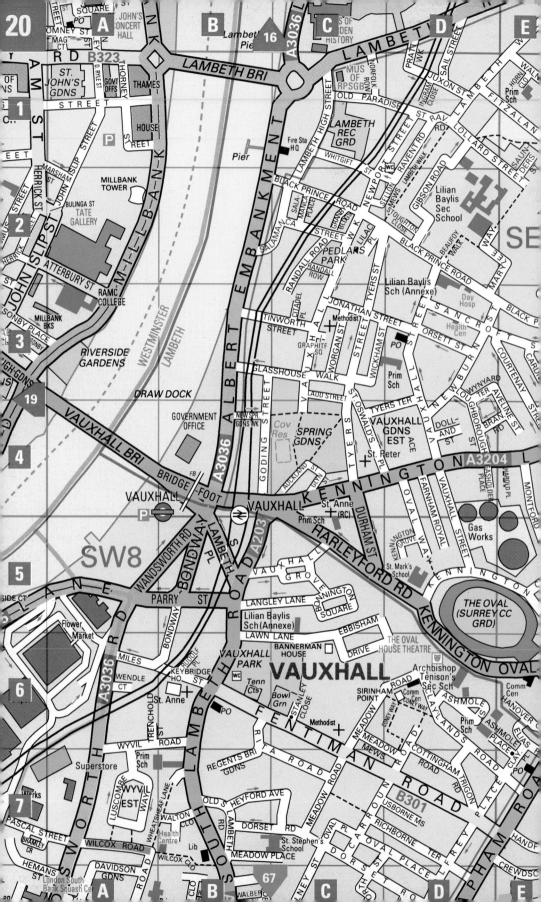

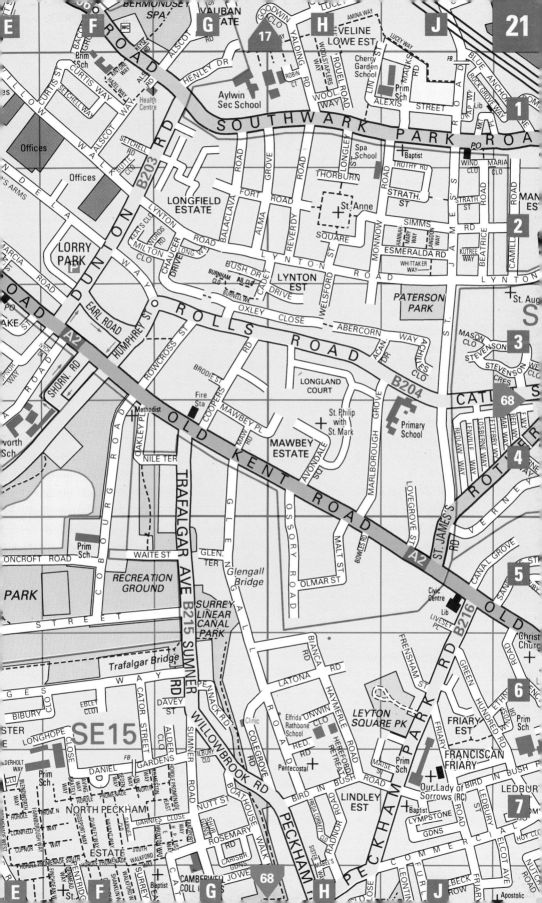

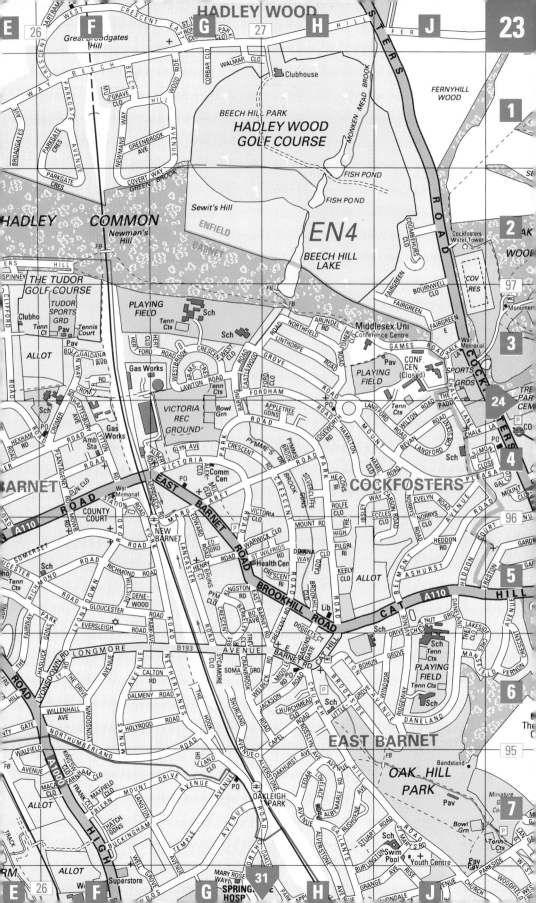

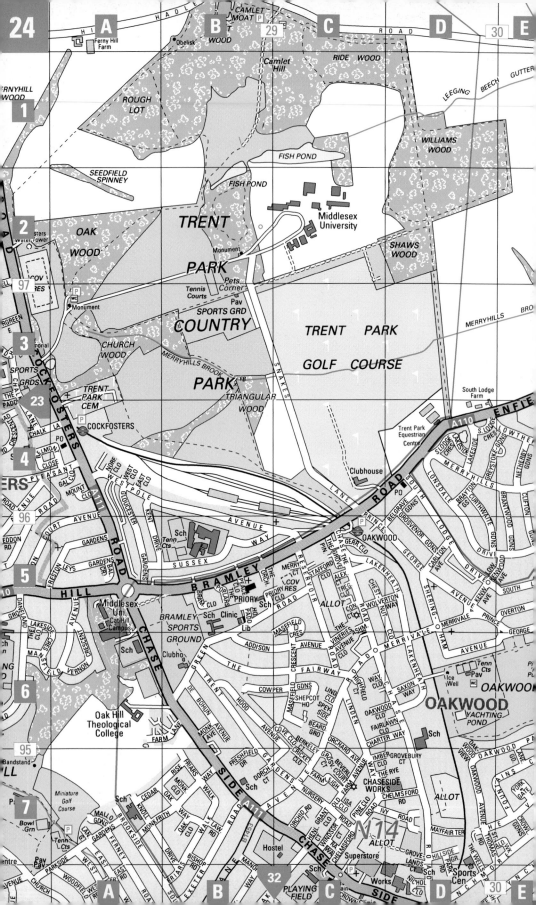

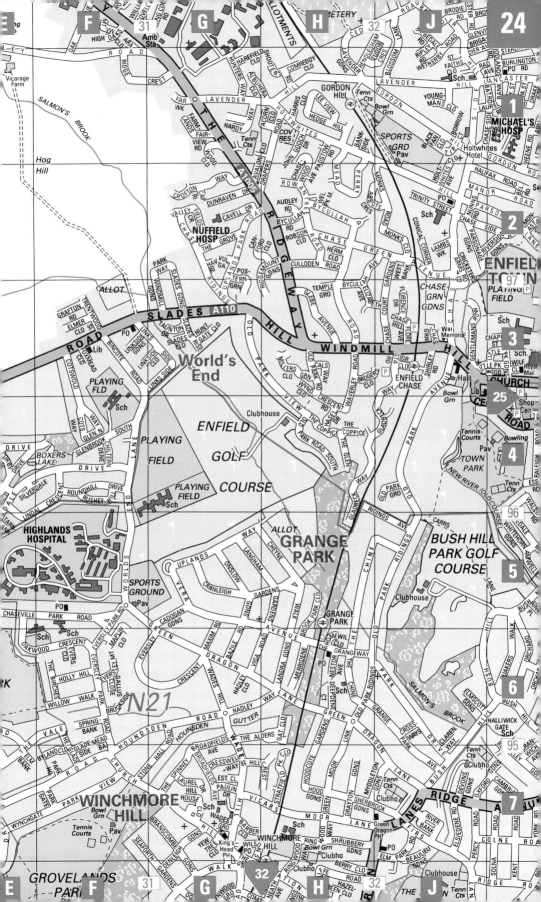

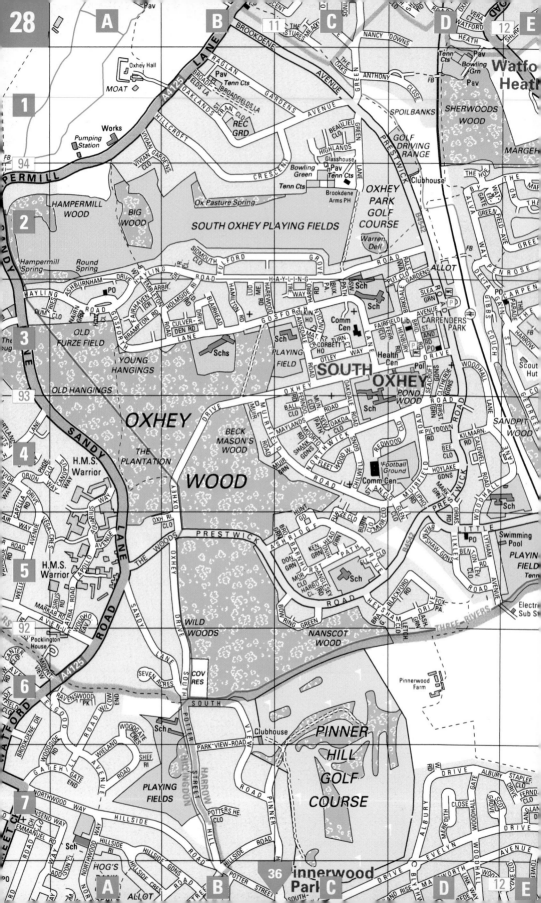

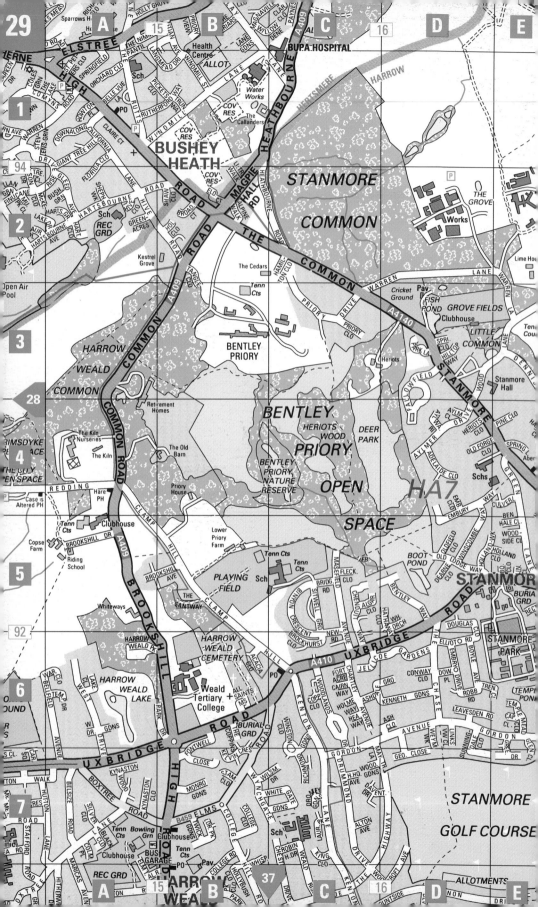

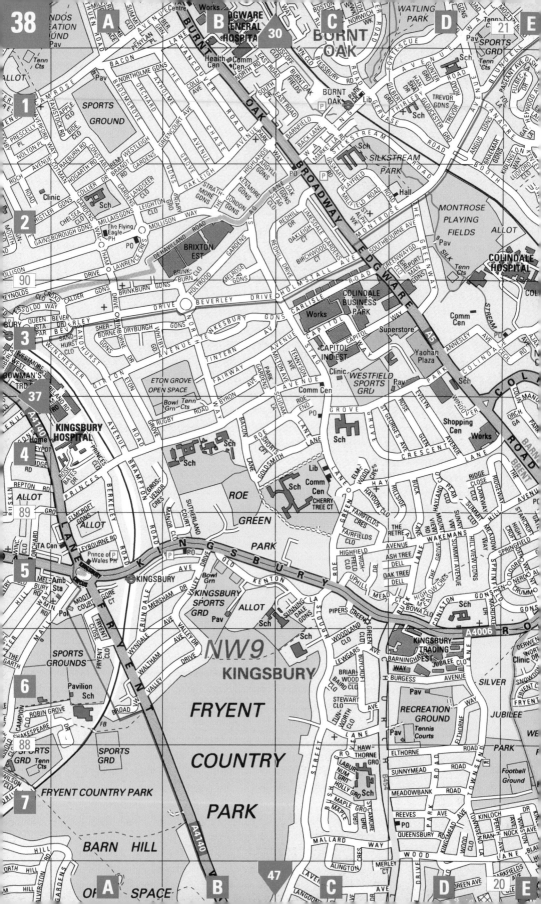

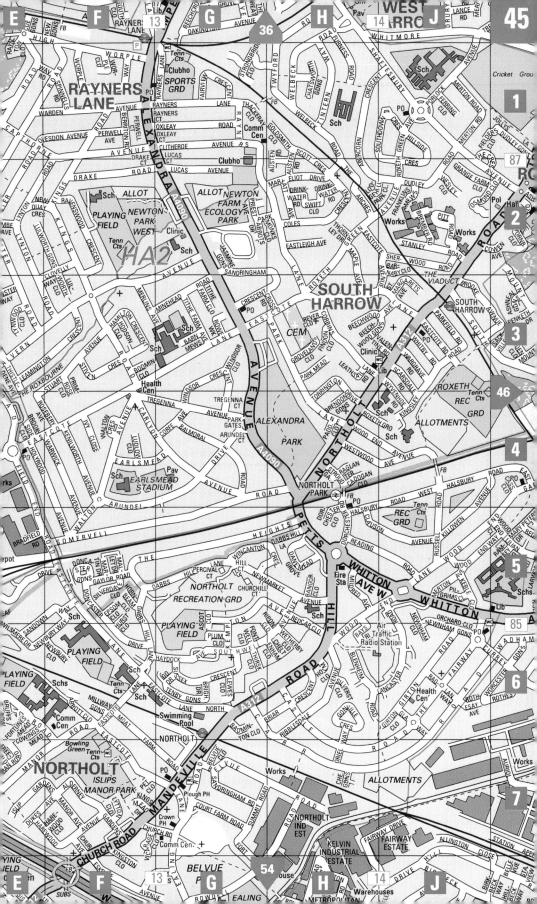

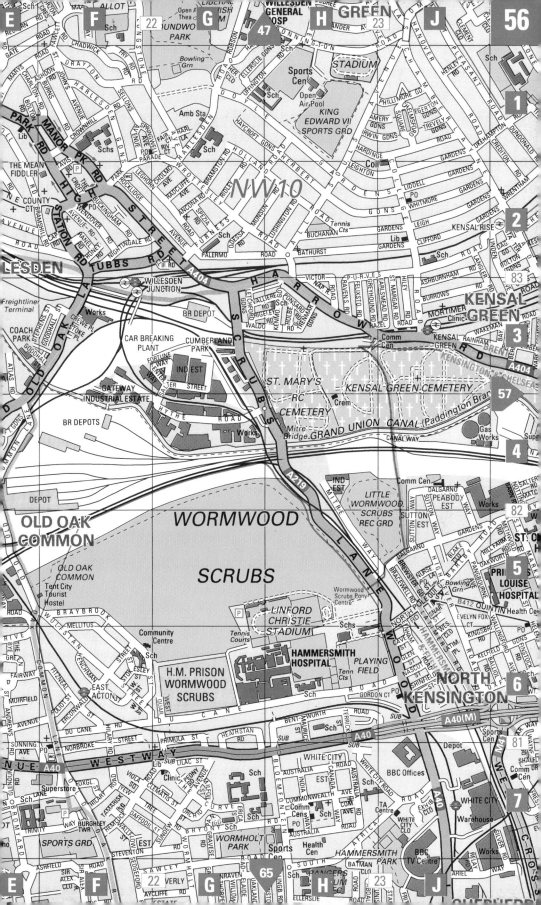

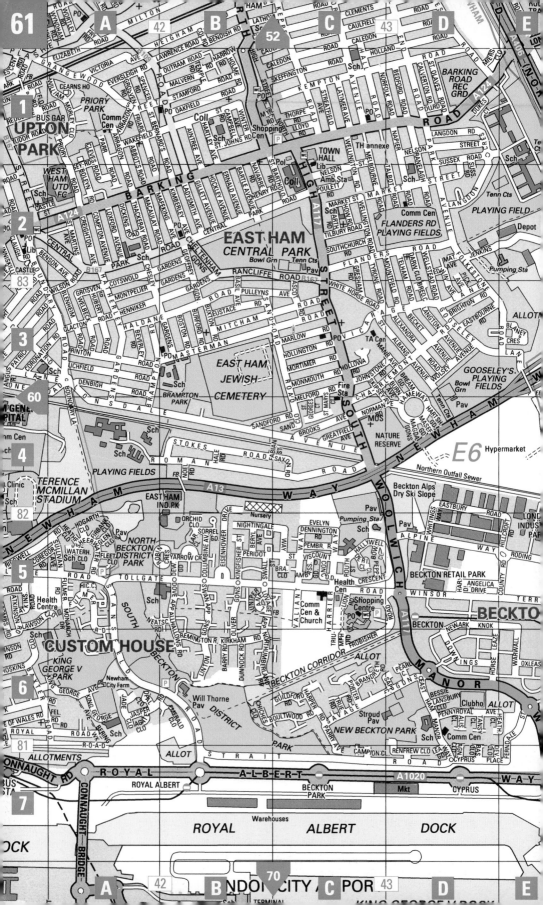

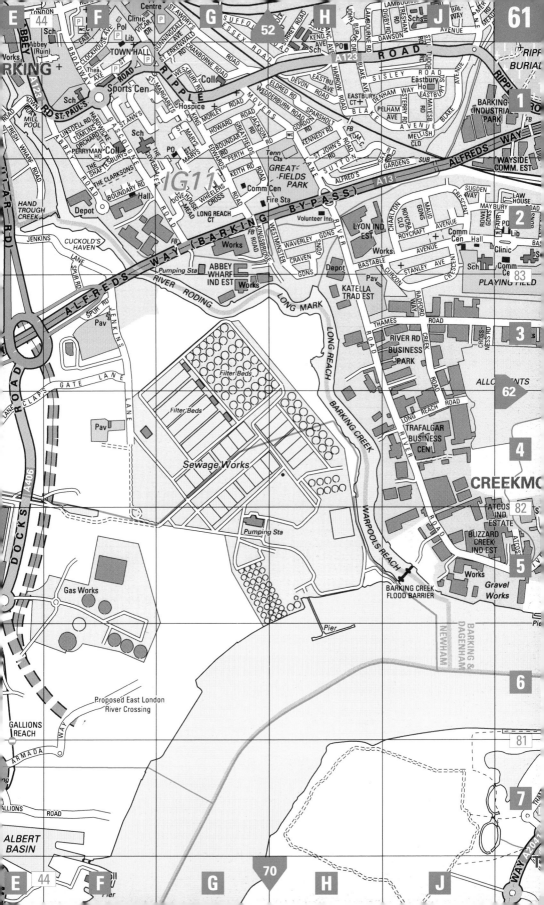

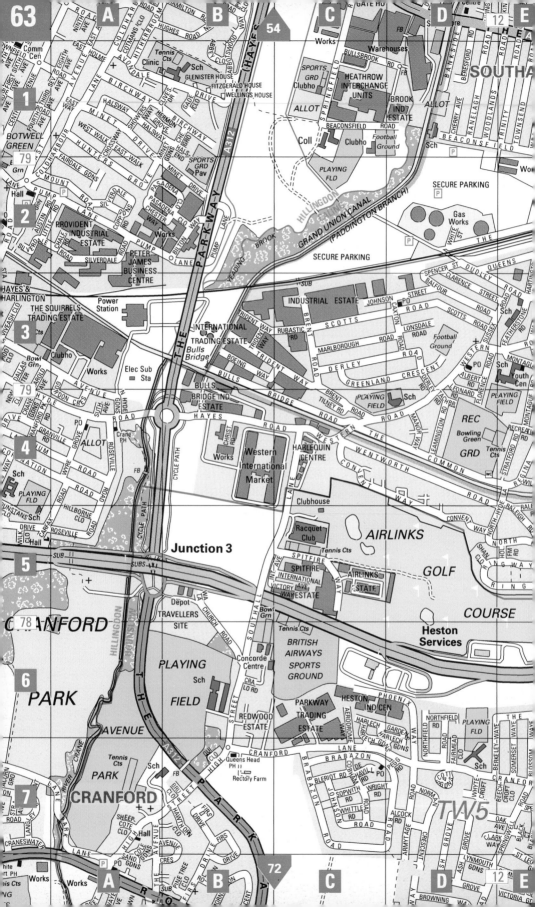

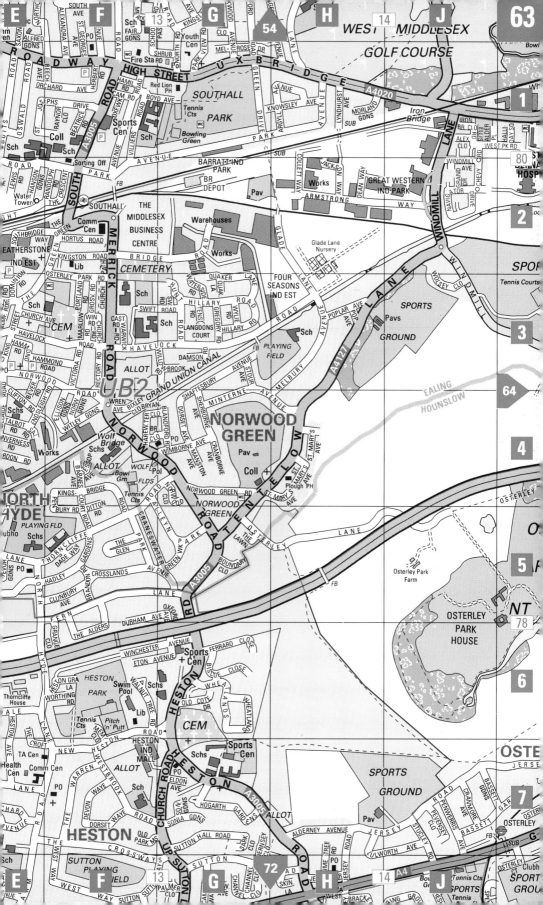

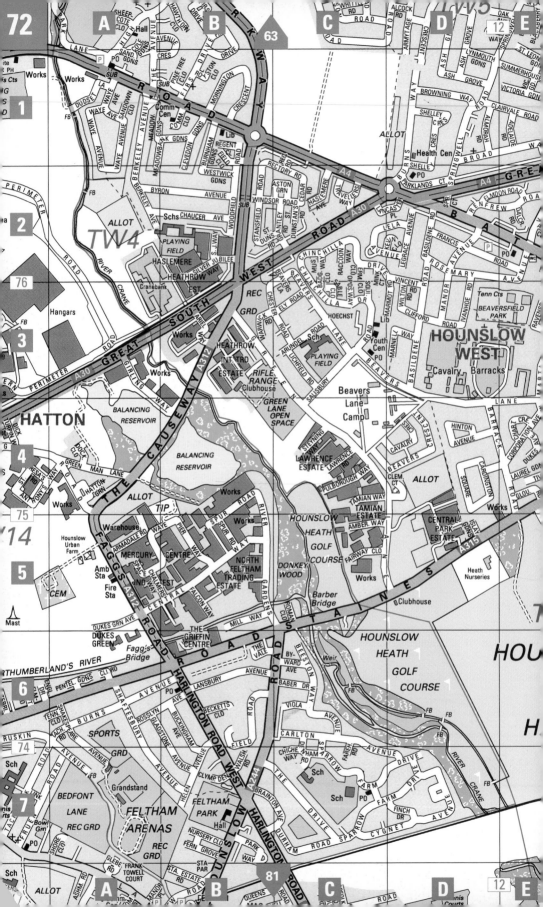

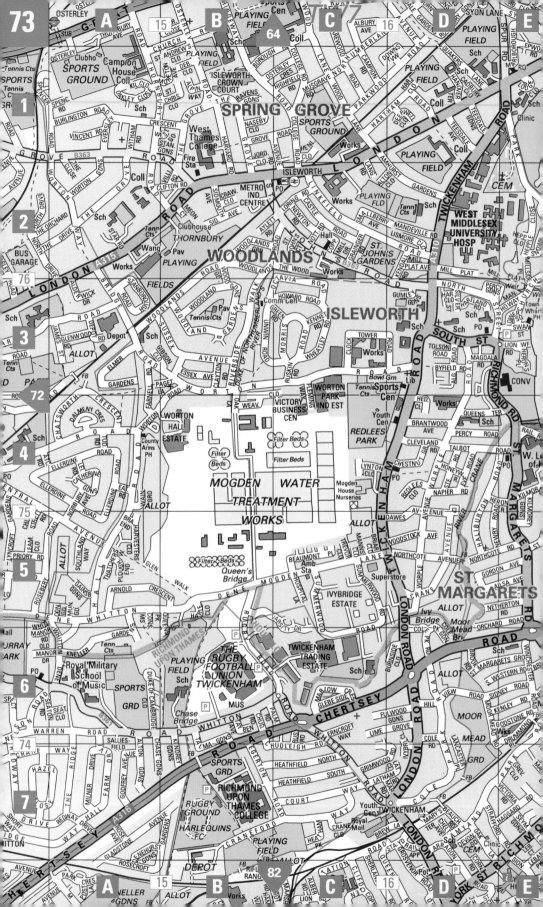

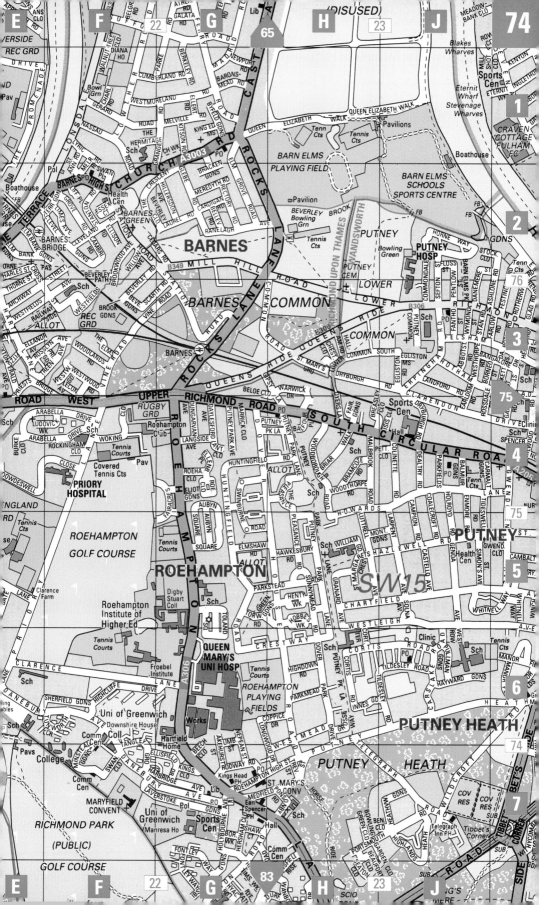

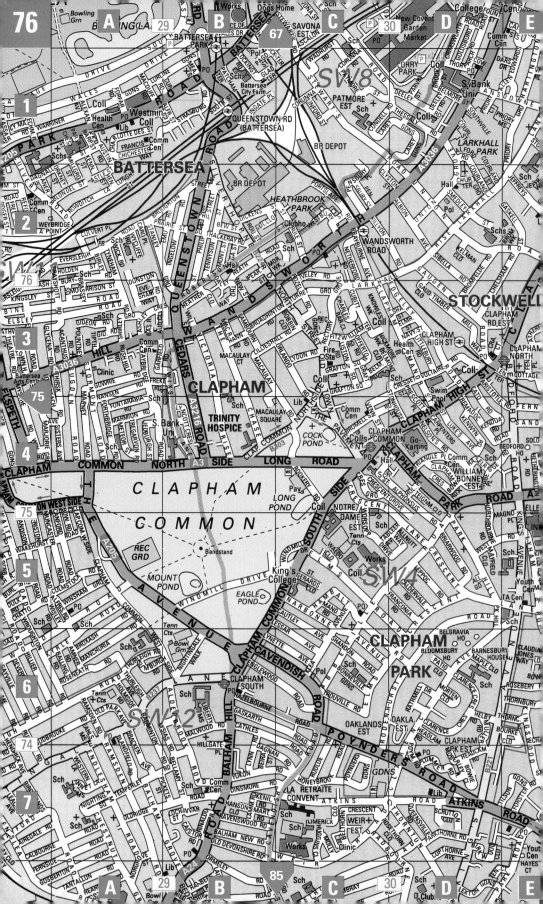

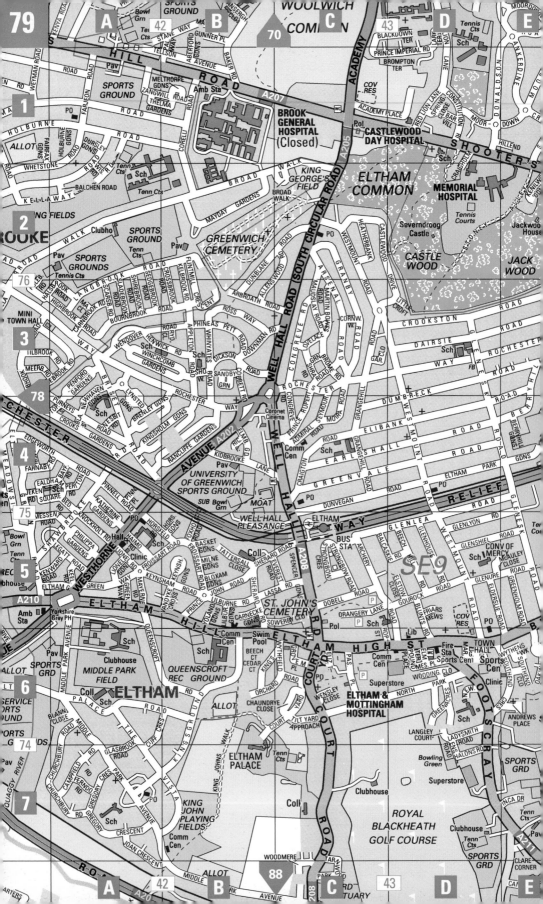

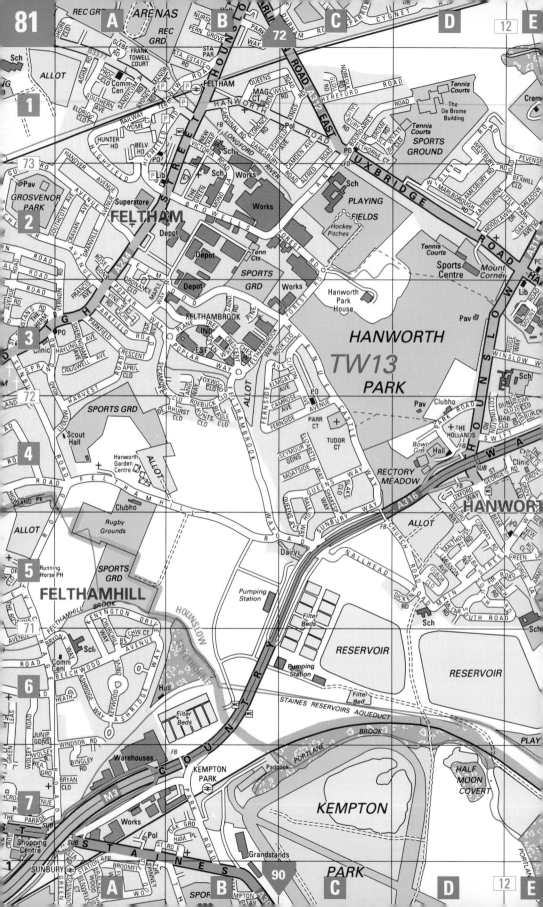

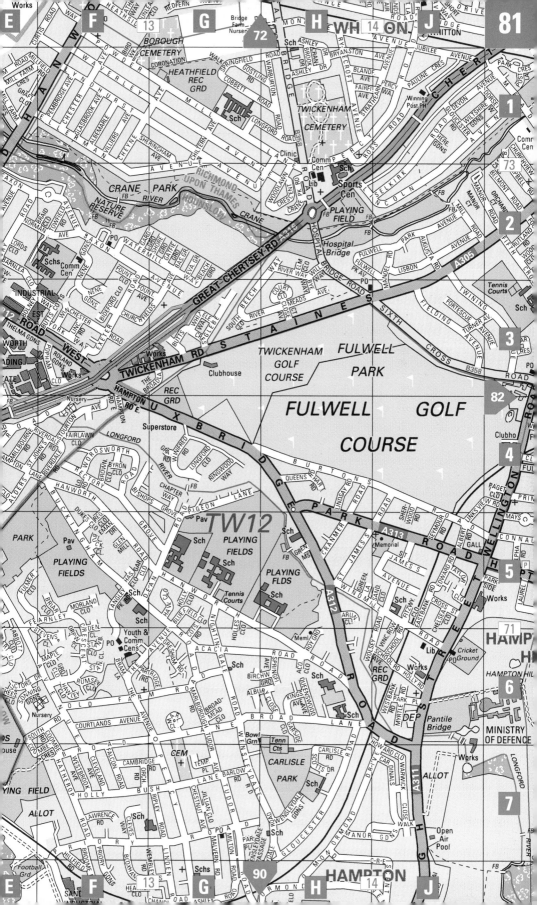

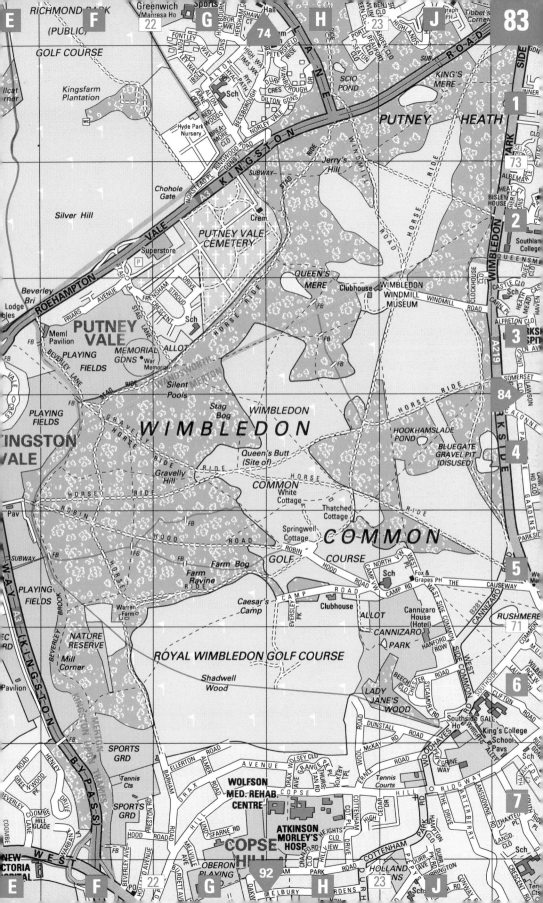

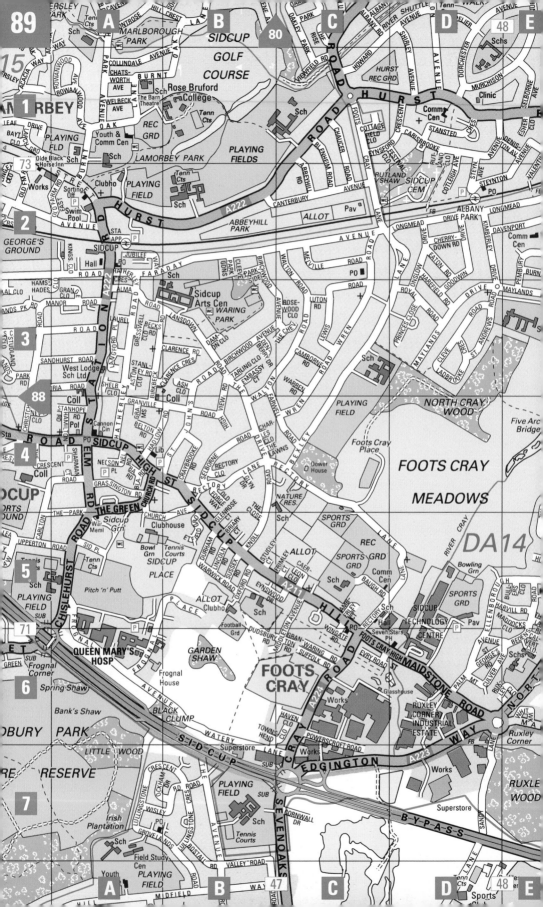

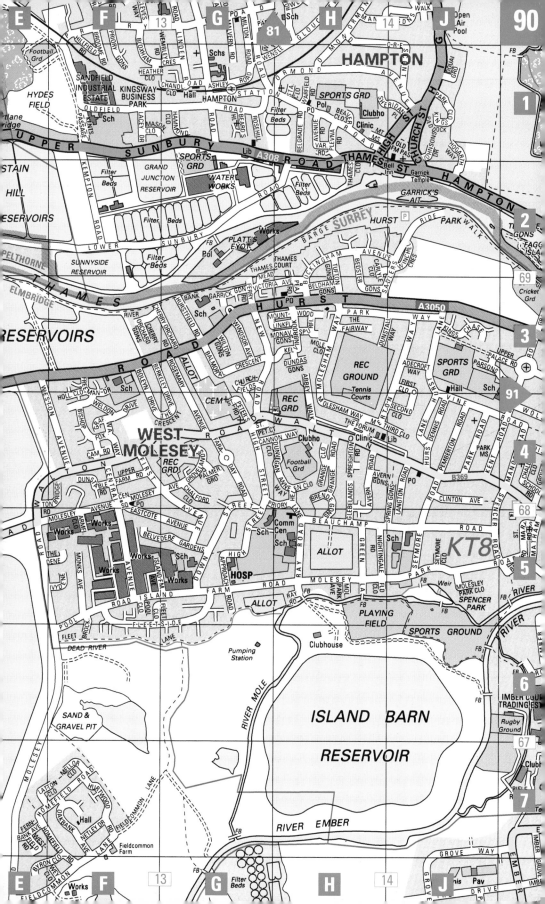

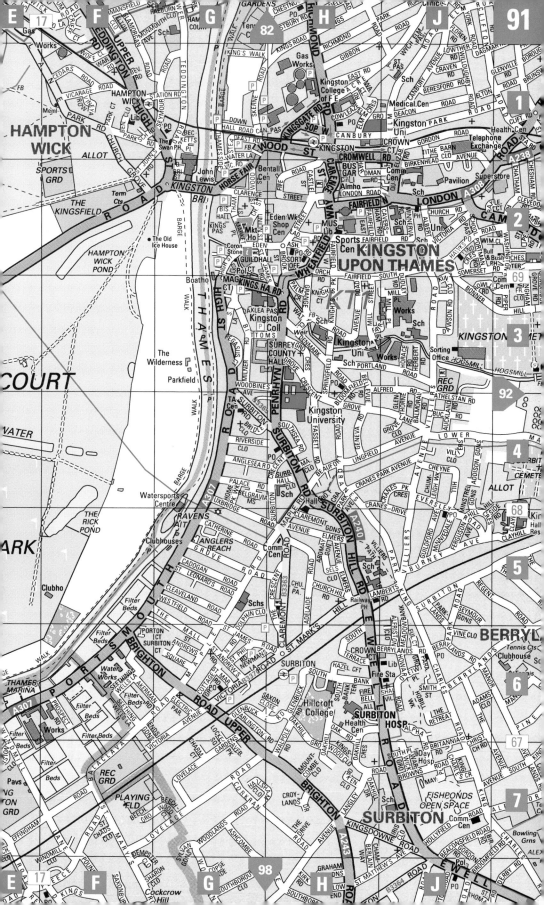

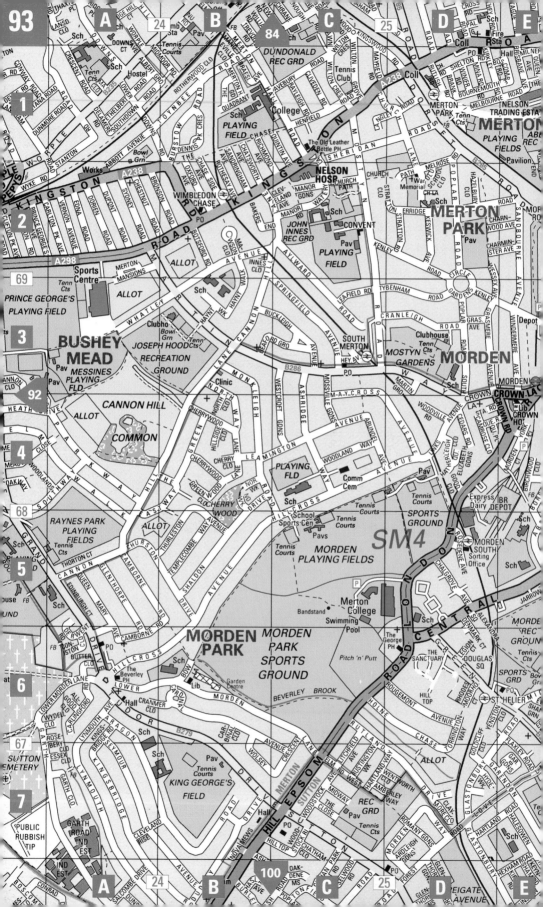

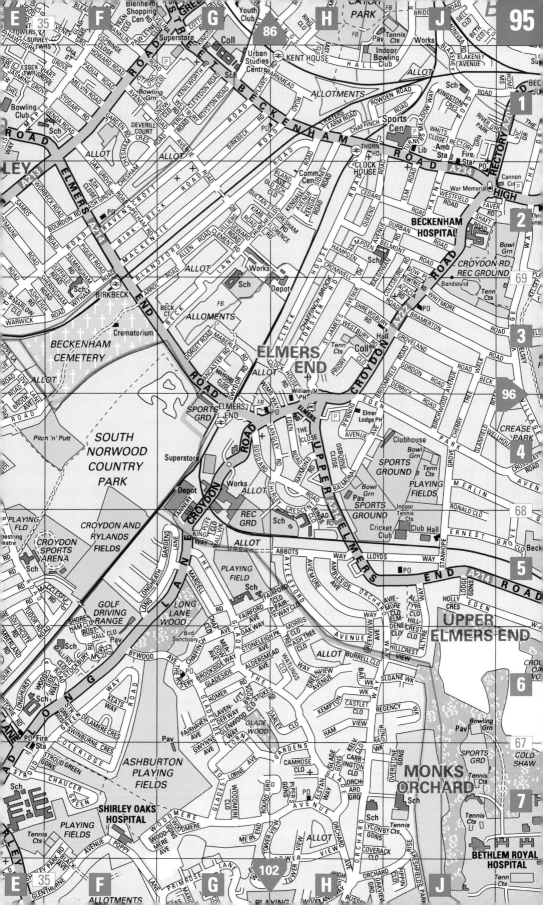

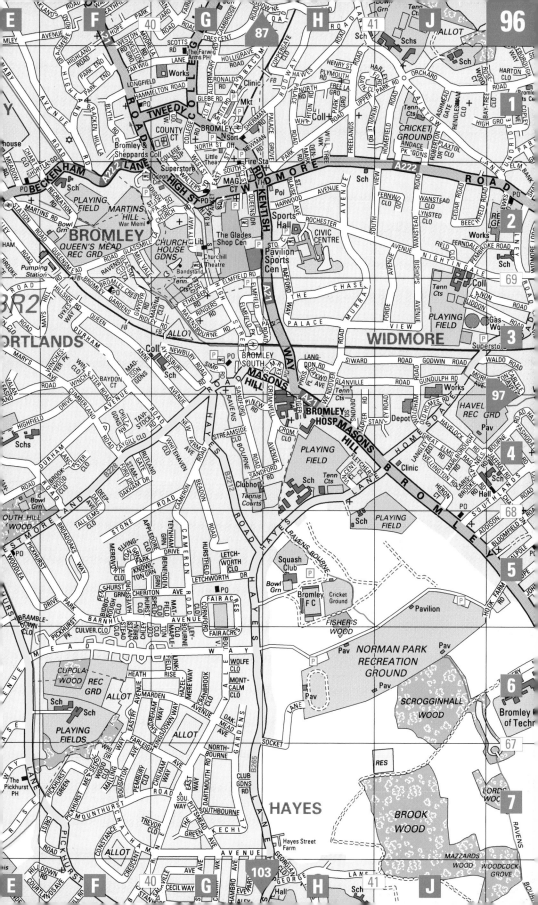

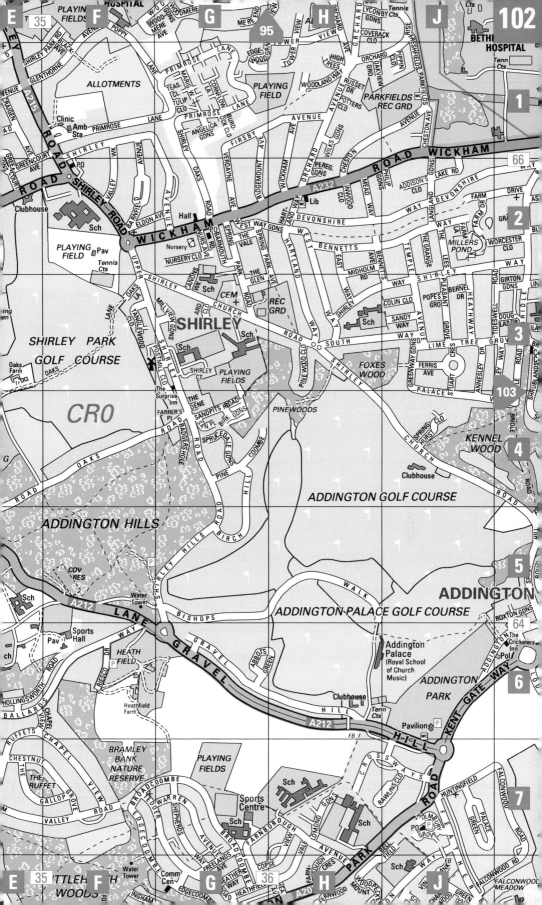

WEST END THEATRES & CINEMAS

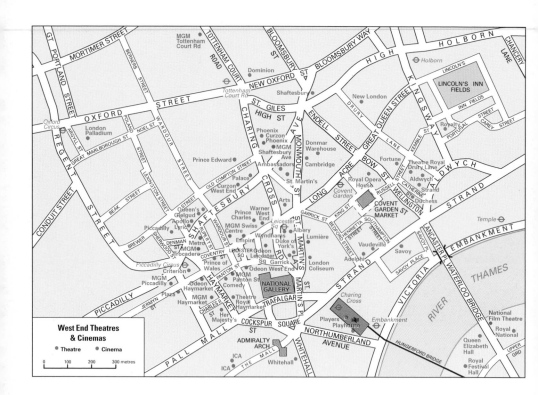

THEATRES

Adelphi *0171 334 0055*
Albery *0171 369 1730*
Aldwych *0171 416 6003*
Ambassadors *0171 836 1171*
Apollo *0171 494 5070*
Arts *0171 836 2132*
Cambridge *0171 494 5054*
Comedy *0171 369 1731*
Criterion *0171 369 1747*
Dominion *0171 580 8845*
Donmar Warehouse
  0171 867 1150
Duchess *0171 494 5075*
Duke of York's *0171 836 5122*
Fortune *0171 836 2238*
Garrick *0171 494 5085*
Gielgud *0171 494 5065*

Her Majesty's *0171 494 5400*
ICA *0171 930 3647*
London Coliseum *0171 632 8300*
London Palladium
  0171 494 5020
Lyric *0171 494 5045*
New London *0171 405 0072*
Palace *0171 434 0909*
Phoenix *0171 369 1733*
Piccadilly *0171 369 1734*
Players *0171 839 1134*
Playhouse *0171 839 4401*
Prince Edward *0171 734 8951*
Prince of Wales *0171 839 5987*
Queen Elizabeth Hall
  0171 928 3002
Queen's *0171 494 5041*

Royal Festival Hall
  0171 928 8800
Royal National *0171 928 2252*
Royal Opera House
  0171 304 4000
Royalty *0171 494 5090*
St. Martin's *0171 836 1443*
Savoy *0171 836 8888*
Shaftesbury *0171 379 5399*
Strand *0171 930 8800*
Theatre Royal, Drury Lane
  0171 494 5062
Theatre Royal, Haymarket
  0171 930 8800
Vaudeville *0171 836 9987*
Whitehall *0171 369 1735*
Wyndhams *0171 369 1736*

CINEMAS

Curzon Phoenix *0171 369 1721*
Curzon West End *0171 369 1722*
Empire *0171 437 1234*
ICA *0171 930 3647*
Lumière *0171 836 0691*
Metro *0171 437 0757*
MGM Haymarket *0171 839 1527*
MGM Panton St *0171 930 0631*
MGM Piccadilly *0171 437 3561*
MGM ShaftesburyAvenue
  0171 836 6279
MGM Swiss Centre *0171 439 4470*

MGM Tottenham Court Rd
  0171 636 6148
MGM Trocadero *0171 434 0031*
National Film Theatre
  0171 928 3232
Odeon Haymarket
  01426 915353
Odeon Leicester Sq
  01426 915683
Odeon Mezzanine
(Odeon Leicester Sq)
  01426 915683

Odeon West End
  01426 915574
Plaza *0171 437 1234*
Prince Charles *0171 437 8181*
Warner West End
  0171 437 4347

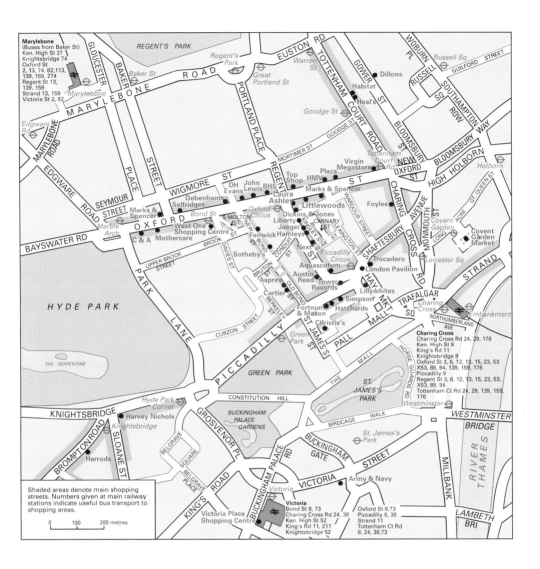

SHOPS

Aquascutum *0171 734 6090*
Army & Navy *0171 834 1234*
Asprey *0171 493 6767*
Austin Reed *0171 734 6789*
BHS (Oxford St) *0171 629 2011*
C & A *0171 629 7272*
Cartier *0171 493 6962*
Christie's *0171 839 9060*
Covent Garden Market
  0171 836 9137
DH Evans *0171 629 8800*
Debenhams *0171 580 3000*
Dickins & Jones *0171 734 7070*
Dillons *0171 636 1577*
Fenwick *0171 629 9161*
Fortnum & Mason
  0171 734 8040
Foyles *0171 437 5660*

Habitat (Tottenham Court Rd)
  0171 631 3880
Hamleys *0171 734 3161*
Harrods *0171 730 1234*
Harvey Nichols
  0171 235 5000
Hatchards *0171 439 9921*
Heal's *0171 636 1666*
HMV *0171 631 3423*
Jaeger *0171 437 7722*
John Lewis *0171 629 7711*
Laura Ashley (Regent St)
  0171 355 1363
Liberty *0171 734 1234*
Lillywhites *0171 930 3181*
Littlewoods *0171 629 7847*
London Pavilion
  0171 437 1838

Marks & Spencer
  (Marble Arch) *0171 935 7954*
Marks & Spencer (Oxford St)
  0171 437 7722
Mothercare *0171 580 1688*
Next (Regent St) *0171 434 2515*
Plaza on Oxford St
  0171 637 8811
Selfridges *0171 629 1234*
Simpson *0171 734 2002*
Sotheby's *0171 493 8080*
Top Shop & Top Man
  0171 636 7700
Tower Records *0171 439 2500*
Trocadero *0171 439 1791*
Victoria Place Shopping
  Centre *0171 931 8811*
Virgin Megastore *0171 580 5822*

INDEX TO PLACES OF INTEREST

Admiralty Arch — 15 J1
Agnew Galleries — 15 F1
Albert Memorial — 14 E3
Alexandra Palace — 40 D3
Angel Centre, The — 8 F2
Angel Information Centre — 58 H1
Anthony d'Offay Gallery — 11 E4
Apollo Victoria — 15 F6
Apothecaries' Hall — 12 G4
Apsley House, Wellington Museum — 15 C3
Armourers' and Brasiers' Hall — 13 B2
Arsenal Football Club — 49 H4
Ashby Windmill — 76 E6
Avery Hill Park, Eltham — 79 F6
Baden Powell House — 18 D1
Baker Street — 7 A6
Bank of England — 13 B4
Bank of England Museum — 13 C4
Bankside Gallery — 12 H6
Banqueting House — 16 A2
Barbican Arts and Conference Centre — 13 A1
Barnes Common — 74 G3
Battersea Park — 66 J7
Bentley Priory, Harrow — 29 B3
Bermondsey Market — 17 D4
Bethnal Green Museum of Childhood — 59 F3
Big Ben — 16 B4
Billingsgate Fish Market — 69 B1
Blackheath — 78 D1
Bloomsbury Square — 12 B2
Borough Market — 17 B2
Brentford Football Club — 64 G6
British Dental Association Museum, Wimpole St. — 11 D2
British Library — 12 A2
British Medical Association — 7 J5
British Museum — 12 A2
British Travel Centre — 15 H1
Broadgate Ice and Arena — 13 D2
Brockwell Park — 76 H6
Brompton Oratory, Brompton Rd. — 14 G6
Bruce Castle Museum, Tottenham — 41 B1
Brunel Engine House, Railway Ave. — 68 F2
Buckingham Palace — 15 E4
Burlington Arcade, Burlington Gdns. — 11 F6
Bushy Park — 91 C1
Business Design Centre — 58 G1
Cabaret Mechanical Theatre, Covent Garden Market — 12 B5
Cabinet Office — 16 A3
Cabinet War Rooms — 15 J3
Camden Lock (Waterbuses) — 49 B7
Camden Lock Market — 49 B7
Camley Street Natural Park — 8 A1
Carlyle's House — 18 G6
Carnaby Street — 11 F4
Caxton Hall — 15 H5
Cenotaph, The — 16 A3
Central Criminal Court (Old Bailey) — 12 H3
Centrepoint — 11 J3
Charing Cross Road — 11 J4
Charlton Athletic Football Club — 69 J5
Charterhouse — 12 H1
Chelsea Antique Market — 18 G5
Chelsea Flower Show, Royal Hospital Grounds — 19 B5
Chelsea Football Club — 18 A7
Chelsea Old Town Hall — 18 G4
Chelsea Physic Garden — 18 J5
Chinatown, Gerrard Street — 11 J5
Chiswick House — 65 E6
Church Farm House Museum, Hendon — 38 H3
City University — 8 G4
Clapham Common — 76 A4
Clarence House — 15 G3
Cleopatra's Needle — 12 C6
Clissold Park — 50 A2
Clothworkers' Hall — 13 E5

Coliseum, The — 12 A6
College of Arms — 12 J5
Conference Forum, The — 13 G3
Court Dress Collection, Kensington Palace — 14 B2
Courtauld Institute Galleries — 12 C5
Covent Garden — 12 B5
Crafts Council Gallery, Waterloo Pl. — 15 H1
Crystal Palace Football Club — 95 B4
Crystal Palace National Sport Centre — 86 D6
Crystal Palace Park — 86 C5
Cuming Museum — 20 J2
Custom House — 13 D6
Cutty Sark — 69 C6
Danson Park, Welling — 80 C4
Department of Trade and Industry — 15 J5
Department of Transport and Environment — 15 J6
Design Centre — 11 H6
Design Museum — 17 G3
Dickens House, Doughty St. — 8 D6
Doctor Johnson's House, Gough Sq. — 12 F3
Dominion — 11 J3
Downing Street — 16 A3
Drapers' Hall — 13 C3
Dulwich College Picture Gallery — 77 B7
Dulwich Park — 77 C7
Ealing Common — 64 H1
Earls Court Exhibition Centre — 66 D5
Eel Pie Island — 82 D1
Eltham Palace — 79 B7
Epping Forest — 26 J1
Eros — 11 H6
Faraday Museum (The Royal Institution), Albemarle St. — 11 F6
Fenton House, Hampstead — 48 F3
Festival Pleasure Gardens, Battersea Park — 19 B7
Finsbury Park — 40 H7
Fishmongers' Hall — 13 C6
Fitzroy Square — 7 F6
Flamstead House Museum, Greenwich — 69 D7
Fleet Street — 12 F4
Florence Nightingale Museum — 16 C4
Flower Market — 20 A5
Foreign Office — 16 A3
Fortnum and Mason — 15 G1
Freightliners City Farm — 49 G6
Freud Museum, Maresfield Gdns. — 48 G6
Fulham Football Club — 75 A1
Fulham Palace — 75 B2
Geological Museum — 14 F6
George Inn, Borough High St. — 17 B2
Gipsy Moth IV — 69 C6
Golders Hill Park — 48 D2
Goldsmiths' Hall — 12 J3
Gray's Inn — 12 D1
Green Park — 15 E3
Greenwich Park — 69 D7
Greenwich Pier — 69 C6
Grocers' Hall — 13 B4
Guildhall — 13 B3
Gunnersbury Park, Ealing — 64 J4
H.M. Treasury — 16 A3
H.M.S. 'Belfast' — 17 E1
H.M.S. 'President' — 12 F5
Haberdashers' Hall — 13 A3
Hackney Marshes — 50 J4
Haggerston City Farm — 9 H2
Ham House — 82 F1
Hamleys — 11 F5
Hammersmith Palais — 65 J4
Hampstead Heath — 48 G2
Hampton Court Palace — 91 B3
Harrods — 14 J5
Harrow School — 46 B1
Hay's Galleria — 17 D1

Hayward Gallery — 16 D1
Heinz Gallery, R.I.B.A. — 11 B3
Hogarths House, Hogarth La. — 65 E6
Holland Park — 66 C2
Home Office — 15 H4
Horniman Museum — 86 E1
Horse Guards Parade — 16 A2
Hospital Museum, Chelsea Royal Hospital — 19 B4
Hounslow Heath — 72 E6
Houses of Parliament — 16 B4
Hyde Park — 14 G1
Hyde Park Corner — 15 C3
Imperial College, University of London — 14 E5
Imperial War Museum — 16 F6
Institute of Contemporary Arts — 15 J2
Ironmongers' Hall — 12 J2
Ismaili Centre — 18 F1
Jack Straw's Castle P.H. — 48 F3
Jewel Tower, Houses of Parliament — 16 A5
Jewish Museum — 7 J5
Jubilee Gardens — 16 C3
Keats House, Hampstead — 48 H4
Kempton Park Racecourse — 81 C7
Kensington Gardens — 14 D2
Kensington Palace — 14 B2
Kenwood House, Hampstead — 48 H1
Kew Bridge Steam Museum — 64 H3
Kew Gardens — 64 G5
Kew Observatory — 73 E3
Kings Road, Chelsea — 18 F5
Lambeth Palace — 16 C6
Lancaster House — 15 F3
Leadenhall Market — 13 D4
Leicester Square — 11 J6
Leighton House, Holland Park Rd. — 66 C3
Lesnes Abbey (ruins) — 71 D4
Leyton Orient Football Club — 51 B3
Liberty — 11 F4
Lincoln's Inn — 12 D3
Linley Sambourne House, Stafford Ter. — 66 D2
Little Venice (Waterbuses) — 10 C1
Livesey Museum — 68 E6
Lloyds of London — 13 D4
London Brass Rubbing Centre, St. Martin-in-the-Fields Church — 12 A6
London Bridge — 17 C1
London Central Mosque — 6 H4
London Diamond Centre — 11 E4
London Dungeon — 17 C2
London Palladium — 11 F4
London Peace Pagoda, Battersea Park — 19 A6
London Silver Vaults — 12 E2
London Stone — 13 B5
London Toy and Model Museum, Craven Hill — 10 D5
London Transport Museum, Covent Gdn. — 12 B5
London Zoo — 7 B1
Lord's Cricket Ground and Museum — 6 F3
Madame Tussaud's — 7 B6
Mall Galleries — 15 J1
Mansion House — 13 B4
Marble Arch — 11 A5
Marble Hill House, Twickenham — 73 F7
Marlborough House — 15 G2
Master Mariners' Hall, H.Q.S. 'Wellington' — 12 E6
Mercers' Hall — 13 B4
Merchant Taylors' Hall — 13 C4
Methodist Central Hall — 15 J4
Middlesex Guildhall — 16 A4
Millbank Tower — 20 A2
Millwall Football Club — 68 F5
Ministry of Agriculture, Fisheries and Food — 16 B1
Ministry of Defence — 16 A2

Monument, The	13	C5
Morden College	78	G2
Museum of Garden History	16	C6
Museum of Instruments, Royal College of Music	14	E5
Museum of London	12	J2
Museum of Mankind, Burlington Gdns.	11	F6
Museum of the Moving Image (M.O.M.I.)	16	D1
Museum of the Royal Pharmaceutical Society of Great Britain (R.P.S.G.B.)	16	C6
Music Information Centre	11	C4
Musical Museum, High St., Brentford	64	H6
National Army Museum	19	A5
National Gallery	11	J6
National Maritime Museum	69	D6
National Portrait Gallery	11	J6
National Postal Museum	12	H3
National Westminster Tower	13	D3
Natural History Museum	14	E6
Nelson's Column	16	A1
New Covent Garden Market	67	D7
New Scotland Yard	15	H5
North Woolwich Station Museum	70	D2
Northern Ireland Tourist Board	15	E1
Notting Hill Carnival, Ladbroke Gro.	57	B6
Old Admiralty Buildings (M.o.D.)	15	J2
Old County Hall	16	C3
Old Curiosity Shop	12	C4
Old Deer Park, Richmond	73	G3
Olympia	66	B3
Operating Theatre Museum	17	C2
Orleans House Gallery, Twickenham	82	E1
Oscar Wilde's House	19	A5
Osterley Park House	63	J5
Oval, The (Cricket Ground)	20	D5
Oxford Circus	11	F4
Oxford Street	11	A4
P.S. 'Tattershall Castle'	16	B2
Pall Mall	15	G2
Passmore Edwards Museum	51	F6
Passport Office	15	G5
Patent Office	12	E3
Percival David Foundation of Chinese Art, Gordon Sq.	7	J6
Peter Pan Statue	14	E1
Petticoat Lane (Market)	13	E2
Petts Wood	97	G3
Photographers' Gallery, Great Newport Street	11	J5
Piccadilly Circus	11	H6
Planetarium	7	B6
Pollock's Toy Museum	11	G1
Pomeroy Purdy Gallery	17	H3
Primrose Hill	57	J1
Prince Henry's Room	12	E4
Public Record Office	12	E3
Public Record Office Museum	12	E4
Q.P.R. Football Club	65	H1
Queen Elizabeth Hall and Purcell Room	16	D1
Queen Elizabeth II Conference Centre	15	J4
Queen Elizabeth's Hunting Lodge, Epping Forest	26	F7
Queen Victoria Memorial	15	F4
Queen's Gallery	15	E4
Queen's Ice Rink	10	B6
Queen's Tower	14	E5
Queens Club (Tennis Centre)	66	B5
R.A.A.B. Gallery	19	J3
R.A.F. Museum, Hendon	38	F2
Regent Street	11	E3
Regent's Park	6	J2
Richmond Palace (remains)	73	F5
Richmond Park	83	A1
Roman Bath, Strand	12	D5
Rotunda Museum of Artillery, Woolwich	70	C5
Royal Academy of Arts	11	F6
Royal Academy of Dramatic Art (R.A.D.A.)	11	H1
Royal Academy of Music	7	C6
Royal Albert Hall	14	E4
Royal Botanic Gardens	64	G5
Royal College of Art	14	E4
Royal College of Music	14	E5
Royal College of Surgeons	12	D3
Royal Courts of Justice	12	D4
Royal Exchange (L.I.F.F.E.)	13	C4
Royal Festival Hall	16	D2
Royal Geographical Society	14	F4
Royal Horticultural Society (New Hall)	15	H6
Royal Horticultural Society (Old Hall)	19	H1
Royal Mews	15	E5
Royal National Theatre	16	D1
Royal Naval College	69	D6
Royal Opera House	12	B4
Saatchi Collection	57	E1
St. Bartholomew-the-Great Church, Cloth Fair	12	H2
St. Bride's Church and Crypt Museum	12	G4
St. Bride's Printing Library, Bride La.	12	G4
St. Clement Danes Church, Strand	12	D4
St. James's Palace	15	G2
St. James's Park	15	H3
St. John's Gate and Museum of the Order of St. John	8	G6
St. Katharine's Dock	17	H1
St. Lawrence Jewry Church, Gresham St.	13	A3
St. Martin-in-the-Fields Church, Trafalgar Square	12	A6
St. Mary at Hill Church, Lovat La.	13	D5
St. Mary-le-Bow Church	13	A4
St. Paul's Cathedral	12	J4
Salters' Hall	13	A2
Salvation Army International Headquarters, Queen Victoria St.	12	J5
Schooner Kathleen and May	17	B1
Science Museum	14	F6
Science Reference Library	12	E2
Scottish Tourist Board	15	J1
Selfridges	11	C4
Serpentine Gallery	14	F2
Serpentine, The	14	G2
Shakespeare Globe Museum	16	J1
Shell Centre	16	D2
Sherlock Holmes Museum	7	A6
Sir John Soane's Museum, Lincoln's Inn Fields	12	C3
Skinners' Hall, Dowgate Hill	13	B5
Smithfield Central Market	12	G2
Soho	11	H5
Somerset House	12	C5
Sotheby's	11	E5
South Bank	16	D1
South London Art Gallery, Peckham Rd.	77	B1
Southwark Cathedral	17	B1
Southwark Park	68	F4
Speaker's Corner	11	A5
Spitalfields Community Farm	9	H6
Stepping Stones Farm	59	G5
Stock Exchange	13	C4
Strand, The	16	A1
Surrey Docks Farm	68	J2
Syon House, Brentford	73	F1
Tate Gallery	20	A2
Technology Showcase	12	H5
Telecom Tower	11	F1
Temple Bar	12	E4
Temple of Mithras, Victoria St.	13	A4
Temple, The	12	E5
Thames Flood Barrier	70	A2
Thames House	20	A1
Theatre Museum, Tavistock Street	12	B5
Theatre Royal, Drury La.	12	B4
Tottenham Hotspur Football Club	33	C7
Tower Bridge Museum and Exhibitions	17	F2
Tower Hill	13	F6
Tower Pier	17	E1
Tower of London	13	F6
Toynbee Hall	13	G3
Trafalgar Square	16	A1
Trent Park, Enfield	24	B2
Trinity House	13	F5
Trocadero	11	H6
Twickenham Rugby Ground	73	B6
University College London	7	H5
University of London	7	J6
Victoria Coach Station	19	D2
Victoria Embankment Gardens	16	B1
Victoria Park	59	H1
Victoria Tower, Houses of Parliament	16	A5
Victoria and Albert Museum	14	F6
Vintners' Hall	13	A5
Wallace Collection	11	C3
Walworth City Farm	20	H4
Waterlow Park, Highgate	49	B1
Wellington Arch	15	C3
Wellington Museum	15	C3
Wembley Conference Centre	46	J4
Wembley Stadium	47	A5
Wesley's House	9	C5
West Ham United Football Club	61	A2
Westminster Abbey	16	A5
Westminster Abbey Museum	16	A5
Westminster Cathedral	15	F6
Westminster City Hall	15	G5
Westminster Pier	16	B3
Whitbread Brewery	13	A1
Whitbread Shire Horse Stables, Garrett St.	9	A5
Whitechapel Art Gallery	13	G3
Whitehall	16	A2
William Morris Gallery, Lloyd Park	42	A3
Wimbledon (All England Tennis Club)	84	B4
Wimbledon Common	83	F4
Wimbledon Football Club*	95	B4
Woolwich Common	70	C7
World Trade Centre	13	G6
Y.H.A., Carter Lane	12	H4
Y.H.A., Earl's Court	18	A3
Y.H.A., Holland House	66	C2
Y.H.A., Oxford Street	11	G4
Y.M.C.A.	11	J3
Y.W.C.A.	11	J3
Zamana Gallery, Ismaili Centre	18	F1

* Play at Crystal Palace Football Club

INDEX TO PLACE NAMES

Abbey Wood SE2	71	B3
Acton W3	65	A1
Addington, Croy.	102	J5
Addiscombe, Croy.	102	C1
Aldborough Hatch, Ilf.	43	H3
Aldersbrook E12	51	H2
Alperton, Wem.	55	H1
Anerley SE20	95	E2
Arkley, Barn.	22	G5
Avery Hill SE9	79	F6
Balham SW12	84	J1
Banstead, Bans.	93	E2
Barbican EC2	**13**	**A2**
Barking, Bark.	61	E1
Barkingside, Ilf.	43	E3
Barnes SW13	74	G2
Barnet, Barn.	23	C3
Barnet Gate, Barn.	22	F6
Barnsbury N1	49	G6
Battersea SW11	76	A2
Bayswater W2	**10**	**C4**
Bayswater W2	57	E6
Beacontree, Dag.	53	D3
Beacontree Heath, Dag.	53	G1
Beckenham, Beck.	96	B1
Beckton E6	61	D5
Beddington, Wall.	101	D2
Beddington Corner, Mitch.	94	A7
Bedford Park W4	65	D3
Belgravia SW1	**19**	**C1**
Belgravia SW1	67	A3
Bell Green SE6	86	J3
Bellingham SE6	87	A3
Belmont, Har.	37	D2
Belsize Park NW3	48	H6
Belvedere, Belv.	71	H4
Benhilton, Sutt.	100	E2
Bermondsey SE1	**17**	**F5**
Bermondsey SE1	68	C3
Berrylands, Surb.	91	J6
Bethnal Green E2	59	D2
Bexley, Bex.	80	G6
Bexleyheath, Bexh.	80	F5
Bickley, Brom.	97	C3
Blackfen, Sid.	79	J7
Blackheath SE3	78	E1
Blackheath Park SE3	78	G4
Bloomsbury WC1	**12**	**A1**
Bloomsbury WC1	58	D5
Borehamwood, Borwd.	22	B3
Borough, The SE1	**16**	**J4**
Borough, The SE1	67	J2
Bow E3	59	J2
Bowes Park N22	32	E6
Brentford, Brent.	64	F6
Brimsdown, Enf.	25	H3
Brixton SW2	76	E4
Broad Green, Croy.	94	G6
Broadgate EC2	**13**	**C1**
Brockley SE4	77	H5
Bromley E3	60	B4
Bromley, Brom.	96	F2
Bromley Common, Brom.	97	C7
Bromley Park, Brom.	96	E1
Brompton SW3	**14**	**G6**
Brompton SW3	66	H3
Brondesbury NW2	48	A6
Brondesbury Park NW6	48	A7
Brunswick Park N11	31	J2
Buckhurst Hill, Buck.H.	26	H7
Burnt Oak, Edg.	30	C7
Bush Hill Park, Enf.	25	B5
Bushey Heath, Wat.	29	B1
Bushey Mead SW20	93	A3
Camberwell SE5	67	J7
Camden Town NW1	58	C1
Canning Town E16	60	G6
Canons Park, Edg.	29	H7
Carpenders Park, Wat.	28	F2
Carshalton, Cars.	100	H5
Carshalton on the Hill, Cars.	101	A7
Castelnau SW13	65	G6
Catford SE6	87	B1
Chadwell Heath, Rom.	44	D6
Charlton SE7	69	J6
Cheam, Sutt.	100	A6
Chelsea SW3	**18**	**E5**
Chelsea SW3	66	G6
Chessington, Chess.	98	H6
Chigwell, Chig.	35	E3
Childs Hill NW2	48	D2
Chingford E4	34	B1
Chingford Green E4	34	F1
Chingford Hatch E4	34	D4
Chipping Barnet, Barn.	23	B4
Chislehurst, Chis.	88	D7
Chislehurst West, Chis.	88	D5
Chiswick W4	65	D6
Church End N3	39	C1
Church End NW10	47	E6
Clapham SW4	76	B3
Clapham Park SW4	76	C6
Claygate, Esher	98	B7
Clayhall, Ilf.	43	C2
Clerkenwell EC1	**8**	**G6**
Clerkenwell EC1	58	H4
Cockfosters, Barn.	23	H4
Coldblow, Bex.	89	J2
Collier Row, Rom.	44	G1
Collier's Wood SW19	84	G7
Coombe, Kings.T.	83	C7
Copse Hill SW20	83	G7
Cottenham Park SW20	92	G1
Cranbrook, Ilf.	52	C1
Cranford, Houns.	63	A7
Cricklewood NW2	48	A3
Crouch End N8	40	C6
Croydon, Croy.	102	A2
Cubitt Town E14	69	C3
Custom House E16	61	A6
Dagenham, Dag.	53	G6
Dalston E8	50	B7
Dartmouth Park NW5	49	B3
Debden, Loug.	27	G3
Deptford SE8	68	J5
Dollis Hill NW2	47	H3
Dormer's Wells, Sthl.	54	H7
Downham, Brom.	87	F4
Ducks Island, Barn.	23	A6
Dulwich SE21	77	B7
Ealing W5	55	F7
Earls Court SW5	66	C5
Earlsfield SW18	84	F1
East Acton W3	56	E7
East Barnet, Barn.	23	H6
East Dulwich SE22	77	D6
East Finchley N2	39	G4
East Ham E6	61	B2
East Molesey, E.Mol.	91	A3
East Sheen SW14	74	D4
East Wickham, Well.	89	A3
Eastcote, Pnr.	36	C6
Eastcote Village, Pnr.	36	B5
Eden Park, Beck.	96	A5
Edgware, Edg.	30	B5
Edmonton N9	33	D4
Elmers End, Beck.	95	G3
Elmstead, Chis.	88	A5
Eltham SE9	79	A6
Enfield, Enf.	25	C3
Enfield Highway, Enf.	25	F2
Enfield Town, Enf.	25	A2
Epsom, Epsom	83	C7
Falconwood, Well.	79	G3
Farnborough, Orp.	104	E5
Feltham, Felt.	81	A2
Finchley N3	39	E1
Finsbury EC1	**8**	**F3**
Finsbury EC1	58	H3
Finsbury Park N4	49	G1
Forest Gate E7	51	G5
Forest Hill SE23	86	G1
Friday Hill E4	34	D2
Friern Barnet N11	31	H4
Fullwell Cross, Ilf.	43	G1
Furzedown SW17	85	A5
Gants Hill, Ilf.	43	D5
Golders Green NW11	39	D7
Goodmayes, Ilf.	53	B2
Gospel Oak NW5	49	A4
Grange Hill, Chig.	35	G6
Grange Park N21	24	H5
Greenford, Grnf.	54	H3
Greenwich SE10	69	D6
Grove Park SE12	87	G2
Grove Park W4	65	C7
Gunnersbury W4	65	B4
Hackbridge, Wall.	101	B2
Hackney E8	50	E6
Hackney Wick E9	50	J5
Hadley, Barn.	23	C2
Haggerston E2	**9**	**H1**
Haggerston E2	59	C2
Hainault, Chig.	35	J4
Hale End E4	34	D6
Ham, Rich.	82	F3
Hammersmith W6	65	J5
Hampstead NW3	48	G4
Hampstead Garden Suburb N2	39	F5
Hampton, Hmptn.	90	H1
Hampton Hill, Hmptn.	82	A6
Hampton Wick, Kings.T.	91	E1
Hanwell W7	64	C1
Hanworth, Felt.	81	D4
Harlesden NW10	56	E2
Harringay N8	40	G5
Harrow, Har.	37	A7
Harrow on the Hill, Har.	46	B1
Harrow Weald, Har.	37	B1
Hatch End, Pnr.	28	E7
Hayes, Brom.	96	H7
Headstone, Har.	36	J4
Hendon NW4	38	H4
Herne Hill SE24	76	J5
Heston, Houns.	63	F7
High Barnet, Barn.	23	A2
High Beach, Loug.	26	G1
Higham Hill E17	41	H2
Highams Park E4	34	D5
Highbury N5	49	H5
Highgate N6	40	B7
Highwood Hill NW7	30	G2
Hinchley Wood, Esher	98	C3
Hither Green SE13	78	E6
Holborn WC2	**12**	**C3**
Holborn WC2	58	F6
Holders Hill NW4	39	A2
Holloway N7	49	E4
Homerton E9	50	H5
Honor Oak SE23	77	F6
Honor Oak Park SE4	77	J6
Hornsey N8	40	F3
Hounslow, Houns.	72	F4
Hounslow, West Houns.	72	D3
Hoxton N1	**9**	**D2**
Hoxton N1	59	A2
Hyde, The NW9	38	F5
Ilford, Ilf.	52	F3
Isleworth, Islw.	73	C3
Islington N1	58	G1
Joydens Wood, Bex.	89	J5
Kennington SE11	**20**	**E6**
Kennington SE11	67	G6
Kensal Green NW10	56	J3
Kensal Rise NW6	57	A2
Kensal Town W10	57	A4
Kensington W8	66	C1
Kentish Town NW5	49	C6
Kenton, Har.	37	E5
Kew, Rich.	65	A6
Kidbrooke SE3	78	J2
Kilburn NW6	57	C2
King's Cross N1	58	D1
Kingsbury NW9	38	B6
Kingston upon Thames, Kings.T.	91	H2
Kingston Vale SW15	74	E6
Ladywell SE13	78	A5
Lambeth SE1	**16**	**D5**
Lambeth SE1	67	F3
Lamorbey, Sid.	88	J1
Lampton, Houns.	72	H1
Lea Bridge E5	50	G3
Lee SE12	78	F6
Lessness Heath, Belv.	71	H5
Lewisham SE13	78	B3
Leyton E11	51	B1
Leytonstone E11	42	D7
Limehouse E14	59	H7
Lisson Grove NW8	**6**	**F5**
Little Ealing W5	64	F4
Long Ditton, Surb.	98	F1
Longlands, Chis.	88	F3
Loughton, Loug.	27	C5
Lower Clapton E5	50	F4
Lower Edmonton N9	33	C1
Lower Holloway N7	49	F5
Lower Sydenham SE26	86	G4
Loxford, Ilf.	52	F5
Maida Hill W9	57	C4
Maida Vale W9	**6**	**B5**
Maida Vale W9	57	E4

Place	Pg	Ref	Place	Pg	Ref	Place	Pg	Ref
Manor Park E12	52	B5	Putney Heath SW15	74	J6	Surbiton , Surb.	91	H7
Mark's Gate, Rom.	44	E2	Putney Vale SW15	83	F3	Sutton, Sutt.	100	D6
Marylebone NW1	**10**	**H1**	Queensbury, Har.	37	G3	Sydenham SE26	86	E5
Marylebone NW1	57	H4	Rayners Lane, Har.	45	F1	Teddington, Tedd.	82	D6
Mayfair W1	**11**	**D6**	Raynes Park SW20	92	H3	Thames Ditton, T.Ditt.	91	D7
Mayfair W1	58	A7	Redbridge, Ilf.	43	C6	Thamesmead SE28	71	A1
Merry Hill, Wat.	28	H1	**Regent's Park NW1**	**7**	**D2**	Thamesmead North SE28	62	D6
Merton SW19	93	D1	Regent's Park NW1	58	B3	Thamesmead West SE18	70	F3
Merton Park SW19	93	D2	Richmond, Rich.	73	H6	Thornton Heath, Th.Hth.	94	H4
Mile End E1	59	H3	Roehampton SW15	74	G5	Tokyngton, Wem.	47	B6
Mill Hill NW7	30	G5	Rosehill, Sutt.	100	E1	Tolworth, Surb.	99	A2
Millwall E14	69	B3	Rotherhithe SE16	68	G3	Tooting Graveney SW17	84	H6
Mitcham, Mitch.	94	A3	Rowley Green, Barn.	22	F4	Tottenham N17	41	B1
Monken Hadley, Barn.	23	C1	Roxeth, Har.	46	A2	Tottenham Hale N17	41	D3
Monks Orchard, Croy.	95	J7	Ruislip Manor, Ruis.	45	A2	Totteridge N20	31	B1
Morden, Mord.	93	D3	Rush Green, Rom.	44	J7	Tufnell Park N7	49	D4
Morden Park, Mord.	93	B6	St. Helier, Cars.	93	G7	Tulse Hill SE21	85	J1
Mortlake SW14	74	C3	**St. James's SW1**	**15**	**G2**	Twickenham, Twick.	82	D2
Motspur Park, N.Mal.	92	G6	St. James's SW1	67	C1	Underhill , Barn.	23	D5
Mottingham SE9	87	J2	St. John's SE8	78	A2	Upper Clapton E5	50	E1
Muswell Hill N10	40	B3	**St. John's Wood NW8**	**6**	**E3**	Upper Edmonton N18	33	D5
Neasden NW2	47	E3	St. John's Wood NW8	57	F2	Upper Elmers End Beck.	95	J5
New Barnet, Barn.	23	E4	**St. Luke's EC1**	**9**	**A5**	Upper Holloway N19	49	C3
New Beckenham, Beck.	86	J6	St. Luke's EC1	58	J4	Upper Norwood SE19	86	A7
New Charlton SE7	69	J4	St. Margarets, Twick.	73	D5	Upper Sydenham SE26	86	D4
New Cross SE14	77	H1	**St. Pancras WC1**	**8**	**A4**	Upper Tooting SW17	84	H3
New Cross Gate SE14	77	G1	St. Pancras WC1	58	E3	Upper Walthamstow E17	42	C4
New Eltham SE9	88	D2	Sands End SW6	75	F1	Upton E7	51	H7
New Malden, N.Mal.	92	D3	Selhurst SE25	95	B6	Upton Park E6	60	J1
New Southgate N11	32	D4	Seven Kings, Ilf.	43	H7	**Vauxhall SW8**	**20**	**C6**
Newbury Park, Ilf.	43	G5	Sewardstone E4	26	C1	Vauxhall SW8	67	D6
Newington SE17	**20**	**J1**	Sewardstonebury E4	26	E4	Waddon, Croy.	101	G2
Newington SE17	67	J3	Shacklewell N16	50	C4	Walham Green SW6	66	E7
Nine Elms SW8	**19**	**G7**	Shadwell E1	59	F7	Wallington, Wall.	101	C5
Noel Park N22	40	G2	Shepherd's Bush W12	65	J1	Walthamstow E17	42	B2
Norbiton, Kings.T.	92	B2	Shirley, Croy.	102	G3	**Walworth SE17**	**20**	**J3**
Norbury SW16	94	F1	Shooter's Hill SE18	79	F1	Walworth SE17	68	A5
Nork, Bans.	93	A1	**Shoreditch E1**	**9**	**F6**	Wandsworth SW18	75	C5
North Acton W3	56	D4	Shoreditch E1	59	C4	Wanstead E11	42	G7
North Cheam, Sutt.	100	A3	Shortlands, Brom.	96	E3	Wapping E1	68	D1
North Cray, Sid.	89	F3	Sidcup, Sid.	88	J4	Watford Heath, Wat.	28	D1
North Finchley N12	31	G5	Silvertown E16	69	J2	Wealdstone, Har.	37	C3
North Harrow, Har.	36	G6	Snaresbrook E11	42	E5	Welling, Well.	80	A3
North Hyde, Sthl.	63	E4	**Soho W1**	**11**	**H5**	Wembley, Wem.	46	H5
North Kensington W10	56	J6	Soho W1	58	C6	Wembley Park , Wem.	46	J2
North Sheen, Rich.	74	A2	**Somers Town NW1**	**7**	**J2**	West Barnes, N.Mal.	92	H4
North Wembley, Wem.	46	E2	Somers Town NW1	58	D3	**West Brompton SW10**	**18**	**A5**
North Woolwich E16	70	B2	South Acton W3	65	B3	West Brompton SW10	66	D6
Northolt, Nthlt.	45	E7	South Beddington, Wall.	101	D6	West Dulwich SE21	86	A3
Northumberland Heath, Erith	71	J7	South Chingford E4	33	J5	West Ewell, Epsom	99	E7
			South Croydon, S.Croy.	101	J6	West Green N15	40	J4
Norwood Green, Sthl.	63	G4	South Hackney E9	59	F1	West Ham E15	51	F7
Norwood New Town SE19	85	J6	South Hampstead NW6	48	E7	West Hampstead NW6	48	E5
Notting Hill W11	57	B6	South Harrow, Har.	45	H3	West Harrow, Har.	36	J7
Nunhead SE15	77	F3	South Kensington SW7	18	C2	West Heath SE2	71	D6
Oakleigh Park N20	31	G1	South Kensington SW7	66	E3	West Kilburn W9	57	C3
Oakwood N14	24	D6	South Lambeth SW8	76	E1	West Molesey, W.Mol.	90	F4
Old Bexley, Bex.	80	H7	South Norwood SE25	95	C3	West Norwood SE27	85	J3
Old Ford E3	59	J1	South Oxhey, Wat.	28	C3	West Wickham, W.Wick.	103	C2
Old Malden, Wor.Pk.	99	D1	South Ruislip, Ruis.	45	C4	Westbourne Green W2	57	D5
Old Oak Common NW10	56	E5	South Tottenham N15	41	B5	**Westminster SW1**	**15**	**F5**
Orpington, Orp.	104	J1	South Wimbledon SW19	84	D7	Westminster SW1	67	C3
Osidge N14	32	B1	South Woodford E18	42	F2	Weston Green, T.Ditt.	98	C1
Osterley, Islw.	64	A7	Southall, Sthl.	63	D1	Whetstone N20	31	E2
Paddington W2	**10**	**C2**	Southborough, Brom.	97	C6	**Whitechapel E1**	**13**	**H4**
Paddington W2	57	E5	Southend SE6	87	C4	Whitechapel E1	59	D6
Palmers Green N13	32	G3	Southfields SW18	84	D1	Whitton , Twick.	72	H7
Park Langley, Beck.	96	C5	Southgate N14	32	C2	Widmore, Brom.	96	J3
Park Royal NW10	56	A2	**Southwark SE1**	**16**	**H2**	Willesden NW10	47	F6
Parsons Green SW6	75	C1	Southwark SE1	67	H1	Willesden Green NW10	47	H6
Peckham SE15	68	C7	Spring Grove, Islw.	73	B2	Wimbledon SW19	84	B6
Penge SE20	86	F7	Stamford Hill N16	50	C1	Wimbledon Park SW19	84	C3
Pentonville N1	**8**	**E2**	Stanmore, Stan.	29	D5	Winchmore Hill N21	24	F7
Pentonville N1	58	G2	Stepney E1	59	F5	Wood Green N22	40	E1
Perivale, Grnf.	55	F1	Stockwell SW9	76	D3	Woodford, Wdf.Grn.	34	H6
Petersham, Rich.	82	H1	Stoke Newington N16	50	B2	Woodford Bridge, Wdf.Grn.	35	G5
Petts Wood, Orp.	97	G5	Stonebridge NW10	56	B1	Woodford Green, Wdf.Grn.	34	G5
Pimlico SW1	**19**	**F3**	Stoneleigh, Epsom	99	G5	Woodford Wells , Wdf.Grn.	34	G3
Pimlico SW1	67	B5	**Strand WC2**	**12**	**A5**	Woodlands, Islw.	73	B2
Pinner, Pnr.	36	E4	Strand WC2	58	E7	Woodmansterne , Bans.	93	H1
Pinner Green, Pnr.	36	C2	Stratford E15	51	C6	Woodside, Croy.	95	C6
Pinnerwood Park, Pnr.	36	C1	Strawberry Hill, Twick.	82	B3	Woolwich SE18	70	C5
Plaistow E13	60	H3	Streatham SW16	85	E4	Worcester Park, Wor.Pk.	99	F2
Plaistow, Brom.	87	F6	Streatham Hill SW2	85	F1	World's End, Enf.	24	A2
Plumstead SE18	70	H5	Streatham Park SW16	85	C4	Wrythe, The, Cars.	100	H2
Ponders End, Enf.	25	G5	Streatham Vale SW16	85	D7	Yeading, Hayes	54	B3
Poplar E14	60	B7	Stroud Green N8	40	F6			
Poverest, Orp.	97	J5	Sudbury, Wem.	46	D5			
Preston, Wem.	46	G1	Summerstown SW17	84	E4			
Primrose Hill NW8	57	J1	Sunbury, Sun.	90	B3			
Putney SW15	74	J5	Sundridge, Brom.	87	J6			

General Abbreviations

All	Alley	Embk	Embankment	Pas	Passage
Allot	Allotments	Est	Estate	Pav	Pavilion
Amb	Ambulance	Ex	Exchange	Pk	Park
App	Approach	FB	Footbridge	Pl	Place
Arc	Arcade	FC	Football Club	Prec	Precinct
Ave	Avenue	Fld	Field	Prom	Promenade
Bdy	Broadway	Flds	Fields	Quad	Quadrant
Bldgs	Buildings	Fm	Farm	Pt	Point
Bowl	Bowling	Gall	Gallery	RC	Roman Catholic
Bri	Bridge	Gar	Garage	Rd	Road
C of E	Church of England	Gdn	Garden	Rds	Roads
Cath	Cathedral	Gdns	Gardens	Rec	Recreation
Cem	Cemetery	Govt	Government	Res	Reservoir
Cen	Central, Centre	Gra	Grange	Ri	Rise
Cft	Croft	Grd	Ground	S	South
Ch	Church	Grds	Grounds	Sch	School
Chyd	Churchyard	Grn	Green	Shop	Shopping
Cin	Cinema	Gro	Grove	Sq	Square
Circ	Circus	Gros	Groves	St	Street
Clo	Close	Ho	House	St.	Saint
Co	County	Hos	Houses	Sta	Station
Coll	College	Hosp	Hospital	SUB	Subway
Comm	Community	Ind	Industrial	Swim	Swimming
Conv	Convent	Junct	Junction	TA	Territorial Army
Cor	Corner	La	Lane	Tenn	Tennis
Cors	Corners	Las	Lanes	Ter	Terrace
Coron	Coroners	Lo	Lodge	Thea	Theatre
Cotts	Cottages	Lwr	Lower	Trd	Trading
Cov	Covered	Mag	Magistrates	Twr	Tower
Crem	Crematorium	Mans	Mansions	Twrs	Towers
Cres	Crescent	Meml	Memorial	Vill	Villas
Ct	Court	Mkt	Market	Vw	View
Ctyd	Courtyard	Mkts	Markets	W	West
Dep	Depot	Ms	Mews	Wd	Wood
Dr	Drive	Mt	Mount	Wds	Woods
Dws	Dwellings	Mus	Museum	Wf	Wharf
E	East	N	North	Wk	Walk
Ed	Education	PH	Public House	Wks	Works
Elec	Electricity	Par	Parade	Yd	Yard

Abbreviations of District Names

Bark.	Barking	Felt.	Feltham	S.Croy.	South Croydon
Barn.	Barnet	Grnf.	Greenford	Sid.	Sidcup
Beck.	Beckenham	Har.	Harrow	Stan.	Stanmore
Belv.	Belvedere	Hmptn.	Hampton	Sthl.	Southall
Bex.	Bexley	Houns.	Hounslow	Sun.	Sunbury-on-Thames
Bexh.	Bexleyheath	Ilf.	Ilford	Surb.	Surbiton
Borwd.	Borehamwood	Islw.	Isleworth	Sutt.	Sutton
Brent.	Brentford	Kes.	Keston	T.Ditt.	Thames Ditton
Brom.	Bromley	Kings.T.	Kingston upon Thames	Tedd.	Teddington
Buck.H.	Buckhurst Hill	Loug.	Loughton	Th.Hth.	Thornton Heath
Cars.	Carshalton	Mitch.	Mitcham	Twick.	Twickenham
Chess.	Chessington	Mord.	Morden	W.Mol.	West Molesey
Chig.	Chigwell	N.Mal.	New Malden	W.Wick	West Wickham
Chis.	Chislehurst	Nthlt.	Northolt	Wall.	Wallington
Croy.	Croydon	Nthwd.	Northwood	Walt.	Walton-on-Thames
Dag.	Dagenham	Orp.	Orpington	Wat.	Watford
Dart.	Dartford	Pnr.	Pinner	Wdf.Grn.	Woodford Green
E.Mol.	East Molesey	Rain.	Rainham	Well.	Welling
Edg.	Edgware	Rich.	Richmond	Wem.	Wembley
Enf.	Enfield	Rom.	Romford	Wor.Pk.	Worcester Park
Epp.	Epping	Ruis.	Ruislip		

NOTES

This index contains some street names in standard text which are followed by another street named in italics. In these cases the street in standard text does not actually appear on the map due to insufficient space but can be located close to the street named in italics.

A.C. Ct., T.Ditt. 91 D6
Harvest La.
Abberley Ms. SW4 76 B3
Cedars Rd.
Abbess Clo. E6 61 B5
Oliver Gdns.
Abbess Clo. SW2 85 G1
Abbeville Rd. N8 40 D4
Barrington Rd.
Abbeville Rd. SW4 76 C6
Abbey Ave., Wem. 55 H2
Abbey Clo., Hayes 63 B1
Abbey Clo., Nthlt. 54 F3
Invicta Gro.
Abbey Cres., Belv. 71 G4
Abbey Dr. SW17 85 A5
Church La.
Abbey Gdns. NW8 6 C2
Abbey Gdns. NW8 57 F2
Abbey Gdns. W6 66 B6
Abbey Gro. SE2 71 B4
Abbey La. E15 60 C2
Abbey La., Beck. 87 A7
Abbey Manufacturing 55 J1
Est., Wem.
Abbey Ms. E17 42 A5
Leamington Ave.
**Abbey Orchard St. 15 J5
SW1**
Abbey Orchard St. 67 D3
SW1
Abbey Par. W5 55 J3
Hanger La.
Abbey Pk., Beck. 87 A7
Abbey Rd. E15 60 D2
Abbey Rd. NW6 48 E7
Abbey Rd. NW8 57 E1
Abbey Rd. NW10 56 B2
Abbey Rd. SE2 71 D4
Abbey Rd. SW19 84 F7
Abbey Rd., Bark. 52 E7
Abbey Rd., Belv. 71 G4
Abbey Rd., Bexh. 80 E4
Abbey Rd., Croy. 101 H3
Abbey Rd., Enf. 25 B5
Abbey Rd., Ilf. 43 G5
Abbey Rd. Est. NW8 57 E1
Abbey St. E13 60 G4
Abbey St. SE1 17 E5
Abbey St. SE1 68 C3
Abbey Ter. SE2 71 C4
Abbey Vw. NW7 30 F3
Abbey Wk., W.Mol. 90 H3
Abbey Way SE2 71 D2
Wolvercote Rd.
Abbey Wf. Ind. Est., 61 G2
Bark.
Abbey Wd. Rd. SE2 71 B4
Abbeydale Rd., Wem. 56 A1
Abbeyfield Rd. SE16 68 F4
Abbeyfields Clo. 56 A3
NW10
Abbeyhill Rd., Sid. 89 C2
Abbot St. E8 50 C6
Abbots Clo. N1 49 J6
Alwyne Rd.
Abbots Clo., Orp. 104 F1
Abbots Clo., Ruis. 45 D3
Abbots Cres., Enf. 24 H2
Abbots Dr., Har. 45 G2
Abbots Gdns. N2 39 G4
Abbots Grn., Croy. 102 G6
Abbots La. SE1 17 E2
**Abbots Manor Est. 19 D3
SW1**
Abbots Pk. SW2 85 G1
Abbot's Pl. NW6 57 E1
Abbots Pl. W8 14 A6
Abbot's Rd. E6 61 H4
Abbots Ter. N8 40 E6
Abbots Way, Beck. 95 H5
Abbotsbury Clo. E15 60 C2
Abbotsbury Clo. W14 66 C2
Abbotsbury Rd.
Abbotsbury Gdns., 36 C6
Pnr.
Abbotsbury Ms. SE15 77 F3
Abbotsbury Rd. W14 66 B2
Abbotsbury Rd., 103 F3
Brom.
Abbotsbury Rd., 93 E5
Mord.
Abbotsford Ave. N15 40 J4
Abbotsford Gdns., 34 G7
Wdf.Grn.
Abbotsford Rd., Ilf. 53 A2

Abbotshall Ave. N14 32 C3
Abbotshall Rd. SE6 87 D1
Abbotsleigh Clo., 100 E7
Sutt.
Abbotsleigh Rd. 85 C4
SW16
Abbotsmede Clo., 82 C2
Twick.
Abbotstone Rd. SW15 74 J3
Abbotswell Rd. SE4 77 J5
Abbotswood Clo., 71 E3
Belv.
Coptefield Dr.
Abbotswood Gdns., 43 C3
Ilf.
Abbotswood Rd. 85 D3
SW16
Abbotswood Way, 63 B1
Hayes
Abbott Ave. SW20 93 A1
Abbott Clo., Hmptn. 81 E6
Abbott Clo., Nthlt. 45 F6
Abbott Rd. E14 60 C6
Abbotts Clo., Rom. 44 H3
Abbotts Cres. E4 34 D4
Abbotts Dr., Wem. 46 E2
Abbotts Pk. Rd. E10 42 C7
Abbotts Rd., Barn. 23 E4
Abbotts Rd., Mitch. 94 C4
Abbotts Rd., Sthl. 63 E1
Abbotts Rd., Sutt. 100 B4
Abbotts Wk., Bexh. 71 D7
Abchurch La. EC4 13 C5
Abchurch La. EC4 59 A7
Abchurch Yd. EC4 13 B5
Abdale Rd. W12 65 H1
Aberavon Rd. E3 59 H3
Abercairn Rd. SW16 85 C7
Aberconway Rd., 93 E3
Mord.
Abercorn Clo. NW7 31 B7
Abercorn Clo. NW8 6 C3
Abercorn Clo. NW8 57 F3
Abercorn Cres., Har. 45 H2
Abercorn Gdns., Har. 37 G7
Abercorn Gdns., Rom. 44 B6
Abercorn Pl. NW8 6 C3
Abercorn Pl. NW8 57 F3
Abercorn Rd. NW7 31 B7
Abercorn Rd., Stan. 29 F7
Abercorn Way SE1 21 H3
Abercorn Way SE1 68 D5
Abercrombie St. SW11 75 H2
Aberdare Clo., 103 C2
W.Wick.
Aberdare Gdns. NW6 48 E7
Aberdare Gdns. NW7 31 A7
Aberdeen La. N5 49 J5
Aberdeen Par. N18 33 E5
Angel Rd.
Aberdeen Pk. N5 49 J5
Aberdeen Pk. Ms. N5 49 J4
Aberdeen Pl. NW8 6 E5
Aberdeen Pl. NW8 57 G4
Aberdeen Rd. N5 49 J4
Aberdeen Rd. N18 33 E5
Aberdeen Rd. NW10 47 F5
Aberdeen Rd., Croy. 101 J4
Aberdeen Rd., Har. 37 C2
Aberdeen Ter. SE3 77 D2
Aberdour Rd., Ilf. 53 B3
Aberdour St. SE1 21 D1
Aberdour St. SE1 68 B4
Aberfeldy St. E14 60 C6
Aberford Gdns. SE18 79 B1
Aberford Rd., Borwd. 22 A2
Aberfoyle Rd. SW16 85 D6
Abergeldie Rd. SE12 78 H6
Abernethy Rd. SE13 78 E4
Abersham Rd. E8 50 C5
Abery St. SE18 70 H4
Abingdon Clo. NW1 49 D6
Camden Sq.
Abingdon Clo. SE1 21 G2
Abingdon Clo. SW19 84 F6
Abingdon Rd. N3 39 F2
Abingdon Rd. SW16 94 E2
Abingdon Rd. W8 66 D3
Abingdon St. SW1 16 A5
Abingdon St. SW1 67 E3
Abingdon Vill. W8 66 D3
Abinger Clo., Bark. 53 A4
Abinger Clo., Brom. 97 B3
Abinger Clo., Wall. 101 E5
Abinger Gdns., Islw. 73 B3
Sussex Ave.
Abinger Gro. SE8 68 J6

Abinger Ms. W9 57 D4
Warlock Rd.
Abinger Rd. W4 65 E3
Ablett St. SE16 68 F5
Abney Gdns. N16 50 C2
*Stoke Newington
High St.*
Aboyne Dr. SW20 92 G2
Aboyne Est. SW17 84 G3
Aboyne Rd. NW10 47 D3
Aboyne Rd. SW17 84 G3
Abridge Rd., Chig. 27 G6
Abridge Way, Bark. 62 B2
Abyssinia Clo. SW11 75 H4
Cairns Rd.
Acacia Ave. N17 33 A7
Acacia Ave., Brent. 64 E7
Acacia Ave., Mitch. 94 B2
Acacia Ave., Ruis. 45 A1
Acacia Ave., Wem. 46 H5
Acacia Clo. SE20 95 D2
Selby Rd.
Acacia Clo., Orp. 97 G5
Acacia Clo., Stan. 29 B6
Acacia Dr., Sutt. 100 C1
Acacia Gdns. NW8 6 F1
Acacia Gdns., 103 C2
W.Wick.
Acacia Gro. SE21 86 A2
Acacia Gro., N.Mal. 92 E3
Acacia Pl. NW8 6 F1
Acacia Rd. E11 51 E2
Acacia Rd. E17 41 H6
Acacia Rd. N22 40 G1
Acacia Rd. NW8 6 F1
Acacia Rd. NW8 57 G2
Acacia Rd. SW16 94 E1
Acacia Rd. W3 56 C7
Acacia Rd., Beck. 95 J3
Acacia Rd., Enf. 25 A1
Acacia Rd., Hmptn. 81 G6
Acacia Rd., Mitch. 94 A2
Acacia Way, Sid. 88 J1
Academy Gdns., 102 C1
Croy.
Academy Gdns., Nthlt. 54 D2
Academy Pl. SE18 79 C1
Academy Rd. SE18 79 C1
Acanthus Dr. SE1 21 H3
Acanthus Rd. SW11 76 A3
Accommodation Rd. 39 C7
NW11
Acer Ave., Hayes 54 E5
Jolly's La.
Acfold Rd. SW6 75 E1
Achilles Clo. SE1 21 J3
Achilles Clo. SE1 68 D5
Achilles Rd. NW6 48 D5
Achilles St. SE14 68 H7
Achilles Way W1 15 C2
Acklam Rd. W10 57 C5
Portobello Rd.
Acklington Dr. NW9 38 E1
Ackmar Rd. SW6 75 D1
Ackroyd Dr. E3 59 J5
Ackroyd Rd. SE23 77 G7
Ackworth Clo. N9 25 F7
Turin Rd.
Acland Cres. SE5 77 A4
Acland Rd. NW2 47 H6
Acol Cres., Ruis. 45 B5
Acol Rd. NW6 48 D7
Aconbury Rd., Dag. 62 B1
Acorn Clo. E4 34 B5
The Lawns
Acorn Clo., Chis. 88 F5
Acorn Clo., Enf. 24 H1
Acorn Clo., Stan. 29 E7
Acorn Ct., Ilf. 43 H6
Acorn Gdns. SE19 95 C1
Acorn Gdns. W3 56 D5
Acorn Par. SE15 68 E7
Carlton Gro.
Acorn Wk. SE16 68 H1
Acorn Way SE23 86 G3
Acorn Way, Orp. 104 E4
Acorns, The, Chig. 35 H4
Acorns Clo., Hmptn. 81 H6
Acre La. SW2 76 E4
Acre La., Cars. 101 A4
Acre La., Wall. 101 A4
Acre Path, Nthlt. 45 E6
Arnold Rd.
Acre Rd. SW19 84 G6
Acre Rd., Dag. 53 H7
Acre Rd., Kings.T. 91 H1

Acris St. SW18 75 F5
Acton Clo. N9 33 D2
Acton La. NW10 56 C3
Acton La. W3 65 C2
Acton La. W4 65 C4
Acton Ms. E8 59 C1
Acton Pk. Ind. Est. W3 65 D2
Acton St. WC1 8 C4
Acton St. WC1 58 F3
Acuba Rd. SW18 84 E1
Acworth Clo. N9 25 F7
Turin Rd.
Ada Gdns. E14 60 D6
Ada Gdns. E15 60 F1
Ada Pl. E2 59 D1
Ada Rd. SE5 68 B7
Ada Rd., Wem. 46 F3
Ada St. E8 59 E1
Adair Clo. SE25 95 E3
Adair Rd. W10 57 B4
Adair Twr. W10 57 B4
Appleford Rd.
Adam & Eve Ct. W1 11 G3
Adam & Eve Ms. W8 66 D3
Adam St. SW7 18 D1
Adam Pl. N16 50 C2
*Stoke Newington
High St.*
Adam St. WC2 12 B6
Adam St. WC2 58 E7
Adam Wk. SW6 65 J7
Adams Clo. N3 31 D7
Falkland Ave.
Adams Clo. NW9 47 B2
Adams Clo., Surb. 91 J6
Adams Ct. EC2 13 C3
Adams Gdns. Est. 68 F2
SE16
St. Marychurch St.
Adams Pl. E14 69 B1
North Colonnade
Adams Pl. N7 49 F5
Georges Rd.
Adams Rd. N17 41 A2
Adams Rd., Beck. 95 H5
Adams Row W1 11 C6
Adams Row W1 58 A7
Adams Sq., Bexh. 80 E3
Regency Way
Adams Way, Croy. 95 C6
Adamson Rd. E16 60 G6
Adamson Rd. NW3 48 G7
Adamsrill Clo., Enf. 25 A5
Adamsrill Rd. SE26 86 H4
Adare Wk. SW16 85 F3
Adastral Est. NW9 38 E1
Adcock Wk., Orp. 104 J4
Borkwood Pk.
Adderley Gdns. SE9 88 D4
Adderley Gro. SW11 76 A5
Culmstock Rd.
Adderley Rd., Har. 37 C1
Adderley St. E14 60 C6
Addington Ct. SW14 74 D3
Addington Dr. N12 31 F6
Addington Gro. SE26 86 H4
Addington Rd. E3 60 A3
Addington Rd. E16 60 E4
Addington Rd. N4 40 G6
Addington Rd., Croy. 101 G1
Addington Rd., 103 C4
W.Wick.
Addington Sq. SE5 21 A7
Addington Sq. SE5 68 A6
Addington St. SE1 16 D4
Addington Village 102 J6
Rd., Croy.
Addis Clo., Enf. 25 G1
Addiscombe Ave., 95 D7
Croy.
Addiscombe Clo., 37 F5
Har.
Addiscombe Ct. Rd., 102 B1
Croy.
Addiscombe Gro., 102 B2
Croy.
Addiscombe Rd., 102 B2
Croy.
Addison Ave. N14 24 B6
Addison Ave. W11 66 B3
Addison Ave., Houns. 72 J1
Addison Bri. Pl. W14 66 C4
Addison Clo., Nthwd. 36 A1
Addison Clo., Orp. 97 F6
Addison Cres. W14 66 B3
Addison Dr. SE12 78 H6
Eltham Rd.
Addison Gdns. W14 66 A3

Addison Gdns., Surb. 91 J4
Addison Gro. W4 65 E3
Addison Pl. W11 66 B1
Addison Pl., Sthl. 54 G7
Longford Ave.
Addison Rd. E11 42 G6
Addison Rd. E17 42 B5
Addison Rd. SE25 95 D4
Addison Rd. W14 66 B3
Addison Rd., Brom. 96 J5
Addison Rd., Enf. 25 F1
Addison Rd., Ilf. 43 F1
Addison Rd., Tedd. 82 E6
Addison Way NW11 39 C4
Addison Way, Hayes 54 A6
Addison's Clo., Croy. 102 J2
Addle Hill EC4 12 H4
Addle St. EC2 13 A2
Adecroft Way, W.Mol. 90 J3
Adela Ave., N.Mal. 92 H5
Adela St. W10 57 B4
Kensal Rd.
Adelaide Ave. SE4 77 J4
Adelaide Clo., Stan. 29 D4
Adelaide Cotts. W7 64 C2
Adelaide Gdns., Rom. 44 E5
Adelaide Gro. W12 65 G1
Adelaide Rd. E10 51 C3
Adelaide Rd. NW3 48 G7
Adelaide Rd. SW18 75 D5
Putney Bri. Rd.
Adelaide Rd. W13 64 D1
Adelaide Rd., Chis. 88 E5
Adelaide Rd., Houns. 72 E1
Adelaide Rd., Ilf. 52 E2
Adelaide Rd., Rich. 73 J4
Adelaide Rd., Sthl. 63 E4
Adelaide Rd., Surb. 91 H5
Adelaide Rd., Tedd. 82 C6
Adelaide St. WC2 12 A6
Adelaide Ter., Brent. 64 G5
Adelaide Wk. SW9 76 G4
Sussex Wk.
Adelina Gro. E1 59 F5
Adelina Ms. SW12 85 D1
King's Ave.
Adeline Pl. WC1 11 J2
Adeline Pl. WC1 58 D5
Adelphi Ter. WC2 12 B6
Adelphi Ter. WC2 58 E7
Aden Gro. N16 50 A4
Aden Rd., Enf. 25 H4
Aden Rd., Ilf. 43 E7
Aden Ter. N16 50 A4
Adeney Clo. W6 66 A6
Adenmore Rd. SE6 78 A7
Adie Rd. W6 65 J3
Adine Rd. E13 60 H4
Adler St. E1 13 H3
Adler St. E1 59 D6
Adley St. E5 50 H4
Admaston Rd. SE18 70 F6
Admiral Pl. SE16 68 H1
Admiral Seymour Rd. SE9 79 C4
Admiral Sq. SW10 75 F1
Admiral St. SE8 78 A1
Admirals Clo. E18 42 H4
Admirals Wk. NW3 48 F3
Admirals Way E14 69 A2
Admiralty Rd., Tedd. 82 C6
Adolf St. SE6 87 B4
Adolphus Rd. N4 49 H2
Adolphus St. SE8 68 J7
Adomar Rd., Dag. 53 D3
Adpar St. W2 10 E1
Adpar St. W2 57 G5
Adrian Ave. NW2 47 H1
North Circular Rd.
Adrian Ms. SW10 18 B5
Adrian Ms. SW10 66 E6
Adrienne Ave., Sthl. 54 F3
Advance Rd. SE27 85 J4
Adys Rd. SE15 77 C3
Aerodrome Rd. NW4 38 G3
Aerodrome Rd. NW9 38 F3
Aerodrome Way, Houns. 63 C6
Aeroville NW9 38 E2
Affleck St. N1 8 D2
Afghan Rd. SW11 75 H2
Agamemnon Rd. NW6 48 C5
Agar Clo., Surb. 98 J2
Agar Gro. NW1 49 C7
Agar Gro. Est. NW1 49 C7
Agar Pl. NW1 49 C7
Agar St. WC2 12 A6
Agar St. WC2 58 E7
Agate Clo. E16 61 A6
Agate Rd. W6 65 J3
Agatha Clo. E1 68 E1
Prusom St.
Agaton Rd. SE9 88 F2
Agave Rd. NW2 47 J4
Agdon St. EC1 8 G5
Agdon St. EC1 58 H4
Agincourt Rd. NW3 48 J4
Agnes Ave., Ilf. 52 E4
Agnes Clo. E6 61 D7
Agnes Gdns., Dag. 53 D4
Agnes Rd. W3 65 F1
Agnes St. E14 59 J6
Agnew Rd. SE23 77 G7
Agricola Pl., Enf. 25 C5
Aidan Clo., Dag. 53 E4
Aileen Wk. E15 51 F7
Devenay Rd.
Ailsa Ave., Twick. 73 D5
Ailsa Rd., Twick. 73 E5
Ailsa St. E14 60 C5
Ainger Ms. NW3 48 J7
Ainger Rd.
Ainger Rd. NW3 48 J7
Ainsdale Clo., Orp. 104 G1
Ainsdale Cres., Pnr. 36 G3
Ainsdale Rd. W5 55 G4
Ainsdale Rd., Wat. 28 C3
Ainsley Ave., Rom. 44 H6
Ainsley Clo. N9 33 B1
Ainsley St. E2 59 E3
Ainslie Wk. SW12 76 B7
Balham Gro.
Ainslie Wd. Cres. E4 34 B5
Ainslie Wd. Gdns. E4 34 B5
Ainslie Wd. Rd. E4 34 A5
Ainsty Est. SE16 68 G2
Needleman St.
Ainsworth Clo. NW2 47 G3
Ainsworth Rd. E9 50 F7
Ainsworth Rd., Croy. 101 H2
Ainsworth Way NW8 57 F1
Aintree Ave. E6 61 B1
Aintree Cres., Ilf. 43 F2
Aintree Est. SW6 66 B7
Dawes Rd.
Aintree Rd., Grnf. 55 E2
Aintree St. SW6 66 B7
Air St. W1 11 G6
Air St. W1 58 C7
Airdrie Clo. N1 49 F7
Airdrie Clo., Hayes 54 E5
Glencoe Rd.
Airedale Ave. W4 65 F4
Airedale Ave. S. W4 65 F5
Netheravon Rd. S.
Airedale Rd. SW12 75 J7
Airedale Rd. W5 64 F3
Airlie Gdns. W8 66 D1
Campden Hill Rd.
Airlie Gdns., Ilf. 52 E1
Airlinks Est., Houns. 63 C5
Airthrie Rd., Ilf. 53 B2
Aisgill Ave. W14 66 C5
Aisher Rd. SE28 62 C7
Aislibie Rd. SE12 78 E4
Aitken Clo. E8 59 D1
Pownall Rd.
Aitken Rd. SE6 87 B2
Aitken Rd., Barn. 22 J5
Ajax Ave. NW9 38 E3
Ajax Rd. NW6 48 C5
Akabusi Clo., Croy. 95 D6
Akehurst St. SW15 74 G6
Akenside Rd. NW3 48 G5
Akerman Rd. SW9 76 H2
Akerman Rd., Surb. 91 F6
Alabama St. SE18 70 G7
Alacross Rd. W5 64 F2
Alan Dr., Barn. 23 B6
Alan Gdns., Rom. 44 G7
Alan Hocken Way E15 60 E2
Manor Rd.
Alan Rd. SW19 84 B5
Alandale Dr., Pnr. 36 B2
Alanthus Clo. SE12 78 F5
Alaska St. SE1 16 E2
Alba Clo., Hayes 54 D4
Ramulis Dr.
Alba Gdns. NW11 39 B6
Alba Pl. W11 57 C6
Portobello Rd.
Albacore Cres. SE13 78 B6
Alban Cres., Borwd. 22 A1
Albany, The W1 11 F6
Albany, The, Wdf.Grn. 34 F4
Albany Clo. N15 40 H4
Albany Clo. SW14 74 B4
Albany Clo., Bex. 80 C7
Albany Ct. E4 26 B6
Chelwood Clo.
Albany Ctyd. W1 11 G6
Albany Cres., Edg. 30 A7
Albany Cres., Esher 98 B6
Albany Mans. SW11 66 H7
Albert Bri. Rd.
Albany Ms. N1 49 G7
Barnsbury Pk.
Albany Ms. SE5 21 A6
Albany Ms., Kings.T. 82 G6
Albany Ms., Sutt. 100 E5
Camden Rd.
Albany Pk. Ave., Enf. 25 F1
Albany Pk. Rd., Kings.T. 82 G6
Albany Pas., Rich. 73 J5
Albany Pl. N7 49 G4
Benwell Rd.
Albany Pl., Brent. 64 H6
Albany Rd. E10 42 A7
Albany Rd. E12 52 A4
Albany Rd. E17 41 H6
Albany Rd. N4 40 F6
Albany Rd. N18 33 E5
Albany Rd. SE5 21 B6
Albany Rd. SE5 68 A6
Albany Rd. SW19 84 E5
Albany Rd. W13 55 E7
Albany Rd., Belv. 71 F6
Albany Rd., Bex. 80 C7
Albany Rd., Brent. 64 G6
Albany Rd., Chis. 88 E5
Albany Rd., N.Mal. 92 D4
Albany Rd., Rich. 73 J5
Albert Rd.
Albany Rd., Rom. 44 F6
Albany St. NW1 7 D1
Albany St. NW1 58 B2
Albany Vw., Buck.H. 34 G1
Albatross St. SE18 70 H7
Albatross Way SE16 68 G2
Needleman St.
Albemarle SW19 84 A2
Albemarle App., Ilf. 43 E6
Albemarle Gdns., Ilf. 43 E6
Albemarle Gdns., N.Mal. 92 D4
Albemarle Pk., Stan. 29 F5
Albemarle Rd., Barn. 23 H7
Albemarle Rd., Beck. 96 B1
Albemarle St. W1 11 E6
Albemarle St. W1 58 B7
Albemarle Way EC1 8 G6
Albermarle Ave., Twick. 81 F1
Alberon Gdns. NW11 39 C4
Albert Ave. E4 34 A4
Albert Ave. SW8 67 F7
Albert Bri. SW3 18 H6
Albert Bri. SW3 66 H6
Albert Bri. SW11 18 H7
Albert Bri. SW11 66 H7
Albert Bri. Rd. SW11 18 H7
Albert Bri. Rd. SW11 66 H7
Albert Carr Gdns. SW16 85 E5
Albert Clo. E9 59 E1
Northiam St.
Albert Clo. N22 40 D1
Albert Ct. SW7 14 E4
Albert Ct. SW7 66 G2
Albert Cres. E4 34 A4
Albert Dr. SW19 84 B2
Albert Embk. SE1 20 B4
Albert Embk. SE1 67 E5
Albert Gdns. E1 59 G6
Albert Gro. SW20 93 A1
Albert Hall Mans. SW7 14 E4
Albert Mans. SW11 75 J1
Albert Bri. Rd.
Albert Ms. W8 14 C5
Albert Pl. N3 39 D1
Albert Pl. N17 41 C3
High Rd.
Albert Pl. W8 14 B4
Albert Pl. W8 66 E2
Albert Rd. E10 51 C2
Albert Rd. E16 70 B1
Albert Rd. E17 42 A5
Albert Rd. E18 42 H3
Albert Rd. N4 49 F1
Albert Rd. N15 41 B6
Albert Rd. N22 40 C1
Albert Rd. NW4 39 A4
Albert Rd. NW6 57 C2
Albert Rd. NW7 30 F5
Albert Rd. SE9 88 B3
Albert Rd. SE20 86 G6
Albert Rd. SE25 95 D4
Albert Rd. W5 55 E4
Albert Rd., Barn. 23 G4
Albert Rd., Belv. 71 F5
Albert Rd., Bex. 80 G6
Albert Rd., Brom. 97 A5
Albert Rd., Buck.H. 35 A2
Albert Rd., Dag. 53 G1
Albert Rd., Hmptn. 81 J5
Albert Rd., Har. 36 J3
Albert Rd., Houns. 72 G4
Albert Rd., Ilf. 52 E3
Albert Rd., Kings.T. 91 J2
Albert Rd., Mitch. 93 J3
Albert Rd., N.Mal. 92 F4
Albert Rd., Rich. 73 H5
Albert Rd., Sthl. 63 D3
Albert Rd., Sutt. 100 G5
Albert Rd., Tedd. 82 C6
Albert Rd., Twick. 82 C1
Albert Rd. Est., Belv. 71 F5
Albert Sq. E15 51 E5
Albert Sq. SW8 67 F7
Albert St. N12 31 F5
Albert St. NW1 58 B1
Albert Ter. NW1 58 A1
Albert Ter. NW10 56 D1
Albert Ter., Buck.H. 35 A2
Albert Ter. Ms. NW1 58 A1
Regents Pk. Rd.
Albert Wk. E16 70 D2
Pier Rd.
Alberta Ave., Sutt. 100 B4
Alberta Est. SE17 20 H3
Alberta Est. SE17 67 H5
Alberta Rd., Enf. 25 C6
Alberta Rd., Erith 80 J1
Alberta St. SE17 20 G3
Alberta St. SE17 67 H5
Albion Ave. N10 40 A1
Albion Ave. SW8 76 D2
Albion Clo. W2 10 H5
Albion Dr. E8 50 C7
Albion Est. SE16 68 F2
Albion Gdns. W6 65 H4
Albion Gro. N16 50 B4
Albion Hill, Loug. 26 J5
Albion Ms. N1 49 G7
Albion Ms. NW6 48 C7
Kilburn High Rd.
Albion Ms. W2 10 H5
Albion Ms. W2 57 H6
Albion Pk., Loug. 27 A5
Albion Pl. EC1 12 G1
Albion Pl. EC1 58 H5
Albion Pl. SE25 95 D3
High St.
Albion Rd. E17 42 C3
Albion Rd. N16 50 A4
Albion Rd. N17 41 D2
Albion Rd., Bexh. 80 F4
Albion Rd., Houns. 72 G4
Albion Rd., Kings.T. 92 C1
Albion Rd., Sutt. 100 G6
Albion Rd., Twick. 82 B1
Albion Sq. E8 50 C7
Albion St. SE16 68 F2
Albion St. W2 10 H4
Albion St. W2 57 H6
Albion St., Croy. 101 H1
Albion Ter. E8 50 C7
Albion Vill. Rd. SE26 86 F3
Albion Way EC1 12 J2
Albion Way SE13 78 C4
Albion Way, Wem. 47 B3
North End Rd.
Albrighton Rd. SE22 77 B3
Albuhera Clo., Enf. 24 G1
Albury Ave., Bexh. 80 E2
Albury Ave., Islw. 64 C7
Albury Clo., Hmptn. 81 G6
Albury Dr., Pnr. 36 C1
Albury Ms. E12 51 J1
Albury Rd., Chess. 98 H5
Albury St. SE8 69 A6
Albyfield, Brom. 97 C3
Albyn Rd. SE8 78 A1
Alcester Cres. E5 50 E2
Alcester Rd., Wall. 101 B4
Alcock Clo., Wall. 101 D7
Alcock Rd., Houns. 63 D7
Alconbury Rd. E5 50 D2
Alcorn Clo., Sutt. 100 D2
Alcott Clo. W7 55 C5
Westcott Cres.

Alcuin Ct., Stan. 29 F6
Aldborough Rd., Dag. 53 J6
Aldborough Rd. N., Ilf. 43 J5
Aldborough Rd. S., Ilf. 52 H1
Aldbourne Rd. W12 65 F1
Aldbridge St. SE17 21 E3
Aldbridge St. SE17 68 B5
Aldburgh Ms. W1 11 C3
Aldbury Ave., Wem. 47 B7
Aldbury Ms. N9 25 A7
Aldebert Ter. SW8 67 E7
Aldeburgh Clo. E5 50 E2 *Southwold Rd.*
Aldeburgh Pl., Wdf.Grn. 34 G4
Aldeburgh St. SE10 69 G5
Alden Ave. E15 60 F4
Aldenham St. NW1 7 G2
Aldenham St. NW1 58 C2
Aldensley Rd. W6 65 H3
Alder Clo. SE15 21 G6
Alder Clo. SE15 68 C6
Alder Gro. NW2 47 G2
Alder Ms. N19 49 C2 *Bredgar Rd.*
Alder Rd. SW14 74 D3
Alder Rd., Sid. 88 J3
Alderbrook Rd. SW12 76 B6
Alderbury Rd. SW13 65 G6
Aldergrove Gdns., Houns. 72 E2 *Bath Rd.*
Alderholt Way SE15 21 E7
Alderman Ave., Bark. 62 A3
Alderman Judge Mall, Kings.T. 91 H2 *Eden St.*
Aldermanbury EC2 13 A3
Aldermanbury EC2 58 J6
Aldermanbury Sq. EC2 13 A2
Aldermans Hill N13 32 E4
Alderman's Wk. EC2 13 D2
Aldermary Rd., Brom. 96 G1
Aldermoor Rd. SE6 86 J3
Alderney Ave., Houns. 63 H7
Alderney Gdns., Nthlt. 45 F7
Alderney Rd. E1 59 G4
Alderney St. SW1 19 E3
Alderney St. SW1 67 B4
Alders, The N21 24 G6
Alders, The, Felt. 81 E4
Alders, The, Houns. 63 F6
Alders, The, W.Wick. 103 B1
Alders Ave., Wdf.Grn. 34 E6
Alders Clo. E11 51 H2 *Aldersbrook Rd.*
Alders Clo. W5 64 G3
Alders Clo., Edg. 30 C5
Alders Gro., E.Mol. 91 A5 *Esher Rd.*
Alders Rd., Edg. 30 C5
Aldersbrook Ave., Enf. 25 B2
Aldersbrook Dr., Kings.T. 82 J6
Aldersbrook La. E12 52 C3
Aldersbrook Rd. E11 51 H2
Aldersbrook Rd. E12 51 H2
Aldersey Gdns., Bark. 52 G6
Aldersford Clo. SE4 77 G5
Aldersgate St. EC1 12 J1
Aldersgate St. EC1 58 J5
Aldersgrove Ave. SE9 87 J3
Aldershot Rd. NW6 57 C1
Aldersmead Ave., Croy. 95 G6
Aldersmead Rd., Beck. 86 H7
Alderson Pl., Sthl. 63 J1
Alderson St. W10 57 B4 *Kensal Rd.*
Alderton Clo. NW10 47 D3
Alderton Clo., Loug. 27 D4
Alderton Cres. NW4 38 H5
Alderton Hall La., Loug. 27 D4
Alderton Hill, Loug. 27 B5
Alderton Ri., Loug. 27 D4
Alderton Rd. SE24 76 J3
Alderton Rd., Croy. 95 C7
Alderton Way NW4 38 H5
Alderton Way, Loug. 27 C5
Alderville Rd. SW6 75 C2
Alderwick Dr., Houns. 73 A3
Alderwood Rd. SE9 79 G6
Aldford St. W1 15 B1
Aldford St. W1 67 A1
Aldgate EC3 13 F4
Aldgate EC3 59 B6
Aldgate Ave. E1 13 F3
Aldgate High St. EC3 13 F4
Aldgate High St. EC3 59 C6
Aldine Ct. W12 65 J1 *Aldine St.*
Aldine Pl. W12 65 J1 *Uxbridge Rd.*
Aldine St. W12 65 J1
Aldington Clo., Dag. 44 C7
Aldington Rd. SE18 70 A3
Aldis Ms. SW17 84 H5 *Aldis St.*
Aldis St. SW17 84 H5
Aldred Rd. NW6 48 D5
Aldren Rd. SW17 84 F3
Aldrich Ter. SW18 84 F2 *Lidiard Rd.*
Aldriche Way E4 34 C6
Aldridge Ave., Edg. 30 B3
Aldridge Ave., Ruis. 45 D2
Aldridge Ave., Stan. 37 H1
Aldridge Ri., N.Mal. 92 E7
Aldridge Rd. Vill. W11 57 C5
Aldridge Wk. N14 24 E7
Aldrington Rd. SW16 85 C4
Aldsworth Clo. W9 6 A6
Aldsworth Clo. W9 57 E4
Aldwick Clo. SE9 88 G3
Aldwick Rd., Croy. 101 F3
Aldworth Gro. SE13 78 C6
Aldworth Rd. E15 51 E7
Aldwych WC2 12 C5
Aldwych WC2 58 F7
Aldwych Ave., Ilf. 43 F4
Alers Rd., Bexh. 80 D5
Aleston Beck Rd. E16 61 A6 *Fulmer Rd.*
Alexa Ct. W8 66 D4 *Lexham Gdns.*
Alexander Ave. NW10 47 H7
Alexander Clo., Barn. 23 G4
Alexander Clo., Brom. 103 G1
Alexander Clo., Sid. 79 H6
Alexander Clo., Sthl. 63 J1
Alexander Clo., Twick. 82 C2
Alexander Ms. W2 10 A3
Alexander Pl. SW7 18 G1
Alexander Pl. SW7 66 H4
Alexander Rd. N19 49 E3
Alexander Rd., Bexh. 80 D2
Alexander Rd., Chis. 88 E5
Alexander Sq. SW3 18 G1
Alexander Sq. SW3 66 H4
Alexander St. W2 57 D6
Alexandra Ave. N22 40 D1
Alexandra Ave. SW11 76 A1
Alexandra Ave. W4 65 D7
Alexandra Ave., Har. 45 F1
Alexandra Ave., Sthl. 54 F7
Alexandra Ave., Sutt. 100 D3
Alexandra Clo., Har. 45 G3 *Alexandra Ave.*
Alexandra Cotts. SE14 77 J1
Alexandra Ct. N14 24 C5
Alexandra Ct., Wem. 46 J4
Alexandra Cres., Brom. 87 F6
Alexandra Dr. SE19 86 B5
Alexandra Dr., Surb. 92 A7
Alexandra Est. NW8 57 E1
Alexandra Gdns. N10 40 B4
Alexandra Gdns. W4 65 E7
Alexandra Gdns., Houns. 72 H2
Alexandra Gro. N4 49 H1
Alexandra Gro. N12 31 E5
Alexandra Ms. N2 39 J3 *Fortis Grn.*
Alexandra Palace Way N22 40 C4
Alexandra Pk. Rd. N10 40 B2
Alexandra Pk. Rd. N22 40 C1
Alexandra Pl. NW8 57 F1
Alexandra Pl. SE25 95 A5
Alexandra Pl., Croy. 102 B1 *Alexandra Rd.*
Alexandra Rd. E6 61 D3
Alexandra Rd. E10 51 C3
Alexandra Rd. E17 41 J6
Alexandra Rd. E18 42 H3
Alexandra Rd. N8 40 G3
Alexandra Rd. N9 25 E7
Alexandra Rd. N10 40 B1
Alexandra Rd. N15 41 A5
Alexandra Rd. NW4 39 A4
Alexandra Rd. NW8 48 F7
Alexandra Rd. SE26 86 G6
Alexandra Rd. SW14 74 D3
Alexandra Rd. SW19 84 C6
Alexandra Rd. W4 65 D2
Alexandra Rd., Brent. 64 G6
Alexandra Rd., Croy. 102 B1
Alexandra Rd., Enf. 25 G4
Alexandra Rd., Houns. 72 H2
Alexandra Rd., Kings.T. 83 A7
Alexandra Rd., Mitch. 84 H7
Alexandra Rd., Rich. 73 J2
Alexandra Rd., Rom. (Chadwell Heath) 44 D6
Alexandra Rd., T.Ditt. 91 C5
Alexandra Rd., Twick. 73 F6
Alexandra Sq., Mord. 93 D5
Alexandra St. E16 60 G5
Alexandra St. SE14 68 H7
Alexandra Wk. SE19 86 B5
Alexandria Rd. W13 55 D7
Alexis St. SE16 21 J1
Alexis St. SE16 68 D4
Alfearn Rd. E5 50 F4
Alford Grn., Croy. 103 D6
Alford Pl. N1 9 A2
Alford Rd. SW8 76 D1
Alford Rd., Erith 71 J5
Alfoxton Ave. N15 40 H4
Alfred Gdns., Sthl. 54 E7
Alfred Ms. W1 11 H1
Alfred Ms. W1 58 D5
Alfred Pl. WC1 11 H1
Alfred Pl. WC1 58 D5
Alfred Prior Ho. E12 52 D4
Alfred Rd. E15 51 F5
Alfred Rd. SE25 95 D5
Alfred Rd. W2 57 D5
Alfred Rd. W3 65 C1
Alfred Rd., Belv. 71 F5
Alfred Rd., Buck.H. 35 A2
Alfred Rd., Felt. 81 C2
Alfred Rd., Kings.T. 91 H3
Alfred Rd., Sutt. 100 F5
Alfred St. E3 59 J3
Alfred St. E16 60 F7
Alfreda St. SW11 76 B1
Alfred's Gdns., Bark. 61 H2
Alfreds Way, Bark. 61 F3
Alfreds Way Ind. Est., Bark. 62 A1
Alfreton Clo. SW19 84 A3
Alfriston Ave., Croy. 94 E7
Alfriston Ave., Har. 36 G6
Alfriston Clo., Surb. 91 J5
Alfriston Rd. SW11 75 J5
Algar Clo., Islw. 73 D3 *Algar Rd.*
Algar Clo., Stan. 29 C5
Algar Rd., Islw. 73 D3
Algarve Rd. SW18 84 E1
Algernon Rd. NW4 38 G6
Algernon Rd. NW6 57 D1
Algernon Rd. SE13 78 B3
Algers Clo., Loug. 27 A5
Algers Mead, Loug. 27 A5
Algers Rd., Loug. 27 A5
Algiers Rd. SE13 78 A4
Alibon Gdns., Dag. 53 G5
Alibon Rd., Dag. 53 F5
Alice Gilliatt Ct. W14 66 C5
Alice La. E3 59 J1
Alice Ms., Tedd. 82 C5 *Luther Rd.*
Alice St. SE1 17 D6
Alice St. SE1 68 B3
Alice Thompson Clo. SE12 87 J2
Alice Walker Clo. SE24 76 H4 *Shakespeare Rd.*
Alice Way, Houns. 72 H4
Alicia Ave., Har. 37 E4
Alicia Clo., Har. 37 F4
Alicia Gdns., Har. 37 E4
Alie St. E1 13 G4
Alie St. E1 59 C6
Alington Cres. NW9 47 C1
Alison Clo. E6 61 D6
Alison Clo., Croy. 102 G1 *Shirley Oaks Rd.*
Aliwal Rd. SW11 75 H4
Alkerden Rd. W4 65 E5
Alkham Rd. N16 50 C1
All Hallows Rd. N17 41 B1
All Saints Clo. N9 33 D2
All Saints Dr. SE3 78 E2
All Saints Ms., Stan. 29 B6 *Uxbridge Rd.*
All Saints Pas. SW18 75 E5 *Wandsworth High St.*
All Saints Rd. SW19 84 F7
All Saints Rd. W3 65 C3
All Saints Rd. W11 57 C6
All Saints Rd., Sutt. 100 E3
All Saints St. N1 8 C1
All Saints St. N1 58 F2
All Saints Twr. E10 42 B7
All Souls Ave. NW10 56 H2
All Souls Pl. W1 11 E2
Allan Barclay Clo. N15 41 C6 *High Rd.*
Allan Clo., N.Mal. 92 D5
Allan Way W3 56 C5
Allandale Ave. N3 39 B3
Allard Cres. (Bushey), Wat. 28 J1
Allard Gdns. SW4 76 D5
Allardyce St. SW4 76 F4
Allbrook Clo., Tedd. 82 B5
Allcroft Rd. NW5 49 A5
Allen Clo., Sun. 90 B1
Allen Ct., Grnf. 46 C5
Allen Edwards Dr. SW8 76 E1
Allen Pl., Twick. 82 D1 *Church St.*
Allen Rd. E3 59 J2
Allen Rd. N16 50 B4
Allen Rd., Beck. 95 G2
Allen Rd., Croy. 101 F1
Allen Rd., Sun. 90 B1
Allen St. W8 66 D3
Allenby Clo., Grnf. 54 G3
Allenby Rd. SE23 86 H3
Allenby Rd., Sthl. 54 G3
Allendale Ave., Sthl. 54 G6
Allendale Clo. SE5 77 A1 *Daneville Rd.*
Allendale Clo. SE26 86 G5
Allendale Rd., Grnf. 46 E6
Allens Rd., Enf. 25 F5
Allensbury Pl. NW1 49 D7
Allenswood Rd. SE9 79 B3
Allerford Ct., Har. 36 H5
Allerford Rd. SE6 87 B3
Allerton Rd. N16 49 J2
Allerton Wk. N7 49 F2 *Durham Rd.*
Allestree Rd. SW6 66 B7
Alleyn Cres. SE21 86 A2
Alleyn Pk. SE21 86 A2
Alleyn Pk., Sthl. 63 G5
Alleyn Rd. SE21 86 A3
Alleyndale Rd., Dag. 53 C2
Allfarthing La. SW18 75 E6
Allgood Clo., Mord. 93 A6
Allgood St. E2 9 G2
Allgood St. E2 59 C2
Allhallows La. EC4 13 B6
Allhallows Rd. E6 61 B5
Alliance Clo., Wem. 46 G4 *Milford Gdns.*
Alliance Rd. E13 60 J4
Alliance Rd. SE18 71 A6
Alliance Rd. W3 56 B4
Allied Ind. Est. W3 65 E2
Allied Way W3 65 E2 *Larden Rd.*
Allingham Clo. W7 55 C7
Allingham St. N1 8 J1
Allingham St. N1 58 J2
Allington Ave. N17 33 B6
Allington Clo. SW19 84 A5 *High St. Wimbledon*
Allington Clo., Grnf. 45 J7
Allington Ct. SW19 84 A5 *High St. Wimbledon*
Allington Ct., Enf. 25 G5
Allington Rd. NW4 38 H5
Allington Rd. W10 57 B2
Allington Rd., Har. 36 J5
Allington Rd., Orp. 104 G2
Allington St. SW1 15 E6
Allington St. SW1 67 B3
Allison Clo. SE10 78 C1 *Dartmouth Hill*
Allison Gro. SE21 86 B1
Allison Rd. N8 40 G5
Allison Rd. W3 56 C6
Allitsen Rd. NW8 6 G2
Allitsen Rd. NW8 57 H2
Allnutt Way SW4 76 D5
Alloa Rd. SE8 68 H5
Alloa Rd., Ilf. 53 A2
Allonby Gdns., Wem. 46 F1
Alloway Rd. E3 59 H3

Allsop Pl. NW1 — 7 A6
Allsop Pl. NW1 — 57 J4
Allum Way N20 — 31 F1
Allwood Clo. SE26 — 86 G4
Alma Ave. E4 — 34 C7
Alma Cres., Sutt. — 100 B5
Alma Gro. SE1 — **21 G2**
Alma Gro. SE1 — 68 C4
  Harrow Rd.
Alma Pl. NW10 — 56 H3
  Harrow Rd.
Alma Pl. SE19 — 86 C7
  Church Rd.
Alma Pl., Th.Hth. — 94 G5
Alma Pl. N10 — 32 B7
Alma Rd. SW18 — 75 F4
Alma Rd., Cars. — 100 H5
Alma Rd., Enf. — 25 H3
Alma Rd., Esher — 98 B1
Alma Rd., Sid. — 89 A3
Alma Rd., Sthl. — 54 E7
Alma Row, Har. — 37 A1
Alma Sq. NW8 — **6 D3**
Alma Sq. NW8 — 57 F3
Alma St. E15 — 51 D6
Alma St. NW5 — 49 B6
Alma Ter. SW18 — 75 G7
Almack Rd. E5 — 50 F4
Almeida St. N1 — 49 H7
Almer Rd. SW20 — 83 G7
Almeric Rd. SW11 — 75 J4
Almington St. N4 — 49 E1
Almond Ave. W5 — 64 H3
Almond Ave., Cars. — 100 J2
Almond Clo. SE15 — 77 D2
Almond Clo., Brom. — 97 D7
Almond Gro., Brent. — 64 E7
Almond Rd. N17 — 33 D7
Almond Rd. SE16 — 68 E4
Almond Way, Borwd. — 22 B4
Almond Way, Brom. — 97 D7
Almond Way, Har. — 36 H2
Almond Way, Mitch. — 94 D5
Almonds Ave., — 34 G2
  Buck.H.
Almorah Rd. N1 — 50 A7
Almorah Rd., Houns. — 72 D1
Alnwick Gro., Mord. — 93 E4
  Bordesley Rd.
Alnwick Rd. E16 — 60 J6
Alnwick Rd. SE12 — 78 H7
Alperton La., Grnf. — 55 G2
Alperton La., Wem. — 55 G2
Alperton St. W10 — 57 B4
Alpha Clo. NW1 — **6 H4**
Alpha Gro. E14 — 69 A2
Alpha Pl. NW6 — 57 D2
Alpha Pl. SW3 — **18 H5**
Alpha Pl. SW3 — 66 H6
Alpha Rd. E4 — 34 A3
Alpha Rd. N18 — 33 D6
Alpha Rd. SE14 — 77 J1
Alpha Rd., Croy. — 102 B1
Alpha Rd., Enf. — 25 H4
Alpha Rd., Surb. — 91 J6
Alpha Rd., Tedd. — 82 A5
Alpha St. SE15 — 77 D2
Alphabet Sq. E3 — 60 A5
  Hawgood St.
Alphea Clo. SW19 — 84 H7
  Courtney Rd.
Alpine Ave., Surb. — 99 C2
Alpine Clo., Croy. — 102 B3
Alpine Copse, Brom. — 97 D2
Alpine Rd. SE16 — 68 F4
Alpine Rd., Walt. — 90 A7
Alpine Vw., Sutt. — 100 H5
Alpine Wk., Stan. — 29 B2
Alpine Way E6 — 61 D5
Alric Ave. NW10 — 47 D7
Alric Ave., N.Mal. — 92 E3
Alroy Rd. N4 — 40 G7
Alsace Rd. SE17 — **21 D3**
Alsace Rd. SE17 — 68 B5
Alscot Rd. SE1 — **21 G1**
Alscot Rd. SE1 — 68 C4
Alscot Way SE1 — **21 F1**
Alscot Way SE1 — 68 C4
Alsike Rd. SE2 — 71 D3
Alsike Rd., Erith — 71 E3
Alsom Ave., Wor.Pk. — 99 F4
Alston Clo., Surb. — 91 E7
Alston Rd. N18 — 33 E5
Alston Rd. SW17 — 84 G4
Alston Rd., Barn. — 23 B3
Alt Gro. SW19 — 84 C7
  St. George's Rd.
Altair Clo. N17 — 33 C6
Altash Way SE9 — 88 C2

Altenburg Ave. W13 — 64 E3
Altenburg Gdns. SW11 — 75 J4
Altham Rd., Pnr. — 28 E7
Althea St. SW6 — 75 E2
Althorne Gdns. E18 — 42 F4
Althorne Way, Dag. — 53 G2
Althorp Rd. SW17 — 84 J1
Althorpe Gro. SW11 — 75 G1
  Westbridge Rd.
Althorpe Ms. SW11 — 75 G1
  Westbridge Rd.
Althorpe Rd., Har. — 36 J5
Altmore Ave. E6 — 52 C7
Alton Ave., Stan. — 29 C7
Alton Clo., Bex. — 89 E1
Alton Clo., Islw. — 73 C2
Alton Gdns., Beck. — 87 A7
Alton Gdns., Twick. — 73 A6
Alton Rd. N17 — 41 A3
Alton Rd. SW15 — 83 G1
Alton Rd., Croy. — 101 G3
Alton Rd., Rich. — 73 H4
Alton St. E14 — 60 B5
Altyre Clo., Beck. — 95 J5
Altyre Rd., Croy. — 102 A2
Altyre Way, Beck. — 95 J6
Alva Way, Wat. — 28 D2
Alvanley Gdns. NW6 — 48 E5
Alverston Gdns. SE25 — 95 B5
Alverstone Ave. SW19 — 84 D2
Alverstone Ave., Barn. — 23 H7
Alverstone Gdns. SE9 — 88 F1
Alverstone Rd. E12 — 52 D4
Alverstone Rd. NW2 — 47 J7
Alverstone Rd., — 92 F4
  N.Mal.
Alverstone Rd., Wem. — 46 J1
Alverton St. SE8 — 68 J5
Alveston Ave., Har. — 37 E3
Alvey Est. SE17 — **21 D2**
Alvey St. SE17 — **21 D3**
Alvey St. SE17 — 68 B5
Alvia Gdns., Sutt. — 100 F4
Alvington Cres. E8 — 50 C5
Alway Ave., Epsom — 99 C5
Alwold Cres. SE12 — 78 H6
Alwyn Ave. W4 — 65 D5
Alwyn Clo., Croy. — 103 B7
Alwyn Gdns. NW4 — 38 G4
Alwyn Gdns. W3 — 56 H6
Alwyne La. N1 — 49 H7
  Alwyne Vill.
Alwyne Pl. N1 — 49 J6
Alwyne Rd. N1 — 49 J7
Alwyne Rd. SW19 — 84 C6
Alwyne Rd. W7 — 55 B7
Alwyne Sq. N1 — 49 J6
Alwyne Vill. N1 — 49 H7
Alyth Gdns. NW11 — 39 D6
Alzette Ho. E2 — 59 G2
  Mace St.
Amalgamated Dr., — 64 D6
  Brent.
Amanda Clo., Ilf. — 35 G6
Amazon St. E1 — 59 E6
  Hessel St.
Ambassador Clo., — 72 E2
  Houns.
Ambassador Gdns. E6 — 61 C5
Ambassador Sq. E14 — 69 B4
Ambassador's Ct. — **15 G2**
SW1
Amber Ave. E17 — 41 H1
Amber Gro. NW2 — 48 A1
  Prayle Gro.
Amber St. E15 — 51 D6
  Salway Rd.
Amberden Ave. N3 — 39 D3
Ambergate St. SE17 — **20 H3**
Ambergate St. SE17 — 67 H5
Amberley Clo., Orp. — 104 J5
  Warnford Rd.
Amberley Clo., Pnr. — 36 F3
Amberley Ct., Sid. — 89 C5
Amberley Gdns., Enf. — 25 B7
Amberley Gdns., — 99 F4
  Epsom
Amberley Gro. SE26 — 86 E5
Amberley Gro., Croy. — 95 C7
Amberley Rd. E10 — 42 A7
Amberley Rd. N13 — 32 F2
Amberley Rd. SE2 — 71 D6
Amberley Rd. W9 — 57 D5
Amberley Rd., Buck.H. — 34 J1
Amberley Rd., Enf. — 25 C7
Amberley Way, — 72 C5
  Houns.
Amberley Way, Mord. — 93 C7

Amberley Way, Rom. — 44 H4
Amberwood Ri., — 92 E6
  N.Mal.
Amblecote Clo. SE12 — 87 H3
Amblecote Meadows — 87 H3
  SE12
Amblecote Rd. SE12 — 87 H3
Ambler Rd. N4 — 49 H3
Ambleside, Brom. — 87 D6
Ambleside Ave. — 85 D4
  SW16
Ambleside Ave., Beck. — 95 H5
Ambleside Clo. E9 — 50 F5
  Churchill Wk.
Ambleside Clo. E10 — 42 B7
  Clyde Pl.
Ambleside Cres., Enf. — 25 G3
Ambleside Gdns., Ilf. — 43 B4
Ambleside Gdns., — 100 F6
  Sutt.
Ambleside Gdns., — 46 G1
  Wem.
Ambleside Rd. NW10 — 47 F7
Ambleside Rd., Bexh. — 80 G2
Ambrosden Ave. SW1 — **15 G6**
Ambrose Ave. NW11 — 39 B7
Ambrose Clo. E6 — 61 B5
  Lovage App.
Ambrose Clo., Orp. — 104 J3
  Stapleton Rd.
Ambrose Ms. SW11 — 75 J2
  Abercrombie St.
Ambrose St. SE16 — 68 E4
Ambrose Wk. E3 — 60 A2
  Malmesbury Rd.
Amelia St. SE17 — **20 J3**
Amelia St. SE17 — 67 H5
Amen Cor. EC4 — **12 H4**
Amen Cor. SW17 — 84 J6
Amen Ct. EC4 — **12 H3**
America Sq. EC3 — **13 F5**
America St. SE1 — **16 J2**
Amerland Rd. SW18 — 75 C5
Amersham Ave. N18 — 33 A6
Amersham Gro. SE14 — 77 J1
Amersham Rd. SE14 — 77 J1
Amersham Rd., Croy. — 94 J6
Amersham Vale SE14 — 68 J7
Amery Gdns. NW10 — 56 H1
Amery Rd., Har. — 46 D2
Amesbury Ave. SW2 — 85 E2
Amesbury Clo., — 99 J1
  Wor.Pk.
Amesbury Dr. E4 — 26 B6
Amesbury Rd., Brom. — 97 A3
Amesbury Rd., Dag. — 53 D7
Amesbury Rd., Felt. — 81 D2
Amethyst Rd. E15 — 51 D4
Amherst Ave. W13 — 55 F6
Amherst Dr., Orp. — 97 J4
Amherst Rd. W13 — 55 F6
Amhurst Gdns., Islw. — 73 C1
Amhurst Pk. N16 — 41 A7
Amhurst Pas. E8 — 50 D5
Amhurst Rd. E8 — 50 E5
Amhurst Rd. N16 — 50 C4
Amhurst Ter. E8 — 50 D4
Amhurst Wk. SE28 — 71 A1
  Pitfield Cres.
Amidas Gdns., Dag. — 53 B4
Amiel St. E1 — 59 F4
Amies St. SW11 — 75 J3
Amina Way SE16 — **17 H6**
Amis Ave., Epsom — 99 A6
Amity Gro. SW20 — 92 J1
Amity Rd. E15 — 60 F1
Ammanford Gdn. — 38 E6
  NW9
  Ruthin Clo.
Amner Rd. SW11 — 76 A6
Amoco Ho. W5 — 55 H3
Amor Rd. W6 — 65 J3
Amott Rd. SE15 — 77 D3
Amoy Pl. E14 — 60 A6
Ampere Way, Croy. — 94 F7
Ampleforth Rd. SE2 — 71 B2
Ampthill Sq. Est. NW1 — **7 G2**
Ampton Pl. WC1 — **8 C4**
Ampton Pl. WC1 — 58 F3
Ampton St. WC1 — **8 C4**
Ampton St. WC1 — 58 F3
Amroth Clo. SE23 — 86 D5
Amsterdam Rd. E14 — 69 C3
Amwell Clo., Enf. — 25 A5
Amwell Ct. Est. N4 — 49 J1
Amwell St. EC1 — **8 E3**

Amwell St. EC1 — 58 G3
Amyand Cotts., Twick. — 73 E6
  Amyand Pk. Rd.
Amyand La., Twick. — 73 E7
  Marble Hill Gdns.
Amyand Pk. Gdns., — 73 E7
  Twick.
  Amyand Pk. Rd.
Amyand Pk. Rd., — 73 D7
  Twick.
Amyruth Rd. SE4 — 78 A5
Anatola Rd. N19 — 49 B2
  Dartmouth Pk. Hill
Ancaster Cres., N.Mal. — 92 G6
Ancaster Ms., Beck. — 95 G3
  Ancaster Rd.
Ancaster Rd., Beck. — 95 G3
Ancaster St. SE18 — 70 H7
Anchor & Hope La. — 69 J4
  SE7
Anchor Ms. SW12 — 76 B6
  Hazelbourne Rd.
Anchor St. SE16 — 68 E4
Anchor Yd. EC1 — **9 A5**
Anchorage Clo. SW19 — 84 D5
Ancill Clo. W6 — 66 B6
Ancona Rd. NW10 — 56 G2
Ancona Rd. SE18 — 70 G5
Andace Pk. Gdns., — 96 J1
  Brom.
Andalus Rd. SW9 — 76 E3
Ander Clo., Wem. — 46 G4
Anderson Clo. W3 — 56 D6
Anderson Ho., Bark. — 61 G2
  The Coverdales
Anderson Pl., Houns. — 72 H4
Anderson Rd. E9 — 50 G6
Anderson Rd., — 43 A3
  Wdf.Grn.
Anderson St. SW3 — **18 J3**
Anderson St. SW3 — 66 J5
Anderson Way, Belv. — 71 H2
Anderton Clo. SE5 — 77 A3
Andover Clo., Grnf. — 54 H4
  Ruislip Rd.
Andover Pl. NW6 — **6 A1**
Andover Pl. NW6 — 57 E2
Andover Rd. N7 — 49 F2
Andover Rd., Orp. — 104 H2
Andover Rd., Twick. — 82 A1
Andre St. E8 — 50 D5
Andrew Borde St. — **11 J3**
WC2
Andrew Clo., Ilf. — 35 G6
Andrew Pl. SW8 — 76 D1
  Cowthorpe Rd.
Andrew St. E14 — 60 C6
Andrews Clo. E6 — 61 B6
  Linton Gdns.
Andrews Clo., Buck.H. — 34 J2
Andrews Clo., Har. — 37 A7
  Bessborough Rd.
Andrews Clo., Wor.Pk. — 99 J2
Andrews Crosse WC2 — **12 E4**
Andrews Pl. SE9 — 79 E6
Andrew's Rd. E8 — 59 E1
Andrews Wk. SE17 — **20 H6**
Andwell Clo. SE2 — 71 B2
Anerley Gro. SE19 — 86 C7
Anerley Hill SE19 — 86 C6
Anerley Pk. SE20 — 86 D7
Anerley Pk. Rd. SE20 — 86 E7
Anerley Rd. SE19 — 86 D7
Anerley Rd. SE20 — 86 D7
Anerley Sta. Rd. SE20 — 95 E1
Anerley St. SW11 — 75 J2
Anerley Vale SE19 — 86 C7
Anfield Clo. SW12 — 76 C7
  Belthorn Cres.
Angel All. E1 — **13 G3**
Angel Clo. N18 — 33 C5
Angel Ct. EC2 — **13 C3**
Angel Ct. SW1 — **15 G2**
Angel Ct. SW17 — 84 J4
Angel Hill, Sutt. — 100 E3
  Sutton Common Rd.
Angel Hill Dr., Sutt. — 100 E3
Angel La. E15 — 51 D6
Angel Ms. N1 — **8 F2**
Angel Ms. N1 — 58 G2
Angel Pas. EC4 — **13 B6**
Angel Pl. N18 — 33 D5
  Angel Clo.
Angel Pl. SE1 — **17 B3**
Angel Rd. N18 — 33 D5
Angel Rd., Har. — 37 B6
Angel Rd., T.Ditt. — 91 D7
Angel Rd. Wks. N18 — 33 F5

Angel St. EC1 — **12 J3**
Angel St. EC1 — 58 J6
Angel Wk. W6 — 65 J5
Angelfield, Houns. — 72 H4
Angelica Dr. E6 — 61 D5
Angelica Gdns., Croy. — 102 G1
Angell Pk. Gdns. SW9 — 76 G3
Angell Rd. SW9 — 76 G3
Angerstein La. SE3 — 78 F1
Angle Grn., Dag. — 53 C1
  Burnside Rd.
Anglers Clo., Rich. — 82 F4
  Locksmeade Rd.
Angler's La. NW5 — 49 B6
Angles Rd. SW16 — 85 E4
Anglesea Ave. SE18 — 70 E4
Anglesea Rd. SE18 — 70 E4
Anglesea Rd., Kings.T. — 91 G4
Anglesey Ct. Rd., Cars. — 101 A6
Anglesey Gdns., Cars. — 101 A6
Anglesey Rd., Enf. — 25 E4
Anglesey Rd., Wat. — 28 C5
Anglesmede Cres., Pnr. — 36 E3
Anglesmede Way, Pnr. — 36 E3
Anglia Ho. E14 — 59 H6
Anglia Wk. E6 — 61 D1
  Napier Rd.
Anglo Rd. E3 — 59 J2
Angrave Ct. E8 — 59 C1
Angrave Pas. E8 — 59 C1
  Haggerston Rd.
Angus Clo., Chess. — 99 A5
Angus Dr., Ruis. — 45 C4
Angus Gdns. NW9 — 38 D1
Angus Rd. E13 — 60 J3
Angus St. SE14 — 68 H7
Anhalt Rd. SW11 — **18 H7**
Anhalt Rd. SW11 — 66 H7
Ankerdine Cres. SE18 — 79 E1
Anlaby Rd., Tedd. — 82 B5
Anley Rd. W14 — 66 A2
Anmersh Gro., Stan. — 37 G1
Ann La. SW10 — **18 E7**
Ann La. SW10 — 66 G7
Ann St. SE18 — 70 F5
Anna Clo. E8 — 59 C1
Anna Neagle Clo. E7 — 51 G4
  Dames Rd.
Annabel Clo. E14 — 60 B6
Annandale Rd. SE10 — 69 F5
Annandale Rd. W4 — 65 E5
Annandale Rd., Croy. — 102 D2
Annandale Rd., Sid. — 79 H7
Anne Boleyn's Wk., Kings.T. — 82 H5
Anne Boleyn's Wk., Sutt. — 100 A7
Anne Case Ms., N.Mal. — 92 D3
  Sycamore Gro.
Anne St. E13 — 60 G4
Anne Way, Ilf. — 35 F6
Anne Way, W.Mol. — 90 H4
Annesley Ave. NW9 — 38 D3
Annesley Clo. NW10 — 47 E3
Annesley Dr., Croy. — 102 J4
Annesley Rd. SE3 — 78 H1
Annesley Wk. N19 — 49 C2
  Macdonald Rd.
Annett Rd., Walt. — 90 A7
Annette Clo., Har. — 37 B2
  Spencer Rd.
Annette Cres. N1 — 49 J7
  Essex Rd.
Annette Rd. N7 — 49 F3
Annie Besant Clo. E3 — 59 J1
Anning St. EC2 — **9 E5**
Annington Rd. N2 — 39 J3
Annis Rd. E9 — 50 H6
Ann's Clo. SW1 — **15 A4**
Ann's Pl. E1 — **13 F2**
Annsworthy Ave., Th.Hth. — 95 A3
  Grange Pk. Rd.
Annsworthy Cres. SE25 — 95 A2
  Grange Rd.
Ansdell Rd. SE15 — 77 F2
Ansdell St. W8 — **14 B5**
Ansdell St. W8 — 66 E3
Ansdell Ter. W8 — **14 B5**
Ansell Gro., Cars. — 101 A1

Ansell Rd. SW17 — 84 H3
Anselm Clo., Croy. — 102 C3
  Park Hill Ri.
Anselm Rd. SW6 — 66 D6
Anselm Rd., Pnr. — 28 F7
Ansford Rd., Brom. — 87 C5
Ansleigh Pl. W11 — 57 A7
Anson Clo., Rom. — 44 H2
Anson Rd. N7 — 49 C4
Anson Rd. NW2 — 47 H5
Anson Ter., Nthlt. — 45 H6
  Blenheim Rd.
Anstey Rd. SE15 — 77 D3
Anstey Wk. N15 — 40 H4
Anstice Clo. W4 — 65 E2
Anstridge Path SE9 — 79 G6
  Anstridge Rd.
Anstridge Rd. SE9 — 79 G6
Antelope Rd. SE18 — 70 C3
Anthony Clo. NW7 — 30 E4
Anthony Clo., Wat. — 28 C1
Anthony Rd. SE25 — 95 D6
Anthony Rd., Grnf. — 55 B2
Anthony Rd., Well. — 80 A1
Anthony St. E1 — 59 E6
  Commercial Rd.
Antigua Clo. SE19 — 86 A5
  Salters Hill
Antill Rd. E3 — 59 H3
Antill Rd. N15 — 41 D4
Antill Ter. E1 — 59 G6
Antlers Hill E4 — 26 B4
Anton Cres., Sutt. — 100 D3
Anton St. E8 — 50 D5
Antoneys Clo., Pnr. — 36 D2
Antrim Gro. NW3 — 48 J6
Antrim Mans. NW3 — 48 J6
  Antrim Rd.
Antrim Rd. NW3 — 48 J6
Antrobus Clo., Sutt. — 100 C5
Antrobus Rd. W4 — 65 C4
Anvil Rd., Sun. — 90 A4
Anworth Clo., Wdf.Grn. — 34 H6
Apex Clo., Beck. — 96 B1
Apex Cor. NW7 — 30 D4
Apex Twr., N.Mal. — 92 E3
Aplin Way, Islw. — 73 B1
Apollo Ave., Brom. — 96 H1
Apollo Ave., Nthwd. — 28 A5
  Rodway Rd.
Apollo Pl. SW10 — **18 E7**
Apollo Way SE28 — 70 G3
  Broadwater Rd.
Apothecary St. EC4 — **12 G4**
Appach Rd. SW2 — 76 G5
Apple Garth, Brent. — 64 G4
Apple Gro., Chess. — 98 H4
Apple Gro., Enf. — 25 B3
Apple Mkt., Kings.T. — 91 G2
  Eden St.
Apple Tree Yd. SW1 — **15 G1**
Appleby Clo. E4 — 34 B6
Appleby Clo. N15 — 41 A5
Appleby Clo., Twick. — 82 A2
Appleby Rd. E8 — 50 D7
Appleby Rd. E16 — 60 F6
Appleby St. E2 — **9 F2**
Appleby St. E2 — 59 C2
Appledore Ave., Ruis. — 45 C3
Appledore Ave., Bexh. — 80 J1
Appledore Clo. SW17 — 84 J2
Appledore Clo., Brom. — 96 F5
Appledore Clo., Edg. — 38 A1
Appledore Cres., Sid. — 88 H3
Appleford Rd. W10 — 57 B4
Applegarth, Croy. — 103 B7
Applegarth Dr., Ilf. — 43 J4
Applegarth Rd. SE28 — 71 B1
Applegarth Rd. W14 — 66 A3
Appleton Gdns., N.Mal. — 92 G6
Appleton Rd. SE9 — 79 B3
Appleton Rd., Loug. — 27 E3
Appleton Sq., Mitch. — 93 H1
Appletree Gdns., Barn. — 23 H4
Applewood Clo. N20 — 31 H1
Applewood Clo. NW2 — 47 H3
Appold St. EC2 — **13 D1**
Appold St. EC2 — 59 B5
Apprentice Way E5 — 50 E4
  Clarence Rd.
Approach, The NW4 — 39 A5
Approach, The W3 — 56 D6
Approach, The, Enf. — 25 E2

Approach, The, Orp. — 104 J2
Approach Clo. N16 — 50 B5
  Cowper Rd.
Approach Rd. E2 — 59 F2
Approach Rd. SW20 — 92 J2
Approach Rd., Barn. — 23 F4
Approach Rd., W.Mol. — 90 G5
Aprey Gdns. NW4 — 38 J4
April Clo. W7 — 55 B7
April Clo., Felt. — 81 A3
April Clo., Orp. — 104 J5
  Briarswood Way
April Glen SE23 — 86 G3
April St. E8 — 50 C4
Apsley Clo., Har. — 36 J5
Apsley Rd. SE25 — 95 E4
Apsley Rd., N.Mal. — 92 C3
Apsley Way NW2 — 47 G2
Apsley Way W1 — **15 C3**
Aquarius Way, Nthwd. — 28 A5
Aquila St. NW8 — **6 F1**
Aquila St. NW8 — 57 G2
Aquinas St. SE1 — **16 F2**
Arabella Dr. SW15 — 74 E4
Arabia Clo. E4 — 26 C7
Arabin Rd. SE4 — 77 H4
Aragon Ave., T.Ditt. — 91 C5
Aragon Clo., Brom. — 104 C1
  Seymour Dr.
Aragon Dr., Ilf. — 35 F7
Aragon Dr., Ruis. — 45 D1
Aragon Ms. E1 — **17 H1**
Aragon Rd., Kings.T. — 82 H7
Aragon Rd., Mord. — 93 A6
Aran Dr., Stan. — 29 F4
Arandora Cres., Rom. — 44 H1
Arbery Rd. E3 — 59 H3
Arbor Clo., Beck. — 96 B2
Arbor Ct. N16 — 50 A2
  Lordship Rd.
Arbor Rd. E4 — 34 D3
Arbour Rd., Enf. — 25 G4
Arbour Sq. E1 — 59 G6
Arbroath Grn., Wat. — 28 A3
Arbroath Rd. SE9 — 79 B3
Arbury Ter. SE26 — 86 E3
  Oaksford Ave.
Arbuthnot La., Bex. — 80 E6
Arbuthnot Rd. SE14 — 77 G2
Arbutus St. E8 — 59 C1
Arcade, The EC2 — **13 D2**
Arcadia Ave. N3 — 39 D1
Arcadia St. E14 — 60 A6
Arcadian Ave., Bex. — 80 E6
Arcadian Clo., Bex. — 80 E6
Arcadian Gdns. N22 — 32 F7
Arcadian Rd., Bex. — 80 E6
Arch St. SE1 — **16 J6**
Arch St. SE1 — 67 J3
Archangel St. SE16 — 68 G2
Archbishops Pl. SW2 — 76 F6
Archdale Rd. SE22 — 77 C5
Archel Rd. W14 — 66 C6
Archer Clo., Kings.T. — 82 H7
Archer Rd. W11 — 75 G1
  Vicarage Cres.
Archer Ms., Hmptn. — 81 J6
  Windmill Rd.
Archer Rd. SE25 — 95 E4
Archer St. W1 — **11 H5**
Archers Dr., Enf. — 25 F2
Archers Wk. SE15 — 77 C1
  Exeter Rd.
Archery Clo. W2 — **10 H4**
Archery Clo. W2 — 57 H6
Archery Clo., Har. — 37 C3
Archery Rd. SE9 — 79 C5
Arches, The SW6 — 75 C2
  Munster Rd.
Arches, The WC2 — **16 B1**
Arches, The, Har. — 45 H2
Archibald Ms. W1 — **11 D6**
Archibald Ms. W1 — 58 A7
Archibald Rd. N7 — 49 D4
Archibald St. E3 — 60 A4
Archway Clo. N19 — 49 C2
  St. Johns Way
Archway Clo. SW19 — 84 E4
Archway Clo., Wall. — 101 D3
Archway Mall N19 — 49 C2
  Magdala Ave.
Archway Rd. N6 — 39 J5
Archway Rd. N19 — 49 C1
Archway St. SW13 — 74 E3
Arcola St. E8 — 50 C5
Arctic St. NW5 — 49 A5
  Gillies St.
Arcus Rd., Brom. — 87 E6

Ardbeg Rd. SE24 — 77 A5
Arden Clo., Har. — 46 A3
Arden Ct. Gdns. N2 — 39 G6
Arden Cres. E14 — 69 A4
Arden Cres., Dag. — 53 C7
Arden Est. N1 — 9 D2
Arden Est. N1 — 59 B2
Arden Gro., Orp. — 104 H4
Arden Mhor, Pnr. — 36 B4
Arden Rd. N3 — 39 B3
Arden Rd. W13 — 55 F7
Ardent Clo. SE25 — 95 B3
Ardfern Ave. SW16 — 94 G3
Ardfillan Rd. SE6 — 87 D1
Ardgowan Rd. SE6 — 78 E7
Ardilaun Rd. N5 — 49 J4
Ardingly Clo., Croy. — 102 F3
Ardleigh Gdns., Sutt. — 93 D7
Ardleigh Ho., Bark. — 61 F1
  St. Ann's
Ardleigh Ms., Ilf. — 52 E3
  Bengal Rd.
Ardleigh Rd. E17 — 41 J1
Ardleigh Rd. N1 — 50 B6
Ardleigh Ter. E17 — 41 J1
Ardley Clo. NW10 — 47 E3
Ardley Clo. SE6 — 86 H3
Ardlui Rd. SE27 — 85 J2
Ardmay Gdns., Surb. — 91 H5
Ardmere Rd. SE13 — 78 D6
Ardmore La., Buck.H. — 26 J1
Ardmore Rd. SE6 — 87 D2
Ardra Rd. N9 — 33 G3
Ardrossan Gdns., Wor.Pk. — 99 G3
Ardshiel Clo. SW15 — 75 A3
  Bemish Rd.
Ardwell Ave., Ilf. — 43 F5
Ardwell Rd. SW2 — 85 E2
Ardwick Rd. NW2 — 48 D4
Argall Ave. E10 — 41 G7
Argent St. SE1 — 16 H3
Argenta Way NW10 — 47 B7
Argon Ms. SW6 — 66 D7
Argus Clo., Rom. — 44 H1
Argus Way W3 — 65 B3
Argus Way, Nthlt. — 54 E3
Argyle Ave., Houns. — 72 G6
Argyle Clo. W13 — 55 D4
Argyle Pas. N17 — 41 C1
  Argyle Rd.
Argyle Pl. W6 — 65 H4
Argyle Rd. E1 — 59 G4
Argyle Rd. E15 — 51 E5
Argyle Rd. E16 — 60 H6
Argyle Rd. N12 — 31 D5
Argyle Rd. N17 — 41 D1
Argyle Rd. N18 — 33 D4
Argyle Rd. W13 — 55 D5
Argyle Rd., Barn. — 22 J4
Argyle Rd., Grnf. — 55 C3
Argyle Rd., Har. — 36 H6
Argyle Rd., Houns. — 72 H5
Argyle Rd., Ilf. — 52 D2
Argyle Rd., Tedd. — 82 B5
Argyle Sq. WC1 — 8 B3
Argyle Sq. WC1 — 58 E3
Argyle St. WC1 — 8 A3
Argyle St. WC1 — 58 E3
Argyle Wk. WC1 — 8 A4
Argyll Ave., Sthl. — 63 H1
Argyll Clo. SW9 — 76 F3
  Dalyell Rd.
Argyll Gdns., Edg. — 38 B2
Argyll Rd. W8 — 66 D2
Argyll St. W1 — 11 F4
Argyll St. W1 — 58 C6
Arica Rd. SE4 — 77 H4
Ariel Rd. NW6 — 48 D6
Ariel Way W12 — 65 J1
Aristotle Rd. SW4 — 76 D3
Arkell Gro. SE19 — 85 H7
Arkindale Rd. SE6 — 87 C3
Arkley Cres. E17 — 41 J5
Arkley Dr., Barn. — 22 G3
Arkley La., Barn. — 22 G3
Arkley Rd. E17 — 41 J5
Arkley Vw., Barn. — 22 H4
Arklow Rd. SE14 — 68 J6
Arkwright Rd. NW3 — 48 F5
Arlesford Rd. SW9 — 76 E3
Arlesey Clo. SW15 — 75 B6
  Lytton Gro.
Arlingford Rd. SW2 — 76 G5
Arlington N12 — 31 D3
Arlington Ave. N1 — 9 A1
Arlington Ave. N1 — 58 J1
Arlington Clo., Sid. — 79 H7

Arlington Clo., Sutt.	100	D2
Arlington Clo., Twick.	73	F6
Arlington Dr., Cars.	100	J2
Arlington Gdns. W4	65	C5
Arlington Gdns., Ilf.	52	D1
Arlington Lo. SW2	76	F4
Arlington Ms., Twick.	73	E6
Arlington Rd.		
Arlington Rd. N14	32	B2
Arlington Rd. NW1	58	B1
Arlington Rd. W13	55	E6
Arlington Rd., Rich.	82	G2
Arlington Rd., Surb.	91	G6
Arlington Rd., Tedd.	82	C4
Arlington Rd., Twick.	73	F6
Arlington Rd.,	34	G7
Wdf.Grn.		
Arlington Sq. N1	58	J1
Arlington St. SW1	**15**	**F1**
Arlington St. SW1	57	C1
Arlington Way EC1	**8**	**F3**
Arlington Way EC1	58	G3
Arliss Way, Nthlt.	54	C1
Arlow Rd. N21	32	G1
Armada Ct. SE8	69	A6
Watergate St.		
Armada St. SE8	69	A6
Armada Way E6	61	F7
Armadale Clo. N17	41	E4
Armadale Rd. SW6	66	D7
Armadale Rd., Felt.	72	A5
Armagh Rd. E3	59	J1
Armfield Clo., W.Mol.	90	F5
Armfield Cres., Mitch.	93	J2
Armfield Rd., Enf.	25	A1
Arminger Rd. W12	65	H1
Armitage Rd. NW11	48	B1
Armitage Rd. SE10	69	F5
Armour Clo. N7	49	F6
Roman Way		
Armoury Rd. SE8	78	B2
Armoury Way SW18	75	D5
Armstead Wk., Dag.	53	G7
Armstrong Ave.,	34	E6
Wdf.Grn.		
Armstrong Clo. E6	61	C6
Porter Rd.		
Armstrong Clo., Dag.	53	D1
Palmer Rd.		
Armstrong Clo., Pnr.	36	A6
Armstrong Clo., Walt.	90	A6
Sunbury La.		
Armstrong Cres.,	23	G3
Barn.		
Armstrong Rd. SW7	**14**	**E6**
Armstrong Rd. SW7	66	G3
Armstrong Rd. W3	65	F1
Armstrong Rd., Felt.	81	E5
Armstrong Way, Sthl.	63	H2
Armytage Rd., Houns.	63	D7
Arnal Cres. SW18	75	B7
Arndale Cen., The	75	E6
SW18		
Arndale Wk. SW18	75	E5
Garratt La.		
Arne Gro., Orp.	104	J3
Arne St. WC2	**12**	**B4**
Arne St. WC2	58	E6
Arne Wk. SE3	78	F4
Arneway St. SW1	**15**	**J6**
Arneways Ave., Rom.	44	D4
Arnewood Clo. SW15	83	G1
Arney's La., Mitch.	94	A6
Arngask Rd. SE6	78	D7
Arnhem Way SE22	77	B5
East Dulwich Gro.		
Arnison Rd., E.Mol.	91	A4
Arnold Circ. E2	**9**	**F4**
Arnold Circ. E2	59	C3
Arnold Clo., Har.	37	J7
Arnold Cres., Islw.	73	A5
Arnold Dr., Chess.	98	G6
Mansfield Rd.		
Arnold Est. SE1	**17**	**G4**
Arnold Est. SE1	68	C2
Arnold Gdns. N13	32	H5
Arnold Rd. E3	60	A3
Arnold Rd. N15	41	C3
Arnold Rd. SW17	84	J7
Arnold Rd., Dag.	53	F7
Arnold Rd., Nthlt.	45	D6
Arnos Gro. N14	32	D4
Arnos Rd. N11	32	C5
Arnott Clo. SE28	62	C7
Applegarth Rd.		
Arnott Clo. W4	65	D4
Fishers La.		
Arnould Ave. SE5	77	A4
Arnsberg Way, Bexh.	80	G4
Arnside Gdns., Wem.	46	G1
Arnside Rd., Bexh.	80	G1
Arnside St. SE17	**21**	**A5**
Arnside St. SE17	67	J6
Arnulf St. SE6	87	B4
Arnulls Rd. SW16	85	G6
Arodene Rd. SW2	76	F6
Arragon Gdns. SW16	85	E7
Arragon Gdns.,	103	B3
W.Wick.		
Arragon Rd. E6	61	A1
Arragon Rd. SW18	84	D1
Bodmin St.		
Arragon Rd., Twick.	73	D7
Arran Clo., Wall.	101	C4
Arran Dr. E12	52	A1
Arran Ms. W5	64	J1
Arran Rd. SE6	87	B2
Arran Wk. N1	49	J7
Arras Ave., Mord.	93	F5
Arrol Rd., Beck.	95	F3
Arrow Rd. E3	60	B3
Arrowscout Wk.,	54	E3
Nthlt.		
Argus Way		
Arrowsmith Clo., Chig.	35	J5
Arrowsmith Path,	35	H5
Chig.		
Arrowsmith Rd., Chig.	35	H5
Arrowsmith Rd.,	27	B3
Loug.		
Arsenal Rd. SE9	79	C2
Arterberry Rd. SW20	83	J7
Artesian Clo. NW10	47	D7
Artesian Rd. W2	57	D6
Arthingworth St. E15	60	E1
Arthur Ct. W2	**10**	**A3**
Arthur Gro. SE18	70	F4
Arthur Henderson Ho.	75	C2
SW6		
Arthur Rd. E6	61	C2
Arthur Rd. N7	49	F4
Arthur Rd. N9	33	C2
Arthur Rd. SW19	84	B5
Arthur Rd., Kings.T.	83	A7
Arthur Rd., N.Mal.	92	H5
Arthur Rd., Rom.	44	D6
Arthur St. EC4	**13**	**C5**
Arthurdon Rd. SE4	78	A5
Artichoke Hill E1	59	E7
Pennington St.		
Artichoke Pl. SE5	77	A1
Camberwell Ch. St.		
Artillery Clo., Ilf.	43	F6
Horns Rd.		
Artillery La. E1	**13**	**E2**
Artillery La. E1	59	B5
Artillery Pas. E1	59	B5
Sandy's Row		
Artillery Pl. SE18	70	C4
Artillery Pl. SW1	**15**	**H6**
Artillery Row SW1	**15**	**H6**
Artillery Row SW1	67	D3
Artington Clo., Orp.	104	F4
Artizan St. E1	**13**	**E3**
Arundel Ave., Mord.	93	C4
Arundel Clo. E15	51	E4
Arundel Clo. SW11	75	H5
Chivalry Rd.		
Arundel Clo., Bex.	80	F6
Arundel Clo., Croy.	101	H3
Arundel Clo., Hmptn.	61	H5
Arundel Ct. N12	31	H6
Arundel Clo., Har.	45	G4
Arundel Dr., Borwd.	22	B5
Arundel Dr., Har.	45	F4
Arundel Dr., Wdf.Grn.	34	G7
Arundel Gdns. N21	32	G1
Arundel Gdns. W11	57	C7
Arundel Gdns., Edg.	30	D7
Arundel Gdns., Ilf.	53	A2
Arundel Great Ct. WC2	**12**	**D5**
Arundel Gro. N16	50	B5
Arundel Pl. N1	49	G6
Arundel Rd., Barn.	23	H3
Arundel Rd., Croy.	95	A6
Arundel Rd., Houns.	72	C3
Arundel Rd., Kings.T.	92	B2
Arundel Rd., Sutt.	100	B7
Arundel Sq. N7	49	G6
Arundel St. WC2	**12**	**D5**
Arundel St. WC2	58	F7
Arundel Ter. SW13	65	H6
Arvon Rd. N5	49	G5
Ascalon St. SW8	67	C7
Ascham Dr. E4	34	B7
Rushcroft Rd.		
Ascham End E17	41	H1
Ascham St. NW5	49	C5
Aschurch Rd., Croy.	95	C7
Ascot Clo., Borwd.	22	A5
Ascot Clo., Ilf.	35	H6
Ascot Clo., Nthlt.	45	G6
Ascot Gdns., Sthl.	54	F4
Ascot Rd. E6	61	C3
Ascot Rd. N15	41	A5
Ascot Rd. N18	33	D4
Ascot Rd. SW17	85	A6
Ascot Rd., Orp.	97	J4
Ascott Ave. W5	64	H2
Ash Clo. SE20	95	F2
Ash Clo., Cars.	100	J2
Ash Clo., Edg.	30	C4
Ash Clo., N.Mal.	92	D2
Ash Clo., Orp.	97	G5
Ash Clo., Sid.	89	B3
Ash Clo., Stan.	29	D6
Ash Ct., Epsom	99	C4
Ash Gro. E8	59	E1
Ash Gro. N13	32	J3
Ash Gro. NW2	48	A4
Ash Gro. SE20	95	F2
Ash Gro. W5	64	H2
Ash Gro., Enf.	25	B7
Ash Gro., Houns.	72	D1
Ash Gro., Sthl.	54	G5
Ash Gro., Wem.	46	D4
Ash Gro., W.Wick.	103	C2
Ash Hill Clo.	28	H1
(Bushey), Wat.		
Ash Hill Dr., Pnr.	36	C3
Ash Island, E.Mol.	91	A3
Ash La., Croy.	101	H4
Ash Rd. E15	51	E5
Ash Rd., Croy.	103	A2
Ash Rd., Orp.	104	J7
Ash Rd., Sutt.	93	B7
Ash Row, Brom.	97	D7
Ash Tree Clo., Croy.	95	H6
Ash Tree Clo., Surb.	98	H1
Ash Tree Dell NW9	38	D5
Ash Tree Way, Croy.	95	H5
Ash Wk. SW2	85	F1
Ash Wk., Wem.	46	F3
Ashbourne Ave. E18	42	H4
Ashbourne Ave. N20	31	J2
Ashbourne Ave. NW11	39	C5
Ashbourne Ave.,	71	E7
Bexh.		
Ashbourne Ave., Har.	46	A2
Ashbourne Clo. N12	31	E4
Ashbourne Clo. W5	56	A5
Ashbourne Ct. E5	50	H4
Daubeney Rd.		
Ashbourne Gro. NW7	30	D5
Ashbourne Gro. SE22	77	C5
Ashbourne Gro. W4	65	E5
Ashbourne Ri., Orp.	104	G4
Ashbourne Rd. W5	55	J4
Ashbourne Rd., Mitch.	85	A6
Ashbourne Ter. SW19	84	D7
Ashbourne Way	39	C5
NW11		
Ashbourne Ave.		
Ashbridge Rd. E11	42	E7
Ashbridge St. NW8	**6**	**G6**
Ashbridge St. NW8	57	H4
Ashbrook Rd. N19	49	D1
Ashbrook Rd., Dag.	53	H3
Ashburn Gdns. SW7	**18**	**C1**
Ashburn Gdns. SW7	66	F4
Ashburn Pl. SW7	**18**	**C1**
Ashburn Pl. SW7	66	F4
Ashburnham Ave.,	37	C6
Har.		
Ashburnham Clo. N2	39	G3
Ashburnham Clo.,	28	A3
Wat.		
Ashburnham Dr.		
Ashburnham Dr., Wat.	28	A3
Ashburnham Gdns.,	37	C7
Har.		
Ashburnham Gro.	69	B7
SE10		
Ashburnham Pl. SE10	69	B7
Ashburnham Retreat	69	B7
SE10		
Ashburnham Rd.	56	J3
NW10		
Ashburnham Rd.	**18**	**D7**
SW10		
Ashburnham Rd.	66	F7
SW10		
Ashburnham Rd.,	71	J4
Belv.		
Ashburnham Rd.,	82	E2
Rich.		
Ashburton Ave., Croy.	102	E1
Ashburton Ave., Ilf.	52	H4
Ashburton Clo., Croy.	102	D1
Ashburton Ct., Pnr.	36	D3
Ashburton Gdns.,	102	D2
Croy.		
Ashburton Gro. N7	49	G4
Ashburton Rd. E16	60	G6
Ashburton Rd., Croy.	102	D2
Ashburton Rd., Ruis.	45	A2
Ashburton Ter. E13	60	G2
Grasmere Rd.		
Ashbury Gdns., Rom.	44	D5
Ashbury Rd. SW11	75	J3
Ashby Ave., Chess.	99	A6
Ashby Gro. N1	49	J7
Ashby Ms. SE4	77	J2
Ashby Rd. N15	41	D5
Ashby Rd. SE4	77	J2
Ashby St. EC1	**8**	**H4**
Ashby Wk., Croy.	94	J6
Ashchurch Gro. W12	65	G3
Ashchurch Pk. Vill.	65	G3
W12		
Ashchurch Ter. W12	65	G3
Ashcombe Ave., Surb.	91	G7
Ashcombe Gdns.,	30	A4
Edg.		
Ashcombe Pk. NW2	47	E3
Ashcombe Rd. SW19	84	D5
Ashcombe Rd., Cars.	101	A6
Ashcombe Sq., N.Mal.	92	C3
Ashcombe St. SW6	75	E2
Ashcroft, Pnr.	28	G6
Ashcroft Ave., Sid.	80	A6
Ashcroft Cres., Sid.	80	A6
Ashcroft Rd. E3	59	H3
Ashcroft Rd., Chess.	98	J3
Ashcroft Sq. W6	65	J4
King St.		
Ashdale Clo., Twick.	72	J7
Ashdale Gro., Stan.	29	C6
Ashdale Rd. SE12	87	H1
Ashdale Way, Twick.	72	J7
Ashdale Clo.		
Ashdene SE15	77	E1
Carlton Gro.		
Ashdene, Pnr.	36	C3
Ashdon Clo., Wdf.Grn.	34	H6
Ashdon Rd. NW10	56	F1
Ashdown Clo., Beck.	96	B2
Ashdown Clo., Bex.	80	J7
Wansunt Rd.		
Ashdown Cres. NW5	49	A5
Queens Cres.		
Ashdown Rd., Enf.	25	F3
Ashdown Rd.,	91	H2
Kings.T.		
Ashdown Wk. E14	69	A4
Charnwood Gdns.		
Ashdown Wk., Rom.	44	H2
Ashdown Way SW17	85	A2
Ashen Gro. SW19	84	D3
Ashenden Rd. E5	50	H5
Asher Way E1	**17**	**J1**
Asher Way E1	68	C1
Ashfield Ave., Felt.	81	B1
Ashfield Clo., Beck.	87	A7
Brackley Rd.		
Ashfield Clo., Rich.	82	H1
Ashfield La., Chis.	88	E5
Ashfield Par. N14	32	D1
Ashfield Rd. N4	40	J6
Ashfield Rd. N14	32	C3
Ashfield Rd. W3	65	F1
Ashfield St. E1	59	E5
Ashfields, Loug.	27	C2
Ashford Ave. N8	40	E4
Ashford Ave., Hayes	54	D6
Ashford Clo. E17	41	J6
Ashford Cres., Enf.	25	F2
Ashford Grn., Wat.	28	D5
Ashford Rd. E6	52	D6
Ashford Rd. E18	42	H2
Ashford Rd. NW2	48	A4
Ashford St. N1	**9**	**D3**
Ashgrove Rd., Brom.	72	C2
Ashgrove Rd., Ilf.	52	J1
Ashingdon Clo. E4	34	C3
Ashington Rd. SW6	75	C2
Ashlake Rd. SW16	85	E4
Ashland Pl. W1	**11**	**B1**
Ashland Pl. W1	58	A5
Ashlar Pl. SE18	70	E4
Masons Hill		
Ashleigh Gdns., Sutt.	100	E2

Ashleigh Rd. SE20 95 E3
Ashleigh Rd. SW14 74 L3
Ashley Ave., Ilf. 43 E2
Ashley Ave., Mord. 93 D5
Chalgrove Ave.
Ashley Clo. NW4 38 J2
Ashley Clo., Pnr. 36 B2
Ashley Cres. N22 40 G2
Ashley Cres. SW11 76 A3
Ashley Dr., Borwd. 22 C5
Ashley Dr., Islw. 64 B6
Ashley Dr., Twick. 81 H1
Ashley Gdns. N13 32 J4
Ashley Gdns. SW1 **15 G6**
Ashley Gdns., Orp. 104 H5
Ashley Gdns., Rich. 82 G2
Ashley Gdns., Wem. 46 H2
Ashley Gro., Loug. 27 B3
Staples Rd.
Ashley La. NW4 38 J2
Ashley La., Croy. 101 H4
Ashley Pl. SW1 **15 F6**
Ashley Pl. SW1 67 C3
Ashley Rd. E4 34 A5
Ashley Rd. E7 51 J7
Ashley Rd. N17 41 D3
Ashley Rd. N19 49 E1
Ashley Rd., Enf. 25 F2
Ashley Rd., Hmptn. 90 G1
Ashley Rd., Rich. 73 H3
Jocelyn Rd.
Ashley Rd., T.Ditt. 91 C6
Ashley Rd., Th.Hth. 94 F4
Ashley Wk. NW7 30 J7
Ashlin Rd. E15 51 D4
Ashling Rd., Croy. 102 D1
Ashlone Rd. SW15 74 J3
Ashlyns Way, Chess. 98 G6
Ashmead N14 24 C5
Ashmead Gate, Brom. 96 J1
Ashmead Rd. SE8 78 A2
Ashmead Rd., Felt. 81 A1
Ashmere Ave., Beck. 96 D2
Ashmere Clo., Sutt. 99 J5
Ashmere Gro. SW2 76 E4
Ashmill St. NW1 **10 G1**
Ashmill St. NW1 57 H5
Ashmole Pl. SW8 **20 D6**
Ashmole Pl. SW8 67 F6
Ashmole St. SW8 **20 D6**
Ashmole St. SW8 67 F6
Ashmore Ct., Houns. 63 G6
Wheatlands
Ashmore Gro., Well. 79 G3
Ashmore Rd. W9 57 C2
Ashmount Rd. N15 41 C5
Ashmount Rd. N19 40 C7
Ashmount Ter. W5 64 G4
Murray Rd.
Ashneal Gdns., Har. 46 A3
Ashness Gdns., Grnf. 46 E6
Ashness Rd. SW11 75 J5
Ashridge Clo., Har. 37 F6
Ashridge Dr., Wat. 28 B5
Ashridge Gdns. N13 32 D5
Ashridge Gdns., Pnr. 36 E4
Ashridge Way, Mord. 93 C3
Ashridge Way, Sun. 81 A6
Ashtead Rd. E5 41 D7
Ashton Clo., Sutt. 100 D4
Ashton Gdns., 72 F4
Houns.
Ashton Gdns., Rom. 44 E6
Ashton Rd. E15 51 D5
Ashton St. E14 60 C7
Ashtree Ave., Mitch. 93 G2
Ashtree Clo., Orp. 104 E4
Broadwater Gdns.
Ashurst Clo. SE20 95 E1
Ashurst Dr., Ilf. 43 E6
Ashurst Rd. N12 31 H5
Ashurst Rd., Barn. 23 J5
Ashurst Wk., Croy. 102 E2
Ashvale Rd. SW17 84 J5
Ashville Rd. E11 51 D2
Ashwater Rd. SE12 87 G1
Ashwell Clo. E6 61 B6
Northumberland Rd.
Ashwin St. E8 50 C6
Ashwood Gdns., 103 B6
Croy.
Ashwood Rd. E4 34 D3
Ashworth Clo. SE5 77 A2
Denmark Hill
Ashworth Rd. W9 **6 B4**
Ashworth Rd. W9 57 E3

Aske St. N1 **9 D3**
Askern Clo., Bexh. 80 D4
Askew Cres. W12 65 F2
Askew Rd. W12 65 F1
Askham Ct. W12 65 G1
Askham Rd. W12 65 G1
Askill Dr. SW15 75 B5
Keswick Rd.
Asland Rd. E15 60 D1
Aslett St. SW18 75 E7
Asmara Rd. NW2 48 B5
Asmuns Hill NW11 39 D5
Asmuns Pl. NW11 39 C5
Aspen Clo. N19 49 C2
Hargrave Pk.
Aspen Clo. W5 64 J2
Aspen Copse, Brom. 97 C2
Aspen Dr., Wem. 46 D4
Aspen Gdns. W6 65 H5
Aspen Gdns., Mitch. 94 A5
Aspen Grn., Erith 71 F3
Aspen La., Nthlt. 54 E3
Aspen Way E14 60 D7
Aspen Way, Felt. 81 B3
Aspenlea Rd. W6 66 A6
Aspern Gro. NW3 48 H5
Aspinall Rd. SE4 77 G3
Aspinden Rd. SE16 68 E4
Aspley Rd. SW18 75 E5
Aspley Way NW2 47 G2
Asplins Rd. N17 41 D1
Asquith Clo., Dag. 53 C1
Crystal Way
Ass Ho. La., Har. 28 H4
Assam St. E1 13 H3
Assata Ms. N1 49 H6
St. Paul's Rd.
Assembly Pas. E1 59 F5
Assembly Wk., Cars. 93 H7
Assurance Cotts., 71 F5
Belv.
Heron Hill
Astall Clo., Har. 37 B1
Sefton Ave.
Astbury Rd. SE15 77 F1
Aste St. E14 69 C2
Astell St. SW3 **18 H3**
Astell St. SW3 66 H5
Asteys Row N1 49 H7
River Pl.
Asthall Gdns., Ilf. 43 F4
Astle St. SW11 76 A2
Astley Ave. NW2 47 J5
Aston Ave., Har. 37 F7
Aston Clo., Sid. 89 A3
Aston Grn., Houns. 72 C2
Aston Ms., Rom. 44 C7
Reynolds Ave.
Aston Rd. SW20 92 J2
Aston Rd. W5 55 G6
Aston Rd., Esher 98 B5
Aston St. E14 59 H6
Astonville St. SW18 84 D1
Astor Ave., Rom. 44 J6
Astor Clo., Kings.T. 83 B6
Astoria Wk. SW9 76 G3
Astrop Ms. W6 65 J3
Astrop Ter. W6 65 J2
Astwood Ms. SW7 **18 B1**
Astwood Ms. SW7 66 E4
Asylum Rd. SE15 68 E7
Atalanta St. SW6 75 A1
Atbara Ct., Tedd. 82 E6
Atbara Rd., Tedd. 82 E6
Atcham Rd., Houns. 72 J4
Atcost Rd., Bark. 62 A5
Atheldene Rd. SW18 75 F7
Athelstan Rd., 91 J4
Kings.T.
Athelstane Gro. E3 59 J2
Athelstane Ms. N4 49 G1
Stroud Grn. Rd.
Athelstone Rd., Har. 37 A2
Athena Clo., Har. 46 B2
Byron Hill Rd.
Athenaeum Pl. N10 40 B3
Fortis Grn. Rd.
Athenaeum Rd. N20 31 F1
Athenlay Rd. SE15 77 G5
Athens Gdns. W9 57 D4
Elgin Ave.
Atherden Rd. E5 50 F4
Atherfold Rd. SW9 76 E3
Atherley Way, Houns. 72 F7
Atherstone Ms. SW7 **18 D1**
Atherstone Ms. SW7 66 F4
Atherton Dr. SW19 84 A4

Atherton Heights, 46 F6
Wem.
Atherton Ms. E7 51 F6
Atherton Pl., Har. 37 A3
Atherton Pl., Sthl. 54 H7
Longford Ave.
Atherton Rd. E7 51 F6
Atherton Rd. SW13 65 G7
Atherton Rd., Ilf. 43 B2
Atherton St. SW11 75 H2
Athlon Rd., Wem. 55 G2
Athlone, Esher 98 B6
Athlone Clo. E5 50 E4
Goulton Rd.
Athlone Rd. SW2 76 F7
Athlone St. NW5 49 A6
Athol Clo., Pnr. 36 B1
Athol Gdns., Pnr. 36 B1
Athol Rd., Erith 71 J5
Athol Sq. E14 60 C6
Athole Gdns., Enf. 25 B5
Atholl Rd., Ilf. 44 A7
Atkins Dr., W.Wick. 103 D2
Atkins Rd. E10 42 B6
Atkins Rd. SW12 76 D7
Atkinson Rd. E16 60 J5
Atlantic Rd. SW9 76 G4
Atlas Gdns. SE7 69 J4
Atlas Ms. E8 50 C6
Tyssen St.
Atlas Ms. N7 49 F6
Atlas Rd. E13 60 G2
Atlas Rd. NW10 56 E3
Atlas Rd., Wem. 47 C4
Atley Rd. E3 60 A1
Atlip Rd., Wem. 55 H1
Atney Rd. SW15 75 B4
Atria Rd., Nthwd. 28 A5
Atterbury Rd. N4 40 G6
Atterbury St. SW1 **20 A2**
Atterbury St. SW1 67 E4
Attewood Ave. NW10 47 E3
Attewood Rd., Nthlt. 45 E6
Attfield Clo. N20 31 G2
Attlee Clo., Hayes 54 B3
Attlee Clo., Th.Hth. 94 J5
Kynaston Ave.
Attlee Clo., Hayes 54 B3
Attlee Rd. SE28 62 B7
Attlee Rd., Hayes 54 A3
Attlee Ter. E17 42 B4
Attneave St. WC1 **8 E4**
Atwater Clo. SW2 85 G1
Atwell Clo. E10 42 B6
Belmont Pk. Rd.
Atwell Rd. SE15 77 D2
Rye La.
Atwood Ave., Rich. 74 A2
Atwood Rd. W6 65 H4
Aubert Pk. N5 49 G4
Aubert Rd. N5 49 H4
Aubrey Pl. NW8 **6 C2**
Aubrey Rd. E17 42 A3
Aubrey Rd. N8 40 E5
Aubrey Rd. W8 66 C1
Aubrey Wk. W8 66 C1
Aubyn Hill SE27 85 J4
Aubyn Sq. SW15 74 G4
Auckland Clo. SE19 95 B1
Auckland Gdns. SE19 95 B1
Auckland Hill SE27 85 J4
Auckland Ri. SE19 95 B1
Auckland Rd. E10 51 B3
Auckland Rd. SE19 95 C1
Auckland Rd. SW11 75 H4
Auckland Rd., Ilf. 52 E1
Auckland Rd., 91 J4
Kings.T.
Auckland St. SE11 **20 C4**
Auden Pl. NW1 58 A1
Manley Ave.
Audleigh Pl., Chig. 35 D6
Audley Clo. SW11 76 A3
Audley Clo., Borwd. 22 A3
Audley Ct. E18 42 F4
Audley Ct., Pnr. 36 C2
Audley Gdns., Ilf. 52 J2
Audley Gdns., Loug. 27 F2
Audley Pl., Sutt. 100 E7
Audley Rd. NW4 38 G6
Audley Rd. W5 55 J5
Audley Rd., Enf. 24 H2
Audley Rd., Rich. 73 J5
Audley Sq. W1 **15 C1**
Audrey Clo., Beck. 96 B6
Audrey Gdns., Wem. 46 E2
Audrey Rd., Ilf. 52 E3
Audrey St. E2 **9 J1**
Audrey St. E2 59 D2

Audric Clo., Kings.T. 92 A1
Augurs La. E13 60 H3
Augusta Clo., W.Mol. 90 F3
Freeman Dr.
Augusta Rd., Twick. 81 J2
Augusta St. E14 60 B6
Augustine Rd. W14 66 A3
Augustine Rd., Har. 36 H1
Augustus Clo., Brent. 64 G7
Augustus Rd. SW19 84 A1
Augustus St. NW1 **7 E2**
Augustus St. NW1 58 B2
Aulton Pl. SE11 **20 F4**
Aultone Way, Cars. 100 J3
Aultone Way, Sutt. 100 E2
Aurelia Gdns., Croy. 94 E6
Aurelia Rd., Croy. 94 E6
Auriga Ms. N16 50 A5
Auriol Clo., Wor.Pk. 99 E3
Auriol Pk. Rd.
Auriol Dr., Grnf. 46 A7
Auriol Pk. Rd., 99 E3
Wor.Pk.
Auriol Rd. W14 66 B4
Austell Gdns. NW7 30 E3
Austen Clo. SE28 71 B1
Austen Clo., Loug. 27 G3
Austen Ho. NW6 57 D3
Austen Rd., Har. 45 H2
Austin Ave., Brom. 97 B5
Austin Clo. SE23 77 J7
Austin Clo., Twick. 73 F5
Austin Ct. E6 60 J1
Kings Rd.
Austin Friars EC2 **13 C3**
Austin Friars EC2 59 A6
Austin Friars Pas. EC2 **13 C3**
Austin Friars Sq. EC2 **13 C3**
Austin Rd. SW11 76 A1
Austin St. E2 **9 F4**
Austin St. E2 59 C3
Austral Clo., Sid. 88 J3
Austral St. SE11 **20 G1**
Austral St. SE11 67 H4
Australia Rd. W12 56 H7
Austyn Gdns., Surb. 99 B1
Autumn Clo., Enf. 25 D1
Autumn St. E3 60 A1
Avalon Clo. W13 55 D5
Avalon Clo., Enf. 24 G2
Avalon Rd. SW6 75 E1
Avalon Rd. W13 55 D4
Avard Gdns., Orp. 104 F4
Isabella Dr.
Avarn Rd. SW17 84 J6
Ave Maria La. EC4 **12 H4**
Ave Maria La. EC4 58 H6
Avebury Ct. N1 59 A1
Poole St.
Avebury Pk., Surb. 91 G7
Avebury Rd. E11 51 D1
Southwest Rd.
Avebury Rd. SW19 93 C1
Avebury Rd., Orp. 104 G3
Avebury St. N1 59 A1
Poole St.
Aveline St. SE11 **20 E4**
Aveline St. SE11 67 G5
Aveling Pk. Rd. E17 42 A2
Avenell Rd. N5 49 H3
Avening Rd. SW18 75 D7
Brathway Rd.
Avening Ter. SW18 75 D6
Avenons Rd. E13 60 G4
Avenue, The E4 34 D6
Avenue, The 51 F2
(Leytonstone) E11
Avenue, The 42 H6
(Wanstead) E11
Avenue, The N3 39 D2
Sylvan Ave.
Avenue, The N8 40 G3
Avenue, The N10 40 C2
Avenue, The N11 32 B5
Avenue, The N17 41 B2
Avenue, The NW6 57 A1
Avenue, The SE7 69 J7
Avenue, The SE10 69 D7
Avenue, The SW4 76 A5
Avenue, The SW11 75 J7
Bellevue Rd.
Avenue, The SW18 75 H7
Avenue, The W4 65 E3
Avenue, The W13 55 E7
Avenue, The, Barn. 23 B3
Avenue, The, Beck. 96 B1
Avenue, The, Bex. 80 D6
Avenue, The, Brom. 97 A3

Avenue, The, Cars. 101 A7
Avenue, The, Croy. 102 B3
Avenue, The, Epsom 99 H7
Avenue, The, Esher 98 B6
Avenue, The, Hmptn. 81 F6
Avenue, The, Har. 37 C1
Avenue, The, Houns. 72 H5
Avenue, The, Houns. 72 A1
  (Cranford)
Avenue, The, Islw. 64 A7
  Jersey Rd.
Avenue, The, Kes. 104 A3
Avenue, The, Loug. 27 A6
Avenue, The, Orp. 104 J2
Avenue, The, Orp. 89 B7
  (St. Paul's Cray)
Avenue, The, Pnr. 36 F6
Avenue, The, Pnr. 28 F6
  (Hatch End)
Avenue, The, Rich. 73 J2
Avenue, The, Sun. 90 B1
Avenue, The, Surb. 91 J6
Avenue, The, Sutt. 99 H7
  (Cheam)
Avenue, The, Twick. 73 E5
Avenue, The, Wem. 46 H1
Avenue, The, W.Wick. 96 C7
Avenue, The, Wor.Pk. 99 F2
Avenue Clo. N14 24 C6
Avenue Clo. NW8 57 H1
Avenue Clo., Houns. 72 A1
  The Ave.
Avenue Cres. W3 65 B2
Avenue Cres., Houns. 63 B7
Avenue Elmers, Surb. 91 H5
Avenue Gdns. SE25 95 F1
Avenue Gdns. SW14 74 E3
Avenue Gdns. W3 65 B2
Avenue Gdns., Houns. 63 A7
  The Ave.
Avenue Gdns., Tedd. 82 C7
Avenue Gate, Loug. 26 J6
Avenue Ind. Est. E4 33 J6
Avenue Ms. N10 40 B3
Avenue Pk. Rd. SE27 85 H2
Avenue Rd. E7 51 H4
Avenue Rd. N6 40 C7
Avenue Rd. N12 31 F4
Avenue Rd. N14 24 B7
Avenue Rd. N15 41 A5
Avenue Rd. NW3 48 G7
Avenue Rd. NW8 48 G7
Avenue Rd. NW10 56 F2
Avenue Rd. SE20 95 F1
Avenue Rd. SE25 95 C2
Avenue Rd. SW16 94 D2
Avenue Rd. SW20 92 H1
Avenue Rd. W3 65 B2
Avenue Rd., Beck. 95 G1
Avenue Rd., Belv. 71 J4
Avenue Rd., Bexh. 80 E4
Avenue Rd., Brent. 64 F5
Avenue Rd., Erith 71 J7
Avenue Rd., Hmptn. 90 H1
Avenue Rd., Islw. 73 C1
Avenue Rd., Kings.T. 91 H3
Avenue Rd., N.Mal. 92 E4
Avenue Rd., Pnr. 36 E3
Avenue Rd., Rom. 53 B1
  (Chadwell Heath)
Avenue Rd., Sthl. 63 F2
Avenue Rd., Tedd. 82 D7
Avenue Rd., Wall. 101 C7
Avenue Rd., Wdf.Grn. 34 J6
Avenue S., Surb. 91 J7
Avenue Ter., N.Mal. 92 C3
  Kingston Rd.
Averil Gro. SW16 85 H6
Averill St. W6 66 A6
Avern Gdns., W.Mol. 90 H4
Avern Rd., W.Mol. 90 H4
Avery Fm. Row SW1 19 D2
Avery Gdns., Ilf. 43 C5
Avery Hill Rd. SE9 79 G6
Avery Row W1 11 E5
Avery Row W1 58 B7
Avey La., Loug. 26 H1
Aviary Clo. E16 60 F5
Aviemore Clo., Beck. 95 J5
Aviemore Way, Beck. 95 H5
Avignon Rd. SE4 77 G3
Avington Gro. SE20 86 F7
Avington Way SE15 21 F7
Avis Sq. E1 59 G6
Avoca Rd. SW17 85 A4
Avocet Ms. SE28 70 G3
Avon Clo., Hayes 54 C4
Avon Clo., Sutt. 100 F4

Avon Clo., Wor.Pk. 99 G2
Avon Ct., Grnf. 54 H4
  Braund Ave.
Avon Ms., Pnr. 36 F1
Avon Path, S.Croy. 101 J6
Avon Rd. E17 42 D3
Avon Rd. SE4 78 A3
Avon Rd., Grnf. 54 G4
Avon Way E18 42 G3
Avondale Ave. N12 31 E5
Avondale Ave. NW2 47 E3
Avondale Ave., Barn. 31 J1
Avondale Ave., Esher 98 D3
Avondale Ave., 99 F1
  Wor.Pk.
Avondale Clo., Loug. 27 C7
Avondale Ct. E11 51 E1
Avondale Ct. E16 60 E5
  Avondale Rd.
Avondale Ct. E18 42 H1
Avondale Cres., Enf. 25 H3
Avondale Cres., Ilf. 43 A5
Avondale Dr., Hayes 63 A1
Avondale Dr., Loug. 27 C7
Avondale Gdns., 72 F5
  Houns.
Avondale Ms., Brom. 87 G6
  Avondale Rd.
Avondale Pk. Gdns. 57 B7
  W11
Avondale Pk. Rd. W11 57 B7
Avondale Ri. SE15 77 C3
Avondale Rd. E16 60 E5
Avondale Rd. E17 42 A7
Avondale Rd. N3 39 F1
Avondale Rd. N13 32 G2
Avondale Rd. N15 40 H5
Avondale Rd. SE9 88 B2
Avondale Rd. SW14 74 D3
Avondale Rd. SW19 84 E5
Avondale Rd., Brom. 87 E6
Avondale Rd., Har. 37 C3
Avondale Rd., S.Croy. 101 J7
Avondale Rd., Well. 80 C2
Avondale Sq. SE1 21 H4
Avondale Sq. SE1 68 D5
Avonley Rd. SE14 68 F7
Avonmore Rd. W14 66 B4
  Avonmore Rd.
Avonmore Rd. W14 66 B4
Avonmouth St. SE1 16 J5
Avonmouth St. SE1 67 J3
Avonwick Rd., Houns. 72 H2
Avril Way E4 34 C5
Avro Way, Wall. 101 E7
Awlfield Ave. N17 41 A1
Awliscombe Rd., 79 J2
  Well.
Axe St., Bark. 61 F1
Axholme Ave., Edg. 38 A1
Axminster Cres., Well. 80 C1
Axminster Rd. N7 49 E3
Aybrook St. W1 11 B2
Aybrook St. W1 58 A5
Aycliffe Clo., Brom. 97 C4
Aycliffe Rd. W12 65 F1
Ayles Rd., Hayes 54 B3
Aylesbury Clo. E7 51 F6
  Atherton Rd.
Aylesbury Est. SE17 21 C4
Aylesbury Rd. SE17 21 C4
Aylesbury Rd. SE17 68 A5
Aylesbury Rd., Brom. 96 G3
Aylesbury St. EC1 8 G6
Aylesbury St. EC1 58 H4
Aylesbury St. NW10 47 D3
Aylesford Ave., Beck. 95 H5
Aylesford St. SW1 19 H4
Aylesford St. SW1 67 D5
Aylesham Rd., Orp. 97 J7
Aylestone Ave. NW6 48 A7
Aylett Rd. SE25 95 E4
  Belfast Rd.
Aylett Rd., Islw. 73 B2
Ayley Cft., Enf. 25 D5
Ayliffe Clo., Kings.T. 92 A4
  Cambridge Gdns.
Aylmer Clo., Stan. 29 D4
Aylmer Dr., Stan. 29 D4
Aylmer Rd. E11 51 F1
Aylmer Rd. N2 39 H5
Aylmer Rd. W12 65 F2
Aylmer Rd., Dag. 53 E3
Ayloffe Rd., Dag. 53 F6
Aylton Est. SE16 68 F2
  Renforth St.
Aylward Rd. SE23 86 G2

Aylward Rd. SW20 93 C2
Aylward St. E1 59 F6
Aylwards Ri., Stan. 29 D4
Aylwyn Est. SE1 17 E5
Aylwyn Est. SE1 68 B3
Aynhoe Rd. W14 66 A4
Aynscombe La. SW14 74 C3
Aynscombe Path 74 C2
  SW14
  Thames Bank
Ayr Ct. W3 56 A5
  Monks Dr.
Ayres Clo. E13 60 G3
Ayres Cres. NW10 47 D7
Ayres St. SE1 17 A3
Ayres St. SE1 67 J2
Ayrsome Rd. N16 50 B3
Ayrton Rd. SW7 14 E5
Aysgarth Rd. SE21 77 B6
Aytoun Pl. SW9 76 F2
Aytoun Rd. SW9 76 F2
Azalea Clo. W7 64 C1
Azalea Ct., Wdf.Grn. 34 E7
  Bridle Path
Azalea Wk., Pnr. 36 B5
Azalea Wk., Sthl. 63 J2
  Navigator Dr.
Azenby Rd. SE15 77 C2
Azile Everitt Ho. SE18 70 F5
  Vicarage Pk.
Azof St. SE10 69 E4

B

Baalbec Rd. N5 49 H5
Babbacombe Clo., 98 G5
  Chess.
Babbacombe Gdns., 43 B4
  Ilf.
Babbacombe Rd., 96 G1
  Brom.
Baber Dr., Felt. 72 C6
Babington Ri., Wem. 47 A6
Babington Rd. NW4 47 A3
Babington Rd. SW16 85 D5
Babington Rd., Dag. 53 C5
Babmaes St. SW1 15 H1
Bacchus Wk. N1 9 D2
Baches St. N1 9 C4
Baches St. N1 59 A3
Back Ch. La. E1 13 J4
Back Ch. La. E1 59 D7
Back Hill EC1 8 E6
Back Hill EC1 58 G4
Back La. N8 40 E5
Back La. NW3 48 F4
  Heath St.
Back La., Bex. 80 G7
Back La., Brent. 64 G6
Back La., Edg. 38 C1
Back La., Rich. 82 F3
Back La., Rom. 44 E7
  St. Chad's Rd.
Back Rd., Sid. 89 A4
Backhouse Pl. SE17 21 E2
Bacon Gro. SE1 17 F6
Bacon Gro. SE1 68 C3
Bacon La. NW9 38 B4
Bacon La., Edg. 38 A1
Bacon St. E1 9 G5
Bacon St. E1 59 C4
Bacon St. E2 9 G5
Bacon St. E2 59 C4
Bacons La. N6 49 A1
Bacton NW5 49 A5
Bacton St. E2 59 F3
  Roman Rd.
Baddow Clo., Dag. 62 G1
Baddow Clo., 35 A6
  Wdf.Grn.
Baden Pl. SE1 17 B3
Baden Powell Clo., 98 J2
  Surb.
Baden Rd. N8 40 D4
Baden Rd., Ilf. 52 E5
Badger Clo., Felt. 81 A3
  Sycamore Clo.
Badger Clo., Houns. 72 C3
Badgers Clo., Enf. 24 H3
Badgers Clo., Har. 37 A6
Badgers Copse, Orp. 104 J2
Badgers Copse, 99 F2
  Wor.Pk.
Badgers Cft. N20 31 B1
Badgers Cft. SE9 88 D3
Badgers Hole, Croy. 102 G4
Badgers Wk., N.Mal. 92 E2
Badlis Rd. E17 42 A2

Badminton Clo., 22 A2
  Borwd.
Badminton Clo., Har. 37 B4
Badminton Clo., Nthlt. 45 G7
Badminton Rd. SW12 76 A6
Badsworth Rd. SE5 76 J1
Bagley's La. SW6 75 E1
Bagleys Spring, Rom. 44 E3
Bagshot Ct. SE18 79 D1
  Prince Imperial Rd.
Bagshot Rd., Enf. 25 C7
Bagshot St. SE17 21 E4
Bagshot St. SE17 68 B5
Baildon St. SE8 69 A7
  Watson's St.
Bailey Clo. E4 34 C4
Bailey Pl. SE26 86 G6
Baillies Wk. W5 64 G2
  Liverpool Rd.
Bainbridge Rd., Dag. 53 F4
Bainbridge St. WC1 11 J3
Bainbridge St. WC1 58 D6
Baird Ave., Sthl. 54 H7
Baird Clo. NW9 38 C6
Baird Gdns. SE19 86 B4
Baird Rd., Enf. 25 E4
Baird St. EC1 9 A5
Baizdon Rd. SE3 78 E2
Baker La., Mitch. 94 A2
Baker Pas. NW10 56 E1
  Acton La.
Baker Rd. NW10 56 E1
Baker Rd. SE18 79 B1
Baker St. NW1 7 A6
Baker St. NW1 57 J4
Baker St. W1 11 A1
Baker St. W1 57 J5
Baker St., Enf. 25 A3
Bakers Ave. E17 42 B6
Bakers Ct. SE25 95 B3
Bakers End SW20 93 B2
Bakers Fld. N7 49 D4
  Crayford Rd.
Bakers Hill E5 50 E1
Bakers Hill, Barn. 23 E2
Bakers La. N6 39 J6
Baker's Ms. W1 11 B3
Bakers Ms., Orp. 104 J6
Bakers Pas. NW3 48 F4
  Heath St.
Baker's Rents E2 9 F4
Bakers Row E15 60 E2
Baker's Row EC1 8 E6
Baker's Row EC1 58 G4
Bakery Pl. SW11 75 J4
  Altenburg Gdns.
Bakewell Ct. E5 50 H3
  Mandeville St.
Bakewell Way, N.Mal. 92 E2
Bala Gdn. NW9 38 E6
  Snowdon Dr.
Balaam St. E13 60 G4
Balaams La. N14 32 D2
Balaclava Rd. SE1 21 G2
Balaclava Rd. SE1 68 C4
Balaclava Rd., Surb. 91 F7
Balben Path E9 50 G7
  Speldhurst Rd.
Balcaskie Rd. SE9 79 C5
Balchen Rd. SE3 79 A2
Balchier Rd. SE22 77 E6
Balcombe Clo., 80 D4
  Bexh.
Balcombe St. NW1 6 J5
Balcombe St. NW1 57 J4
Balcon Way, Borwd. 22 C1
Balcorne St. E9 50 F7
Balder Ri. SE12 87 H2
Balderton St. W1 11 C4
Balderton St. W1 58 A6
Baldock St. E3 60 B2
Baldry Gdns. SW16 85 E6
Baldwin Cres. SE5 76 J1
Baldwin St. EC1 9 B4
Baldwin Ter. N1 8 J1
Baldwin Ter. N1 58 J2
Baldwin's Gdns. EC1 12 E1
Baldwin's Gdns. EC1 58 G5
Baldwins Hill, Loug. 27 C2
Baldwyn Gdns. W3 56 D7
Balfe St. N1 8 B2
Balfe St. N1 58 E2
Balfern Gro. W4 65 E5
Balfern St. SW11 75 H2
Balfour Ave. W7 64 C1
Balfour Gro. N20 31 J3
Balfour Ho. W10 57 A5
  St. Charles Sq.

Balfour Ms. N9 33 D3
The Bdy.
Balfour Ms. W1 15 C1
Balfour Pl. SW15 74 H4
Balfour Pl. W1 11 C6
Balfour Rd. N5 49 J4
Balfour Rd. SE25 95 D5
Balfour Rd. SW19 84 E7
Balfour Rd. W3 56 C5
Balfour Rd. W13 64 D2
Balfour Rd., Brom. 97 A5
Balfour Rd., Cars. 100 J7
Balfour Rd., Har. 37 A5
Balfour Rd., Houns. 72 H3
Balfour Rd., Ilf. 52 E2
Balfour Rd., Sthl. 63 D3
Balfour St. SE17 21 B1
Balfour St. SE17 68 A4
Balgonie Rd. E4 34 D1
Balgowan Clo., N.Mal. 92 E4
Balgowan Rd., Beck. 95 H3
Balgowan St. SE18 70 J4
Balham Gro. SW12 76 A7
Balham High Rd. SW12 85 A3
Balham High Rd. SW17 85 A3
Balham Hill SW12 76 B7
Balham New Rd. SW12 76 B7
Balham Pk. Rd. SW12 84 J1
Balham Rd. N9 33 D2
Balham Sta. Rd. SW12 85 B1
Balkan Wk. E1 59 E7
Pennington St.
Ballamore Rd., Brom. 87 G3
Ballance Rd. E9 50 G6
Ballantine St. SW18 75 F4
Ballard Clo., Kings.T. 83 D7
Ballards Clo., Dag. 62 H1
Ballards Fm. Rd., Croy. 102 D6
Ballards Fm. Rd., S.Croy. 102 D6
Ballards La. N3 39 D1
Ballards La. N12 31 F6
Ballards Ms., Edg. 30 A6
Ballards Ri., S.Croy. 102 D6
Ballards Rd. NW2 47 G2
Ballards Rd., Dag. 62 H2
Ballards Way, Croy. 102 E6
Ballards Way, S.Croy. 102 D6
Ballast Quay SE10 69 D5
Ballater Clo., Wat. 28 C4
Ballater Rd. SW2 76 E4
Ballater Rd., S.Croy. 102 C5
Ballina St. SE23 77 G7
Ballingdon Rd. SW11 76 A6
Ballinger Pt. E3 60 B3
Bromley High St.
Balliol Ave. E4 34 E4
Balliol Rd. N17 41 B1
Balliol Rd. W10 57 A6
Balliol Rd., Well. 80 B2
Balloch Rd. SE6 87 D1
Ballogie Ave. NW10 47 E4
Ballow Clo. SE5 68 B7
Harris St.
Balls Pond Pl. N1 50 A6
Balls Pond Rd.
Balls Pond Rd. N1 50 A6
Balmain Clo. W5 64 G1
Balmer Rd. E3 59 J2
Balmes Rd. N1 59 A1
Balmoral Ave., Beck. 95 H4
Balmoral Clo. SW15 75 A6
Westleigh Ave.
Balmoral Cres., W.Mol. 90 G3
Balmoral Dr., Borwd. 22 D5
Balmoral Dr., Hayes 54 A5
Balmoral Dr., Sthl. 54 F4
Balmoral Gdns. W13 64 D3
Balmoral Gdns., Bex. 80 F7
Balmoral Gdns., Ilf. 52 J1
Balmoral Gro. N7 49 F6
Balmoral Ms. W12 65 F3
Balmoral Rd. E7 51 J4
Balmoral Rd. E10 51 B2
Balmoral Rd. NW2 47 H6
Balmoral Rd., Har. 45 G4
Balmoral Rd., Kings.T. 91 J4
Balmoral Rd., Wor.Pk. 99 H3
Balmore Cres., Barn. 24 A5
Balmore St. N19 49 B2
Balmuir Gdns. SW15 74 J4
Balnacraig Ave. NW10 47 E4
Balniel Gate SW1 19 J3
Balniel Gate SW1 67 D5
Baltic Clo. SW19 84 G7
Baltic Ct. SE16 68 G2
Timber Pond Rd.
Baltic St. EC1 8 J6
Baltic St. EC1 58 J4
Baltimore Pl., Well. 79 J2
Balvernie Gro. SW18 75 C7
Bamber Ho., Bark. 61 F1
St. Margarets
Bamborough Gdns. W12 65 J2
Bamford Ave., Wem. 55 J1
Bamford Ct. E15 51 B5
Clays La.
Bamford Rd., Bark. 52 F6
Bamford Rd., Brom. 87 C5
Bampfylde Clo., Wall. 101 C3
Bampton Rd. SE23 86 G3
Banavie Gdns., Beck. 96 C1
Banbury Clo., Enf. 24 H1
Holtwhites Hill
Banbury Ct. WC2 12 A5
Banbury Ct., Sutt. 100 D7
Banbury Enterprise Cen., Croy. 101 H2
Factory La.
Banbury Rd. E9 50 G7
Banbury Rd. E17 33 H7
Banbury St. SW11 75 H2
Banbury Wk., Nthlt. 54 G2
Brabazon Rd.
Banchory Rd. SE3 69 H7
Bancroft Ave. N2 39 H5
Bancroft Ave., Buck.H. 34 G2
Bancroft Ct., Nthlt. 54 C1
Bancroft Gdns., Har. 36 J1
Bancroft Gdns., Orp. 104 J1
Bancroft Rd. E1 59 G3
Bancroft Rd., Har. 36 J1
Bandon Ri., Wall. 101 D5
Bangalore St. SW15 74 J3
Bangor Clo., Nthlt. 45 H5
Banim St. W6 65 H4
Banister Rd. W10 57 A3
Bank, The N6 49 B1
Cholmeley Pk.
Bank Ave., Mitch. 93 G2
Bank End SE1 17 A1
Bank End SE1 67 J1
Bank La. SW15 74 E5
Bank La., Kings.T. 82 H7
Bankfoot Rd., Brom. 87 E4
Bankhurst Rd. SE6 77 J7
Banks La., Bexh. 80 F4
Banks Rd., Borwd. 22 C2
Banksia Rd. N18 33 F5
Banksian Wk., Islw. 73 B1
The Gro.
Bankside SE1 12 J6
Bankside SE1 58 J7
Bankside, Enf. 24 H1
Bankside, S.Croy. 102 C6
Bankside, Sthl. 63 D1
Bankside Ave., Nthlt. 54 A2
Townson Ave.
Bankside Clo., Cars. 100 H6
Bankside Dr., T.Ditt. 98 E1
Bankside Way SE19 86 B6
Lunham Rd.
Bankton Rd. SW2 76 G4
Bankwell Rd. SE13 78 E4
Banner St. EC1 9 A6
Banner St. EC1 58 J4
Bannerman Ho. SW8 20 C6
Bannerman Ho. SW8 67 F6
Banning St. SE10 69 E5
Bannister Clo. SW2 85 G1
Ewen Cres.
Bannister Clo., Grnf. 46 A5
Bannister Ho. E9 50 G5
Homerton High St.
Bannockburn Rd. SE18 70 H4
Banstead Gdns. N9 33 B3
Banstead Rd., Cars. 100 H6
Banstead St. SE15 77 F3
Banstead Way, Wall. 101 E5
Banstock Rd., Edg. 30 B6
Banton Clo., Enf. 25 E2
Central Ave.
Bantry St. SE5 68 A7
Banwell Rd., Bex. 80 D6
Woodside La.
Banyard Rd. SE16 68 E3
Southwark Pk. Rd.
Baptist Gdns. NW5 49 A6
Queens Cres.
Barandon Wk. W11 57 A7
Whitchurch Rd.
Barb Ms. W6 65 J3
Barbara Brosnan Ct. NW8 6 E2
Barbara Hucklesby Clo. N22 40 H2
Russell Ave.
Barbauld Rd. N16 50 B3
Barber Clo. N21 24 G7
Barber's All. E13 60 H3
Barbers Rd. E15 60 B2
Barbican, The EC2 12 J1
Barbican, The EC2 58 J5
Barbican Rd., Grnf. 54 H6
Barbon Clo. WC1 12 B1
Barbot Clo. N9 33 D3
Barchard St. SW18 75 E5
Barchester Clo. W7 64 C1
Barchester Rd., Har. 37 A2
Barchester St. E14 60 B5
Barclay Clo. SW6 66 D7
Barclay Oval, Wdf.Grn. 34 G4
Barclay Path E17 42 C5
Barclay Rd.
Barclay Rd. E11 51 E1
Barclay Rd. E13 60 J4
Barclay Rd. E17 42 C5
Barclay Rd. N18 33 A6
Barclay Rd. SW6 66 D7
Barclay Rd., Croy. 102 A3
Barclay Way SE22 77 D7
Lordship La.
Barcombe Ave. SW2 85 E2
Bard Rd. W10 57 A7
Barden St. SE18 70 H7
Bardfield Ave., Rom. 44 D3
Bardney Rd., Mord. 93 E4
Bardolph Rd. N7 49 E4
Bardolph Rd., Rich. 73 J3
St. Georges Rd.
Bardsey Pl. E1 59 F5
Bardsey Wk. N1 49 J6
Marquess Est.
Bardsley Clo., Croy. 102 C3
Bardsley La. SE10 69 C6
Barfett St. W10 57 C4
Barfield Ave. N20 31 J2
Barfield Rd. E11 51 F1
Barfield Rd., Brom. 97 D3
Barfields, Loug. 27 D4
Barfields Gdns., Loug. 27 D4
Barfields
Barfields Path, Loug. 27 D4
Barford Clo. NW4 38 G1
Barford St. N1 58 G1
Barforth Rd. SE15 77 E3
Barfreston Way SE20 95 E1
Bargate Clo. SE18 70 J5
Bargate Clo., N.Mal. 92 G7
Barge Ho. Rd. E16 70 E2
Barge Ho. St. SE1 16 F1
Barge Wk., E.Mol. 91 A3
Barge Wk., Kings.T. 91 G2
Barge Wk., Walt. 90 C3
Bargery Rd. SE6 87 B1
Bargrove Clo. SE20 86 D7
Bargrove Cres. SE6 86 J2
Elm La.
Barham Clo., Brom. 104 B1
Barham Clo., Chis. 88 E5
Barham Clo., Rom. 44 H2
Barham Clo., Wem. 46 E6
Barham Rd. SW20 83 G7
Barham Rd., Chis. 88 E5
Barham Rd., S.Croy. 101 J4
Baring Clo. SE12 87 G2
Baring Rd. SE12 78 G7
Baring Rd., Barn. 23 G4
Baring Rd., Croy. 102 D1
Baring St. N1 59 A1
Bark Pl. W2 10 A5
Bark Pl. W2 57 E7
Barker Dr. NW1 49 C7
Barker St. SW10 18 C5
Barker St. SW10 66 F6
Barker Wk. SW16 85 D3
Mount Ephraim Rd.
Barker Way SE22 86 D1
Dulwich Common
Barkham Rd. N17 33 A7
Barking Ind. Pk., Bark. 61 J1
Barking Rd. E6 61 A2
Barking Rd. E13 60 G4
Barking Rd. E16 60 E5
Barkis Way SE16 68 E5
Egan Way
Barkston Gdns. SW5 18 A2
Barkston Gdns. SW5 66 E4
Barkway Ct. N4 49 J3
Queens Dr.
Barkwood Clo., Rom. 44 J5
Barkworth Rd. SE16 68 E5
Credon Rd.
Barlborough St. SE14 68 G7
Barlby Gdns. W10 57 A4
Barlby Rd. W10 56 J5
Barley La., Ilf. 44 A7
Barley La., Rom. 44 B4
Barley Mow Pas. EC1 12 H2
Barley Mow Pas. W4 65 D5
Heathfield Ter.
Barleycorn Way E14 59 J7
Barleyfields Clo., Rom. 44 B6
Barlow Clo., Wall. 101 E6
Cobham Clo.
Barlow Pl. W1 11 E6
Barlow Rd. NW6 48 C6
Barlow Rd. W3 65 B1
Barlow Rd., Hmptn. 81 G7
Barlow St. SE17 21 C2
Barmeston Rd. SE6 87 B2
Barmor Clo., Har. 36 H2
Barmouth Ave., Grnf. 55 C2
Barmouth Rd. SW18 75 F6
Barmouth Rd., Croy. 102 G2
Barn Clo., Nthlt. 54 C2
Barn Cres., Stan. 29 F6
Barn Elms Pk. SW15 74 J2
Barn Hill, Wem. 47 A1
Barn Ms., Har. 45 G3
Barn Ri., Wem. 47 A1
Barn St. N16 50 B3
Stoke Newington Ch. St.
Barn Way, Wem. 47 A1
Barnabas Ct. N21 24 G5
Cheyne Wk.
Barnabas Rd. E9 50 G5
Barnaby Clo., Har. 45 J2
Barnaby Pl. SW7 18 E2
Barnaby Pl. SW7 66 G4
Barnaby Way, Chig. 35 D3
Barnard Clo. SE18 70 D3
Barnard Clo., Chis. 97 G1
Barnard Clo., Sun. 81 B7
Oak Gro.
Barnard Clo., Wall. 101 D7
Alcock Clo.
Barnard Gdns., Hayes 54 B4
Barnard Gdns., N.Mal. 92 G4
Barnard Gro. E15 51 F7
Vicarage La.
Barnard Hill N10 40 B1
Barnard Ms. SW11 75 H4
Barnard Rd. SW11 75 H4
Barnard Rd., Enf. 25 E2
Barnard Rd., Mitch. 94 A3
Barnardo Dr., Ilf. 43 F4
Civic Way
Barnardo St. E1 59 G6
Devonport St.
Barnard's Inn EC1 12 E3
Barnby St. E15 60 E1
Barnby St. NW1 7 G3
Barnby St. NW1 58 C3
Barncroft Clo., Loug. 27 C5
Barncroft Grn., Loug. 27 D5
Barncroft Rd., Loug. 27 D5
Barnehurst Ave., Bexh. 80 J1
Barnehurst Ave., Erith 80 J1
Barnehurst Clo., Erith 80 J1
Barnehurst Rd., Bexh. 80 J2
Barnes All., Hmptn. 90 J2
Hampton Ct. Rd.
Barnes Ave. SW13 65 G7
Barnes Ave., Sthl. 63 F4
Barnes Bri. SW13 74 E2
Barnes Bri. W4 74 E2
Barnes Clo. E12 52 A4
Barnes Ct. E16 60 J5
Ridgwell Rd.
Barnes Ct., Wdf.Grn. 35 A5
Barnes End, N.Mal. 92 G5
Barnes High St. SW13 74 F2
Barnes Ho., Bark. 61 G1
St. Marys
Barnes Rd. N18 33 F4
Barnes Rd., Ilf. 52 F5
Barnes St. E14 59 H6
Barnes Ter. SE8 68 J5
Barnesbury Ho. SW4 76 D6

Barnet Bypass, Barn.	22	E1
Barnet Dr., Brom.	104	B2
Barnet Gate La., Barn.	22	F6
Barnet Gro. E2	**9**	**H3**
Barnet Gro. E2	59	D3
Barnet Hill, Barn.	23	C4
Barnet Ho. N20	31	F2
Barnet La. N20	31	C1
Barnet La., Barn.	23	D6
Barnet Rd. (Arkley), Barn.	22	D6
Barnet Trd. Est., Barn.	23	C3
Barnet Way NW7	30	D3
Barnet Wd. Rd., Brom.	103	H2
Barnett St. E1	59	E6
Cannon St. Rd.		
Barney Clo. SE7	69	J5
Barnfield, N.Mal.	92	E6
Barnfield Ave., Croy.	102	F2
Barnfield Ave., Kings.T.	82	H5
Barnfield Ave., Mitch.	94	B4
Barnfield Clo. N4	40	E7
Crouch Hill		
Barnfield Gdns. SE18	70	E6
Plumstead Common Rd.		
Barnfield Gdns., Kings.T.	82	H5
Barnfield Pl. E14	69	A4
Barnfield Rd. SE18	70	E6
Barnfield Rd. W5	55	F4
Barnfield Rd., Belv.	71	F6
Barnfield Rd., Edg.	38	C1
Barnfield Wd. Clo., Beck.	96	D6
Barnfield Wd. Rd., Beck.	96	D6
Barnham Rd., Grnf.	54	J3
Barnham St. SE1	**17**	**E3**
Barnham St. SE1	68	B2
Barnhill, Pnr.	36	C5
Barnhill Ave., Brom.	96	F5
Barnhill La., Hayes	54	B4
Barnhill Rd., Hayes	54	B4
Barnhill Rd., Wem.	47	C3
Barnhurst Path, Wat.	28	C5
Barningham Way NW9	38	D6
Barnlea Clo., Felt.	81	E2
Barnmead Gdns., Dag.	53	F5
Barnmead Rd., Beck.	95	H1
Barnmead Rd., Dag.	53	F5
Barnsbury Clo., N.Mal.	92	C4
Barnsbury Cres., Surb.	99	B1
Barnsbury Gro. N7	49	F6
Barnsbury La., Surb.	99	B2
Barnsbury Pk. N1	49	G7
Barnsbury Rd. N1	**8**	**E1**
Barnsbury Rd. N1	58	G2
Barnsbury Sq. N1	49	G7
Barnsbury St. N1	49	G7
Barnsbury Ter. N1	49	F7
Barnscroft SW20	92	H3
Barnsdale Ave. E14	69	B4
Barnsdale Rd. W9	57	C4
Barnsley St. E1	59	E4
Barnstaple Rd., Ruis.	45	C3
Popham St.		
Barnwell Rd. SW2	76	G5
Barnwood Clo. W9	**6**	**A6**
Barnwood Clo. W9	57	E4
Barnwood Ct. E16	69	G1
North Woolwich Rd.		
Baron Gdns., Ilf.	43	F3
Baron Gro., Mitch.	93	H4
Baron Rd., Dag.	53	D1
Baron St. N1	**8**	**E2**
Baron St. N1	58	G2
Baron Wk. E16	60	F5
Malmesbury Rd.		
Baron Wk., Mitch.	93	H4
Baroness Rd. E2	**9**	**G3**
Baronet Gro. N17	41	D1
St. Paul's Rd.		
Baronet Rd. N17	41	D1
Barons, The, Twick.	73	E6
Barons Ct. Rd. W14	66	B5
Barons Gate, Barn.	23	H6
Barons Keep W14	66	B5
Barons Mead, Har.	37	B4
Barons Pl. SE1	**16**	**F4**
Barons Pl. SE1	67	G2
Barons Wk., Croy.	95	H6
Baronsfield Rd., Twick.	73	E6
Baronsmead Rd. SW13	74	G1
Baronsmede W5	64	J2
Barque Ms. SE8	69	A6
Watergate St.		
Barrack Rd., Houns.	72	D4
Barracks La., Barn.	23	B3
High St.		
Barratt Ave. N22	40	F2
Barratt Ind. Pk., Sthl.	63	G2
Tudor Rd.		
Barrenger Rd. N10	39	J1
Barrett Rd. E17	42	C4
Barrett St. W1	**11**	**C4**
Barrett St. W1	58	A6
Barretts Grn. Rd. NW10	56	C3
Barretts Gro. N16	50	B5
Barrhill Rd. SW2	85	E2
Barrie Est. W2	10	E5
Barrie Twr. W3	65	C2
Barriedale SE14	77	H2
Barrier App. SE7	70	A3
Barringer Sq. SW17	85	A4
Barrington Clo. NW5	49	A5
Grafton Rd.		
Barrington Clo., Ilf.	43	C1
Hurstleigh Gdns.		
Barrington Clo., Loug.	27	F4
Barrington Rd.		
Barrington Grn., Loug.	27	F4
Barrington Rd. E12	52	D6
Barrington Rd. N8	40	D5
Barrington Rd. SW9	76	H3
Barrington Rd., Bexh.	80	D2
Barrington Rd., Loug.	27	F4
Barrington Rd., Sutt.	100	D1
Barrington Vill. SE18	79	D1
Barrow Ave., Cars.	100	J7
Barrow Clo. N21	32	H3
Barrow Hedges Clo., Cars.	100	H7
Barrow Hedges Way, Cars.	100	H7
Barrow Hill Rd. NW8	**6**	**G2**
Barrow Hill Rd. NW8	57	H2
Barrow Pt. Ave., Pnr.	36	E2
Barrow Pt. La., Pnr.	36	E2
Barrow Rd. SW16	85	D6
Barrow Rd., Croy.	101	G5
Barrow Wk., Brent.	64	F5
Glenhurst Rd.		
Barrow Way N7	49	F3
Barrowdene Clo., Pnr.	36	E2
Paines La.		
Barrowell Grn. N21	32	H2
Barrowfield Clo. N9	33	E3
Barrowgate Rd. W4	65	C5
Barrs Rd. NW10	47	D7
Barry Ave. N15	41	C6
Craven Pk. Rd.		
Barry Ave., Bexh.	71	E7
Barry Clo., Orp.	104	H3
Barry Rd. E6	61	B6
Barry Rd. NW10	47	C7
Barry Rd. SE22	77	D6
Barset Rd. SE15	77	F3
Barson Clo. SE20	86	F7
Barston Rd. SE27	85	J2
Barstow Cres. SW2	85	F1
Barter St. WC1	**12**	**B2**
Barter St. WC1	58	E5
Barters Wk., Pnr.	36	E3
High St.		
Barth Rd. SE18	70	H4
Bartholomew Clo. EC1	**12**	**J2**
Bartholomew Clo. EC1	58	J5
Bartholomew Rd. SW18	75	F4
Bartholomew La. EC2	**13**	**C4**
Bartholomew Pl. EC1	**12**	**J2**
Bartholomew Rd. NW5	49	C6
Bartholomew Sq. E1	59	E4
Coventry Rd.		
Bartholomew Sq. EC1	**9**	**A5**
Bartholomew Sq. EC1	58	J4
Bartholomew St. SE1	**17**	**C6**
Bartholomew St. SE1	68	A3
Bartholomew Vill. NW5	49	C6
Bartle Ave. E6	61	B2
Bartle Rd. W11	57	B6
Bartlett Clo. E14	60	A6
Bartlett Ct. EC4	**12**	**F3**
Bartlett St., S.Croy.	102	A5
Barton Ave., Rom.	53	H1
Barton Clo. E6	61	C6
Brandreth Rd.		
Barton Clo. E9	50	F5
Churchill Wk.		
Barton Clo. SE15	77	E3
Kirkwood Rd.		
Barton Clo., Bexh.	80	E5
Barton Clo., Chig.	35	F2
Barton Grn., N.Mal.	92	D2
Barton Meadows, Ilf.	81	D1
Barton Rd. W14	66	B5
Barton Rd., Sid.	89	E6
Barton St. SW1	**16**	**A5**
Barton Way, Borwd.	22	A2
Barville Clo. SE4	77	H4
St. Norbert Rd.		
Barwick Rd. E7	51	H4
Barwood Ave., W.Wick.	103	B1
Basden Gro., Felt.	81	G2
Basedale Rd., Dag.	53	B7
Baseing Clo. E6	61	D7
Bashley Rd. NW10	56	D4
Basil Ave. E6	61	B2
Basil Gdns., Croy.	102	G1
Primrose La.		
Basil St. SW3	**14**	**J5**
Basil St. SW3	66	J3
Basildene Rd., Houns.	72	D3
Basildon Ave., Ilf.	43	D1
Basildon Rd. SE2	71	A5
Basildon Rd., Bexh.	80	E2
Basing Clo., T.Ditt.	91	C7
Basing Ct. SE15	77	C1
Basing Dr., Bex.	80	F6
Basing Hill NW11	48	C1
Basing Hill, Wem.	46	J2
Basing Ho., Bark.	61	G1
St. Margarets		
Basing Ho. Yd. E2	**9**	**E3**
Basing Pl. E2	**9**	**E3**
Basing St. W11	57	C6
Basing Way N3	39	D3
Basing Way, T.Ditt.	91	C7
Basingdon Way SE5	77	A4
Basingfield Rd., T.Ditt.	91	C7
Basinghall Ave. EC2	**13**	**B2**
Basinghall Ave. EC2	59	A5
Basinghall St. EC2	**13**	**B3**
Basinghall St. EC2	58	J5
Basire St. N1	58	A1
Baskerville Rd. SW18	75	H7
Basket Gdns. SE9	79	B5
Baslow Clo., Har.	37	A1
Baslow Wk. E5	50	G4
Overbury St.		
Basnett Rd. SW11	76	A3
Basque Ct. SE16	68	G2
Poolmans St.		
Bassano St. SE22	77	C5
Bassant Rd. SE18	70	J6
Bassein Pk. Rd. W12	65	F2
Basset Ho., Dag.	62	B1
Bassett Gdns., Islw.	63	J7
Bassett Rd. W10	57	A6
Bassett St. NW5	49	A6
Bassetts Clo., Orp.	104	E3
Bassetts Way, Orp.	104	E4
Bassingham Rd. SW18	75	F7
Bassingham Rd., Wem.	46	G6
Basswood Clo. SE15	77	E3
Linden Gro.		
Bastable Ave., Bark.	61	H2
Bastion Rd. SE2	71	A5
Baston Manor Rd., Brom.	103	H3
Baston Rd., Brom.	103	H1
Bastwick St. EC1	**8**	**J5**
Bastwick St. EC1	58	J4
Basuto Rd. SW6	75	D1
Batavia Clo., Sun.	90	C1
Batavia Ms. SE14	68	H7
Goodwood Rd.		
Batavia Rd. SE14	68	H7
Batavia Rd., Sun.	90	B1
Batchelor St. N1	**8**	**F1**
Batchelor St. N1	58	G2
Bate St. E14	59	J7
Three Colt St.		
Bateman Clo., Bark.	52	F6
Glenny Rd.		
Bateman Ho. SE17	**20**	**G6**
Bateman Rd. E4	34	A6
Bateman St. W1	**11**	**H4**
Bateman's Bldgs. W1	**11**	**H4**
Bateman's Row EC2	**9**	**E5**
Bateman's Row EC2	59	B4
Bates Cres. SW16	85	C7
Bates Cres., Croy.	101	G5
Bateson St. SE18	70	H4
Gunning St.		
Bath Clo. SE15	68	E7
Asylum Rd.		
Bath Ct. EC1	**8**	**E6**
Bath Ho. Rd., Croy.	101	E1
Bath Pas., Kings.T.	91	G2
St. James Rd.		
Bath Pl., Barn.	23	C3
Bath Rd. E7	52	A6
Bath Rd. N9	33	E2
Bath Rd. W4	65	E4
Bath Rd., Houns.	72	D2
Bath Rd., Mitch.	93	G3
Bath Rd., Rom.	44	E6
Bath St. EC1	**9**	**A4**
Bath St. EC1	58	J3
Bath Ter. SE1	**16**	**J6**
Bath Ter. SE1	67	J3
Bathgate Rd. SW19	84	A3
Baths Rd., Brom.	92	A4
Bathurst Ave. SW19	93	E1
Brisbane Ave.		
Bathurst Gdns. NW10	56	H2
Bathurst Ms. W2	**10**	**F5**
Bathurst Rd., Ilf.	52	E1
Bathurst St. W2	**10**	**F5**
Bathurst St. W2	57	G7
Bathway SE18	70	D4
Batley Pl. N16	50	C3
Batley Rd. N16	50	C3
Stoke Newington High St.		
Batley Rd., Enf.	25	A1
Batman Clo. W12	65	H1
Batoum Gdns. W6	65	J3
Batson St. W12	65	G2
Batsworth Rd., Mitch.	93	G3
Batten Clo. E6	61	C6
Savage Gdns.		
Batten St. SW11	75	H3
Battenburg Wk. SE19	86	B5
Brabourne Clo.		
Battersby Rd. SE6	87	D2
Battersea Bri. SW3	**18**	**F7**
Battersea Bri. SW3	66	G7
Battersea Bri. SW11	**18**	**F7**
Battersea Bri. SW11	66	H7
Battersea Bri. Rd. SW11	66	H7
Battersea Ch. Rd. SW11	75	G1
Battersea High St. SW11	75	G1
Battersea Pk. SW11	66	J7
Battersea Pk. Rd. SW8	76	B1
Battersea Pk. Rd. SW11	76	H2
Battersea Ri. SW11	75	G5
Battersea Sq. SW11	75	G1
Battersea High St.		
Battery Rd. SE28	70	H2
Battishill Gdns. N1	49	H7
Waterloo Ter.		
Battishill St. N1	49	H7
Waterloo Ter.		
Battle Bri. La. SE1	**17**	**D2**
Battle Bri. La. SE1	68	B1
Battle Bri. Rd. NW1	**8**	**A2**
Battle Bri. Rd. NW1	58	E2
Battle Clo. SW19	84	F6
North Rd.		
Battle Rd., Belv.	71	J4
Battle Rd., Erith	71	J4
Battledean Rd. N5	49	H5
Batty St. E1	**13**	**J3**
Batty St. E1	59	D6
Baudwin Rd. SE6	87	E2
Baugh Rd., Sid.	89	C5
Baulk, The SW18	75	D7
Bavant Rd. SW16	94	F2
Bavaria Rd. N19	49	E2
Bavent Rd. SE5	76	J2
Bawdale Rd. SE22	77	C5
Bawdsey Ave., Ilf.	43	J4

Bawtree Rd. SE14 68 H7
Bawtry Rd. N20 31 J3
Baxendale N20 31 F2
Baxendale St. E2 9 H3
Baxendale St. E2 59 D3
Baxter Rd. E16 60 J6
Baxter Rd. N1 50 A6
Baxter Rd. N18 33 E4
Baxter Rd. NW10 56 E4
Baxter Rd., Ilf. 52 E5
Bay Ct. W5 64 H3
Popes La.
Bay Tree Clo., Brom. 96 J1
Baydon Ct., Brom. 96 F3
Bayes Clo. SE26 86 F5
Bayford Rd. SE9 79 A4
Bayford Ms. E8 50 E7
Bayford St.
Bayford Rd. NW10 57 A3
Bayford St. E8 50 E7
Bayham Pl. NW1 58 C1
Bayham Rd. W4 65 D3
Bayham Rd. W13 55 E7
Bayham Rd., Mord. 93 E4
Bayham St. NW1 58 C1
Bayley St. WC1 11 H2
Bayley St. WC1 58 D5
Bayley Wk. SE2 71 E5
Woolwich Rd.
Baylin Rd. SW18 75 E6
Garratt La.
Baylis Rd. SE1 16 E4
Baylis Rd. SE1 67 G2
Bayliss Ave. SE28 62 D7
Bayne Clo. E6 61 C6
Savage Gdns.
Baynes Clo., Enf. 25 D1
Baynes Ms. NW3 48 G6
Belsize La.
Baynes St. NW1 49 C7
Baynham Clo., Bex. 80 F6
Bayonne Rd. W6 66 B6
Bayshill Ri., Nthlt. 45 H6
Bayston Rd. N16 50 C3
Bayswater Rd. W2 10 A6
Bayswater Rd. W2 57 E7
Baytree Clo., Sid. 88 J1
Baytree Rd. SW2 76 F4
Bazalgette Clo., 92 D5
N.Mal.
Bazalgette Gdns., 92 D5
N.Mal.
Bazely St. E14 60 C7
Bazile Rd. N21 24 G6
Beach Gro., Felt. 81 G2
Beacham Clo. SE7 70 A5
Beachborough Rd., 87 C4
Brom.
Beachcroft Rd. E11 51 E3
Beachcroft Way N19 49 D1
Beachy Rd. E3 51 A7
Beacon Gro., Cars. 101 A4
Beacon Hill N7 49 E5
Beacon Rd. SE13 78 D6
Beacons Clo. E6 61 B5
Oliver Gdns.
Beaconsfield Clo. N11 32 A5
Beaconsfield Clo. SE3 69 G6
Beaconsfield Clo. W4 65 C5
Beaconsfield Rd. E10 51 C2
Beaconsfield Rd. E16 60 F4
Beaconsfield Rd. E17 41 J6
Beaconsfield Rd. N9 33 D3
Beaconsfield Rd. N11 32 A3
Beaconsfield Rd. N15 41 B4
Beaconsfield Rd. 47 F6
NW10
Beaconsfield Rd. SE3 69 F7
Beaconsfield Rd. SE9 88 B2
Beaconsfield Rd. SE17 21 C4
Beaconsfield Rd. 68 A6
SE17
Beaconsfield Rd. W4 65 D3
Beaconsfield Rd. W5 64 F2
Beaconsfield Rd., 97 A3
Brom.
Beaconsfield Rd., 95 A6
Croy.
Beaconsfield Rd., 98 B7
Esher
Beaconsfield Rd., 63 C1
Hayes
Beaconsfield Rd., 92 D2
N.Mal.
Beaconsfield Rd., 63 D1
Sthl.
Beaconsfield Rd., 91 J7
Surb.

Beaconsfield Rd., 73 E6
Twick.
Beaconsfield Ter., 44 D6
Rom.
Beaconsfield Ter. Rd. 66 B3
W14
Beaconsfield Wk. E6 61 D6
East Ham
Manor Way
Beaconsfield Wk. SW6 75 C1
Parsons Grn. La.
Beacontree Ave. E17 42 D1
Beacontree Rd. E11 42 F7
Beadlow Clo., Cars. 93 G6
Olveston Wk.
Beadman Pl. SE27 85 H4
Beadman St.
Beadman St. SE27 85 H4
Beadnell Rd. SE23 86 G1
Beadon Rd. W6 65 J4
Beadon Rd., Brom. 96 G4
Beaford Gro. SW20 93 B3
Beagle Clo., Felt. 81 B4
Beak St. W1 11 G5
Beak St. W1 58 C7
Beal Clo., Well. 80 A1
Beal Rd., Ilf. 52 D2
Beale Clo. N13 32 H5
Beale Pl. E3 59 J2
Beale Rd. E3 59 J1
Beam Ave., Dag. 62 H1
Beaminster Gdns., Ilf. 43 E2
Beamish Dr. 28 J1
(Bushey), Wat.
Beamish Rd. N9 33 D1
Bean Rd., Bexh. 80 D4
Beanacre Clo. E9 50 J6
Beanshaw SE9 88 D4
Beansland Gro., 44 E2
Rom.
Bear All. EC4 12 G3
Bear Clo., Rom. 44 H6
Fernden Way
Bear Gdns. SE1 16 J1
Bear Gdns. SE1 67 J1
Bear La. SE1 16 H2
Bear La. SE1 67 H1
Bear Rd., Felt. 81 D5
Bear St. WC2 11 J5
Beard Rd., Kings.T. 82 J5
Beardell St. SE19 86 C6
Beardow Gro. N14 24 C6
Beard's Hill, Hmptn. 90 G1
Beard's Hill Clo., 90 G1
Hmptn.
Beard's Hill
Beardsfield E13 60 G1
Valetta Gro.
Beardsley Way W3 65 D2
Bearfield Rd., Kings.T. 82 H7
Bearstead Ri. SE4 77 J5
Bearstead Ter., Beck. 87 A4
Copers Cope Rd.
Beatrice Ave. SW16 94 F2
Beatrice Ave., Wem. 46 H5
Beatrice Clo. E13 60 G4
Chargeable La.
Beatrice Clo., Pnr. 36 A4
Reid Clo.
Beatrice Ct., Buck.H. 35 A2
Beatrice Ct., Wem. 46 J4
Beatrice Pl. W8 14 A6
Beatrice Pl. W8 66 E3
Beatrice Rd. E17 42 A5
Beatrice Rd. N4 40 G7
Beatrice Rd. N9 25 F7
Beatrice Rd. SE1 21 J2
Beatrice Rd. SE1 68 D4
Beatrice Rd., Rich. 73 J5
Albert Rd.
Beatson Wk. SE16 68 H1
Beattock Ri. N10 40 B4
Beatty Rd. N16 50 B4
Beatty Rd., Stan. 29 F6
Beatty St. NW1 7 F1
Beatty St. NW1 58 C2
Beattyville Gdns., Ilf. 43 D3
Beauchamp Clo. W4 65 C3
Church Path
Beauchamp Pl. SW3 14 H5
Beauchamp Pl. SW3 66 H3
Beauchamp Rd. E7 51 H7
Beauchamp Rd. SE19 95 A1
Beauchamp Rd. SW11 75 H4
Beauchamp Rd., 90 H5
E.Mol.
Beauchamp Rd., Sutt. 100 D4

Beauchamp Rd., 73 D7
Twick.
Beauchamp Rd., 90 H5
W.Mol.
Beauchamp St. EC1 12 E2
Beauchamp Ter. SW15 74 H3
Dryburgh Rd.
Beauclerc Rd. W6 65 H3
Beauclerk Clo., Felt. 81 B1
Florence Rd.
Beaufort E6 61 D5
Newark Knok
Beaufort Ave., Har. 37 D4
Beaufort Clo. E4 34 B6
Higham Sta. Ave.
Beaufort Clo. SW15 74 H7
Beaufort Clo. W5 55 J5
Beaufort Clo., Rom. 44 J4
Beaufort Ct., Rich. 82 F4
Beaufort Rd.
Beaufort Dr. NW11 39 D4
Beaufort Gdns. NW4 38 J6
Beaufort Gdns. SW3 14 H5
Beaufort Gdns. SW3 66 H3
Beaufort Gdns. SW16 85 F7
Beaufort Gdns., 72 E1
Houns.
Beaufort Gdns., Ilf. 52 D1
Beaufort Ms. SW6 66 C6
Lillie Rd.
Beaufort Pk. NW11 39 D4
Beaufort Rd. W5 55 J5
Beaufort Rd., Kings.T. 91 H4
Beaufort Rd., Rich. 82 F4
Beaufort Rd., Twick. 73 F7
Beaufort St. SW3 18 F6
Beaufort St. SW3 66 G6
Beaufort Way, Epsom 97 B7
Beaufoy Rd. N17 33 B7
Beaufoy Wk. SE11 **20 D2**
Beaufoy Wk. SE11 67 F4
Beaulieu Ave. SE26 86 E4
Beaulieu Clo. NW9 38 E3
Beaulieu Clo. SE5 77 A3
Beaulieu Clo., Houns. 72 F5
Beaulieu Clo., Mitch. 94 A1
Beaulieu Clo., Twick. 73 G6
Beaulieu Clo., Wat. 28 C1
Beaulieu Dr., Pnr. 36 D6
Beaulieu Gdns. N21 24 J7
Beaulieu Pl. W4 65 C3
Rothschild Rd.
Beaumanor Gdns. SE9 88 D4
Beanshaw
Beaumaris Dr., 35 A7
Wdf.Grn.
Beaumont Ave. W14 66 C5
Beaumont Ave., Har. 36 H6
Beaumont Ave., Rich. 73 J3
Beaumont Ave., 46 F5
Wem.
Beaumont Clo., 83 A7
Kings.T.
Beaumont Cres. W14 66 C5
Beaumont Gdns. NW3 48 D3
Beaumont Gro. E1 59 G4
Beaumont Ms. W1 11 C1
Beaumont Pl. W1 7 G5
Beaumont Pl. W1 58 C4
Beaumont Pl., Barn. 23 C1
Beaumont Pl., Islw. 73 C5
Beaumont Ri. N19 40 D7
Beaumont Rd. E10 42 B7
Beaumont Rd. E13 60 H3
Beaumont Rd. SE19 85 J6
Beaumont Rd. SW19 75 B7
Beaumont Rd. W4 65 C3
Beaumont Rd., Orp. 97 G6
Beaumont Sq. E1 59 G4
Beaumont St. W1 11 C1
Beaumont St. W1 58 A5
Beaumont Wk. NW3 48 J7
Beauvais Ter., Nthlt. 54 D3
Beauval Rd. SE22 77 C6
Beaver Clo. SE20 86 D7
Lullington Rd.
Beaver Clo., Hmptn. 90 H1
Beaver Gro., Nthlt. 54 E3
Jetstar Way
Beaverbank Rd. SE9 88 G1
Beavers Cres., Houns. 72 D4
Beavers La., Houns. 72 C2
Beaverwood Rd., 88 H6
Chis.
Beavor La. W6 65 G4
Bebbington Rd. SE18 70 H4
Beblets Clo., Orp. 104 J5
Bec Clo., Ruis. 45 D3

Beccles Dr., Bark. 52 H6
Beccles St. E14 59 J7
Beck Clo. SE13 78 B1
Beck La., Beck. 95 G3
Beck La., Beck. 95 G3
Beck River Pk., Beck. 96 A1
Rectory Rd.
Beck Rd. E8 59 E1
Beck Way, Beck. 95 J3
Beckenham Gdns. N9 33 B3
Beckenham Gro., 96 D2
Brom.
Beckenham Hill Rd. 87 C5
SE6
Beckenham Hill Rd., 87 B5
Beck.
Beckenham La., 96 E2
Brom.
Beckenham Pl. Pk., 87 B7
Beck.
Beckenham Rd., Beck. 95 G1
Beckenham Rd., 96 B7
W.Wick.
Beckers, The N16 50 D3
Rectory Rd.
Becket Ave. E6 61 D3
Becket Clo. SE25 95 D6
Becket Fold, Har. 37 C5
Courtfield Cres.
Becket Rd. N18 33 F4
Becket St. SE1 17 B5
Beckett Clo. NW10 47 D6
Beckett Clo. SW16 85 D2
Beckett Clo., Belv. 71 E3
Tunstock Way
Beckett Wk., Beck. 86 H6
Becketts Clo., Felt. 72 B6
Becketts Clo., Orp. 104 J3
Becketts Pl., Kings.T. 91 G1
Beckford Dr., Orp. 97 H7
Beckford Pl. SE17 21 A4
Beckford Rd., Croy. 95 C6
Becklow Gdns. W12 65 G2
Becklow Rd.
Becklow Rd. W12 65 F2
Becks Rd., Sid. 89 A3
Beckton Retail Pk. E6 61 D5
Beckton Rd. E16 60 F5
Beckway Rd. SW16 94 D2
Beckway St. SE17 21 D2
Beckway St. SE17 68 A4
Beckwith Rd. SE24 77 A6
Beclands Rd. SW17 85 A6
Becmead Ave. SW16 85 D4
Becmead Ave., Har. 37 E5
Becondale Rd. SE19 86 B5
Becontree Ave., Dag. 53 B4
Bective Pl. SW15 75 C4
Bective Rd.
Bective Rd. E7 51 G4
Bective Rd. SW15 75 B4
Becton Pl., Erith 71 H7
Bedale St. SE1 17 B2
Bedale St. SE1 68 A1
Beddington Fm. Rd. 94 E7
Croy.
Beddington Gdns., 101 A6
Cars.
Beddington Gdns., 101 B6
Wall.
Beddington Grn., Orp. 97 J1
Beddington Gro., 101 D5
Wall.
Beddington La., Croy. 94 C5
Beddington Path, Orp. 97 J1
Beddington Rd., Ilf. 43 J3
Beddington Rd., Orp. 97 H1
Beddington Trd. Pk. 101 E1
W., Croy.
Beddington Fm. Rd.
Bede Clo., Pnr. 36 D1
Bede Rd., Rom. 44 C6
Bedenham Way SE15 21 F7
Bedens Rd., Sid. 89 E6
Bedfont Clo., Mitch. 94 A2
Bedford Ave. WC1 11 J2
Bedford Ave. WC1 58 D5
Bedford Ave., Barn. 23 C5
Bedford Ave., Hayes 54 B6
Bedford Clo. N10 32 A7
Bedford Cor. W4 65 E4
The Ave.
Bedford Ct. WC2 12 A6
Bedford Gdns. W8 66 D1
Bedford Hill SW12 85 B1
Bedford Hill SW16 85 B1
Bedford Ho. SW4 76 E4
Bedford Pk., Croy. 101 J1

Bedford Pl. WC1	**12**	**A1**
Bedford Pl., WC1	58	E5
Bedford Pl., Croy.	102	A1
Bedford Rd. E6	61	D1
Bedford Rd. E17	42	A2
Bedford Rd. E18	42	G2
Bedford Rd. N2	39	H3
Bedford Rd. N8	40	D6
Bedford Rd. N9	25	E7
Bedford Rd. N15	41	B4
Bedford Rd. N22	40	E1
Bedford Rd. NW7	30	E2
Bedford Rd. SW4	76	E3
Bedford Rd. W4	65	D3
Bedford Rd. W13	55	E7
Bedford Rd., Har.	36	J6
Bedford Rd., Ilf.	52	E3
Bedford Rd., Sid.	88	H3
Bedford Rd., Twick.	82	A3
Bedford Rd., Wor.Pk.	99	J2
Bedford Row WC1	**12**	**D1**
Bedford Row WC1	58	F5
Bedford Sq. WC1	**11**	**J2**
Bedford Sq. WC1	58	D5
Bedford St. WC2	**12**	**A5**
Bedford St. WC2	58	E7
Bedford Way WC1	**7**	**J6**
Bedford Way WC1	58	D4
Bedfordbury WC2	**12**	**A6**
Bedgebury Gdns. SW19	84	B2
Bedgebury Rd. SE9	79	A4
Bedivere Rd., Brom.	87	G3
Bedlow Way, Croy.	101	F4
Bedonwell Rd. SE2	71	E6
Bedonwell Rd., Belv.	71	E6
Bedonwell Rd., Bexh.	80	F1
Bedser Clo., Th.Hth.	94	J3
Norbury Ave.		
Bedser Dr., Grnf.	46	A5
Bedster Gdns., W.Mol.	90	H2
Bedwardine Rd. SE19	86	B7
Bedwell Rd. N17	41	B1
Bedwell Rd., Belv.	71	G5
Bedwin Way SE16	68	E5
Catlin St.		
Beeby Rd. E16	60	H5
Beech Ave. N20	31	H1
Beech Ave. W3	65	E1
Beech Ave., Brent.	64	E7
Beech Ave., Buck.H.	34	H2
Beech Ave., Ruis.	45	B1
Beech Ave., Sid.	80	A7
Beech Clo. N9	25	D6
Beech Clo. SE8	68	J6
Clyde St.		
Beech Clo. SW15	74	G7
Beech Clo. SW19	83	J6
Beech Clo., Cars.	100	J2
Beech Clo., Sun.	90	D2
Harfield Rd.		
Beech Copse, Brom.	97	C2
Beech Copse, S.Croy.	102	B5
Beech Ct. E17	42	D3
Beech Ct. SE9	79	B6
Beech Ct., Ilf.	52	D3
Riverdene Rd.		
Beech Dell, Kes.	104	C4
Beech Dr. N2	39	J2
Beech Gdns. W5	64	H2
Beech Gdns., Dag.	53	H7
Beech Gro., Ilf.	35	H6
Beech Gro., Mitch.	94	D5
Beech Gro., N.Mal.	92	D3
Beech Hall Cres. E4	34	D7
Beech Hall Rd. E4	34	C7
Beech Hill, Barn.	23	F1
Beech Hill Ave., Barn.	23	F1
Beech Ho., Croy.	103	B6
Beech Ho. Rd., Croy.	102	A3
Beech La., Buck.H.	34	H2
Beech Lawns N12	31	G5
Beech Rd. N11	32	E6
Beech Rd. SW16	94	E2
Beech Row, Rich.	82	H4
Beech St. EC2	**12**	**J1**
Beech St. EC2	58	J5
Beech St., Rom.	44	J4
Beech Tree Glade E4	34	F1
Forest Side		
Beech Wk. NW7	30	E6
Beech Way NW10	47	D7
Beech Way, Twick.	81	G3
Beechcroft, Chis.	88	D7
Beechcroft Ave. NW11	39	C7
Beechcroft Ave., Har.	36	G7
Beechcroft Ave., N.Mal.	92	C1
Beechcroft Ave., Sthl.	63	F1
Beechcroft Clo., Houns.	63	E7
Beechcroft Clo., Orp.	104	G4
Beechcroft Gdns., Wem.	46	J3
Beechcroft Rd. E18	42	H2
Beechcroft Rd. SW14	74	C3
Elm Rd.		
Beechcroft Rd. SW17	84	H2
Beechcroft Rd., Chess.	98	J4
Beechcroft Rd., Orp.	104	G4
Beechdale N21	32	F2
Beechdale Rd. SW2	76	F6
Beechen Cliff Way, Islw.	73	C1
Henley Clo.		
Beechen Gro., Pnr.	36	F3
Beeches Ave., Cars.	100	H7
Beeches Clo. SE20	95	F1
Genoa Rd.		
Beeches Rd. SW17	84	H3
Beeches Rd., Sutt.	100	B1
Beechfield Cotts., Brom.	96	J2
Widmore Rd.		
Beechfield Gdns., Rom.	44	J7
Beechfield Rd. N4	40	J6
Beechfield Rd. SE6	86	J1
Beechfield Rd., Brom.	96	J2
Beechhill Rd. SE9	79	D5
Beechmont Clo., Brom.	87	E5
Beechmore Gdns., Sutt.	100	A2
Beechmore Rd. SW11	75	J1
Beechmount Ave. W7	55	A5
Beecholme Ave., Mitch.	94	B1
Beecholme Est. E5	50	E3
Prout Rd.		
Beechtree Clo., Stan.	29	F5
Beechtree Pl., Sutt.	100	E5
St. Nicholas Way		
Beechvale Clo. N12	31	H5
Beechway, Bex.	80	D6
Beechwood Ave. N3	39	C3
Beechwood Ave., Grnf.	54	H3
Beechwood Ave., Har.	45	H3
Beechwood Ave., Orp.	104	H5
Beechwood Ave., Rich.	74	A1
Beechwood Ave., Sun.	81	A6
Beechwood Ave., Th.Hth.	94	H4
Beechwood Clo. NW7	30	D5
Beechwood Clo., Surb.	91	G7
Beechwood Ct., Cars.	100	J4
Beechwood Ct., Sun.	81	A6
Beechwood Cres., Bexh.	80	D3
Beechwood Dr., Kes.	104	A4
Beechwood Dr., Wdf.Grn.	34	F5
Beechwood Gdns. NW10	55	J3
St. Annes Gdns.		
Beechwood Gdns., Har.	45	H3
Beechwood Gdns., Ilf.	43	C5
Beechwood Gro. W3	56	E7
East Acton La.		
Beechwood Gro., Surb.	91	F7
Beechwood Ms. N9	33	D2
Winchester Rd.		
Beechwood Pk. E18	42	G3
Beechwood Ri., Chis.	88	E4
Beechwood Rd. E8	50	C6
Beechwood Rd. N8	40	D4
Beechwoods Ct. SE19	86	C5
Crystal Palace Par.		
Beechworth Clo. NW3	48	D2
Beecroft Rd. SE4	77	H5
Beehive La., Ilf.	43	C5
Beehive Pas. EC3	**13**	**D4**
Beehive Pl. SW9	76	G3
Beeken Dene, Orp.	104	F4
Isabella Dr.		
Beeleigh Rd., Mord.	93	E4
Beeston Clo. E8	50	D5
Ferncliff Rd.		
Beeston Rd., Barn.	23	G6
Beeston Way, Felt.	72	C6
Beethoven St. W10	57	B3
Beeton Clo., Pnr.	28	G7
Begbie Rd. SE3	78	J1
Beggars Hill, Epsom	99	E6
Beggars Roost La., Sutt.	100	D6
Begonia Pl., Hmptn.	81	G6
Gresham Rd.		
Begonia Rd. W12	56	F6
Du Cane Rd.		
Beira St. SW12	76	B7
Bekesbourne St. E14	59	H6
Ratcliffe La.		
Belcroft Clo., Brom.	87	F7
Hope Pk.		
Beldham Gdns., W.Mol.	90	H3
Belfairs Dr., Rom.	44	C7
Belfairs Grn., Wat.	28	D5
Heysham Dr.		
Belfast Rd. N16	50	C2
Belfast Rd. SE25	95	E4
Belfont Wk. N7	49	E4
Belford Gro. SE18	70	D4
Belfort Rd. SE15	77	F2
Belgrade Rd. N16	50	B4
Belgrade Rd., Hmptn.	90	H1
Belgrave Clo. N14	24	C5
Prince George Ave.		
Belgrave Clo. W3	65	C2
Avenue Rd.		
Belgrave Cres., Sun.	90	B1
Belgrave Gdns. N14	24	D5
Belgrave Gdns. NW8	57	E1
Belgrave Gdns., Stan.	29	F5
Copley Rd.		
Belgrave Ms. N. SW1	**15**	**B4**
Belgrave Ms. N. SW1	67	A3
Belgrave Ms. S. SW1	**15**	**C5**
Belgrave Ms. S. SW1	67	A3
Belgrave Ms. W. SW1	**15**	**B5**
Belgrave Ms. W. SW1	67	A3
Belgrave Pl. SW1	**15**	**C5**
Belgrave Pl. SW1	67	A3
Belgrave Rd. E10	51	C1
Belgrave Rd. E11	51	G2
Belgrave Rd. E13	60	J3
Belgrave Rd. E17	42	A5
Belgrave Rd. SE25	95	D4
Belgrave Rd. SW1	**19**	**F2**
Belgrave Rd. SW1	67	B4
Belgrave Rd. SW13	65	F7
Belgrave Rd., Houns.	72	F3
Belgrave Rd., Ilf.	52	C1
Belgrave Rd., Mitch.	93	G3
Belgrave Rd., Sun.	90	B1
Belgrave Sq. SW1	**15**	**B5**
Belgrave Sq. SW1	67	A3
Belgrave St. E1	59	G5
Belgrave Ter., Wdf.Grn.	34	G3
Belgrave Wk., Mitch.	**93**	**G3**
Belgrave Yd. SW1	**15**	**D6**
Belgravia Gdns., Brom.	87	E6
Belgravia Ho. SW4	76	D6
Belgravia Ms., Kings.T.	91	G4
Belgrove St. WC1	**8**	**B3**
Belgrove St. WC1	58	E3
Belham Wk. SE5	77	A1
D'Eynsford Rd.		
Belinda Rd. SW9	76	H3
Belitha Vill. N1	49	F7
Bell Clo., Pnr.	36	C2
Bell Ct., Surb.	99	B2
Barnsbury La.		
Bell Dr. SW18	75	B7
Bell Fm. Ave., Dag.	53	J3
Bell Grn. SE26	86	J3
Bell Grn. La. SE26	86	J5
Bell Hill, Croy.	101	J3
Surrey St.		
Bell Ho. Rd., Rom.	53	J1
Bell Inn Yd. EC3	**13**	**C4**
Bell La. E1	**13**	**F2**
Bell La. E1	59	C5
Bell La. E16	69	G1
Bell La. NW4	38	C4
Bell La., Twick.	82	D1
Bell La., Wem.	46	G2
Lumen Rd.		
Bell Meadow SE19	86	B4
Dulwich Wd. Ave.		
Bell Rd., E.Mol.	91	A5
Bell Rd., Enf.	25	A1
Bell Rd., Houns.	72	H3
Bell St. NW1	**10**	**G1**
Bell St. NW1	57	H5
Bell Water Gate SE18	70	E4
Bell Wf. La. EC4	**13**	**A5**
Bell Yd. WC2	**12**	**E4**
Bell Yd. WC2	58	G6
Bellamy Clo. W14	66	C5
Aisgill Ave.		
Bellamy Clo., Edg.	30	C3
Bellamy Dr., Stan.	37	E1
Bellamy Rd. E4	34	B6
Bellamy Rd., Enf.	25	A2
Bellamy St. SW12	76	B7
Bellasis Ave. SW2	85	E2
Belle Staines Pleasaunce E4	34	A2
Belle Vue, Grnf.	55	A1
Belle Vue Est. NW4	38	J4
Belle Vue La. (Bushey), Wat.	29	A1
Belle Vue Rd. E17	42	D2
Bellefields Rd. SW9	76	F3
Bellegrove Clo., Well.	79	J2
Bellegrove Rd., Well.	79	H2
Bellenden Rd. SE15	77	C3
Belleville Rd. SW11	75	H5
Bellevue Ms. N11	32	A5
Bellevue Rd.		
Bellevue Pk., Th.Hth.	94	J3
Bellevue Pl. E1	59	F4
Bellevue Rd. N11	32	A4
Bellevue Rd. SW13	74	G2
Bellevue Rd. SW17	84	H1
Bellevue Rd. W13	55	E4
Bellevue Rd., Bexh.	80	F5
Bellevue Rd., Kings.T.	91	H3
Bellew St. SW17	84	F3
Bellfield, Croy.	102	J7
Bellfield Ave., Har.	29	A5
Bellflower Clo. E6	61	B5
Sorrel Gdns.		
Bellgate Ms. NW5	49	B3
York Ri.		
Bellingham Grn. SE6	87	A3
Bellingham Rd. SE6	87	C3
Bello Clo. SE24	76	H7
Bellot St. SE10	69	E5
Bellring Clo., Belv.	71	G6
Bells All. SW6	75	D2
Bells Gdn. Est. SE15	68	D7
Buller Clo.		
Bells Hill, Barn.	23	A5
Belltrees Gro. SW16	85	F5
Bellwood Rd. SE15	77	G4
Belmarsh Rd. SE28	70	H2
Western Way		
Belmont Ave. N9	33	D1
Belmont Ave. N13	32	E5
Belmont Ave. N17	40	J3
Belmont Ave., Barn.	23	J5
Belmont Ave., N.Mal.	92	G5
Belmont Ave., Sthl.	63	E3
Belmont Ave., Well.	79	H2
Belmont Ave., Wem.	55	J1
Belmont Circle, Har.	37	E2
Kenton La.		
Belmont Clo. E4	34	D5
Belmont Clo. N20	31	E1
Belmont Clo. SW4	76	C3
Belmont Clo., Barn.	23	J4
Belmont Clo., Wdf.Grn.	34	H4
Belmont Ct. NW11	39	C5
Belmont Gro. SE13	78	D3
Belmont Gro.		
Belmont Hall Ct. SE13	78	D3
Belmont Hill SE13	78	C3
Belmont La., Chis.	88	G5
Belmont La., Stan.	29	F7
Belmont Pk. SE13	78	D4
Belmont Pk. Clo. SE13	78	D4
Belmont Pk.		
Belmont Pk. Rd. E10	42	B6
Belmont Ri., Sutt.	100	C7
Belmont Rd. N15	40	J4
Belmont Rd. N17	40	J3
Belmont Rd. SE25	95	E5
Belmont Rd. SW4	76	C3

Belmont Rd. W4 65 D4
Belmont Rd., Beck. 95 J2
Belmont Rd., Chis. 88 E5
Belmont Rd., Erith 71 G7
Belmont Rd., Har. 37 C3
Belmont Rd., Ilf. 52 F3
Belmont Rd., Twick. 82 A2
Belmont Rd., Wall. 101 B5
Belmont St. NW1 49 A7
Belmont Ter. W4 65 D4
Belmont Rd.
Belmor, Borwd. 22 A5
Belmore Ave., Hayes 54 A6
Belmore La. N7 49 D5
Belmore St. SW8 76 D1
Beloe Clo. SW15 74 G3
Belper Ct. E5 50 G4
Pedro St.
Belsham St. E9 50 F6
Belsize Ave. N13 32 F6
Belsize Ave. NW3 48 G6
Belsize Ave. W13 64 E3
Belsize Cres. NW3 48 G5
Belsize Gdns., Sutt. 100 E4
Belsize Gro. NW3 48 H6
Belsize La. NW3 48 G6
Belsize La. NW3 48 G6
Belsize La.
Belsize Ms. NW3 48 G6
Belsize Pk. NW3 48 G6
Belsize Pk. Gdns. 48 H6
NW3
Belsize Pk. Ms. NW3 48 G6
Belsize La.
Belsize Pl. NW3 48 G6
Belsize La.
Belsize Rd. NW6 57 E1
Belsize Rd., Har. 29 A7
Belsize Sq. NW3 48 G6
Belsize Ter. NW3 48 G6
Belson Rd. SE18 70 C4
Beltane Dr. SW19 84 A3
Belthorn Cres. SW12 76 C7
Belton Rd. E7 51 H7
Belton Rd. E11 51 E4
Belton Rd. N17 41 B3
Belton Rd. NW2 47 G6
Belton Rd., Sid. 89 A4
Belton Way E3 60 A5
Beltran Rd. SW6 75 E2
Beltwood Rd., Belv. 71 J4
Belvedere Ave. SW19 84 B5
Belvedere Ave., Ilf. 34 E2
Belvedere Bldgs. SE1 16 H4
Belvedere Clo., Tedd. 82 B5
Belvedere Ct. N2 39 G5
Belvedere Dr. SW19 84 B5
Belvedere Gdns., 90 F5
W.Mol.
Belvedere Gro. SW19 84 B5
Belvedere Ho., Felt. 81 A1
Belvedere Ind. Est., 71 J3
Belv.
Belvedere Ms. SE15 77 F3
Belvedere Pl. SE1 16 H4
Belvedere Rd. E10 50 H1
Belvedere Rd. SE1 16 D3
Belvedere Rd. SE1 67 F2
Belvedere Rd. SE2 71 D1
Belvedere Rd. SE19 86 C7
Belvedere Rd. W7 64 B3
Belvedere Rd., Bexh. 80 F3
Belvedere Sq. SW19 84 B5
Belvedere Strand NW9 38 F2
Belvedere Way, Har. 37 H6
Belvoir Clo. SE9 88 B3
Belvoir Rd. SE22 77 D7
Belvue Clo., Nthlt. 45 G7
Belvue Rd., Nthlt. 45 G7
Bembridge Clo. NW6 48 B7
Bemerton Est. N1 49 E7
Bemerton St. N1 58 F1
Bemish Rd. SW15 75 A3
Bempton Dr., Ruis. 45 B2
Bemsted Rd. E17 41 J3
Ben Hale Clo., Stan. 29 E4
Ben Jonson Rd. E1 59 G5
Ben Smith Way SE16 17 J5
Ben Tillet Clo., Bark. 53 A7
Benares Rd. SE18 70 J4
Benbow Rd. W6 65 H3
Benbow St. SE8 69 A6
Benbury Clo., Brom. 87 C5
Bench Fld., S.Croy. 102 C6
Bencroft Rd. SW16 85 C7
Bencurtis Pk., 103 D3
W.Wick.
Bendall Ms. NW1 10 H1
Bendemeer Rd. SW15 75 A3

Bendish Rd. E6 52 B7
Bendmore Ave. SE2 71 A5
Bendon Valley SW18 75 E7
Benedict Clo., Belv. 71 E3
Tunstock Way
Benedict Clo., Orp. 104 H3
Benedict Rd. SW9 76 F3
Benedict Rd., Mitch. 93 G3
Benedict Way N2 39 F3
Beneden Grn., Brom. 96 F5
Benett Gdns. SW16 94 E2
Benfleet Clo., Sutt. 100 F3
Bengal Rd., Ilf. 52 E4
Bengarth Dr., Har. 37 A2
Bengarth Rd., Nthlt. 54 D1
Bengeworth Rd. SE5 76 J3
Bengeworth Rd., Har. 46 D4
Benham Clo. SW11 75 G3
Benham Clo., Chess. 98 F6
Mansfield Rd.
Benham Gdns., 72 F4
Houns.
Benham Rd. W7 55 B5
Benhams Pl. NW3 48 F4
Holly Wk.
Benhill Ave., Sutt. 100 E4
Benhill Rd. SE5 68 A7
Benhill Rd., Sutt. 100 F3
Benhill Wd. Rd., Sutt. 100 F4
Benhilton Gdns., 100 E3
Sutt.
Benhurst Ct. SW16 85 G5
Benhurst La. SW16 85 G5
Benin St. SE13 78 D7
Benjafield Clo. N18 33 E4
Brettenham Rd.
Benjamin Clo. E8 59 D1
Benjamin St. EC1 12 G1
Benjamin St. EC1 58 H5
Benledi St. E14 60 D6
Benn St. E9 50 H6
Bennerley Rd. SW11 75 H5
Bennet's Hill EC4 12 H5
Bennett Clo., Kings.T. 91 F1
Bennett Clo., Well. 80 A2
Bennett Gro. SE13 78 B1
Bennett Pk. SE3 78 F3
Bennett Rd. E13 60 J4
Bennett Rd. N16 50 B4
Bennett Rd., Rom. 44 E6
Bennett St. SW1 15 F1
Bennett St. W4 65 E6
Bennetts Ave., Croy. 102 H2
Bennetts Ave., Grnf. 55 B1
Bennetts Castle La., 53 C4
Dag.
Bennetts Clo. N17 33 C6
Bennetts Copse, Chis. 88 B6
Bennetts Way, Croy. 102 H2
Bennetts Yd. SW1 15 J6
Benningholme Rd., 30 E6
Edg.
Bennington Rd. N17 41 B1
Bennington Rd., 34 E7
Wdf.Grn.
Benn's Wk., Rich. 73 H4
Rosedale Rd.
Benrek Clo., Ilf. 43 F1
Bensbury Clo. SW15 74 J7
Bensham Clo., 94 J4
Th.Hth.
Bensham Gro., 94 J2
Th.Hth.
Bensham La., Croy. 94 H7
Bensham La., Th.Hth. 94 H4
Bensham Manor Rd., 94 J4
Th.Hth.
Bensley Clo. N11 31 J5
Benson Ave. E6 60 J2
Benson Clo., Houns. 72 G4
Benson Quay E1 59 F7
Garnet St.
Benson Rd. SE23 86 F1
Benson Rd., Croy. 101 G3
Bentfield Gdns. SE9 87 J3
Aldersgrove Ave.
Benthal Rd. N16 50 D2
Bentham Rd. E9 50 G6
Bentham Rd. SE28 62 B7
Bentham Wk. NW10 47 C5
Bentinck Ms. W1 11 C3
Bentinck Pl. NW8 6 G2
Bentinck St. W1 11 C3
Bentinck St. W1 58 A6
Bentley Dr., Ilf. 43 F6
Bentley Rd. N1 50 B6
Tottenham Rd.
Bentley Way, Stan. 29 D5

Bentley Way, 34 G3
Wdf.Grn.
Benton Rd., Ilf. 52 G1
Benton Rd., Wat. 28 D5
Bentons La. SE27 85 J4
Bentons Ri. SE27 86 A5
Bentry Clo., Dag. 53 E2
Bentry Rd., Dag. 53 E2
Bentworth Rd. W12 56 H6
Benwell Ct., Sun. 90 A1
Benwell Rd. N7 49 G4
Benwick Clo. SE16 68 E4
Benworth St. E3 59 J3
Benyon Rd. N1 59 A1
Southgate Rd.
Berber Rd. SW11 75 J5
Bercta Rd. SE9 88 F2
Bere St. E1 59 G7
Cranford St.
Berenger Wk. SW10 18 E7
Berens Rd. NW10 57 A3
Berens Way, Chis. 97 J4
Beresford Ave. N20 31 J2
Beresford Ave. W7 55 A5
Beresford Ave., Surb. 99 B1
Beresford Ave., 73 F6
Twick.
Beresford Ave., Wem. 55 J1
Beresford Dr., Brom. 97 B3
Beresford Dr., 34 J4
Wdf.Grn.
Beresford Gdns., Enf. 25 B4
Beresford Gdns., 72 F5
Houns.
Beresford Gdns., 44 E5
Rom.
Beresford Rd. E4 34 E1
Beresford Rd. E17 42 B1
Beresford Rd. N2 39 H3
Beresford Rd. N5 50 A5
Beresford Rd. N8 40 G5
Beresford Rd., Har. 37 A5
Beresford Rd., 91 J1
Kings.T.
Beresford Rd., N.Mal. 92 C4
Beresford Rd., Sthl. 63 D1
Beresford Rd., Sutt. 100 C7
Beresford Sq. SE18 70 E4
Beresford St. SE18 70 E3
Beresford Ter. N5 49 J5
Berestede Rd. W6 65 F5
Bergen Sq. SE16 68 H3
Norway Gate
Berger Clo., Orp. 97 G6
Berger Rd. E9 50 G6
Berghem Ms. W14 66 A3
Blythe Rd.
Bergholt Ave., Ilf. 43 B5
Bergholt Cres. N16 41 B7
Bergholt Ms. NW1 49 C7
Rossendale Way
Bering Wk. E16 61 A6
Berkeley Ave., Bexh. 80 D1
Berkeley Ave., Grnf. 46 B6
Berkeley Ave., Houns. 72 A1
Berkeley Ave., Ilf. 43 D2
Berkeley Clo., Borwd. 22 A5
Berkeley Clo., 82 H7
Kings.T.
Berkeley Clo., Orp. 97 H7
Berkeley Clo., Ruis. 45 A3
Berkeley Ct. N14 24 C6
Berkeley Ct., Wall. 101 C4
Berkeley Cres., Barn. 23 G5
Berkeley Gdns. N21 25 A7
Berkeley Gdns. W8 66 D1
Brunswick Gdns.
Berkeley Gdns., Esher 98 D6
Berkeley Ho. E3 60 A3
Wellington Way
Berkeley Ms. W1 11 A4
Berkeley Pl. SW19 84 A6
Berkeley Rd. N8 40 D5
Berkeley Rd. N15 41 A6
Berkeley Rd. NW9 38 A4
Berkeley Rd. SW13 74 G1
Berkeley Sq. W1 11 E6
Berkeley Sq. W1 58 B7
Berkeley St. W1 15 E1
Berkeley St. W1 67 B1
Berkeley Wk. N7 49 F2
Durham Rd.
Berkeley Waye, 63 D7
Houns.
Berkhampstead Rd., 71 G5
Belv.
Berkhamsted Ave., 46 J6
Wem.

Berkley Dr., W.Mol. 90 F3
Berkley Gro. NW1 48 J7
Berkley Rd.
Berkley Rd. E12 52 B5
Berkley Rd. NW1 48 J7
Berkshire Gdns. N13 32 G6
Berkshire Gdns. N18 33 E5
Berkshire Rd. E9 50 J6
Berkshire Sq., Mitch. 94 E4
Berkshire Way
Berkshire Way, Mitch. 94 E4
Bermans Way NW10 47 E4
Bermondsey Sq. SE1 17 E5
Bermondsey St. SE1 17 D2
Bermondsey St. SE1 68 B2
Bermondsey Wall E. 17 J4
SE16
Bermondsey Wall E. 68 D2
SE16
Bermondsey Wall W. 17 H3
SE16
Bermondsey Wall W. 68 D2
SE16
Bernal Clo. SE28 62 D7
Haldane Rd.
Bernard Ashley Dr. 69 H5
SE7
Bernard Ave. W13 64 E3
Bernard Cassidy St. 60 F5
E16
Bernard Gdns. SW19 84 C5
Bernard Rd. N15 41 C5
Bernard Rd., Rom. 44 J7
Bernard Rd., Wall. 101 B5
Bernard St. WC1 8 A6
Bernard St. WC1 58 E4
Bernards Clo., Ilf. 35 F7
Bernays Clo., Stan. 29 F6
Bernays Gro. SW9 76 F4
Berne Rd., Th.Hth. 94 H5
Bernel Dr., Croy. 102 J3
Berners Dr. W13 55 D6
Berners Ms. W1 11 G2
Berners Ms. W1 58 C5
Berners Pl. W1 11 G3
Berners Pl. W1 58 C6
Berners Rd. N1 58 G1
Berners Rd. N22 40 G1
Berners St. W1 11 G2
Berners St. W1 58 C5
Berney Rd., Croy. 95 A7
Bernville Way, Har. 37 J5
Kenton Rd.
Bernwell Rd. E4 34 E3
Berridge Grn., Edg. 30 B7
Berridge Rd. SE19 86 B5
Berriman Rd. N7 49 F3
Berriton Rd., Har. 45 F1
Berry Clo. N21 32 H1
Berry Clo. NW10 47 E7
Berry Ct., Houns. 72 F5
Berry Hill, Stan. 29 G4
Berry La. SE21 86 A4
Berry Pl. EC1 8 H4
Berry St. EC1 8 H5
Berry St. EC1 64 H3
Berry Way W5 34 C2
Greenbank Clo.
Berrydale Rd., Hayes 54 E4
Berryfield Clo. E17 42 B4
Berryfield Clo., Brom. 97 B3
Berryfield Rd. SE17 20 H3
Berryfield Rd. SE17 67 H5
Berryhill SE9 79 E4
Berryhill Gdns. SE9 79 E4
Berrylands SW20 92 J3
Berrylands, Surb. 91 J6
Berrylands Rd., Surb. 91 J6
Berryman Clo., Dag. 53 C3
Bennetts Castle La.
Berrymans La. SE26 86 G4
Berrymead Gdns. W3 65 C2
Berrymede Rd. W4 65 D3
Bert Rd., Th.Hth. 94 J5
Bertal Rd. SW17 84 G4
Berthon St. SE8 69 A7
Bertie Rd. NW10 47 G6
Bertie Rd. SE26 86 G6
Bertram Cotts. SW19 84 D7
Hartfield Rd.
Bertram Rd. NW4 38 G6
Bertram Rd., Enf. 25 D4
Bertram Rd., Kings.T. 83 A7
Bertram St. N19 49 B2
Bertram Way, Enf. 25 C4
Bertrand St. SE13 78 B3
Bertrand Way SE28 62 G7

Berwick Ave., Hayes 54 D6
Berwick Clo., Stan. 29 C7
Gordon Ave.
Berwick Cres., Sid. 79 H6
Berwick Rd. E16 60 H6
Berwick Rd. N22 40 H1
Berwick Rd., Well. 80 B1
Berwick St. W1 11 G3
Berwick St. W1 58 C6
Berwyn Ave., Houns. 72 H1
Berwyn Rd. SE24 85 H1
Berwyn Rd., Rich. 74 B4
Beryl Ave. E6 61 B5
Beryl Rd. W6 66 A5
Berystede, Kings.T. 83 B7
Besant Ct. N1 50 A5
Mildmay Gro.
Besant Rd. NW2 48 B4
Besant Wk. N7 49 F2
Newington Barrow Way
Besant Way NW10 47 C5
Besley St. SW16 85 C7
Bessborough Gdns. SW1 19 J3
Bessborough Gdns. SW1 67 D5
Bessborough Pl. SW1 19 H3
Bessborough Pl. SW1 67 D5
Bessborough Rd. SW15 83 G1
Bessborough Rd., Har. 46 A1
Bessborough St. SW1 19 H3
Bessborough St. SW1 67 D5
Bessemer Rd. SE5 76 J2
Bessie Lansbury Clo. E6 61 D6
Bessingby Rd., Ruis. 45 B2
Bessingham Wk. SE4 77 G4
Frendsbury Rd.
Besson St. SE14 77 F1
Bessy St. E2 59 F3
Roman Rd.
Bestwood St. SE8 68 G4
Beswick Ms. NW6 48 E6
Lymington Rd.
Betchworth Clo., Sutt. 100 G5
Turnpike La.
Betchworth Rd., Ilf. 52 H2
Betham Rd., Grnf. 55 A3
Bethecar Rd., Har. 37 B5
Bethel Rd., Well. 80 C3
Bethell Ave. E16 60 F4
Bethell Ave., Ilf. 43 D7
Bethersden Clo., Beck. 86 J7
Bethnal Grn. Rd. E1 9 F5
Bethnal Grn. Rd. E1 59 C4
Bethnal Grn. Rd. E2 9 J4
Bethnal Grn. Rd. E2 59 C4
Bethune Ave. N11 31 J4
Bethune Rd. N16 41 A7
Bethune Rd. NW10 56 D4
Bethwin Rd. SE5 20 H7
Bethwin Rd. SE5 67 H7
Betjeman Clo., Pnr. 36 G4
Betony Clo., Croy. 102 G1
Primrose La.
Betoyne Ave. E4 34 E4
Betstyle Rd. N11 32 B4
Betterton Dr., Sid. 89 E2
Betterton St. WC2 12 A4
Betterton St. WC2 58 E6
Bettons Pk. E15 60 E1
Bettridge Rd. SW6 75 C2
Betts Clo., Beck. 95 H2
Kendall Rd.
Betts Rd. E16 60 H7
Victoria Dock Rd.
Betts St. E1 59 E7
The Highway
Betts Way SE20 95 E1
Betts Way, Surb. 98 E1
Beulah Ave., Th.Hth. 94 F4
Beulah Rd.
Beulah Clo., Edg. 30 B3
Beulah Cres., Th.Hth. 94 J2
Beulah Gro., Croy. 94 J6
Beulah Hill SE19 85 H6
Beulah Path E17 42 B5
Addison Rd.
Beulah Rd. E17 42 B5
Beulah Rd. SW19 84 C7
Beulah Rd., Sutt. 100 D4
Beulah Rd., Th.Hth. 94 J3
Bev Callender Clo. SW8 76 B3
Daley Thompson Way
Bevan Ave., Bark. 53 A7
Bevan Ct., Croy. 101 G5
Bevan Rd. SE2 71 B5
Bevan Rd., Barn. 23 J4
Bevan St. N1 58 J1
Bevenden St. N1 9 C3
Bevenden St. N1 59 A3
Bevercote Wk., Belv. 71 F6
Osborne Rd.
Beveridge Rd. NW10 47 E7
Curzon Cres.
Beverley NW8 6 G4
Beverley Ave. SW20 92 F1
Beverley Ave., Houns. 72 F4
Beverley Ave., Sid. 79 J7
Beverley Clo. N21 32 J1
Beverley Clo. SW11 75 G4
Maysoule Rd.
Beverley Clo. SW13 74 F2
Beverley Clo., Chess. 98 F4
Beverley Clo., Enf. 25 B4
Beverley Ct. N14 24 C7
Beverley Ct. SE4 77 J3
Beverley Cres., Wdf.Grn. 42 H1
Beverley Dr., Edg. 38 A3
Beverley Gdns. NW11 39 B7
Beverley Gdns. SW13 74 F3
Beverley Gdns., Stan. 37 D1
Beverley Gdns., Wem. 46 J1
Beverley Gdns., Wor.Pk. 99 G1
Green La.
Beverley La. SW15 83 F3
Beverley La., Kings.T. 83 E7
Beverley Ms. E4 34 D6
Beverley Rd.
Beverley Path SW13 74 F2
Beverley Rd. E4 34 D6
Beverley Rd. E6 61 A3
Beverley Rd. SE20 95 E2
Wadhurst Clo.
Beverley Rd. SW13 74 F3
Beverley Rd. W4 65 F5
Beverley Rd., Bexh. 80 J2
Beverley Rd., Brom. 104 B2
Beverley Rd., Dag. 53 E4
Beverley Rd., Kings.T. 91 F1
Beverley Rd., Mitch. 94 D4
Beverley Rd., N.Mal. 92 G4
Beverley Rd., Ruis. 45 A2
Beverley Rd., Sthl. 63 E4
Beverley Rd., Wor.Pk. 99 J2
Beverley Way SW20 92 F1
Beverley Way, N.Mal. 92 F1
Beversbrook Rd. N19 49 D3
Beverstone Rd. SW2 76 F5
Beverstone Rd., Th.Hth. 94 G4
Bevill Allen Clo. SW17 84 J5
Bevin Clo. SE16 68 H1
Bevin Rd., Hayes 54 A3
Bevin Way WC1 8 E3
Bevington Rd. W10 57 B5
Bevington Rd., Beck. 96 B2
Bevington St. SE16 17 J4
Bevington St. SE16 68 D2
Bevis Marks EC3 13 E3
Bevis Marks EC3 59 B6
Bewcastle Gdns., Enf. 24 E4
Bewdley St. N1 49 G7
Bewick St. SW8 76 B2
Bewley St. E1 59 E7
Bewlys Rd. SE27 85 H5
Bexhill Clo., Felt. 81 E2
Bexhill Rd. N11 32 D5
Bexhill Rd. SE4 77 J6
Bexhill Rd. SW14 74 C3
Bexhill Wk. E15 60 E2
Mitre Rd.
Bexley Gdns. N9 33 A3
Bexley Gdns., Rom. 44 B5
Bexley High St., Bex. 80 G7
Bexley La., Sid. 89 C4
Bexley Rd. SE9 79 E5
Bexley Rd., Erith 71 J7
Beynon Rd., Cars. 100 J5
Bianca Rd. SE15 21 H6
Bianca Rd. SE15 68 C6
Bibsworth Rd. N3 39 C2
Bibury Clo. SE15 21 E6
Bibury Clo. SE15 68 B6
Bicester Rd., Rich. 74 A3
Bickenhall St. W1 11 A1
Bickenhall St. W1 57 J5
Bickersteth Rd. SW17 84 J6
Bickerton Rd. N19 49 C2
Bickley Cres., Brom. 97 B4
Bickley Pk. Rd., Brom. 97 B3
Bickley Rd. E10 42 B7
Bickley Rd., Brom. 97 A2
Bickley St. SW17 84 H5
Bicknell Rd. SE5 76 J3
Bicknoller Rd., Enf. 25 B1
Bicknor Rd., Orp. 97 H7
Bidborough Clo., Brom. 96 F5
Bidborough St. WC1 8 A4
Bidborough St. WC1 58 E3
Biddenden Way SE9 88 D4
Bidder St. E16 60 E5
Biddestone Rd. N7 49 F4
Biddulph Rd. W9 6 A4
Biddulph Rd. W9 57 E3
Bideford Ave., Grnf. 55 E2
Bideford Clo., Edg. 38 A1
Bideford Clo., Felt. 81 F3
Bideford Gdns., Enf. 25 B7
Bideford Rd., Brom. 87 F3
Bideford Rd., Ruis. 45 B3
Bideford Rd., Well. 71 B7
Bidwell Gdns. N11 32 C7
Bidwell St. SE15 77 E1
Big Hill E5 50 E1
Bigbury Rd. N17 33 B7
Barkham Rd.
Biggerstaff Rd. E15 60 C1
Biggerstaff St. N4 49 G2
Biggin Ave., Mitch. 93 J1
Biggin Hill SE19 94 H1
Biggin Way SE19 85 H7
Bigginwood Rd. SW16 85 H7
Biggs Row SW15 75 A3
Felsham Rd.
Bigland St. E1 59 E6
Bignell Rd. SE18 70 E5
Bignold Rd. E7 51 G4
Bigwood Rd. NW11 39 E5
Bill Hamling Clo. SE9 88 C2
Billet Clo., Rom. 44 D3
Billet Rd. E17 41 G1
Billet Rd., Rom. 44 B4
Billing Pl. SW10 18 B7
Billing Pl. SW10 66 E7
Billing Rd. SW10 18 B7
Billing Rd. SW10 66 E7
Billing St. SW10 18 B7
Billing St. SW10 66 E7
Billingford Clo. SE4 77 G4
Billington Rd. SE14 68 G7
Billiter Sq. EC3 13 E4
Billiter St. EC3 13 E4
Billiter St. EC3 59 B6
Billockby Clo., Chess. 98 J6
Billson St. E14 69 C4
Bilsby Gro. SE9 88 A4
Bilton Rd., Grnf. 55 D1
Bilton Way, Enf. 25 H1
Bilton Way, Hayes 63 B2
Bina Gdns. SW5 18 C2
Bina Gdns. SW5 66 F4
Bincote Rd., Enf. 24 F3
Binden Rd. W12 65 F3
Bindon Grn., Mord. 93 E4
Bayham Rd.
Binfield Rd. SW4 76 E1
Binfield Rd., S.Croy. 102 C5
Bingfield St. N1 58 E1
Bingham Pl. W1 11 B1
Bingham Rd., Croy. 102 D1
Bingham St. N1 50 A6
Bingley Rd. E16 60 J6
Bingley Rd., Grnf. 54 J4
Bingley Rd., Sun. 81 A7
Binney St. W1 11 C4
Binney St. W1 58 A6
Binns Rd. W4 65 E5
Binsey Wk. SE2 71 C2
Binyon Cres., Stan. 29 C5
Birbeck Gdns., Wdf.Grn. 34 F2
Birbetts Rd. SE9 88 C2
Birch Ave. N13 32 J3
Birch Clo. E16 60 E5
Birch Clo. N19 49 C2
Hargrave Pk.
Birch Clo. SE15 77 D2
Birch Clo., Brent. 64 E7
Birch Clo., Buck.H. 35 A3
Birch Clo., Rom. 44 H3
Birch Clo., Tedd. 82 D5
Birch Gdns., Dag. 53 J3
Birch Grn. NW9 30 E7
Clayton Fld.
Birch Gro. SE12 78 F7
Birch Gro. W3 65 A1
Birch Gro., Well. 80 A4
Birch Hill, Croy. 102 G5
Birch Mead, Orp. 104 D2
Birch Pk., Har. 28 J7
Birch Rd., Felt. 81 D5
Birch Rd., Rom. 44 H3
Birch Row, Brom. 97 D7
Birch Tree Ave., W.Wick. 103 F5
Birch Tree Way, Croy. 102 E2
Birch Wk., Borwd. 22 A1
Grove Rd.
Birch Wk., Erith 71 J6
Birch Wk., Mitch. 94 B1
Bircham Path SE4 77 G4
St. Norbert Rd.
Birchanger Rd. SE25 95 D5
Birchdale Gdns., Rom. 44 D7
Birchdale Rd. E7 51 J5
Birchdene Dr. SE28 71 A1
Birchen Clo. NW9 47 D2
Birchen Gro. NW9 47 D2
Birchend Clo., S.Croy. 102 A6
Sussex Rd.
Birches, The N21 24 F6
Birches, The SE7 69 H6
Birches, The, Orp. 104 D4
Birches Clo., Mitch. 93 J3
Birches Clo., Pnr. 36 E5
Birchfield St. E14 60 A7
Birchin La. EC3 13 C4
Birchin La. EC3 59 A6
Birchington Clo., Bexh. 80 H1
Birchington Rd. N8 40 D6
Birchington Rd. NW6 57 D1
Birchington Rd., Surb. 91 J7
Birchlands Ave. SW12 75 J7
Birchmead Ave., Pnr. 36 C4
Birchmere Row SE3 78 F2
Birchmore Wk. N5 49 J3
Highbury Quad.
Birchville Ct. (Bushey), Wat. 29 B1
Heathbourne Rd.
Birchway, Hayes 63 A1
Birchwood Ave. N10 40 A3
Birchwood Ave., Beck. 95 J4
Birchwood Ave., Sid. 89 B2
Birchwood Ave., Wall. 101 A3
Birchwood Clo., Mord. 93 E4
Birchwood Ct. N13 32 H5
Birchwood Ct., Edg. 38 C2
Birchwood Dr. NW3 48 E3
Birchwood Gro., Hmptn. 81 G6
Birchwood Rd. SW17 85 B5
Birchwood Rd., Orp. 97 G4
Bird in Bush Rd. SE15 21 H7
Bird in Bush Rd. SE15 68 D7
Bird St. W1 11 C4
Bird Wk., Twick. 81 F1
Bird-in-hand La., Brom. 97 A2
Bird-in-hand Pas. SE23 86 F2
Dartmouth Rd.
Birdbrook Clo., Dag. 53 J7
Birdbrook Rd. SE3 78 J3
Birdcage Wk. SW1 15 G4
Birdcage Wk. SW1 67 C2
Birdham Clo., Brom. 97 B5
Birdhurst Ave., S.Croy. 102 A4
Birdhurst Gdns., S.Croy. 102 A4
Birdhurst Ri., S.Croy. 102 B5
Birdhurst Rd. SW18 75 F4
Birdhurst Rd. SW19 84 H6
Birdhurst Rd., S.Croy. 102 B5
Birdlip Clo. SE15 21 D6
Birdlip Clo. SE15 68 B6
Birds Fm. Ave., Rom. 44 H1
Birdsfield La. E3 59 J1
Birdwood Clo., Tedd. 82 B4
Birkbeck Ave. W3 56 C7
Birkbeck Ave., Grnf. 54 J1
Birkbeck Gdns., Wdf.Grn. 34 F2
Birkbeck Gro. W3 65 D2
Birkbeck Hill SE21 85 H2
Birkbeck Ms. E8 50 C5
Sandringham Rd.
Birkbeck Pl. SE21 85 J1
Birkbeck Rd. E8 50 C5
Birkbeck Rd. N8 40 E4
Birkbeck Rd. N12 31 F5

Birkbeck Rd. N17	41	C1
Birkbeck Rd. NW7	30	F5
Birkbeck Rd. SW19	84	E5
Birkbeck Rd. W3	65	D1
Birkbeck Rd. W5	64	F4
Birkbeck Rd., Beck.	95	F2
Birkbeck Rd., Enf.	25	A1
Birkbeck Rd., Ilf.	43	G5
Birkbeck Rd., Sid.	89	A3
Birkbeck St. E2	59	E3
Cambridge Heath Rd.		
Birkbeck Way, Grnf.	54	J1
Birkdale Ave., Pnr.	36	G3
Birkdale Clo., Orp.	97	G7
Birkdale Gdns., Croy.	102	G4
Birkdale Gdns., Wat.	28	D3
Birkdale Rd. SE2	71	A4
Birkdale Rd. W5	55	H4
Birkenhead Ave., Kings.T.	91	J2
Birkenhead St. WC1	**8**	**B3**
Birkenhead St. WC1	58	E3
Birkhall Rd. SE6	87	D1
Birkwood Clo. SW12	76	D7
Birley Rd. N20	31	F2
Birley St. SW11	76	A2
Birnam Rd. N4	49	F2
Birse Cres. NW10	47	E4
Birstall Grn., Wat.	28	D4
Birstall Rd. N15	41	B5
Biscay Rd. W6	66	A5
Biscoe Clo., Houns.	63	G6
Biscoe Way SE13	78	D3
Bisenden Rd., Croy.	102	B2
Bisham Clo., Cars.	93	J7
Bisham Gdns. N6	49	A1
Bishop Butt Clo., Orp.	104	J3
Stapleton Rd.		
Bishop Fox Way, E.Mol.	90	F4
Bishop Ken Rd., Har.	37	C2
Bishop Kings Rd. W14	66	B4
Bishop Rd. N14	24	B7
Bishop St. N1	58	J1
Bishop Way NW10	47	E7
Bishop Wilfred Wd. Clo. SE18	77	D2
Moncrieff St.		
Bishop's Ave. E13	60	H1
Bishop's Ave. SW6	75	A2
Bishops Ave., Brom.	96	J2
Bishops Ave., Rom.	44	C6
Bishops Ave., The N2	39	G7
Bishops Bri. W2	**10**	**D3**
Bishops Bri. W2	57	F5
Bishops Bri. Rd. W2	**10**	**B3**
Bishops Bri. Rd. W2	57	E6
Bishops Clo. E17	42	B4
Bishops Clo. N19	49	C3
Wyndham Cres.		
Bishops Clo. SE9	88	F2
Bishops Clo., Barn.	23	A6
Bishops Clo., Enf.	25	E2
Central Ave.		
Bishops Clo., Rich.	82	G3
Bishops Clo., Sutt.	100	D3
Bishop's Ct. EC4	**12**	**G3**
Bishop's Ct. WC2	**12**	**E3**
Bishops Dr., Nthlt.	54	E1
Bishops Gro. N2	39	G6
Bishops Gro., Hmptn.	81	F4
Bishop's Hall, Kings.T.	91	G2
Bishops Hill, Walt.	90	A7
Bishop's Pk. Rd. SW6	75	A2
Bishops Pk. Rd. SW16	94	E1
Bishops Rd. N6	40	A6
Bishops Rd. SW6	75	B1
Bishops Rd. W7	64	B2
Bishops Rd., Croy.	94	H7
Bishops Ter. SE11	**20**	**F1**
Bishops Ter. SE11	67	G4
Bishops Wk., Chis.	97	F1
Bishops Wk., Croy.	102	G5
Bishop's Wk., Pnr.	36	E3
High St.		
Bishops Way E2	59	E2
Bishopsford Rd., Mord.	93	F7
Bishopsgate EC2	**13**	**E2**
Bishopsgate EC2	59	B6
Bishopsgate Chyd. EC2	**13**	**D3**
Bishopsthorpe Rd. SE26	86	G4
Bishopswood Rd. N6	39	J7
Bisley Clo., Wor.Pk.	99	J1
Bispham Rd. NW10	55	J3
Bisson Rd. E15	60	C2
Bisterne Ave. E17	42	D3
Bittacy Clo. NW7	31	A6
Bittacy Hill NW7	31	A6
Bittacy Pk. Ave. NW7	31	A6
Bittacy Ri. NW7	30	J6
Bittacy Rd. NW7	31	A6
Bittern St. SE1	**16**	**J4**
Bittoms, The, Kings.T.	91	G3
Bixley Clo., Sthl.	63	F4
Black Boy La. N15	40	J5
Black Fan Clo., Enf.	24	J1
Black Friars Ct. EC4	**12**	**G5**
Black Friars La. EC4	**12**	**G5**
Black Friars La. EC4	58	H6
Black Gates, Pnr.	36	F3
Church La.		
Black Horse Ct. SE1	**17**	**C5**
Black Lion La. W6	65	G4
Black Path E10	41	G7
Black Prince Rd. SE1	**20**	**B2**
Black Prince Rd. SE1	67	F4
Black Prince Rd. SE11	**20**	**D2**
Black Prince Rd. SE11	67	F4
Black Swan Yd. SE1	**17**	**D3**
Blackall St. EC2	**9**	**D5**
Blackberry Fm. Clo., Houns.	63	E7
Blackbird Hill NW9	47	C2
Blackbird Yd. E2	**9**	**G3**
Blackborne Rd., Dag.	53	G6
Blackbrook La., Brom.	97	D3
Blackburn Rd. NW6	48	E6
Blackburne's Ms. W1	**11**	**B5**
Blackburne's Ms. W1	58	E7
Blackbush Ave., Rom.	44	D5
Blackbush Clo., Sutt.	100	E7
Blackett St. SW15	75	A3
Blackfen Rd., Sid.	79	H6
Blackford Rd., Wat.	28	D5
Blackford's Path SW15	74	G7
Roehampton High St.		
Blackfriars Bri. EC4	**12**	**G6**
Blackfriars Bri. EC4	58	H7
Blackfriars Bri. SE1	**12**	**G6**
Blackfriars Bri. SE1	58	H7
Blackfriars Pas. EC4	**12**	**G5**
Blackfriars Rd. SE1	**16**	**G1**
Blackfriars Rd. SE1	67	H1
Blackheath Ave. SE10	69	D7
Blackheath Gro. SE3	78	F2
Blackheath Hill SE10	78	C1
Blackheath Pk. SE3	78	F3
Blackheath Ri. SE13	78	C2
Blackheath Rd. SE10	78	B1
Blackheath Vale SE3	78	E1
Blackheath Village SE3	78	F2
Blackhorse La. E17	41	G4
Blackhorse La., Croy.	95	D7
Blackhorse Ms. E17	41	G3
Blackhorse Rd.		
Blackhorse Rd. E17	41	G4
Blackhorse Rd. SE8	68	H5
Blackhorse Rd., Sid.	89	A4
Blackland Ter. SW3	**18**	**J2**
Blackland Rd. SW3	66	J4
Blacklands Rd. SE6	87	C4
Blackmore Ave., Sthl.	64	A1
Blackmore Rd., Buck.H.	27	B7
Blackmores Gro., Tedd.	82	D6
Blackness La., Kes.	104	A7
Blackpool Rd. SE15	77	E2
Blacks Rd. W6	65	J4
Queen Caroline St.		
Blackshaw Pl. N1	50	B7
Hertford Rd.		
Blackshaw Rd. SW17	84	F4
Blacksmith Clo., Rom.	44	C6
Blackstock Ms. N4	49	H2
Blackstock Rd.		
Blackstock Rd. N4	49	H2
Blackstock Rd. N5	49	H2
Blackstone Est. E8	50	D7
Blackstone Rd. NW2	47	J5
Blackthorn Ct., Houns.	63	E7
Blackthorn Gro., Bexh.	80	E3
Blackthorn St. E3	60	A4
Blackthorne Ave., Croy.	102	F1
Blackthorne Dr. E4	34	D4
Blacktree Ms. SW9	76	G3
Blackwall La. SE10	69	E5
Blackwall Tunnel E14	69	D1
Blackwall Tunnel App. SE10	69	E2
Blackwall Tunnel Northern App. E3	60	A2
Blackwall Tunnel Northern App. E14	60	C4
Blackwall Way E14	60	C7
Blackwater Clo. E7	51	F5
Tower Hamlets Rd.		
Blackwater Rd., Sutt.	100	E4
High St.		
Blackwater St. SE22	77	C5
Blackwell Clo. E5	50	H4
Blackwell Clo., Har.	29	A7
Blackwell Gdns., Edg.	30	A3
Blackwood St. SE17	**21**	**B3**
Blackwood St. SE17	68	A5
Blade Ms. SW15	75	C4
Deodar Rd.		
Bladindon Dr., Bex.	80	C7
Bladon Gdns., Har.	36	H6
Blagdens Clo. N14	32	C2
Blagdens La. N14	32	D2
Blagdon Rd. SE13	78	B6
Blagdon Rd., N.Mal.	93	F4
Blagdon Wk., Tedd.	82	F6
Blagrove Rd. W10	57	B5
Blair Ave. NW9	38	E7
Blair Clo. N1	49	J6
Blair Clo., Sid.	79	H5
Blair St. E14	60	C6
Blairderry Rd. SW2	85	E2
Blairhead Dr., Wat.	28	B3
Blake Ave., Bark.	61	H1
Blake Clo. W10	56	J5
Blake Clo., Cars.	93	H7
Blake Clo., Well.	79	H1
Blake Gdns. SW6	75	E1
Blake Hall Cres. E11	51	G1
Blake Hall Rd. E11	42	G7
Blake Ho., Beck.	87	A6
Blake Rd. E16	60	F4
Blake Rd. N11	32	C7
Blake Rd., Croy.	102	B2
Blake Rd., Mitch.	93	H3
Blake St. SE8	69	A6
Watergate St.		
Blakeden Dr., Esher	98	C6
Blakehall Rd., Cars.	100	J6
Blakemore Rd. SW16	85	E3
Blakemore Rd., Th.Hth.	94	F5
Blakemore Way, Belv.	71	E3
Blakeney Ave., Beck.	95	J1
Blakeney Clo. E8	50	D5
Ferncliff Rd.		
Blakeney Clo. N20	31	F1
Blakeney Clo. NW1	49	D7
Rossendale Way		
Blakeney Rd., Beck.	95	J1
Blakenham Rd. SW17	84	J4
Blaker Ct. SE7	69	J7
Fairlawn		
Blaker Rd. E15	60	C1
Blakes Ave., N.Mal.	92	F5
Blake's Grn., W.Wick.	103	C1
Blakes La., N.Mal.	92	F5
Blakes Rd. SE15	**21**	**E7**
Blakes Rd. SE15	68	B7
Blakes Ter., N.Mal.	93	G5
Blakesley Ave. W5	55	F6
Blakesley Wk. SW20	93	C2
Blakesware Gdns. N9	25	A7
Blakewood Clo., Felt.	81	C4
Blanch Clo. SE15	68	F7
Culmore Rd.		
Blanchard Clo. SE9	88	B3
Blanchard Way E8	50	D6
Blanche St. E16	60	F4
Blanchedowne SE5	77	A4
Blanchland Rd., Mord.	93	E5
Bland St. SE9	79	A4
Blandfield Rd. SW12	76	A6
Blandford Ave., Beck.	95	H2
Blandford Ave., Twick.	81	H1
Blandford Clo. N2	39	F5
Blandford Clo., Croy.	101	E3
Wandle Rd.		
Blandford Clo., Rom.	44	H4
Blandford Cres. E4	26	C7
Blandford Rd. W4	65	E3
Blandford Rd. W5	64	G2
Blandford Rd., Beck.	95	F2
Blandford Rd., Sthl.	63	G4
Blandford Rd., Tedd.	82	A5
Blandford Sq. NW1	**6**	**H6**
Blandford Sq. NW1	57	H4
Blandford St. W1	**11**	**A3**
Blandford St. W1	57	J6
Blandford Waye, Hayes	54	C6
Blaney Cres. E6	61	E3
Blanmerle Rd. SE9	88	E1
Blann Clo. SE9	79	A6
Blantyre St. SW10	**18**	**E7**
Blantyre St. SW10	66	G7
Blantyre Wk. SW10	**18**	**E7**
Blashford NW3	48	J7
Blashford St. SE13	78	D7
Blasker Wk. E14	69	A5
Blawith Rd., Har.	37	B4
Blaydon Clo. N17	33	E7
Blaydon Wk. N17	33	E7
Bleak Hill La. SE18	70	J6
Blean Gro. SE20	86	F7
Bleasdale Ave., Grnf.	55	D2
Blechynden St. W10	57	A7
Bramley Rd.		
Bleddyn Clo., Sid.	80	C6
Bledlow Clo. SE28	62	C7
Bledlow Ri., Grnf.	54	J2
Bleeding Heart Yd. EC1	**12**	**F2**
Blegborough Rd. SW16	85	C6
Blendon Dr., Bex.	80	D6
Blendon Path, Brom.	87	F7
Hope Pk.		
Blendon Rd., Bex.	80	C6
Blendon Ter. SE18	70	F5
Blendworth Way SE15	**21**	**E7**
Blenheim Ave., Ilf.	43	D6
Blenheim Clo. N21	32	J1
Elm Pk. Rd.		
Blenheim Clo. SW20	92	J3
Blenheim Clo., Grnf.	55	A2
Leaver Gdns.		
Blenheim Clo., Rom.	44	J4
Blenheim Clo., Wall.	101	C7
Blenheim Ct. N19	49	E2
Marlborough Rd.		
Blenheim Ct., Sid.	88	G3
Blenheim Cres. W11	57	B7
Blenheim Cres., S.Croy.	101	J7
Blenheim Dr., Well.	79	J1
Blenheim Gdns. NW2	47	J5
Blenheim Gdns. SW2	76	F6
Blenheim Gdns., Kings.T.	83	B7
Blenheim Gdns., Wall.	101	C6
Blenheim Gdns., Wem.	46	H3
Blenheim Gro. SE15	77	D2
Blenheim Pas. NW8	**6**	**C1**
Blenheim Ri. N15	41	C4
Talbot Rd.		
Blenheim Rd. E6	61	A3
Blenheim Rd. E15	51	E4
Blenheim Rd. E17	41	G3
Blenheim Rd. NW8	**6**	**D1**
Blenheim Rd. NW8	57	F2
Blenheim Rd. SE20	86	F7
Maple Rd.		
Blenheim Rd. SW20	92	J3
Blenheim Rd. W4	65	E3
Blenheim Rd., Barn.	23	A3
Blenheim Rd., Brom.	97	B4
Blenheim Rd., Har.	36	H6
Blenheim Rd., Nthlt.	45	H6
Blenheim Rd., Sid.	89	C1
Blenheim Rd., Sutt.	100	D3
Blenheim St. W1	**11**	**D4**
Blenheim Ter. NW8	**6**	**C1**
Blenheim Ter. NW8	57	F2
Blenkarne Rd. SW11	75	J6
Bleriot Rd., Houns.	63	C7
Blessbury Rd., Edg.	38	C1
Blessington Clo. SE13	78	D3
Blessington Rd. SE13	78	D4
Bletchingley Clo., Th.Hth.	94	H4
Bletchley Ct. N1	**9**	**B2**
Bletchley St. N1	**9**	**A2**
Bletchley St. N1	58	J2
Bletsoe Wk. N1	**9**	**A1**
Blincoe Clo. SW19	84	A2
Blind La., Loug.	26	E2
Bliss Cres. SE13	78	B2
Coldbath St.		
Blissett St. SE10	78	C1
Blisworth Clo., Hayes	54	E4
Braunston Dr.		
Blithbury Rd., Dag.	53	B6

Name	Page	Grid
Blithdale Rd. SE2	71	A4
Blithfield St. W8	**14**	**A6**
Blithfield St. W8	66	E3
Blockley Rd., Wem.	46	E2
Bloemfontein Ave. W12	65	H1
Bloemfontein Rd. W12	56	H7
Blomfield Rd. W9	**10**	**B1**
Blomfield Rd. W9	57	E5
Blomfield St. EC2	**13**	**C2**
Blomfield St. EC2	59	A5
Blomfield Vill. W2	**10**	**B2**
Blomfield Vill. W2	57	E5
Blomville Rd., Dag.	53	E3
Blondel St. SW11	76	A2
Blondin Ave. W5	64	F4
Blondin St. E3	60	A2
Bloom Gro. SE27	85	H3
Bloom Pk. Rd. SW6	66	C7
Bloomburg St. SW1	**19**	**G2**
Bloomfield Cres., Ilf.	43	E6
Bloomfield Pl. W1	**11**	**E5**
Bloomfield Rd. N6	40	A6
Bloomfield Rd. SE18	70	E5
Bloomfield Rd., Brom.	97	A5
Bloomfield Rd., Kings.T.	91	H4
Bloomfield Ter. SW1	**19**	**C3**
Bloomfield Ter. SW1	67	A5
Bloomhall Rd. SE19	86	A5
Bloomsbury Clo. W5	55	J7
Bloomsbury Ct. WC1	**12**	**B2**
Bloomsbury Ct., Pnr.	36	F3
Bloomsbury Ho. SW4	76	D6
Bloomsbury Pl. SW18	75	F5
Fullerton Rd.		
Bloomsbury Pl. WC1	**12**	**B1**
Bloomsbury Sq. WC1	**12**	**B2**
Bloomsbury Sq. WC1	58	E5
Bloomsbury St. WC1	**11**	**J2**
Bloomsbury St. WC1	58	D5
Bloomsbury Way WC1	**12**	**A3**
Bloomsbury Way WC1	58	E5
Blore Clo. SW8	76	D1
Thessaly Rd.		
Blore Ct. W1	**11**	**H5**
Blossom Clo. W5	64	H2
Blossom Clo., Dag.	62	F1
Blossom Clo., S.Croy.	102	C5
Melville Ave.		
Blossom St. E1	**9**	**E6**
Blossom St. E1	59	B4
Blossom Waye, Houns.	63	E7
Blount St. E14	59	H5
Bloxam Gdns. SE9	79	B5
Bloxhall Rd. E10	50	J1
Bloxham Cres., Hmptn.	81	F7
Bloxworth Clo., Wall.	101	C3
Blucher Rd. SE5	67	J7
Blue Anchor All., Rich.	73	H4
Kew Rd.		
Blue Anchor La. SE16	**21**	**J1**
Blue Anchor La. SE16	68	D4
Blue Anchor Yd. E1	**13**	**H5**
Blue Anchor Yd. E1	59	D7
Blue Ball Yd. SW1	**15**	**F2**
Bluebell Clo. SE26	86	C4
Bluebell Clo., Orp.	104	F2
Bluebell Clo., Wall.	101	B1
Bluefield Clo., Hmptn.	81	G5
Bluegates, Epsom	99	G7
Bluehouse Rd. E4	34	E3
Blundell Rd., Edg.	38	D1
Blundell St. N7	49	E7
Blunden Clo., Dag.	53	C1
Blunt Rd., S.Croy.	102	A5
Blunts Rd. SE9	79	D5
Blurton Rd. E5	50	F4
Blyth Clo. E14	69	D4
Manchester Rd.		
Blyth Clo., Twick.	73	C6
Grimwood Rd.		
Blyth Rd. E17	41	J7
Blyth Rd. SE28	62	C7
Blyth Rd., Brom.	96	F1
Blythe Clo. SE6	77	J7
Blythe Clo., Twick.	73	C7
Grimwood Rd.		
Blythe Hill SE6	77	J7
Blythe Hill, Orp.	97	J1
Blythe Hill La. SE6	77	J7
Blythe Rd. W14	66	A3

Name	Page	Grid
Blythe St. E2	59	E3
Blythe Vale SE6	86	J1
Blythswood Rd., Ilf.	53	A1
Blythwood Rd. N4	40	E7
Blythwood Rd., Pnr.	36	D1
Boades Ms. NW3	48	G4
New End		
Boadicea St. N1	58	F1
Copenhagen St.		
Boakes Clo. NW9	38	C4
Roe Grn.		
Boardman Ave. E4	26	B5
Boar's Head Yd., Brent.	64	G7
Brent Way		
Boathouse Wk. SE15	**21**	**G7**
Boathouse Wk. SE15	68	D7
Boathouse Wk., Rich.	73	G1
Kew Rd.		
Bob Anker Clo. E13	60	G3
Chesterton Rd.		
Bob Marley Way SE24	76	G4
Mayall Rd.		
Bobbin Clo. SW4	76	C3
Bockhampton Rd., Kings.T.	82	J7
Bocking St. E8	59	E1
Boddicott Clo. SW19	84	B2
Bodiam Clo., Enf.	25	A2
Bodiam Rd. SW16	85	D7
Bodley Clo., N.Mal.	92	E5
Bodley Manor Way SW2	76	G7
Papworth Way		
Bodley Rd., N.Mal.	92	D6
Bodmin Clo., Har.	45	F3
Bodmin Gro., Mord.	93	E4
Bodmin St. SW18	84	D1
Bodnant Gdns. SW20	92	H3
Bodney Rd. E8	50	E5
Boeing Way, Sthl.	63	B3
Boevey Path, Belv.	71	F5
Orchard Ave.		
Bogey La., Orp.	104	C7
Bognor Gdns., Wat.	28	C5
Bowring Grn.		
Bognor Rd., Well.	80	D1
Bohemia Pl. E8	50	F6
Bohun Gro., Barn.	23	H6
Boileau Rd. SW13	65	G7
Boileau Rd. W5	55	J6
Bolden St. SE8	78	B2
Bolderwood Way, W.Wick.	103	B2
Boldmere Rd., Pnr.	36	C7
Boleyn Ave., Enf.	25	E1
Boleyn Clo. E17	42	A4
Boleyn Ct., Buck.H.	34	G1
Boleyn Dr., Ruis.	45	D2
Boleyn Dr., W.Mol.	90	F3
Boleyn Gdns., Dag.	53	J7
Boleyn Gdns., W.Wick.	103	B2
Boleyn Gro., W.Wick.	103	C2
Boleyn Rd. E6	61	A2
Boleyn Rd. E7	51	G7
Boleyn Rd. N16	50	B5
Boleyn Way, Barn.	23	F3
Boleyn Way, Ilf.	35	F6
Bolina Rd. SE16	68	F5
Bolingbroke Gro. SW11	75	J6
Bolingbroke Rd. W14	66	A3
Bolingbroke Wk. SW11	75	G1
Bolliger Ct. NW10	56	C4
Park Royal Rd.		
Bollo Bri. Rd. W3	65	B3
Bollo La. W3	65	B2
Bollo La. W4	65	C4
Bolney St. SW8	67	F7
Bolney Way, Felt.	81	E3
Bolsover St. W1	58	B4
Bolstead Rd., Mitch.	94	B1
Bolt Ct. EC4	**12**	**F4**
Boltmore Clo. NW4	39	A3
Bolton Clo. SE20	95	D2
Selby Rd.		
Bolton Clo., Chess.	98	G6
Bolton Cres. SE5	**20**	**G7**
Bolton Cres. SE5	67	H6
Bolton Gdns. NW10	57	A2
Bolton Gdns. SW5	**18**	**A3**
Bolton Gdns. SW5	66	E5
Bolton Gdns., Brom.	87	F6
Bolton Gdns., Tedd.	82	D6

Name	Page	Grid
Bolton Gdns. Ms. SW10	**18**	**B3**
Bolton Gdns. Ms. SW10	66	E5
Bolton Rd. E15	51	F6
Bolton Rd. N18	33	C5
Bolton Rd. NW8	57	E1
Bolton Rd. NW10	56	E1
Bolton Rd. W4	65	C7
Bolton Rd., Chess.	98	G6
Bolton Rd., Har.	36	J4
Bolton St. W1	**15**	**E1**
Bolton St. W1	67	B1
Bolton Wk. N7	49	F2
Durham Rd.		
Boltons, The SW10	**18**	**C3**
Boltons, The SW10	66	F5
Boltons, The, Wem.	46	C4
Boltons, The, Wdf.Grn.	34	G4
Bombay St. SE16	68	E4
Bomore Rd. W11	57	B7
Bon Marche Ter. SE27	86	B4
Gipsy Rd.		
Bonar Pl., Chis.	88	B7
Sundridge Ave.		
Bonar Rd. SE15	68	D7
Bonchester Clo., Chis.	88	D7
Bonchurch Clo., Sutt.	100	E7
Bonchurch Rd. W10	57	B5
Bonchurch Rd. W13	64	E1
Bond Ct. EC4	**13**	**B4**
Bond Gdns., Wall.	101	C4
Bond Rd., Mitch.	93	H2
Bond Rd., Surb.	98	J1
Bond St. E15	51	E5
Bond St. W4	65	E4
Chiswick Common Rd.		
Bond St. W5	55	G7
Bondfield Rd. E6	61	B5
Bondfield Rd., Hayes	54	A3
Bonding Yd. Wk. SE16	68	H3
Finland St.		
Bondway SW8	**20**	**B5**
Bondway SW8	67	E6
Boneta Rd. SE18	70	C3
Bonfield Rd. SE13	78	C4
Bonham Gdns., Dag.	53	D2
Bonham Rd. SW2	76	F5
Bonham Rd., Dag.	53	D2
Bonheur Rd. W4	65	D2
Bonhill St. EC2	**9**	**C6**
Bonhill St. EC2	59	A4
Boniface Gdns., Har.	28	H7
Boniface Wk., Har.	28	H7
Bonner Hill Rd., Kings.T.	91	J3
Bonner Rd. E2	59	F2
Bonner St. E2	59	F2
Bonnersfield Clo., Har.	37	C6
Bonnersfield La., Har.	37	C6
Bonneville Gdns. SW4	76	C6
Bonnington Sq. SW8	**20**	**C5**
Bonnington Sq. SW8	67	F6
Bonnington Twr., Brom.	97	B6
Bonny St. NW1	49	C7
Bonser Rd., Twick.	82	C2
Bonsor St. SE5	68	B7
Bonville Gdns. NW4	38	G4
Handowe Clo.		
Bonville Rd., Brom.	87	F5
Book Ms. WC2	**11**	**J4**
Booker Clo. E14	59	J5
Wallwood St.		
Booker Rd. N18	33	D5
Boone Ct. N9	33	F3
Boone St. SE13	78	E4
Boones Rd. SE13	78	E4
Boord St. SE10	69	E3
Boot St. N1	**9**	**D4**
Boot St. N1	59	B3
Booth Clo. SE28	62	B7
Booth Rd. NW9	38	D2
Booth Rd., Croy.	101	H2
Waddon New Rd.		
Boothby Rd. N19	49	D2
Booth's Pl. W1	**11**	**G2**
Bordars Rd. W7	55	B5
Bordars Wk. W7	55	B5
Borden Ave., Enf.	25	A4
Border Cres. SE26	86	E5
Border Gdns., Croy.	103	B4
Border Rd. SE26	86	E5
Bordergate, Mitch.	93	J1
Borders La., Loug.	27	D4

Name	Page	Grid
Bordesley Rd., Mord.	93	E4
Bordon Wk. SW15	74	G1
Boreas Wk. N1	8	H2
Boreham Ave. E16	60	G6
Boreham Clo. E11	51	C1
Hainault Rd.		
Boreham Rd. N22	40	J1
Borehamwood Ind. Pk., Borwd.	22	D2
Borer's Pas. E1	**13**	**E3**
Borgard Rd. SE18	70	C4
Borkwood Pk., Orp.	104	J4
Borkwood Way, Orp.	104	H4
Borland Rd. SE15	77	F4
Borland Rd., Tedd.	82	E6
Borneo St. SW15	74	J3
Borough High St. SE1	**17**	**A4**
Borough High St. SE1	67	J2
Borough Hill, Croy.	101	H3
Borough Rd. SE1	**16**	**H5**
Borough Rd. SE1	67	H3
Borough Rd., Islw.	73	B1
Borough Rd., Kings.T.	92	A1
Borough Rd., Mitch.	93	H2
Borough Sq. SE1	**16**	**J4**
Borrett Clo. SE17	**20**	**J4**
Borrodaile Rd. SW18	75	E6
Borrowdale Ave., Har.	37	D2
Borrowdale Clo., Ilf.	43	B4
Borrowdale Ct., Enf.	24	J1
Borthwick Ms. E15	51	E4
Borthwick Rd.		
Borthwick Rd. E15	51	E4
Borthwick Rd. NW9	38	F6
West Hendon Bdy.		
Borthwick St. SE8	69	A5
Borwick Ave. E17	41	J3
Bosbury Rd. SE6	87	C3
Boscastle Rd. NW5	49	B3
Bosco Clo., Orp.	104	J4
Strickland Way		
Boscobel Pl. SW1	**19**	**C1**
Boscobel Pl. SW1	67	A4
Boscobel St. NW8	**6**	**F4**
Boscobel St. NW8	57	G4
Boscombe Ave. E10	42	D7
Boscombe Clo. E5	50	H5
Boscombe Gdns. SW16	85	E6
Boscombe Rd. SW17	85	A6
Boscombe Rd. SW19	93	D1
Boscombe Rd. W12	65	G2
Boscombe Rd., Wor.Pk.	99	J1
Bosgrove E4	34	C1
Boss St. SE1	**17**	**F3**
Bostal Row, Bexh.	80	F3
Harlington Rd.		
Bostall Heath SE2	71	B5
Bostall Hill SE2	71	A5
Bostall Hill Rd. SE2	71	C6
Bostall La. SE2	71	B5
Bostall Manorway SE2	71	B4
Bostall Pk. Ave., Bexh.	71	E7
Bostall Rd., Orp.	89	B7
Boston Gdns. W4	65	E6
Boston Gdns., Brent.	64	D4
Boston Manor Rd., Brent.	64	E4
Boston Pk. Rd., Brent.	64	F5
Boston Pl. NW1	**6**	**J6**
Boston Pl. NW1	57	J4
Boston Rd. E6	61	B3
Boston Rd. E17	42	A6
Boston Rd. W7	64	B1
Boston Rd., Croy.	94	F6
Boston Rd., Edg.	30	C7
Boston Vale W7	64	D4
Bostonthorpe Rd. W7	64	B2
Boswell Ct. WC1	**12**	**B1**
Boswell Rd., Th.Hth.	94	J4
Boswell St. WC1	**12**	**B1**
Boswell St. WC1	58	E5
Bosworth Clo. E17	41	J1
Bosworth Rd. N11	32	D6
Bosworth Rd. W10	57	B4
Bosworth Rd., Barn.	23	D3
Bosworth Rd., Dag.	53	G3
Botany Bay La., Chis.	97	F2
Boteley Clo. E4	34	D2
Botha Rd. E13	60	H5
Botham Clo., Edg.	30	C7
Pavilion Way		
Bothwell Clo. E16	60	F5
Bothwell St. W6	66	A6
Delorme St.		
Botolph All. EC3	**13**	**D5**

Street	Map	Ref
Botolph La. EC3	13	D5
Botsford Rd. SW20	93	B2
Botts Ms. W2	57	D6
Chepstow Rd.		
Botts Pas. W2	57	D6
Chepstow Rd.		
Boucher Clo., Tedd.	82	C5
Boughton Ave., Brom.	96	F7
Boughton Rd. SE28	70	H3
Boulcott St. E1	59	G6
Boulevard, The SW17	85	A2
Balham High Rd.		
Boulevard, The, Pnr.	36	G4
Pinner Rd.		
Boulogne Rd., Croy.	94	J6
Boulton Ho., Brent.	64	H5
Boulton Rd., Dag.	53	E3
Boultwood Rd. E6	61	C6
Bounces La. N9	33	E2
Bounces Rd. N9	33	E2
Boundaries Rd. SW12	84	J2
Boundaries Rd., Felt.	81	C1
Boundary Clo. SE20	95	D2
Haysleigh Gdns.		
Boundary Clo., Ilf.	52	H4
Loxford La.		
Boundary Clo., Kings.T.	92	B3
Boundary Clo., Sthl.	63	G5
Boundary La. E13	61	A3
Boundary La. SE17	21	A6
Boundary La. SE17	67	J6
Boundary Par. N8	40	E6
Boundary Pas. E2	9	F5
Boundary Rd. E13	60	J2
Boundary Rd. E17	41	J7
Boundary Rd. N9	25	F6
Boundary Rd. N22	40	H3
Boundary Rd. NW8	57	F1
Boundary Rd. SW19	84	G6
Boundary Rd., Bark.	61	G1
Boundary Rd., Cars.	101	A7
Boundary Rd., Pnr.	36	D7
Boundary Rd., Sid.	79	H5
Boundary Rd., Wall.	101	B6
Boundary Rd., Wem.	46	H3
Boundary Row SE1	16	G3
Boundary St. E2	9	F4
Boundary St. E2	59	C4
Boundary Way, Croy.	103	A5
Boundfield Rd. SE6	87	E3
Bounds Grn. Rd. N11	32	C6
Bounds Grn. Rd. N22	32	E7
Bourchier St. W1	11	H5
Bourdon Pl. W1	11	E5
Bourdon Rd. SE20	95	F2
Bourdon St. W1	11	D6
Bourdon St. W1	58	B7
Bourke Clo. NW10	47	E6
Mayo Rd.		
Bourke Clo. SW4	76	E6
Bourlet Clo. W1	11	F2
Bourn Ave. N15	41	A4
Bourn Ave., Barn.	23	G5
Bournbrook Rd. SE3	79	A3
Bourne, The N14	32	D1
Bourne Ave. N14	32	E2
Bourne Ave., Ruis.	45	C5
Bourne Ct., Ruis.	45	B5
Bourne Dr., Mitch.	93	G2
Bourne Est. EC1	12	E1
Bourne Est. EC1	58	G5
Bourne Gdns. E4	34	B4
Bourne Hill N13	32	F2
Bourne Hill Clo. N13	32	F2
Bourne Hill		
Bourne Mead, Bex.	80	J5
Bourne Pl. W4	65	D5
Dukes Ave.		
Bourne Rd. E7	51	F3
Bourne Rd. N8	40	E6
Bourne Rd., Bex.	80	H7
Bourne Rd., Brom.	97	A4
Bourne St. SW1	19	B2
Bourne St. SW1	67	A4
Bourne St., Croy.	101	H2
Waddon New Rd.		
Bourne Ter. W2	10	A1
Bourne Ter. W2	57	E5
Bourne Vale, Brom.	103	F1
Bourne Vw., Grnf.	46	C6
Bourne Way, Brom.	103	E2
Bourne Way, Epsom	99	C4
Bourne Way, Sutt.	100	C5
Bournemead Ave., Nthlt.	54	A2
Bournemead Clo., Nthlt.	54	A3
Bournemead Way, Nthlt.	54	B2
Bournemouth Rd. SE15	77	D2
Bournemouth Rd. SW19	93	D1
Bourneside Cres. N14	32	D1
Bourneside Gdns. SE6	87	C5
Bournevale Rd. SW16	85	E4
Bournewood Rd. SE18	71	A7
Bournville Rd. SE6	78	A7
Bournwell Clo., Barn.	23	J3
Bourton Clo., Hayes	63	A1
Avondale Dr.		
Bousfield Rd. SE14	77	G2
Boutflower Rd. SW11	75	H4
Bouverie Gdns., Har.	37	G6
Bouverie Ms. N16	50	B2
Bouverie Rd.		
Bouverie Pl. W2	10	F3
Bouverie Pl. W2	57	G6
Bouverie Rd. N16	50	B1
Bouverie Rd., Har.	36	J6
Bouverie St. EC4	12	F4
Bouverie St. EC4	58	G6
Boveney Rd. SE23	77	G7
Bovill Rd. SE23	77	G7
Bovingdon Ave., Wem.	47	A6
Bovingdon Clo. N19	49	C2
Junction Rd.		
Bovingdon La. NW9	38	E1
Bovingdon Rd. SW6	75	E1
Bovingdon Sq., Mitch.	94	E4
Leicester Ave.		
Bow Bri. Est. E3	60	B2
Bow Chyd. EC4	13	A4
Bow Common La. E3	59	H4
Bow Ind. Est. E15	51	B7
Bow La. EC4	13	A4
Bow La. EC4	58	J6
Bow La. N12	31	F7
Bow La., Mord.	93	B6
Bow Rd. E3	59	J3
Bow St. E15	51	E5
Bow St. WC2	12	B4
Bow St. WC2	58	E6
Bowater Clo. NW9	38	D5
Bowater Clo. SW2	76	E6
Bowater Pl. SE3	69	H7
Bowater Rd. SE18	70	A3
Bowden St. SE11	20	F3
Bowden St. SE11	67	G5
Bowditch SE8	68	J5
Bowdon Rd. E17	42	A7
Bowen Dr. SE21	86	B3
Bowen Rd., Har.	36	J7
Bowen St. E14	60	B6
Bower Ave. SE10	78	E1
Bower Clo., Nthlt.	54	C2
Bower St. E1	59	G6
Bowerdean St. SW6	75	E1
Bowerman Ave. SE14	68	H6
Bowers Wk. E6	61	C6
Northumberland Rd.		
Bowes Clo., Sid.	80	B6
Bowes Rd. N11	32	B5
Bowes Rd. N13	32	E5
Bowes Rd. W3	56	E7
Bowes Rd., Dag.	53	C4
Bowfell Rd. W6	65	J6
Bowford Ave., Bexh.	80	E1
Bowhill Clo. SW9	20	F7
Bowhill Clo. SW9	67	G7
Bowie Clo. SW4	76	D7
Bowland Rd. SW4	76	D4
Bowland Rd., Wdf.Grn.	34	J2
Bowland Yd. SW1	15	A4
Bowles Rd. SE1	21	H5
Bowley La. SE19	86	C5
Bowley Rd. SE19	86	C6
Farquhar Rd.		
Bowling Grn. Clo. SW15	74	H7
Bowling Grn. Ct. EC2	9	E6
Bowling Grn. Ct. EC2	59	B4
Bowling Grn. La. EC1	8	F5
Bowling Grn. La. EC1	58	G4
Bowling Grn. Pl. SE1	17	B3
Bowling Grn. Pl. SE1	68	A2
Bowling Grn. Row SE18	70	C3
Samuel St.		
Bowling Grn. St. SE11	20	E5
Bowling Grn. St. SE11	67	G6
Bowling Grn. Wk. N1	9	D3
Bowls, The, Chig.	35	H4
Bowls Clo., Stan.	29	E5
Bowman Ave. E16	60	F7
Bowman Ms. SW18	84	C1
Bowmans Clo. W13	64	E1
Bowmans Lea SE23	77	G7
Bowmans Meadow, Wall.	101	B3
Bowmans Ms. E1	13	H5
Bowmans Ms. N7	49	E3
Seven Sisters Rd.		
Bowmans Pl. N7	49	E3
Holloway Rd.		
Bowman's Trd. Est. NW9	37	J3
Westmoreland Rd.		
Bowmead SE9	88	C2
Bowmore Wk. NW1	49	D7
St. Paul's Cres.		
Bowness Clo. E8	50	C6
Beechwood Rd.		
Bowness Cres. SW15	83	E5
Bowness Dr., Hours.	72	E4
Bowness Rd. SE6	78	B7
Bowness Rd., Bexh.	80	H2
Bowood Rd. SW11	76	A5
Bowood Rd., Enf.	25	G2
Bowring Grn., Wat.	28	C5
Bowrons Ave., Wem.	46	G7
Bowyer Clo. E6	61	C5
Bowyer Pl. SE5	21	A7
Bowyer Pl. SE5	67	J7
Bowyer St. SE5	21	A7
Bowyer St. SE5	67	J7
Box La., Bark.	62	B2
Boxall Rd. SE21	77	B6
Boxgrove Rd. SE2	71	B2
Boxley Rd., Mord.	93	F4
Boxley St. E16	69	H1
Boxmoor Rd., Har.	37	E4
Boxoll Rd., Dag.	53	F4
Boxted Clo., Buck.H.	35	B1
Boxtree La., Har.	36	J1
Boxtree Rd., Har.	29	A7
Boxworth Gro. N1	58	F1
Richmond Ave.		
Boyard Rd. SE18	70	E5
Boyce St. SE1	16	E2
Boyce Way E13	60	G4
Boycroft Ave. NW9	38	C6
Boyd Ave., Sthl.	63	F1
Boyd Clo., Kings.T.	83	A7
Crescent Rd.		
Boyd Rd. SW19	84	G6
Boyd St. E1	13	J4
Boyd St. E1	59	D6
Boydell Ct. NW8	48	G7
St. John's Wd. Pk.		
Boyfield St. SE1	16	H4
Boyfield St. SE1	67	H2
Boyland Rd., Brom.	87	F5
Boyle Ave., Stan.	29	D6
Boyle Fm. Rd., T.Ditt.	91	D6
Boyle St. W1	11	F5
Boyne Ave. NW4	39	A4
Boyne Rd. SE13	78	C3
Boyne Rd., Dag.	53	G3
Boyne Ter. Ms. W11	66	C1
Boyseland Ct., Edg.	30	C2
Boyson Rd. SE17	21	B5
Boyson Rd. SE17	68	A6
Boythorn Way SE16	68	E5
Credon Rd.		
Boyton Clo. E1	59	G4
Stayners Rd.		
Boyton Clo. N8	40	E3
Boyton Rd. N8	40	E3
Brabant Ct. EC3	13	D5
Brabant Rd. N22	40	F2
Brabazon Ave., Wall.	101	E7
Brabazon Rd., Hours.	63	C7
Brabazon Rd., Nthlt.	54	G2
Brabazon St. E14	60	B6
Brabourn Gro. SE15	77	F2
Brabourne Clo. SE19	86	B5
Brabourne Cres., Bexh.	71	F6
Brabourne Heights NW7	30	E3
Brabourne Ri., Beck.	96	C5
Bracewell Ave., Grnf.	46	D6
Bracewell Rd. W10	56	J5
Bracewood Gdns., Croy.	102	C3
Bracey St. N4	49	E2
Bracken, The E4	34	C1
Hortus Rd.		
Bracken Ave. SW12	76	A6
Bracken Ave., Croy.	103	A3
Bracken Clo. E6	61	C5
Bracken Clo., Twick.	72	G7
Hedley Rd.		
Bracken Dr., Chig.	35	E6
Bracken End, Islw.	73	A5
Bracken Gdns. SW13	74	G2
Bracken Hill Clo., Brom.	96	F1
Bracken Hill La.		
Bracken Hill La., Brom.	96	F1
Bracken Ind. Est., Ilf.	35	J7
Bracken Ms., Rom.	44	H6
Brackenbridge Dr., Ruis.	45	D3
Brackenbury Gdns. W6	65	H3
Brackenbury Rd. N2	39	F3
Brackenbury Rd. W6	65	H3
Brackendale N21	32	F2
Brackendale Clo., Hours.	72	H1
Brackenfield Clo. E5	50	E4
Tiger Way		
Brackens, The, Enf.	25	B7
Brackenwood, Sun.	90	A1
Brackley Clo., Wall.	101	E7
Brackley Rd. W4	65	E5
Brackley Rd., Beck.	86	J7
Brackley Sq., Wdf.Grn.	35	A7
Brackley St. EC1	13	A1
Brackley Ter. W4	65	E5
Bracklyn Ct. N1	9	B1
Bracklyn St. N1	9	B1
Bracklyn St. N1	59	A2
Bracknell Clo. N22	40	G1
Bracknell Gdns. NW3	48	E4
Bracknell Gate NW3	48	E5
Bracknell Way NW3	48	E4
Bracondale Rd. SE2	71	A4
Brad St. SE1	16	F2
Bradbourne Rd., Bex.	80	G7
Bradbourne St. SW6	75	D2
Bradbury Clo., Borwd.	22	B1
Bradbury Clo., Sthl.	63	F4
Bradbury St. N16	50	B5
Braddon Rd., Rich.	73	J3
Braddyll St. SE10	69	E5
Braden St. W9	6	A6
Bradenham Ave., Well.	80	A4
Bradenham Clo. SE17	21	B5
Bradenham Clo. SE17	68	A6
Bradenham Rd., Har.	37	E4
Bradfield Dr., Bark.	53	A5
Bradfield Rd. E16	69	G2
Bradfield Rd., Ruis.	45	E5
Bradford Clo. SE26	86	E4
Coombe Rd.		
Bradford Clo., Brom.	104	C1
Bradford Dr., Epsom	99	F6
Bradford Rd. W3	65	E2
Warple Way		
Bradford Rd., Ilf.	52	G1
Bradgate Rd. SE6	78	A6
Brading Cres. E11	51	H2
Brading Rd. SW2	76	F7
Brading Rd., Croy.	94	F6
Bradiston Rd. W9	57	C3
Bradley Clo. N7	49	F6
Sutterton St.		
Bradley Gdns. W13	55	E6
Bradley Ms. SW17	84	J1
Bellevue Rd.		
Bradley Rd. N22	40	F2
Bradley Rd. SE19	85	J6
Bradley's Clo. N1	8	F1
Bradman Row, Edg.	30	C7
Pavilion Way		
Bradmead SW8	67	B7
Bradmore Ho. E1	59	F5
Jamaica St.		
Bradmore Pk. Rd. W6	65	H4
Bradshaws Clo. SE25	95	D3
Bradstock Rd. E9	50	G6
Bradstock Rd., Epsom	99	G5
Bradwell Ave., Dag.	53	G2
Bradwell Clo. E18	42	F4
Bradwell Ms. N18	33	D4
Lyndhurst Rd.		
Bradwell Rd., Buck.H.	35	B1
Bradwell St. E1	59	G3
Brady Ave., Loug.	27	F2
Brady St. E1	59	E4
Bradymead E6	61	E6
Warwall		

Braemar Ave. N22 40 E1
Braemar Ave. NW10 47 D3
Braemar Ave. SW19 84 D2
Braemar Ave., Bexh. 80 J4
Braemar Ave., Th.Hth. 94 G3
Braemar Ave., Wem. 46 G7
Braemar Gdns. NW9 38 D1
Braemar Gdns., Sid. 88 G3
Braemar Gdns., 103 C1
 W.Wick.
Braemar Rd. E13 60 F4
Braemar Rd. N15 41 B5
Braemar Rd., Brent. 64 G6
Braemar Rd., Wor.Pk. 99 H3
Braes St. N1 49 H7
Braeside, Beck. 87 A5
Braeside Ave. SW19 93 B1
Braeside Clo., Pnr. 28 G7
 The Ave.
Braeside Cres., Bexh. 80 J4
Braeside Rd. SW16 85 C7
Braesyde Clo., Belv. 71 F4
Brafferton Rd., Croy. 101 J4
Braganza St. SE17 20 G4
Braganza St. SE17 67 H5
Braham St. E1 13 G4
Braham St. E1 59 C6
Braid Ave. W3 56 E6
Braid Clo., Felt. 81 F2
Braidwood Rd. SE6 87 D1
Braidwood St. SE1 17 D2
Brailsford Clo., Mitch. 84 H7
Brailsford Rd. SW2 76 H5
Brainton Ave., Felt. 72 B7
Braintree Ave., Ilf. 43 B4
Braintree Rd., Dag. 53 G3
Braintree Rd., Ruis. 45 B4
Braintree St. E2 59 F4
Braithwaite Ave., 44 G7
 Rom.
Braithwaite Gdns., 37 F1
 Stan.
Braithwaite Rd., Enf. 25 J3
Bramah Grn. SW9 76 G1
Bramalea Clo. N6 40 A6
Bramall Clo. E15 51 F5
 Idmiston Rd.
Bramber Ct. W5 64 H4
 Sterling Pl.
Bramber Rd. N12 31 H5
Bramber Rd. W14 66 C6
Bramble Clo., Croy. 103 A4
Bramble Clo., Stan. 29 G7
Bramble Cft., Erith 71 J4
Bramble Gdns. W12 56 F7
 Wallflower St.
Bramble La., Hmptn. 81 F6
Brambleacres Clo., 100 D7
 Sutt.
Bramblebury Rd. SE18 70 F5
Brambledown Clo., 96 E5
 W.Wick.
Brambledown Rd., 101 A7
 Cars.
Brambledown Rd., 102 B7
 S.Croy.
Brambledown Rd., 101 B7
 Wall.
Brambles, The, Chig. 35 F6
Brambles Clo., Islw. 64 E7
Bramblewood Clo., 100 J1
 Cars.
Bramblings, The E4 34 D4
Bramcote Ave., Mitch. 93 J4
Bramcote Gro. SE16 68 F5
Bramcote Rd. SW15 74 H4
Bramdean Cres. SE12 87 G1
Bramdean Gdns. SE12 87 G1
Bramerton Rd., Beck. 95 J3
Bramerton St. SW3 18 G5
Bramerton St. SW3 66 H6
Bramfield Ct. N4 49 J2
 Queens Dr.
Bramfield Rd. SW11 75 H6
Bramford Ct. N14 32 D2
Bramford Rd. SW18 75 F4
Bramham Gdns. SW5 18 A3
Bramham Gdns. SW5 66 E5
Bramham Gdns., 98 G4
 Chess.
Bramhope La. SE7 69 H6
Bramlands Clo. SW11 75 H3
Bramley Clo. E17 41 H2
Bramley Clo. N14 24 B5
Bramley Clo., Hayes 54 A7
 Orchard Rd.
Bramley Clo., Orp. 104 E1
Bramley Clo., S.Croy. 101 H5

Bramley Clo., Twick. 72 J6
Bramley Ct., Well. 80 B1
Bramley Cres. SW8 19 J7
Bramley Cres., Ilf. 43 D6
Bramley Gdns., Wat. 28 C5
Bramley Hill, S.Croy. 101 H5
Bramley Rd. N14 24 B5
Bramley Rd. W5 64 F3
Bramley Rd. W10 57 A7
Bramley Rd., Sutt. 100 G5
Bramley Way, Houns. 72 F5
Bramley Way, 103 B2
 W.Wick.
Brampton Clo. E5 50 E2
Brampton Gdns. N15 40 J5
 Brampton Rd.
Brampton Gro. NW4 38 H4
Brampton Gro., Har. 37 D4
Brampton Gro., Wem. 46 J1
Brampton La. NW4 38 J4
Brampton Pk. Rd. N8 40 G3
Brampton Rd. E6 61 A4
Brampton Rd. N15 40 J5
Brampton Rd. NW9 38 A4
Brampton Rd. SE2 71 C6
Brampton Rd., Bexh. 80 D3
Brampton Rd., Croy. 95 C7
Brampton Rd., Wat. 28 D5
Bramsham Gdns., 28 D5
 Wat.
Bramshaw Ri., N.Mal. 92 E6
Bramshaw Rd. E9 50 G6
Bramshill Clo., Chig. 35 H5
 Tine Rd.
Bramshill Gdns. NW5 49 B3
Bramshill Rd. NW10 56 E2
Bramshot Ave. SE7 69 G6
Bramshot Way, Wat. 28 A2
Bramston Clo., Ilf. 35 J6
Bramston Rd. NW10 56 G2
Bramston Rd. SW17 84 F3
Bramwell Clo., Sun. 90 D2
Brancaster Rd. E12 52 C4
Brancaster Rd. SW16 85 E3
Brancaster Rd., Ilf. 43 G6
Brancepeth Gdns., 34 G2
 Buck.H.
Branch Hill NW3 48 F3
Branch Pl. N1 59 A1
Branch Rd. E14 59 H7
Brancker Clo., Wall. 101 E7
 Brown Clo.
Brancker Rd., Har. 37 G3
Brancroft Way, Enf. 25 H1
Brand St. SE10 69 C7
Brandlehow Rd. SW15 75 C4
Brandon Est. SE17 20 H6
Brandon Est. SE17 67 H6
Brandon Rd. E17 42 C3
Brandon Rd. N7 49 E7
Brandon Rd., Sthl. 63 F5
Brandon Rd., Sutt. 100 E4
Brandon St. SE17 21 A2
Brandon St. SE17 67 J4
Brandram Rd. SE13 78 E3
Brandreth Rd. E6 61 C6
Brandreth Rd. SW17 85 B2
Brandries, The, Wall. 101 D3
Brandville Gdns., Ilf. 43 E4
Brandy Way, Sutt. 100 D7
Branfield Clo. SW17 84 F3
Brangbourne Rd., 87 C5
 Brom.
Brangton Rd. SE11 20 D4
Brangton Rd. SE11 67 F5
Brangwyn Cres. SW19 93 F2
Branksea St. SW6 66 B7
Branksome Ave. N18 33 C6
Branksome Rd. SW2 76 E4
Branksome Rd. SW19 93 D1
Branksome Way, Har. 37 H6
Branksome Way, 92 C1
 N.Mal.
Bransby Rd., Chess. 98 H7
Branscombe Gdns. 24 G7
 N21
Branscombe St. SE13 78 B3
Bransdale Clo. NW6 57 E1
 West End La.
Bransgrove Rd., Edg. 37 J1
Branston Cres., Orp. 104 G1
Branstone Rd., Rich. 73 J1
Brants Wk. W7 55 B4
Brantwood Ave., Erith 71 J7
Brantwood Ave., Islw. 73 D4
Brantwood Clo. E17 42 B3
Brantwood Gdns., Enf. 24 E4
Brantwood Gdns., Ilf. 43 B4

Brantwood Rd. N17 33 C6
Brantwood Rd. SE24 76 J5
Brantwood Rd., Bexh. 80 H2
Brasher Clo., Grnf. 46 A5
 Lilian Board Way
Brass Tally All. SE16 68 G2
 Middleton Dr.
Brassey Rd. NW6 48 C6
Brassey Sq. SW11 76 A3
Brassie Ave. W3 56 E6
Brasted Clo. SE26 86 F4
Brasted Clo., Bexh. 80 D5
Brathway Rd. SW18 75 D7
Bratley St. E1 9 H6
Braund Ave., Grnf. 54 H4
Braundton Ave., Sid. 88 J1
Braunston Dr., Hayes 54 E4
Bravington Pl. W9 57 C4
 Bravington Rd.
Bravington Rd. W9 57 C3
Brawne Ho. SE17 20 H6
Braxfield Rd. SE4 77 H4
Braxted Pk. SW16 85 F6
Bray NW3 48 H7
Bray Clo., Borwd. 22 C1
Bray Cres. SE16 68 G2
 Marlow Way
Bray Dr. E16 60 F7
 Bowman Ave.
Bray Pas. E16 60 F7
 Bowman Ave.
Bray Pl. SW3 18 J2
Bray Pl. SW3 66 J4
Bray Rd. NW7 31 A7
Brayards Rd. SE15 77 E2
Braybourne Dr., Islw. 64 C7
Braybrook St. W12 56 F5
Braybrooke Gdns. 86 C7
 SE19
 Fox Hill
Brayburne Ave. SW4 76 C2
Braycourt Ave., Walt. 90 B7
Braydon Rd. N16 41 D7
Brayfield Ter. N1 49 G7
 Lofting Rd.
Brayford Sq. E1 59 H6
 Summercourt Rd.
Brayton Gdns., Enf. 24 D4
Braywood Rd. SE9 79 G4
Brazil Clo., Croy. 94 E7
Breach La., Dag. 62 G3
Bread St. EC4 13 A5
Bread St. EC4 58 J7
Breakspears Rd. SE4 77 J3
Bream Clo. N17 41 E4
Bream Gdns. E6 61 D3
Bream St. E3 51 A7
Breamore Clo. SW15 83 G1
Breamore Rd., Ilf. 52 J2
Bream's Bldgs. EC4 12 E3
Bream's Bldgs. EC4 58 G6
Breamwater Gdns., 82 E3
 Rich.
Brearley Clo., Edg. 30 C7
 Pavilion Way
Breasley Clo. SW15 74 H4
Brechin Pl. SW7 18 D2
Breck Rd. NW6 48 F4
Brecknock Rd. N7 49 D5
Brecknock Rd. N19 49 C4
Brecknock Rd. Est. N7 49 C4
Brecon Clo., Mitch. 94 E3
Brecon Clo., Wor.Pk. 99 J2
 Cotswold Way
Brecon Rd. W6 66 B6
Brecon Rd., Enf. 25 F4
Brede Clo. E6 61 D3
Bredgar Rd. N19 49 C2
Bredhurst Clo. SE20 86 F6
Bredon Rd. SE5 76 J3
Bredon Rd., Croy. 95 C7
Breer St. SW6 75 E3
Breezers Hill E1 13 J6
Brember Rd., Har. 45 J2
Bremner Rd. SW7 14 D5
Brenchley Clo., Brom. 96 F6
Brenchley Clo., Chis. 97 D1
Brenchley Gdns. SE23 77 F6
Brenchley Rd., Orp. 97 H1
Brenda Rd. SW17 84 J2
Brende Gdns., W.Mol. 90 H4
Brendon Ave. NW10 47 E4
Brendon Gdns., Har. 45 H4
Brendon Gdns., Ilf. 43 H5
Brendon Rd. SE9 88 G2
Brendon Rd., Dag. 53 F1
Brendon St. W1 10 H3
Brendon St. W1 57 H6
Brendon Way, Enf. 25 B7

Brenley Clo., Mitch. 94 A3
Brenley Gdns. SE9 79 A4
Brent Clo., Bex. 89 E1
Brent Cres. NW10 55 J2
Brent Cross Shop. 38 J7
 Cen. NW4
Brent Grn. NW4 38 J5
Brent Grn. Wk., Wem. 47 C3
Brent Lea, Brent. 64 F7
Brent Pk. NW10 47 D5
Brent Pk. Rd. NW4 38 H7
Brent Pl., Barn. 23 D5
Brent Rd. E16 60 G5
Brent Rd. SE18 70 E7
Brent Rd., Brent. 64 F6
Brent Rd., Sthl. 63 C3
Brent St. NW4 38 J4
Brent Ter. NW2 47 J1
Brent Vw. Rd. NW9 38 G6
Brent Way N3 31 D6
Brent Way, Brent. 64 G7
Brent Way, Wem. 47 B6
Brentcot Clo. W13 55 E4
Brentfield NW10 47 B7
Brentfield Clo. NW10 47 D6
 Normans Mead
Brentfield Gdns. NW2 39 A7
 Hendon Way
Brentfield Rd. NW10 47 D6
Brentford Business 64 F7
 Cen., Brent.
Brentford Clo., Hayes 54 D4
Brentham Way W5 55 G4
Brenthouse Rd. E9 50 D4
Brenthurst Rd. NW10 47 F6
Brentmead Clo. W7 55 B7
Brentmead Gdns. 55 J2
 NW10
Brentmead Pl. NW11 39 A6
 North Circular Rd.
Brenton St. E14 59 H6
Brentside, Brent. 64 F6
Brentside Clo. W13 55 D4
Brentside Executive 64 E6
 Cen., Brent.
Brentvale Ave., Sthl. 64 A1
Brentvale Ave., Wem. 55 J1
Brentwick Gdns., 64 H4
 Brent.
Brentwood Clo. SE9 88 F1
Brentwood Ho. SE18 70 A7
 Shooter's Hill Rd.
Brereton Rd. N17 33 C7
Bressenden Pl. SW1 15 E5
Bressenden Pl. SW1 67 B3
Bressey Gro. E18 42 F2
Brett Clo. N16 50 B2
 Yoakley Rd.
Brett Clo., Nthlt. 54 D3
 Broomcroft Ave.
Brett Ct. N9 33 F2
Brett Cres. NW10 47 D7
Brett Gdns., Dag. 53 E7
Brett Rd. E8 SW15 75 A6
 Putney Heath La.
Brett Pas. E8 50 E5
 Kenmure Rd.
Brett Rd. E8 50 E5
Brett Rd., Barn. 22 J5
Brettell St. SE17 21 C4
Brettenham Ave. E17 42 A1
 Penrhyn Ave.
Brettenham Rd. E17 42 A2
Brettenham Rd. N18 33 D4
Brewer St. W1 11 G5
Brewer St. W1 58 C7
Brewer's Grn. SW1 15 G5
Brewers Hall Gdns. 13 A2
 EC2
Brewers La., Rich. 73 G5
 George St.
Brewery Clo., Wem. 46 D5
Brewery La., Twick. 73 C7
Brewery Rd. N7 49 E7
Brewery Rd. SE18 70 G5
Brewery Rd., Brom. 104 B1
Brewhouse La. E1 68 E1
Brewhouse Rd. SE18 70 C4
Brewhouse St. SW15 75 B3
Brewhouse Wk. SE16 68 H1
Brewhouse Yd. EC1 8 G5
Brewood Rd., Dag. 53 B6
Brewster Gdns. W10 56 J5
Brewster Ho. E14 59 J7
Brewster Rd. E10 51 B1
Brian Rd., Rom. 44 C5
Briant St. SE14 77 G1
Briants Clo., Pnr. 36 F2

Briar Ave. SW16 85 F7
Briar Clo. N2 39 E2
Briar Clo. N13 32 J3
Briar Clo., Buck.H. 35 A2
Briar Clo., Hmptn. 81 F5
Briar Clo., Islw. 73 C5
Briar Ct., Sutt. 99 J4
Briar Cres., Nthlt. 45 H6
Briar Gdns., Brom. 103 F1
Briar La., Croy. 103 B4
Briar Pas. SW16 94 E3
Pollards Cres.
Briar Pl. SW16 94 F3
Briar Rd.
Briar Rd. NW2 47 J4
Briar Rd. SW16 94 E3
Briar Rd., Har. 37 F5
Briar Rd., Twick. 82 B1
Briar Wk. SW15 74 H4
Briar Wk. W10 57 B4
Droop St.
Briar Wk., Edg. 30 C7
Briarbank Rd. W13 55 D6
Briardale Gdns. NW3 48 D3
Briarfield Ave. N3 39 E2
Briars Clo. N17 33 E7
Briarswood Way, Orp. 104 J5
Briarwood Clo. NW9 38 C6
Briarwood Dr., Nthwd. 36 A2
Briarwood Rd. SW4 76 D5
Briarwood Rd., Epsom 99 G6
Briary Clo. NW3 48 H7
Fellows Rd.
Briary Ct., Sid. 89 B5
Briary Gdns., Brom. 87 H5
Briary Gro., Edg. 38 B2
Briary La. N9 33 C3
Brick Ct. EC4 12 E4
Brick Fm. Clo., Rich. 74 B1
Brick La. E1 9 G4
Brick La. E1 59 C4
Brick La. E2 9 G6
Brick La. E2 59 C3
Brick La., Enf. 25 E2
Brick La., Stan. 29 G7
Honeypot La.
Brick St. W1 15 D2
Brick St. W1 67 B1
Brickfield Clo., Brent. 64 F7
Brickfield Cotts. SE18 70 J6
Brickfield Fm. Gdns., Orp. 104 F4
Brickfield La., Barn. 22 F6
Brickfield Rd. SW19 84 E4
Brickfield Rd., Th.Hth. 94 H1
Brickfields, Har. 46 A2
Bricklayer's Arms SE1 21 E1
Brickwood Clo. SE26 86 E3
Brickwood Rd., Croy. 102 B2
Bride Ct. EC4 12 G4
Bride La. EC4 12 G4
Bride St. N7 49 F6
Brideale Clo. SE15 68 C7
Colegrove Rd.
Bridewain St. SE1 17 F5
Bridewain St. SE1 68 C3
Bridewell Pl. E1 68 E1
Brewhouse La.
Bridewell Pl. EC4 12 G4
Bridford Ms. W1 11 E1
Bridge, The, Har. 37 C4
Bridge App. NW1 49 A7
Bridge Ave. W6 65 H5
Bridge Ave. W7 55 A5
Bridge Clo. W10 57 A6
Kingsdown Clo.
Bridge Clo., Enf. 25 E2
Bridge Dr. N13 32 F4
Bridge End E17 42 C1
Bridge Gdns., E.Mol. 91 A4
Bridge Gate N21 24 J7
Bridge Ho. Quay E14 69 C1
Prestons Rd.
Bridge La. NW11 39 B4
Bridge La. SW11 75 H1
Bridge Pk. SW18 75 D5
Bridge Pl. SW1 19 E1
Bridge Pl. SW1 67 B4
Bridge Pl., Croy. 102 A1
Bridge Rd. E6 52 C7
Bridge Rd. E15 60 D1
Bridge Rd. E17 41 J7
Bridge Rd. N9 33 D3
The Bdy.
Bridge Rd. N22 40 E1
Bridge Rd. NW10 47 E6
Bridge Rd., Beck. 86 J7
Bridge Rd., Bexh. 80 E2
Bridge Rd., Chess. 98 G5
Bridge Rd., Croy. 101 J3
Duppas Hill Rd.
Bridge Rd., E.Mol. 91 A5
Bridge Rd., Houns. 73 A3
Bridge Rd., Islw. 73 A3
Bridge Rd., Sthl. 63 F2
Bridge Rd., Sutt. 100 E6
Bridge Rd., Twick. 73 E6
Bridge Rd., Wall. 101 B5
Bridge Rd., Wem. 47 A3
Bridge Row, Croy. 102 A1
Cross Rd.
Bridge St. SW1 16 A4
Bridge St. SW1 67 E2
Bridge St. W4 65 D4
Bridge St., Pnr. 36 E3
Bridge St., Rich. 73 G5
Bridge Ter. E15 51 D7
Bridge Vw. W6 65 J5
Bridge Way N11 32 C3
Pymmes Grn. Rd.
Bridge Way NW11 39 C5
Bridge Way, Twick. 72 J7
Bridge Way, Wem. 46 H7
Bridge Wf. Rd., Islw. 73 E3
Church St.
Bridge Yd. SE1 17 C1
Bridgefield Rd., Sutt. 100 D6
Bridgefoot SE1 20 B4
Bridgefoot SE1 67 E5
Bridgeford St. SW18 84 F3
Bridgeland Rd. E16 60 G7
Bridgeman Rd. N1 49 F7
Bridgeman Rd. W4 65 C3
Bridgeman Rd., Tedd. 82 D6
Bridgeman St. NW8 6 G2
Bridgeman St. NW8 57 H2
Bridgen Rd., Bex. 80 E6
Bridgend Rd. SW18 75 F4
Bridgenhall Rd., Enf. 25 C1
Bridgeport Pl. E1 17 J1
Bridges Ct. SW11 75 G3
Bridges La., Croy. 101 E4
Bridges Pl. SW6 75 C1
Bridges Rd. SW19 84 E6
Bridges Rd., Stan. 29 C5
Bridges Rd. Ms. SW19 84 E6
Bridges Rd.
Bridgetown Clo. SE19 86 B5
St. Kitts Ter.
Bridgeview Ct., Ilf. 35 G6
Bridgewater Clo., Chis. 97 H3
Bridgewater Gdns., Edg. 37 J2
Bridgewater Rd., Ruis. 45 A4
Bridgewater Rd., Wem. 46 F6
Bridgewater Sq. EC2 12 J1
Bridgewater St. EC2 12 J1
Bridgeway, Bark. 52 J7
Bridgeway St. NW1 7 G2
Bridgeway St. NW1 58 C2
Bridgewood Clo. SE20 86 E7
Bridgewood Rd. SW16 85 D7
Bridgewood Rd., Wor.Pk. 99 G3
Bridgwater Rd. E15 60 C1
Bridle Clo., Epsom 99 D5
Bridle Clo., Kings.T. 91 G4
Bridle Clo., Sun. 90 A3
Forge La.
Bridle La. W1 11 G5
Bridle La., Twick. 73 E6
Crown Rd.
Bridle Path, Croy. 101 E3
Bridle Path, Wdf.Grn. 34 E7
Bridle Rd., Croy. 103 A3
Bridle Rd., Esher 98 E6
Bridle Rd., Pnr. 36 C6
Bridle Way, Croy. 103 A5
Bridle Way, Orp. 104 F4
Bridle Way, The, Wall. 101 C4
Bridlington Rd. N9 25 E7
Bridlington Rd., Wat. 28 D3
Bridport Ave., Rom. 44 H6
Bridport Pl. N1 9 C1
Bridport Pl. N1 59 A1
Bridport Rd. N18 33 B5
Bridport Rd., Grnf. 54 H1
Bridport Rd., Th.Hth. 94 G3
Bridport Ter. SW8 76 D1
Wandsworth Rd.
Bridstow Pl. W2 57 D6
Talbot Rd.
Brief St. SE5 76 H1
Brierley, Croy. 103 B6
Brierley Ave. N9 33 F1
Brierley Clo. SE25 95 D4
Brierley Rd. E11 51 D4
Brierley Rd. SW12 85 C2
Brierly Gdns. E2 59 F2
Royston St.
Brig Ms. SE8 69 A6
Watergate St.
Brigade Clo., Har. 46 A2
Brigade St. SE3 78 F2
Royal Par.
Briggeford Clo. E5 50 D2
Geldeston Rd.
Bright Clo., Belv. 71 D4
Bright St. E14 60 B6
Brightfield Rd. SE12 78 F5
Brightling Rd. SE4 77 J6
Brightlingsea Pl. E14 59 J7
Brightman Rd. SW18 84 G1
Brighton Ave. E17 41 J5
Brighton Dr., Nthlt. 45 G6
Brighton Gro. SE14 77 H1
New Cross Rd.
Brighton Rd. E6 61 D3
Brighton Rd. N2 39 F2
Brighton Rd. N16 50 B4
Brighton Rd., S.Croy. 101 J5
Brighton Rd., Surb. 91 F6
Brighton Rd., Sutt. 100 F7
Brighton Ter. SW9 76 F4
Brightside, The, Enf. 25 G1
Brightside Rd. SE13 78 D6
Brightwell Cres. SW17 84 J5
Brigstock Rd., Belv. 71 H4
Brigstock Rd., Th.Hth. 94 G5
Brill Pl. NW1 7 J2
Brill Pl. NW1 58 D2
Brim Hill N2 39 F4
Brimpsfield Clo. SE2 71 B3
Brimsdown Ave., Enf. 25 H2
Brimsdown Ind. Est., Enf. 25 J2
Brindle Gate, Sid. 88 H1
Brindley Clo., Bexh. 80 H3
Brindley St. SE14 77 J1
Brindley Way, Brom. 87 G5
Brindley Way, Sthl. 54 H7
Brindwood Rd. E4 33 J3
Brinkburn Clo. SE2 71 A4
Brinkburn Clo., Edg. 38 B2
Brinkburn Gdns., Edg. 38 A3
Brinkley Rd., Wor.Pk. 99 H2
Brinklow Cres. SE18 70 E7
Brinklow Ho. W2 57 E5
Brinkworth Rd., Ilf. 43 B3
Brinkworth Way E9 50 J6
Brinsdale Rd. NW4 39 A3
Brinsley Rd., Har. 37 A2
Brinsley St. E1 59 E6
Watney St.
Brinsworth Clo., Twick. 82 A1
Brinton Wk. SE1 16 G2
Brion Pl. E14 60 C5
Brisbane Ave. SW19 93 E1
Brisbane Rd. E10 51 B2
Brisbane Rd. W13 64 D2
Brisbane Rd., Ilf. 43 E7
Brisbane St. SE5 68 A7
Briscoe Clo. E11 51 F2
Briscoe Rd. SW19 84 G6
Briset Rd. SE9 79 A3
Briset St. EC1 12 G1
Briset Way N7 49 F2
Bristol Gdns. W9 6 B6
Bristol Gdns. W9 57 E4
Bristol Ms. W9 6 B6
Bristol Pk. Rd. E17 41 H4
Hervey Pk. Rd.
Bristol Rd. E7 51 J6
Bristol Rd., Grnf. 54 H1
Bristol Rd., Mord. 93 F5
Briston Gro. N8 40 E6
Bristow Rd. SE19 86 B5
Bristow Rd., Bexh. 80 E1
Bristow Rd., Croy. 101 E4
Bristow Rd., Houns. 72 H3
Britannia Clo. SW4 76 D4
Bowland Rd.
Britannia Clo., Nthlt. 54 D3
Britannia La., Twick. 72 J7
Britannia Rd. E14 69 A4
Britannia Rd. N12 31 F3
Britannia Rd. SW6 66 E7
Britannia Rd., Ilf. 52 E3
Britannia Rd., Surb. 91 J7
Britannia Row N1 58 H1
Britannia St. WC1 8 C3
Britannia St. WC1 58 F3
Britannia Wk. N1 9 B3
Britannia Way NW10 56 B4
Britannia Way SW6 75 E1
Britannia Rd.
British Gro. W4 65 F5
British Gro. Pas. W4 65 F5
British Gro. S. W4 65 F5
British Gro. Pas.
British Legion Rd. E4 34 F2
British St. E3 59 J3
Brittain Rd., Dag. 53 E3
Britten Clo. NW11 48 E1
Britten Dr., Sthl. 54 G6
Britten St. SW3 18 G4
Britten St. SW3 66 H5
Brittenden Clo., Orp. 104 H6
Britten's Ct. E1 59 E7
The Highway
Britton St. EC1 8 G6
Britton St. EC1 58 H4
Brixham Cres., Ruis. 45 A1
Brixham Gdns., Ilf. 52 H5
Brixham Rd., Well. 80 D1
Brixham St. E16 70 C1
Brixton Est., Edg. 38 B2
Brixton Hill SW2 76 E7
Brixton Hill Pl. SW2 76 E7
Brixton Hill
Brixton Oval SW2 76 G4
Brixton Rd. SW9 76 G3
Brixton Sta. Rd. SW9 76 G3
Brixton Water La. SW2 76 G5
Broad Ct. WC2 12 B4
Broad Grn. Ave., Croy. 94 H7
Broad La. EC2 13 D2
Broad La. EC2 59 B5
Broad La. N8 40 F5
Tottenham La.
Broad La. N15 41 C4
Broad La., Hmptn. 81 F7
Broad Lawn SE9 88 D2
Broad Oak, Wdf.Grn. 34 H5
Broad Oak Clo. E4 34 A5
Royston Ave.
Broad Sanctuary SW1 15 J4
Broad Sanctuary SW1 67 D2
Broad St., Dag. 53 G7
Broad St., Tedd. 82 C6
Broad St. Ave. EC2 13 D2
Broad St. Pl. EC2 13 C2
Broad Vw. NW9 38 A6
Broad Wk. N21 32 F2
Broad Wk. NW1 7 C1
Broad Wk. SE3 78 J2
Broad Wk. W1 15 B1
Broad Wk. W1 67 A1
Broad Wk., Houns. 72 D1
Broad Wk., Rich. 64 J7
Broad Wk., The W8 14 C3
Broad Wk., The W8 66 F1
Broad Wk., The, E.Mol. 91 C4
Broad Wk. La. NW11 39 C7
Broad Yd. EC1 8 G6
Broadbent Clo. N6 49 B1
Broadbent St. W1 11 D5
Broadberry Ct. N18 33 E6
Broadbridge Clo. SE3 69 G7
Broadcoombe, S.Croy. 102 F7
Broadcroft Ave., Stan. 37 G2
Broadcroft Rd., Orp. 97 G7
Broadfield Clo. NW2 47 J3
Broadfield Clo., Croy. 101 F2
Progress Way
Broadfield Ct. (Bushey), Wat. 29 B2
Broadfield La. NW1 49 E7
Broadfield Rd. SE6 78 E7
Broadfield Sq., Enf. 25 E2
Broadfield Way, Buck.H. 34 J3
Broadfields, E.Mol. 91 A6
Broadfields, Har. 36 H1
Broadfields Ave. N21 24 G7
Broadfields Ave., Edg. 30 B4
Broadfields Heights, Edg. 30 B4
Broadfields La., Wat. 28 B1
Broadfields Way NW10 47 F5
Broadgate E13 60 J2
Broadgate Circle EC2 13 D1

Broadgate Rd. E16   61 A6
Fulmer Rd.
Broadgates Ave.,   23 E1
Barn.
Broadgates Rd. SW18   84 G1
Ellerton Rd.
Broadhead Strand   38 F1
NW9
Broadheath Dr., Chis.   88 C5
Broadhinton Rd. SW4   76 B3
Broadhurst Ave., Edg.   30 B4
Broadhurst Ave., Ilf.   52 J4
Broadhurst Clo. NW6   48 F6
Broadhurst Gdns.
Broadhurst Clo., Rich.   73 J5
Lower Gro. Rd.
Broadhurst Gdns.   48 E6
NW6
Broadhurst Gdns.,   35 F4
Chig.
Broadhurst Gdns.,   45 C2
Ruis.
Broadlands, The, Felt.   81 F3
Broadlands Ave.   85 E2
SW16
Broadlands Ave., Enf.   25 E3
Broadlands Clo. N6   40 A7
Broadlands Clo.   85 E2
SW16
Broadlands Clo., Enf.   25 F3
Broadlands Rd. N6   39 J7
Broadlands Rd.,   87 H4
Brom.
Broadlands Way,   92 F6
N.Mal.
Broadlawns Ct., Har.   37 C1
Broadley St. NW8   **10 F1**
Broadley St. NW8   57 G5
Broadley Ter. NW1   **6 H1**
Broadley Ter. NW1   57 H4
Broadmayne SE17   **21 B3**
Broadmead SE6   87 A3
Broadmead Ave.,   92 G7
Wor.Pk.
Broadmead Clo.,   81 G6
Hmptn.
Broadmead Clo., Pnr.   28 E7
Broadmead Est.,   34 J7
Wdf.Grn.
Broadmead Rd.,   54 E4
Hayes
Broadmead Rd.,   54 E4
Nthlt.
Broadmead Rd.,   34 G6
Wdf.Grn.
Broadoaks, Surb.   99 B1
Broadoaks Way,   96 F5
Brom.
Broadstone Pl. W1   **11 B2**
Broadview Rd. SW16   85 D7
Broadwalk E18   42 F3
Broadwalk, Har.   36 G5
Broadwall SE1   **16 F1**
Broadwall SE1   67 G1
Broadwater Gdns.,   104 E4
Orp.
Broadwater Rd. N17   41 B1
Broadwater Rd. SE28   70 F3
Broadwater Rd. SW17   84 H4
Broadway E15   51 D7
Broadway N20   31 F2
Broadway SW1   **15 H5**
Broadway SW1   67 D3
Broadway, Bark.   52 F7
Broadway, Bexh.   80 E4
Broadway, Grnf.   54 J4
Broadway, Surb.   99 B1
Broadway, The E4   34 C6
Broadway, The E13   60 H2
Broadway, The N8   40 E6
Broadway, The N9   33 D3
Broadway, The N22   40 G2
Broadway, The NW7   30 E5
Broadway, The SW19   84 D7
Broadway, The W5   55 G7
Broadway, The W7   64 B1
Broadway, The W13   64 D1
Broadway, The, Croy.   101 E4
Croydon Rd.
Broadway, The, Dag.   53 F2
Whalebone La. S.
Broadway, The,   99 G5
Epsom
Broadway, The, Har.   37 B2
Broadway, The, Loug.   27 F4
Broadway, The, Pnr.   28 F7
Broadway, The, Sthl.   54 D7
Broadway, The, Stan.   29 F5

Broadway, The, Sutt.   100 B6
Broadway, The, T.Ditt.   98 B1
Hampton Ct. Way
Broadway, The, Wem.   46 H3
East La.
Broadway, The,   34 H6
Wdf.Grn.
Broadway Ave., Croy.   95 A5
Broadway Ave.,   73 E6
Twick.
Broadway Clo.,   34 H6
Wdf.Grn.
Broadway Ct. SW19   84 D6
The Bdy.
Broadway Gdns.,   93 H4
Mitch.
Broadway Mkt. E8   59 E1
Broadway Ms. E5   41 C7
Broadway Ms. N13   32 F5
Elmdale Rd.
Broadway Ms. N21   32 H1
Compton Rd.
Broadwick St. W1   **11 G5**
Broadwick St. W1   58 C6
Brocas Clo. NW3   48 H7
Fellows Rd.
Brock Pl. E3   60 B4
Brock Rd. E13   60 H5
Brock St. SE15   77 E3
Evelina Rd.
Brockdish Ave., Bark.   52 J5
Brockenhurst, W.Mol.   90 F6
Brockenhurst Ave.,   99 E1
Wor.Pk.
Brockenhurst Gdns.   30 E6
NW7
Brockenhurst Gdns.,   52 F5
Ilf.
Brockenhurst Rd.,   95 E7
Croy.
Brockenhurst Way   94 D2
SW16
Brocket Clo., Chig.   35 J5
Brocket Way, Chig.   35 H5
Brockham Clo. SW19   84 C5
Brockham Cres.,   103 D7
Croy.
Fairview Pl.
Brockham Dr. SW2   76 F7
Brockham Dr., Ilf.   43 E6
Brockham St. SE1   **17 A5**
Brockham St. SE1   67 J3
Brockhurst Clo., Stan.   29 C6
Brockill Cres. SE4   77 H4
Brocklebank Rd. SE7   69 H4
Brocklebank Rd.   75 F7
SW18
Brocklehurst St. SE14   68 G7
Brocklesby Rd. SE25   95 E4
Brockley Ave., Stan.   29 H3
Brockley Clo., Stan.   29 H4
Brockley Cross SE4   77 H3
Endwell Rd.
Brockley Footpath   77 F4
SE15
Brockley Gdns. SE4   77 J2
Brockley Gro. SE4   77 J5
Brockley Hall Rd. SE4   77 H5
Brockley Hill, Stan.   29 F1
Brockley Ms. SE4   77 H5
Brockley Pk. SE23   77 H7
Brockley Ri. SE23   77 H7
Brockley Rd. SE4   77 J3
Brockley Vw. SE23   77 H7
Brockley Way SE4   77 G5
Brocklesbie, Stan.   29 H4
Brockman Ri., Brom.   87 D4
Brocks Dr., Sutt.   100 B3
Brockshot Clo., Brent.   64 G5
Brockway Clo. E11   51 E2
Brockwell Clo., Orp.   97 J4
Brockwell Pk. Gdns.   76 G7
SE24
Brockworth Clo. SE15   **21 E6**
Brockworth Clo. SE15   68 B6
Broderick Gro. SE2   71 B4
Brodewater Rd.,   22 B2
Borwd.
Brodia Rd. N16   50 B3
Brodie Rd. E4   34 C1
Brodie St. SE1   **21 G3**
Brodlove La. E1   59 G7
Brodrick Rd. SW17   84 H2
Brograve Gdns., Beck.   96 B2
Broke Wk. E8   59 D1
Marlborough Ave.
Broken Wf. EC4   **12 J5**
Brokesley St. E3   59 J3

Bromar Rd. SE5   77 B3
Bromborough Grn.,   28 C5
Wat.
Brome Rd. SE9   79 C3
Bromefield, Stan.   37 F1
Bromehead St. E1   59 F6
Commercial Rd.
Bromell's Rd. SW4   76 C4
Bromfelde Rd. SW4   76 D3
Bromfelde Wk. SW4   76 E2
Bromfield St. N1   58 G2
Bromhall Rd., Dag.   53 B6
Bromhedge SE9   88 C3
Bromholm Rd. SE2   71 B3
Bromley Ave., Brom.   87 E7
Bromley Common,   96 J4
Brom.
Bromley Cres., Brom.   96 F3
Bromley Gdns., Brom.   96 F3
Bromley Gro., Brom.   96 D2
Bromley Hall Rd. E14   60 C5
Bromley High St. E3   60 B3
Bromley Hill, Brom.   87 E6
Bromley La., Chis.   88 F7
Bromley Pk., Brom.   87 D4
Bromley Hill
Bromley Rd. E10   42 B6
Bromley Rd. E17   42 A2
Bromley Rd. N17   41 C1
Bromley Rd. N18   33 A3
Bromley Rd. SE6   87 B2
Bromley Rd., Beck.   96 B2
Bromley Rd., Brom.   96 B2
Bromley Rd.   87 D4
(Downham), Brom.
Bromley Rd., Chis.   97 E1
Bromley St. E1   59 G5
Brompton Arc. SW3   14 J4
Brompton Clo. SE20   95 D2
Brompton Clo.,   72 F5
Houns.
Brompton Gro. N2   39 H4
Brompton Pk. Cres.   **18 A6**
SW6
Brompton Pk. Cres.   66 E6
SW6
Brompton Pl. SW3   66 H3
Brompton Rd. SW1   **14 J4**
Brompton Rd. SW1   66 J2
Brompton Rd. SW3   **18 G1**
Brompton Rd. SW3   66 H4
Brompton Rd. SW7   **14 G6**
Brompton Rd. SW7   66 H3
Brompton Sq. SW3   **14 G5**
Brompton Sq. SW3   66 H3
Bromwich Ave. N6   49 A2
Bromyard Ave. W3   56 E7
Bromyard Ho. SE15   68 E7
Commercial Way
Brondesbury Ct. NW2   48 A6
Brondesbury Ms. NW6   48 D7
Willesden La.
Brondesbury Pk. NW2   47 J7
Brondesbury Pk. NW6   48 A7
Brondesbury Rd. NW6   57 C2
Brondesbury Vill.   57 C2
NW6
Bronsart Rd. SW6   66 B7
Bronson Rd. SW20   93 A2
Bronte Clo. E7   51 G4
Bective Rd.
Bronte Clo., Ilf.   43 D4
Bronte Ho. NW6   57 D3
Bronti Clo. SE17   **21 A4**
Bronti Clo. SE17   67 J5
Bronze St. SE8   69 A7
Brook Ave., Dag.   53 H7
Brook Ave., Edg.   30 B6
Brook Ave., Wem.   47 A3
Brook Clo. NW7   31 B7
Frith Ct.
Brook Clo. SW20   92 H3
Brook Clo. W3   65 A1
West Lo. Ave.
Brook Clo., Borwd.   22 B2
Brook Rd.
Brook Clo., Chis.   97 D1
Brook Cres. E4   34 A4
Brook Cres. N9   33 E4
Brook Dr. SE11   **16 F6**
Brook Dr. SE11   67 G3
Brook Dr., Har.   36 J4
Brook Gdns. E4   34 B4
Brook Gdns. SW13   74 F3
Brook Gdns., Kings.T.   92 C1
Brook Gate W1   **11 A6**

Brook Grn. W6   65 J3
Brook Ind. Est., Hayes   63 D1
Brook La. SE3   78 H2
Brook La., Bex.   80 D6
Brook La., Brom.   87 G6
Brook La. N., Brent.   64 G5
Brook Mead, Epsom   99 E6
Brook Meadow N12   31 E3
Brook Meadow Clo.,   34 E6
Wdf.Grn.
Brook Ms. N. W2   **10 D5**
Brook Par., Chig.   35 E3
High Rd.
Brook Pk. Clo. N21   24 H6
Brook Pl., Barn.   23 D5
Brook Ri., Chig.   35 D3
Brook Rd. N8   40 E4
Brook Rd. N22   40 F3
Brook Rd. NW2   47 F2
Brook Rd., Borwd.   22 A1
Brook Rd., Buck.H.   34 G2
Brook Rd., Ilf.   43 H6
Brook Rd., Loug.   27 B4
Brook Rd., Surb.   98 H2
Brook Rd., Th.Hth.   94 J4
Brook Rd., Twick.   73 D6
Brook Rd. S., Brent.   64 G6
Brook St. N17   41 C2
High Rd.
Brook St. W1   **11 D5**
Brook St. W1   58 A7
Brook St. W2   **10 F5**
Brook St. W2   57 G7
Brook St., Belv.   71 H5
Brook St., Erith   71 H6
Brook St., Kings.T.   91 H2
Brook Wk. N2   39 G1
Old Fm. Rd.
Brook Wk., Edg.   30 D6
Brook Way, Chig.   35 D3
Brookbank Ave. W7   55 A5
Brookbank Rd. SE13   78 A3
Brookdale N11   32 C4
Brookdale Rd. E17   42 A3
Brookdale Rd. SE6   78 B6
Brookdale Rd., Bex.   80 E6
Brookdene Rd. SE18   70 J4
Brooke Ave., Har.   45 J3
Brooke Rd. E5   50 D3
Brooke Rd. E17   42 C4
Brooke Rd. N16   50 C3
Brooke St. EC1   **12 E2**
Brooke St. EC1   58 G5
Brookend Rd., Sid.   88 H1
Brookehowse Rd. SE6   87 A2
Brooke's Ct. EC1   **12 E1**
Brookes Mkt. EC1   **12 E1**
Brookfield N6   49 A3
Brookfield Ave. E17   42 C4
Brookfield Ave. NW7   30 H6
Brookfield Ave. W5   55 G4
Brookfield Ave., Sutt.   100 H4
Brookfield Clo. NW7   30 H6
Brookfield Ct., Grnf.   54 J3
Brookfield Ct., Har.   37 H5
Brookfield Cres. NW7   30 H6
Brookfield Cres., Har.   37 H5
Brookfield Gdns.,   98 C6
Esher
Brookfield Pk. NW5   49 B3
Brookfield Path,   34 E6
Wdf.Grn.
Brookfield Rd. E9   50 H6
Brookfield Rd. N9   33 D3
Brookfield Rd. W4   65 D2
Brookfields, Enf.   25 G4
Brookfields Ave.,   93 H5
Mitch.
Brookhill Clo. SE18   70 E5
Brookhill Clo., Barn.   23 H5
Brookhill Rd. SE18   70 E4
Brookhill Rd., Barn.   23 G5
Brookhouse Gdns. E4   34 E4
Brooking Rd. E7   51 H5
Brookland Clo. NW11   39 E4
Brookland Garth   39 E4
NW11
Brookland Hill NW11   39 E4
Brookland Ri. NW11   39 D4
Brooklands Ave.   84 E2
SW19
Brooklands Ave., Sid.   88 G2
Brooklands Dr., Grnf.   55 F1
Brooklands Pk. SE3   78 G3
Brooklands Rd., T.Ditt.   98 C1
Brooklands St. SW8   76 D1
Brooklea Clo. NW9   38 E1
Brooklyn Ave. SE25   95 E4

Brooklyn Ave., Loug.	27	B4
Brooklyn Clo., Cars.	100	H2
Brooklyn Gro. SE25	95	E4
Brooklyn Rd. SE25	95	E4
Brooklyn Rd., Brom.	97	A5
Brookmead Ave., Brom.	97	C5
Brookmead Rd., Croy.	94	C6
Brookmeads Est., Mitch.	93	H5
Brookmill Rd. SE8	78	A1
Brooks Ave. E6	61	C4
Brooks Clo. SE9	88	D2
Brooks Ct. E15	51	B5
Clays La.		
Brooks La. W4	65	A6
Brook's Ms. W1	**11**	**D5**
Brook's Ms. W1	58	B7
Brooks Rd. E13	60	G1
Brooks Rd. W4	65	A5
Brooksbank St. E9	50	F6
Brooksby Ms. N1	49	G7
Brooksby St.		
Brooksby St. N1	49	G7
Brooksby's Wk. E9	50	G5
Brookscroft Rd. E17	42	B1
Brookshill, Har.	29	A5
Brookshill Ave., Har.	29	A5
Brookshill Dr., Har.	29	A5
Brookside N21	24	F6
Brookside, Barn.	23	H6
Brookside, Cars.	101	A6
Brookside, Ilf.	35	F6
Brookside, Orp.	97	J7
Brookside Clo., Barn.	23	B6
Brookside Clo., Felt.	81	A3
Sycamore Clo.		
Brookside Clo., Har.	37	G5
Brookside Clo. (Kenton), Har.	45	E4
Brookside Cres., Wor.Pk.	99	G1
Green La.		
Brookside Rd. N9	33	E4
Brookside Rd. N19	49	C2
Junction Rd.		
Brookside Rd. NW11	39	B6
Brookside Rd., Hayes	54	C7
Brookside S., Barn.	24	A7
Brookside Wk. N3	39	A3
Brookside Wk. N12	31	D6
Brookside Wk. NW4	39	B4
Brookside Wk. NW11	39	B4
Brookside Way, Croy.	95	G6
Brooksville Ave. NW6	57	B1
Brookvale, Erith	80	H1
Brookview Rd. SW16	85	C5
Brookville Rd. SW6	66	C7
Brookway SE3	78	G3
Brookwood Ave. SW13	74	F3
Brookwood Clo., Brom.	96	F4
Brookwood Rd. SW18	84	C1
Brookwood Rd., Houns.	72	H1
Broom Clo., Brom.	97	B6
Manor Way		
Broom Clo., Tedd.	82	G7
Broom Gdns., Croy.	103	A3
Broom Lock, Tedd.	82	F6
Broom Mead, Bexh.	80	G5
Broom Pk., Tedd.	82	G7
Broom Rd., Croy.	103	A3
Broom Rd., Tedd.	82	E5
Broom Water, Tedd.	82	F6
Broom Water W., Tedd.	82	F6
Broomcroft Ave., Nthlt.	54	C3
Broome Rd., Hmptn.	81	F7
Broome Way SE5	67	J7
Broomfield E17	41	J7
Broomfield, Sun.	90	A1
Broomfield Ave. N13	32	F5
Broomfield Ave., Loug.	27	C6
Broomfield Rd.		
Broomfield La. N13	32	E4
Broomfield Pl. W13	64	E1
Broomfield Rd.		
Broomfield Rd. N13	32	E5
Broomfield Rd. W13	64	E1
Broomfield Rd., Beck.	95	H4
Broomfield Rd., Bexh.	80	G5
Broomfield Rd., Rich.	73	J1
Broomfield Rd., Rom.	44	D7
Broomfield Rd., Surb.	98	J1

Broomfield Rd., Tedd.	82	F6
Melbourne Rd.		
Broomfield St. E14	60	A5
Broomgrove Gdns., Edg.	38	A1
Broomgrove Rd. SW9	76	F2
Broomhill Ri., Bexh.	80	G5
Broomhill Rd. SW18	75	D5
Broomhill Rd., Ilf.	53	A2
Broomhill Rd., Wdf.Grn.	34	G6
Broomhill Wk., Wdf.Grn.	34	F7
Broomhouse La. SW6	75	D2
Broomhouse Rd. SW6	75	D2
Broomloan La., Sutt.	100	D2
Broomsleigh St. NW6	48	C5
Broomwood Rd. SW11	75	J6
Broseley Gro. SE26	86	H5
Broster Gdns. SE25	95	C3
Brough Clo. SW8	67	E7
Kenchester Clo.		
Brougham Rd. E8	59	D1
Brougham Rd. W3	56	C6
Brougham St. SW11	75	J2
Reform St.		
Broughinge Rd., Borwd.	22	A2
Broughton Ave. N3	39	B3
Broughton Ave., Rich.	82	E3
Broughton Dr. SW9	76	G4
Broughton Gdns. N6	40	C6
Broughton Rd. SW6	75	E2
Broughton Rd. W13	55	E7
Broughton Rd., Orp.	104	G2
Broughton Rd., Th.Hth.	94	G6
Broughton St. SW8	76	A2
Brouncker Rd. W3	65	C2
Browells La., Felt.	81	B2
Brown Clo., Wall.	101	E7
Brown Hart Gdns. W1	**11**	**C5**
Brown Hart Gdns. W1	58	A7
Brown St. W1	**10**	**J3**
Brown St. W1	57	J6
Brownfield St. E14	60	B6
Brownhill Rd. SE6	78	B7
Browning Ave. W7	55	C6
Browning Ave., Sutt.	100	H4
Browning Ave., Wor.Pk.	99	H1
Browning Clo. W9	**6**	**D6**
Browning Clo., Hmptn.	81	F4
Browning Clo., Well.	79	H1
Browning Est. SE17	**21**	**A3**
Browning Est. SE17	67	J5
Browning Ho. W12	56	J6
Wood La.		
Browning Ms. W1	**11**	**C2**
Browning Rd. E11	42	F7
Browning Rd. E12	52	C6
Browning St. SE17	**21**	**A3**
Browning St. SE17	67	J5
Browning Way, Houns.	72	D1
Brownlea Gdns., Ilf.	53	A2
Brownlow Ms. WC1	**8**	**D6**
Brownlow Ms. WC1	58	F4
Brownlow Rd. E7	51	H4
Woodford Rd.		
Brownlow Rd. E8	59	C1
Brownlow Rd. N3	31	E7
Brownlow Rd. N11	32	E6
Brownlow Rd. NW10	47	E7
Brownlow Rd. W13	64	D1
Brownlow Rd., Borwd.	22	A4
Brownlow Rd., Croy.	102	B4
Brownlow St. WC1	**12**	**D2**
Brown's Bldgs. EC3	**13**	**E4**
Browns La. NW5	49	B5
Browns Rd. E17	42	A3
Browns Rd., Surb.	91	J7
Brownspring Dr. SE9	88	E4
Brownswell Rd. N2	39	G2
Brownswood Rd. N4	49	H3
Broxash Rd. SW11	76	A6
Broxbourne Ave. E18	42	H4
Broxbourne Rd. E7	51	G3
Broxbourne Rd., Orp.	104	J1
Broxholm Rd. SE27	85	G3
Broxted Rd. SE6	86	J2
Broxwood Way NW8	57	H1
Bruce Castle Rd. N17	41	C1

Bruce Clo. W10	57	B5
Ladbroke Gro.		
Bruce Clo., Well.	80	B1
Bruce Gdns. N20	31	J3
Balfour Gro.		
Bruce Gro. N17	41	B1
Bruce Hall Ms. SW17	85	A4
Brudenell Rd.		
Bruce Rd. E3	60	B3
Bruce Rd. NW10	47	D7
Bruce Rd. SE25	95	A4
Bruce Rd., Barn.	23	B3
St. Albans Rd.		
Bruce Rd., Har.	37	B2
Bruce Rd., Mitch.	85	A7
Bruckner St. W10	57	C3
Brudenell Rd. SW17	84	J3
Bruffs Meadow, Nthlt.	45	E6
Bruges Pl. NW1	49	C7
Randolph St.		
Brumfield Rd., Epsom	99	C5
Brummel Clo., Bexh.	80	J3
Brundley Way, Brom.	87	G5
Brune St. E1	**13**	**F2**
Brune St. E1	59	C5
Brunel Clo. SE19	86	C6
Brunel Clo., Houns.	63	B7
Brunel Clo., Nthlt.	54	F3
Brunel Est. W2	57	D5
Brunel Pl., Sthl.	54	H6
Brunel Rd. SE16	68	F2
Brunel Rd. W3	56	E5
Brunel Rd., Wdf.Grn.	35	B4
Brunel St. E16	60	F6
Victoria Dock Rd.		
Brunel Wk. N15	41	B4
Brunel Wk., Twick.	72	G7
Stephenson Rd.		
Brunner Clo. NW11	39	E5
Brunner Rd. E17	41	H5
Brunner Rd. W5	55	G4
Bruno Pl., Wem.	47	C2
Brunswick Ave. N11	32	A3
Brunswick Cen. WC1	**8**	**A5**
Brunswick Clo., Bexh.	80	D4
Brunswick Clo., Pnr.	36	E6
Brunswick Clo., T.Ditt.	98	C1
Brunswick Clo., Twick.	82	A3
Brunswick Ct. SE1	**17**	**E3**
Brunswick Ct. SE1	68	B2
Brunswick Ct., Barn.	23	G5
Brunswick Cres. N11	32	A3
Brunswick Gdns. W5	55	H4
Brunswick Gdns. W8	66	D1
Brunswick Gdns., Ilf.	35	F7
Brunswick Gro. N11	32	A3
Brunswick Ind. Pk. N11	32	B4
Brunswick Ms. SW16	85	D6
Potters La.		
Brunswick Ms. W1	**11**	**A3**
Brunswick Pk. SE5	77	A1
Brunswick Pk. Gdns. N11	32	A2
Brunswick Pk. Rd. N11	32	A2
Brunswick Pl. N1	**9**	**C4**
Brunswick Pl. N1	59	A3
Brunswick Pl. SE19	86	D7
Brunswick Quay SE16	68	G3
Brunswick Rd. E10	51	C1
Brunswick Rd. E14	60	C6
Brunswick Rd. N15	41	B4
Brunswick Rd. W5	55	G4
Brunswick Rd., Bexh.	80	D4
Brunswick Rd., Kings.T.	92	A1
Brunswick Rd., Sutt.	100	E4
Brunswick Sq. N17	33	C6
Brunswick Sq. WC1	**8**	**B5**
Brunswick Sq. WC1	58	E4
Brunswick St. E17	42	C5
Brunswick Vill. SE5	77	B1
Brunswick Way N11	32	B4
Brunton Pl. E14	59	H6
Brushfield St. E1	**13**	**E1**
Brushfield St. E1	59	B5
Brussels Rd. SW11	75	G4
Bruton Clo., Chis.	88	C7
Bullers Wd. Dr.		
Bruton La. W1	**11**	**E6**
Bruton La. W1	58	B7
Bruton Pl. W1	**11**	**E6**
Bruton Pl. W1	58	B7
Bruton Rd., Mord.	93	F4
Bruton St. W1	**11**	**E6**
Bruton St. W1	58	B7
Bruton Way W13	55	D5

Bryan Ave. NW10	47	H7
Bryan Clo., Sun.	81	A7
Bryan Rd. SE16	68	J2
Bryanston Ave., Twick.	81	H1
Bryanston Clo., Sthl.	63	F4
Bryanston Ms. E. W1	**10**	**J2**
Bryanston Ms. W. W1	**10**	**J2**
Bryanston Pl. W1	**10**	**J2**
Bryanston Pl. W1	57	J5
Bryanston Sq. W1	**10**	**J2**
Bryanston Sq. W1	57	J5
Bryanston St. W1	**10**	**J4**
Bryanston St. W1	57	J6
Bryanstone Rd. N8	40	D5
Bryant Clo., Barn.	23	C5
Bryant Ct. E2	**9**	**F1**
Bryant Rd., Nthlt.	54	C3
Bryant St. E15	51	D7
Bryantwood Rd. N7	49	G5
Bryce Rd., Dag.	53	C4
Brycedale Cres. N14	32	C4
Bryden Clo. SE26	86	H5
Brydges Pl. WC2	**12**	**A6**
Brydges Rd. E15	51	D5
Brydon Wk. N1	58	E1
Outram Pl.		
Bryett Rd. N7	49	E3
Brymay Clo. E3	60	A2
Bryn-y-Mawr Rd., Enf.	25	C4
Brynmaer Rd. SW11	75	J1
Bryony Rd. W12	56	G7
Buchan Rd. SE15	77	F3
Buchanan Clo., Borwd.	22	C2
Banks Rd.		
Buchanan Gdns. NW10	56	H2
Bucharest Rd. SW18	75	F7
Buck Hill Wk. W2	**10**	**F6**
Buck La. NW9	38	D4
Buck St. NW1	49	B7
Buck Wk. E17	42	D4
Foresters Dr.		
Buckden Clo. SE12	78	F6
Upwood Rd.		
Buckfast Rd., Mord.	93	E4
Buckfast St. E2	**9**	**J4**
Buckfast St. E2	59	D3
Buckhold Rd. SW18	75	D6
Buckhurst Ave., Cars.	100	H1
Buckhurst St. E1	59	E4
Buckhurst Way, Buck.H.	35	A4
Buckingham Arc. WC2	**12**	**B6**
Buckingham Ave. N20	23	F7
Buckingham Ave., Felt.	72	B6
Buckingham Ave., Grnf.	55	D1
Buckingham Ave., Th.Hth.	94	G1
Buckingham Ave., Well.	79	H4
Buckingham Ave., W.Mol.	90	H3
Buckingham Clo. W5	55	F5
Buckingham Clo., Enf.	25	B2
Buckingham Clo., Hmptn.	81	F5
Buckingham Clo., Orp.	97	H7
Buckingham Ct. NW4	38	G3
Buckingham Dr., Chis.	88	E5
Buckingham Gdns., Edg.	29	H7
Buckingham Gdns., Th.Hth.	94	G2
Buckingham Gdns., W.Mol.	90	H2
Buckingham Ave.		
Buckingham Gate SW1	**15**	**F4**
Buckingham Gate SW1	67	B3
Buckingham La. SE23	77	H7
Buckingham Ms. NW10	56	F2
Buckingham Rd.		
Buckingham Ms. SW1	**15**	**F5**
Buckingham Palace Rd. SW1	**19**	**D2**
Buckingham Palace Rd. SW1	67	B4
Buckingham Pl. SW1	**15**	**F5**
Buckingham Rd. E10	51	B3
Buckingham Rd. E11	42	J5

Buckingham Rd. E15 51 F5
Buckingham Rd. E18 42 F1
Buckingham Rd. N1 50 B6
Buckingham Rd. N22 40 E1
Buckingham Rd. NW10 56 F2
Buckingham Rd., Borwd. 22 D4
Buckingham Rd., Edg. 29 J7
Buckingham Rd., Hmptn. 81 F4
Buckingham Rd., Har. 37 A5
Buckingham Rd., Ilf. 52 G2
Buckingham Rd., Kings.T. 91 J4
Buckingham Rd., Mitch. 94 E5
Buckingham Rd., Rich. 82 G2
Buckingham St. WC2 12 B6
Buckland Cres. NW3 48 G7
Buckland Ri., Pnr. 36 C1
Buckland Rd. E10 51 C2
Buckland Rd., Chess. 98 J5
Buckland Rd., Orp. 104 H4
Buckland St. N1 9 C2
Buckland St. N1 59 A2
Buckland Wk., Mord. 93 F4
Buckland Way, Wor.Pk. 99 J1
Bucklands Rd., Tedd. 82 F6
Buckle St. E1 13 G3
Buckleigh Ave. SW20 93 C3
Buckleigh Rd. SW16 85 D6
Buckleigh Way SE19 95 C1
Buckler Gdns. SE9 88 C3
Southold Ri.
Bucklers All. SW6 66 D6
Haldane Rd.
Bucklers Way, Cars. 100 J3
Bucklersbury EC4 13 B4
Bucklersbury EC4 59 A6
Fendyke Rd.
Buckles Ct., Belv. 71 D3
Buckley Rd. NW6 48 C7
Buckley St. SE1 16 E2
Buckmaster Rd. SW11 75 H4
Bucknall St. WC2 11 J3
Bucknall St. WC2 58 D6
Bucknell Clo. SW2 76 F4
Buckner Rd. SW2 76 F4
Buckrell Rd. E4 34 D2
Buckstone Clo. SE23 77 F6
Buckstone Rd. N18 33 D5
Buckters Rents SE16 68 H1
Buckthorne Rd. SE4 77 H6
Budd Clo. N12 31 E4
Buddings Circ., Wem. 47 C3
Budd's All., Twick. 73 F5
Arlington Clo.
Budge Row EC4 13 B5
Budge's Wk. W2 14 C1
Budge's Wk. W2 57 G7
Budich Ct., Ilf. 53 A2
Budleigh Cres., Well. 80 C1
Budoch Dr., Ilf. 53 A2
Buer Rd. SW6 75 H2
Bugsby's Way SE7 69 G4
Bugsby's Way SE10 69 F4
Bulganak Rd., Th.Hth. 94 J4
Bulinga St. SW1 20 A2
Bulinga St. SW1 67 D4
Bull All., Well. 80 B3
Welling High St.
Bull Inn Ct. WC2 12 B6
Bull La. N18 33 B5
Bull La., Chis. 88 G7
Bull La., Dag. 53 H3
Bull Rd. E15 60 F2
Bull Wf. La. EC4 13 A5
Bull Yd. SE15 77 D1
Peckham High St.
Bullace Row SE5 76 J1
Camberwell Rd.
Bullards Pl. E2 59 G3
Bullbanks Rd., Belv. 71 J4
Bullen St. SW11 75 H2
Buller Clo. SE15 68 D7
Buller Rd. N17 41 D2
Buller Rd. N22 40 G2
Buller Rd. NW10 57 A3
Chamberlayne Rd.
Buller Rd., Bark. 52 H7
Buller Rd., Th.Hth. 95 A2
Bullers Clo., Sid. 89 E5
Bullers Wd. Dr., Chis. 88 C7
Bullescroft Rd., Edg. 30 A3
Bullhead Rd., Borwd. 22 D4

Bullied Way SW1 19 E2
Bullivant St. E14 60 C6
Bull's All. SW14 74 D2
Bulls Bri. Ind. Est., Sthl. 63 B3
Bulls Bri. Rd., Sthl. 63 B3
Bulls Gdns. SW3 18 H1
Bull's Head Pas. EC3 13 D4
Bulmer Gdns., Har. 37 G7
Bulmer Ms. W11 57 D7
Ladbroke Rd.
Bulmer Pl. W11 66 D1
Bulow Ct. SW6 75 E2
Bulstrode Ave., Houns. 72 F2
Bulstrode Gdns., Houns. 72 F3
Bulstrode Pl. W1 11 C2
Bulstrode Rd., Houns. 72 G3
Bulstrode St. W1 11 C3
Bulstrode St. W1 58 A6
Bulwer Ct. Rd. E11 51 D1
Bulwer Gdns., Barn. 23 F4
Bulwer Rd.
Bulwer Rd. E11 42 D7
Bulwer Rd. N18 33 B4
Bulwer Rd., Barn. 23 E4
Bulwer St. W12 65 J1
Bunces La., Wdf.Grn. 34 F7
Bungalow Rd. SE25 95 B4
Bungalows, The SW16 85 B7
Bungalows, The, Wall. 101 B5
Bunhill Row EC1 9 B5
Bunhill Row EC1 59 A4
Bunhouse Pl. SW1 19 B3
Bunhouse Pl. SW1 67 A5
Bunkers Hill NW11 39 F7
Bunkers Hill, Belv. 71 G4
Bunkers Hill, Sid. 89 F3
Bunning Way N7 49 E7
Bunns La. NW7 30 E6
Bunsen St. E3 59 H2
Kenilworth Rd.
Bunting Clo. N9 33 G1
Bunting Clo., Mitch. 93 J5
Buntingbridge Rd., Ilf. 43 G5
Bunton St. SE18 70 D3
Creton St.
Bunyan Rd. E17 41 H3
Buonaparte Ms. SW1 19 H3
Burbage Clo. SE1 17 B6
Burbage Clo. SE1 68 A3
Burbage Rd. SE21 77 A7
Burbage Rd. SE24 76 J6
Burberry Clo., N.Mal. 92 E2
Burbridge Way N17 41 C2
Burcham St. E14 60 B6
Burcharbro Rd. SE2 71 D6
Burchell Rd. E10 51 B1
Burchell Rd. SE15 77 E1
Burchett Way, Rom. 44 F6
Burcote Rd. SW18 75 G7
Burden Clo., Brent. 64 F5
Burden Way E11 51 H2
Brading Cres.
Burdenshott Ave., Rich. 74 B4
Burder Clo. N1 50 B6
Burder Rd. N1 50 B6
Balls Pond Rd.
Burdett Ave. SW20 92 G1
Burdett Clo., Sid. 89 E5
Burdett Ms. NW3 48 G6
Belsize Cres.
Burdett Ms. W2 10 A3
Burdett Rd. E3 59 H4
Burdett Rd. E14 59 J5
Burdett Rd., Croy. 95 A6
Burdett Rd., Rich. 73 J2
Burdett St. SE1 16 E5
Burdetts Rd., Dag. 62 F1
Burdock Clo., Croy. 102 G1
Burdock Rd. N17 41 D3
Burdon La., Sutt. 100 B7
Burfield Clo. SW17 84 G4
Burford Clo., Dag. 53 C3
Burford Clo., Ilf. 43 F4
Burford Gdns. N13 32 F3
Burford Rd. E6 61 B3
Burford Rd. E15 51 D7
Burford Rd. SE6 86 J2
Burford Rd., Brent. 64 H5
Burford Rd., Brom. 97 B4
Burford Rd., Sutt. 100 D2
Burford Rd., Wor.Pk. 92 F7

Burford Wk. SW6 66 E7
Cambria St.
Burford Way, Croy. 103 C6
Burge St. SE1 17 C6
Burges Ct. E6 52 D7
Burges Rd. E6 52 B7
Burgess Ave. NW9 38 D6
Burgess Clo., Felt. 81 E4
Burgess Hill NW2 48 D4
Burgess Rd. E15 51 E4
Burgess Rd., Sutt. 100 E4
Burgess St. E14 60 A5
Burgh St. N1 8 H1
Burgh St. N1 58 H2
Burghill Rd. SE26 86 H4
Burghley Ave., N.Mal. 92 D1
Burghley Ave., Borwd. 22 C5
Burghley Pl., Mitch. 93 J5
Burghley Rd. E11 51 E1
Burghley Rd. N8 40 G3
Burghley Rd. NW5 49 B4
Burghley Rd. SW19 84 A4
Burghley Twr. W3 56 F7
Burgon St. EC4 12 H4
Burgos Gro. SE10 78 B1
Burgoyne Rd. N4 40 H6
Burgoyne Rd. SE25 95 C4
Burgoyne Rd. SW9 76 F3
Burham Clo. SE20 86 F7
Maple Rd.
Burhill Gro., Pnr. 36 E2
Burke Clo. SW15 74 E4
Burke St. E16 60 F6
Burland Rd. SW11 75 J5
Burleigh Ave., Sid. 79 J5
Burleigh Ave., Wall. 101 A3
Burleigh Gdns. N14 32 C1
Burleigh Ho. W10 57 A5
St. Charles Sq.
Burleigh Pl. SW15 75 A5
Burleigh Pl., Mitch. 93 J5
Burleigh Rd., Enf. 25 B4
Burleigh Rd., Sutt. 100 B1
Burleigh St. WC2 12 B5
Burleigh Wk. SE6 87 C1
Muirkirk Rd.
Burleigh Way, Enf. 25 A3
Church St.
Burley Clo. E4 34 A5
Burley Clo. SW16 94 D2
Burley Rd. E16 60 G5
Burlington Arc. W1 11 F6
Burlington Ave., Rich. 74 A1
Burlington Ave., Rom. 44 H6
Burlington Clo. E6 61 B6
Northumberland Rd.
Burlington Clo. W9 57 C4
Burlington Clo., Orp. 104 E2
Burlington Gdns. W1 11 F6
Burlington Gdns. W1 58 C7
Burlington Gdns. W3 65 C5
Burlington Gdns. W4 65 C5
Burlington Gdns., Rom. 44 E7
Burlington La. W4 65 E7
Burlington Ms. W3 65 C1
Burlington Pl. SW6 75 B2
Burlington Rd.
Burlington Pl., Wdf.Grn. 34 H3
Burlington Ri., Barn. 31 H1
Burlington Rd. N10 40 A2
Tetherdown
Burlington Rd. N17 41 D1
Burlington Rd. SW6 75 B2
Burlington Rd. W4 65 C5
Burlington Rd., Enf. 25 A1
Burlington Rd., Islw. 73 A1
Burlington Rd., N.Mal. 92 F4
Burlington Rd., Th.Hth. 94 J2
Burma Ms. N16 50 A4
Burma Rd. N16 50 A4
Burmester Rd. SW17 84 F3
Burn Side N9 33 F3
Burnaby Cres. W4 65 C6
Burnaby Gdns. W4 65 B6
Burnaby St. SW10 66 F7
Burnbrae Clo. N12 31 E6
Burnbury Rd. SW12 85 C1
Burncroft Ave., Enf. 25 F2
Burne Jones Ho. W14 66 C4
Burne St. NW1 10 G1
Burne St. NW1 57 H5
Burnell Ave., Rich. 82 F5
Burnell Ave., Well. 80 A2
Burnell Gdns., Stan. 37 G1

Burnell Rd., Sutt. 100 E4
Burnell Wk. SE1 21 G3
Burnels Ave. E6 61 D3
Burness Clo. N7 49 F6
Roman Way
Burnett Clo. E9 50 F5
Burney Ave., Surb. 91 J5
Burney Dr., Loug. 27 E2
Burney St. SE10 69 C7
Burnfoot Ave. SW6 75 B1
Burnfoot Ct. SE22 86 E1
Burnham NW3 48 H7
Burnham Clo. SE1 21 G3
Burnham Clo., Har. 37 D4
Burnham Clo., NW4 38 J4
Burnham Cres. E11 42 A4
Burnham Dr., Wor.Pk. 100 A2
Burnham Gdns., Croy. 95 C7
Burnham Gdns., Houns. 72 B3
Burnham Rd. E4 33 J5
Burnham Rd., Dag. 53 B7
Burnham Rd., Mord. 93 E5
Burnham Rd., Sid. 89 E2
Burnham St. E2 59 F3
Burnham St., Kings.T. 92 A1
Burnham Way SE26 86 J5
Burnham Way W13 64 E4
Burnhill Rd., Beck. 96 A2
Burnley Clo., Wat. 28 C5
Burnley Rd. NW10 47 F5
Burnley Rd. SW9 76 F2
Burns Ave., Felt. 72 A6
Burns Ave., Rom. 44 C7
Burns Ave., Sid. 80 A6
Burns Ave., Sthl. 54 G7
Burns Clo. SW19 84 G6
North Rd.
Burns Clo., Well. 79 J1
Burns Rd. NW10 56 F1
Burns Rd. SW11 75 J2
Burns Rd. W13 64 E2
Burns Rd., Wem. 55 H2
Burns Way, Houns. 72 D2
Burnsall St. SW3 18 H3
Burnsall St. SW3 66 H5
Burnside Clo. SE16 68 G1
Burnside Clo., Barn. 23 D3
Burnside Clo., Twick. 73 D6
Burnside Cres., Wem. 55 G1
Burnside Rd., Dag. 53 C2
Burnt Ash Hill SE12 78 F6
Burnt Ash La., Brom. 87 G7
Burnt Ash Rd. SE12 78 F5
Burnt Oak Bdy., Edg. 30 B7
Burnt Oak Flds., Edg. 38 C1
Burnt Oak La., Sid. 89 A2
Burnthwaite Rd. SW6 66 C7
Burntwood Clo. SW18 84 G1
Burntwood Gra. Rd. 84 G1
SW18
Burntwood La. SW17 84 F3
Burntwood Vw. SE19 86 C5
Bowley La.
Buross St. E1 59 E6
Commercial Rd.
Burr Clo. E1 17 H1
Burr Clo., Bexh. 80 F3
Burr Rd. SW18 84 D1
Burrage Gro. SE18 70 F4
Burrage Pl. SE18 70 E5
Burrage Rd. SE18 70 F4
Burrard Rd. E16 60 H6
Burrard Rd. NW6 48 D5
Burrell Clo., Croy. 95 H6
Burrell Clo., Edg. 30 B2
Burrell Row, Beck. 96 A2
High St.
Burrell St. SE1 16 G1
Burrell St. SE1 67 H1
Burrell Twr. E10 42 A7
Burrells Wf. Sq. E14 69 B5
Burritt Rd., Kings.T. 92 A2
Burroughs, The NW4 38 H4
Burroughs Gdns. NW4 38 H4
Burrow Clo., Chig. 35 J5
Burrow Rd.
Burrow Grn., Chig. 35 J5
Burrow Rd., Chig. 35 J5
Burrow Wk. SE21 76 J7
Rosendale Rd.
Burrows Ms. SE1 16 G3
Burrows Rd. NW10 56 J3
Bursdon Clo., Sid. 88 J2
Bursland Rd., Enf. 25 G4
Burslem St. E1 13 J4
Burslem St. E1 59 D6
Burstock Rd. SW15 75 B5

Burston Rd. SW15	75	A5
Burstow Rd. SW20	93	B1
Burt Rd. E16	69	J1
Burtenshaw Rd., T.Ditt.	91	D7
Burtley Clo. N4	49	J1
Burton Clo., Chess.	98	G3
Burton Gdns., Houns.	72	F1
Burton Gro. SE17	**21**	**B4**
Burton La. SW9	76	G2
Burton Ms. SW1	**19**	**C2**
Burton Pl. WC1	**7**	**J4**
Burton Rd. E18	42	H3
Burton Rd. NW6	48	C7
Burton Rd. SW9	76	H2
Burton Rd., Kings.T.	82	H7
Burton Rd., Loug.	27	F4
Burton St. WC1	**7**	**J4**
Burton St. WC1	58	D3
Burtonhole Clo. NW7	31	A4
Burtonhole La. NW7	30	J5
Burtons Rd., Hmptn.	81	H4
Burtwell La. SE27	86	A4
Burwash Ho. SE1	**17**	**C4**
Burwash Rd. SE18	70	G5
Burwell Ave., Grnf.	46	B6
Burwell Clo. E1	59	E6
Bigland St.		
Burwell Rd. E10	50	H1
Burwell Wk. E3	60	A4
Burwood Ave., Brom.	103	H2
Burwood Ave., Pnr.	36	B5
Burwood Clo., Surb.	99	A1
Burwood Ho. W2	**10**	**H3**
Burwood Pl. W2	57	H6
Bury Clo. SE16	68	G1
Rotherhithe St.		
Bury Ct. EC3	**13**	**E3**
Bury Gro., Mord.	93	E5
Bury Pl. WC1	**12**	**A2**
Bury Pl. WC1	58	E5
Bury Rd. E4	26	E4
Bury Rd. N22	40	G3
Bury Rd., Dag.	53	H5
Bury St. EC3	**13**	**E4**
Bury St. EC3	59	B6
Bury St. N9	25	C7
Bury St. SW1	**15**	**G1**
Bury St. SW1	67	C1
Bury St. W. N9	25	A7
Bury Wk. SW3	**18**	**G2**
Bury Wk. SW3	66	H4
Busbridge Ho. E14	60	A5
Brabazon St.		
Busby Ms. NW5	49	D6
Busby Pl. NW5	49	D6
Busby St. E2	**9**	**G5**
Bush Clo., Ilf.	43	G5
Bush Cotts. SW18	75	D5
Putney Bri. Rd.		
Bush Ct. W12	66	A2
Bush Gro. NW9	38	C7
Bush Gro., Stan.	29	G7
Bush Hill N21	24	J7
Bush Hill Rd. N21	25	A6
Bush Hill Rd., Har.	37	J6
Bush Ind. Est. NW10	56	D4
Bush La. EC4	**13**	**B5**
Bush Rd. E8	59	E1
Bush Rd. E11	42	F7
Bush Rd. SE8	68	G4
Bush Rd., Buck.H.	35	A4
Bush Rd., Rich.	64	J6
Bushbaby Clo. SE1	**17**	**D6**
Bushberry Rd. E9	50	H6
Bushell Clo. SW2	85	F2
Bushell Grn. (Bushey), Wat.	29	A2
Bushell St. E1	**17**	**J2**
Bushell Way, Chis.	88	D5
Bushey Ave. E18	42	F3
Bushey Ave., Orp.	97	G7
Bushey Clo. E4	34	C3
Bushey Ct. SW20	92	H3
Bushey Down SW12	85	B2
Bedford Hill		
Bushey Hill Rd. SE5	77	B1
Bushey La., Sutt.	100	D3
Bushey Lees, Sid.	79	J6
Fen Gro.		
Bushey Rd. E13	60	J2
Bushey Rd. N15	41	B6
Bushey Rd. SW20	92	H3
Bushey Rd., Croy.	103	A2
Bushey Rd., Sutt.	100	D4
Bushey Way, Beck.	96	D6
Bushfield Clo., Edg.	30	B2
Bushfield Cres., Edg.	30	B2
Bushfields, Loug.	27	D5
Bushgrove Rd., Dag.	53	D4
Bushmead Clo. N15	41	C4
Copperfield Dr.		
Bushmoor Cres. SE18	70	F7
Bushnell Rd. SW17	85	B2
Bushway, Dag.	53	D4
Bushwood E11	51	F1
Bushwood Dr. SE1	**21**	**G2**
Bushwood Dr. SE1	68	C4
Bushwood Rd., Rich.	65	A6
Bushy Pk., Tedd.	91	C1
Bushy Pk. Gdns., Tedd.	82	A5
Bushy Pk. Rd., Tedd.	82	E7
Bushy Rd., Tedd.	82	C6
Butcher Row E1	59	G7
Butcher Row E14	59	G7
Butchers Rd. E16	60	G6
Bute Ave., Rich.	82	H2
Bute Ct., Wall.	101	C5
Bute Rd.		
Bute Gdns. W6	66	A4
Bute Gdns., Wall.	101	C5
Bute Gdns. W., Wall.	101	C5
Bute Rd., Croy.	101	G1
Bute Rd., Ilf.	43	E5
Bute Rd., Wall.	101	C4
Bute St. SW7	**18**	**E1**
Bute St. SW7	66	G4
Bute Wk. N1	50	A6
Marquess Rd.		
Butler Ave., Har.	37	A7
Butler Pl. SW1	**15**	**H5**
Butler Rd. NW10	47	F7
Curzon Cres.		
Butler Rd., Dag.	53	B4
Butler Rd., Har.	36	J7
Butler St. E2	59	F3
Knottisford St.		
Butter Hill, Cars.	101	A3
Butter Hill, Wall.	101	A3
Butterfield Clo. SE16	68	E2
Wilson Gro.		
Butterfield Clo., Twick.	73	C6
Rugby Rd.		
Butterfield Sq. E6	61	C6
Guildford Rd.		
Butterfields E17	42	C5
Butterfly La. SE9	79	E6
Butterfly Wk. SE5	77	A1
Denmark Hill		
Butteridges Clo., Dag.	62	F1
Buttermere Clo., Mord.	93	A6
Buttermere Dr. SW15	75	B5
Buttermere Wk. E8	50	C6
Butterwick W6	65	J4
Butterworth Gdns., Wdf.Grn.	34	G5
Harts Gro.		
Buttesland St. N1	**9**	**C3**
Buttesland St. N1	59	A3
Buttfield Clo., Dag.	53	H6
Buttmarsh Clo. SE18	70	E5
Butts, The, Brent.	64	F6
Butts, The, Sun.	90	C3
Elizabeth Gdns.		
Butts Cotts., Felt.	81	F3
Butts Cres., Felt.	81	G3
Butts Piece, Nthlt.	54	B2
Longhook Gdns.		
Butts Rd., Brom.	87	E5
Buttsbury Rd., Ilf.	52	G5
Buxted Clo. E8	50	C7
Buxted Rd. N12	31	H5
Buxton Clo., Wdf.Grn.	35	A6
Buxton Ct. N1	**9**	**A3**
Buxton Cres., Sutt.	100	B4
Buxton Dr. E11	42	E4
Buxton Dr., N.Mal.	92	D2
Buxton Gdns. W3	56	B7
Buxton Path, Wat.	28	C3
Buxton Rd. E4	26	D7
Buxton Rd. E6	61	B3
Buxton Rd. E15	51	E5
Buxton Rd. E17	41	H4
Buxton Rd. N19	49	D1
Buxton Rd. NW2	47	H6
Buxton Rd. SW14	74	E3
Buxton Rd., Ilf.	43	H6
Buxton Rd., Th.Hth.	94	H5
Buxton St. E1	**9**	**G6**
Buxton St. E1	59	C4
Buzzard Creek Ind. Est., Bark.	61	J5
By the Wd., Wat.	28	D2
Byam St. SW6	75	F2
Byards Cft. SW16	94	D1
Byatt Wk., Hmptn.	81	E6
Victors Dr.		
Bychurch End, Tedd.	82	C5
Church Rd.		
Bycroft Rd., Sthl.	54	G4
Bycroft St. SE20	86	G7
Parish La.		
Bycullah Ave., Enf.	24	H3
Bycullah Rd., Enf.	24	H2
Bye, The W3	56	E6
Bye Way, The, Har.	37	C1
Bye Ways, Twick.	81	H3
Byegrove Rd. SW19	84	G6
Byeway, The SW14	74	C3
Byeway, The, Epsom	99	F4
Byeways, The, Surb.	82	A7
Byfeld Gdns. SW13	74	G1
Byfield Rd., Islw.	73	D3
Byford Clo. E15	51	E7
Bygrove, Croy.	103	B6
Bygrove St. E14	60	B6
Byland Clo. N21	24	F7
Byland Clo. SE2	71	B3
Finchale Rd.		
Bylands Clo. SE16	68	G1
Rotherhithe St.		
Byne Rd. SE26	86	F6
Byne Rd., Cars.	100	H2
Bynes Rd., S.Croy.	102	A7
Byng Pl. WC1	**7**	**H6**
Byng Pl. WC1	58	D4
Byng Rd., Barn.	23	A3
Byng St. E14	69	A2
Bynon Ave., Bexh.	80	F3
Byre, The N14	24	B6
Farm La.		
Byre Rd. N14	24	A6
Farm La.		
Byrne Rd. SW12	85	B1
Byron Ave. E12	52	B6
Byron Ave. E18	42	F3
Byron Ave. NW9	38	B4
Byron Ave., Borwd.	22	A5
Byron Ave., Houns.	72	A2
Byron Ave., N.Mal.	92	G5
Byron Ave., Sutt.	100	G4
Byron Ave. E., Sutt.	100	G4
Byron Clo. E8	59	D1
Byron Clo. SE28	71	C1
Byron Clo., Hmptn.	81	F4
Byron Ct. W9	57	D4
Lanhill Rd.		
Byron Ct., Enf.	24	H2
Bycullah Rd.		
Byron Dr. N2	39	G6
Byron Gdns., Sutt.	100	G4
Byron Hill Rd., Har.	46	A1
Byron Ho., Beck.	87	B6
Byron Ms. W9	57	D4
Shirland Rd.		
Byron Rd. E10	51	B1
Byron Rd. E17	42	A3
Byron Rd. NW2	47	H2
Byron Rd. NW7	30	G5
Byron Rd. W5	64	J1
Byron Rd., Har.	37	C2
Byron Rd. (Wealdstone), Har.	37	B6
Byron Rd., Wem.	46	F2
Byron St. E14	60	C6
St. Leonards Rd.		
Byron Way, Nthlt.	54	E3
Bysouth Clo., Ilf.	43	E1
Bythorn St. SW9	76	F4
Byton Rd. SW17	84	J6
Byward Ave., Felt.	72	C6
Byward St. EC3	**13**	**E6**
Byward St. EC3	59	B7
Bywater Pl. SE16	68	H1
Bywater St. SW3	**18**	**J3**
Bywater St. SW3	66	J5
Bywell Pl. W1	**11**	**F2**
Bywood Ave., Croy.	95	F6
Byworth Wk. N19	49	D1
Courtauld Rd.		

C

C.I. Twr., N.Mal.	92	E3
Cabbell St. NW1	**10**	**G2**
Cabbell St. NW1	57	H5
Cabinet Way E4	33	J6
Cable Pl. SE10	78	C1
Diamond Ter.		
Cable St. E1	**13**	**J5**
Cable St. E1	59	D7
Cabot Sq. E14	69	A1
Cabot Way E6	61	A1
Parr La.		
Cabul Rd. SW11	75	H2
Cactus Wk. W12	56	F7
Du Cane Rd.		
Cadbury Clo., Islw.	73	D1
Cadbury Way SE16	**17**	**G6**
Caddington Clo., Barn.	23	H5
Caddington Rd. NW2	48	B3
Caddis Clo., Stan.	29	C7
Daventer Dr.		
Cade Rd. SE10	78	D1
Cadell Clo. E2	**9**	**G2**
Cader Rd. SW18	75	F6
Cadet Dr. SE1	**21**	**G3**
Cadet Dr. SE1	68	C5
Cadet Pl. SE10	69	E5
Cadiz Rd., Dag.	53	J7
Cadiz St. SE17	**21**	**A4**
Cadiz St. SE17	67	J5
Cadley Ter. SE23	86	F2
Cadmer Clo., N.Mal.	92	E4
Cadogan Clo., Beck.	96	D1
Albemarle Rd.		
Cadogan Clo., Har.	45	H4
Cadogan Clo., Tedd.	82	B5
Cadogan Ct., Sutt.	100	E6
Cadogan Gdns. E18	42	H3
Cadogan Gdns. N3	39	E1
Cadogan Gdns. N21	24	F5
Cadogan Gdns. SW3	**19**	**A1**
Cadogan Gdns. SW3	66	J4
Cadogan Gate SW1	**19**	**A1**
Cadogan Gate SW1	66	J4
Cadogan La. SW1	**15**	**B6**
Cadogan La. SW1	67	A3
Cadogan Pl. SW1	**15**	**A5**
Cadogan Pl. SW1	66	J3
Cadogan Rd., Surb.	91	G5
Cadogan Sq. SW1	**15**	**A6**
Cadogan Sq. SW1	66	J3
Cadogan St. SW3	**18**	**J2**
Cadogan St. SW3	66	J4
Cadogan Ter. E9	50	J6
Cadoxton Ave. N15	41	C6
Cadwallon Rd. SE9	88	E2
Caedmon Rd. N7	49	F4
Caerleon Clo., Sid.	89	C5
Caerleon Ter. SE2	71	B4
Blithdale Rd.		
Caernarvon Clo., Mitch.	94	E3
Caernarvon Dr., Ilf.	43	D1
Caesars Wk., Mitch.	93	J5
Cage Rd. E16	60	E5
Malmesbury Rd.		
Cahill St. EC1	**9**	**A6**
Cahir St. E14	69	B4
Caird St. W10	57	B3
Cairn Ave. W5	64	G1
Cairn Way, Stan.	29	C6
Cairndale Clo., Brom.	87	F7
Cairnfield Ave. NW2	47	E3
Cairngorm Clo., Tedd.	82	D5
Vicarage Rd.		
Cairns Ave., Wdf.Grn.	35	B6
Cairns Rd. SW11	75	H5
Cairo New Rd., Croy.	101	H2
Cairo Rd. E17	42	A4
Caishowe Rd., Borwd.	22	B1
Caistor Ms. SW12	76	B7
Caistor Rd.		
Caistor Pk. Rd. E15	60	F1
Caistor Rd. SW12	76	B7
Caithness Gdns., Sid.	79	J6
Caithness Rd. W14	66	A3
Caithness Rd., Mitch.	85	B7
Calabria Rd. N5	49	H6
Calais Gate SE5	76	H1
Calais St.		
Calais St. SE5	76	H1
Calbourne Rd. SW12	75	J7
Calcott Wk. SE9	88	B4
Caldbeck Ave., Wor.Pk.	99	G2
Caldecot Rd. SE5	76	J2
Caldecott Way E5	50	G3
Calder Ave., Grnf.	55	C2
Calder Clo., Enf.	25	B3
Calder Gdns., Edg.	38	A3
Calder Rd., Mord.	93	F5
Calderon Pl. W10	56	J5
St. Quintin Gdns.		
Calderon Rd. E11	51	C4
Caldervale Rd. SW4	75	D5

Calderwood St. SE18	70 D4	Camberwell Pas. SE5	76 J1
Caldicot Grn. NW9	38 E6	Camberwell Grn.	
Snowdon Dr.		Camberwell Rd. SE5	**21 A6**
Caldwell Rd., Wat.	28 D4	Camberwell Rd. SE5	67 J6
Caldwell St. SW9	67 F7	Camberwell Sta. Rd.	76 J1
Caldy Rd., Belv.	71 H3	SE5	
Caldy Wk. N1	49 J6	Cambeys Rd., Dag.	53 H5
Marquess Est.		Camborne Av. W13	64 E2
Cale St. SW3	**18 G3**	Camborne Ms. W11	57 B6
Cale St. SW3	66 H5	St. Marks Rd.	
Caleb St. SE1	**16 J3**	Camborne Rd. SW18	75 D7
Caledon Rd. E6	61 B1	Camborne Rd., Croy.	95 D7
Caledon Rd., Wall.	101 A4	Camborne Rd., Mord.	93 A5
Caledonia St. N1	**8 B2**	Camborne Rd., Sid.	89 C3
Caledonia St. N1	58 E2	Camborne Rd., Sutt.	100 D7
Caledonian Clo., Ilf.	53 B1	Camborne Rd., Well.	79 J2
Caledonian Rd. N1	**8 B2**	Camborne Way,	72 G1
Caledonian Rd. N1	58 E2	Houns.	
Caledonian Rd. N7	49 F4	Cambourne Av. N9	25 G7
Caledonian Wf. Rd.	69 D4	Cambray Rd. SW12	85 C1
E14		Cambray Rd., Orp.	97 J7
Caletock Way SE10	69 F5	Cambria Clo., Houns.	72 G4
Calico Row SW11	75 F3	Cambria Clo., Sid.	88 G1
York Pl.		Cambria Ct., Felt.	72 B7
Calidore Clo. SW2	76 F6	Hounslow Rd.	
Endymion Rd.		Cambria Rd. SE5	76 J3
California La.	29 A1	Cambria St. SW6	66 E7
(Bushey), Wat.		Cambrian Av., Ilf.	43 H5
California Rd., N.Mal.	92 C3	Cambrian Clo. SE27	85 H3
Callaby Ter. N1	50 A6	Cambrian Rd. E10	42 A7
Wakeham St.		Cambrian Rd., Rich.	73 J6
Callaghan Clo. SE13	78 E4	Cambridge Av. NW6	57 D2
Glenton Rd.		Cambridge Av., Grnf.	46 C5
Callander Rd. SE6	87 B2	Cambridge Av.,	92 E2
Callard Av. N13	32 H5	N.Mal.	
Callcott Rd. NW6	48 C7	Cambridge Av., Well.	79 J4
Callcott St. W8	66 D1	Cambridge Barracks	70 C4
Hillgate Pl.		Rd. SE18	
Callendar Rd. SW7	**14 E5**	Cambridge Circ. WC2	**11 J4**
Callendar Rd. SW7	66 G3	Cambridge Circ. WC2	58 D6
Callingham Clo. E14	59 J5	Cambridge Clo. NW10	47 C3
Wallwood St.		Cambridge Clo. SW20	92 H1
Callis Rd. E17	41 J6	Cambridge Clo.,	72 E4
Callow St. SW3	**18 D5**	Houns.	
Callow St. SW3	66 G6	Cambridge Cotts.,	65 A6
Calmington Rd. SE5	**21 E4**	Rich.	
Calmington Rd. SE5	68 B5	Cambridge Cres. E2	59 E2
Calmont Rd., Brom.	87 D6	Cambridge Cres.,	82 D5
Calne Av., Ilf.	43 E1	Tedd.	
Calonne Rd. SW19	84 A4	Cambridge Dr. SE12	78 G5
Calshot St. N1	**8 C1**	Cambridge Dr., Ruis.	45 D2
Calshot St. N1	58 F2	Cambridge Gdns. N10	40 A1
Calshot Way, Enf.	24 H3	Cambridge Gdns. N13	32 G5
Calthorpe Gdns., Edg.	29 H5	Cambridge Gdns. N17	33 A7
Jesmond Way		Great Cambridge Rd.	
Calthorpe Gdns.,	100 F3	Cambridge Gdns. N21	25 A7
Sutt.		Cambridge Gdns.	57 D2
Calthorpe St. WC1	**8 D5**	NW6	
Calthorpe St. WC1	58 F4	Cambridge Gdns. W10	57 A6
Calton Av. SE21	77 B6	Cambridge Gdns., Enf.	25 D2
Calton Rd., Barn.	23 F6	Cambridge Gdns.,	92 A2
Calverley Clo., Beck.	87 B6	Kings.T.	
Calverley Cres., Dag.	53 G2	Cambridge Gate NW1	**7 E5**
Calverley Gdns., Har.	37 G7	Cambridge Gate Ms.	**7 E5**
Calverley Gro. N19	49 D1	NW1	
Calverley Rd., Epsom	99 G6	Cambridge Grn. SE9	88 E1
Calvert Av. E2	**9 E4**	Cambridge Gro. SE20	95 E1
Calvert Av. E2	59 B3	Cambridge Gro. W6	65 H4
Calvert Clo., Belv.	71 G4	Cambridge Gro. Rd.,	92 A3
Calvert Clo., Sid.	89 E6	Kings.T.	
Calvert Rd. SE10	69 F5	Cambridge Heath Rd.	59 E4
Calvert Rd., Barn.	23 A2	E1	
Calvert St. NW1	58 A1	Cambridge Heath Rd.	59 F4
Chalcot Rd.		E2	
Calverton SE5	**21 D5**	Cambridge Mans.	75 J1
Calverton Rd. E6	61 D1	SW11	
Calvert's Bldgs. SE1	**17 B2**	Cambridge Rd.	
Calvin St. E1	**9 F6**	Great Cambridge Rd.	
Calvin St. E1	59 C4	Cambridge Par., Enf.	25 D1
Calydon Rd. SE7	69 H5	Cambridge Pk. E11	42 G7
Calypso Way SE16	68 J4	Cambridge Pk., Twick.	73 H6
Cam Rd. E15	60 D1	Cambridge Pk. Rd. E11	42 F7
Camac Rd., Twick.	82 A1	Cambridge Pl. W8	**14 B4**
Cambalt Rd. SW15	75 A5	Cambridge Pl. W8	66 E2
Camberley Av. SW20	92 H2	Cambridge Rd. E4	34 D1
Camberley Av., Enf.	25 B4	Cambridge Rd. E11	42 F6
Camberley Clo., Sutt.	100 A3	Cambridge Rd. NW6	57 D2
Cambert Way SE3	78 H4	Cambridge Rd. SE20	95 E3
Camberwell Ch. St.	77 A1	Cambridge Rd. SW11	75 J1
SE5		Cambridge Rd. SW13	74 F2
Camberwell Glebe	77 B1	Cambridge Rd. SW20	92 H1
SE5		Cambridge Rd. W7	64 C2
Camberwell Grn. SE5	77 A1	Cambridge Rd., Bark.	52 F7
Camberwell Gro. SE5	77 A1	Cambridge Rd., Brom.	87 G7
Camberwell New Rd.	**20 F7**	Cambridge Rd., Cars.	100 H4
SE5		Cambridge Rd.,	81 F7
Camberwell New Rd.	67 G6	Hmptn.	
SE5		Cambridge Rd., Har.	36 G5

Cambridge Rd.,	72 E4	Camlan Rd., Brom.	87 F4
Houns.		Camlet St. E2	**9 F5**
Cambridge Rd., Ilf.	52 H1	Camlet St. E2	59 C4
Cambridge Rd.,	92 A2	Camlet Way, Barn.	23 D2
Kings.T.		Camley St. NW1	**7 J1**
Cambridge Rd., Mitch.	94 B3	Camley St. NW1	49 D7
Cambridge Rd.,	92 D4	Camm Gdns., Kings.T.	91 J2
N.Mal.		Church Rd.	
Cambridge Rd., Rich.	65 A7	Camm Gdns., T.Ditt.	91 B7
Cambridge Rd., Sid.	88 H4	Camomile Av.,	93 J1
Cambridge Rd., Sthl.	63 F1	Mitch.	
Cambridge Rd., Tedd.	82 C4	Camomile St. EC3	**13 D3**
Cambridge Rd.,	73 G6	Camomile St. EC3	59 B6
Twick.		Camp Rd. SW19	83 H5
Cambridge Rd., Walt.	90 B6	Camp Vw. SW19	83 H5
Cambridge Rd.,	90 F4	Campana Rd. SW6	75 D1
W.Mol.		Campbell Av., Ilf.	43 E4
Cambridge Rd. Est.,	92 A2	Campbell Clo. SE18	79 D1
Kings.T.		Moordown	
Cambridge Rd. N. W4	65 B5	Campbell Clo. SW16	85 D5
Cambridge Rd. S. W4	65 B5	Campbell Clo., Ruis.	36 A6
Oxford Rd. S.		Campbell Clo., Twick.	82 A4
Cambridge Row SE18	70 E5	Campbell Ct. N17	41 C1
Cambridge Sq. W2	**10 G3**	Campbell Cft., Edg.	30 A5
Cambridge Sq. W2	57 H6	Campbell Gordon	47 H4
Cambridge St. SW1	**19 E3**	Way NW2	
Cambridge St. SW1	67 B4	Campbell Rd. E3	60 A3
Cambridge Ter. N13	32 G5	Campbell Rd. E6	61 B1
Cambridge Ter. NW1	**7 D4**	Campbell Rd. E15	51 F4
Cambridge Ter. Ms.	**7 E4**	Trevelyan Rd.	
NW1		Campbell Rd. E17	41 J4
Cambus Clo., Hayes	54 E5	Campbell Rd. N17	41 C1
Cambus Rd. E16	60 G5	Campbell Rd. W7	55 B7
Camdale Rd. SE18	70 J7	Campbell Rd., Croy.	94 H7
Camden Av., Felt.	81 C2	Campbell Rd., E.Mol.	91 C3
Camden Av., Hayes	54 D7	Hampton Ct. Rd.	
Camden Clo., Chis.	97 F1	Campbell Rd., Twick.	82 A1
Camden Est. SE15	77 C1	Campbell Wk. N1	58 E1
Camden Gdns. NW1	49 B7	Outram Pl.	
Kentish Town Rd.		Campdale Rd. N7	49 D3
Camden Gdns., Sutt.	100 E5	Campden Cres., Dag.	53 B4
Camden Gdns.,	94 H3	Campden Cres.,	46 E3
Th.Hth.		Wem.	
Camden Gro., Chis.	88 E6	Campden Gro. W8	66 D2
Camden High St. NW1	58 B1	Campden Hill W8	66 D2
Camden Hill Rd. SE19	86 B6	Campden Hill Gdns.	66 D1
Camden La. N7	49 D6	W8	
Camden Lock Pl. NW1	49 B7	Campden Hill Pl. W11	66 C1
Chalk Fm. Rd.		Holland Pk. Av.	
Camden Ms. NW1	49 C7	Campden Hill Rd. W8	66 D1
Camden Pk. Rd. NW1	49 D6	Campden Hill Sq. W8	66 C1
Camden Pk. Rd., Chis.	88 C7	Campden Ho. Clo. W8	66 D2
Camden Pas. N1	58 H1	Hornton St.	
Camden Rd. E11	42 H6	Campden Rd., S.Croy.	102 B5
Camden Rd. E17	41 J6	Campden St. W8	66 D1
Camden Rd. N7	49 E4	Campen Clo. SW19	84 B2
Camden Rd. NW1	49 C7	Queensmere Rd.	
Camden Rd., Bex.	89 E1	Camperdown St. E1	**13 G4**
Camden Rd., Cars.	100 J4	Campfield Rd. SE9	79 A7
Camden Rd., Sutt.	100 D5	Campion Clo. E6	61 C7
Camden Row SE3	78 E2	Campion Clo., Croy.	102 B4
Camden Sq. NW1	49 D6	Campion Clo., Har.	37 J6
Camden Sq. SE15	77 C1	Campion Pl. SE28	71 B1
Exeter Rd.		Campion Rd. SW15	74 J4
Camden St. NW1	49 C7	Campion Rd., Islw.	73 C1
Camden Ter. NW1	49 D6	Campion Ter. NW2	48 A4
North Vill.		Camplin Rd., Har.	37 H5
Camden Wk. N1	58 H1	Camplin St. SE14	68 G7
Camden Way, Chis.	88 C7	Campsbourne, The N8	40 E4
Camden Way, Th.Hth.	94 H3	Rectory Gdns.	
Camdenhurst St. E14	59 H6	Campsbourne Rd. N8	40 E3
Camel Rd. E16	70 A1	Campsey Gdns., Dag.	53 B7
Camelford Wk. W11	57 B6	Campsey Rd., Dag.	53 B7
Lancaster Rd.		Campsfield Rd. N8	40 E3
Camellia Ct., Wdf.Grn.	34 E7	Campsbourne Rd.	
Bridle Path		Campshill Pl. SE13	78 C5
Camellia Pl., Twick.	72 H7	Campshill Rd.	
Camellia St. SW8	67 E7	Campshill Rd. SE13	78 C5
Camelot Clo. SE28	71 B1	Campus Rd. E17	41 J6
Camelot Clo. SW19	84 D4	Camrose Av., Edg.	37 J2
Camelot St. SE15	68 E7	Camrose Av., Erith	71 H6
Bird in Bush Rd.		Camrose Av., Felt.	81 B4
Camera Pl. SW10	**18 E5**	Camrose Clo., Croy.	95 H7
Camera Pl. SW10	66 G6	Camrose Clo., Mord.	93 D4
Cameron Clo. N18	33 E4	Camrose St. SE2	71 A5
Cameron Clo. N20	31 H2	Canada Av. N18	32 J6
Myddelton Pk.		Canada Cres. W3	56 C4
Cameron Pl. E1	59 E6	Canada Est. SE16	68 F3
Varden St.		Canada Gdns. SE13	78 C5
Cameron Rd. SE6	86 J2	Monument Gdns.	
Cameron Rd., Brom.	96 G4	Canada Rd. W3	56 C5
Cameron Rd., Croy.	94 H6	Canada Sq. E14	69 B1
Cameron Rd., Ilf.	52 H1	Canada St. SE16	68 G2
Cameron Sq., Mitch.	93 H1	Canada Way W12	56 H7
Camerton Clo. E8	50 C6	Canadian Av. SE6	87 B1
Buttermere Wk.		Canal App. SE8	68 H5
Camilla Rd. SE16	68 E4	Canal Clo. E1	59 H4
Camille Clo. SE25	95 D3		

Name	Page	Grid
Canal Gro. SE15	21	J5
Canal Gro. SE15	68	D6
Canal Head SE15	77	D1
Peckham High St.		
Canal Rd. E3	59	H4
Canal St. SE5	21	B6
Canal St. SE5	68	A6
Canal Wk. N1	59	A1
Canal Wk. SE26	86	F5
Canal Wk., Croy.	95	C6
Canal Way NW1	58	A1
Regents Pk. Rd.		
Canal Way NW10	56	D2
Canal Way W10	57	A4
Canal Way, Wem.	55	J1
Canal Way Wk. W10	57	B4
Kensal Rd.		
Canary Wf. E14	69	A1
Canberra Clo. NW4	38	G3
Canberra Dr., Nthlt.	54	C3
Canberra Rd. E6	61	C1
Barking Rd.		
Canberra Rd. SE7	69	J6
Canberra Rd. W13	64	D1
Canberra Rd., Bexh.	71	D6
Canbury Ave., Kings.T.	91	J1
Canbury Ms. SE26	86	D3
Wells Pk. Rd.		
Canbury Pk. Rd., Kings.T.	91	H1
Canbury Pas., Kings.T.	91	G1
Cancell Rd. SW9	76	G1
Candahar Rd. SW11	75	H2
Candler St. N15	41	A6
Candover St. W1	11	F2
Candy St. E3	59	J1
Cane Clo., Wall.	101	E7
Kingsford Ave.		
Caney Ms. NW2	48	A2
Claremont Rd.		
Canfield Dr., Ruis.	45	B5
Canfield Gdns. NW6	48	E7
Canfield Pl. NW6	48	F6
Canfield Gdns.		
Canfield Rd., Wdf.Grn.	35	B7
Canford Ave., Nthlt.	54	E1
Canford Clo., Enf.	24	G2
Canford Gdns., N.Mal.	92	E6
Canford Rd. SW11	76	A5
Canham Rd. SE25	95	B3
Canham Rd. W3	65	E2
Canmore Gdns. SW16	85	C7
Cann Hall Rd. E11	51	E4
Canning Cres. N22	40	F1
Canning Cross SE5	77	B2
Canning Pas. W8	14	C5
Canning Pl. W8	14	C5
Canning Pl. W8	66	F3
Canning Pl. Ms. W8	14	C5
Canning Rd. E15	60	E2
Canning Rd. E17	41	H4
Canning Rd. N5	49	H3
Canning Rd., Croy.	102	C2
Canning Rd., Har.	37	B3
Cannington Rd., Dag.	53	C6
Cannizaro Rd. SW19	83	J5
Cannon Clo. SW20	92	J3
Cannon Clo., Hmptn.	81	H6
Hanworth Rd.		
Cannon Dr. E14	60	A7
Cannon Hill N14	32	D3
Cannon Hill NW6	48	D5
Cannon Hill La. SW20	93	B3
Cannon La. NW3	48	G3
Cannon La., Pnr.	36	E5
Cannon Pl. NW3	48	F3
Cannon Pl. SE7	70	B5
Cannon Rd. N14	32	E3
Cannon Rd., Bexh.	80	E1
Cannon St. EC4	12	J4
Cannon St. EC4	58	J6
Cannon St. Rd. E1	59	E6
Cannon Way, W.Mol.	90	G4
Cannonbury Ave., Pnr.	36	D6
Canon Ave., Rom.	44	C5
Canon Beck Rd. SE16	68	F2
Canon Mohan Clo. N14	24	B6
Farm La.		
Canon Rd., Brom.	96	J3
Canon Row SW1	16	A3
Canon Row SW1	67	E2
Canon St. N1	58	J1
Canon Trd. Est., The, Wem.	47	B4
Canonbie Rd. SE23	77	F7
Canonbury Cres. N1	49	J7
Canonbury Gro. N1	49	J7
Canonbury La. N1	49	H7
Canonbury Pk. N. N1	49	J6
Canonbury Pk. S. N1	49	J6
Canonbury Pl. N1	49	H6
Canonbury Rd. N1	49	H6
Canonbury Rd., Enf.	25	B1
Canonbury Sq. N1	49	H7
Canonbury St. N1	49	J7
Canonbury Vill. N1	49	H7
Canonbury Yd. N1	58	J1
New N. Rd.		
Canons Clo. N2	39	G7
Canons Clo., Edg.	29	J6
Canons Cor., Edg.	29	H4
Canons Dr., Edg.	29	H5
Canons Wk., Croy.	102	G3
Canonsleigh Rd., Dag.	53	B7
Canopus Way, Nthwd.	28	A4
Canrobert St. E2	59	E3
Cantelowes Rd. NW1	49	D6
Canterbury Ave., Ilf.	43	B7
Canterbury Ave., Sid.	89	C2
Canterbury Clo. E6	61	C6
Harper Rd.		
Canterbury Clo., Beck.	96	B1
Canterbury Clo., Chig.	35	J3
Canterbury Clo., Grnf.	54	H6
Canterbury Cres. SW9	76	G3
Canterbury Gro. SE27	85	G4
Canterbury Pl. SE17	20	H2
Canterbury Pl. SE17	67	H4
Canterbury Rd. E10	42	C7
Canterbury Rd. NW6	57	C2
Canterbury Rd., Borwd.	22	A2
Canterbury Rd., Croy.	94	G7
Canterbury Rd., Felt.	81	E3
Canterbury Rd., Har.	36	H5
Canterbury Rd., Mord.	93	E7
Canterbury Ter. NW6	57	D2
Cantley Gdns. SE19	95	C1
Cantley Gdns., Ilf.	43	F6
Cantley Rd. W7	64	D3
Canton St. E14	60	A6
Cantrell Rd. E3	59	J4
Cantwell Rd. SE18	70	E7
Canute Gdns. SE16	68	G4
Canvey St. SE1	16	H1
Cape Rd., Bark.	52	F6
North St.		
Cape Rd. N17	41	D3
High Cross Rd.		
Cape Yd. E1	17	J1
Capel Ave., Wall.	101	F5
Capel Clo. N20	31	F3
Capel Clo., Brom.	104	C1
Capel Ct. EC2	13	C4
Capel Ct. SE20	95	F1
Melvin Rd.		
Capel Gdns., Ilf.	52	J4
Capel Gdns., Pnr.	36	F4
Capel Pt. E7	51	H4
Capel Rd. E7	51	H4
Capel Rd. E12	52	A4
Capel Rd., Barn.	23	H6
Capener's Clo. SW1	15	B4
Capern Rd. SW18	84	F1
Cargill Rd.		
Capital Business Cen., Wem.	55	G1
Capital Interchange Way, Brent.	65	A5
Capital Pl., Croy.	101	F5
Stafford Rd.		
Capitol Ind. Est. NW9	38	C3
Capitol Way NW9	38	C3
Capland St. NW8	6	F5
Capland St. NW8	57	G4
Caple Rd. NW10	56	F2
Capper St. WC1	7	G6
Capper St. WC1	58	C4
Caprea Clo., Hayes	54	D5
Triandra Way		
Capri Rd., Croy.	102	C1
Capstan Clo., Rom.	44	B6
Capstan Ride, Enf.	24	G2
Crofton Way		
Capstan Rd. SE8	68	J4
Capstan Sq. E14	69	C2
Capstan Way SE16	68	H1
Capstone Rd., Brom.	87	F4
Capthorne Ave., Har.	45	E1
Capworth St. E10	51	A1
Caradoc Clo. W2	57	D6
Caradoc St. SE10	69	E5
Caradon Clo. E11	51	E2
Brockway Clo.		
Caradon Way N15	41	A4
Caravel Ms. SE8	69	A6
Watergate St.		
Caravelle Gdns., Nthlt.	54	D3
Javelin Way		
Carberry Rd. SE19	86	B6
Carbery Ave. W3	64	J2
Carbis Clo. E4	34	D1
Carbis Rd. E14	59	J6
Carbuncle Pas. Way N17	41	D2
Carburton St. W1	11	E1
Carburton St. W1	58	B5
Cardale St. E14	69	C3
Plevna St.		
Carden Rd. SE15	77	E3
Cardiff Rd. W7	64	D3
Cardiff Rd., Enf.	25	E4
Cardiff St. SE18	70	H7
Cardigan Gdns., Ilf.	53	A2
Cardigan Rd. E3	59	J2
Cardigan Rd. SW13	74	G2
Cardigan Rd. SW19	84	F6
Cardigan Rd., Rich.	73	H6
Cardigan St. SE11	20	E3
Cardigan St. SE11	67	G5
Cardigan Wk. N1	49	J7
Ashby Gro.		
Cardinal Ave., Borwd.	22	B3
Cardinal Ave., Kings.T.	82	H5
Cardinal Ave., Mord.	93	B6
Cardinal Bourne St. SE1	17	C6
Cardinal Bourne St. SE1	68	A3
Cardinal Clo., Chis.	97	G1
Cardinal Clo., Mord.	93	B6
Cardinal Clo., Wor.Pk.	99	G4
Cardinal Cres., N.Mal.	92	C2
Cardinal Dr., Ilf.	35	F6
Cardinal Pl. SW15	75	A4
Cardinal Rd., Felt.	81	B1
Cardinal Rd., Ruis.	45	D1
Cardinal Way, Har.	37	B3
Wolseley Rd.		
Cardinals Wk. E4	81	J7
Hmptn.		
Cardinals Way N19	49	D1
Cardine Ms. SE15	68	E7
Cardington Sq., Houns.	72	D4
Cardington St. NW1	7	G3
Cardington St. NW1	58	C3
Cardozo Rd. N7	49	E5
Cardrew Ave. N12	31	G5
Cardrew Clo. N12	31	G5
Cardross St. W6	65	H3
Cardwell Rd. N7	49	E4
Cardwell Rd. SE18	70	C4
Carew Clo. N7	49	F2
Carew Rd. N17	41	D2
Carew Rd. W13	64	F2
Carew Rd., Mitch.	94	A2
Carew Rd., Th.Hth.	94	H3
Carew Rd., Wall.	101	C6
Carew St. SE5	76	J2
Carey Ct., Bexh.	80	H5
Carey Gdns. SW8	76	C1
Carey La. EC2	12	J3
Carey Pl. SW1	19	H2
Carey Rd., Dag.	53	E4
Carey St. WC2	12	D4
Carey St. WC2	58	F6
Carey Way, Wem.	47	C4
Carfax Pl. SW4	76	D4
Holwood Pl.		
Carfree Clo. N1	49	G7
Bewdley St.		
Cargill Rd. SW18	84	E1
Cargreen Pl. SE25	95	C4
Cargreen Rd.		
Cargreen Rd. SE25	95	C4
Carholme Rd. SE23	86	J1
Carisbrook Rd., Stan.	37	G2
Carisbrooke Ave., Bex.	89	D1
Carisbrooke Clo., Enf.	25	C1
Carisbrooke Gdns. SE15	21	G7
Carisbrooke Rd. E17	41	H4
Carisbrooke Rd., Brom.	96	J4
Carisbrooke Rd., Mitch.	94	D4
Carker's La. NW5	49	B5
Carleton Ave., Wall.	101	D7
Carleton Clo., Esher	98	A1
Carleton Rd. N7	49	D5
Carlile Clo. E3	59	J2
Carlingford Gdns., Mitch.	84	J7
Carlingford Rd. N15	40	H3
Carlingford Rd. NW3	48	G4
Carlingford Rd., Mord.	93	A6
Carlisle Ave. EC3	13	F4
Carlisle Ave. W3	56	E6
Carlisle Clo., Kings.T.	92	A1
Carlisle Gdns., Har.	37	G7
Carlisle Gdns., Ilf.	43	B6
Carlisle La. SE1	16	D6
Carlisle La. SE1	67	F3
Carlisle Ms. NW8	10	F1
Carlisle Ms. NW8	57	G5
Carlisle Pl. N11	32	B4
Carlisle Pl. SW1	15	F6
Carlisle Pl. SW1	67	C3
Carlisle Rd. E10	51	A1
Carlisle Rd. N4	40	G7
Carlisle Rd. NW6	57	B1
Carlisle Rd. NW9	38	C3
Carlisle Rd., Hmptn.	81	H7
Carlisle Rd., Sutt.	100	C5
Carlisle St. W1	11	H4
Carlisle Wk. E8	50	C6
Laurel St.		
Carlisle Way SW17	85	A5
Carlos Pl. W1	11	C5
Carlos Pl. W1	58	A7
Carlow St. NW1	7	F1
Carlton Ave. N14	24	D5
Carlton Ave., Felt.	72	C6
Carlton Ave., Har.	37	E5
Carlton Ave., S.Croy.	102	B7
Carlton Ave. E., Wem.	46	G2
Carlton Ave. W., Wem.	46	E2
Carlton Clo. NW3	48	D2
Carlton Clo., Borwd.	22	D4
Carlton Clo., Chess.	98	G6
Carlton Clo., Edg.	30	A5
Carlton Ct. SW9	76	H1
Carlton Ct., Ilf.	43	G3
Carlton Cres., Sutt.	100	B4
Carlton Dr. SW15	75	A5
Carlton Dr., Ilf.	43	G3
Carlton Gdns. SW1	15	H2
Carlton Gdns. SW1	67	D1
Carlton Gdns. W5	55	F6
Carlton Gro. SE15	77	E1
Carlton Hill NW8	6	B1
Carlton Hill NW8	57	E2
Carlton Ho. Ter. SW1	15	H2
Carlton Ho. Ter. SW1	67	D1
Carlton Pk. Ave. SW20	93	J2
Carlton Rd. E11	51	F1
Carlton Rd. E12	52	A4
Carlton Rd. E17	41	H1
Carlton Rd. N4	40	G7
Carlton Rd. N11	32	A5
Carlton Rd. SW14	74	C3
Carlton Rd. W4	65	D2
Carlton Rd. W5	55	F7
Carlton Rd., Erith	71	H6
Carlton Rd., N.Mal.	92	E2
Carlton Rd., Sid.	88	J5
Carlton Rd., S.Croy.	102	A6
Carlton Rd., Walt.	90	B7
Carlton Rd., Well.	80	B3
Carlton Sq. E1	59	G4
Argyle Rd.		
Carlton St. SW1	11	H6
Carlton Ter. E11	42	H5
Carlton Ter. N18	33	A3
Carlton Ter. SE26	86	F3
Carlton Twr. Pl. SW1	15	A5
Carlton Twr. Pl. SW1	66	J3
Carlton Vale NW6	57	D2
Carlwell St. SW17	84	H5
Carlyle Ave., Brom.	97	A3
Carlyle Ave., Sthl.	54	F7
Carlyle Clo. N2	39	F6
Carlyle Clo. NW10	56	D1
Carlyle Clo., W.Mol.	90	H2
Carlyle Gdns., Sthl.	54	F7
Carlyle Pl. SW15	75	A4
Carlyle Rd. E12	52	B4
Carlyle Rd. SE28	62	B7
Carlyle Rd. W5	64	F4
Carlyle Rd., Croy.	102	D2
Carlyle Sq. SW3	18	F4
Carlyle Sq. SW3	66	G5
Carlyon Ave., Har.	45	F4

Carlyon Clo., Wem. 55 H1
Carlyon Rd., Hayes 54 C5
Carlyon Rd., Wem. 55 H2
Carmalt Gdns. SW15 74 J4
Carmarthen Gdn. NW9 38 E6
Snowdon Dr.
Carmel Ct. W8 14 A3
Carmel Ct., Wem. 47 B2
Carmelite Clo., Har. 36 J1
Carmelite Rd., Har. 36 J1
Carmelite St. EC4 12 F5
Carmelite St. EC4 58 G7
Carmelite Wk., Har. 36 J1
Carmelite Way, Har. 36 J2
Hampden Rd.
Carmen St. E14 60 B6
Carmichael Clo. SW11 75 G3
Darien Rd.
Carmichael Clo., Ruis. 45 A4
Carmichael Ms. SW18 75 G6
Heathfield Rd.
Carmichael Rd. SE25 95 D4
Carminia Rd. SW17 85 B2
Carnaby St. W1 11 F4
Carnaby St. W1 58 C6
Carnac St. SE27 86 A4
Carnanton Rd. E17 42 D1
Carnarvon Ave., Enf. 25 C3
Carnarvon Rd. E10 42 C6
Carnarvon Rd. E15 51 F6
Carnarvon Rd. E18 42 F2
Carnarvon Rd., Barn. 23 B3
Carnation St. SE2 71 B5
Carnbrook Rd. SE3 79 A3
Carnecke Gdns. SE9 79 B5
Carnegie Clo., Surb. 98 J2
Fullers Ave.
Carnegie Pl. SW19 84 A3
Carnegie St. N1 58 F1
Carnforth Clo., Epsom 99 B6
Carnforth Rd. SW16 85 D7
Carnie Lo. SW17 85 B3
Manville Rd.
Carnoustie Dr. N1 49 F7
Carnwath Rd. SW6 75 D3
Carol St. NW1 58 C1
Carolina Rd., Th.Hth. 94 H2
Caroline Clo. N10 40 B2
Alexandra Pk. Rd.
Caroline Clo. SW16 85 F4
Caroline Clo. W2 10 B6
Caroline Clo., Croy. 102 B4
Brownlow Rd.
Caroline Clo., Islw. 64 B7
Caroline Ct., Stan. 29 D6
The Chase
Caroline Gdns. SE15 68 E7
Caroline Pl. SW11 76 A2
Caroline Pl. W2 10 B5
Caroline Pl. W2 57 E7
Caroline Pl. Ms. W2 10 B6
Caroline Rd. SW19 84 C7
Caroline St. E1 59 G6
Caroline Ter. SW1 19 B2
Caroline Ter. SW1 67 A4
Caroline Wk. W6 66 B6
Laundry Rd.
Carpenders Ave., Wat. 28 E3
Carpenter Gdns. N21 32 H2
Carpenter St. W1 11 D6
Carpenters Ct., Twick. 82 B2
Carpenters Pl. SW4 76 D4
Carpenters Rd. E15 51 A6
Carr Rd. E17 41 J2
Carr Rd., Nthlt. 45 G6
Carr St. E14 59 H5
Carrara Wk. SW9 76 G4
Somerleyton Rd.
Carriage Dr. E. SW11 19 C7
Carriage Dr. E. SW11 67 A7
Carriage Dr. N. SW11 19 C6
Carriage Dr. N. SW11 66 J7
Carriage Dr. S. SW11 75 J1
Carriage Dr. W. SW11 66 J7
Carrick Dr., Ilf. 43 F1
Carrick Gdns. N17 33 B7
Flexmere Rd.
Carrick Ms. SE8 69 A6
Watergate St.
Carrill Way, Belv. 71 D4
Carrington Ave., Borwd. 22 B5
Carrington Ave., Houns. 72 H5
Carrington Clo., Barn. 22 G5
Carrington Clo., Borwd. 22 C5
Carrington Clo., Croy. 95 H7
Carrington Gdns. E7 51 H4
Woodford Rd.
Carrington Rd., Rich. 74 A4
Carrington Sq., Har. 28 J7
Carrington St. W1 15 D2
Carrol Clo. NW5 49 B4
Carroll Clo. E15 51 F5
Carroll Hill, Loug. 27 C3
Carron Clo. E14 60 B6
Carronade Pl. SE28 70 F3
Carroun Rd. SW8 20 C7
Carroun Rd. SW8 67 F7
Carrow Rd., Dag. 53 B7
Carroway La., Grnf. 55 A3
Cowgate Rd.
Carrs La. N21 24 J5
Carshalton Gro., Sutt. 100 G4
Carshalton Pk. Rd., Cars. 100 J6
Carshalton Pl., Cars. 101 A4
Carshalton Rd., Cars. 100 H5
Carshalton Rd., Mitch. 94 A4
Carshalton Rd., Sutt. 100 F5
Carslake Rd. SW15 74 J6
Carson Rd. E16 60 G4
Carson Rd. SE21 85 J2
Carson Rd., Barn. 23 J4
Carstairs Rd. SE6 87 C3
Carston Clo. SE12 78 F5
Carswell Clo., Ilf. 43 A4
Roding La. S.
Carswell Rd. SE6 78 C7
Cart La. E4 26 D7
Carter Clo., Wall. 101 D7
Hermes Way
Carter La. EC4 12 H4
Carter La. EC4 58 H6
Carter Pl. SE17 21 A4
Carter Pl. SE17 67 J5
Carter Rd. E13 60 H1
Carter Rd. SW19 84 G6
Carter St. SE17 20 J5
Carter St. SE17 67 J6
Carteret St. SW1 15 H4
Carteret St. SW1 67 D2
Carteret Way SE8 68 H4
Carterhatch Rd., Enf. 25 F1
Carters Clo., Wor.Pk. 100 A2
Carters Hill Clo. SE9 87 J1
Carters La. SE23 86 H2
Carters Yd. SW18 75 D5
Wandsworth High St.
Carthew Rd. W6 65 H3
Carthew Vill. W6 65 H3
Carthusian St. EC1 12 J1
Carthusian St. EC1 58 J5
Cartier Circle E14 69 B1
Carting La. WC2 12 B6
Carting La. WC2 58 E7
Cartmel Clo. N17 33 E7
Heybourne Rd.
Cartmel Rd., Bexh. 80 G1
Cartmell Gdns., Mord. 93 F5
Carton St. W1 11 A3
Cartwright Gdns. WC1 8 A4
Cartwright Gdns. WC1 58 E3
Cartwright Rd., Dag. 53 E7
Cartwright St. E1 13 G6
Cartwright St. E1 59 C7
Carver Rd. SE24 76 J6
Carville Cres., Brent. 64 H4
Cary Rd. E11 51 E4
Carysfort Rd. N8 40 D5
Carysfort Rd. N16 50 A3
Cascade Ave. N10 40 C4
Cascade Clo., Buck.H. 35 A2
Cascade Rd.
Cascade Rd., Buck.H. 35 A2
Casella Rd. SE14 68 G7
Casewick Rd. SE27 85 G5
Casimir Rd. E5 50 E3
Casino Ave. SE24 77 A5
Caspian St. SE5 21 B7
Caspian St. SE5 68 A7
Caspian Wk. E16 61 A6
King George Ave.
Cassandra Clo., Nthlt. 46 A4
Casselden Rd. NW10 47 D7
Cassidy Rd. SW6 66 D7
Cassilda Rd. SE2 71 A4
Cassilis Rd., Twick. 73 E5
Cassiobury Rd. E17 41 H5
Cassland Rd. E9 50 G7
Cassland Rd., Th.Hth. 95 A4
Casslee Rd. SE6 77 J7
Casson St. E1 13 H2
Casson St. E1 59 D5
Castalia Sq. E14 69 C2
Roserton St.
Castalia St. E14 69 C2
Plevna St.
Castell Rd., Loug. 27 F1
Castellain Rd. W9 6 A5
Castellain Rd. W9 57 E4
Castellane Clo., Stan. 29 C7
Daventer Dr.
Castello Ave. SW15 74 J5
Castelnau SW13 74 G1
Castelnau Pl. SW13 65 H6
Castelnau
Castelnau Row SW13 65 H6
Lonsdale Rd.
Casterbridge NW6 57 E1
Casterbridge Rd. SE3 78 G3
Casterton St. E8 50 E6
Wilton Way
Castile Rd. SE18 70 D4
Castillon Rd. SE6 87 E2
Castlands Rd. SE6 86 J2
Castle Ave. E4 34 D5
Castle Baynard St. EC4 12 H5
Castle Clo. E9 50 H5
Swinnerton St.
Castle Clo. SW19 84 A3
Castle Clo., Brom. 96 E3
Castle Ct. EC3 13 C4
Castle Dr., Ilf. 43 B6
Castle La. SW1 15 F5
Castle La. SW1 67 C3
Castle Ms. N12 31 F5
Castle Rd.
Castle Ms. NW1 49 B6
Castle Rd.
Castle Par., Epsom 99 G7
Ewell Bypass
Castle Pl. NW1 49 B6
Castle Rd.
Castle Pl. W4 65 E4
Windmill Rd.
Castle Pt. E6 60 J2
Castle Rd. N12 31 F5
Castle Rd. NW1 49 B6
Castle Rd., Dag. 62 B1
Castle Rd., Enf. 25 H1
Castle Rd., Islw. 73 C2
Castle Rd., Nthlt. 45 H6
Castle Rd., Sthl. 63 F3
Castle St. E6 60 J2
Castle St., Kings.T. 91 H2
Castle Wk., Sun. 90 C3
Elizabeth Gdns.
Castle Way SW19 84 A3
Castle Way, Felt. 81 C4
Castle Yd. N6 40 A7
North Rd.
Castle Yd. SE1 16 H1
Castle Yd., Rich. 73 G5
Hill St.
Castlebar Hill W5 55 E5
Castlebar Ms. W5 55 F5
Castlebar Pk. W5 55 E4
Castlebar Rd. W5 55 F6
Castlecombe Dr. SW19 75 A7
Castlecombe Rd. SE9 88 B4
Castledine Rd. SE20 86 E7
Castleford Ave. SE9 88 E1
Castlegate, Rich. 73 J3
Castlehaven Rd. NW1 49 B7
Castleleigh Ct., Enf. 25 A5
Castlemaine Ave., S.Croy. 102 C5
Castlemaine Twr. SW11 75 J2
Castlereagh St. W1 10 H3
Castleton Ave., Wem. 46 H4
Castleton Clo., Croy. 95 H6
Castleton Rd. E17 42 D2
Castleton Rd. SE9 88 A4
Castleton Rd., Ilf. 53 A1
Castleton Rd., Mitch. 94 D4
Castleton Rd., Ruis. 45 D1
Castletown Rd. W14 66 B5
Castleview Gdns., Ilf. 43 B6
Castlewood Dr. SE9 79 C2
Castlewood Rd. N15 41 D6
Castlewood Rd. N16 41 D7
Castlewood Rd., Barn. 23 G3
Castor La. E14 60 B7
Cat Hill, Barn. 23 J5
Caterham Ave., Ilf. 43 C2
Caterham Rd. SE13 78 C3
Catesby St. SE17 21 C2
Catesby St. SE17 68 A4
Catford Bdy. SE6 78 B7
Catford Hill SE6 86 J1
Catford Ms. SE6 78 B7
Holbeach Rd.
Catford Rd. SE6 78 A7
Cathall Rd. E11 51 D2
Cathay St. SE16 68 E2
Cathay Wk., Nthlt. 54 G2
Brabazon Rd.
Cathcart Dr., Orp. 104 H2
Cathcart Hill N19 49 C3
Cathcart Rd. SW10 18 B5
Cathcart Rd. SW10 66 E6
Cathcart St. NW5 49 B6
Cathedral Pl. EC4 12 J4
Cathedral St. SE1 17 B1
Cathedral St. SE1 68 A1
Catherall Rd. N5 49 J3
Catherine Clo. SE16 68 G1
Rotherhithe St.
Catherine Ct. N14 24 C5
Conisbee Ct.
Catherine Gdns., Houns. 73 A4
Catherine Griffiths Ct. EC1 8 F5
Catherine Gro. SE10 78 B1
Catherine Pl. SW1 15 F5
Catherine Pl. SW1 67 C3
Catherine Rd., Surb. 91 G5
Catherine St. WC2 12 C5
Catherine St. WC2 58 F7
Catherine Wheel All. E1 13 E2
Catherine Wheel Rd., Brent. 64 G7
Catherine Wheel Yd. SW1 15 F2
Cathles Rd. SW12 76 B6
Cathnor Hill Ct. W12 65 H3
Cathnor Rd. W12 65 H2
Catlin St. SE16 21 J4
Catlin St. SE16 68 D5
Catling Clo. SE23 86 F3
Catlins La., Pnr. 36 B3
Cato Rd. SW4 76 D3
Cato St. W1 10 H2
Cator La., Beck. 95 J1
Rectory Grn.
Cator Rd. SE26 86 G6
Cator Rd., Cars. 100 J5
Cator St. SE15 68 C6
Cattistock Rd. SE9 88 B5
Cattley Clo., Barn. 23 B4
Wood St.
Catton St. WC1 12 C2
Catton St. WC1 58 F5
Caulfield Rd. E6 61 B1
Caulfield Rd. SE15 77 E2
Causeway, The N2 39 H4
Causeway, The SW18 75 E5
Causeway, The SW19 83 J5
Causeway, The, Cars. 101 A3
Causeway, The, Chess. 98 H4
Causeway, The, Esher 98 C7
Causeway, The, Felt. 72 A4
Causeway, The, Tedd. 82 C6
Broad St.
Causeyware Rd. N9 25 E7
Causton Rd. N6 40 B7
Causton St. SW1 19 J2
Causton St. SW1 67 D4
Cautley Ave. SW4 76 C5
Cavalier Clo., Rom. 44 D4
Cavalry Cres., Houns. 72 D4
Cavalry Gdns. SW15 75 C5
Upper Richmond Rd.
Cavaye Pl. SW10 18 D4
Cave Rd. E13 60 H2
Cave Rd., Rich. 82 F4
Cavell Dr., Enf. 24 G2
Cavell Rd. N17 33 A7
Cavell St. E1 59 E5
Cavendish Ave. N3 39 D2
Cavendish Ave. NW8 6 F2
Cavendish Ave. NW8 57 G2
Cavendish Ave. W13 55 D5
Cavendish Ave., Erith 71 J7
Cavendish Ave., Har. 46 A4
Cavendish Ave., N.Mal. 92 G5
Cavendish Ave., Ruis. 45 B5
Cavendish Ave., Sid. 80 A7
Cavendish Ave., Well. 79 J3
Cavendish Ave., Wdf.Grn. 42 H1

Cavendish Clo. N18 33 E5
Cavendish Rd.
Cavendish Clo. NW6 48 C7
Cavendish Rd.
Cavendish Clo. NW8 6 F3
Cavendish Clo. NW8 57 G3
Cavendish Ct. EC3 13 E3
Cavendish Cres., Borwd. 22 A4
Cavendish Dr. E11 51 D1
Cavendish Dr., Edg. 29 J6
Cavendish Dr., Esher 98 B5
Cavendish Gdns., Bark. 52 H5
Cavendish Gdns., Ilf. 52 D1
Cavendish Gdns., Rom. 44 E5
Cavendish Ms. N. W1 11 E1
Cavendish Ms. S. W1 11 E2
Cavendish Pl. W1 11 E3
Cavendish Pl. W1 58 B6
Cavendish Rd. E4 34 C7
Cavendish Rd. N4 40 G6
Cavendish Rd. N18 33 E5
Cavendish Rd. NW6 48 B7
Cavendish Rd. SW12 76 B6
Cavendish Rd. SW19 84 G7
Cavendish Rd. W4 74 C1
Cavendish Rd., Barn. 22 J3
Cavendish Rd., Croy. 101 H1
Cavendish Rd., N.Mal. 92 E5
Cavendish Rd., Sutt. 100 F7
Cavendish Sq. W1 11 E3
Cavendish Sq. W1 58 B6
Cavendish St. N1 9 B2
Cavendish St. N1 59 A2
Cavendish Way, W.Wick. 103 B1
Cavenham Gdns., Ilf. 52 G3
Caverleigh Way, Wor.Pk. 99 G1
Caversham Ave. N13 32 G3
Caversham Ave., Sutt. 100 B2
Caversham Flats SW3 18 J5
Caversham Rd. N15 40 J4
Caversham Rd. NW5 49 C6
Caversham Rd., Kings.T. 91 J2
Caversham St. SW3 18 J5
Caversham St. SW3 66 J6
Caverswall St. W12 56 J6
Caveside Clo., Chis. 97 D1
Cawdor Cres. W7 64 D4
Cawnpore St. SE19 86 B5
Caxton Gro. E3 60 A3
Caxton Ms., Brent. 64 G6
The Butts
Caxton Rd. N22 40 F2
Caxton Rd. SW19 84 F5
Caxton Rd. W12 66 A1
Caxton Rd., Sthl. 63 D3
Caxton St. SW1 15 G5
Caxton St. SW1 67 C3
Caxton St. N. E16 60 F7
Victoria Dock Rd.
Caygill Clo., Brom. 96 F4
Cayley Clo., Wall. 101 E7
Brabazon Ave.
Cayton Pl. EC1 9 B4
Cayton Rd., Grnf. 55 B2
Cayton St. EC1 9 B4
Cazenove Rd. E17 42 A1
Cazenove Rd. N16 50 C2
Cearns Ho. E6 61 A1
Cecil Ave., Bark. 52 G7
Cecil Ave., Enf. 25 C4
Cecil Ave., Wem. 46 J5
Cecil Clo., Chess. 98 G4
Cecil Ct. WC2 12 A6
Cecil Ct., Barn. 23 A3
Cecil Pk., Pnr. 36 E4
Cecil Pl., Mitch. 93 J5
Cecil Rd. E11 51 E3
Cecil Rd. E13 60 G1
Cecil Rd. E17 42 A1
Cecil Rd. N10 40 B2
Cecil Rd. N14 32 C1
Cecil Rd. NW9 38 D3
Cecil Rd. NW10 56 E1
Cecil Rd. SW19 84 E7
Cecil Rd. W3 56 C5
Cecil Rd., Croy. 94 E6
Cecil Rd., Enf. 24 J4
Cecil Rd., Har. 37 B3
Cecil Rd., Houns. 72 J2
Cecil Rd., Ilf. 52 E4
Cecil Rd., Rom. 44 D7
Cecil Rd., Sutt. 100 C6
Cecil Way, Brom. 103 G1
Cecile Pk. N8 40 E6
Cecilia Clo. N2 39 F3
Cecilia Rd. E8 50 C5
Cedar Ave., Barn. 23 H7
Cedar Ave., Enf. 25 F2
Cedar Ave., Rom. 44 E5
Cedar Ave., Ruis. 45 C6
Cedar Ave., Sid. 80 A7
Cedar Ave., Twick. 72 H6
Cedar Clo. SE21 85 J1
Cedar Clo. SW15 83 D4
Cedar Clo., Borwd. 22 B4
Cedar Clo., Brom. 104 B3
Cedar Clo., Buck.H. 35 A2
Cedar Clo., Cars. 100 J6
Cedar Clo., E.Mol. 91 B4
Cedar Rd.
Cedar Clo., Rom. 44 J4
Cedar Copse, Brom. 97 C2
Cedar Ct. E8 50 C7
Cedar Ct. N1 49 J7
Essex Rd.
Cedar Ct. SE9 79 B6
Cedar Ct. SW19 84 A3
Cedar Cres., Brom. 104 B3
Cedar Dr. N2 39 H4
Cedar Dr., Pnr. 28 G7
Cedar Gdns., Sutt. 100 F6
Cedar Gro. W5 64 H3
Cedar Gro., Bex. 80 C6
Cedar Gro., Sthl. 54 G5
Cedar Heights, Rich. 82 H1
Cedar Ho., Croy. 103 B6
Cedar Lawn Ave., Barn. 23 B5
Cedar Mt. SE9 88 A1
Cedar Pk. Gdns., Rom. 44 D7
Cedar Ri. N14 24 A7
Cedar Rd. N17 41 C1
Cedar Rd. NW2 47 J4
Cedar Rd., Brom. 96 J2
Cedar Rd., Croy. 102 A2
Cedar Rd., E.Mol. 91 B4
Cedar Rd., Houns. 72 C2
Cedar Rd., Rom. 44 J4
Cedar Rd., Sutt. 100 F6
Cedar Rd., Tedd. 82 D5
Cedar Ter., Rich. 73 H4
Cedar Tree Gro. SE27 85 H5
Cedar Vista, Rich. 73 H1
Kew Rd.
Cedar Way NW1 49 D7
Cedarcroft Rd., Chess. 98 J4
Cedarhurst Dr. SE9 78 J5
Cedarne Rd. SW6 66 E7
Cedars, The, Buck.H. 34 G1
Cedars, The, Tedd. 82 C6
Adelaide Rd.
Cedars Ave. E17 42 A5
Cedars Ave., Mitch. 94 A4
Cedars Clo. NW4 39 A3
Cedars Ct. N9 33 B2
Church St.
Cedars Ms. SW4 76 B4
Cedars Rd.
Cedars Pl. SE7 69 J5
Floyd Rd.
Cedars Rd. E15 51 E6
Cedars Rd. N9 33 D2
Church St.
Cedars Rd. N21 32 H2
Cedars Rd. SW4 76 B3
Cedars Rd. SW13 74 F2
Cedars Rd. W4 65 C6
Cedars Rd., Beck. 95 H2
Cedars Rd., Croy. 101 E3
Cedars Rd., Kings.T. 91 F1
Cedars Rd., Mord. 93 D4
Cedarville Gdns. SW16 85 F6
Cedra Ct. N16 50 D1
Cedric Rd. SE9 88 F3
Celadon Clo., Enf. 25 H3
Celandine Clo. E14 60 A5
Celandine Dr. SE28 71 B1
Celandine Way E15 60 E3
Celbridge Ms. W2 10 B3
Celestial Gdns. SE13 78 D4
Celia Rd. N19 49 C4
Celtic Ave., Brom. 96 E3
Celtic St. E14 60 B5
Cemetery La. SE7 70 B6
Cemetery Rd. E7 51 F4
Cemetery Rd. N17 33 B7
Cemetery Rd. SE2 71 B7
Cenacle Clo. NW3 48 D3
Centaur St. SE1 16 D5
Centaur St. SE1 67 F3
Centaurs Business Pk., Islw. 64 D6
Centenary Rd., Enf. 25 J4
Centenary Trd. Est., Enf. 25 J4
Central Ave. E11 51 D2
Central Ave. N2 39 G2
Central Ave. N9 33 B3
Central Ave. SW11 67 A7
Central Ave., Enf. 25 E2
Central Ave., Hayes 54 A7
Central Ave., Houns. 72 J4
Central Ave., Pnr. 36 F6
Central Ave., Wall. 101 E5
Central Ave., Well. 79 J2
Central Ave., W.Mol. 90 F4
Central Circ. NW4 38 H5
Hendon Way
Central Gdns., Mord. 93 F5
Central Hill SE19 86 A5
Central Mkts. EC1 12 H2
Central Mkts. EC1 58 J5
Central Par., Felt. 72 C7
Sparrow Fm. Dr.
Central Pk. Ave., Dag. 53 H3
Central Pk. Est., Houns. 72 D5
Central Pk. Rd. E6 61 A2
Central Pl. SE25 95 E4
Portland Rd.
Central Rd., Mord. 93 D6
Central Rd., Wem. 46 E5
Central Rd., Wor.Pk. 99 G1
Central Sq. NW11 39 D5
Central Sq., Wem. 46 H5
Station Gro.
Central Sq., W.Mol. 90 F4
Central St. EC1 8 J3
Central St. EC1 58 J3
Central Way SE28 71 A1
Central Way, Cars. 100 H7
Central Way, Felt. 72 A5
Centre, The, Felt. 81 A2
Highfield Rd.
Centre Ave. W3 65 D1
Centre Ave. W10 56 J3
Harrow Rd.
Centre Common Rd., Chis. 88 F6
Centre Rd. E7 51 G2
Centre Rd. E11 51 G2
Centre Rd., Dag. 62 H2
Centre St. E2 59 E2
Centre Way E17 34 C7
Centre Way N9 33 F2
Centreway NW7 30 G7
Centreway, Ilf. 52 F2
Centric Clo. NW1 58 B1
Oval Rd.
Centurion Clo. N7 49 F7
Centurion La. E3 59 J2
Libra Rd.
Centurion Way, Erith 71 G3
Century Rd. E17 41 H3
Cephas Ave. E1 59 F4
Cephas St. E1 59 F4
Ceres Rd. SE18 70 J4
Cerise Rd. SE15 77 D1
Cerne Clo., Hayes 54 C7
Cerne Rd., Mord. 93 F6
Cerney Ms. W2 10 E5
Cervantes Ct. W2 10 B4
Cester St. E2 59 D1
Whiston Rd.
Ceylon Rd. W14 66 A3
Chadacre Ave., Ilf. 43 C3
Chadacre Rd., Epsom 99 H6
Chadbourn St. E14 60 B5
Chadd Dr., Brom. 97 B3
Chadd Grn. E13 60 G1
Chadville Gdns., Rom. 44 D5
Chadway, Dag. 53 C1
Chadwell Ave., Rom. 44 B7
Chadwell Heath La., Rom. 44 B4
Chadwell St. EC1 8 F3
Chadwell St. EC1 58 G3
Chadwick Ave. E4 34 D4
Chadwick Clo., Tedd. 82 D6
Chadwick Rd. E11 42 E7
Chadwick Rd. NW10 56 F1
Chadwick Rd. SE15 77 C2
Chadwick Rd., Ilf. 52 E3
Chadwick St. SW1 15 H6
Chadwick St. SW1 67 D3
Chadwick Way SE28 62 D7
Chadwin Ms. E13 60 H5
Chadwin Rd. E13 60 H5
Chadworth Way, Esher 98 A5
Chaffinch Ave., Croy. 95 G6
Chaffinch Clo. N9 33 G1
Chaffinch Clo., Croy. 95 G5
Chaffinch Clo., Surb. 99 A3
Chaffinch Rd., Beck. 95 H1
Chafford Way, Rom. 44 C4
Chagford St. NW1 6 J6
Chagford St. NW1 57 J4
Chailey Ave., Enf. 25 C2
Chailey Clo., Houns. 72 D1
Springwell Rd.
Chailey St. E5 50 F3
Chalcombe Rd. SE2 71 B3
Chalcot Clo., Sutt. 100 D7
Chalcot Cres. NW1 57 J1
Chalcot Gdns. NW3 48 J6
Chalcot Rd. NW1 49 A7
Chalcot Sq. NW1 49 A7
Chalcott Gdns., Surb. 98 F1
Chalcroft Rd. SE13 78 E5
Chaldon Path, Th.Hth. 94 H4
Chaldon Rd. SW6 66 B7
Chale Rd. SW2 76 E6
Chalet Est. NW7 30 G4
Chalfont Ave., Wem. 47 B6
Chalfont Ct. NW9 38 F3
Chalfont Grn. N9 33 B3
Chalfont Rd. N9 33 B3
Chalfont Rd. SE25 95 C3
Chalfont Rd., Hayes 63 A2
Chalfont Wk., Pnr. 36 C2
Willows Clo.
Chalfont Way W13 64 E3
Chalford Clo., W.Mol. 90 G4
Chalford Rd. SE21 86 A3
Chalford Wk., Wdf.Grn. 43 A1
Chalgrove Ave., Mord. 93 D5
Chalgrove Cres., Ilf. 43 B2
Chalgrove Gdns. N3 39 B3
Chalgrove Rd. E9 50 F6
Morning La.
Chalgrove Rd. N17 41 E1
Chalgrove Rd., Sutt. 100 G7
Chalice Clo., Wall. 101 D6
Lavender Vale
Chalk Cres. SE12 87 H3
Chalk Fm. Rd. NW1 49 A7
Chalk Hill Rd. W6 66 A4
Shortlands
Chalk La., Barn. 23 J3
Chalk Pit Way, Sutt. 100 F5
Chalk Rd. E13 60 H5
Chalkenden Clo. SE20 86 E7
Chalkhill Rd., Wem. 47 A3
Chalklands, The, Wem. 47 C3
The Leadings
Chalkstone Clo., Well. 80 A1
Chalkwell Pk. Ave., Enf. 25 B4
Challice Way SW2 85 F1
Challin St. SE20 95 F1
Challis Rd., Brent. 64 G5
Challoner Clo. N2 39 G2
Challoner Cres. W14 66 C5
Challoner St.
Challoner St. W14 66 C5
Challoners Clo., E.Mol. 91 A4
Chalmers Wk. SE17 20 H6
Chalmers Way, Felt. 72 A5
Chaloner Ct. SE1 17 B3
Chalsey Rd. SE4 77 J4
Chalton Dr. N2 39 F6
Chalton St. NW1 7 G1
Chalton St. NW1 58 C2
Chamber St. E1 13 G5
Chamber St. E1 59 C7
Chamberlain Clo. SE28 70 G3
Broadwater Rd.
Chamberlain Cotts. SE5 77 A1
Camberwell Gro.
Chamberlain Cres., W.Wick. 103 B1
Chamberlain La., Pnr. 36 A4
Chamberlain Pl. E17 41 H3
Chamberlain Rd. N2 39 F2
Chamberlain Rd. N9 33 D3
Chamberlain Rd. W13 64 D2
Midhurst Rd.
Chamberlain St. NW1 48 J7
Regents Pk. Rd.

Chamberlain Wk., Felt.	81 E4	Chapel La., Chig.	35 J3
Burgess Clo.		Chapel La., Pnr.	36 D3
Chamberlain Way, Pnr.	36 B3	Chapel La., Rom.	44 D7
		Chapel Mkt. N1	**8 E1**
Chamberlain Way, Surb.	91 H7	Chapel Mkt. N1	58 G2
		Chapel Path E11	42 H6
Chamberlayne Rd. NW10	56 J1	Chapel Pl. EC2	**9 D4**
		Chapel Pl. N1	**8 F1**
Chambers Gdns. N2	39 G1	White Hart La.	
Chambers La. NW10	47 H7	Chapel Pl. N17	33 C7
Chambers Rd. N7	49 E4	Chapel Pl. W1	**11 D4**
Chambers St. SE16	**17 H4**	Chapel Pl. W1	58 B6
Chambers St. SE16	68 D2	Chapel Rd. SE27	85 H4
Chambord St. E2	**9 G4**	Chapel Rd. W13	64 E1
Chambord St. E2	59 C3	Chapel Rd., Bexh.	80 G4
Champion Cres. SE26	86 H4	Chapel Rd., Houns.	72 H3
Champion Gro. SE5	77 A3	Chapel Rd., Ilf.	52 D3
Champion Hill SE5	77 A3	Chapel Rd., Twick.	73 E7
Champion Hill Est. SE5	77 B3	Orleans Rd.	
		Chapel Side W2	**10 A5**
Champion Pk. SE5	77 A2	Chapel Side W2	57 E7
Champion Rd. SE26	86 H4	Chapel Stones N17	41 C1
Champness Clo. SE27	86 A4	King's Rd.	
Rommany Rd.		Chapel St. E15	51 D7
Champneys Clo., Sutt.	100 C7	Chapel St. NW1	**10 G2**
		Chapel St. NW1	57 H5
Chance St. E1	**9 F5**	Chapel St. SW1	**15 C4**
Chance St. E1	59 C4	Chapel St. SW1	67 A3
Chance St. E2	**9 F5**	Chapel St., Enf.	25 A3
Chance St. E2	59 C4	Chapel Ter., Loug.	27 B4
Chancel St. SE1	**16 G2**	Forest Rd.	
Chancel St. SE1	67 H1	Chapel Vw., S.Croy.	102 F6
Chancellor Gro. SE21	85 J2	Chapel Wk. NW4	38 H4
Chancellor Pas. E14	69 A1	Wellesley Rd.	
South Colonnade		Chapel Wk., Croy.	101 J2
Chancellor Pl. NW9	38 F2	King's Rd.	
Chancellors Rd. W6	65 J5	Chapel Way N7	49 F3
Chancellors St. W6	65 J5	Sussex Way	
Chancelot Rd. SE2	71 B4	Chapel Yd. SW18	75 D5
Chancery La. WC2	**12 E3**	Wandsworth High St.	
Chancery La. WC2	58 G6		
Chancery La., Beck.	96 B2	Chapelmount Rd., Wdf.Grn.	35 C6
Chanctonbury Clo. SE9	88 E3		
		Chaplin Clo. SE1	**16 F3**
Chanctonbury Gdns., Sutt.	100 E7	Chaplin Clo. SE1	67 G2
		Chaplin Rd. E15	60 E1
Chanctonbury Way N12	31 D4	Chaplin Rd. N17	41 C3
		Chaplin Rd. NW2	47 G6
Chandler Ave. E16	60 G5	Chaplin Rd., Dag.	53 E7
Chandler Clo., Hmptn.	90 G1	Chaplin Rd., Wem.	46 F6
Chandler Rd., Loug.	27 E1	Chapman Cres., Har.	37 H5
Chandler St. E1	68 E1	Chapman Rd. E9	50 J6
Wapping La.		Chapman Rd., Belv.	71 G5
Chandlers Ms. E14	69 A2	Chapman Rd., Croy.	101 G1
Chandlers Way SW2	76 G7	Chapman St. E1	59 E7
Chandos Ave. E17	42 A2	Chapman's La. SE2	71 C4
Chandos Ave. N14	32 C3	Chapmans La., Belv.	71 D4
Chandos Ave. N20	31 F1	Chapmans Pk. Ind. Est. NW10	47 F6
Chandos Ave. W5	64 G4		
Chandos Clo., Buck.H.	34 H2	Chapone Pl. W1	**11 H4**
Chandos Cres., Edg.	29 J7	Chapter Clo. W4	65 C3
Chandos Par., Edg.	29 J7	Beaumont Rd.	
Chandos Pl. WC2	**12 A6**	Chapter Ho. Ct. EC4	**12 H4**
Chandos Pl. WC2	58 E7	Chapter Rd. NW2	47 G5
Chandos Rd. E15	51 D5	Chapter Rd. SE17	**20 H4**
Chandos Rd. N2	39 G2	Chapter Rd. SE17	67 H5
Chandos Rd. N17	41 B2	Chapter St. SW1	**19 H2**
Chandos Rd. NW2	47 J5	Chapter St. SW1	67 A4
Chandos Rd., Har.	36 J5	Chapter Way, Hmptn.	81 G4
Chandos Rd., Pnr.	36 D7	Chara Pl. W4	65 D6
Chandos St. W1	**11 E2**	Charcroft Gdns., Enf.	25 G4
Chandos St. W1	58 B5	Chardin Rd. W4	65 E4
Chandos Way NW11	48 E1	Elliott Rd.	
Change All. EC3	**13 C4**	Chardmore Rd. N16	50 D1
Channel Clo., Houns.	72 G1	Chardwell Clo. E6	61 B6
Channel Gate Rd. NW10	56 F3	Northumberland Rd.	
		Charecroft Way W12	66 A2
Old Oak La.		Charfield Ct. W9	**6 A6**
Channelsea Rd. E15	60 D1	Charford Rd. E16	60 G5
Chant Sq. E15	51 D7	Chargeable La. E13	60 F4
Chant St. E15	51 D7	Chargeable St. E16	60 F4
Chantrey Rd. SW9	76 F3	Chargrove Clo. SE16	68 G2
Chantry Clo., Har.	37 J5	Marlow Way	
Chantry Clo., Sid.	89 E5	Charing Clo., Orp.	104 J4
Ellenborough Rd.		Charing Cross WC2	**16 A1**
Chantry La., Brom.	97 A5	Charing Cross Rd. WC2	**11 J4**
Bromley Common		Charing Cross Rd. WC2	58 D6
Chantry Pl., Har.	36 H1		
Chantry Pt. W9	57 C4	Charlbert St. NW8	**6 G1**
Chantry Rd., Chess.	98 J5	Charlbert St. NW8	57 H2
Chantry Rd., Har.	36 H1	Charlbury Ave., Stan.	29 G5
Chantry St. N1	58 H1	Charlbury Gdns., Ilf.	52 E2
Chapel Ct. N2	39 H3	Charlbury Gro. W5	55 F6
Chapel Ct. SE1	**17 B3**	Charldane Rd. SE9	88 E3
		Charlecote Gro. SE26	86 E3
Chapel Fm. Rd. SE9	88 C3	Charlecote Rd., Dag.	53 E3
Chapel Ho. St. E14	69 B5	Charlemont Rd. E6	61 C3

Charles Barry Clo. SW4	76 C3	Charnwood Ave. SW19	93 D2
Charles Burton Ct. E5	50 H5	Charnwood Clo., N.Mal.	92 E4
Ashenden Rd.			
Charles Clo., Sid.	89 B4	Charnwood Dr. E18	42 H3
Charles Cres., Har.	37 A7	Charnwood Gdns. E14	69 A4
Charles Dickens Ho. E2	59 E3	Charnwood Pl. N20	31 F3
		Charnwood Rd. SE25	95 A5
Charles Grinling Wk. SE18	70 D4	Charnwood St. E5	50 E2
		Charrington Rd., Croy.	101 H2
Charles Ho. N17	33 C7		
Charles La. NW8	**6 G1**	Drayton Rd.	
Charles Pl. NW1	**7 G4**	Charrington St. NW1	**7 H1**
Charles Rd. E7	51 J7	Charrington St. NW1	58 D2
Lens Rd.		Charsley Rd. SE6	87 B2
Charles Rd. SW19	93 D1	Chart Clo., Brom.	96 E1
Charles Rd. W13	55 D6	Chart Clo., Croy.	95 F6
Charles Rd., Rom.	53 H6	Stockbury Rd.	
Charles II St. SW1	**15 H1**	Chart St. N1	**9 C3**
Charles II St. SW1	67 D1	Chart St. N1	59 A3
Charles Sevright Dr. NW7	31 A5	Charter Ave., Ilf.	52 G1
		Charter Ct., N.Mal.	92 E3
Charles Sq. N1	**9 C4**	Charter Cres., Houns.	72 E4
Charles St. E16	70 A1	Charter Dr., Bex.	80 E7
Charles St. SW13	74 E2	Charter Rd., Kings.T.	92 B3
Charles St. W1	**15 D1**	Charter Rd., The, Wdf.Grn.	34 E6
Charles St. W1	67 B1		
Charles St., Croy.	101 J3	Charter Sq., Kings.T.	92 B2
Charles St., Enf.	25 C5	Charter Way N3	39 C4
Charles St., Houns.	72 E2	Regents Pk. Rd.	
Charlesfield SE9	87 J3	Charter Way N14	24 C6
Charleston Clo., Felt.	81 A3	Charterhouse Ave., Wem.	46 F4
Charleston St. SE17	**21 A2**		
Charleston St. SE17	67 H4	Charterhouse Bldgs. EC1	**8 H6**
Charleville Circ. SE26	86 D5		
Charleville Rd. W14	66 B5	Charterhouse Ms. EC1	**12 H1**
Charlieville Rd., Erith	71 J7	Charterhouse Sq. EC1	**12 H1**
Northumberland Pk.		Charterhouse Sq. EC1	58 H5
Charlmont Rd. SW17	84 J6	Charterhouse St. EC1	**12 G2**
Charlotte Clo., Bexh.	80 E5	Charterhouse St. EC1	58 G5
Charlotte Despard Ave. SW11	76 A1	Charteris Rd. N4	49 G1
		Charteris Rd. NW6	57 C1
Charlotte Ms. W1	**11 G1**	Charteris Rd., Wdf.Grn.	34 H7
Charlotte Ms. W14	66 B4		
Munden St.		Charters Clo. SE19	86 B5
Charlotte Pl. NW9	38 C5	Chartfield Ave. SW15	74 H5
Uphill Dr.		Chartfield Sq. SW15	75 A5
Charlotte Pl. SW1	**19 F2**	Chartfield Ave.	
Charlotte Pl. W1	**11 G2**	Chartham Gro. SE27	85 G3
Charlotte Rd. EC2	**9 D4**	Royal Circ.	
Charlotte Rd. EC2	59 B4	Chartham Rd. SE25	95 E3
Charlotte Rd. SW13	74 F1	Chartley Ave. NW2	47 E3
Charlotte Rd., Dag.	53 H6	Chartley Ave., Stan.	29 C6
Charlotte Rd., Wall.	101 C6	Charton Clo., Belv.	71 F6
Charlotte Row SW4	76 C3	Chartridge Clo., Barn.	22 G5
North St.		Chartwell Clo. SE9	88 F2
Charlotte Sq., Rich.	73 J6	Chartwell Clo., Croy.	102 A1
Greville Rd.		Tavistock Rd.	
Charlotte St. W1	**11 G1**	Chartwell Clo., Grnf.	54 H1
Charlotte St. W1	58 C5	Chartwell Dr., Orp.	104 G5
Charlotte Ter. N1	58 F1	Chartwell Pl., Sutt.	100 C3
Charlton Ch. La. SE7	69 J5	Chartwell Way SE20	95 E1
Charlton Cres., Bark.	61 J2	Charwood NW16	85 G4
Charlton Dene SE7	69 J7	Chase, The E12	52 H4
Charlton Kings Rd. NW5	49 D5	Chase, The SW4	76 B3
		Chase, The SW16	85 F7
Charlton La. SE7	70 A5	Chase, The SW20	93 H3
Charlton Pk. La. SE7	70 A7	Chase, The, Bexh.	80 H3
Charlton Pk. Rd. SE7	70 A6	Chase, The, Brom.	96 H3
Charlton Pl. N1	**8 G1**	Chase, The, Chig.	35 F4
Charlton Pl. N1	58 H2	Chase, The, Edg.	38 B1
Charlton Rd. N9	33 G1	Chase, The, Pnr.	36 F4
Charlton Rd. NW10	56 E1	Chase, The, Pnr. (Eastcote)	36 C6
Charlton Rd. SE3	69 H7		
Charlton Rd. SE7	69 J6	Chase, The, Rom. (Chadwell Heath)	44 E6
Charlton Rd., Har.	37 G5		
Charlton Rd., Wem.	46 J1	Chase, The, Stan.	29 D5
Charlton Way SE3	78 E1	Chase, The, Sun.	90 B1
Charlwood Clo., Har.	29 B7	Chase, The, Wall.	101 E5
Kelvin Cres.		Chase Ct. Gdns., Enf.	24 J3
Charlwood Pl. SW1	**19 G2**	Chase Gdns. E4	34 A4
Charlwood Pl. SW1	67 C4	Chase Gdns., Twick.	73 A6
Charlwood Rd. SW15	75 A4	Chase Grn., Enf.	24 J3
Charlwood Sq., Mitch.	93 G3	Chase Grn. Ave., Enf.	24 H2
Charlwood St. SW1	**19 G3**	Chase Hill, Enf.	24 J3
Charlwood St. SW1	67 C5	Chase La., Chig.	35 J3
Charlwood Ter. SW15	75 A4	Chase La., Ilf.	43 G5
Cardinal Pl.		Chase Ridings, Enf.	24 G2
Charminster Ave. SW19	93 D2	Chase Rd. N14	24 C5
		Chase Rd. NW10	56 D4
Charminster Ct., Surb.	91 G6	Chase Rd. W3	56 D4
Charminster Rd. SE9	88 A4	Chase Side N14	24 A5
Charminster Rd., Wor.Pk.	100 A1	Chase Side, Enf.	24 J2
		Chase Side Ave. SW20	93 B2
Charmouth Rd., Well.	80 B1	Chase Side Cres., Enf.	24 J1
Charnock Rd. E5	50 E3	Chase Side Pl., Enf.	24 J3
		Chase Side	

Chase Way N14 32 B2
Chasefield Rd. SW17 84 J4
Chaseley Dr. W4 74 B1
 Wellesley Rd.
Chaseley St. E14 59 H6
Chasemore Gdns., 101 H5
 Croy.
 Thorneloe Gdns.
Chaseville Pk. Rd. N21 24 E5
Chasewood Ave., Enf. 24 H2
Chatfield Rd. SW11 75 F3
Chatfield Rd., Croy. 101 H1
Chatham Ave., Brom. 96 F7
Chatham Clo. NW11 39 D5
Chatmore Clo., Sutt. 93 C7
Chatham Pl. E9 50 F6
Chatham Rd. E17 41 H3
Chatham Rd. E18 42 F2
 Grove Hill
Chatham Rd. SW11 75 J6
Chatham Rd., Kings.T. 92 A2
Chatham Rd., Orp. 104 F5
Chatham St. SE17 **21 B1**
Chatham St. SE17 68 A4
Chatsfield Pl. W5 55 H6
Chatsworth Ave. NW4 38 J2
Chatsworth Ave. 93 B1
 SW20
Chatsworth Ave., 87 H5
 Brom.
Chatsworth Ave., Sid. 89 A1
Chatsworth Ave., 46 J5
 Wem.
Chatsworth Clo. NW4 38 J2
Chatsworth Clo., 22 A3
 Borwd.
Chatsworth Clo., 103 F2
 W.Wick.
Chatsworth Ct. W8 66 D4
 Pembroke Rd.
Chatsworth Cres., 73 A4
 Houns.
Chatsworth Dr., Enf. 25 D7
Chatsworth Est. E5 50 G4
 Elderfield Rd.
Chatsworth Gdns. W3 65 B1
Chatsworth Gdns., 45 H1
 Har.
Chatsworth Gdns., 92 F5
 N.Mal.
Chatsworth Pl., Mitch. 93 J3
Chatsworth Pl., Tedd. 82 D4
Chatsworth Ri. W5 55 J5
Chatsworth Rd. E5 50 F3
Chatsworth Rd. E15 51 F5
Chatsworth Rd. NW2 48 A6
Chatsworth Rd. W4 65 C6
Chatsworth Rd. W5 55 J4
Chatsworth Rd., Croy. 102 A4
Chatsworth Rd., Hayes 54 B4
Chatsworth Rd., Sutt. 100 A5
Chatsworth Way SE27 85 H3
Chatterton Rd. N4 49 H3
Chatterton Rd., Brom. 97 A4
Chatto Rd. SW11 75 J5
Chaucer Ave., Hayes 54 A5
Chaucer Ave., Houns. 72 B2
Chaucer Ave., Rich. 74 A3
Chaucer Clo. N11 32 C5
Chaucer Ct. N16 50 B4
Chaucer Dr. SE1 **21 G2**
Chaucer Dr. SE1 68 C4
Chaucer Gdns., Sutt. 100 D3
Chaucer Grn., Croy. 95 F7
Chaucer Rd. E7 51 G6
Chaucer Rd. E11 42 G6
Chaucer Rd. E17 42 C2
Chaucer Rd. SE24 76 G5
Chaucer Rd. W3 65 C1
Chaucer Rd., Sid. 89 C1
Chaucer Rd., Sutt. 100 D4
Chaucer Rd., Well. 71 G3
Chaucer Way SW19 84 G6
Chauncey Clo. N9 33 D3
Chaundrye Clo. SE9 79 B6
Chauntler Rd. E16 60 H7
 Victoria Dock Rd.
Cheam Common Rd., 99 H2
 Wor.Pk.
Cheam Mans., Sutt. 100 B7
Cheam Pk. Way, Sutt. 100 B6
Cheam Rd., Sutt. 100 C6
Cheam St. SE15 77 E3
 Evelina Rd.
Cheapside EC2 **12 J4**
Cheapside EC2 58 J6
Cheddar Waye, Hayes 54 B6
Cheddington Rd. N18 33 B3

Chedworth Clo. E16 60 F6
 Hallsville Rd.
Cheeseman Clo., 81 E6
 Hmptn.
Cheesemans Ter. W14 66 C5
Chelford Rd., Brom. 87 D5
Chelmer Cres., Bark. 62 B2
Chelmer Rd. E9 50 G5
Chelmsford Clo. E6 61 C6
 Guildford Rd.
Chelmsford Clo. W6 66 A6
Chelmsford Gdns., Ilf. 43 B7
Chelmsford Rd. E11 51 D1
Chelmsford Rd. E17 42 A6
Chelmsford Rd. E18 42 F1
Chelmsford Rd. N14 24 C7
Chelmsford Sq. NW10 56 J1
Chelsea Bri. SW1 **19 D5**
Chelsea Bri. SW1 67 B6
Chelsea Bri. SW8 **19 D5**
Chelsea Bri. SW8 67 B6
Chelsea Bri. Rd. SW1 **19 B3**
Chelsea Bri. Rd. SW1 67 A5
Chelsea Cloisters SW3 66 H4
 Lucan Pl.
Chelsea Clo. NW10 56 D1
 Winchelsea Rd.
Chelsea Clo., Edg. 38 A2
Chelsea Clo., Hmptn. 81 J6
Chelsea Embk. SW3 **18 H6**
Chelsea Embk. SW3 66 H6
Chelsea Gdns., Sutt. 100 B4
Chelsea Harbour Dr. 75 F1
 SW10
Chelsea Manor Gdns. **18 H4**
 SW3
Chelsea Manor Gdns. 66 H5
 SW3
Chelsea Manor St. **18 H4**
 SW3
Chelsea Manor St. 66 H5
 SW3
Chelsea Pk. Gdns. **18 E5**
 SW3
Chelsea Pk. Gdns. 66 G6
 SW3
Chelsea Sq. SW3 **18 F3**
Chelsea Sq. SW3 66 G5
Chelsea Wf. SW10 66 G7
 Lots Rd.
Chelsfield Ave. N9 25 G7
Chelsfield Gdns. SE26 86 F3
Chelsfield Grn. N9 25 G7
 Chelsfield Ave.
Chelsham Rd. SW4 76 D3
Chelsham Rd., 102 A6
 S.Croy.
Chelston App., Ruis. 45 A2
Chelston Rd., Ruis. 45 A1
Chelsworth Dr. SE18 70 G6
Cheltenham Ave., 73 D7
 Twick.
Cheltenham Clo. 92 C3
 N.Mal.
 Northcote Rd.
Cheltenham Clo., 45 H6
 Nthlt.
Cheltenham Gdns. E6 61 B2
Cheltenham Gdns., 27 B6
 Loug.
Cheltenham Pl. W3 65 B1
Cheltenham Pl., Har. 37 H4
Cheltenham Rd. E10 42 C6
Cheltenham Rd. SE15 77 F4
Cheltenham Ter. SW3 **19 A3**
Cheltenham Ter. SW3 66 J5
Chelverton Rd. SW15 75 A4
Chelwood Clo. E4 26 B6
Chelwood Gdns., 74 A2
 Rich.
Chelwood Wk. SE4 77 H4
Chenappa Clo. E13 60 G3
Chenduit Way, Stan. 29 C5
Cheney Rd. NW1 **8 A2**
Cheney Rd. NW1 58 E2
Cheney Row E17 41 J1
Cheney St., Pnr. 36 C5
Cheneys Rd. E11 51 E3
Chenies, The, Orp. 97 H6
Chenies Ms. WC1 **7 H6**
Chenies Pl. NW1 **7 J1**
Chenies Pl. NW1 58 D2
Chenies St. WC1 **11 H1**
Chenies St. WC1 58 D5
Cheniston Gdns. W8 **14 A5**
Cheniston Gdns. W8 66 E3
Chepstow Clo. SW15 75 B6
 Lytton Gro.

Chepstow Cres. W11 57 D7
Chepstow Cres., Ilf. 43 H6
Chepstow Gdns., 54 F6
 Sthl.
Chepstow Pl. W2 57 D6
Chepstow Ri., Croy. 102 B3
Chepstow Rd. W2 57 D6
Chepstow Rd. W7 64 D3
Chepstow Rd., Croy. 102 B3
Chepstow Vill. W11 57 C7
Chepstow Way SE15 68 C7
 Exeter Rd.
Chequer St. EC1 **9 A6**
Chequers Clo., Orp. 97 J4
Chequers Gdns. N13 32 H5
Chequers La., Dag. 62 F5
Chequers Rd., Loug. 27 D5
Chequers Way N13 32 H5
Cherbury Clo. SE28 62 D6
Cherbury St. N1 **9 C2**
Cherbury St. N1 59 A2
Cherchefelle Ms. 29 E5
 Stan.
Cherimoya Gdns., 90 H3
 W.Mol.
 Kelvinbrook
Cherington Rd. W7 64 C1
Cheriton Ave., Brom. 96 F5
Cheriton Ave., Ilf. 43 C2
Cheriton Clo. W5 55 F5
Cheriton Dr. SE18 70 G7
Cheriton Sq. SW17 85 A2
Cherry Ave. E17 42 B5
 Eden Rd.
Cherry Clo. SW2 76 G7
 Tulse Hill
Cherry Clo. W5 64 G3
Cherry Clo., Cars. 100 J2
Cherry Clo., Mord. 93 B4
Cherry Cres., Brent. 64 E7
Cherry Gdn. St. SE16 68 E2
Cherry Gdns., Dag. 53 F5
Cherry Gdns., Nthlt. 45 H7
Cherry Garth, Brent. 64 G5
Cherry Gro., Hayes 63 B1
Cherry Hill, Barn. 23 E6
Cherry Hill Gdns., 101 F4
 Croy.
Cherry Laurel Wk. 76 F6
 SW2
 Beechdale Rd.
Cherry Orchard 102 A2
 Gdns., Croy.
 Oval Rd.
Cherry Orchard 90 F3
 Gdns., W.Mol.
Cherry Orchard Rd., 104 B2
 Brom.
Cherry Orchard Rd., 102 A2
 Croy.
Cherry Orchard Rd., 90 F3
 W.Mol.
Cherry Tree Clo., 46 C4
 Wem.
Cherry Tree Ct. NW9 38 C4
Cherry Tree Dr. SW16 85 E3
Cherry Tree Ri., 34 J4
 Buck.H.
Cherry Tree Rd. E15 51 E4
 Wingfield Rd.
Cherry Tree Rd. N2 39 J4
Cherry Tree Wk. EC1 **9 A6**
Cherry Tree Wk., 95 J4
 Beck.
Cherry Tree Wk., 103 F4
 W.Wick.
Cherry Tree Way, 29 E6
 Stan.
Cherry Wk., Brom. 103 G1
Cherry Way, Epsom 99 D6
Cherry Wd. Way W5 56 A5
 Hanger Vale La.
Cherrycot Hill, Orp. 104 G4
Cherrycot Ri., Orp. 104 F4
Cherrycroft Gdns., 28 F7
 Pnr.
 Westfield Pk.
Cherrydown Ave. E4 33 J3
Cherrydown Clo. E4 33 J3
Cherrydown Rd., Sid. 89 D2
Cherrydown Wk. 44 H2
 Rom.
Cherrywood Clo., 83 A7
 Kings.T.
Cherrywood Dr. SW15 75 A5
Cherrywood La., 93 B4
 Mord.

Cherston Gdns., Loug. 27 D4
 Cherston Rd.
Cherston Rd., Loug. 27 D4
Chertsey Dr., Sutt. 100 B2
Chertsey Rd. E11 51 D2
Chertsey Rd., Ilf. 52 G4
Chertsey Rd., Twick. 81 J1
Chertsey St. SW17 85 A5
Chervil Clo., Felt. 81 A3
Chervil Ms. SE28 71 B1
Cherwell Ct., Epsom 99 C4
Cheryls Clo. SW6 75 E1
Cheseman St. SE26 86 E3
Chesfield Rd., 82 H7
 Kings.T.
Chesham Ave., Orp. 97 E6
Chesham Clo. SW1 **15 B6**
Chesham Cres. SE20 95 F2
Chesham Ms. SW1 **15 B5**
Chesham Ms. SW1 67 A3
Chesham Pl. SW1 **15 B6**
Chesham Pl. SW1 67 A3
Chesham Rd. SE20 95 F2
Chesham Rd. SW19 84 G5
Chesham Rd., 92 A2
 Kings.T.
Chesham St. NW10 47 D3
Chesham St. SW1 **15 B6**
Chesham St. SW1 67 A3
Chesham Ter. W13 64 E2
Cheshire Clo. SE4 77 J2
Cheshire Clo., Mitch. 94 E3
Cheshire Gdns., 98 G6
 Chess.
Cheshire Rd. N22 32 F6
Cheshire St. E2 **9 G5**
Cheshire St. E2 59 C4
Chesholm Rd. N16 50 B3
Cheshunt Rd. E7 51 H6
Cheshunt Rd., Belv. 71 G5
Chesilton Rd. SW6 75 C1
Chesley Gdns. E6 61 A2
Chesney Cres., Croy. 103 C7
Chesney St. SW11 76 A1
Chesnut Est. N17 41 C3
 Chesnut Rd.
Chesnut Gro. N17 41 C3
 Chesnut Rd.
Chesnut Rd. N17 41 C3
Chessington Ave. N3 39 B3
Chessington Ave., 71 E7
 Bexh.
Chessington Clo., 99 C6
 Epsom
Chessington Ct., Pnr. 36 F4
Chessington Hall 98 G7
 Gdns., Chess.
Chessington Hill Pk., 99 A5
 Chess.
Chessington Lo. N3 39 C3
Chessington Rd., 99 B6
 Epsom
Chessington Way, 103 B2
 W.Wick.
Chesson Rd. W14 66 C6
Chesswood Way, Pnr. 36 D2
Chester Ave., Rich. 73 J6
Chester Ave., Twick. 81 F1
Chester Clo. SW1 **15 D4**
Chester Clo. SW1 67 B2
Chester Clo. SW13 74 H3
Chester Clo., Loug. 27 F1
Chester Clo., Sutt. 100 D2
 Broomloan La.
Chester Clo. N. NW1 **7 E3**
Chester Clo. S. NW1 **7 E4**
Chester Cotts. SW1 **19 B2**
Chester Ct. NW1 **7 E3**
Chester Ct. SE5 68 A7
Chester Cres. E8 50 C6
 Ridley Rd.
Chester Dr., Har. 36 H2
Chester Gdns. W13 55 E6
Chester Gdns., Enf. 25 E6
Chester Gdns., Mord. 93 F6
Chester Gate NW1 **7 D4**
Chester Gate NW1 58 B3
Chester Grn., Loug. 27 F1
Chester Ms. SW1 **15 D5**
Chester Ms. SW1 67 B3
Chester Path, Loug. 27 F1
Chester Pl. NW1 **7 D3**
Chester Rd. E7 52 A7
Chester Rd. E11 42 H6
Chester Rd. E16 60 E4
Chester Rd. E17 41 G5
Chester Rd. N9 33 E1
Chester Rd. N17 41 A3

Chester Rd. N19 49 B2
Chester Rd. NW1 7 C4
Chester Rd. NW1 58 A3
Chester Rd. SW19 83 J6
Chester Rd., Borwd. 22 C3
Chester Rd., Chig. 35 D2
Chester Rd., Houns. 72 B3
Chester Rd., Ilf. 52 J1
Chester Rd., Loug. 27 E2
Chester Rd., Sid. 79 H5
Chester Row SW1 19 B2
Chester Row SW1 67 A4
Chester Sq. SW1 19 C1
Chester Sq. SW1 67 A4
Chester Sq. Ms. SW1 15 D6
Chester St. E2 9 J5
Chester St. SW1 15 C5
Chester St. SW1 67 A3
Chester Ter. NW1 7 D3
Chester Way SE11 20 F2
Chester Way SE11 67 G4
Chesterfield Dr., Esher 98 D2
Chesterfield Gdns. N4 40 H5
Chesterfield Gdns. 69 D7
SE10
Crooms Hill
Chesterfield Gdns. W1 15 D1
Chesterfield Gdns. W1 67 B1
Chesterfield Gro. SE22 77 C5
Chesterfield Hill W1 15 D1
Chesterfield Hill W1 67 B1
Chesterfield Rd. E10 42 C6
Chesterfield Rd. N3 31 D6
Chesterfield Rd. W4 65 C6
Chesterfield Rd., Barn. 23 A5
Chesterfield Rd., 99 D7
Epsom
Chesterfield St. W1 15 D1
Chesterfield St. W1 67 B1
Chesterfield Wk. SE10 78 D1
Chesterfield Way SE15 68 F7
Chesterfield Way, 63 A2
Hayes
Chesterford Gdns. 48 E4
NW3
Chesterford Ho. SE18 70 A7
Shooter's Hill Rd.
Chesterford Rd. E12 52 C5
Chesters, The, N.Mal. 92 A4
Chesterton Clo. SW18 75 D5
Ericcson Clo.
Chesterton Clo., Grnf. 54 H2
Chesterton Rd. E13 60 G3
Chesterton Rd. W10 57 A5
Chesterton Ter. E13 60 G3
Chesterton Ter., 92 A2
Kings.T.
Chesthunte Rd. N17 40 J1
Chestnut All. SW6 66 C6
Lillie Rd.
Chestnut Ave. E7 51 H4
Chestnut Ave. N8 40 E5
Chestnut Ave. SW14 74 D3
Thornton Rd.
Chestnut Ave., Brent. 64 G4
Chestnut Ave., 35 A3
Buck.H.
Chestnut Ave., E.Mol. 91 C3
Chestnut Ave., Edg. 29 H6
Chestnut Ave., Epsom 99 E4
Chestnut Ave., Esher 91 A7
Chestnut Ave., Hmptn. 81 G7
Chestnut Ave., Tedd. 91 C2
Chestnut Ave., Wem. 46 E5
Chestnut Ave., 103 E5
W.Wick.
Chestnut Ave. N. E17 42 C4
Chestnut Ave. S. E17 42 C4
Chestnut Clo. N14 24 C5
Chestnut Clo. N16 50 A2
Lordship Gro.
Chestnut Clo. SE6 87 C5
Chestnut Clo. SW16 85 G4
Chestnut Clo., Buck.H. 35 A3
Chestnut Clo., Cars. 100 J1
Chestnut Ct. SW6 66 C6
North End Rd.
Chestnut Dr. E11 42 G6
Chestnut Dr., Bexh. 80 D3
Chestnut Dr., Har. 29 C7
Chestnut Dr., Pnr. 36 D6
Chestnut Gro. SE20 86 E7
Hawthorn Gro.
Chestnut Gro. SW12 76 A7
Chestnut Gro. W5 64 G3
Chestnut Gro., Barn. 23 J5
Chestnut Gro., Ilf. 35 H6

Chestnut Gro., Islw. 73 D4
Chestnut Gro., Mitch. 94 D5
Chestnut Gro., N.Mal. 92 D3
Chestnut Gro., 102 E7
S.Croy.
Chestnut Gro., Wem. 46 E5
Chestnut La. N20 31 B1
Chestnut Ri. SE18 70 H5
Chestnut Rd. SE27 85 H3
Chestnut Rd. SW20 93 A2
Chestnut Rd., Kings.T. 82 H7
Chestnut Rd., Twick. 82 B2
Chestnut Wk., 34 G5
Wdf.Grn.
Chestnut Way, Felt. 81 B3
Cheston Ave., Croy. 102 H2
Chettle Clo. SE1 17 B5
Chettle Ct. N8 49 A5
Chetwode Rd. SW17 84 J3
Chetwood Wk. E6 61 B5
Oliver Gdns.
Chetwynd Ave., Barn. 31 J1
Chetwynd Rd. NW5 49 B4
Cheval Pl. SW7 14 H5
Cheval Pl. SW7 66 H3
Cheval St. E14 69 A3
Cheveney Wk., Brom. 96 G3
Marina Clo.
Chevening Rd. NW6 57 A2
Chevening Rd. SE10 69 F5
Chevening Rd. SE19 86 A6
Chevenings, The, Sid. 89 C3
Cheverton Rd. N19 49 D1
Chevet St. E9 50 H5
Kenworthy Rd.
Cheviot Clo., Enf. 25 A2
Cheviot Gdns. NW2 48 A2
Cheviot Gate NW2 48 B2
Cheviot Rd. SE27 85 G5
Cheviot Way, Ilf. 43 H4
Chevron Clo. E16 60 G6
Chevy Rd., Sthl. 63 J2
Chewton Rd. E17 41 H4
Cheyne Ave. E18 42 F3
Cheyne Ave., Twick. 81 F1
Cheyne Wk.
Cheyne Clo. NW4 38 J6
Cheyne Wk.
Cheyne Clo., Brom. 104 B3
Cedar Cres.
Cheyne Ct. SW3 18 J5
Cheyne Gdns. SW3 18 H5
Cheyne Gdns. SW3 66 H6
Cheyne Hill, Surb. 91 J4
Cheyne Ms. SW3 18 H6
Cheyne Path W7 55 C6
Copley Clo.
Cheyne Pl. SW3 18 J5
Cheyne Row SW3 18 G6
Cheyne Row SW3 66 H6
Cheyne Wk. N21 24 H5
Cheyne Wk. NW4 38 J6
Cheyne Wk. SW3 18 H6
Cheyne Wk. SW3 66 H6
Cheyne Wk. SW10 18 E7
Cheyne Wk. SW10 66 G7
Cheyne Wk., Croy. 102 D2
Cheyneys Ave., Edg. 29 G6
Chichele Gdns., Croy. 102 C4
Brownlow Rd.
Chichele Rd. NW2 48 A5
Chicheley Gdns., Har. 28 J7
Chicheley Rd., Har. 28 J7
Chicheley St. SE1 16 D3
Chicheley St. SE1 67 F2
Chichester Clo. E6 61 B6
Chichester Clo. SE3 78 J1
Chichester Clo., 81 F6
Hmptn.
Maple Clo.
Chichester Ct., Stan. 37 H3
Chichester Gdns., Ilf. 43 B7
Chichester Ms. SE27 85 H5
Chichester Rents WC2 12 E3
Chichester Rd. E11 51 E3
Chichester Rd. N9 33 D2
Chichester Rd. NW6 57 D2
Chichester Rd. W2 10 B1
Chichester Rd. W2 57 E5
Chichester Rd., Croy. 102 B3
Chichester St. SW1 19 G4
Chichester St. SW1 67 C5
Chichester Way E14 69 D4
Chichester Way, Felt. 72 C7
Chicksand St. E1 13 G2
Chicksand St. E1 59 C5
Chiddingfold N12 31 D3
Chiddingstone Ave., 71 F7
Bexh.

Chiddingstone St. 75 D2
SW6
Chieveley Rd., Bexh. 80 H4
Chignell Pl. W13 64 D1
The Bdy.
Chigwell Hill E1 59 E7
Pennington St.
Chigwell Hurst Ct., Pnr. 36 D2
Chigwell La., Loug. 27 F4
Chigwell Pk. Dr., Chig. 35 D3
Chigwell Ri., Chig. 35 D2
Chigwell Rd. E18 42 H3
Chigwell Rd., 35 A7
Wdf.Grn.
Chilcot Clo. E14 60 B6
Grundy St.
Childebert Rd. SW17 85 B2
Childeric Rd. SE14 68 H7
Childerley St. SW6 75 A1
Fulham Palace Rd.
Childers, The, 35 C5
Wdf.Grn.
Childers St. SE8 68 H6
Childs La. SE19 86 B6
Westow St.
Child's Pl. SW5 66 D4
Child's St. SW5 66 D4
Child's Wk. SW5 66 D4
Child's Pl.
Childs Way NW11 39 C5
Chilham Clo., Bex. 80 F7
Chilham Clo., Grnf. 55 D2
Chilham Rd. SE9 88 B4
Chilham Way, Brom. 96 G7
Chillerton Rd. SW17 85 A5
Chillingworth Gdns., 82 C3
Twick.
Tower Rd.
Chillingworth Rd. N7 49 G5
Liverpool Rd.
Chilmark Gdns., 92 F7
N.Mal.
Chilmark Rd. SW16 94 D2
Chiltern Ave., Twick. 81 G1
Chiltern Clo., Croy. 102 B3
Cotswold Way
Chiltern Dene, Enf. 24 F4
Chiltern Dr., Surb. 92 A6
Chiltern Gdns. NW2 48 A3
Chiltern Gdns., Brom. 96 F4
Chiltern Rd. E3 60 A4
Knapp Rd.
Chiltern Rd., Ilf. 43 H4
Chiltern Rd., Pnr. 36 C5
Chiltern St. W1 11 B1
Chiltern St. W1 58 A5
Chiltern Way, 34 G3
Wdf.Grn.
Chilthorne Clo. SE6 77 J7
Ravensbourne
Pk. Cres.
Chilton Ave. W5 64 G4
Chilton Gro. SE8 68 G4
Chilton Rd., Edg. 30 A6
Manor Pk. Cres.
Chilton Rd., Rich. 74 A3
Chilton St. E2 9 G5
Chilton St. E2 59 C4
Chiltonian Ind. Est. 78 F6
SE12
Chiltons, The E18 42 G2
Grove Hill
Chilver St. SE10 69 F5
Chilwell Gdns., Wat. 28 C4
Chilworth Ct. SW19 84 A1
Chilworth Gdns., 100 F3
Sutt.
Chilworth Ms. W2 10 E4
Chilworth Ms. W2 57 G6
Chilworth St. W2 10 D4
Chilworth St. W2 57 F6
Chimes Ave. N13 32 G5
Chinbrook Cres. SE12 87 H3
Chinbrook Rd.
Chinbrook Est. SE9 88 A3
Chinbrook Rd. SE12 87 H3
Chinchilla Dr., Houns. 72 C2
Chine, The N10 40 C4
Chine, The N21 24 H6
Chine, The, Wem. 46 E5
Ching Ct. WC2 12 A4
Chingdale Rd. E4 34 E3
Chingford Ave. E4 34 A3
Chingford Hall Est. E4 33 J6
Chingford Ind. Est. E4 33 H5
Chingford La., 34 E4
Wdf.Grn.

Chingford Mt. Rd. E4 34 A4
Chingford Rd. E4 34 A6
Chingford Rd. E17 42 B1
Chingley Clo., Brom. 87 E6
Chinnor Cres., Grnf. 54 H2
Chip St. SW4 76 D3
Stonhouse St.
Chipka St. E14 69 C2
Chipley St. SE14 68 H6
Nynehead St.
Chipmunk Gro., Nthlt. 54 E3
Argus Way
Chippendale St. E5 50 G3
Chippenham Ave., 47 B5
Wem.
Chippenham Gdns. 57 D3
NW6
Chippenham Ms. W9 57 D4
Chippenham Rd. W9 57 D4
Chipping Clo., Barn. 23 B3
St. Albans Rd.
Chipstead Ave., 94 H4
Th.Hth.
Chipstead Clo. SE19 86 C7
Chipstead Gdns. NW2 47 H2
Chipstead St. SW6 75 D1
Chirk Clo., Hayes 54 E4
Braunston Dr.
Chisenhale Rd. E3 59 H2
Chisholm Rd., Croy. 102 B2
Chisholm Rd., Rich. 73 J6
Chisledon Wk. E9 50 J6
Trowbridge Est.
Chislehurst Ave. N12 31 F7
Chislehurst Rd., 97 A2
Brom.
Chislehurst Rd., Chis. 97 C1
Chislehurst Rd., Orp. 97 H6
Chislehurst Rd., Rich. 73 H5
Chislehurst Rd., Sid. 89 A5
Chislet Clo., Beck. 87 A7
Abbey La.
Chisley Rd. N15 41 B6
Chiswell Sq. SE3 78 H2
Brook La.
Chiswell St. EC1 13 B1
Chiswell St. EC1 59 A5
Chiswick Bri. SW14 74 C2
Chiswick Bri. W4 74 C2
Chiswick Clo., Croy. 101 F3
Chiswick Common 65 D4
Rd. W4
Chiswick Ct., Pnr. 36 F3
Chiswick Gdns. W4 74 C1
Hartington Rd.
Chiswick High Rd. W4 65 A5
Chiswick High Rd., 65 A5
Brent.
Chiswick Ho. Grds. W4 65 D6
Chiswick La. W4 65 E5
Chiswick La. S. W4 65 F5
Chiswick Mall W4 65 F6
Chiswick Mall W6 65 G5
Chiswick Quay W4 74 C1
Chiswick Rd. N9 33 D2
Chiswick Rd. W4 65 C4
Chiswick Sq. W4 65 E6
Hogarth Roundabout
Chiswick Staithe W4 74 C1
Chiswick Vill. W4 65 B6
Chiswick Wf. W4 65 F6
Chitty St. W1 11 G1
Chitty St. W1 58 C5
Chitty's La., Dag. 53 D2
Chivalry Rd. SW11 75 H5
Chivers Rd. E4 34 B4
Choats Manor Way, 62 B4
Bark.
Renwick Rd.
Choats Rd., Dag. 62 E3
Chobham Gdns. SW19 84 A2
Chobham Rd. E15 51 D5
Cholmeley Cres. N6 40 B7
Cholmeley Pk. N6 49 B1
Cholmley Gdns. NW6 48 D6
Fortune Grn. Rd.
Cholmley Rd., T.Ditt. 91 E6
Cholmondeley Ave. 56 G2
NW10
Cholmondeley Wk., 73 F5
Rich.
Choppins Ct. E1 68 E1
Wapping La.
Chopwell Clo. E15 51 D7
Bryant St.
Chorleywood Cres., 97 J2
Orp.
Choumert Gro. SE15 77 D2

Choumert Rd. SE15 77 C3
Choumert Sq. SE15 77 D2
Chrisp St. E14 60 B5
Christ Ch. Rd. SW14 74 B5
Christ Ch. Rd., Beck. 96 A2
  Fairfield Rd.
Christ Ch., Surb. 91 J7
Christchurch Ave. N12 31 F6
Christchurch Ave. 57 A1
  NW6
Christchurch Ave., Har. 37 C4
Christchurch Ave., 82 D5
  Tedd.
Christchurch Ave., 46 H6
  Wem.
Christchurch Clo. 84 G7
  SW19
Christchurch Gdns. 37 D4
  Har.
Christchurch Grn., 46 H6
  Wem.
Christchurch Hill NW3 48 G3
Christchurch Ind. 37 C4
  Cen., Har.
Christchurch La., 23 B2
  Barn.
Christchurch Pk., Sutt.100 F7
Christchurch Pas. 48 G3
  NW3
  Christchurch Hill
Christchurch Pas., 23 B3
  Barn.
  Christchurch La.
Christchurch Rd. N8 40 E6
Christchurch Rd. SW2 85 F1
Christchurch Rd. 93 G1
  SW19
Christchurch Rd., Ilf. 52 E1
Christchurch Rd., Sid. 88 J4
Christchurch Sq. E9 59 F1
  Victoria Pk. Rd.
Christchurch St. SW3 18 J5
Christchurch St. SW3 66 J6
Christchurch Ter. SW3 18 J5
Christchurch Way 69 E5
  SE10
Christian Ct. SE16 68 J1
Christian Flds. SW16 85 G7
Christian St. E1 13 J3
Christian St. E1 59 D6
Christie Dr., Croy. 95 D5
Christie Gdns., Rom. 44 B6
Christie Rd. E9 50 H6
Christina Clo. N4 49 H1
  Adolphus Rd.
Christina Sq. N4 49 H1
  Adolphus Rd.
Christina St. EC2 9 D5
Christopher Ave. W7 64 D3
Christopher Clo. SE16 68 G2
Christopher Clo., Sid. 79 J5
Christopher Gdns., 53 D5
  Dag.
  Wren Rd.
Christopher Pl. NW1 7 J4
Christopher Rd., Sthl. 63 B4
Christopher St. EC2 9 C6
Christopher St. EC2 59 A4
Christopher's Ms. W11 66 B1
  Penzance St.
Chryssell Rd. SW9 67 G7
Chubworthy St. SE14 68 H6
Chudleigh Cres., Ilf. 52 H4
Chudleigh Gdns., 100 F3
  Sutt.
Chudleigh Rd. NW6 48 A7
Chudleigh Rd. SE4 77 J5
Chudleigh Rd., Twick. 73 B6
Chudleigh St. E1 59 G6
Chudleigh Way, Ruis. 45 A1
Chulsa Rd. SE26 86 E5
Chumleigh St. SE5 21 D5
Chumleigh St. SE5 68 B6
Chumleigh Wk., Surb. 91 J4
Church All., Croy. 94 H7
  Handcroft Rd.
Church App. SE21 86 A3
Church Ave. E4 34 D6
Church Ave. NW1 49 B6
  Kentish Town Rd.
Church Ave. SW14 74 D3
Church Ave., Beck. 96 A1
Church Ave., Nthlt. 45 F7
Church Ave., Pnr. 36 E6
Church Ave., Sid. 89 A5
Church Ave., Sthl. 63 E3
Church Clo. N20 31 H3
Church Clo. W8 14 A3

Church Clo., Edg. 30 C5
Church Clo., Loug. 27 C2
Church Ct., Rich. 73 G5
  George St.
Church Cres. E9 50 G7
Church Cres. N3 39 C1
Church Cres. N10 40 B4
Church Cres. N20 31 H3
Church Dr. NW9 47 D1
Church Dr., Har. 36 F6
Church Dr., W.Wick. 103 E3
Church Elm La., Dag. 53 G6
Church End E17 42 B4
Church End NW4 38 H3
Church Fm. La., Sutt. 100 B6
Church Gdns. W5 64 G2
Church Gdns., Wem. 46 D4
Church Gate W6 75 B3
Church Gro. SE13 78 B4
Church Gro., Kings.T. 91 F1
Church Hill E17 42 A4
Church Hill N21 24 F7
Church Hill SE18 70 C3
Church Hill SW19 84 C5
Church Hill, Cars. 100 J5
Church Hill, Har. 46 B1
Church Hill, Loug. 27 C3
Church Hill Rd. E17 42 B4
Church Hill Rd., Barn. 23 H6
Church Hill Rd., Surb. 91 H5
Church Hill Rd., Sutt. 100 A4
Church Hyde SE18 70 H6
  Old Mill Rd.
Church La. E11 51 E1
Church La. E17 42 B4
Church La. N2 39 F3
Church La. N8 40 F4
Church La. N9 33 D2
Church La. N17 41 B1
Church La. NW9 38 C6
Church La. SW17 85 B5
Church La. SW19 93 C1
Church La. W5 64 F2
Church La., Brom. 104 B1
Church La., Chess. 98 J6
Church La., Chis. 97 F1
Church La., Dag. 53 H6
Church La., Enf. 25 A3
Church La., Har. 37 C1
Church La., Loug. 27 C3
Church La., Pnr. 36 E3
Church La., Rich. 82 H1
  Petersham Rd.
Church La., Tedd. 82 C5
Church La., T.Ditt. 91 C6
Church La., Twick. 82 D1
Church La., Wall. 101 D3
Church Manor Est. 67 G7
  SW9
  Vassall Rd.
Church Manorway SE2 71 A5
Church Meadow, 98 F2
  Surb.
Church Mt. N2 39 G5
Church Pas., Barn. 23 C4
  Wood St.
Church Pas., Surb. 91 H5
  Adelaide Rd.
Church Path E11 42 G5
Church Path E17 42 B4
  St. Mary Rd.
Church Path N5 49 H5
Church Path N12 31 F5
Church Path N17 33 B7
  White Hart La.
Church Path N20 31 F4
Church Path NW10 47 E7
Church Path SW14 74 D3
  North Worple Way
Church Path SW19 93 C2
Church Path W4 65 C3
Church Path W7 64 B1
  Station Rd.
Church Path, Croy. 101 J2
  Keeley Rd.
Church Path, Mitch. 93 H3
Church Path, Sthl. 63 F3
Church Pl. SW1 11 G6
Church Pl. W5 64 G2
Church Pl., Mitch. 93 H3
Church Pl., Twick. 82 E1
  Church St.
Church Ri. SE23 86 G2
Church Ri., Chess. 98 J6
Church Rd. E10 51 A1
Church Rd. E12 52 B5
Church Rd. E17 41 H2
Church Rd. N6 40 A6

Church Rd. N17 41 B1
Church Rd. NW4 38 H4
Church Rd. NW10 47 E7
Church Rd. SE19 95 B1
Church Rd. SW13 74 F2
Church Rd. SW19 84 B5
  (Wimbledon)
Church Rd. W3 65 C1
Church Rd. W7 55 A7
Church Rd., Bark. 52 F6
Church Rd., Bexh. 80 F3
Church Rd., Brom. 96 G2
Church Rd., Brom. 96 E3
  (Shortlands)
Church Rd., Buck.H. 34 H1
Church Rd., Croy. 101 H2
Church Rd., E.Mol. 91 A4
Church Rd., Enf. 25 F6
Church Rd., Epsom 99 D7
  (West Ewell)
Church Rd., Erith 71 J5
Church Rd., Esher 98 C6
Church Rd., Felt. 81 D5
Church Rd., Houns. 63 B5
  (Cranford)
Church Rd., Houns. 63 G7
  (Heston)
Church Rd., Ilf. 43 H6
Church Rd., Islw. 73 A1
Church Rd., Kes. 104 A7
Church Rd., Kings.T. 91 F2
Church Rd., Loug. 26 G3
Church Rd., Mitch. 93 G3
Church Rd., Nthlt. 54 D2
Church Rd., Orp. 104 F5
  (Farnborough)
Church Rd., Rich. 73 H4
Church Rd. (Ham), 82 G4
  Rich.
Church Rd., Sid. 89 A4
Church Rd., Sthl. 63 F3
Church Rd., Stan. 29 E5
Church Rd., Surb. 98 F1
Church Rd., Sutt. 100 B6
Church Rd., Tedd. 82 B4
Church Rd., Wall. 101 C3
Church Rd., Well. 80 B2
Church Rd., Wor.Pk. 99 E2
Church Rd. Merton 93 G1
  SW19
Church Row NW3 48 F4
Church Row, Chis. 97 F1
Church St. E15 60 E2
Church St. E16 70 E1
Church St. N9 33 C2
Church St. NW8 10 F1
Church St. NW8 57 G5
Church St. W2 10 F1
Church St. W2 57 G5
Church St. W4 65 F6
Church St., Croy. 101 H3
Church St., Dag. 53 H6
Church St., Enf. 24 J3
Church St., Hmptn. 90 J2
Church St., Islw. 73 A3
Church St., Kings.T. 91 G2
Church St., Sun. 90 A3
Church St., Sutt. 100 E5
  High St.
Church St., Twick. 82 D1
Church St. Est. NW8 6 F6
Church St. Est. NW8 57 G4
Church St. N. E15 60 E1
Church St. Pas. E15 60 E1
  Church St.
Church Stretton Rd., 72 J5
  Houns.
Church Ter. NW4 38 H3
Church Ter. SE13 78 E3
Church Ter. SW8 76 D2
Church Ter., Rich. 73 G5
Church Vale N2 39 J3
Church Vale SE23 86 F2
Church Wk. N6 49 A3
  Swains La.
Church Wk. N16 50 A4
Church Wk. NW2 48 C3
Church Wk. NW4 38 J3
Church Wk. NW9 47 D2
Church Wk. SW13 74 G1
Church Wk. SW15 74 H5
  St. Margarets Cres.
Church Wk. SW16 94 C2
Church Wk. SW20 92 J3
Church Wk., Brent. 64 F6
Church Wk., Rich. 73 G5
  Red Lion St.
Church Wk., T.Ditt. 91 C6

Church Way N20 31 G3
Church Way, Barn. 23 J4
  Mount Pleasant
Church Way, Edg. 30 A6
  Station Rd.
Churchbury Clo., Enf. 25 B2
Churchbury La., Enf. 25 A3
Churchbury Rd. SE9 79 A1
Churchbury Rd., Enf. 25 A2
Churchcroft Clo. SW12 76 A7
  Endlesham Rd.
Churchdown, Brom. 87 E4
Churchfield Ave. N12 31 F6
Churchfield Clo., Har. 36 J4
Churchfield Rd. W3 65 C1
Churchfield Rd. W7 64 B2
Churchfield Rd. W13 64 E1
Churchfield Rd., Well. 80 A3
Churchfields E18 42 G1
Churchfields SE10 69 C6
  Roan St.
Churchfields, Loug. 27 B4
Churchfields, W.Mol. 90 G3
Churchfields Ave., 81 F3
  Felt.
Churchfields Rd., 95 G2
  Beck.
Churchill Ave., Har. 37 E6
Churchill Ct. W5 55 J4
Churchill Ct., Nthlt. 45 G5
Churchill Gdns. W3 56 A6
Churchill Gdns. Est. 19 F4
  SW1
Churchill Gdns. Est. 67 C5
  SW1
Churchill Gdns. Rd. 19 E4
  SW1
Churchill Gdns. Rd. 67 B5
  SW1
Churchill Ms. 34 F6
  Wdf.Grn.
  High Rd.
Churchill Pl. E14 69 B1
Churchill Pl., Har. 37 B4
  Sandridge Clo.
Churchill Rd. E16 60 J6
Churchill Rd. NW2 47 H6
Churchill Rd. NW5 49 B4
Churchill Rd., Edg. 29 J6
Churchill Rd., S.Croy. 101 J7
Churchill Ter. E4 34 A4
Churchill Wk. E9 50 F5
Churchill Way, Brom. 96 G3
  Ethelbert Rd.
Churchill Way, Sun. 81 A5
Churchley Rd. SE26 86 E4
Churchmead Clo., 23 H6
  Barn.
Churchmead Rd. 47 G6
  NW10
Churchmore Rd. SW16 94 C1
Churchview Rd., 82 A1
  Twick.
Churchway NW1 7 J3
Churchway NW1 58 D3
Churchwell Path E9 50 F6
  Morning La.
Churchyard Row SE11 20 H1
Churston Ave. E13 60 H1
Churston Clo. SW2 85 H1
  Tulse Hill
Churston Dr., Mord. 93 A5
Churston Gdns. N11 32 C6
Churton Pl. SW1 19 G2
Churton St. SW1 19 G2
Churton St. SW1 67 C4
Chusan Pl. E14 59 J6
  Commercial Rd.
Chyngton Clo., Sid. 88 J3
Cibber Rd. SE23 86 G2
Cicada Rd. SW18 75 F6
Cicely Rd. SE15 77 D1
Cinderford Way, 87 E4
  Brom.
Cinema Par. W5 55 J4
  Ashbourne Rd.
Cinnamon Row SW11 75 F3
Cinnamon St. E1 68 E1
Cintra Pk. SE19 86 C7
Circle, The NW2 47 E3
Circle, The NW7 30 D5
Circle Gdns. SW19 93 D2
Circuits, The, Pnr. 36 C4
Circular Rd. N17 41 C3
Circular Way SE18 70 C6
Circus Ms. W1 10 J1
Circus Pl. EC2 13 C2
Circus Rd. NW8 6 E3

Circus Rd. NW8	57	G3
Circus St. SE10	69	C7
Cirencester St. W2	**10**	**A1**
Cirencester St. W2	57	E5
Cissbury Ring N. N12	31	C5
Cissbury Ring S. N12	31	C5
Cissbury Rd. N15	41	A5
Citadel Pl. SE11	**20**	**C3**
Citizen Rd. N7	49	G3
Citron Ter. SE15	77	E3
Nunhead La.		
City Gdn. Row N1	**8**	**H2**
City Gdn. Row N1	58	H2
City Rd. EC1	**8**	**G2**
City Rd. EC1	58	H2
Civic Way, Ilf.	43	F4
Civic Way, Ruis.	45	D5
Clabon Ms. SW1	**14**	**J6**
Clabon Ms. SW1	66	J3
Clack St. SE16	68	F2
Clacton Rd. E6	61	A3
Clacton Rd. E17	41	H6
Clacton Rd. N17	41	C2
Sperling Rd.		
Claigmar Gdns. N3	39	E1
Claire Ct. N12	31	F3
Claire Ct., Pnr.	28	F7
Westfield Pk.		
Claire Ct., Wat.	29	A1
Claire Pl. E14	69	A3
Clairvale Rd., Houns.	72	D1
Clairview Rd. SW16	85	B5
Clairville Gdns. W7	64	B1
Clairville Pt. SE23	86	G3
Clamp Hill, Stan.	29	A4
Clancarty Rd. SW6	75	D2
Clandon Clo. W3	65	B2
Avenue Rd.		
Clandon Clo., Epsom	99	F6
Clandon Gdns. N3	39	D3
Clandon Rd., Ilf.	52	H2
Clandon St. SE8	78	A2
Clanfield Way SE15	**21**	**E7**
Clanricarde Gdns. W2	57	D7
Clap La., Dag.	53	H3
Clapham Common N.	75	J4
Side SW4		
Clapham Common S.	76	B6
Side SW4		
Clapham Common	75	J4
W. Side SW4		
Clapham Cres. SW4	76	D4
Clapham High St. SW4	76	D4
Clapham Junct. Est.	75	H4
SW11		
Clapham Manor St.	76	C3
SW4		
Clapham Pk. Est. SW4	76	D6
Clapham Pk. Rd. SW4	76	D4
Clapham Rd. SW9	76	E3
Clapham Rd. Est. SW4	76	D3
Claps Gate La. E6	61	E4
Royal Docks Rd.		
Claps Gate La., Bark.	61	E4
Royal Docks Rd.		
Clapton Common E5	41	C7
Clapton Pas. E5	50	F5
Lower Clapton Rd.		
Clapton Sq. E5	50	F5
Clapton Ter. N16	50	D1
Oldhill St.		
Clapton Way E5	50	D4
Clara Pl. SE18	70	D4
Clare Clo. N2	39	F3
Thomas More Way		
Clare Cor. SE9	79	E7
Clare Gdns. E7	51	G4
Clare Gdns. W11	57	B6
Westbourne Pk. Rd.		
Clare Gdns., Bark.	52	J6
Clare Gdns., Stan.	29	F5
Clare La. N1	49	J7
Clare Lawn Ave. SW14	74	D5
Clare Mkt. WC2	**12**	**C4**
Clare Ms. SW6	66	E7
Waterford Rd.		
Clare Pl. SW15	74	F6
Minstead Gdns.		
Clare Rd. E11	42	D6
Clare Rd. NW10	47	G7
Clare Rd. SE14	77	J2
Clare Rd., Grnf.	46	A6
Clare Rd., Houns.	72	F3
Clare St. E2	59	E2
Clare Way, Bexh.	80	E1
Claredale St. E2	**9**	**J2**
Claredale St. E2	59	E2
Claremont Ave., Har.	37	H5

Claremont Ave.,	92	H5
N.Mal.		
Claremont Ave., Sun.	90	B1
Claremont Clo. E16	70	D1
Claremont Clo. N1	**8**	**E2**
Claremont Clo. N1	58	G2
Claremont Clo. SW2	85	F1
Garden La.		
Claremont Clo., Orp.	104	D4
Hilda Vale Rd.		
Claremont Gdns., Ilf.	52	H2
Claremont Gdns.,	91	H5
Surb.		
Claremont Gro. W4	65	E7
Edensor Gdns.		
Claremont Gro.,	34	J6
Wdf.Grn.		
Claremont Pk. N3	39	B1
Claremont Rd. E7	51	H5
Claremont Rd. E11	51	D3
Claremont Rd. E17	41	H2
Claremont Rd. N6	40	B7
Claremont Rd. NW2	38	J7
Claremont Rd. W9	57	C2
Claremont Rd. W13	55	D5
Claremont Rd., Brom.	97	B4
Claremont Rd., Croy.	102	D1
Claremont Rd., Esher	98	B7
Claremont Rd., Har.	37	B2
Claremont Rd., Surb.	91	H6
Claremont Rd., Tedd.	82	C5
Claremont Rd., Twick.	73	E6
Claremont Sq. N1	**8**	**E2**
Claremont Sq. N1	58	G2
Claremont St. E16	70	D1
Claremont St. N18	33	D6
Claremont St. SE10	69	B6
Claremont Way NW2	47	J1
Clarence Ave. SW4	76	D7
Clarence Ave., Brom.	97	B4
Clarence Ave., Ilf.	43	D6
Clarence Ave., N.Mal.	92	B2
Clarence Cres. SW4	76	D6
Clarence Cres., Sid.	89	B3
Clarence Gdns. NW1	**7**	**E4**
Clarence Gdns. NW1	58	B3
Clarence La. SW15	74	E6
Clarence Ms. E5	50	E5
Clarence Pas. NW1	**8**	**A2**
Clarence Pl. E5	50	E5
Clarence Rd. E5	50	E4
Clarence Rd. E12	52	A5
Clarence Rd. E16	60	E4
Clarence Rd. E17	41	G2
Clarence Rd. N15	40	J5
Clarence Rd. N22	32	E7
Clarence Rd. NW6	48	C7
Clarence Rd. SE9	88	B2
Clarence Rd. SW19	84	E6
Clarence Rd. W4	65	A5
Clarence Rd., Bexh.	80	E4
Clarence Rd., Brom.	97	A3
Clarence Rd., Croy.	95	A7
Clarence Rd., Enf.	25	E5
Clarence Rd., Rich.	73	J1
Clarence Rd., Sid.	89	B3
Clarence Rd., Sutt.	100	E4
Clarence Rd., Tedd.	82	C6
Clarence Rd., Wall.	101	B5
Clarence St.,	91	H2
Kings.T.		
Clarence St., Rich.	73	H4
Clarence St., Sthl.	63	D3
Clarence Ter. NW1	**7**	**A5**
Clarence Ter., Houns.	72	H4
Clarence Wk. SW4	76	E2
Clarence Way NW1	49	B7
Clarence Way Est.	49	B7
NW1		
Clarendon Clo. W2	**10**	**G5**
Clarendon Cres. W11	57	B7
Clarendon Rd.		
Clarendon Cres.,	82	A3
Twick.		
Clarendon Cross W11	57	B7
Portland Rd.		
Clarendon Dr. SW15	74	J3
Clarendon Gdns.	38	G3
NW4		
Clarendon Gdns. W9	**6**	**D6**
Clarendon Gdns. W9	57	F4
Clarendon Gdns., Ilf.	52	C1
Clarendon Gdns.,	46	G3
Wem.		
Clarendon Gro. NW1	**7**	**H3**
Clarendon Gro.,	93	J3
Mitch.		
Clarendon Ms. W2	**10**	**G5**

Clarendon Ms.,	22	A3
Borwd.		
Clarendon Rd.		
Clarendon Pl. W2	**10**	**G5**
Clarendon Pl. W2	57	H7
Clarendon Ri. SE13	78	C3
Clarendon Rd. E11	51	D1
Clarendon Rd. E17	42	B6
Clarendon Rd. E18	42	G3
Clarendon Rd. N8	40	F3
Clarendon Rd. N15	40	H4
Clarendon Rd. N18	33	D6
Clarendon Rd. N22	40	F2
Clarendon Rd. SW19	84	H7
Clarendon Rd. W5	55	H4
Clarendon Rd. W11	57	B7
Clarendon Rd.,	22	A3
Borwd.		
Clarendon Rd., Croy.	101	H2
Clarendon Rd., Har.	37	B6
Clarendon Rd., Wall.	101	C6
Clarendon St. SW1	**19**	**E3**
Clarendon St. SW1	67	B5
Clarendon Ter. W9	**6**	**D5**
Clarendon Wk. W11	57	B6
Lancaster Rd.		
Clarendon Way N21	24	J6
Clarendon Way, Chis.	97	J3
Clarens St. SE6	86	J2
Claret Gdns. SE25	95	B4
Clareville Gro. SW7	**18**	**D2**
Clareville Gro. SW7	66	F4
Clareville Rd., Orp.	104	F2
Clareville St. SW7	**18**	**D2**
Clareville St. SW7	66	F4
Clarewood Wk. SW9	76	G4
Somerleyton Rd.		
Clarges Ms. W1	**15**	**D1**
Clarges Ms. W1	67	B1
Clarges St. W1	**15**	**E1**
Clarges St. W1	67	B1
Claribel Rd. SW9	76	H2
Claridge Rd., Dag.	53	D1
Clarina Rd. SE20	86	G7
Evelina Rd.		
Clarissa Rd., Rom.	44	D7
Clarissa St. E8	59	C1
Clark St. E1	59	E5
Clark Way, Houns.	63	D7
Clarke Path N16	50	D1
Braydon Rd.		
Clarkes Ave., Wor.Pk.	100	A1
Clarke's Ms. W1	**11**	**C1**
Clarks Pl. EC2	59	B6
Clarks Rd., Ilf.	52	G2
Clarkson Rd. E16	60	F6
Clarkson St. E2	59	E3
Clarksons, The, Bark.	61	F2
Claude Rd. E10	51	C2
Claude Rd. E13	60	H1
Claude Rd. SE15	77	E2
Claude St. E14	69	A4
Claudia Jones Way	76	E6
SW2		
Claudia Pl. SW19	84	B1
Claughton Rd. E13	60	J2
Clauson Ave., Nthlt.	45	H5
Clave St. E1	68	E1
Cinnamon St.		
Clavell St. SE10	69	C6
Claverdale Rd. SW2	76	F7
Clavering Ave. SW13	65	H6
Clavering Clo., Twick.	92	B2
Clavering Rd. E12	52	A1
Claverings Ind. Est. N9	33	G2
Claverley Gro. N3	39	E1
Claverley Vill. N3	31	E7
Claverley Gro.		
Claverton St. SW1	**19**	**G4**
Claverton St. SW1	67	C5
Claxton Gro. W6	66	A5
Clay Ave., Mitch.	94	B2
Clay La., Edg.	30	B2
Clay Rd., The, Loug.	27	A1
Clay St. W1	**11**	**A2**
Claybank Gro. SE13	78	B3
Algernon Rd.		
Claybourne Ms. SE19	86	B7
Church Rd.		
Claybridge Rd. SE12	87	J4
Claybrook Clo. N2	39	G3
Long La.		
Claybrook Rd. W6	66	A6
Claybury Bdy., Ilf.	43	B3
Claybury Rd.,	35	B7
Wdf.Grn.		
Claydon Dr., Croy.	101	E4

Clayfarm Rd. SE9	88	F2
Claygate Cres., Croy.	103	C6
Claygate La., Esher	98	D3
Claygate La., T.Ditt.	98	D1
Claygate Lo. Clo.,	98	B7
Esher		
Claygate Rd. W13	64	E3
Clayhall Ave., Ilf.	43	B3
Clayhill, Surb.	92	A5
Clayhill Cres. SE9	88	A4
Claylands Pl. SW8	**20**	**E7**
Claylands Pl. SW8	67	G7
Claylands Rd. SW8	**20**	**D6**
Claylands Rd. SW8	67	F6
Claymill Ho. SE18	70	F5
Claymore Clo., Mord.	93	D7
Claypole Rd. E15	60	C2
Clayponds Ave.,	64	H4
Brent.		
Clayponds Gdns. W5	64	G4
Clayponds La., Brent.	64	H5
Clays La. E15	51	B5
Clay's La., Loug.	27	D1
Clays La. Clo. E15	51	B5
Clayside, Chig.	35	F5
Clayton Ave., Wem.	46	H7
Clayton Clo. E6	61	C6
Brandreth Rd.		
Clayton Cres., Brent.	64	G5
Clayton Fld. NW9	30	E7
Clayton Rd. SE15	77	D1
Clayton Rd., Chess.	98	F4
Clayton Rd., Islw.	73	B3
Clayton Rd., Rom.	53	J1
Clayton St. SE11	**20**	**E5**
Clayton St. SE11	67	G6
Claywood Clo., Orp.	97	H7
Clayworth Clo., Sid.	80	B6
Cleanthus Clo. SE18	79	E1
Cleanthus Rd.		
Cleanthus Rd. SE18	79	E1
Clearbrook Way E1	59	G6
West Arbour St.		
Clearwell Dr. W9	**6**	**B6**
Clearwell Dr. W9	57	E4
Cleave Ave., Orp.	104	H6
Cleaveland Rd., Surb.	91	G5
Cleaver Sq. SE11	**20**	**F5**
Cleaver Sq. SE11	67	G5
Cleaver St. SE11	**20**	**F3**
Cleaver St. SE11	67	G5
Cleaverholme Clo.	95	E6
SE25		
Cleeve Hill SE23	86	E1
Cleeve Pk. Gdns., Sid.	89	B2
Clegg St. E1	68	E1
Prusom St.		
Clegg St. E13	60	G2
Cleland Path, Loug.	27	E1
Clematis St. W12	56	G7
Clemence St. E14	59	J5
Clement Clo. NW6	47	J7
Clement Clo. W4	65	D4
Acton La.		
Clement Rd. SW19	84	B5
Clement Rd., Beck.	95	G2
Clementhorpe Rd.,	53	C6
Dag.		
Clementina Rd. E10	50	J1
Clementine Clo. W13	64	E2
Balfour Rd.		
Clements Ave. E16	60	G7
Clements La. EC4	—	—
Clements Ct., Houns.	72	D5
Clement's Inn WC2	**12**	**D4**
Clement's Inn WC2	58	F6
Clement's Inn Pas.	**12**	**D4**
WC2		
Clements La. EC4	**13**	**C5**
Clements La. EC4	59	A7
Clements La., Ilf.	52	E3
Clements Pl., Brent.	64	G5
Clements Rd. E6	52	B7
Clements Rd. SE16	**17**	**J6**
Clements Rd. SE16	68	D3
Clements Rd., Ilf.	52	E3
Clendon Way SE18	70	G4
Polthorne Gro.		
Clenham St. SE1	**17**	**A3**
Clensham La., Sutt.	100	D2
Clenston Ms. W1	**10**	**J3**
Clephane Rd. N1	49	J6
Clere St. EC2	**9**	**C5**
Clerkenwell Clo. EC1	**8**	**F5**
Clerkenwell Clo. EC1	58	G4
Clerkenwell Grn. EC1	**8**	**F6**
Clerkenwell Grn. EC1	58	G4
Clerkenwell Rd. EC1	**8**	**E6**

Clerkenwell Rd. EC1 58 G4
Clerks Piece, Loug. 27 C3
Clermont Rd. E9 59 F1
Cleve Rd. NW6 48 D7
Cleve Rd., Sid. 89 D3
Clevedon Clo. N16 50 C3
Smalley Clo.
Clevedon Gdns., Houns. 72 B1
Clevedon Rd. SE20 95 G1
Clevedon Rd., Kings.T. 92 A2
Clevedon Rd., Twick. 73 G6
Cleveland Ave. SW20 93 C2
Cleveland Ave. W4 65 F4
Cleveland Ave., Hmptn. 81 F7
Cleveland Cres., Borwd. 22 C5
Cleveland Gdns. N4 40 J5
Cleveland Gdns. NW2 48 A2
Cleveland Gdns. SW13 74 F2
Cleveland Gdns. W2 10 C4
Cleveland Gdns. W2 57 F6
Cleveland Gdns., Wor.Pk. 99 E2
Cleveland Gro. E1 59 F4
Cleveland Way
Cleveland Ms. W1 11 F1
Cleveland Pk. Ave. E17 42 A4
Cleveland Pk. Cres. E17 42 A4
Cleveland Pl. SW1 15 G1
Cleveland Ri., Mord. 93 A7
Cleveland Rd. E18 42 G3
Cleveland Rd. N1 50 A7
Cleveland Rd. N9 25 E7
Cleveland Rd. SW13 74 F2
Cleveland Rd. W4 65 C3
Antrobus Rd.
Cleveland Rd. W13 55 D5
Cleveland Rd., Ilf. 52 E3
Cleveland Rd., Islw. 73 D4
Cleveland Rd., N.Mal. 92 E4
Cleveland Rd., Well. 79 J2
Cleveland Rd., Wor.Pk. 99 E2
Cleveland Row SW1 15 F2
Cleveland Row SW1 67 C1
Cleveland Sq. W2 10 C4
Cleveland Sq. W2 57 F6
Cleveland St. W1 7 E6
Cleveland St. W1 58 B4
Cleveland Ter. W2 10 C4
Cleveland Ter. W2 57 F6
Cleveland Way E1 59 F4
Cleveley Clo. SE7 70 A4
Cleveley Cres. W5 55 H2
Cleveleys Rd. E5 50 E3
Cleverley Est. W12 65 G1
Cleves Rd. E6 61 A1
Cleves Rd., Rich. 82 F3
Cleves Wk., Ilf. 35 F7
Cleves Way, Hmptn. 81 F7
Cleves Way, Ruis. 45 D1
Clewer Cres., Har. 37 A1
Clichy Est. E1 59 F5
Clifden Rd. E5 50 F5
Clifden Rd., Brent. 64 G6
Clifden Rd., Twick. 82 C1
Cliff Rd. NW1 49 D6
Cliff Ter. SE8 78 A2
Cliff Vill. NW1 49 D6
Cliff Wk. E16 60 F4
Cliffe Rd., S.Croy. 102 A5
Cliffe Wk., Sutt. 100 F5
Turnpike La.
Clifford Ave. SW14 74 B3
Clifford Ave., Chis. 88 C6
Clifford Ave., Ilf. 43 E1
Clifford Ave., Wall. 101 C4
Clifford Clo., Nthlt. 54 E1
Clifford Dr. SW9 76 H4
Clifford Gdns. NW10 56 J2
Clifford Rd. E16 60 F4
Clifford Rd. E17 42 C2
Clifford Rd. N9 25 F6
Clifford Rd. SE25 95 D4
Clifford Rd., Barn. 23 E3
Clifford Rd., Houns. 72 D3
Clifford Rd., Rich. 82 G2
Clifford Rd., Wem. 55 G1
Clifford St. W1 11 F6
Clifford St. W1 58 C7
Clifford Way NW10 47 F4
Clifford's Inn Pas. EC4 12 E4
Cliffview Rd. SE13 78 A3
Clifton Ave. E17 41 G3
Clifton Ave. N3 39 C1
Clifton Ave. W12 65 F2
Clifton Ave., Felt. 81 C3
Clifton Ave., Stan. 37 E2
Clifton Ave., Wem. 46 J6
Clifton Clo., Orp. 104 F5
Clifton Ct. NW8 6 E5
Clifton Cres. SE15 68 E7
Clifton Est. SE15 77 E1
Consort Rd.
Clifton Gdns. N15 41 C6
Clifton Gdns. NW11 39 C6
Clifton Gdns. W4 65 D4
Chiswick High Rd.
Clifton Gdns. W9 6 C6
Clifton Gdns. W9 57 F4
Clifton Gdns., Enf. 24 E4
Clifton Gro. E8 50 D6
Clifton Hill NW8 6 B1
Clifton Hill NW8 57 E2
Clifton Pk. Ave. SW20 92 J2
Clifton Pl. SE16 68 F2
Canon Beck Rd.
Clifton Pl. W2 10 F4
Clifton Pl. W2 57 G6
Clifton Ri. SE14 68 H7
Clifton Rd. E7 52 A6
Clifton Rd. E16 60 E5
Clifton Rd. N3 39 F1
Clifton Rd. N8 40 D6
Clifton Rd. N22 40 C1
Clifton Rd. NW10 56 G2
Clifton Rd. SE25 95 A4
Clifton Rd. SW19 84 A6
Clifton Rd. W9 6 D5
Clifton Rd. W9 57 F4
Clifton Rd., Grnf. 54 J4
Clifton Rd., Har. 37 J5
Clifton Rd., Ilf. 43 G6
Clifton Rd., Islw. 73 A2
Clifton Rd., Kings.T. 82 J7
Clifton Rd., Loug. 27 B4
Clifton Rd., Sid. 88 H4
Clifton Rd., Sthl. 63 E4
Clifton Rd., Tedd. 82 B4
Clifton Rd., Wall. 101 B5
Clifton Rd., Well. 80 C3
Clifton St. EC2 13 D1
Clifton St. EC2 59 B5
Clifton Ter. N4 49 G2
Clifton Vill. W9 10 B1
Clifton Vill. W9 57 F5
Clifton Wk. E6 61 B5
Tollgate Rd.
Clifton Way SE15 68 F7
Clifton Way, Borwd. 22 A1
Clifton Way, Wem. 55 H1
Clinch Ct. E16 60 G5
Brent Rd.
Cline Rd. N11 32 C6
Clinger Ct. N1 59 B1
Pitfield St.
Clink St. SE1 17 B1
Clink St. SE1 67 J1
Clinton Ave., E.Mol. 90 J4
Clinton Ave., Well. 80 A4
Clinton Cres., Ilf. 35 H6
Clinton Rd. E3 59 H3
Clinton Rd. E7 51 G4
Clinton Rd. N15 41 A4
Clipper Clo. SE16 68 G2
Kinburn St.
Clipper Way SE13 78 C4
Clippesby Clo., Chess. 98 J6
Clipstone Ms. W1 7 F6
Clipstone Ms. W1 58 C5
Clipstone Rd., Houns. 72 G3
Clipstone St. W1 11 E1
Clipstone St. W1 58 B5
Clissold Clo. N2 39 J3
Clissold Ct. N4 49 J2
Clissold Cres. N16 50 A4
Clissold Rd. N16 50 A3
Clitheroe Ave., Har. 45 G1
Clitheroe Gdns., Wat. 28 D3
Clitheroe Rd. SW9 76 E2
Clitherow Ave. W7 64 D3
Clitherow Pas., Brent. 64 E5
Clitherow Rd.
Clitherow Rd., Brent. 64 E5
Clitterhouse Cres. NW2 47 J1
Clitterhouse Rd. NW2 47 J1
Clive Ave. N18 33 D6
Claremont St.
Clive Ct. W9 6 D5
Clive Pas. SE21 86 A3
Clive Rd.
Clive Rd. SE21 86 A3
Clive Rd. SW19 84 H6
Clive Rd., Belv. 71 G4
Clive Rd., Enf. 25 D4
Clive Rd., Felt. 72 A6
Clive Rd., Twick. 82 C4
Clive Way, Enf. 25 D4
Cliveden Clo. N12 31 F4
Woodside Ave.
Cliveden Pl. SW1 19 B1
Cliveden Pl. SW1 67 A4
Cliveden Rd. SW19 93 C1
Clivedon Ct. W13 55 E5
Clivedon Rd. E4 34 E5
Clivesdale Dr., Hayes 63 A1
Cloak La. EC4 13 B5
Cloak La. EC4 58 J7
Clock Ho. Rd., Beck. 95 H3
Clock Twr. Ms. N1 58 J1
Arlington Ave.
Clock Twr. Pl. N7 49 E6
Clock Twr. Rd., Islw. 73 C3
Clockhouse Ave., Bark. 61 F1
Clockhouse Clo. SW19 83 J3
Cloister Clo., Tedd. 82 E5
Cloister Gdns. SE25 95 E6
Cloister Gdns., Edg. 30 C5
Cloister Rd. NW2 48 C3
Cloister Rd. W3 56 C5
Cloisters, The SW9 76 G1
Cloisters Ave., Brom. 97 C5
Cloisters Mall, Kings.T. 91 G2
Union St.
Clonard Way, Pnr. 28 G6
Clonbrock Rd. N16 50 B4
Cloncurry St. SW6 75 A2
Clonmel Clo., Har. 46 A2
Clonmel Rd., Tedd. 82 A4
Clonmell Rd. N17 41 A3
Clonmell Rd. SW6 66 C7
Clonmore St. SW18 84 C1
Cloonmore Ave., Orp. 104 J4
Clorane Gdns. NW3 48 D3
Close, The E4 34 C7
Beech Hall Rd.
Close, The N14 32 D2
Close, The N20 31 C2
Close, The SE3 78 D2
Heath La.
Close, The, Barn. 23 J6
Close, The, Beck. 95 H4
Close, The, Bex. 80 G6
Close, The, Har. 36 J2
Harrow Vw.
Close, The, Islw. 73 A2
Close, The, Mitch. 93 J4
Close, The, N.Mal. 92 C2
Close, The, Orp. 97 H6
Close, The, Pnr. 36 C7
(Eastcote)
Close, The, Pnr. 36 F7
(Rayners La.)
Close, The, Rich. 74 B3
Close, The, Rom. 44 E6
Close, The, Sid. 89 B4
Close, The, Sutt. 93 C7
Close, The, Wem. 47 C3
(Barnhill Rd.)
Close, The, Wem. 46 H6
(Lyon Pk. Ave.)
Cloth Ct. EC1 12 H2
Cloth Fair EC1 12 H2
Cloth Fair EC1 58 H5
Cloth St. EC1 12 J1
Clothier St. E1 59 B6
Cutler St.
Clothworkers Rd. SE18 70 G7
Cloudesdale Rd. SW17 85 B2
Cloudesley Pl. N1 58 G1
Cloudesley Rd. N1 58 G1
Cloudesley Rd., Bexh. 80 F1
Cloudesley Sq. N1 58 G1
Cloudesley St. N1 58 G1
Clouston Clo., Wall. 101 E5
Clova Rd. E7 51 F6
Clove Cres. E14 60 D7
Clove Hitch Quay SW11 75 F3
Cotton Row
Clove St. E13 60 G4
Barking Rd.
Clovelly Ave. NW9 38 F4
Clovelly Clo., Pnr. 36 B3
Clovelly Gdns. SE19 95 C1
Clovelly Gdns., Enf. 25 B7
Clovelly Gdns., Rom. 44 H1
Clovelly Rd. N8 40 D4
Clovelly Rd. W4 65 D2
Clovelly Rd. W5 64 F2
Clovelly Rd., Bexh. 71 E6
Clovelly Rd., Houns. 72 F2
Clovelly Way E1 59 F6
Jamaica St.
Clovelly Way, Har. 45 F2
Clovelly Way, Orp. 97 J6
Clover Clo. E11 51 D2
Clover Ms. SW3 19 A5
Clover Way, Wall. 101 A1
Cloverdale Gdns., Sid. 79 J6
Cloverleys (Park Hill), Loug. 27 A5
Clowders Rd. SE6 86 J3
Clowser Clo., Sutt. 100 F5
Turnpike La.
Cloyster Wd., Edg. 29 G7
Cloysters Grn. E1 17 H1
Club Gdns. Rd., Brom. 96 G7
Club Row E1 9 F5
Club Row E1 59 C4
Club Row E2 9 F5
Club Row E2 59 C4
Clunbury Ave., Sthl. 63 F5
Clunbury St. N1 9 C2
Clunbury St. N1 59 A2
Cluny Est. SE1 17 D5
Cluny Ms. SW5 66 D4
Cluny Pl. SE1 17 D5
Cluse Ct. N1 8 J1
Clutton St. E14 60 B5
Clydach Rd., Enf. 25 C4
Clyde Circ. N15 41 B4
Clyde Pl. E10 42 B7
Clyde Rd. N15 41 B4
Clyde Rd. N22 40 D1
Clyde Rd., Croy. 102 C2
Clyde Rd., Sutt. 100 D5
Clyde Rd., Wall. 101 C6
Clyde St. SE8 68 J6
Clyde Ter. SE23 86 F2
Clyde Vale SE23 86 F2
Clydesdale, Enf. 25 G4
Clydesdale Ave., Stan. 37 G3
Clydesdale Clo., Borwd. 22 D5
Clydesdale Gdns., Rich. 74 B4
Clydesdale Rd. W11 57 C6
Clymping Dene, Felt. 72 B7
Clyston St. SW8 76 C2
Coach & Horses Yd. W1 11 F5
Coach Ho. La. N5 49 H4
Highbury Hill
Coach Ho. La. SW19 84 A4
Coach Ho. Ms. SE23 77 F6
Coach Ho. Yd. SW18 75 E4
Ebner St.
Coachhouse Ms. SE20 86 E7
Coal Wf. Rd. W12 66 A2
Shepherds Bush Pl.
Coaldale Wk. SE21 76 J7
Lairdale Clo.
Coalecroft Rd. SW15 74 J4
Coate St. E2 9 J2
Coate St. E2 59 D2
Coates Hill Rd., Brom. 97 D2
Coates Wk., Brent. 64 H5
Burford Rd.
Cobb Clo., Borwd. 22 C5
Cobb St. E1 13 F2
Cobb St. E1 59 C5
Cobbett Rd. SE9 79 B3
Cobbett Rd., Twick. 81 G1
Cobbett St. SW8 67 F7
Cobbetts Ave., Ilf. 43 A5
Cobblers Wk., E.Mol. 91 E1
Cobblers Wk., Hmptn. 90 J1
High St.
Cobblers Wk., Kings.T. 91 D1
Cobblers Wk., Tedd. 82 A7
Cobblestone Pl., Croy. 101 J1
Oakfield Rd.
Cobbold Est. NW10 47 F6
Cobbold Rd. E11 51 F3
Cobbold Rd. NW10 47 F6
Cobbold Rd. W12 65 F2
Cobb's Rd., Houns. 72 F4
Cobden Rd. E11 51 E3
Cobden Rd. SE25 95 D5
Cobden Rd., Orp. 104 G4
Cobham Ave., N.Mal. 92 G5
Cobham Clo. SW11 75 H6
Cobham Clo., Brom. 97 B7

Cobham Clo., Wall. 101 E6
Cobham Ho., Bark. 61 F1
St. Margarets
Cobham Pl., Bexh. 80 E5
Cobham Rd. E17 42 C1
Cobham Rd. N22 40 H3
Cobham Rd., Houns. 63 C7
Cobham Rd., Ilf. 52 H2
Cobham Rd., Kings.T. 92 A2
Cobland Rd. SE12 87 J4
Coborn Rd. E3 59 J3
Coborn St. E3 59 J3
Cobourg Rd. SE5 21 F5
Cobourg Rd. SE5 68 C6
Cobourg St. NW1 7 G4
Cobourg St. NW1 58 C3
Coburg Clo. SW1 19 G1
Coburg Cres. SW2 85 F1
Coburg Gdns., Ilf. 43 A2
Coburg Rd. N22 40 F3
Cochrane Ms. NW8 6 F2
Cochrane Rd. SW19 84 C7
Cochrane St. NW8 6 F2
Cochrane St. NW8 57 G2
Cock Hill E1 13 E2
Cock La. EC1 12 G2
Cock La. EC1 58 H5
Cockayne Way SE8 68 H4
Windlass Pl.
Cockfosters Rd., Barn. 23 J3
Cockpit Steps SW1 15 J4
Cockpit Yd. WC1 12 D1
Cocks Cres., N.Mal. 92 F4
Cocksett Ave., Orp. 104 H6
Cockspur Ct. SW1 15 J1
Cockspur St. SW1 15 J1
Cockspur St. SW1 67 D1
Cocksure La., Sid. 89 G3
Code St. E1 9 G6
Code St. E1 59 C4
Codicote Ter. N4 49 J2
Green Las.
Codling Clo. E1 17 J1
Codling Way, Wem. 46 G4
Codrington Hill SE23 77 H7
Codrington Ms. W11 57 B6
Blenheim Cres.
Cody Clo., Har. 37 G3
Cody Clo., Wall. 101 D7
Alcock Clo.
Cody Rd. E16 60 E4
Coe Ave. SE25 95 D6
Coe's All., Barn. 23 B4
Wood St.
Cofers Circle, Wem. 47 B3
Cogan Ave. E17 41 H1
Coin St. SE1 16 E1
Coin St. SE1 67 G1
Coity Rd. NW5 49 A6
Coke St. E1 13 H3
Coke St. E1 59 D6
Cokers La. SE21 86 A1
Perifield
Colas Ms. NW6 57 D1
Birchington Rd.
Colbeck Ms. SW7 18 B2
Colbeck Ms. SW7 66 E4
Colbeck Rd., Har. 36 J7
Colberg Pl. N16 41 B7
Colborne Way, Wor.Pk. 99 J3
Colburn Ave., Pnr. 28 E6
Colburn Way, Sutt. 100 G3
Colby Rd. SE19 86 B5
Colchester Ave. E12 52 C3
Colchester Dr., Pnr. 36 D5
Colchester Rd. E10 42 C7
Colchester Rd. E17 42 A6
Colchester Rd., Edg. 30 C7
Colchester Rd., Nthwd. 36 A2
Colchester St. E1 13 G3
Cold Blow La. SE14 68 G7
Cold Blows, Mitch. 94 A3
Cold Harbour E14 69 C2
Coldbath Sq. EC1 8 E5
Coldbath St. SE13 78 B1
Coldershaw Rd. W13 64 D1
Coldfall Ave. N10 39 J2
Coldharbour La. SE5 76 J3
Coldharbour La. SW9 76 G4
Coldharbour Pl. SE5 76 J2
Denmark Hill
Coldharbour Rd., Croy. 101 G5
Coldharbour Way, Croy. 101 G5
Coldstream Gdns. SW18 75 C6
Cole Clo. SE28 71 B1
Cole Gdns., Houns. 63 A7
Cole Pk. Gdns., Twick. 73 D6
Cole Pk. Rd., Twick. 73 D7
Cole Pk. Vw., Twick. 73 D6
Cole Rd., Twick. 73 D6
Cole St. SE1 17 A4
Cole St. SE1 67 J2
Colebeck Ms. N1 49 H6
Colebert Ave. E1 59 F4
Colebrook Clo. SW15 75 A7
West Hill
Colebrook Gdns., Loug. 27 E2
Colebrook Ho. E14 60 B6
Brabazon St.
Colebrook La., Loug. 27 E2
Colebrook Path, Loug. 27 E2
Colebrook La.
Colebrook Rd. SW16 94 E1
Colebrook Way N11 32 B5
Colebrooke Ave. W13 55 E6
Colebrooke Dr. E11 42 H7
Colebrooke Pl. N1 58 H1
St. Peters St.
Colebrooke Ri., Brom. 96 E2
Colebrooke Row N1 8 G2
Colebrooke Row N1 58 H2
Coleby Path SE5 68 A7
Harris St.
Coledale Dr., Stan. 37 F1
Coleford Rd. SW18 75 F5
Colegrave Rd. E15 51 D5
Colegrove Rd. SE15 21 G6
Colegrove Rd. SE15 68 C6
Coleherne Ct. SW5 18 B4
Coleherne Ct. SW5 66 E5
Coleherne Ms. SW10 18 A4
Coleherne Ms. SW10 66 E5
Coleherne Rd. SW10 18 A4
Coleherne Rd. SW10 66 E5
Colehill Gdns. SW6 75 B2
Fulham Palace Rd.
Colehill La. SW6 75 B1
Coleman Clo. SE25 95 D2
Warminster Rd.
Coleman Flds. N1 58 J1
Coleman Rd. SE5 21 D7
Coleman Rd. SE5 68 B7
Coleman Rd., Belv. 71 G4
Coleman Rd., Dag. 53 E6
Coleman St. EC2 13 B3
Coleman St. EC2 59 A6
Colemans Heath SE9 88 D3
Colenso Rd. E5 50 F4
Colenso Rd., Ilf. 52 H1
Colepits Wd. Rd. SE9 79 G5
Coleraine Rd. N8 40 G3
Coleraine Rd. SE3 69 F6
Coleridge Ave. E12 52 B6
Coleridge Ave., Sutt. 100 H4
Coleridge Clo. SW8 76 B2
Coleridge Gdns. NW6 48 F7
Fairhazel Gdns.
Coleridge La. N8 40 E6
Coleridge Rd.
Coleridge Rd. E17 41 J4
Coleridge Rd. N4 49 G2
Coleridge Rd. N8 40 D6
Coleridge Rd. N12 31 F5
Coleridge Rd., Croy. 95 F6
Coleridge Sq. W13 55 D6
Berners Dr.
Coleridge Wk. NW11 39 D4
Coleridge Way, Hayes 54 A6
Coles Cres., Har. 45 H2
Coles Grn., Loug. 27 D1
Coles Grn., Wat. (Bushey) 28 J1
Coles Grn. Ct. NW2 47 G2
Coles Grn. Rd. NW2 47 G1
Colesburg Rd., Beck. 95 J3
Coleshill Rd., Tedd. 82 B6
Colestown St. SW11 75 H2
Colet Clo. N13 32 H6
Colet Gdns. W14 66 A5
Coley St. WC1 8 D6
Coley St. WC1 58 F4
Colfe Rd. SE23 86 H1
Colin Clo. NW9 38 E4
Colin Clo., Croy. 102 J3
Colin Clo., W.Wick. 103 F3
Colin Cres. NW9 38 F4
Colin Dr. NW9 38 F5
Colin Gdns. NW9 38 F5
Colin Pk. Rd. NW9 38 E3
Colin Rd. NW10 47 G6
Colina Ms. N15 40 H5
Harringay Rd.
Colina Rd. N15 40 H5
Colindale Ave. NW9 38 D3
Colindale Business Pk. NW9 38 C3
Colindeep Gdns. NW4 38 G5
Colindeep La. NW9 38 E3
Colinette Rd. SW15 74 J4
Colinton Rd., Ilf. 53 B2
Coliston Pas. SW18 75 D7
Coliston Rd.
Coliston Rd. SW18 75 D7
Collamore Ave. SW18 84 H1
Collapit Clo., Har. 36 H6
Collard Ave., Loug. 27 F2
Collard Grn., Loug. 27 F2
Collard Ave.
College App. SE10 69 C6
College Ave., Har. 37 B1
College Clo. E9 50 F5
Median Rd.
College Clo. N18 33 C5
College Clo., Har. 29 B7
College Clo., Twick. 82 A1
Meadway
College Cres. NW3 48 G6
College Cross N1 49 G7
College Dr., Ruis. 36 A7
College Gdns. E4 26 B7
College Gdns. N18 33 C5
College Gdns. SE21 86 B1
College Gdns. SW17 84 H2
College Gdns., Enf. 25 A1
College Gdns., Ilf. 43 B5
College Gdns., N.Mal. 92 F5
College Grn. SE19 86 B7
College Gro. NW1 58 D1
St. Pancras Way
College Hill EC4 13 A5
College Hill Rd., Har. 29 B7
College La. NW5 49 B4
College Ms. SW1 16 A5
College Ms. SW18 75 E5
St. Ann's Hill
College Pk. Clo. SE13 78 D4
College Pk. Rd. N17 33 C6
College Rd.
College Pl. E17 42 E4
College Pl. NW1 58 C1
College Pl. SW10 66 F7
Hortensia Rd.
College Pt. E15 51 F6
Wolffe Gdns.
College Rd. E17 42 C5
College Rd. N17 33 C6
College Rd. N21 32 G2
College Rd. NW10 56 J2
College Rd. SE19 86 C5
College Rd. SE21 77 B7
College Rd. SW19 84 G6
College Rd. W13 55 E6
College Rd., Brom. 96 G1
College Rd., Croy. 102 A2
College Rd., Enf. 25 A1
College Rd., Har. (Harrow on the Hill) 37 B6
College Rd., Har. (Harrow Weald) 37 B1
College Rd., Islw. 73 C1
College Rd., Wem. 46 G1
College Row E9 50 G5
Homerton High St.
College Slip, Brom. 96 G1
College St. EC4 13 B5
College Ter. E3 59 J3
College Ter. N3 39 C2
Hendon La.
College Vw. SE9 88 A1
College Wk., Kings.T. 91 H2
Grange Rd.
College Yd. NW5 49 B4
College La.
Collent St. E9 50 F6
Colless Rd. N15 41 C5
Collett Rd. SE16 17 J6
Collett Rd. SE16 68 D3
Collett Way, Sthl. 63 H1
Collier Clo., Epsom 99 A6
Collier Dr., Edg. 38 A2
Collier Row La., Rom. 44 H1
Collier Row Rd., Rom. 44 G1
Collier St. N1 8 C2
Collier St. N1 58 F2
Colliers Shaw, Kes. 104 A5
Colliers Water La., Th.Hth. 94 G5
Collindale Ave., Erith 71 H6
Collindale Ave., Sid. 89 A1
Collingbourne Rd. W12 65 H1
Collingham Gdns. SW5 18 B2
Collingham Gdns. SW5 66 E4
Collingham Pl. SW5 18 A2
Collingham Pl. SW5 66 E4
Collingham Rd. SW5 18 B1
Collingham Rd. SW5 66 E4
Collings Clo. N22 32 F6
Whittington Rd.
Collingtree Rd. SE26 86 F4
Collingwood Ave. N10 40 A3
Collingwood Ave., Surb. 99 C1
Collingwood Clo. SE20 95 E1
Collingwood Clo., Twick. 72 G7
Collingwood Rd. E17 42 A6
Collingwood Rd. N15 41 B4
Collingwood Rd., Mitch. 93 H2
Collingwood Rd., Sutt. 100 C3
Collingwood St. E1 59 E4
Collins Ave., Stan. 37 H2
Collins Dr., Ruis. 45 C2
Collins Rd. N5 49 J4
Collins Sq. SE3 78 F2
Tranquil Vale
Collins St. SE3 78 E2
Collin's Yd. N1 58 H1
Islington Grn.
Collinson St. SE1 16 J4
Collinson Wk. SE1 16 J4
Collinwood Ave., Enf. 25 F3
Collinwood Gdns., Ilf. 43 C5
Colls Rd. SE15 77 F1
Collyer Ave., Croy. 101 E4
Collyer Pl. SE15 77 D1
Peckham High St.
Collyer Rd., Croy. 101 E4
Colman Rd. E16 60 J5
Colmar Clo. E1 59 G4
Alderney Rd.
Colmer Pl., Har. 29 A7
Colmer Rd. SW16 94 E1
Colmore Ms. SE15 77 E1
Colmore Rd., Enf. 25 F4
Colnbrook St. SE1 16 G6
Colnbrook St. SE1 67 H3
Colne Ct., Epsom 99 C4
Colne Ho., Bark. 52 E6
Colne Rd. E5 50 H4
Colne Rd. N21 24 J7
Colne Rd., Twick. 82 B1
Colne St. E13 60 G3
Grange Rd.
Colney Hatch La. N10 32 A7
Colney Hatch La. N11 31 J6
Cologne Rd. SW11 75 G4
Colomb St. SE10 69 E5
Colombo Rd., Ilf. 52 F1
Colombo St. SE1 16 G2
Colombo St. SE1 67 H1
Colonial Ave., Twick. 72 J5
Colonnade WC1 8 B6
Colonnade WC1 58 E4
Colonnade Wk. SW1 19 D2
Colonnades, The W2 10 B3
Colson Gdns., Loug. 27 E4
Colson Rd.
Colson Path, Loug. 27 D4
Colson Rd., Croy. 102 B2
Colson Rd., Loug. 27 D4
Colson Way SW16 85 C4
Colsterworth Rd. N15 41 C4
Colston Ave., Cars. 100 H4
Colston Clo., Cars. 100 J4
West St.
Colston Rd. E7 52 A6
Colston Rd. SW14 74 C4
Coltness Cres. SE2 71 B5
Colton Gdns. N17 40 J3
Colton Rd., Har. 37 B5
Columbia Ave., Edg. 38 B1
Columbia Ave., Ruis. 45 B1
Columbia Ave., Wor.Pk. 92 F7
Columbia Ctyd. E14 69 A1
West India Ave.
Columbia Rd. E2 9 F3
Columbia Rd. E2 59 C3
Columbia Rd. E13 60 F4

Columbia Sq. SW14 74 C4
Upper Richmond Rd. W.
Columbine Ave. E6 61 B5
Columbine Ave., 101 H7
S.Croy.
Columbine Way SE13 78 C2
Columbus Gdns., 36 A1
Nthwd.
Colva Wk. N19 49 B2
Chester Rd.
Colvestone Cres. E8 50 C5
Colview Ct. SE9 88 A1
Mottingham La.
Colville Est. N1 59 B1
Colville Gdns. W11 57 C6
Colville Hos. W11 57 C6
Colville Ms. W11 57 C6
Lonsdale Rd.
Colville Pl. W1 **11 G2**
Colville Rd. E11 51 C3
Colville Rd. E17 41 H2
Colville Rd. N9 33 E1
Colville Rd. W3 65 B3
Colville Sq. W11 57 C6
Colville Ter. W11 57 C6
Colvin Clo. SE26 86 F5
Colvin Gdns. E4 34 C3
Colvin Gdns. E11 42 H4
Colvin Gdns., Ilf. 43 F1
Colvin Rd. E6 52 B7
Colvin Rd., Th.Hth. 94 G5
Colwell Rd. SE22 77 C5
Colwick Clo. N6 40 D7
Colwith Rd. W6 65 J6
Colwood Gdns. SW19 84 G7
Colworth Gro. SE17 **21 A2**
Colworth Rd. E11 42 E6
Colworth Rd., Croy. 102 D1
Colwyn Ave., Grnf. 55 C2
Colwyn Clo. SW16 85 C5
Colwyn Cres., Houns. 72 J1
Colwyn Grn. NW9 38 E6
Snowdon Dr.
Colwyn Rd. NW2 47 H3
Colyer Clo. SE9 88 E2
Colyers La., Erith 80 J1
Colyton Clo., Well. 80 D1
Colyton Clo., Wem. 46 F6
Bridgewater Rd.
Colyton Rd. SE22 77 E5
Colyton Way N18 33 D5
Combe Ave. SE3 69 F7
Combe Lea, Brom. 97 B3
Combe Lo. SE7 69 J6
Elliscombe Rd.
Combe Ms. SE3 69 F7
Combedale Rd. SE10 69 G5
Combemartin Rd. 75 B7
SW18
Comber Clo. NW2 47 H3
Comber Gro. SE5 67 J7
Combermere Rd. SW9 76 F3
Combermere Rd., 93 E5
Mord.
Comberton Rd. E5 50 E2
Combeside SE18 71 H3
Combwell Cres. SE2 71 A3
Comely Bank Rd. E17 42 C5
Comeragh Ms. W14 66 B5
Comeragh Rd. W14 66 B5
Comerford Rd. SE4 77 H4
Comet Pl. SE8 69 A7
Comet St. SE8 69 A7
Commerce Rd. N22 40 F1
Commerce Rd., Brent. 64 F6
Commerce Way, 101 F2
Croy.
Commercial Rd. E1 **13 H3**
Commercial Rd. E1 59 D6
Commercial Rd. E14 59 H6
Commercial Rd. N17 33 B6
Commercial Rd. N18 33 B5
Commercial St. E1 **9 F6**
Commercial St. E1 59 C4
Commercial Way 56 B2
NW10
Commercial Way SE15 68 C7
Commerell St. SE10 69 E5
Commodity Quay E1 **13 G6**
Commodore Sq. 75 F1
SW10
Commodore St. E1 59 H4
Common, The W5 55 H7
Common, The, Rich. 82 G3
Common, The, Sthl. 63 C4

Common, The, Stan. 29 B2
Common La., Esher 98 D7
Common Rd. SW13 74 G3
Common Rd., Esher 98 D6
Common Rd., Stan. 29 A3
Commondale SW15 74 J3
Commonfield La. 84 H5
SW17
Tooting Gro.
Commonside, Kes. 103 J4
Commonside E., 94 A3
Mitch.
Commonside W., 93 J3
Mitch.
Commonwealth Ave. 56 H7
W12
Commonwealth Rd. 33 D7
N17
Commonwealth Way 71 B5
SE2
Community Clo., 72 B1
Houns.
Community Rd. E15 51 D5
Community Rd., Grnf. 54 J1
Como Rd. SE23 86 H2
Compass Hill, Rich. 73 G6
Compayne Gdns. NW6 48 E7
Compton Ave. E6 61 A2
Compton Ave. N1 49 H6
Compton Ave. N6 39 H7
Compton Clo. E3 60 A5
Compton Clo. NW1 **7 E4**
Compton Clo. W13 55 D6
Compton Clo., Edg. 30 C7
Pavilion Way
Compton Ct. SE19 86 B5
Victoria Cres.
Compton Cres. N17 32 J7
Compton Cres. W4 65 C6
Compton Cres., 98 H6
Chess.
Compton Cres., Nthlt. 54 D1
Compton Pas. EC1 **8 H5**
Compton Pl. WC1 **8 A5**
Compton Pl., Wat. 28 E3
Compton Ri., Pnr. 36 E5
Compton Rd. N1 49 H6
Compton Rd. N21 32 G1
Compton Rd. NW10 57 A3
Compton Rd. SW19 84 C6
Compton Rd., Croy. 102 E1
Compton St. EC1 **8 G5**
Compton St. EC1 58 H4
Compton Ter. N1 49 H6
Comredly Clo., Enf. 24 H1
Comus Pl. SE17 **21 D2**
Comus Pl. SE17 68 B4
Comyn Rd. SW11 75 H4
Comyns, The 28 J1
(Bushey), Wat.
Comyns Clo. E16 60 F5
Comyns Rd., Dag. 53 G7
Conant Ms. E1 **13 H5**
Concanon Rd. SW2 76 F4
Concert Hall App. SE1 **16 D2**
Concert Hall App. SE1 67 F1
Concord Clo., Nthlt. 54 D3
Britannia Clo.
Concord Rd. W3 56 B4
Concord Rd., Enf. 25 E5
Concorde Clo., Houns. 72 H2
Lampton Rd.
Concorde Dr. E6 61 C5
Concourse, The N9 33 D2
New Rd.
Concourse, The NW9 38 F1
Long Mead
Condell Rd. SW8 76 C1
Conder St. E14 59 H6
Conderton Rd. SE5 76 J3
Condor Path, Nthlt. 54 G2
Brabazon Rd.
Condover Cres. SE18 70 E7
Condray Pl. SW11 66 H7
Conduit Ct. WC2 **12 A5**
Conduit La. N18 33 F5
Conduit La., Croy. 102 D5
Conduit La., Enf. 25 H6
Morson Rd.
Conduit La., S.Croy. 102 D5
Conduit Ms. W2 **10 E4**
Conduit Ms. W2 57 G6
Conduit Pas. W2 **10 E4**
Conduit Pl. W2 **10 E4**
Conduit Pl. W2 57 G6
Conduit Rd. SE18 70 E5
Conduit St. W1 **11 E5**
Conduit St. W1 58 B7

Conduit Way NW10 47 C7
Conewood St. N5 49 H3
Coney Acre SE21 85 J1
Coney Burrows E4 34 E2
Wyemead Cres.
Coney Hill Rd., 103 E2
W.Wick.
Coney Way SW8 **20 D6**
Coney Way SW8 67 F6
Coneygrove Path, 45 E6
Nthlt.
Arnold Rd.
Conference Clo. E4 34 C2
Greenbank Clo.
Conference Rd. SE2 71 C4
Congleton Gro. SE18 70 F5
Congo Rd. SE18 70 G5
Congress Rd. SE2 71 C4
Congreve Rd. SE9 79 C3
Congreve St. SE17 **21 D2**
Congreve St. SE17 68 B4
Congreve Wk. E16 61 A5
Fulmer Rd.
Conical Cor., Enf. 24 J2
Conifer Clo., Orp. 104 G4
Conifer Gdns. SW16 85 E3
Conifer Gdns., Enf. 25 A6
Conifer Gdns., Sutt. 100 E3
Conifer Way, Hayes 54 A7
Conifer Way, Wem. 46 F3
Conifers Clo., Tedd. 82 F7
Coniger Rd. SW6 75 D2
Coningham Ms. W12 65 G1
Percy Rd.
Coningham Rd. W12 65 H1
Coningsby Cotts. W5 64 G2
Coningsby Rd.
Coningsby Gdns. E4 34 B6
Coningsby Rd. N4 40 H7
Coningsby Rd. W5 64 G2
Conington Rd. SE13 78 B2
Conisbee Ct. N14 24 C5
Conisborough Cres. 87 C3
SE6
Coniscliffe Rd. N13 32 J3
Coniston Ave., Bark. 52 H7
Coniston Ave., Grnf. 55 E3
Coniston Ave., Well. 79 H3
Coniston Clo. N20 31 F3
Coniston Clo. SW13 65 F7
Lonsdale Rd.
Coniston Clo. SW20 93 A6
Coniston Clo. W4 65 C7
Coniston Clo., Bark. 52 H7
Coniston Ave.
Coniston Clo., Bexh. 80 J1
Coniston Gdns. N9 33 F1
Coniston Gdns. NW9 38 D5
Coniston Gdns., Ilf. 43 B4
Coniston Gdns., Pnr. 36 A4
Coniston Gdns., Sutt. 100 G6
Coniston Gdns., 46 F1
Wem.
Coniston Ho. SE5 **20 J7**
Coniston Rd. N10 40 B2
Coniston Rd. N17 33 D6
Coniston Rd., Bexh. 80 J1
Coniston Rd., Brom. 87 D6
Coniston Rd., Croy. 95 D7
Coniston Rd., Twick. 72 H6
Coniston Wk. E9 50 F5
Clifden Rd.
Coniston Way, Chess. 98 H3
Conistone Way N7 49 E7
Conlan St. W10 57 B4
Conley Rd. NW10 47 E6
Conley St. SE10 69 E5
Pelton Rd.
Connaught Ave. E4 26 D7
Connaught Ave. 74 C3
SW14
Connaught Ave., 31 J1
Barn.
Connaught Ave., Enf. 25 B2
Connaught Ave., 72 E5
Houns.
Connaught Ave., 27 A4
Loug.
Connaught Bri. E16 61 A7
Connaught Clo. E10 50 H2
Connaught Clo. W2 **10 G4**
Connaught Clo., Enf. 25 B2
Connaught Clo., Sutt. 100 G6
Connaught Dr. NW11 39 D4
Connaught Gdns. N10 40 B5
Connaught Gdns. N13 32 H4
Connaught Gdns., 93 F4
Mord.

Connaught Hill, Loug. 27 A4
Connaught La., Ilf. 52 G2
Connaught Rd.
Connaught Ms. SE18 70 D5
Connaught Ms. W2 **10 J4**
Connaught Ms., Ilf. 52 G2
Connaught Rd.
Connaught Pl. W2 **10 J4**
Connaught Pl. W2 57 J7
Connaught Rd. E4 26 E7
Connaught Rd. E11 51 D1
Connaught Rd. E16 70 A1
Connaught Bri.
Connaught Rd. E17 42 A5
Connaught Rd. N4 40 G7
Connaught Rd. NW10 56 E1
Connaught Rd. SE18 70 D5
Connaught Rd. W13 55 E7
Connaught Rd., Barn. 23 A6
Connaught Rd., Har. 37 C1
Connaught Rd., Ilf. 52 G2
Connaught Rd., 92 E4
N.Mal.
Connaught Rd., Rich. 73 J5
Albert Rd.
Connaught Rd., Sutt. 100 G2
Connaught Rd., Tedd. 82 A5
Connaught Sq. W2 **10 J4**
Connaught Sq. W2 57 J6
Connaught St. W2 **10 H4**
Connaught St. W2 57 H6
Connaught Way N13 32 H4
Connell Cres. W5 55 J4
Connemara Clo., 22 D6
Borwd.
Percheron Rd.
Connington Cres. E4 34 D3
Connor Rd., Dag. 53 F4
Connor St. E9 59 G1
Lauriston Rd.
Conolly Rd. W7 64 B1
Conrad Dr., Wor.Pk. 99 J1
Conrad Ho. N16 50 B5
Cons St. SE1 **16 F3**
Consfield Ave., N.Mal. 92 G4
Consort Ms., Islw. 73 A5
Consort Rd. SE15 77 E1
Constable Clo. NW11 39 E6
Constable Cres. N15 41 D5
Constable Gdns., Edg. 38 A1
Constable Gdns., Islw. 73 A5
Constable Wk. SE21 86 C3
Ferrings
Constance Cres., 96 F7
Brom.
Constance Rd., Croy. 94 H7
Constance Rd., Enf. 25 B6
Constance Rd., Sutt. 100 F4
Constance Rd., Twick. 72 H1
Constance St. E16 70 B1
Albert Rd.
Constantine Rd. NW3 48 H4
Constitution Hill SW1 **15 D3**
Constitution Hill SW1 67 B2
Constitution Ri. SE18 79 D1
Consul Ave., Dag. 62 J4
Content St. SE17 **21 A2**
Content St. SE17 67 J4
Contessa Clo., Orp. 104 H5
Convair Wk., Nthlt. 54 D3
Kittiwake Rd.
Convent Gdns. W5 64 F4
Convent Gdns. W11 57 C6
Kensington Pk. Rd.
Convent Hill SE19 85 J6
Convent Way, Sthl. 63 C4
Conway Clo., Stan. 29 D6
Conway Cres., Grnf. 55 B2
Conway Cres., Rom. 44 C6
Conway Dr., Sutt. 100 E6
Conway Gdns., Mitch. 94 D4
Conway Gdns., Wem. 37 F1
Conway Gro. W3 56 D5
Conway Ms. W1 **7 F6**
Conway Rd. N14 32 E3
Conway Rd. N15 40 H5
Conway Rd. NW2 47 J2
Conway Rd. SE18 70 D4
Conway Rd. SW20 92 J1
Conway Rd., Felt. 81 J3
Conway Rd., Houns. 72 F7
Conway St. W1 **7 F6**
Conway St. W1 58 C4
Conway Wk., Hmptn. 81 F6
Fearnley Cres.
Conybeare NW3 48 H7
King Henry's Rd.

Conyer St. E3	59	H2
Conyers Clo., Wdf.Grn.	34	E6
Conyers Rd. SW16	85	D5
Conyers Way, Loug.	27	E3
Cooden Clo. N17	33	C6
Brantwood Rd.		
Cookes Clo. E11	51	F2
Cookes La., Sutt.	100	B6
Marlow Way		
Cookham Cres. SE16	68	G2
Cookham Dene Clo., Chis.	97	G1
Cookhill Rd. SE2	71	B2
Cooks Clo. E14	69	A1
Westferry Circ.		
Cooks Clo., Rom.	44	J1
Cook's Rd. E15	60	B2
Cooks Rd. SE17	**20**	**G5**
Cooks Rd. SE17	67	H6
Cool Oak La. NW9	38	E7
Coolfin Rd. E16	60	G6
Coolgardie Ave. E4	34	D5
Coolgardie Ave., Chig.	35	D3
Coolhurst Rd. N8	40	D6
Coomassie Rd. W9	57	C4
Bravington Rd.		
Coombe Ave., Croy.	102	B4
Coombe Bank, Kings.T.	92	E1
Coombe Clo., Edg.	37	J2
Coombe Clo., Houns.	72	G4
Coombe Cor. N21	32	H1
Coombe Cres., Hmptn.	81	E7
Coombe Dr., Kings.T.	83	D7
Coombe Dr., Ruis.	45	B1
Coombe End, Kings.T.	83	D7
Coombe Gdns. SW20	92	G2
Coombe Gdns., N.Mal.	92	F4
Coombe Heights, Kings.T.	83	E7
Coombe Hill Glade, Kings.T.	83	E7
Coombe Hill Rd., Kings.T.	83	E7
Coombe Ho. Chase, N.Mal.	92	D1
Coombe La. SW20	92	F1
Coombe La., Croy.	102	E5
Coombe La. W., Kings.T.	92	B1
Coombe Lea, Brom.	97	B3
Coombe Neville, Kings.T.	83	D7
Coombe Pk., Kings.T.	83	D5
Coombe Ridings, Kings.T.	83	C5
Coombe Ri., Kings.T.	92	C1
Coombe Rd. N22	40	G2
Coombe Rd. NW10	47	D3
Coombe Rd. SE26	86	E4
Coombe Rd. W4	65	E5
Coombe Rd. W13	64	E3
Northcroft Rd.		
Coombe Rd., Croy.	101	J4
Coombe Rd., Hmptn.	81	F6
Coombe Rd., Kings.T.	92	A1
Coombe Rd., N.Mal.	92	E2
Coombe Wk., Sutt.	100	E3
Coombe Wd. Rd., Kings.T.	83	C5
Coombefield Clo., N.Mal.	92	E5
Coombehurst Clo., Barn.	23	J2
Coomber Way, Croy.	94	D7
Coombes Rd., Dag.	62	F1
Coombewood Dr., Rom.	44	G6
Coombs St. N1	**8**	**H2**
Coombs St. N1	58	H2
Coomer Ms. SW6	66	C6
Coomer Pl.		
Coomer Pl. SW6	66	C6
Coomer Rd. SW6	66	C6
Coomer Pl.		
Cooms Wk., Edg.	38	C1
East Rd.		
Cooper Ave. E17	41	H1
Cooper Clo. SE1	**16**	**F4**
Cooper Ct. E15	51	B5
Clays La.		
Cooper Cres., Cars.	100	J3
Cooper Rd. NW10	47	G5

Cooper Rd., Croy.	101	H4
Cooper St. E16	60	F5
Lawrence St.		
Coopers Clo. E1	59	F4
Coopers Cres., Borwd.	22	C1
Coopers La. E10	51	B1
Coopers La. NW1	**7**	**J2**
Coopers La. NW1	58	D2
Cooper's La. SE12	87	H2
Coopers Rd. SE1	**21**	**G4**
Coopers Rd. SE1	68	C5
Cooper's Row EC3	**13**	**F5**
Cooper's Yd. SE19	86	B6
Westow Hill		
Coopersale Clo., Wdf.Grn.	34	J7
Navestock Cres.		
Coopersale Rd. E9	50	G5
Nicholas Rd.		
Coote Gdns., Dag.	53	F3
Coote Rd., Bexh.	80	F1
Coote Rd., Dag.	53	F3
Cope Pl. W8	66	D3
Cope St. SE16	68	G4
Copeland Dr. E14	69	A4
Copeland Rd. E17	42	B5
Copeland Rd. SE15	77	D2
Copeman Clo. SE26	86	F5
Copenhagen Gdns. W4	65	D2
Copenhagen Pl. E14	59	J6
Copenhagen St. N1	58	E1
Copers Cope Rd., Beck.	86	J7
Copford Clo., Wdf.Grn.	35	B6
Copford Wk. N1	58	J1
Popham St.		
Copinger Wk., Edg.	38	B1
North Rd.		
Copland Ave., Wem.	46	G5
Copland Clo., Wem.	46	F5
Copland Rd., Wem.	46	H6
Copleston Ms. SE15	77	C2
Copleston Rd.		
Copleston Pas. SE15	77	C2
Copleston Rd. SE15	77	C3
Copley Clo. SE17	20	H6
Copley Clo. W7	55	C4
Copley Dene, Brom.	97	A1
Copley Pk. SW16	85	F6
Copley Rd., Stan.	29	F5
Copley St. E1	59	G5
Stepney Grn.		
Copnor Way SE15	**21**	**E7**
Coppard Gdns., Chess.	98	F6
Mansfield Rd.		
Copped Hall SE21	86	A2
Glazebrook Clo.		
Coppelia Rd. SE3	78	F4
Coppen Rd., Dag.	44	F7
Copper Beech Clo. NW3	48	G6
Daleham Ms.		
Copper Beech Clo., Ilf.	43	D1
Copper Beech Ct., Loug.	27	D1
Copper Beeches, Islw.	73	A1
Eversley Cres.		
Copper Clo. SE19	86	C7
Copper Mead Clo. NW2	47	J3
Copper Mill Dr., Islw.	73	C2
Copper Mill La. SW17	84	F4
Copperas St. SE8	69	B6
Copperbeech Clo. NW3	48	G5
Akenside Rd.		
Copperdale Rd., Hayes	63	A2
Copperfield, Chig.	35	G5
Copperfield App., Chig.	35	G6
Copperfield Ct., Pnr.	36	F4
Copperfield Dr. N15	41	C4
Copperfield Ms. N18	33	B5
Copperfield Rd. E3	59	H4
Copperfield Rd. SE28	62	C6
Copperfield St. SE1	**16**	**H3**
Copperfield St. SE1	67	H2
Copperfield Way, Chis.	88	F6
Copperfield Way, Pnr.	36	F4
Coppergate Clo., Brom.	96	H1
Coppermill La. E17	41	F6
Coppetts Clo. N12	31	H7

Coppetts Rd. N10	31	J7
Coppice, The, Enf.	24	H4
Coppice Clo. SW20	92	J3
Coppice Clo., Stan.	29	C6
Coppice Dr. SW15	74	G6
Coppice Wk. N20	31	D3
Coppice Way E18	42	F4
Coppies Gro. N11	32	B4
Copping Clo., Croy.	102	B4
Tipton Dr.		
Coppins, The, Croy.	103	B6
Coppins, The, Har.	29	B6
Coppock Clo. SW11	75	H2
Coppsfield, W.Mol.	90	G3
Hurst Rd.		
Copse, The E4	34	F1
Copse Ave., W.Wick.	103	B3
Copse Clo. SE7	69	H6
Copse Glade, Surb.	98	G1
Copse Hill SW20	92	G1
Copse Hill, Sutt.	100	E7
Coptefield Dr., Belv.	71	D3
Copthall Ave. EC2	**13**	**C3**
Copthall Ave. EC2	59	A6
Copthall Bldgs. EC2	**13**	**C3**
Copthall Clo. EC2	**13**	**B3**
Copthall Dr. NW7	30	G7
Copthall Gdns. NW7	30	G7
Copthall Gdns., Twick.	82	C1
Copthorne Ave. SW12	76	D7
Copthorne Ave., Brom.	104	C2
Copthorne Ave., Ilf.	35	E6
Coptic St. WC1	**12**	**A2**
Coptic St. WC1	58	E5
Copwood Clo. N12	31	G4
Coral Clo., Rom.	44	C3
Coral Row SW11	75	F3
Gartons Way		
Coral St. SE1	**16**	**F4**
Coral St. SE1	67	G2
Coraline Clo., Sthl.	54	F3
Coralline Wk. SE2	71	C2
Coram St. WC1	**8**	**A6**
Coram St. WC1	58	E4
Coran Clo. N9	25	G7
Corban Rd., Houns.	72	G3
Corbar Clo., Barn.	23	G1
Corbet Clo., Wall.	101	A1
Corbet Ct. EC3	**13**	**C4**
Corbet Pl. E1	**13**	**F1**
Corbett Gro. N22	32	E7
Bounds Grn. Rd.		
Corbett Ho., Wat.	28	C3
Corbett Rd. E11	42	J6
Corbett Rd. E17	42	C3
Corbetts La. SE16	68	F4
Rotherhithe New Rd.		
Corbetts Pas. SE16	68	F4
Rotherhithe New Rd.		
Corbicum E11	42	E7
Corbiere Ct. SW19	84	A6
Thornton Rd.		
Corbiere Ho. N1	59	B1
Corbins La., Har.	45	H3
Corbridge Cres. E2	59	E2
Corby Cres., Enf.	24	E4
Corby Rd. NW10	56	D2
Corby Way E3	60	A4
Knapp Rd.		
Corbylands Rd., Sid.	79	H7
Corbyn St. N4	49	E1
Cord Way E14	69	A3
Mellish St.		
Cordelia Clo. SE24	76	H4
Cordelia St. E14	60	B6
Cording St. E14	60	B5
Chrisp St.		
Cordova Rd. E3	59	H3
Cordwainers Wk. E13	60	G2
Clegg St.		
Cordwell Rd. SE13	78	E5
Corelli Rd. SE3	79	B1
Corfe Ave., Har.	45	G4
Corfe Twr. W3	65	C2
Corfield St. E2	59	E3
Corfton Rd. W5	55	H6
Coriander Ave. E14	60	D6
Corinium Clo., Wem.	46	J4
Corinne Rd. N19	49	C4
Cork Sq. E1	68	E1
Smeaton St.		
Cork St. W1	**11**	**F6**
Cork St. W1	58	C7
Cork St. Ms. W1	**11**	**F6**
Cork Tree Way E4	33	H5
Corker Wk. N7	49	F2
Corkran Rd., Surb.	91	G7

Corkscrew Hill, W.Wick.	103	C2
Corlett St. NW1	**10**	**G1**
Cormont Rd. SE5	76	H1
Cormorant Clo. E17	33	H7
Banbury Rd.		
Cormorant Rd. E7	51	F5
Cornbury Rd., Edg.	29	G7
Cornelia St. N7	49	F6
Cornell Clo., Sid.	89	E6
Corner Grn. SE3	78	G2
Corner Ho. St. WC2	**16**	**A1**
Corner Mead NW9	30	F7
Corney Rd. W4	65	E6
Cornflower La., Croy.	102	G2
Cornflower Ter. SE22	77	E6
Cornford Clo., Brom.	96	G5
Cornford Gro. SW12	85	B2
Cornhill EC3	**13**	**C4**
Cornhill EC3	59	A6
Cornish Ct. N9	25	E7
Cornish Gro. SE20	95	E1
Cornish Ho. SE17	**20**	**G6**
Cornish Ho., Brent.	64	J5
Cornmill La. SE13	78	C3
Cornmow Dr. NW10	47	G4
Cornshaw Rd., Dag.	53	D1
Cornthwaite Rd. E5	50	F3
Cornwall Ave. E2	59	F3
Cornwall Ave. N3	31	D7
Cornwall Ave. N22	40	E1
Cornwall Ave., Esher	98	C7
The Causeway		
Cornwall Ave., Sthl.	54	F5
Cornwall Ave., Well.	79	H3
Cornwall Clo., Bark.	52	J6
Cornwall Cres. W11	57	B6
Cornwall Dr., Orp.	89	C7
Cornwall Gdns. NW10	47	H6
Cornwall Gdns. SW7	**14**	**B6**
Cornwall Gdns. SW7	66	E3
Cornwall Gdns. Wk. SW7	**14**	**B6**
Cornwall Gro. W4	65	E5
Cornwall Ms. S. SW7	**14**	**C6**
Cornwall Ms. S. SW7	66	F3
Cornwall Ms. W. SW7	**14**	**B6**
Cornwall Rd. N4	40	G7
Cornwall Rd. N15	41	A5
Cornwall Rd. N18	33	D5
Fairfield Rd.		
Cornwall Rd. SE1	**16**	**E1**
Cornwall Rd. SE1	67	G1
Cornwall Rd., Croy.	101	H2
Cornwall Rd., Har.	36	J6
Cornwall Rd., Pnr.	28	F7
Cornwall Rd., Sutt.	100	C7
Cornwall Rd., Twick.	73	D7
Cornwall St. E1	59	E7
Watney St.		
Cornwall Ter. NW1	**7**	**A6**
Cornwall Ter. Ms. NW1	**7**	**A6**
Cornwallis Ave. N9	33	E2
Cornwallis Ave. SE9	88	G2
Cornwallis Gro. N9	33	E2
Cornwallis Rd. E17	41	G4
Cornwallis Rd. N9	33	E2
Cornwallis Rd. N19	49	E2
Cornwallis Rd., Dag.	53	D4
Cornwallis Wk. SE9	79	C3
Cornwood Clo. N2	39	G5
Cornwood Dr. E1	59	F6
Cornworthy Rd., Dag.	53	C5
Corona Rd. SE12	78	G7
Coronation Ave. N16	50	C3
Victorian Rd.		
Coronation Clo., Bex.	80	D6
Coronation Clo., Ilf.	43	F4
Coronation Rd. E13	60	J3
Coronation Rd. NW10	55	J3
Coronation Wk., Twick.	81	G1
Coronet St. N1	**9**	**D4**
Coronet St. N1	59	B3
Corporation Ave., Houns.	72	E4
Corporation Row EC1	**8**	**F5**
Corporation Row EC1	58	G4
Corporation St. E15	60	E2
Corporation St. N7	49	E5
Corrance Rd. SW2	76	E4
Corri Ave. N14	32	D4
Corrib Dr., Sutt.	100	H5
Corringham Ct. NW11	39	E7
Corringham Rd.		
Corringham Rd. NW11	39	D7

Corringham Rd., Wem.	47	A2
Corringway NW11	39	E7
Corringway W5	55	J5
Corscombe Clo., Kings.T.	83	C5
Corsehill St. SW16	85	C6
Corsham St. N1	**9**	**C4**
Corsham St. N1	59	A3
Corsica St. N5	49	H6
Corsley Way E9	50	J6
Trowbridge Est.		
Cortayne Rd. SW6	75	C2
Cortis Rd. SW15	74	H6
Cortis Ter. SW15	74	H6
Corunna Rd. SW8	76	C1
Corunna Ter. SW8	76	C1
Corvette Sq. SE10	69	D6
Feathers Pl.		
Coryton Path W9	57	C4
Ashmore Rd.		
Cosbycote Ave. SE24	76	J5
Cosdach Ave., Wall.	101	D7
Cosedge Cres., Croy.	101	G5
Cosgrove Clo. N21	32	J2
Cosgrove Clo., Hayes	54	E4
Kingsash Dr.		
Cosmo Pl. WC1	**12**	**B1**
Cosmur Clo. W12	65	F3
Cossall Wk. SE15	77	E1
Cosser St. SE1	**16**	**E5**
Cosser St. SE1	67	G3
Costa St. SE15	77	D2
Coston Wk. SE4	77	G4
Frendsbury Rd.		
Costons Ave., Grnf.	55	A3
Costons La., Grnf.	55	A3
Cosway St. NW1	**10**	**H1**
Cosway St. NW1	57	H5
Cotall St. E14	60	A6
Coteford Clo., Loug.	27	E2
Coteford Clo., Pnr.	36	A5
Coteford St. SW17	84	J4
Cotelands, Croy.	102	B3
Cotesbach Rd. E5	50	F3
Cotesmore Gdns., Dag.	53	C4
Cotford Rd., Th.Hth.	94	J4
Cotham St. SE17	**21**	**A2**
Cotherstone Rd. SW2	85	F1
Cotleigh Ave., Bex.	89	D2
Cotleigh Rd. NW6	48	D7
Cotman Clo. NW11	39	F6
Cotman Clo. SW15	74	J6
Westleigh Ave.		
Cotman Gdns., Edg.	38	A2
Cotmans Clo., Hayes	63	A1
Coton Rd., Well.	80	A3
Cotsford Ave., N.Mal.	92	C5
Cotswold Clo., Kings.T.	83	B6
Cotswold Gdns. E6	61	A3
Cotswold Gdns. NW2	44	A2
Cotswold Gdns., Ilf.	43	G7
Cotswold Gate NW2	48	B1
Cotswold Gdns.		
Cotswold Grn., Enf.	24	F4
Cotswold Way		
Cotswold Ms. SW11	75	G1
Battersea High St.		
Cotswold Ri., Orp.	97	J6
Cotswold Rd., Hmptn.	81	G6
Cotswold St. SE27	85	H4
Norwood High St.		
Cotswold Way, Enf.	24	F3
Cotswold Way, Wor.Pk.	99	J2
Cottage Ave., Brom.	104	B1
Cottage Fld. Clo., Sid.	89	C1
Cottage Grn. SE5	**21**	**C7**
Cottage Grn. SE5	68	A7
Cottage Gro. SW9	76	E3
Cottage Gro., Surb.	91	G6
Cottage Homes NW7	30	G4
Cottage Homes Chalet Est. NW7	30	G4
Cottage Pl. SW3	**14**	**G6**
Cottage Pl. SW3	66	H3
Cottage Rd., Epsom	99	D7
Cottage St. E14	60	B7
Cottage Wk. N16	50	C3
Smalley Clo.		
Cottage Wk. SE15	68	C7
Sumner Est.		
Cottenham Dr. NW9	38	F3
Cottenham Dr. SW20	83	H7
Cottenham Par. SW20	92	H2
Durham Rd.		

Cottenham Pk. Rd. SW20	92	H1
Cottenham Pl. SW20	83	H7
Cottenham Rd. E17	41	J4
Cotterill Rd., Surb.	98	H2
Cottesbrook St. SE14	68	H7
Nynehead St.		
Cottesmore Ave., Ilf.	43	D2
Cottesmore Gdns. W8	**14**	**B5**
Cottesmore Gdns. W8	66	E3
Cottimore Cres., Walt.	90	B7
Cottimore La., Walt.	90	B7
Cottimore Ter., Walt.	90	B7
Cottingham Chase, Ruis.	45	A3
Cottingham Rd. SE20	86	G7
Cottingham Rd. SW8	**20**	**D7**
Cottingham Rd. SW8	76	D1
Cottington Clo. SE11	**20**	**G2**
Cottington Clo. SE11	67	H4
Cottington Rd., Felt.	81	D4
Cottington St. SE11	**20**	**F3**
Cottle St. SE16	68	F2
St. Marychurch St.		
Cotton Ave. W3	56	D6
Cotton Hill, Brom.	87	D4
Cotton Row SW11	75	G3
Cotton St. E14	60	C7
Cottongrass Clo., Croy.	102	G1
Cornflower La.		
Cottons Gdns. E2	**9**	**E3**
Cottons La. SE1	**17**	**C1**
Couchmore Ave., Esher	98	B2
Couchmore Ave., Ilf.	43	C2
Coulgate St. SE4	77	H3
Coulson Clo., Dag.	44	C7
Coulson St. SW3	**18**	**J3**
Coulson St. SW3	66	J5
Coulter Rd. W6	65	H3
Coultree Clo., Hayes	54	E4
Berrydale Rd.		
Councillor St. SE5	67	J7
Counter Ct. SE1	**17**	**B2**
Counter St. SE1	**17**	**D2**
Countess Rd. NW5	49	C5
Countisbury Ave., Enf.	25	C7
Country Way, Felt.	81	B6
Country Way, Sun.	81	A7
County Gdns., Bark.	61	H2
River Rd.		
County Gate SE9	88	F3
County Gate, Barn.	23	E6
County Gro. SE5	76	J1
County Rd. E6	61	E5
County Rd., Th.Hth.	94	H2
County St. SE1	**17**	**A6**
County St. SE1	67	J3
Coupland Pl. SE18	70	F5
Courcy Rd. N8	40	G3
Courland Gro. SW8	76	D2
Courland St. SW8	76	D1
Course, The SE9	88	D3
Court, The, Ruis.	45	E4
Court Ave., Belv.	71	F5
Court Clo., Har.	37	G3
Court Clo., Twick.	81	H3
Court Clo., Wall.	101	D7
Court Clo. Ave., Twick.	81	H3
Court Cres., Chess.	98	G5
Court Downs Rd., Beck.	96	B2
Court Dr., Croy.	101	F4
Court Dr., Stan.	29	H4
Court Dr., Sutt.	100	H4
Court Fm. Ave., Epsom	99	D5
Court Fm. Rd. SE9	88	A2
Court Fm. Rd., Nthlt.	45	G7
Court Ho. Gdns. N3	31	D6
Court La. SE21	77	B6
Court La. Gdns. SE21	77	B7
Court Mead, Nthlt.	54	F3
Court Par., Wem.	46	E3
Court Rd. SE9	79	C6
Court Rd. SE25	95	C2
Court Rd., Sthl.	63	F4
Court St. E1	59	E5
Durward St.		
Court St., Brom.	96	G2
Court Way NW9	38	E4
Court Way W3	56	C5
Court Way, Ilf.	43	F3
Court Way, Twick.	73	C7
Court Yd. SE9	79	C6

Courtauld Clo. SE28	71	A1
Pitfield Cres.		
Courtauld Rd. N19	49	D1
Courtenay Ave. N6	39	H7
Courtenay Ave., Har.	28	J7
Courtenay Dr., Beck.	96	D2
Courtenay Gdns., Har.	36	A3
Courtenay Ms. E17	41	H5
Courtenay Pl.		
Courtenay Pl. E17	41	H5
Courtenay Rd. E11	51	F3
Courtenay Rd. E17	41	G4
Courtenay Rd. SE20	86	G7
Courtenay Rd., Wem.	46	G3
Courtenay Rd., Wor.Pk.	99	J3
Courtenay Sq. SE11	**20**	**E4**
Courtenay St. SE11	**20**	**E3**
Courtenay St. SE11	67	G5
Courtens Ms., Stan.	29	F7
Courtfield W5	55	F5
Courtfield Ave., Har.	37	C5
Courtfield Cres., Har.	37	C5
Courtfield Gdns. SW5	**18**	**B2**
Courtfield Gdns. SW5	66	E4
Courtfield Gdns. W13	55	D6
Courtfield Ms. SW5	**18**	**B2**
Courtfield Ri., W.Wick.	103	D3
Courtfield Rd. SW7	**18**	**C1**
Courtfield Rd. SW7	66	F4
Courthill Rd. SE13	78	C4
Courthope Rd. NW3	48	J4
Courthope Rd. SW19	84	B5
Courthope Rd., Grnf.	55	A2
Courthope Vill. SW19	84	B7
Courthouse Rd. N12	31	E6
Courtland Ave. E4	34	F2
Courtland Ave. NW7	30	D3
Courtland Ave. SW16	85	F7
Courtland Ave., Ilf.	52	C2
Courtland Dr., Chig.	35	E3
Courtland Gro. SE28	62	D7
Courtland Rd. E6	61	B1
Harrow Rd.		
Courtlands, Rich.	74	A5
Courtlands Ave. SE12	78	H1
Courtlands Ave., Brom.	103	E1
Courtlands Ave., Hmptn.	81	F6
Courtlands Ave., Rich.	74	B2
Courtlands Dr., Epsom	99	E6
Courtlands Rd., Surb.	92	A7
Courtleet Dr., Erith	80	H1
Courtleigh Gdns. NW11	39	B4
Courtman Rd. N17	32	J7
Courtmead Clo. SE24	76	J6
Courtnell St. W2	57	D6
Courtney Cres., Cars.	100	J7
Courtney Pl., Croy.	101	G3
Courtney Rd.		
Courtney Rd. N7	49	G5
Bryantwood Rd.		
Courtney Rd. SW19	84	H7
Courtney Rd., Croy.	101	G3
Courtrai Rd. SE23	77	H6
Courtside N8	40	D6
Courtway, Wdf.Grn.	34	J5
Courtway, The, Wat.	28	E2
Courtyard, The E1	59	E7
Courtyard, The N1	49	F7
Barnsbury Ter.		
Cousin La. EC4	**13**	**B6**
Couthurst Rd. SE3	69	H6
Coutts Ave., Chess.	98	F5
Coutts Cres. NW5	49	A3
Coval Gdns. SW14	74	B4
Coval La. SW14	74	B4
Coval Rd. SW14	74	B4
Covelees Wall E6	61	E6
Warwall		
Covent Gdn. WC2	**12**	**B5**
Covent Gdn. WC2	58	E7
Coventry Clo. E6	61	C6
Harper Rd.		
Coventry Clo. NW6	57	D1
Kilburn High Rd.		
Coventry Cross E3	60	C4
Gillender St.		
Coventry Rd. E1	59	E4
Coventry Rd. E2	59	E4
Coventry Rd. SE25	95	D4
Coventry Rd., Ilf.	52	E2
Coventry St. W1	**11**	**H6**
Coventry St. W1	58	D7

Coverack Clo. N14	24	C6
Coverack Clo., Croy.	95	H7
Coverdale Clo., Stan.	29	E5
Coverdale Gdns., Croy.	102	C3
Park Hill Ri.		
Coverdale Rd. NW2	48	A7
Coverdale Rd. W12	65	H2
Coverdales, The, Bark.	61	G2
Coverley Clo. E1	**13**	**J1**
Coverley Clo. E1	59	D5
Covert, The, Orp.	97	H6
Covert Rd., Chig.	35	J6
Covert Way, Barn.	23	F2
Coverton Rd. SW17	84	H5
Covet Wd. Clo., Orp.	97	J6
Covington Gdns. SW16	85	H7
Covington Way SW16	85	F6
Cow La., Grnf.	55	A2
Oldfield La. S.		
Cow Leaze E6	61	D6
Downings		
Cowan Clo. E6	61	B5
Oliver Gdns.		
Cowbridge La., Bark.	52	E7
Cowbridge Rd., Har.	37	J4
Cowcross St. EC1	**12**	**G1**
Cowcross St. EC1	58	H5
Cowden Rd., Orp.	97	J7
Cowden St. SE6	87	A4
Cowdenbeath Path N1	58	F1
Bingfield St.		
Cowdrey Clo., Enf.	25	B2
Cowdrey Rd. SW19	84	E5
Cowdry Rd. E9	50	H6
Wick Rd.		
Cowen Ave., Har.	45	J2
Cowgate Rd., Grnf.	55	A2
Cowick Rd. SW17	84	J4
Cowings Mead, Nthlt.	45	E6
Cowland Ave., Enf.	25	F4
Cowleaze Rd., Kings.T.	91	H1
Cowley La. E11	51	E3
Cathall Rd.		
Cowley Pl. NW4	38	J5
Cowley Rd. E11	42	H5
Cowley Rd. SW9	76	G1
Cowley Rd. SW14	74	E3
Cowley Rd. W3	65	F1
Cowley Rd., Ilf.	43	C7
Cowley St. SW1	**16**	**A5**
Cowling Clo. W11	66	B1
Wilsham St.		
Cowper Ave. E6	52	B7
Cowper Ave., Sutt.	100	F4
Cowper Clo., Brom.	97	A4
Cowper Clo., Well.	80	A5
Cowper Gdns. N14	24	B6
Cowper Gdns., Wall.	101	C6
Cowper Rd. N14	32	B1
Cowper Rd. N16	50	B5
Cowper Rd. N18	33	D5
Cowper Rd. SW19	84	F6
Cowper Rd. W3	65	D1
Cowper Rd. W7	55	C7
Cowper Rd., Belv.	71	G4
Cowper Rd., Brom.	97	A4
Cowper Rd., Kings.T.	82	J5
Cowper St. EC2	**9**	**C5**
Cowper St. EC2	59	A4
Cowper Ter. W10	57	A4
St. Marks Rd.		
Cowslip Rd. E18	42	H2
Cowthorpe Rd. SW8	76	D1
Cox La., Chess.	98	H4
Cox La., Epsom	99	B4
Coxmount Rd. SE7	70	A5
Cox's Wk. SE21	86	D1
Coxson Pl. SE1	**17**	**F2**
Coxwell Rd. SE18	70	G5
Coxwell Rd. SE19	86	B7
Coxwold Path, Chess.	98	H7
Garrison La.		
Crab Hill, Beck.	87	D7
Crabbs Cft. Clo., Orp.	104	F5
Ladycroft Way		
Crabtree Ave., Rom.	44	D4
Crabtree Ave., Wem.	55	H2
Crabtree Ct. E15	51	B5
Clays La.		
Crabtree La. SW6	66	A7
Crabtree Manorway N., Belv.	71	J2
Crabtree Manorway S., Belv.	71	J3

Crabtree Wk. SE15 77 C1
Lisford St.
Crace St. NW1 7 H3
Craddock Rd., Enf. 25 C3
Craddock St. NW5 49 A6
Prince of Wales Rd.
Cradley Rd. SE9 88 G1
Craig Gdns. E18 42 F2
Craig Pk. Rd. N18 33 E5
Craig Rd., Rich. 82 F4
Craigen Ave., Croy. 102 E1
Craigerne Rd. SE3 69 H7
Craigholm SE18 79 D2
Craigmuir Pk., Wem. 55 J1
Craignair Rd. SW2 76 G7
Craignish Ave. SW16 94 F2
Craigs Ct. SW1 16 A1
Craigton Rd. SE9 79 C4
Craigweil Clo., Stan. 29 G5
Craigweil Dr., Stan. 29 G5
Craigwell Ave., Felt. 81 A3
Craik Ct. NW6 57 C2
Carlton Vale
Crail Row SE17 21 C2
Cramer St. W1 11 C2
Cramond Clo. W6 66 B6
Crampton Rd. SE20 86 F6
Crampton St. SE17 20 J3
Crampton St. SE17 67 J4
Cranberry Clo., Nthlt. 54 D2
Parkfield Ave.
Cranberry La. E16 60 E4
Cranborne Ave., Sthl. 63 G4
Cranborne Rd., Bark. 61 G1
Cranborne Waye, Hayes 54 B6
Cranbourn All. WC2 11 J5
Cranbourn Pas. SE16 68 E2
Marigold St.
Cranbourn St. WC2 11 J5
Cranbourn St. WC2 58 D7
Cranbourne Ave. E11 42 H4
Cranbourne Ave., Surb. 99 A3
Cranbourne Clo. SW16 94 E3
Cranbourne Dr., Pnr. 36 D5
Cranbourne Gdns. NW11 39 B5
Cranbourne Gdns., Ilf. 43 F3
Cranbourne Rd. E12 52 B5
High St. N.
Cranbourne Rd. E15 51 C4
Cranbourne Rd. N10 40 B2
Cranbrook Clo., Brom. 96 G6
Cranbrook Dr., Twick. 81 H1
Cranbrook Est. E2 59 G2
Cranbrook Ms. E17 41 J5
Cranbrook Pk. N22 40 F1
Cranbrook Pt. E16 69 G1
Cranbrook Ri., Ilf. 43 C6
Cranbrook Rd. SE8 78 A1
Cranbrook Rd. SW19 84 B7
Cranbrook Rd. W4 65 E5
Cranbrook Rd., Barn. 23 G6
Cranbrook Rd., Bexh. 80 F1
Cranbrook Rd., Houns. 72 F4
Cranbrook Rd., Ilf. 43 D5
Cranbrook Rd., Th.Hth. 94 J2
Cranbrook St. E2 59 G2
Roman Rd.
Cranbury Rd. SW6 75 E2
Crane Ave. W3 56 C7
Crane Ave., Islw. 73 D5
Crane Clo., Dag. 53 G6
Crane Ct. EC4 12 F4
Crane Ct., Epsom 99 C4
Crane Gro. N7 49 G6
Crane Lo. Rd., Houns. 63 B6
Crane Mead SE16 68 G4
Crane Pk. Rd., Twick. 81 H2
Crane Rd., Twick. 82 B1
Crane St. SE10 69 D5
Park Row
Crane Way, Twick. 72 J7
Cranebrook, Twick. 81 J2
Manor Rd.
Craneford Clo., Twick. 73 C7
Craneford Way, Twick. 73 B7
Cranes Dr., Surb. 91 H4
Cranes Pk., Surb. 91 H4
Cranes Pk. Ave., Surb. 91 H4
Cranes Pk. Cres., Surb. 91 J4
Cranes Way, Borwd. 22 C5
Craneswater Pk., Sthl. 63 F5
Cranfield Clo. SE27 85 J3
Dunelm Gro.
Cranfield Dr. NW9 30 E7
Cranfield Rd. SE4 77 J3
Cranfield Row SE1 16 F5
Cranford Ave. N13 32 E5
Cranford Clo. SW20 83 H7
Cranford Cotts. E1 59 G7
Cranford St.
Cranford La. (Heston), Houns. 63 B7
Cranford St. E1 59 G7
Cranford Way N8 40 F5
Cranhurst Rd. NW2 47 J5
Cranleigh Clo. SE20 95 E2
Cranleigh Clo., Bex. 80 H5
Cranleigh Gdns. N21 24 G5
Cranleigh Gdns. SE25 95 B3
Cranleigh Gdns., Bark. 52 G7
Cranleigh Gdns., Har. 37 H5
Cranleigh Gdns., Kings.T. 82 J6
Cranleigh Gdns., Loug. 27 C6
Cranleigh Gdns., Sthl. 54 F6
Cranleigh Gdns., Sutt. 100 E2
Cranleigh Ms. SW11 75 H2
Cranleigh Rd. N15 40 J5
Cranleigh Rd. SW19 93 C3
Cranleigh St. NW1 7 G2
Cranleigh St. NW1 58 C2
Cranley Dene Ct. N10 40 B4
Cranley Dr., Ilf. 43 F7
Cranley Gdns. N10 40 B4
Cranley Gdns. N13 32 F3
Cranley Gdns. SW7 18 D3
Cranley Gdns. SW7 66 F5
Cranley Gdns., Wall. 101 C7
Cranley Ms. SW7 18 D3
Cranley Ms. SW7 66 F5
Cranley Pl. SW7 18 E2
Cranley Pl. SW7 66 G4
Cranley Rd. E13 60 H5
Cranley Rd., Ilf. 43 F6
Cranmer Ave. W13 64 E3
Cranmer Clo., Mord. 93 A6
Cranmer Clo., Ruis. 45 D1
Cranmer Clo., Stan. 29 F7
Cranmer Ct. SW3 18 H2
Cranmer Ct. SW4 76 D3
Cranmer Ct., Hmptn. 81 H5
Cranmer Rd.
Cranmer Fm. Clo., Mitch. 93 J4
Cranmer Gdns., Dag. 53 J4
Cranmer Rd. E7 51 H4
Cranmer Rd. SW9 20 F7
Cranmer Rd. SW9 67 G7
Cranmer Rd., Croy. 101 H3
Cranmer Rd., Edg. 30 B3
Cranmer Rd., Hmptn. 81 H5
Cranmer Rd., Kings.T. 82 H5
Cranmer Rd., Mitch. 93 J4
Cranmer Ter. SW17 84 G5
Cranmore Ave., Islw. 63 J7
Cranmore Rd., Brom. 87 F3
Cranmore Rd., Chis. 88 C5
Cranmore Way N10 40 C4
Cranston Clo., Houns. 72 E2
Cranston Est. N1 9 C2
Cranston Est. N1 59 A2
Cranston Gdns. E4 34 B5
Cranston Rd. SE23 86 H1
Cranswick Rd. SE16 68 E5
Crantock Rd. SE6 87 B2
Cranwell Clo. E3 60 B4
Cranwich Ave. N21 25 A7
Cranwich Rd. N16 41 A7
Cranwood St. EC1 9 C4
Cranwood St. EC1 59 A3
Cranworth Cres. E4 34 D1
Cranworth Gdns. SW9 76 G1
Craster Rd. SW2 76 F7
Crathie Rd. SE12 78 H6
Crathorn St. SE13 78 C3
Loampit Vale
Cravan Ave., Felt. 81 A2
Craven Ave. W5 55 F7
Craven Ave., Sthl. 54 F5
Craven Clo., Hayes 54 A6
Craven Gdns. SW19 84 D5
Craven Gdns., Bark. 61 H2
Craven Gdns., Ilf. 43 G2
Craven Hill W2 10 D5
Craven Hill W2 57 F7
Craven Hill Gdns. W2 10 C5
Craven Hill Gdns. W2 57 F7
Craven Hill Ms. W2 10 D5
Craven Hill Ms. W2 57 F7
Craven Ms. SW11 76 A3
Taybridge Rd.
Craven Pk. NW10 56 E1
Craven Pk. Ms. NW10 56 E1
Craven Pk. Rd. N15 41 C6
Craven Pk. Rd. NW10 56 E1
Craven Pas. WC2 16 A1
Craven Rd. NW10 56 D1
Craven Rd. W2 10 D5
Craven Rd. W2 57 F6
Craven Rd. W5 55 F7
Craven Rd., Croy. 102 E1
Craven Rd., Kings.T. 91 J1
Craven St. WC2 16 A1
Craven St. WC2 67 E1
Craven Ter. W2 10 D5
Craven Ter. W2 57 F7
Craven Wk. N16 41 D7
Crawford Ave., Wem. 46 G5
Crawford Clo., Islw. 73 B2
Crawford Est. SE5 76 J2
Crawford Gdns. N13 32 H3
Crawford Gdns., Nthlt. 54 F3
Crawford Ms. W1 10 J2
Crawford Pas. EC1 8 E6
Crawford Pl. W1 10 H3
Crawford Pl. W1 57 H6
Crawford Rd. SE5 76 J1
Crawford St. W1 10 H2
Crawford St. W1 57 J5
Crawley Rd. E10 51 B1
Crawley Rd. N22 40 J2
Crawley Rd., Enf. 25 B7
Crawshaw Ct. SW9 76 G1
Eythorne Rd.
Crawthew Gro. SE22 77 C4
Cray Rd., Belv. 71 G6
Cray Rd., Sid. 89 C7
Craybrooke Rd., Sid. 89 B4
Craybury End SE9 88 F2
Crayford Clo. E6 61 B5
Neatscourt Rd.
Crayford Rd. N7 49 D4
Crayke Hill, Chess. 98 H7
Crealock Gro., Wdf.Grn. 34 F5
Crealock St. SW18 75 E6
Creasy Est. SE1 17 D6
Crebor St. SE22 77 D6
Credenhall Dr., Brom. 104 C1
Lower Gravel Rd.
Credenhill St. SW16 85 C6
Crediton Hill NW6 48 E5
Crediton Rd. E16 60 G6
Pacific Rd.
Crediton Rd. NW10 57 A1
Crediton Way, Esher 98 D5
Credon Rd. E13 60 J2
Credon Rd. SE16 68 E5
Creechurch La. EC3 13 E4
Creechurch La. EC3 59 B6
Creechurch Pl. EC3 13 E4
Creed La. EC4 12 H4
Creek, The, Sun. 90 A5
Creek Rd. SE8 69 A6
Creek Rd. SE10 69 B6
Creek Rd., Bark. 61 J3
Creek Rd., E.Mol. 91 B4
Creekside SE8 69 B7
Creeland Gro. SE6 86 J1
Catford Hill
Crefeld Clo. W6 66 A6
Creffield Rd. W3 55 J7
Creffield Rd. W5 55 J7
Creighton Ave. E6 61 A2
Creighton Ave. N2 39 H3
Creighton Ave. N10 39 J2
Creighton Rd. N17 33 B7
Creighton Rd. NW6 57 A2
Creighton Rd. W5 64 G3
Cremer St. E2 9 F2
Cremer St. E2 59 C2
Cremorne Est. SW10 18 E7
Cremorne Rd. SW10 18 D7
Cremorne Rd. SW10 66 F7
Crescent, The E17 41 H5
Crescent, The EC3 13 F5
Crescent, The N11 32 A4
Crescent, The NW2 47 H3
Crescent, The SW13 74 F2
Crescent, The SW19 84 D3
Crescent, The W3 56 E6
Crescent, The, Barn. 23 E3
Crescent, The, Beck. 96 A1
Crescent, The, Bex. 80 C7
Crescent, The, Croy. 95 A5
Crescent, The, Har. 45 J1
Crescent, The, Ilf. 43 D6
Crescent, The, Loug. 27 A5
Crescent, The, N.Mal. 92 C2
Crescent, The, Sid. 88 J4
Crescent, The, Sthl. 63 F2
Crescent, The, Surb. 91 H5
Crescent, The, Sutt. 100 G5
Crescent, The, Wat. (Aldenham) 28 H2
Crescent, The, Wem. 46 D2
Crescent, The, W.Mol. 90 G4
Crescent, The, W.Wick. 96 E6
Crescent Dr., Orp. 97 E6
Crescent Gdns. SW19 84 D3
Crescent Gdns., Ruis. 36 B7
Crescent Gro. SW4 76 C4
Crescent Gro., Mitch. 93 H4
Crescent La. SW4 76 C4
Crescent Pl. SW3 18 G1
Crescent Pl. SW3 66 H4
Crescent Ri. N22 40 D1
Crescent Ri., Barn. 23 H5
Crescent Rd. E4 26 E7
Crescent Rd. E6 60 J1
Crescent Rd. E10 51 B2
Crescent Rd. E13 60 G1
Crescent Rd. E18 42 J2
Crescent Rd. N3 39 C1
Crescent Rd. N8 40 D6
Crescent Rd. N9 33 D1
Crescent Rd. N11 31 J4
Crescent Rd. N15 40 H3
Carlingford Rd.
Crescent Rd. N22 40 D1
Crescent Rd. SE18 70 E5
Crescent Rd. SW20 93 A1
Crescent Rd., Barn. 23 G4
Crescent Rd., Beck. 96 B2
Crescent Rd., Brom. 87 G7
Crescent Rd., Dag. 53 H3
Crescent Rd., Enf. 24 H4
Crescent Rd., Kings.T. 83 A7
Crescent Rd., Sid. 88 J3
Crescent Row EC1 8 J6
Crescent Stables SW15 75 B4
Upper Richmond Rd.
Crescent St. N1 49 F7
Crescent Vw., Loug. 27 A5
Crescent Way N12 31 H6
Crescent Way SE4 78 A3
Crescent Way SW16 85 F6
Crescent Way, Orp. 104 H5
Crescent W., Barn. 23 F1
Crescent Wd. Rd. SE26 86 D3
Cresford Rd. SW6 75 E1
Crespigny Rd. NW4 38 H6
Cressage Clo., Sthl. 54 G4
Cresset Rd. E9 50 F6
Cresset St. SW4 76 D3
Cressfield Clo. NW5 49 A5
Cressida Rd. N19 49 C1
Cressingham Gro., Sutt. 100 F4
Cressingham Rd. SE13 78 C3
Cressingham Rd., Edg. 30 D6
Cressington Clo. N16 50 B5
Wordsworth Rd.
Cresswell Gdns. SW5 18 C3
Cresswell Gdns. SW5 66 F5
Cresswell Pk. SE3 78 F3
Cresswell Pl. SW10 18 C3
Cresswell Pl. SW10 66 F5
Cresswell Rd. SE25 95 D4
Cresswell Rd., Felt. 81 E4
Cresswell Rd., Twick. 73 G6
Cresswell Way N21 24 G7
Cressy Ct. E1 59 F5
Cressy Pl.
Cressy Ct. W6 65 H3
Cressy Pl. E1 59 F5
Cressy Rd. NW3 48 J5
Crest, The N13 32 G4
Crest, The NW4 38 J5
Crest, The, Surb. 92 A5
Crest Gdns., Ruis. 45 C3
Crest Rd. NW2 47 F3
Crest Rd., Brom. 96 F7
Crest Rd., S.Croy. 102 E7
Crest Vw., Pnr. 36 D4
Crest Vw. Dr., Orp. 97 E5
Crestbrook Ave. N13 32 H3
Crestfield St. WC1 8 B3
Crestfield St. WC1 58 E3
Creston Way, Wor.Pk. 100 A1
Crestway SW15 74 G6

Crestwood Way, Hphhouns.	72 F5	Crofton Ter. E5 *Studley Clo.*	50 H5	Crondall St. N1	59 A2	Crossway SE28	62 C6
Creswick Rd. W3	56 B7	Crofton Ter., Rich.	73 J4	Crook Log, Bexh.	80 D3	Crossway SW20	92 J4
Creswick Wk. E3 *Malmesbury Rd.*	60 A3	Crofton Way, Barn. *Wycherley Cres.*	23 E6	Crooke Rd. SE8	68 H5	Crossway, Dag.	53 C3
Creswick Wk. NW11	39 C4	Crofton Way, Enf.	24 G2	Crooked Billet SW19 *Woodhayes Rd.*	83 J6	Crossway, Enf.	25 B7
Creton St. SE18	70 D3	Croftongate Way SE4	77 H5	Crooked Billet	34 A7	Crossway, Hayes	63 A1
Crewdson Rd. SW9	67 G7	Crofts Rd., Har.	37 D6	Roundabout E17		Crossway, Orp.	97 G4
Crewe Pl. NW10	56 F3	**Crofts St. E1**	**13 H6**	Crooked Usage N3	39 B3	Crossway, Ruis.	45 C4
Crews St. E14	69 A4	Crofts St. E1	59 D7	Crookham Rd. SW6	75 C1	Crossway, Wdf.Grn.	34 J4
Crewys Rd. NW2	48 C2	Croftway NW3	48 D4	Crookston Rd. SE9	79 D3	Crossway, The SE9	88 A2
Crewys Rd. SE15	77 E2	Croftway, Rich.	82 E3	Croombs Rd. E16	60 J5	Crossway, The W13	55 D4
Crichton Ave., Wall.	101 D5	Crogsland Rd. NW1	49 A7	Crooms Hill SE10	69 C7	Crossways N21	24 J6
Crichton Rd., Cars.	100 J7	Croham Clo., S.Croy.	102 B7	Crooms Hill Gro. SE10	69 C7	Crossways, S.Croy.	102 H7
Cricket Grn., Mitch.	93 J3	Croham Manor Rd., S.Croy.	102 B7	**Cropley St. N1**	**9 B1**	Crossways, The, Hphhouns.	63 F7
Cricket Grd. Rd., Chis.	97 E1	Croham Mt., S.Croy.	102 B7	Cropley St. N1	59 A2	Crossways, The, Wem.	47 A2
Cricket La., Beck.	86 H5	Croham Pk. Ave., S.Croy.	102 B5	Croppath Rd., Dag.	53 G4		
Cricketers Arms Rd., Enf.	24 J2	Croham Rd., S.Croy.	102 A5	**Cropthorne Ct. W9**	**6 D4**	Crossways Rd., Beck.	96 A4
Cricketers Clo. N14	24 C7	Croham Valley Rd., S.Croy.	102 C6	Crosby Clo., Felt.	81 E4	Crossways Rd., Mitch.	94 B3
Cricketers Clo., Chess.	98 G4	Croindene Rd. SW16	94 E1	**Crosby Ct. SE1**	**17 B3**	Croston St. E8	59 D1
Cricketers Ct. SE11	**20 G2**	Cromartie Rd. N19	40 D7	Crosby Rd. E7	51 G6	Crothall Clo. N13	32 F3
Cricketfield Rd. E5	50 E4	Cromarty Rd., Edg.	30 B2	Crosby Rd., Dag.	62 H2	Crouch Ave., Bark.	62 B2
Cricklade Ave. SW2	85 E2	Crombie Clo., Ilf.	43 C5	**Crosby Row SE1**	**17 B3**	Crouch Clo., Beck.	87 A6
Cricklewood Bdy. NW2	47 J3	Crombie Rd., Sid.	88 G1	Crosby Sq. EC3	68 A2	*Abbey La.*	
Cricklewood La. NW2	48 A4	Cromer Pl., Orp.	104 G1	**Crosby Sq. EC3**	**13 D4**	Crouch Cft. SE9	88 D3
Cricklewood Trd. Est. NW2	48 B3	*Andover Rd.*		Crosby Wk. E8	50 C6	Crouch End Hill N8	40 D7
Cridland St. E15 *Church St.*	60 F1	Cromer Rd. E10 *James La.*	42 D6	*Laurel St.*		Crouch Hall Rd. N8	40 D6
Crieff Ct., Tedd.	82 F7	Cromer Rd. N17	41 D2	Crosby Wk. SW2 *Taybridge Rd.*	76 G7	Crouch Hill N4	40 E7
Crieff Rd. SW18	75 F6	Cromer Rd. SE25	95 E3	Crosland Pl. SW11 *Taybridge Rd.*	76 A3	Crouch Hill N8	40 E6
Criffel Ave. SW2	85 D2	Cromer Rd. SW17	85 A6	Cross Ave. SE10	69 D6	Crouch Rd. NW10	47 D7
Crimscott St. SE1	**17 E6**	Cromer Rd., Barn.	23 F4	Cross Deep, Twick.	82 C3	Crouchman Clo. SE26	86 C3
Crimscott St. SE1	68 B3	Cromer Rd., Rom.	44 J6	Cross Deep Gdns., Twick.	82 C2	Crow La., Rom.	44 F7
Crimsworth Rd. SW8	76 D1	Cromer Rd., Rom. (Chadwell Heath)	44 E6	**Cross Keys Clo. W1**	**11 C2**	Crowborough Path, Wat. *Prestwick Rd.*	28 C2
Crinan St. N1	**8 B1**	Cromer Rd., Wdf.Grn.	34 G4	**Cross Keys Sq. EC1**	**12 J2**	Crowborough Rd. SW17	85 A6
Crinan St. N1	58 E2	**Cromer St. WC1**	**8 B4**	Cross Lances Rd., Hphhouns.	72 H4	Crowden Way SE28	62 C7
Cringle St. SW8	**19 F7**	Cromer St. WC1	58 E3	**Cross La. EC3**	**13 D6**	Crowder St. E1	59 E7
Cringle St. SW8	67 C7	Cromer Ter. E8 *Ferncliff Rd.*	50 D5	Cross La. N8	40 F3	Crowhurst Clo. SW9	76 G2
Cripplegate St. EC2	**12 J1**	Cromer Vill. Rd. SW18	75 C6	Cross La., Bex.	80 F7	Crowland Gdns. N14	24 E7
Crisp Rd. W6	65 J5	Cromford Clo., Orp.	104 H3	Cross Rd. E4	34 E1	Crowland Rd. N15	41 C5
Crispe Ho., Bark. *Dovehouse Mead*	61 G2	Cromford Path E5 *Overbury St.*	50 G4	Cross Rd. N11	32 B5	Crowland Rd., Th.Hth.	95 A4
Crispen Rd., Felt.	81 E4	Cromford Rd. SW18	75 D5	Cross Rd. N22	32 G7	Crowland Ter. N1	50 A7
Crispian Clo. NW10	47 E4	Cromford Way, N.Mal.	92 D1	Cross Rd. SE5	77 B2	Crowland Wk., Mord.	93 E6
Crispin Clo., Croy. *Harrington Clo.*	101 E2	Cromlix Clo., Chis.	97 E2	Cross Rd. SW19	84 D7	Crowlands Ave., Rom.	44 H6
Crispin Cres., Croy.	101 D2	**Crompton St. W2**	**6 E6**	Cross Rd., Brom.	104 B2	Crowley Cres., Croy.	101 G5
Crispin Rd., Edg.	30 C6	Crompton St. W2	57 G4	Cross Rd., Croy.	102 A1	Crowline Wk. N1 *Clephane Rd.*	50 A6
Crispin St. E1	**13 F2**	Cromwell Ave. N6	49 B1	Cross Rd., Enf.	25 C4	Crowmarsh Gdns. SE23 *Tyson Rd.*	77 F7
Crispin St. E1	59 C5	Cromwell Ave. W6	65 H4	Cross Rd., Felt.	81 E4	Crown Arc., Kings.T. *Union St.*	91 G2
Cristowe Rd. SW6	75 C4	Cromwell Ave., Brom.	96 H3	Cross Rd., Har.	37 A4	Crown Clo. E3	60 A1
Criterion Ms. N19 *St. Johns Vill.*	49 D2	Cromwell Ave., N.Mal.	92 F5	Cross Rd., Har. (South Harrow)	45 H3	Crown Clo. NW6	48 E6
Crockerton Rd. SW17	84 J2	**Cromwell Clo. E1**	**17 J1**	Cross Rd., Har. (Wealdstone)	37 D2	Crown Clo. NW7	30 F2
Crockham Way SE9	88 D4	Cromwell Clo. N2	39 G4	Cross Rd., Kings.T.	82 J7	Crown Clo., Wal.T.	90 C7
Crocus Clo., Croy. *Cornflower La.*	102 G1	Cromwell Clo. W3 *High St.*	65 C1	Cross Rd., Rom.	44 G4	**Crown Ct. EC2**	**13 A4**
Crocus Fld., Barn.	23 C6	Cromwell Clo., Brom.	96 H4	Cross Rd., Rom. (Chadwell Heath)	44 C7	Crown Ct. SE12	78 H6
Croft, The NW10	56 F2	Cromwell Cres. SW5	66 D4	Cross Rd., Sid.	89 B4	**Crown Ct. WC2**	**12 B4**
Croft, The W5	55 H5	**Cromwell Gdns. SW7**	**14 F6**	*Sidcup Hill*		Crown Ct., Brom. *Victoria Rd.*	97 A5
Croft, The, Barn.	23 B4	Cromwell Gdns. SW7	66 G3	Cross Rd., Sutt.	100 G5	Crown Dale SE19	85 H6
Croft, The, Hphhouns.	63 E6	Cromwell Gro. W6	65 J3	Cross Rd., Wdf.Grn.	35 C6	Crown Hill, Croy.	101 J2
Croft, The, Loug.	27 D2	Cromwell Ind. Est. E10	50 H1	Cross Rds., Loug.	26 H2	Crown La. N14	32 C1
Croft, The, Pnr. *Rayners La.*	36 F7	**Cromwell Ms. SW7**	**18 F1**	Cross St. N1	58 H1	Crown La. SW16	85 G5
Croft, The, Ruis.	45 C4	Cromwell Ms. SW7	66 G4	Cross St. SW13	74 E2	Crown La., Brom.	97 A5
Croft, The, Wem.	46 F5	Cromwell Pl. N6	49 B1	Cross St., Hmptn.	81 J5	Crown La., Chis.	97 F1
Croft Ave., W.Wick.	103 C1	**Cromwell Pl. SW7**	**18 F1**	Cross Way, Pnr.	36 B2	Crown La., Mord.	93 D3
Croft Clo. NW7	30 E3	Cromwell Pl. SW7	66 G4	Cross Way, The, Har.	37 B2	Crown La. Gdns. SW16 *Crown La.*	85 G5
Croft Clo., Belv.	71 F5	Cromwell Pl. SW14	74 C3	Crossbow Rd., Chig.	35 J5		
Croft Clo., Chis.	88 C4	Cromwell Pl. W3 *Grove Pl.*	65 C1	Crossbrook Rd. SE3	79 B2	Crown La. Spur, Brom.	97 A6
Croft Gdns. W7	64 D2	Cromwell Rd. E7	51 J7	Crossfield Rd. N17	40 J3	Crown Ms. E13 *Waghorn Rd.*	60 J1
Croft Lo. Clo., Wdf.Grn.	34 H6	Cromwell Rd. E17	42 C5	Crossfield Rd. NW3	48 G6		
Croft Rd. SW16	94 G1	Cromwell Rd. N3	39 F2	Crossfield St. SE8	69 A7	Crown Ms. W6	65 G4
Croft Rd. SW19	84 F7	Cromwell Rd. N10	32 A7	Crossfields, Loug.	27 E5	**Crown Office Row EC4**	**12 E5**
Croft Rd., Brom.	87 G6	Cromwell Rd. SW5	66 E4	Crossford St. SW9	76 E2	**Crown Pas. SW1**	**15 G2**
Croft Rd., Enf.	25 H1	**Cromwell Rd. SW7**	**18 E1**	Crossgate, Edg.	30 A3	Crown Pl. NW5 *Kentish Town Rd.*	49 B6
Croft Rd., Sutt.	100 H5	Cromwell Rd. SW7	66 E4	Crossgate, Grnf.	46 E6		
Croft St. SE8	68 H4	Cromwell Rd. SW9	76 F1	Crossland Rd., Th.Hth.	94 H5	Crown Pt. Par. SE19 *Beulah Hill*	85 H6
Croft Way NW3 *Ferncroft Ave.*	48 D4	Cromwell Rd. SW19	84 D5	Crosslands Ave. W5	64 J1		
Croft Way, Sid.	88 H3	Cromwell Rd., Beck.	95 H2	Crosslands Ave., Sthl.	63 F5	Crown Rd. N10	32 A7
Croftdown Rd. NW5	49 A3	Cromwell Rd., Croy.	95 A7	Crosslands Rd., Epsom	99 D6	Crown Rd. N17	33 D7
Crofters Clo., Islw. *Ploughmans End*	73 A5	Cromwell Rd., Felt.	81 B1	**Crosslet St. SE17**	**21 C1**	Crown Rd., Borwd.	22 A1
Crofters Ct. SE8	68 H4	Cromwell Rd., Hphhouns.	72 G4	Crossley St. N7	49 G6	Crown Rd., Enf.	25 E4
Crofters Way NW1	58 D1	Cromwell Rd., Kings.T.	91 H1	Crossmead SE9	88 C1	Crown Rd., Ilf.	43 G4
Crofton Ave. W4	65 C7	Cromwell Rd., Tedd.	82 D6	Crossmead Ave., Grnf.	54 G3	Crown Rd., Mord.	93 D4
Crofton Ave., Bex.	80 D7	Cromwell Rd., Wem.	55 H2	**Crossmount Ho. SE5**	**21 A7**	Crown Rd., N.Mal.	92 C1
Crofton Ave., Orp.	104 F2	Cromwell Rd., Wor.Pk.	99 D3	Crossness La. SE28 *Bayliss Ave.*	62 D7	Crown Rd., Sutt.	100 D4
Crofton La., Orp.	104 G2	Cromwell St., Hphhouns.	72 G4	Crossness Rd., Bark.	61 J3	Crown Rd., Twick.	73 E6
Crofton Pk. Rd. SE4	77 J6	Crondace Rd. SW6	75 D1	Crossthwaite Ave. SE5	77 A4	**Crown St. SE5**	**21 A7**
Crofton Rd. E13	60 H4	**Crondall St. N1**	**9 D2**	**Crosswall EC3**	**13 F5**	Crown St. SE5	67 J7
Crofton Rd. SE5	77 B1			Crosswall EC3	59 C7	Crown St. W3	65 B1
Crofton Rd., Orp.	104 D3			Crossway N12	31 G6	Crown St., Dag.	53 J6
				Crossway N16	50 B5	Crown St., Har.	46 A1
				Crossway N22	32 H7	Crown Ter., Rich.	73 J4
				Crossway NW9	38 F4		

Crown Wk., Wem. 46 J3
Crown Wds. La. SE9 79 F2
Crown Wds. La. SE18 79 E2
Crown Wds. Way SE9 79 G5
Crown Yd., Houns. 72 J3
  High St.
Crowndale Rd. NW1 **7 G1**
Crowndale Rd. NW1 58 C2
Crownfield Ave., Ilf. 43 H6
Crownfield Rd. E15 51 D4
Crownhill Rd. NW10 56 F1
Crownhill Rd., 35 B7
  Wdf.Grn.
Crownmead Way, 44 H4
  Rom.
Crownstone Rd. SW2 76 G5
Crowntree Clo., Islw. 64 C6
Crows Rd. E15 60 D3
Crowshott Ave., Stan. 37 F2
Crowther Ave., Brent. 64 H4
Crowther Rd. SE25 95 D4
Crowthorne Clo. SW18 84 C1
Crowthorne Rd. W10 57 A6
Croxden Clo., Edg. 37 J3
Croxden Wk., Mord. 93 F6
Croxford Gdns. N22 32 H7
Croxley Rd. W9 57 C3
Croxted Clo. SE21 76 J7
Croxted Rd. SE21 76 J7
Croxted Rd. SE24 76 J7
Croyde Ave., Grnf. 54 J3
Croyde Clo., Sid. 79 G7
Croydon Flyover, 101 H4
  The, Croy.
  Duppas Hill Rd.
Croydon Gro., Croy. 101 H1
Croydon Rd. E13 60 F4
Croydon Rd. SE20 95 E2
Croydon Rd., Beck. 95 H3
Croydon Rd., Brom. 103 J3
Croydon Rd., Croy. 101 B4
Croydon Rd., Kes. 104 C3
Croydon Rd., Mitch. 94 A4
Croydon Rd., Wall. 101 B4
Croydon Rd., W.Wick. 103 E3
Croyland Rd. N9 33 D1
Croylands Dr., Surb. 91 H7
Croysdale Ave., Sun. 90 A3
Crozier Ter. E9 50 G5
Crucible Clo., Rom. 44 B6
Crucifix La. SE1 **17 D3**
Crucifix La. SE1 68 B2
Cruden Ho. SE17 **20 G6**
Cruden St. N1 58 H1
Cruikshank Rd. E15 51 E4
Cruikshank St. WC1 **8 E3**
Cruikshank St. WC1 58 G3
Crummock Gdns. 38 E5
  NW9
Crumpsall St. SE2 71 C4
Crundale Ave. NW9 38 A5
Crunden Rd., S.Croy. 102 A7
Crusader Gdns., Croy. 102 B3
  Cotelands
Crusoe Rd., Mitch. 84 J7
Crutched Friars EC3 **13 E5**
Crutched Friars EC3 59 B7
Crutchley Rd. SE6 87 E2
Crystal Ct. SE19 86 C5
  College Rd.
Crystal Palace Par. 86 C6
  SE19
Crystal Palace Pk. Rd. 86 D5
  SE26
Crystal Palace Rd. 77 C6
  SE22
Crystal Palace Sta. 86 D6
  Rd. SE19
  Anerley Hill
Crystal Ter. SE19 86 A6
Crystal Vw. Ct., Brom. 87 D4
  Winlaton Rd.
Crystal Way, Dag. 53 C1
Crystal Way, Har. 37 C5
Cuba Dr., Enf. 25 F2
Cuba St. E14 69 A2
Cubitt Sq., Sthl. 63 J1
  Windmill Ave.
Cubitt Steps E14 69 A1
  Cabot Sq.
Cubitt St. WC1 **8 D4**
Cubitt St. WC1 58 H1
Cubitt St., Croy. 101 F5
Cubitt Ter. SW4 76 C3
Cubitts Yd. WC2 **12 B5**
Cuckoo Ave. W7 55 B4
Cuckoo Dene W7 55 A5
Cuckoo Hall La. N9 25 F7

Cuckoo Hill, Pnr. 36 C3
Cuckoo Hill Dr., Pnr. 36 C3
Cuckoo Hill Rd., Pnr. 36 C4
Cuckoo La. W7 55 B7
Cudas Clo., Epsom 99 F4
Cuddington Ave., 99 F3
  Wor.Pk.
Cudham St. SE6 78 C7
Cudworth St. E1 59 E4
Cuff Cres. SE9 79 A6
Cuff Pt. E2 **9 F3**
Culford Gdns. SW3 **19 A2**
Culford Gdns. SW3 66 J4
Culford Gro. N1 50 B6
Culford Ms. N1 50 B6
  Southgate Rd.
Culford Rd. N1 50 B7
Culgaith Gdns., Enf. 24 E4
Cullen Way NW10 56 C4
Culling Rd. SE16 68 F3
  Lower Rd.
Cullington Clo., Har. 37 D4
Cullingworth Rd. 47 G5
  NW10
Culloden Clo. SE14 60 C6
Culloden Rd., Enf. 24 H2
Culloden St. E14 60 C6
Cullum St. EC3 **13 D5**
Culmington Rd. W13 64 F1
Culmington Rd., 101 J7
  S.Croy.
Culmore Cross SW12 85 B1
Culmore Rd. SE15 68 E7
Culmstock Rd. SW11 76 A5
Culpeper Clo., Ilf. 35 E6
Culross Clo. N15 40 J4
Culross St. W1 **11 B6**
Culross St. W1 58 A7
Culsac Rd., Surb. 98 H2
Culver Gro., Stan. 37 F2
Culverden Rd. SW12 85 C2
Culverden Rd., Wat. 28 B3
Culverhouse Gdns. 85 F3
  SW16
Culverlands Clo., 29 E4
  Stan.
Culverley Rd. SE6 87 B1
Culvers Ave., Cars. 100 H4
Culvers Retreat, Cars. 100 J1
Culvers Way, Cars. 100 J3
Culverstone Clo., 96 F6
  Brom.
Culvert Pl. SW11 76 A2
Culvert Rd. N15 41 B5
Culvert Rd. SW11 75 J1
Culworth St. NW8 **6 G2**
Cumberland Ave. 56 B3
  NW10
Cumberland Ave., 79 H3
  Well.
Cumberland Clo. E8 50 C6
Cumberland Clo. 84 A7
  SW20
  Lansdowne Rd.
Cumberland Clo., Ilf. 43 F1
  Carrick Dr.
Cumberland Clo., 73 E6
  Twick.
  Westmorland Clo.
Cumberland Cres. 66 B4
  W14
Cumberland Dr., 71 E7
  Bexh.
Cumberland Dr., 98 J3
  Chess.
Cumberland Dr., 98 D2
  Esher
Cumberland Gdns. 39 A2
  NW4
Cumberland Gdns. **8 D3**
  WC1
Cumberland Gate W1 **10 J5**
Cumberland Gate W1 57 J7
Cumberland Mkt. NW1 **7 E3**
Cumberland Mkt. NW1 58 B3
Cumberland Mkt. Est. **7 E3**
  NW1
Cumberland Mills Sq. 69 D5
  E14
  Saunders Ness Rd.
Cumberland Pk. W3 56 C7
Cumberland Pl. NW1 **7 D3**
Cumberland Pl. SE6 87 F1
Cumberland Pl., Sun. 90 A4
Cumberland Rd. E12 52 A4
Cumberland Rd. E13 60 H5
Cumberland Rd. E17 41 H2
Cumberland Rd. N9 33 F1
Cumberland Rd. N22 40 F2

Cumberland Rd. SE25 95 E6
Cumberland Rd. 74 F1
  SW13
Cumberland Rd. W3 56 C7
Cumberland Rd. W7 64 C2
Cumberland Rd., 96 E4
  Brom.
Cumberland Rd., Har. 36 H5
Cumberland Rd., Rich. 65 A7
Cumberland Rd., 37 J3
  Stan.
Cumberland St. SW1 **19 E3**
Cumberland St. SW1 67 B5
Cumberland Ter. NW1 **7 D2**
Cumberland Ter. Ms. **7 D2**
  NW1
Cumberlow Ave. SE25 95 C3
Cumberton Rd. N17 41 A1
Cumbrae Gdns., Surb. 98 F1
Cumbrian Gdns. NW2 48 A2
Cumming St. N1 **8 D2**
Cumming St. N1 58 F2
Cumnor Gdns., 99 G6
  Epsom
Cumnor Rd., Sutt. 100 F6
Cunard Pl. EC3 **13 E4**
Cunard Rd. NW10 56 D3
Cunard Wk. SE16 68 G4
  Trident St.
Cundy Rd. E16 60 J6
Cundy St. SW1 **19 C2**
Cundy St. SW1 67 A4
Cundy St. Est. SW1 **19 C2**
Cunliffe Rd., Wor.Pk. 99 F3
Cunliffe St. SW16 85 C6
Cunningham Clo., 44 C5
  Rom.
  Chadwell Heath La.
Cunningham Clo., 103 B2
  W.Wick.
Cunningham Pk., Har. 36 J5
Cunningham Pl. NW8 **6 E5**
Cunningham Rd. N15 41 D4
Cunnington St. W4 65 C4
Cupar Rd. SW11 76 B1
Cupola Clo., Brom. 87 H5
Cureton St. SW1 **19 J2**
Cureton St. SW1 67 D4
Curfew Ho., Bark. 61 F1
  St. Ann's
Curlew Clo. SE28 62 D7
Curlew Ct., Surb. 98 J3
Curlew St. SE1 **17 F3**
Curlew St. SE1 68 C2
Curnick's La. SE27 85 J4
  Chapel Rd.
Curnock Est. NW1 58 C1
  Plender St.
Curran Ave., Sid. 79 J5
Curran Ave., Wall. 101 A3
Currey Rd., Grnf. 45 J6
Curricle St. W3 65 A1
Currie Hill Clo. SW19 84 C4
Curry Ri. NW7 31 A6
Cursitor St. EC4 **12 E3**
Cursitor St. EC4 58 G6
Curtain Rd. EC2 **9 E4**
Curtain Rd. EC2 59 B3
Curthwaite Gdns., Enf. 24 D4
Curtis Dr. W3 56 D6
Curtis Fld. Rd. SW16 85 F4
Curtis La., Wem. 46 H5
  Station Gro.
Curtis Rd., Epsom 99 C4
Curtis Rd., Houns. 72 E7
Curtis St. SE1 **21 F1**
Curtis St. SE1 68 C4
Curtis Way SE1 **21 F1**
Curtis Way SE28 62 B7
  Tawney Rd.
Curve, The W12 56 G7
Curwen Ave. E7 51 H4
  Woodford Rd.
Curwen Rd. W12 65 G2
Curzon Ave., Enf. 25 G5
Curzon Ave., Stan. 37 D1
Curzon Clo., Orp. 104 G4
Curzon Cres. NW10 47 E7
Curzon Cres., Bark. 61 J2
Curzon Gate W1 **15 C2**
Curzon Pl. W1 **15 C2**
Curzon Pl., Pnr. 36 C5
Curzon Rd. N10 40 B2
Curzon Rd. W5 55 E4
Curzon Rd., Th.Hth. 94 G6
Curzon St. W1 **15 C2**

Curzon St. W1 67 A1
Cusack Clo., Twick. 82 C4
  Waldegrave Rd.
Cut, The SE1 **16 F3**
Cut, The SE1 67 G2
Cutcombe Rd. SE5 76 J2
Cuthbert Gdns. SE25 95 B3
Cuthbert Rd. E17 42 C3
Cuthbert Rd. N18 33 D5
  Fairfield Rd.
Cuthbert Rd., Croy. 101 H2
Cuthbert St. W2 **10 E1**
Cuthbert St. W2 57 G4
Cuthill Wk. SE5 77 A1
  Kerfield Pl.
Cutler St. E1 **13 E3**
Cutler St. E1 59 B6
Cutlers Gdns. E1 **13 E3**
Cutlers Sq. E14 69 A4
  Britannia Rd.
Cutthroat All., Rich. 82 F2
  Ham St.
Cuxton Clo., Bexh. 80 E5
Cyclamen Clo., 81 G6
  Hmptn.
  Gresham Rd.
Cyclamen Way, 99 C5
  Epsom
Cyclops Ms. E14 69 A4
Cygnet Ave., Felt. 72 C7
Cygnet Clo. NW10 47 D5
Cygnet Clo., Borwd. 22 C1
Cygnet St. E1 **9 G5**
Cygnets, The, Felt. 81 E4
Cymbeline Ct., Har. 37 C6
Cynthia St. N1 **8 D2**
Cynthia St. N1 58 F2
Cyntra Pl. E8 50 E7
  Mare St.
Cypress Ave., Twick. 72 J7
Cypress Gro., Ilf. 35 H6
Cypress Pl. W1 **7 G6**
Cypress Rd. SE25 95 B2
Cypress Rd., Har. 37 A2
Cyprus Ave. N3 39 B2
Cyprus Gdns. N3 39 B2
Cyprus Pl. E2 59 F2
Cyprus Pl. E6 61 D7
Cyprus Rd. N3 39 C2
Cyprus Rd. N9 33 C2
Cyprus St. E2 59 F2
Cyrena Rd. SE22 77 C6
Cyril Mans. SW11 75 J1
Cyril Rd., Bexh. 80 E2
Cyrus St. EC1 **8 H5**
Cyrus St. EC1 58 H4
Czar St. SE8 69 A6

D

Dabbs Hill La., Nthlt. 45 G5
Dabin Cres. SE10 78 C1
Dacca St. SE8 68 J6
Dace Rd. E3 60 A1
Dacre Ave., Ilf. 43 D2
Dacre Clo., Chig. 35 F4
Dacre Clo., Grnf. 54 H2
Dacre Gdns. SE13 78 E4
Dacre Gdns., Borwd. 22 D5
Dacre Gdns., Chig. 35 F4
Dacre Pk. SE13 78 E3
Dacre Pl. SE13 78 E3
Dacre Rd. E11 51 F1
Dacre Rd. E13 60 H1
Dacre Rd., Croy. 94 E7
Dacre St. SW1 **15 H5**
Dacre St. SW1 67 D3
Dacres Rd. SE23 86 G3
Dade Way, Sthl. 83 F5
Daerwood Clo., Brom. 104 C1
Daffodil Clo., Croy. 102 G1
  Primrose La.
Daffodil Pl., Hmptn. 81 G6
  Gresham Rd.
Daffodil St. W12 56 F7
Dafforne Rd. SW17 84 J3
Dagenham Ave., Dag. 62 E1
Dagenham Rd. E10 50 J1
Dagenham Rd., Dag. 53 H3
Dagmar Ave., Wem. 46 J4
Dagmar Gdns. NW10 57 A2
Dagmar Pas. N1 58 H1
  Cross St.
Dagmar Rd. N4 40 G7
Dagmar Rd. N15 41 A4
  Cornwall Rd.
Dagmar Rd. N22 40 D1
Dagmar Rd. SE5 77 B1

Dagmar Rd. SE25 95 B5
Dagmar Rd., Dag. 53 J7
Dagmar Rd., Kings.T. 91 J1
Dagmar Rd., Sthl. 63 E3
Dagmar Ter. N1 58 H1
Dagnall Pk. SE25 95 B6
Dagnall Rd. SE25 95 B5
Dagnall St. SW11 75 J2
Dagnan Rd. SW12 76 B7
Dagonet Gdns., Brom. 87 G3
Shroffold Rd.
Dagonet Rd., Brom. 87 G3
Dahlia Gdns., Mitch. 94 D4
Dahlia Rd. SE2 71 B4
Dahomey Rd. SW16 85 C6
Daimler Way, Wall. 101 E7
Daines Clo. E12 52 C3
Colchester Ave.
Dainford Clo., Brom. 87 D5
Dainton Clo., Brom. 96 H1
Daintry Clo., Har. 37 D4
Daintry Way E9 50 J6
Eastway
Dairsie Rd. SE9 79 D3
Dairy Clo., Th.Hth. 94 J2
Dairy La. SE18 70 C4
Rideout St.
Dairy Ms. SW9 76 E3
Dairy Wk. SW19 84 B4
Daisy Clo., Croy. 102 G1
Primrose La.
Daisy La. SW6 75 D3
Daisy Rd. E18 42 H2
Dakota Gdns., Nthlt. 54 E3
Argus Way
Dalberg Rd. SW2 76 G5
Dalberg Way SE2 71 D3
Lanridge Rd.
Dalby Rd. SW18 75 F4
Dalby St. NW5 49 B6
Dalcross Rd., Houns. 72 E2
Dale, The, Kes. 104 A4
Dale Ave., Edg. 37 J1
Dale Ave., Houns. 72 E3
Dale Clo. SE3 78 G3
Dale Clo., Barn. 23 E6
Dale Clo., Pnr. 36 B1
Dale Gdns., Wdf.Grn. 34 H4
Dale Grn. Rd. N11 32 B3
Dale Gro. N12 31 F5
Dale Pk. Ave., Cars. 100 J2
Dale Pk. Rd. SE19 94 J1
Dale Rd. NW5 49 A5
Grafton Rd.
Dale Rd. SE17 20 H6
Dale Rd. SE17 67 H6
Dale Rd., Grnf. 54 H5
Dale Rd., Sutt. 100 C4
Dale Row W11 57 B6
St. Marks Rd.
Dale St. W4 65 E5
Dale Vw. Ave. E4 34 C2
Dale Vw. Cres. E4 34 C2
Dale Vw. Gdns. E4 34 D3
Dale Wd. Rd., Orp. 97 H7
Dalebury Rd. SW17 84 H2
Daleham Gdns. NW3 48 G5
Daleham Ms. NW3 48 G6
Dalehead NW1 7 F2
Dalehead NW1 58 C2
Dales Path, Borwd. 22 D5
Farriers Way
Dales Rd., Borwd. 22 D5
Daleside Gdns., Chig. 35 F3
Daleside Rd. SW16 85 B5
Daleside Rd., Epsom 99 D6
Daleview Rd. N15 41 B6
Dalewood Gdns., 99 H2
Wor.Pk.
Daley St. E9 50 G6
Daley Thompson 76 B3
Way SW8
Dalgarno Gdns. W10 56 J5
Dalgarno Gdns. Est. 56 J4
W10
Dalgarno Way W10 56 J4
Dalgleish St. E14 59 H6
Daling Way E3 59 H2
Dalkeith Gro., Stan. 29 G5
Dalkeith Rd. SE21 85 J1
Dalkeith Rd., Ilf. 52 F3
Dallas Rd. NW4 38 G7
Dallas Rd. SE26 86 E4
Dallas Rd. W5 55 J5
Dallas Rd., Sutt. 100 B6
Dallin Rd. SE18 70 E7
Dallin Rd., Bexh. 80 D4
Dalling Rd. W6 65 H4

Dallinger Rd. SE12 78 F6
Dallington St. EC1 8 H5
Dallington St. EC1 58 H4
Dalmain Rd. SE23 86 G1
Dalmally Rd., Croy. 95 C7
Dalmeny Ave. N7 49 D4
Dalmeny Ave. SW16 94 G2
Dalmeny Clo., Wem. 46 F6
Dalmeny Cres., 73 A4
Houns.
Dalmeny Rd. N7 49 D3
Dalmeny Rd., Barn. 23 F6
Dalmeny Rd., Cars. 101 A4
Dalmeny Rd., Erith 80 H1
Dalmeny Rd., Wor.Pk. 99 H3
Dalmeyer Rd. NW10 47 F6
Dalmore Ave., Esher 98 C6
Dalmore Rd. SE21 85 J2
Dalrymple Rd. SE4 77 H4
Dalston Cross Shop. 50 C6
Cen. E8
Kingsland High St.
Dalston La. E8 50 C6
Dalton Ave., Mitch. 93 H2
Dalton Clo., Orp. 104 H3
Dalton Rd., Har. 37 A2
Athelstone Rd.
Dalton St. SE27 85 H2
Dalwood St. SE5 77 B1
Daly Ct. E15 51 C5
Clays La.
Dalyell Rd. SW9 76 F3
Damascene Wk. SE21 85 J1
Lovelace Rd.
Damask Cres. E16 60 E4
Cranberry La.
Dame St. N1 8 J1
Dame St. N1 58 J2
Damer Ter. SW10 66 F7
Tadema Rd.
Dames Rd. E7 51 G3
Damien St. E1 59 E6
Damon Clo., Sid. 89 B3
Damsonwood Clo., 63 G3
Sthl.
Dan Leno Wk. SW6 66 E7
Britannia Rd.
Danbrook Rd. SW16 94 E1
Danbury Clo., Rom. 44 D3
Danbury Ms., Wall. 101 B4
Danbury Rd., Loug. 27 B7
Danbury St. N1 8 H1
Danbury St. N1 58 H2
Danbury Way, 34 J6
Wdf.Grn.
Danby St. SE15 77 C3
Dancer Rd. SW6 75 C1
Dancer Rd., Rich. 74 A3
Dando Cres. SE3 78 H3
Dandridge Clo. SE10 69 F5
Dane Clo., Bex. 80 G7
Dane Clo., Orp. 104 G5
Dane Pl. E3 59 H2
Roman Rd.
Dane Rd. N18 33 F4
Dane Rd. SW19 93 F1
Dane Rd. W13 64 F1
Dane Rd., Ilf. 52 F5
Dane Rd., Sthl. 54 E7
Dane St. WC1 12 C2
Danebury, Croy. 103 B6
Danebury Ave. SW15 74 E6
Daneby Rd. SE6 87 B3
Danecourt Gdns., 102 C3
Croy.
Danecroft Rd. SE24 76 J5
Danehill Wk., Sid. 89 A3
Hatherley Rd.
Danehurst Gdns., Ilf. 43 B5
Danehurst St. SW6 75 B1
Daneland, Barn. 23 J5
Danemead Gro., Nthlt. 45 H5
Danemere St. SW15 74 J3
Danes Ct., Wem. 47 B3
Danes Gate, Har. 37 B3
Danes Rd., Rom. 44 J7
Danesbury Rd., Felt. 81 B1
Danescombe SE12 87 G1
Winn Rd.
Danescourt Cres., 100 F2
Sutt.
Danescroft NW4 39 A5
Danescroft Ave. NW4 39 A5
Danescroft Gdns. NW4 39 A5
Danesdale Rd. E9 50 H6
Danesfield SE5 21 D5
Daneswood Ave. SE6 87 C3

Danethorpe Rd., 46 G6
Wem.
Danetree Clo., Epsom 99 C7
Danetree Rd., Epsom 99 C7
Danette Gdns., Dag. 53 F2
Daneville Rd. SE5 77 A1
Dangan Rd. E11 42 A5
Daniel Bolt Clo. E14 60 B5
Uamvar St.
Daniel Clo. N18 33 F4
Daniel Clo. SW17 84 H6
Daniel Gdns. SE15 21 F7
Daniel Gdns. SE15 68 C7
Daniel Pl. NW4 38 H6
Daniel Rd. W5 55 J7
Daniels Rd. SE15 77 F3
Dansey Pl. W1 11 H5
Dansington Rd., Well. 80 A4
Danson Cres., Well. 80 B3
Danson La., Well. 80 A4
Danson Mead, Well. 80 C3
Danson Pk., Bexh. 80 C4
Danson Rd., Bex. 80 D5
Danson Rd., Bexh. 80 D5
Dante Pl. SE11 20 H2
Dante Rd. SE11 20 G1
Dante Rd. SE11 67 H4
Danube St. SW3 18 H3
Danvers Rd. N8 40 D4
Danvers St. SW3 18 F6
Danvers St. SW3 66 G6
Danziger Way, Borwd. 22 C1
Daphne Gdns. E4 34 C3
Gunners Gro.
Daphne St. SW18 75 F6
Daplyn St. E1 13 H1
D'Arblay St. W1 11 G4
D'Arblay St. W1 58 C6
Darby Cres., Sun. 90 C2
Darby Gdns., Sun. 90 C2
Darcy Ave., Wall. 101 C4
Darcy Clo. N20 31 G2
D'Arcy Dr., Har. 37 G4
Darcy Gdns., Dag. 62 F1
D'Arcy Gdns., Har. 37 H4
Darcy Rd. SW16 94 E2
D'Arcy Rd., Sutt. 100 A4
Dare Gdns., Dag. 53 E3
Grafton Rd.
Darell Rd., Rich. 74 A3
Darenth Rd. N16 41 C7
Darenth Rd., Well. 80 A1
Darfield Rd. SE4 77 J5
Darfield Way W10 57 A6
Darfur St. SW15 75 A3
Dargate Clo. SE19 86 C7
Chipstead Clo.
Darien Rd. SW11 75 G3
Darlan Rd. SW6 66 C7
Darlaston Rd. SW19 84 A7
Darley Clo., Croy. 95 H6
Darley Dr., N.Mal. 92 D2
Darley Gdns., Mord. 93 F6
Darley Rd. N9 33 C1
Darley Rd. SW11 75 J6
Darling Rd. SE4 78 A3
Darling Row E1 59 E4
Darlington Rd. SE27 85 H5
Darmaine Clo., 101 J7
S.Croy.
Churchill Rd.
Darnley Ho. E14 59 H6
Camdenhurst St.
Darnley Rd. E9 50 F6
Darnley Rd., Wdf.Grn. 42 G1
Darnley Ter. W11 66 B1
St. James Gdns.
Darrell Rd. SE22 77 D5
Darren Clo. N4 40 F7
Darrick Wd. Rd., Orp. 104 G2
Darris Clo., Hayes 54 E4
Darsley Dr. SW8 76 E1
Dart St. W10 57 B3
Dartford Ave. N9 25 F6
Dartford Rd., Bex. 89 J1
Dartford St. SE17 21 A5
Dartford St. SE17 67 J6
Dartmoor Wk. E14 69 A4
Charnwood Gdns.
Dartmouth Clo. W11 57 D6
Dartmouth Gro. SE10 78 C1
Dartmouth Hill SE10 78 C1
Dartmouth Pk. Ave. 49 B3
NW5
Dartmouth Pk. Hill 49 B1
N19
Dartmouth Pk. Hill 49 C3
NW5

Dartmouth Pk. Rd. 49 B4
NW5
Dartmouth Pl. SE23 86 F2
Dartmouth Rd.
Dartmouth Pl. W4 65 E6
Dartmouth Rd. E16 60 G6
Fords Pk. Rd.
Dartmouth Rd. NW2 48 A6
Dartmouth Rd. NW4 38 G6
Dartmouth Rd. SE23 86 F2
Dartmouth Rd. SE26 86 E3
Dartmouth Rd., Brom. 96 G7
Dartmouth Rd., Ruis. 45 A3
Dartmouth Row SE10 78 C1
Dartmouth St. SW1 15 J4
Dartmouth St. SW1 67 D2
Dartnell Rd., Croy. 95 C7
Dartrey Wk. SW10 18 E7
Darville Rd. N16 50 C3
Darwell Clo. E6 61 D2
Darwin Clo. N11 32 B3
Darwin Clo., Orp. 104 G5
Darwin Dr., Sthl. 54 H6
Darwin Gdns., Wat. 28 C5
Darwin Rd. N22 40 H1
Darwin Rd. W5 64 F5
Darwin Rd., Well. 79 J3
Darwin St. SE17 21 C1
Darwin St. SE17 68 A4
Daryngton Dr., Grnf. 55 A2
Dashwood Clo., 80 G5
Bexh.
Dashwood Rd. N8 40 F6
Dassett Rd. SE27 85 H5
Datchelor Pl. SE5 77 A1
Datchet Rd. SE6 86 J3
Datchworth Ct. N4 49 J3
Queens Dr.
Date St. SE17 21 A4
Date St. SE17 67 J5
Daubeney Gdns. N17 32 J7
Daubeney Rd. E5 50 H4
Daubeney Rd. N17 32 J7
Daubeney Twr. SE8 68 J4
Dault Rd. SW18 75 F6
Davema Clo., Chis. 97 D1
Davenant Rd. N19 49 D2
Davenant Rd., Croy. 101 H4
Duppas Hill Rd.
Davenant St. E1 13 J2
Davenant St. E1 59 D5
Davenport Clo., Tedd. 82 D6
Davenport Rd. SE6 78 C6
Davenport Rd., Sid. 89 D2
Daventer Dr., Stan. 29 C7
Daventry Ave. E17 42 A5
Daventry St. NW1 10 G1
Daventry St. NW1 57 H5
Davern Clo. SE10 69 F4
Davey Clo. N7 49 F6
Davey Rd. E9 51 A7
White Post La.
Davey St. SE15 21 G6
Davey St. SE15 68 C6
David Ave., Grnf. 55 B3
David Ms. W1 11 B1
David Rd., Dag. 53 E2
David St. E15 51 D6
Davidge St. SE1 16 H4
Davidge St. SE1 67 H2
Davids Rd. SE23 86 F1
David's Way, Ilf. 35 H7
Davidson Gdns. SW8 67 E7
Davidson La., Har. 37 C7
Grove Hill
Davidson Rd., Croy. 102 B1
Davies Clo., Croy. 95 C6
Davies La. E11 51 E2
Davies Ms. W1 11 D5
Davies St. W1 11 D5
Davies St. W1 58 B7
Davington Gdns., 53 B5
Dag.
Davington Rd., Dag. 53 B6
Davinia Clo., Wdf.Grn. 35 C6
Deacon Way
Davis Rd. W3 65 F1
Davis Rd., Chess. 99 A4
Davis St. E13 60 H2
Davisville Rd. W12 65 G2
Dawes Ave., Islw. 73 D5
Dawes Ho. SE17 21 B2
Dawes Rd. SW6 66 B7
Dawes St. SE17 21 C3
Dawes St. SE17 68 A5
Dawlish Ave. N13 32 E4
Dawlish Ave. SW18 84 E2
Dawlish Ave., Grnf. 55 D2

Dawlish Dr., Ilf. 52 H4
Dawlish Dr., Pnr. 36 E5
Dawlish Dr., Ruis. 45 A2
Dawlish Rd. E10 51 C1
Dawlish Rd. N17 41 D3
Dawlish Rd. NW2 48 A6
Dawn Clo., Houns. 72 E3
Dawnay Gdns. SW18 84 G2
Dawnay Rd. SW18 84 F2
Dawpool Rd. NW2 47 F2
Daws Hill E4 26 C2
Daws La. NW7 30 F5
Dawson Ave., Bark. 52 J7
Dawson Clo. SE18 70 F4
Dawson Gdns., Bark. 52 J7
  Dawson Ave.
Dawson Heights Est. 77 D7
  SE22
Dawson Pl. W2 57 D7
Dawson Rd. NW2 47 J5
Dawson Rd., Kings.T. 91 J3
Dawson St. E2 9 G2
Dawson St. E2 59 C2
Dax Ct., Sun. 90 C3
  Thames St.
Daybrook Rd. SW19 93 E2
Daylesford Ave. SW15 74 G4
Daymer Gdns., Pnr. 36 B4
Days La., Sid. 79 H7
Daysbrook Rd. SW2 85 F2
Dayton Gro. SE15 77 F1
De Beauvoir Cres. N1 59 B1
De Beauvoir Est. N1 59 A1
De Beauvoir Rd. N1 59 B1
De Beauvoir Sq. N1 50 B7
De Bohun Ave. N14 24 B6
De Brome Rd., Felt. 81 C1
De Crespigny Pk. SE5 77 A2
De Frene Rd. SE26 86 G4
De Havilland Rd., Edg. 38 A2
De Havilland Rd., 63 C7
  Houns.
De Havilland Rd., 101 E7
  Wall.
De Laune St. SE17 **20 G4**
De Laune St. SE17 67 H5
De Luci Rd., Erith 71 J5
De Lucy St. SE2 71 B4
De Montfort Rd. SW16 85 E3
De Morgan Rd. SW6 75 E3
De Quincey Rd. N17 41 A1
De Vere Cotts. W8 **14 C5**
De Vere Gdns. W8 **14 C4**
De Vere Gdns. W8 66 F2
De Vere Gdns., Ilf. 52 C2
De Vere Ms. W8 **14 C5**
De Walden St. W1 **11 C2**
Deacon Ms. N1 50 A7
Deacon Rd. NW2 47 G5
Deacon Rd., Kings.T. 91 J1
Deacon Way SE17 **20 J1**
Deacon Way SE17 67 J4
Deacon Way, 35 C7
  Wdf.Grn.
Deacons Clo., Borwd. 22 A4
Deacons Clo., Pnr. 36 B2
Deacons Leas, Orp. 104 G4
Deacons Wk., Hmptn. 81 F4
  Bishops Gro.
Deal Porters Way 68 F3
  SE16
Deal Rd. SW17 85 A6
Deal St. E1 **13 H1**
Deal St. E1 59 D5
Deal's Gateway SE10 78 B1
  Blackheath Rd.
Dealtry Rd. SW15 74 J4
Dean Bradley St. SW1 **16 A6**
Dean Bradley St. SW1 67 E3
  Churchill Wk.
Dean Clo. E9 50 F5
Dean Clo. SE16 68 G1
  Surrey Water Rd.
Dean Clo., Wem. 46 E3
Dean Dr., Stan. 37 H2
Dean Farrar St. SW1 **15 J5**
Dean Farrar St. SW1 67 D3
Dean Gdns. E17 42 D4
Dean Rd. NW2 47 J6
Dean Rd., Croy. 102 A4
Dean Rd., Hmptn. 81 F5
Dean Rd., Houns. 72 H5
Dean Ryle St. SW1 **20 A1**
Dean Ryle St. SW1 67 E3
Dean Stanley St. SW1 **16 A6**
Dean Stanley St. SW1 67 E3
Dean St. E7 51 G5
Dean St. W1 **11 H3**

Dean St. W1 58 D6
Dean Trench St. SW1 **16 A6**
Dean Wk., Edg. 30 C6
  Deansbrook Rd.
Dean Way, Sthl. 63 H2
Deancross St. E1 59 F6
Deane Ave., Ruis. 45 B5
Deane Cft. Rd., Pnr. 36 C6
Deane Way, Ruis. 36 B6
Deanery Clo. N2 39 H4
Deanery Rd. E15 51 E6
Deanery St. W1 **15 C1**
Deanery St. W1 67 A1
Deanhill Rd. SW14 74 B4
Deans Bldgs. SE17 **21 C2**
Deans Bldgs. SE17 68 A4
Deans Clo. W4 65 B6
Deans Clo., Croy. 102 C3
Deans Clo., Edg. 30 C6
Deans Ct. EC4 **12 H4**
Deans Dr. N13 32 H6
Deans Dr., Edg. 30 D5
Dean's Gate Clo. SE23 86 G3
Deans La., Edg. 30 C6
Deans Ms. W1 **11 E3**
Dean's Pl. SW1 **19 H3**
Dean's Pl. SW1 67 D5
Deans Rd. W7 64 C1
Deans Rd., Sutt. 100 E3
Deans Way, Edg. 30 C5
Dean's Yd. SW1 **15 J5**
Deansbrook Clo., Edg. 30 C6
Deansbrook Rd., Edg. 30 B7
Deanscroft Ave. NW9 47 C2
Deansway N2 39 G4
Deansway N3 33 B3
Dearn Gdns., Mitch. 93 H3
Dearne Clo., Stan. 29 D5
Deason St. E15 60 C1
  High St.
Debden Clo., Wdf.Grn. 35 A7
Debden Ind. Group, 27 G4
  Loug.
Debnams Rd. SE16 68 F4
  Rotherhithe New Rd.
Deborah Clo., Islw. 73 B1
Deburgh Rd. SW19 84 F7
Decima St. SE1 **17 D5**
Decima St. SE1 68 B3
Deck Clo. SE16 68 G2
  Thame Rd.
Decoy Ave. NW11 39 B5
Dee Rd., Rich. 73 J4
Dee St. E14 60 C6
Deeley Rd. SW8 76 D1
Deena Clo. W3 55 J6
Deepdale SW19 84 A4
Deepdale Ave., Brom. 96 F4
Deepdene W5 55 J4
Deepdene Ave., 102 C3
  Croy.
Deepdene Clo. E11 42 G4
Deepdene Ct. N21 24 H6
Deepdene Gdns. SW2 76 F7
Deepdene Path, Loug. 27 D4
Deepdene Rd. SE5 77 A4
Deepdene Rd., Loug. 27 D4
Deepdene Rd., Well. 80 A3
Deepwell Clo., Islw. 73 D1
Deepwood La., Grnf. 55 A3
  Cowgate Rd.
Deer Pk. Clo., Kings.T. 83 B7
Deer Pk. Gdns., Mitch. 93 G3
Deer Pk. Rd. SW19 93 E2
Deer Pk. Way, 103 E2
  W.Wick.
Deerbrook Rd. SE24 85 H1
Deerdale Rd. SE24 76 J4
Deerhurst Clo., Felt. 81 A4
Deerhurst Rd. NW2 48 A6
Deerhurst Rd. SW16 85 F5
Deerings Dr., Pnr. 36 A5
Deerleap Gro. E4 26 B5
Deeside Rd. SW17 84 G3
Defiance Wk. SE18 70 C3
  Antelope Rd.
Defiant Way, Wall. 101 E7
Defoe Ave., Rich. 65 A7
Defoe Clo. SE16 68 J2
  Vaughan St.
Defoe Clo. SW17 84 H6
Defoe Rd. N16 50 B2
Degema Rd., Chis. 88 E5
Dehar Cres. NW9 38 F7
Dekker Rd. SE21 77 B6
Delacourt Rd. SE3 69 H7
  Old Dover Rd.

Delafield Rd. SE7 69 H5
Delaford Rd. SE16 68 E5
Delaford St. SW6 66 B7
Delamere Cres., Croy. 95 F6
Delamere Gdns. NW7 30 D6
Delamere Rd. SW20 93 A1
Delamere Rd. W5 64 H1
Delamere Rd., Borwd. 22 B1
Delamere Rd., Hayes 54 D7
Delamere Ter. W2 **10 B1**
Delamere Ter. W2 57 E5
Delancey Pas. NW1 58 B1
  Delancey St.
Delancey St. NW1 58 B1
Delaware Rd. W9 **6 A5**
Delaware Rd. W9 57 E4
Delawyk Cres. SE24 76 J6
Delcombe Ave., 99 J1
  Wor.Pk.
Delft Way SE22 77 B5
  East Dulwich Gro.
Delhi Rd., Enf. 25 C7
Delhi St. N1 58 E1
Delia St. SW18 75 E7
Dell, The SE2 71 A5
Dell, The SE19 95 C1
Dell, The, Brent. 64 F6
Dell, The, Felt. 72 B7
  Harlington Rd. W.
Dell, The, Pnr. 36 D2
Dell, The, Wem. 46 E5
Dell, The, Wdf.Grn. 34 H3
Dell Clo. E15 60 D1
Dell Clo., Wall. 101 C4
Dell Clo., Wdf.Grn. 34 H3
Dell La., Epsom 99 G5
Dell Rd., Epsom 99 G6
Dell Wk., N.Mal. 92 E2
Dell Way W13 55 F6
Della Path E5 50 E3
  Napoleon Rd.
Dellbow Rd., Felt. 72 B5
  Central Way
Dellfield Clo., Beck. 87 C7
  Foxgrove Rd.
Dellors Clo., Barn. 23 A5
Dellow Clo., Ilf. 43 G7
Dellow St. E1 59 E7
Dells Clo. E4 26 B7
Dell's Ms. SW1 **19 G2**
Dellwood Gdns., Ilf. 43 D3
Delmare Clo. SW9 76 F4
  Brighton Ter.
Delme Cres. SE3 78 H2
Delmey Clo., Croy. 102 C3
  Radcliffe Rd.
Deloraine St. SE8 78 A1
Delorme St. W6 66 A6
Delta Clo., Wor.Pk. 99 F3
Delta Ct. NW2 47 G2
Delta Gain, Wat. 28 D2
Delta Gro., Nthlt. 54 D3
Delta Rd., Wor.Pk. 99 E3
Delta St. E2 **9 H3**
Delvan Clo. SE18 70 D7
  Ordnance Rd.
Delverton Rd. SE17 **20 H4**
Delverton Rd. SE17 67 H5
Delvino Rd. SW6 75 D1
Demesne Rd., Wall. 101 D4
Demeta Clo., Wem. 47 C3
Dempster Clo., Surb. 91 F7
Dempster Rd. SW18 75 F5
Den Clo., Beck. 96 D3
Den Rd., Brom. 96 D3
Denberry Dr., Sid. 89 B3
Denbigh Clo. NW10 47 E7
Denbigh Clo., Chis. 88 C6
Denbigh Clo., Sthl. 54 F6
  Denbigh Rd.
Denbigh Clo., Sutt. 100 C5
Denbigh Gdns., Rich. 73 J5
Denbigh Ms. SW1 **19 F2**
Denbigh Pl. SW1 **19 F3**
Denbigh Pl. SW1 67 C5
Denbigh Rd. E6 61 A3
Denbigh Rd. W11 57 C7
Denbigh Rd. W13 55 E7
Denbigh Rd., Houns. 72 H2
Denbigh Rd., Sthl. 54 F6
Denbigh St. SW1 **19 F2**
Denbigh St. SW1 67 C4
Denbigh Ter. W11 57 C7
Denbridge Rd., Brom. 97 C2
Dene, The W13 55 E5
Dene, The, Croy. 102 G4

Dene, The, Wem. 46 H4
Dene, The, W.Mol. 90 F5
Dene Ave., Houns. 72 F3
Dene Ave., Sid. 80 B7
Dene Clo. SE4 77 H3
Dene Clo., Brom. 103 F1
Dene Clo., Wor.Pk. 99 F2
Dene Gdns., Stan. 29 F5
Dene Gdns., T.Ditt. 98 D2
Dene Rd. N11 31 J1
Dene Rd., Buck.H. 35 A1
Denehurst Gdns. NW4 38 J6
Denehurst Gdns. W3 65 B1
Denehurst Gdns., 74 A4
  Rich.
Denehurst Gdns., 73 A7
  Twick.
Denehurst Gdns., 34 H4
  Wdf.Grn.
Denewood, Barn. 23 F5
Denewood Rd. N6 39 J6
Dengie Wk. N1 58 J1
  Basire St.
Denham Cres., Mitch. 93 J4
Denham Dr., Esher 98 D5
Denham Dr., Ilf. 43 F6
Denham Rd. N20 31 J3
Denham Rd., Felt. 72 C6
Denham St. SE10 69 G5
Denham Way, Bark. 61 H1
Denham Way, Borwd. 22 C1
Denholme Rd. W9 57 C3
Denison Clo. N2 39 F3
Denison Rd. SW19 84 G6
Denison Rd. W5 55 F4
Deniston Ave., Bex. 89 E1
Denleigh Gdns. N21 32 G1
Denleigh Gdns., T.Ditt. 91 B6
Denman Dr. NW11 39 D5
Denman Dr. N. NW11 39 D5
Denman Dr. S. NW11 39 D5
Denman Rd. SE15 77 C1
Denman St. W1 **11 H6**
Denmark Ave. SW19 84 B7
Denmark Ct., Mord. 93 D5
Denmark Gdns., Cars. 100 J3
Denmark Gro. N1 **8 E1**
Denmark Gro. N1 58 G2
Denmark Hill SE5 77 A1
Denmark Hill Dr. NW9 38 F4
Denmark Hill Est. SE5 77 A4
Denmark Pl. WC2 **11 J3**
Denmark Rd. N8 40 G4
Denmark Rd. NW6 57 C2
Denmark Rd. SE5 76 J1
Denmark Rd. SE25 95 D5
Denmark Rd. SW19 84 A6
Denmark Rd. W13 55 E7
Denmark Rd., Brom. 96 H1
Denmark Rd., Cars. 100 J3
Denmark Rd., 91 H3
  Kings.T.
Denmark Rd., Twick. 82 A3
Denmark St. E11 51 E3
  High Rd. Leytonstone
Denmark St. E13 60 H5
Denmark St. N17 41 E1
Denmark St. WC2 **11 J4**
Denmark St. WC2 58 D6
Denmark Wk. SE27 76 D6
Denmead Ho. SW15 74 F6
  Highcliffe Dr.
Denmead Rd., Croy. 101 H1
Denmead Way SE15 68 C7
  Pentridge St.
Dennan Rd., Surb. 98 J1
Denne Ter. E8 59 C1
Denner Rd. E4 34 A2
Dennett Rd., Croy. 101 G1
Dennetts Gro. SE14 77 G2
  Dennetts Rd.
Dennetts Rd. SE14 77 F1
Denning Ave., Croy. 101 G4
Denning Clo. NW8 **6 D3**
Denning Clo., Hmptn. 81 D6
Denning Rd. NW3 48 G4
Dennington Clo. E5 50 E2
  Detmold Rd.
Dennington Pk. Rd. 48 D6
  NW6
Denningtons, The, 99 E2
  Wor.Pk.
Dennis Ave., Wem. 46 J5
Dennis Gdns., Stan. 29 F5
Dennis La., Stan. 29 E3

Dennis Pk. Cres. SW20	93 B1	Derwent Ave. N18	33 A5
Dennis Reeve Clo., Mitch.	93 J1	Derwent Ave. NW7	30 D6
Dennis Rd., E.Mol.	90 J4	Derwent Ave. NW9	38 E5
Dennis Way SW4	76 D3	Derwent Ave. SW15	83 E4
Gauden Rd.		Derwent Ave., Barn.	31 J1
Dennison Pt. E15	51 C7	Derwent Ave., Pnr.	28 E6
Denny Clo. E6	61 B5	Derwent Clo., Esher	98 B6
Linton Gdns.		Derwent Cres. N20	31 F3
Denny Cres. SE11	**20 F3**	Derwent Cres., Bexh.	80 G2
Denny Gdns., Dag.	53 B7	Derwent Cres., Stan.	37 F2
Canonsleigh Rd.		Derwent Dr., Orp.	97 G7
Denny Rd. N9	33 E1	Derwent Gdns., Ilf.	43 B4
Denny St. SE11	**20 F3**	Derwent Gdns., Wem.	37 F7
Denny St. SE11	67 G5	Derwent Gro. SE22	77 C4
Densham Rd. E15	60 E1	Derwent Ri. NW9	38 E6
Densole Clo., Beck.	95 H1	Derwent Rd. N13	32 F4
Kings Hall Rd.		Derwent Rd. SE20	95 D2
Densworth Gro. N9	33 F2	Derwent Rd. SW20	93 A6
Denton Clo., Barn.	22 J5	Derwent Rd. W5	64 F3
Denton Rd. N8	40 F5	Derwent Rd., Sthl.	54 F6
Denton Rd. N18	33 B4	Derwent Rd., Twick.	72 H6
Denton Rd., Twick.	73 G6	Derwent St. SE10	69 E5
Denton Rd., Well.	71 C7	Derwent Wk., Wall.	101 B7
Denton St. SW18	75 E6	Derwent Yd. W5	64 F3
Denton Way E5	50 G3	Northfield Ave.	
Dents Rd. SW11	75 J6	Derwentwater Rd. W3	65 C1
Denver Clo., Orp.	97 H6	**Desborough St. W2**	**10 A1**
Denver Rd. N16	41 B7	Desenfans Rd. SE21	77 B6
Denyer St. SW3	**18 H2**	Desford Rd. E16	60 E4
Denyer St. SW3	66 H4	Desmond St. SE14	68 H6
Denzil Rd. NW10	47 F5	Despard Rd. N19	49 C1
Deodar Rd. SW15	75 B4	Detling Rd., Brom.	87 G5
Deodara Clo. N20	31 H3	Detmold Rd. E5	50 F2
Depot Rd., Houns.	73 A3	Devalls Clo. E6	61 D7
Deptford Bri. SE8	78 A1	Devana End, Cars.	100 J3
Deptford Bdy. SE8	78 A1	Devas Rd. SW20	92 J1
Deptford Ch. St. SE8	69 A6	Devas St. E3	60 B4
Deptford Ferry Rd. E14	69 A4	Devenay Rd. E15	51 F7
Deptford Grn. SE8	69 A6	Devenish Rd. SE2	71 A2
Deptford High St. SE8	69 A6	Deventer Cres. SE22	77 B5
Deptford Strand SE8	68 J4	East Dulwich Gro.	
Deptford Wf. SE8	68 J4	**Deverell St. SE1**	**17 B6**
Derby Ave. N12	31 F5	Deverell St. SE1	68 A3
Derby Ave., Har.	37 A1	**Devereux Ct. WC2**	**12 E4**
Derby Ave., Rom.	44 J6	Devereux Rd. SW11	75 J6
Derby Ct. E5	50 G4	Deverill St. SE20	95 F1
Overbury St.		Devizes St. N1	59 A1
Derby Est., Houns.	72 G4	Poole St.	
Derby Gate SW1	**16 A3**	Devon Ave., Twick.	81 J1
Derby Hill SE23	86 F2	Devon Clo. N17	41 C3
Derby Hill Cres. SE23	86 F2	Devon Clo., Buck.H.	34 H2
Derby Rd. E7	52 A7	Devon Clo., Grnf.	55 F1
Derby Rd. E9	59 G1	Devon Gdns. N4	40 H6
Derby Rd. E18	42 F1	Devon Ri. N2	39 G4
Derby Rd. N18	33 F5	Devon Rd., Bark.	61 H1
Derby Rd. SW14	74 B4	Devon St. SE15	68 E6
Derby Rd. SW19	84 D7	Devon Way, Chess.	98 F5
Russell Rd.		Devon Way, Epsom	99 B5
Derby Rd., Croy.	101 H2	Devon Waye, Houns.	63 F7
Derby Rd., Enf.	25 E5	Devoncroft Gdns., Twick.	73 D7
Derby Rd., Grnf.	54 H1	Devonia Gdns. N18	32 J6
Derby Rd., Houns.	72 H4	**Devonia Rd. N1**	**8 H1**
Derby Rd., Surb.	99 A1	Devonia Rd. N1	58 H2
Derby Rd., Sutt.	100 C6	Devonport Gdns., Ilf.	43 C6
Derby St. W1	**15 C2**	Devonport Ms. W12	65 H1
Derbyshire St. E2	**9 J4**	Devonport Rd.	
Derbyshire St. E2	59 D3	Devonport Rd. W12	65 H2
Dereham Pl. EC2	**9 E4**	Devonport St. E1	59 G6
Dereham Rd., Bark.	52 J6	Devons Est. E3	60 B3
Derek Ave., Epsom	99 A6	Devons Rd. E3	60 A5
Derek Ave., Wall.	101 B3	Devonshire Ave., Sutt.	100 F7
Derek Ave., Wem.	47 B7	Devonshire Clo. E15	51 E4
Derek Clo., Epsom	99 B5	Devonshire Clo. N13	32 G3
Derek Walcott Clo. SE24	76 H4	**Devonshire Clo. W1**	**11 D1**
Shakespeare Rd.		Devonshire Clo. W1	58 B5
Dericote St. E8	59 D1	Devonshire Cres. NW7	31 A7
Derifall Clo. E6	61 C5	Devonshire Dr. SE10	69 B7
Dering Pl., Croy.	101 J4	Devonshire Dr., Surb.	98 G2
Dering Rd., Croy.	101 J4	Devonshire Gdns. N17	32 J6
Dering St. W1	**11 D4**	Devonshire Gdns. N21	24 J7
Dering St. W1	58 B6	Devonshire Gdns. W4	65 C7
Derinton Rd. SW17	84 J4	Devonshire Gro. SE15	68 E6
Derley Rd., Sthl.	63 C3	Devonshire Hill La. N17	32 H6
Dermody Gdns. SE13	78 D5	Devonshire Ms. W4	65 E5
Dermody Rd. SE13	78 D5	Glebe St.	
Deronda Rd. SE24	85 H1	**Devonshire Ms. N. W1**	**11 D1**
Derrick Gdns. SE7	69 J4	**Devonshire Ms. S. W1**	**11 D1**
Anchor & Hope La.		**Devonshire Ms. W. W1**	**7 D6**
Derrick Rd., Beck.	95 J3	Devonshire Ms. W. W1	58 A4
Derry Rd., Croy.	101 E3	Devonshire Pas. W4	65 E5
Derry St. W8	**14 A4**	Duke Rd.	
Derry St. W8	66 E2	Devonshire Pl. NW2	48 D3
Dersingham Ave. E12	52 C6	**Devonshire Pl. W1**	**7 C6**
Dersingham Rd. NW2	48 B3		

Devonshire Pl. W1	58 A4	Dickerson St. NW5	49 B6
Devonshire Pl. W4	65 E5	Dickensons La. SE25	95 D5
Dalby St.		Dickensons Pl. SE25	95 D6
Devonshire Pl. Ms. W1	**7 C6**	Dickerage La., N.Mal.	92 C3
Devonshire Rd. E15	51 E4	Dickerage Rd., Kings.T.	92 C1
Janson Rd.		Dickerage Rd., N.Mal.	92 C1
Devonshire Rd. E16	60 H6	Dickson Fold, Pnr.	36 D4
Devonshire Rd. E17	42 A6	Dickson Rd. SE9	79 B3
Devonshire Rd. N9	33 F1	Didsbury Clo. E6	61 C1
Devonshire Rd. N13	32 F4	Barking Rd.	
Devonshire Rd. N17	32 J6	Digby Cres. N4	49 J2
Devonshire Rd. NW7	31 A7	Digby Gdns., Dag.	62 G1
Devonshire Rd. SE9	88 B2	Digby Pl., Croy.	102 C3
Devonshire Rd. SE23	86 F1	Digby Rd. E9	50 G5
Devonshire Rd. SW19	84 H7	Digby Rd., Bark.	52 J7
Devonshire Rd. W4	65 E5	Digby St. E2	59 F3
Devonshire Rd. W5	64 F3	**Dighton Ct. SE5**	**20 J6**
Devonshire Rd., Bexh.	80 E4	Dighton Rd. SW18	75 F5
Devonshire Rd., Cars.	101 A4	Digswell St. N7	49 G6
Devonshire Rd., Croy.	95 A7	Holloway Rd.	
Devonshire Rd., Felt.	61 E3	Dilhorne Clo. SE12	87 H3
Devonshire Rd., Har.	37 A6	**Dilke St. SW3**	**19 A5**
Devonshire Rd., Ilf.	43 G7	Dilke St. SW3	66 J6
Devonshire Rd., Pnr. (Eastcote)	36 C6	Dillwyn Clo. SE26	86 H4
Devonshire Rd., Pnr. (Hatch End)	36 F1	Dilston Clo., Nthlt.	54 C3
Devonshire Rd., Sthl.	54 G5	Yeading La.	
Devonshire Rd., Sutt.	100 F7	Dilston Gro. SE16	68 F4
Devonshire Row EC2	**13 E2**	Abbeyfield Rd.	
Devonshire Row Ms. W1	**7 E6**	Dilton Gdns. SW15	83 H1
Devonshire Sq. EC2	**13 E2**	Dimes Pl. W6	65 H4
Devonshire Sq., Brom.	96 H4	King St.	
Devonshire St. W1	**11 C1**	Dimmock Dr., Grnf.	46 A5
Devonshire St. W1	58 B5	Dimond Clo. E7	51 G4
Devonshire St. W4	65 E5	Dimsdale Dr. NW9	47 C1
Devonshire Ter. W2	**10 D4**	Dimsdale Dr., Enf.	25 D6
Devonshire Ter. W2	57 F6	Dimsdale Wk. E13	60 G1
Devonshire Way, Croy.	102 H2	Stratford Rd.	
Devonshire Way, Hayes	54 B6	Dimson Cres. E3	60 A4
Dewar St. SE15	77 D3	Wellington Way	
Dewberry Gdns. E6	61 B5	Dingle Clo., Barn.	22 F6
Dewberry St. E14	60 C5	Dingle Gdns. E14	60 A7
Dewey Rd. N1	**8 E1**	Dingley La. SW16	85 D2
Dewey Rd. N1	58 G2	**Dingley Pl. EC1**	**9 A4**
Dewey Rd., Dag.	53 H6	Dingley Pl. EC1	58 J3
Dewey St. SW17	84 J5	**Dingley Rd. EC1**	**8 J4**
Dewhurst Rd. W14	66 A3	Dingley Rd. EC1	58 J3
Dewsbury Clo., Pnr.	36 E6	Dingonhill Clo., Hayes	54 B7
Dewsbury Ct. W4	65 C4	Dingwall Ave., Croy.	101 J2
Chiswick Rd.		Dingwall Gdns. NW11	39 D6
Dewsbury Gdns., Wor.Pk.	99 G3	Dingwall Pl., Croy.	102 A2
Dewsbury Rd. NW10	47 G5	Dingwall Rd.	
Dewsbury Ter. NW1	58 B1	Dingwall Rd. SW18	75 F7
Camden High St.		Dingwall Rd., Croy.	102 A1
Dexter Rd., Barn.	23 A6	Dinmont St. E2	59 E2
Deyncourt Rd. N17	40 J1	Coate St.	
Deynecourt Gdns. E11	42 J4	Dinsdale Gdns. SE25	95 B5
D'Eynsford Rd. SE5	77 A1	Dinsdale Gdns., Barn.	23 E5
Diadem Ct. W1	**11 H4**	Dinsdale Rd. SE3	69 F6
Dial Wk., The W8	**14 B3**	Dinsmore Rd. SW12	76 B7
Diameter Rd., Orp.	97 E7	Dinton Rd. SW19	84 G6
Diamond Clo., Dag.	53 C1	Dinton Rd., Kings.T.	82 J7
Diamond Rd., Ruis.	45 D4	Diploma Ave. N2	39 H4
Diamond St. SE15	68 B7	Dirleton Rd. E15	60 F1
Diamond Ter. SE10	78 C1	Disbrowe Rd. W6	66 B6
Diana Clo. E18	42 H1	Discovery Wk. E1	68 E1
Diana Gdns., Surb.	98 J2	Waterman Way	
Diana Ho. SW13	74 F1	Dishforth La. NW9	38 E1
Diana Pl. NW1	**7 E5**	**Disney Pl. SE1**	**17 A3**
Diana Pl. NW1	58 B4	**Disney St. SE1**	**17 A3**
Diana Rd. E17	41 J3	Dison Clo., Enf.	25 G1
Dianna Way, Barn.	23 H5	Disraeli Clo. SE28	71 C1
Dianthus Clo. SE2	71 B5	Disraeli Clo. W4	65 D4
Carnation St.		Acton La.	
Dibden St. N1	58 J1	Disraeli Gdns. SW15	75 C4
Dibdin Clo., Sutt.	100 D3	Fawe Pk. Rd.	
Dibdin Rd., Sutt.	100 D3	Disraeli Rd. E7	51 G6
Dicey Ave. NW2	47 J4	Disraeli Rd. NW10	56 D2
Dickens Ave. N3	39 F1	Disraeli Rd. SW15	75 B4
Dickens Clo., Rich.	82 H2	Disraeli Rd. W5	64 G1
Dickens Dr., Chis.	88 F6	**Diss St. E2**	**9 F3**
Dickens Est. SE1	**17 H4**	Diss St. E2	59 C3
Dickens Est. SE1	68 C2	**Distaff La. EC4**	**12 J7**
Dickens Est. SE16	**17 H5**	Distaff La. EC4	58 J7
Dickens Est. SE16	68 C2	Distillery La. W6	65 J5
Dickens La. N18	33 B5	Fulham Palace Rd.	
Dickens Ri., Chig.	35 E3	Distillery Rd. W6	65 J5
Dickens Rd. E6	61 A2	Distillery Wk., Brent.	64 H6
Dickens Sq. SE1	**17 A5**	Pottery Rd.	
Dickens Sq. SE1	67 J3	**Distin St. SE11**	**20 E2**
Dickens St. SW8	76 B2	District Rd., Wem.	46 E5
Dickenson Rd. N8	40 E7	Ditch All. SE10	78 B1
Dickenson Rd., Felt.	81 D7	Ditchburn St. E14	60 C7
		Ditchfield Rd., Hayes	54 E4
		Dittisham Rd. SE9	87 B6
		Ditton Clo., T.Ditt.	91 D7
		Ditton Gra. Clo., Surb.	98 G1

Ditton Gra. Dr., Surb.	98	G1
Ditton Hill, Surb.	98	F1
Ditton Hill Rd., Surb.	98	F1
Ditton Lawn, T.Ditt.	98	D1
Ditton Pl. SE20	95	E1
Hartfield Gro.		
Ditton Reach, T.Ditt.	91	E6
Ditton Rd., Bexh.	80	D5
Ditton Rd., Sthl.	63	F5
Ditton Rd., Surb.	98	G2
Divis Way SW15	74	H6
Dover Pk. Dr.		
Dixon Clark Ct. N1	49	H6
Canonbury Rd.		
Dixon Clo. E6	61	C6
Brandreth Rd.		
Dixon Pl., W.Wick.	103	B1
Dixon Rd. SE14	77	H1
Dixon Rd. SE25	95	B3
Dixon's All. SE16	68	E2
West La.		
Dobbin Clo., Har.	37	D2
Dobell Rd. SE9	79	C5
Dobree Ave. NW10	47	H7
Dobson Clo. NW6	48	G7
Dock Hill Ave. SE16	68	G2
Dock Rd. E16	60	F7
Dock Rd., Brent.	64	G7
Dock St. E1	**13**	**H5**
Dock St. E1	59	D7
Dockers Tanner Rd. E14	69	A4
Dockhead SE1	**17**	**G4**
Dockhead SE1	68	C2
Dockland St. E16	70	D1
Dockley Rd. SE16	**17**	**H6**
Dockley Rd. SE16	68	D3
Dockwell Clo., Felt.	72	A4
Doctor Johnson Ave. SW17	85	B3
Doctors Clo. SE26	86	F5
Docwra's Bldgs. N1	50	B6
Dod St. E14	60	A6
Dodbrooke Rd. SE27	85	G3
Doddington Gro. SE17	**20**	**G5**
Doddington Gro. SE17	67	H6
Doddington Pl. SE17	**20**	**G5**
Doddington Pl. SE17	67	H6
Dodsley Pl. N9	33	F3
Dodson St. SE1	**16**	**F4**
Dodson St. SE1	67	G2
Doel Clo. SW19	84	F7
Dog Kennel Hill SE22	77	B3
Dog Kennel Hill Est. SE22	77	B3
Dog La. NW10	47	E4
Doggets Ct., Barn.	23	H5
Doggett Rd. SE6	78	A7
Doherty Rd. E13	60	G4
Dolben St. SE1	**16**	**H2**
Dolben St. SE1	67	H1
Dolby Ct. EC4	58	J7
Garlick Hill		
Dolby Rd. SW6	75	C2
Dolland St. SE11	**20**	**D4**
Dolland St. SE11	67	F5
Dollis Ave. N3	39	C1
Dollis Brook Wk., Barn.	23	B6
Dollis Cres., Ruis.	45	C1
Dollis Hill Ave. NW2	47	H3
Dollis Hill Est. NW2	47	G3
Dollis Hill La. NW2	47	F4
Dollis Ms. N3	39	C1
Dollis Pk.		
Dollis Pk. N3	39	C1
Dollis Rd. N3	39	B1
Dollis Rd. NW7	31	B7
Dollis Valley Grn. Wk. N20	31	F2
Totteridge La.		
Dollis Valley Grn. Wk., Barn.	23	B6
Leeside		
Dollis Valley Way, Barn.	23	C5
Dolman Rd. W4	65	D4
Dolman St. SW4	76	F4
Dolphin Clo. SE16	68	G2
Kinburn St.		
Dolphin Clo. SE28	62	D6
Dolphin Clo., Surb.	91	G6
Dolphin Ct. NW11	39	B6
Dolphin La. E14	60	B7
Dolphin Rd., Nthlt.	54	F1
Dolphin Sq. SW1	**19**	**G4**
Dolphin Sq. SW1	67	C5
Dolphin Sq. W4	65	E7

Dolphin St., Kings.T.	91	H1
Wood La.		
Dombey St. WC1	**12**	**C1**
Dombey St. WC1	58	F5
Dome Hill Pk. SE26	86	C4
Domett Clo. SE5	77	A4
Domfe Pl. E5	50	F4
Rushmore Rd.		
Domingo St. EC1	**8**	**J5**
Dominion Rd., Croy.	95	C7
Dominion Rd., Sthl.	63	E3
Dominion St. EC2	**13**	**C1**
Domonic Dr. SE9	88	E4
Domville Clo. N20	31	G2
Don Phelan Clo. SE5	77	A1
Donald Dr., Rom.	44	C5
Donald Rd. E13	60	H1
Donald Rd., Croy.	94	F6
Donaldson Rd. NW6	57	C1
Donaldson Rd. SE18	79	D1
Doncaster Dr., Nthlt.	45	F5
Doncaster Gdns. N4	40	J6
Stanhope Gdns.		
Doncaster Gdns., Nthlt.	45	F5
Doncaster Grn., Wat.	28	C5
Doncaster Rd. N9	25	E7
Doncel Ct. E4	26	D7
Donegal St. N1	**8**	**D2**
Donegal St. N1	58	F2
Doneraile St. SW6	75	A2
Dongola Rd. E13	60	H3
Dongola Rd. N17	41	B3
Dongola Rd. W. E13	60	H3
Balaam St.		
Donington Ave., Ilf.	43	F5
Donkey All. SE22	77	D7
Donkey La., Enf.	25	D2
Donne Ct. SE24	76	J6
Burbage Rd.		
Donne Pl. SW3	**18**	**H1**
Donne Pl. SW3	66	H4
Donne Pl., Mitch.	94	B4
Donne Rd., Dag.	53	C2
Donnefield Ave., Edg.	29	H7
Donnington Rd. NW10	47	H7
Donnington Rd., Har.	37	F5
Donnington Rd., Wor.Pk.	99	G2
Donnybrook Rd. SW16	85	C7
Donovan Ave. N10	40	B3
Doon St. SE1	**16**	**E1**
Doone Clo., Tedd.	82	D6
Dora Rd. SW19	84	D5
Dora St. E14	59	J6
Doral Way, Cars.	100	J5
Doran Gro. SE18	70	H7
Doran Mans. N2	39	J5
Great N. Rd.		
Doran Wk. E15	51	C7
Dorchester Ave. N13	32	J4
Dorchester Ave., Bex.	76	J4
Dorchester Ave., Har.	36	J6
Dorchester Clo., Nthlt.	45	H5
Dorchester Clo., Orp.	89	A7
Grovelands Rd.		
Dorchester Ct. N14	24	B7
Dorchester Ct. SE24	76	J5
Dorchester Dr. SE24	76	J5
Dorchester Gdns. E4	34	A4
Dorchester Gdns. NW11	39	D4
Dorchester Gro. W4	65	E5
Dorchester Ms. N.Mal.	92	D4
Elm Rd.		
Dorchester Rd., Mord.	93	E7
Dorchester Rd., Nthlt.	45	H5
Dorchester Rd., Wor.Pk.	99	J1
Dorchester Way, Har.	37	J6
Dorchester Waye, Hayes	54	B6
Dorcis Ave., Bexh.	80	E2
Dordrecht Rd. W3	65	E1
Dore Ave. E12	52	D5
Doric Way NW1	**7**	**H3**
Doric Way NW1	58	D3
Dorien Rd. SW20	93	A2
Doris Ave., Erith	80	J1
Doris Rd. E7	51	G7
Dorking Clo. SE8	68	J6
Dorking Clo., Wor.Pk.	100	A2
Dorlcote Rd. SW18	75	H7

Dorma Trd. Est. E10	50	G1
Dorman Pl. N9	33	D2
Balham Rd.		
Dorman Wk. NW10	47	D5
Garden Way		
Dorman Way NW8	57	G1
Dormay St. SW18	75	E5
Dormer Clo. E15	51	F6
Dormer Clo., Barn.	23	A5
Dormers Ave., Sthl.	54	G6
Dormers Ri., Sthl.	54	H7
Dormers Wells La., Sthl.	54	G6
Dornberg Clo. SE3	69	G7
Dornberg Rd. SE3	69	H7
Banchory Rd.		
Dorncliffe Rd. SW6	75	B2
Dorney NW3	48	H7
Dorney Ri., Orp.	97	J4
Dorney Way, Houns.	72	E5
Dornfell St. NW6	48	C5
Dornton Rd. SW12	85	B2
Dornton Rd., S.Croy.	102	A5
Dorothy Ave., Wem.	46	H7
Dorothy Evans Clo., Bexh.	80	H4
Dorothy Gdns., Dag.	53	B4
Dorothy Rd. SW11	75	J3
Dorrington Ct. SE25	95	B2
Dorrington Pt. E3	60	B3
Bromley High St.		
Dorrington St. EC1	**12**	**E1**
Dorrington St. EC1	58	G5
Dorrit Ms. N18	33	B5
Dorrit Way, Chis.	88	F6
Dors Clo. NW9	47	D1
Dorset Ave., Sthl.	63	G4
Dorset Ave., Well.	79	J4
Dorset Bldgs. EC4	**12**	**G4**
Dorset Clo. NW1	**10**	**J1**
Dorset Dr., Edg.	29	J6
Dorset Est. E2	**9**	**G3**
Dorset Est. E2	59	C3
Dorset Gdns., Mitch.	94	F4
Dorset Ms. SW1	**15**	**D5**
Dorset Pl. E15	51	D6
Dorset Pl. SW1	**19**	**H3**
Dorset Ri. EC4	**12**	**G4**
Dorset Ri. EC4	58	H6
Dorset Rd. E7	51	J7
Dorset Rd. N15	41	A4
Dorset Rd. N22	40	E1
Dorset Rd. SE9	88	B2
Dorset Rd. SW1	**15**	**D5**
Dorset Rd. SW8	67	E7
Dorset Rd. SW19	93	D1
Dorset Rd. W5	64	F3
Dorset Rd., Beck.	95	G3
Dorset Rd., Har.	36	J6
Dorset Rd., Mitch.	93	H2
Dorset Sq. NW1	**6**	**J6**
Dorset Sq. NW1	57	J4
Dorset St. W1	**11**	**A2**
Dorset St. W1	57	J5
Dorset Way, Twick.	82	A1
Dorset Way, Houns.	63	F7
Dorville Cres. W6	65	H3
Dorville Rd. SE12	78	F5
Dothill Rd. SE18	70	G7
Douai Gro., Hmptn.	90	J1
Doubleday Rd., Loug.	27	F3
Doughty Ms. WC1	**8**	**C6**
Doughty Ms. WC1	58	F4
Doughty St. WC1	**8**	**C5**
Doughty St. WC1	58	F4
Douglas Ave. E17	42	A1
Douglas Ave., N.Mal.	92	H4
Douglas Ave., Wem.	46	H7
Douglas Clo., Stan.	29	D5
Douglas Clo., Wall.	101	E6
Douglas Cres., Hayes	54	C4
Douglas Dr., Croy.	103	A3
Douglas Pl. E14	69	C5
Manchester Rd.		
Douglas Rd. E4	26	E7
Douglas Rd. E16	60	G5
Douglas Rd. N1	49	J7
Douglas Rd. N22	40	G1
Douglas Rd. NW6	57	C1
Douglas Rd., Houns.	72	H3
Douglas Rd., Ilf.	44	A7
Douglas Rd., Kings.T.	92	B2
Douglas Rd., Surb.	98	J2
Douglas Rd., Well.	80	B1
Douglas Sq., Mord.	93	D6
Douglas St. SW1	**19**	**H2**

Douglas St. SW1	67	D4
Douglas Way SE8	68	J7
Doulton Ms. NW6	48	E6
Lymington Rd.		
Dounesforth Gdns. SW18	84	E1
Douro Pl. W8	**14**	**B5**
Douro Pl. W8	66	E3
Douro St. E3	60	A2
Douthwaite Sq. E1	**17**	**J1**
Dove App. E6	61	B5
Dove Clo., Nthlt.	54	D4
Wayfarer Rd.		
Dove Ct. EC2	**13**	**B4**
Dove Ho. Gdns. E4	34	A2
Dove Ms. SW5	**18**	**C2**
Dove Ms. SW5	66	F4
Dove Pk., Pnr.	28	G7
Dove Rd. N1	50	A6
Dove Row E2	59	D1
Dove Wk. SW1	**19**	**B3**
Dovecot Clo., Pnr.	36	B5
Dovecote Ave. N22	40	G3
Dovecott Gdns. SW14	74	D3
North Worple Way		
Dovedale Ave., Har.	37	F6
Dovedale Ave., Ilf.	43	D2
Dovedale Clo., Well.	80	A1
Dovedale Ri., Mitch.	84	J7
Dovedale Rd. SE22	77	E5
Dovedon Clo. N14	32	E2
Dovehouse Mead, Bark.	61	G2
Dovehouse St. SW3	**18**	**G3**
Dovehouse St. SW3	66	G5
Dover Clo., Rom.	44	J2
Dover Ct. Est. N1	50	A6
Dove Rd.		
Dover Gdns., Cars.	100	J3
Dover Ho. Rd. SW15	74	G4
Dover Pk. Dr. SW15	74	H6
Dover Rd. E12	51	J2
Dover Rd. N9	33	F2
Dover Rd. SE19	86	A6
Dover Rd., Rom.	44	E6
Dover St. W1	**11**	**E6**
Dover St. W1	58	B7
Dover Yd. W1	**15**	**E1**
Dovercourt Ave., Th.Hth.	94	G5
Dovercourt Gdns., Stan.	29	H5
Dovercourt La., Sutt.	100	F3
Dovercourt Rd. SE22	77	B6
Doverfield Rd. SW2	76	E6
Doveridge Gdns. N13	32	H4
Doves Clo., Brom.	104	B3
Doveton Rd., S.Croy.	102	A5
Doveton St. E1	59	F4
Malcolm Rd.		
Dowanhill Rd. SE6	87	D1
Dowdeswell Clo. SW15	74	E4
Dowding Pl., Stan.	29	D6
Dowgate Hill EC4	**13**	**B5**
Dowgate Hill EC4	59	A7
Dowland St. W10	57	B3
Dowlas St. SE5	**21**	**D7**
Dowlas St. SE5	68	B7
Dowlerville Rd., Orp.	104	J4
Dowman Clo. SW19	93	E1
Nelson Gro. Rd.		
Down Clo., Nthlt.	54	B2
Down Hall Rd., Kings.T.	91	G1
Down Pl. W6	65	H5
Down Rd., Tedd.	82	E6
Down St. W1	**15**	**D2**
Down St. W1	67	B1
Down St., W.Mol.	90	G5
Down St. Ms. W1	**15**	**D2**
Down Way, Nthlt.	54	B3
Downage NW4	38	J3
Downalong (Bushey), Wat.	29	A1
Downbarns Rd., Ruis.	45	D3
Downbury Ms. SW18	75	D6
Merton Rd.		
Downderry Rd., Brom.	87	D3
Downe Clo., Well.	71	C7
Downe Ms., Mitch.	93	J2
Downend SE18	70	E7
Moordown		
Downers Cotts. SW4	76	C4
The Pavement		
Downes Clo., Twick.	73	E6
St. Margarets Rd.		

Downes Ct. N21 32 G1
Downfield, Wor.Pk. 99 F1
Downfield Clo. W9 6 A6
Downfield Clo. W9 57 E4
Downham Rd. N1 50 A7
Downham Way, Brom. 87 D5
Downhills Ave. N17 41 A3
Downhills Pk. Rd. N17 40 J3
Downhills Way N17 40 J2
Downhurst Ave. NW7 30 D5
Downing Clo., Har. 36 J3
Downing Dr., Grnf. 55 A1
Downing Rd., Dag. 62 F1
Downing St. SW1 16 A3
Downing St. SW1 67 E2
Downings E6 61 D6
Downland Clo. N20 31 F1
Downleys Clo. SE9 88 B2
Downman Rd. SE9 79 B3
Downs, The SW20 84 A7
Downs Ave., Chis. 88 C5
Downs Ave., Pnr. 36 F6
Downs Bri. Rd., Beck. 96 D1
Downs Hill, Beck. 87 D7
Downs Pk. Rd. E5 50 D5
Downs Pk. Rd. E8 50 C5
Downs Rd. E5 50 D4
Downs Rd., Beck. 96 B2
Downs Rd., Enf. 25 B4
Downs Rd., Th.Hth. 94 J1
Downs Vw., Islw. 73 C1
Downs Way, Orp. 104 H5
Southlands Ave.
Downsbury Ms. SW18 75 D5
Merton Rd.
Downsell Rd. E15 51 C4
Downsfield Rd. E17 41 H6
Downshall Ave., Ilf. 43 H6
Downshire Hill NW3 48 G4
Downside, Sun. 90 A1
Downside, Twick. 82 C3
Downside Clo. SW19 84 F6
Downside Cres. NW3 48 H5
Downside Cres. W13 55 D4
Downside Rd., Sutt. 100 G6
Downside Wk., Nthlt. 54 F3
Invicta Gro.
Downsview Gdns. SE19 85 J7
Downsview Rd. SE19 85 J7
Downsway, Orp. 104 H5
Southlands Ave.
Downton Ave. SW2 85 E2
Downtown Rd. SE16 68 H2
Downway N12 31 H7
Dowrey St. N1 58 G1
Richmond Ave.
Dowsett Rd. N17 41 C2
Dowson Clo. SE5 77 A4
Doyce St. SE1 16 J3
Doyle Gdns. NW10 56 G1
Doyle Rd. SE25 95 D4
D'Oyley St. SW1 19 B1
D'Oyley St. SW1 67 A4
Doynton St. N19 49 B2
Draco St. SE17 20 J5
Draco St. SE17 67 J6
Dragmire La., Mitch. 93 G4
Dragoon Rd. SE8 68 J5
Dragor Rd. NW10 56 C4
Drake Clo. SE16 68 G2
Middleton Dr.
Drake Ct. SE19 86 C5
Drake Ct., Har. 45 F1
Drake Cres. SE28 62 C6
Drake Rd. SE4 78 A3
Drake Rd., Chess. 99 A5
Drake Rd., Croy. 94 F7
Drake Rd., Har. 45 F2
Drake Rd., Mitch. 94 A6
Drake St. WC1 12 C2
Drake St., Enf. 25 A1
Drakefell Rd. SE4 77 H3
Drakefell Rd. SE14 77 G2
Drakefield Rd. SW17 85 A3
Drakely Ct. N5 49 H4
Highbury Hill
Drakes Ctyd. NW6 57 C1
Kilburn High Rd.
Drakes Wk. E6 61 D2
Talbot Rd.
Drakewood Rd. SW16 85 D7
Draper Clo., Belv. 71 F4
Drapers Rd. E15 51 D4
Drapers Rd. N17 41 C3
Drapers Rd., Enf. 24 H2
Drappers Way SE16 21 J1
Drawdock Rd. SE10 69 D1
Drawell Clo. SE18 70 H5
Drax Ave. SW20 83 G7
Draxmont SW19 84 B6
Dray Gdns. SW2 76 F5
Draycot Rd. E11 42 H6
Draycot Rd., Surb. 99 A1
Draycott Ave. SW3 18 H1
Draycott Ave. SW3 66 H4
Draycott Ave., Har. 37 E6
Draycott Clo., Har. 37 E6
Draycott Ms. SW6 75 C2
New Kings Rd.
Draycott Pl. SW3 18 J2
Draycott Pl. SW3 66 J4
Draycott Ter. SW3 19 A2
Draycott Ter. SW3 66 J4
Drayford Clo. W9 57 C4
Drayside Ms., Sthl. 63 F2
Kingston Rd.
Drayson Ms. W8 66 D2
Drayton Ave. W13 55 D7
Drayton Ave., Loug. 27 C6
Drayton Ave., Orp. 104 E1
Drayton Bri. Rd. W7 55 C7
Drayton Bri. Rd. W13 55 D6
Drayton Clo., Houns. 72 F5
Bramley Way
Drayton Clo., Ilf. 52 G1
Drayton Gdns. N21 24 H7
Drayton Gdns. SW10 18 D3
Drayton Gdns. SW10 66 F5
Drayton Gdns. W13 55 D7
Drayton Grn. W13 55 D7
Drayton Grn. Rd. W13 55 E7
Drayton Gro. W13 55 D7
Drayton Pk. N5 49 G5
Drayton Rd. E11 51 D1
Drayton Rd. N17 41 B2
Drayton Rd. NW10 56 F1
Drayton Rd. W13 55 D7
Drayton Rd., Borwd. 22 A4
Drayton Rd., Croy. 101 H2
Drayton Waye, Har. 37 E6
Dreadnought St. SE10 69 E3
Dresden Clo. NW6 48 E6
Dresden Rd. N19 49 C1
Dressington Ave. SE4 78 A6
Drew Ave. NW7 31 B6
Drew Gdns., Grnf. 46 C6
Drew Rd. E16 70 B1
Drewstead Rd. SW16 85 D2
Driffield Rd. E3 59 H2
Drift, The, Brom. 104 A3
Drift Way, Rich. 82 J1
Driftway, The, Mitch. 94 A1
Drinkwater Rd., Har. 45 H2
Drive, The E4 26 D7
Drive, The E17 42 B3
Drive, The E18 42 G4
Drive, The N3 31 D7
Drive, The N6 39 J5
Fordington Rd.
Drive, The N11 32 C6
Drive, The NW10 56 F1
Longstone Ave.
Drive, The NW11 39 B7
Drive, The SW16 94 F3
Drive, The SW20 83 J7
Drive, The W3 56 C6
Drive, The, Bark. 52 J7
Drive, The, Barn. 23 B3
Drive, The, Barn. (New Barnet) 23 F6
Drive, The, Beck. 96 A2
Drive, The, Bex. 80 C6
Drive, The, Buck.H. 26 J7
Drive, The, Chis. 97 J3
Drive, The, Edg. 30 A5
Drive, The, Enf. 25 A1
Drive, The, Epsom 99 F6
Drive, The, Erith 71 H7
Drive, The, Felt. 72 C7
Drive, The, Har. 36 G7
Drive, The, Houns. 72 J2
Drive, The, Ilf. 43 B6
Drive, The, Islw. 73 A2
Drive, The, Kings.T. 83 C7
Drive, The, Loug. 27 B3
Drive, The, Mord. 93 F5
Drive, The, Orp. 104 J2
Drive, The, Rom. 44 J1
Drive, The, Sid. 89 B3
Drive, The, Surb. 91 H7
Drive, The, Th.Hth. 95 A4
Drive, The, Wem. 47 C2
Drive, The, W.Wick. 96 D7
Driveway, The E17 42 B6
Hoe St.
Droitwich Clo. SE26 86 D3
Dromey Gdns., Har. 29 C7
Dromore Rd. SW15 75 B6
Dronfield Gdns., Dag. 53 C5
Droop St. W10 57 B4
Drove Way, Loug. 27 E2
Drover La. SE15 68 E7
Drovers Pl. SE15 68 E7
Drovers Rd., S.Croy. 102 A5
Druce Rd. SE21 77 B6
Druid St. SE1 17 E3
Druid St. SE1 68 B2
Druids Way, Brom. 96 D4
Drum St. E1 13 G3
Drumaline Ridge, Wor.Pk. 99 E2
Drummond Cres. NW1 7 H3
Drummond Cres. NW1 58 D3
Drummond Dr., Stan. 29 C7
Drummond Gate SW1 19 J3
Drummond Gate SW1 67 D5
Drummond Pl., Rich. 73 H4
Drummond Pl., Twick. 73 E7
Drummond Rd. E11 42 J6
Drummond Rd. SE16 68 E3
Drummond Rd., Croy. 101 J2
Drummond St. NW1 7 F5
Drummond St. NW1 58 C4
Drummonds, The, Buck.H. 34 H2
Drummonds Pl., Rich. 73 H4
Drury Cres., Croy. 101 G2
Drury Ind. Est. NW10 47 C5
Drury La. WC2 12 B3
Drury La. WC2 58 E6
Drury Rd., Har. 36 J7
Drury Way NW10 47 D5
Dryad St. SW15 75 A3
Dryburgh Gdns. NW9 38 A3
Dryburgh Rd. SW15 74 H3
Dryden Ave. W7 55 C6
Dryden Clo., Ilf. 35 J6
Dryden Ct. SE11 20 F2
Dryden Rd. SW19 84 F6
Dryden Rd., Enf. 25 B6
Dryden Rd., Har. 46 C4
Dryden Rd., Well. 79 H1
Dryden St. WC2 12 B4
Dryfield Clo. NW10 47 C6
Dryfield Rd., Edg. 30 C6
Dryfield Wk. SE8 69 A6
New King St.
Dryhill Rd., Belv. 71 F6
Dryland Ave., Orp. 104 J4
Drylands Rd. N8 40 E6
Drysdale Ave. E4 26 B7
Drysdale Pl. N1 9 E3
Drysdale St. N1 9 E3
Drysdale St. N1 59 B3
Du Burstow Ter. W7 64 B2
Du Cane Clo. W12 56 J6
Du Cane Rd.
Du Cane Ct. SW17 85 A1
Du Cane Rd. W12 56 F6
Du Cros Dr., Stan. 29 G6
Du Cros Rd. W3 65 E1
The Vale
Dublin Cres. E8 59 D1
Ducal St. E2 9 G4
Duchess Ms. W1 11 E2
Duchess of Bedford's Wk. W8 66 D2
Duchess St. W1 11 E2
Duchess St. W1 58 B5
Duchy St. SE1 16 F1
Duchy St. SE1 67 G1
Ducie St. SW4 76 F4
Duck La. W1 11 H4
Duck Lees La., Enf. 25 H4
Duckett Rd. N4 40 G6
Duckett St. E1 59 G4
Ducks Wk., Twick. 73 F5
Dudden Hill La. NW10 47 F4
Duddington Clo. SE9 88 A4
Dudley Ave., Har. 37 F3
Dudley Ct. NW11 39 C4
Dudley Dr., Mord. 100 B1
Dudley Dr., Ruis. 45 B5
Dudley Gdns. W13 64 E2
Dudley Gdns., Har. 46 A1
Dudley Rd. E17 42 A2
Dudley Rd. N3 39 E2
Dudley Rd. NW6 57 B2
Dudley Rd. SW19 84 D6
Dudley Rd., Har. 45 J2
Dudley Rd., Ilf. 52 E4
Dudley Rd., Kings.T. 91 J3
Dudley Rd., Rich. 73 J2
Dudley Rd., Sthl. 63 D2
Dudley Rd., Walt. 90 A6
Dudley St. W2 10 E2
Dudlington Rd. E5 50 F2
Dudmaston Ms. SW3 18 F3
Dudsbury Rd., Sid. 89 B6
Dudset La., Houns. 72 A1
Duff St. E14 60 B6
Dufferin Ave. EC1 9 B6
Dufferin St. EC1 9 A6
Dufferin St. EC1 58 J4
Duffield Clo., Har. 37 C5
Duffield Dr. N15 41 C4
Copperfield Dr.
Dufour's Pl. W1 11 G4
Duke Gdns., Ilf. 43 G4
Duke Rd.
Duke Hill St. SE1 17 C1
Duke Hill St. SE1 68 A1
Duke Humphrey Rd. SE3 78 E1
Duke of Cambridge Clo., Twick. 73 A6
Duke of Edinburgh Rd., Sutt. 100 G2
Duke of Wellington Pl. SW1 15 C3
Duke of Wellington Pl. SW1 67 A2
Duke of York St. SW1 15 G1
Duke of York St. SW1 67 C1
Duke Rd. W4 65 D5
Duke Rd., Ilf. 43 G4
Duke Shore Pl. E14 59 J7
Narrow St.
Duke St. SW1 15 G1
Duke St. SW1 67 C1
Duke St. W1 11 C3
Duke St. W1 58 A6
Duke St., Rich. 73 G5
Duke St., Sutt. 100 G4
Dukes Ave. N3 39 E1
Dukes Ave. N10 40 C3
Dukes Ave. W4 65 D5
Dukes Ave., Edg. 29 J6
Dukes Ave., Har. 36 F6
Dukes Ave., Har. (Wealdstone) 37 B4
Dukes Ave., Houns. 72 E4
Dukes Ave., Kings.T. 82 F4
Dukes Ave., N.Mal. 92 F3
Dukes Ave., Nthlt. 45 E7
Dukes Ave., Rich. 82 F4
Dukes Clo., Hmptn. 81 F5
Dukes Clo., Kings.T. 82 G4
Dukes Ct. E6 61 D1
Dukes Grn. Ave., Felt. 72 A5
Dukes La. W8 66 E2
Duke's Meadows W4 74 C2
Great Chertsey Rd.
Dukes Ms. N10 40 B3
Dukes Ave.
Duke's Ms. W1 11 C3
Dukes Orchard, Bex. 89 J1
Duke's Pas. E17 42 C3
Marlowe Rd.
Dukes Pl. EC3 13 E4
Dukes Pl. EC3 59 B6
Dukes Rd. E6 61 D1
Dukes Rd. W3 56 A4
Duke's Rd. WC1 7 J4
Duke's Rd. WC1 58 D3
Dukes Way, W.Wick. 103 E3
Duke's Yd. W1 11 C5
Dukesthorpe Rd. SE26 86 G4
Dulas St. N4 49 F1
Everleigh St.
Dulford St. W11 57 B7
Dulka Rd. SW11 75 J5
Dulverton Rd. SE9 88 F2
Dulverton Rd., Ruis. 45 A1
Dulwich Common SE21 86 B1
Dulwich Common SE22 86 C1
Dulwich Lawn Clo. SE22 77 C5
Melbourne Gro.
Dulwich Oaks, The SE21 86 C3
Dulwich Rd. SE24 76 G5
Dulwich Village SE21 77 B6
Dulwich Wd. Ave. SE19 86 B4
Dulwich Wd. Pk. SE19 86 B4
Dumbarton Rd. SW2 76 E6

Dumbleton Clo., 92 B1
Kings.T.
Gloucester Rd.
Dumbreck Rd. SE9 79 C4
Dumont Rd. N16 50 B3
Dumpton Pl. NW1 49 A7
Gloucester Ave.
Dunbar Ave. SW16 94 G2
Dunbar Ave., Beck. 95 H4
Dunbar Ave., Dag. 53 G3
Dunbar Clo., Hayes 54 A5
Dunbar Ct., Sutt. 100 G5
Dunbar Gdns., Dag. 53 G5
Dunbar Rd. E7 51 G6
Dunbar Rd. N22 40 G1
Dunbar Rd., N.Mal. 92 C4
Dunbar St. SE27 85 J3
Dunblane Clo., Edg. 30 B2
Tayside Dr.
Dunblane Rd. SE9 79 B2
Dunboyne Rd. NW3 48 J5
Dunbridge St. E2 **9 H5**
Dunbridge St. E2 59 D4
Duncan Clo., Barn. 23 F4
Duncan Gro. W3 56 E6
Duncan Rd. E8 59 E1
Duncan Rd., Rich. 73 H4
Duncan St. N1 **8 G1**
Duncan St. N1 58 H2
Duncan Ter. N1 **8 G2**
Duncan Ter. N1 58 H2
Duncannon St. WC2 **12 A6**
Duncannon St. WC2 58 E7
Dunch St. E1 59 E6
Watney St.
Duncombe Hill SE23 77 H7
Duncombe Rd. N19 49 D1
Duncrievie Rd. SE13 78 D6
Duncroft SE18 70 H7
Dundalk Rd. SE4 77 H3
Dundas Gdns., W.Mol. 90 H3
Dundas Rd. SE15 77 F2
Dundee Rd. E13 60 H2
Dundee Rd. SE25 95 E5
Dundee St. E1 68 E1
Dundela Gdns., 99 H4
Wor.Pk.
Dundonald Clo. E6 61 B6
Northumberland Rd.
Dundonald Rd. NW10 57 A1
Dundonald Rd. SW19 84 B7
Dunedin Rd. E10 51 B3
Dunedin Rd., Ilf. 52 F1
Dunedin Way, Hayes 54 C4
Dunelm Gro. SE27 85 J4
Dunelm St. E1 59 G6
Dunfield Gdns. SE6 87 B5
Dunfield Rd. SE6 87 B5
Dunford Rd. N7 49 F4
Dungarvan Ave. SW15 74 G4
Dunheved Clo., 94 G6
Th.Hth.
Dunheved Rd. N., 94 G6
Th.Hth.
Dunheved Rd. S., 94 G6
Th.Hth.
Dunheved Rd. W., 94 G6
Th.Hth.
Dunholme Grn. N9 33 C3
Dunholme La. N9 33 C3
Dunholme Rd.
Dunholme Rd. N9 33 C3
Dunkeld Rd. SE25 95 A4
Dunkeld Rd., Dag. 53 B2
Dunkery Rd. SE9 88 A4
Dunkirk St. SE27 85 J4
Waring St.
Dunlace Rd. E5 50 F4
Dunleary Clo., Houns. 72 F7
Dunley Dr., Croy. 103 B7
Dunlin Ho. W13 55 C4
Dunloe Ave. N17 41 A3
Dunloe St. E2 **9 G2**
Dunloe St. E2 59 C2
Dunlop Pl. SE16 **17 G6**
Dunlop Pl. E16 69 G1
Dunmore Pt. E2 **9 F4**
Dunmore Rd. NW6 57 B1
Dunmore Rd. SW20 92 J1
Dunmow Clo., Felt. 81 D4
Dunmow Clo., Loug. 27 B6
Dunmow Clo., Rom. 44 C5
Dunmow Ho., Dag. 62 B1
Dunmow Rd. E15 51 D4
Dunmow Wk. N1 58 J1
Popham St.
Dunn Mead NW9 30 F7
Field Mead

Dunn St. E8 50 C5
Dunnock Clo. N9 33 G1
Dunnock Clo., Borwd. 22 A4
Siskin Clo.
Dunnock Rd. E6 61 B6
Dunollie Pl. NW5 49 C5
Dunollie Rd.
Dunollie Rd. NW5 49 C5
Dunoon Rd. SE23 77 F7
Dunraven Dr., Enf. 24 G2
Dunraven Rd. W12 65 G1
Dunraven St. W1 **11 A5**
Dunsany Rd. W14 66 A3
Dunsfold Way, Croy. 103 B7
Dunsford Way SW15 74 H6
Dover Pk. Dr.
Dunsmore Clo., Hayes 54 E4
Kingsash Dr.
Dunsmore Rd., Walt. 90 B6
Dunsmure Rd. N16 50 B1
Dunspring La., Ilf. 43 E2
Dunstable Ms. W1 **11 C1**
Dunstable Rd., Rich. 73 H4
Dunstable Rd., W.Mol. 90 F4
Dunstall Rd. SW20 83 H6
Dunstall Way, W.Mol. 90 H3
Dunstan Clo. N2 39 F3
Thomas More Way
Dunstan Rd. NW11 48 C1
Dunstans Gro. SE22 77 E6
Dunstans Rd. SE22 77 D7
Dunster Ave., Mord. 100 A1
Dunster Clo., Barn. 23 A4
Dunster Clo., Rom. 44 J2
Dunster Ct. EC3 **13 D5**
Dunster Dr. NW9 47 C1
Dunster Gdns. NW6 48 C7
Dunster Way, Har. 45 E4
Dunsterville Way SE1 **17 C4**
Dunston Rd. E8 59 C1
Dunston Rd. SW11 76 A3
Dunston St. E8 59 C1
Dunton Clo., Surb. 98 H1
Dunton Rd. E10 42 B7
Dunton Rd. SE1 **21 F2**
Dunton Rd. SE1 68 C4
Duntshill Rd. SW18 84 E1
Dunvegan Clo., 90 H4
W.Mol.
Dunvegan Rd. SE9 79 C4
Dunwich Rd., Bexh. 80 F1
Dunworth Ms. W11 57 C6
Portobello Rd.
Duplex Ride SW1 **15 A4**
Dupont Rd. SW20 93 A2
Dupont St. E14 59 H5
Maroon St.
Duppas Ave., Croy. 101 H4
Violet La.
Duppas Hill La., Croy. 101 H4
Duppas Hill Rd.
Duppas Hill Rd., Croy. 101 G4
Duppas Hill Ter., 101 H3
Croy.
Duppas Rd., Croy. 101 G3
Dupree Rd. SE7 69 H5
Dura Den Clo., Beck. 87 B7
Durand Clo., Cars. 100 J1
Durand Gdns. SW9 76 F1
Durand Way NW10 47 C7
Durands Wk. SE16 68 H2
Salter Rd.
Durant St. E2 **9 H3**
Durant St. E2 59 D3
Durants Pk. Ave., Enf. 25 G4
Durants Rd., Enf. 25 F4
Durban Gdns., Dag. 53 J7
Durban Rd. E15 60 E3
Durban Rd. E17 41 J1
Durban Rd. N17 33 B6
Durban Rd. SE27 85 J4
Durban Rd., Beck. 95 J2
Durban Rd., Ilf. 52 H1
Durbin Rd., Chess. 98 H4
Durdans Rd., Sthl. 54 F6
Durell Gdns., Dag. 53 D5
Durell Rd., Dag. 53 D5
Durford Cres. SW15 83 H1
Durham Ave., Brom. 96 F4
Durham Ave., Houns. 63 F6
Durham Ave., 35 A5
Wdf.Grn.
Durham Clo. SW20 92 H2
Durham Rd.
Durham Hill, Brom. 87 F4
Durham Ho. St. WC2 **12 B6**
Durham Pl. SW3 **18 J4**

Durham Pl., Ilf. 52 F4
Eton Rd.
Durham Ri. SE18 70 F5
Durham Rd. E12 52 A4
Durham Rd. E16 60 E4
Durham Rd. N2 39 H3
Durham Rd. N7 49 F2
Durham Rd. N9 33 D2
Durham Rd. SW20 92 H1
Durham Rd. W5 64 G3
Durham Rd., Borwd. 22 C3
Durham Rd., Brom. 96 F3
Durham Rd., Dag. 53 J5
Durham Rd., Felt. 72 C7
Durham Rd., Har. 36 H5
Durham Rd., Sid. 89 B5
Durham Row E1 59 H5
Durham St. SE11 **20 C4**
Durham St. SE11 67 F5
Durham Ter. W2 **10 A3**
Durham Ter. W2 57 E6
Durham Wf., Brent. 64 F7
High St.
Durley Ave., Pnr. 36 E7
Durley Rd. N16 41 B7
Durlston Rd. E5 50 D2
Durlston Rd., Kings.T. 82 H6
Durnell Way, Loug. 27 C3
Durnford St. N15 41 B5
Durnford St. SE10 69 C6
Greenwich Ch. St.
Durning Rd. SE19 86 A5
Durnsford Ave. SW19 84 D2
Durnsford Rd. N11 40 D2
Durnsford Rd. SW19 84 D2
Durrant Way, Orp. 104 G5
Durrell Rd. SW6 75 C1
Durrington Ave. SW20 92 J1
Durrington Pk. Rd. 92 J1
SW20
Durrington Rd. E5 50 H4
Dursley Clo. SE3 78 J2
Dursley Gdns. SE3 79 A1
Dursley Rd. SE3 78 J2
Durward St. E1 59 E5
Durweston Ms. W1 **11 A1**
Durweston St. W1 **11 A2**
Dury Rd., Barn. 23 C2
Dutch Gdns., Kings.T. 83 B6
Windmill Ri.
Dutch Yd. SW18 75 D5
Wandsworth High St.
Duthie St. E14 60 C7
Dutton St. SE10 78 C1
Duxberry Clo., Brom. 97 B5
Southborough La.
Dwight Ct. SW6 75 B2
Burlington Rd.
Dye Ho. La. E3 60 A1
Dyer's Bldgs. EC1 **12 E2**
Dyers Hall Rd. E11 51 E2
Dyers La. SW15 74 H4
Dykes Way, Brom. 96 F3
Dylan Rd. SE24 76 H4
Dylan Rd., Belv. 71 G3
Dylan Thomas Ho. N8 40 F4
Dylways SE5 77 A4
Dymchurch Clo., Ilf. 43 D3
Dymchurch Clo., Orp. 104 H4
Dymes Path SW19 84 A2
Queensmere Rd.
Dymock St. SW6 75 E3
Dymond Est. SW17 84 H3
Glenburnie Rd.
Dyne Rd. NW6 48 B7
Dyneley Rd. SE12 87 J4
Dynevor Rd. N16 50 C3
Dynevor Rd., Rich. 73 H5
Dynham Rd. NW6 48 D7
Dyott St. WC1 **11 J3**
Dyott St. W1 58 D6
Dysart Ave., Kings.T. 82 F5
Dysart St. EC2 **9 D6**
Dyson Rd. E11 42 E6
Dyson Rd. E15 51 F6
Dysons Rd. N18 33 E5

E

Eade Rd. N4 40 J7
Eagans Clo. N2 39 H3
Market Pl.
Eagle Ave., Rom. 44 E6
Eagle Clo. SE16 68 F5
Varcoe Rd.
Eagle Clo., Enf. 25 F4
Eagle Ct. EC1 **12 G1**
Eagle Ct. EC1 58 H5

Eagle Dr. NW9 38 E2
Eagle Hill SE19 86 A6
Eagle La. E11 42 G4
Eagle Ms. N1 50 B6
Tottenham Rd.
Eagle Pl. SW1 **11 G6**
Eagle Pl. SW7 **18 D3**
Eagle Pl. SW7, Wem. 46 G7
Eagle St. WC1 **12 C2**
Eagle St. WC1 58 E5
Eagle Ter., Wdf.Grn. 34 H7
Eagle Wf. Rd. N1 **9 A1**
Eagle Wf. Rd. N1 58 J2
Eaglesfield Rd. SE18 79 E2
Ealdham Sq. SE9 78 J4
Ealing Clo., Borwd. 22 C4
Ealing Downs Ct., 55 D3
Grnf.
Perivale La.
Ealing Grn. W5 64 G1
Ealing Pk. Gdns. W5 64 F4
Ealing Rd., Brent. 64 G4
Ealing Rd., Nthlt. 54 G1
Ealing Rd., Wem. 46 H6
Ealing Village W5 55 H6
Eamont St. NW8 **6 G1**
Eamont St. NW8 57 H2
Eardley Cres. SW5 66 D5
Eardley Pt. SE18 70 E4
Wilmount St.
Eardley Rd. SW16 85 C5
Eardley Rd., Belv. 71 G5
Earl Ri. SE18 70 G4
Earl Rd. SE1 **21 F3**
Earl Rd. SE1 68 C5
Earl Rd. SW14 74 C4
Elm Rd.
Earl St. EC2 **13 C1**
Earl St. EC2 59 A5
Earldom Rd. SW15 74 J4
Earle Gdns., Kings.T. 82 H7
Earlham Gro. E7 51 F5
Earlham Gro. N22 32 F7
Earlham St. WC2 **11 J4**
Earlham St. WC2 58 D6
Earls Ct. Gdns. SW5 **18 A2**
Earls Ct. Gdns. SW5 66 E4
Earls Ct. Rd. SW5 66 D4
Earls Ct. Rd. W8 66 D4
Earls Ct. Sq. SW5 **18 A3**
Earls Ct. Sq. SW5 66 E5
Earls Cres., Har. 37 B4
Earl's Path, Loug. 26 J2
Earls Ter. W8 66 C3
Earls Wk. W8 66 D3
Earls Wk., Dag. 53 B4
Earlsdown Ho., Bark. 61 G2
Wheelers Cross
Earlsferry Way N1 49 F7
Earlsfield Rd. SW18 84 F1
Earlshall Rd. SE9 79 C4
Earlsmead, Har. 45 F4
Earlsmead Rd. N15 41 C5
Earlsmead Rd. NW10 56 J3
Earlsthorpe Ms. SW12 76 A6
Earlsthorpe Rd. SE26 86 G4
Earlstoke St. EC1 **8 G3**
Earlston Gro. E9 59 E1
Earlswood Ave., 94 G5
Th.Hth.
Earlswood Clo. SE10 69 E5
Earlswood St.
Earlswood Gdns., Ilf. 43 D3
Earlswood St. SE10 69 E5
Early Ms. NW1 58 B1
Arlington Rd.
Earnshaw St. WC2 **11 J3**
Earnshaw St. WC2 58 D6
Earsby St. W14 66 B4
Easby Cres., Mord. 93 E6
Easebourne Rd., Dag. 53 C5
Easedale Ho., Islw. 73 C5
Easley's Ms. W1 **11 C3**
East Acton La. W3 56 E7
East Arbour St. E1 59 G6
East Ave. E12 52 B7
East Ave. E17 42 B4
East Ave., Hayes 63 A1
East Ave., Sthl. 54 A2
East Ave., Wall. 101 F5
East Bank N16 41 B7
East Barnet Rd., Barn. 23 G4
East Churchfield Rd. 65 D1
W3
East Clo. W5 56 A4
East Clo., Barn. 24 A4
East Clo., Grnf. 54 J2
East Ct., Wem. 46 F1

East Cres. N11 31 J4
East Cres., Enf. 25 B5
East Cross Route E3 50 J7
East Dulwich Gro. 77 B5
SE22
East Dulwich Rd. 77 D4
SE15
East Dulwich Rd. SE22 77 C4
East End Rd. N2 39 E3
East End Rd. N3 39 C2
East End Way, Pnr. 36 E3
East Entrance, Dag. 62 H2
East Ferry Rd. E14 69 B4
East Gdns. SW17 84 H6
East Ham Ind. Est. E6 61 A4
East Ham Manor Way 61 D6
E6
East Harding St. EC4 12 F3
East Heath Rd. NW3 48 F3
East Hill SW18 75 E5
East Hill, Wem. 47 A2
East Holme, Hayes 63 A1
East India Dock Rd. 60 A6
E14
East India Dock Wall 60 D7
Rd. E14
East La. SE16 17 H4
East La. SE16 68 D2
East La., Kings.T. 91 G3
East La., Wem. 46 E3
East Mascalls SE7 69 J6
Mascalls Rd.
East Mead, Ruis. 45 D3
East Mt. St. E1 59 E5
East Pk. Clo., Rom. 44 D5
East Pas. EC1 12 J1
East Pier E1 68 E1
Wapping High St.
East Pl. SE27 85 J4
Pilgrim Hill
East Poultry Ave. EC1 12 G2
East Rd. E15 60 G1
East Rd. N1 9 C3
East Rd. N1 59 A3
East Rd. SW19 84 F6
East Rd., Barn. 32 A1
East Rd., Edg. 38 B1
East Rd., Kings.T. 91 H1
East Rd., Rom. 44 E5
(Chadwell Heath)
East Rd., Well. 80 B2
East Rochester Way 79 G4
SE9
East Rochester Way, 80 D6
Bex.
East Rochester Way, 79 G4
Sid.
East Row E11 42 G6
East Row W10 57 B4
East Sheen Ave. SW14 74 D5
East Smithfield E1 13 G6
East Smithfield E1 59 C7
East St. SE17 21 A3
East St. SE17 67 J5
East St., Bark. 52 F7
East St., Bexh. 80 G4
East St., Brent. 64 F7
East St., Brom. 96 G2
East Surrey Gro. SE15 68 C7
East Tenter St. E1 13 G4
East Tenter St. E1 59 C6
East Twrs., Pnr. 36 D5
East Vw. E4 34 C5
East Vw., Barn. 23 C2
East Wk. NW7 30 G7
Northway
East Wk., Barn. 24 A7
East Wk., Hayes 63 A1
East Way E11 42 H5
East Way, Brom. 96 G7
East Way, Croy. 102 H2
East Way, Hayes 63 A1
East Way, Ruis. 45 A1
East Woodside, Bex. 89 E1
Maiden Erlegh Ave.
Eastbank Rd., Hmptn. 81 J5
Eastbourne Ave. W3 56 D6
Eastbourne Gdns. 74 C3
SW14
Eastbourne Ms. W2 10 D3
Eastbourne Ms. W2 10 D3
Eastbourne Rd. E6 61 D3
Eastbourne Rd. E15 60 E1
Eastbourne Rd. N15 41 B5
Eastbourne Rd. SW17 85 A6
Eastbourne Rd. W4 65 C6
Eastbourne Rd., Brent. 64 G3
Eastbourne Rd., Felt. 81 D2

Eastbourne Ter. W2 10 D3
Eastbourne Ter. W2 57 F6
Eastbournia Ave. N9 33 E3
Eastbrook Ave. N9 25 J1
Eastbrook Ave., Dag. 53 J4
Eastbrook Rd. SE3 78 H1
Eastbury Ave., Bark. 61 H1
Eastbury Ave., Enf. 25 B1
Eastbury Ct., Bark. 61 H1
Eastbury Gro. W4 65 E5
Eastbury Ho., Bark. 61 J1
Eastbury Rd. E6 61 D4
Eastbury Rd., Kings.T. 82 H7
Eastbury Rd., Orp. 97 G6
Eastbury Sq., Bark. 61 J1
Eastbury Ter. E1 59 G4
Eastcastle St. W1 11 F3
Eastcastle St. W1 58 C6
Eastcheap EC3 13 C5
Eastcheap EC3 59 A7
Eastcombe Ave. SE7 69 H6
Eastcote, Orp. 104 J1
Eastcote Ave., Grnf. 46 D6
Eastcote Ave., Har. 45 H2
Eastcote Ave., W.Mol. 90 F5
Eastcote High Rd., 36 A6
Pnr.
Eastcote La., Har. 45 J4
Eastcote La., Nthlt. 45 F5
Eastcote La. N., Nthlt. 45 F6
Eastcote Rd., Har. 45 J3
Eastcote Rd., Pnr. 36 D5
Eastcote Rd., Ruis. 36 A6
Eastcote Rd., Well. 79 G2
Eastcote St. SW9 76 F2
Eastcote Vw., Pnr. 36 C4
Eastcroft Rd., Epsom 99 E7
Eastdown Pk. SE13 78 D4
Eastern Ave. E11 42 H6
Eastern Ave., Ilf. 43 E6
Eastern Ave., Pnr. 36 D7
Eastern Ave., Rom. 44 C4
Eastern Ave. W., Rom. 44 E4
Eastern Ind. Est., Erith 71 F7
Eastern Rd. E13 60 H2
Eastern Rd. E17 42 C5
Eastern Rd. N2 39 J3
Eastern Rd. N22 40 E1
Eastern Rd. SE4 78 A4
Eastern Way SE2 71 E1
Eastern Way SE28 71 A2
Eastern Way, Erith 71 E1
Easternville Gdns., Ilf. 43 F6
Eastfield Gdns., Dag. 53 G4
Eastfield Rd. E17 42 A4
Eastfield Rd. N8 40 E3
Eastfield Rd., Dag. 53 F4
Eastfields, Pnr. 36 C5
Eastfields Rd. W3 56 C5
Eastfields Rd., Mitch. 94 A2
Eastgate Clo. SE28 62 D6
Eastglade, Pnr. 36 F3
Eastholm NW11 39 E4
Eastlake Rd. SE5 76 J2
Eastlands Cres. SE21 77 C6
Eastleigh Ave., Har. 45 H2
Eastleigh Clo. NW2 47 E3
Eastleigh Clo., Sutt. 100 E7
Eastleigh Rd., Bexh. 80 J2
Eastleigh Wk. SW15 74 G7
Alton Rd.
Eastman Rd. W3 65 D2
Eastmead Ave., Grnf. 54 H3
Eastmead Clo., Brom. 97 B2
Eastmearn Rd. SE21 85 J2
Eastmoor Pl. SE7 70 A3
Eastmoor St.
Eastmoor St. SE7 70 A3
Eastney Rd., Croy. 101 H1
Eastney St. SE10 69 D5
Eastnor Rd. SE9 88 F1
Easton Gdns., Borwd. 22 D4
Easton St. WC1 8 E4
Eastry Ave., Brom. 96 F6
Eastry Rd., Erith 71 G6
Eastside Rd. NW11 39 C4
Eastview Ave. SE18 70 H7
Eastville Ave. NW11 39 C6
Eastway E9 50 J6
Eastway E10 51 A4
Eastway, Mord. 93 A5
Eastway, Wall. 101 C4
Eastwell Clo., Beck. 86 H7
Eastwood Clo. E18 42 G2
The Viaduct
Eastwood Rd. E18 42 G2
Eastwood Rd. N10 40 A2

Eastwood Rd., Ilf. 44 A7
Eastwood St. SW16 85 C6
Eatington Rd. E10 42 D5
Eaton Clo. SW1 19 B2
Eaton Clo. SW1 67 A4
Eaton Clo., Stan. 29 E4
Eaton Dr. SW9 76 H4
Eaton Dr., Kings.T. 83 A7
Eaton Gdns., Dag. 53 E7
Eaton Gate SW1 19 B1
Eaton Gate SW1 67 A4
Eaton La. SW1 15 E6
Eaton La. SW1 67 B3
Eaton Ms. N. SW1 15 B6
Eaton Ms. N. SW1 67 A3
Eaton Ms. S. SW1 15 D6
Eaton Ms. S. SW1 67 A4
Eaton Ms. W. SW1 19 C1
Eaton Ms. W. SW1 67 A4
Eaton Pk. Rd. N13 32 G2
Eaton Pl. SW1 15 B6
Eaton Pl. SW1 67 A3
Eaton Ri. E11 42 J5
Eaton Ri. W5 55 F5
Eaton Rd. NW4 38 J3
Eaton Rd., Enf. 25 B3
Eaton Rd., Houns. 73 A4
Eaton Rd., Sid. 89 D2
Eaton Rd., Sutt. 100 G6
Eaton Row SW1 15 D6
Eaton Row SW1 67 B3
Eaton Sq. SW1 19 C1
Eaton Sq. SW1 67 A4
Eaton Ter. SW1 19 B1
Eaton Ter. SW1 67 A4
Eaton Ter. Ms. SW1 19 B1
Eaton Wk. SE15 68 C7
Sumner Est.
Eatons Mead E4 34 A2
Eatonville Rd. SW17 84 J2
Eatonville Vill. SW17 84 J2
Eatonville Rd.
Ebbisham Dr. SW8 20 C6
Ebbisham Dr. SW8 67 F6
Ebbisham Rd., 99 J2
Wor.Pk.
Ebbsfleet Rd. NW2 48 B5
Ebdon Way SE3 78 H3
Ebenezer St. N1 9 B3
Ebenezer St. N1 59 A3
Ebenezer Wk. SW16 94 C1
Meopham Rd.
Ebley Clo. SE15 21 F6
Ebner St. SW18 75 E5
Ebor St. E1 9 F5
Ebor St. E1 59 C4
Ebrington Rd., Har. 37 G6
Ebsworth St. SE23 77 G2
Eburne Rd. N7 49 E3
Ebury Bri. SW1 19 D3
Ebury Bri. SW1 67 B5
Ebury Bri. Est. SW1 19 D3
Ebury Bri. Est. SW1 67 B5
Ebury Bri. Rd. SW1 19 C4
Ebury Bri. Rd. SW1 67 A5
Ebury Clo., Kes. 104 B3
Ebury Ms. SE27 85 H3
Ebury Ms. SW1 19 D1
Ebury Ms. SW1 67 B4
Ebury Ms. E. SW1 15 D6
Ebury Sq. SW1 19 C2
Ebury Sq. SW1 67 A4
Ebury St. SW1 19 C2
Ebury St. SW1 67 A4
Eccles Rd. SW11 75 J4
Ecclesbourne Clo. 32 G5
N13
Ecclesbourne Gdns. 32 G5
N13
Ecclesbourne Rd. N1 49 J7
Ecclesbourne Rd., 94 J5
Th.Hth.
Eccleston Bri. SW1 19 E1
Eccleston Bri. SW1 67 B4
Eccleston Clo., Barn. 23 J4
Eccleston Clo., Orp. 104 G1
Eccleston Cres., Rom. 44 A7
Eccleston Ms. SW1 15 C6
Eccleston Ms. SW1 67 A3
Eccleston Pl. SW1 19 D1
Eccleston Pl. SW1 67 B4
Eccleston Rd. W13 55 D7
Eccleston Sq. SW1 19 E2
**Eccleston Sq. Ms. 19 E2
SW1**
Eccleston St. SW1 15 C6
Eccleston St. SW1 67 B4

Ecclestone Ct., Wem. 46 H5
St. John's Rd.
Ecclestone Ms., Wem. 46 H5
Ecclestone Pl., Wem. 46 J5
Echo Heights E4 34 B1
Eckford St. N1 8 E1
Eckford St. N1 58 G2
Eckstein Rd. SW11 75 H4
Eclipse Rd. E13 60 H5
Ector Rd. SE6 87 E2
Edbrooke Rd. W9 57 D4
Eddiscombe Rd. SW6 75 C2
Eddy Clo., Rom. 44 H6
Eddystone Rd. SE4 77 H5
Ede Clo., Houns. 72 F3
Eden Clo. W8 66 D3
Adam & Eve Ms.
Eden Clo., Wem. 55 G1
Eden Gro. E17 42 B5
Eden Gro. N7 49 F5
Eden Ms. SW17 84 F3
Huntspill
Eden Pk. Ave., Beck. 95 H4
Eden Rd. E17 42 B5
Eden Rd. SE27 85 H5
Eden Rd., Beck. 95 H4
Eden Rd., Bex. 89 J4
Eden Rd., Croy. 102 A4
Eden St., Kings.T. 91 G2
Eden Wk., Kings.T. 91 H2
Eden Wk.
Eden Way, Beck. 95 J5
Edenbridge Rd. E9 50 G2
Edenbridge Rd., Enf. 25 B6
Edencourt Rd. SW16 85 B6
Edenfield Gdns., 99 F3
Wor.Pk.
Edenham Way W10 57 C5
Elkstone Rd.
Edenhurst Ave. SW6 75 C3
Edensor Gdns. W4 65 E7
Edensor Rd. W4 65 E7
Edenvale Rd., Mitch. 85 A7
Edenvale St. SW6 75 E2
Ederline Ave. SW16 94 F3
Edgar Rd. E3 60 B3
Edgar Rd., Houns. 72 F7
Edgar Rd., Rom. 44 D7
Edgarley Ter. SW6 75 H1
Edgbaston Rd., Wat. 28 B3
Holmside Ri.
Edge Hill SE18 70 E6
Edge Hill SW19 84 A7
Edge Hill Ave. N3 39 D4
Edge Hill Ct. SW19 84 A7
Edge St. W8 66 D1
Kensington Ch. St.
Edgeborough Way, 88 A7
Brom.
Edgebury, Chis. 88 E4
Edgebury Wk., Chis. 88 F4
Edgehill Rd.
Edgecombe Ho. 84 B1
SW19
Edgecoombe, S.Croy. 102 F7
Edgecoombe Clo., 83 D7
Kings.T.
Edgecot Gro. N15 41 A5
Oulton Rd.
Edgecote Clo. W3 65 C1
Cheltenham Pl.
Edgefield Ave., Bark. 52 J7
Edgehill Gdns., Dag. 53 G4
Edgehill Rd. W13 55 F5
Edgehill Rd., Chis. 88 F3
Edgehill Rd., Mitch. 94 B1
Edgel St. SW18 75 E4
Ferrier St.
Edgeley La. SW4 76 D3
Edgeley Rd.
Edgeley Rd. SW4 76 D3
Edgepoint Clo. SE27 85 H5
Knights Hill
Edgewood Dr., Orp. 104 J5
Edgewood Grn., Croy. 102 G1
Edgeworth Ave. NW4 38 G5
Edgeworth Clo. NW4 38 G5
Edgeworth Cres. NW4 38 G5
Edgeworth Rd. SE9 78 A4
Edgeworth Rd., Barn. 23 H4
Edgington Rd. SW16 85 D6
Edgington Way, Sid. 89 C7
Edgware Ct., Edg. 30 A6
Cavendish Dr.
Edgware Rd. NW2 47 H1
Edgware Rd. NW9 38 C2
Edgware Rd. W2 6 E6

Edgware Rd. W2　57 G4
Edgware Way, Edg.　29 J4
Edgwarebury Gdns.,　30 A5
　Edg.
Edgwarebury La., Edg. 30 A2
Edinburgh Clo. E2　59 F2
　Russia La.
Edinburgh Ct. SW20　93 A5
Edinburgh Dr., Rom.　44 J4
　Eastern Ave. W.
Edinburgh Gate SW1　14 J4
Edinburgh Gate SW1　66 J2
Edinburgh Ho. W9　6 B3
Edinburgh Ho. W9　57 E3
Edinburgh Rd. E13　60 H2
Edinburgh Rd. E17　42 A5
Edinburgh Rd. N18　33 D5
Edinburgh Rd. W7　64 C2
Edinburgh Rd., Sutt.　100 F2
Edington Rd. SE2　71 B3
Edington Rd., Enf.　25 F2
Edis St. NW1　58 A1
Edison Dr., Sthl.　54 H6
Edison Gro. SE18　70 J7
Edison Rd. N8　40 D6
Edison Rd., Brom.　96 G2
Edison Rd., Enf.　25 J2
Edison Rd., Well.　79 J1
Edith Gdns., Surb.　92 B7
Edith Gro. SW10　18 C6
Edith Gro. SW10　66 F6
Edith Rd. E6　52 A7
Edith Rd. E15　51 D5
　Chandos Rd.
Edith Rd. N11　32 D7
Edith Rd. SE25　95 A5
Edith Rd. SW19　84 E6
Edith Rd. W14　66 B4
Edith Rd., Rom.　44 D6
Edith Row SW6　75 E1
Edith St. E2　9 H1
Edith Ter. SW10　18 C7
Edith Ter. SW10　66 F7
Edith Vill. W14　66 C5
Edith Yd. SW10　18 D7
Edithna St. SW9　76 E3
Edmansons Clo. N17　41 B1
　Bruce Gro.
Edmeston Clo. E9　50 H6
Edmonds Ct., W.Mol.　90 H4
　Avern Rd.
Edmund Rd., Mitch.　93 H3
Edmund Rd., Well.　80 A3
Edmund St. SE5　21 B7
Edmund St. SE5　68 A7
Edmunds Clo., Hayes 54 C5
Edmunds Wk. N2　39 H4
Edna Rd. SW20　93 A2
Edna St. SW11　75 H1
Edric Rd. SE14　68 G7
Edrich Ho. SW4　76 E1
Edrick Rd., Edg.　30 C6
Edrick Wk., Edg.　30 C6
Edridge Rd., Croy.　101 J3
Edulf Rd., Borwd.　22 B1
Edward Ave. E4　34 B6
Edward Ave., Mord.　93 G5
Edward Clo. N9　25 C7
Edward Clo., Hmptn.　81 J3
　Edward Rd.
Edward Clo., Nthlt.　54 C2
Edward Ct. E16　60 G5
　Alexandra St.
Edward Gro., Barn.　23 G5
　Edward Rd.
Edward Ms. NW1　7 E2
Edward Pl. SE8　68 J6
Edward Rd. E17　41 G4
Edward Rd. SE20　86 G7
Edward Rd., Barn.　23 G5
Edward Rd., Brom.　87 H7
Edward Rd., Chis.　88 E5
Edward Rd., Croy.　95 B7
Edward Rd., Hmptn.　81 J5
Edward Rd., Har.　36 J3
Edward Rd., Nthlt.　54 C2
Edward Rd., Rom.　44 D6
Edward Sq. N1　58 F1
　Caledonian Rd.
Edward Sq. SE16　68 H1
　Rotherhithe St.
Edward St. E16　60 G4
Edward St. SE8　68 J6
Edward St. SE14　68 H7
Edward Temme Ave.　51 F7
　E15
Edward Tyler Rd.　87 J2
　SE12

Edwardes Sq. W8　66 C3
Edward's Ave., Ruis.　45 B6
Edwards Clo., Wor.Pk. 100 A2
Edwards Cotts. N1　49 H6
　Compton Ave.
Edwards Dr. N11　32 D7
　Gordon Rd.
Edwards La. N16　50 A2
Edwards Ms. W1　11 B4
Edwards Ms. W1　58 A6
Edwards Rd., Belv.　71 G4
Edwin Ave. E6　61 D2
Edwin Clo., Bexh.　71 F6
Edwin Pl., Croy.　102 A1
　Cross Rd.
Edwin Rd., Edg.　30 D6
Edwin Rd., Twick.　82 B1
Edwin St. E1　59 F4
Edwin St. E16　60 G5
Edwina Gdns., Ilf.　43 B5
Edwins Mead E9　50 H4
　Lindisfarne Way
Edwyn Clo., Barn.　22 J6
Eel Brook Studios　66 D7
　SW6
　Moore Pk. Rd.
Effie Pl. SW6　66 D7
Effie Rd. SW6　66 D7
Effingham Clo., Sutt. 100 E7
Effingham Rd. N8　40 G5
Effingham Rd. SE12　78 E5
Effingham Rd., Croy.　94 F7
Effingham Rd., Surb.　91 E7
Effort St. SW17　84 H5
Effra Par. SW2　76 G5
Effra Rd. SW2　76 G4
Effra Rd. SW19　84 D6
Egan Way SE16　68 E5
Egbert St. NW1　58 A1
Egerton Clo., Pnr.　36 A2
Egerton Cres. SW3　18 H1
Egerton Cres. SW3　66 H4
Egerton Dr. SE10　78 B1
Egerton Gdns. NW4　38 H4
Egerton Gdns. NW10　56 J1
Egerton Gdns. SW3　14 G6
Egerton Gdns. SW3　66 H4
Egerton Gdns. W13　55 E6
Egerton Gdns., Ilf.　52 J3
Egerton Gdns. Ms.　14 H6
**　SW3**
Egerton Gdns. Ms.　66 H3
　SW3
Egerton Pl. SW3　14 H6
Egerton Pl. SW3　66 H3
Egerton Rd. N16　41 C7
Egerton Rd. SE25　95 B3
Egerton Rd., N.Mal.　92 F4
Egerton Rd., Twick.　73 B7
Egerton Rd., Wem.　46 J7
Egerton Ter. SW3　14 H6
Egerton Ter. SW3　66 H3
Egham Clo. SW19　84 B2
　Winterfold Clo.
Egham Clo., Sutt.　100 B2
Egham Cres., Sutt.　100 A3
Egham Rd. E13　60 H5
Eglantine Rd. SW18　75 F5
Egleston Rd., Mord.　93 E6
Eglington Ct. SE17　20 J5
Eglington Rd. E4　26 D7
Eglinton Hill SE18　70 E6
Eglinton Rd. SE18　70 E6
Egliston Ms. SW15　74 J3
Egliston Rd. SW15　74 J3
Eglon Ms. NW1　48 J7
　Berkley Rd.
Egmont Ave., Surb.　98 J1
Egmont Rd., N.Mal.　92 F4
Egmont Rd., Surb.　98 J1
Egmont Rd., Sutt.　100 F7
Egmont Rd., Walt.　90 B7
Egmont St. SE14　68 G7
Egremont Rd. SE27　85 G3
Eider Clo. E7　51 F5
　Cormorant Rd.
Eighteenth Rd., Mitch. 94 E4
Eighth Ave. E12　52 C4
Eighth Ave., Hayes　63 A1
Eileen Rd. SE25　95 A5
Eisenhower Dr. E6　61 B5
Elaine Gro. NW5　49 A5
Elam Clo. SE5　76 H2
Elam St. SE5　76 H2
Eland Rd. SW11　75 J3
Eland Rd., Croy.　101 H3
Elba Pl. SE17　21 A1
Elbe St. SW6　75 F2

Elberon Ave., Croy.　94 C6
Elborough Rd. SE25　95 D5
Elborough St. SW18　84 D1
Elbury Dr. E16　60 G6
Elcho St. SW11　66 H7
Elcot Ave. SE15　68 D7
Elder Ave. N8　40 E5
Elder Ct. (Bushey),　29 E7
　Wat.
Elder Oak Clo. SE20　95 E1
Elder Rd. SE27　85 J5
Elder St. E1　9 F6
Elder St. E1　59 C5
Elder Wk. N1　58 H1
　Essex Rd.
Elderberry Gro. SE27　85 J5
　Linton Gro.
Elderberry Rd. W5　64 H2
Elderfield Rd. E5　50 G4
Elderfield Wk. E11　42 H5
Elderslie Clo., Beck.　96 A5
Elderslie Rd. SE9　79 D5
Elderton Rd. SE26　86 H4
Eldertree Pl., Mitch.　94 C1
　Eldertree Way
Eldertree Way, Mitch.　94 C1
Elderwood Pl. SE27　85 J5
　Elder Rd.
Eldon Ave., Borwd.　22 A2
Eldon Ave., Croy.　102 F2
Eldon Ave., Houns.　63 G7
Eldon Gro. NW3　48 G5
Eldon Pk. SE25　95 E4
　Lincoln Rd.
Eldon Rd. E17　41 J4
Eldon Rd. N9　33 F2
Eldon Rd. N22　40 H1
Eldon Rd. W8　14 B6
Eldon Rd. W8　66 E3
Eldon St. EC2　13 C2
Eldon St. EC2　59 A5
Eldon Way NW10　56 B2
Eldonwall Trd. Est.　47 G1
　NW2
Eldred Rd., Bark.　61 H1
Eldridge Clo., Felt.　81 A1
Eleanor Clo. N15　41 C3
Eleanor Clo. SE16　68 G2
Eleanor Cres. NW7　31 A4
Eleanor Gdns., Barn.　23 A5
　Chesterfield Rd.
Eleanor Gdns., Dag.　53 F3
　Nicholas Rd.
Eleanor Gro. SW13　74 E3
Eleanor Rd. E8　50 E6
Eleanor Rd. E15　51 F6
Eleanor Rd. N11　32 E6
Eleanor St. E3　60 A3
Eleanor Wk. SE18　70 C4
　Samuel St.
Electric Ave. SW9　76 G4
Electric La. SW9　76 G4
Electric Par., Surb.　91 G6
Elephant & Castle　20 H1
**　SE1**
Elephant & Castle SE1 67 H3
Elephant La. SE16　68 F2
Elephant Rd. SE17　20 J1
Elephant Rd. SE17　67 J4
Elers Rd. W13　64 F2
Eleven Acre Ri., Loug. 27 C3
Eley Est. N18　33 H4
Eley Rd. N18　33 F4
Elf Row E1　59 F7
Elfin Gro., Tedd.　82 C5
　Broad St.
Elfindale Rd. SE24　76 J5
Elford Clo. SE3　78 J4
Elfort Rd. N5　49 G4
Elfrida Cres. SE6　87 A4
Elfwine Rd. W7　55 B5
Elgal Clo., Orp.　104 E5
　Orchard Rd.
Elgar Ave. NW10　47 D6
　Mitchellbrook Way
Elgar Ave. SW16　94 E3
Elgar Ave. W5　64 H2
Elgar Ave., Surb.　99 A1
Elgar Clo. SE8　69 A7
　Comet St.
Elgar Clo., Buck.H.　35 A2
Elgar St. SE16　68 H2
Elgin Ave. W9　57 D4
Elgin Ave., Har.　37 G7
Elgin Cres. W11　57 B7
Elgin Est. W9　57 D4
Elgin Ms. W11　57 B6
　Ladbroke Gro.

Elgin Ms. N. W9　6 B3
Elgin Ms. S. W9　6 B3
Elgin Rd. N22　40 C7
Elgin Rd., Croy.　102 C2
Elgin Rd., Ilf.　52 H1
Elgin Rd., Sutt.　100 F3
Elgin Rd., Wall.　101 C6
Elgood Clo. W11　57 B7
　Avondale Pk. Rd.
Elham Clo., Brom.　88 A7
Elia Ms. N1　8 G2
Elia Ms. N1　58 H2
Elia St. N1　8 G2
Elia St. N1　58 H2
Elias Pl. SW8　20 E6
Elias Pl. SW8　67 G6
Elibank Rd. SE9　79 C4
Elim Est. SE1　17 D5
Elim Est. SE1　68 A3
Elim Way E13　60 F3
Eliot Bank SE23　86 E2
Eliot Cotts. SE3　78 E2
　Eliot Pl.
Eliot Dr., Har.　45 H2
Eliot Gdns. SW15　74 G4
Eliot Hill SE13　78 C2
Eliot Pk. SE13　78 C2
Eliot Pl. SE3　78 E2
Eliot Rd., Dag.　53 D4
Eliot Vale SE3　78 D2
Elizabeth Ave. N1　49 J7
Elizabeth Ave., Enf.　24 H3
Elizabeth Ave., Ilf.　52 G2
Elizabeth Blackwell　40 G1
　Ho. N22
　Progress Way
Elizabeth Bri. SW1　19 D2
Elizabeth Bri. SW1　67 B4
Elizabeth Clo. E14　60 B6
　Grundy St.
Elizabeth Clo. W9　6 D6
Elizabeth Clo., Barn.　23 A3
Elizabeth Clo., Rom.　44 H1
Elizabeth Clyde Clo.　41 B4
　N15
Elizabeth Cotts., Rich. 73 J1
Elizabeth Ct. E15　15 J6
Elizabeth Est. SE17　21 B5
Elizabeth Est. SE17　68 A6
Elizabeth Fry Rd. E8　50 E7
　Lamb La.
Elizabeth Gdns. W3　65 F1
Elizabeth Gdns., Stan. 29 F6
Elizabeth Gdns., Sun.　90 C3
Elizabeth Ms. NW3　48 J6
Elizabeth Pl. N15　41 A4
Elizabeth Ride N9　25 E7
Elizabeth Rd. E6　61 A1
Elizabeth Rd. N15　41 B5
Elizabeth Sq. SE16　59 H7
　Rotherhithe St.
Elizabeth St. SW1　19 C1
Elizabeth St. SW1　67 A4
Elizabeth Ter. SE9　79 C6
Elizabeth Way SE19　86 A7
Elizabeth Way, Felt.　81 C4
Elkington Rd. E13　60 H4
Elkstone Rd. W10　57 C5
Ella Rd. N8　40 E7
Ellaline Rd. W6　66 A6
Ellanby Cres. N18　33 H4
Elland Rd. SE15　77 F4
Ellement Clo., Pnr.　36 D5
Ellen Clo., Brom.　97 A3
Ellen Ct. N9　33 F2
　Densworth Gro.
Ellen St. E1　13 J4
Ellen St. E1　59 D6
Ellenborough Pl.　74 G4
　SW15
Ellenborough Rd. N22 40 J1
Ellenborough Rd., Sid. 89 D7
Elleray Rd., Tedd.　82 C6
Ellerby St. SW6　75 A1
Ellerdale Clo. NW3　48 F4
　Ellerdale Rd.
Ellerdale Rd. NW3　48 F5
Ellerdale St. SE13　78 B4
Ellerdine Rd., Houns.　73 A4
Ellerker Gdns., Rich.　73 H5
Ellerman Ave., Twick. 81 F1
Ellerslie Gdns. NW10　56 G1
Ellerslie Rd. W12　65 H1
Ellerslie Sq. Ind. Est.　76 E4
　SW2
Ellerton Gdns., Dag.　53 C7
Ellerton Rd. SW13　74 G1
Ellerton Rd. SW18　84 G1

Ellerton Rd. SW20 83 G7
Ellerton Rd., Dag. 53 C7
Ellerton Rd., Surb. 98 J2
Ellery Rd. SE19 86 A7
Ellery St. SE15 77 E2
Ellesborough Clo., 28 C5
Wat.
Ellesmere Ave. NW7 30 D3
Ellesmere Ave., Beck. 96 B2
Ellesmere Clo. E11 42 F5
Ellesmere Gdns., Ilf. 43 B5
Ellesmere Gro., Barn. 23 C5
Ellesmere Rd. E3 59 H2
Ellesmere Rd. NW10 47 G5
Ellesmere Rd. W4 65 D6
Ellesmere Rd., Grnf. 54 J4
Ellesmere Rd., Twick. 73 F6
Ellesmere St. E14 60 B6
Ellingfort Rd. E8 50 E7
Ellingham Rd. E15 51 D4
Ellingham Rd. W12 65 G2
Ellingham Rd., Chess. 98 G6
Ellington Rd. N10 40 B4
Ellington Rd., Houns. 72 H2
Ellington St. N7 49 G6
Elliot Ave., Ruis. 45 B2
Elliot Clo. E15 51 E7
Elliot Rd. NW4 38 H6
Elliot Rd., Stan. 29 D6
Elliott Clo., Wem. 46 J3
Elliott Rd. SW9 67 H7
Elliott Rd. W4 65 E4
Elliott Rd., Brom. 97 A4
Elliott Rd., Th.Hth. 94 H4
Elliott Sq. NW3 48 H7
Elliott's Pl. N1 58 H1
St. Peters St.
Elliotts Row SE11 20 G1
Elliotts Row SE11 67 H4
Ellis Clo. SE9 88 F2
Ellis Ct. W7 55 C5
Ellis Ms. SE7 69 J6
Ellis Rd., Mitch. 93 J6
Ellis Rd., Sthl. 63 J1
Ellis St. SW1 19 A1
Ellis St. SW1 66 J4
Elliscombe Rd. SE7 69 J5
Ellisfield Dr. SW15 74 F7
Ellison Gdns., Sthl. 63 F4
Ellison Rd. SW13 74 F2
Ellison Rd. SW16 85 D7
Ellison Rd., Sid. 88 G1
Elliston Ho. SE18 70 D4
Wellington St.
Ellora Rd. SW16 85 D5
Ellsworth St. E2 59 E3
Ellwood Ct. W9 6 A6
Elm Ave. W5 64 H1
Elm Ave., Ruis. 45 A1
Elm Bank N14 24 E7
Elm Bank, Brom. 97 A2
Elm Bank Gdns. 74 E2
SW13
Elm Clo. E11 42 H6
Elm Clo. N19 49 C2
Hargrave Pk.
Elm Clo. NW4 39 A5
Elm Clo. SW20 92 J4
Grand Dr.
Elm Clo., Buck.H. 35 A2
Elm Clo., Cars. 100 J1
Elm Clo., Har. 36 H6
Elm Clo., Hayes 54 A6
Elm Clo., Rom. 44 H1
Elm Clo., S.Croy. 102 B6
Elm Clo., Surb. 92 C7
Elm Clo., Twick. 81 H2
Elm Ct. EC4 12 E5
Elm Ct., Mitch. 93 J2
Armfield Cres.
Elm Cres. W5 64 H1
Elm Cres., Kings.T. 91 H1
Elm Cft., Sutt. 100 A3
Elm Dr., Har. 36 H6
Elm Dr., Sun. 90 C2
Elm Friars Wk. NW1 49 D7
Maiden La.
Elm Gdns. N2 39 F3
Elm Gdns., Esher 98 C6
Elm Gdns., Mitch. 94 D4
Elm Grn. W3 56 E6
Elm Gro. N8 40 E6
Elm Gro. NW2 48 A4
Elm Gro. SE15 77 C2
Elm Gro. SW19 84 B7
Elm Gro., Har. 36 G7
Elm Gro., Kings.T. 91 H1
Elm Gro., Orp. 104 J1

Elm Gro., Sutt. 100 E4
Elm Gro., Wdf.Grn. 34 F5
Elm Gro. Par., Wall. 101 A3
Butter Hill
Elm Gro. Rd. SW13 74 G2
Elm Gro. Rd. W5 64 H2
Elm La. SE6 86 J2
Elm Ms., Rich. 73 J6
Grove Rd.
Elm Pk. SW2 76 F6
Elm Pk., Stan. 29 E5
Elm Pk. Ave. N15 41 C5
Elm Pk. Ct., Pnr. 36 C3
Elm Pk. Gdns. NW4 39 A5
Elm Pk. Gdns. SW10 18 E4
Elm Pk. Gdns. SW10 66 G5
Elm Pk. La. SW3 18 E4
Elm Pk. La. SW3 66 G5
Elm Pk. Mans. SW10 18 D5
Elm Pk. Rd. E10 50 H1
Elm Pk. Rd. N3 31 C7
Elm Pk. Rd. N21 24 J7
Elm Pk. Rd. SE25 95 C3
Elm Pk. Rd. SW3 18 E5
Elm Pk. Rd. SW3 66 G6
Elm Pk. Rd., Pnr. 36 C2
Elm Pl. SW7 18 E3
Elm Pl. SW7 66 G5
Elm Quay Ct. SW8 19 H6
Elm Quay Ct. SW8 67 D6
Elm Rd. E7 51 F6
Elm Rd. E11 51 D2
Elm Rd. E17 42 C5
Elm Rd. N22 40 H1
Granville Rd.
Elm Rd. SW14 74 C3
Elm Rd., Barn. 23 C4
Elm Rd., Beck. 95 J2
Elm Rd., Chess. 98 H4
Elm Rd., Epsom 99 F6
Elm Rd., Esher 98 C6
Elm Rd., Kings.T. 91 J1
Elm Rd., N.Mal. 92 D3
Elm Rd., Rom. 44 H2
Elm Rd., Sid. 89 A4
Elm Rd., Th.Hth. 95 A4
Elm Rd., Wall. 101 A1
Elm Rd., Wem. 46 H5
Elm Rd. W., Sutt. 93 C7
Elm Row NW3 48 F3
Elm St. WC1 8 D6
Elm St. WC1 58 F4
Elm Ter. NW2 48 D3
Elm Ter. NW3 48 H4
Constantine Rd.
Elm Ter. SE9 79 D6
Elm Ter., Har. 37 A1
Elm Tree Ave., Esher 91 A7
Elm Tree Clo. NW8 6 E3
Elm Tree Clo. NW8 57 G3
Elm Tree Clo., Nthlt. 54 F2
Elm Tree Rd. NW8 6 E3
Elm Tree Rd. NW8 57 G3
Elm Wk. NW3 48 D2
Elm Wk. SW20 92 J4
Elm Wk., Orp. 104 C3
Elm Way N11 32 A6
Elm Way NW10 47 E4
Elm Way, Epsom 99 D5
Elm Way, Wor.Pk. 99 J3
Elmar Rd. N15 41 A4
Elmbank Ave., Barn. 22 J4
Elmbank Way W7 55 A5
Elmbourne Dr., Belv. 71 H4
Elmbourne Rd. SW17 85 A3
Elmbridge Ave., Surb. 92 B5
Elmbridge Clo., Ruis. 36 A6
Elmbridge Wk. E8 50 D7
Wilman Gro.
Elmbrook Clo., Sun. 90 B1
Elmbrook Gdns. SE9 79 B4
Elmbrook Rd., Sutt. 100 C4
Elmcourt Rd. SE27 85 H2
Elmcroft Ave. E11 42 H5
Elmcroft Ave. N9 25 E6
Elmcroft Ave. NW11 39 C7
Elmcroft Ave., Sid. 79 J7
Elmcroft Clo. E11 42 H4
Elmcroft Clo. N8 40 F5
Elmcroft Clo. W5 55 G6
Elmcroft Clo., Chess. 98 H3
Elmcroft Cres. NW11 39 A7
Elmcroft Cres., Har. 36 G3
Elmcroft Dr., Chess. 98 H3
Elmcroft Gdns. NW9 38 A5
Elmcroft St. E5 50 H4
Elmdale Rd. N13 32 F5
Elmdene, Surb. 99 C1

Elmdene Clo., Beck. 95 J5
Elmdene Rd. SE18 70 E5
Elmdon Rd., Houns. 72 D2
Elmer Clo., Enf. 24 F3
Elmer Gdns., Edg. 30 B7
Elmer Gdns., Islw. 73 A3
Elmer Rd. SE6 78 C7
Elmers Dr., Tedd. 82 E6
St. Mark's Rd.
Elmers End Rd. SE20 95 F2
Elmers End Rd., Beck. 95 F3
Elmers Rd. SE25 95 D7
Elmerside Rd., Beck. 95 H4
Elmfield Ave. N8 40 E5
Elmfield Ave., Mitch. 94 A1
Elmfield Ave., Tedd. 82 C5
Elmfield Clo., Har. 46 B2
Elmfield Pk., Brom. 96 G3
Elmfield Rd. E4 34 C2
Elmfield Rd. E17 41 G5
Elmfield Rd. N2 39 G3
Elmfield Rd. SW17 85 A2
Elmfield Rd., Brom. 96 G3
Elmfield Rd., Sthl. 63 E3
Elmgate Ave., Felt. 81 B3
Elmgate Gdns., Edg. 30 D5
Elmgreen Clo. E15 60 E1
Church St. N.
Elmgrove Cres., Har. 37 C5
Elmgrove Gdns., Har. 37 D5
Elmgrove Rd., Croy. 95 E7
Elmgrove Rd., Har. 37 C5
Elmhall Gdns. E11 42 H6
Elmhurst, Belv. 71 E6
Elmhurst Ave. N2 39 G3
Elmhurst Ave., Mitch. 85 A7
Elmhurst Dr. E18 42 G2
Elmhurst Gdns. E18 42 H1
Elmhurst Rd. E7 51 H7
Elmhurst Rd. N17 41 B2
Elmhurst Rd. SE9 88 B2
Elmhurst St. SW4 76 D3
Elmhurst Way, Loug. 27 C7
Elmington Clo., Bex. 80 H6
Elmington Est. SE5 21 C7
Elmington Est. SE5 68 A7
Elmington Rd. SE5 77 A1
Elmira St. SE13 78 B3
Elmlee Clo., Chis. 88 C6
Elmley Clo. E6 61 B5
Northumberland Rd.
Elmley St. SE18 70 G4
Elmore Clo., Wem. 55 H2
Elmore Rd. E11 51 C3
Elmore St. N1 50 A7
Elmores, Loug. 27 D3
Elms, The SW13 74 F3
Elms Ave. N10 40 B3
Elms Ave. NW4 39 A5
Elms Ct., Wem. 46 D4
Elms Cres. SW4 76 C6
Elms Gdns., Dag. 53 F4
Elms Gdns., Wem. 46 D4
Elms La., Wem. 46 D3
Elms Ms. W2 10 E5
Elms Ms. W2 57 G7
Elms Pk. Ave., Wem. 46 D4
Elms Rd. SW4 76 C5
Elms Rd., Har. 29 B7
Elms Wk. SE3 78 F4
Elmscott Gdns. N21 24 J6
Elmscott Rd., Brom. 87 E5
Elmscroft N8 40 F5
Tottenham La.
Elmsdale Rd. E17 41 J4
Elmshaw Rd. SW15 74 G5
Elmshurst Cres. N2 39 F4
Elmside, Croy. 103 B6
Elmside Rd., Wem. 47 A3
Elmsleigh Ave., Har. 37 E4
Elmsleigh Rd., Twick. 82 A2
Elmslie Clo., Wdf.Grn. 35 C6
Elmslie Pt. E3 59 J5
Ackroyd Dr.
Elmstead Ave., Chis. 88 C5
Elmstead Ave., Wem. 46 H1
Elmstead Clo. N20 31 D2
Elmstead Clo., 99 E5
Epsom
Elmstead Cres., Well. 71 C6
Elmstead Gdns., 99 G3
Wor.Pk.
Elmstead Glade, Chis. 88 C6
Elmstead La., Chis. 88 B7
Elmstead Rd., Ilf. 52 H2
Elmstone Rd. SW6 75 D1
Elmsworth Ave., 72 H2
Houns.

Elmton Way E5 50 D3
Rendlesham Rd.
Elmtree Rd., Tedd. 82 B4
Elmwood Ave. N13 32 E5
Elmwood Ave., 22 B4
Borwd.
Elmwood Ave., Felt. 81 A2
Elmwood Ave., Har. 37 D5
Elmwood Clo., 99 G7
Epsom
Elmwood Clo., Wall. 101 A2
Elmwood Ct., Wem. 46 D3
Elmwood Cres. NW9 38 C4
Elmwood Dr., Bex. 80 E7
Elmwood Dr., Epsom 99 G6
Elmwood Gdns. W7 55 B6
Elmwood Rd. SE24 77 A5
Elmwood Rd. W4 65 C6
Elmwood Rd., Croy. 94 H7
Elmwood Rd., Mitch. 93 J3
Elmworth Gro. SE21 86 A2
Elnathan Ms. W9 6 B6
Elphinstone Rd. E17 41 J2
Elphinstone St. N5 49 H4
Avenell Rd.
Elrington Rd. E8 50 D6
Elrington Rd., Wdf. 80 B2
Elsa Rd., Well. 80 B2
Elsa St. E1 59 H5
Elsdale St. E9 50 F6
Elsden Ms. E2 59 F2
Old Ford Rd.
Elsden Rd. N17 41 C1
Elsenham Rd. E12 52 D5
Elsenham St. SW18 84 C1
Elsham Rd. E11 51 E3
Elsham Rd. W14 66 B2
Elsham Ter. W14 66 B2
Elsie Rd. SE22 77 C4
Elsiedene Rd. N21 24 J7
Elsiemaud Rd. SE4 77 J5
Elsinore Rd. SE23 86 H1
Elsinore Way, Rich. 74 B3
Lower Richmond Rd.
Elsley Rd. SW11 75 J3
Elspeth Rd. SW11 75 J4
Elspeth Rd., Wem. 46 H5
Elsrick Ave., Mord. 93 D5
Chalgrove Ave.
Elstan Way, Croy. 95 H7
Elsted St. SE17 21 C2
Elsted St. SE17 68 A4
Elstow Clo. SE9 79 D5
Elstow Clo., Ruis. 36 D7
Elstow Gdns., Dag. 62 E1
Elstow Rd., Dag. 53 E7
Elstree Gdns. N9 33 E1
Elstree Gdns., Belv. 71 E4
Elstree Gdns., Ilf. 52 F5
Elstree Hill, Brom. 87 E7
Elstree Way, Borwd. 22 B3
Elswick Rd. SE13 78 B2
Elswick St. SW6 75 F2
Elsworthy, T.Ditt. 91 B6
Elsworthy Ri. NW3 48 H7
Elsworthy Rd. NW3 57 G1
Elsworthy Ter. NW3 48 H7
Elsynge Rd. SW18 75 G5
Eltham Grn. SE9 78 J5
Eltham Grn. Rd. SE9 78 J4
Eltham High St. SE9 79 C6
Eltham Hill SE9 79 A5
Eltham Palace Rd. SE9 78 J4
Eltham Pk. Gdns. SE9 79 D4
Eltham Rd. SE9 78 D5
Eltham Rd. SE12 78 G5
Elthiron Rd. SW6 75 D1
Elthorne Ave. W7 64 C2
Elthorne Ct., Felt. 81 C1
Elthorne Pk. Rd. W7 64 C2
Elthorne Rd. N19 49 D2
Elthorne Rd. NW9 38 D7
Elthorne Way NW9 38 D6
Elthruda Rd. SE13 78 D6
Eltisley Rd., Ilf. 52 E4
Elton Ave., Barn. 23 C6
Elton Ave., Grnf. 46 B6
Elton Ave., Wem. 46 E5
Elton Clo., Kings.T. 82 F7
Elton Ho. E3 59 J1
Elton Pl. N16 50 B5
Elton Rd., Kings.T. 91 J1
Eltringham St. SW18 75 F4
Elvaston Ms. SW7 14 D6
Elvaston Ms. SW7 66 F3
Elvaston Pl. SW7 14 C6
Elvaston Pl. SW7 66 F3
Elveden Pl. NW10 56 A2
Elveden Rd. NW10 56 A2

Elvendon Rd. N13	32	E6
Elver Gdns. E2	**9**	**J2**
Elverson Rd. SE8	78	B2
Elverton St. SW1	**19**	**H1**
Elverton St. SW1	67	D4
Elvington Grn., Brom.	96	F5
Elvington La. NW9	38	E1
Elvino Rd. SE26	86	G5
Elvis Rd. NW2	47	J6
Elwill Way, Beck.	96	C4
Elwin St. E2	**9**	**H3**
Elwin St. E2	59	D3
Elwood St. N5	49	H3
Elwyn Gdns. SE12	78	G7
Ely Clo., N.Mal.	92	F2
Ely Ct. EC1	**12**	**F2**
Ely Gdns., Borwd.	22	D5
Ely Gdns., Dag.	53	J3
Ely Gdns., Ilf.	43	B7
Canterbury Ave.		
Ely Pl. EC1	**12**	**F2**
Ely Pl., Wdf.Grn.	35	D6
Ely Rd. E10	42	C7
Ely Rd., Croy.	95	A5
Ely Rd., Houns.	72	C3
(Hounslow W.)		
Elyne Rd. N4	40	G6
Elysian Ave., Orp.	97	H6
Elysium Pl. SW6	75	C2
Fulham Pk. Gdns.		
Elysium St. SW6	75	C2
Fulham Pk. Gdns.		
Elystan Pl. SW3	**18**	**H3**
Elystan Pl. SW3	66	H5
Elystan St. SW3	**18**	**G2**
Elystan St. SW3	66	H4
Elystan Wk. N1	58	G1
Cloudesley Rd.		
Emanuel Ave. W3	56	C6
Emanuel Dr., Hmptn.	81	F5
Emba St. SE16	**17**	**J4**
Emba St. SE16	68	D2
Embankment SW15	75	A2
Embankment, The,	82	D1
Twick.		
Embankment Gdns. SW3	**19**	**A5**
Embankment Gdns. SW3	66	J6
Embankment Pl. WC2	**16**	**B1**
Embankment Pl. WC2	67	E1
Embassy Ct., Sid.	89	B3
Embassy Ct., Well.	80	B3
Ember Clo., Orp.	97	F7
Ember Fm. Ave., E.Mol.	91	A6
Ember Fm. Way, E.Mol.	91	A6
Ember Gdns., T.Ditt.	91	B7
Ember La., E.Mol.	91	A6
Ember La., Esher	91	A7
Embercourt Rd., T.Ditt.	91	B6
Emberton SE5	**21**	**D5**
Embleton Rd. SE13	78	B4
Embleton Rd., Wat.	28	A3
Embleton Wk., Hmptn.	81	F6
Fearnley Cres.		
Embley Pt. E5	50	E4
Tiger Way		
Embry Clo., Stan.	29	D4
Embry Dr., Stan.	29	D6
Embry Way, Stan.	29	D4
Emden St. SW6	75	E1
Emerald Clo. E16	61	B6
Emerald Gdns., Dag.	53	G1
Emerald St. WC1	**12**	**C1**
Emerald St. WC1	58	F5
Emerson Gdns., Har.	37	J6
Emerson Rd., Ilf.	43	D7
Emerson St. SE1	**16**	**J1**
Emerson St. SE1	67	J1
Emerton Rd., Bexh.	80	E4
Emery Hill St. SW1	**15**	**G6**
Emery Hill St. SW1	67	C3
Emery St. SE1	**16**	**F5**
Emes Rd., Erith	71	J7
Emily Pl. N7	49	G4
Emlyn Gdns. W12	65	E2
Emlyn Rd. W12	65	E2
Emma Rd. E13	60	F2
Emma St. E2	59	E2
Emmanuel Rd. SW12	85	C1
Emmaus Way, Chig.	35	D5
Emmott Ave., Ilf.	43	F5
Emmott Clo. E1	59	H4
Emmott Clo. NW11	39	F6

Emms Pas., Kings.T.	91	G2
High St.		
Emperor's Gate SW7	**14**	**B6**
Emperor's Gate SW7	66	E3
Empire Ave. N18	32	J5
Empire Ct., Wem.	47	B3
Empire Rd., Grnf.	55	E1
Empire Way, Wem.	46	J4
Empire Wf. Rd. E14	69	D4
Empire Yd. N7	49	E3
Holloway Rd.		
Empress Ave. E4	34	B7
Empress Ave. E12	51	J2
Empress Ave., Ilf.	52	C2
Empress Ave., Wdf.Grn.	34	F7
Empress Dr., Chis.	88	E6
Empress Pl. SW6	66	D5
Empress St. SE17	**21**	**A5**
Empress St. SE17	67	J6
Empson St. E3	60	B4
Emsworth Clo. N9	33	F1
Emsworth Rd., Ilf.	43	E2
Emsworth St. SW2	85	E2
Emu Rd. SW8	76	B2
Ena Rd. SW16	94	E3
Enbrook St. W10	57	B3
End Way, Surb.	92	A7
Endale Clo., Cars.	100	J2
Endeavour Way SW19	84	E4
Endeavour Way, Bark.	62	A2
Endeavour Way, Croy.	94	D7
Endell St. WC2	**12**	**A3**
Endell St. WC2	58	E6
Enderby St. SE10	69	E5
Enderley Clo., Har.	37	B1
Enderley Rd., Har.	37	B1
Endersby Rd., Barn.	22	J5
Endersleigh Gdns. NW4	38	G4
Endlebury Rd. E4	34	C2
Endlesham Rd. SW12	76	A7
Endsleigh Gdns. WC1	**7**	**H5**
Endsleigh Gdns. WC1	58	D4
Endsleigh Gdns., Ilf.	52	C2
Endsleigh Gdns., Surb.	91	F6
Endsleigh Pl. WC1	**7**	**J5**
Endsleigh Pl. WC1	58	D4
Endsleigh Rd. W13	55	D7
Endsleigh Rd., Sthl.	63	E4
Endsleigh St. WC1	**7**	**J5**
Endsleigh St. WC1	58	D4
Endwell Rd. SE4	77	H2
Endymion Rd. N4	40	G7
Endymion Rd. SW2	76	F6
Enfield Rd. N1	50	B7
Enfield Rd. W3	65	B2
Enfield Rd., Brent.	64	G5
Enfield Rd., Enf.	24	E4
Enfield Wk., Brent.	64	G5
Enfield Rd.		
Enford St. W1	**10**	**J1**
Enford St. W1	57	J5
Engadine Clo., Croy.	102	C3
Engadine St. SW18	84	C1
Engate St. SE13	78	C4
Engel Pk. NW7	30	J6
Engineer Clo. SE18	70	D6
Engineers Way, Wem.	47	A4
Englands La. NW3	48	J6
Englands La., Loug.	27	D2
Englefield Clo., Croy.	94	J6
Queen's Rd.		
Englefield Clo., Orp.	97	J4
Englefield Cres., Orp.	97	J4
Englefield Rd. N1	50	A7
Englehart Rd. SE6	78	B7
Englewood Rd. SW12	76	B6
English Grds. SE1	**17**	**D2**
Enid St. SE16	37	J4
Enid St. SE16	**17**	**G5**
Enid St. SE16	68	C3
Enmore Ave. SE25	95	D5
Enmore Gdns. SW14	74	D5
Enmore Rd. SE25	95	D5
Enmore Rd. SW15	74	J4
Enmore Rd., Sthl.	54	G4
Ennerdale Ave., Stan.	37	F3
Ennerdale Clo. (Cheam), Sutt.	100	C4
Ennerdale Dr. NW9	38	E5
Ennerdale Gdns., Wem.	46	F1
Ennerdale Ho. E3	59	J4

Ennerdale Rd., Bexh.	80	G1
Ennerdale Rd., Rich.	73	J2
Ennersdale Rd. SE13	78	D5
Ennis Rd. N4	49	G1
Ennis Rd. SE18	70	F6
Ennismore Ave. W4	65	F4
Ennismore Ave., Grnf.	46	B6
Ennismore Gdns. SW7	**14**	**G5**
Ennismore Gdns. SW7	66	H2
Ennismore Gdns., T.Ditt.	91	B6
Ennismore Gdns. Ms. SW7	**14**	**G5**
Ennismore Gdns. Ms. SW7	66	H3
Ennismore Ms. SW7	**14**	**G5**
Ennismore Ms. SW7	66	H3
Ennismore St. SW7	**14**	**G5**
Ennismore St. SW7	66	H3
Ensign Dr. N13	32	J3
Ensign St. E1	**13**	**H5**
Ensign St. E1	59	D7
Enslin Rd. SE9	79	D7
Ensor Ms. SW7	**18**	**E3**
Enstone Rd., Enf.	25	H3
Enterprise Clo., Croy.	101	G1
Enterprise Way NW10	56	G3
Enterprise Way SW18	75	D4
Enterprise Way, Tedd.	82	C5
Enterprize Way SE8	68	J4
Epirus Ms. SW6	66	D7
Epirus Rd.		
Epirus Rd. SW6	66	C7
Epping Clo. E14	69	A4
Epping Clo., Rom.	44	H3
Epping Glade E4	26	C6
Epping New Rd., Buck.H.	34	G3
Epping New Rd., Loug.	26	J3
Epping Pl. N1	49	G6
Liverpool Rd.		
Epping Way E4	26	B6
Epple Rd. SW6	75	C1
Epsom Clo., Bexh.	80	H3
Epsom Clo., Nthlt.	45	F5
Epsom Rd. E10	42	C6
Epsom Rd., Croy.	101	G4
Epsom Rd., Ilf.	43	J6
Epsom Rd., Mord.	93	D6
Epsom Rd., Sutt.	93	C7
Epstein Rd. SE28	71	A1
Epworth Rd., Islw.	73	E1
Epworth St. EC2	**9**	**C6**
Epworth St. EC2	59	A4
Erasmus St. SW1	**19**	**J2**
Erasmus St. SW1	67	D4
Erconwald St. W12	56	F6
Eresby Dr., Beck.	103	A1
Eresby Pl. NW6	48	D7
Eric Clo. E7	51	G4
Eric Rd. E7	51	G4
Eric Rd. NW10	47	F6
Church Rd.		
Eric Rd., Rom.	44	D7
Eric St. E3	59	J4
Erica Gdns., Croy.	103	A3
Erica St. W12	56	G7
Ericcson Clo. SW18	75	D5
Eridge Rd. W4	65	D3
Erin Clo., Brom.	87	E7
Erindale SE18	70	G6
Erindale Ter. SE18	70	G6
Erith Cres., Rom.	44	J1
Erith Rd., Belv.	71	G5
Erith Rd., Bexh.	80	H4
Erith Rd., Erith	80	J1
Erlanger Rd. SE14	77	J4
Erlesmere Gdns. W13	64	D3
Ermine Clo., Houns.	72	C2
Ermine Ho. N17	33	C7
Ermine Rd. N15	41	C6
Ermine Rd. SE13	78	B4
Ermine Side, Enf.	25	D5
Ermington Rd. SE9	88	F2
Ernald Ave. E6	61	B2
Erncroft Way, Twick.	73	C6
Ernest Ave. SE27	85	H4
Ernest Clo., Beck.	96	A5
Ernest Gdns. W4	65	B6
Ernest Gro., Beck.	95	J5
Ernest Rd., Kings.T.	92	B2
Ernest Sq., Kings.T.	92	B2
Ernest St. E1	59	G4
Ernle Rd. SW20	83	H7
Ernshaw Pl. SW15	75	B5
Carlton Dr.		
Erpingham Rd. SW15	74	J3

Erridge Rd. SW19	93	D2
Errington Rd. W9	57	C4
Errol Gdns., Hayes	54	B4
Errol Gdns., N.Mal.	92	G4
Errol St. EC1	**9**	**A6**
Errol St. EC1	58	J4
Erskine Clo., Sutt.	100	H3
Erskine Cres. N17	41	E4
Erskine Hill NW11	39	D5
Erskine Ms. NW3	48	J7
Erskine Rd.		
Erskine Rd. E17	41	J4
Erskine Rd. NW3	48	J7
Erskine Rd., Sutt.	100	G4
Erwood Rd. SE7	70	B5
Esam Way SW16	85	G5
Escot Way, Barn.	22	J5
Escott Gdns. SE9	88	B4
Escreet Gro. SE18	70	D4
Esher Ave., Rom.	44	J6
Esher Ave., Sutt.	100	A3
Esher Ave., Walt.	90	A6
Esher Bypass, Chess.	98	F4
Esher Bypass, Esher	98	E7
Esher Clo., Bex.	89	E1
Esher Gdns. SW19	84	A2
Esher Ms., Mitch.	93	J3
Esher Rd., E.Mol.	91	A6
Esher Rd., Ilf.	52	H3
Esk Rd. E13	60	G4
Eskdale Ave., Nthlt.	54	F1
Eskdale Clo., Wem.	46	G2
Eskdale Rd., Bexh.	80	G2
Eskmont Ridge SE19	86	B7
Esmar Cres. NW9	38	G7
Esme Ho. NW15	74	F4
Ludovick Wk.		
Esmeralda Rd. SE1	**21**	**J2**
Esmeralda Rd. SE1	68	D4
Esmond Rd. NW6	57	C1
Esmond Rd. W4	65	D4
Esmond St. SW15	75	B4
Esparto St. SW18	75	E7
Essenden Rd., Belv.	71	G5
Essenden Rd., S.Croy.	102	B7
Essendine Rd. W9	57	D3
Essex Ave., Islw.	73	B3
Essex Clo. E17	41	H4
Essex Clo., Mord.	93	A7
Essex Clo., Rom.	44	H4
Essex Clo., Ruis.	45	D1
Essex Ct. EC4	**12**	**E4**
Essex Ct. SW13	74	F2
Essex Gdns. N4	40	H6
Essex Gro. SE19	86	A6
Essex Ho. E14	60	B6
Giraud St.		
Essex Pk. N3	31	E6
Essex Pk. Ms. W3	65	E1
Essex Pl. W4	65	C4
Essex Rd. E4	34	E1
Essex Rd. E10	42	C6
Essex Rd. E12	52	B5
Essex Rd. E17	41	H6
Essex Rd. E18	42	H2
Essex Rd. N1	58	H1
Essex Rd. NW10	47	E7
Essex Rd. W3	56	C7
Essex Rd. W4	65	D4
Belmont Rd.		
Essex Rd., Bark.	52	G7
Essex Rd., Borwd.	22	A3
Essex Rd., Dag.	53	J3
Essex Rd., Enf.	25	A4
Essex Rd., Rom.	44	G4
Essex Rd., Rom. (Chadwell Heath)	44	C7
Essex Rd. S. E11	42	D7
Essex St. E7	51	G5
Essex St. WC2	**12**	**E5**
Essex Twr. SE20	95	E1
Essex Vill. W8	66	D2
Essex Wf. E5	50	F2
Essian St. E1	59	H5
Essoldo Way, Edg.	37	J3
Estate Way E10	50	J1
Estcourt Rd. SE25	95	E6
Estcourt Rd. SW6	66	C7
Este Rd. SW11	75	H3
Estella Ave., N.Mal.	92	H4
Estelle Rd. NW3	48	J4
Esterbrooke St. SW1	**19**	**H2**
Esterbrooke St. SW1	67	D4
Esther Clo. N21	24	G7
Esther Rd. E11	42	E7
Estreham Rd. SW16	85	D6
Estridge Clo., Houns.	72	G4
Eswyn Rd. SW17	84	J4

Etchingham Pk. Rd. N3 — 31 E7
Etchingham Rd. E15 — 51 C4
Eternit Wk. SW6 — 74 J1
Etfield Gro., Sid. — 89 B5
Ethel Rd. E16 — 60 H6
Ethel St. SE17 — 21 A2
Ethelbert Clo., Brom. — 96 G3
Ethelbert Gdns., Ilf. — 43 C5
Ethelbert Rd. SW20 — 93 A1
Ethelbert Rd., Brom. — 96 G3
Ethelbert Rd., Erith — 71 J7
Hengist Rd.
Ethelbert St. SW12 — 85 B1
Fernlea Rd.
Ethelburga St. SW11 — 75 H1
Ethelden Rd. W12 — 65 H1
Etheldene Ave. N10 — 40 C4
Etheridge Grn., Loug. — 27 F3
Etheridge Rd.
Etheridge Rd. NW2 — 38 J7
Etheridge Rd., Loug. — 27 E2
Etherley Rd. N15 — 40 J5
Etherow St. SE22 — 77 D6
Etherstone Grn. SW16 — 85 G4
Etherstone Rd.
Etherstone Rd. SW16 — 85 G4
Ethnard Rd. SE15 — 68 E6
Ethronvi Rd., Bexh. — 80 E3
Etloe Rd. E10 — 51 A2
Eton Ave. N12 — 31 F7
Eton Ave. NW3 — 48 G7
Eton Ave., Barn. — 23 H6
Eton Ave., Houns. — 63 F6
Eton Ave., N.Mal. — 92 D5
Eton Ave., Wem. — 46 E5
Eton College Rd. NW3 — 48 J6
Eton Ct. NW3 — 48 G7
Eton Ave.
Eton Ct., Wem. — 46 F4
Eton Ave.
Eton Garages NW3 — 48 H6
Lambolle Pl.
Eton Gro. NW9 — 38 A3
Eton Gro. SE13 — 78 E3
Eton Hall NW3 — 48 J6
Eton College Rd.
Eton Pl. NW3 — 49 A7
Haverstock Hill
Eton Ri. NW3 — 48 J6
Eton College Rd.
Eton Rd. NW3 — 48 J7
Eton Rd., Ilf. — 52 F5
Eton St., Rich. — 73 H5
Eton Vill. NW3 — 48 J6
Etta St. SE8 — 68 H6
Ettrick St. E14 — 60 C6
Etwell Pl., Surb. — 91 J6
Eugenia Rd. SE16 — 68 F4
Eureka Rd., Kings.T. — 92 A2
Washington Rd.
Europa Pl. EC1 — 8 J4
Europe Rd. SE18 — 70 C3
Eustace Rd. E6 — 61 B3
Eustace Rd. SW6 — 66 D7
Eustace Rd., Rom. — 44 D7
Euston Gro. NW1 — 7 H4
Euston Gro. NW1 — 58 D3
Euston Rd. N1 — 58 B4
Euston Rd. NW1 — 7 E6
Euston Rd. NW1 — 58 B4
Euston Rd., Croy. — 101 G1
Euston Sq. NW1 — 7 H4
Euston Sq. NW1 — 58 D3
Euston Sta. Colonnade NW1 — 7 H4
Euston St. NW1 — 7 G4
Euston St. NW1 — 58 C3
Eva Rd., Rom. — 44 C7
Evandale Rd. SW9 — 76 G2
Evangelist Rd. NW5 — 49 B4
Evans Clo. E8 — 50 C6
Buttermere Wk.
Evans Gro., Felt. — 81 G2
Evans Rd. SE6 — 87 E2
Evanston Ave. E4 — 34 C7
Evanston Gdns., Ilf. — 43 B6
Eve Rd. E11 — 51 E4
Eve Rd. E15 — 60 E2
Eve Rd. N17 — 41 B3
Eve Rd., Islw. — 73 D4
Evelina Rd. SE15 — 77 F3
Evelina Rd. SE20 — 86 G7
Eveline Lowe Est. SE16 — 17 H6
Eveline Lowe Est. SE16 — 68 D3

Eveline Rd., Mitch. — 93 J1
Evelyn Ave. NW9 — 38 D3
Evelyn Clo., Twick. — 72 H7
Evelyn Ct. N1 — 9 B2
Evelyn Dennington Rd. E6 — 61 C5
Evelyn Dr., Pnr. — 28 D7
Evelyn Fox Ct. W10 — 56 J5
Evelyn Gdns. SW7 — 18 E4
Evelyn Gdns. SW7 — 66 G5
Evelyn Gdns., Rich. — 73 H4
Kew Rd.
Evelyn Gro. W5 — 64 J1
Evelyn Gro., Sthl. — 54 F6
Evelyn Rd. E17 — 42 C4
Evelyn Rd. SW19 — 84 E5
Evelyn Rd. W4 — 65 D3
Evelyn Rd., Barn. — 23 J4
Evelyn Rd., Rich. — 73 H3
Evelyn Rd., Rich. (Ham) — 82 F3
Ham St.
Evelyn St. SE8 — 68 H5
Evelyn Ter., Rich. — 73 H3
Evelyn Wk. N1 — 9 B2
Evelyn Wk. N1 — 59 A2
Evelyn Way, Wall. — 101 D4
Evelyn Yd. W1 — 11 H3
Evening Hill, Beck. — 87 C7
Evenwood Clo. SW15 — 75 B5
Everard Ave., Brom. — 103 G1
Everard Way, Wem. — 46 H3
Everatt Clo. SW18 — 75 C6
Amerland Rd.
Everdon Rd. SW13 — 65 G6
Everest Pl. E14 — 60 C5
Everest Rd. SE9 — 79 C5
Everett Wk., Belv. — 71 F5
Osborne Rd.
Everglade Strand NW9 — 38 F1
Everilda St. N1 — 58 F1
Evering Rd. E5 — 50 D3
Evering Rd. N16 — 50 D3
Everington Rd. N10 — 39 J2
Everington St. W6 — 66 A6
Everitt Rd. NW10 — 56 D3
Everleigh St. N4 — 49 F1
Eversfield Gdns. NW7 — 30 E6
Eversfield Rd., Rich. — 73 J2
Eversholt St. NW1 — 7 G1
Eversholt St. NW1 — 58 C2
Evershot Rd. N4 — 49 F1
Eversleigh Rd. E6 — 61 A1
Eversleigh Rd. N3 — 31 C7
Eversleigh Rd. SW11 — 75 J3
Eversleigh Rd., Barn. — 23 F5
Eversley Ave., Wem. — 47 A2
Eversley Clo. N21 — 24 F6
Eversley Cres. N21 — 24 F6
Eversley Cres., Islw. — 73 A1
Eversley Mt. N21 — 24 F6
Eversley Pk. SW19 — 83 H5
Eversley Pk. Rd. N21 — 24 F6
Eversley Rd. SE7 — 69 H6
Eversley Rd. SE19 — 86 A7
Eversley Rd., Surb. — 91 J4
Eversley Way, Croy. — 103 A4
Everthorpe Rd. SE15 — 77 C3
Everton Bldgs. NW1 — 7 F4
Everton Dr., Stan. — 37 J3
Everton Rd., Croy. — 102 D1
Evesham Ave. E17 — 42 A2
Evesham Clo., Grnf. — 54 H2
Evesham Clo., Sutt. — 100 D7
Evesham Grn., Mord. — 93 E6
Evesham Rd. E15 — 51 F7
Evesham Rd. N11 — 32 C5
Evesham Rd., Felt. — 72 C7
Sparrow Fm. Dr.
Evesham Rd., Mord. — 93 E6
Evesham St. W11 — 57 A7
Evesham Wk. SE5 — 77 A2
Love Wk.
Evesham Wk. SW9 — 76 G2
Evesham Way SW11 — 76 A3
Evesham Way, Ilf. — 43 D3
Evry Rd., Sid. — 89 C6
Ewald Rd. SW6 — 75 C2
Ewanrigg Ter., Wdf.Grn. — 34 J5
Ewart Gro. N22 — 40 G1
Ewart Pl. E3 — 59 J2
Ewart Rd. SE23 — 77 G7
Ewe Clo. N7 — 49 E6
Ewell Bypass, Epsom — 99 G6
Ewell Ct. Ave., Epsom — 99 E5
Ewell Pk. Way, Epsom — 99 G6

Ewell Rd., Surb. — 91 H5
Ewell Rd., Surb. (Long Ditton) — 91 E7
Ewell Rd., Sutt. — 100 A7
Ewellhurst Rd., Ilf. — 43 B2
Ewelme Rd. SE23 — 86 F1
Ewen Cres. SW2 — 76 G7
Ewer St. SE1 — 16 J2
Ewer St. SE1 — 67 J1
Ewhurst Ho. E1 — 59 F5
Jamaica St.
Ewhurst Rd. SE4 — 77 J6
Exbury Rd. SE6 — 87 A2
Excel Ct. WC2 — 11 J6
Excelsior Clo., Kings.T. — 92 A2
Washington Rd.
Excelsior Gdns. SE13 — 78 C2
Exchange Arc. EC2 — 13 E1
Exchange Arc. EC2 — 59 B5
Exchange Ct. WC2 — 12 B6
Exchange Pl. EC2 — 13 D1
Exchange Pl. EC2 — 59 B5
Exchange Sq. EC2 — 13 D1
Exchange Sq. EC2 — 59 B5
Exeter Clo. E6 — 61 C6
Harper Rd.
Exeter Gdns., Ilf. — 52 B1
Exeter Ho. SW15 — 74 J6
Putney Heath
Exeter Ms. NW6 — 48 E6
West Hampstead Ms.
Exeter Rd. E16 — 60 G5
Exeter Rd. E17 — 42 A5
Exeter Rd. N9 — 33 F2
Exeter Rd. N14 — 32 B1
Exeter Rd. NW2 — 48 B5
Exeter Rd. SE15 — 77 C1
Exeter Rd., Croy. — 95 B7
Exeter Rd., Dag. — 53 H6
Exeter Rd., Enf. — 25 G3
Exeter Rd., Felt. — 81 F3
Exeter Rd., Har. — 45 E2
Exeter Rd., Well. — 79 J2
Exeter St. WC2 — 12 B5
Exeter St. WC2 — 58 E7
Exeter Way SE14 — 68 J7
Exford Gdns. SE12 — 87 H1
Exford Rd. SE12 — 87 H2
Exhibition Clo. W12 — 56 J7
Exhibition Rd. SW7 — 14 F5
Exhibition Rd. SW7 — 66 G2
Exmoor Clo., Ilf. — 43 F1
Exmoor St. W10 — 57 A5
Exmouth Mkt. EC1 — 8 E5
Exmouth Mkt. EC1 — 58 G4
Exmouth Ms. NW1 — 7 G4
Exmouth Pl. E8 — 50 E7
Exmouth Rd. E17 — 41 J5
Exmouth Rd., Brom. — 96 H3
Exmouth Rd., Ruis. — 45 C3
Exmouth Rd., Well. — 80 C1
Exmouth St. E1 — 59 F6
Commercial Rd.
Exning Rd. E16 — 60 F4
Exon St. SE17 — 21 D2
Exon St. SE17 — 68 B4
Express Dr., Ilf. — 53 B1
Exton Cres. NW10 — 47 C7
Exton Gdns., Dag. — 53 C5
Exton St. SE1 — 16 E2
Exton St. SE1 — 67 G1
Eyebright Clo., Croy. — 102 G1
Primrose La.
Eyhurst Clo. NW2 — 47 C3
Eylewood Rd. SE27 — 85 J5
Eynella Rd. SE22 — 77 C7
Eynham Rd. W12 — 56 J6
Eynsford Clo., Orp. — 97 F7
Eynsford Cres., Bex. — 89 C1
Eynsford Rd., Ilf. — 52 H2
Eynsham Dr. SE2 — 71 A4
Eynswood Dr., Sid. — 89 B5
Eyot Gdns. W6 — 65 F5
Eyot Grn. W4 — 65 F6
Chiswick Mall
Eyre Ct. NW8 — 6 E1
Eyre St. Hill EC1 — 8 E6
Eythorne Rd. SW9 — 76 G1
Ezra St. E2 — 9 G3
Ezra St. E2 — 59 C3

F

Faber Gdns. NW4 — 38 G5
Fabian Rd. SW6 — 66 C7
Fabian St. E6 — 61 C4
Factory La. N17 — 41 C2

Factory La., Croy. — 101 G1
Factory Pl. E14 — 69 B5
Factory Rd. E16 — 70 B1
Factory Sq. SW16 — 85 E6
Factory Yd. W7 — 64 B1
Uxbridge Rd.
Faggs Rd., Felt. — 72 A5
Fair Acres, Brom. — 96 G5
Fair St. SE1 — 17 E3
Fair St., Houns. — 72 J3
High St.
Fairacre, N.Mal. — 92 E3
Fairacres SW15 — 74 G5
Fairbairn Grn. SW9 — 76 G1
Fairbank Ave., Orp. — 104 E2
Fairbanks Rd. N17 — 41 C3
Fairbourne Rd. N17 — 41 B3
Fairbridge Rd. N19 — 49 D2
Fairbrook Clo. N13 — 32 G5
Fairbrook Rd. N13 — 32 G6
Fairburn Clo., Borwd. — 22 A1
Fairburn Ct. SW15 — 75 B5
Mercier Rd.
Fairby Rd. SE12 — 78 H5
Fairchild Clo. SW11 — 75 G2
Wye St.
Fairchild Pl. EC2 — 9 E6
Fairchild St. EC2 — 9 E6
Fairclough St. E1 — 13 J4
Fairclough St. E1 — 59 D6
Faircross Ave., Bark. — 52 F6
Fairdale Gdns. SW15 — 74 H4
Fairdale Gdns., Hayes — 63 A2
Fairfax Gdns. SE3 — 73 J1
Fairfax Pl. NW6 — 48 F7
Fairfax Rd. N8 — 40 G4
Fairfax Rd. NW6 — 48 F7
Fairfax Rd. W4 — 65 E3
Fairfax Rd., Tedd. — 82 D6
Fairfax Way N10 — 32 A7
Cromwell Rd.
Fairfield Ave. NW4 — 38 H6
Fairfield Ave., Edg. — 30 B6
Fairfield Ave., Twick. —
Fairfield Ave., Wat. — 28 C3
Fairfield Clo. N12 — 31 F4
Fairfield Clo., Enf. — 25 H4
Scotland Grn. Rd. N.
Fairfield Clo., Epsom — 99 E5
Fairfield Clo., Mitch. — 84 H7
Fairfield Clo., Sid. — 79 J6
Fairfield Ct. NW10 — 56 G1
Fairfield Cres., Edg. — 30 B6
Fairfield Dr. SW18 — 75 E5
Fairfield Dr., Grnf. — 55 F1
Fairfield Dr., Har. — 36 J3
Fairfield E., Kings.T. — 91 H2
Fairfield Gdns. N8 — 40 E5
Elder Ave.
Fairfield Gro. SE7 — 70 A6
Fairfield Ind. Est., Kings.T. — 92 A3
Fairfield N., Kings.T. — 91 H2
Fairfield Path, Croy. — 102 A3
Fairfield Pl., Kings.T. — 91 H3
Fairfield Rd. E3 — 60 A2
Fairfield Rd. E17 — 41 H2
Fairfield Rd. N8 — 40 E5
Fairfield Rd. N18 — 33 D4
Fairfield Rd. W7 — 64 D3
Southdown Ave.
Fairfield Rd., Beck. — 96 A2
Fairfield Rd., Bexh. — 80 F2
Fairfield Rd., Brom. — 87 G7
Fairfield Rd., Croy. — 102 B3
Fairfield Rd., Ilf. — 52 E6
Fairfield Rd., Kings.T. — 91 H2
Fairfield Rd., Orp. — 97 G6
Fairfield Rd., Sthl. — 54 F6
Fairfield Rd., Wdf.Grn. — 34 G6
Fairfield S., Kings.T. — 91 H3
Fairfield St. SW18 — 75 E5
Fairfield Way, Barn. — 23 D5
Fairfield Way, Epsom — 99 F5
Fairfield W., Kings.T. — 91 H2
Fairfields Clo. NW9 — 38 C5
Fairfields Cres. NW9 — 38 C5
Fairfields Rd., Houns. — 72 J3
Fairfoot Rd. E3 — 60 A4
Fairford Ave., Croy. — 95 G5
Fairford Clo., Croy. — 95 G5
Fairford Gdns., Wor.Pk. — 99 F2
Fairgreen, Barn. — 23 J3
Fairgreen E., Barn. — 23 J3
Fairgreen Rd., Th.Hth. — 94 H5
Fairhaven Ave., Croy. — 95 G6
Fairhaven Cres., Wat. — 28 A3

Fairhazel Gdns. NW6 48 E6
Fairholme Clo. N3 39 B4
Fairholme Gdns. N3 39 B3
Fairholme Rd. W14 66 B5
Fairholme Rd., Croy. 94 G7
Fairholme Rd., Har. 37 C5
Fairholme Rd., Ilf. 43 C7
Fairholme Rd., Sutt. 100 C6
Fairholt Clo. N16 50 B1
Fairholt Rd.
Fairholt St. SW7 14 H5
Fairland Rd. E15 51 F6
Fairlands Ave., 34 G2
Buck.H.
Fairlands Ave., Sutt. 100 D2
Fairlands Ave., 94 F4
Th.Hth.
Fairlands Ct. SE9 79 D6
North Pk.
Fairlawn SE7 69 J6
Fairlawn Ave. N2 39 H4
Fairlawn Ave. W4 65 C4
Fairlawn Ave., Bexh. 80 D2
Fairlawn Clo. N14 24 C6
Fairlawn Clo., Esher 98 C6
Fairlawn Clo., Felt. 81 F4
Fairlawn Clo., 83 C6
Kings.T.
Fairlawn Dr., Wdf.Grn. 34 G7
Fairlawn Gdns., Sthl. 54 F7
Fairlawn Gro. W4 65 C4
Fairlawn Pk. SE26 86 H5
Fairlawn Rd. SW19 84 C7
Fairlawns, Sun. 90 A3
Fairlawns, Twick. 73 F6
Fairlea Pl. W5 55 F5
Fairlie Gdns. SE23 77 F7
Fairlight Ave. E4 34 D2
Fairlight Ave. NW10 56 E2
Fairlight Ave., 34 G6
Wdf.Grn.
Fairlight Clo. E4 34 D2
Fairlight Clo., Wor.Pk. 99 J4
Fairlight Rd. SW17 84 G4
Fairlop Gdns., Ilf. 35 F7
Fairlop Rd. E11 42 D7
Fairlop Rd., Ilf. 43 F2
Fairmead, Brom. 97 C4
Fairmead, Surb. 99 B1
Fairmead Clo., Brom. 97 C4
Fairmead Clo., Houns. 63 D7
Fairmead Clo., N.Mal. 92 D3
Fairmead Cres., Edg. 30 C3
Fairmead Gdns., Ilf. 43 B5
Fairmead Rd. N19 49 D3
Fairmead Rd., Croy. 101 F1
Fairmead Rd., Loug. 26 H5
Fairmead Side, Loug. 26 J5
Fairmeads, Loug. 27 E2
Fairmile Ave. SW16 85 D5
Fairmont Clo., Belv. 71 F5
Lullingstone Rd.
Fairmount Rd. SW2 76 F6
Fairoak Clo., Orp. 97 E7
Fairoak Dr. SE9 79 G5
Fairseat Clo. 29 B2
(Bushey), Wat.
Hive Rd.
Fairstead Wk. N1 58 J1
Popham Rd.
Fairthorn Rd. SE7 69 G5
Fairview Ave., Wem. 46 G6
Fairview Clo. E17 41 H1
Fairview Clo., Chig. 35 H4
Fairview Cres., Har. 45 G1
Fairview Dr., Chig. 35 H4
Fairview Dr., Orp. 104 G4
Fairview Gdns., 42 H1
Wdf.Grn.
Fairview Pl. SW2 76 F7
Fairview Rd. N15 41 C5
Fairview Rd. SW16 94 F1
Fairview Rd., Chig. 35 H4
Fairview Rd., Enf. 24 G1
Fairview Rd., Sutt. 100 G5
Fairview Way, Edg. 30 A4
Fairwater Ave., Well. 80 A4
Fairway SW20 92 J3
Fairway, Bexh. 80 E5
Fairway, Orp. 97 G5
Fairway, Wdf.Grn. 34 J5
Fairway, The N13 32 J3
Fairway, The N14 24 B6
Fairway, The NW7 30 D3
Fairway, The W3 56 E6
Fairway, The, Barn. 23 E6
Fairway, The, Brom. 97 C5

Fairway, The, N.Mal. 92 D1
Fairway, The, Nthlt. 45 J4
Fairway, The, Ruis. 45 C4
Fairway, The, Wem. 46 B5
Fairway, The, W.Mol. 90 H3
Fairway Ave. NW9 38 B3
Fairway Ave., Borwd. 22 B2
Fairway Clo. NW11 39 F7
Fairway Clo., Croy. 95 H5
Fairway Clo., Epsom 99 C4
Fairway Clo., Houns. 72 C5
Fairway Ct. NW7 30 D3
The Fairway
Fairway Dr., Grnf. 45 H7
Fairway Est., Grnf. 45 J7
Fairway Gdns., Beck. 96 D6
Fairway Gdns., Ilf. 52 F5
Fairways, Stan. 37 H2
Fairways, Tedd. 82 G7
Fairweather Clo. N15 41 B4
Fairweather Rd. N16 41 D6
Fairwyn Rd. SE26 86 H4
Fakenham Clo., Nthlt. 45 G6
Goodwood Dr.
Fakruddin St. E1 9 J6
Fakruddin St. E1 59 D4
Falcon Ave., Brom. 97 B4
Falcon Clo. SE1 16 H1
Falcon Clo. SE1 59 D4
Falcon Cres., Enf. 25 G5
Falcon Gro. SW11 75 H3
Falcon Ho. W13 55 C4
Falcon La. SW11 75 H3
Falcon Rd. SW11 75 H2
Falcon Rd., Enf. 25 G5
Falcon Rd., Hmptn. 81 F7
Falcon St. E13 60 F4
Falcon Ter. SW11 75 H3
Falcon Trd. Est. NW10 47 E4
Falcon Way E11 42 G4
Falcon Way E14 69 B4
Falcon Way NW9 38 E2
Falcon Way, Felt. 72 B5
Falcon Way, Har. 37 H5
Falconberg Ct. W1 11 J3
Falconberg Ms. W1 11 H3
Falconer Wk. N7 49 F2
Newington
Barrow Way
Falconwood Ave., 79 G2
Well.
Falconwood Par., 79 H4
Well.
Falconwood Rd., 103 A7
Croy.
Falcourt Clo., Sutt. 100 E5
Falkirk Gdns., Wat. 28 D5
Blackford Rd.
Falkirk Ho. W9 6 B3
Falkirk Ho. W9 57 E3
Falkirk St. N1 9 E2
Falkirk St. N1 59 B2
Falkland Ave. N3 31 D7
Falkland Ave. N11 32 A4
Falkland Pk. Ave. 95 B3
SE25
Falkland Pl. NW5 49 C5
Falkland Rd.
Falkland Rd. N8 40 G4
Falkland Rd. NW5 49 C5
Falkland Rd., Barn. 23 B2
Fallaize Ave., Ilf. 52 E4
Riverdene Rd.
Falloden Way NW11 39 D4
Fallow Clo., Chig. 35 J5
Fallow Ct. Ave. N12 31 F7
Fallow Flds., Loug. 26 J4
Fallowfield, Stan. 29 D4
Fallowfield Ct., Stan. 29 D3
Stanmore Hill
Fallsbrook Rd. SW16 85 B6
Falmer Rd. E17 42 B3
Falmer Rd. N15 40 J5
Falmer Rd., Enf. 25 B4
Falmouth Ave. E4 34 D5
Falmouth Clo. N22 32 F7
Truro Rd.
Falmouth Clo. SE12 78 F5
Falmouth Gdns., Ilf. 43 A4
Falmouth Rd. SE1 17 A6
Falmouth Rd. SE1 67 J3
Falmouth St. E15 51 D5
Fambridge Clo. SE26 86 J4
Fambridge Rd., Dag. 53 G1
Fane St. W14 66 C6
North End Rd.
Fann St. EC1 8 J6
Fann St. EC1 58 J4
Fanshaw St. N1 9 D3

Fanshaw St. N1 59 B3
Fanshawe Ave., Bark. 52 F6
Fanshawe Cres., Dag. 53 E5
Fanshawe Rd., Rich. 82 F4
Fanthorpe St. SW15 74 J3
Faraday Ave., Sid. 89 A2
Faraday Clo. N7 49 F6
Bride St.
Faraday Rd. E15 51 F6
Faraday Rd. SW19 84 D6
Faraday Rd. W3 56 C7
Faraday Rd. W10 57 B5
Faraday Rd., Sthl. 54 H7
Faraday Rd., Well. 80 A3
Faraday Rd., W.Mol. 90 G4
Faraday Way SE18 70 A3
Faraday Way, Croy. 101 F1
Ampere Way
Fareham Rd., Felt. 72 C7
Fareham St. W1 11 H3
Farewell Pl., Mitch. 93 H1
Faringdon Ave., 97 D7
Brom.
Faringford Rd. E15 51 E7
Farjeon Rd. SE3 79 A1
Farleigh Ave., Brom. 96 F6
Farleigh Pl. N16 50 C4
Farleigh Rd.
Farleigh Rd. N16 50 C4
Farley Dr., Ilf. 52 H1
Farley Pl. SE25 95 D4
Farley Rd. SE6 78 C7
Farley Rd., S.Croy. 102 D7
Farlington Pl. SW15 74 H7
Roehampton La.
Farlow Rd. SW15 74 J3
Farlton Rd. SW18 75 E7
Farm Ave. NW2 48 B3
Farm Ave. SW16 85 E4
Farm Ave., Har. 36 F7
Farm Ave., Wem. 46 F6
Farm Clo., Barn. 22 H5
Farm Clo., Buck.H. 34 J3
Farm Clo., Dag. 53 J7
Farm Clo., Sthl. 54 H7
Farm Clo., Sutt. 100 G7
Farm Clo., W.Wick. 103 E3
Farm Ct. NW4 38 G3
Farm Dr., Croy. 102 J2
Farm End E4 26 E5
Farm La. N14 24 A6
Farm La. SW6 66 D6
Farm La., Croy. 102 J2
Farm Pl. W8 66 D1
Uxbridge St.
Farm Rd. N21 32 J1
Farm Rd., Edg. 30 B6
Farm Rd., Houns. 81 E1
Farm Rd., Mord. 93 E5
Farm Rd., Sutt. 100 G7
Farm St. W1 11 D6
Farm St. W1 58 B7
Farm Vale, Bex. 80 H6
Farm Wk. NW11 39 C5
Farm Way, Buck.H. 34 J4
Farm Way, Wor.Pk. 99 J3
Farman Gro., Nthlt. 54 D3
Wayfarer Rd.
Farmborough Clo., 37 A7
Har.
Pool Rd.
Farmcote Rd. SE12 87 G1
Farmdale Rd. SE10 69 G5
Farmdale Rd., Cars. 100 H7
Farmer Rd. E10 51 B1
Farmer St. W8 66 D1
Uxbridge St.
Farmers Rd. SE5 67 H7
Farmfield Rd., Brom. 87 E5
Farmhouse Rd. SW16 85 C7
Farmilo Rd. E17 41 J7
Farmington Ave., 100 G3
Sutt.
Farmland Wk., Chis. 88 E5
Farmlands, Enf. 24 G1
Farmlands, Pnr. 36 A4
Farmlands, The, Nthlt. 45 G6
Moat Fm. Rd.
Farmleigh N14 24 C7
Farmstead Rd. SE6 87 B4
Farmstead Rd., Har. 37 A1
Farmway, Dag. 53 C3
Farnaby Rd. SE9 78 J4
Farnaby Rd., Brom. 87 D7
Farnan Ave. E17 42 A2
Farnan Rd. SW16 85 E5
Farnborough Ave. 41 H3
E17

Farnborough Ave., 102 G7
S.Croy.
Farnborough Clo., 47 B2
Wem.
Chalkhill Rd.
Farnborough 104 C3
Common, Orp.
Farnborough Cres., 103 F1
Brom.
Saville Row
Farnborough Hill, 104 G5
Orp.
Farnborough Way 21 E7
SE15
Farnborough Way, 104 E5
Orp.
Farncombe St. SE16 17 J4
Farncombe St. SE16 68 D2
Farndale Ave. N13 32 H3
Farndale Cres., Grnf. 54 J3
Farnell Ms. SW5 18 A3
Farnell Rd., Islw. 73 A4
Farnham Clo. N20 23 F7
Farnham Gdns. SW20 92 H1
Farnham Pl. SE1 16 H2
Farnham Rd., Ilf. 43 J7
Farnham Rd., Well. 80 C2
Farnham Royal SE11 20 D4
Farnham Royal SE11 67 F5
Farningham Rd. N17 33 D7
Farnley Rd. E4 26 E7
Farnley Rd. SE25 95 A4
Faro Clo., Brom. 97 D2
Faroe Rd. W14 66 A3
Farorna Wk., Enf. 24 G1
Farquhar Rd. SE19 86 C5
Farquhar Rd. SW19 84 D3
Farquharson Rd., 101 J1
Croy.
Farr Ave., Bark. 62 A2
Farr Rd., Enf. 25 A1
Farrance Rd., Rom. 44 E6
Farrance St. E14 60 A6
Farrans Ct., Har. 37 E7
Farrant Ave. N22 40 G2
Farrell Ho. E1 59 F6
Devonport St.
Farren Rd. SE23 86 H2
Farrer Ms. N8 40 C4
Farrer Rd.
Farrer Rd. N8 40 C4
Farrer Rd., Har. 37 H5
Farrier Clo., Sun. 90 A4
Farrier Rd., Nthlt. 54 G2
Farrier St. NW1 49 B7
Farriers Way, Borwd. 22 D5
Farringdon La. EC1 8 F6
Farringdon Rd. EC1 8 E5
Farringdon Rd. EC1 58 G4
Farringdon St. EC4 12 G3
Farringdon St. EC4 58 H5
Farrington Pl., Chis. 88 G7
Farrins Rents SE16 68 H1
Farrow La. SE14 68 F7
Farrow Pl. SE16 68 H3
Ropemaker Rd.
Farthing All. SE1 17 H4
Farthing Flds. E1 68 E1
Raine St.
Farthing St., Orp. 104 C7
Farthings, The, 92 A1
Kings.T.
Brunswick Rd.
Farthings Clo. E4 34 E3
Farthings Clo., Pnr. 36 B6
Farwell Rd., Sid. 89 B3
Farwig La., Brom. 96 F1
Fashion St. E1 13 G2
Fashion St. E1 59 C5
Fashoda Rd., Brom. 96 J4
Fassett Rd. E8 50 D6
Fassett Rd., Kings.T. 91 H4
Fassett Sq. E8 50 D6
Fauconberg Rd. W4 65 C6
Faulkner Clo., Dag. 44 D7
Faulkner St. SE14 77 F1
Faulkner's All. EC1 12 G1
Fauna Clo., Rom. 44 C6
Faunce St. SE17 20 G4
Favart Rd. SW6 75 D1
Faversham Ave. E4 34 E4
Faversham Ave., Enf. 25 A6
Faversham Rd. SE6 77 J7
Faversham Rd., Beck. 95 D2
Faversham Rd., 93 E6
Mord.
Fawcett Clo. SW11 75 G2

Fawcett Est. E5	50	D1
Fawcett Rd. NW10	47	F7
Fawcett Rd., Croy.	101	J3
Fawcett St. SW10	**18**	**C6**
Fawcett St. SW10	66	E6
Fawcus Clo., Esher	98	C6
Dalmore Ave.		
Fawe Pk. Rd. SW15	75	C4
Fawe St. E14	60	B5
Fawley Rd. NW6	48	E5
Fawn Rd. E13	60	J2
Fawn Rd., Chig.	35	J5
Fawnbrake Ave. SE24	76	H5
Fawood Ave. NW10	47	D7
Faygate Cres., Bexh.	80	G5
Faygate Rd. SW2	85	F2
Fayland Ave. SW16	85	C5
Fearnley Cres.,	81	E5
Hmptn.		
Fearon St. SE10	69	G5
Featherbed La., Croy.	102	J7
Feathers Pl. SE10	69	D6
Featherstone Ave.	86	E2
SE23		
Featherstone Gdns.,	22	C4
Borwd.		
Featherstone Ind.	63	E2
Est., Sthl.		
Featherstone Rd.	30	H6
NW7		
Featherstone Rd.,	63	E3
Sthl.		
Featherstone St. EC1	**9**	**B5**
Featherstone St. EC1	59	A4
Featherstone Ter.,	63	E3
Sthl.		
Featley Rd. SW9	76	H3
Federal Rd., Grnf.	55	F2
Federation Rd. SE2	71	B4
Fee Fm. Rd., Esher	98	C7
Felbridge Ave., Stan.	31	H3
Felbridge Clo. SW16	85	G4
Felbrigge Rd., Ilf.	52	J2
Felday Rd. SE13	78	B6
Felden Clo., Pnr.	28	E7
Felden St. SW6	75	C1
Feldman Clo. N16	50	D1
Oldhill St.		
Felgate Ms. W6	65	H4
Felhampton Rd. SE9	88	E2
Felhurst Cres., Dag.	53	H4
Felix Ave. N8	40	E6
Felix Rd. W13	55	D7
Felix Rd., Walt.	90	A6
Felix St. E2	59	E2
Hackney Rd.		
Felixstowe Rd. N9	33	D3
Felixstowe Rd. N17	41	C3
Felixstowe Rd. NW10	56	H3
Felixstowe Rd. SE2	71	B3
Fell Rd., Croy.	101	J3
Fell Wk., Edg.	38	B1
East Rd.		
Fellbrigg Rd. SE22	77	C5
Fellbrigg St. E1	59	E4
Headlam St.		
Fellbrook, Rich.	82	E3
Fellowes Clo., Hayes	54	D4
Paddington Clo.		
Fellowes Rd., Cars.	100	H3
Fellows Ct. E2	**9**	**F2**
Fellows Rd. NW3	48	G7
Felltram Way SE7	69	G4
Felmersham Clo. SW4	76	D4
Haselrigge Rd.		
Felmingham Rd. SE20	95	F2
Fels Clo., Dag.	53	H3
Fels Fm. Ave., Dag.	53	J3
Felsberg Rd. SW2	76	E6
Felsham Rd. SW15	75	A3
Felspar Clo. SE18	70	J5
Felstead Ave., Ilf.	43	D1
Felstead Gdns. E14	69	C5
Ferry St.		
Felstead Rd. E11	42	G7
Felstead Rd., Loug.	27	B7
Felstead St. E9	50	J6
Felsted Rd. E16	61	A6
Feltham Ave., E.Mol.	91	B4
Feltham Rd., Mitch.	93	J2
Felthambrook Ind.	81	B3
Est., Felt.		
Felthambrook Way,	81	B3
Felt.		
Felthamhill Rd., Felt.	81	A4
Felton Clo., Orp.	97	E6
Felton Gdns., Bark.	61	H1
Sutton Rd.		
Felton Lea, Sid.	88	J5
Felton Rd. W13	64	F2
Camborne Ave.		
Felton Rd., Bark.	61	H2
Sutton Rd.		
Felton St. N1	59	A1
Fen Ct. EC3	13	D5
Fen Gro., Sid.	79	J6
Fen St. E16	60	F7
Victoria Dock Rd.		
Fencepiece Rd., Chig.	35	F5
Fencepiece Rd., Ilf.	35	F6
Fenchurch Ave. EC3	**13**	**D4**
Fenchurch Ave. EC3	59	B6
Fenchurch Bldgs. EC3	**13**	**E4**
Fenchurch Pl. EC3	**13**	**E5**
Fenchurch St. EC3	**13**	**D5**
Fenchurch St. EC3	59	B7
Fendall Rd., Epsom	99	C5
Fendall St. SE1	**17**	**E6**
Fendall St. SE1	68	B3
Fendt Clo. E16	60	F7
Bowman Ave.		
Fendyke Rd., Belv.	71	D3
Fenelon Pl. W14	66	C4
Fenham Rd. SE15	68	D7
Fenman Ct. N17	41	E1
Shelbourne Rd.		
Fenman Gdns., Ilf.	53	B1
Fenn Clo., Brom.	87	G6
Fenn St. E9	50	F5
Fennel Clo. E16	60	E4
Cranberry La.		
Fennel Clo., Croy.	102	G1
Primrose La.		
Fennel St. SE18	70	D6
Fenner Clo. SE16	68	E4
Layard Rd.		
Fenner Sq. SW11	75	G3
Thomas Baines Rd.		
Fenning St. SE1	**17**	**D3**
Fenstanton Ave. N12	31	G6
Fenswood Clo., Bex.	80	G6
Rochester Dr.		
Fentiman Rd. SW8	**20**	**C6**
Fentiman Rd. SW8	67	E6
Fenton Clo. E8	50	C6
Laurel St.		
Fenton Clo. SW9	76	F2
Fenton Clo., Chis.	88	C5
Fenton Rd. N17	32	J7
Fentons Ave. E13	60	H2
Fenwick Clo. SE18	70	D6
Ritter St.		
Fenwick Gro. SE15	77	D3
Fenwick Pl. SW9	76	E3
Fenwick Rd. SE15	77	D3
Ferdinand Pl. NW1	49	A7
Ferdinand St.		
Ferdinand St. NW1	49	A7
Fergus Rd. N5	49	H5
Calabria Rd.		
Ferguson Ave., Surb.	91	J5
Ferguson Clo., Brom.	96	D3
Ferguson Dr. W3	56	D6
Ferme Pk. Rd. N4	40	F7
Ferme Pk. Rd. N8	40	E5
Fermor Rd. SE23	86	H1
Fermoy Rd. W9	57	C4
Fermoy Rd., Grnf.	54	H4
Fern Ave., Mitch.	94	D4
Fern Dene W13	55	E5
Templewood		
Fern Gro., Felt.	72	B7
Fern La., Houns.	63	F5
Fern St. E3	60	A4
Fernbank, Buck.H.	34	H1
Fernbank Ave., Walt.	90	E7
Fernbank Ave., Wem.	46	C4
Fernbrook Ave., Sid.	79	H5
Blackfen Rd.		
Fernbrook Cres. SE13	78	E6
Fernbrook Rd.		
Fernbrook Dr., Har.	36	H7
Fernbrook Rd. SE13	78	E6
Ferncliff Rd. E8	50	D5
Ferncroft Ave. N12	31	H6
Ferncroft Ave. NW3	48	D3
Ferncroft Ave., Ruis.	45	C2
Ferndale, Brom.	96	J2
Ferndale Ave. E17	42	D5
Ferndale Ave.,	72	E3
Houns.		
Ferndale Ct. SE3	69	F7
Ferndale Rd. E7	51	H7
Ferndale Rd. E11	51	E2
Ferndale Rd. N15	41	C6
Ferndale Rd. SE25	95	E5
Ferndale Rd. SW4	76	F4
Ferndale Rd. SW9	76	E4
Ferndale Rd., Rom.	44	J2
Ferndale St. E6	61	E7
Ferndale Ter., Har.	37	C4
Ferndale Way, Orp.	104	G5
Fernden Way, Rom.	44	H6
Ferndene Rd. SE24	76	J4
Ferndown, Nthwd.	36	A2
Ferndown Ave., Orp.	104	G1
Ferndown Clo., Pnr.	28	E7
Ferndown Clo., Sutt.	100	G6
Ferndown Rd. SE9	79	A7
Ferndown Rd., Wat.	28	C3
Ferney Rd., Barn.	24	A7
Fernhall Dr., Ilf.	43	A5
Fernham Rd., Th.Hth.	36	A2
Fernhead Rd. W9	57	C3
Fernhill Ct. E17	42	D2
Fernhill Gdns.,	82	G5
Kings.T.		
Fernhill St. E16	70	C1
Fernholme Rd. SE15	77	G5
Fernhurst Gdns., Edg.	30	A6
Fernhurst Rd. SW6	75	B1
Fernhurst Rd., Croy.	95	D7
Fernlea Rd. SW12	85	B1
Fernlea Rd., Mitch.	94	A2
Fernleigh Clo., Croy.	101	G4
Stafford Rd.		
Fernleigh Ct., Har.	36	H2
Fernleigh Ct., Wem.	46	H2
Fernleigh Rd. N21	32	G2
Ferns Rd. E15	51	F6
Fernsbury St. WC1	**8**	**E4**
Fernshaw Rd. SW10	**18**	**C6**
Fernshaw Rd. SW10	66	F6
Fernside NW11	48	D2
Finchley Rd.		
Fernside, Buck.H.	34	H1
Fernside Ave. NW7	30	D3
Fernside Ave., Felt.	81	B4
Fernside Rd. SW12	84	J1
Fernthorpe Rd. SW16	85	C6
Ferntower Rd. N5	50	A5
Fernways, Ilf.	52	E4
Cecil Rd.		
Fernwood Ave. SW16	85	D4
Fernwood Ave., Wem.	46	F5
Bridgewater Rd.		
Fernwood Clo., Brom.	96	J2
Fernwood Cres. N20	31	J3
Ferranti Clo. SE18	70	A3
Ferraro Clo., Houns.	63	G6
Ferrers Ave., Wall.	101	D4
Ferrers Rd. SW16	85	D5
Ferrestone Rd. N8	40	F4
Ferriby Clo. N1	49	G7
Bewdley St.		
Ferrier Pt. E16	60	H5
Forty Acre La.		
Ferrier St. SW18	75	E4
Ferring Clo., Har.	45	J1
Ferrings SE21	86	B2
Ferris Ave., Croy.	102	J3
Ferris Rd. SE22	77	D4
Ferron Rd. E5	50	E3
Ferry App. SE18	70	D3
Ferry La. N17	41	E4
Ferry La. SW13	65	F6
Ferry La., Brent.	64	H6
Ferry La., Rich.	64	J6
Ferry Pl. SE18	70	D3
Woolwich High St.		
Ferry Rd. SW13	65	G7
Ferry Rd., Tedd.	82	E5
Ferry Rd., T.Ditt.	91	E6
Ferry Rd., Twick.	82	E1
Ferry Rd., W.Mol.	90	G3
Ferry Sq., Brent.	64	G6
Ferry St. E14	69	C5
Ferryhills Clo., Wat.	28	C3
Ferrymead Ave., Grnf.	54	G3
Ferrymead Dr., Grnf.	54	G3
Ferrymead Gdns.,	54	J2
Grnf.		
Ferrymoor, Rich.	82	E3
Festing Rd. SW15	75	A3
Festival Clo., Bex.	89	D1
Fetter La. EC4	**12**	**F4**
Fetter La. EC4	58	G6
Ffinch St. SE8	69	A7
Field Clo. E4	34	B6
Field Clo., Brom.	96	J2
Field Clo., Buck.H.	34	J3
Field Clo., Chess.	98	F5
Field Clo., Houns.	72	B1
Field Clo., W.Mol.	90	H5
Field Ct. WC1	**12**	**D2**
Field End, Barn.	22	H4
Field End, Nthlt.	45	D6
Field End, Ruis.	45	C6
Field End, Twick.	82	C4
Field End Rd., Pnr.	36	B5
Field End Rd., Ruis.	45	C1
Field La., Brent.	64	F7
Field La., Tedd.	82	D5
Field Mead NW7	30	E7
Field Mead NW9	30	E7
Field Pl., N.Mal.	92	F6
Field Rd. E7	51	G4
Field Rd. N17	41	A3
Field Rd. W6	66	B5
Field Rd., Felt.	72	B6
Field St. WC1	**8**	**C3**
Field St. WC1	58	F3
Field Way NW10	47	C7
Twybridge Way		
Field Way, Croy.	103	B7
Field Way, Grnf.	54	H1
Fieldend Rd. SW16	94	C1
Fielders Clo., Enf.	25	B4
Woodfield Clo.		
Fielders Clo., Har.	45	J1
Fieldfare Rd. SE28	62	C7
Fieldgate La., Mitch.	93	H3
Fieldgate St. E1	**13**	**J2**
Fieldgate St. E1	59	D5
Fieldhouse Rd. SW12	85	C1
Fielding Ave., Twick.	81	J3
Fielding Ho. NW6	57	D3
Fielding Rd. W4	65	D3
Fielding Rd. W14	66	A3
Fielding St. SE17	**21**	**A5**
Fielding St. SE17	67	J6
Fieldings, The SE23	86	F1
Fields Est. E8	50	D7
Fields Pk. Cres., Rom.	44	C5
Fieldsend Rd., Sutt.	100	B5
Fieldside Clo., Orp.	104	F4
State Fm. Ave.		
Fieldside Rd., Brom.	87	D5
Fieldview SW18	84	G1
Fieldway, Dag.	53	C3
Fieldway, Orp.	97	G6
Fieldway Cres. N5	49	G5
Fiennes Clo., Dag.	53	C1
Fiesta Dr., Dag.	62	J4
Fife Rd. E16	60	G5
Fife Rd. N22	32	H7
Fife Rd. SW14	74	C5
Fife Rd., Kings.T.	91	H2
Fife Ter. N1	**8**	**D1**
Fifield Path SE23	86	G3
Bampton Rd.		
Fifth Ave. E12	52	C4
Fifth Ave. W10	57	B2
Fifth Cross Rd., Twick.	82	A2
Fifth Way, Wem.	47	B4
Fig Tree Clo. NW10	56	E1
Craven Pk.		
Figges Rd., Mitch.	85	A7
Filby Rd., Chess.	98	J3
Filey Ave. N16	50	D1
Filey Clo., Sutt.	100	F7
Filey Waye, Ruis.	45	A2
Fillebrook Ave., Enf.	25	B2
Fillebrook Rd. E11	51	D1
Filmer Rd. SW6	75	B1
Filston Rd., Erith	71	H5
Riverdale Rd.		
Finborough Rd. SW10	**18**	**A4**
Finborough Rd. SW10	66	E5
Finborough Rd. SW17	84	A6
Finch Ave. SE27	86	A4
Finch Clo. NW10	47	D5
Finch Clo., Barn.	23	D5
Brent Pl.		
Finch Dr., Felt.	72	D7
Finch La. EC3	**13**	**C4**
Finchale Rd. SE2	71	A3
Finchdale Rd. SE2	71	A3
Finchdean Way SE15	68	C7
Daniel Gdns.		
Finchingfield Ave.,	34	J7
Wdf.Grn.		
Finchley Ct. N3	31	E6
Finchley La. NW4	38	J4
Finchley Pk. N12	31	F4
Finchley Pl. NW8	**6**	**E1**
Finchley Pl. NW8	57	G2
Finchley Rd. NW2	48	E5
Finchley Rd. NW3	48	E5
Finchley Rd. NW8	48	E5
Finchley Rd. NW11	39	C4
Finchley Way N3	31	D7

Finck St. SE1 | **16 D4**
Finck St. SE1 | 67 F2
Finden Rd. E7 | 51 H5
Findhorn Ave., Hayes | 54 B5
Findhorn St. E14 | 60 C6
Findon Clo. SW18 | 75 D6
  Wimbledon Pk. Rd.
Findon Clo., Har. | 45 H3
Findon Rd. N9 | 33 E1
Findon Rd. W12 | 65 G2
Fingal St. SE10 | 69 F5
Finland Quay SE16 | 68 H3
Finland Rd. SE4 | 77 H3
Finland St. SE16 | 68 H3
Finlay St. SW6 | 75 A1
Finlays Clo., Chess. | 99 A5
Finnis St. E2 | 59 E3
Finnymore Rd., Dag. | 53 E7
Finsbury Ave. EC2 | **13 C2**
Finsbury Circ. EC2 | **13 C2**
Finsbury Circ. EC2 | 59 A5
Finsbury Cotts. N22 | 32 E7
  Clarence Rd.
Finsbury Est. EC1 | **8 F4**
Finsbury Est. EC1 | 58 G3
Finsbury Ho. N22 | 40 E1
Finsbury Mkt. EC2 | **9 D6**
Finsbury Mkt. EC2 | 59 B4
Finsbury Pk. Ave. N4 | 40 J6
Finsbury Pk. Rd. N4 | 49 H2
Finsbury Pavement | **13 C1**
EC2
Finsbury Pavement | 59 A5
EC2
Finsbury Rd. N22 | 40 F1
Finsbury Sq. EC2 | **9 C6**
Finsbury Sq. EC2 | 59 A5
Finsbury St. EC2 | **13 B1**
Finsbury St. EC2 | 59 A5
Finsbury Way, Bex. | 80 F6
Finsen Rd. SE5 | 76 J3
Finstock Rd. W10 | 57 A6
Finucane Ri. | 28 J2
  (Bushey), Wat.
Fir Clo., Walt. | 90 A7
Fir Dene, Orp. | 104 C3
Fir Gro., N.Mal. | 92 F6
Fir Rd., Felt. | 81 D5
Fir Rd., Sutt. | 100 C1
Fir Tree Clo. SW16 | 85 C5
Fir Tree Clo. W5 | 55 H6
Fir Tree Clo., Epsom | 99 F4
Fir Tree Clo., Orp. | 104 J5
  Highfield Ave.
Fir Tree Gdns., Croy. | 103 A4
Fir Tree Gro., Cars. | 100 J3
Fir Tree Rd., Houns. | 72 E4
Fir Tree Wk., Dag. | 53 J3
  Wheel Fm. Dr.
Fir Tree Wk., Enf. | 25 A3
Fir Trees Clo. SE16 | 68 H1
Firbank Clo. E16 | 61 A5
Firbank Clo., Enf. | 24 J4
  Gladbeck Way
Firbank Rd. SE15 | 77 E2
Fircroft Ave., Chess. | 98 J4
Fircroft Gdns., Har. | 46 B3
Fircroft Rd. SW17 | 84 J2
Firdene, Surb. | 99 C1
Fire Bell All., Surb. | 91 H6
Fire Sta. All., Barn. | 23 C2
  Christchurch La.
Firecrest Dr. NW3 | 48 E3
Firefly Clo., Wall. | 101 E7
  Defiant Way
Firhill Rd. SE6 | 87 A4
Firs, The N20 | 31 G1
Firs, The W5 | 55 G5
Firs Ave. N10 | 40 A3
Firs Ave. N11 | 31 J6
Firs Ave. SW14 | 74 C4
Firs Clo. N10 | 40 A3
  Firs Ave.
Firs Clo. SE23 | 77 G7
Firs Clo., Esher | 98 B6
Firs Clo., Mitch. | 94 B2
Firs Dr., Houns. | 72 B1
Firs Dr., Loug. | 27 D1
Firside Gro., Sid. | 88 J1
First Ave. E12 | 52 B4

First Ave. E13 | 60 G3
First Ave. E17 | 42 A5
First Ave. N18 | 33 F4
First Ave. NW4 | 38 J4
First Ave. SW14 | 74 E3
First Ave. W3 | 65 F1
First Ave. W10 | 57 C4
First Ave., Bexh. | 71 C7
First Ave., Dag. | 62 H2
First Ave., Enf. | 25 C5
First Ave., Rom. | 44 C5
First Ave., Walt. | 90 B6
First Ave., Wem. | 46 G2
First Ave., W.Mol. | 90 F4
First Clo., W.Mol. | 90 J3
First Cross Rd., Twick. | 82 B2
First St. SW3 | **18 H1**
First St. SW3 | 66 H4
First Way, Wem. | 47 B4
Firstway SW20 | 92 J2
Firswood Ave., Epsom | 99 F5
Firth Gdns. SW6 | 75 B1
Firtree Ave., Mitch. | 94 A2
Fish St. Hill EC3 | **13 C6**
Fish St. Hill EC3 | 59 A7
Fisher Clo., Croy. | 102 C1
  Grant Rd.
Fisher Clo., Grnf. | 54 G3
  Gosling Clo.
Fisher Rd., Har. | 37 C2
Fisher St. E16 | 60 G5
Fisher St. WC1 | **12 C2**
Fisher St. WC1 | 58 F5
  Locksmeade Rd.
Fisherman Clo., Rich. | 82 F4
Fishermans Dr. SE16 | 68 G2
Fisherman's Wk. E14 | 69 A1
  Cabot Sq.
Fishers Ct. SE14 | 77 G1
  Besson St.
Fishers La. W4 | 65 D4
Fishers Way, Belv. | 71 J1
Fishersdene, Esher | 98 B6
Fisherton St. NW8 | **6 F5**
Fisherton St. NW8 | **6 E5**
Fisherton St. NW8 | 57 G4
Fisherton St. Est. NW8 | 57 G4
Fishponds Rd. SW17 | 84 H4
Fishponds Rd., Kes. | 104 A5
Fisons Rd. E16 | 69 G1
Fitzalan Rd. N3 | 39 B3
Fitzalan Rd., Esher | 98 B7
Fitzalan St. SE11 | **20 E1**
Fitzalan St. SE11 | 67 F4
Fitzgeorge Ave. W14 | 66 B4
Fitzgerald Ave., | 92 D1
  N.Mal.
Fitzgerald Ave. SW14 | 74 E3
Fitzgerald Rd. E11 | 42 G5
Fitzgerald Rd. SW14 | 74 D3
Fitzgerald Rd., T.Ditt. | 91 D6
Fitzhardinge St. W1 | **11 B3**
Fitzhardinge St. W1 | 58 A6
Fitzhugh Gro. SW18 | 75 G6
Fitzhugh Gro. Est. | 75 G6
SW18
Fitzjames Ave. W14 | 66 B4
Fitzjames Ave., Croy. | 102 D2
Fitzjohn Ave., Barn. | 23 B5
Fitzjohn's Ave. NW3 | 48 G5
Fitzmaurice Pl. W1 | **15 E1**
Fitzmaurice Pl. W1 | 67 B1
Fitzneal St. W12 | 56 F6
Fitzroy Clo. N6 | 48 J1
Fitzroy Ct. W1 | **7 G6**
Fitzroy Cres. W4 | 65 D7
Fitzroy Gdns. SE19 | 86 B7
Fitzroy Ms. W1 | **7 F6**
Fitzroy Pk. N6 | 48 J2
Fitzroy Rd. NW1 | 58 A1
Fitzroy Sq. W1 | **7 F6**
Fitzroy Sq. W1 | 58 C4
Fitzroy St. W1 | **7 F6**
Fitzroy St. W1 | 58 C4
Fitzroy Yd. NW1 | 58 A1
  Fitzroy Rd.
Fitzstephen Rd., Dag. | 53 B5
Fitzwarren Gdns. N19 | 49 C1
Fitzwilliam Ave., Rich. | 73 J2
Fitzwilliam Rd. SW4 | 76 C3
Fitzwygram Clo., | 81 J5
  Hmptn.
Five Acre NW9 | 38 F1

Five Bell All. E14 | 59 J7
  Three Colt St.
Five Elms Rd., Brom. | 103 H3
Five Elms Rd., Dag. | 53 F3
Five Ways Rd. SW9 | 76 G2
Fiveacre Clo., Th.Hth. | 94 G6
Fladbury Rd. N15 | 41 A6
Fladgate Rd. E11 | 42 E6
Flag Clo., Croy. | 102 G1
  Primrose La.
Flag Wk., Pnr. | 36 A6
  Eastcote Rd.
Flambard Rd., Har. | 37 D6
Flamborough Rd., | 45 A3
  Ruis.
Flamborough St. E14 | 59 H6
Flamingo Gdns., Nthlt. | 54 E3
  Jetstar Way
Flamstead Gdns., | 53 C7
  Dag.
  Flamstead Rd.
Flamstead Rd., Dag. | 53 C7
Flamstead Ave., Wem. | 47 A6
Flamsteed Rd. SE7 | 70 B5
Flanchford Rd. W12 | 65 F3
Flanders Cres. SW17 | 84 J7
Flanders Rd. E6 | 61 C2
Flanders Rd. W4 | 65 E4
Flanders Way E9 | 50 G6
Flank St. E1 | **13 H5**
  New End Sq.
Flask Cotts. NW3 | 48 G4
Flask Wk. NW3 | 48 F4
Flaxen Rd. E4 | 34 B3
Flaxley Rd., Mord. | 93 E6
Flaxman Ct. W1 | **11 H4**
Flaxman Rd. SE5 | 76 H3
Flaxman Ter. WC1 | **7 J4**
Flaxman Ter. WC1 | 58 D3
Flaxmore Pl., Beck. | 96 D6
Flaxton Rd. SE18 | 70 G7
Flecker Clo., Stan. | 29 C5
Fleece Rd., Surb. | 98 F1
Fleece Wk. N7 | 49 E6
  Manger Rd.
Fleeming Clo. E17 | 41 J2
  Pennant Ter.
Fleeming Rd. E17 | 41 J2
Fleet Clo., W.Mol. | 90 G5
Fleet La., W.Mol. | 90 F6
Fleet Rd. NW3 | 48 H5
Fleet Sq. WC1 | **8 D4**
Fleet St. EC4 | **12 F4**
Fleet St. EC4 | 58 G6
Fleet St. Hill E1 | **9 H6**
Fleetside, W.Mol. | 90 F5
Fleetway W. | 55 E2
  Business Pk., Grnf.
Fleetwood Clo. E16 | 61 A5
Fleetwood Clo., | 98 G7
  Chess.
Fleetwood Clo., Croy. | 102 B3
  Chepstow Ri.
Fleetwood Ct. E6 | 61 C5
  Evelyn Dennington Rd.
Fleetwood Gro. W3 | 56 E7
  East Acton La.
Fleetwood Rd. NW10 | 47 G5
Fleetwood Rd., | 92 B3
  Kings.T.
Fleetwood Sq., | 92 B3
  Kings.T.
Fleetwood St. N16 | 50 B7
  Stoke Newington
  Ch. St.
Fleetwood Way, Wat. | 28 C4
Fleming Ave., Ruis. | 45 B2
Fleming Ct. W2 | **10 E1**
Fleming Ct., Croy. | 101 G5
Fleming Mead, Mitch. | 84 H7
Fleming Rd. SE17 | **20 H5**
Fleming Rd. SE17 | 67 H6
Fleming Rd., Sthl. | 54 H6
Fleming Way SE28 | 62 D7
Fleming Way, Islw. | 73 C3
Flempton Rd. E10 | 50 H1
Fletcher La. E10 | 42 C7
Fletcher Path SE8 | 69 A7
  New Butt La.
Fletcher Rd. W4 | 65 C3
Fletcher Rd., Chig. | 35 J5
Fletcher St. E1 | **13 J5**
Fletcher St. E1 | 59 D7
Fletchers Clo., Brom. | 96 H4
Fletching Rd. E5 | 50 F3
Fletching Rd. SE7 | 69 J6
Fletton Rd. N11 | 32 E7
Fleur de Lis St. E1 | **9 E6**

Fleur de Lis St. E1 | 59 B4
Fleur Gates SW19 | 75 A7
  Princes Way
Flexmere Gdns. N17 | 41 A1
  Flexmere Rd.
Flexmere Rd. N17 | 41 A1
Flight App. NW9 | 38 F2
  Lanacre Ave.
Flimwell Clo., Brom. | 87 E5
Flint St. SE17 | **21 C2**
Flint St. SE17 | 68 A4
Flintmill Cres. SE3 | 79 B2
Flinton St. SE17 | **21 E3**
Flinton St. SE17 | 68 B5
Flitcroft St. WC2 | **11 J4**
Flockton St. SE16 | 17 H4
Flodden Rd. SE5 | 76 J1
Flood La., Twick. | 82 D1
  Church La.
Flood Pas. SE18 | 70 C4
  Samuel St.
Flood St. SW3 | **18 H4**
Flood St. SW3 | 66 H5
Flood Wk. SW3 | **18 H5**
Flood Wk. SW3 | 66 H6
Flora Clo. E14 | 60 B6
Flora Gdns. W6 | 65 H4
  Ravenscourt Rd.
Flora Gdns., Rom. | 44 C6
Flora St., Belv. | 71 F5
  Victoria Rd.
Floral St. WC2 | **12 A5**
Floral St. WC2 | 58 E7
Florence Ave., Enf. | 24 J3
Florence Ave., Mord. | 93 F5
Florence Clo., Walt. | 90 B7
  Florence Rd.
Florence Dr., Enf. | 24 J3
Florence Gdns. W4 | 65 C6
Florence Nightingale | 50 A6
  Ho. N1
  Clephane Rd.
Florence Rd. E6 | 60 J1
Florence Rd. E13 | 60 F2
Florence Rd. N4 | 49 G1
Florence Rd. SE2 | 71 C3
Florence Rd. SE14 | 77 J1
Florence Rd. SW19 | 84 E6
Florence Rd. W4 | 65 D3
Florence Rd. W5 | 55 H7
Florence Rd., Beck. | 95 H2
Florence Rd., Brom. | 96 G1
Florence Rd., Felt. | 81 B1
Florence Rd., Kings.T. | 82 J7
Florence Rd., Sthl. | 63 D4
Florence Rd., Walt. | 90 B7
Florence St. E16 | 60 F4
Florence St. N1 | 49 H7
Florence St. NW4 | 38 J4
Florence Ter. SE14 | 77 J1
Florfield Rd. E8 | 50 E6
  Reading La.
Florian Ave., Sutt. | 100 G4
Florian Rd. SW15 | 75 B4
Florida Clo. (Bushey), | 29 A2
  Wat.
Florida Rd., Th.Hth. | 94 H1
Florida St. E2 | **9 J4**
Florida St. E2 | 59 D3
Floriston Clo., Stan. | 37 E1
Floriston Gdns., Stan. | 37 E1
Floss St. SW15 | 74 J2
Flower & Dean Wk. E1 | **13 G2**
Flower La. NW7 | 30 F5
Flower Wk., The SW7 | **14 D4**
Flower Wk., The SW7 | 66 F2
Flowersmead SW17 | 85 A2
Floyd Rd. SE7 | 69 J5
Fludyer St. SE13 | 78 E4
Folair Way SE16 | 68 E5
  Catlin St.
Foley Ms., Esher | 98 B7
Foley Rd., Esher | 98 B7
Foley St. W1 | **11 F2**
Foley St. W1 | 58 C5
Folgate St. E1 | **13 E1**
Foliot St. W12 | 56 F6
Folkestone Rd. E6 | 61 D2
Folkestone Rd. E17 | 42 B4
Folkestone Rd. N18 | 33 D4
Folkingham La. NW9 | 38 D1
Folkington Cor. N12 | 31 C5
Follett St. E14 | 60 C6
Folly La. E17 | 41 H1
Folly Ms. W11 | 57 C6
  Kensington Pk. Rd.
Folly Wall E14 | 69 C2

Font Hills N2 39 F2
Fontaine Rd. SW16 85 F7
Fontayne Ave., Chig. 35 F4
Fontenoy Rd. SW12 85 B2
Fonteyne Gdns., 43 A2
Wdf.Grn.
Lechmere Ave.
Fonthill Clo. SE20 95 D2
Selby Rd.
Fonthill Ms. N4 49 G2
Lennox Rd.
Fonthill Rd. N4 49 F1
Fontley Way SW15 74 G7
Fontwell Clo., Har. 29 B7
Fontwell Clo., Nthlt. 45 G6
Fontwell Dr., Brom. 97 D5
Football La., Har. 46 B1
Footpath, The SW15 74 G5
Parkstead Rd.
Foots Cray High St., 89 C6
Sid.
Foots Cray La., Sid. 89 C1
Footscray Rd. SE9 79 D6
Footway, The SW15 79 F7
Forbes Clo. NW2 47 G2
Forbes Ct. SE19 86 B5
Forbes St. E1 13 J4
Forbes Way, Ruis. 45 B2
Forburg Rd. N16 50 D1
Ford Clo., Har. 37 A7
Ford Clo., Th.Hth. 94 H5
Ford End, Wdf.Grn. 34 H6
Ford Rd. E3 59 H1
Ford Rd., Dag. 53 F7
Ford Sq. E1 59 E5
Ford St. E3 59 H1
Ford St. E16 60 F6
Forde Ave., Brom. 96 J3
Fordel Rd. SE6 87 D1
Fordham Clo., Barn. 23 H3
Fordham Rd., Barn. 23 G3
Fordham St. E1 13 J3
Fordham St. E1 59 D6
Fordhook Ave. W5 55 J7
Fordingley Rd. W9 57 C3
Fordington Rd. N6 39 J5
Fordmill Rd. SE6 87 A2
Fords Gro. N21 32 J1
Fords Pk. Rd. E16 60 G6
Fordwich Clo., Orp. 97 J7
Fordwych Rd. NW2 48 B4
Fordyce Rd. SE13 78 C6
Fordyke Rd., Dag. 53 F2
Fore St. EC2 13 A2
Fore St. EC2 58 J5
Fore St. N9 33 D4
Fore St. N18 33 C6
Fore St., Pnr. 36 A5
Fore St. Ave. EC2 13 B2
Foreland Ct. NW4 39 A1
Foreland St. SE18 70 G4
Plumstead Rd.
Foreman Ct. W6 65 J4
Hammersmith Bdy.
Foremark Clo., Ilf. 35 J6
Foreshore SE8 68 J4
Forest, The E11 42 E4
Forest App. E4 26 E7
Forest App., Wdf.Grn. 34 G2
Forest Ave. E4 26 E7
Forest Ave., Chig. 35 D5
Forest Business Pk. 41 H7
E17
Forest Clo. E11 42 F5
Forest Clo., Chis. 97 D1
Forest Clo., Wdf.Grn. 34 H4
Forest Ct. E4 34 F1
Forest Ct. E11 42 E4
Forest Cft. SE23 86 E2
Forest Dr. E12 52 A3
Forest Dr., Kes. 104 B4
Forest Dr., Wdf.Grn. 34 D7
Forest Dr. E. E11 42 D7
Forest Dr. W. E11 42 C7
Forest Edge, Buck.H. 34 J4
Forest Gdns. N17 41 C2
Forest Gate NW9 38 E5
Forest Glade E4 34 E4
Forest Glade E11 42 E6
Forest Gro. E8 50 C6
Forest Heights, 34 G2
Buck.H.
Forest Hill Rd. SE22 77 E5
Forest Hill Rd. SE23 77 F6
Forest Ind. Est., Ilf. 43 H1
Forest La. E7 51 G5
Forest La. E15 51 E6

Forest La., Chig. 35 D5
Forest Mt. Rd., 34 D7
Wdf.Grn.
Forest Ridge, Beck. 96 A3
Forest Ridge, Kes. 104 B4
Forest Ri. E17 42 D5
Forest Rd. E7 51 G4
Forest Rd. E8 50 C6
Forest Rd. E11 42 D7
Forest Rd. E17 41 F4
Forest Rd. N9 33 E1
Forest Rd., Felt. 81 C2
Forest Rd., Ilf. 43 H1
Forest Rd., Loug. 27 A3
Forest Rd., Rich. 65 A7
Forest Rd., Rom. 44 H3
Forest Rd., Sutt. 100 D1
Forest Rd., Wdf.Grn. 34 G3
Forest Side E4 26 F7
Forest Side E7 51 H4
Capel Rd.
Forest Side, Buck.H. 34 J1
Forest Side, Wor.Pk. 99 F1
Forest St. E7 51 G5
Forest Vw. E4 26 D7
Forest Vw. E11 42 F7
Forest Vw. Ave. E10 42 D5
Forest Vw. Rd. E12 52 B4
Forest Vw. Rd. E17 42 C1
Forest Vw. Rd., Loug. 24 A4
Forest Way N19 49 C2
Hargrave Pk.
Forest Way, Loug. 27 B3
Forest Way, Orp. 97 J5
Forest Way, Sid. 79 G7
Forest Way, Wdf.Grn. 34 H4
Forestdale N14 32 D4
Forester Rd. SE15 77 E4
Foresters Clo., Wall. 101 D7
Foresters Cres., 80 H4
Bexh.
Foresters Dr. E17 42 D4
Foresters Dr., Wall. 101 D6
Forestholme Clo. 86 F2
SE23
Forfar Rd. N22 40 H1
Forfar Rd. SW11 76 A1
Forge Clo., Brom. 103 G1
Forge Dr., Esher 98 D7
Forge La., Felt. 81 E5
Forge La., Sun. 90 A3
Forge La., Sutt. 100 B7
Forge Pl. NW1 49 A6
Malden Cres.
Forman Pl. N16 50 C4
Farleigh Rd.
Formby Ave., Stan. 37 F3
Formosa St. W9 6 B6
Formosa St. W9 57 E4
Formunt Clo. E16 60 F5
Vincent St.
Forres Gdns. NW11 39 D6
Forrest Gdns. SW16 94 F3
Forrester Path SE26 86 F4
Forset St. W1 10 H3
Forset St. W1 57 H6
Forstal Clo., Brom. 96 G3
Ridley Rd.
Forster Rd. E17 41 H6
Forster Rd. N17 41 C3
Forster Rd. SW2 76 E7
Forster Rd., Beck. 95 H3
Forster Rd., Croy. 94 J7
Windmill Rd.
Forsters Clo., Rom. 44 F6
Forsters Way, Hayes 54 B6
Forston St. N1 9 B1
Forsyte Cres. SE19 95 B1
Forsyth Gdns. SE17 20 H5
Forsyth Gdns. SE17 67 H6
Forsyth Pl., Enf. 25 B5
Forsythia Clo., Ilf. 52 E5
Fort Rd. SE1 21 G2
Fort Rd. SE1 68 C4
Fort Rd., Nthlt. 45 G7
Fort St. E1 13 E2
Fort St. E1 59 B5
Fort St. E16 69 H1
Forterie Gdns., Ilf. 53 A3
Fortescue Ave. E8 50 E7
Mentmore Ter.
Fortescue Ave., 81 J3
Twick.
Fortescue Rd. SW19 84 G7
Fortescue Rd., Edg. 38 C1
Fortess Gro. NW5 49 B5
Fortess Rd. NW5 49 B5

Fortess Wk. NW5 49 B5
Fortess Rd.
Forthbridge Rd. SW11 76 A4
Fortis Clo. E16 60 J6
Fortis Grn. N2 39 H4
Fortis Grn. N10 40 A3
Fortis Grn. Ave. N2 39 J3
Fortis Grn. Rd. N10 40 A3
Fortismere Ave. N10 40 A3
Fortnam Rd. N19 49 D2
Fortnums Acre, Stan. 29 C6
Fortrose Gdns. SW2 85 D1
New Pk. Rd.
Fortuna Clo. N7 49 F6
Vulcan Way
Fortune Gate Rd. 56 E1
NW10
Fortune Grn. Rd. NW6 48 D4
Fortune St. EC1 9 A6
Fortune St. EC1 58 J4
Fortune Wk. SE28 70 G3
Broadwater Rd.
Fortune Way NW10 56 G3
Fortunes Mead, Nthlt. 45 E6
Forty Acre La. E16 60 G5
Forty Ave., Wem. 46 J3
Forty Clo., Wem. 46 J3
Forty La., Wem. 47 B2
Forum, The, W.Mol. 90 H4
Forum Way, Edg. 30 A6
High St.
Forumside, Edg. 30 A6
High St.
Forval Clo., Mitch. 93 J5
Forward Dr., Har. 37 C4
Fosbury Ms. W2 10 B6
Amberley Rd.
Foscote Ms. W9 57 D5
Foscote Rd. NW4 38 H5
Foskett Rd. SW6 75 C2
Foss Ave., Croy. 101 G5
Foss Rd. SW17 84 G4
Fossdene Rd. SE7 69 H5
Fossdyke Clo., Hayes 54 F5
Fosse Way W13 55 D5
Fossil Rd. SE13 78 A3
Fossington Rd., Belv. 71 D4
Fossway, Dag. 53 C2
Foster La. EC2 12 J3
Foster La. EC2 58 J6
Foster Rd. E13 60 G4
Foster Rd. W3 56 E7
Foster Rd. W4 65 D5
Foster St. NW4 38 J4
Foster Wk. NW4 38 J4
New Brent St.
Fosters Clo. E18 42 H1
Fosters Clo., Chis. 88 C5
Fothergill Clo. E13 60 G2
Fotheringham Rd., 25 C4
Enf.
Foubert's Pl. W1 11 F4
Foubert's Pl. W1 58 C6
Foulden Rd. N16 50 C4
Foulis Ter. SW7 18 F3
Foulis Ter. SW7 66 G5
Foulser Rd. SW17 84 A3
Foulsham Rd., Th.Hth. 94 J3
Founders Ct. EC2 13 B3
Founders Gdns. SE19 85 J7
Foundry Clo. SE16 68 H1
Foundry Ms. NW1 7 G5
Fount St. SW8 67 D7
Fountain Ct. EC4 12 E5
Fountain Dr. SE19 86 C4
Fountain Ms. N5 49 J4
Kelross Rd.
Fountain Pl. SW9 76 G1
Fountain Rd. SW17 84 G5
Fountain Rd., Th.Hth. 94 J2
Fountain Sq. SW1 19 D1
Fountains Ave., Felt. 81 F3
Fountains Clo., Felt. 81 F3
Fountains Cres. N14 24 E7
Fountayne Rd. N15 41 D4
Fountayne Rd. N16 50 D2
Four Seasons Cres. 100 C2
Sutt.
Kimpton Rd.
Four Seasons Ind. 63 H3
Est., Sthl.
Four Wents, The E4 34 D2
Kings Rd.
Fouracres, Enf. 25 H1
Fourland Wk., Edg. 30 C6
Fournier St. E1 13 G1
Fournier St. E1 59 C5
Fourth Ave. E12 52 C4

Fourth Ave. W10 57 B3
Fourth Ave., Rom. 53 J1
Fourth Cross Rd., 82 A2
Twick.
Fourth Way, Wem. 47 C4
Fowey Ave., Ilf. 43 A5
Fowey Clo. E1 68 E1
Kennet St.
Fowler Clo. SW11 75 G3
Fowler Rd. E7 51 G4
Fowler Rd. N1 49 H7
Halton Rd.
Fowler Rd., Mitch. 94 A2
Fowlers Clo., Sid. 89 E5
Thursland Rd.
Fowlers Wk. W5 55 G4
Fownes St. SW11 75 H3
Fox and Knot St. EC1 12 H1
Fox Clo. E1 59 F4
Fox Clo. E16 60 G5
Fox Hill SE19 86 C7
Fox Hill, Kes. 103 H5
Fox Hill Gdns. SE19 86 C7
Fox Hollow Dr., Bexh. 80 D3
Fox Ho. Rd., Belv. 71 H4
Fox La. N13 32 E2
Fox La. W5 55 H4
Fox La., Kes. 103 H5
Fox Rd. E16 60 F5
Foxberry Rd. SE4 77 H3
Foxborough Gdns. 78 A6
SE4
Foxbourne Rd. SW17 85 A2
Foxbury Ave., Chis. 88 G6
Foxbury Clo., Brom. 87 H6
Foxbury Rd., Brom. 87 G6
Foxcombe, Croy. 103 B6
Foxcombe Clo. E6 61 A2
Boleyn Rd.
Foxcombe Rd. SW15 83 G1
Alton Rd.
Foxcote SE5 21 E4
Foxcroft Rd. SE18 79 E1
Foxes Dale SE3 78 G3
Foxes Dale, Brom. 96 D3
Foxfield Rd., Orp. 104 G2
Foxglove Gdns. E11 42 J4
Foxglove La., Chess. 99 A4
Foxglove St. W12 56 F7
Foxglove Way, Wall. 101 B1
Foxgrove N14 32 E3
Foxgrove Ave., Beck. 87 B7
Foxgrove Path, Wat. 28 D5
Foxgrove Rd., Beck. 87 B7
Foxham Rd. N19 49 D3
Foxhole Rd. SE9 79 B5
Foxholt Gdns. NW10 47 C7
Foxhome Clo., Chis. 88 D6
Foxlands Cres., Dag. 53 J5
Foxlands Rd., Dag. 53 J5
Foxlees, Wem. 46 D4
Foxley Clo. E8 50 D5
Ferncliff Rd.
Foxley Clo., Loug. 27 E2
Foxley Rd. SW9 20 F7
Foxley Rd. SW9 67 G7
Foxley Rd., Th.Hth. 94 H4
Foxley Sq. SW9 67 H7
Cancell Rd.
Foxleys, Wat. 28 E3
Foxmead Clo., Enf. 24 F3
Foxmore St. SW11 75 J1
Fox's Path, Mitch. 93 H2
Foxwell St. SE4 77 H3
Foxwood Clo., Felt. 81 B3
Foxwood Rd. SE3 78 F4
Foyle Rd. N17 41 D1
Foyle Rd. SE3 69 F6
Framfield Clo. N12 31 D3
Framfield Ct., Enf. 25 B6
Framfield Rd. N5 49 H5
Framfield Rd. W7 55 C6
Framfield Rd., Mitch. 85 A7
Framlingham Clo. E5 50 F2
Detmold Rd.
Framlingham Cres. 88 B4
SE9
Frampton Clo., Sutt. 100 D7
Frampton Pk. Est. E9 50 F6
Frampton Pk. Rd. E9 50 F6
Frampton Rd., Houns. 72 E5
Frampton St. NW8 6 F6
Frampton St. NW8 57 G4
Francemary Rd. SE4 78 A5
Frances Rd. E4 34 A6
Frances St. SE18 70 C4
Franche Ct. Rd. SW17 84 F3
Francis Ave., Bexh. 80 G2

Francis Ave., Felt. 81 A3
Francis Ave., Ilf. 52 G2
Francis Barber Clo. SW16 85 F4
Well Clo.
Francis Chichester Way SW11 76 A1
Francis Clo. E14 69 D4
Saunders Ness Rd.
Francis Clo., Epsom 99 D4
Francis Gro. SW19 84 C6
Francis Rd. E10 51 C1
Francis Rd. N2 39 J4
Lynmouth Rd.
Francis Rd., Croy. 94 H6
Francis Rd., Grnf. 55 E2
Francis Rd., Har. 37 D5
Francis Rd., Houns. 72 D2
Francis Rd., Ilf. 52 G2
Francis Rd., Pnr. 36 C5
Francis Rd., Wall. 101 C6
Francis St. E15 51 E5
Francis St. SW1 19 F1
Francis St. SW1 67 C4
Francis St., Ilf. 52 G2
Francis Ter. N19 49 C3
Junction Rd.
Franciscan Rd. SW17 84 J5
Francklyn Gdns., Edg. 30 A3
Franconia Rd. SW4 76 D5
Frank Bailey Wk. E12 52 D5
Gainsborough Ave.
Frank Dixon Clo. SE21 86 B1
Frank Dixon Way SE21 86 B1
Frank St. E13 60 G4
Frank Trowell Ct., Felt. 81 A1
Frankburton Clo. SE7 69 H5
Victoria Way
Frankfurt Rd. SE24 76 J5
Frankham St. SE8 69 A7
Frankland Clo. SE16 68 F4
Frankland Clo., Wdf.Grn. 34 J5
Frankland Rd. E4 34 A5
Frankland Rd. SW7 14 E6
Frankland Rd. SW7 66 G3
Franklin Clo. N20 23 F7
Franklin Clo. SE27 85 H3
Franklin Clo., Kings.T. 92 A3
Franklin Cres., Mitch. 94 C4
Franklin Ho. NW9 38 F7
Franklin Pas. SE9 79 B3
Phineas Pett Rd.
Franklin Rd. SE20 86 F7
Franklin Rd., Bexh. 80 E1
Franklin Sq. W14 66 C5
Marchbank Rd.
Franklin St. E3 60 B3
St. Leonards St.
Franklin St. N15 41 B6
Franklin Way, Croy. 101 E1
Franklins Ms., Har. 45 J2
Franklin's Row SW3 19 A3
Franklin's Row SW3 66 J5
Franklyn Gdns., Ilf. 35 G6
Franklyn Rd. NW10 47 F7
Franklyn Rd., Walt. 90 A6
Franks Ave., N.Mal. 92 C4
Frankswood Ave., Orp. 97 E5
Franlaw Cres. N13 32 J4
Fransfield Gro. SE26 86 E3
Frant Clo. SE20 86 F7
Frant Rd., Th.Hth. 94 H5
Franthorne Way SE6 87 B2
Fraser Clo. E6 61 B6
Linton Gdns.
Fraser Clo., Bex. 89 J1
Dartford Rd.
Fraser Ho., Brent. 64 J5
Fraser Rd. E17 42 B5
Fraser Rd. N9 33 E3
Fraser Rd., Erith 71 J5
Fraser Rd., Grnf. 55 E1
Fraser St. W4 65 E5
Frating Cres., Wdf.Grn. 34 H6
Frazer Ave., Ruis. 45 C5
Frazier St. SE1 16 E4
Frazier St. SE1 67 G2
Frean St. SE16 17 H5
Frean St. SE16 68 D3
Fred Wigg Twr. E11 51 F2
Freda Corbett Clo. SE15 21 H7
Frederic Ms. SW1 15 A4
Frederic St. E17 41 H5
Frederica Rd. E4 26 D7
Frederica St. N7 49 F7
Caledonian Rd.
Frederick Clo. W2 10 H5
Frederick Clo. W2 57 H7
Frederick Clo., Sutt. 100 C4
Frederick Cres. SW9 67 H7
Frederick Cres., Enf. 25 F2
Frederick Gdns., Sutt. 100 C5
Frederick Pl. SE18 70 E5
Frederick Rd. SE17 20 H5
Frederick Rd., Sutt. 100 C5
Frederick Sq. SE16 59 H7
Rotherhithe St.
Frederick St. WC1 8 C4
Frederick St. WC1 58 F3
Frederick Ter. E8 59 C1
Haggerston Rd.
Frederick's Pl. EC2 13 B4
Fredericks Pl. N12 31 F4
Frederick's Row EC1 8 G3
Freedom Clo. E17 41 H4
Freedom Rd. N17 41 A2
Freedom St. SW11 75 J2
Freegrove Rd. N7 49 E5
Freeland Pk. NW4 39 B2
Freeland Rd. W5 55 J7
Freelands Gro., Brom. 96 H1
Freelands Rd., Brom. 96 H1
Freeling St. N1 49 F7
Caledonian Rd.
Freeman Clo., Nthlt. 45 E7
Freeman Dr., W.Mol. 90 F3
Freeman Rd., Mord. 93 G5
Freemantle Ave., Enf. 25 G5
Freemasons Rd. E16 60 H5
Freemasons Rd., Croy. 102 B1
Freesia Clo., Orp. 104 J5
Briarswood Way
Freethorpe Clo. SE19 95 B1
Freke Rd. SW11 76 A3
Fremantle Rd., Belv. 71 G4
Fremantle Rd., Ilf. 43 F2
Fremantle St. SE17 21 D3
Fremantle St. SE17 68 B5
Fremont St. E9 59 F1
French Ordinary Ct. EC3 59 B7
Crutched Friars
French Pl. E1 9 E5
French St., Sun. 90 C2
Frendsbury Rd. SE4 77 H4
Frensham Clo., Sthl. 54 F4
Frensham Ct., Mitch. 93 G3
Phipps Bri. Rd.
Frensham Dr. SW15 83 F3
Frensham Dr., Croy. 103 C7
Frensham Rd. SE9 88 G2
Frensham St. SE15 21 J6
Frensham St. SE15 68 D6
Frere St. SW11 75 H2
Fresh Wf. Rd., Bark. 61 E1
Freshfield Clo. SE13 78 D4
Marischal Rd.
Freshfield Dr. N14 24 B7
Freshfields, Croy. 95 J7
Freshford St. SW18 84 F3
Freshwater Clo. SW17 85 A6
Freshwater Rd. SW17 85 A6
Freshwater Rd., Dag. 53 D1
Freshwell Ave., Rom. 44 C4
Freshwood Clo., Beck. 96 B1
Freston Gdns., Barn. 23 J5
Freston Pk. N3 39 C2
Freston Rd. W10 57 A7
Freston Rd. W11 57 A7
Freta Rd., Bexh. 80 F5
Frewin Rd. SW18 84 G1
Friar Ms. SE27 85 H3
Prioress Rd.
Friar Rd., Hayes 54 D4
Friar St. EC4 12 H4
Friars, The, Chig. 35 H4
Friars Ave. N20 31 H3
Friars Ave. SW15 83 F3
Friars Clo. E4 34 C3
Friars Clo. N2 39 G4
Friars Clo., Nthlt. 54 D3
Broomcroft Ave.
Friars Gdns. W3 56 D6
St. Dunstans Ave.
Friars Gate Clo., Wdf.Grn. 34 G4
Friars La., Rich. 73 G5
Friars Mead E14 69 C3
Friars Ms. SE9 79 D5
Friars Pl. La. W3 56 D7
Friars Rd. E6 61 A1
Friars Stile Pl., Rich. 73 H6
Friars Stile Rd.
Friars Stile Rd., Rich. 73 H6
Friars Wk. N14 24 B7
Friars Wk. SE2 71 D5
Friars Way W3 56 D6
Friary Clo. N12 31 H5
Friary Ct. SW1 15 G2
Friary Est. SE15 21 J6
Friary Est. SE15 68 D6
Friary La., Wdf.Grn. 34 G4
Friary Rd. N12 31 G4
Friary Rd. SE15 21 J6
Friary Rd. SE15 68 D7
Friary Rd. W3 56 C6
Friary Way N12 31 H4
Friday Hill E4 34 E2
Friday Hill E. E4 34 E3
Friday Hill W. E4 34 E2
Friday Rd., Mitch. 84 J7
Friday St. EC4 12 J5
Friday St. EC4 58 J7
Frideswide Pl. NW5 49 C5
Islip St.
Friend St. EC1 8 G3
Friend St. EC1 58 H3
Friendly St. SE8 78 A2
Friendly St. Ms. SE8 78 A2
Friendly St.
Friends Rd., Croy. 102 A3
Friendship Wk., Nthlt. 54 D3
Wayfarer Rd.
Friern Barnet La. N11 31 J4
Friern Barnet La. N20 31 F2
Friern Barnet Rd. N11 31 J5
Friern Ct. N20 31 G3
Friern Mt. Dr. N20 23 F7
Friern Pk. N12 31 F5
Friern Rd. SE22 77 D7
Friern Watch Ave. N12 31 F4
Frigate Ms. SE8 69 A6
Watergate St.
Frimley Clo. SW19 84 B2
Frimley Clo., Croy. 103 C7
Frimley Ct., Sid. 89 C5
Frimley Cres., Croy. 103 C7
Frimley Gdns., Mitch. 93 H3
Frimley Rd., Chess. 98 G5
Frimley Rd., Ilf. 52 H3
Frimley Way E1 59 G4
Frimley Way, Wall. 101 E5
Frinton Clo., Wat. 28 B2
Frinton Dr., Wdf.Grn. 34 D7
Frinton Ms., Ilf. 43 D6
Bramley Cres.
Frinton Rd. E6 61 A3
Frinton Rd. N15 41 B6
Frinton Rd. SW17 85 A6
Frinton Rd., Sid. 89 E2
Friston Path, Chig. 35 H5
Manford Way
Friston St. SW6 75 E2
Friswell Pl., Bexh. 80 G4
Frith Ct. NW7 31 B7
Frith La. NW7 31 B7
Frith Rd. E11 51 C4
Frith Rd., Croy. 101 J2
Frith St. W1 11 H4
Frith St. W1 58 D6
Fritham Clo., N.Mal. 92 E6
Frithville Gdns. W12 65 J1
Frizlands La., Dag. 53 H4
Frobisher Clo., Pnr. 36 D7
Frobisher Pas. E14 69 A1
North Colonnade
Frobisher Rd. E6 61 C6
Frobisher Rd. N8 40 G4
Frobisher St. SE10 69 E6
Froghall La., Chig. 35 G4
Frogley Rd. SE22 77 C4
Frogmore SW18 75 D5
Frogmore Clo., Sutt. 100 A3
Frogmore Gdns., Sutt. 100 B4
Frognal NW3 48 F5
Frognal Ave., Har. 37 C4
Frognal Ave., Sid. 89 A5
Frognal Clo. NW3 48 F5
Frognal Ct. NW3 48 F6
Frognal Gdns. NW3 48 F4
Frognal La. NW3 48 E5
Frognal Par. NW3 48 F6
Frognal Ct.
Frognal Pl., Sid. 89 A6
Frognal Ri. NW3 48 F3
Frognal Way NW3 48 F4
Froissart Rd. SE9 79 A5
Frome Rd. N15 40 H3
Westbury Ave.
Frome St. N1 8 J1
Frome St. N1 58 J2
Fromondes Rd., Sutt. 100 B5
Frostic Wk. E1 13 H2
Froude St. SW8 76 B2
Fry Rd. E6 52 A7
Fry Rd. NW10 56 F1
Fryatt Rd. N17 33 A7
Fryatt St. E14 60 E6
Orchard Pl.
Fryent Clo. NW9 38 A5
Fryent Cres. NW9 38 E6
Fryent Flds. NW9 38 E6
Fryent Gro. NW9 38 E6
Fryent Way NW9 38 A5
Frye's Bldgs. N1 8 F1
Frying Pan All. E1 13 F2
Fryston Ave., Croy. 102 D2
Fuchsia St. SE2 71 B5
Fulbeck Dr. NW9 38 E1
Fulbeck Way, Har. 36 J2
Fulbourne Rd. E17 42 C1
Fulbourne St. E1 59 E5
Durward St.
Fulbrook Ms. N19 49 C4
Junction Rd.
Fulbrook Rd. N19 49 C4
Junction Rd.
Fulbrooks Ave., Wor.Pk. 99 F1
Fulford Gro., Wat. 28 B2
Fulford Rd., Epsom 99 D7
Fulford St. SE16 68 E2
Paradise St.
Fulham Bdy. SW6 66 D7
Fulham Ct. SW6 66 D7
Fulham Rd.
Fulham High St. SW6 75 B2
Fulham Palace Rd. SW6 66 A6
Fulham Palace Rd. W6 65 J5
Fulham Pk. Gdns. SW6 75 C2
Fulham Pk. Rd. SW6 75 C2
Fulham Rd. SW3 18 E4
Fulham Rd. SW3 66 G5
Fulham Rd. SW6 75 B2
Fulham Rd. SW10 18 D5
Fulham Rd. SW10 66 G5
Fuller Clo. E2 9 H5
Fuller Clo., Orp. 104 J5
Fuller Rd., Dag. 53 B3
Fuller St. NW4 38 J4
Fullers Ave., Surb. 98 J2
Fullers Ave., Wdf.Grn. 34 F7
Fullers Rd. E18 42 F1
Fullers Way N., Surb. 98 J3
Fullers Way S., Chess. 98 H4
Fullers Wd., Croy. 103 A5
Fullerton Rd. SW18 75 F5
Fullerton Rd., Croy. 95 C7
Fullwell Ave., Ilf. 43 C1
Fullwoods Ms. N1 9 C3
Fulmar Ct., Surb. 91 J6
Fulmead St. SW6 75 E1
Fulmer Clo., Hmptn. 81 E5
Fulmer Rd. E16 61 A5
Fulmer Way W13 64 E3
Fulready Rd. E10 42 D5
Fulstone Clo., Houns. 72 F4
Fulthorp Rd. SE3 78 F2
Fulton Ms. W2 10 C5
Fulton Rd., Wem. 47 A3
Fulwell Cross, Ilf. 43 G2
Fulwell Pk. Ave., Twick. 81 H2
Fulwell Rd., Tedd. 82 A4
Fulwood Ave., Wem. 55 J2
Fulwood Gdns., Twick. 73 C6
Fulwood Pl. WC1 12 D2
Fulwood Wk. SW19 84 B1
Furber St. W6 65 H3
Furham Feild, Pnr. 28 G7
Furley Rd. SE15 68 D7
Furlong Clo., Wall. 101 A1
Furlong Rd. N7 49 G6
Furmage St. SW18 75 E7
Furneaux Ave. SE27 85 H5
Furness Rd. NW10 56 G2
Furness Rd. SW6 75 E2
Furness Rd., Har. 36 H7
Furness Rd., Mord. 93 E7
Furnival St. EC4 12 E3
Furnival St. EC4 58 G6
Furrow La. E9 50 F5

Fursby Ave. N3	31	D6
Further Acre NW9	38	F2
Further Grn. Rd. SE6	78	E7
Furtherfield Clo., Croy.	94	G6
Furze Clo., Wat.	28	C5
Furze Fm. Clo., Rom.	44	E2
Furze Rd., Th.Hth.	94	J3
Furze St. E3	60	A5
Furzedown Dr. SW17	85	B5
Furzedown Rd. SW17	85	B5
Furzefield Clo., Chis.	88	E6
Furzefield Rd. SE3	69	H7
Furzehill Rd., Borwd.	22	A3
Furzewood, Sun.	90	A1
Fuschia Ct., Wdf.Grn.	34	E7
Bridle Path		
Fyfe Way, Brom.	96	G2
Widmore Rd.		
Fyfield Clo., Brom.	96	D4
Fyfield Ct. E7	51	G6
Fyfield Rd. E17	42	D3
Fyfield Rd. SW9	76	G3
Fyfield Rd., Enf.	25	B3
Fyfield Rd., Wdf.Grn.	34	J7
Fynes St. SW1	**19**	**H1**
Fynes St. SW1	67	D4

G

Gable Clo. SE26	86	E4
Lawrie Pk. Ave.		
Gable Clo., Pnr.	28	G7
Gable Ct. SE26	86	E5
Lawrie Pk. Ave.		
Gables Clo. SE5	77	B1
Gables Clo. SE12	87	G1
Gabriel Clo., Felt.	81	D4
Gabriel St. SE23	77	G7
Gabrielle Clo., Wem.	46	J3
Gabrielle Ct. NW3	48	G6
Gaddesden Ave., Wem.	46	J6
Gade Clo., Hayes	63	B1
Gadesden Rd., Epsom	99	C6
Gadsbury Clo. NW9	38	F6
Gadwall Clo. E16	60	H6
Freemasons Rd.		
Gadwall Way SE28	70	G2
Goldfinch Rd.		
Gage Rd. E16	60	E5
Malmesbury Rd.		
Gage St. WC1	**12**	**B1**
Gainford St. N1	58	G1
Richmond Ave.		
Gainsborough Ave. E12	52	D5
Gainsborough Clo., Beck.	87	A7
Gainsborough Clo., Esher	98	B1
Lime Tree Ave.		
Gainsborough Ct. N12	31	E5
Gainsborough Ct. W12	65	J2
Lime Gro.		
Gainsborough Gdns. NW3	48	G3
Gainsborough Gdns. NW11	39	C7
Gainsborough Gdns., Edg.	37	J2
Gainsborough Gdns., Grnf.	46	B5
Gainsborough Gdns., Islw.	73	A5
Gainsborough Ms. SE26	86	E3
Panmure Rd.		
Gainsborough Rd. E11	42	E7
Gainsborough Rd. E15	60	E3
Gainsborough Rd. N12	31	E5
Gainsborough Rd. W4	65	F4
Gainsborough Rd., Dag.	53	B4
Gainsborough Rd., N.Mal.	92	D6
Gainsborough Rd., Rich.	73	J2
Gainsborough Rd., Wdf.Grn.	35	B6
Gainsborough Sq., Bexh.	80	D3
Regency Way		
Gainsford Rd. E17	41	J4
Gainsford St. SE1	**17**	**F3**
Gainsford St. SE1	68	C2
Gairloch Rd. SE5	77	B2

Gaisford St. NW5	49	C6
Gaitskell Rd. SE9	88	F1
Galahad Rd., Brom.	87	G3
Galata Rd. SW13	65	G7
Galatea Sq. SE15	77	E3
Scylla Rd.		
Galbraith St. E14	69	C3
Galdana Ave., Barn.	23	F3
Gale Clo., Hmptn.	81	E6
Stewart Clo.		
Gale Clo., Mitch.	93	G3
Gale St. E3	60	A5
Gale St., Dag.	53	C5
Galeborough Ave., Wdf.Grn.	34	D7
Galen Pl. WC1	**12**	**B2**
Galena Rd. W6	65	H4
Gales Gdns. E2	59	E3
Gales Way, Wdf.Grn.	35	B7
Galesbury Rd. SW18	75	F6
Galgate Clo. SW19	84	B1
Gallants Fm. Rd., Barn.	23	H7
Galleon Clo. SE16	68	G2
Kinburn St.		
Gallery Gdns., Nthlt.	54	D2
Gallery Rd. SE21	86	A1
Galleyhall Rd. SE16	68	E4
Gallia Rd. N5	49	H5
Galliard Clo. N9	25	F6
Galliard Rd. N9	33	D1
Gallions Clo., Bark.	62	A3
Gallions Rd. E16	61	E7
Gallions Rd. SE7	69	H4
Gallon Clo. SE7	69	J4
Gallop, The, S.Croy.	102	E7
Gallosson Rd. SE18	70	H4
Galloway Path, Croy.	102	A4
St. Peter's Rd.		
Galloway Rd. W12	65	G1
Gallus Clo. N21	24	F6
Gallus Sq. SE3	78	H3
Galpins Rd., Th.Hth.	94	E5
Galsworthy Ave., Rom.	44	B7
Galsworthy Cres. SE28	71	B1
Galsworthy Cres. SE3	78	J1
Merriman Rd.		
Galsworthy Rd. NW2	48	B4
Galsworthy Rd., Kings.T.	83	B7
Galsworthy Ter. N16	50	B3
Hawksley Rd.		
Galton St. W10	57	B3
Galva Clo., Barn.	24	A4
Galvani Way, Croy.	101	F1
Ampere Way		
Galveston Rd. SW15	75	C5
Galway St. EC1	**9**	**A4**
Galway St. EC1	58	J3
Gambetta St. SW8	76	B2
Gambia St. SE1	**16**	**H2**
Gambole Rd. SW17	84	H4
Games Rd., Barn.	23	J3
Gamlen Rd. SW15	75	A4
Gander Grn. La., Sutt.	100	B2
Gandhi Clo. E17	42	A6
Gane Clo., Wall.	101	E7
Kingsford Ave.		
Ganton St. W1	**11**	**F5**
Ganton Wk., Wat.	28	E4
Woodhall La.		
Gantshill Cres., Ilf.	43	D5
Gantshill Cross, Ilf.	43	D6
Eastern Ave.		
Gap Rd. SW19	84	D5
Garage Rd. W3	56	A6
Garbutt Pl. W1	**11**	**C1**
Gard St. EC1	8	H3
Garden Ave., Bexh.	80	G3
Garden Ave., Mitch.	85	B7
Garden City, Edg.	30	A6
Garden Clo. E4	34	A5
Garden Clo. SE12	87	H3
Garden Clo. SW15	74	H7
Garden Clo., Barn.	22	H4
Garden Clo., Hmptn.	81	F5
Garden Clo., Nthlt.	54	E1
Garden Clo., Wall.	101	E5
Garden Ct. EC4	**12**	**E5**
Garden Ct. SE15	77	C1
Sumner Est.		
Garden Ct., Rich.	73	J1
Lichfield Rd.		
Garden Ct., W.Mol.	90	H4
Avern Rd.		
Garden La. SW2	85	F1
Garden La., Brom.	87	H6

Garden Ms. W2	57	D7
Linden Gdns.		
Garden Rd. NW8	**6**	**D3**
Garden Rd. NW8	57	F3
Garden Rd. SE20	95	F1
Garden Rd., Brom.	87	H7
Garden Rd., Rich.	74	A3
Garden Rd., Walt.	90	B6
Garden Row SE1	**16**	**G6**
Garden Row SE1	67	H3
Garden St. E1	59	G5
Garden Ter. SW1	**19**	**H3**
Garden Wk. EC2	**9**	**D4**
Garden Wk., Beck.	95	J1
Hayne Rd.		
Garden Way NW10	47	C6
Gardeners Clo. N11	32	A4
Gardeners La. EC4	**12**	**J5**
Gardeners Rd., Croy.	101	H1
Gardenia Rd., Enf.	25	B6
Gardenia Way, Wdf.Grn.	34	H5
Harts Gro.		
Gardens, The SE22	77	D4
Gardens, The, Beck.	96	C1
Gardens, The, Har.	36	J6
Gardens, The, Pnr.	36	F6
Gardiner Ave. NW2	47	J5
Gardner Clo. E11	42	H6
Gardner Gro., Felt.	81	F2
Gardner Rd. E13	60	H4
Gardnor Rd. NW3	48	G4
Flask Wk.		
Garendon Gdns., Mord.	93	E7
Garendon Rd., Mord.	93	D7
Gareth Clo., Wor.Pk.	100	A2
Burnham Dr.		
Gareth Gro., Brom.	87	G4
Garfield Rd. E4	34	D1
Garfield Rd. E13	60	F4
Garfield Rd. SW11	76	A3
Garfield Rd. SW19	84	F5
Garfield Rd., Enf.	25	F4
Garfield Rd., Twick.	82	D1
York St.		
Garford St. E14	60	A7
Garganey Wk. SE28	62	C7
Garibaldi St. SE18	70	H4
Garland Rd. SE18	70	G7
Garland Rd., Stan.	37	H1
Garlands Ct., Croy.	102	A4
Chatsworth Rd.		
Garlick Hill EC4	**13**	**A5**
Garlick Hill EC4	58	J7
Garlies Rd. SE23	86	H3
Garlinge Rd. NW2	48	C6
Garman Clo. N18	33	A5
Garman Rd. N17	33	F7
Garnault Ms. EC1	**8**	**F4**
Garnault Pl. EC1	**8**	**F4**
Garner Rd. E17	42	C1
Garner St. E2	**9**	**J2**
Garnet Rd. NW10	47	E6
Garnet Rd., Th.Hth.	94	J4
Garnet St. E1	59	F7
Garnet Wk. E6	61	B5
Kingfisher St.		
Garnet Way E17	41	H1
McEntee Ave.		
Garnett Clo. SE9	79	C3
Garnett Rd. NW3	48	J5
Garnham Clo. N16	50	C2
Garnham St.		
Garnham St. N16	50	C2
Garnies Clo. SE15	**21**	**F7**
Garrad's Rd. SW16	85	D3
Garrard Clo., Bexh.	80	G3
Garrard Clo., Chis.	88	E5
Garrard Wk. NW10	47	E6
Garnet Rd.		
Garratt Clo., Croy.	101	E4
Garratt La. SW17	84	G4
Garratt La. SW18	75	E5
Garratt Rd., Edg.	30	A7
Garratt Ter. SW17	84	H4
Garratt Clo. W3	56	D5
Jenner Ave.		
Garrett St. EC1	**9**	**A5**
Garrick Ave. NW11	39	B6
Garrick Clo. SW18	75	F4
Garrick Clo. W5	55	H4
Garrick Clo., Islw.	73	D3
Byfield Rd.		
Garrick Clo., Rich.	73	G5
The Grn.		
Garrick Cres., Croy.	102	B2
Garrick Dr. NW4	38	J2

Garrick Dr. SE28	70	G3
Broadwater Rd.		
Garrick Gdns., W.Mol.	90	G3
Garrick Pk. NW4	39	A2
Garrick Rd. NW9	38	F6
Garrick Rd., Grnf.	54	H4
Garrick Rd., Rich.	74	A2
Garrick St. WC2	**12**	**A5**
Garrick St. WC2	58	E7
Garrick Way NW4	39	A4
Garrison Clo. SE18	70	D7
Red Lion La.		
Garrison La., Chess.	98	G7
Garside Clo. SE28	70	G3
Goosander Way		
Garside Clo., Hmptn.	81	H6
Garsington Ms. SE4	77	J3
Garter Way SE16	68	G2
Poolmans St.		
Garth, The, Hmptn.	81	H6
Uxbridge Rd.		
Garth, The, Har.	37	J6
Garth Clo. W4	65	D5
Garth Clo., Kings.T.	82	J5
Garth Clo., Mord.	93	A7
Garth Clo., Ruis.	45	D1
Garth Ct. W4	65	D5
Garth Rd.		
Garth Ms. W5	55	H4
Greystoke Gdns.		
Garth Rd. NW2	48	C2
Garth Rd. W4	65	D6
Garth Rd., Kings.T.	82	J5
Garth Rd., Mord.	93	A7
Garth Rd. Ind. Est., Mord.	93	A7
Garthland Dr., Barn.	22	H5
Garthorne Rd. SE23	77	G7
Garthside, Rich.	82	H5
Garthway N12	31	H6
Gartmoor Gdns. SW19	84	C1
Gartmore Rd., Ilf.	52	J2
Garton Pl. SW18	75	F6
Gartons Clo., Enf.	25	F4
Gartons Way SW11	75	F3
Garvary Rd. E16	60	H4
Garway Rd. W2	**10**	**A4**
Garway Rd. W2	57	E6
Gascoigne Gdns., Wdf.Grn.	34	E7
Gascoigne Pl. E2	**9**	**F3**
Gascoigne Pl. E2	59	C3
Gascoigne Rd., Bark.	61	F1
Gascony Ave. NW6	48	D7
Gascoyne Rd. E9	50	G7
Gaselee St. E14	60	C7
Gasholder Pl. SE11	**20**	**D4**
Gaskarth Rd. SW12	76	B6
Gaskarth Rd., Edg.	38	C1
Gaskell Rd. N6	39	H4
Gaskell St. SW4	76	E2
Gaskin St. N1	58	H1
Gaspar Clo. SW5	**18**	**B1**
Gaspar Ms. SW5	**18**	**B1**
Gassiot Rd. SW17	84	J4
Gassiot Way, Sutt.	100	G3
Gastein Rd. W6	66	A6
Gaston Bell Clo., Rich.	73	J3
Gaston Rd., Mitch.	94	A3
Gataker St. SE16	68	E3
Gatcombe Rd. N19	49	D3
Gate Clo., Borwd.	22	C1
Gate End, Nthwd.	28	A7
Gate Ms. SW7	**14**	**H4**
Gate Ms. SW7	66	H2
Gate St. WC2	**12**	**C1**
Gateforth St. NW8	6	G6
Gateforth St. NW8	57	H4
Gatehouse Clo., Kings.T.	83	C7
Gateley Rd. SW9	76	F3
Gates Grn. Rd., Kes.	103	H4
Gates Grn. Rd., W.Wick.	103	F3
Gatesborough St. EC2	**9**	**D5**
Gateshead Rd., Borwd.	22	A1
Gateside Rd. SW17	84	J3
Gatestone Rd. SE19	86	B6
Gateway SE17	**21**	**A5**
Gateway SE17	67	J6
Gateway Ind. Est. NW10	56	F3
Gateway Ms. E8	50	C5
Shacklewell La.		
Gateways, The SW3	**18**	**H2**
Gatfield Gro., Felt.	81	G2
Gathorne Rd. N22	40	G2

Gathorne St. E2	59 G2	
Mace St.		
Gatley Ave., Epsom	99 B5	
Gatliff Rd. SW1	**19 D4**	
Gatliff Rd. SW1	67 B5	
Gatling Rd. SE2	71 A5	
Gatting Clo., Edg.	30 C7	
Pavilion Way		
Gatton Rd. SW17	84 H4	
Gattons Way, Sid.	89 F4	
Gatward Clo. N21	24 H6	
Gatward Grn. N9	33 C2	
Gatwick Rd. SW18	75 C7	
Gauden Clo. SW4	76 D3	
Gauden Rd. SW4	76 D2	
Gaumont Ter. W12	65 J2	
Lime Gro.		
Gaunt St. SE1	**16 H5**	
Gaunt St. SE1	67 J3	
Gauntlet Clo., Nthlt.	45 E7	
Gauntlett Ct., Wem.	46 E5	
Gauntlett Rd., Sutt.	100 G5	
Gautrey Rd. SE15	77 F2	
Gautrey Sq. E6	61 C6	
Truesdale Rd.		
Gavel St. SE17	**21 C1**	
Gaverick St. E14	69 A4	
Gavestone Cres. SE12	78 H7	
Gavestone Rd. SE12	78 H7	
Gaviller Pl. E5	50 E4	
Clarence Rd.		
Gavin St. SE18	70 H4	
Gavina Clo., Mord.	93 G5	
Gawber St. E2	59 F3	
Gawsworth Clo. E15	51 E5	
Ash Rd.		
Gawthorne Ave. NW7	31 B5	
Lane App.		
Gay Clo. NW2	47 H5	
Gay Gdns., Dag.	53 J4	
Gay Rd. E15	60 D2	
Gay St. SW15	75 A3	
Waterman St.		
Gaydon Ho. W2	**10 A1**	
Gaydon Ho. W2	57 E5	
Gaydon La. NW9	38 E1	
Gayfere Rd., Epsom	99 G5	
Gayfere Rd., Ilf.	43 C3	
Gayfere St. SW1	**16 A6**	
Gayfere St. SW1	67 E3	
Gayford Rd. W12	65 F2	
Gayhurst SE17	**21 C5**	
Gayhurst Rd. E8	50 D7	
Gaylor Rd., Nthlt.	45 F5	
Gaynes Hill Rd., Wdf.Grn.	35 B6	
Gaynesford Rd. SE23	86 G2	
Gaynesford Rd., Cars.	100 J7	
Gaysham Ave., Ilf.	43 D5	
Gaysham Hall, Ilf.	43 E3	
Gayton Ct., Har.	37 C6	
Gayton Cres. NW3	48 G4	
Gayton Rd. NW3	48 G4	
Gayton Rd. SE2	71 C3	
Florence Rd.		
Gayton Rd., Har.	37 C6	
Gayville Rd. SW11	75 J6	
Gaywood Clo. SW2	85 F1	
Gaywood Est. SE1	**16 H6**	
Gaywood Rd. E17	42 A3	
Gaywood St. SE1	**16 H6**	
Gaza St. SE17	**20 G4**	
Geariesville Gdns., Ilf.	43 E4	
Geary Rd. NW10	47 G5	
Geary St. N7	49 F5	
GEC Est., Wem.	46 G3	
Geddes Pl., Bexh.	80 G4	
Market Pl.		
Gedeney Rd. N17	40 J1	
Gedling Pl. SE1	**17 G5**	
Gedling Pl. SE1	68 C3	
Gee St. EC1	**8 J5**	
Gee St. EC1	58 J4	
Geere Rd. E15	60 F1	
Gees Ct. W1	**11 C4**	
Geffrye Ct. N1	**9 E2**	
Geffrye St. E2	**9 F2**	
Geffrye St. E2	59 C2	
Geldart Rd. SE15	68 E7	
Geldeston Rd. E5	50 D2	
Gellatly Rd. SE14	77 F2	
Gemini Gro., Nthlt.	54 E3	
Javelin Way		
General Gordon Pl. SE18	70 E4	
General Wolfe Rd. SE10	78 D1	

Genesta Rd. SE18	70 E6	
Geneva Dr. SW9	76 G4	
Geneva Gdns., Rom.	44 E5	
Geneva Rd., Kings.T.	91 H4	
Geneva Rd., Th.Hth.	94 J5	
Genever Clo. E4	34 A5	
Genista Rd. N18	33 E5	
Genoa Ave. SW15	74 J5	
Genoa Rd. SE20	95 F1	
Genotin Rd., Enf.	25 A3	
Genotin Ter., Enf.	25 A3	
Genotin Rd.		
Gentian Row SE13	78 C1	
Sparta St.		
Gentlemans Row, Enf.	24 J3	
Gentry Gdns. E13	60 G4	
Whitwell Rd.		
Geoffrey Clo. SE5	76 J2	
Geoffrey Gdns. E6	61 B2	
Geoffrey Rd. SE4	77 J3	
George Beard Rd. SE8	68 J4	
George Comberton Wk. E12	52 D5	
Gainsborough Ave.		
George Ct. WC2	**12 B6**	
George Cres. N10	32 A7	
George Downing Est. N16	50 C2	
Cazenove Rd.		
George V Ave., Pnr.	36 F1	
George V Clo., Pnr.	36 G3	
George V Ave.		
George V Way, Grnf.	55 E1	
George Gros. Rd. SE20	95 D1	
George Inn Yd. SE1	**17 B2**	
George La. E18	42 G2	
George La. SE13	78 C6	
George La., Brom.	103 H1	
George Lansbury Ho. N22	40 G1	
Progress Way		
George Loveless Ho. E2	**9 G3**	
George Ms. NW1	**7 F4**	
George Ms., Enf.	25 A3	
Sydney Rd.		
George Rd. E4	34 A6	
George Rd., Kings.T.	83 B7	
George Rd., N.Mal.	92 F4	
George Row SE16	**17 H4**	
George Row SE16	68 D2	
George Sq. SW19	93 C3	
Mostyn Rd.		
George St. E16	60 F6	
George St. EC4	**13 B4**	
George St. W1	**10 J3**	
George St. W1	57 J6	
George St. W7	64 B1	
The Bdy.		
George St., Bark.	52 F7	
George St., Croy.	101 J2	
George St., Houns.	72 F2	
George St., Rich.	73 G5	
George St., Sthl.	63 E4	
George St., Sutt.	100 E5	
George Wyver Clo. SW19	75 B7	
Beaumont Rd.		
George Yd. EC3	**13 C4**	
George Yd. W1	**11 C5**	
George Yd. W1	58 A7	
George's Rd. N7	49 F5	
Georges Rd., Brom.	97 C3	
Georges Sq. SW6	66 C6	
North End Rd.		
Georgetown Clo. SE19	86 A6	
St. Kitts Ter.		
Georgette Pl. SE10	69 C7	
King George St.		
Georgeville Gdns., Ilf.	43 E4	
Georgia Rd., N.Mal.	92 C4	
Georgia Rd., Th.Hth.	94 H1	
Georgian Clo., Brom.	96 H7	
Georgian Clo., Stan.	29 D7	
Georgian Ct., Wem.	47 A6	
Georgian Way, Har.	46 A2	
Georgiana St. NW1	58 C1	
Georgina Gdns. E2	**9 G3**	
Geraint Rd., Brom.	87 G4	
Gerald Ms. SW1	**19 C1**	
Gerald Rd. E16	60 F4	
Gerald Rd. SW1	**19 C1**	
Gerald Rd. SW1	67 A4	
Gerald Rd., Dag.	53 F2	
Geraldine Rd. SW18	75 F5	
Geraldine Rd. W4	65 A6	
Geraldine St. SE11	**16 G6**	

Geraldine St. SE11	67 H3	
Gerard Ave., Houns.	72 G7	
Redfern Ave.		
Gerard Rd. SW13	74 F1	
Gerard Rd., Har.	37 D6	
Gerards Clo. SE16	68 F5	
Gerda Rd. SE9	88 F2	
Germander Way E15	60 E3	
Gernon Rd. E3	59 H2	
Geron Way NW2	47 H2	
Gerrard Gdns., Pnr.	36 A5	
Gerrard Pl. W1	**11 J5**	
Gerrard Rd. N1	**8 G1**	
Gerrard Rd. N1	58 H2	
Gerrard St. W1	**11 J5**	
Gerrard St. W1	58 D7	
Gerrards Clo. N14	24 C5	
Gerridge St. SE1	**16 F5**	
Gerridge St. SE1	67 G3	
Gerry Raffles Sq. E15	51 D6	
Salway Rd.		
Gertrude Rd., Belv.	71 G4	
Gertrude St. SW10	**18 D6**	
Gertrude St. SW10	66 F6	
Gervase Clo., Wem.	47 C3	
Gervase Rd., Edg.	38 C1	
Gervase St. SE15	68 E7	
Ghent St. SE6	87 A2	
Ghent Way E8	50 C6	
Giant Tree Hill (Bushey), Wat.	29 A1	
Gibbard Ms. SW19	84 A5	
Gibbins Rd. E15	51 C7	
Gibbon Rd. SE15	77 F2	
Gibbon Rd. W3	56 E7	
Gibbon Rd., Kings.T.	91 H1	
Gibbon Wk. SW15	74 G4	
Swinburne Rd.		
Gibbons Rd. NW10	47 E6	
Gibbs Ave. SE19	86 A5	
Gibbs Clo. SE19	86 A5	
Gibbs Couch, Wat.	28 D3	
Gibbs Grn. W14	66 C5	
Gibbs Grn., Edg.	30 C5	
Gibbs Rd. N18	33 F4	
Gibbs Sq. SE19	86 A5	
Gibraltar Wk. E2	**9 G4**	
Gibraltar Wk. E2	59 C3	
Gibson Clo. E1	59 F4	
Colebert Ave.		
Gibson Clo., Chess.	98 F6	
Gibson Clo., Islw.	73 A3	
Gibson Gdns. N16	50 C2	
Northwold Rd.		
Gibson Rd. SE11	**20 D2**	
Gibson Rd. SE11	67 F4	
Gibson Rd., Dag.	53 C1	
Gibson Rd., Sutt.	100 E5	
Gibson Sq. N1	58 G1	
Gibson St. SE10	69 E5	
Gibson's Hill SW16	85 G7	
Gideon Clo., Belv.	71 H4	
Gideon Rd. SW11	76 A3	
Giesbach Rd. N19	49 C2	
Giffard Rd. N18	33 B5	
Giffin St. SE8	69 A7	
Gifford Gdns. W7	55 A5	
Gifford St. N1	49 E7	
Gift La. E15	60 F1	
Giggs Hill Gdns., T.Ditt.	98 D1	
Giggs Hill Rd., T.Ditt.	91 D7	
Gilbert Gro., Edg.	38 D1	
Gilbert Ho. SE8	69 A6	
McMillan St.		
Gilbert Pl. WC1	**12 A2**	
Gilbert Rd. SE11	**20 F2**	
Gilbert Rd. SE11	67 G4	
Gilbert Rd. SW19	84 F7	
Gilbert Rd., Belv.	71 G3	
Gilbert Rd., Brom.	87 G7	
Gilbert Rd., Pnr.	36 D4	
Gilbert St. E15	51 E4	
Gilbert St. W1	**11 C4**	
Gilbert St. W1	58 A6	
Gilbert St., Houns.	72 J3	
High St.		
Gilbey Rd. SW17	84 H4	
Gilbourne Rd. SE18	70 J6	
Gilda Ave., Enf.	25 H5	
Gilda Cres. N16	50 D1	
Gildea St. W1	**11 E2**	
Gilden Cres. NW5	49 A5	
Gilders Rd., Chess.	98 J7	
Giles Coppice SE19	86 C4	
Gilkes Cres. SE21	77 B6	
Gilkes Pl. SE21	77 B6	
Gill Ave. E16	60 G6	

Gill St. E14	59 J7	
Gillan Grn., Wat. (Bushey)	28 J2	
Gillender St. E3	60 C4	
Gillender St. E14	60 C4	
Gillespie Rd. N5	49 G3	
Gillett Ave. E6	61 B2	
Gillett Pl. N16	50 B5	
Gillett St.		
Gillett Rd., Th.Hth.	95 A4	
Gillett St. N16	50 B5	
Gillfoot NW1	**7 F2**	
Gillfoot NW1	58 C2	
Gillham Ter. N17	33 D6	
Gillian Pk. Rd., Sutt.	100 C1	
Gillian St. SE13	78 B5	
Gillies St. NW5	49 A5	
Gilling Ct. NW3	48 H6	
Gillingham Ms. SW1	**19 F1**	
Gillingham Rd. NW2	48 B3	
Gillingham Row SW1	**19 F1**	
Gillingham St. SW1	**19 E1**	
Gillingham St. SW1	67 C4	
Gillison Wk. SE16	**17 J5**	
Gillman Dr. E15	60 F1	
Gillum Clo., Barn.	31 J1	
Gilmore Rd. SE13	78 D4	
Gilpin Ave. SW14	74 D4	
Gilpin Clo., Mitch.	93 H2	
Gilpin Cres. N18	33 C5	
Gilpin Cres., Twick.	72 H7	
Gilpin Rd. E5	50 H4	
Gilsland Rd., Th.Hth.	95 A4	
Gilstead Ho., Bark.	62 B2	
Gilstead Rd. SW6	75 E2	
Gilston Rd. SW10	**18 D4**	
Gilston Rd. SW10	66 F5	
Gilton Rd. SE6	87 E3	
Giltspur St. EC1	**12 H3**	
Giltspur St. EC1	58 H6	
Gilwell Clo. E4	26 B4	
Antlers Hill		
Gilwell La. E4	26 D4	
Gilwell Pk. E4	26 D3	
Gippeswyck Clo., Pnr.	36 D1	
Uxbridge Rd.		
Gipsy Hill SE19	86 B5	
Gipsy La. SW15	74 G3	
Gipsy Rd. SE27	85 J4	
Gipsy Rd., Well.	80 D1	
Gipsy Rd. Gdns. SE27	85 J4	
Giralda Clo. E16	61 A5	
Fulmer Rd.		
Giraud St. E14	60 B6	
Girdlers Rd. W14	66 A4	
Girdlestone Wk. N19	49 C2	
Girdwood Rd. SW18	75 B7	
Girling Way, Felt.	72 A3	
Gironde Rd. SW6	66 C7	
Girton Ave. NW9	38 A3	
Girton Clo., Nthlt.	45 J6	
Girton Gdns., Croy.	103 A3	
Girton Rd. SE26	86 G5	
Girton Rd., Nthlt.	45 J6	
Girton Vill. W10	57 A6	
Cambridge Gdns.		
Gisburn Rd. N8	40 F4	
Gissing Wk. N1	49 G7	
Lofting Rd.		
Given Wilson Wk. E13	60 F2	
Stride Rd.		
Glacier Way, Wem.	55 G2	
Gladbeck Way, Enf.	24 H5	
Gladding Rd. E12	52 A4	
Glade, The N21	24 F6	
Glade, The SE7	69 J7	
Glade, The, Brom.	97 A2	
Glade, The, Croy.	95 G5	
Glade, The, Enf.	24 G2	
Chase Ridings		
Glade, The, Epsom	99 G5	
Glade, The, Ilf.	43 C1	
Glade, The, W.Wick.	103 B3	
Glade, The, Wdf.Grn.	34 H3	
Glade Clo., Surb.	98 G2	
Glade Ct., Ilf.	43 C1	
The Glade		
Glade Gdns., Croy.	95 H7	
Glade La., Sthl.	63 H2	
Glades Pl., Brom.	96 G2	
Widmore Rd.		
Glades Shop. Cen., The, Brom.	96 G2	
Gladeside N21	24 F7	
Gladeside, Croy.	95 G7	
Gladesmore Rd. N15	41 C6	
Gladeswood Rd., Belv.	71 H4	

Gladiator St. SE23 77 H7
Glading Ter. N16 50 C3
Gladioli Clo., Hmptn. 81 G6
Gresham Rd.
Gladsdale Dr., Pnr. 36 B4
Gladsmuir Rd. N19 49 C1
Gladsmuir Rd., Barn. 23 B2
Gladstone Ave. E12 52 B7
Gladstone Ave. N22 40 G2
Gladstone Ave., Felt. 72 A6
Gladstone Ave., Twick. 73 A7
Gladstone Ms. SE20 86 F7
Gladstone Pk. Gdns. NW2 47 H4
Gladstone Pl. E3 59 J2
Roman Rd.
Gladstone Pl., Barn. 23 A4
Gladstone Rd. SW19 84 D7
Gladstone Rd. W4 65 D3
Acton La.
Gladstone Rd., Buck.H. 34 H1
Gladstone Rd., Croy. 95 A7
Gladstone Rd., Kings.T. 92 A3
Gladstone Rd., Orp. 104 F5
Gladstone Rd., Sthl. 63 E2
Gladstone Rd., Surb. 98 G2
Gladstone St. SE1 16 G5
Gladstone St. SE1 67 H3
Gladstone Ter. SE27 85 J4
Gladstone Ter. SW8 76 B1
Gladstone Way, Har. 37 B3
Gladwell Rd. N8 40 F6
Gladwell Rd., Brom. 87 G6
Gladwyn Rd. SW15 75 A3
Gladys Rd. NW6 48 D7
Glaisher St. SE10 69 C7
Straightsmouth
Glamis Pl. E1 59 F7
Glamis Rd. E1 59 F7
Glamis Way, Nthlt. 45 J6
Glamorgan Clo., Mitch. 94 E3
Glamorgan Rd., Kings.T. 82 F7
Glanfield Rd., Beck. 95 J4
Glanleam Rd., Stan. 29 G4
Glanville Rd. SW2 76 E5
Glanville Rd., Brom. 96 H3
Glasbrook Ave., Twick. 81 F1
Glasbrook Rd. SE9 79 A7
Glaserton Rd. N16 41 B7
Glasford St. SW17 84 J6
Glasgow Ho. W9 6 B2
Glasgow Ho. W9 57 E2
Glasgow Rd. E13 60 H2
Glasgow Rd. N18 33 E5
Aberdeen Rd.
Glasgow Ter. SW1 19 F4
Glasgow Ter. SW1 67 C5
Glass St. E2 59 E4
Coventry Rd.
Glass Yd. SE18 70 D3
Glasse Clo. W13 55 D7
Glasshill St. SE1 16 H3
Glasshill St. SE1 67 H2
Glasshouse All. EC4 12 F4
Glasshouse Flds. E1 59 G7
Glasshouse St. W1 11 G6
Glasshouse St. W1 58 C7
Glasshouse Wk. SE11 20 B3
Glasshouse Wk. SE11 67 E5
Glasshouse Yd. EC1 8 J6
Glasslyn Rd. N8 40 D5
Glassmill La., Brom. 96 F2
Glastonbury Ave., Wdf.Grn. 35 A7
Glastonbury Rd. N9 33 D1
Glastonbury Rd., Mord. 93 D7
Glastonbury St. NW6 48 C5
Glaucus St. E3 60 B5
Glazbury Rd. W14 66 B4
Glazebrook Clo. SE21 86 A2
Glazebrook Rd., Tedd. 82 C7
Glebe, The SE3 78 E3
Glebe, The SW16 85 D4
Glebe, The, Chis. 97 F1
Glebe, The, Wor.Pk. 99 F1
Glebe Ave., Enf. 24 H3
Glebe Ave., Har. 37 H3
Glebe Ave., Mitch. 93 H2
Glebe Ave., Ruis. 45 B6
Glebe Ave., Wdf.Grn. 34 G6
Glebe Clo. W4 65 E5
Glebe St.
Glebe Cotts., Sutt. 100 E4
Vale Rd.
Glebe Ct. W7 55 A7
Glebe Ct., Mitch. 93 J3
Glebe Ct., Stan. 29 F5
Glebe Rd.
Glebe Cres. NW4 38 J4
Glebe Cres., Har. 37 H3
Glebe Gdns., N.Mal. 92 E7
Glebe Ho. Dr., Brom. 103 H1
Glebe Hyrst SE19 86 C4
Giles Coppice
Glebe La., Barn. 22 G5
Glebe La., Har. 37 H4
Glebe Path, Mitch. 93 H3
Glebe Pl. SW3 18 G5
Glebe Pl. SW3 66 H6
Glebe Rd. E8 50 C7
Middleton Rd.
Glebe Rd. N3 39 F1
Glebe Rd. N8 40 F4
Glebe Rd. NW10 47 F6
Glebe Rd. SW13 74 G2
Glebe Rd., Brom. 96 G1
Glebe Rd., Cars. 100 J6
Glebe Rd., Dag. 53 H6
Glebe Rd., Stan. 29 F5
Glebe Side, Twick. 73 C7
Glebe St. W4 65 E5
Glebe Ter. E3 60 A3
Bow Rd.
Glebe Way, Felt. 81 G3
Glebe Way, W.Wick. 103 C2
Glebelands, W.Mol. 90 H5
Glebelands Ave. E18 42 G2
Glebelands Ave., Ilf. 43 G7
Glebelands Clo. SE5 77 B3
Grove Hill Rd.
Glebelands Rd., Felt. 72 A7
Glebeway, Wdf.Grn. 34 J5
Gledhow Gdns. SW5 18 C2
Gledhow Gdns. SW5 66 F4
Gledstanes Rd. W14 66 B5
Gleed Ave. (Bushey), Wat. 29 A2
Gleeson Dr., Orp. 104 J5
Glegg Pl. SW15 75 A4
Glen, The, Brom. 96 E2
Glen, The, Croy. 102 G3
Glen, The, Enf. 24 H4
Glen, The, Orp. 104 C3
Glen, The, Pnr. 36 B5
Glen, The, Pnr. (Eastcote) 36 E7
Glen, The, Sthl. 63 F5
Glen, The, Wem. 46 G4
Glen Albyn Rd. SW19 84 A2
Glen Cres., Wdf.Grn. 34 H6
Glen Gdns., Croy. 101 H3
Glen Mill, Hmptn. 81 F5
Glen Ri., Wdf.Grn. 34 H6
Glen Rd. E13 60 J4
Glen Rd. E17 41 J5
Glen Rd., Chess. 98 H3
Glen Wk., Islw. 73 A5
Glena Mt., Sutt. 100 F4
Glenaffric Ave. E14 69 D4
Glenalmond Rd., Har. 37 H4
Glenalvon Way SE18 70 B4
Glenarm Rd. E5 50 F5
Glenavon Clo., Esher 98 D6
Glenavon Rd. E15 51 E7
Glenbarr Clo. SE9 79 E3
Dumbreck Rd.
Glenbow Rd., Brom. 87 E6
Glenbrook N., Enf. 24 F4
Glenbrook Rd. NW6 48 D5
Glenbrook S., Enf. 24 F4
Glenbuck Ct., Surb. 91 G6
Glenbuck Rd.
Glenbuck Rd., Surb. 91 G6
Glenburnie Rd. SW17 84 H3
Glencairn Dr. W5 55 F4
Glencairn Rd. SW16 85 E7
Glencairne Clo. E16 61 A5
Glencoe Ave., Ilf. 43 G7
Glencoe Dr., Dag. 53 G4
Glencoe Rd., Hayes 54 D4
Glencourse Grn., Wat. 28 D4
Caldwell Rd.
Glendale Ave. N22 32 G7
Glendale Ave., Edg. 30 A4
Glendale Ave., Rom. 44 C7
Glendale Clo. SE9 79 D3
Dumbreck Rd.
Glendale Dr. SW19 84 C5
Glendale Gdns., Wem. 46 G1
Glendale Ms., Beck. 96 B1
Glendale Rd., Erith 71 J4
Glendale Way SE28 62 C7
Glendall St. SW9 76 F4
Glendarvon St. SW15 75 A3
Glendevon Clo., Edg. 30 B3
Tayside Dr.
Glendish Rd. N17 41 D1
Glendor Gdns. NW7 30 D4
Glendower Gdns. SW14 74 D3
Glendower Rd.
Glendower Pl. SW7 18 E1
Glendower Pl. SW7 66 G4
Glendower Rd. E4 34 D1
Glendower Rd. SW14 74 D3
Glendown Rd. SE2 71 A5
Glendun Rd. W3 56 E7
Gleneagle Ms. SW16 85 D5
Ambleside Ave.
Gleneagle Rd. SW16 85 D6
Gleneagles, Stan. 29 E6
Gleneagles Clo., Orp. 104 G1
Gleneagles Clo., Stan. 29 E6
Gleneagles Clo., Wat. 28 D4
Gleneagles Grn., Orp. 104 G1
Tandridge Dr.
Gleneagles Twr., Sthl. 54 J6
Gleneldon Ms. SW16 85 E4
Gleneldon Rd. SW16 85 E4
Glenelg Rd. SW2 76 E5
Glenesk Rd. SE9 79 D3
Glenfarg Rd. SE6 87 D1
Glenfield Rd. SW12 85 C1
Glenfield Rd. W13 64 E2
Glenfield Ter. W13 64 E1
Glenfinlas Way SE5 20 H7
Glenfinlas Way SE5 67 H7
Glenforth St. SE10 69 F5
Glengall Causeway E14 69 A3
Westferry Rd.
Glengall Gro. E14 69 C3
Glengall Rd. NW6 57 C1
Glengall Rd. SE15 21 G5
Glengall Rd. SE15 68 C5
Glengall Rd., Bexh. 80 E3
Glengall Rd., Edg. 30 B3
Glengall Rd., Wdf.Grn. 34 G6
Glengall Ter. SE15 21 G5
Glengall Ter. SE15 68 C6
Glengarnock Ave. E14 69 C4
Glengarry Rd. SE22 77 B5
Glenham Dr., Ilf. 43 E5
Glenhaven Ave., Borwd. 22 A3
Glenhead Clo. SE9 79 E3
Dumbreck Rd.
Glenhill Clo. N3 39 D2
Glenhouse Rd. SE9 79 D5
Glenhurst Ave. NW5 49 A4
Glenhurst Ave., Bex. 89 F1
Glenhurst Ct. SE19 86 C5
Glenhurst Ri. SE19 85 J7
Glenhurst Rd. N12 31 G5
Glenhurst Rd., Brent. 64 F6
Glenilla Rd. NW3 48 H6
Glenister Ho., Hayes 63 B1
Glenister Pk. Rd. SW16 85 D7
Glenister Rd. SE10 69 F5
Glenister St. E16 70 D1
Glenlea Rd. SE9 79 D5
Glenloch Rd. NW3 48 H6
Glenloch Rd., Enf. 25 F2
Glenluce Rd. SE3 69 G6
Glenlyon Rd. SE9 79 D5
Glenmere Ave. NW7 30 G7
Glenmore Rd. NW3 48 H6
Glenmore Rd., Well. 70 J7
Glenmore Way, Bark. 62 A3
Glenmount Path SE18 70 F5
Raglan Rd.
Glennie Rd. SE27 85 G3
Glenny Rd., Bark. 52 F6
Glenorchy Clo., Hayes 54 E5
Glenparke Rd. E7 51 H6
Glenrosa St. SW6 75 F2
Glenrose Ct., Sid. 89 B5
Glenroy St. W12 56 J6
Glensdale Rd. SE4 77 J3
Glenshiel Rd. SE9 79 D5
Glenside, Chig. 35 E6
Glentanner Way SW17 84 G3
Aboyne Rd.
Glentham Gdns. SW13 65 H6
Glentham Rd.
Glentham Rd. SW13 65 G6
Glenthorne Ave., Croy. 102 E1
Glenthorne Clo., Sutt. 100 D1
Glenthorne Gdns., Ilf. 43 D3
Glenthorne Gdns., Sutt. 100 D1
Glenthorne Rd. E17 41 H5
Glenthorne Rd. N11 31 J5
Glenthorne Rd. W6 65 H4
Glenthorne Rd., Kings.T. 91 J4
Glenthorpe Rd., Mord. 93 A5
Glenton Rd. SE13 78 E4
Glentrammon Ave., Orp. 104 J6
Glentrammon Clo., Orp. 104 J5
Glentrammon Gdns., Orp. 104 J6
Glentrammon Rd., Orp. 104 J6
Glentworth St. NW1 7 A6
Glentworth St. NW1 57 J4
Glenure Rd. SE9 79 D5
Glenview SE2 71 D6
Glenview Rd., Brom. 97 A2
Glenville Gro. SE8 68 J7
Glenville Ms. SW18 75 E7
Glenville Rd., Kings.T. 92 A1
Glenwood Ave. NW9 47 E1
Glenwood Clo., Har. 37 C5
Glenwood Gdns., Ilf. 43 D5
Glenwood Gro. NW9 47 C1
Glenwood Rd. N15 40 H5
Glenwood Rd. NW7 30 E3
Glenwood Rd. SE6 86 J1
Glenwood Rd., Epsom 99 G6
Glenwood Rd., Houns. 73 A3
Glenwood Way, Croy. 95 G6
Glenworth Ave. E14 69 D4
Gliddon Rd. W14 66 B4
Glimpsing Grn., Erith 71 E3
Global App. E3 60 B2
Hancock Rd.
Globe Pond Rd. SE16 68 H1
Globe Rd. E1 59 G4
Globe Rd. E2 59 F3
Globe Rd. E15 51 F5
Globe Rd., Wdf.Grn. 34 J6
Globe Robe Wk. E14 69 C4
East Ferry Rd.
Globe St. SE1 17 B4
Globe St. SE1 68 A2
Globe Ter. E2 59 F3
Globe Rd.
Globe Yd. W1 11 D4
Gloster Rd., N.Mal. 92 E4
Gloucester Ave. NW1 49 A7
Gloucester Ave., Sid. 88 H2
Gloucester Ave., Well. 79 J4
Gloucester Circ. SE10 69 C7
Gloucester Clo. NW10 47 D7
Gloucester Clo., T.Ditt. 98 D1
Gloucester Ct. EC3 13 E6
Gloucester Ct., Rich. 65 A7
Gloucester Cres. NW1 58 B1
Gloucester Dr. N4 49 H2
Gloucester Dr. NW11 39 D4
Gloucester Gdns. NW11 39 C7
Gloucester Gdns. W2 10 B3
Gloucester Gdns., Barn. 24 A4
Gloucester Gdns., Ilf. 43 B7
Gloucester Gdns., Sutt. 100 E2
Gloucester Gate NW1 7 D1
Gloucester Gate NW1 58 B2
Gloucester Gate Ms. NW1 7 D1
Gloucester Gro., Edg. 38 D1
Gloucester Gro. Est. SE15 68 B6
Gloucester Ho. N7 49 E3
Gloucester Ho. NW6 57 D2
Gloucester Ms. W2 10 D4
Gloucester Ms. W2 57 F6
Gloucester Ms. W. W2 10 C4
Gloucester Par., Sid. 80 A5
Gloucester Pl. NW1 6 J5
Gloucester Pl. NW1 57 J4
Gloucester Pl. W1 11 A1
Gloucester Pl. W1 57 J5
Gloucester Pl. Ms. W1 11 A2
Gloucester Rd. E10 42 A7
Gloucester Rd. E11 42 H5
Gloucester Rd. E12 52 C3

Gloucester Rd. E17 41 G2
Gloucester Rd. N17 41 A3
Gloucester Rd. N18 33 C5
Gloucester Rd. SW7 14 C5
Gloucester Rd. SW7 66 F3
Gloucester Rd. W3 65 C2
Gloucester Rd. W5 64 F2
Gloucester Rd., Barn. 23 E5
Gloucester Rd., Belv. 71 F5
Gloucester Rd., Croy. 102 A1
Gloucester Rd., Felt. 81 C1
Gloucester Rd., Hmptn. 81 H7
Gloucester Rd., Har. 36 H5
Gloucester Rd., Houns. 72 E4
Gloucester Rd., Kings.T. 92 A2
Gloucester Rd., Rich. 65 A7
Gloucester Rd., Tedd. 82 B5
Gloucester Rd., Twick. 81 J1
Gloucester Sq. E2 59 D1
Whiston Rd.
Gloucester Sq. W2 10 F4
Gloucester Sq. W2 57 G6
Gloucester St. SW1 19 F4
Gloucester St. SW1 67 C5
Gloucester Ter. W2 10 B3
Gloucester Ter. W2 57 E6
Gloucester Wk. W8 66 D2
Gloucester Way EC1 8 F4
Gloucester Way EC1 58 G3
Glover Dr. N18 33 F6
Glover Rd., Pnr. 36 D6
Gloxinia Wk., Hmptn. 81 G6
The Ave.
Glycena Rd. SW11 75 J3
Glyn Ave., Barn. 23 G4
Glyn Clo. SE25 95 B2
Glyn Ct. SW16 85 G3
Glyn Dr., Sid. 89 B4
Glyn Rd. E5 50 G4
Glyn Rd., Enf. 25 F4
Glyn Rd., Wor.Pk. 100 A2
Glyn St. SE11 20 C4
Glynde Ms. SW3 14 H6
Glynde Rd., Bexh. 80 D3
Glynde St. SE4 77 J6
Glyndebourne Pk., Orp. 104 E2
Glyndon Rd. SE18 70 F4
Glynfield Rd. NW10 47 E7
Glynne Rd. N22 40 G2
Glynwood Dr. SE23 86 F3
Goat La., Surb. 98 E2
Goat Rd., Mitch. 93 J7
Goat St. SE1 17 F3
Goat Wf., Brent. 64 H6
Goaters All. SW6 66 C7
Dawes Rd.
Godalming Ave., Wall. 101 E5
Godalming Rd. E14 60 B5
Godbold Rd. E15 60 E3
Goddard Rd., Beck. 95 G4
Goddards Way, Ilf. 52 G1
Godfrey Ave., Nthlt. 54 E1
Godfrey Ave., Twick. 73 A7
Godfrey Hill SE18 70 B4
Godfrey Rd. SE18 70 C4
Godfrey St. E15 60 C2
Abbey La.
Godfrey St. SW3 18 H3
Godfrey St. SW3 66 H5
Godfrey Way, Houns. 72 F7
Goding St. SE11 20 B4
Goding St. SE11 67 E5
Godley Rd. SW18 84 G1
Godliman St. EC4 12 J4
Godliman St. EC4 58 J6
Godman Rd. SE15 77 E2
Godolphin Clo. N13 32 H6
Godolphin Pl. W3 56 D7
Vyner Rd.
Godolphin Rd. W12 65 H1
Godson Rd., Croy. 101 G3
Godson St. N1 8 E1
Godstone Rd., Sutt. 100 F4
Godstone Rd., Twick. 73 D6
Godstow Rd. SE2 71 B2
Godwin Clo. N1 9 A1
Godwin Clo., Epsom 99 C6
Godwin Ct. NW1 7 G1
Godwin Rd. E7 51 H4
Godwin Rd., Brom. 96 J3
Goffers Rd. SE3 78 E2
Goidel Clo., Wall. 101 D4
Golborne Gdns. W10 57 C4
Golborne Rd.
Golborne Ms. W10 57 B5
Portobello Rd.
Golborne Rd. W10 57 B5
Gold Hill, Edg. 30 D6
Gold La., Edg. 30 D6
Golda Clo., Barn. 23 A6
Goldbeaters Gro., Edg. 30 E6
Goldcliff Clo., Mord. 93 D7
Goldcrest Clo. E16 61 A5
Sheerwater Rd.
Goldcrest Clo. SE28 62 C7
Goldcrest Ms. W5 55 G5
Montpelier Ave.
Goldcrest Way (Bushey), Wat. 28 J1
Golden Ct., Rich. 73 G5
George St.
Golden La. EC1 8 J6
Golden La. EC1 58 J4
Golden La. Est. EC1 8 J6
Golden Manor W7 55 B7
Golden Plover Clo. E16 60 H6
Maplin Rd.
Golden Sq. W1 11 G5
Golden Sq. W1 58 C7
Golden Yd. NW3 48 F4
Heath St.
Golders Clo., Edg. 30 B5
Golders Gdns. NW11 39 B7
Golders Grn. Cres. NW11 39 C7
Golders Grn. Rd. NW11 39 B6
Golders Manor Dr. NW11 39 A6
Golders Pk. Clo. NW11 48 D1
Golders Ri. NW4 39 A5
Golders Way NW11 39 C7
Goldfinch Rd. SE28 70 G3
Goldfinch Way, Borwd. 22 A4
Siskin Clo.
Goldhawk Ms. W12 65 H2
Devonport Rd.
Goldhawk Rd. W6 65 F4
Goldhawk Rd. W12 65 G3
Goldhaze Clo., Wdf.Grn. 35 A7
Goldhurst Ter. NW6 48 E7
Golding Clo., Chess. 98 F6
Mansfield Rd.
Golding St. E1 13 J4
Golding St. E1 59 D6
Goldingham Ave., Loug. 27 F2
Goldings Ri., Loug. 27 D1
Goldings Rd., Loug. 27 D1
Goldington Cres. NW1 7 H1
Goldington Cres. NW1 58 D2
Goldington Cres. Gdns. NW1 58 D2
Goldington St. NW1 7 H1
Goldington St. NW1 58 D2
Goldman Clo. E2 9 H5
Goldman Clo. E2 59 D4
Goldney Rd. W9 57 D4
Goldsborough Cres. E4 34 B2
Goldsborough Rd. SW8 76 D1
Goldsdown Clo., Enf. 25 H2
Goldsdown Rd., Enf. 25 G2
Goldsmid St. SE18 70 H5
Sladedale Rd.
Goldsmith Ave. E12 52 B6
Goldsmith Ave. NW9 38 E5
Goldsmith Ave. W3 56 D7
Goldsmith Ave., Rom. 44 G7
Goldsmith Clo. W3 65 E1
East Acton La.
Goldsmith Clo., Har. 45 H1
Goldsmith La. NW9 38 B4
Goldsmith Rd. E10 51 A1
Goldsmith Rd. E17 41 G2
Goldsmith Rd. N11 31 J5
Goldsmith Rd. SE15 77 D1
Goldsmith Rd. W3 65 D1
Goldsmith St. EC2 13 A3
Goldsmith's Row E2 9 J1
Goldsmith's Row E2 59 D2
Goldsmith's Sq. E2 9 J1
Goldsmith's Sq. E2 59 D2
Goldsworthy Gdns. SE16 68 F4
Goldwell Rd., Th.Hth. 94 F4
Goldwin Clo. SE14 77 F1
Goldwing Clo. E16 60 G6
Golf Clo., Stan. 29 F7
Golf Club Dr., Kings.T. 83 D7
Golf Rd. W5 55 J6
Boileau Rd.
Golf Rd., Brom. 97 D3
Golf Side, Twick. 82 A3
Golfe Rd., Ilf. 52 G3
Golfside Clo. N20 31 H3
Golfside Clo., N.Mal. 92 E2
Goliath Clo., Wall. 101 E7
Avro Way
Gollogly Ter. SE7 69 J5
Gomer Gdns., Tedd. 82 D6
Gomer Pl., Tedd. 82 D6
Gomm Rd. SE16 68 F3
Gomshall Ave., Wall. 101 E5
Gondar Gdns. NW6 48 C5
Gonson Pl. SE8 69 A6
Gonson St. SE8 69 B6
Gonston Clo. SW19 84 B2
Boddicott Clo.
Gonville Cres., Nthlt. 45 H6
Gonville Rd., Th.Hth. 94 F5
Gonville St. SW6 75 B3
Putney Bri. App.
Goodall Rd. E11 51 C3
Gooden Ct., Har. 46 B3
Goodenough Rd. SW19 84 C7
Goodge Pl. W1 11 G2
Goodge St. W1 11 G2
Goodge St. W1 58 C5
Goodhall St. NW10 56 E3
Goodhart Pl. E14 59 H7
Goodhart Way, W.Wick. 96 E7
Goodhew Rd., Croy. 95 D6
Gooding Clo., N.Mal. 92 C4
Goodinge Clo. N7 49 E6
Goodman Cres. SW2 85 D2
Goodman Rd. E10 42 C7
Goodmans Ct., Wem. 46 G4
Goodman's Flds. E1 13 H4
Goodman's Stile E1 13 H3
Goodman's Stile E1 59 D6
Goodmans Yd. E1 13 F5
Goodmans Yd. E1 59 C7
Goodmayes Ave., Ilf. 53 A1
Goodmayes La., Ilf. 53 A2
Goodmayes Rd., Ilf. 53 A1
Goodrich Rd. SE22 77 C6
Goods Way NW1 8 A1
Goods Way NW1 58 E2
Goodson Rd. NW10 47 E7
Goodway Gdns. E14 60 D6
Goodwin Clo. SE16 17 G6
Goodwin Clo. SE16 68 D3
Goodwin Clo., Mitch. 93 G3
Goodwin Dr., Sid. 89 D3
Goodwin Gdns., Croy. 101 H6
Goodwin Rd. N9 33 F1
Goodwin Rd. W12 65 G2
Goodwin Rd., Croy. 101 H5
Goodwin St. N4 49 G2
Fonthill Rd.
Goodwins Ct. WC2 12 A5
Goodwood Clo., Mord. 93 D4
Goodwood Clo., Stan. 29 F5
Goodwood Dr., Nthlt. 45 G6
Goodwood Path, Borwd. 22 A3
Stratfield Rd.
Goodwood Rd. SE14 68 H7
Goodwyn Ave. NW7 30 E5
Goodwyns Vale N10 40 A1
Goodyers Gdns. NW4 39 A5
Goosander Way SE28 70 G3
Goose Sq. E6 61 C6
Harper Rd.
Gooseacre La., Har. 37 G5
Gooseley La. E6 61 D3
Goossens Clo., Sutt. 100 F5
Turnpike La.
Gophir La. EC4 13 B5
Gopsall St. N1 59 A1
Gordon Ave. E4 34 E6
Gordon Ave. SW14 74 E4
Gordon Ave., Stan. 29 C7
Gordon Ave., Twick. 73 D5
Gordon Clo. E17 42 A6
Gordon Clo. N19 49 C1
Highgate Hill
Gordon Ct. W12 56 H6
Gordon Cres., Croy. 102 B1
Gordon Cres., Hayes 63 A3
Gordon Gdns., Edg. 38 B2
Gordon Gro. SE5 76 H2
Gordon Hill, Enf. 24 J1
Gordon Ho. Rd. NW5 49 A4
Gordon Pl. W8 66 D2
Gordon Rd. E4 26 E7
Gordon Rd. E11 42 G6
Gordon Rd. E15 51 C4
Gordon Rd. E18 42 H1
Gordon Rd. N3 31 C7
Gordon Rd. N9 33 E2
Gordon Rd. N11 32 D7
Gordon Rd. SE15 77 E2
Gordon Rd. W4 65 B6
Gordon Rd. W5 55 F7
Gordon Rd. W13 55 E7
Gordon Rd., Bark. 61 H1
Gordon Rd., Beck. 95 J3
Gordon Rd., Belv. 71 J4
Gordon Rd., Cars. 100 J6
Gordon Rd., Enf. 25 A1
Gordon Rd., Esher 98 B7
Gordon Rd., Har. 37 B3
Gordon Rd., Houns. 72 J4
Gordon Rd., Ilf. 52 G3
Gordon Rd., Kings.T. 91 J1
Gordon Rd., Rich. 73 J2
Gordon Rd., Rom. 44 F6
Gordon Rd., Sid. 79 H5
Gordon Rd., Sthl. 63 E4
Gordon Rd., Surb. 91 J7
Gordon Sq. WC1 7 H5
Gordon Sq. WC1 58 D4
Gordon St. E13 60 G3
Grange Rd.
Gordon St. WC1 7 H5
Gordon St. WC1 58 D4
Gordon Way, Barn. 23 C4
Gordon Way, Brom. 96 G1
Gordonbrock Rd. SE4 78 A5
Gordondale Rd. SW19 84 D2
Gore Ct. NW9 38 A5
Gore Rd. E9 59 F1
Gore Rd. SW20 92 J2
Gore St. SW7 14 D5
Gore St. SW7 66 F3
Gorefield Pl. NW6 57 D2
Goresbrook Rd., Dag. 62 B1
Gorham Pl. W11 57 B7
Mary Pl.
Goring Clo., Rom. 44 J1
Goring Gdns., Dag. 53 C4
Goring Rd. N11 32 E6
Goring St. EC3 13 E3
Goring St. EC3 59 B6
Goring Way, Grnf. 54 J2
Gorleston Rd. N15 41 A5
Gorleston St. W14 66 B4
Gorman Rd. SE18 70 C4
Gorringe Pk. Ave., Mitch. 84 J7
Gorse Ri. SW17 85 A5
Gorse Rd., Croy. 103 A3
Gorst Rd. NW10 56 C4
Gorst Rd. SW11 75 J6
Gorsuch Pl. E2 9 F3
Gorsuch St. E2 9 F3
Gorsuch St. E2 59 C3
Gosberton Rd. SW12 84 J1
Gosbury Hill, Chess. 98 H4
Gosfield Rd., Dag. 53 G2
Gosfield St. W1 11 F1
Gosfield St. W1 58 C5
Gosford Gdns., Ilf. 43 C5
Gosforth La., Wat. 28 A3
Gosforth Path, Wat. 28 A3
Gosforth La.
Goslett Yd. WC2 11 J4
Gosling Clo., Grnf. 54 G3
Gosling Way SW9 76 G1
Gospatrick Rd. N17 32 J7
Gospel Oak Est. NW5 48 J5
Gosport Rd. E17 41 J5
Gosport Way SE15 21 F7
Gossage Rd. SE18 70 G5
Ancona Rd.
Gosset St. E2 9 G4
Gosset St. E2 59 C3
Gosshill Rd., Chis. 97 D2
Gossington Clo., Chis. 88 E4
Beechwood Ri.
Gosterwood St. SE8 68 H6
Gostling Rd., Twick. 81 G1
Goston Gdns., Th.Hth. 94 G3
Goswell Rd. EC1 8 G2
Goswell Rd. EC1 58 H2
Gothic Rd., Twick. 82 A2
Goudhurst Rd., Brom. 87 E5

Gough Rd. E15   51 F4
Gough Rd., Enf.   25 E2
Gough Sq. EC4   **12 F3**
Gough St. WC1   **8 D5**
Gough St. WC1   58 F4
Gough Wk. E14   60 A6
  Saracen St.
Gould Ct. SE19   86 B5
Gould Rd., Twick.   82 B1
Gould Ter. E8   50 E5
  Kenmure Rd.
Goulston St. E1   **13 F3**
Goulston St. E1   59 C6
Goulton Rd. E5   50 E4
Gourley Pl. N15   41 B5
  Gourley St.
Gourley St. N15   41 B5
Gourock Rd. SE9   79 D5
Govan St. E2   59 D1
  Whiston Rd.
Govier Clo. E15   51 E7
Gowan Ave. SW6   75 B1
Gowan Rd. NW10   47 H6
Gower Ct. WC1   **7 H5**
Gower Ms. WC1   **11 J2**
Gower Ms. WC1   58 D5
Gower Pl. WC1   **7 G5**
Gower Pl. WC1   58 C4
Gower Rd. E7   51 G6
Gower Rd., Islw.   64 C6
Gower St. WC1   **7 H6**
Gower St. WC1   58 C4
Gower's Wk. E1   **13 H3**
Gower's Wk. E1   59 D6
Gowland Pl., Beck.   95 J2
Gowlett Rd. SE15   77 D3
Gowrie Rd. SW11   76 A3
Graburn Way, E.Mol.   91 A3
Grace Ave., Bexh.   80 F2
Grace Clo. SE9   88 A3
Grace Clo., Borwd.   22 D1
Grace Clo., Edg.   30 C7
  Pavilion Way
Grace Clo., Ilf.   35 J6
Grace Jones Clo. E8   50 D6
  Parkholme Rd.
Grace Path SE26   86 F4
  Silverdale
Grace Rd., Croy.   94 J6
Grace St. E3   60 B3
Gracechurch St. EC3   **13 C5**
Gracechurch St. EC3   59 C4
Gracedale Rd. SW16   85 B5
Gracefield Gdns.   85 E3
  SW16
Grace's All. E1   **13 H5**
Graces Ms. SE5   77 A2
Graces Rd. SE5   77 B2
Gradient, The SE26   86 D4
Graeme Rd., Enf.   25 A2
Graemesdyke Ave.   74 B3
  SW14
Grafton Clo. W13   55 D6
Grafton Clo., Houns.   81 E1
Grafton Clo., Wor.Pk.   99 E3
Grafton Cres. NW1   49 B6
Grafton Gdns. N4   40 J6
Grafton Gdns., Dag.   53 E2
Grafton Ho. E3   60 A3
  Wellington Way
Grafton Ms. W1   **7 F6**
Grafton Pk. Rd.,   99 E2
  Wor.Pk.
Grafton Pl. NW1   **7 H4**
Grafton Pl. NW1   58 D3
Grafton Rd. NW5   49 A5
Grafton Rd. W3   56 C7
Grafton Rd., Croy.   101 G1
Grafton Rd., Dag.   53 E1
Grafton Rd., Enf.   24 F3
Grafton Rd., Har.   36 J5
Grafton Rd., N.Mal.   92 E3
Grafton Rd., Wor.Pk.   99 D4
Grafton Sq. SW4   76 C3
Grafton St. W1   **11 E6**
Grafton St. W1   58 B7
Grafton Ter. NW5   48 J5
Grafton Way W1   **7 F6**
Grafton Way W1   58 C4
Grafton Way WC1   **7 G6**
Grafton Way WC1   58 C4
Grafton Way, W.Mol.   90 F4
Grafton Yd. NW5   49 B6
  Prince of Wales Rd.
Graftons, The NW2   48 D3
  Hermitage La.
Graham Ave. W13   64 E2
Graham Ave., Mitch.   94 A1

Graham Clo., Croy.   103 A2
Graham Gdns., Surb.   98 H1
Graham Rd. E8   50 D6
Graham Rd. E13   60 G3
Graham Rd. N15   40 H3
Graham Rd. NW4   38 H6
Graham Rd. SW19   84 C7
Graham Rd. W4   65 D3
Graham Rd., Bexh.   80 G4
Graham Rd., Hmptn.   81 G4
Graham Rd., Har.   37 B3
Graham Rd., Mitch.   94 A1
Graham St. N1   **8 H2**
Graham St. N1   58 H2
Graham Ter. SW1   **19 B2**
Graham Ter. SW1   67 A4
Grahame Pk. Est. NW9   30 F7
Grahame Pk. Way   30 F7
  NW7
Grahame Pk. Way   38 F2
  NW9
Grainger Clo., Nthlt.   45 J5
  Lancaster Rd.
Grainger Rd. N22   40 J1
Grainger Rd., Islw.   73 C2
Gramer Clo. E11   51 D2
Grampian Clo., Orp.   97 J6
  Cotswold Ri.
Grampian Gdns. NW2   48 B1
Granard Ave. SW15   74 H5
Granard Rd. SW12   75 J7
Granary Clo. N9   25 F7
  Turin Rd.
Granary St. NW1   58 D1
Granby Bldgs. SE11   **20 C2**
Granby Rd. SE9   79 C2
Granby St. E2   **9 H5**
Granby St. E2   59 C4
Granby Ter. NW1   **7 F2**
Granby Ter. NW1   58 C2
Grand Ave. EC1   **12 H1**
Grand Ave. N10   40 A4
Grand Ave., Surb.   92 B5
Grand Ave., Wem.   47 A5
Grand Ave. E., Wem.   47 A6
  Victoria Ave.
Grand Depot Rd. SE18   70 D5
Grand Dr. SW20   92 J2
Grand Dr., Sthl.   63 E2
Grand Par. Ms. SW15   75 B5
  Upper Richmond Rd.
Grand Union Cres. E8   59 D1
Grand Union Ind. Est.   56 B2
  NW10
Grand Union Wk.   49 B7
  NW1
Grand Wk. E1   59 H4
  Solebay St.
Granden Rd. SW16   94 E2
Grandison Rd. SW11   75 J5
Grandison Rd.,   99 J2
  Wor.Pk.
Granfield St. SW11   75 G1
Grange, The N2   39 G2
  Central Ave.
Grange, The N20   31 F1
Grange, The SE1   **17 F5**
Grange, The SE1   68 C3
Grange, The SW19   84 A6
Grange, The, Croy.   102 J2
Grange, The, Wem.   47 A7
Grange, The, Wor.Pk.   99 D3
Grange Ave. N12   31 F5
Grange Ave. N20   23 B7
Grange Ave. SE25   95 B2
Grange Ave., Barn.   31 H1
Grange Ave., Stan.   37 E2
Grange Ave., Twick.   82 B2
Grange Ave.,   34 G6
  Wdf.Grn.
Grange Clo., Edg.   30 C5
Grange Clo., Houns.   63 F6
Grange Clo., Sid.   89 A3
Grange Clo., W.Mol.   90 H4
Grange Clo., Wdf.Grn.   34 G7
Grange Ct. E8   50 C7
  Queensbridge Rd.
Grange Ct. WC2   **12 D4**
Grange Ct., Chig.   35 F2
Grange Ct., Loug.   27 A5
Grange Ct., Nthlt.   54 C2
Grange Cres. SE28   62 C6
Grange Cres., Chig.   35 G5
Grange Dr., Chis.   88 B2
Grange Fm. Clo., Har.   45 J2
Grange Gdns. N14   32 D1
Grange Gdns. NW3   48 E3
Grange Gdns. SE25   95 B2

Grange Gdns., Pnr.   36 E3
Grange Gro. N1   49 J6
Grange Hill SE25   95 B2
Grange Hill, Edg.   30 C5
Grange Ho., Bark.   61 G1
  St. Margarets
Grange La. SE21   86 C2
Grange Mans., Epsom   99 F7
Grange Ms. SE10   69 D7
  Crooms Hill
Grange Pk. W5   64 H1
Grange Pk. Ave. N21   24 J6
Grange Pk. Pl. SW20   83 H7
Grange Pk. Rd. E10   51 B1
Grange Pk. Rd.,   95 A4
  Th.Hth.
Grange Pl. NW6   48 D7
Grange Rd. E10   51 A1
Grange Rd. E13   60 F3
Grange Rd. E17   41 H5
Grange Rd. N6   40 A6
Grange Rd. N17   33 D6
Grange Rd. N18   33 D6
Grange Rd. NW10   47 H6
Grange Rd. SE1   **17 E6**
Grange Rd. SE1   68 B3
Grange Rd. SE19   95 A2
Grange Rd. SE25   95 A3
Grange Rd. SW13   74 G1
Grange Rd. W4   65 B5
Grange Rd. W5   64 G1
Grange Rd., Chess.   98 H3
Grange Rd., Edg.   30 D6
Grange Rd., Har.   37 D6
  (Greenhill)
Grange Rd.,Har.   46 A2
  (Roxeth)
Grange Rd., Ilf.   52 E4
Grange Rd., Kings.T.   91 H3
Grange Rd., Orp.   104 F2
Grange Rd., Sthl.   63 E2
Grange Rd., Sutt.   100 D7
Grange Rd., Th.Hth.   95 A4
Grange Rd., W.Mol.   90 H4
Grange Vale, Sutt.   100 E7
Grange Wk. SE1   **17 E5**
Grange Wk. SE1   68 B3
Grange Way N12   31 E4
Grange Yd. SE1   **17 F6**
Grange Yd. SE1   68 C3
Grangecliffe Gdns.   95 B2
  SE25
Grangecourt Rd. N16   50 B1
Grangehill Pl. SE9   79 C3
  Westmount Rd.
Grangehill Rd. SE9   79 C4
Grangemill Rd. SE6   87 A3
Grangemill Way SE6   87 A2
Grangeview Rd. N20   31 F1
Grangeway NW6   48 D7
  Messina Ave.
Grangeway, Wdf.Grn.   34 J4
Grangeway, The N21   24 H6
Grangeway Gdns., Ilf.   43 B5
Grangewood, Bex.   89 F1
  Hurst Rd.
Grangewood Clo.,   36 A5
  Pnr.
Grangewood La.,   86 J6
  Beck.
Grangewood St. E6   61 A1
Granham Gdns. N9   33 C2
Granite St. SE18   70 J5
Granleigh Rd. E11   51 E2
Gransden Ave. E8   50 E7
Gransden Rd. W12   65 F2
  Wendell Rd.
Grant Clo. N14   24 C7
Grant Pl., Croy.   102 C1
Grant Rd. SW11   75 G4
Grant Rd., Croy.   102 C1
Grant Rd., Har.   37 B3
Grant St. E13   60 G3
Grant St. N1   **8 E1**
Grant Way, Islw.   64 D7
Grantbridge St. N1   **8 H1**
Grantbridge St. N1   58 H2
Grantchester Clo.,   46 C3
  Har.
Grantham Clo., Edg.   29 H3
Grantham Gdns.,   44 F6
  Rom.
Grantham Grn.,   22 C5
  Borwd.
Grantham Pl. W1   **15 D2**
Grantham Rd. E12   52 D4
Grantham Rd. SW9   76 E3
Grantham Rd. W4   65 E7

Grantley Rd., Houns.   72 C2
Grantley St. E1   59 G3
Grantock Rd. E17   42 D1
Granton Rd. SW16   94 C1
Granton Rd., Ilf.   53 A1
Granton Rd., Sid.   89 C6
Grants Clo. NW7   30 J7
Grantully Rd. W9   **6 A4**
Grantully Rd. W9   57 E3
Granville Ave. N9   33 F3
Granville Ave., Felt.   81 A2
Granville Ave.,   72 G5
  Houns.
Granville Clo., Croy.   102 B2
Granville Ct. N1   59 A1
Granville Gdns. SW16   94 F1
Granville Gdns. W5   64 J1
Granville Gro. SE13   78 C3
Granville Ms., Sid.   89 A4
Granville Pk. SE13   78 C3
Granville Pl. N12   31 F7
  (North Finchley)
  High Rd.
Granville Pl. W1   **11 B4**
Granville Pl. W1   58 A6
Granville Rd. E17   42 B6
Granville Rd. E18   42 H2
Granville Rd. N4   40 F6
Granville Rd. N12   31 E6
Granville Rd. N13   32 F6
  Russell Rd.
Granville Rd. N22   40 H1
Granville Rd. NW2   48 C2
Granville Rd. NW6   57 D2
Granville Rd. SW18   75 C7
Granville Rd. SW19   84 D7
  Russell Rd.
Granville Rd., Barn.   22 J4
Granville Rd., Ilf.   52 E1
Granville Rd., Sid.   89 A4
Granville Rd., Well.   80 C3
Granville Sq. SE15   **21 E7**
Granville Sq. WC1   **8 D4**
Granville Sq. WC1   58 F3
Granville St. WC1   **8 D4**
Granville St. WC1   58 F3
Grape St. WC2   **12 A3**
Graphite Sq. SE11   **20 C3**
Grasdene Rd. SE18   71 A7
Grasmere Ave. SW15   83 D4
Grasmere Ave. SW19   93 D3
Grasmere Ave. W3   56 D7
Grasmere Ave.,   72 H6
  Houns.
Grasmere Ave., Orp.   104 E3
Grasmere Ave., Wem.   37 F7
Grasmere Clo., Loug.   27 C2
Grasmere Ct. N22   32 F6
  Palmerston Rd.
Grasmere Gdns., Har.   37 D2
Grasmere Gdns., Ilf.   43 C5
Grasmere Gdns.,   104 E3
  Orp.
Grasmere Rd. E13   60 G2
Grasmere Rd. N10   40 B1
Grasmere Rd. N17   33 D6
Grasmere Rd. SE25   95 E6
Grasmere Rd. SW16   85 F5
Grasmere Rd., Bexh.   80 J1
Grasmere Rd., Brom.   96 F1
Grasmere Rd., Orp.   104 E3
Grass Pk. N3   39 C1
Grassington Rd., Sid.   89 A4
Grassmount SE23   86 J2
Grassway, Wall.   101 C4
Grasvenor Ave., Barn.   23 E6
Grately Way SE15   **21 F7**
Gratton Rd. W14   66 B3
Gratton Ter. NW2   48 A3
Gravel Hill N3   39 C2
Gravel Hill, Bexh.   80 H5
Gravel Hill, Croy.   102 H5
Gravel Hill Clo., Bexh.   80 H5
Gravel La. E1   **13 F3**
Gravel La., Chig.   27 J4
Gravel Pit La. SE9   79 F5
Gravel Rd., Brom.   104 B3
Gravel Rd., Twick.   82 B1
Graveley Ave.,   22 C4
  Borwd.
Gravelly Ride SW19   83 F4
Gravelwood Clo.,   88 F3
  Chis.
Graveney Gro. SE20   86 F5
Graveney Rd. SW17   84 H4
Gravesend Rd. W12   56 G7
Gray Ave., Dag.   53 F1
Gray St. SE1   **16 F4**

Grayham Cres., N.Mal.	92	D4
Grayham Rd., N.Mal.	92	D4
Grayland Clo., Brom.	97	A1
Grayling Clo. E16	60	E4
Cranberry La.		
Grayling Rd. N16	50	A2
Gray's Inn Pl. WC1	**12**	**D2**
Gray's Inn Rd. WC1	**8**	**B3**
Gray's Inn Rd. WC1	58	E3
Gray's Inn Sq. WC1	**12**	**E1**
Gray's Yd. W1	**11**	**C3**
Grayscroft Rd. SW16	85	D7
Grayshott Rd. SW11	76	A2
Grayswood Gdns. SW20	92	H2
Farnham Gdns.		
Graywood Ct. N12	31	F7
Grazebrook Rd. N16	50	A2
Grazeley Clo., Bexh.	80	J5
Grazeley Ct. SE19	86	B4
Gipsy Hill		
Great Acre Ct. SW4	76	D4
St. Alphonsus Rd.		
Great Bell All. EC2	**13**	**B3**
Great Brownings SE21	86	C4
Great Bushey Dr. N20	31	E1
Great Cambridge Rd. N9	33	A3
Great Cambridge Rd. N17	33	A7
Great Cambridge Rd. N18	33	A4
Great Cambridge Rd., Enf.	25	D3
Great Castle St. W1	**11**	**E3**
Great Castle St. W1	58	B6
Great Cen. Ave., Ruis.	45	C5
Great Cen. St. NW1	**10**	**J1**
Great Cen. St. NW1	57	J5
Great Cen. Way NW10	47	C4
Great Chapel St. W1	**11**	**H3**
Great Chapel St. W1	58	D6
Great Chertsey Rd. W4	74	C2
Great Chertsey Rd., Felt.	81	G3
Great Ch. La. W6	66	A5
Great College St. SW1	**16**	**A5**
Great College St. SW1	67	E3
Great Cross Ave. SE10	69	E7
Great Cumberland Ms. W1	**10**	**J4**
Great Cumberland Pl. W1	**11**	**A3**
Great Cumberland Pl. W1	57	J6
Great Dover St. SE1	**17**	**B4**
Great Dover St. SE1	68	A2
Great Eastern Rd. E15	51	D7
Great Eastern St. EC2	**9**	**D4**
Great Eastern St. EC2	59	B3
Great Eastern Wk. EC2	**13**	**.D2**
Great Elms Rd., Brom.	96	J4
Great Fld. NW9	38	E1
Great George St. SW1	**15**	**J4**
Great George St. SW1	67	D2
Great Guildford St. SE1	**16**	**J2**
Great Guildford St. SE1	67	J1
Great Harry Dr. SE9	88	D3
Great James St. WC1	**12**	**C1**
Great James St. WC1	58	F5
Great Marlborough St. W1	**11**	**F4**
Great Marlborough St. W1	58	C6
Great Maze Pond SE1	**17**	**C3**
Great Maze Pond SE1	68	A1
Great New St. EC4	**12**	**F3**
Great Newport St. WC2	**11**	**J5**
Great N. Rd. N2	39	H4
Great N. Rd. N6	39	J5
Great N. Rd., Barn.	23	C2
Great N. Way NW4	38	H1
Great Oaks, Chig.	35	F4
Great Ormond St. WC1	**12**	**B1**
Great Ormond St. WC1	58	E5
Great Owl Rd., Chig.	35	D3
Great Percy St. WC1	**8**	**D3**
Great Percy St. WC1	58	J3
Great Peter St. SW1	**15**	**H6**
Great Peter St. SW1	67	D3

Great Portland St. W1	11	E1
Great Portland St. W1	58	B4
Great Pulteney St. W1	**11**	**G5**
Great Queen St. WC2	**12**	**B4**
Great Queen St. WC2	58	E6
Great Russell St. WC1	**11**	**J3**
Great Russell St. WC1	58	D6
Great St. Helens EC3	**13**	**D3**
Great St. Thomas Apostle EC4	**13**	**A5**
Great Scotland Yd. SW1	**16**	**A1**
Great Scotland Yd. SW1	67	E1
Great Smith St. SW1	**15**	**J5**
Great Smith St. SW1	67	D3
Great Spilmans SE22	77	B5
Great Strand NW9	38	F1
Great Suffolk St. SE1	**15**	**H2**
Great Suffolk St. SE1	67	H1
Great Sutton St. EC1	**8**	**H6**
Great Sutton St. EC1	58	A4
Great Swan All. EC2	**13**	**B3**
Great Thrift, Orp.	97	F4
Great Titchfield St. W1	**11**	**F1**
Great Titchfield St. W1	58	C5
Great Twr. St. EC3	**13**	**D5**
Great Twr. St. EC3	59	B7
Great Trinity La. EC4	**13**	**A5**
Great Turnstile WC1	**12**	**D2**
Great W. Rd. W4	65	B5
Great W. Rd. W6	65	G5
Great W. Rd., Brent.	65	B5
Great W. Rd., Houns.	72	E2
Great W. Rd., Islw.	64	A7
Great Western Ind. Pk., Sthl.	63	H2
Great Western Rd. W9	57	C5
Great Western Rd. W11	57	C5
Great Winchester St. EC2	**13**	**C3**
Great Winchester St. EC2	59	A6
Great Windmill St. W1	**11**	**H5**
Great Windmill St. W1	58	D7
Great Yd. SE1	**17**	**E3**
Greatdown Rd. W7	55	C4
Greatfield Ave. E6	61	C4
Greatfield Clo. N19	49	C4
Warrender Rd.		
Greatfield Clo. SE4	78	A4
Greatfields Rd., Bark.	61	G1
Greatham Wk. SW15	83	G1
Bessborough Rd.		
Greatorex St. E1	**13**	**H1**
Greatorex St. E1	59	D5
Greatwood, Chis.	88	D7
Greaves Clo., Bark.	52	H7
Norfolk Rd.		
Greaves Pl. SW17	84	H4
Grebe Clo. E7	51	F5
Cormorant Rd.		
Grebe Clo. E17	33	H7
Banbury Rd.		
Grecian Cres. SE19	85	H6
Gredo Ho., Bark.	62	B3
Greek Ct. W1	**11**	**J4**
Greek St. W1	**11**	**J4**
Greek St. W1	58	D6
Greek Yd. WC2	**12**	**A5**
Green, The E4	34	C1
Green, The E11	42	H6
Green, The E15	51	E6
Green, The N9	33	D2
Green, The N14	32	D3
Green, The N21	24	G7
Green, The SW19	84	A5
Green, The W3	56	E6
Green, The W5	64	G1
The Gro.		
Green, The, Bexh.	80	G1
Green, The, Brom.	96	G7
Green, The, Cars.	101	A4
Green, The, Esher	98	C6
Green, The, Felt.	81	B2
Green, The, Houns.	63	G6
Heston Rd.		
Green, The, Mord.	93	B4
Green, The, N.Mal.	92	C3
Green, The, Orp.	89	B7
(St. Paul's Cray)		
The Ave.		
Green, The, Rich.	73	G5

Green, The, Sid.	89	A4
Green, The, Sthl.	63	E3
Green, The, Sutt.	100	E3
Green, The, Twick.	82	B2
Green, The, Well.	79	H4
Green, The, Wem.	46	D2
Green, The, Wdf.Grn.	34	G5
Green Acres, Croy.	102	C3
Green Ave. NW7	30	D4
Green Ave. W13	64	E3
Green Bank E1	68	E1
Green Bank N12	31	E4
Green Clo. NW9	38	C6
Green Clo. NW11	39	F7
Green Clo., Brom.	96	E3
Green Clo., Cars.	100	J2
Green Clo., Felt.	81	E5
Green Cft., Edg.	30	C5
Deans La.		
Green Dale SE22	77	B5
Green Dale Clo. SE22	77	B5
Green Dale		
Green Dragon Ct. SE1	**17**	**B1**
Green Dragon La. N21	24	G5
Green Dragon La., Brent.	64	H5
Green Dragon Yd. E1	**13**	**H2**
Green Dr., Sthl.	63	G1
Green End N21	32	H2
Green End, Chess.	98	H4
Green Gdns., Orp.	104	F5
Green Hill SE18	70	C5
Green Hill, Buck.H.	34	J1
Green Hill Ter. SE18	70	C5
Green Hundred Rd. SE15	**21**	**J6**
Green Hundred Rd. SE15	68	D6
Green La. E4	26	D3
Green La. NW4	39	A4
Green La. SE9	88	E1
Green La. SE20	86	G7
Green La. SW16	85	F7
Green La. W7	64	B2
Green La., Chig.	35	F1
Green La., Chis.	88	E3
Green La., Dag.	53	D2
Green La., Edg.	29	J4
Green La., Felt.	81	E5
Green La., Har.	46	B3
Green La., Houns.	72	B3
Green La., Ilf.	52	F2
Green La., Mord.	93	D6
Green La., N.Mal.	92	C5
Green La., Stan.	29	E4
Green La., Th.Hth.	94	H1
Green La., Wat.	28	C1
Green La., W.Mol.	90	H5
Green La., Wor.Pk.	99	G1
Green La. Gdns., Th.Hth.	94	H2
Green Las. N4	40	H7
Green Las. N8	40	H3
Green Las. N13	32	F6
Green Las. N15	40	H3
Green Las. N16	49	J3
Green Las. N21	32	H2
Green Lawns, Ruis.	45	C1
Green Leaf Ave., Wall.	101	D4
Green Man Gdns. W13	55	D7
Green Man La. W13	55	D7
Green Man La., Felt.	72	A4
Green Moor Link N21	24	H7
Green Pt. E15	51	E6
Green Pond Clo. E17	41	H3
Green Pond Rd. E17	41	H3
Green Ride, Loug.	26	G5
Green Rd. N14	24	B6
Green Rd. N20	31	F3
Green Shield Ind. Est. E16	69	G1
Green St. E7	51	H6
Green St. E13	51	J7
Green St. W1	**11**	**A5**
Green St. W1	57	J7
Green St., Enf.	25	F2
Green St., Sun.	90	A1
Green Vale W5	55	J4
Green Vale, Bexh.	80	D5
Green Verges, Stan.	29	G7
Green Vw., Chess.	98	J7
Green Wk. NW4	39	A5
Green Wk. SE1	**17**	**D6**
Green Wk., Hmptn.	81	F6
Orpwood Clo.		

Green Wk., Sthl.	63	G5
Green Wk., Wdf.Grn.	35	B6
Green Wk. The E4	34	C1
Green Way SE9	79	A5
Green Way, Brom.	97	B6
Green Way, Sun.	90	A4
Green Wrythe Cres. Cars.	100	H1
Green Wrythe La., Cars.	93	G6
Greenacre Gdns. E17	42	C4
Greenacre Sq. SE16	68	G2
Fishermans Dr.		
Greenacre Wk. N14	32	E3
Greenacres SE9	79	D6
Greenacres (Bushey), Wat.	29	A2
Greenacres Clo., Nthlt.	45	F5
Eastcote La.		
Greenacres Clo., Orp.	104	F4
State Fm. Ave.		
Greenacres Dr., Stan.	29	E6
Greenaway Gdns. NW3	48	E4
Greenbank Ave., Wem.	46	D5
Greenbank Clo. E4	34	C2
Greenbank Cres. NW4	39	B4
Greenbay Rd. SE7	70	A7
Greenberry St. NW8	**6**	**G2**
Greenberry St. NW8	57	H2
Greenbrook Ave., Barn.	23	F1
Greencoat Pl. SW1	**19**	**G1**
Greencoat Pl. SW1	67	C4
Greencoat Row SW1	**15**	**G6**
Greencourt Ave., Croy.	102	E2
Greencourt Ave., Edg.	38	B1
Greencourt Gdns., Croy.	102	E1
Greencourt Rd., Orp.	97	G5
Greencrest Pl. NW2	47	H3
Dollis Hill La.		
Greencroft Ave., Ruis.	45	C2
Greencroft Clo. E6	61	B5
Neatscourt Rd.		
Greencroft Gdns. NW6	48	E7
Greencroft Gdns., Enf.	25	B3
Greencroft Rd., Houns.	72	F1
Greenend Rd. W4	65	E2
Greenfarm Clo., Orp.	104	J5
Greenfell St. SE10	69	E3
Greenfield Ave., Surb.	92	B7
Greenfield Ave., Wat.	28	D2
Greenfield Gdns. NW2	48	B2
Greenfield Gdns., Dag.	62	D1
Greenfield Gdns., Orp.	97	G7
Greenfield Rd. E1	**13**	**J2**
Greenfield Rd. E1	59	D5
Greenfield Rd. N15	41	B5
Greenfield Rd., Dag.	53	C7
Greenfield Way, Har.	36	H3
Greenfields, Loug.	27	D4
Greenfields Clo., Loug.	27	D4
Greenford Ave. W7	55	B4
Greenford Ave., Sthl.	54	F7
Greenford Gdns., Grnf.	54	H3
Greenford Rd., Grnf.	54	J6
Greenford Rd., Har.	46	C4
Greenford Rd., Sthl.	54	J6
Greenford Rd., Sutt.	100	E4
Greengate, Grnf.	46	E6
Greengate St. E13	60	H2
Greenhalgh Wk. N2	39	F4
Greenham Clo. SE1	**16**	**E4**
Greenham Clo. SE1	67	G2
Greenham Rd. N10	40	A2
Greenheys Dr. E18	42	F3
Greenhill NW3	48	G4
Hampstead High St.		
Greenhill, Sutt.	100	F2
Greenhill, Wem.	47	B2
Greenhill Gdns., Nthlt.	54	F7
Greenhill Gro. E12	52	B4
Greenhill Pk. NW10	56	E1
Greenhill Pk., Barn.	23	E5
Greenhill Rents EC1	**12**	**G1**
Greenhill Rd. NW10	56	E1

Greenhill Rd., Har.	37	B6
Greenhill Ter., Nthlt.	54	F2
Greenhill Way, Har.	37	B6
Greenhill Way, S.Croy.	102	G4
Greenhill Way, Wem.	47	B2
Greenhills Ter. N1	50	A6
Baxter Rd.		
Greenhithe Clo., Sid.	79	H7
Greenholm Rd. SE9	79	E5
Greenhurst Rd. SE27	85	G5
Greening St. SE2	71	C4
Greenland Cres., Sthl.	63	C3
Greenland Ms. SE8	68	G5
Trundleys Rd.		
Greenland Pl. NW1	58	B1
Greenland Rd.		
Greenland Quay SE16	68	G4
Greenland Rd. NW1	58	B1
Greenland Rd., Barn.	22	A6
Greenland St. NW1	58	B1
Camden High St.		
Greenlaw Gdns., N.Mal.	92	F7
Greenlaw St. SE18	70	D3
Greenlea Trd. Pk. SW19	93	G1
Greenleaf Clo. SW2	76	G7
Tulse Hill		
Greenleaf Rd. E6	60	J1
Redclyffe Rd.		
Greenleaf Rd. E17	41	J3
Greenleafe Dr., Ilf.	43	E3
Greenman St. N1	49	J7
Greenmoor Rd., Enf.	25	F2
Greenoak Way SW19	84	A4
Greenock Rd. SW16	94	D1
Greenock Rd. W3	65	B3
Greens Clo., The, Loug.	27	D2
Green's Ct. W1	**11**	**H5**
Green's End SE18	70	E4
Greenshank Clo. E17	33	H7
Banbury Rd.		
Greenside, Bex.	89	E1
Greenside, Dag.	53	C1
Greenside Clo. N20	31	G2
Greenside Rd. W12	65	G3
Greenside Rd., Croy.	94	G7
Greenstead Ave., Wdf.Grn.	34	J7
Greenstead Clo., Wdf.Grn.	34	J6
Greenstead Gdns.		
Greenstead Gdns. SW15	74	G5
Greenstead Gdns., Wdf.Grn.	34	J6
Greensted Rd., Loug.	27	B7
Greenstone Ms. E11	42	G6
Greenvale Rd. SE9	79	C4
Greenview Ave., Beck.	95	H6
Greenview Ave., Croy.	95	H6
Greenway N14	32	E2
Greenway N20	31	D2
Greenway SW20	92	J4
Greenway, Chis.	88	D5
Greenway, Dag.	53	C2
Greenway, Har.	37	H5
Greenway, Hayes	54	A3
Greenway, Pnr.	36	B5
Greenway, Wall.	101	C4
Greenway, Wdf.Grn.	34	J5
Greenway, The NW9	38	D2
Greenway, The, Har.	37	B1
Greenway, The, Houns.	72	F4
Greenway, The, Pnr.	36	F6
Greenway Ave. E17	42	D4
Greenway Clo. N4	49	J2
Greenway Clo. N11	32	A6
Greenway Clo. N15	41	C4
Copperfield Dr.		
Greenway Clo. N20	31	D2
Greenway Clo. NW9	38	D2
Greenway Gdns. NW9	38	D2
Greenway Gdns., Croy.	102	J3
Greenway Gdns., Grnf.	54	G3
Greenway Gdns., Har.	37	B2
Greenways, Beck.	96	A2
Greenways, Esher	98	B4
Greenways, The, Twick.	73	D6
Greenwell St. W1	**7**	**E6**

Greenwell St. W1	58	B4
Greenwich Ch. St. SE10	69	C6
Greenwich Cres. E6	61	B5
Swan App.		
Greenwich High Rd. SE10	78	B1
Greenwich Ind. Est. SE7	69	H4
Greenwich Mkt. SE10	69	C6
Greenwich Pk. SE10	69	D7
Greenwich Pk. St. SE10	69	D5
Greenwich S. St. SE10	78	B1
Greenwich Vw. Pl. E14	69	B3
Greenwood Ave., Dag.	53	H4
Greenwood Ave., Enf.	25	H2
Greenwood Clo., Mord.	93	B4
Greenwood Clo., Orp.	97	H6
Greenwood Clo., Sid.	89	A2
Hurst Rd.		
Greenwood Clo., T.Ditt.	98	D1
Greenwood Ct. SW1	**19**	**G4**
Greenwood Dr. E4	34	C5
Avril Way		
Greenwood Gdns. N13	32	H3
Greenwood Gdns., Ilf.	35	F7
Greenwood La., Hmptn.	81	H5
Greenwood Pk., Kings.T.	83	E7
Greenwood Pl. NW5	49	B5
Highgate Rd.		
Greenwood Rd. E8	50	D6
Greenwood Rd. E13	60	F2
Maud Rd.		
Greenwood Rd., Croy.	94	H7
Greenwood Rd., Islw.	73	C3
Greenwood Rd., Mitch.	94	D3
Greenwood Rd., T.Ditt.	98	D1
Greenwood Ter. NW10	56	D1
Greer Rd., Har.	36	J1
Greet St. SE1	**16**	**F2**
Greet St. SE1	67	G1
Gregor Ms. SE3	69	G7
Gregory Cres. SE9	79	A7
Gregory Pl. W8	**14**	**A3**
Gregory Pl. W8	66	E2
Gregory Rd., Rom.	44	D4
Gregory Rd., Sthl.	63	G3
Gregson Clo., Borwd.	22	C1
Greig Clo. N8	40	E5
Greig Ter. SE17	**20**	**H5**
Grena Gdns., Rich.	73	J4
Grena Rd., Rich.	73	J4
Grenaby Ave., Croy.	95	A7
Grenaby Rd., Croy.	95	A7
Grenada Rd. SE7	69	J7
Grenade St. E14	59	J7
Grenadier St. E16	70	D1
Grendon Gdns., Wem.	47	A2
Grendon St. NW8	**6**	**G5**
Grendon St. NW8	57	H4
Grenfell Gdns., Har.	37	H7
Grenfell Rd. W11	57	A7
Grenfell Rd., Mitch.	84	J6
Grenfell Twr. W11	57	A7
Grenfell Wk. W11	57	A7
Whitchurch Rd.		
Grennell Clo., Sutt.	100	G2
Grennell Rd., Sutt.	100	F3
Grenoble Gdns. N13	32	G6
Grenville Clo. N3	39	C1
Grenville Clo., Surb.	99	C1
Grenville Gdns., Wdf.Grn.	42	J1
Grenville Ms. SW7	**18**	**D1**
Grenville Ms. SW7	66	F4
Grenville Ms., Hmptn.	81	H5
Grenville Pl. NW7	**30**	**D5**
Grenville Pl. SW7	**14**	**C6**
Grenville Pl. SW7	66	F3
Grenville Rd. N19	49	E1
Grenville St. WC1	**8**	**B6**
Grenville St. WC1	58	E4
Gresham Ave. N20	31	J4
Gresham Clo., Bex.	80	E6
Gresham Clo., Enf.	24	J3
Gresham Dr., Rom.	44	B5
Gresham Gdns. NW11	48	B1
Gresham Rd. E6	61	C2
Gresham Rd. E16	60	H6
Gresham Rd. NW10	47	D5

Gresham Rd. SE25	95	D4
Gresham Rd. SW9	76	G3
Gresham Rd., Beck.	95	H2
Gresham Rd., Edg.	29	J6
Gresham Rd., Hmptn.	81	G6
Gresham Rd., Houns.	72	J1
Gresham St. EC2	**13**	**A3**
Gresham St. EC2	58	J6
Gresham Way SW19	84	D3
Gresley Clo. N15	41	A4
Clinton Rd.		
Gresley Rd. N19	49	C1
Gresse St. W1	**11**	**H3**
Gresse St. W1	58	D5
Gressenhall Rd. SW18	75	C6
Gresswell Clo., Sid.	89	A3
Greswell St. SW6	75	A1
Gretton Rd. N17	33	B7
Greville Clo., Twick.	73	E7
Greville Hall NW6	**6**	**B1**
Greville Hall NW6	57	E2
Greville Pl. NW6	**6**	**B1**
Greville Pl. NW6	57	E2
Greville Rd. NW6	**6**	**A1**
Greville Rd. NW6	57	E2
Greville Rd., Rich.	73	J6
Greville St. EC1	**12**	**F2**
Greville St. EC1	58	G5
Grey Clo. NW11	39	F6
Grey Eagle St. E1	**9**	**G6**
Grey Eagle St. E1	59	C5
Greycoat Pl. SW1	**15**	**H6**
Greycoat Pl. SW1	67	D3
Greycoat St. SW1	**15**	**H6**
Greycoat St. SW1	67	D3
Greycot Rd., Beck.	87	A5
Greyfell Clo., Stan.	29	E5
Coverdale Clo.		
Greyfriars Pas. EC1	**12**	**H3**
Greyhound Hill NW4	38	G3
Greyhound La. SW16	85	D6
Greyhound Rd. N17	41	B3
Greyhound Rd. NW10	56	H3
Greyhound Rd. W6	66	A6
Greyhound Rd. W14	66	B6
Greyhound Rd., Sutt.	100	F5
Greyhound Ter. SW16	94	C1
Greys Pk. Clo., Kes.	104	A5
Greystead Rd. SE23	77	F7
Greystoke Ave., Pnr.	36	G3
Greystoke Gdns. W5	55	H4
Greystoke Gdns., Enf.	24	D4
Greystoke Pk. Ter. W5	55	G3
Greystoke Pl. EC4	**12**	**E3**
Greystone Gdns., Har.	37	F6
Greystone Gdns., Ilf.	37	F2
Greyswood St. SW16	85	B6
Grierson Rd. SE23	77	G7
Griffin Clo. NW10	47	H5
Griffin Manor Way SE28	70	G3
Griffin Rd. N17	41	B2
Griffin Rd. SE18	70	G5
Griffin Way, Sun.	90	A2
Griffith Clo., Dag.	53	C1
Gibson Rd.		
Griffiths Clo., Wor.Pk.	99	H2
Griffiths Rd. SW19	84	D7
Griggs App., Ilf.	52	F2
Griggs Pl. SE1	**17**	**E5**
Griggs Rd. E10	42	C6
Grilse Clo. N9	33	E4
Parr Clo.		
Grimsby St. E2	**9**	**G6**
Grimsdyke Cres., Barn.	22	J3
Grimsdyke Rd., Pnr.	28	E7
Grimsel Path SE5	**20**	**H7**
Grimshaw Clo. N6	40	A7
Grimston Rd. SW6	75	C2
Grimwade Ave., Croy.	102	D3
Grimwade Clo. SE15	77	F3
Grimwade Cres. SE15	77	F3
Evelina Rd.		
Grimwood Rd., Twick.	73	C7
Grindal St. SE1	**16**	**E4**
Grindall Clo., Croy.	101	H4
Hillside Rd.		
Grindley Gdns., Croy.	96	B6
Grinling Pl. SE8	69	A6
Grinstead Rd. SE8	68	H5
Grittleton Ave., Wem.	46	B6
Grittleton Rd. W9	57	D4
Grizedale Ter. SE23	86	E2
Eliot Bank		
Grocer's Hall Ct. EC2	**13**	**B4**

Grogan Clo., Hmptn.	81	F6
Groom Cres. SW18	75	G7
Groom Pl. SW1	**15**	**C5**
Groom Pl. SW1	67	A3
Groombridge Clo., Well.	80	A5
Groombridge Rd. E9	50	G7
Groomfield Clo. SW17	85	A4
Grooms Dr., Pnr.	36	A5
Grosmont Rd. SE18	70	J6
Grosse Way SW15	74	H6
Grosvenor Ave. N5	49	J5
Grosvenor Ave. SW14	74	E3
Grosvenor Ave., Cars.	100	J6
Grosvenor Ave., Har.	36	H6
Grosvenor Ave., Rich.	73	H5
Grosvenor Rd.		
Grosvenor Clo., Loug.	27	E1
Grosvenor Cotts. SW1	**19**	**B1**
Grosvenor Ct. N14	24	C7
Grosvenor Cres. NW9	38	A4
Grosvenor Cres. SW1	**15**	**C4**
Grosvenor Cres. SW1	67	A2
Grosvenor Cres. Ms. SW1	**15**	**B4**
Grosvenor Cres. Ms. SW1	67	A2
Grosvenor Dr., Loug.	27	E2
Grosvenor Est. SW1	**19**	**J1**
Grosvenor Est. SW1	67	D4
Grosvenor Gdns. E6	61	A3
Grosvenor Gdns. N10	40	D3
Grosvenor Gdns. N14	24	D4
Grosvenor Gdns. NW2	47	J5
Grosvenor Gdns. NW11	39	C6
Grosvenor Gdns. SW1	**15**	**E6**
Grosvenor Gdns. SW1	67	B3
Grosvenor Gdns. SW14	74	E3
Grosvenor Gdns., Kings.T.	82	G6
Grosvenor Gdns., Wall.	101	C7
Grosvenor Gdns., Wdf.Grn.	34	G6
Grosvenor Gdns. Ms. E. SW1	**15**	**E5**
Grosvenor Gdns. Ms. N. SW1	**15**	**D6**
Grosvenor Gdns. Ms. S. SW1	**15**	**E6**
Grosvenor Gate W1	**11**	**A6**
Grosvenor Hill SW19	84	B6
Grosvenor Hill W1	**11**	**D5**
Grosvenor Hill W1	58	B7
Grosvenor Pk. SE5	**20**	**J6**
Grosvenor Pk. SE5	67	J7
Grosvenor Pk. Rd. E17	42	A5
Grosvenor Path, Loug.	27	E1
Grosvenor Pl. SW1	**15**	**C4**
Grosvenor Pl. SW1	67	A2
Grosvenor Ri. E. E17	42	B5
Grosvenor Rd. E6	61	A1
Grosvenor Rd. E7	51	H6
Grosvenor Rd. E10	51	C1
Grosvenor Rd. E11	42	G5
Grosvenor Rd. N3	31	C7
Grosvenor Rd. N9	33	E1
Grosvenor Rd. N10	40	B1
Grosvenor Rd. SE25	95	D4
Grosvenor Rd. SW1	**19**	**F5**
Grosvenor Rd. SW1	67	B6
Grosvenor Rd. W4	65	B5
Grosvenor Rd. W7	64	D1
Grosvenor Rd., Belv.	71	G6
Grosvenor Rd., Bexh.	80	D5
Grosvenor Rd., Borwd.	22	A3
Grosvenor Rd., Brent.	64	G6
Grosvenor Rd., Dag.	53	F1
Grosvenor Rd., Houns.	72	F1
Grosvenor Rd., Ilf.	52	F3
Grosvenor Rd., Orp.	97	H6
Grosvenor Rd., Rich.	73	H5
Grosvenor Rd., Sthl.	63	F3
Grosvenor Rd., Twick.	73	D7
Grosvenor Rd., Wall.	101	B6
Grosvenor Rd., W.Wick.	103	B1
Grosvenor Sq. W1	**11**	**C5**
Grosvenor Sq. W1	58	A7
Grosvenor St. W1	**11**	**D5**
Grosvenor St. W1	58	B7
Grosvenor Ter. SE5	**20**	**J6**
Grosvenor Ter. SE5	67	J6
Grosvenor Wf. Rd. E14	69	D4

Grote's Bldgs. SE3	78	E2
Grote's Pl. SE3	78	E2
Groton Rd. SW18	84	E2
Grotto Pas. W1	**11**	**C1**
Grotto Rd., Twick.	82	C2
Grove, The E15	51	E6
Grove, The N3	39	D1
Grove, The N4	40	F7
Grove, The N6	49	A1
Grove, The N8	40	D5
Grove, The N13	32	G5
Grove, The N14	24	C5
Grove, The NW9	38	D5
Grove, The NW11	39	B7
Grove, The W5	64	G1
Grove, The, Bexh.	80	D4
Grove, The, Edg.	30	B4
Grove, The, Enf.	24	G2
Grove, The, Grnf.	54	J6
Grove, The, Islw.	73	B1
Grove, The, Sid.	89	E5
Grove, The, Tedd.	82	D4
Grove, The, Twick.	73	E6
Bridge Rd.		
Grove, The, Walt.	90	B7
Grove, The, W.Wick.	103	B3
Grove Ave. N3	31	D7
Grove Ave. N10	40	C2
Grove Ave. W7	55	B6
Grove Ave., Pnr.	36	E5
Grove Ave., Sutt.	100	D6
Grove Rd.		
Grove Ave., Twick.	82	C1
Grove Clo. SE23	86	H1
Grove Clo., Brom.	103	G2
Grove Clo., Felt.	81	E4
Grove Clo., Kings.T.	91	J4
Grove Cotts. SW3	**18**	**H5**
Grove Cotts. SW3	66	H6
Grove Ct. SE3	78	G1
Grove Ct., E.Mol.	91	A5
Walton Rd.		
Grove Cres. E18	42	F2
Grove Cres. NW9	38	C4
Grove Cres. SE5	77	B2
Grove Cres., Felt.	81	E4
Grove Cres., Kings.T.	91	H3
Grove Cres., Walt.	90	B7
Grove Cres. Rd. E15	51	D6
Grove End E18	42	F2
Grove Hill		
Grove End La., Esher	98	A1
Grove End Rd. NW8	**6**	**E3**
Grove End Rd. NW8	57	G2
Grove Fm. Ind. Est.,	93	J5
Mitch.		
Grove Footpath,	91	H4
Surb.		
Grove Gdns. E15	51	E6
Grove Gdns. NW4	38	G5
Grove Gdns. NW8	**6**	**H4**
Grove Gdns., Dag.	53	J3
Grove Gdns., Tedd.	82	D4
Grove Grn. Rd. E11	51	C3
Grove Hall Ct. NW8	**6**	**D3**
Grove Hill E18	42	F2
Grove Hill, Har.	37	B7
Grove Hill Rd. SE5	77	B3
Grove Hill Rd., Har.	37	B7
Grove Ho. Rd. N8	40	E4
Grove La. SE5	77	B2
Grove La., Chig.	35	J3
Grove La., Kings.T.	91	H4
Grove Mkt. Pl. SE9	79	C6
Grove Ms. W6	65	J3
Grove Ms. W11	57	C6
Portobello Rd.		
Grove Pk. E11	42	H6
Grove Pk. NW9	38	C4
Grove Pk. SE5	77	B2
Grove Pk. Ave. E4	34	B7
Grove Pk. Bri. W4	65	C7
Grove Pk. Gdns. W4	65	C7
Grove Pk. Ms. W4	65	C7
Grove Pk. Rd. N15	41	B4
Grove Pk. Rd. SE9	87	J3
Grove Pk. Rd. W4	65	B7
Grove Pk. Ter. W4	65	B7
Grove Pas. E2	59	E2
The Oval		
Grove Pas., Tedd.	82	D5
Grove Pl. NW3	48	G4
Christchurch Hill		
Grove Pl. W3	65	C1
Grove Pl. W5	64	G1
The Gro.		
Grove Pl., Bark.	61	F1
Clockhouse Ave.		

Grove Rd. E3	59	G1
Grove Rd. E4	34	C4
Grove Rd. E11	42	F7
Grove Rd. E17	42	B6
Grove Rd. E18	42	F2
Grove Rd. N11	32	B5
Grove Rd. N12	31	G5
Grove Rd. N15	41	B5
Grove Rd. NW2	47	J6
Grove Rd. SW13	74	F2
Grove Rd. SW19	84	F7
Grove Rd. W3	65	C1
Grove Rd. W5	55	G7
Grove Rd., Barn.	23	H3
Grove Rd., Belv.	71	F6
Grove Rd., Bexh.	80	J4
Grove Rd., Borwd.	22	A1
Grove Rd., Brent.	64	F5
Grove Rd., E.Mol.	91	A4
Grove Rd., Edg.	30	A6
Grove Rd., Houns.	72	G4
Grove Rd., Islw.	73	B1
Grove Rd., Mitch.	94	A3
Grove Rd., Pnr.	36	F5
Grove Rd., Rich.	73	J6
Grove Rd., Rom.	44	B7
Grove Rd., Surb.	91	G5
Grove Rd., Sutt.	100	D6
Grove Rd., Th.Hth.	94	G4
Grove Rd., Twick.	82	A3
Grove St. N18	33	C5
Grove St. SE8	68	J4
Grove Ter. NW5	49	B3
Grove Ter., Tedd.	82	D4
Grove Vale SE22	77	B4
Grove Vale, Chis.	88	D6
Grove Vill. E14	60	B7
Grove Way, Esher	90	J7
Grovebury Ct. N14	24	D7
Grovebury Rd. SE2	71	B2
Grovedale Rd. N19	49	D2
Groveland Ave. SW16	85	F7
Groveland Ct. EC4	**13**	**A4**
Groveland Rd., Beck.	95	J3
Groveland Way,	92	C5
N.Mal.		
Grovelands, W.Mol.	90	G4
Grovelands Clo. SE5	77	B2
Grovelands Clo., Har.	46	A3
Grovelands Ct. N14	24	D7
Grovelands Rd. N13	32	F4
Grovelands Rd. N15	41	D6
Grovelands Rd., Orp.	89	A7
Groveside Clo. W3	56	B6
Groveside Clo., Cars.	100	H2
Groveside Rd. E4	34	E2
Groveway SW9	76	F1
Groveway, Dag.	53	D4
Groveway, Wem.	47	C5
Grovewood, Rich.	73	J1
Sandycombe Rd.		
Grummant Rd. SE15	77	C1
Grundy St. E14	60	B6
Gruneisen Rd. N3	31	E7
Gubyon Ave. SE24	76	H5
Guerin Sq. E3	59	J3
Malmesbury Rd.		
Guernsey Clo., Houns.	72	G1
Guernsey Gro. SE24	76	J7
Guernsey Rd. E11	51	D1
Guibal Rd. SE12	78	H7
Guild Rd. SE7	70	A5
Guildersfield Rd.	85	E7
SW16		
Guildford Gro. SE10	78	B1
Guildford Rd. E6	61	C6
Guildford Rd. E17	42	C1
Guildford Rd. SW8	76	E1
Guildford Rd., Croy.	95	A6
Guildford Rd., Ilf.	52	H2
Guildford Way, Wall.	101	E5
Guildhall Bldgs. EC2	**13**	**B3**
Guildhouse St. SW1	**19**	**F1**
Guildhouse St. SW1	67	C4
Guildown Ave. N12	31	E4
Guildsway E17	41	J1
Guilford Ave., Surb.	91	J5
Guilford Pl. WC1	**8**	**C6**
Guilford Pl. WC1	58	F4
Guilford St. WC1	**8**	**B6**
Guilford St. WC1	58	E4
Guilford Vill., Surb.	91	J6
Alpha Rd.		
Guilsborough Clo.	47	E7
NW10		
Guinness Bldgs. SE1	**17**	**D6**
Guinness Bldgs. SE1	68	B4
Guinness Clo. E9	50	H7

Guinness Sq. SE1	**21**	**D1**
Guinness Trust	**20**	**G3**
Bldgs. SE11		
Guinness Trust	67	H5
Bldgs. SE11		
Guinness Trust	**18**	**J2**
Bldgs. SW3		
Guinness Trust Est.	50	B1
N16		
Guinness Trust Est.	76	H4
SW9		
Guion Rd. SW6	75	C2
Gull Clo., Wall.	101	E7
Gulland Wk. N1	49	J6
Marquess Est.		
Gulliver Clo., Nthlt.	54	F1
Gulliver Rd., Sid.	88	H2
Gulliver St. SE16	68	J3
Gumleigh Rd. W5	64	F4
Gumley Gdns., Islw.	73	D3
Gumping Rd., Orp.	104	F1
Gun St. E1	**13**	**F2**
Gun St. E1	59	C5
Gundulph Rd., Brom.	96	J3
Gunmakers La. E3	59	H1
Gunnell Clo., Croy.	95	D6
Gunner La. SE18	70	D5
Gunners Gro. E4	34	C3
Gunners Rd. SW18	84	G2
Gunnersbury Ave. W3	65	A3
Gunnersbury Ave. W4	64	J1
Gunnersbury Ave. W5	64	J1
Gunnersbury Clo. W4	65	B5
Grange Rd.		
Gunnersbury Ct. W3	65	B2
Bollo La.		
Gunnersbury Cres.	65	A2
W3		
Gunnersbury Dr. W5	64	J2
Gunnersbury Gdns.	65	A2
W3		
Gunnersbury La. W3	65	A3
Gunnersbury Ms. W4	65	B5
Chiswick High Rd.		
Gunnersbury Pk. W3	64	J4
Gunnersbury Pk. W5	64	J4
Gunning St. SE18	70	H4
Gunpowder Sq. EC4	**12**	**F3**
Gunpowder Sq. EC4	58	G6
Gunstor Rd. N16	50	B4
Gunter Gro. SW10	**18**	**C6**
Gunter Gro. SW10	66	F6
Gunter Gro., Edg.	38	D1
Gunterstone Rd. W14	66	B4
Gunthorpe St. E1	**13**	**G2**
Gunthorpe St. E1	59	C5
Gunton Rd. E5	50	E2
Gunton Rd. SW17	85	A6
Gunwhale Clo. SE16	68	G1
Gurdon Rd. SE7	69	G5
Gurnell Gro. W13	55	C4
Gurney Clo. E15	51	E5
Gurney Rd.		
Gurney Clo. E17	41	G1
Gurney Clo., Bark.	52	E6
Gurney Cres., Croy.	101	F1
Gurney Dr. N2	39	F4
Gurney Rd. E15	51	E5
Gurney Rd., Cars.	101	A3
Gurney Rd., Nthlt.	54	B3
Guthrie St. SW3	**18**	**G3**
Gutter La. EC2	**13**	**A3**
Gutter La. EC2	58	J6
Guy Rd., Wall.	101	D3
Guy St. SE1	**17**	**C3**
Guy St. SE1	68	A2
Guyatt Gdns., Mitch.	94	A2
Ormerod Gdns.		
Guyscliff Rd. SE13	78	C5
Gwalior Rd. SW15	75	A3
Felsham Rd.		
Gwendolen Ave.	75	A4
SW15		
Gwendolen Clo.	75	A5
SW15		
Gwendoline Ave. E13	60	H1
Gwendwr Rd. W14	66	B5
Gwillim Clo., Sid.	80	A5
Gwydor Rd., Beck.	95	G4
Gwydyr Rd., Brom.	96	F3
Gwyn Clo. SW6	66	F7
Gwynne Ave., Croy.	95	G5
Gwynne Pk. Ave.,	35	C6
Wdf.Grn.		
Gwynne Pl. WC1	**8**	**D4**
Gwynne Rd. SW11	75	G2
Gylcote Clo. SE5	77	A4
Gyles Pk., Stan.	29	F7

Gyllyngdune Gdns.,	52	J3
Ilf.		
H		
Ha-Ha Rd. SE18	70	C6
Haarlem Rd. W14	66	A3
Haberdasher Pl. N1	**9**	**C3**
Haberdasher St. N1	**9**	**C3**
Haberdasher St. N1	59	A3
Habgood Rd., Loug.	27	B3
Haccombe Rd. SW19	84	F6
Hackbridge Grn.,	101	A2
Wall.		
Hackbridge Pk.	101	A2
Gdns., Cars.		
Hackbridge Rd., Wall.	101	A2
Hackford Rd. SW9	76	F1
Hackforth Clo., Barn.	22	H5
Hackington Cres.,	87	A6
Beck.		
Hackney Clo., Borwd.	22	D5
Hackney Gro. E8	50	E6
Reading La.		
Hackney Rd. E2	**9**	**F3**
Hackney Rd. E2	59	C3
Hadden Rd. SE28	70	H3
Hadden Way, Grnf.	46	A6
Haddington Rd.,	87	D4
Brom.		
Haddo St. SE10	69	C6
Haddon Clo., Borwd.	22	A2
Haddon Clo., Enf.	25	D6
Haddon Clo., N.Mal.	92	F5
Haddon Gro., Sid.	79	J7
Haddon Rd., Sutt.	100	E4
Haddonfield SE8	68	G4
Hadfield Clo., Sthl.	54	F3
Adrienne Ave.		
Hadleigh Clo. E1	59	F4
Mantus Rd.		
Hadleigh Rd. N9	25	E7
Hadleigh St. E2	59	F3
Hadleigh Wk. E6	61	B6
Dunnock Rd.		
Hadley Clo. N21	24	G6
Hadley Common,	23	D2
Barn.		
Hadley Gdns. W4	65	D3
Hadley Gdns., Sthl.	63	F5
Hadley Grn., Barn.	23	C2
Hadley Grn. Rd.,	23	C2
Barn.		
Hadley Grn. W., Barn.	23	B2
Hadley Gro., Barn.	23	B2
Hadley Highstone,	23	C1
Barn.		
Hadley Ridge, Barn.	23	C3
Hadley Rd., Barn.	23	E3
(New Barnet)		
Hadley Rd., Belv.	71	F4
Hadley Rd., Mitch.	94	D4
Hadley St. NW1	49	B6
Hadley Way N21	24	G6
Hadlow Pl. SE19	86	D7
Hadlow Rd., Sid.	89	A4
Hadlow Rd., Well.	71	C7
Hadrian Clo., Wall.	101	E7
De Havilland Rd.		
Hadrian Est. E2	**9**	**J2**
Hadrian St. SE10	69	E5
Hadrians Ride, Enf.	25	C5
Hadyn Pk. Rd. W12	65	G2
Hafer Rd. SW11	75	J4
Hafton Rd. SE6	87	E1
Haggard Rd., Twick.	73	D7
Haggerston Rd. E8	50	C7
Hague St. E2	**9**	**J4**
Haig Rd., Stan.	29	F5
Haig Rd. E. E13	60	J3
Haig Rd. W. E13	60	J3
Haigville Gdns., Ilf.	43	E4
Hailes Clo. SW19	84	F6
North Rd.		
Hailey Rd., Erith	71	G2
Haileybury Ave., Enf.	25	C6
Hailsham Ave. SW2	85	F2
Hailsham Clo., Surb.	91	G7
Hailsham Dr., Har.	37	A3
Hailsham Rd. SW17	85	A6
Hailsham Ter. N18	32	J5
Haimo Rd. SE9	79	A5
Hainault Ct. E17	42	D4
Hainault Gore, Rom.	44	E5
Hainault Gro., Chig.	35	F4
Hainault Rd. E11	51	C1
Hainault Rd., Chig.	35	E3
Hainault Rd., Rom.	44	J2

Hainault Rd., Rom. 44 F6
(Chadwell Heath)
Hainault Rd., Rom. 44 B3
(Hainault)
Hainault St. SE9 88 E1
Hainault St., Ilf. 52 F2
Hainford Clo. SE4 77 G4
Haining Clo. W4 65 A5
Wellesley Rd.
Hainthorpe Rd. SE27 85 H3
Halberd Ms. E5 50 E2
Knightland Rd.
Halbutt Gdns., Dag. 53 F3
Halbutt St., Dag. 53 F4
Halcomb St. N1 59 B1
Halcot Ave., Bexh. 80 H5
Halcrow St. E1 59 E5
Newark St.
Haldan Rd. E4 34 C6
Haldane Clo. N10 32 B7
Haldane Pl. SW18 84 E1
Haldane Rd. E6 61 A3
Haldane Rd. SE28 62 D7
Haldane Rd. SW6 66 C7
Haldane Rd., Sthl. 54 J7
Haldon Clo., Chig. 35 H5
Haldon Rd. SW18 75 C5
Hale, The E4 34 D7
Hale, The N17 41 D3
Hale Clo. E4 34 C3
Hale Clo., Edg. 30 C5
Hale Clo., Orp. 104 F4
Hale Dr. NW7 30 C6
Hale End Clo., Ruis. 36 A6
Hale End Rd. E4 34 D6
Hale End Rd. E17 42 D1
Hale End Rd., 34 D7
Wdf.Grn.
Hale Gdns. N17 41 D3
Hale Gdns. W3 65 A1
Hale Gro. Gdns. NW7 30 D5
Hale La. NW7 30 D5
Hale La., Edg. 30 B5
Hale Path SE27 85 H4
Hale Rd. E6 61 B4
Hale Rd. N17 41 D3
Hale St. E14 60 B7
Hale Wk. W7 55 B5
Benham Rd.
Halefield Rd. N17 41 D1
Hales St. SE8 69 A7
Deptford High St.
Halesowen Rd., Mord. 93 E7
Halesworth Clo. E5 50 F2
Theydon Rd.
Halesworth Rd. SE13 78 B3
Haley Rd. NW4 38 J6
Half Acre, Brent. 64 G6
Half Acre Rd. W7 64 B1
Half Moon Ct. EC1 12 J2
Half Moon Cres. N1 8 D1
Half Moon Cres. N1 58 F2
Half Moon La. SE24 76 J6
Half Moon Pas. E1 13 G4
Half Moon St. W1 15 E1
Half Moon St. W1 67 B1
Halford Rd. E10 42 D5
Halford Rd. SW6 66 D6
Halford Rd., Rich. 73 H5
Halfway St., Sid. 79 G7
Haliburton Rd., 73 D5
Twick.
Haliday Wk. N1 50 A6
Balls Pond Rd.
Halidon Clo. E9 50 F5
Urswick Rd.
Halifax Rd., Enf. 24 J2
Halifax Rd., Grnf. 54 H1
Halifax St. SE26 86 E4
Halifield Dr., Belv. 71 E3
Haling Gro., S.Croy. 101 J7
Haling Pk. Gdns., 101 H6
S.Croy.
Haling Pk. Rd., 101 H6
S.Croy.
Haling Rd., S.Croy. 102 A6
Halkin Arc. SW1 15 B5
Halkin Ms. SW1 15 B5
Halkin Pl. SW1 15 B5
Halkin Pl. SW1 67 A3
Halkin St. SW1 15 C4
Halkin St. SW1 67 A2
Hall, The SE3 78 G3
Hall Ave. N18 33 A6
Weir Hall Ave.
Hall Clo. W5 55 H5
Hall Ct., Tedd. 82 C5
Teddington Pk.

Hall Dr. SE26 86 F5
Hall Dr. W7 55 B6
Hall Fm. Clo., Stan. 29 E4
Hall Fm. Dr., Twick. 73 A7
Hall Gdns. E4 33 J4
Hall Gate NW8 6 D3
Hall La. E4 33 H5
Hall La. NW4 38 G1
Hall Oak Wk. NW6 48 C6
Maygrove Rd.
Hall Pl. W2 6 E6
Hall Pl. W2 57 G4
Hall Pl. Cres., Bex. 80 J5
Hall Rd. E6 61 C1
Hall Rd. E15 51 D4
Hall Rd. NW8 6 D4
Hall Rd. NW8 57 F3
Hall Rd., Islw. 73 A5
Hall Rd., Rom. 44 C6
Hall St. EC1 8 H3
Hall St. EC1 58 H3
Hall St. N12 31 F5
Hall Vw. SE9 88 A2
Hallam Clo., Chis. 88 C5
Hallam Gdns., Pnr. 28 E7
Hallam Ms. W1 11 E1
Hallam Rd. N15 40 H4
Hallam Rd. SW15 74 H3
Hallam St. W1 7 E6
Hallam St. W1 58 B5
Halley Gdns. SE13 78 D4
Halley Rd. E7 51 J6
Halley Rd. E12 52 A6
Halley St. E14 59 H5
Hallfield Est. W2 10 C4
Halliards, The, Walt. 90 A6
Felix Rd.
Halliday Sq., Sthl. 64 A1
Halliford St. N1 49 J7
Hallingbury Ct. E17 42 B3
Halliwell Rd. SW2 76 F6
Halliwick Rd. N10 40 A1
Hallmark Trd. Est. 47 C4
NW10
Great Cen. Way
Hallmead Rd., Sutt. 100 E3
Hallowell Ave., Croy. 101 E4
Hallowell Clo., Mitch. 94 A3
Hallowes Cres., Wat. 28 A3
Hayling Rd.
Hallsville Rd. E16 60 F6
Hallswelle Rd. NW11 39 C5
Hallywell Cres. E6 61 C5
Halons Rd. SE9 79 D7
Halpin Pl. SE17 21 C2
Halsbrook Rd. SE3 78 J3
Halsbury Clo., Stan. 29 E4
Halsbury Rd. W12 65 G1
Halsbury Rd. E., Nthlt. 45 J4
Halsbury Rd. W., 45 H5
Nthlt.
Halsend, Hayes 63 B1
Halsey Ms. SW3 18 J1
Halsey St. SW3 18 J1
Halsey St. SW3 66 J4
Halsham Cres., Bark. 52 J6
Halsmere Rd. SE5 76 H1
Halstead Ct. N1 9 C2
Halstead Gdns. N21 33 A1
Halstead Rd. E11 42 G5
Halstead Rd. N21 33 A1
Halstead Rd., Enf. 25 B4
Halston Clo. SW11 75 J6
Halstow Rd. NW10 57 A3
Halstow Rd. SE10 69 G5
Halsway, Hayes 63 A1
Halt Robin La., Belv. 71 H4
Halt Robin Rd.
Halt Robin Rd., Belv. 71 G4
Halter Clo., Borwd. 22 D5
Clydesdale Clo.
Halton Cross St. N1 58 H1
Halton Rd.
Halton Rd. N1 49 H7
Ham, The, Brent. 64 F7
Ham Clo., Rich. 82 F3
Ham Common, Rich. 82 G3
Ham Fm. Rd., Rich. 82 G4
Ham Gate Ave., Rich. 82 H4
Ham Pk. Rd. E7 51 G7
Ham Pk. Rd. E15 51 F7
Ham Ridings, Rich. 82 J5
Ham St., Rich. 82 E1
Ham Vw., Croy. 95 H6
Ham Yd. W1 11 H5
Hambalt Rd. SW4 76 C5
Hamble Ct., Kings.T. 82 G7
Hamble St. SW6 75 E3

Hamble Wk., Nthlt. 54 G2
Brabazon Rd.
Hambleden Pl. SE21 86 B1
Hambledon Gdns. 95 C3
SE25
Hambledon Rd. SW18 75 C7
Hambledown Rd., Sid. 79 G7
Hambleton Clo., 99 J2
Wor.Pk.
Cotswold Way
Hambridge Way SW2 76 G7
Hambro Ave., Brom. 103 G1
Hambro Rd. SW16 85 D6
Hambrook Rd. SE25 95 E3
Hambrough Rd., Sthl. 63 E3
Hamden Cres., Dag. 53 H3
Hamelin St. E14 60 C6
St. Leonards Rd.
Hameway E6 61 D4
Hamfrith Rd. E15 51 F6
Hamilton Ave. N9 25 D7
Hamilton Ave., Ilf. 43 E4
Hamilton Ave., Surb. 99 A2
Hamilton Ave., Sutt. 100 B1
Hamilton Clo. N17 41 C3
Hamilton Clo. NW8 6 E4
Hamilton Clo. NW8 57 G3
Hamilton Clo. SE16 68 H2
Somerford Way
Hamilton Clo., Barn. 23 H4
Hamilton Clo., Stan. 29 C2
Hamilton Ct. W5 55 J7
Hamilton Ct. W9 6 C3
Hamilton Cres. N13 32 G4
Hamilton Cres., Har. 45 F3
Hamilton Cres., 72 H5
Houns.
Hamilton Gdns. NW8 6 D3
Hamilton Gdns. NW8 57 F3
Hamilton La. N5 49 H4
Hamilton Pk.
Hamilton Ms. W1 15 D3
Hamilton Pk. N5 49 H4
Hamilton Pk. W. N5 49 H4
Hamilton Pl. W1 15 C2
Hamilton Pl. W1 67 A1
Hamilton Pl., Sun. 81 B7
Hamilton Rd. E15 60 E3
Hamilton Rd. E17 41 H2
Hamilton Rd. N2 39 F3
Hamilton Rd. N9 25 D7
Hamilton Rd. NW10 47 G5
Hamilton Rd. NW11 39 A7
Hamilton Rd. SE27 86 A4
Hamilton Rd. SW19 84 E7
Hamilton Rd. W4 65 E2
Hamilton Rd. W5 55 H7
Hamilton Rd., Barn. 23 H4
Hamilton Rd., Bexh. 80 E2
Hamilton Rd., Brent. 64 G6
Hamilton Rd., Har. 37 B5
Hamilton Rd., Hayes 54 B7
Hamilton Rd., Ilf. 52 E4
Hamilton Rd., Sid. 89 A4
Hamilton Rd., Sthl. 63 F1
Hamilton Rd., Th.Hth. 95 A3
Hamilton Rd., Twick. 82 B1
Hamilton Rd., Wat. 28 B3
Hamilton Sq. SE1 17 C3
Hamilton St. SE8 69 A6
Deptford High St.
Hamilton Ter. NW8 6 B2
Hamilton Ter. NW8 57 E2
Hamilton Way N3 31 D6
Hamilton Way N13 32 H4
Hamlea Clo. SE12 78 G5
Hamlet, The SE5 77 A3
Hamlet Clo. SE13 78 E4
Old Rd.
Hamlet Gdns. W6 65 G4
Hamlet Rd. SE19 86 C7
Hamlet Sq. NW2 48 B3
Cricklewood Trd. Est.
Hamlet Sq. NW11 48 B3
The Vale
Hamlet Way SE1 17 C3
Hamlets Way E3 59 J4
Hamlin Cres., Pnr. 36 C5
Hamlyn Clo., Edg. 29 H3
Hamlyn Gdns. SE19 86 B7
Hammelton Grn. 76 H1
SW9
Cromwell Rd.
Hammelton Rd., 96 F1
Brom.
Hammers La. NW7 30 G5
Hammersmith Bri. 65 H5
SW13

Hammersmith Bri. 65 J5
Rd. W6
Hammersmith Bdy. 65 J4
W6
Hammersmith 65 J5
Flyover W6
Hammersmith Gro. 65 J2
W6
Hammersmith Rd. W6 66 A4
Hammersmith Rd. 66 A4
W14
Hammersmith Ter. W6 65 G5
Hammet Clo., Hayes 54 D5
Willow Tree La.
Hammett St. EC3 13 F5
Hammond Ave., 94 B2
Mitch.
Hammond Clo., Barn. 23 B5
Hammond Clo., Grnf. 46 A5
Lilian Board Way
Hammond Clo., 90 G1
Hmptn.
Hammond Rd., Enf. 25 E2
Hammond Rd., Sthl. 63 E3
Hammond St. NW5 49 C6
Hammond Way SE28 62 B7
Oriole Way
Hamonde Clo., Edg. 30 B2
Hampden Ave., Beck. 95 H2
Hampden Clo. NW1 7 J2
Hampden Gurney St. 10 J4
W1
Hampden La. N17 41 C1
Hampden Rd. N8 40 G4
Hampden Rd. N10 32 A7
Hampden Rd. N17 41 D1
Hampden Rd. N19 49 D2
Holloway Rd.
Hampden Rd., Beck. 95 H2
Hampden Rd., Har. 36 J1
Hampden Rd., 92 A3
Kings.T.
Hampden Sq. N14 32 B1
Osidge La.
Hampden Way N14 32 B2
Hampshire Clo. N18 33 E5
Hampshire Hog La. 65 H4
W6
King St.
Hampshire Rd. N22 32 F7
Hampshire St. NW5 49 D6
Torriano Ave.
Hampson Way SW8 76 F1
Hampstead Clo. SE28 71 B1
Hampstead Gdns. 39 D6
NW11
Hampstead Gdns., 44 B5
Rom.
Hampstead Grn. NW3 48 H5
Hampstead Gro. NW3 48 F3
Hampstead High St. 48 F4
NW3
Hampstead Hill Gdns. 48 G4
NW3
Hampstead La. N6 39 G7
Hampstead La. NW3 48 G1
Hampstead Rd. NW1 7 F2
Hampstead Rd. NW1 58 C2
Hampstead Sq. NW3 48 F3
Hampstead Way 39 C5
NW11
Hampton Clo. NW6 57 D3
Hampton Clo. SW20 83 J7
Hampton Ct. N1 49 H6
Upper St.
Hampton Ct. Ave., 91 A5
E.Mol.
Hampton Ct. Palace, 91 B3
E.Mol.
Hampton Ct. Par., 91 B4
E.Mol.
Creek Rd.
Hampton Ct. Rd., 91 C3
E.Mol.
Hampton Ct. Rd., 90 J2
Hmptn.
Hampton Ct. Rd., 91 F2
Kings.T.
Hampton Ct. Way, 91 B6
E.Mol.
Hampton Ct. Way, 98 B2
T.Ditt.
Hampton Fm. Ind. 81 E3
Est., Felt.
Hampton La., Felt. 81 E4
Hampton Mead, 27 E3
Loug.
Hampton Ri., Har. 37 H6

Hampton Rd. E4 33 J5
Hampton Rd. E7 51 H5
Hampton Rd. E11 51 D1
Hampton Rd., Croy. 94 J6
Hampton Rd., Ilf. 52 E4
Hampton Rd., Tedd. 82 A5
Hampton Rd., Twick. 82 A3
Hampton Rd., Wor.Pk. 99 G2
Hampton Rd. E., Felt. 81 F3
Hampton Rd. W., Felt. 81 E2
Hampton St. SE1 20 H2
Hampton St. SE1 67 J4
Hampton St. SE17 20 H2
Hampton St. SE17 67 H4
Hamshades Clo., Sid. 88 J3
Hanah Ct. SW19 84 A7
Hanameel St. E16 69 H1
Hanbury Ms. N1 58 J1
Mary St.
Hanbury Rd. N17 41 E2
Hanbury Rd. W3 65 B2
Hanbury St. E1 13 G1
Hanbury St. E1 59 C5
Hancock Ct., Borwd. 22 C2
Banks Rd.
Hancock Rd. E3 60 C3
Hancock Rd. SE19 86 A6
Hand Ct. WC1 12 D2
Handa Wk. N1 50 A6
Clephane Rd.
Handcroft Rd., Croy. 94 H7
Handel Clo., Edg. 29 J6
Handel Pl. NW10 47 D6
Mitchellbrook Way
Handel St. WC1 8 A5
Handel St. WC1 58 E4
Handel Way, Edg. 30 A7
Handen Rd. SE12 78 E5
Handforth Rd. SW9 20 E7
Handforth Rd. SW9 67 G7
Handforth Rd., Ilf. 52 E3
Winston Way
Handley Rd. E9 59 F1
Handowe Clo. NW4 38 G4
Hands Wk. E16 60 G6
Butchers Rd.
Handside Clo., Wor.Pk. 100 A1
Carters Clo.
Handsworth Ave. E4 34 D6
Handsworth Rd. N17 41 A3
Handsworth Way, Wat. 28 A3
Handtrough Way, Bark. 61 E2
Fresh Wf. Rd.
Hanford Clo. SW18 84 D1
Hanford Row SW19 83 J6
Hangar Ruding, Wat. 28 F3
Hanger Grn. W5 56 A4
Hanger La. W5 55 H2
Hanger Vale La. W3 55 J6
Hanger Vale La. W5 55 J6
Hanger Vw. Way W3 56 A6
Hankey Pl. SE1 17 C4
Hankey Pl. SE1 68 A2
Hankins La. NW7 30 E2
Hanley Pl., Beck. 87 A7
Hanley Rd. N4 49 E1
Hanmer Wk. N7 49 F2
Newington Barrow Way
Hannah Clo. NW10 47 C4
Hannah Clo., Beck. 96 C3
Hannah Mary Way SE1 21 J2
Hannah Ms., Wall. 101 C7
Hannay Wk. SW16 85 D2
Dingley La.
Hannell Rd. SW6 66 B7
Hannen Rd. SE27 85 H3
Norwood High St.
Hannibal Rd. E1 59 F5
Hannibal Way, Croy. 101 F5
Hannington Rd. SW4 76 B3
Hanover Ave., Felt. 81 A1
Hanover Clo., Rich. 65 A7
Hanover Clo., Sutt. 100 B4
Hanover Ct. W12 65 G1
Uxbridge Rd.
Hanover Dr., Chis. 88 F4
Hanover Gdns. SE11 20 E6
Hanover Gdns. SE11 67 G6
Hanover Gdns., Ilf. 35 F7
Hanover Gate NW1 6 H4
Hanover Gate NW1 57 H3
Hanover Pk. SE15 77 D1
Hanover Pl. WC2 12 B4
Hanover Rd. N15 41 C4
Hanover Rd. NW10 47 J7
Hanover Rd. SW19 84 F7
Hanover Sq. W1 11 E4
Hanover Sq. W1 58 B6
Hanover St. W1 11 E4
Hanover St. W1 58 B6
Hanover St., Croy. 101 H3
Abbey Rd.
Hanover Ter. NW1 6 H4
Hanover Ter. NW1 57 H3
Hanover Ter., Islw. 73 D1
Hanover Ter. Ms. NW1 6 H4
Hanover Way, Bexh. 80 D3
Hanover W. Ind. Est. NW10 56 D3
Acton La.
Hanover Yd. N1 8 H1
Hans Cres. SW1 14 J5
Hans Cres. SW1 66 J3
Hans Pl. SW1 15 A5
Hans Pl. SW1 66 J3
Hans Rd. SW3 14 J5
Hans Rd. SW3 66 J3
Hans St. SW1 15 A6
Hansard Ms. W14 66 A2
Holland Rd.
Hansart Way, Enf. 24 G1
The Ridgeway
Hanselin Clo., Stan. 29 C5
Chenduit Way
Hansha Dr., Edg. 38 D1
Hansler Gro., E.Mol. 91 A5
Hansler Rd. SE22 77 C5
Hansol Rd., Bexh. 80 E5
Hanson Clo. SW12 76 B7
Hanson Clo., Beck. 87 B6
Hanson Clo., Loug. 27 F2
Hanson Dr.
Hanson Dr., Loug. 27 F2
Hanson Gdns., Sthl. 63 E2
Hanson Grn., Loug. 27 F2
Hanson Dr.
Hanson St. W1 11 F1
Hanson St. W1 58 C5
Hanway Pl. W1 11 H3
Hanway Rd. W7 55 A6
Hanway St. W1 11 H3
Hanway St. W1 58 D6
Hanworth Rd., Felt. 81 B1
Hanworth Rd., Hmptn. 81 F4
Hanworth Rd., Houns. 81 E1
Hanworth Rd., Sun. 81 A7
Hanworth Ter., Houns. 72 H4
Hanworth Trd. Est., Felt. 81 E3
Hapgood Clo., Grnf. 46 A5
Harben Rd. NW6 48 F7
Harberson Rd. E15 60 F1
Harberson Rd. SW12 85 B1
Harberton Rd. N19 49 C1
Harbet Rd. N18 33 G5
Harbet Rd. W2 10 F2
Harbet Rd. W2 57 G5
Harbex Clo., Bex. 80 H7
Harbinger Rd. E14 69 B4
Harbledown Rd. SW6 75 D1
Harbord Clo. SE5 77 A2
De Crespigny Pk.
Harbord St. SW6 75 A1
Harborne Clo., Wat. 28 C5
Harborough Ave., Sid. 79 H7
Harborough Rd. SW16 85 F4
Harbour Ave. SW10 75 F1
Harbour Ex. Sq. E14 69 B2
Harbour Rd. SE5 76 J3
Harbridge Ave. SW15 74 F7
Harbut Rd. SW11 75 G4
Harcombe Rd. N16 50 B3
Harcourt Ave. E12 52 C4
Harcourt Ave., Edg. 30 C3
Harcourt Ave., Sid. 80 C6
Harcourt Ave., Wall. 101 B4
Harcourt Clo., Islw. 73 D3
Harcourt Fld., Wall. 101 B4
Harcourt Rd. E15 60 F2
Harcourt Rd. N22 40 D1
Harcourt Rd. SE4 77 H4
Harcourt Rd. SW19 84 D7
Russell Rd.
Harcourt Rd., Bexh. 80 E4
Harcourt Rd., Th.Hth. 94 F6
Harcourt Rd., Wall. 101 B4
Harcourt St. W1 10 H2
Harcourt St. W1 57 H5
Harcourt Ter. SW10 18 B4
Harcourt Ter. SW10 66 E5
Hardcastle Clo., Croy. 95 C6
Hardcourts Clo., W.Wick. 103 B3
Hardel Ri. SW2 85 H1
Hardel Wk. SW2 76 G7
Papworth Way
Hardens Manorway SE7 70 A3
Harders Rd. SE15 77 E2
Hardess St. SE24 76 J3
Herne Hill Rd.
Hardie Clo. NW10 47 D5
Hardie Rd., Dag. 53 J3
Harding Clo. SE17 20 J6
Harding Ho., Hayes 54 A6
Harding Rd., Bexh. 80 F2
Hardinge Rd. N18 33 B5
Hardinge Rd. NW10 56 H1
Hardinge St. E1 59 F6
Hardings La. SE20 86 G6
Hardman Rd. SE7 69 H5
Hardman Rd., Kings.T. 91 H2
Hardwick Clo., Stan. 29 F5
Hardwick Grn. W13 55 E5
Hardwick St. EC1 8 F4
Hardwick St. EC1 58 G3
Hardwicke Ave., Houns. 72 G1
Hardwicke Rd. N13 32 E6
Hardwicke Rd. W4 65 C4
Hardwicke Rd., Rich. 82 F4
Hardwicke St., Bark. 61 F1
Hardwicks Way SW18 75 D5
Buckhold Rd.
Hardwidge St. SE1 17 D3
Hardy Ave., Ruis. 45 B5
Hardy Clo. SE16 68 G2
Middleton Dr.
Hardy Clo., Pnr. 36 D7
Hardy Rd. SE3 69 F6
Hardy Rd. SW19 84 E7
Hardy Way, Enf. 24 G1
Hare & Billet Rd. SE3 78 D1
Hare Ct. EC4 12 E4
Hare La., Esher 98 A5
Hare Marsh E2 9 H5
Hare Pl. EC4 12 F4
Hare Row E2 59 E2
Hare St. SE18 70 D3
Hare Wk. N1 9 E2
Hare Wk. N1 59 B2
Harebell Dr. E6 61 D5
Harecastle Clo., Hayes 54 E4
Braunston Dr.
Harecourt Rd. N1 49 J6
Haredale Rd. SE24 76 J4
Haredon Clo. SE23 77 F7
Harefield, Esher 98 B3
Harefield Clo., Enf. 24 G1
Harefield Ms. SE4 77 J3
Harefield Rd. N8 40 D5
Harefield Rd. SE4 77 J3
Harefield Rd. SW16 85 F7
Harefield Rd., Sid. 89 D2
Haresfield Rd., Dag. 53 G6
Harewood Ave. NW1 6 H6
Harewood Ave. NW1 57 H4
Harewood Ave., Nthlt. 45 E7
Harewood Clo., Nthlt. 45 F7
Harewood Dr., Ilf. 43 C2
Harewood Pl. W1 11 E4
Harewood Rd. SW19 84 H6
Harewood Rd., Islw. 64 C7
Harewood Rd., S.Croy. 102 B6
Harewood Rd., Wat. 28 B2
Harewood Row NW1 10 H1
Harewood Ter., Sthl. 63 F4
Harfield Gdns. SE5 77 B3
Harfield Rd., Sun. 90 D2
Harford Clo. E4 26 B7
Harford Rd. E4 26 B7
Harford St. E1 59 H4
Harford Wk. N2 39 G4
Hargood Clo., Har. 37 H6
Hargood Rd. SE3 78 J1
Hargrave Pk. N19 49 C2
Hargrave Pl. N7 49 D5
Brecknock Rd.
Hargrave Rd. N19 49 C2
Hargwyne St. SW9 76 F3
Haringey Pk. N8 40 E6
Haringey Pas. N4 40 H5
Warham Rd.
Haringey Pas. N8 40 H4
Haringey Rd. N8 40 E4
Harington Ter. N9 33 A3
Harington Ter. N18 33 A3
Harkett Clo., Har. 37 C2
Byron Rd.
Harkett Ct., Har. 37 C2
Harland Ave., Croy. 102 C3
Harland Ave., Sid. 88 G3
Harland Rd. SE12 87 G1
Harlands Gro., Orp. 104 E4
Pinecrest Gdns.
Harlech Gdns., Houns. 63 C6
Harlech Rd. N14 32 E3
Harlech Twr. W3 65 C2
Harlequin Ave., Brent. 64 D6
Harlequin Clo., Islw. 73 B5
Harlequin Rd., Tedd. 82 E7
Harlescott Rd. SE15 77 G4
Harlesden Gdns. NW10 56 F1
Harlesden La. NW10 56 G1
Harlesden Rd. NW10 56 G1
Harleston Clo. E5 50 F2
Theydon Rd.
Harley Clo., Wem. 46 G6
Harley Ct. E11 42 G7
Blake Hall Rd.
Harley Cres., Har. 37 A4
Harley Gdns. SW10 18 D4
Harley Gdns. SW10 66 F5
Harley Gdns., Orp. 104 H4
Harley Gro. E3 59 J3
Harley Pl. W1 11 D2
Harley Pl. W1 58 B5
Harley Rd. NW3 48 G7
Harley Rd. NW10 56 E2
Harley Rd., Har. 37 A4
Harley St. W1 7 D6
Harley St. W1 58 B5
Harleyford, Brom. 96 J1
Harleyford Rd. SE11 20 C5
Harleyford Rd. SE11 67 F6
Harleyford St. SE11 20 E6
Harleyford St. SE11 67 G6
Harlington Rd., Bexh. 80 E3
Harlington Rd. E., Felt. 72 B7
Harlington Rd. W., Felt. 72 B6
Harlow Rd. N13 33 A3
Harlyn Dr., Pnr. 36 B3
Harman Ave., Wdf.Grn. 34 F6
Harman Clo. E4 34 D4
Harman Clo. NW2 48 B3
Harman Dr. NW2 48 B3
Harman Dr., Sid. 79 J6
Harman Rd., Enf. 25 C5
Harmony Clo. NW11 39 B5
Harmony Way NW4 38 J4
Bell La.
Harmood Gro. NW1 49 B7
Clarence Way
Harmood Pl. NW1 49 B7
Harmood St.
Harmood St. NW1 49 B6
Harmsworth St. SE17 20 G4
Harmsworth St. SE17 67 H5
Harmsworth Way N20 31 C1
Harnage Rd., Brent. 64 E7
Harness Rd. SE28 71 A2
Harold Ave., Belv. 71 F5
Harold Est. SE1 17 E6
Harold Est. SE1 68 B3
Harold Gibbons Ct. SE7 69 J6
Victoria Way
Harold Pl. SE11 20 E4
Harold Rd. E4 34 C4
Harold Rd. E11 51 E1
Harold Rd. E13 60 H1
Harold Rd. N8 40 F5
Harold Rd. N15 41 C5
Harold Rd. NW10 56 D3
Harold Rd. SE19 86 A7
Harold Rd., Sutt. 100 G4
Harold Rd., Wdf.Grn. 42 G1
Haroldstone Rd. E17 41 G5
Harp All. EC4 12 G3
Harp Island Clo. NW10 47 D2
Harp La. EC3 13 D6
Harp Rd. W7 55 B4
Harpenden Rd. E12 51 J2
Harpenden Rd. SE27 85 H2
Harper Rd. E6 61 C6
Harper Rd. SE1 17 A5
Harper Rd. SE1 67 J3
Harpley Sq. E1 59 F3
Harpour Rd., Bark. 52 F6
Harpsden St. SW11 76 A1
Harpur Ms. WC1 12 C1
Harpur St. WC1 12 C1

Harpur St. WC1	58	F5
Harraden Rd. SE3	78	J1
Harrier Ms. SE28	70	G3
Harrier Rd. NW9	38	E2
Harrier Way E6	61	C5
Harries Rd., Hayes	54	C4
Harriet Clo. E8	59	D1
Harriet Gdns., Croy.	102	D2
Harriet St. SW1	**15**	**A4**
Harriet Wk. SW1	**15**	**A4**
Harriet Wk. SW1	66	J2
Harringay Gdns. N8	40	H4
Harringay Rd. N15	40	H5
Harrington Clo. NW10	47	D3
Harrington Clo., Croy.	101	E2
Harrington Gdns. SW7	**18**	**B2**
Harrington Gdns. SW7	66	F4
Harrington Hill E5	50	E1
Harrington Rd. E11	51	E1
Harrington Rd. SE25	95	D4
Harrington Rd. SW7	**18**	**F1**
Harrington Rd. SW7	66	G4
Harrington Sq. NW1	**7**	**F2**
Harrington Sq. NW1	58	C2
Harrington St. NW1	**7**	**F2**
Harrington St. NW1	58	C3
Harrington Way SE18	70	A3
Harriott Clo. SE10	69	F4
Harris Clo., Enf.	24	H1
Harris Clo., Houns.	72	G1
Harris Rd., Bexh.	80	E1
Harris Rd., Dag.	53	F5
Harris St. E17	41	J7
Harris St. SE5	68	A7
Harrison Rd., Dag.	53	H6
Harrison St. WC1	**8**	**B4**
Harrison St. WC1	58	E3
Harrisons Ri., Croy.	101	H3
Harrogate Rd., Wat.	28	C3
Harrold Rd., Dag.	53	B5
Harrow Ave., Enf.	25	C6
Harrow Clo., Chess.	98	G7
Harrow Dr. N9	33	C1
Harrow Flds. Gdns., Har.	46	B3
Harrow La. E14	60	C7
Harrow Manorway SE2	71	C3
Harrow Pk., Har.	46	B2
Harrow Pas., Kings.T.	91	G2
Market Pl.		
Harrow Pl. E1	**13**	**F3**
Harrow Pl. E1	59	B6
Harrow Rd. E6	61	B1
Harrow Rd. E11	51	E3
Harrow Rd. NW10	56	H3
Harrow Rd. W2	57	B4
Harrow Rd. W9	57	B4
Harrow Rd. W10	57	B4
Harrow Rd., Bark.	61	H1
Harrow Rd., Cars.	100	H5
Harrow Rd., Ilf.	52	F4
Harrow Rd., Wem.	46	C4
Harrow Vw., Har.	36	J1
Harrow Vw., Hayes	54	A6
Harrow Vw. Rd. W5	55	E4
Harrow Way, Wat.	28	E3
Harrow Weald Pk., Har.	29	A6
Harroway Rd. SW11	75	G2
Harrowby St. W1	**10**	**H3**
Harrowby St. W1	57	H6
Harrowdene Clo., Wem.	46	G4
Harrowdene Gdns., Tedd.	82	D6
Harrowdene Rd., Wem.	46	G5
Harrowes Meade, Edg.	30	A3
Harrowgate Rd. E9	50	H6
Hart Cres., Chig.	35	J5
Hart Gro. W5	65	A1
Hart Gro., Sthl.	54	G5
Hart St. EC3	**13**	**E5**
Harte Rd., Houns.	72	F2
Hartfield Ave., Borwd.	22	A5
Hartfield Ave., Nthlt.	54	B2
Hartfield Clo., Borwd.	22	A5
Hartfield Cres. SW19	84	C7
Hartfield Cres., W.Wick.	103	G3
Hartfield Gro. SE20	95	F1
Hartfield Rd. SW19	84	C6
Hartfield Rd., Chess.	98	G5
Hartfield Rd., W.Wick.	103	G4
Hartfield Ter. E3	60	A2
Hartford Ave., Har.	37	D3
Hartford Rd., Bex.	80	G6
Hartford Rd., Epsom	99	A6
Hartforde Rd., Borwd.	22	A2
Hartham Clo. N7	49	E5
Hartham Clo., Islw.	73	D1
Hartham Rd. N7	49	E5
Hartham Rd. N17	41	C2
Hartham Rd., Islw.	73	C1
Harting Rd. SE9	88	B4
Hartington Clo., Har.	46	B4
Hartington Ct. W4	65	B7
Hartington Rd. E16	60	H6
Hartington Rd. E17	41	H6
Hartington Rd. SW8	76	E1
Hartington Rd. W4	65	B7
Hartington Rd. W13	55	C7
Hartington Rd., Sthl.	63	E3
Hartington Rd., Twick.	73	E7
Hartismere Rd. SW6	66	C7
Hartlake Rd. E9	50	G6
Hartland Clo., Edg.	30	A2
Hartland Dr., Edg.	30	A2
Hartland Dr., Ruis.	45	B3
Hartland Rd. E15	51	F7
Hartland Rd. N11	31	J5
Hartland Rd. NW1	49	B7
Hartland Rd. NW6	57	C2
Hartland Rd., Hmptn.	81	H4
Hartland Rd., Islw.	73	D3
Hartland Rd., Mord.	93	D7
Hartland Way, Croy.	102	H2
Hartland Way, Mord.	93	C7
Hartlands Clo., Bex.	80	F6
Hartley Ave. E6	61	B1
Hartley Ave. NW7	30	F5
Hartley Clo. NW7	30	F5
Hartley Clo., Brom.	97	C2
Hartley Rd. E11	51	F1
Hartley Rd., Croy.	94	H7
Hartley Rd., Well.	71	C7
Hartley St. E2	59	F3
Hartnoll St. N7	49	F5
Eden Gro.		
Harton Clo., Brom.	97	A1
Harton Rd. N9	33	E2
Harton St. SE8	78	A1
Harts Gro., Wdf.Grn.	34	G5
Harts La. SE14	68	H7
Harts La., Bark.	52	E6
Hartsbourne Ave. (Bushey), Wat.	28	J2
Hartsbourne Clo. (Bushey), Wat.	29	A2
Hartsbourne Rd. (Bushey), Wat.	29	A2
Hartshorn All. EC3	**13**	**E4**
Hartshorn Gdns. E6	61	D4
Hartslock Dr. SE2	71	D2
Hartsmead Rd. SE9	88	C2
Hartsway, Enf.	25	F4
Hartswood Grn. (Bushey), Wat.	29	A2
Hartswood Rd. W12	65	F2
Hartsworth Clo. E13	60	F2
Hartville Rd. SE18	70	H4
Hartwell Dr. E4	34	C6
Hartwell St. E8	50	C6
Dalston La.		
Harvard Hill W4	65	B5
Wolseley Gdns.		
Harvard La. W4	65	B5
Harvard Rd.		
Harvard Rd. SE13	78	C5
Harvard Rd. W4	65	B5
Harvard Rd., Islw.	73	B1
Harvel Cres. SE2	71	D5
Harvest Bank Rd., W.Wick.	103	F3
Harvest La., T.Ditt.	91	D6
Harvest Rd., Felt.	81	A4
Harvesters Clo., Islw.	73	A5
Harvey Gdns. E11	51	F1
Harvey Rd.		
Harvey Gdns. SE7	69	J5
Harvey Gdns., Loug.	27	E3
Harvey Ho., Brent.	64	H5
Harvey Pt. E16	60	H5
Fife Rd.		
Harvey Rd. E11	51	E1
Harvey Rd. N8	40	F5
Harvey Rd. SE5	77	A1
Harvey Rd., Houns.	72	F7
Harvey Rd., Ilf.	52	E5
Harvey Rd., Nthlt.	45	C7
Harvey Rd., Walt.	90	A7
Harvey St. N1	59	A1
Harvill Rd., Sid.	89	D5
Harvington Wk. E8	50	D7
Wilman Gro.		
Harvist Est. N7	49	G4
Harvist Rd. NW6	57	A2
Harwater Dr., Loug.	27	C2
Harwell Pas. N2	39	J4
Harwich La. EC2	**13**	**E1**
Harwich La. EC2	59	B5
Harwood Ave., Brom.	96	H2
Harwood Ave., Mitch.	93	H3
Harwood Clo., Wem.	46	G4
Harrowdene Rd.		
Harwood Rd. SW6	66	D7
Harwood Ter. SW6	75	E1
Harwoods Yd. N21	24	G7
Wades Hill		
Hascombe Ter. SE5	77	A2
Haselbury Rd. N9	33	B3
Haselbury Rd. N18	33	B4
Haseley End SE23	77	F7
Tyson Rd.		
Haselrigge Rd. SW4	76	D4
Haseltine Rd. SE26	86	J4
Haselwood Dr., Enf.	24	H4
Haskard Rd., Dag.	53	D4
Haskell Ho. NW10	56	D1
Hasker St. SW3	**18**	**H1**
Hasker St. SW3	66	H4
Haslam Ave., Sutt.	100	B1
Haslam Clo. N1	49	G7
Haslemere Ave. NW4	39	A6
Haslemere Ave. SW18	84	E2
Haslemere Ave. W7	64	D3
Haslemere Ave. W13	64	D3
Haslemere Ave., Barn.	31	J1
Haslemere Ave., Houns.	72	C2
Haslemere Ave., Mitch.	93	G2
Haslemere Clo., Hmptn.	81	F5
Haslemere Clo., Wall.	101	E5
Stafford Rd.		
Haslemere Gdns. N3	39	C3
Haslemere Heathrow Est., Houns.	72	B2
Haslemere Rd. N8	40	D7
Haslemere Rd. N21	32	H2
Haslemere Rd., Bexh.	80	F2
Haslemere Rd., Ilf.	52	J2
Haslemere Rd., Th.Hth.	94	H5
Hasler Clo. SE28	62	B7
Hasluck Gdns., Barn.	23	E6
Hassard St. E2	**9**	**G2**
Hassendean Rd. SE3	69	H6
Hassett Rd. E9	50	G6
Hassock Wd., Kes.	104	A4
Hassocks Clo. SE26	86	E3
Hassocks Rd. SW16	94	C1
Hassop Rd. NW2	48	A4
Hassop Wk. SE9	88	B4
Hasted Rd. SE7	70	A5
Hastings Ave., Ilf.	43	F4
Hastings Clo. SE15	68	D7
Hastings Clo., Barn.	23	F4
Leicester Rd.		
Hastings Ho. SE18	70	C4
Cardwell Rd.		
Hastings Rd. N11	32	C5
Hastings Rd. N17	41	A3
Hastings Rd. W13	55	E7
Hastings Rd., Brom.	104	B1
Hastings Rd., Croy.	102	C1
Hastings St. WC1	**8**	**A4**
Hastings St. WC1	58	E3
Hastoe Clo., Hayes	54	E4
Kingsash Dr.		
Hat and Mitre Ct. EC1	**8**	**H6**
Hatch, The, Enf.	25	G1
Hatch Gro., Rom.	44	E4
Hatch La. E4	34	D4
Hatch Pl., Kings.T.	82	J5
Hatch Rd. SW16	94	E2
Hatch Side, Chig.	35	D5
Hatcham Pk. Ms. SE14	77	G1
Hatcham Pk. Rd.		
Hatcham Pk. Rd. SE14	77	G1
Hatcham Rd. SE15	68	F6
Hatchard Rd. N19	48	E2
Hatchcroft NW4	38	H3
Hatchwood Clo., Wdf.Grn.	34	F4
Sunset Ave.		
Hatcliffe Clo. SE3	78	F3
Hatcliffe St. SE10	69	F5
Woolwich Rd.		
Hatfield Clo. SE14	68	G7
Hatfield Clo., Ilf.	43	E3
Hatfield Clo., Mitch.	93	G4
Hatfield Mead, Mord.	93	D5
Central Rd.		
Hatfield Rd. E15	51	E5
Hatfield Rd. W4	65	D2
Hatfield Rd. W13	64	D1
Hatfield Rd., Dag.	53	E6
Hatfields SE1	**16**	**F1**
Hatfields SE1	67	G1
Hatfields, Loug.	27	E3
Hathaway Clo., Brom.	104	C1
Hathaway Clo., Stan.	29	D5
Hathaway Cres. E12	53	D5
Hathaway Gdns. W13	55	C5
Hathaway Gdns., Rom.	44	D5
Hathaway Rd., Croy.	94	H7
Hatherleigh Clo., Chess.	98	G5
Hatherleigh Clo., Mord.	93	D4
Hatherleigh Rd., Ruis.	45	A2
Hatherley Cres., Sid.	89	A2
Hatherley Gdns. E6	61	A2
Hatherley Gdns. N8	40	E6
Hatherley Gro. W2	**10**	**A3**
Hatherley Gro. W2	57	E6
Hatherley Ms. E17	42	A4
Hatherley Rd. E17	41	J4
Hatherley Rd., Rich.	73	J1
Hatherley Rd., Sid.	89	A4
Hatherley St. SW1	**19**	**G2**
Hathern Gdns. SE9	88	D4
The Knole		
Hatherop Rd., Hmptn.	81	F7
Hathorne Clo. SE15	77	E2
Hathway St. SE15	77	F2
Gibbon Rd.		
Hathway Ter. SE14	77	F2
Gibbon Rd.		
Hatley Ave., Ilf.	43	F4
Hatley Clo. N11	31	J5
Hatley Rd. N4	49	F2
Hatteraick St. SE16	68	F2
Brunel Rd.		
Hattersfield Clo., Belv.	71	F4
Hatton Clo. SE18	70	G7
Hatton Ct. E5	50	H4
Gilpin Rd.		
Hatton Gdn. EC1	**12**	**F1**
Hatton Gdn. EC1	58	G4
Hatton Gdns., Mitch.	93	J3
Hatton Grn., Felt.	72	A4
Hatton Ho. E1	**13**	**J5**
Hatton Pl. EC1	**12**	**F1**
Hatton Pl. EC1	58	G4
Hatton Rd., Croy.	101	G1
Hatton Row NW8	**6**	**F6**
Hatton St. NW8	**6**	**F6**
Hatton Wall EC1	**12**	**E1**
Hatton Wall EC1	58	G5
Haunch of Venison Yd. W1	**11**	**D4**
Havana Rd. SW19	84	D2
Havannah St. E14	69	A2
Havant Rd. E17	42	C3
Havant Way SE15	**21**	**F7**
Havelock Pl., Har.	37	B6
Havelock Rd. N17	41	D2
Havelock Rd. SW19	84	F5
Havelock Rd., Belv.	71	F4
Havelock Rd., Brom.	96	J4
Havelock Rd., Croy.	102	C2
Havelock Rd., Har.	37	B3
Havelock Rd., Sthl.	63	E3
Havelock St. N1	58	E1
Havelock St., Ilf.	52	E2
Havelock Ter. SW8	67	B7
Havelock Wk. SE23	86	F1
Haven, The, Rich.	74	A3
Haven Clo. SE9	88	C3
Haven Clo. SW19	84	A3
Haven Clo., Sid.	89	C6
Haven Grn. W5	55	G6
Haven Grn. Ct. W5	55	G6
Haven La. W5	55	H6
Haven Pl. W5	55	G7
The Bdy.		
Haven St. NW1	49	B7
Castlehaven Rd.		
Haven Ter. W5	55	J7
The Bdy.		
Havenhurst Ri., Enf.	24	G2

Havenwood, Wem. 47 B3
Haverfield Gdns., 65 A7
Rich.
Haverfield Rd. E3 59 H3
Haverford Way, Edg. 37 J1
Haverhill Rd. E4 34 C1
Haverhill Rd. SW12 64 C1
Havering Gdns., Rom. 44 C5
Havering St. E1 59 G6
Devonport St.
Havering Way, Bark. 62 B3
Haversfield Est., 64 H5
Brent.
Haversham Clo., 73 G6
Twick.
Haverstock Hill NW3 48 J6
Haverstock Rd. NW5 49 A5
Haverstock St. N1 8 H2
Haverstock St. N1 58 H2
Haverthwaite Rd., 104 G2
Orp.
Havil St. SE5 68 B7
Havisham Pl. SE19 85 H6
Hawarden Gro. SE24 76 J7
Hawarden Hill NW2 47 G3
Hawarden Rd. E17 41 G4
Hawbridge Rd. E11 51 D1
Hawes La., W.Wick. 103 C1
Hawes Rd. N18 33 E6
Hawes Rd., Brom. 96 H1
Hawes St. N1 49 H7
Haweswater Ho., Islw. 73 C5
Hawgood St. E3 60 A5
Hawkdene E4 26 B6
Hawke Pk. Rd. N22 40 H3
Hawke Pl. SE16 68 G2
Middleton Dr.
Hawke Rd. SE19 86 B6
Hawker Clo., Wall. 101 E7
Kingsford Ave.
Hawkes Rd., Mitch. 93 H1
Hawkesbury Rd. 74 H5
SW15
Hawkesfield Rd. SE23 86 H2
Hawkesley Clo., 82 D4
Twick.
Hawkewood Rd., Sun. 90 A3
Hawkhurst Gdns., 98 H4
Chess.
Hawkhurst Rd. SW16 94 D1
Hawkhurst Way, 92 D5
N.Mal.
Hawkhurst Way, 103 B2
W.Wick.
Hawkins Clo., Borwd. 22 C2
Banks Rd.
Hawkins Clo., Har. 37 A7
Hawkins Rd., Tedd. 82 E6
Hawkley Gdns. SE27 85 H2
Hawkridge Clo., Rom. 44 E6
Hawks Ms. SE10 69 C7
Luton Pl.
Hawks Rd., Kings.T. 91 J2
Hawksbrook La., 96 B6
Beck.
Hawkshaw Clo. SW2 76 E7
Tierney Rd.
Hawkshead Clo., 87 E7
Brom.
Hawkshead Rd. 47 F7
NW10
Hawkshead Rd. W4 65 E2
Hawkslade Rd. SE15 77 G5
Hawksley Rd. N16 50 A3
Hawksmoor Clo. E6 61 B6
Allhallows Rd.
Hawksmoor Ms. E1 59 E7
Cable St.
Hawksmoor St. W6 66 A6
Hawksmouth E4 26 B7
Hawkstone Rd. SE16 68 F4
Hawkwell Wk. N1 58 J1
Basire St.
Hawkwood Cres. E4 26 B6
Hawkwood La., Chis. 97 F1
Hawkwood Mt. E5 50 E1
Hawlands Dr., Pnr. 36 E7
Hawley Clo., Hmptn. 81 F6
Hawley Cres. NW1 49 B7
Hawley Ms. NW1 49 B7
Hawley St.
Hawley Rd. N18 33 G5
Hawley Rd. NW1 49 B7
Hawley St. NW1 49 B7
Hawstead Rd. SE6 78 B6
Hawsted, Buck.H. 26 H7
Hawthorn Ave. N13 32 E5
Hawthorn Ave., Cars. 101 A7

Hawthorn Ave., Rich. 73 H2
Kew Rd.
Hawthorn Ave., 94 H1
Th.Hth.
Hawthorn Clo., 81 G5
Hmptn.
Hawthorn Clo., Houns. 63 B7
Hawthorn Clo., Orp. 97 G6
Hawthorn Ct., Rich. 74 B1
Hawthorn Cres. SW17 85 A5
Hawthorn Dr., Har. 36 G6
Hawthorn Dr., 103 E4
W.Wick.
Hawthorn Gdns. W5 64 G3
Hawthorn Gro. SE20 86 E7
Hawthorn Gro., Barn. 22 F6
Hawthorn Hatch, 64 E7
Brent.
Hawthorn Ms. NW7 39 B1
Holders Hill Rd.
Hawthorn Pl., Erith 71 J5
Hawthorn Rd. N8 40 D3
Hawthorn Rd. N18 33 C6
Hawthorn Rd. NW10 47 G7
Hawthorn Rd., Bexh. 80 F4
Hawthorn Rd., Brent. 64 E7
Hawthorn Rd., 35 A4
Buck.H.
Hawthorn Rd., Sutt. 100 H5
Hawthorn Rd., Wall. 101 B7
Hawthorn Wk. W10 57 B4
Droop St.
Hawthorn Way N9 33 B2
Hawthorndene Clo., 103 F2
Brom.
Hawthorndene Rd., 103 F2
Brom.
Hawthorne Ave., Har. 37 D6
Hawthorne Ave., 93 G2
Mitch.
Hawthorne Ave., Ruis. 36 B7
Hawthorne Clo. N1 50 B6
Hawthorne Clo., 97 C3
Brom.
Hawthorne Clo., Sutt. 100 E2
Aultone Way
Hawthorne Fm. Ave., 54 E1
Nthlt.
Hawthorne Gro. NW9 38 C7
Hawthorne Ms., Grnf. 54 J6
Greenford Rd.
Hawthorne Rd. E17 42 A3
Hawthorne Rd., Brom. 97 C3
Hawthornes Cen., 37 C4
Har.
Hawthorns, Wdf.Grn. 34 G3
Hawthorns, The, 99 F6
Epsom
Ewell Bypass
Hawthorns, The, 27 D4
Loug.
Hawtrey Ave., Nthlt. 54 D2
Hawtrey Dr., Ruis. 36 A7
Hawtrey Rd. NW3 48 H7
Haxted Rd., Brom. 96 H1
North Rd.
Hay Clo. E15 51 E7
Hay Clo., Borwd. 22 C2
Banks Rd.
Hay Currie St. E14 60 B6
Hay Hill W1 11 E6
Hay Hill W1 58 B7
Hay La. NW9 38 C4
Hay St. E2 59 D1
Haycroft Gdns. NW10 56 G1
Haycroft Rd. SW2 76 E5
Haycroft Rd., Surb. 98 G3
Hayday Rd. E16 60 G5
Hayden Way, Rom. 44 J2
Haydens Pl. W11 57 C6
Portobello Rd.
Haydns Ms. W3 56 C6
Emanuel Ave.
Haydock Ave., Nthlt. 45 G6
Haydock Grn., Nthlt. 45 G6
Haydock Ave.
Haydon Clo. NW9 38 C4
Haydon Clo., Enf. 25 B6
Mortimer Dr.
Haydon Dr., Pnr. 36 B4
Haydon Pk. Rd. SW19 84 D5
Haydon Rd., Dag. 53 C2
Haydon St. EC3 13 F5
Haydon Wk. E1 13 G5
Haydons Rd. SW19 84 E5
Hayes Chase, 96 D6
W.Wick.
Hayes Clo., Brom. 103 G2

Hayes Ct. SW2 85 E1
Hayes Cres. NW11 39 C5
Hayes Cres., Sutt. 100 A4
Hayes Gdn., Brom. 103 G2
Hayes Hill, Brom. 103 E1
Hayes Hill Rd., Brom. 103 F1
Hayes La., Beck. 96 C3
Hayes La., Brom. 96 G5
Hayes Mead Rd., 103 E1
Brom.
Hayes Pl. NW1 6 H6
Hayes Rd., Brom. 96 G4
Hayes Rd., Sthl. 63 B4
Hayes St., Brom. 103 H1
Hayes Way, Beck. 96 C4
Hayes Wd. Ave., 103 H1
Brom.
Hayesford Pk. Dr., 96 F5
Brom.
Hayfield Pas. E1 59 F4
Stepney Grn.
Hayfield Yd. E1 59 F4
Mile End Rd.
Haygarth Pl. SW19 84 A5
Haygreen Clo., 83 B6
Kings.T.
Hayland Clo. NW9 38 D4
Hayles St. SE11 20 G1
Hayles St. SE11 67 H4
Haylett Gdns., 91 G4
Kings.T.
Anglesea Rd.
Hayling Ave., Felt. 81 A3
Hayling Rd., Wat. 28 A3
Hayman St. N1 49 H7
Cross St.
Haymarket SW1 11 H6
Haymarket SW1 58 D7
Haymarket Arc. SW1 11 H6
Haymer Gdns., 99 G3
Wor.Pk.
Haymerle Rd. SE15 21 H6
Haymerle Rd. SE15 68 D6
Haymill Clo., Grnf. 55 C3
Hayne Rd., Beck. 95 J2
Hayne St. EC1 12 H1
Haynes Clo. N17 33 E7
Haynes Clo. SE3 78 E3
Haynes La. SE19 86 B6
Haynes Rd., Wem. 46 H7
Haynt Wk. SW20 93 B3
Hay's La. SE1 17 D2
Hay's Ms. W1 15 D1
Hay's Ms. W1 67 B1
Haysleigh Gdns. 95 D2
SE20
Hayter Rd. SW2 76 E5
Hayton Clo. E8 50 C6
Buttermere Wk.
Hayward Clo. SW19 84 E1
Hayward Gdns. SW15 74 J6
Hayward Rd. N20 31 F2
Hayward's Pl. EC1 8 G6
Haywood Clo., Pnr. 36 D2
Haywood Ri., Orp. 104 H4
Haywood Rd., Brom. 97 A4
Hayworth Clo., Enf. 25 H2
Green St.
Hazel Bank, Surb. 99 C1
Hazel Clo. N13 33 A3
Hazel Clo. N19 49 C2
Hargrave Pk.
Hazel Clo. SE15 77 D2
Copeland Rd.
Hazel Clo., Brent. 64 E7
Hazel Clo., Croy. 102 G1
Primrose La.
Hazel Clo., Mitch. 94 D4
Hazel Clo., Twick. 72 J7
Hazel Gdns., Edg. 30 B4
Hazel Gro. SE26 86 G4
Hazel Gro., Enf. 25 D6
Dimsdale Dr.
Hazel Gro., Orp. 104 E2
Hazel Gro., Rom. 44 E3
Hazel Gro., Wem. 55 H1
Carlyon Rd.
Hazel Gro. Est. SE26 86 G4
Hazel La., Rich. 82 H2
Hazel Mead, Barn. 22 H5
Hazel Rd. E15 51 E5
Wingfield Rd.
Hazel Rd. NW10 56 H3
Hazel Wk., Brom. 97 D6
Hazel Way E4 33 J6
Hazel Way SE1 21 F1
Hazelbank Rd. SE6 87 D2

Hazelbourne Rd. 76 B6
SW12
Hazelbrouck Gdns., 35 G7
Ilf.
Hazelbury Clo. SW19 93 D2
Hazelbury Grn. N9 33 B3
Hazelbury La. N9 33 B3
Hazelcroft, Pnr. 28 H6
Hazeldean Rd. NW10 47 D7
Hazeldene Dr., Pnr. 36 C3
Hazeldene Rd., Ilf. 53 B2
Hazeldene Rd., Well. 80 C2
Hazeldon Rd. SE4 77 H5
Hazeleigh Gdns., 35 B5
Wdf.Grn.
Hazelgreen Clo. N21 32 H1
Hazelhurst, Beck. 96 D1
Hazelhurst Rd. SW17 84 F4
Hazell Cres., Rom. 44 H1
Hazellville Rd. N19 40 D7
Hazelmere Clo., Nthlt. 54 F2
Hazelmere Dr., Nthlt. 54 F2
Hazelmere Rd. NW6 57 C1
Hazelmere Rd., Nthlt. 54 F2
Hazelmere Rd., Orp. 97 F4
Hazelmere Wk., Nthlt. 54 F2
Hazelmere Way, 96 G6
Brom.
Hazeltree La., Nthlt. 54 E3
Hazelwood, Loug. 27 A5
Hazelwood Ave., 93 E4
Mord.
Hazelwood Clo. W5 64 H2
Hazelwood Clo., Har. 36 H4
Hazelwood Ct. NW10 47 E3
Neasden La. N.
Hazelwood Cres. N13 32 G4
Hazelwood Cres. W10 57 B4
Hazelwood Cft., Surb. 91 H6
Hazelwood Dr., Pnr. 36 B2
Hazelwood La. N13 32 G4
Hazelwood Pk. Clo., 35 H5
Chig.
Hazelwood Rd. E17 41 H5
Hazelwood Rd., Enf. 25 C6
Hazlebury Rd. SW6 75 E2
Hazledean Rd., Croy. 102 A2
Hazledene Rd. W4 65 C6
Hazlemere Gdns., 99 G1
Wor.Pk.
Hazlewell Rd. SW15 74 H5
Hazlitt Ms. W14 66 B3
Hazlitt Rd.
Hazlitt Rd. W14 66 B3
Head St. E1 59 G6
Headcorn Pl., Th.Hth. 94 F4
Headcorn Rd.
Headcorn Rd. N17 33 C1
Headcorn Rd., Brom. 87 G5
Headcorn Rd., 94 F4
Th.Hth.
Headfort Pl. SW1 15 C4
Headfort Pl. SW1 67 A2
Headingley Clo., Ilf. 35 J6
Headington Rd. 84 F2
SW18
Headlam Rd. SW4 76 D6
Headlam St. E1 59 E4
Headley App., Ilf. 43 E5
Headley Ave., Wall. 101 F5
Headley Clo., Epsom 99 A6
Headley Ct. SE26 86 F5
Headley Dr., Croy. 103 B7
Headley Dr., Ilf. 43 E6
Head's Ms. W11 57 D6
Artesian Rd.
Headstone Dr., Har. 37 B3
Headstone Gdns., Har. 36 J4
Headstone La., Har. 28 H7
Headstone Rd., Har. 37 B5
Headway Clo., Rich. 82 F4
Locksmeade Rd.
Heald St. SE14 77 J1
Healey Dr., Orp. 104 J4
Healey St. NW1 49 B6
Heanor Ct. E5 50 G3
Pedro St.
Hearn Ri., Nthlt. 54 D1
Hearn St. EC2 9 E6
Hearn St. EC2 58 H5
Hearne Rd. W4 65 A6
Hearn's Bldgs. SE17 21 C2
Hearnville Rd. SW12 85 A1
Heath, The W7 64 B1
Lower Boston Rd.
Heath Ave., Bexh. 71 D6
Heath Brow NW3 48 F3
North End Way

Name	Page	Grid
Heath Clo. NW11	39	E7
Heath Clo. W5	55	J4
Heath Ct., Houns.	72	F4
Heath Dr. NW3	48	E4
Heath Dr. SW20	92	J4
Heath Gdns., Twick.	82	C1
Heath Gro. SE20	86	F7
Maple Rd.		
Heath Hurst Rd. NW3	48	H4
Heath La. SE3	78	D2
Heath Mead SW19	84	A3
Heath Pk. Dr., Brom.	97	B3
Heath Ri. SW15	75	A6
Heath Ri., Brom.	96	F6
Heath Rd. SW8	76	B2
Heath Rd., Bex.	89	J1
Heath Rd., Har.	36	J7
Heath Rd., Houns.	72	H4
Heath Rd., Rom.	44	D7
Heath Rd., Th.Hth.	94	J3
Heath Rd., Twick.	82	C1
Heath Side NW3	48	G4
Heath Side, Orp.	104	F1
Heath St. NW3	48	F3
Heath Vw. N2	39	F4
Heath Vw. Clo. N2	39	F4
Heath Vill. SE18	70	J5
Heath Way, Erith	80	J1
Heatham Pk., Twick.	73	C7
Heathbourne Rd.	29	B1
(Bushey), Wat.		
Heathcock Ct. WC2	58	E7
Strand		
Heathcote Ave., Ilf.	43	C2
Heathcote Gro. E4	34	C3
Heathcote Rd., Twick.	73	E6
Heathcote St. WC1	**8**	**C5**
Heathcote St. WC1	58	F4
Heathcroft NW11	48	E1
Heathcroft W5	55	J4
Heathdale Ave.,	72	E3
Houns.		
Heathdene Dr., Belv.	71	H4
Heathdene Rd. SW16	85	F7
Heathdene Rd., Wall.	101	A7
Heathedge SE26	86	E2
Heather Clo. E6	61	E6
Heather Clo. SW8	76	B3
Heather Clo., Hmptn.	90	F1
Heather Clo., Islw.	73	A5
Harvesters Clo.		
Heather Dr., Enf.	24	H2
Chasewood Ave.		
Heather Gdns. NW11	39	B6
Heather Gdns., Sutt.	100	D6
Heather Pk. Dr.,	47	A7
Wem.		
Heather Rd. NW2	47	F2
Heather Rd. SE12	87	G2
Heather Wk. W10	57	B4
Droop St.		
Heather Wk., Edg.	30	B5
Heather Way, Stan.	29	C6
Heatherbank SE9	79	C2
Heatherbank, Chis.	97	D2
Heatherdale Clo.,	83	B7
Kings.T.		
Heatherdene Clo. N12	39	F1
Bow La.		
Heatherdene Clo.,	93	H4
Mitch.		
Heatherlands, Sun.	81	A6
Heatherley Dr., Ilf.	43	B3
Heatherset Gdns.	85	F7
SW16		
Heatherside Rd.,	99	D7
Epsom		
Heatherside Rd., Sid.	89	D3
Wren Rd.		
Heatherwood Clo. E12	51	J2
Heathfield E4	34	C3
Heathfield, Chis.	88	F6
Heathfield Ave. SW18	75	G7
Heathfield Rd.		
Heathfield Clo. E16	61	A5
Heathfield Clo., Kes.	103	J5
Heathfield Dr., Mitch.	93	H1
Heathfield Gdns.	39	A6
NW11		
Heathfield Gdns.	75	G6
SW18		
Heathfield Rd.		
Heathfield Gdns. W4	65	C5
Heathfield Gdns.,	102	A4
Croy.		
Coombe Rd.		
Heathfield La., Chis.	88	E6
Heathfield N., Twick.	73	C7
Heathfield Pk. NW2	47	J6
Heathfield Pk. Dr.,	44	B5
Rom.		
Barley La.		
Heathfield Rd. SW18	75	F6
Heathfield Rd. W3	65	B2
Heathfield Rd., Bexh.	80	F4
Heathfield Rd., Brom.	87	F7
Heathfield Rd., Croy.	102	A4
Heathfield Rd., Kes.	103	J5
Heathfield S., Twick.	73	C7
Heathfield Sq. SW18	75	G7
Heathfield St. W11	57	B7
Portland Rd.		
Heathfield Ter. SE18	70	H6
Heathfield Ter. W4	65	C5
Heathfields Ct.,	72	E5
Houns.		
Frampton Rd.		
Heathgate NW11	39	E6
Heathland Rd. N16	50	B1
Heathlands Clo.,	82	C1
Twick.		
Heathlands Way,	72	E5
Houns.		
Frampton Rd.		
Heathlee Rd. SE3	78	F4
Heathley End, Chis.	88	F6
Heathmans Rd. SW6	75	C1
Heathrow International	72	B3
Trd. Est., Houns.		
Heaths Clo., Enf.	25	B2
Heathside, Esher	98	B3
Heathside, Houns.	72	F7
Heathside Ave., Bexh.	80	E2
Heathside Clo., Esher	98	B3
Heathstan Rd. W12	56	G6
Heathview Ct. SW19	84	A2
Heathview Dr. SE2	71	D6
Heathview Gdns.	74	J7
SW15		
Heathview Rd.,	94	G4
Th.Hth.		
Heathville Rd. N19	40	E7
Heathwall St. SW11	75	J3
Heathway SE3	69	G7
Heathway, Croy.	102	J3
Heathway, Dag.	53	F3
Heathway, Wdf.Grn.	34	J4
Heathwood Gdns.	70	B4
SE7		
Heaton Clo. E4	34	C3
Friars Clo.		
Heaton Rd. SE15	77	D3
Heaton Rd., Mitch.	85	A7
Heaver Rd. SW11	75	G3
Wye St.		
Heavitree Rd. SE18	70	G5
Hebden Ct. E2	59	C1
Laburnum St.		
Hebdon Rd. SW17	84	H3
Heber Rd. NW2	48	A5
Heber Rd. SE22	77	C6
Hebron Rd. W6	65	H3
Hecham Clo. E17	41	H2
Heckfield Pl. SW6	66	D7
Fulham Rd.		
Heckford St. E1	59	G7
The Highway		
Hector St. SE18	70	H4
Heddington Gro. N7	49	F5
Heddon Clo., Islw.	73	D4
Heddon Ct. Ave.,	23	J5
Barn.		
Heddon Rd., Barn.	23	J5
Heddon St. W1	**11**	**F5**
Heddon St. W1	58	C7
Hedge Hill, Enf.	24	H1
Hedge La. N13	32	H3
Hedge Wk. SE6	87	B5
Lushington Rd.		
Hedgeley, Ilf.	43	C4
Hedgemans Rd., Dag.	53	D7
Hedgemans Way,	53	E6
Dag.		
Hedgerley Gdns.,	54	J2
Grnf.		
Hedgers Gro. E9	50	H6
Hedgewood Gdns., Ilf.	43	D4
Hedgley St. SE12	78	F5
Hedingham Clo. N1	49	J7
Popham Rd.		
Hedingham Rd., Dag.	53	B5
Hedley Rd., Twick.	72	G7
Hedley Row N5	50	A5
Poets Rd.		
Heenan Clo., Bark.	52	F6
Glenny Rd.		
Heene Rd., Enf.	25	A1
Heigham Rd. E6	52	B7
Heighton Gdns., Croy.	101	H5
Heights, The SE7	69	J5
Heights, The, Beck.	87	C7
Heights, The, Loug.	27	C2
Heights, The, Nthlt.	45	F5
Heights Clo. SW20	83	H7
Heiron St. SE17	**20**	**H6**
Heiron St. SE17	67	H6
Helby Rd. SW4	76	D6
Helder Gro. SE12	78	F7
Helder St., S.Croy.	102	A6
Heldmann Clo.,	73	A4
Houns.		
Helen Ave., Felt.	72	B7
Helen Clo. N2	39	F3
Thomas More Way		
Helen Clo., W.Mol.	90	H4
Helen St. SE18	70	E4
Wilmount St.		
Helena Clo., Wall.	101	E7
Kingsford Ave.		
Helena Pl. E9	59	F1
Fremont St.		
Helena Rd. E13	60	F2
Helena Rd. E17	42	A5
Helena Rd. NW10	47	H5
Helena Rd. W5	55	G5
Helena Sq. SE16	59	H7
Rotherhithe St.		
Helen's Pl. E2	59	F3
Roman Rd.		
Helenslea Ave. NW11	48	C1
Helix Gdns. SW2	76	F6
Helix Rd.		
Helix Rd. SW2	76	F6
Hellings St. E1	**17**	**J2**
Helme Clo. SW19	84	C5
Helmet Row EC1	**9**	**A5**
Helmet Row EC1	58	J4
Helmsdale Clo., Hayes	54	E4
Berrydale Rd.		
Helmsdale Rd. SW16	94	D1
Helmsley Pl. E8	50	E7
Helsinki Sq. SE16	68	H3
Finland St.		
Helston Clo., Pnr.	28	F7
Helvetia St. SE6	86	J2
Hemans St. SW8	67	D7
Hemberton Rd. SW9	76	E3
Hemery Rd., Grnf.	46	A5
Lilian Board Way		
Heming Rd., Edg.	30	B7
Hemingford Rd. N1	58	F1
Hemingford Rd., Sutt.	99	J4
Hemington Ave. N11	31	J5
Hemlock Rd. W12	56	F7
Hemming Clo.,	90	G1
Hmptn.		
Chandler Clo.		
Hemming St. E1	**9**	**J6**
Hemming St. E1	59	D4
Hemp Wk. SE17	**21**	**C1**
Hempstead Clo.,	34	G2
Buck.H.		
Hempstead Rd. E17	42	D2
Hemsby Rd., Chess.	98	J6
Hemstal Rd. NW6	48	D7
Hemswell Dr. NW9	38	E1
Hemsworth Ct. N1	**9**	**D1**
Hemsworth St. N1	**9**	**D1**
Hemsworth St. N1	59	B2
Hemus Pl. SW3	**18**	**H4**
Hen & Chicken Ct. EC4	58	G6
Fleet St.		
Henbury Way, Wat.	28	D3
Henchman St. W12	56	F6
Hendale Ave. NW4	38	G3
Henderson Clo. NW10	47	C6
Henderson Dr. NW8	**6**	**E5**
Henderson Rd. E7	51	J6
Henderson Rd. N9	33	E1
Henderson Rd. SW18	75	H7
Henderson Rd., Croy.	95	A6
Henderson Rd., Hayes	54	A3
Hendham Rd. SW17	84	H2
Hendon Ave. N3	39	B1
Hendon La. N3	39	B3
Hendon Pk. Row	39	C6
NW11		
Hendon Rd. N9	33	D2
Hendon Way NW2	39	A7
Hendon Way NW4	38	H6
Hendon Wd. La. NW7	22	F7
Hendre Rd. SE1	**21**	**E2**
Hendren Clo., Grnf.	46	A5
Dimmock Dr.		
Hendrick Ave. SW12	75	J7
Heneage La. EC3	**13**	**E4**
Heneage St. E1	**13**	**G1**
Heneage St. E1	59	C5
Henfield Clo. N19	49	C1
Henfield Clo., Bex.	80	G6
Henfield Rd. SW19	93	C1
Hengelo Gdns., Mitch.	93	G3
Hengist Rd. SE12	78	H7
Hengist Rd., Erith	71	H7
Hengist Way, Brom.	96	D4
Hengrave Rd. SE23	77	F7
Hengrove Ct., Bex.	89	E1
Hurst Rd.		
Henley Ave., Sutt.	100	B3
Henley Clo., Grnf.	54	J2
Henley Clo., Islw.	73	C1
Henley Ct. N14	24	C7
Henley Dr. SE1	**21**	**G1**
Henley Dr. SE1	68	C4
Henley Dr., Kings.T.	83	F7
Henley Gdns., Pnr.	36	B3
Henley Gdns., Rom.	44	E5
Henley Rd. E16	70	C2
Henley Rd. N18	33	B4
Henley Rd. NW10	56	J1
Henley Rd., Ilf.	52	F4
Henley St. SW11	76	A2
Henley Way, Felt.	81	D5
Conway Rd.		
Hennel Clo. SE23	86	F3
Henniker Gdns. E6	61	A3
Henniker Ms. SW3	**18**	**E5**
Henniker Rd. E15	51	E5
Henniker Rd. E15	51	D5
Henning St. SW11	75	H1
Henningham Rd. N17	41	A1
Henrietta Ms. WC1	**8**	**B5**
Henrietta Pl. W1	**11**	**D3**
Henrietta Pl. W1	58	B6
Henrietta St. E15	51	C5
Henrietta St. WC2	**12**	**B5**
Henrietta St. WC2	58	E7
Henriques St. E1	**13**	**J3**
Henriques St. E1	59	D6
Henry Cooper Way	88	A3
SE9		
Henry Darlot Dr. NW7	31	A5
Henry Dickens Ct.	57	A7
W11		
Henry Jackson Rd.	75	A3
SW15		
Henry Rd. E6	61	B2
Henry Rd. N4	49	J1
Henry Rd., Barn.	23	G5
Henry St., Brom.	96	H1
Henry's Ave.,	34	F5
Wdf.Grn.		
Henry's Wk., Ilf.	35	G7
Henryson Rd. SE4	78	A5
Hensford Gdns. SE26	86	E4
Wells Pk. Rd.		
Henshall St. N1	50	A6
Henshaw St. SE17	**21**	**B1**
Henshaw St. SE17	68	A4
Henshawe Rd., Dag.	53	D3
Henshill Pt. E3	60	B3
Bromley High St.		
Henslowe Rd. SE22	77	D5
Henson Ave. NW2	47	J5
Henson Clo., Orp.	104	J2
Henson Path, Har.	37	G3
Brancker Rd.		
Henson Pl., Nthlt.	54	C1
Henstridge Pl. NW8	57	H2
Henty Clo. SW11	66	H7
Henty Wk. SW15	74	H5
Henville Rd., Brom.	96	J1
Henwick Rd. SE9	79	A3
Henwood Rd. SE16	68	F3
Gomm Rd.		
Henwood Side,	35	C6
Wdf.Grn.		
Love La.		
Hepburn Gdns., Brom.	103	E1
Hepburn Ms. SW11	75	J5
Webbs Rd.		
Hepple Clo., Islw.	73	E2
Hepplestone Clo.	74	H6
SW15		
Dover Pk. Dr.		
Hepscott Rd. E9	51	A6
Hepworth Ct., Bark.	53	A5
Hepworth Gdns.,	53	A5
Bark.		
Hepworth Rd. SW16	85	E7
Hepworth Wk. NW3	48	H5
Haverstock Hill		

Heracles Clo., Wall.	101	E7
Gull Clo.		
Herald Gdns., Wall.	101	B3
Herald St. E2	59	E4
Three Colts La.		
Herald's Ct. SE11	**20**	**G2**
Herald's Pl. SE11	**20**	**F1**
Herbal Hill EC1	**8**	**F6**
Herbal Hill EC1	58	G4
Herbert Cres. SW1	**15**	**A5**
Herbert Gdns. NW10	56	H1
Herbert Gdns. W4	65	B6
Magnolia Rd.		
Herbert Gdns., Rom.	44	D7
Herbert Pl. SE18	70	E6
Plumstead Common Rd.		
Herbert Rd. E12	52	B4
Herbert Rd. E17	41	J7
Herbert Rd. N11	32	E7
Herbert Rd. N15	41	C5
Herbert Rd. NW9	38	G6
Herbert Rd. SE18	70	D7
Herbert Rd. SW19	84	C7
Herbert Rd., Bexh.	80	E2
Herbert Rd., Brom.	97	A5
Herbert Rd., Ilf.	52	H2
Herbert Rd., Kings.T.	91	J3
Herbert Rd., Sthl.	63	F1
Herbert St. E13	60	G2
Herbert St. NW5	49	A6
Herbert Ter. SE18	70	E6
Herbert Rd.		
Herbrand St. WC1	**8**	**A5**
Herbrand St. WC1	58	E4
Hercules Pl. N7	49	E3
Hercules St.		
Hercules Rd. SE1	**16**	**D6**
Hercules Rd. SE1	67	F3
Hercules St. N7	49	E3
Hercules Twr. SE14	68	H6
Milton Ct. Rd.		
Hereford Ave., Barn.	31	J1
Hereford Gdns. SE13	78	E5
Longhurst Rd.		
Hereford Gdns., Ilf.	43	B7
Hereford Gdns., Pnr.	36	E5
Hereford Gdns.,	81	J1
Twick.		
Hereford Ho. NW6	57	D2
Hereford Ms. W2	57	D6
Hereford Rd.		
Hereford Pl. SE14	68	J7
Hereford Retreat	**21**	**H7**
SE15		
Hereford Rd. E11	42	H5
Hereford Rd. W2	57	D6
Hereford Rd. W3	56	B7
Hereford Rd. W5	64	F3
Hereford Rd., Felt.	81	C1
Hereford Sq. SW7	**18**	**D2**
Hereford Sq. SW7	66	F4
Hereford St. E2	59	D4
Hereford Way, Chess.	98	F5
Herent Dr., Ilf.	43	B4
Hereward Gdns. N13	32	G5
Hereward Grn., Loug.	27	F1
Hereward Rd. SW17	84	H4
Herga Ct., Har.	46	B3
Herga Rd., Har.	37	C4
Heriot Ave. E4	34	A2
Heriot Rd. NW4	38	J5
Heriots Clo., Stan.	29	D4
Heritage Hill, Kes.	103	J5
Heritage Vw., Har.	46	C3
Herlwyn Gdns. SW17	84	J4
Hermes Pt. W9	57	D4
Harrow Rd.		
Hermes St. N1	**8**	**E2**
Hermes Wk., Nthlt.	54	G2
Hotspur Rd.		
Hermes Way, Wall.	101	D7
Hermiston Ave. N8	40	E5
Hermit Pl. NW6	57	E1
Belsize Rd.		
Hermit Rd. E16	60	F4
Hermit St. EC1	**8**	**G3**
Hermit St. EC1	58	H3
Hermitage, The SE23	86	F1
Hermitage, The SW13	74	
Hermitage, The, Rich.	73	H5
Hermitage Clo. E18	42	F4
Hermitage Clo., Enf.	24	H2
Hermitage Clo., Esher	98	D6
Hermitage Ct. E18	42	G4
Hermitage Ct. NW2	48	D3
Hermitage La.		
Hermitage Gdns.	48	D3
NW2		

Hermitage Gdns.	85	J7
SE19		
Hermitage La. N18	33	A5
Great Cambridge Rd.		
Hermitage La. NW2	48	D3
Hermitage La. SE25	95	D6
Hermitage La. SW16	85	F7
Hermitage La., Croy.	95	D6
Hermitage Path	94	E1
SW16		
Hermitage Rd. N4	40	H7
Hermitage Rd. N15	40	H7
Hermitage Rd. SE19	85	J7
Hermitage St. W2	**10**	**E2**
Hermitage Wk. E18	42	F4
Hermitage Wall E1	**17**	**J2**
Hermitage Wall E1	68	D1
Hermitage Way, Stan.	37	D1
Hermon Gro., Hayes	63	A1
Hermon Hill E11	42	G5
Hermon Hill E18	42	H3
Herndon Rd. SW18	75	F5
North Circular Rd.		
Herne Hill SE24	76	J5
Herne Hill Rd. SE24	76	J3
Herne Ms. N18	33	D4
Lyndhurst Rd.		
Herne Pl. SE24	76	H5
Herne Rd., Surb.	98	G2
Heron Clo. E17	41	J2
Heron Clo. NW10	47	E6
Heron Clo., Buck.H.	34	G1
Heron Ct., Brom.	96	J4
Heron Cres., Sid.	88	H3
Heron Hill, Belv.	71	F5
Heron Ms., Ilf.	52	E2
Balfour Rd.		
Heron Pl. SE16	68	H1
Heron Quay E14	69	A1
Heron Rd. SE24	76	J4
Heron Rd., Croy.	102	B2
Tunstall Rd.		
Heron Rd., Twick.	73	D4
Heron Sq., Rich.	73	G5
Bridge St.		
Herondale Ave.	84	G1
SW18		
Herongate Rd. E12	51	J2
Herons, The E11	42	F6
Heron's Pl., Islw.	73	E3
Herons Ri., Barn.	23	H4
Heronsforde W13	55	F6
Heronsgate, Edg.	30	A5
Heronslea Dr., Stan.	29	H5
Heronway, Wdf.Grn.	34	J4
Herrick Rd. N5	49	J3
Herrick St. SW1	**19**	**J2**
Herrick St. SW1	67	D4
Herries St. W10	57	B2
Herringham Rd. SE7	69	J3
Herrongate Clo., Enf.	25	C2
Hersant Clo. NW10	56	G1
Herschell Rd. SE23	77	H7
Hersham Clo. SW15	74	G7
Hertford Ave. SW14	74	D5
Hertford Clo., Barn.	23	G3
Hertford Pl. W1	**7**	**F6**
Hertford Rd. N1	59	B1
Hertford Rd. N2	39	H3
Hertford Rd. N9	33	D2
Hertford Rd., Bark.	52	E7
Hertford Rd., Barn.	23	F3
Hertford Rd., Enf.	25	F2
Hertford Rd., Ilf.	43	H6
Hertford Sq., Mitch.	94	E4
Hertford Way		
Hertford St. W1	**15**	**C2**
Hertford St. W1	67	A1
Hertford Wk., Belv.	71	G5
Hoddesdon Rd.		
Hertford Way, Mitch.	94	E4
Hertslet Rd. N7	49	F3
Hertsmere Rd. E14	60	A7
Hervey Clo. N3	39	D1
Hervey Pk. Rd. E17	41	H4
Hervey Rd. SE3	78	H1
Hesa Rd., Hayes	54	A6
Hesketh Pl. W11	57	B7
Hesketh Rd. E7	51	G3
Heslop Rd. SW12	84	J1
Hesper Ms. SW5	**18**	**A3**
Hesper Ms. SW5	66	E5
Hesperus Cres. E14	69	B4
Hessel Rd. W13	64	D2
Hessel St. E1	59	E6
Hester Rd. N18	33	D5
Hester Rd. SW11	66	H7

Hester Ter., Rich.	74	A3
Chilton Rd.		
Hestercombe Ave.	75	B2
SW6		
Heston Ave., Houns.	63	E6
Heston Gra. La.,	63	F6
Houns.		
Heston Ind. Cen.,	63	C6
Houns.		
Heston Ind. Mall,	63	F7
Houns.		
Heston Rd., Houns.	63	G6
Heston St. SE14	78	A1
Heswell Grn., Wat.	28	A3
Fairhaven Cres.		
Hetherington Rd. SW4	76	E4
Hetley Gdns. SE19	86	C7
Fox Hill		
Hetley Rd. W12	65	H1
Heton Gdns. NW4	38	G4
Hevelius Clo. SE10	69	F5
Hever Cft. SE9	88	D4
Hever Gdns., Brom.	97	D2
Heverham Rd. SE18	70	H4
Heversham Rd.,	80	G2
Bexh.		
Hewer St. W10	57	A5
Hewett Clo., Stan.	29	E4
Hewett Rd., Dag.	53	C5
Hewett St. EC2	**9**	**E6**
Hewish Rd. N18	33	B4
Hewison St. E3	59	J2
Hewitt Ave. N22	40	H2
Hewitt Clo., Croy.	103	B3
Oak Ave.		
Hewitt Rd. N8	40	G5
Hewlett Rd. E3	59	H2
Hexagon, The N6	48	J1
Hexal Rd. SE6	87	E3
Hexham Gdns., Islw.	64	D7
Hexham Rd. SE27	85	J2
Hexham Rd., Barn.	23	E4
Hexham Rd., Mord.	100	E1
Heybourne Rd. N17	33	E7
Heybridge Ave.	85	E7
SW16		
Heybridge Dr., Ilf.	43	G2
Heybridge Way E10	41	H7
Heyford Ave. SW8	**20**	**B7**
Heyford Ave. SW8	67	E7
Heyford Ave. SW20	93	C3
Heyford Rd., Mitch.	93	H2
Heygate St. SE17	**20**	**J2**
Heygate St. SE17	67	J4
Heylyn Sq. E3	59	J3
Malmesbury Rd.		
Heynes Rd., Dag.	53	C4
Heysham Dr., Wat.	28	C5
Heysham La. NW3	48	E3
Heysham Rd. N15	41	A6
Heythorp St. SW18	84	C1
Heywood Ave. NW9	38	E1
Heyworth Rd. E5	50	E4
Heyworth Rd. E15	51	F4
Hibbert Rd. E17	41	J7
Hibbert Rd., Har.	37	C2
Hibbert St. SW11	75	F3
Hibernia Gdns.,	72	G4
Houns.		
Hibernia Rd., Houns.	72	G4
Hichisson Rd. SE15	77	F5
Hickin Clo. SE7	70	A4
Hickin St. E14	69	C3
Plevna St.		
Hickling Rd., Ilf.	52	E5
Hickman Ave. E4	34	C6
Hickman Clo. E16	61	A5
Hickman Rd., Rom.	44	C7
Hickmore Wk. SW4	76	C3
Hickory Clo. N9	25	D7
Hicks Ave., Grnf.	55	A2
Hicks Clo. SW11	75	H3
Hicks St. SE8	68	H5
Hidcote Gdns. SW20	92	H3
Hide Pl. SW1	**19**	**H2**
Hide Pl. SW1	67	D4
Hide Rd., Har.	36	J4
Hides St. N7	49	F6
Sheringham Rd.		
Higgins Wk., Hmptn.	81	E6
Abbott Rd.		
High Beech, S.Croy.	102	B7
High Beech Rd., Loug.	27	B4
High Beeches, Sid.	89	E5
High Bri. SE10	69	D5
Eastney St.		
High Broom Cres.,	96	B7
W.Wick.		

High Cedar Dr. SW20	83	H7
High Coombe Pl.,	83	D7
Kings.T.		
High Cross Cen. N15	41	D4
High Cross Rd. N17	41	D3
High Dr., N.Mal.	92	C1
High Elms, Chig.	35	H4
High Elms, Wdf.Grn.	34	G5
High Foleys, Esher	98	E7
High Gables, Loug.	27	A5
High Gro. SE18	70	G7
High Gro., Brom.	96	J1
High Hill Est. E5	50	E1
Mount Pleasant La.		
High Holborn WC1	**12**	**A3**
High Holborn WC1	58	E6
High La. W7	55	A5
High Lawns, Har.	46	B3
High Level Dr. SE26	86	D4
High Mead, Chig.	35	F2
High Mead, Har.	37	B5
High Mead, W.Wick.	103	D2
High Meadow Clo.,	36	B4
Pnr.		
Daymer Gdns.		
High Meadow Cres.	38	D5
NW9		
High Meadows, Chig.	35	G5
High Meads Rd. E16	61	A6
Fulmer Rd.		
High Mt. NW4	38	G6
High Pk. Ave., Rich.	74	A1
High Pk. Rd., Rich.	74	A1
High Path SW19	93	E1
High Pt. N6	40	A7
High Pt. SE9	88	E3
High Rd. E18	42	G1
High Rd. N2	39	G1
High Rd. N11	32	B5
High Rd. N12	31	F4
High Rd. N15	41	C6
High Rd. N17	41	C3
High Rd. N20	31	F2
High Rd. N22	32	F6
High Rd. NW10	47	F6
(Willesden)		
High Rd., Buck.H.	34	H3
High Rd., Chig.	35	D5
High Rd., Har.	29	B7
(Harrow Weald)		
High Rd., Ilf.	52	F2
High Rd., Loug.	26	J6
High Rd., Pnr.	36	B5
High Rd., Rom.	53	A1
High Rd., Wat.	29	A1
(Bushey)		
High Rd., Wem.	46	H5
High Rd., Wdf.Grn.	34	F6
High Rd. Leyton E10	42	B6
High Rd. Leyton E15	51	C4
High Rd. Leytonstone	51	E4
E11		
High Rd. Leytonstone	51	E4
E15		
High Silver, Loug.	27	A4
High St. E11	42	G5
High St. E13	60	G2
High St. E15	60	C2
High St. E17	41	H5
High St. N8	40	E4
High St. N14	32	D2
High St. NW7	30	H5
High St. NW10	56	F2
(Harlesden)		
High St. SE20	86	F7
High St. SE25	95	C4
(South Norwood)		
High St. SW6	75	B3
High St. W3	65	B1
High St. W5	55	G7
High St., Barn.	23	B3
High St., Beck.	96	A2
High St., Brent.	64	H6
High St., Brom.	96	G2
High St., Cars.	100	J4
High St., Chis.	88	E6
High St., Croy.	101	J3
High St., Edg.	30	A6
High St., Enf.	25	F4
(Ponders End)		
High St., Esher	98	C6
(Claygate)		
High St., Felt.	81	A3
High St., Hmptn.	90	H1
High St., Har.	37	B2
High St., Har.	46	B1
(Wealdstone)		
High St., Houns.	72	H3

High St., Houns. (Cranford) 63 A7
High St., Ilf. 43 F3
High St., Kings.T. 91 G3
High St., Kings.T. (Hampton Wick) 91 F1
High St., N.Mal. 92 E4
High St., Orp. (Farnborough) 104 E5
High St., Orp. (Green St Grn.) 104 J7
High St., Pnr. 36 E3
High St., Sthl. 63 F1
High St., Sutt. 100 E4
High St., Sutt. (Cheam) 100 B6
High St., Tedd. 82 C5
High St., T.Ditt. 91 D7
High St., Th.Hth. 94 J4
High St., Twick. (Whitton) 72 J7
High St., Wem. 46 J4
High St., W.Mol. 90 G4
High St., W.Wick. 103 B1
High St. Colliers Wd. SW19 84 G7
High St. Ms. SW19 84 B5
High St. N. E6 52 B7
High St. N. E12 52 B5
High St. S. E6 61 C2
High St. Wimbledon SW19 84 A5
High Timber St. EC4 12 J5
High Timber St. EC4 58 J7
High Tor Clo., Brom. 87 H7 *Babbacombe Rd.*
High Tree Ct. W7 55 B7
High Trees SW2 85 G1
High Trees, Barn. 23 H5
High Trees, Croy. 102 H1
High Vw., Pnr. 36 C3
High Vw. Clo. SE19 95 C2
High Vw. Clo., Loug. 26 J5
High Vw. Rd. E18 42 F3
High Vw. Rd., Sid. 89 B4
High Worple, Har. 36 E7
Higham Hill Rd. E17 41 H1
Higham Pl. E17 41 H3
Higham Rd. N17 41 A3
Higham Rd., Wdf.Grn. 34 G6
Higham Sta. Ave. E4 34 A6
Higham St. E17 41 H3
Highams Lo. Business Cen. E17 41 G3
Highams Pk. Ind. Est. E4 34 C6
Highbanks Clo., Well. 71 B7
Highbanks Rd., Pnr. 28 G6
Highbarrow Rd., Croy. 95 D7
Highbridge Rd., Bark. 61 E1
Highbrook Rd. SE3 79 A3
Highbury Ave., Th.Hth. 94 G2
Highbury Clo., N.Mal. 92 C4
Highbury Clo., W.Wick. 103 B2
Highbury Cor. N5 49 H6
Highbury Cres. N5 49 H5
Highbury Est. N5 49 J5
Highbury Gdns., Ilf. 52 H2
Highbury Gra. N5 49 J4
Highbury Gro. N5 49 H6
Highbury Hill N5 49 G3
Highbury Ms. N7 49 G6 *Holloway Rd.*
Highbury New Pk. N5 49 J5
Highbury Pk. N5 49 H4
Highbury Pk. Ms. N5 49 J4 *Highbury Gra.*
Highbury Pl. N5 49 H6
Highbury Quad. N5 49 J3
Highbury Rd. SW19 84 B5
Highbury Sta. Rd. N1 49 G6
Highbury Ter. N5 49 H5
Highbury Ter. Ms. N5 49 H5
Highclere Rd., N.Mal. 92 D3
Highclere St. SE26 86 H4
Highcliffe Dr. SW15 74 F6
Highcliffe Gdns., Ilf. 43 B5
Highcombe SE7 69 H6
Highcombe Clo. SE9 88 A1
Highcroft NW9 38 E5
Highcroft Ave., Wem. 56 A1
Highcroft Gdns. NW11 39 C6
Highcroft Rd. N19 40 E7
Highcross Way SW15 83 G1
Highdaun Dr. SW16 94 F4
Highdown, Wor.Pk. 99 E2
Highdown Rd. SW15 74 H6
Highfield, Felt. 81 A1
Highfield Ave. NW9 38 C5
Highfield Ave. NW11 39 A7
Highfield Ave., Erith 71 H6
Highfield Ave., Grnf. 46 B5
Highfield Ave., Orp. 104 J5
Highfield Ave., Pnr. 36 F5
Highfield Ave., Wem. 46 H3
Highfield Clo. N22 40 G1
Highfield Clo. NW9 38 C5
Highfield Clo., Surb. 98 F1
Highfield Ct. N14 24 C6
Highfield Dr., Brom. 96 E4
Highfield Dr., Epsom 99 F7
Highfield Dr., W.Wick. 103 B2
Highfield Gdns. NW11 39 B6
Highfield Hill SE19 86 A7
Highfield Rd. N21 32 H2
Highfield Rd. NW11 39 B6
Highfield Rd. W3 56 B5
Highfield Rd., Bexh. 80 F5
Highfield Rd., Brom. 97 C4
Highfield Rd., Chis. 97 J3
Highfield Rd., Felt. 81 A1
Highfield Rd., Islw. 73 C1
Highfield Rd., Surb. 92 C7
Highfield Rd., Sutt. 100 H5
Highfield Rd., Wdf.Grn. 35 B7
Highfields Gro. N6 48 J1
Highgate Ave. N6 40 B7
Highgate Clo. N6 40 A7
Highgate High St. N6 49 A1
Highgate Hill N6 49 B1
Highgate Hill N19 49 B1
Highgate Rd. NW5 49 B4
Highgate Wk. SE23 86 F2
Highgate W. Hill N6 49 A1
Highgrove Clo., Chis. 97 B1
Highgrove Ct., Beck. 87 A7 *Park Rd.*
Highgrove Rd., Dag. 53 C5
Highgrove Way, Ruis. 36 A6
Highland Ave. W7 55 B6
Highland Ave., Dag. 53 J3
Highland Ave., Loug. 27 B6
Highland Cotts., Wall. 101 B4
Highland Ct. E18 42 H1
Highland Cft., Beck. 87 B5
Highland Rd. SE19 86 B6
Highland Rd., Bexh. 80 G5
Highland Rd., Brom. 96 F1
Highlands, Wat. 28 C1
Highlands, The, Edg. 38 B2
Highlands Ave. W3 56 C7
Highlands Clo. N4 40 E7 *Mount Vw. Rd.*
Highlands Clo., Houns. 72 H1
Highlands Gdns., Ilf. 52 C1
Highlands Heath SW15 74 J7
Highlands Rd., Barn. 23 D5
Highlea Clo. NW9 38 E1
Highlever Rd. W10 56 J5
Highmead SE18 70 J7
Highmead Cres., Wem. 46 J7
Highmore Rd. SE3 69 E7
Highshore Rd. SE15 77 C2
Highstone Ave. E11 42 G6
Highview Ave., Edg. 30 C4
Highview Ave., Wall. 101 F5
Highview Gdns. N3 39 B4
Highview Gdns. N11 32 C5
Highview Gdns., Edg. 30 C5
Highview Ho., Rom. 44 E4
Highview Rd. SE19 86 A6
Highview Rd. W13 55 D5
Highway, The E1 13 J6
Highway, The E1 59 D7
Highway, The E14 59 G7
Highway, The, Stan. 37 C1
Highwood, Brom. 96 D3
Highwood Ave. N12 31 F4
Highwood Clo., Orp. 104 F2
Highwood Dr., Orp. 104 F2
Highwood Gdns., Ilf. 43 C5
Highwood Gro. NW7 30 D5
Highwood Hill NW7 30 F2
Highwood La., Loug. 27 D5
Highwood Rd. N19 49 E3
Highworth Rd. N11 32 D6
Hilary Ave., Mitch. 94 A3
Hilary Clo. SW6 18 A7
Hilary Clo. SW6 66 E7
Hilary Clo., Erith 80 H1
Hilary Rd. W12 56 F6
Hilbert Rd., Sutt. 100 A3
Hilborough Way, Orp. 104 G5
Hilda Rd. E6 52 A7
Hilda Rd. E16 60 E4
Hilda Ter. SW9 76 G2
Hilda Vale Clo., Orp. 104 E4
Hilda Vale Rd., Orp. 104 D4
Hildenborough Gdns., Brom. 87 E6
Hildenlea Pl., Brom. 96 E2
Hildreth St. SW12 85 B1
Hildyard Rd. SW6 66 D6
Hiley Rd. NW10 56 J3
Hilgrove Rd. NW6 48 F7
Hiliary Gdns., Stan. 37 F2
Hill Brow, Brom. 97 A1
Hill Clo. NW2 47 H3
Hill Clo. NW11 39 D6
Hill Clo., Barn. 22 J5
Hill Clo., Chis. 88 E5
Hill Clo., Har. 46 B3
Hill Clo., Stan. 29 E4
Hill Ct., Nthlt. 45 G5
Hill Cres. N20 31 E2
Hill Cres., Bex. 89 J1
Hill Cres., Har. 37 D5
Hill Cres., Surb. 91 J5
Hill Cres., Wor.Pk. 99 J2
Hill Crest, Sid. 80 A7
Hill Crest Gdns. N3 39 B4
Hill Dr. NW9 47 C1
Hill Dr. SW16 94 F3
Hill End, Orp. 104 J2 *The App.*
Hill Fm. Rd. W10 56 J5
Hill Ho. Ave., Stan. 29 C7
Hill Ho. Clo. N21 24 G7
Hill Ho. Rd. SW16 85 F5
Hill Path SW16 85 F5 *Valley Rd.*
Hill Ri. N9 25 E6
Hill Ri. NW11 39 E4
Hill Ri. SE23 86 E1 *London Rd.*
Hill Ri., Esher 98 E2
Hill Ri., Grnf. 45 J7
Hill Ri., Rich. 73 G5
Hill Rd. N10 39 J1
Hill Rd. NW8 6 D3
Hill Rd. NW8 57 F2
Hill Rd., Cars. 100 H6
Hill Rd., Har. 37 D5
Hill Rd., Mitch. 94 B1
Hill Rd., Pnr. 36 E6
Hill Rd., Sutt. 100 E5
Hill Rd., Wem. 46 E3
Hill St. W1 15 C1
Hill St. W1 58 A7
Hill St., Rich. 73 G5
Hill Top NW11 39 E4
Hill Top, Loug. 27 D2
Hill Top, Mord. 93 E6
Hill Top Clo., Loug. 27 D3
Hill Top Vw., Wdf.Grn. 35 C6
Hill Vw. Cres., Orp. 104 J1
Hill Vw. Dr., Well. 79 H2
Hill Vw. Gdns. NW9 38 D5
Hill Vw. Rd., Esher 98 D7
Hill Vw. Rd., Orp. 104 J1
Hill Vw. Rd., Twick. 82 D1
Hillary Ri., Barn. 23 D4
Hillary Rd., Sthl. 63 G3
Hillbeck Clo. SE15 68 F7
Hillbeck Way, Grnf. 55 A1
Hillborne Clo., Hayes 63 A5
Hillborough Clo. SW19 84 F7
Hillbrook Rd. SW17 84 J3
Hillbrow, N.Mal. 92 F3
Hillbrow Rd., Brom. 87 E7
Hillbury Ave., Har. 37 E5
Hillbury Rd. SW17 85 B3
Hillcote Ave. SW16 85 G7
Hillcourt Ave. N12 31 E6
Hillcourt Est. N16 50 A1
Hillcourt Rd. SE22 77 E6
Hillcrest N6 40 A7
Hillcrest N21 24 G7
Hillcrest Ave. NW11 39 B5
Hillcrest Ave., Edg. 30 B4
Hillcrest Ave., Pnr. 36 D4
Hillcrest Clo. SE26 86 D4
Hillcrest Clo., Beck. 95 J5
Hillcrest Gdns. NW2 47 G3
Hillcrest Gdns., Esher 98 C3
Hillcrest Rd. E17 42 D2
Hillcrest Rd. E18 42 F2
Hillcrest Rd. W3 65 A1
Hillcrest Rd. W5 55 H5
Hillcrest Rd., Brom. 87 G4
Hillcrest Rd., Loug. 27 A6
Hillcrest Vw., Beck. 95 J6
Hillcroft, Loug. 27 D2
Hillcroft Ave., Pnr. 36 F6
Hillcroft Cres. W5 55 G6
Hillcroft Cres., Ruis. 45 D3
Hillcroft Cres., Wat. 28 A1
Hillcroft Cres., Wem. 46 J4
Hillcroft Rd. E6 61 E5
Hillcroome Rd., Sutt. 100 G6
Hillcross Ave., Mord. 93 A6
Hilldale Rd., Sutt. 100 C4
Hilldown Rd. SW16 85 E7
Hilldown Rd., Brom. 103 E1
Hilldrop Cres. N7 49 D5
Hilldrop Est. N7 49 D5
Hilldrop La. N7 49 D5
Hilldrop Rd. N7 49 D5
Hilldrop Rd., Brom. 87 G6
Hillend SE18 79 E1
Hillersdon Ave. SW13 74 G2
Hillersdon Ave., Edg. 29 J5
Hillery Clo. SE17 21 C2
Hillfield Ave. N8 40 E5
Hillfield Ave. NW9 38 E5
Hillfield Ave., Mord. 93 H6
Hillfield Ave., Wem. 46 H7
Hillfield Clo., Har. 36 J4
Hillfield Ct. NW3 48 H5
Hillfield Pk. N10 40 B3
Hillfield Pk. N21 32 G2
Hillfield Pk. Ms. N10 40 B4
Hillfield Rd. NW6 48 C5
Hillfield Rd., Hmptn. 81 F7
Hillfoot Ave., Rom. 44 J1
Hillfoot Rd., Rom. 44 J1
Hillgate Pl. SW12 76 B7
Hillgate Pl. W8 66 D1
Hillgate St. W8 66 D1
Hilliards Ct. E1 68 E1 *Wapping High St.*
Hilliards St. E1 68 F1 *Wapping High St.*
Hillier Clo., Barn. 23 E6
Hillier Gdns., Croy. 101 G5 *Crowley Cres.*
Hillier Pl., Chess. 98 F6 *Mansfield Rd.*
Hillier Rd. SW11 75 J6
Hilliers La., Croy. 101 E3
Hillingdon Rd., Bexh. 80 J2
Hillingdon St. SE5 20 G6
Hillingdon St. SE5 67 H6
Hillingdon St. SE17 20 J6
Hillingdon St. SE17 67 H6
Hillington Gdns., Wdf.Grn. 43 A2
Hillman St. E8 50 E6
Hillmarton Rd. N7 49 E5
Hillmead Dr. SW9 76 H4
Hillmont Rd., Esher 98 B3
Hillmore Gro. SE26 86 G5
Hillreach SE18 70 C5
Hillrise Rd. N19 40 E7
Hills Ms. W5 55 H7
Hills Pl. W1 11 F4
Hills Rd., Buck.H. 34 H1
Hillsborough Grn., Wat. 28 A3 *Ashburnham Dr.*
Hillsborough Rd. SE22 77 B5
Hillside NW9 38 D4
Hillside NW10 47 C7
Hillside SW19 84 A6
Hillside, Barn. 23 F5
Hillside, Erith 71 J5 *Pembroke Rd.*
Hillside Ave. N11 31 J6
Hillside Ave., Borwd. 22 B4
Hillside Ave., Wem. 46 J4
Hillside Ave., Wdf.Grn. 34 J5
Hillside Clo. NW8 6 B1
Hillside Clo. NW8 57 E2
Hillside Clo., Mord. 93 B4
Hillside Clo., Wdf.Grn. 34 J5
Hillside Cres., Har. 45 J1
Hillside Cres., Nthwd. 36 A1
Hillside Dr., Edg. 30 A6
Hillside Est. N15 41 C6
Hillside Gdns. E17 42 D3
Hillside Gdns. N6 40 A6
Hillside Gdns. SW2 85 G2
Hillside Gdns., Barn. 23 B4
Hillside Gdns., Edg. 29 J4
Hillside Gdns., Har. 37 H7

Hillside Gdns., Nthwd. 28 A7
Hillside Gdns., Wall. 101 C7
Hillside Gro. N14 24 D7
Hillside Gro. NW7 30 G7
Hillside La., Brom. 103 G2
Hillside Pas. SW2 85 F2
Hillside Ri., Nthwd. 28 A7
Hillside Rd. N15 41 B6
Hillside Rd. SW2 85 F2
Hillside Rd. W5 55 H5
Hillside Rd., Brom. 96 F3
Hillside Rd., Croy. 101 H5
Hillside Rd., Nthwd. 28 A7
Hillside Rd., Sthl. 54 G4
Hillside Rd., Surb. 91 J4
Hillside Rd., Sutt. 100 C7
Hillsleigh Rd. W8 66 C1
Hillstowe St. E5 50 F3
Hilltop, Sutt. 93 C7
Hilltop Gdns. NW4 38 H1
Great N. Way
Hilltop Gdns., Orp. 104 H2
Hilltop Rd. NW6 48 D7
Hilltop Way, Stan. 29 D3
Hillview SW20 83 H7
Hillview, Mitch. 94 E4
Hillview Ave., Har. 37 H5
Hillview Clo., Pnr. 28 F6
Hillview Cres., Ilf. 43 C6
Hillview Gdns. NW4 39 A4
Hillview Gdns., Har. 36 G3
Hillview Rd. NW7 31 A4
Hillview Rd., Chis. 88 D5
Hillview Rd., Pnr. 28 F7
Hillview Rd., Sutt. 100 F3
Hillway N6 49 A1
Hillway NW9 38 E7
Hillworth Rd. SW2 76 G7
Hilly Flds. Cres. SE4 78 A3
Hillyard Rd. W7 55 B5
Hillyard St. SW9 76 G1
Hillyfield E17 41 H3
Hillyfields, Loug. 27 D2
Hilsea St. E5 50 F4
Hilton Ave. N12 31 G5
Hilversum Cres. SE22 77 B5
East Dulwich Gro.
Himley Rd. SW17 84 H5
Hinchcliffe Clo., Wall. 101 F7
Roe Way
Hinchley Clo., Esher 98 C3
Hinchley Dr., Esher 98 C3
Hinchley Way, Esher 98 D3
Hinckler Clo., Wall. 101 E7
Kingsford Ave.
Hinckley Rd. SE15 77 D4
Hind Clo., Chig. 35 J5
Hind Ct. EC4 12 F4
Hind Gro. E14 60 A6
Hinde Ms. W1 58 A6
Marylebone La.
Hinde St. W1 11 C3
Hinde St. W1 58 A6
Hindes Rd., Har. 37 A5
Hindhead Clo. N16 50 B1
East Bank
Hindhead Gdns., 54 E1
Nthlt.
Hindhead Grn., Wat. 28 C5
Hindhead Way, Wall. 101 H5
Hindmans Rd. SE22 77 D5
Hindmans Way, Dag. 62 F4
Hindmarsh Clo. E1 13 J5
Hindrey Rd. E5 50 E5
Hindsley's Pl. SE23 86 F2
Hinkler Rd., Har. 37 G3
Hinksey Path SE2 71 D2
Hinstock Rd. SE18 70 F6
Hinton Ave., Houns. 72 D4
Hinton Clo. SE9 88 B1
Hinton Rd. N18 33 B4
Hinton Rd. SE24 76 H3
Hinton Rd., Wall. 101 C6
Hippodrome Ms. W11 57 B7
Portland Rd.
Hippodrome Pl. W11 57 B7
Hiroshima Wk. SE7 69 H3
Hiscocks Ho. NW10 47 C7
Hitcham Rd. E17 41 J7
Hitchin Sq. E3 59 H2
Hither Grn. La. SE13 78 C5
Hitherbroom Rd., 63 A1
Hayes
Hitherfield Rd. SW16 85 F2
Hitherfield Rd., Dag. 53 E2
Hitherlands SW12 85 B2
Hitherwell Dr., Har. 37 A1
Hitherwood Dr. SE19 86 C4

Hive Clo. (Bushey), 29 A2
Wat.
Hive Rd. (Bushey), 29 A2
Wat.
Hoadly Rd. SW16 85 D3
Hobart Clo. N20 31 H2
Hobart Clo., Hayes 54 D4
Hobart Dr., Hayes 54 D4
Hobart Gdns., Th.Hth. 95 A3
Hobart La., Hayes 54 D4
Hobart Pl. SW1 15 D5
Hobart Pl. SW1 67 B3
Hobart Pl., Rich. 73 J6
Chisholm Rd.
Hobart Rd., Dag. 53 D4
Hobart Rd., Hayes 54 D4
Hobart Rd., Ilf. 43 F2
Hobart Rd., Wor.Pk. 99 H3
Hobbayne Rd. W7 55 A6
Hobbes Wk. SW15 74 H5
Hobbs Grn. N2 39 F3
Hobbs Ms., Ilf. 52 J2
Ripley Rd.
Hobbs Rd. SE27 85 J4
Hobday St. E14 60 B5
Hobill Wk., Surb. 91 J6
Hoblands End, Chis. 88 H6
Hobsons Clo., Har. 45 F3
Hoe, The, Wat. 28 D2
Hoe St. E17 42 A5
Hofland Rd. W14 66 A3
Hogan Ms. W2 10 E1
Hogan Way E5 50 D2
Geldeston Rd.
Hogarth Clo. E16 61 A5
Hogarth Clo. W5 55 H5
Hogarth Ct. EC3 13 E5
Hogarth Ct. SE19 86 C4
Fountain Dr.
Hogarth Cres. SW19 93 G1
Hogarth Cres., Croy. 94 J7
Hogarth Gdns., 63 G7
Houns.
Hogarth Hill NW11 39 C4
Hogarth La. W4 65 E6
Hogarth Pl. SW5 18 A2
Hogarth Reach, Loug. 27 C5
Hogarth Rd. SW5 66 E4
Hogarth Rd., Edg. 38 A2
Hogarth Roundabout 65 E6
W4
Hogarth Way, Hmptn. 90 J1
Hogshead Pas. E1 59 E7
Pennington St.
Hogsmill Way, Epsom 99 C5
Holbeach Gdns., Sid. 79 H6
Holbeach Ms. SW12 85 B1
Harberson Rd.
Holbeach Rd. SE6 78 A7
Holbeck Row SE15 68 D7
Holbein Ms. SW1 19 B3
Holbein Ms. SW1 67 A5
Holbein Pl. SW1 19 B2
Holbein Pl. SW1 67 A4
Holberton Gdns. 56 H3
NW10
Holborn EC1 12 E2
Holborn EC1 58 G5
Holborn Circ. EC1 12 F2
Holborn Pl. WC1 12 C2
Holborn Rd. E13 60 H4
Holborn Viaduct EC1 12 F2
Holborn Viaduct EC1 58 G5
Holborn Way, Mitch. 93 J2
Holbrook Clo. N19 49 B1
Dartmouth Pk. Hill
Holbrook Clo., Enf. 25 C1
Holbrook La., Chis. 88 G7
Holbrook Rd. E15 60 F2
Holbrook Way, Brom. 97 C6
Holbrooke Ct. N7 49 E3

Holbrooke Pl., Rich. 73 G5
Hill Ri.
Holburne Clo. SE3 78 J1
Holburne Gdns. SE3 79 A1
Holburne Rd. SE3 78 J1
Holcombe Hill NW7 30 G3
Highwood Hill
Holcombe Rd. N17 41 C3
Holcombe Rd., Ilf. 43 D7
Holcombe St. W6 65 H5
Holcote Clo., Belv. 71 E3
Blakemore Way
Holcroft Rd. E9 50 F7
Holden Ave. N12 31 E5
Holden Ave. NW9 47 C1
Holden Clo., Dag. 53 B3
Holden Pt. E15 51 D6
Waddington Rd.
Holden Rd. N12 31 E5
Holden St. SW11 76 A2
Holdenby Rd. SE4 77 H5
Holdenhurst Ave. N12 31 E7
Holderness Way SE27 85 H5
Holdernesse Rd. SW17 84 J3
Holders Hill Ave. NW4 39 A2
Holders Hill Circ. NW7 31 B7
Dollis Rd.
Holders Hill Cres. NW4 39 A2
Holders Hill Dr. NW4 39 A3
Holders Hill Gdns. 39 B2
NW4
Holders Hill Rd. NW4 39 A2
Holders Hill Rd. NW7 39 B1
Holdgate St. SE7 70 A3
Westmoor St.
Holford Pl. WC1 8 D3
Holford Rd. NW3 48 F3
Holford St. WC1 8 E3
Holford St. WC1 58 G3
Holgate Ave. SW11 75 G3
Holgate Gdns., Dag. 53 G6
Holgate Rd., Dag. 53 G5
Holland Ave. SW20 92 F1
Holland Ave., Sutt. 100 D7
Holland Clo., Barn. 23 G7
Holland Clo., Brom. 103 F2
Holland Clo., Rom. 44 J5
Holland Clo., Stan. 29 E5
Holland Dr. SE23 86 H3
Holland Gdns. W14 66 B3
Holland Gro. SW9 67 G7
Holland Pk. W8 66 C2
Holland Pk. W11 66 B1
Holland Pk. Ave. W11 66 B1
Holland Pk. Ave., Ilf. 43 H6
Holland Pk. Gdns. 66 B2
W14
Holland Pk. Ms. W11 66 C1
Holland Pk. Rd. W14 66 C3
Holland Pl. W8 14 A3
Holland Rd. E6 61 C1
Holland Rd. E15 60 E3
Holland Rd. NW10 56 G1
Holland Rd. SE25 95 D5
Holland Rd. W14 66 A2
Holland Rd., Wem. 46 G6
Holland St. SE1 16 H1
Holland St. SE1 67 H1
Holland St. W8 66 D2
Holland Vill. Rd. W14 66 B2
Holland Wk. N19 49 D1
Duncombe Rd.
Holland Wk. W8 66 C2
Holland Wk., Stan. 29 D5
Holland Way, Brom. 103 F2
Hollands, The, Felt. 81 D4
Hollands, The, 99 F1
Wor.Pk.
Hollar Rd. N16 50 C3
Stoke Newington
High St.
Hollen St. W1 11 G3
Hollen St. W1 58 D6
Holles Clo., Hmptn. 81 G6
Holles St. W1 11 E3
Holles St. W1 58 B6
Holley Rd. W3 65 E4
Hollickwood Ave. N12 31 J6
Holliday Sq. SW11 75 G3
Fowler Rd.
Hollidge Way, Dag. 53 H6
Hollies, The E11 42 G5
Hollies, The N20 31 G1
Hollies Ave., Sid. 88 J2
Hollies Clo. SW16 85 G6
Hollies Clo., Twick. 82 C2
Hollies End NW7 30 H5
Hollies Rd. W5 64 F4

Hollies Way SW12 76 A7
Bracken Ave.
Holligrave Rd., Brom. 96 G1
Hollingbourne Ave., 71 F7
Bexh.
Hollingbourne Gdns. 55 E5
W13
Hollingbourne Rd. 76 J5
SE24
Hollingsworth Rd., 102 E6
Croy.
Hollington Cres., 92 F6
N.Mal.
Hollington Rd. E6 61 C3
Hollington Rd. N17 41 D2
Hollingworth Clo., 90 F4
W.Mol.
Hollingworth Rd., Orp. 97 E7
Hollman Gdns. SW16 85 H6
Hollow, The, Wdf.Grn. 34 F4
Hollow Wk., Rich. 64 H7
Kew Rd.
Holloway Rd. E6 61 C3
Holloway Rd. E11 51 E3
Holloway Rd. N7 49 F3
Holloway Rd. N19 49 C2
Holloway St., Houns. 72 H3
Hollowfield Wk., 45 E6
Nthlt.
Hollows, The, Brent. 64 J6
Kew Bri. Rd.
Holly Ave., Stan. 37 H2
Holly Bush Hill NW3 48 F4
Holly Bush La., 81 F7
Hmptn.
Holly Bush Steps 48 F4
NW3
Heath St.
Holly Bush Vale NW3 48 F4
Heath St.
Holly Clo. NW10 47 E7
Holly Clo., Buck.H. 35 A3
Holly Clo., Felt. 81 E5
Holly Clo., Wall. 101 B7
Holly Cres., Beck. 95 J5
Holly Cres., Wdf.Grn. 34 D7
Holly Dr. E4 26 B7
Holly Fm. Rd., Sthl. 63 E5
Holly Gro. NW9 38 C7
Holly Gro. SE15 77 C2
Holly Gro., Pnr. 36 E1
Holly Hedge Ter. SE13 78 D5
Holly Hill N21 24 F6
Holly Hill NW3 48 F4
Holly Hill Rd., Belv. 71 H5
Holly Hill Rd., Erith 71 J5
Holly Lo. Gdns. N6 49 A1
Holly Ms. SW10 18 D4
Holly Mt. NW3 48 F4
Holly Bush Hill
Holly Pk. N3 39 C3
Holly Pk. N4 40 E7
Holly Pk. Est. N4 40 F7
Blythwood Rd.
Holly Pk. Gdns. N3 39 D3
Holly Pk. Rd. N11 32 A5
Holly Pk. Rd. W7 64 C1
Holly Rd. E11 42 F7
Holly Rd. W4 65 D4
Dolman Rd.
Holly Rd., Hmptn. 81 J6
Holly Rd., Houns. 72 H4
Holly Rd., Twick. 82 D1
Holly St. E8 50 C6
Holly St. Est. E8 50 C7
Holly Ter. N20 31 F2
Holly Vw. Clo. NW4 38 G6
Holly Wk. NW3 48 F4
Holly Wk., Enf. 24 J3
Gentlemans Row
Holly Wk., Rich. 73 H2
Holly Way, Mitch. 94 D4
Hollybank Clo., 81 G5
Hmptn.
Hollyberry La. NW3 48 F4
Holly Wk.
Hollybrake Clo., Chis. 88 G7
Hollybush Clo. E11 42 G5
Hollybush Clo., Har. 37 B1
Hollybush Gdns. E2 59 E3
Hollybush Hill E11 42 F7
Hollybush Pl. E2 59 E3
Bethnal Grn. Rd.
Hollybush Rd., 82 H5
Kings.T.
Hollybush St. E13 60 H3
Hollybush Wk. SW9 76 H4
Hollycroft Ave. NW3 48 D3

Hollycroft Ave., Wem.	46	J2
Hollydale Dr., Brom.	104	C3
Hollydale Rd. SE15	77	F1
Hollydene SE15	77	F1
Hollydown Way E11	51	D3
Hollyfield Ave. N11	31	J5
Hollyfield Rd., Surb.	91	J7
Hollymead, Cars.	100	J3
Hollymount Clo. SE10	78	C1
Hollytree Clo. SW9	84	A1
Hollywood Gdns., Hayes	54	B6
Hollywood Ms. SW10	**18**	**C5**
Hollywood Rd. E4	33	H5
Hollywood Rd. SW10	**18**	**C5**
Hollywood Rd. SW10	66	F6
Hollywood Way, Wdf.Grn.	34	D7
Holm Oak Clo. SW15	75	C6
West Hill		
Holm Oak Ms. SW4	76	E5
King's Ave.		
Holm Wk. SE3	78	G2
Blackheath Pk.		
Holman Rd. SW11	75	G2
Holman Rd., Epsom	99	C5
Holmbridge Gdns., Enf.	25	G4
Holmbrook Dr. NW4	39	A5
Holmbury Ct. SW17	84	J3
Holmbury Ct. SW19	84	H7
Cavendish Rd.		
Holmbury Gro., Croy.	102	J7
Holmbury Pk., Brom.	88	B7
Holmbury Vw. E5	50	E1
Holmbush Rd. SW15	75	B6
Holmcote Gdns. N5	49	J5
Holmcroft Way, Brom.	97	C5
Holmdale Gdns. NW4	39	A5
Holmdale Rd. NW6	48	D5
Holmdale Rd., Chis.	88	F5
Holmdale Ter. N15	41	B7
Holmdene Ave. NW7	30	G6
Holmdene Ave. SE24	76	J3
Holmdene Ave., Har.	36	H3
Holmdene Clo., Beck.	96	C2
Holme Lacey Rd. SE12	78	F6
Holme Rd. E6	61	B1
Holme Way, Stan.	29	C6
Holmead Rd. SW6	66	E7
Holmebury Clo. (Bushey), Wat.	29	B2
Holmefield Ct. NW3	48	H6
Holmes Ave. E17	41	J3
Holmes Ave. NW7	31	B5
Holmes Pl. SW10	**18**	**D5**
Holmes Rd. NW5	49	B6
Holmes Rd. SW19	84	F7
Holmes Rd., Twick.	82	C2
Holmes Ter. SE1	**16**	**E3**
Holmes Ter. SE1	67	G2
Holmesdale Ave. SW14	74	B3
Holmesdale Clo. SE25	95	C3
Holmesdale Rd. N6	40	B7
Holmesdale Rd. SE25	95	A5
Holmesdale Rd., Bexh.	80	D2
Holmesdale Rd., Croy.	95	A5
Holmesdale Rd., Rich.	73	J1
Holmesdale Rd., Tedd.	82	F7
Holmesley Rd. SE23	77	H6
Holmewood Gdns. SW2	76	F7
Holmewood Rd. SE25	95	B3
Holmewood Rd. SW2	76	E7
Holmfield Ave. NW4	39	A5
Holmhurst Rd., Belv.	71	H5
Holmleigh Rd. N16	50	B1
Holms St. E2	**9**	**H1**
Holmshaw Clo. SE26	86	H4
Holmside Ri., Wat.	28	B3
Holmside Rd. SW12	76	A6
Holmsley Clo., N.Mal.	92	F6
Holmstall Ave., Edg.	38	C3
Holmwood Clo., Har.	36	J3
Holmwood Clo., Nthlt.	45	H6
Holmwood Gdns. N3	39	D2
Holmwood Gdns., Wall.	101	B6
Holmwood Gro. NW7	30	D5
Holmwood Rd., Chess.	98	G5
Holmwood Rd., Ilf.	52	H2
Holmwood Vill. SE7	69	G5
Holne Chase N2	39	F6
Holne Chase, Mord.	93	C6

Holness Rd. E15	51	F6
Holroyd Rd. SW15	74	J4
Holstein Way, Erith	71	D3
Holstock Rd., Ilf.	52	F2
Holsworth Clo., Har.	36	J5
Holsworthy Sq. WC1	**8**	**D6**
Holsworthy Way, Chess.	98	F5
Holt, The, Ilf.	35	F6
Holt, The, Wall.	101	C4
Holt Clo. N10	40	A4
Holt Clo. SE28	62	B7
Holt Clo., Chig.	35	J5
Holt Ct. E15	51	C5
Clays La.		
Holt Rd. E16	70	B1
Holt Rd., Wem.	46	E3
Holt Way, Chig.	35	J5
Holton St. E1	59	G4
Holtwhite Ave., Enf.	24	J2
Holtwhites Hill, Enf.	24	H1
Holwell Pl., Pnr.	36	E4
Holwood Pk. Ave., Orp.	104	C4
Holwood Pl. SW4	76	D4
Holybourne Ave. SW15	74	G7
Holyhead Clo. E3	60	A3
Holyhead Clo. E6	61	C5
Valiant Way		
Holyoak Rd. SE11	**20**	**G1**
Holyoak Rd. SE11	67	H4
Holyoake Ct. SE16	68	J2
Bryan Rd.		
Holyoake Wk. N2	39	F3
Holyoake Wk. W5	55	F4
Holyport Rd. SW6	65	J7
Holyrood Ave., Har.	45	E4
Holyrood Gdns., Edg.	38	B3
Holyrood Rd., Barn.	23	F6
Holyrood St. SE1	**17**	**D2**
Holywell Clo. SE3	69	G6
Holywell La. EC2	**9**	**E5**
Holywell La. EC2	59	B4
Holywell Row EC2	**9**	**D6**
Holywell Row EC2	59	B4
Home Clo., Cars.	100	J2
Home Clo., Nthlt.	54	F3
Home Ct., Felt.	81	A1
Home Fm. Clo., T.Ditt.	91	C7
Home Gdns., Dag.	53	J3
Home Lea, Orp.	104	J5
Home Mead, Stan.	37	F1
Home Pk. Rd. SW19	84	C4
Home Pk. Wk., Kings.T.	91	G4
Home Rd. SW11	75	H2
Homecroft Gdns., Loug.	27	E4
Homecroft Rd. N22	40	H1
Homecroft Rd. SE26	86	F5
Homefarm Rd. W7	55	F6
Homefield Ave., Ilf.	43	H5
Homefield Clo. NW10	47	C6
Homefield Clo., Hayes	54	D4
Homefield Gdns. N2	39	G3
Homefield Gdns., Mitch.	93	F2
Homefield Pk., Sutt.	100	E6
Homefield Rd. SW19	84	A6
Homefield Rd. W4	65	F5
Homefield Rd., Brom.	96	J1
Homefield Rd., Edg.	30	D6
Homefield Rd., Walt.	90	E7
Homefield Rd., Wem.	46	D4
Homefield St. N1	**9**	**D2**
Homelands Dr. SE19	86	B3
Homeleigh Rd. SE15	77	G5
Homemead SW12	85	B2
Homemead Rd., Brom.	97	C5
Homemead Rd., Croy.	95	F6
Homer Clo., Bexh.	80	J1
Homer Dr. E14	69	A4
Homer Rd. E9	50	H6
Homer Rd., Croy.	95	G6
Homer Row W1	**10**	**H2**
Homer Row W1	57	H5
Homer St. W1	**10**	**H2**
Homer St. W1	57	H5
Homersham Rd., Kings.T.	92	A2
Homerton Gro. E9	50	G5
Homerton High St. E9	50	F5
Homerton Rd. E9	50	H5
Homerton Row E9	50	F5

Homerton Ter. E9	50	F6
Morning La.		
Homesdale Clo. E11	42	G5
Homesdale Rd., Brom.	96	J4
Homesdale Rd., Orp.	97	H7
Homesfield NW11	39	D5
Homestall Rd. SE22	77	F5
Homestead, The N11	32	B4
Homestead Gdns., Esher	98	B5
Homestead Paddock N14	24	B5
Homestead Pk. NW2	47	F3
Homestead Rd. SW6	66	C7
Homestead Rd., Dag.	53	F2
Homewillow Clo. N21	24	H6
Homewood Clo., Hmptn.	81	F6
Fearnley Cres.		
Homewood Cres., Chis.	88	H6
Honduras St. EC1	**8**	**J5**
Honey Clo., Dag.	53	H6
Honey La. EC2	**13**	**A4**
Honeybourne Rd. NW6	48	E5
Honeybourne Way, Orp.	104	G1
Honeybrook Rd. SW12	76	C7
Honeycroft, Loug.	27	D4
Honeyden Rd., Sid.	89	E6
Honeyman Clo. NW6	48	A7
Honeypot Clo. NW9	37	J4
Honeypot La. NW9	38	A5
Honeypot La., Stan.	29	C7
Honeysett Rd. N17	41	C2
Reform Row		
Honeysuckle Gdns., Croy.	102	G1
Primrose La.		
Honeywell Rd. SW11	75	H6
Honeywood Rd. NW10	56	F2
Honeywood Rd., Islw.	73	D4
Honeywood Wk., Cars.	100	J4
Honister Clo., Stan.	37	E1
Honister Gdns., Stan.	37	E1
Honister Pl., Stan.	37	E1
Honiton Rd. NW6	57	C2
Honiton Rd., Well.	79	J2
Honley Rd. SE6	78	B7
Honor Oak Pk. SE23	77	G6
Honor Oak Ri. SE23	77	F6
Honor Oak Rd. SE23	86	F1
Hood Ave. N14	24	B6
Hood Ave. SW14	74	C5
Hood Clo., Croy.	101	H1
Parson's Mead		
Hood Ct. EC4	**12**	**F4**
Hood Rd. SW20	83	F7
Hood Wk., Rom.	44	H1
Hoodcote Gdns. N21	24	H7
Hook, The, Barn.	23	G6
Hook Fm. Rd., Brom.	97	A5
Hook La., Well.	79	J4
Hook Ri. N., Surb.	99	A3
Hook Ri. S., Surb.	99	A3
Hook Rd., Chess.	98	G5
Hook Rd., Epsom	99	C7
Hook Rd., Surb.	98	H3
Hook Wk., Edg.	30	C6
Hookers Rd. E17	41	G3
Hooking Grn., Har.	36	H5
Hooks Clo. SE15	77	E1
Woods Rd.		
Hooks Hall Dr., Dag.	53	J3
Hooks Way SE22	86	D1
Dulwich Common		
Hookstone Way, Wdf.Grn.	35	A7
Hoop La. NW11	39	C7
Hooper Rd. E16	60	G6
Hooper St. EC1	**13**	**H4**
Hooper St. E1	59	D7
Hooper's Ct. SW3	**14**	**J4**
Hop La. WC2	58	E7
St. Martin's La.		
Hope Clo. SE12	87	H3
Hope Clo., Sutt.	100	F5
Hope Clo., Wdf.Grn.	34	J6
West Gro.		
Hope Pk., Brom.	87	F7
Hope St. SW11	75	G3

Hopedale Rd. SE7	69	H6
Hopefield Ave. NW6	57	B2
Hopes Clo., Houns.	63	G6
Old Cote Dr.		
Hopetown St. E1	**13**	**G2**
Hopewell St. SE5	68	A7
Hopewell Yd. SE5	68	A7
Hopgood St. W12	65	J1
Macfarlane Rd.		
Hopkins Clo. N10	32	A7
Cromwell Rd.		
Hopkins St. W1	**11**	**G4**
Hopkinsons Pl. NW1	58	A1
Fitzroy Rd.		
Hoppers Rd. N13	32	G2
Hoppers Rd. N21	32	G2
Hoppett Rd. E4	34	E2
Hopping La. N1	49	H6
St. Mary's Gro.		
Hoppingwood Ave., N.Mal.	92	E3
Hopton Gdns. SE1	**16**	**H1**
Hopton Gdns., N.Mal.	92	G6
Hopton Rd. SW16	85	E5
Hopton St. SE1	**16**	**H1**
Hopton St. SE1	67	H1
Hopwood Rd. SE17	**21**	**C5**
Hopwood Rd. SE17	68	A6
Hopwood Wk. E8	50	D7
Wilman Gro.		
Horace Ave., Rom.	53	J1
Horace Rd. E7	51	H4
Horace Rd., Ilf.	43	F3
Horace Rd., Kings.T.	91	J3
Horatio Pl. SW19	84	D7
Kingston Rd.		
Horatio St. E2	**9**	**G2**
Horatio St. E2	59	D2
Horatius Way, Croy.	101	F5
Horbury Cres. W11	57	D7
Horbury Ms. W11	57	C7
Ladbroke Rd.		
Horder Rd. SW6	75	B1
Hordle Prom. E. SE15	**21**	**G7**
Hordle Prom. N. SE15	**21**	**F7**
Hordle Prom. S. SE15	68	C7
Pentridge St.		
Hordle Prom. W. SE15	**21**	**E7**
Horizon Way SE7	69	H4
Horley Clo., Bexh.	80	G5
Horley Rd. SE9	88	B4
Hormead Rd. W9	57	C4
Horn La. SE10	69	G4
Horn La. W3	65	C1
Horn La., Bexh.	80	J2
Horn La., Wdf.Grn.	34	G6
Horn Pk. Clo. SE12	78	H5
Horn Pk. La. SE12	78	H5
Hornbeam Clo. SE11	**20**	**E1**
Hornbeam Clo., Borwd.	22	A1
Hornbeam Clo., Buck.H.	35	A3
Hornbeam Rd.		
Hornbeam Clo., Nthlt.	45	E1
Hornbeam Cres., Brent.	64	E7
Hornbeam Gro. E4	34	E3
Hornbeam La. E4	26	E5
Hornbeam La., Bexh.	80	J2
Hornbeam Rd., Buck.H.	35	A3
Hornbeam Rd., Hayes	54	C5
Hornbeam Ter., Cars.	100	H1
Hornbeam Twr. E11	51	D3
Hollydown Way		
Hornbeam Wk., Rich.	82	J2
Hornbeam Way, Brom.	97	D6
Hornbeams Ri. N11	32	A6
Hornblower Clo. SE16	68	H4
Greenland Quay		
Hornbuckle Clo., Har.	46	A2
Hornby Clo. NW3	48	G7
Horncastle Clo. SE12	78	G7
Horncastle Rd. SE12	78	G7
Horndean Clo. SW15	83	G1
Bessborough Rd.		
Horndon Clo., Rom.	44	J1
Horndon Grn., Rom.	44	J1
Horndon Rd., Rom.	44	J1
Horne Way SW15	74	J1
Horner La., Mitch.	93	G2
Hornfair Rd. SE7	69	J6
Horniman Dr. SE23	86	E1
Horning Clo. SE9	88	B4
Horns End, Pnr.	36	C4
Horns Rd., Ilf.	43	G6

Entry	Ref
Hornsey La. N6	49 B1
Hornsey La. Est. N19	40 D7
Hornsey La.	
Hornsey La. Gdns. N6	40 C7
Hornsey Pk. Rd. N8	40 F3
Hornsey Ri. N19	40 D7
Hornsey Ri. Gdns. N19	40 D7
Hornsey Rd. N7	49 F3
Hornsey Rd. N19	49 E1
Hornsey St. N7	49 F5
Hornshay St. SE15	68 F6
Hornton St. W8	66 D2
Horsa Clo., Wall.	101 E7
Kingsford Ave.	
Horsa Rd. SE12	78 J7
Horsa Rd., Erith	71 H7
Horse and Dolphin Yd. W1	**11 J5**
Horse Fair, Kings.T.	91 G2
Wood St.	
Horse Guards Ave. SW1	**16 A2**
Horse Guards Ave. SW1	67 E1
Horse Guards Rd. SW1	**15 J2**
Horse Guards Rd. SW1	67 D1
Horse Leaze E6	61 D6
Horse Ride SW1	**15 H2**
Horse Rd. E7	51 H3
Centre Rd.	
Horse Shoe Cres., Nthlt.	54 G2
Horse Shoe Yd. W1	**11 E5**
Horsebridges Clo., Dag.	62 E1
Horsecroft Rd., Edg.	30 D7
Horseferry Pl. SE10	69 C6
Horseferry Rd. E14	59 G7
Horseferry Rd. SW1	**15 H6**
Horseferry Rd. SW1	67 D4
Horsell Rd. N5	49 G5
Horselydown La. SE1	**17 F3**
Horselydown La. SE1	68 C2
Horsenden Ave., Grnf.	46 B5
Horsenden Cres., Grnf.	46 C5
Horsenden La. N., Grnf.	46 C6
Horsenden La. S., Grnf.	55 D1
Horseshoe Clo. E14	69 C5
Ferry St.	
Horseshoe Clo. NW2	47 H2
Horseshoe Grn., Sutt.	100 E2
Aultone Way	
Horseshoe La. N20	31 A1
Horseshoe La., Enf.	24 J3
Chase Side	
Horsfeld Gdns. SE9	79 B5
Horsfeld Rd. SE9	79 A5
Horsford Rd. SW2	76 F5
Horsham Ave. N12	31 H5
Horsham Rd., Bexh.	80 G6
Horsley Dr., Croy.	103 C7
Horsley Rd. E4	34 C2
Horsley Rd., Brom.	96 H1
Palace Rd.	
Horsley St. SE17	**21 B5**
Horsley St. SE17	68 A6
Horsmonden Clo., Orp.	97 J7
Horsmonden Rd. SE4	77 J5
Hortensia Rd. SW10	**18 C7**
Hortensia Rd. SW10	66 F7
Horticultural Pl. W4	65 D5
Heathfield Ter.	
Horton Ave. NW2	48 B4
Horton Rd. E8	50 E6
Horton St. SE13	78 B3
Hortus Rd. E4	34 C2
Hortus Rd., Sthl.	63 F2
Hosack Rd. SW17	84 J1
Hoser Ave. SE12	87 G2
Hosier La. EC1	**12 G2**
Hosier La. EC1	58 H5
Hoskins Clo. E16	60 J6
Hoskins St. SE10	69 D5
Hospital Bri. Rd., Twick.	72 H7
Hospital La., Islw.	73 C5
Hospital Rd. E9	50 G5
Homerton Row	
Hospital Rd., Houns.	72 G3
Hotham Rd. SW15	74 J3
Hotham Rd. SW19	84 F7
Hotham Rd., W.Mol.	90 G3
Garrick Gdns.	
Hotham Rd. Ms. SW19	84 F7
Haydons Rd.	
Hotham St. E15	60 E1
Hothfield Pl. SE16	68 F3
Lower Rd.	
Hotspur Rd., Nthlt.	54 G2
Hotspur St. SE11	**20 E3**
Hotspur St. SE11	67 G5
Houblon Rd., Rich.	73 H5
Houghton Clo. E8	50 C6
Buttermere Wk.	
Houghton Clo., Hmptn.	81 E6
Houghton Rd. N15	41 C5
West Grn. Rd.	
Houghton St. WC2	**12 D4**
Houlder Cres., Croy.	101 H6
Houndsden Rd. N21	24 F6
Houndsditch EC3	**13 E3**
Houndsditch EC3	59 B6
Houndsfield Rd. N9	25 E7
Hounslow Ave., Houns.	72 H5
Hounslow Gdns., Houns.	72 H5
Hounslow Rd. (Feltham), Felt.	81 B1
Hounslow Rd. (Hanworth), Felt.	81 D4
Hounslow Rd., Twick.	72 H6
Houseman Way SE5	68 A7
Benhill Rd.	
Houston Pl., Esher	98 B1
Lime Tree Ave.	
Houston Rd. SE23	86 H2
Hove Ave. E17	41 J5
Hove Gdns., Sutt.	100 E1
Hoveden Rd. NW2	48 B5
Hoveton Rd. SE28	62 C6
Howard Ave., Bex.	89 C1
Howard Clo. N11	32 A2
Howard Clo. NW2	48 B4
Howard Clo. W3	56 B6
Howard Clo., Hmptn.	81 J6
Howard Dr., Borwd.	22 D4
Howard Ms. N5	49 H4
Hamilton Pk.	
Howard Pl. SW1	**15 F6**
Howard Rd. E6	61 C2
Howard Rd. E11	51 E3
Howard Rd. E17	42 A3
Howard Rd. N15	41 B6
Howard Rd. N16	50 A4
Howard Rd. NW2	48 A4
Howard Rd. SE20	95 F1
Howard Rd. SE25	95 D5
Howard Rd., Bark.	61 G1
Howard Rd., Brom.	87 G7
Howard Rd., Ilf.	52 E4
Howard Rd., Islw.	73 C3
Howard Rd., N.Mal.	92 E3
Howard Rd., Sthl.	54 H6
Howard Rd., Surb.	91 J6
Howard St., T.Ditt.	91 E7
Howard Wk. N2	39 F4
Howard Way, Barn.	23 A5
Sampson Ave.	
Howards Clo., Pnr.	36 B2
Howards Crest Clo., Beck.	96 C2
Howards La. SW15	74 H5
Howards Rd. E13	60 G3
Howarth Ct. E15	51 C5
Taylor Ct.	
Howarth Rd. SE2	71 A5
Howberry Clo., Edg.	29 G6
Howberry Rd., Edg.	29 G6
Howberry Rd., Stan.	29 G6
Howberry Rd., Th.Hth.	95 A1
Howbury Rd. SE15	77 F3
Howcroft Cres. N3	31 D7
Howcroft La., Grnf.	55 A3
Cowgate Rd.	
Howden Clo. SE28	62 D7
Howden Rd. SE25	95 C2
Howden St. SE15	77 D3
Howe Clo., Rom.	44 G1
Howell Clo., Rom.	44 D5
Howell Wk. SE1	**20 H2**
Howes Clo. N3	39 D3
Howgate Rd. SW14	74 D3
Howick Pl. SW1	**15 G6**
Howick Pl. SW1	67 G3
Howie St. SW11	66 H7
Howitt Rd. NW3	48 H6
Howland Ms. E. W1	**11 G1**
Howland St. W1	**11 F1**
Howland St. W1	58 C5
Howland Way SE16	68 H2
Howletts Rd. SE24	76 J6
Howley Pl. W2	**10 D1**
Howley Pl. W2	57 F5
Howley Rd., Croy.	101 H3
Hows St. E2	**9 F1**
Hows St. E2	59 C2
Howsman Rd. SW13	65 G6
Howson Rd. SE4	77 H4
Howson Ter., Rich.	73 H6
Howton Pl. (Bushey), Wat.	29 A1
Hoxton Mkt. N1	**9 D4**
Hoxton Sq. N1	**9 D4**
Hoxton Sq. N1	59 B3
Hoxton St. N1	9 D4
Hoxton St. N1	59 B1
Hoy St. E16	60 F6
Hoylake Gdns., Mitch.	94 C3
Hoylake Gdns., Ruis.	45 B1
Hoylake Gdns., Wat.	28 D4
Hoylake Rd. W3	56 E6
Hoyland Clo. SE15	68 E7
Commercial Way	
Hoyle Rd. SW17	84 H5
Hubbard Dr., Chess.	98 F6
Mansfield Rd.	
Hubbard Rd. SE27	85 J4
Hubbard St. E15	60 E1
Hubbinet Ind. Est., Rom.	44 J3
Hubert Gro. SW9	76 E3
Hubert Rd. E6	61 A3
Huddart St. E3	59 J5
Huddleston Clo. E2	59 F2
Huddleston Rd. N7	49 C3
Huddlestone Rd. E7	51 F4
Huddlestone Rd. NW2	47 H6
Hudson Ct. SW19	84 E7
Hudson Pl. SE18	70 F5
Hudson Rd., Bexh.	80 F2
Hudson's Pl. SW1	**19 F1**
Huggin Ct. EC4	**13 A5**
Huggin Hill EC4	**13 A5**
Hugh Ms. SW1	**19 E2**
Hugh Pl. SW1	**19 H1**
Hugh St. SW1	**19 E2**
Hugh St. SW1	67 B4
Hughan Rd. E15	51 D5
Hughenden Ave., Har.	37 E5
Hughenden Gdns., Nthlt.	54 C3
Hughenden Rd., Wor.Pk.	92 G7
Hughendon Ter. E15	51 C4
Westdown Rd.	
Hughes Rd., Hayes	54 A7
Hughes Wk., Croy.	94 J7
St. Saviours Rd.	
Hugo Rd. N19	49 C4
Hugon Rd. SW6	75 E3
Huguenot Pl. SW18	75 F5
Huguenot Sq. SE15	77 E3
Scylla Rd.	
Hull Clo. SE16	68 G2
Hull St. EC1	**8 J4**
Hullbridge Ms. N1	59 A1
Sherborne St.	
Hulse Ave., Bark.	52 G6
Hulse Ave., Rom.	44 H1
Humber Rd. NW2	47 H2
Humber Rd. SE3	69 F6
Humberstone Rd. E13	60 J3
Humberton Clo. E9	50 H5
Marsh Hill	
Humbolt Rd. W6	66 B6
Hume Ter. E16	60 J6
Prince Regent La.	
Hume Way, Ruis.	36 A6
Humes Ave. W7	64 B3
Humphrey Clo., Ilf.	43 C1
Humphrey St. SE1	**21 F3**
Humphrey St. SE1	68 C5
Humphries Clo., Dag.	53 F4
Hundred Acre NW9	38 F2
Hungerdown E4	34 C1
Hungerford Bri. SE1	**16 C2**
Hungerford Bri. SE1	67 F1
Hungerford Bri. WC2	**16 C2**
Hungerford Bri. WC2	67 F1
Hungerford La. WC2	**16 B1**
Hungerford Rd. N7	49 D6
Hungerford St. E1	59 E6
Commercial Rd.	
Hunsdon Clo., Dag.	53 E6
Hunsdon Rd. SE14	68 G7
Hunslett St. E2	59 F2
Royston St.	
Hunston Rd., Mord.	100 E1
Hunt Rd., Sthl.	63 G3
Hunt St. W11	66 A1
Hunt Way SE22	86 D1
Dulwich Common	
Hunter Clo. SE1	**17 C6**
Hunter Clo. SW12	85 A1
Balham Pk. Rd.	
Hunter Clo., Borwd.	22 C5
Hunter Ho., Felt.	81 A1
Hunter Rd. SW20	92 J1
Hunter Rd., Ilf.	52 E5
Hunter Rd., Th.Hth.	95 A3
Hunter St. WC1	**8 B5**
Hunter St. WC1	58 E4
Hunter Wk. E13	60 G1
Stratford Rd.	
Hunter Wk., Borwd.	22 C5
Ashley Dr.	
Huntercombe Gdns., Wat.	28 C5
Hunters, The, Beck.	96 C1
Hunters Ct., Rich.	73 G5
Friars La.	
Hunters Gro., Har.	37 F4
Hunters Gro., Hayes	63 A1
Hunters Gro., Orp.	104 F4
State Fm. Ave.	
Hunters Hall Rd., Dag.	53 G4
Hunters Hill, Ruis.	45 C3
Hunters Meadow SE19	86 B4
Dulwich Wd. Ave.	
Hunters Rd., Chess.	98 H3
Hunters Sq., Dag.	53 G4
Hunters Way, Croy.	102 B4
Brownlow Rd.	
Hunters Way, Enf.	24 G1
Hunting Gate Clo., Enf.	24 G3
Hunting Gate Dr., Chess.	98 H7
Hunting Gate Ms., Sutt.	100 E3
Hunting Gate Ms., Twick.	82 B1
Colne Rd.	
Huntingdon Clo., Mitch.	94 E4
Huntingdon Gdns. W4	65 C7
Huntingdon Gdns., Wor.Pk.	99 J3
Huntingdon Rd. N2	39 H3
Huntingdon Rd. N9	33 F1
Huntingdon St. E16	60 F6
Huntingdon St. N1	49 F7
Huntingfield, Croy.	102 J7
Huntingfield Rd. SW15	74 G4
Huntings Rd., Dag.	53 G6
Huntley Dr. N3	31 D6
Huntley St. WC1	**7 G6**
Huntley St. WC1	58 C4
Huntley Way SW20	92 G2
Huntly Rd. SE25	95 B4
Hunton St. E1	9 H6
Hunton St. E1	59 D5
Hunt's Clo. SE3	78 G2
Hunt's Ct. WC2	11 J6
Hunts La. E15	60 C2
Hunts Mead, Enf.	25 G3
Hunts Slip Rd. SE21	86 B3
Huntsman St. SE17	**21 C2**
Huntsman St. SE17	68 B4
Huntsmans Clo., Felt.	81 B4
Huntsmead Clo., Chis.	88 C7
Bullers Wd. Dr.	
Huntsmoor Rd., Epsom	99 D5
Huntspill St. SW17	84 F3
Huntsworth Ms. NW1	**7 G6**
Hurley Cres. SE16	68 G2
Marlow Way	
Hurley Rd., Grnf.	54 H6
Hurlingham Ct. SW6	75 C3
Hurlingham Gdns. SW6	75 C3
Hurlingham Rd. SW6	75 C2
Hurlingham Rd., Bexh.	71 F7
Hurlingham Sq. SW6	75 E3
Peterborough Rd.	
Hurlock St. N5	49 H3
Hurlstone Rd. SE25	95 A5
Hurn Ct. Rd., Houns.	72 D2
Renfrew Rd.	
Huron Rd. SW17	85 A2
Hurren Clo. SE3	78 E3

Hurry Clo. E15	51	E7
Hurst Ave. E4	34	A4
Hurst Ave. N6	40	C6
Hurst Clo. E4	34	A3
Hurst Clo. NW11	39	E6
Hurst Clo., Brom.	103	F1
Hurst Clo., Chess.	99	A5
Hurst Clo., Nthlt.	45	F6
Hurst Est. SE2	71	D5
Hurst La. SE2	71	D5
Hurst La., E.Mol.	90	J4
Hurst Ri., Barn.	23	D3
Hurst Rd. E17	42	B3
Hurst Rd. N21	32	G1
Hurst Rd., Bex.	89	C1
Hurst Rd., Buck.H.	35	A1
Hurst Rd., Croy.	102	A5
Hurst Rd., E.Mol.	90	G3
Hurst Rd., Erith	80	J1
Hurst Rd., Sid.	89	A2
Hurst Rd., Walt.	90	C5
Hurst Rd., W.Mol.	90	G3
Hurst Springs, Bex.	89	E1
Hurst St. SE24	76	H6
Hurst Vw. Rd., S.Croy.	102	B7
Hurst Way, S.Croy.	102	B6
Hurstbourne, Esher	98	C6
Hurstbourne Gdns., Bark.	52	H6
Hurstbourne Rd. SE23	86	H1
Hurstcourt Rd., Sutt.	100	E1
Hurstdene Ave., Brom.	103	F1
Hurstdene Gdns. N15	41	B7
Hurstfield, Brom.	96	G5
Hurstfield Rd., W.Mol.	90	G3
Hurstleigh Gdns., Ilf.	43	C1
Hurstmead Ct., Edg.	30	B4
Hurstway Wk. W11	57	A7
Whitchurch Rd.		
Hurstwood Ave. E18	42	H4
Hurstwood Ave., Bex.	89	E1
Hurstwood Dr., Brom.	97	C3
Hurstwood Rd. NW11	39	B4
Hurtwood Rd., Walt.	90	F7
Huson Clo. NW3	48	H7
Husseywell Cres., Brom.	103	G1
Hutchings St. E14	69	A2
Hutchings Wk. NW11	39	E4
Hutchins Clo. E15	51	C7
Gibbins Rd.		
Hutchinson Ter., Wem.	46	G3
Hutton Clo., Grnf.	46	A5
Mary Peters Dr.		
Hutton Clo., Wdf.Grn.	34	H6
Hutton Gdns., Har.	28	J7
Hutton Wk.		
Hutton Gro. N12	31	E5
Hutton La., Har.	28	J7
Hutton Row, Edg.	30	C7
Pavilion Way		
Hutton St. EC4	**12**	**F4**
Hutton Wk., Har.	28	J7
Huxbear St. SE4	77	J5
Huxley Clo., Nthlt.	54	E1
Huxley Dr., Rom.	44	B7
Huxley Gdns. NW10	55	J3
Huxley Par. N18	32	J5
Huxley Pl. N13	32	H3
Huxley Rd. E10	51	C2
Huxley Rd. N18	33	A4
Huxley Rd., Well.	79	J3
Huxley Sayze N18	32	J5
Huxley St. W10	57	B3
Hyacinth Clo., Hmptn.	81	G6
Gresham Rd.		
Hyacinth Ct., Pnr.	36	C3
Tulip Ct.		
Hyacinth Rd. SW15	83	G1
Hycliffe Gdns., Chig.	35	F4
Hyde, The NW9	38	E4
Hyde Clo. E13	60	G1
Pelly Rd.		
Hyde Clo., Barn.	23	C3
Hyde Ct. N20	31	G3
Hyde Cres. NW9	38	E5
Hyde La. SW11	75	H1
Battersea Bri. Rd.		
Hyde Pk. SW7	**14**	**G1**
Hyde Pk. SW7	66	H1
Hyde Pk. W1	**14**	**G1**
Hyde Pk. W1	66	H1
Hyde Pk. W2	**14**	**G1**
Hyde Pk. W2	66	H1

Hyde Pk. Ave. N21	32	J2
Hyde Pk. Cor. W1	**15**	**C3**
Hyde Pk. Cor. W1	67	A2
Hyde Pk. Cres. W2	**10**	**G4**
Hyde Pk. Cres. W2	57	H6
Hyde Pk. Gdns. N21	32	J1
Hyde Pk. Ave.		
Hyde Pk. Gdns. W2	**10**	**F5**
Hyde Pk. Gdns. W2	57	G7
Hyde Pk. Gdns. Ms. W2	**10**	**F5**
Hyde Pk. Gate SW7	**14**	**D4**
Hyde Pk. Gate SW7	66	F2
Hyde Pk. Gate Ms. SW7	**14**	**D4**
Hyde Pk. Pl. W2	**10**	**H5**
Hyde Pk. Sq. W2	**10**	**G4**
Hyde Pk. Sq. W2	57	H6
Hyde Pk. Sq. Ms. W2	**10**	**G4**
Hyde Pk. St. W2	**10**	**G4**
Hyde Pk. St. W2	57	H6
Hyde Rd. N1	59	B1
Hyde Rd., Bexh.	80	F2
Hyde Rd., Rich.	73	J5
Albert Rd.		
Hyde St. SE8	69	A6
Deptford High St.		
Hyde Vale SE10	78	D1
Hyde Wk., Mord.	93	D7
Glastonbury Rd.		
Hyde Way N9	33	C2
Hydefield Clo. N21	33	A1
Hydefield Ct. N9	33	B2
Hydes Pl. N1	49	H7
Compton Ave.		
Hydeside Gdns. N9	33	C2
Hydethorpe Ave. N9	33	C2
Hydethorpe Rd. SW12	85	C1
Hylands Rd. E17	42	D2
Hylton St. SE18	70	J4
Hyndewood SE23	86	G3
Hyndman St. SE15	68	E6
Hynton Rd., Dag.	53	C2
Hyrstdene, S.Croy.	101	H4
Hyson Rd. SE16	68	E4
Galleywall Rd.		
Hythe Ave., Bexh.	71	E7
Hythe Clo. N18	33	D4
Hythe Path, Th.Hth.	95	A3
Buller Rd.		
Hythe Rd. NW10	56	G4
Hythe Rd., Th.Hth.	95	A2
Hyver Hill NW7	22	D6

I

Ian Sq., Enf.	25	G1
Lansbury Rd.		
Ibbetson Path, Loug.	27	E3
Ibbotson Ave. E16	60	F6
Ibbott St. E1	59	F4
Mantus Rd.		
Iberian Ave., Wall.	101	D4
Ibis La. W4	74	C1
Ibscott Clo., Dag.	53	J6
Ibsley Gdns. SW15	83	G1
Ibsley Way, Barn.	23	H5
Iceland Rd. E3	60	A1
Ickburgh Est. E5	50	E3
Ickburgh Rd.		
Ickburgh Rd. E5	50	E3
Ickleton Rd. SE9	88	B4
Icknield Dr., Ilf.	43	E5
Ickworth Pk. Rd. E17	41	H4
Ida Rd. N15	41	A5
Ida St. E14	60	C6
Iden Clo., Brom.	96	E3
Idlecombe Rd. SW17	85	A6
Idmiston Rd. E15	51	F5
Idmiston Rd. SE27	85	J3
Idmiston Rd., Wor.Pk.	92	F7
Idmiston Sq., Wor.Pk.	99	F1
Idol La. EC3	**13**	**D6**
Idonia St. SE8	69	A7
Iffley Rd. W6	65	H3
Ifield Rd. SW10	**18**	**B5**
Ifield Rd. SW10	66	E6
Ightham Rd., Erith	71	G7
Ikea Twr. NW10	47	D5
Ilbert St. W10	57	A3
Ilchester Gdns. W2	**10**	**A5**
Ilchester Gdns. W2	57	E7
Ilchester Pl. W14	66	C3
Ilchester Rd., Dag.	53	B5
Ildersley Gro. SE21	86	A2
Ilderton Rd. SE15	68	F7
Ilderton Rd. SE16	68	E5

Ilex Clo., Sun.	90	C2
Oakington Dr.		
Ilex Ho. N4	40	F7
Ilex Rd. NW10	47	F6
Ilex Way SW16	85	G5
Ilford Hill, Ilf.	52	D3
Ilford La., Ilf.	52	E3
Ilfracombe Gdns., Rom.	44	B7
Ilfracombe Rd., Brom.	87	F3
Iliffe St. SE17	**20**	**H3**
Iliffe St. SE17	67	H5
Iliffe Yd. SE17	**20**	**H3**
Ilkeston Ct. E5	50	G4
Overbury St.		
Ilkley Clo. SE19	86	A6
Ilkley Rd. E16	60	J5
Ilkley Rd., Wat.	28	D5
Illingworth Clo., Mitch.	93	G3
Illingworth Way, Enf.	25	B4
Ilmington Rd., Har.	37	G6
Ilminster Gdns. SW11	75	H4
Imber Clo. N14	24	C7
Imber Clo., Esher	98	A1
Ember La.		
Imber Ct. Ind. Est., E.Mol.	91	A6
Imber Gro., Esher	91	A7
Imber Pk. Rd., Esher	98	A1
Imber St. N1	59	A1
Imperial Ave. N16	50	C3
Victorian Rd.		
Imperial Clo., Har.	36	G6
Imperial College Rd. SW7	**14**	**E5**
Imperial College Rd. SW7	66	G3
Imperial Dr., Har.	36	G7
Imperial Gdns., Mitch.	94	B3
Imperial Ms. E6	60	J2
Central Pk. Rd.		
Imperial Rd. N22	40	E1
Imperial Rd. SW6	75	E1
Imperial Sq. SW6	75	E1
Imperial St. E3	60	C3
Imperial Way, Chis.	88	F3
Imperial Way, Croy.	101	G6
Imperial Way, Har.	37	H6
Inca Dr. SE9	79	E7
Inchmery Rd. SE6	87	B2
Inchwood, Croy.	103	B4
Independent Pl. E8	50	C5
Downs Pk. Rd.		
Independents Rd. SE3	78	F3
Blackheath Village		
Inderwick Rd. N8	40	F5
Indescon Ct. E14	69	A2
India St. EC3	**13**	**F4**
India Way W12	56	H7
Indus Rd. SE7	69	J7
Industry Ter. SW9	76	G3
Canterbury Cres.		
Ingal Rd. E13	60	G4
Ingate Pl. SW8	76	B1
Ingatestone Rd. E12	51	J1
Ingatestone Rd. SE25	95	E5
Ingatestone Rd., Wdf.Grn.	34	H7
Ingelow Rd. SW8	76	B2
Ingersoll Rd. W12	65	H1
Ingestre Pl. W1	**11**	**G4**
Ingestre Rd. E7	51	G4
Ingestre Rd. NW5	49	B4
Ingham Rd. NW6	48	D4
Ingle Clo., Pnr.	36	F3
Inglebert St. EC1	**8**	**E3**
Ingleborough St. SW9	76	G2
Ingleby Clo., Dag.	53	H6
Ingleby Dr., Har.	46	A3
Ingleby Rd. N7	49	E3
Ingleby Rd., Dag.	53	H6
Ingleby Rd., Ilf.	52	E1
Ingleby Way, Chis.	88	D5
Ingledew Rd. SE18	71	G5
Inglehurst Gdns., Ilf.	43	C5
Inglemere Rd. SE23	86	G3
Inglemere Rd., Mitch.	84	J7
Inglesham Wk. E9	50	J6
Trowbridge Est.		
Ingleside Clo., Beck.	87	A7
Ingleside Gro. SE3	69	F6
Inglethorpe St. SW6	75	A4
Ingleton Ave., Well.	80	A5
Ingleton Rd. N18	33	D6
Ingleton St. SW9	76	G2
Ingleway N12	31	G6

Inglewood Clo. E14	69	A4
Inglewood Clo., Ilf.	35	J6
Inglewood Copse, Brom.	97	B2
Inglewood Rd. NW6	48	D5
Inglis Barracks NW7	31	B5
Inglis Rd. W5	55	J7
Inglis Rd., Croy.	102	C1
Inglis St. SE5	76	H1
Ingram Ave. NW11	39	F7
Ingram Clo. SE11	**20**	**D1**
Ingram Clo., Stan.	29	F5
Ingram Rd. N2	39	H4
Ingram Rd., Th.Hth.	94	J1
Ingram Way, Grnf.	55	A1
Ingrave Ho., Dag.	62	B1
Ingrave St. SW11	75	G3
Ingress St. W4	65	E5
Devonshire Rd.		
Inigo Jones Rd. SE7	70	B7
Inigo Pl. WC2	**12**	**A5**
Inkerman Rd. NW5	49	B6
Inks Grn. E4	34	B5
Inman Rd. NW10	56	E1
Inman Rd. SW18	75	F7
Inmans Row, Wdf.Grn.	34	G4
Inner Circle NW1	**7**	**B4**
Inner Circle NW1	58	A3
Inner Pk. Rd. SW19	84	A1
Inner Temple La. EC4	**12**	**E4**
Innes Clo. SW20	93	B2
Innes Gdns. SW15	74	H6
Innes Yd., Croy.	101	J3
High St.		
Inniskilling Rd. E13	60	J2
Inskip Clo. E10	51	B2
Inskip Rd., Dag.	53	D1
Institute Pl. E8	50	E5
Amhurst Rd.		
Instone Clo., Wall.	101	E7
De Havilland Rd.		
Integer Gdns. E11	42	D7
Forest Rd.		
International Ave., Houns.	63	C5
International Trd. Est., Sthl.	63	B3
Inver Clo. E5	50	F2
Theydon Rd.		
Inver Ct. W2	**10**	**B4**
Inveraray Pl. SE18	70	G6
Old Mill Rd.		
Inverclyde Gdns., Rom.	44	D4
Inveresk Gdns., Wor.Pk.	99	F3
Inverforth Clo. NW3	48	F2
North End Way		
Inverforth Rd. N11	32	B5
Inverine Rd. SE7	69	H5
Invermore Pl. SE18	70	F4
Inverness Ave., Enf.	25	E1
Inverness Dr., Ilf.	35	H6
Inverness Gdns. W8	**14**	**A2**
Inverness Ms. W2	**10**	**B5**
Inverness Pl. W2	**10**	**B5**
Inverness Pl. W2	57	E7
Inverness Rd. N18	33	E5
Inverness Rd., Houns.	72	F4
Inverness Rd., Sthl.	63	E4
Inverness Rd., Wor.Pk.	100	A1
Inverness St. NW1	58	B1
Inverness Ter. W2	**10**	**B5**
Inverness Ter. W2	57	E6
Inverton Rd. SE15	77	G4
Invicta Clo., Chis.	88	D5
Invicta Gro., Nthlt.	54	F3
Invicta Rd. SE3	69	G7
Inville Rd. SE17	**21**	**C4**
Inville Rd. SE17	68	A5
Inwood Ave., Houns.	72	J3
Inwood Clo., Croy.	102	H2
Inwood Rd., Houns.	72	H4
Inworth St. SW11	75	H2
Inworth Wk. N1	58	J1
Popham St.		
Ion Sq. E2	**9**	**H2**
Iona Clo. SE6	78	A7
Ipswich Rd. SW17	85	A6
Ireland Pl. N22	32	E7
Whittington Rd.		
Ireland Row E14	59	J6
Commercial Rd.		
Ireland Yd. EC4	**12**	**H4**
Irene Rd. SW6	75	D1
Irene Rd., Orp.	97	J7

Ireton Clo. N10　32 A7
Cromwell Rd.
Ireton St. E3　60 A4
Tidworth Rd.
Iris Ave., Bex.　80 E6
Iris Clo., Croy.　102 G1
Primrose La.
Iris Clo., Surb.　91 J7
Iris Ct., Pnr.　36 C3
Iris Cres., Bexh.　71 F6
Iris Rd., Epsom　99 B5
Iris Way E4　33 J6
Irkdale Ave., Enf.　25 C1
Iron Bri. Clo. NW10　47 E5
Iron Bri. Clo., Sthl.　63 J1
Iron Mill Pl. SW18　75 E6
Garratt La.
Iron Mill Rd. SW18　75 E6
Ironmonger La. EC2　**13 B4**
Ironmonger Pas. EC1　**9 A4**
Ironmonger Row EC1　**9 A4**
Ironmonger Row EC1　58 J3
Ironmongers Pl. E14　69 A4
Spindrift Ave.
Ironside Clo. SE16　68 G2
Kinburn St.
Irvine Ave., Har.　37 D3
Irvine Clo. N20　31 H2
Irvine Way, Orp.　97 J7
Irving Ave., Nthlt.　54 D1
Irving Gro. SW9　76 F2
Irving Rd. W14　66 A3
Irving St. WC2　**11 J6**
Irving St. WC2　58 D7
Irving Way NW9　38 F5
Irwin Ave. SE18　70 H7
Irwin Gdns. NW10　56 H1
Isabel St. SW9　76 F1
Isabella Clo. N14　24 C7
Isabella Dr., Orp.　104 F4
Isabella Rd. E9　50 F5
Isabella St. SE1　**16 G2**
Isabella St. SE1　67 H1
Isambard Ms. E14　69 C3
Isambard Pl. SE16　68 F1
Rotherhithe St.
Isel Way SE22　77 B5
East Dulwich Gro.
Isham Rd. SW16　94 E2
Isis Clo. SW15　74 J4
Isis St. SW18　84 F2
Isla Rd. SE18　70 F6
Island Fm. Ave.,
W.Mol.　90 F5
Island Fm. Rd.,
W.Mol.　90 F5
Island Rd., Mitch.　84 J7
Island Row E14　59 H6
Commercial Rd.
Islay Gdns., Houns.　72 D5
Isledon Rd. N7　49 G3
Islehurst Clo., Chis.　97 D1
Islington Grn. N1　58 H1
Islington High St. N1　**8 G1**
Islington High St. N1　58 H2
Islington Pk. Ms. N1　49 G7
Islington Pk. St.
Islington Pk. St. N1　49 G7
Islip Gdns., Edg.　30 D7
Islip Gdns., Nthlt.　45 E7
Islip Manor Rd., Nthlt.　45 E7
Islip St. NW5　49 C5
Ismailia Rd. E7　51 H7
Isom Clo. E13　60 J4
Belgrave Rd.
Ivanhoe Dr., Har.　37 D3
Ivanhoe Rd. SE5　77 C3
Ivanhoe Rd., Houns.　72 D3
Ivatt Pl. W14　66 C5
Ivatt Way N17　40 H3
Ive Fm. Clo. E10　51 A2
Ive Fm. La. E10　51 A2
Iveagh Ave. NW10　56 A2
Iveagh Clo. E9　59 G1
Iveagh Clo. NW10　56 A2
Ivedon Rd., Well.　80 C2
Iveley Rd. SW4　76 C2
Ivere Dr., Barn.　23 E6
Iverhurst Clo., Bexh.　80 D5
Iverna Ct. W8　66 D3
Iverna Gdns. W8　66 D3
Ivers Way, Croy.　103 B7
Iverson Rd. NW6　48 C6
Ives Rd. E16　51 A2
Ives St. SW3　**18 H1**
Ives St. SW3　66 H4
Ivestor Ter. SE23　77 F7
Ivimey St. E2　**9 J3**

Ivimey St. E2　59 D3
Ivinghoe Clo., Enf.　25 B1
Ivinghoe Rd., Dag.　53 B5
Ivor Gro. SE9　88 E1
Ivor Pl. NW1　**6 J6**
Ivor Pl. NW1　57 J4
Ivor St. NW1　49 C7
Ivory Sq. SW11　75 F3
Gartons Way
Ivorydown, Brom.　87 G4
Ivy Clo., Har.　45 F4
Ivy Clo., Pnr.　36 C7
Ivy Clo., Sun.　90 C2
Ivy Cotts. E14　60 B7
Grove Vill.
Ivy Cres. W4　65 C4
Bollo La.
Ivy Gdns. N8　40 E6
Ivy Gdns., Mitch.　94 D3
Ivy La., Houns.　72 F4
Ivy Pl., Surb.　91 J6
Alpha Rd.
Ivy Rd. E16　60 G6
Pacific Rd.
Ivy Rd. E17　42 A6
Ivy Rd. N14　24 C7
Ivy Rd. NW2　47 J4
Ivy Rd. SE4　77 J4
Ivy Rd. SW17　84 H5
Ivy Rd., Houns.　72 H4
Ivy Rd., Surb.　99 A2
Ivy St. N1　**9 D1**
Ivy St. N1　59 B2
Ivy Wk., Dag.　53 E6
Ivybridge Clo., Twick.　73 D7
Ivybridge Est., Islw.　73 C5
Ivybridge La. WC2　**12 B6**
Ivychurch Clo. SE20　86 F7
Laurel Gro.
Ivychurch La. SE17　**21 E3**
Ivydale Rd. SE15　77 G3
Ivydale Rd., Cars.　100 J2
Ivyday Gro. SW16　85 F3
Ivydene, W.Mol.　90 F5
Ivydene Clo., Sutt.　100 F4
Ivyhouse Rd., Dag.　53 D6
Ivymount Rd. SE27　85 G3
Ixworth Pl. SW3　**18 G3**
Ixworth Pl. SW3　66 H4
Izane Rd., Bexh.　80 F4

J

Jack Barnett Way N22　40 F2
Mayes Rd.
Jack Clow Rd. E15　60 E2
Manor Rd.
Jack Cornwell St. E12　52 D4
Jack Walker Ct. N5　49 H4
Jackass La., Kes.　103 H5
Jacklin Grn.,
Wdf.Grn.　34 G4
Jackman Ms. NW10　47 E3
Jackman St. E8　59 E1
Jackson Rd. N7　49 F4
Jackson Rd., Bark.　61 G1
Jackson Rd., Barn.　23 G6
Jackson Rd., Brom.　104 B2
Jackson St. SE18　70 D6
Jackson Way, Sthl.　63 H2
Jacksons La. N6　40 A7
Jacksons Pl., Croy.　102 A1
Cross Rd.
Jacob St. SE1　**17 H3**
Jacob St. SE1　68 C2
Jacobs Clo., Dag.　53 H4
Jacobs Ho. E13　60 J3
Jacob's Well Ms. W1　**11 C3**
Canford Ave.
Jade Clo. E16　61 A6
Jade Clo. NW2　39 A7
Marble Dr.
Jade Clo., Dag.　53 C1
Jaffe Rd., Ilf.　52 G1
Jaffray Pl. SE27　85 H4
Chapel Rd.
Jaffray Rd., Brom.　97 A4
Jaggard Way SW12　75 J7
Jago Clo. SE18　70 F6
Jago Wk. SE5　68 A7
Lomond Gro.
Jamaica Rd. SE1　**17 G4**
Jamaica Rd. SE1　68 C2
Jamaica Rd. SE16　**17 H5**
Jamaica Rd. SE16　68 D3
Jamaica Rd., Th.Hth.　94 H6
Jamaica St. E1　59 F5

James Ave. NW2　47 J5
James Ave., Dag.　53 F1
James Bedford Clo.,　36 C2
Pnr.
James Boswell Clo.　85 G4
SW16
Curtis Fld. Rd.
James Clo. E13　60 G2
Richmond St.
James Clo. NW11　39 B6
Woodlands
James Collins Clo. W9　57 C4
Fermoy Rd.
James Ct. N1　49 J7
Morton Rd.
James Dudson Ct.　47 C7
NW10
James Gdns. N22　32 H7
James Hammett Ho.　**9 G3**
E2
James Joyce Wk.　76 H4
SE24
Shakespeare Rd.
James La. E10　42 D7
James La. E11　42 D6
James Newman Ct.　88 D3
SE9
Great Harry Dr.
James Pl. N17　41 C1
Ruskin Rd.
James Sinclair Pt. E13　60 J1
James St. W1　**11 C3**
James St. W1　58 A6
James St. WC2　**12 B5**
James St., Bark.　52 F7
James St., Enf.　25 C5
James St., Houns.　73 A3
James Yd. E4　34 D6
Larkshall Rd.
Jameson St. W8　66 D1
James's Cotts., Rich.　65 A7
Kew Rd.
Jamestown Rd. NW1　58 B1
Jamieson Ho., Houns.　72 F6
Jane St. E1　59 E6
Commercial Rd.
Janet St. E14　69 A3
Janeway Pl. SE16　68 E2
Janeway St.
Janeway St. SE16　**17 J4**
Janeway St. SE16　68 D2
Janice Ms., Ilf.　52 E3
Oakfield Rd.
Jansen Wk. SW11　75 G4
Hope St.
Janson Clo. E15　51 E5
Janson Rd.
Janson Clo. NW10　47 E3
Janson Rd. E15　51 E5
Jansons Rd. N15　41 B3
Japan Cres. N4　40 F7
Japan Rd., Rom.　44 D6
Jardine Rd. E1　59 G7
Jarrett Clo. SW2　85 H1
Jarrow Clo., Mord.　93 E5
Jarrow Rd. N17　41 E4
Jarrow Rd. SE16　68 F4
Jarrow Rd., Rom.　44 C6
Jarrow Way E9　50 J5
Jarvis Clo., Barn.　23 A5
Jarvis Rd. SE22　77 B4
Melbourne Gro.
Jarvis Rd., S.Croy.　102 A6
Jasmin Rd., Epsom　99 B6
Jasmine Clo., Ilf.　52 E5
Jasmine Clo., Orp.　104 E2
Jasmine Gdns., Croy.　103 A3
Jasmine Gdns., Har.　45 G2
Jasmine Gro. SE20　95 E1
Jasmine Way, E.Mol.　91 B4
Hampton Ct. Way
Jason Ct. W1　58 A6
Marylebone La.
Jason Wk. SE9　88 D4
Jasper Pas. SE19　86 C6
Jasper Rd. E16　61 A6
Jasper Rd. SE19　86 C6
Jasper Wk. N1　**9 B3**
Javelin Way, Nthlt.　54 D3
Jay Gdns., Chis.　88 C4
Jay Ms. SW7　**14 D4**
Jay Ms. SW7　66 F2
Jaycroft, Enf.　24 G1
The Ridgeway
Jebb Ave. SW2　76 E6
Jebb St. E3　60 A2
Jedburgh Rd. E13　60 J3
Jedburgh St. SW11　76 A4

Jeddo Rd. W12　65 F2
Jefferies Ho. NW10　47 D7
Jefferson Clo. W13　64 E3
Jefferson Clo., Ilf.　43 E5
Jefferson Wk. SE18　70 D6
Kempt St.
Jeffreys Pl. NW1　49 C7
Jeffreys St.
Jeffreys Rd. SW4　76 E2
Jeffreys Rd., Enf.　25 J3
Jeffreys St. NW1　49 C7
Jeffreys Wk. SW4　76 E2
Jeffs Clo., Hmptn.　81 H6
Uxbridge Rd.
Jeffs Rd., Sutt.　100 C4
Jeken Rd. SE9　78 J4
Jelf Rd. SW2　76 G5
Jellicoe Gdns., Stan.　29 C6
Jellicoe Rd. E13　60 G4
Jutland Rd.
Jellicoe Rd. N17　33 A7
Jengar Clo., Sutt.　100 E4
Jenkins La. E6　61 D2
Jenkins La., Bark.　61 E2
Jenkins Rd. E13　60 H4
Jenner Ave. W3　56 D5
Jenner Ho. SE3　69 E6
Jenner Pl. SW13　65 H6
Jenner Rd. N16　50 C3
Jennett Rd., Croy.　101 G3
Jennifer Rd., Brom.　87 E5
Jennings Rd. SE22　77 C6
Jennings Way, Barn.　22 J3
Jenningtree Way,　71 J2
Belv.
Jenny Hammond Clo.　51 F3
E11
Newcomen Rd.
Jenson Way SE19　86 C7
Jenton Ave., Bexh.　80 E1
Jephson Rd. E7　51 J7
Jephson St. SE5　77 A1
Grove La.
Jephtha Rd. SW18　75 D6
Jeppos La., Mitch.　93 J4
Jerdan Pl. SW6　66 D7
Fulham Bdy.
Jeremiah St. E14　60 B6
Jeremys Grn. N18　33 E4
Jermyn St. SW1　**15 G1**
Jermyn St. SW1　67 C1
Jerningham Ave., Ilf.　43 E2
Jerningham Rd. SE14　77 H2
Jerome Cres. NW8　**6 G5**
Jerome Cres. NW8　57 H4
Jerome St. E1　**9 F6**
Jerrard St. N1　**9 E2**
Jerrard St. SE13　78 B3
Jersey Ave., Stan.　37 E2
Jersey Dr., Orp.　97 G6
Jersey Par., Houns.　72 H1
Jersey Rd. E11　51 D1
Jersey Rd. E16　60 J6
Prince Regent La.
Jersey Rd. SW17　85 B6
Jersey Rd. W7　64 D2
Jersey Rd., Houns.　72 H1
Jersey Rd., Ilf.　52 E4
Jersey Rd., Islw.　64 A7
Jersey St. E2　59 E3
Bethnal Grn. Rd.
Jerusalem Pas. EC1　**8 G6**
Jervis Ct. W1　**11 E4**
Jerviston Gdns.　85 G5
SW16
Jesmond Ave., Wem.　46 J6
Jesmond Rd., Croy.　95 C7
Jesmond Way, Stan.　29 H5
Jessam Ave. E5　50 E1
Jessamine Rd. W7　64 B1
Jesse Rd. E10　51 C1
Jessel Dr., Loug.　27 F1
Jessica Rd. SW18　75 F6
Jessop Ave., Sthl.　63 F4
Jessop Rd. SE24　76 H4
Milkwood Rd.
Jessops Way, Croy.　94 C6
Jessup Clo. SE18　70 F4
Jetstar Way, Nthlt.　54 E3
Jevington Way SE12　87 H1
Jewel Rd. E17　42 A3
Jewry St. EC3　**13 F4**
Jewry St. EC3　59 C6
Jew's Row SW18　75 E4
Jews Wk. SE26　86 E4
Jeymer Ave. NW2　47 H5
Jeymer Dr., Grnf.　54 J1
Jeypore Rd. SW18　75 F7

Jillian Clo., Hmptn.	81	G7
Jim Bradley Clo. SE18	70	D4
John Wilson St.		
Joan Cres. SE9	79	A7
Joan Gdns., Dag.	53	E2
Joan Rd., Dag.	53	E1
Joan St. SE1	**16**	**G2**
Joan St. SE1	67	H1
Jocelyn Rd., Rich.	73	H3
Jockey's Flds. WC1	**12**	**D1**
Jockey's Flds. WC1	58	F5
Jodane St. SE8	68	J4
Jodrell Rd. E3	59	J1
Joel St., Nthwd.	36	A3
Joel St., Pnr.	36	A3
Johanna St. SE1	**16**	**E4**
John Adam St. WC2	**12**	**B6**
John Adam St. WC2	58	E7
John Aird Ct. W2	**10**	**D1**
John Ashby Clo. SW2	76	E6
John Barnes Wk. E15	51	F6
Hamfrith Rd.		
John Bradshaw Rd. N14	32	D1
High St.		
John Burns Dr., Bark.	52	H7
John Campbell Rd. N16	50	B5
John Carpenter St. EC4	**12**	**F5**
John Carpenter St. EC4	58	H7
John Cornwall VC Ho. E12	52	D4
John Deed Ind. Est., Mitch.	93	J6
John Felton Rd. SE16	**17**	**H4**
John Felton Rd. SE16	68	D2
John Fisher St. E1	**13**	**H5**
John Fisher St. E1	59	D7
John Gooch Dr., Enf.	24	H1
John Groom's Est., Edg.	30	C4
John Islip St. SW1	**19**	**J3**
John Islip St. SW1	67	D5
John Keats Ho. N22	32	F7
John Maurice Clo. SE17	68	A4
John McKenna Wk. SE16	**17**	**J5**
John Newton Ct., Well.	80	B3
Danson La.		
John Parker Clo., Dag.	53	H7
John Parker Sq. SW11	75	G3
Thomas Baines Rd.		
John Penn St. SE13	78	B1
John Perrin Pl., Har.	37	H7
John Princes St. W1	**11**	**E3**
John Princes St. W1	58	B6
John Rennie Wk. E1	68	E1
Wine Clo.		
John Roll Way SE16	**17**	**J5**
John Roll Way SE16	68	D3
John Ruskin St. SE5	**20**	**G7**
John Ruskin St. SE5	67	H7
John Silkin La. SE8	68	G5
John Spencer Sq. N1	49	H6
John St. E15	60	F1
John St. SE25	95	D4
John St. WC1	**8**	**D6**
John St. WC1	58	F4
John St., Enf.	25	C5
John St., Houns.	72	E2
John Walsh Twr. E11	51	F2
John Wilson St. SE18	70	D4
John Woolley Clo. SE13	78	D4
Johns Ave. NW4	38	J4
Johns La., Mord.	93	F5
John's Ms. WC1	**8**	**D6**
John's Ms. WC1	58	F4
John's Pl. E1	**19**	**E6**
Damien St.		
John's Ter., Croy.	102	B1
Johnson Clo. E8	59	D1
Johnson Rd., Brom.	97	A5
Johnson Rd., Croy.	95	A7
Johnson Rd., Houns.	63	C7
Johnson St. E1	59	F7
Cable St.		
Johnson St., Sthl.	63	C3
Johnsons Clo., Cars.	100	H3
Johnson's Ct. EC4	58	G6
Fleet St.		
Johnsons Dr., Hmptn.	90	J1
Johnson's Pl. SW1	**19**	**F4**
Johnson's Pl. SW1	67	C5
Johnsons Way NW10	56	B4
Johnston Clo. SW9	76	F1
Hackford Rd.		
Johnston Rd., Wdf.Grn.	34	G5
Johnston Ter. NW2	48	A3
Campion Ter.		
Johnstone Rd. E6	61	C3
Joiner St. SE1	**17**	**C2**
Joiner's Arms Yd. SE5	77	A1
Denmark Hill		
Jollys La., Har.	46	A1
Lower Rd.		
Jolly's La., Hayes	54	D5
Jonathan St. SE11	**20**	**C3**
Jonathan St. SE11	67	F5
Jones Rd. E13	60	H4
Holborn Rd.		
Jones St. W1	**11**	**D6**
Jones Wk., Rich.	73	J6
Pyrland Rd.		
Jonquil Gdns., Hmptn.	81	F6
Partridge Rd.		
Jonson Clo., Hayes	54	A5
Jonson Clo., Mitch.	94	B4
Joram Way SE16	68	E5
Egan Way		
Jordan Clo., Dag.	53	H4
Muggeridge Rd.		
Jordan Clo., Har.	45	F3
Hamilton Cres.		
Jordan Rd., Grnf.	55	E1
Jordans Clo., Islw.	73	B1
Joseph Ave. W3	56	D6
Joseph Powell Clo. SW12	76	B6
Hazelbourne Rd.		
Joseph Ray Rd. E11	51	E2
High Rd.		
Leytonstone		
Joseph St. E3	59	J4
Josephine Ave. SW2	76	F5
Joshua St. E14	60	C6
St. Leonards St.		
Joubert St. SW11	75	J2
Jowett St. SE15	68	C7
Joyce Ave. N18	33	C5
Joyce Dawson Way SE28	62	A7
Thamesmere Dr.		
Joyce Page Clo. SE7	70	A6
Lansdowne La.		
Joydon Dr., Rom.	44	B6
Joyners Clo., Dag.	53	F4
Jubb Powell Ho. N15	41	B6
Jubilee Ave. E4	34	C6
Jubilee Ave., Rom.	44	H5
Jubilee Ave., Twick.	72	J7
Jubilee Clo. NW9	38	D6
Jubilee Clo., Pnr.	36	C2
Jubilee Clo., Rom.	44	H5
Jubilee Cres. E14	69	C3
Jubilee Cres. N9	33	D1
Jubilee Dr., Ruis.	45	D4
Jubilee Gdns., Sthl.	54	G6
Jubilee Pl. SW3	**18**	**H3**
Jubilee Pl. SW3	66	H5
Jubilee Rd., Grnf.	55	E1
Jubilee Rd., Sutt.	100	A7
Jubilee St. E1	59	F6
Jubilee Way SW19	93	E1
Jubilee Way, Chess.	90	A4
Jubilee Way, Sid.	89	A2
Judd St. WC1	**8**	**A4**
Judd St. WC1	58	E3
Jude St. E16	60	F6
Judge Wk., Esher	98	B6
Juer St. SW11	66	H7
Julia Gdns., Bark.	62	D2
Julia St. NW5	49	A4
Oak Village		
Julian Ave. W3	56	B7
Julian Clo., Barn.	23	E3
Julian Hill, Har.	46	B2
Julian Pl. E14	69	B5
Julien Rd. W5	64	F4
Junction App. SE13	78	C3
Loampit Vale		
Junction App. SW11	75	H3
Junction Ave. W10	56	J3
Harrow Rd.		
Junction Ms. W2	**10**	**G3**
Junction Pl. W2	**10**	**F3**
Junction Rd. E13	60	H2
Junction Rd. N9	33	D1
Junction Rd. N17	41	D3
Junction Rd. N19	49	C4
Junction Rd. W5	64	G4
Junction Rd., Har.	37	B6
Junction Rd., S.Croy.	102	A5
Junction Rd. E., Rom.	44	E7
Kenneth Rd.		
Junction Rd. W., Rom.	44	E7
Junction Wf. N1	**8**	**J2**
Junction Wf. N1	58	J2
Juniper Clo., Barn.	23	A5
Sellwood Dr.		
Juniper Clo., Wem.	47	A5
Juniper Gdns. SW16	94	C1
Leonard Rd.		
Juniper La. E6	61	B5
Juniper Rd., Ilf.	52	E4
Juniper St. E1	59	F7
Juno Way SE14	68	G6
Jupiter Way N7	49	F6
Jupp Rd. E15	51	D7
Jupp Rd. W. E15	60	C1
Justice Wk. SW3	**18**	**G6**
Justin Clo., Brent.	64	G7
Justin Rd. E4	33	J6
Jute La., Enf.	25	H2
Jutland Clo. N19	49	E1
Sussex Way		
Jutland Rd. E13	60	G4
Jutland Rd. SE6	78	C7
Jutsums Ave., Rom.	44	H6
Jutsums La., Rom.	44	H6
Juxon Clo., Har.	36	H1
Augustine Rd.		
Juxon St. SE11	**20**	**D1**
Juxon St. SE11	67	F4

K

Kaduna Clo., Pnr.	36	B5
Kale Rd., Erith	71	E2
Kambala Rd. SW11	75	G3
Kangley Bri. Rd. SE26	86	J4
Karen Ct. SE4	77	J2
Wickham Rd.		
Karen Ct., Brom.	96	F1
Blyth Rd.		
Karen Ter. E11	51	F2
Montague Rd.		
Karoline Gdns., Grnf.	55	A2
Oldfield La. N.		
Kashgar Rd. SE18	70	J4
Kashmir Rd. SE7	70	A7
Kassala Rd. SW11	75	J1
Katella Trd. Est., Bark.	61	H3
Kates Clo., Barn.	22	G5
Katharine St., Croy.	101	J3
Katherine Gdns. SE9	79	A4
Katherine Gdns., Ilf.	35	F7
Katherine Rd. E6	52	A7
Katherine Rd. E7	51	J6
Katherine Rd., Twick.	82	D1
London Rd.		
Katherine Sq. W11	66	B1
Wilsham Rd.		
Kathleen Ave. W3	56	C5
Kathleen Ave., Wem.	46	H7
Kathleen Rd. SW11	75	J3
Kay Rd. SW9	76	E2
Kay St. E2	**9**	**J1**
Kay St. E2	59	D2
Kay St. E15	51	D7
Kay St., Well.	80	B1
Kayemoor Rd., Sutt.	100	H7
Kean St. WC2	**12**	**C4**
Kean St. WC2	58	F6
Keats Clo. E11	42	H5
Nightingale La.		
Keats Clo. NW3	48	H4
Keats Gro.		
Keats Clo. SE1	**21**	**F2**
Keats Clo. SW19	84	G6
North Rd.		
Keats Clo., Chig.	35	F6
Keats Clo., Enf.	25	G5
Keats Clo., Hayes	54	A5
Keats Gro. NW3	48	H4
Keats Ho., Beck.	87	A6
Keats Pl. EC2	**13**	**B2**
Keats Rd., Belv.	71	J3
Keats Rd., Well.	79	H1
Keats Way, Croy.	95	H6
Keats Way, Grnf.	54	H5
Keble Clo., Nthlt.	45	J5
Keble Clo., Wor.Pk.	99	F1
Keble St. SW17	84	F4
Kechill Gdns., Brom.	96	G7
Kedelston Ct. E5	50	G4
Redwald Rd.		
Kedleston Dr., Orp.	97	J6
Kedleston Wk. E2	59	E3
Middleton St.		
Keedonwood Rd., Brom.	87	E5
Keel Clo. SE16	68	G1
Keeley Rd., Croy.	101	J2
Keeley St. WC2	**12**	**C4**
Keeley St. WC2	58	F6
Keeling Rd. SE9	79	A5
Keely Clo., Barn.	23	H5
Keemor St. SE18	70	D7
Llanover Rd.		
Keens Clo. SW16	85	D5
Keens Rd., Croy.	101	J4
Keens Yd. N1	49	H6
St. Paul's Rd.		
Keetons Rd. SE16	68	E3
Keevil Dr. SW19	75	A7
Keighley Clo. N7	49	E5
Penn Rd.		
Keightley Dr. SE9	88	F1
Keildon Rd. SW11	75	J4
Keir, The SW19	83	J5
West Side Common		
Keir Hardie Est. E5	50	E1
Springfield		
Keir Hardie Ho. W6	65	J6
Lochaline St.		
Keir Hardie Way, Bark.	53	A7
Keir Hardie Way, Hayes	54	A3
Keith Connor Clo. SW8	76	B3
Daley Thompson Way		
Keith Gro. W12	65	G2
Keith Rd. E17	41	J1
Keith Rd., Bark.	61	G2
Kelbrook Rd. SE3	79	B2
Kelby Path SE9	88	E3
Kelceda Clo. NW2	47	G2
Kelfield Gdns. W10	56	J6
Kell St. SE1	**16**	**H5**
Kelland Clo. N8	40	D5
Palace Rd.		
Kelland Rd. E13	60	G4
Kellaway Rd. SE3	78	J2
Kellerton Rd. SE13	78	E5
Kellett Rd. SW2	76	G4
Kelling Gdns., Croy.	94	H7
Kellino St. SW17	84	J4
Kellner Rd. SE28	70	D7
Kelly Ct., Borwd.	22	C2
Banks Rd.		
Kelly Rd. NW7	31	B6
Kelly St. NW1	49	B6
Kelly Way, Rom.	44	E5
Kelman Clo. SW4	76	D2
Kelmore Gro. SE22	77	D4
Kelmscott Clo. E17	41	J2
Kelmscott Gdns. W12	65	G3
Kelmscott Rd. SW11	75	H5
Kelross Pas. N5	49	J4
Kelross Rd.		
Kelross Rd. N5	49	J4
Kelsall Clo. SE3	78	H2
Kelsey La., Beck.	96	A3
Kelsey Pk. Ave., Beck.	96	B2
Kelsey Pk. Rd., Beck.	96	A2
Kelsey Sq., Beck.	96	A2
High St.		
Kelsey St. E2	**9**	**J5**
Kelsey St. E2	59	D4
Kelsey Way, Beck.	96	A3
Kelshall Ct. N4	49	J2
Brownswood Rd.		
Kelsie Way, Ilf.	35	H6
Kelso Pl. W8	**14**	**B5**
Kelso Pl. W8	66	E3
Kelso Rd., Cars.	93	F7
Kelson Ho. E14	69	C3
Kelston Rd., Ilf.	43	E2
Kelvedon Clo., Kings.T.	83	A6
Kelvedon Rd. SW6	66	C7
Kelvedon Way, Wdf.Grn.	35	C6
Kelvin Ave. N13	32	F6
Kelvin Ave., Tedd.	82	B6
Kelvin Clo., Epsom	99	A6
Kelvin Cres., Har.	29	B7

Kelvin Dr., Twick. 73 E6
Kelvin Gdns., Croy. 94 E7
Franklin Way
Kelvin Gdns., Sthl. 54 G6
Kelvin Gro. SE26 86 E3
Kelvin Gro., Chess. 98 H3
Kelvin Ind. Est., Grnf. 45 H7
Kelvin Par., Orp. 104 H1
Kelvin Rd. N5 49 H4
Kelvin Rd., Well. 80 A3
Kelvinbrook, W.Mol. 90 H3
Kelvington Clo., Croy. 95 H7
Kelvington Rd. SE15 77 G5
Kember St. N1 49 F7
Carnoustie Dr.
Kemble Dr., Brom. 104 B3
Kemble Rd. N17 41 D1
Kemble Rd. SE23 86 G1
Kemble Rd., Croy. 101 G3
Kemble St. WC2 12 C4
Kemble St. WC2 58 F6
Kemerton Rd. SE5 76 J3
Kemerton Rd., Beck. 96 B2
Kemerton Rd., Croy. 95 C7
Kemeys St. E9 50 H5
Kemnal Rd., Chis. 88 F7
Kemp Gdns., Croy. 94 J6
St. Saviours Rd.
Kemp Rd., Dag. 53 D1
Kempe Rd. NW6 57 A2
Kempis Way SE22 77 B5
East Dulwich Gro.
Kemplay Rd. NW3 48 G4
Kemp's Ct. W1 11 G4
Kemps Dr. E14 60 A7
Morant St.
Kemps Gdns. SE13 78 C5
Thornford Rd.
Kempsford Gdns. SW5 66 D5
Kempsford Rd. SE11 20 G2
Kempsford Rd. SE11 67 G4
Kempshott Rd. SW16 85 D7
Kempson Rd. SW6 75 D1
Kempt St. SE18 70 D6
Kempthorne Rd. SE8 68 H4
Kempton Ave., Nthlt. 45 G6
Kempton Ave., Sun. 90 B1
Kempton Clo., Erith 71 J6
Kempton Ct., Sun. 90 B1
Kempton Rd. E6 61 C1
Kempton Rd., Hmptn. 90 F2
Kempton Wk., Croy. 95 H6
Kemsing, Bex. 80 E7
Kemsing Clo., Brom. 103 F2
Bourne Way
Kemsing Rd., Th.Hth. 94 J4
Kemsing Rd. SE10 69 G5
Ken Way, Wem. 47 C2
Kenbury St. SE5 76 J2
Kenchester Clo. SW8 67 E7
Kencot Way, Erith 71 F2
Kendal Ave. N18 33 A4
Kendal Ave. W3 56 A4
Kendal Ave., Bark. 52 H7
Kendal Clo. SW9 20 G7
Kendal Clo. SW9 67 H7
Kendal Clo., Wdf.Grn. 34 F2
Kendal Gdns. N18 33 A4
Kendal Gdns., Sutt. 100 F2
Kendal Par. N18 33 A4
Great Cambridge Rd.
Kendal Pl. SW15 75 C5
Upper Richmond Rd.
Kendal Rd. NW10 47 G4
Kendal St. W2 10 H4
Kendal St. W2 57 H6
Kendale Rd., Brom. 87 E5
Kendall Ave., Beck. 95 H2
Kendall Pl. W1 11 B2
Kendall Rd., Beck. 95 H2
Kendall Rd., Islw. 73 D2
Kendalmere Clo. N10 40 B1
Kender St. SE14 77 F1
Kendoa Rd. SW4 76 D4
Kendon Clo. E11 42 H5
The Ave.
Kendra Hall Rd., 101 H7
S.Croy.
Kendrey Gdns., Twick. 73 B6
Kendrick Ms. SW7 18 E1
Kendrick Pl. SW7 18 E2
Kendrick Rd. SW7 66 G4
Kenelm Clo., Har. 46 D3
Kenerne Dr., Barn. 23 B5
Kenilford Rd. SW12 76 B7
Kenilworth Ave. E17 42 A2
Kenilworth Ave. SW19 84 D5
Kenilworth Ave., Har. 45 F4

Kenilworth Clo., 22 C3
Borwd.
Kenilworth Ct. SW15 75 A3
Kenilworth Cres., Enf. 25 B1
Kenilworth Dr., 22 C3
Borwd.
Kenilworth Gdns. 79 E2
SE18
Kenilworth Gdns., Ilf. 52 J2
Kenilworth Gdns., 27 C6
Loug.
Kenilworth Gdns., 54 F3
Sthl.
Kenilworth Gdns., 28 C5
Wat.
Kenilworth Rd. E3 59 H2
Kenilworth Rd. NW6 57 C1
Kenilworth Rd. SE20 95 G1
Kenilworth Rd. W5 64 H1
Kenilworth Rd., Edg. 30 C3
Kenilworth Rd., 99 G5
Epsom
Kenilworth Rd., Orp. 97 F6
Kenley Ave. NW9 38 E1
Kenley Clo., Bex. 80 G7
Kenley Clo., Chis. 97 H3
Kenley Gdns., Th.Hth. 94 H4
Kenley Rd. SW19 93 C2
Kenley Rd., Kings.T. 92 B2
Kenley Rd., Twick. 73 D6
Kenley Wk. W11 57 B7
Princedale Rd.
Kenley Wk., Sutt. 100 A4
Kenlor Rd. SW17 84 G5
Kenmare Dr., Mitch. 84 J7
Kenmare Gdns. N13 32 J4
Kenmare Rd., Th.Hth. 94 G6
Kenmere Gdns., 56 A1
Wem.
Kenmere Rd., Well. 80 C2
Kenmont Gdns. NW10 56 H3
Kenmore Ave., Har. 37 D4
Kenmore Clo., Rich. 65 A7
Kent Rd.
Kenmore Rd., Edg. 38 B2
Kenmore Rd., Har. 37 G3
Kenmure Rd. E8 50 E5
Kennard Rd. E15 51 D7
Kennard Rd. N11 31 J5
Kennard St. E16 70 C1
Kennard St. SW11 76 A1
Kennedy Ave., Enf. 25 F6
Kennedy Clo. E13 60 G2
Kennedy Clo., Orp. 104 G1
Kennedy Clo., Pnr. 28 F6
Kennedy Path W7 55 C4
Harp Rd.
Kennedy Rd. W7 55 B5
Kennedy Rd., Bark. 61 H1
Kennel Hill SE22 77 B3
Kennet Clo. SW11 75 G4
Maysoule Rd.
Kennet Rd. W9 57 C4
Kennet Rd., Islw. 73 C3
Kennet Sq., Mitch. 93 H1
Kennet St. E1 17 J1
Kennet St. E1 68 D1
Kennet Wf. La. EC4 13 A5
Kenneth Ave., Ilf. 52 E4
Kenneth Cres. NW2 47 H5
Kenneth Gdns., Stan. 29 D6
Kenneth More Rd., Ilf. 52 E3
Oakfield Rd.
Kenneth Rd., Rom. 44 D7
Kenneth Robbins Ho. 33 E7
N17
Kennett Dr., Hayes 54 E5
Kenning St. SE16 68 F2
Railway La.
Kenning Ter. N1 59 B1
Kenninghall Rd. E5 50 D3
Kenninghall Rd. N18 33 F5
Kennings Way SE11 20 G3
Kennings Way SE11 67 G5
Kennington Grn. SE11 20 E4
Kennington Gro. SE11 20 D5
Kennington La. SE11 20 C4
Kennington La. SE11 67 E5
Kennington Oval SE11 20 D5
Kennington Oval SE11 67 F6
Kennington Pk. Est. 20 E6
SE11
Kennington Pk. Gdns. 20 G5
SE11
Kennington Pk. Pl. 20 F5
SE11
Kennington Pk. Pl. 67 G6
SE11

Kennington Pk. Rd. 20 F5
SE11
Kennington Pk. Rd. 67 G6
SE11
Kennington Rd. SE1 16 E5
Kennington Rd. SE1 67 G3
Kennington Rd. SE11 20 E1
Kennington Rd. SE11 67 G3
Kenny Rd. NW7 31 B5
Kenrick Pl. W1 11 B2
Kensal Rd. W10 57 A4
Kensington Ave. E12 52 B6
Kensington Ave., 94 G1
Th.Hth.
Kensington Ch. Ct. W8 14 A4
Kensington Ch. Ct. W8 66 E2
Kensington Ch. St. W8 66 D1
Kensington Ch. Wk. 14 A3
W8
Kensington Ch. Wk. 66 E2
W8
Kensington Ct. W8 14 B4
Kensington Ct. W8 66 E2
Kensington Ct. Ms. 14 B4
W8
Kensington Ct. Pl. W8 14 B5
Kensington Ct. Pl. W8 66 E3
Kensington Dr., 43 A2
Wdf.Grn.
Kensington Gdns. W2 14 D2
Kensington Gdns. W2 66 E1
Kensington Gdns., Ilf. 52 C1
Kensington Gdns. Sq. 10 A4
W2
Kensington Gdns. Sq. 57 E6
W2
Kensington Gate W8 14 C5
Kensington Gate W8 66 F3
Kensington Gore SW7 14 E4
Kensington Gore SW7 66 F2
Kensington Hall 66 C5
Gdns. W14
Beaumont Ave.
Kensington High St. 66 D3
W8
Kensington High St. 66 C3
W14
Kensington Mall W8 66 D1
Kensington Palace 14 A1
Gdns. W8
Kensington Palace 66 E1
Gdns. W8
Kensington Pk. Gdns. 57 C7
W11
Kensington Pk. Ms. 57 C6
W11
Kensington Pk. Rd.
Kensington Pk. Rd. 57 C6
W11
Kensington Pl. W8 66 D1
Kensington Rd. SW7 14 C4
Kensington Rd. SW7 66 F2
Kensington Rd. W8 14 B4
Kensington Rd. W8 66 E2
Kensington Rd., Nthlt. 63 G3
Kensington Rd., Rom. 44 J6
Kensington Sq. W8 14 A4
Kensington Sq. W8 66 E2
Kensington Ter., 102 A7
S.Croy.
Sanderstead Rd.
Kent Ave. W13 55 E5
Kent Ave., Dag. 62 G4
Kent Ave., Well. 79 J5
Kent Clo., Mitch. 94 E4
Kent Clo., Orp. 104 H6
Kent Dr., Barn. 24 A4
Kent Dr., Tedd. 82 B5
Kent Gdns. W13 55 E5
Kent Gdns., Ruis. 36 B6
Kent Gate Way, Croy. 102 J6
Kent Ho. La., Beck. 86 H5
Kent Ho. Rd. SE26 86 H5
Kent Ho. Rd., Beck. 86 G7
Kent Pas. NW1 6 J5
Kent Rd. N21 33 A1
Kent Rd. W4 65 C3
Kent Rd., Dag. 53 H5
Kent Rd., E.Mol. 90 J4
Kent Rd., Kings.T. 91 G3
Kent Rd., Rich. 65 A7
Kent Rd., W.Wick. 103 B1
Kent St. E2 9 G1
Kent St. E2 59 C2
Kent St. E13 60 H3
Kent Ter. NW1 6 H4
Kent Ter. NW1 57 H3
Kent Twrs. SE20 86 E7

Kent Vw. Gdns., Ilf. 52 H2
Kent Wk. SW9 76 H4
Moorland Rd.
Kent Way SE15 77 C1
Sumner Est.
Kent Way, Surb. 98 H3
Kent Yd. SW7 14 H4
Kentford Way, Nthlt. 54 E1
Kentish Bldgs. SE1 17 B3
Kentish Rd., Belv. 71 G4
Kentish Town Rd. 49 B7
NW1
Kentish Town Rd. 49 B6
NW5
Kentish Way, Brom. 96 G2
Kentmere Rd. SE18 70 H4
Kenton Ave., Har. 37 C7
Kenton Ave., Sthl. 54 G7
Kenton Ave., Sun. 90 D2
Kenton Gdns., Har. 37 F5
Kenton La., Har. 29 C6
Kenton Pk. Ave., Har. 37 G4
Kenton Pk. Clo., Har. 37 F4
Kenton Pk. Cres., Har. 37 G4
Kenton Pk. Rd., Har. 37 F4
Kenton Rd. E9 50 G6
Kenton Rd., Har. 37 C7
Kenton St. WC1 8 A5
Kenton St. WC1 58 E4
Kents Pas., Hmptn. 90 F1
Kentwode Grn. SW13 65 G7
Kenver Ave. N12 31 G6
Kenward Rd. SE9 78 J5
Kenway, Rom. 44 J2
Kenway Rd. SW5 18 A2
Kenway Rd. SW5 66 E4
Kenwood Ave. N14 24 D5
Kenwood Ave. SE14 77 G1
Besson St.
Kenwood Clo. NW3 48 G1
Kenwood Dr., Beck. 96 C3
Kenwood Gdns. E18 42 H3
Kenwood Gdns., Ilf. 43 G4
Kenwood Rd. N6 39 J6
Kenwood Rd. N9 33 D1
Kenworthy Rd. E9 50 H5
Kenwyn Dr. NW2 47 E3
Kenwyn Rd. SW4 76 D4
Kenwyn Rd. SW20 92 J1
Kenya Rd. SE7 70 A7
Kenyngton Dr., Sun. 81 A5
Kenyngton Pl., Har. 37 F5
Kenyon St. SW6 75 A1
Keogh Rd. E15 51 E6
Kepler Rd. SW4 76 E4
Keppel Rd. E6 52 C7
Keppel Rd., Dag. 53 E4
Keppel Row SE1 16 J2
Keppel St. WC1 11 J1
Keppel St. WC1 58 D5
Kerbela St. E2 9 H5
Kerbey St. E14 60 B6
Kerfield Cres. SE5 77 A1
Grove La.
Kerfield Pl. SE5 77 A1
Kerri Clo., Barn. 22 J4
Kerridge Ct. N1 50 B6
Kingsbury Rd.
Kerrison Pl. W5 64 G1
Kerrison Rd. E15 60 D1
Kerrison Rd. SW11 75 H3
Kerrison Rd. W5 64 G1
Kerry Ave., Stan. 29 G4
Kerry Clo. E16 60 H6
Kerry Ct., Stan. 29 G4
Kerry Path SE14 68 J6
Edward St.
Kersey Gdns. SE9 88 B4
Kersfield Rd. SW15 75 A6
Kershaw Clo. SW18 75 G6
Westover Rd.
Kershaw Rd., Dag. 53 G3
Kersley Ms. SW11 75 J2
Kersley Rd. N16 50 B2
Kersley St. SW11 75 J2
Kerswell Clo. N15 41 B5
Kerwick Clo. N7 49 F7
Sutterton St.
Keslake Rd. NW6 57 A2
Kessock Clo. N17 41 E5
Kesteven Clo., Ilf. 35 J6
Kestlake Rd., Bex. 80 C6
East Rochester Way
Keston Ave., Kes. 103 J5
Keston Clo. N18 33 A3
Keston Clo., Well. 71 C7
Keston Gdns., Kes. 103 J4
Keston Pk. Clo., Kes. 103 C3

Keston Rd. N17 41 A3
Keston Rd. SE15 77 D3
Keston Rd., Th.Hth. 94 F6
Kestrel Ave. E6 61 B5
Swan App.
Kestrel Ave. SE24 76 H5
Kestrel Clo. NW9 38 E2
Kestrel Clo. NW10 47 D5
Kestrel Ho. EC1 8 J3
Kestrel Ho. W13 55 C4
Keswick Ave. SW15 83 E5
Keswick Ave. SW19 93 D2
Keswick Clo., Sutt. 100 F4
Keswick Gdns., Ilf. 43 B5
Keswick Gdns., Wem. 46 H4
Keswick Ms. W5 64 H1
Keswick Rd. SW15 75 B5
Keswick Rd., Bexh. 80 G2
Keswick Rd., Orp. 104 J1
Keswick Rd., Twick. 72 J6
Keswick Rd., W.Wick. 103 E2
Kett Gdns. SW2 76 F5
Kettering St. SW16 85 C6
Kettlebaston Rd. E10 50 J1
Kevan Ho. SE5 67 J7
Wyndham Rd.
Kevelioc Rd. N17 40 J1
Kevin Clo., Houns. 72 C2
Kevington Clo., Orp. 97 J4
Kevington Dr., Chis. 97 H4
Kew Bri., Brent. 64 J6
Kew Bri., Rich. 64 J6
Kew Bri. Ct. W4 65 A5
Kew Bri. Rd., Brent. 64 J6
Kew Cres., Sutt. 100 B3
Kew Foot Rd., Rich. 73 H4
Kew Gdns. Rd., Rich. 64 J7
Kew Grn., Rich. 64 J6
Kew Meadows Path, 74 B1
Rich.
Kew Palace, Rich. 64 H7
Kew Rd., Rich. 73 H4
Key Clo. E1 59 E4
Keybridge Ho. SW8 20 B6
Keybridge Ho. SW8 67 E6
Keyes Rd. NW2 48 A5
Keymer Rd. SW2 85 F2
Keynes Clo. N2 39 J4
Keynsham Ave., 34 E4
Wdf.Grn.
Keynsham Gdns. SE9 79 B5
Keynsham Rd. SE9 79 A5
Keynsham Rd., Mord. 100 E1
Keynsham Wk., 100 E1
Mord.
Hunston Rd.
Keyse Rd. SE1 17 F6
Keysham Ave., 72 A1
Houns.
The Ave.
Keystone Cres. N1 8 B2
Keywood Dr., Sun. 81 A6
Keyworth St. SE1 16 H5
Keyworth St. SE1 67 H3
Kezia St. SE8 68 H5
Trundleys Rd.
Khama Rd. SW17 84 H4
Khartoum Rd. E13 60 H3
Khartoum Rd. SW17 84 G4
Khartoum Rd., Ilf. 52 E5
Khyber Rd. SW11 75 H2
Kibworth St. SW8 67 F7
Kidbrooke Gdns. SE3 78 G2
Kidbrooke Gro. SE3 78 G1
Kidbrooke La. SE9 79 B4
Kidbrooke Pk. Clo. 78 H1
SE3
Kidbrooke Pk. Rd. 78 H1
SE3
Kidbrooke Way SE3 78 H2
Kidd Pl. SE7 70 B5
Kidderminster Pl., 101 H1
Croy.
Kidderminster Rd.
Kidderminster Rd., 101 H1
Croy.
Kidderpore Ave. NW3 48 D4
Kidderpore Gdns. 48 D4
NW3
Kidlington Way NW9 38 E2
Kidron Way E9 59 F1
Clermont Rd.
Kielder Clo., Ilf. 35 J6
Kiffen St. EC2 9 C5
Kilberry Clo., Islw. 73 A1
Kilburn Bldgs. NW6 57 E1
Kilburn High Rd.
Kilburn Gate NW6 6 A1

Kilburn High Rd. NW6 48 C7
Kilburn La. W9 57 B3
Kilburn La. W10 57 A3
Kilburn Pk. Rd. NW6 57 D3
Kilburn Pl. NW6 57 D1
Kilburn Priory NW6 57 E1
Kilburn Sq. NW6 57 D1
Kilburn High Rd.
Kilburn Vale NW6 57 E1
Belsize Rd.
Kildare Clo., Ruis. 45 C1
Kildare Gdns. W2 57 D6
Kildare Rd. E16 60 G5
Kildare Ter. W2 57 D6
Kildare Wk. E14 60 A6
Farrance St.
Kildoran Rd. SW2 76 E5
Kildowan Rd., Ilf. 53 A1
Kilgour Rd. SE23 77 H6
Kilkie St. SW6 75 F2
Killarney Rd. SW18 75 F6
Killearn Rd. SE6 87 D1
Killester Gdns., 99 H4
Wor.Pk.
Killick St. N1 8 C1
Killick St. N1 58 F2
Killieser Ave. SW2 85 E1
Killip Clo. E16 60 F6
Killowen Ave., Nthlt. 45 J5
Killowen Rd. E9 50 G6
Killyon Rd. SW8 76 C2
Killyon Ter. SW8 76 C2
Killyon Rd.
Kilmaine Rd. SW6 66 B7
Kilmarnock Gdns., 53 C3
Dag.
Lindsey Rd.
Kilmarnock Rd., Wat. 28 D4
Kilmarsh Rd. W6 65 J4
Kilmartin Ave. SW16 94 F3
Kilmartin Rd., Ilf. 53 A2
Kilmeston Way SE15 21 G7
Kilmington Rd. SW13 65 G6
Kilmorey Gdns., 73 E4
Twick.
Kilmorey Rd., Twick. 73 E4
Kilmorie Rd. SE23 86 H1
Kiln Pl. NW5 49 A4
Kilner St. E14 60 A5
Kilnside, Esher 98 D7
Kilpatrick Way, Hayes 54 E5
Kilravock St. W10 57 B3
Kilsby Wk., Dag. 53 B6
Rugby Rd.
Kilsha Rd., Walt. 90 B6
Kimbell Gdns. SW6 75 B1
Kimber Rd. SW18 75 D7
Kimberley Ave. E6 61 B2
Kimberley Ave. SE15 77 E2
Kimberley Ave., Ilf. 43 G7
Kimberley Ave., Rom. 44 J6
Kimberley Dr., Sid. 89 D2
Kimberley Gdns. N4 40 H5
Kimberley Gdns., Enf. 25 C3
Kimberley Rd. E4 34 E1
Kimberley Rd. E11 51 D2
Kimberley Rd. E16 60 F4
Kimberley Rd. E17 41 J1
Kimberley Rd. N17 41 D2
Kimberley Rd. N18 33 E6
Kimberley Rd. NW6 57 B1
Kimberley Rd. SW9 76 E2
Kimberley Rd., Beck. 95 G2
Kimberley Rd., Croy. 94 H6
Kimberley Way E4 34 E1
Kimble Rd. SW19 94 F6
Kimbolton Clo. SE12 78 F6
Kimbolton Grn., 22 C4
Borwd.
Kimbolton Row SW3 18 G2
Kimmeridge Gdns. 88 B4
SE9
Kimmeridge Rd. SE9 88 B4
Kimpton Ind. Est., 100 C2
Sutt.
Kimpton Rd. SE5 77 A1
Kimpton Rd., Sutt. 100 C3
Kinburn St. SE16 68 G2
Kincaid Rd. SE15 68 E7
Kincardine Gdns. W9 57 C4
Harrow Rd.
Kinch Gro., Har. 37 J7
Kinder Rd. SE28 62 D7
Kinder St. E1 59 E6
Cannon St. Rd.
Kinfauns Rd. SW2 85 G2
Kinfauns Rd., Ilf. 53 A1
King Alfred Ave. SE6 87 A4

King & Queen Clo. 88 B4
SE9
Beaconsfield Rd.
King & Queen St. 21 A3
SE17
King & Queen St. 67 J5
SE17
King Arthur Clo. SE15 68 F7
King Charles Cres., 91 J7
Surb.
King Charles Rd., 91 J5
Surb.
King Charles St. SW1 16 A3
King Charles St. SW1 67 D2
King Charles Wk. 84 B1
SW19
Princes Way
King David La. E1 59 F7
King Edward Dr., 98 H3
Chess.
Kelvin Gro.
King Edward Ms. 74 G1
SW13
King Edward Rd. E10 51 C1
King Edward Rd. E17 41 H3
King Edward Rd., 23 D4
Barn.
King Edward St. EC1 12 J3
King Edward St. EC1 58 J6
King Edward Wk. SE1 16 F5
King Edward Wk. SE1 67 G3
King Edwards Gdns. 65 A1
W3
King Edwards Gro., 82 E6
Tedd.
King Edwards Rd. E9 59 E1
King Edwards Rd. N9 25 E7
King Edwards Rd., 61 G1
Bark.
King Edward's Rd., 25 G4
Enf.
King Gdns., Croy. 101 H5
King George Ave. E16 61 A6
King George Ave., Ilf. 43 G5
King George Clo., 44 J3
Rom.
King George VI Ave., 93 J4
Mitch.
King George Sq., 73 J6
Rich.
King George St. SE10 69 C7
King Georges Dr., 54 F5
Sthl.
King Harolds Way, 71 D7
Bexh.
King Henry Ms., Orp. 104 J5
Osgood Ave.
King Henry St. N16 50 B5
King Henry's Rd. NW3 48 H7
King Henry's Rd., 92 B3
Kings.T.
King Henry's Wk. N1 50 B6
King James St. SE1 16 H4
King James St. SE1 67 H2
King John Ct. EC2 9 E5
King John St. E1 59 G5
King John's Wk. SE9 88 A1
King Sq. EC1 8 J4
King Stairs Clo. SE16 68 E2
Elephant La.
King St. E13 60 G4
King St. EC2 13 A4
King St. EC2 58 J6
King St. N2 39 G3
King St. N17 41 C1
King St. SW1 15 G2
King St. SW1 67 C1
King St. W3 65 B1
King St. W6 65 G4
King St. WC2 12 A5
King St. WC2 58 E7
King St., Rich. 73 G5
King St., Sthl. 63 E3
King St., Twick. 82 D1
King William IV 86 F6
Gdns. SE20
St. John's Rd.
King William La. SE10 69 E5
Orlop St.
King William St. EC4 13 C6
King William St. EC4 59 A7
King William Wk. 86 F6
SE10
Kingcup Clo., Croy. 102 G1
Primrose La.
Kingdon Rd. NW6 48 D6
Kingfield Rd. W5 55 G4
Kingfield St. E14 69 C4

King & Queen Clo. 62 C7
Kingfisher Clo. SE28 62 C7
Kingfisher Clo. Har. 29 C7
Kingfisher Ct. SW19 84 B2
Queensmere Rd.
Kingfisher Dr., Rich. 82 E4
Kingfisher Sq. SE8 68 J6
Dorking Clo.
Kingfisher St. E6 61 B5
Kingfisher Way NW10 47 D6
Kingfisher Way, Beck. 95 G6
Kingham Clo. SW18 75 F7
Kingham Clo. W11 66 B2
Kinghorn St. EC1 12 J2
Kinglake Est. SE17 21 E3
Kinglake St. SE17 21 D4
Kinglake St. SE17 68 B5
Kingly Ct. W1 11 G5
Kingly St. W1 11 F5
Kingly St. W1 58 C7
Kings Arbour, Sthl. 63 E5
Ringway
Kings Arms Ct. E1 13 H2
Kings Arms Yd. EC2 13 B3
Kings Ave. N10 40 A3
Kings Ave. N21 32 H1
King's Ave. SW4 76 E5
Kings Ave. SW12 85 D1
Kings Ave. W5 55 G6
Kings Ave., Brom. 87 F6
Kings Ave., Buck.H. 35 A2
Kings Ave., Cars. 100 H3
Kings Ave., Grnf. 54 H6
Kings Ave., Houns. 72 H1
Kings Ave., N.Mal. 92 E4
Kings Ave., Rom. 44 F6
Kings Ave., Wdf.Grn. 34 H6
Kings Bench St. SE1 16 H3
Kings Bench Wk. EC4 12 F4
Kings Chase, E.Mol. 90 J3
Kings Clo. E10 42 B7
Kings Clo. NW4 39 A4
Kings College Rd. 48 H7
NW3
Kings Ct. E13 60 H1
Kings Ct. W6 65 G4
King St.
Kings Ct., Wem. 47 B2
Kings Cres. N4 49 J3
Kings Cres. Est. N4 49 J2
King's Cross Rd. WC1 8 C3
King's Cross Rd. WC1 58 F3
Kings Dr., Edg. 29 J4
Kings Dr., Surb. 92 A7
Kings Dr., Tedd. 82 A5
Kings Dr., T.Ditt. 91 E6
Kings Dr., Wem. 47 B2
Kings Fm. Ave., Rich. 74 A4
Kings Gdns. NW6 48 D7
West End La.
Kings Gdns., Ilf. 52 G1
King's Garth Ms. SE23 86 F3
London Rd.
Kings Grn., Loug. 27 B3
Kings Gro. SE15 77 E1
Kings Hall Rd., Beck. 86 H7
Kings Head Hill E4 26 B7
Kings Head Yd. SE1 17 B2
Kings Highway SE18 70 H6
Kings Hill, Loug. 27 B2
Kings Keep, Kings.T. 91 H4
Beaufort Rd.
Kings La., Sutt. 100 G6
Kings Mead Pk., 98 B7
Esher
Kings Ms. SW4 76 E5
King's Ave.
King's Ms. WC1 8 D6
King's Ms. WC1 58 F4
Kings Ms., Chig. 35 F2
King's Orchard SE9 79 B6
Kings Paddock, 90 J1
Hmptn.
King's Pas. E11 42 E7
Kings Pas., Kings.T. 91 G2
Kings Pl. SE1 16 J4
Kings Pl. W4 65 C4
Chiswick High Rd.
Kings Pl., Buck.H. 35 A2
King's Reach Twr. SE1 16 F1
Kings Ride Gate, Rich. 74 A4
Kings Rd. E4 34 D1
Kings Rd. E6 60 J1
Kings Rd. E11 42 E7
King's Rd. N17 41 C1
Kings Rd. N18 33 D6
Kings Rd. N22 40 F1
Kings Rd. NW10 47 H7
Kings Rd. SE25 95 D3

King's Rd. SW1   **18 F5**
King's Rd. SW1   66 G6
King's Rd. SW3   **18 F5**
King's Rd. SW3   66 G6
King's Rd. SW6   66 E7
King's Rd. SW10   66 F7
Kings Rd. SW14   74 D3
Kings Rd. SW19   84 D6
Kings Rd. W5   55 G5
Kings Rd., Bark.   52 F7
North St.
Kings Rd., Barn.   22 J3
Kings Rd., Felt.   81 C1
Kings Rd., Har.   45 F2
Kings Rd., Kings.T.   82 H7
Kings Rd., Mitch.   94 A3
Kings Rd., Orp.   104 J4
Kings Rd., Rich.   73 J6
Kings Rd., Surb.   98 F1
Kings Rd., Tedd.   82 A5
Kings Rd., Twick.   73 E6
King's Scholars' Pas.   **15 F6**
SW1
Plender St.
Kings Ter. NW1   58 C1
Kings Wk., Kings.T.   91 G1
Kings Way, Har.   37 B4
Kingsand Rd. SE12   87 G2
Kingsash Dr., Hayes   54 E4
Kingsbridge Ave. W3   64 J2
Kingsbridge Cres.,   54 F5
Sthl.
Kingsbridge Rd. W10   56 J6
Kingsbridge Rd., Bark.   61 G2
Kingsbridge Rd.,   93 A7
Mord.
Kingsbridge Rd., Sthl.   63 F4
Kingsbridge Rd., Walt.   90 B7
Kingsbury Circle NW9   38 A5
Kingsbury Rd. N1   50 B6
Kingsbury Rd. NW9   38 A5
Kingsbury Ter. N1   50 B6
Kingsbury Trd. Est.   38 D6
NW9
Kingsclere Clo. SW15   74 G7
Kingscliffe Gdns.   84 C1
SW19
Kingscote Rd. W4   65 D3
Kingscote Rd., Croy.   95 E7
Kingscote Rd., N.Mal.   92 D3
Kingscote St. EC4   **12 G5**
Kingscourt Rd. SW16   85 D3
Kingscroft Rd. NW2   48 C6
Kingsdale Gdns. W11   66 A1
Kingsdale Rd. SE18   70 J6
Kingsdale Rd. SE20   86 G7
Kingsdown Ave. W3   56 E7
Kingsdown Ave. W13   64 E2
Kingsdown Clo. W10   57 A6
Kingsdown Rd. E11   51 E3
Kingsdown Rd. N19   49 E3
Kingsdown Rd., Sutt.   100 B5
Kingsdown Way,   96 G7
Brom.
Kingsdowne Rd.,   91 H7
Surb.
Kingsfield Ave., Har.   36 H4
Kingsfield Ho. SE9   88 A3
Kingsfield Rd., Har.   37 A7
Kingsford Ave., Wall.   101 E7
Kingsford St. NW5   48 J5
Kingsgate Ave. N3   39 D3
Kingsgate Clo., Bexh.   80 E1
Kingsgate Pl. NW6   48 D7
Kingsgate Rd. NW6   48 D7
Kingsgate Rd.,   91 H1
Kings.T.
Kingsground SE9   79 B7
Kingshill Ave., Har.   37 E4
Kingshill Ave., Hayes   54 A3
Kingshill Ave., Nthlt.   54 A3
Kingshill Ave.,   92 G7
Wor.Pk.
Kingshill Dr., Har.   37 E2
Kingshold Rd. E9   50 F7
Kingsholm Gdns. SE9   79 A4
Kingshurst Rd. SE12   78 G7
Kingsland NW8   57 H1
Broxwood Way
Kingsland Grn. E8   50 B6
Kingsland High St. E8   50 C6
Kingsland Pas. E8   50 B6
Kingsland Grn.
Kingsland Rd. E2   **9 E3**
Kingsland Rd. E2   59 B3
Kingsland Rd. E8   59 B1
Kingsland Rd. E13   60 J3

Kingslawn Clo. SW15   74 H5
Howards La.
Kingsleigh Pl., Mitch.   93 J3
Chatsworth Pl.
Kingsleigh Wk., Brom.   96 F4
Stamford Dr.
Kingsley Ave. W13   55 D6
Kingsley Ave., Houns.   72 J2
Kingsley Ave., Sthl.   54 G7
Kingsley Ave., Sutt.   100 G4
Kingsley Clo. N2   39 F5
Kingsley Clo., Dag.   53 H4
Kingsley Ct., Edg.   30 B2
Kingsley Dr., Wor.Pk.   99 F2
Badgers Copse
Kingsley Gdns. E4   34 A5
Kingsley Ms. E1   59 E7
Wapping La.
Kingsley Ms. W8   **14 B6**
Kingsley Ms., Chis.   88 E6
Kingsley Pl. N6   40 A7
Kingsley Rd. E7   51 G7
Kingsley Rd. E17   42 C2
Kingsley Rd. N13   32 G4
Kingsley Rd. NW6   57 C1
Kingsley Rd. SW19   84 E5
Kingsley Rd., Croy.   101 G1
Kingsley Rd., Har.   45 J4
Kingsley Rd., Houns.   72 H1
Kingsley Rd., Ilf.   43 F1
Kingsley Rd., Loug.   27 G3
Kingsley Rd., Orp.   104 J6
Kingsley Rd., Pnr.   36 F4
Kingsley St. SW11   75 J3
Kingsley Way N2   39 F5
Kingsley Wd. Dr. SE9   88 C3
Kingslyn Cres. SE19   95 B1
Kingsman Par. SE18   70 C3
Woolwich Ch. St.
Kingsman St. SE18   70 C3
Kingsmead, Barn.   23 D4
Kingsmead, Rich.   73 J6
Kingsmead Ave. N9   33 E1
Kingsmead Ave. NW9   38 D7
Kingsmead Ave.,   94 C3
Mitch.
Kingsmead Ave., Sun.   90 C2
Kingsmead Ave.,   99 A2
Surb.
Kingsmead Ave.,   99 H2
Wor.Pk.
Kingsmead Clo.,   99 D7
Epsom
Kingsmead Clo., Sid.   89 A2
Kingsmead Clo.,   82 E6
Tedd.
Kingsmead Dr., Nthlt.   45 F7
Kingsmead Rd. SW2   85 G2
Kingsmead Way E9   50 H4
Kingsmere Clo. SW15   75 B3
Felsham Rd.
Kingsmere Pk. NW9   47 B1
Kingsmere Rd. SW19   84 A2
Kingsmill Gdns., Dag.   53 F5
Kingsmill Rd., Dag.   53 F5
Kingsmill Ter. NW8   **6 F1**
Kingsmill Ter. NW8   57 G2
Kingsnympton Pk.,   83 B7
Kings.T.
Kingspark Ct. E18   42 G3
Kingsridge SW19   84 J5
Kingsthorpe Rd. SE26   86 G4
Kingston Ave., Sutt.   100 B3
Kingston Bri.,   91 G2
Kings.T.
Kingston Bypass   83 E4
SW15
Kingston Bypass   83 E6
SW20
Kingston Bypass,   98 B2
Esher
Kingston Bypass,   92 G4
N.Mal.
Kingston Bypass,   98 E3
Surb.
Kingston Clo., Nthlt.   45 F7
Kingston Clo., Rom.   44 E3
Kingston Clo., Tedd.   82 E6
Kingston Cr. N4   40 J6
Wiltshire Gdns.
Kingston Cres., Beck.   95 J1
Kingston Gdns., Croy.   101 E3
Wandle Rd.
Kingston Hall Rd.,   91 G3
Kings.T.
Kingston Hill, Kings.T.   92 A1
Kingston Hill Ave.,   44 E3
Rom.

Kingston Hill Pl.,   83 C4
Kings.T.
Kingston La., Tedd.   82 D5
Kingston Pk. Est.,   83 B6
Kings.T.
Kingston Pl., Har.   29 C7
Richmond Gdns.
Kingston Rd. N9   33 D2
Kingston Rd. SW15   83 G2
Kingston Rd. SW19   83 G2
Kingston Rd. SW20   92 J2
Kingston Rd., Barn.   23 G5
Kingston Rd., Epsom   99 E4
Kingston Rd., Ilf.   52 E4
Kingston Rd., Kings.T.   92 B3
Kingston Rd., N.Mal.   92 D4
Kingston Rd., Sthl.   63 F2
Kingston Rd., Surb.   99 B2
Kingston Rd., Tedd.   82 E5
Kingston Rd., Wor.Pk.   99 C3
Kingston Sq. SE19   86 A5
Kingston Vale SW15   83 D4
Kingstown St. NW1   58 A1
Kingswater Pl. SW11   66 H7
Battersea Ch. Rd.
Kingsway N12   31 F6
Kingsway SW14   74 B3
Kingsway WC2   **12 C3**
Kingsway WC2   58 F6
Kingsway, Croy.   101 F5
Kingsway, Enf.   25 E5
Kingsway, N.Mal.   92 J4
Kingsway, Orp.   97 F5
Kingsway, Wem.   46 H4
Kingsway, W.Wick.   103 E3
Kingsway, Wdf.Grn.   34 J5
Kingsway Business   90 F1
Pk., Hmptn.
Kingsway Cres., Har.   36 J4
Kingsway Ind. Est.   33 G6
N18
Kingsway Rd., Sutt.   100 B6
Kingswear Rd. NW5   49 B3
Kingswear Rd., Ruis.   36 A3
Kingswood Ave. NW6   57 B1
Kingswood Ave.,   71 F4
Belv.
Kingswood Ave.,   96 E3
Brom.
Kingswood Ave.,   81 H6
Hmptn.
Kingswood Ave.,   72 F1
Houns.
Kingswood Ave.,   94 G5
Th.Hth.
Kingswood Clo. N20   23 F7
Kingswood Clo. SW8   67 E7
Kenchester Clo.
Kingswood Clo., Enf.   25 B5
Kingswood Clo.,   92 F6
N.Mal.
Motspur Pk.
Kingswood Clo., Orp.   97 G7
Kingswood Clo., Surb.   91 H7
Kingswood Dr. SE19   86 B4
Kingswood Dr., Cars.   100 J1
Kingswood Est. SE21   86 B4
Bowen Dr.
Kingswood Pk. N3   39 C2
Kingswood Pl. SE13   78 E4
Kingswood Rd. SE20   86 F6
Kingswood Rd. SW2   76 E6
Kingswood Rd. SW19   84 C7
Kingswood Rd. W4   65 C3
Kingswood Rd.,   96 D4
Brom.
Kingswood Rd., Ilf.   53 A1
Kingswood Rd., Wem.   47 A3
Kingswood Ter. W4   65 C3
Kingswood Rd.
Kingswood Way,   101 E5
Wall.
Kingsworth Clo.,   95 H5
Beck.
Shirley Cres.
Kingsworthy Clo.,   91 J3
Kings.T.
Kingthorpe Rd. NW10   47 D7
Kingthorpe Ter. NW10   47 C7
Kingwood Rd. SW6   66 B7
Kinlet Rd. SE18   79 F1
Kinloch Dr. NW9   38 D7
Kinloch St. N7   49 F3
Hornsey Rd.
Kinloss Gdns. N3   39 C3
Kinloss Rd., Cars.   93 F7
Kinnaird Ave. W4   65 C7
Kinnaird Ave., Brom.   87 F6

Kinnaird Clo., Brom.   87 F6
Kinnaird Way,   35 C6
Wdf.Grn.
Kinnear Rd. W12   65 F2
Kinnerton Pl. N. SW1   **15 A4**
Kinnerton Pl. S. SW1   **15 A4**
Kinnerton St. SW1   **15 B4**
Kinnerton St. SW1   67 A2
Kinnerton Yd. SW1   **15 A4**
Kinnoul Rd. W6   66 B6
Kinross Ave., Wor.Pk.   99 G2
Kinross Clo., Edg.   30 B2
Tayside Dr.
Kinross Clo., Har.   37 H5
Kinsale Rd. SE15   77 D3
Kintore Way SE1   **21 F7**
Kintyre Clo. SW16   94 F2
Kinveachy Gdns. SE7   70 B5
Kinver Rd. SE26   86 F4
Kipling Dr. SW19   84 G6
Kipling Est. SE1   **17 C4**
Kipling Est. SE1   68 A2
Kipling Pl., Stan.   29 C6
Uxbridge Rd.
Kipling Rd., Bexh.   80 E1
Kipling St. SE1   **17 C4**
Kipling St. SE1   68 A2
Kipling Ter. N9   33 A3
Kippington Dr. SE9   88 A1
Kirby Clo., Epsom   99 F5
Kirby Clo., Ilf.   35 H6
Kirby Clo., Loug.   27 B7
Kirby Est. SE16   68 E3
Kirby Gro. SE1   **17 D3**
Kirby Gro. SE1   68 B2
Kirby St. EC1   **12 F1**
Kirby Way, Walt.   90 C6
Kirchen Rd. W13   55 E7
Kirk La. SE18   70 F6
Kirk Ri., Sutt.   100 E3
Kirk Rd. E17   41 J6
Kirkcaldy Grn., Wat.   28 C3
Trevose Way
Kirkdale SE26   86 F4
Kirkdale Rd. E11   51 E1
Kirkfield Clo. W13   64 E1
Broomfield Rd.
Kirkham Rd. E6   61 B6
Kirkham St. SE18   70 H6
Kirkland Ave., Ilf.   43 D2
Kirkland Clo., Sid.   79 H6
Kirkland Wk. E8   50 C6
Laurel St.
Kirkleas Rd., Surb.   98 H1
Kirklees Rd., Dag.   53 C5
Kirklees Rd., Th.Hth.   94 G5
Kirkley Rd. SW19   93 D1
Kirkman Pl. W1   **11 H2**
Kirkmichael Rd. E14   60 C6
Dee St.
Kirks Pl. E14   59 J5
Rhodeswell Rd.
Kirkside Rd. SE3   69 G6
Kirkstall Ave. N17   41 A4
Kirkstall Gdns. SW2   85 D1
Kirkstall Rd. SW2   85 D1
Kirkstead Ct. E5   50 H3
Mandeville St.
Kirksted Rd., Mord.   100 E1
Kirkstone Way, Brom.   87 E6
Kirkton Rd. N15   41 B4
Kirkwall Pl. E2   59 F3
Kirkwood Rd. SE15   77 E2
Kirn Rd. W13   55 E7
Kirchen Rd.
Kirtley Rd. SE26   86 H4
Kirtling St. SW8   **19 F7**
Kirtling St. SW8   67 C7
Kirton Clo. W4   65 D4
Dolman Rd.
Kirton Gdns. E2   **9 G4**
Kirton Rd. E13   60 J2
Kirton Wk., Edg.   30 C7
Kirwyn Way SE5   **20 H7**
Kirwyn Way SE5   67 H7
Kitcat Ter. E3   60 A3
Kitchener Rd. E7   51 H6
Kitchener Rd. E17   42 B1
Kitchener Rd. N2   39 H3
Kitchener Rd. N17   41 A3
Kitchener Rd., Dag.   53 H6
Kitchener Rd.,   95 A3
Th.Hth.
Kite Yd. SW11   75 J1
Cambridge Rd.
Kitley Gdns. SE19   95 C1
Kitson Rd. SE5   **21 A7**
Kitson Rd. SE5   68 A7

Kitson Rd. SW13	74	G1
Kittiwake Rd., Nthlt.	54	D3
Kitto Rd. SE14	77	G2
Kiver Rd. N19	49	D2
Kiwi Clo., Twick.	73	E6
Crown Rd.		
Klea Ave. SW4	76	C6
Knapdale Clo. SE23	86	E2
Knapmill Rd. SE6	87	A2
Knapmill Way SE6	87	B2
Knapp Clo. NW10	47	E6
Knapp Rd. E3	63	H1
Knapton Ms. SW17	85	A6
Seely Rd.		
Knaresborough Dr. SW18	84	E1
Strathville Rd.		
Knaresborough Pl. SW5	**18**	**A1**
Knaresborough Pl. SW5	66	E4
Knatchbull Rd. NW10	56	D1
Knatchbull Rd. SE5	76	H2
Knebworth Ave. E17	42	A1
Knebworth Path, Borwd.	22	D4
Knebworth Rd. N16	50	B4
Nevill Rd.		
Knee Hill SE2	71	C4
Knee Hill Cres. SE2	71	C4
Kneller Gdns., Islw.	73	A6
Kneller Rd. SE4	77	H4
Kneller Rd., N.Mal.	92	E7
Kneller Rd., Twick.	72	J6
Knighten St. E1	**17**	**J2**
Knightland Rd. E5	50	E2
Knighton Clo., S.Croy.	101	H7
Knighton Clo., Wdf.Grn.	34	H4
Knighton Dr., Wdf.Grn.	34	H4
Knighton La., Buck.H.	34	H2
Knighton Pk. Rd. SE26	86	G5
Knighton Rd. E7	51	G3
Knighton Rd., Rom.	44	J6
Knightrider Ct. EC4	58	J7
Godliman St.		
Knights Arc. SW1	**14**	**J4**
Knights Ave. W5	64	H2
Knights Clo. E9	50	F5
Churchill Wk.		
Knights Ct., Kings.T.	91	H3
Knights Ct., Rom.	44	E6
Knights Hill SE27	85	H5
Knights Hill Sq. SE27	85	H4
Knights Hill		
Knights La. N9	33	D3
Knights Pk., Kings.T.	91	H3
Knights Rd. E16	69	G2
Knights Rd., Stan.	29	F4
Knights Wk. SE11	**20**	**G2**
Knights Way, Ilf.	35	F6
Knightsbridge SW1	**15**	**A3**
Knightsbridge SW1	66	J2
Knightsbridge SW7	**14**	**H4**
Knightsbridge SW7	66	H2
Knightsbridge Grn. SW1	**14**	**J4**
Knightsbridge Grn. SW1	66	J2
Knightswood Clo., Edg.	30	C2
Knightwood Cres., N.Mal.	92	E6
Knivet Rd. SW6	66	D6
Knobs Hill Rd. E15	60	B1
Knockholt Rd. SE9	79	A5
Knole, The SE9	88	D4
Knole Clo., Croy.	95	F6
Stockbury Rd.		
Knole Gate, Sid.	88	H3
Woodside Cres.		
Knoll, The W13	55	F5
Knoll, The, Beck.	96	B1
Knoll, The, Brom.	103	G1
Knoll Ct. SE19	86	C5
Knoll Dr. N14	24	A7
Knoll Ri., Orp.	104	J1
Knoll Rd. SW18	75	F5
Knoll Rd., Bex.	80	G7
Knoll Rd., Sid.	89	B5
Knollmead, Surb.	99	C1
Knolls Clo., Wor.Pk.	99	H3
Knollys Clo. SW16	85	G3
Knollys Rd. SW16	85	F3
Knottisford St. E2	59	F3

Knotts Grn. Ms. E10	42	B6
Knotts Grn. Rd.		
Knotts Grn. Rd. E10	42	B6
Knowle Ave., Bexh.	71	E7
Knowle Clo. SW9	76	G3
Knowle Rd., Brom.	104	B2
Knowle Rd., Twick.	82	B1
Knowles Hill Cres. SE13	78	D5
Knowles Wk. SW4	76	C3
Knowlton Grn., Brom.	96	F5
Knowsley Ave., Sthl.	63	H1
Knowsley Rd. SW11	75	J2
Knox Rd. E7	51	F6
Knox St. W1	**10**	**J1**
Knox St. W1	57	J5
Knoyle St. SE14	68	H6
Chubworthy St.		
Kohat Rd. SW19	84	E5
Kossuth St. SE10	69	E5
Kramer Ms. SW5	66	D5
Kempsford Gdns.		
Kreisel Wk., Rich.	64	J6
Kuala Gdns. SW16	94	F1
Kuhn Way E7	51	G5
Forest La.		
Kydbrook Clo., Orp.	97	F7
Kylemore Clo. E6	61	A2
Parr Rd.		
Kylemore Rd. NW6	48	D7
Kymberley Rd., Har.	37	B6
Kynance Gdns., Stan.	37	F1
Kynance Ms. SW7	**14**	**B6**
Kynance Ms. SW7	66	F3
Kynance Pl. SW7	**14**	**C6**
Kynance Pl. SW7	66	F3
Kynaston Ave. N16	50	C3
Dynevor Rd.		
Kynaston Ave., Th.Hth.	94	J5
Kynaston Clo., Har.	29	A7
Kynaston Cres., Th.Hth.	94	J5
Kynaston Rd. N16	50	B3
Kynaston Rd., Brom.	87	G5
Kynaston Rd., Enf.	25	A1
Kynaston Rd., Th.Hth.	94	J5
Kynaston Wd., Har.	29	A7
Kynnersley Clo., Cars.	100	J3
William St.		
Kynock Rd. N18	33	F4
Kyrle Rd. SW11	75	J6
Kyverdale Rd. N16	41	C7

L

La Tourne Gdns., Orp.	104	F3
Laburnum Ave. N9	33	B2
Laburnum Ave. N17	33	A7
Laburnum Ave., Sutt.	100	H3
Laburnum Clo. E4	33	J6
Laburnum Clo. N11	32	A6
Laburnum Clo. SE15	68	F7
Clifton Way		
Laburnum Ct. E2	59	C1
Laburnum St.		
Laburnum Ct., Stan.	29	F4
Laburnum Cres., Sun.	90	B1
Batavia Rd.		
Laburnum Gdns. N21	32	J2
Laburnum Gdns., Croy.	102	G1
Primrose La.		
Laburnum Gro. N21	32	J2
Laburnum Gro. NW9	38	C7
Laburnum Gro., Houns.	72	F4
Laburnum Gro., N.Mal.	92	D2
Laburnum Gro., Sthl.	54	F4
Laburnum Ho., Dag.	53	G2
Althorne Way		
Laburnum Rd. SW19	84	F7
Laburnum Rd., Mitch.	94	A2
Laburnum St. E2	59	C1
Laburnum Way, Brom.	97	D7
Lacebark Clo., Sid.	79	J7
Lacey Clo. N9	33	D2
Lacey Dr., Edg.	29	H4
Lacey Dr., Hmptn.	90	F1
Lacey Wk. E3	60	A2
Lackington St. EC2	**13**	**C1**
Lackington St. EC2	59	A5

Lacock Clo. SW19	84	F6
Lacon Rd. SE22	77	D4
Lacy Rd. SW15	75	A4
Ladas Rd. SE27	85	J4
Ladbroke Cres. W11	57	B6
Ladbroke Gro.		
Ladbroke Gdns. W11	57	C7
Ladbroke Gro. W10	57	A4
Ladbroke Gro. W11	57	B6
Ladbroke Ms. W11	66	B1
Ladbroke Rd.		
Ladbroke Rd. W11	66	C1
Ladbroke Rd., Enf.	25	C6
Ladbroke Sq. W11	57	C7
Ladbroke Ter. W11	57	C7
Ladbroke Wk. W11	66	C1
Ladbrook Clo., Pnr.	36	F5
Ladbrook Rd. SE25	95	A3
Ladbrooke Cres., Sid.	89	D3
Ladderstile Ride, Kings.T.	83	C5
Ladderswood Way N11	32	C5
Lady Booth Rd., Kings.T.	91	H2
Lady Hay, Wor.Pk.	99	F2
Lady Margaret Rd. N19	49	C4
Lady Margaret Rd. NW5	49	C5
Lady Margaret Rd., Sthl.	54	F5
Lady Somerset Rd. NW5	49	B4
Ladybower Ct. E5	50	H4
Gilpin Rd.		
Ladycroft Gdns., Orp.	104	F5
Ladycroft Rd. SE13	78	B3
Ladycroft Wk., Stan.	37	G1
Ladycroft Way, Orp.	104	F5
Ladyfield Clo., Loug.	27	E4
Ladyfields, Loug.	27	E4
Ladysmith Ave. E6	61	B2
Ladysmith Ave., Ilf.	43	G7
Ladysmith Rd. E16	60	F3
Ladysmith Rd. N17	41	D2
Ladysmith Rd. N18	33	E5
Ladysmith Rd. SE9	79	D6
Ladysmith Rd., Enf.	25	B3
Ladysmith Rd., Har.	37	B2
Ladywell Rd. SE13	78	B5
Ladywell St. E15	60	F1
Plaistow Gro.		
Ladywood Ave., Orp.	97	H5
Ladywood Rd., Surb.	99	A2
Lafone Ave., Felt.	81	C1
Alfred Rd.		
Lafone St. SE1	**17**	**F3**
Lafone St. SE1	68	C2
Lagado Ms. SE16	68	G1
Lagonda Ave., Ilf.	35	J6
Laing Clo., Ilf.	35	G6
Laing Dean, Nthlt.	54	C1
Laings Ave., Mitch.	93	J2
Lainlock Pl., Houns.	72	H1
Spring Gro. Rd.		
Lainson St. SW18	75	D7
Laird Ho. SE5	67	J7
Redcar St.		
Lairdale Clo. SE21	85	J1
Lairs Clo. N7	49	E6
Manger Rd.		
Laitwood Rd. SW12	85	B1
Lake, The (Bushey), Wat.	28	J1
Lake Ave., Brom.	87	G6
Lake Clo. SW19	84	C5
Lake Rd.		
Lake Dr. (Bushey), Wat.	28	J2
Lake Gdns., Dag.	53	G5
Lake Gdns., Rich.	82	E2
Lake Gdns., Wall.	101	B3
Lake Ho. Rd. E11	51	G3
Lake Rd. SW19	84	C5
Lake Rd., Croy.	102	J2
Lake Rd., Rom.	44	D4
Lake Vw., Edg.	29	J5
Lakedale Rd. SE18	70	H5
Lakefield Rd. N22	40	H2
Lakehall Gdns., Th.Hth.	94	H5
Lakehall Rd., Th.Hth.	94	H5
Lakehurst Rd., Epsom	99	E5
Lakeland Clo., Har.	29	A6
Lakenheath N14	24	C5
Laker Pl. SW15	75	B6
Lakes Rd., Kes.	103	J5

Lakeside N3	39	E2
Lakeside W13	55	F6
Edgehill Rd.		
Lakeside, Beck.	96	B3
Lakeside, Enf.	24	D4
Lakeside, Wall.	101	B3
Derek Ave.		
Lakeside Ave., Ilf.	43	A4
Lakeside Clo. SE25	95	D2
Lakeside Clo., Chig.	35	J4
Lakeside Clo., Sid.	80	C5
Lakeside Ct. N4	49	H2
Lakeside Ct., Borwd.	22	A4
Cavendish Cres.		
Lakeside Cres., Barn.	23	J5
Lakeside Dr., Brom.	104	B3
Lakeside Rd. N13	32	F4
Lakeside Rd. W14	66	A3
Lakeside Way, Wem.	47	A4
Lakeswood Rd., Orp.	97	E5
Lakeview Ct. SW19	84	B2
Victoria Dr.		
Lakeview Rd. SE27	85	G5
Lakeview Rd., Well.	80	B4
Lakis Clo. NW3	48	F4
Flask Wk.		
Laleham Ave. NW7	30	D3
Laleham Rd. SE6	78	C7
Lalor St. SW6	75	B2
Lamb La. E8	50	E7
Lamb St. E1	**13**	**F1**
Lamb St. E1	59	C5
Lamb Wk. SE1	**17**	**D4**
Lambarde Ave. SE9	88	D4
Lamberhurst Rd. SE27	85	G4
Lamberhurst Rd., Dag.	53	E1
Lambert Ave., Rich.	74	A3
Lambert Rd. E16	60	H6
Lambert Rd. N12	31	F5
Lambert Rd. SW2	76	E5
Lambert St. N1	49	G7
Lambert Wk., Wem.	46	G3
Clarendon Gdns.		
Lambert Way N12	31	F5
Woodhouse Rd.		
Lamberts Pl., Croy.	102	A1
Lamberts Rd., Surb.	91	H5
Lambeth Bri. SE1	**20**	**B1**
Lambeth Bri. SE1	67	E4
Lambeth Bri. SW1	**20**	**B1**
Lambeth Bri. SW1	67	E4
Lambeth High St. SE1	**20**	**C1**
Lambeth High St. SE1	67	F4
Lambeth Hill EC4	**12**	**J5**
Lambeth Hill EC4	58	J7
Lambeth Palace Rd. SE1	**16**	**C6**
Lambeth Palace Rd. SE1	67	F3
Lambeth Rd. SE1	**16**	**E6**
Lambeth Rd. SE1	67	F3
Lambeth Rd., Croy.	94	G7
Lambeth Wk. SE11	**20**	**D1**
Lambeth Wk. SE11	67	F4
Lamble St. NW5	49	A5
Lambley Rd., Dag.	53	B6
Lambolle Pl. NW3	48	H6
Lambolle Rd. NW3	48	H6
Lambourn Clo. W7	64	C2
Lambourn Rd. SW4	76	B3
Lambourne Ave. SW19	84	C4
Lambourne Gdns. E4	34	A2
Lambourne Gdns., Bark.	52	J7
Lambourne Rd.		
Lambourne Gdns., Enf.	25	C2
Lambourne Gro., Kings.T.	92	B2
Kenley Rd.		
Lambourne Pl. SE3	78	H1
Shooter's Hill Rd.		
Lambourne Rd. E11	42	D7
Lambourne Rd., Bark.	52	H7
Lambourne Rd., Chig.	35	J4
Lambourne Rd., Ilf.	52	H2
Lambrook Ter. SW6	75	B1
Lamb's Bldgs. EC1	**9**	**B6**
Lambs Conduit Pas. WC1	**12**	**C1**
Lamb's Conduit St. WC1	**8**	**C6**
Lamb's Conduit St. WC1	58	F4
Lambs Meadow, Wdf.Grn.	43	A2

192 Lam-Lan

Lambs Ms. N1 58 H1
Colebrooke Row
Lamb's Pas. EC1 13 B1
Lamb's Pas. EC1 59 A5
Lambs Ter. N9 33 A2
Lambs Wk., Enf. 24 J2
Lambscroft Ave. SE9 87 J3
Lambton Pl. W11 57 C6
Westbourne Gro.
Lambton Rd. N19 49 E1
Lambton Rd. SW20 92 J1
Lamerock Rd., Brom. 87 F4
Lamerton Rd., Ilf. 43 E2
Lamerton St. SE8 69 A6
Lamford Clo. N17 33 A7
Lamington St. W6 65 H4
Lamlash St. SE11 20 G1
Lammas Ave., Mitch. 94 A2
Lammas Grn. SE26 86 E3
Lammas Pk. Gdns. W5 64 F1
Lammas Pk. Rd. W5 64 F1
Lammas Rd. E9 50 G7
Lammas Rd. E10 50 H2
Lea Bri. Rd.
Lammas Rd., Rich. 82 F4
Lammermoor Rd. SW12 76 B7
Lamont Rd. SW10 18 D6
Lamont Rd. SW10 66 F6
Lamont Rd. Pas. SW10 18 E6
Lamorbey Clo., Sid. 88 J1
Lamorna Gro., Stan. 37 G1
Lampard Gro. N16 50 C1
Lampern Sq. E2 9 J3
Lampeter Sq. W6 66 B6
Humbolt Rd.
Lamplighter Clo. E1 59 F4
Cleveland Way
Lampmead Rd. SE12 78 F5
Lamport Clo. SE18 70 C4
Lampton Ave., Houns. 72 H1
Lampton Ho. Clo. SW19 84 A4
Lampton Pk. Rd., Houns. 72 H2
Lampton Rd., Houns. 72 H2
Lanacre Ave. NW9 38 D1
Lanark Clo. W5 55 F5
Lanark Pl. W9 6 D5
Lanark Pl. W9 57 F4
Lanark Rd. W9 6 B2
Lanark Rd. W9 57 E2
Lanark Sq. E14 69 B3
Lanata Wk., Hayes 54 D4
Ramulis Dr.
Lanbury Rd. SE15 77 G4
Lancashire Ct. W1 11 E5
Lancaster Ave. E18 42 H4
Lancaster Ave. SE27 85 H2
Lancaster Ave. SW19 84 A5
Lancaster Ave., Bark. 52 H7
Lancaster Ave., Mitch. 94 E5
Lancaster Clo. N1 50 B7
Hertford Rd.
Lancaster Clo. N17 33 D7
Park La.
Lancaster Clo. SE27 85 H2
Lancaster Clo., Brom. 96 F4
Lancaster Clo., Kings.T. 82 G5
Lancaster Cotts., Rich. 73 H6
Lancaster Pk.
Lancaster Ct. SW6 66 C7
Lancaster Ct. W2 10 D6
Lancaster Ct., Walt. 90 A7
Lancaster Dr. E14 69 C1
Prestons Rd.
Lancaster Dr. NW3 48 H6
Lancaster Gdns. SW19 84 B5
Lancaster Gdns. W13 64 E2
Lancaster Gdns., Kings.T. 82 G5
Lancaster Gate W2 10 D6
Lancaster Gate W2 57 F7
Lancaster Gro. NW3 48 G6
Lancaster Ms. W2 10 D5
Lancaster Ms. W2 57 F7
Lancaster Ms., Rich. 73 H6
Richmond Hill
Lancaster Pk., Rich. 73 H5
Lancaster Pl. SW19 84 A5
Lancaster Rd.
Lancaster Pl. WC2 12 C5
Lancaster Pl. WC2 58 F7
Lancaster Pl., Houns. 72 C2
Lancaster Pl., Ilf. 52 F5
Staines Rd.
Lancaster Pl., Twick. 73 D6
Lancaster Rd. E7 51 G7
Lancaster Rd. E11 51 E2
Lancaster Rd. E17 41 G2
Lancaster Rd. N4 40 F7
Lancaster Rd. N11 32 D6
Lancaster Rd. N18 33 C5
Lancaster Rd. NW10 47 G5
Lancaster Rd. SE25 95 C2
Lancaster Rd. SW19 84 A5
Lancaster Rd. W11 57 B6
Lancaster Rd., Barn. 23 G5
Lancaster Rd., Enf. 25 A1
Lancaster Rd., Har. 36 G5
Lancaster Rd., Nthlt. 45 J6
Lancaster Rd., Sthl. 54 E7
Lancaster St. SE1 16 H4
Lancaster St. SE1 67 H2
Lancaster Ter. W2 10 E5
Lancaster Ter. W2 57 G7
Lancaster Wk. W2 14 D1
Lancaster Wk. W2 66 G1
Lance Rd., Har. 36 J7
Lancefield St. W10 57 C3
Lancell St. N16 50 B2
Stoke Newington Ch. St.
Lancelot Ave., Wem. 46 G4
Lancelot Cres., Wem. 46 G4
Lancelot Gdns., Barn. 24 A7
Lancelot Pl. SW7 14 J4
Lancelot Pl. SW7 66 J2
Lancelot Rd., Ilf. 35 H6
Lancelot Rd., Well. 80 A4
Lancelot Rd., Wem. 46 G4
Lancer Sq. W8 14 A3
Lancey Clo. SE7 70 A4
Cleveley Clo.
Lanchester Rd. N6 39 J5
Lancing Gdns. N9 33 C1
Lancing Rd. W13 55 E7
Drayton Grn. Rd.
Lancing Rd., Croy. 94 F6
Lancing Rd., Ilf. 43 G6
Lancing St. NW1 7 H4
Lancresse Ct. N1 59 B1
Landcroft Rd. SE22 77 C5
Landells Rd. SE22 77 C6
Landford Rd. SW15 74 J3
Landgrove Rd. SW19 84 D5
Landmann Way SE14 68 G6
Landon Pl. SW1 14 J5
Landon Pl. SW1 66 J3
Landon Wk. E14 60 B7
Cottage St.
Landons Clo. E14 69 C1
Landor Rd. SW9 76 E3
Landor Wk. W12 65 G2
Landport Way SE15 21 G7
Landra Gdns. N21 24 H6
Landridge Rd. SW6 75 C2
Landrock Rd. N8 40 E6
Landscape Rd., Wdf.Grn. 34 H7
Landseer Ave. E12 52 D5
Landseer Clo. SW19 93 F1
Brangwyn Cres.
Landseer Clo., Edg. 38 A2
Landseer Rd. N19 49 E3
Landseer Rd., Enf. 25 D5
Landseer Rd., N.Mal. 92 D7
Landseer Rd., Sutt. 100 D6
Landstead Rd. SE18 70 G7
Lane, The NW8 6 C2
Lane, The SE3 78 G3
Lane App. NW7 31 B5
Lane Clo. NW2 47 H3
Lane End, Bexh. 80 H3
Lanercost Clo. SW2 85 G2
Lanercost Gdns. N14 24 E7
Lanercost Rd. SW2 85 G2
Lanesborough Pl. SW1 15 C3
Laneside, Chis. 88 E5
Laneside, Edg. 30 C5
Laneside Ave., Dag. 44 F7
Laneway SW15 74 H5
Sunnymead Rd.
Lanfranc Rd. E3 59 H2
Lanfrey Pl. W14 66 C5
North End Rd.
Lang St. E1 59 F4
Langbourne Ave. N6 49 A2
Langbourne Way, Esher 98 D6
Langbrook Rd. SE3 79 A3
Langcroft Clo., Cars. 100 J3
Langdale Ave., Mitch. 93 J3
Langdale Clo. SE17 20 J5
Langdale Clo. SE17 67 J6
Langdale Clo. SW14 74 B4
Clifford Ave.
Langdale Clo., Dag. 53 C1
Langdale Clo., Orp. 104 E3
Grasmere Rd.
Langdale Cres., Bexh. 71 G7
Langdale Gdns., Grnf. 55 E3
Langdale Rd. SE10 69 C7
Langdale Rd., Th.Hth. 94 G4
Langdale St. E1 59 E6
Burslem St.
Langdon Ct. NW10 56 E1
Langdon Cres. E6 61 D2
Langdon Dr. NW9 47 C1
Langdon Pk. Rd. N6 40 C7
Langdon Pl. SW14 74 C3
Rosemary La.
Langdon Rd. E6 61 D1
Langdon Rd., Brom. 96 H3
Langdon Rd., Mord. 93 F5
Langdon Shaw, Sid. 88 J5
Langdon Wk., Mord. 93 F5
Langdon Rd.
Langdon Way SE1 21 J2
Langford Clo. E8 50 D5
Langford Clo. N15 41 B6
Langford Clo. NW8 6 D1
Langford Ct. NW8 6 D2
Langford Cres., Barn. 23 J4
Langford Grn. SE5 77 B3
Langford Pl. NW8 6 D1
Langford Pl. NW8 57 F2
Langford Pl., Sid. 89 A3
Langford Rd. SW6 75 E2
Gilstead Rd.
Langford Rd., Barn. 23 H4
Langford Rd., Wdf.Grn. 34 J6
Langfords, Buck.H. 35 A2
Langham Clo. N15 40 H3
Langham Rd.
Langham Dr., Rom. 44 B6
Langham Gdns. N21 24 G5
Langham Gdns. W13 55 E7
Langham Gdns., Edg. 30 C7
Langham Gdns., Rich. 82 F4
Langham Gdns., Wem. 46 F2
Langham Ho. Clo., Rich. 82 G4
Langham Pl. N15 40 H3
Langham Pl. W1 11 E2
Langham Pl. W1 58 B5
Langham Pl. W4 65 E6
Hogarth Roundabout
Langham Rd. N15 40 H3
Langham Rd. SW20 92 J1
Langham Rd., Edg. 30 C6
Langham Rd., Tedd. 82 E5
Langham St. W1 11 E2
Langham St. W1 58 B5
Langhedge Clo. N18 33 C6
Langhedge La.
Langhedge La. N18 33 C5
Langhedge La. Ind. Est. N18 33 C6
Langholm Clo. SW12 76 D7
King's Ave.
Langholme (Bushey), Wat. 28 J1
Langhorne Rd., Dag. 53 G7
Langland Cres., Stan. 37 G2
Langland Dr., Pnr. 28 E7
Langland Gdns. NW3 48 E5
Langland Gdns., Croy. 102 J2
Langler Rd. NW10 56 J2
Langley Ave., Ruis. 45 B2
Langley Ave., Surb. 98 G1
Langley Ave., Wor.Pk. 100 A1
Langley Ct. SE9 79 D6
Langley Ct. WC2 12 A5
Langley Ct., Beck. 96 B5
Langley Cres. E11 42 H7
Langley Cres., Dag. 53 C7
Langley Cres., Edg. 30 C3
Langley Dr. E11 42 H7
Langley Dr. W3 65 B2
Langley Gdns., Brom. 96 J4
Langley Gdns., Dag. 53 D7
Langley Gdns., Orp. 97 E6
Langley Gro., N.Mal. 92 E2
Langley La. SW8 20 B5
Langley La. SW8 67 E6
Langley Meadow, Loug. 27 G2
Langley Pk. NW7 30 E6
Langley Pk. Rd., Sutt. 100 F5
Langley Rd. SW19 93 C1
Langley Rd., Beck. 95 H4
Langley Rd., Islw. 73 C2
Langley Rd., Surb. 91 H7
Langley Rd., Well. 71 C6
Langley Row, Barn. 23 C1
Langley St. WC2 12 A4
Langley St. WC2 58 E6
Langley Way, W.Wick. 103 D1
Langmead St. SE27 85 H4
Beadman St.
Langmore Ct., Bexh. 80 D3
Regency Way
Langroyd Rd. SW17 84 J2
Langside Ave. SW15 74 G4
Langside Cres. N14 32 D3
Langston Hughes Clo. SE24 76 H4
Shakespeare Rd.
Langston Rd., Loug. 27 F5
Langthorn Ct. EC2 13 C3
Langthorne Rd. E11 51 C3
Langthorne St. SW6 75 A1
Langton Ave. E6 61 D3
Langton Ave. N20 23 F7
Langton Clo. WC1 8 D5
Langton Ri. SE23 77 E7
Langton Rd. NW2 47 J3
Langton Rd. SW9 67 H7
Langton Rd., Har. 28 J7
Langton Rd., W.Mol. 90 J5
Langton St. SW10 18 D6
Langton St. SW10 66 F6
Langton Way SE3 78 F1
Langton Way, Croy. 102 B3
Langtry Rd. NW8 57 E1
Langtry Rd., Nthlt. 54 D2
Langtry Wk. NW8 48 F7
Alexandra Pl.
Langwood Chase, Tedd. 82 F6
Langworth Dr., Hayes 54 A6
Lanhill Rd. W9 57 D4
Lanier Rd. SE13 78 C6
Lanigan Dr., Houns. 72 H5
Lankaster Gdns. N2 39 G1
Lankers Dr., Har. 36 F6
Lankton Clo., Beck. 96 C1
Lannoy Rd. SE9 88 F1
Lanrick Rd. E14 60 D6
Lanridge Rd. SE2 71 D3
Lansbury Ave. N18 33 A5
Lansbury Ave., Bark. 53 A7
Lansbury Ave., Felt. 72 B6
Lansbury Ave., Rom. 44 E5
Lansbury Clo. NW10 47 C5
Lansbury Est. E14 60 B6
Lansbury Gdns. E14 60 C6
Lansbury Rd., Enf. 25 G1
Lansbury Way N18 33 B5
Lansbury Ave.
Lansdell Rd., Mitch. 94 A2
Lansdown Rd. E7 51 J7
Lansdown Rd., Sid. 89 B3
Lansdowne Ave., Bexh. 71 C7
Lansdowne Ave., Orp. 104 E1
Lansdowne Clo. SW20 84 A7
Lansdowne Clo., Twick. 82 C1
Lion Rd.
Lansdowne Ct., Wor.Pk. 99 G2
Lansdowne Cres. W11 57 C7
Lansdowne Dr. E8 50 D6
Lansdowne Gdns. SW8 76 E1
Lansdowne Grn. SW8 76 E1
Hartington Rd.
Lansdowne Gro. NW10 47 E4
Lansdowne Hill SE27 85 H3
Lansdowne La. SE7 70 A5
Lansdowne Ms. SE7 70 A5
Lansdowne Ms. W11 66 C1
Lansdowne Rd.
Lansdowne Pl. SE1 17 C5
Lansdowne Pl. SE19 86 C7
Lansdowne Ri. W11 57 B7
Lansdowne Rd. E4 34 A2
Lansdowne Rd. E11 51 F2
Lansdowne Rd. E17 42 A6
Lansdowne Rd. E18 42 G3

Lansdowne Rd. N3 31 C7
Lansdowne Rd. N10 40 C2
Lansdowne Rd. N17 41 D1
Lansdowne Rd. SW20 83 J7
Lansdowne Rd. W11 57 B7
Lansdowne Rd., 87 G7
Brom.
Lansdowne Rd., Croy. 101 J2
Lansdowne Rd., 99 C7
Epsom
Lansdowne Rd., Har. 37 B7
Lansdowne Rd., 72 H3
Houns.
Lansdowne Rd., Ilf. 52 J1
Lansdowne Rd., Stan. 29 F6
Lansdowne Row W1 **15 E1**
Lansdowne Ter. WC1 **8 B6**
Lansdowne Ter. WC1 58 E4
Lansdowne Wk. W11 66 C1
Lansdowne Way SW8 76 D1
Lansdowne Wd. Clo. 85 H3
SE27
Lansfield Ave. N18 33 D4
Lant St. SE1 **16 J3**
Lant St. SE1 67 J2
Lantern Clo. SW15 74 G4
Lantern Clo., Wem. 46 G5
Lanterns Ct. E14 59 A3
Lanvanor Rd. SE15 77 F2
Lapford Clo. W9 57 C4
Lapponum Wk., Hayes 54 E4
Lochan Clo.
Lapse Wd. Wk. SE23 86 E2
Lapstone Gdns., Har. 37 F6
Lapwing Ct., Surb. 99 A3
Chaffinch Clo.
Lara Clo. SE13 78 C6
Lara Clo., Chess. 98 H7
Larbert Rd. SW16 85 C7
Larch Ave. W3 65 E1
Larch Clo. N11 32 A7
Larch Clo. N19 49 C2
Bredgar Rd.
Larch Clo. SE8 68 J6
Clyde St.
Larch Clo. SW12 85 B1
Larch Cres., Epsom 99 B6
Larch Cres., Hayes 54 C4
Larch Dr. W4 65 A5
Gunnersbury Ave.
Larch Grn. NW9 38 E1
Clayton Fld.
Larch Ms. N19 49 C2
Bredgar Rd.
Larch Rd. NW2 47 J4
Larch Tree Way, Croy. 103 A3
Larch Way, Brom. 97 D7
Larchdene, Orp. 104 D2
Larches, The N13 32 J3
Larches Ave. SW14 74 D4
Larchwood Rd. SE9 88 E2
Larcom St. SE17 **21 A2**
Larcom St. SE17 67 J4
Larcombe Clo., Croy. 102 C4
Larden Rd. W3 65 E1
Largewood Ave., 98 J2
Surb.
Larissa St. SE17 **21 C3**
Lark Row E2 59 F1
Larkbere Rd. SE26 86 H4
Larken Dr. (Bushey), 28 J1
Wat.
Larkfield Ave., Har. 37 E3
Larkfield Clo., Brom. 103 F2
Larkfield Rd., Rich. 73 H4
Larkfield Rd., Sid. 88 J3
Larkhall Ct., Rom. 44 J2
Larkhall La. SW4 76 D2
Larkhall Ri. SW4 76 C3
Larkhill Ter. SE18 70 D7
Larks Gro., Bark. 52 H7
Larksfield Gro., Enf. 25 E1
Larkshall Cres. E4 34 C4
Larkshall Rd. E4 34 C5
Larkspur Clo. E6 61 B5
Larkspur Clo. N17 33 A7
Fryatt Rd.
Larkspur Way, Epsom 99 B5
Larkswood Ct. E4 34 D5
Larkswood Ri., Pnr. 66 A6
Larkswood Rd. E4 34 A4
Larkway Clo. NW9 38 D4
Larnach Rd. W6 66 A6
Larpent Ave. SW15 74 J5
Larwood Clo., Grnf. 46 A5
Lascelles Ave., Har. 37 A7
Lascelles Clo. E11 51 D2

Lascotts Rd. N22 32 F6
Lassa Rd. SE9 79 B5
Lassell St. SE10 69 D5
Lasterton St. E8 50 E6
Wilton Way
Latchett Rd. E18 42 H1
Latchingdon Ct. E17 41 G4
Latchingdon Gdns., 35 B6
Wdf.Grn.
Latchmere Clo., Rich. 82 H5
Latchmere La., 82 J6
Kings.T.
Latchmere Pas. SW11 75 H2
Cabul Rd.
Latchmere Rd. SW11 75 J2
Latchmere Rd., 82 H7
Kings.T.
Latchmere St. SW11 75 J2
Lateward Rd., Brent. 64 G6
Latham Clo. E6 61 B6
Latham Clo. 73 D7
Oliver Gdns.
Latham Clo., Twick. 73 D7
Latham Ho. E1 59 G6
Latham Rd., Bexh. 80 G5
Latham Rd., Twick. 73 C7
Lathams Way, Croy. 101 F1
Lathkill Clo., Enf. 25 C7
Lathom Rd. E6 52 B7
Latimer SE17 21 D4
Latimer Ave. E6 61 C1
Latimer Clo., Pnr. 36 C1
Latimer Clo., Wor.Pk. 99 H4
Latimer Clo., Pnr. 36 C1
Latimer Pl. W10 56 J6
Latimer Rd. E7 51 H4
Latimer Rd. N15 41 B6
Latimer Rd. SW19 84 E6
Latimer Rd. W10 56 J5
Latimer Rd., Barn. 23 E3
Latimer Rd., Croy. 101 H3
Abbey Rd.
Latimer Rd., Tedd. 82 C5
Latimer St. E1 59 G5
Stepney Way
Latona Rd. SE15 **21 H6**
Latona Rd. SE15 68 D6
Latton Clo., Walt. 90 E7
Latymer Ct. W6 66 A4
Latymer Rd. N9 33 C2
Latymer Way N9 33 A2
Laud St. SE11 **20 C3**
Laud St., Croy. 101 J3
Lauder Clo., Nthlt. 54 D2
Lauderdale Dr., Rich. 82 G3
Lauderdale Rd. W9 **6 A4**
Lauderdale Rd. W9 57 E3
Laughton Ct., Borwd. 22 D2
Banks Rd.
Laughton Rd., Nthlt. 54 D1
Launcelot Rd., Brom. 87 G4
Launcelot St. SE1 **16 E4**
Launceston Gdns., 55 F1
Grnf.
Launceston Pl. W8 **14 C5**
Launceston Pl. W8 66 F3
Launceston Rd., Grnf. 55 F1
Launch St. E14 69 C3
Laundry La. N1 58 J1
Greenman St.
Laundry Rd. W6 66 B6
Laura Clo. E11 42 J5
Laura Clo., Enf. 25 B5
Laura Pl. E5 50 F4
Lauradale Rd. N2 39 J4
Laurel Ave., Twick. 82 C1
Laurel Bank Gdns. 75 C2
SW6
New Kings Rd.
Laurel Bank Rd., Enf. 24 J1
Laurel Clo. N19 49 C2
Hargrave Pk.
Laurel Clo. SW17 84 H5
Laurel Clo., Ilf. 35 F6
Laurel Clo., Sid. 89 A3
Laurel Cres., Croy. 103 A3
Laurel Dr. N21 24 G7
Laurel Gdns. E4 26 B7
Laurel Gdns. NW7 30 D3
Laurel Gdns. W7 64 B1
Laurel Gdns., Houns. 72 E4
Laurel Gro. SE20 86 E7
Laurel Gro. SE26 86 G4
Laurel Pk., Har. 29 C7
Laurel Rd. SW13 74 G2
Laurel Rd. SW20 92 H1
Laurel Rd., Hmptn. 82 A5
Laurel St. E8 50 C6
Laurel Vw. N12 31 E3

Laurel Way E18 42 F4
Laurel Way N20 31 D3
Laurence Ms. W12 65 G2
Askew Rd.
Laurence Pountney **13 B5**
Hill EC4
Laurence Pountney **13 B5**
La. EC4
Laurie Gro. SE14 77 H1
Laurie Rd. W7 55 B5
Laurier Rd. NW5 49 B3
Laurier Rd., Croy. 95 C7
Laurimel Clo., Stan. 29 E6
September Way
Laurino Pl. (Bushey), 28 J2
Wat.
Lauriston Rd. E9 59 G1
Lauriston Rd. SW19 84 A6
Lausanne Rd. N8 40 G4
Lausanne Rd. SE15 77 F1
Lavell St. N16 50 A4
Lavender Ave. NW9 47 C1
Lavender Ave., Mitch. 93 H1
Lavender Ave., 99 J3
Wor.Pk.
Lavender Clo. SW3 **18 F6**
Lavender Clo., Cars. 101 B4
Lavender Ct., W.Mol. 90 H3
Molesham Way
Lavender Gdns. SW11 75 J4
Lavender Gdns., Enf. 24 H1
Lavender Gro. E8 50 D7
Lavender Gro., Mitch. 93 H1
Lavender Hill SW11 75 J4
Lavender Hill, Enf. 24 G1
Lavender Pl., Ilf. 52 E5
Lavender Rd. SE16 68 H1
Lavender Rd. SW15 75 G3
Lavender Rd., Cars. 101 A4
Lavender Rd., Croy. 94 F6
Lavender Rd., Enf. 25 A1
Lavender Rd., Epsom 99 B5
Lavender Rd., Sutt. 100 G4
Lavender St. E15 51 E6
Manbey Gro.
Lavender Sweep 75 J4
SW11
Lavender Ter. SW11 75 H3
Falcon Rd.
Lavender Vale, Wall. 101 D6
Lavender Wk. SW11 75 J4
Lavender Wk., Mitch. 94 A3
Lavender Way, Croy. 95 G6
Lavengro Rd. SE27 85 J2
Lavenham Rd. SW18 84 C2
Lavernock Rd., Bexh. 80 G2
Lavers Rd. N16 50 B3
Laverstoke Gdns. 74 F7
SW15
Laverton Ms. SW5 **18 B2**
Laverton Pl. SW5 **18 B2**
Laverton Pl. SW5 66 E4
Lavidge Rd. SE9 88 B2
Lavina Gro. N1 8 C1
Lavington Rd. W13 64 E1
Lavington Rd., Croy. 101 F3
Lavington St. SE1 **16 H2**
Lavington St. SE1 67 H1
Law Ho., Bark. 62 A2
Law St. SE1 **17 C5**
Law St. SE1 68 A3
Lawdons Gdns., 101 H4
Croy.
Lawford Rd. N1 50 B7
Lawford Rd. NW5 49 C6
Lawford Rd. W4 65 C7
Lawless St. E14 60 B7
Lawley Rd. N14 24 B7
Lawley St. E5 50 F4
Lawn, The, Sthl. 63 G5
Lawn Clo. N9 25 C7
Lawn Clo., Brom. 87 H6
Lawn Clo., N.Mal. 92 E2
Lawn Cres., Rich. 74 A2
Lawn Fm. Gro., Rom. 44 E4
Lawn Gdns. W7 64 B1
Lawn Ho. Clo. E14 69 C2
Lawn La. SW8 **20 B6**
Lawn La. SW8 67 E6
Lawn Pl. SE15 77 C1
Sumner Est.
Lawn Rd. NW3 48 J5
Lawn Rd., Beck. 86 J7
Lawn Ter. SE3 78 E3
Lawn Vale, Pnr. 36 E2
Lawnfield NW6 48 A7
Coverdale Rd.
Lawns, The E4 34 A5

Lawns, The SE3 78 E3
Lee Ter.
Lawns, The SE19 95 A1
Lawns, The, Pnr. 28 H7
Lawns, The, Sid. 89 B4
Lawns, The, Sutt. 100 B7
Lawnside SE3 78 F4
Lawrence Ave. E12 52 D4
Lawrence Ave. E17 41 G1
Lawrence Ave. N13 32 H4
Lawrence Ave. NW7 30 E4
Lawrence Ave., 92 D6
N.Mal.
Lawrence Bldgs. N16 50 C3
Lawrence Campe 31 G3
Clo. N20
Friern Barnet La.
Lawrence Clo. E3 60 A3
Lawrence Clo. N15 41 B3
Lawrence Rd.
Lawrence Clo. NW7 30 E5
Lawrence Cres., Dag. 53 H3
Lawrence Cres., Edg. 38 A2
Lawrence Est., Houns. 72 C4
Lawrence Gdns. NW7 30 F3
Lawrence Hill E4 34 A2
Lawrence La. EC2 **13 A4**
Lawrence Pl. N1 58 E1
Outram Pl.
Lawrence Rd. E6 61 B1
Lawrence Rd. E13 60 H1
Lawrence Rd. N15 41 B4
Lawrence Rd. N18 33 E4
Lawrence Rd. SE25 95 C4
Lawrence Rd. W5 64 G4
Lawrence Rd., Hmptn. 81 F7
Lawrence Rd., Houns. 72 C4
Lawrence Rd., Pnr. 36 D6
Lawrence Rd., Rich. 82 F4
Lawrence Rd., 103 G4
W.Wick.
Lawrence St. E16 60 F5
Lawrence St. NW7 30 F5
Lawrence St. SW3 **18 G6**
Lawrence St. SW3 66 H6
Lawrence Way NW10 47 C3
Lawrence Weaver 93 E6
Clo., Mord.
Green La.
Lawrie Pk. Ave. SE26 86 E5
Lawrie Pk. Cres. SE26 86 E5
Lawrie Pk. Gdns. SE26 86 E4
Lawrie Pk. Rd. SE26 86 E6
Lawson Clo. E16 60 J5
Lawson Clo. SW19 84 A3
Lawson Est. SE1 **17 B6**
Lawson Gdns., Pnr. 36 B3
Lawson Rd., Enf. 25 F1
Lawson Rd., Sthl. 54 F4
Lawton Rd. E10 51 D1
Lawton Rd., Barn. 23 G3
Lawton Rd., Loug. 27 E2
Laxcon Clo. NW10 47 C5
Laxey Rd., Orp. 104 J6
Laxley Clo. SE5 **20 H7**
Laxley Clo. SE5 67 H7
Laxton Pl. NW1 **7 E5**
Layard Rd. SE16 68 E4
Layard Rd., Enf. 25 C1
Layard Rd., Th.Hth. 95 A2
Layard Sq. SE16 68 E4
Laycock St. N1 49 G6
Layer Gdns. W3 56 A7
Layfield Clo. NW4 38 H7
Layfield Cres. NW4 38 H7
Layfield Rd. NW4 38 H7
Layhams Rd., Kes. 103 F5
Layhams Rd., 103 D3
W.Wick.
Laymarsh Clo., Belv. 71 F3
Laymead Clo., Nthlt. 45 E6
Laystall St. EC1 **8 E6**
Laystall St. EC1 58 G4
Layton Cres., Croy. 101 G5
Layton Rd. N1 **8 F1**
Layton Rd. N1 58 G2
Layton Rd., Brent. 64 G5
Layton Rd., Houns. 72 H4
Laytons Bldgs. SE1 **17 B3**
Layzell Wk. SE9 88 A1
Mottingham La.
Lazar Wk. N7 49 F2
Briset Way
Le May Ave. SE12 87 H3
Lea Bri. Rd. E5 50 E3
Lea Bri. Rd. E10 42 A7
Lea Bri. Rd. E17 42 D5
Lea Gdns., Wem. 46 J4

Lea Hall Rd. E10 | 51 A1
Lea Rd., Beck. | 96 A2
  Fairfield Rd.
Lea Rd., Enf. | 25 A1
Lea Rd., Sthl. | 63 E4
Lea Side Ind. Est., Enf. | 25 J3
Lea Valley Rd. E4 | 25 G5
Lea Valley Rd., Enf. | 25 G5
Lea Valley Viaduct E4 | 33 G5
Lea Valley Viaduct | 33 G5
  N18
Lea Vw. Hos. E5 | 50 E1
  Springfield
Leabank Clo., Har. | 46 B3
Leabank Sq. E9 | 51 A6
Leabank Vw. N15 | 41 D6
Leabourne Rd. N16 | 41 D6
Leacroft Ave. SW12 | 75 J7
Leadale Ave. E4 | 33 J2
Leadale Rd. N15 | 41 D6
Leadale Rd. N16 | 41 D6
Leadenhall Mkt. EC3 | **13 D4**
Leadenhall Pl. EC3 | **13 D4**
Leadenhall St. EC3 | **13 D4**
Leadenhall St. EC3 | 59 B6
Leader Ave. E12 | 52 D5
Leadings, The, Wem. | 47 C3
Leaf Clo., T.Ditt. | 91 B5
Leaf Gro. SE27 | 85 G5
Leafield Clo. SW16 | 85 H6
Leafield La., Sid. | 89 F4
Leafield Rd. SW20 | 93 C3
Leafield Rd., Sutt. | 100 D2
Leafy Gro., Kes. | 103 J5
Leafy Oak Rd. SE12 | 87 J4
Leafy Way, Croy. | 102 C2
Leake St. SE1 | **16 D3**
Leake St. SE1 | **16 D3**
Leake St. SE1 | 67 F2
Lealand Rd. N15 | 41 C6
Leamington Ave. E17 | 42 A5
Leamington Ave., | 87 J5
  Brom.
Leamington Ave., | 93 B4
  Mord.
Leamington Ave., | 104 H4
  Orp.
Leamington Clo. E12 | 52 C5
Leamington Clo., | 87 J5
  Brom.
Leamington Clo., | 72 J5
  Houns.
Leamington Cres., | 45 E3
  Har.
Leamington Gdns., Ilf. | 52 J2
Leamington Pk. W3 | 56 D5
Leamington Rd., Sthl. | 63 D4
Leamington Rd. Vill. | 57 C5
  W11
Leamore St. W6 | 65 H4
Leamouth Rd. E6 | 61 B6
Leamouth Rd. E14 | 60 D6
Leander Ct. SE8 | 78 A1
Leander Rd. SW2 | 76 F7
Leander Rd., Nthlt. | 54 G2
Leander Rd., Th.Hth. | 94 F4
Learoyd Gdns. E6 | 61 D7
Leas Clo., Chess. | 98 J7
Leas Dale SE9 | 88 D3
Leas Grn., Chis. | 88 J6
Leaside Ave. N10 | 40 A3
Leaside Rd. E5 | 50 F1
Leasowes Rd. E10 | 51 A1
Leather Bottle La., | 71 F4
  Belv.
  St. Augustine's Rd.
Leather Clo., Mitch. | 94 A2
Leather Gdns. E15 | 60 E1
  Abbey Rd.
Leather La. EC1 | **12 E1**
Leather La. EC1 | 58 G4
Leatherbottle Grn., | 71 F3
  Erith
Leatherdale St. E1 | 59 F4
  Portelet Rd.
Leatherhead Clo. N16 | 50 B1
Leathermarket St. | **17 D4**
  SE1
Leathermarket St. SE1 | 68 B2
Leathersellers Clo., | 23 B4
  Barn.
  The Ave.
Leathsail Rd., Har. | 45 H3
Leathwaite Rd. SW11 | 75 J4
Leathwell Rd. SE8 | 78 B2
Leaveland Clo., Beck. | 96 A4

Leaver Gdns., Grnf. | 55 A2
Leavesden Rd., Stan. | 29 D6
Leaway E10 | 50 G1
Lebanon Ave., Felt. | 81 D5
Lebanon Ct., Twick. | 73 E7
Lebanon Gdns. SW18 | 75 D5
Lebanon Pk., Twick. | 73 E7
Lebanon Rd. SW18 | 75 D5
Lebanon Rd., Croy. | 102 B1
Lebrun Sq. SE3 | 78 H3
Lechmere App., | 42 J2
  Wdf.Grn.
Lechmere Ave., Chig. | 35 F4
Lechmere Ave., | 43 A2
  Wdf.Grn.
Lechmere Rd. NW2 | 47 H6
Leckford Rd. SW18 | 84 F2
Leckwith Ave., Bexh. | 71 E6
Leconfield Ave. SW13 | 74 F3
Leconfield Rd. N5 | 50 A4
Leda Rd. SE18 | 70 C3
Ledbury Est. SE15 | 68 E7
Ledbury Ms. N. W11 | 57 D7
  Ledbury Rd.
Ledbury Ms. W. W11 | 57 D7
  Ledbury Rd.
Ledbury Pl., Croy. | 101 J4
  Ledbury Rd.
Ledbury Rd. W11 | 57 C6
Ledbury Rd., Croy. | 101 J4
Ledbury St. SE15 | **21 J7**
Ledbury St. SE15 | 68 D7
Ledrington Rd. SE19 | 86 D6
  Anerley Hill
Ledway Dr., Wem. | 37 J7
Lee Ave., Rom. | 44 E6
Lee Bri. SE13 | 78 C3
Lee Ch. St. SE13 | 78 E4
Lee Clo. E17 | 41 G1
Lee Conservancy Rd. | 50 J5
  E9
Lee Grn. SE12 | 78 F5
Lee Gro., Chig. | 35 D2
Lee High Rd. SE12 | 78 F4
Lee High Rd. SE13 | 78 D4
Lee Pk. SE3 | 78 F4
Lee Pk. Way N9 | 33 H3
Lee Pk. Way N18 | 33 G5
Lee Rd. NW7 | 31 A7
Lee Rd. SE3 | 78 F3
Lee Rd. SW19 | 93 E1
Lee Rd., Enf. | 25 D6
Lee Rd., Grnf. | 55 F1
Lee St. E8 | 59 C1
Lee Ter. SE3 | 78 E3
Lee Ter. SE13 | 78 E3
Lee Valley Trd. Est. | 33 G5
  N18
Lee Vw., Enf. | 24 H1
Leechcroft Ave., Sid. | 79 J5
Leechcroft Rd., Wall. | 101 A3
Leecroft Rd., Barn. | 23 B5
Leeds Pl. N4 | 49 F2
  Tollington Pk.
Leeds Rd., Ilf. | 52 G1
Leeds St. N18 | 33 D5
Leefern Rd. W12 | 65 G2
Leegate SE12 | 78 F5
Leeke St. WC1 | **8 C3**
Leeke St. WC1 | 58 F3
Leeland Rd. W13 | 64 D1
Leeland Ter. W13 | 64 D1
Leeland Way NW10 | 47 F4
Leerdam Dr. E14 | 69 C3
Lees, The, Croy. | 102 J2
Lees Pl. W1 | **11 B5**
Lees Pl. W1 | 58 A7
Leeside, Barn. | 23 B5
Leeside Cres. NW11 | 39 B6
Leeside Rd. N17 | 33 E6
Leeson Rd. SE24 | 76 G4
Leesons Hill, Chis. | 97 H3
Leesons Way, Orp. | 97 J2
Leeward Gdns. SW19 | 84 C5
Leeway SE8 | 68 J5
Leeway Clo., Pnr. | 28 F7
  Woodridings Clo.
Leewood Clo. SE12 | 78 F6
  Upwood Rd.
Lefevre Wk. E3 | 59 J1
  Old Ford Rd.
Lefroy Rd. W12 | 65 F2
Legard Rd. N5 | 49 H3
Legatt Rd. SE9 | 79 A5
Leggatt Rd. E15 | 60 C2
Legge St. SE13 | 78 C5

Leghorn Rd. NW10 | 56 F2
Leghorn Rd. SE18 | 70 G5
Legion Clo. N1 | 49 G7
Legion Ct., Mord. | 93 D6
Legion Rd., Grnf. | 54 J1
Legion Way N12 | 31 H7
  Downway
Legon Ave., Rom. | 53 J1
Legrace Ave., Houns. | 72 D2
Leicester Ave., Mitch. | 94 E4
Leicester Clo., | 99 J4
  Wor.Pk.
Leicester Ct. WC2 | **11 J5**
Leicester Gdns., Ilf. | 43 H7
Leicester Pl. WC2 | **11 J5**
Leicester Rd. E11 | 42 H5
Leicester Rd. N2 | 39 H3
Leicester Rd. NW10 | 47 D7
Leicester Rd., Barn. | 23 E5
Leicester Rd., Croy. | 95 B7
Leicester Sq. WC2 | **11 J6**
Leicester Sq. WC2 | 58 D7
Leicester St. WC2 | **11 J5**
Leigh Ave., Ilf. | 43 A4
Leigh Clo., N.Mal. | 92 D4
Leigh Ct., Borwd. | 22 D2
  Banks Rd.
Leigh Ct., Har. | 46 B1
Leigh Cres., Croy. | 103 B7
Leigh Gdns. NW10 | 56 J2
Leigh Hunt Dr. N14 | 32 D1
Leigh Orchard Clo. | 85 F3
  SW16
Leigh Hunt St. SE1 | **16 J3**
Leigh Pl. EC1 | 58 G5
  Baldwin's Gdns.
Leigh Pl., Well. | 80 A2
Leigh Rd. E6 | 52 D6
Leigh Rd. E10 | 42 C7
Leigh Rd. N5 | 49 H4
Leigh Rd., Houns. | 73 A4
Leigh Rodd, Wat. | 28 F3
Leigh St. WC1 | **8 A5**
Leigh St. WC1 | 58 E4
Leigham Ave. SW16 | 85 E3
Leigham Ct. Rd. SW16 | 85 E2
Leigham Dr., Islw. | 64 B7
Leigham Vale SW2 | 85 G2
Leigham Vale SW16 | 85 F3
Leighton Ave. E12 | 52 D5
Leighton Ave., Pnr. | 36 E3
Leighton Clo., Edg. | 38 A2
Leighton Cres. NW5 | 49 C5
  Leighton Gro.
Leighton Gdns. NW10 | 56 H2
Leighton Gro. NW5 | 49 C5
Leighton Pl. NW5 | 49 C5
Leighton Rd. NW5 | 49 C5
Leighton Rd. W13 | 64 D2
Leighton Rd., Enf. | 25 C5
Leighton Rd., Har. | 37 A2
Leighton St. E., Croy. | 101 H1
Leighton St. W., | 101 H1
  Croy.
Leinster Ave. SW14 | 74 C3
Leinster Gdns. W2 | **10 C4**
Leinster Gdns. W2 | 57 F6
Leinster Ms. W2 | **10 C6**
Leinster Ms. W2 | 57 F7
Leinster Pl. W2 | **10 B4**
Leinster Pl. W2 | 57 F6
Leinster Rd. N10 | 48 B4
Leinster Rd. NW6 | 57 D3
  Stafford Rd.
Leinster Sq. W2 | 57 D6
Leinster Ter. W2 | **10 C5**
Leinster Ter. W2 | 57 F7
Leith Clo. NW9 | 47 D1
Leith Rd. N22 | 40 H1
Leith Yd. NW6 | 57 D1
  Quex Rd.
Leithcote Gdns. SW16 | 85 F4
Leithcote Path SW16 | 85 F3
Lela Ave., Houns. | 72 C2
Lelitia Clo. E8 | 59 D1
  Pownall Rd.
Leman St. E1 | **13 G4**
Leman St. E1 | 59 C6
Lemark Clo., Stan. | 29 F5
Lemmon Rd. SE10 | 69 E6
Lemna Rd. E11 | 42 E7
Lemonwell Ct. SE9 | 79 F5
Lemsford Clo. N15 | 41 D5
Lemsford Ct. N4 | 49 J2
  Brownswood Rd.
Lemsford Ct., Borwd. | 22 C4
Lemuel St. SW18 | 75 E6
  St. Ann's Hill

Lena Gdns. W6 | 65 J3
Lena Kennedy Clo. E4 | 34 C6
Lenanton Steps E14 | 69 A2
  Manilla St.
Lendal Ter. SW4 | 76 D3
Lenelby Rd., Surb. | 99 A1
Lenham Rd. SE12 | 78 F4
Lenham Rd., Bexh. | 71 F6
Lenham Rd., Sutt. | 100 E4
Lenham Rd., Th.Hth. | 95 A2
Lennard Ave., | 103 E2
  W.Wick.
Lennard Clo., | 103 E2
  W.Wick.
Lennard Rd. SE20 | 86 G6
Lennard Rd., Beck. | 86 H7
Lennard Rd., Brom. | 104 C1
Lennard Rd., Croy. | 101 J1
Lennon Rd. NW2 | 47 J6
Lennox Gdns. NW10 | 47 F4
Lennox Gdns. SW1 | **14 J6**
Lennox Gdns. SW1 | 66 J3
Lennox Gdns., Croy. | 101 H4
Lennox Gdns., Ilf. | 52 C1
Lennox Gdns. Ms. | **14 J6**
  SW1
Lennox Gdns. Ms. | 66 J3
  SW1
Lennox Rd. E17 | 41 J6
Lennox Rd. N4 | 49 F2
Lenor Clo., Bexh. | 80 E4
Lens Rd. E7 | 51 J7
Lensbury Way SE2 | 71 C3
Lenthall Pl. SW7 | **18 C1**
Lenthall Rd. E8 | 50 C7
Lenthall Rd., Loug. | 27 G4
Lenthorp Rd. SE10 | 69 F4
Lentmead Rd., Brom. | 87 F3
Lenton Ri., Rich. | 73 H3
  Evelyn Ter.
Lenton St. SE18 | 70 G4
Lenville Way SE16 | **21 J4**
Leo St. SE15 | 68 E7
Leo Yd. EC1 | **8 H6**
Leof Cres. SE6 | 87 B5
Leominster Rd., Mord. | 93 F6
Leominster Wk., | 93 F6
  Mord.
Leonard Ave., Mord. | 93 F5
Leonard Rd. E4 | 34 A6
Leonard Rd. E7 | 51 G4
Leonard Rd. N9 | 33 C3
Leonard Rd. SW16 | 94 C1
Leonard Rd., Sthl. | 63 D3
Leonard Robbins | 62 B7
  Path SE28
  Tawney Rd.
Leonard St. EC2 | **9 C5**
Leonard St. EC2 | 59 A4
Leontine Clo. SE15 | 68 D7
Leopards Ct. EC1 | **12 E1**
Leopold Ave. SW19 | 84 C5
Leopold Ms. E9 | 59 F1
  Fremont St.
Leopold Rd. E17 | 42 A5
Leopold Rd. N2 | 39 G3
Leopold Rd. N18 | 33 E5
Leopold Rd. NW10 | 47 E7
Leopold Rd. SW19 | 84 C4
Leopold Rd. W5 | 64 J1
Leopold St. E3 | 59 J5
Lepe Clo., Brom. | 87 E4
  Winlaton Rd.
Leppoc Rd. SW4 | 76 D5
Leroy St. SE1 | **17 D6**
Leroy St. SE1 | 68 B4
Lescombe Clo. SE23 | 86 H3
Lescombe Rd. SE23 | 86 H3
Lesley Clo., Bex. | 80 H7
Leslie Gdns., Sutt. | 100 D6
Leslie Gro., Croy. | 102 A1
Leslie Pk. Rd., Croy. | 102 B1
Leslie Rd. E11 | 51 C4
Leslie Rd. E16 | 60 H6
Leslie Rd. N2 | 39 G3
Leslie Smith Sq. | 70 D6
  SE18
  Nightingale Vale
Lessar Ave. SW4 | 76 B5
Lessing St. SE23 | 77 H7
Lessingham Ave. | 84 J4
  SW17
Lessingham Ave., Ilf. | 43 D3
Lessington Ave., | 44 J6
  Rom.
Lessness Ave., Bexh. | 71 D7
Lessness Pk., Belv. | 71 F5

Lessness Rd., Belv.	71 G5
Stapley Rd.	
Lessness Rd., Mord.	93 F6
Lester Ave. E15	60 E4
Leswin Pl. N16	50 C3
Leswin Rd.	
Leswin Rd. N16	50 C3
Letchford Gdns. NW10	56 G3
Letchford Ms. NW10	56 G3
Letchford Gdns.	
Letchford Ter., Har.	36 H1
Letchworth Clo., Brom.	96 G5
Letchworth Clo., Wat.	28 D5
Letchworth Dr., Brom.	96 G5
Letchworth St. SW17	84 J4
Lethbridge Clo. SE13	78 C1
Lett Rd. E15	51 D7
Letterstone Rd. SW6	66 C7
Varna Rd.	
Lettice St. SW6	75 C1
Lettsom St. SE5	77 B2
Lettsom Wk. E13	60 G2
Stratford Rd.	
Leucha Rd. E17	41 H5
Levana Clo. SW19	84 B1
Levehurst Way SW4	76 E2
Leven Clo., Wat.	28 D5
Leven Rd. E14	60 C5
Levendale Rd. SE23	86 H2
Lever St. EC1	**8 H4**
Lever St. EC1	58 H3
Leverett St. SW3	**18 H1**
Leverholme Gdns. SE9	88 D3
Leverson St. SW16	85 C6
Leverton Pl. NW5	49 C5
Leverton St.	
Leverton St. NW5	49 C5
Levett Gdns., Ilf.	52 J4
Levett Rd., Bark.	52 H6
Levine Gdns., Bark.	62 D2
Levison Way N19	49 D2
Grovedale Rd.	
Lewes Clo., Nthlt.	45 G6
Lewes Rd. N12	31 H5
Lewes Rd., Brom.	97 A2
Lewesdon Clo. SW19	84 A1
Leweston Pl. N16	41 C7
Lewey Ho. E3	59 J4
Lewgars Ave. NW9	38 C6
Lewin Rd. SW14	74 D3
Lewin Rd. SW16	85 D6
Lewin Rd., Bexh.	80 E5
Lewis Ave. E17	42 A1
Lewis Cres. NW10	47 C5
Lewis Gdns. N2	39 G2
Lewis Gro. SE13	78 C3
Lewis Rd., Mitch.	93 G2
Lewis Rd., Rich.	73 G5
Red Lion St.	
Lewis Rd., Sid.	89 C3
Lewis Rd., Sthl.	63 E2
Lewis Rd., Sutt.	100 E4
Lewis Rd., Well.	80 C3
Lewis St. NW1	49 B6
Lewisham High St. SE13	78 B6
Lewisham Hill SE13	78 C2
Lewisham Pk. SE13	78 C5
Lewisham Rd. SE13	78 B1
Lewisham St. SW1	**15 J4**
Lewisham Way SE4	78 A2
Lewisham Way SE14	77 J1
Lexden Dr., Rom.	44 B6
Lexden Rd. W3	65 B1
Lexden Rd., Mitch.	94 D4
Lexham Gdns. W8	66 D4
Lexham Gdns. Ms. W8	**14 B6**
Lexham Ho., Bark.	61 G1
St. Margarets	
Lexham Wk. W8	66 D4
Lexham Wk. W8	**14 B6**
Lexington St. W1	**11 G5**
Lexington St. W1	58 C7
Lexington Way, Barn.	23 A4
Lexton Gdns. SW12	85 D1
Ley St., Ilf.	52 E2
Leyborne Ave. W13	64 E2
Leyborne Pk., Rich.	74 A1
Leybourne Clo., Brom.	96 G6
Leybourne Rd. E11	51 F1
Leybourne Rd. NW1	49 B7
Leybourne Rd. NW9	38 A5
Leybourne St. NW1	49 B7
Hawley St.	
Leybridge Ct. SE12	78 G5
Leyburn Clo. E17	42 C4
Leyburn Gdns., Croy.	102 C2
Leyburn Gro. N18	33 D6
Leyburn Rd. N18	33 D6
Leycroft Clo., Loug.	27 D5
Leyden St. E1	**13 F2**
Leydon Clo. SE16	68 G1
Lagado Ms.	
Leyes Rd. E16	60 J6
Leyfield, Wor.Pk.	99 E1
Leyland Ave., Enf.	25 H2
Leyland Gdns., Wdf.Grn.	34 J5
Leyland Rd. SE12	78 F5
Leylang Rd. SE14	68 G7
Leys, The N2	39 F4
Leys, The, Har.	37 H6
Leys Ave., Dag.	62 J1
Leys Clo., Dag.	53 J7
Leys Clo., Har.	37 A5
Leys Gdns., Barn.	24 A5
Leys Rd. E., Enf.	25 H1
Leys Rd. W., Enf.	25 H1
Leysdown Ave., Bexh.	80 J4
Leysdown Rd. SE9	88 B2
Leysfield Rd. W12	65 G3
Leyspring Rd. E11	51 F1
Leyswood Dr., Ilf.	43 H5
Leythe Rd. W3	65 C2
Leyton Business Cen. E10	51 A2
Leyton Gra. E10	51 B1
Leyton Gra. Est. E10	51 A1
Leyton Grn. Rd. E10	42 C6
Leyton Ind. Village E10	41 G7
Leyton Pk. Rd. E10	51 C3
Leyton Rd. E15	51 D5
Leyton Rd. SW19	84 F7
Leyton Way E11	42 E7
Leytonstone Rd. E15	51 E6
Leywick St. E15	60 E2
Lezayre Rd., Orp.	104 J6
Liardet St. SE14	68 H6
Liberia Rd. N5	49 H6
Liberty Ave. SW19	93 F1
Liberty Ms. SW12	76 B6
Liberty St. SW9	76 F1
Libra Rd. E3	59 J1
Libra Rd. E13	60 G2
Library Pl. E1	59 E7
Cable St.	
Library St. SE1	**16 G4**
Library St. SE1	67 H2
Library Way, Twick.	72 J7
Nelson Rd.	
Lichfield Gdns., Rich.	73 H4
Lichfield Gro. N3	39 D1
Lichfield Rd. E3	59 H3
Lichfield Rd. E6	61 A3
Lichfield Rd. N9	33 D2
Winchester Rd.	
Lichfield Rd. NW2	48 B4
Lichfield Rd., Dag.	53 B4
Lichfield Rd., Houns.	72 C3
Lichfield Rd., Nthwd.	36 A3
Lichfield Rd., Rich.	73 J1
Lichfield Rd., Wdf.Grn.	34 E4
Lichfield Sq., Rich.	73 H4
Lichfield Gdns.	
Lichlade Clo., Orp.	104 J4
Lidbury Rd. NW7	31 B6
Lidcote Gdns. SW9	76 G2
Liddell Clo., Har.	37 G3
Liddell Gdns. NW10	56 J2
Liddell Rd. NW6	48 D6
Lidding Rd., Har.	37 G5
Liddington Rd. E15	60 F1
Liddon Rd. E13	60 H3
Liddon Rd., Brom.	96 J3
Liden Clo. E17	50 J1
Hitcham Rd.	
Lidfield Rd. N16	50 A4
Lidiard Rd. SW18	84 F2
Lidlington Pl. NW1	7 G2
Lidlington Pl. NW1	**58 C2**
Lidyard Rd. N19	49 C1
Liffler Rd. SE18	70 H5
Liffords Pl. SW13	75 A4
Lifford St. SW15	74 F2
Lightcliffe Rd. N13	32 G4
Lightermans Rd. E14	69 A2
Lightfoot Rd. N8	40 E5
Lightley Clo., Wem.	46 J7
Stanley Ave.	
Ligonier St. E2	**9 F5**
Lilac Clo. E4	33 J6
Lilac Gdns. W5	64 G3
Lilac Gdns., Croy.	103 A3
Lilac Pl. SE11	**20 C2**
Lilac Pl. SE11	67 F4
Lilac St. W12	56 G7
Lilburne Gdns. SE9	79 B5
Lilburne Rd. SE9	79 B5
Lilburne Wk. NW10	47 C6
Pitfield Way	
Lile Cres. W7	55 B5
Lilestone Est. NW8	**6 E6**
Lilestone St. NW8	**6 G5**
Lilestone St. NW8	57 H4
Lilford Rd. SE5	76 H2
Lilian Barker Clo. SE12	78 G5
Lilian Board Way, Grnf.	46 A5
Lilian Clo. N16	50 B3
Barbauld Rd.	
Lilian Gdns., Wdf.Grn.	42 H1
Lilian Rd. SW16	94 C1
Lillechurch Rd., Dag.	53 B6
Lilleshall Rd., Mord.	93 G5
Lilley Clo. E1	57 H1
Lilley La. NW7	30 D5
Lillian Ave. W3	65 A2
Lillian Rd. SW13	65 G6
Lillie Rd. SW6	66 A6
Lillie Rd., West Dr.	66 D6
Lillieshall Rd. SW4	76 B3
Lillington Gdns. Est. SW1	**19 G2**
Lilliput Ave., Nthlt.	54 E1
Lily Clo. W14	66 A4
Gliddon Rd.	
Lily Gdns., Wem.	55 F2
Lily Pl. EC1	**12 F1**
Lily Pl. EC1	58 G5
Lily Rd. E17	42 A6
Lilyville Rd. SW6	75 C1
Limbourne Ave., Dag.	44 F7
Limburg Rd. SW11	75 J4
Lime Clo. E1	**17 J1**
Lime Clo. E1	68 D1
Lime Clo., Brom.	97 B4
Lime Clo., Buck.H.	35 A3
Lime Clo., Cars.	100 J2
Lime Clo., Har.	37 D2
Lime Clo., Rom.	44 J4
Lime Ct., Mitch.	93 G2
Lime Cres., Sun.	90 C2
Lime Gro. N20	31 C1
Lime Gro. W12	65 J2
Lime Gro., Ilf.	35 J6
Lime Gro., N.Mal.	92 D3
Lime Gro., Orp.	104 E2
Lime Gro., Ruis.	36 B6
Lime Gro., Sid.	79 J6
Lime Gro., Twick.	73 C6
Lime Rd., Rich.	73 J4
St. Mary's Gro.	
Lime Row, Erith	71 F3
Northwood Pl.	
Lime St. E17	41 H4
Lime St. EC3	**13 D5**
Lime St. EC3	59 B7
Lime St. Pas. EC3	**13 D5**
Lime Ter. W7	55 B7
Manor Ct. Rd.	
Lime Tree Ave., Esher	98 A1
Lime Tree Ave., T.Ditt.	98 A1
Lime Tree Gro., Croy.	102 J3
Lime Tree Pl., Mitch.	94 B1
Lime Tree Rd., Houns.	72 H1
Lime Tree Wk. (Bushey), Wat.	29 B1
Lime Tree Wk., W.Wick.	103 F4
Lime Wk. E15	60 E1
Church St. N.	
Limeburner La. EC4	**12 G4**
Limeburner La. EC4	58 H6
Limecroft Clo., Epsom	99 D7
Limedene Clo., Pnr.	36 D1
Limeharbour E14	69 B3
Limehouse Causeway E14	59 J7
Limehouse Flds. Est. E14	59 H5
Limerick Clo. SW12	76 C7
Limerston St. SW10	**18 D5**
Limerston St. SW10	66 F6
Limes, The W2	57 D7
Linden Gdns.	
Limes, The, Brom.	104 B2
Limes Ave. E11	42 H4
Limes Ave. N12	31 F4
Limes Ave. NW7	30 E6
Limes Ave. NW11	39 B7
Limes Ave. SE20	86 E7
Limes Ave. SW13	74 F2
Limes Ave., Cars.	100 J1
Limes Ave., Chig.	35 F5
Limes Ave., Croy.	101 G3
Limes Ave., The N11	32 B5
Limes Gdns. SW18	75 D6
Limes Gro. SE13	78 C4
Limes Pl., Croy.	95 A7
Limes Rd., Beck.	96 B2
Limes Rd., Croy.	95 A6
Limes Row, Orp.	104 E5
Orchard Rd.	
Limes Wk. SE15	77 E4
Limes Wk. W5	64 G2
Chestnut Gro.	
Limesdale Gdns., Edg.	38 C2
Limesfield Rd. SW14	74 E3
White Hart La.	
Limesford Rd. SE15	77 G4
Limestone Wk., Erith	71 D3
Alsike Rd.	
Limetree Clo. SW2	85 F1
Limetree Wk. SW17	85 A5
Church La.	
Limewood Clo. W13	55 E6
St. Stephens Rd.	
Limewood Ct., Ilf.	43 C5
Beehive La.	
Limewood Rd., Erith	71 J7
Limpsfield Ave. SW19	84 A2
Limpsfield Ave., Th.Hth.	94 F5
Linacre Ct. W6	66 A5
Linacre Rd. NW2	47 H6
Linberry Wk. SE8	68 H4
Carteret Way	
Linchmere Rd. SE12	78 F7
Lincoln Ave. N14	32 C3
Lincoln Ave. SW19	84 A3
Lincoln Ave., Twick.	81 H2
Lincoln Clo. SE25	95 D6
Woodside Grn.	
Lincoln Clo., Grnf.	54 J1
Lincoln Clo., Har.	36 F5
Lincoln Ct. N16	41 A7
Lincoln Ct., Borwd.	22 D5
Lincoln Cres., Enf.	25 B5
Lincoln Dr., Wat.	28 C3
Lincoln Gdns., Ilf.	43 B7
Lincoln Grn. Rd., Orp.	97 J5
Lincoln Ms. NW6	57 C1
Willesden La.	
Lincoln Ms. SE21	86 A1
Lincoln Rd. E7	52 A6
Lincoln Rd. E13	60 H4
Lincoln Rd. E18	42 G1
Grove Rd.	
Lincoln Rd. N2	39 H3
Lincoln Rd. SE25	95 E3
Lincoln Rd., Enf.	25 B4
Lincoln Rd., Felt.	81 F3
Lincoln Rd., Har.	36 F5
Lincoln Rd., Mitch.	94 E5
Lincoln Rd., N.Mal.	92 C3
Lincoln Rd., Sid.	89 B5
Lincoln Rd., Wem.	46 G6
Lincoln Rd., Wor.Pk.	99 H1
Lincoln St. E11	51 E2
Lincoln St. SW3	**18 J2**
Lincoln St. SW3	66 J4
Lincoln Way, Enf.	25 E5
Lincolns, The NW7	30 F3
Lincoln's Inn Flds. WC2	**12 C3**
Lincoln's Inn Flds. WC2	58 F6
Lincombe Rd., Brom.	87 F3
Lind Rd., Sutt.	100 F5
Lind St. SE8	78 A2
Lindal Cres., Enf.	24 E5
Lindal Rd. SE4	77 J5
Lindales, The N17	33 C6
Brantwood Rd.	
Lindbergh Rd., Wall.	101 E7
Linden Ave. NW10	57 A2
Linden Ave., Enf.	25 D1
Linden Ave., Houns.	72 H5
Linden Ave., Ruis.	45 A1
Linden Ave., Th.Hth.	94 H4
Linden Ave., Wem.	46 J5
Linden Clo. N14	24 C6
Linden Clo., Ruis.	45 A1
Linden Clo., Stan.	29 E5
Linden Clo., T.Ditt.	91 C7

Linden Ct. W12	65 J1	
Linden Cres., Grnf.	46 C6	
Linden Cres., Kings.T.	91 J2	
Linden Cres., Wdf.Grn.	34 H6	
Linden Gdns. W2	57 D7	
Linden Gdns. W4	65 E5	
Linden Gdns., Enf.	25 D1	
Linden Gro. SE15	77 E3	
Linden Gro. SE26	86 F6	
Linden Gro., N.Mal.	92 E3	
Linden Gro., Tedd.	82 C5	
Waldegrave Rd.		
Linden Lawns, Wem.	46 J4	
Linden Lea N2	39 F5	
Linden Leas, W.Wick.	103 G2	
Linden Ms. N1	50 A5	
Mildmay Gro.		
Linden Ms. W2	57 D7	
High St.		
Linden Rd. E17	41 J5	
Linden Rd. N10	40 B4	
Linden Rd. N11	31 J2	
Linden Rd. N15	40 J4	
Linden Rd., Hmptn.	81 G7	
Linden Way N14	24 C6	
Lindenfield, Chis.	97 E2	
Lindens, The N12	31 G5	
Lindens, The W4	74 C1	
Hartington Rd.		
Lindens, The, Croy.	103 C6	
Lindens, The, Loug.	27 C5	
Lindeth Clo., Stan.	29 F6	
Old Ch. La.		
Lindfield Gdns. NW3	48 F5	
Lindfield Rd. W5	55 F4	
Lindfield Rd., Croy.	95 C6	
Lindfield St. E14	60 A6	
Lindisfarne Rd. SW20	83 G7	
Lindisfarne Rd., Dag.	53 C3	
Lindisfarne Way E9	50 H4	
Lindley Est. SE15	21 H7	
Lindley Rd. E10	51 B2	
Lindley St. E1	59 F5	
Lindo St. SE15	77 F2	
Selden Rd.		
Lindore Rd. SW11	75 J4	
Lindores Rd., Cars.	93 F7	
Lindrop St. SW6	75 F2	
Lindsay Clo., Chess.	98 H7	
Lindsay Dr., Har.	37 H6	
Lindsay Rd., Hmptn.	81 H4	
Lindsay Rd., Wor.Pk.	99 H2	
Lindsay Sq. SW1	**19 J4**	
Lindsay Sq. SW1	67 D5	
Lindsell St. SE10	78 C1	
Lindsey Clo., Brom.	97 A3	
Lindsey Clo., Mitch.	94 E4	
Lindsey Ms. N1	49 J7	
Lindsey Rd., Dag.	53 C4	
Lindsey St. EC1	**12 H1**	
Lindsey St. EC1	58 H5	
Lindum Rd., Tedd.	82 F7	
Lindway SE27	85 H5	
Lindwood Clo. E6	61 B5	
Northumberland Rd.		
Linfield Clo. NW4	38 J3	
Linford E17	42 C3	
Linford St. SW8	76 C1	
Ling Rd. E16	60 G5	
Ling Rd., Erith	71 J6	
Lingards Rd. SE13	78 C4	
Lingey Clo., Sid.	88 J2	
Lingfield Ave., Kings.T.	91 H4	
Lingfield Clo., Enf.	25 B6	
Lingfield Cres. SE9	79 G4	
Lingfield Gdns. N9	25 E7	
Lingfield Rd. SW19	84 A6	
Lingfield Rd., Wor.Pk.	99 J3	
Lingham St. SW9	76 E2	
Lingholm Way, Barn.	23 A4	
Lingmere Clo., Chig.	35 F2	
Lingrove Gdns., Buck.H.	34 H2	
Beech La.		
Lings Coppice SE21	86 A2	
Lingwell Rd. SW17	84 H3	
Lingwood Gdns., Islw.	64 B7	
Lingwood Rd. E5	41 D7	
Linhope St. NW1	**6 J5**	
Linhope St. NW1	57 J4	
Link, The W3	56 B6	
Link, The, Enf.	25 H1	
Link, The, Nthlt.	45 F5	
Eastcote La.		
Link, The, Pnr.	36 C7	

Link, The, Wem.	46 F1	
Nathans Rd.		
Link La., Wall.	101 D6	
Link Rd. N11	32 A4	
Link Rd., Dag.	62 H2	
Link Rd., Wall.	101 A1	
Link St. E9	50 F5	
Link Way, Brom.	97 B7	
Link Way, Dag.	53 C4	
Link Way, Pnr.	36 D1	
Linkfield, Brom.	96 G6	
Linkfield, W.Mol.	90 H3	
Linkfield Rd., Islw.	73 C2	
Linklea Clo. NW9	30 E7	
Links, The E17	41 H4	
Links Ave., Mord.	93 D4	
Links Dr. N20	31 D1	
Links Gdns. SW16	85 G7	
Links Rd. NW2	47 F2	
Links Rd. W3	56 A6	
Links Rd., W.Wick.	103 C1	
Links Rd., Wdf.Grn.	34 G5	
Links Side, Enf.	24 F3	
Links Vw. N3	31 C7	
Links Vw. Clo., Stan.	29 D6	
Links Vw. Rd., Croy.	103 A3	
Links Vw. Rd., Hmptn.	81 J5	
Links Way, Beck.	96 A6	
Linkside N12	31 C6	
Linkside, Chig.	35 F5	
Linkside, N.Mal.	92 E2	
Linkside Clo., Enf.	24 F3	
Linkside Gdns., Enf.	24 F3	
Linksway NW4	39 A2	
Linkway N4	40 J7	
Linkway SW20	92 H3	
Linkway, Rich.	82 E3	
Linkway, The, Barn.	23 E6	
Linkwood Wk. NW1	49 D7	
Maiden La.		
Linley Cres., Rom.	44 H3	
Linley Rd. N17	41 B2	
Linnell Clo. NW11	39 E6	
Linnell Dr. NW11	39 E6	
Linnell Rd. N18	33 D5	
Fairfield Rd.		
Linnell Rd. SE5	77 B2	
Linnet Clo. N9	33 G1	
Linnet Clo. SE28	62 C7	
Linnet Ms. SW12	76 A7	
Linnett Clo. E4	34 C4	
Linom Rd. SW4	76 E4	
Linscott Rd. E5	50 F4	
Linsdell Rd., Bark.	61 F1	
Linsey St. SE16	**21 H1**	
Linsey St. SE16	68 D4	
Linslade Clo., Houns.	72 E5	
Frampton Rd.		
Linslade Clo., Pnr.	36 B3	
Linstead Ct. SE9	79 H6	
Linstead St. NW6	48 D7	
Linstead Way SW18	75 B7	
Linster Gro., Borwd.	22 C5	
Lintaine Clo. W6	66 B6	
Moylan Rd.		
Linthorpe Ave., Wem.	46 F6	
Linthorpe Rd. N16	41 B7	
Linthorpe Rd., Barn.	23 H3	
Linton Clo., Well.	80 B1	
Anthony Rd.		
Linton Gdns. E6	61 B6	
Linton Gro. SE27	85 H5	
Linton Rd., Bark.	52 F7	
Linton St. N1	58 J1	
Lintons, The, Bark.	52 F7	
Linver Rd. SW6	75 C2	
Linwood Clo. E6	61 B5	
Northumberland Rd.		
Linwood Clo. SE5	77 C2	
Linwood Way SE15	**21 F7**	
Linzee Rd. N8	40 E4	
Lion Ave., Twick.	82 C1	
Lion La.		
Lion Clo. SE4	78 A6	
Lion Ct., Borwd.	22 C1	
Lion Gate Gdns., Rich.	73 J3	
Lion Pk. Ave., Chess.	99 A4	
Lion Rd. E6	61 C5	
Lion Rd. N9	33 D2	
Lion Rd., Bexh.	80 F4	
Lion Rd., Croy.	94 J5	
Pawson's Rd.		
Lion Rd., Twick.	82 C1	
Lion Way, Brent.	64 G7	
Lion Wf. Rd., Islw.	73 E3	
Lion Yd. SW4	76 D4	
Tremadoc Rd.		

Lionel Gdns. SE9	79 A5	
Lionel Ms. W10	57 B5	
Telford Rd.		
Lionel Rd. SE9	79 A5	
Lionel Rd., Brent.	64 H3	
Lions Clo. SE9	87 J3	
Liphook Cres. SE23	77 F7	
Liphook Rd., Wat.	28 D4	
Lippitts Hill, Loug.	26 E1	
Lipton Clo. SE28	62 C7	
Aisher Rd.		
Lipton Rd. E1	59 G6	
Bower St.		
Lisbon Ave., Twick.	81 J2	
Lisburne Rd. NW3	48 J4	
Lisford St. SE15	77 C1	
Lisgar Ter. W14	66 C4	
Liskeard Clo., Chis.	88 F6	
Liskeard Gdns. SE3	78 G1	
Lisle St. WC2	**11 J5**	
Lisle St. WC2	58 D7	
Lismore Circ. NW5	49 A5	
Wellesley Rd.		
Lismore Clo., Islw.	73 D2	
Lismore Rd. N17	41 A3	
Lismore Rd., S.Croy.	102 B6	
Lismore Wk. N1	49 J6	
Clephane Rd.		
Liss Way SE15	**21 G7**	
Lissenden Gdns. NW5	49 A4	
Lisson Grn. Est. NW8	**6 G4**	
Lisson Grn. Est. NW8	57 H3	
Lisson Gro. NW1	**6 F5**	
Lisson Gro. NW1	57 H4	
Lisson Gro. NW8	**6 F5**	
Lisson Gro. NW8	57 G4	
Lisson St. NW1	**10 G1**	
Lisson St. NW1	57 H5	
Lister Clo. W3	56 D5	
Lister Clo., Mitch.	93 H1	
Lister Gdns. N18	32 J5	
Lister Ho. SE3	69 E6	
Lister Ms. N7	49 F4	
Lister Rd. E11	51 E1	
Lister St. E13	60 G3	
Sewell St.		
Lister Wk. SE28	62 D7	
Haldane Rd.		
Liston Rd. N17	41 D1	
Liston Rd. SW4	76 C3	
Liston Way, Wdf.Grn.	34 J7	
Listowel Clo. SW9	**20 F7**	
Listowel Rd., Dag.	53 G3	
Listria Pk. N16	50 B2	
Litchfield Ave. E15	51 E6	
Litchfield Ave., Mord.	93 C7	
Litchfield Gdns. NW10	47 G6	
Litchfield Rd., Sutt.	100 F4	
Litchfield St. WC2	**11 J5**	
Litchfield St. WC2	58 D7	
Litchfield Way NW11	39 E5	
Lithos Rd. NW3	48 F6	
Little Acre, Beck.	96 A3	
Little Albany St. NW1	**7 E4**	
Little Argyll St. W1	**11 F4**	
Little Birches, Sid.	88 H2	
Little Boltons, The SW10	**18 B3**	
Little Boltons, The SW10	66 E5	
Little Bornes SE21	86 B4	
Little Britain EC1	**12 H2**	
Little Britain EC1	58 H5	
Little Brownings SE23	86 E2	
Little Bury St. N9	33 A1	
Little Cedars N12	31 F4	
Woodside Ave.		
Little Chester St. SW1	**15 D5**	
Little Chester St. SW1	67 B3	
Little College St. SW1	**16 A5**	
Little Ct., W.Wick.	103 G2	
Little Dean's Yd. SW1	**16 A5**	
Little Dimocks SW12	85 B2	
Little Dorrit Ct. SE1	**17 A3**	
Little Dorrit Ct. SE1	67 J2	
Little Dragons, Loug.	27 A4	
Little Ealing La. W5	64 F4	
Little Edward St. NW1	**7 E3**	
Little Essex St. WC2	**12 E5**	
Little Ferry Rd., Twick.	82 E1	
Ferry Rd.		
Little Friday Rd. E4	34 E2	
Little Gearies, Ilf.	43 E4	
Little George St. SW1	**16 A4**	

Little Gra., Grnf.	55 D3	
Perivale La.		
Little Grn., Rich.	73 G4	
Little Grn. St. NW5	49 B4	
College La.		
Little Halliards, Walt.	90 A6	
Felix Rd.		
Little Heath SE7	70 B5	
Little Heath, Rom.	44 B4	
Little Heath Rd., Bexh.	80 E1	
Little Ilford La. E12	52 C4	
Little Marlborough St. W1	**11 F4**	
Little Moss La., Pnr.	36 E2	
Little New St. EC4	**12 F3**	
Little Newport St. WC2	**11 J5**	
Little Newport St. WC2	58 D7	
Little Orchard Clo., Pnr.	36 E2	
Barrow Pt. La.		
Little Oxhey La., Wat.	28 D5	
Little Pk. Dr., Felt.	81 D2	
Little Pk. Gdns., Enf.	24 J3	
Little Plucketts Way, Buck.H.	34 J1	
Little Portland St. W1	**11 E3**	
Little Portland St. W1	58 C6	
Little Queens Rd., Tedd.	82 C6	
Little Redlands, Brom.	97 D3	
Little Rd., Croy.	102 B1	
Lower Addiscombe Rd.		
Little Russell St. WC1	**12 A2**	
Little Russell St. WC1	58 E5	
Little St. James's St. SW1	**15 F2**	
Little St. James's St. SW1	67 C1	
Little St. Leonards SW14	74 C3	
Little Sanctuary SW1	**15 J4**	
Little Smith St. SW1	**15 J5**	
Little Somerset St. E1	**13 F4**	
Little Strand NW9	38 F2	
Little Thrift, Orp.	97 F4	
Little Titchfield St. W1	**11 F2**	
Little Trinity La. EC4	**13 A5**	
Little Turnstile WC1	**12 C2**	
Littlebrook Clo., Croy.	95 G6	
Littlebury Rd. SW4	76 D3	
Littlecombe SE7	69 H6	
Littlecombe Clo. SW15	75 A6	
Littlecote Clo. SW19	75 A7	
Littlecote Pl., Pnr.	36 F1	
Littlecroft SE9	79 D3	
Littledale SE2	71 A6	
Littlefield Clo. N19	49 C4	
Tufnell Pk. Rd.		
Littlefield Clo., Kings.T.	91 H2	
Fairfield W.		
Littlefield Rd., Edg.	30 C7	
Littlegrove, Barn.	23 H6	
Littleheath Rd., S.Croy.	102 E7	
Littlejohn Rd. W7	55 C6	
Littlemead, Esher	98 A4	
Littlemede SE9	88 C3	
Littlemoor Rd., Ilf.	52 G3	
Littlemore Rd. SE2	71 A2	
Littlers Clo. SW19	93 G1	
Runnymede		
Littlestone Clo., Beck.	87 A6	
Abbey La.		
Littleton Ave. E4	34 F1	
Littleton Cres., Har.	46 C2	
Littleton Rd., Har.	46 C2	
Littleton St. SW18	84 F2	
Littlewood SE13	78 C5	
Littlewood Clo. W13	64 E3	
Littleworth Ave., Esher	98 A5	
Littleworth Common Rd., Esher	98 A3	
Littleworth La., Esher	98 A4	
Littleworth Pl., Esher	98 A4	
Littleworth Rd., Esher	98 A5	
Livermere Rd. E8	59 C1	
Liverpool Gro. SE17	**21 B4**	
Liverpool Gro. SE17	68 A5	
Liverpool Rd. E10	42 C6	
Liverpool Rd. E16	60 E5	
Liverpool Rd. N1	49 G7	
Liverpool Rd. N7	49 G5	

Liverpool Rd. W5	64	G2
Liverpool Rd., Kings.T.	83	A7
Liverpool Rd., Th.Hth.	94	J3
Liverpool St. EC2	**13**	**D2**
Liverpool St. EC2	59	B5
Livesey Pl. SE15	**21**	**J5**
Livingston College Twrs. E10	42	C6
Livingstone Pl. E14	69	C5
Ferry St.		
Livingstone Rd. E15	60	C1
Livingstone Rd. E17	42	B6
Livingstone Rd. N13	32	E6
Livingstone Rd. SW11	75	G3
Winstanley Rd.		
Livingstone Rd., Houns.	72	J4
Livingstone Rd., Sthl.	54	D7
Livingstone Rd., Th.Hth.	94	J2
Livingstone Wk. SW11	75	G3
Livonia St. W1	**11**	**G4**
Lizard St. EC1	**9**	**A4**
Lizard St. EC1	58	J3
Lizban St. SE3	69	H7
Llanelly Rd. NW2	48	C2
Llanover Rd. SE18	70	D6
Llanover Rd., Wem.	46	G3
Llanthony Rd., Mord.	93	G6
Llanvanor Rd. NW2	48	C2
Llewellyn St. SE16	**17**	**J4**
Lloyd Ave. SW16	94	E1
Lloyd Baker St. WC1	**8**	**D4**
Lloyd Baker St. WC1	58	F3
Lloyd Ct., Pnr.	36	D5
Lloyd Pk. Ave., Croy.	102	C4
Lloyd Rd. E6	61	C1
Lloyd Rd. E17	41	G4
Lloyd Rd., Dag.	53	F6
Lloyd Rd., Wor.Pk.	99	J3
Lloyd Sq. WC1	**8**	**E3**
Lloyd Sq. WC1	58	G3
Lloyd St. WC1	**8**	**E3**
Lloyd St. WC1	58	G3
Lloyd's Ave. EC3	**13**	**E4**
Lloyd's Ave. EC3	59	B6
Lloyds Pl. SE3	78	E2
Lloyd's Row EC1	**8**	**G4**
Lloyds Way, Beck.	95	H5
Loampit Hill SE13	78	A2
Loampit Vale SE13	78	B3
Loanda Clo. E8	59	C1
Clarissa St.		
Loats Rd. SW2	76	E6
Lobelia Clo. E6	61	B5
Sorrel Gdns.		
Locarno Rd. W3	65	C1
High St.		
Locarno Rd., Grnf.	54	J4
Lochaber Rd. SE13	78	E4
Lochaline St. W6	65	J6
Lochan Clo., Hayes	54	E4
Lochinvar St. SW12	76	B7
Lochmere Clo., Erith	71	H6
Lochnagar St. E14	60	C5
Lock Chase SE3	78	E3
Lock Clo., Sthl.	63	J2
Navigator Dr.		
Lock Rd., Rich.	82	F4
Lockesfield Pl. E14	69	B5
Lockesley Dr., Orp.	97	J6
Lockesley Sq., Surb.	91	G6
Locket Rd., Har.	37	B3
Lockfield Ave., Enf.	25	H2
Lockhart Clo. N7	49	F6
Lockhart Clo., Enf.	25	E5
Derby Rd.		
Lockhart St. E3	59	J4
Lockhurst St. E5	50	G4
Lockie Pl. SE25	95	D3
Lockier Wk., Wem.	46	G3
Hutchinson Ter.		
Lockington Rd. SW8	78	B1
Lockmead Rd. N15	41	D6
Lockmead Rd. SE13	78	C3
Locks La., Mitch.	93	J1
Lockside E14	59	H7
Northey St.		
Locksley Est. E14	59	J6
Locksley St. E14	59	J5
Locksmeade Rd., Rich.	82	F4
Lockwood Clo. SE26	86	G4
Lockwood Ind. Pk. N17	41	E3

Lockwood Sq. SE16	68	E3
Lockwood Way E17	41	G2
Lockwood Way, Chess.	99	A5
Lockyer Est. SE1	**17**	**C3**
Lockyer St. SE1	**17**	**C4**
Loddiges Rd. E9	50	F7
Loder St. SE15	68	F7
Lodge Ave. SW14	74	E3
Lodge Ave., Croy.	101	G3
Lodge Ave., Dag.	62	A1
Lodge Ave., Har.	37	H4
Lodge Clo. N18	32	J5
Lodge Clo., Edg.	29	J6
Lodge Clo., Islw.	73	E1
Lodge Clo., Wall.	101	A1
Lodge Ct., Wem.	46	H5
Lodge Dr. N13	32	G4
Lodge Gdns., Beck.	95	J5
Lodge Hill SE2	71	B7
Lodge Hill, Ilf.	43	B4
Lodge Hill, Well.	71	B7
Lodge La. N12	31	F5
Lodge La., Bex.	80	D6
Lodge La., Croy.	103	A6
Lodge Pl., Sutt.	100	E5
Lodge Rd. NW8	**6**	**F4**
Lodge Rd. NW8	57	G3
Lodge Rd., Brom.	87	H7
Lodge Rd., Croy.	94	H6
Lodge Rd., Sutt.	100	E5
Throwley Way		
Lodge Rd., Wall.	101	B5
Lodge Vill., Wdf.Grn.	34	F7
Lodgehill Pk. Clo., Har.	45	H2
Lodore Gdns. NW9	38	E5
Lodore St. E14	60	C6
Lofthouse Pl., Chess.	98	F6
Mansfield Rd.		
Loftie St. SE16	**17**	**J4**
Loftie St. SE16	68	D2
Lofting Rd. N1	49	F7
Loftus Rd. W12	65	H1
Logan Clo., Enf.	25	G1
Logan Clo., Houns.	72	F3
Logan Ms. W8	66	D4
Logan Pl. W8	66	D4
Logan Rd. N9	33	E2
Logan Rd., Wem.	46	H2
Loggetts, The SE21	86	A3
Logs Hill, Chis.	88	B7
Logs Hill Clo., Chis.	97	B1
Lolesworth Clo. E1	**13**	**G2**
Lollard St. SE11	67	G4
Lollard St. SE11	**20**	**D1**
Loman St. SE1	**16**	**H3**
Loman St. SE1	67	H2
Lomas Clo., Croy.	103	C7
Lomas St. E1	**13**	**J1**
Lomas St. E1	59	D5
Lombard Ave., Enf.	25	F1
Lombard Ave., Ilf.	52	H1
Lombard Business Pk. SW19	93	E2
Lombard Ct. EC3	**13**	**C5**
Lombard La. EC4	**12**	**F4**
Lombard Rd. N11	32	B5
Lombard Rd. SW11	75	G2
Lombard Rd. SW19	93	E2
Lombard St. EC3	**13**	**C4**
Lombard St. EC3	59	A6
Lombard Wall SE7	69	H3
Lombardy Pl. W2	**10**	**A6**
Lomond Clo. N15	41	B5
Lomond Clo., Wem.	46	J7
Lomond Gdns., S.Croy.	102	H7
Lomond Gro. SE5	**21**	**B7**
Lomond Gro. SE5	68	A7
Lomond Ho. SE5	77	A1
Lomond Gro.		
Loncroft Rd. SE5	**21**	**E5**
Loncroft Rd. SE5	68	B6
Londesborough Rd. N16	50	B4
London Bri. EC4	**17**	**C1**
London Bri. EC4	59	A7
London Bri. SE1	**17**	**C1**
London Bri. SE1	68	A1
London Bri. St. SE1	**17**	**C2**
London Bri. St. SE1	68	A1
London Bri. Wk. SE1	**17**	**C1**
London City Airport E16	70	B1
London Flds. E8	50	E7

London Flds. E. Side E8	50	E7
London Flds. W. Side E8	50	D7
London Ind. Pk. E6	61	E5
London La. E8	50	E7
London La., Brom.	87	F7
London Ms. W2	**10**	**F4**
London Rd. E13	60	G2
London Rd. SE1	**16**	**G5**
London Rd. SE1	67	H3
London Rd. SE23	86	E1
London Rd. SW16	94	F1
London Rd. SW17	84	J7
London Rd., Bark.	52	E7
London Rd., Brent.	73	C2
London Rd., Brom.	87	F7
London Rd., Croy.	94	G5
London Rd., Enf.	25	A4
London Rd., Epsom	99	G7
London Rd., Har.	46	B2
London Rd., Houns.	72	J3
London Rd., Islw.	73	C2
London Rd., Kings.T.	91	J2
London Rd., Mitch.	93	H4
London Rd., Mitch. (Mitcham Junct.)	94	A7
London Rd., Mord.	93	D5
London Rd., Rom.	44	G6
London Rd., Stan.	29	F5
London Rd., Sutt.	99	J3
London Rd., Th.Hth.	94	G5
London Rd., Twick.	73	D7
London Rd., Wall.	101	B4
London Rd., Wem.	46	H5
London Stile W4	65	A5
Wellesley Rd.		
London St. EC3	**13**	**E5**
London St. W2	**10**	**E3**
London St. W2	57	G6
London Wall EC2	**13**	**A2**
London Wall EC2	58	J5
Long Acre WC2	12	A5
Long Acre WC2	58	E7
Long Ct. WC2	**11**	**J6**
Long Deacon Rd. E4	34	E1
Long Dr. W3	56	G6
Long Dr., Grnf.	54	H1
Long Dr., Ruis.	45	D4
Long Elmes, Har.	36	H1
Long Fld. NW9	30	E7
Long Grn., Chig.	35	H4
Long Hedges, Houns.	72	G1
Great W. Rd.		
Long La. EC1	**12**	**H1**
Long La. EC1	58	H5
Long La. N2	39	F2
Long La. N3	31	E7
Long La. SE1	**17**	**B4**
Long La. SE1	68	A2
Long La., Bexh.	71	B4
Long La., Croy.	95	E6
Long Leys E4	34	B6
Long Mark Rd. E16	61	A5
Fulmer Rd.		
Long Mead NW9	38	F1
Long Meadow NW5	49	D5
Torriano Ave.		
Long Meadow Clo., W.Wick.	96	C7
Long Pond Rd. SE3	78	E1
Long Reach Ct., Bark.	61	G2
Long Reach Rd., Bark.	61	J4
Long Rd. SW4	76	B4
Long St. E2	**9**	**F3**
Long St. E2	59	C3
Long Wk. SE1	**17**	**E5**
Long Wk. SE18	70	E6
Long Wk. SW13	74	E2
The Ter.		
Long Wk., N.Mal.	92	C3
Long Yd. WC1	**8**	**C6**
Long Yd. WC1	58	F4
Longacre Pl., Cars.	101	A6
Beddington Gdns.		
Longacre Rd. E17	42	D1
Longbeach Rd. SW11	75	J3
Longberrys NW2	48	C3
Longboat Row, Sthl.	54	F6
Longbridge Rd., Bark.	52	E6
Longbridge Rd., Dag.	53	A4
Longbridge Way SE13	78	C5
Longcliffe Path, Wat.	28	A3
Gosforth La.		
Longcroft SE9	88	C3
Longcroft Ri., Loug.	27	D5
Longcrofte Rd., Edg.	29	G7

Longdon Wd., Kes.	104	B3
Longdown Rd. SE6	87	A4
Longfellow Rd. E17	41	J6
Longfellow Rd., Wor.Pk.	99	G1
Longfellow Way SE1	**21**	**G2**
Longfield, Brom.	96	F1
Longfield, Loug.	26	J5
Longfield Ave. E17	41	H4
Longfield Ave. NW7	30	G7
Longfield Ave. W5	55	F7
Longfield Ave., Wall.	101	A1
Longfield Ave., Wem.	46	H1
Longfield Cres. SE26	86	F3
Longfield Dr. SW14	74	B5
Longfield Dr., Mitch.	84	H7
Longfield Est. SE1	**21**	**G2**
Longfield Est. SE1	68	C4
Longfield Rd. W5	55	F6
Longfield St. SW18	75	D7
Longfield Wk. W5	55	F6
Longford Ave., Sthl.	54	G7
Longford Clo., Hmptn.	81	G4
Longford Clo., Hayes	54	D7
Longford Gdns.		
Longford Ct. E5	50	G4
Pedro St.		
Longford Ct. NW4	39	A4
Longford Ct., Epsom	99	C4
Longford Gdns., Hayes	54	D7
Longford Gdns., Sutt.	100	F3
Longford Rd., Twick.	81	G1
Longford St. NW1	**7**	**E5**
Longford St. NW1	58	B4
Longford Wk. SW2	76	G7
Papworth Way		
Longhayes Ave., Rom.	44	D4
Longheath Gdns., Croy.	95	F5
Longhedge Ho. SE26	86	C4
Longhedge St. SW11	76	A2
Longhill Rd. SE6	87	D2
Longhook Gdns., Nthlt.	54	A2
Longhope Clo. SE15	**21**	**F6**
Longhope Clo. SE15	68	B6
Longhurst Rd. SE13	78	D5
Longhurst Rd., Croy.	95	E6
Longland Ct. SE1	**21**	**H3**
Longland Dr. N20	31	E3
Longlands Ct. W11	57	C7
Portobello Rd.		
Longlands Ct., Mitch.	94	A1
Summerhill Way		
Longlands Pk. Cres., Sid.	88	H3
Longlands Rd., Sid.	88	H3
Longleat Rd., Enf.	25	B5
Longleigh La. SE2	71	C6
Longleigh La., Bexh.	71	C6
Longlents Ho. NW10	56	D1
Shrewsbury Cres.		
Longley Ave., Wem.	55	J1
Longley Rd. SW17	84	H6
Longley Rd., Croy.	94	H7
Longley Rd., Har.	36	J5
Longley St. SE1	**21**	**H1**
Longley St. SE1	68	C4
Longley Way NW2	47	J3
Longmead, Chis.	97	D2
Longmead Dr., Sid.	89	D2
Longmead Rd. SW17	84	J5
Longmead Rd., T.Ditt.	91	H7
Longmeadow Rd., Sid.	88	H1
Longmoor Pt. SW15	83	H1
Norley Vale		
Longmoore St. SW1	**19**	**F2**
Longmoore St. SW1	67	C4
Longmore Ave., Barn.	23	F6
Longnor Rd. E1	59	G3
Longridge La., Sthl.	54	H6
Longridge Rd. SW5	66	D4
Longs Ct., Rich.	73	G4
Crown Ter.		
Longshaw Rd. E4	34	D3
Longshore SE8	68	J4
Longstaff Cres. SW18	75	D6
Longstaff Rd. SW18	75	D6
Longstone Ave. NW10	47	F7
Longstone Rd. SW17	85	B5
Longthornton Rd. SW16	94	C2

Longton Ave. SE26 86 D4
Longton Gro. SE26 86 E4
Longville Rd. SE11 20 H1
Longwood Dr. SW15 74 G6
Longwood Gdns., Ilf. 43 C4
Longworth Clo. SE28 62 D6
Loning, The NW9 38 E4
Lonsdale Ave. E6 61 A3
Lonsdale Ave., Rom. 44 J6
Lonsdale Ave., Wem. 46 H5
Lonsdale Clo. E6 61 B4
Lonsdale Ave.
Lonsdale Clo. SE9 88 A3
Lonsdale Clo., Edg. 29 J5
Orchard Dr.
Lonsdale Clo., Pnr. 28 E7
Lonsdale Cres., Ilf. 43 E6
Lonsdale Dr., Enf. 24 D4
Lonsdale Gdns., 94 F4
Th.Hth.
Lonsdale Ms., Rich. 74 A1
Lonsdale Pl. N1 49 G7
Barnsbury St.
Lonsdale Rd. E11 42 F7
Lonsdale Rd. NW6 57 C1
Lonsdale Rd. SE25 95 E4
Lonsdale Rd. SW13 74 F1
Lonsdale Rd. W4 65 F4
Lonsdale Rd. W11 57 C6
Lonsdale Rd., Bexh. 80 F2
Lonsdale Rd., Sthl. 63 D3
Lonsdale Sq. N1 58 G1
Loobert Rd. N15 41 B3
Looe Gdns., Ilf. 43 E3
Loop Rd., Chis. 88 F6
Lopen Rd. N18 33 B4
Loraine Clo., Enf. 25 F5
Loraine Rd. N7 49 F4
Loraine Rd. W4 65 B6
Lord Ave., Ilf. 43 C4
Lord Chancellor Wk., 92 C1
Kings.T.
Lord Gdns., Ilf. 43 B4
Lord Hills Bri. W2 10 B2
Lord Hills Rd. W2 10 B1
Lord Hills Rd. W2 57 E5
Lord Holland La. SW9 76 G1
Myatt's Flds. S.
Lord Napier Pl. W6 65 G5
Upper Mall
Lord N. St. SW1 16 A6
Lord N. St. SW1 67 E3
Lord Roberts Ms. 66 E7
SW6
Moore Pk. Rd.
Lord Roberts Ter. 70 D5
SE18
Lord St. E16 70 B1
Lord Warwick St. 70 C3
SE18
Lorden Wk. E2 9 H4
Lord's Clo. SE21 85 J2
Lords Clo., Felt. 81 E2
Lord's Vw. NW8 6 F4
Lordship Gro. N16 50 A2
Lordship La. N17 40 J1
Lordship La. N22 40 G2
Lordship La. SE22 77 C6
Lordship La. Est. 86 D1
SE22
Lordship Pk. N16 49 J2
Lordship Pk. Ms. N16 49 J2
Allerton Rd.
Lordship Pl. SW3 18 G6
Lordship Rd. N16 50 A1
Lordship Rd., Nthlt. 45 E7
Lordship Ter. N16 50 A2
Lordsmead Rd. N17 41 B1
Lorenzo St. WC1 8 C2
Lorenzo St. WC1 58 F3
Loretto Gdns., Har. 37 H4
Lorian Clo. N12 31 E4
Loring Rd. N20 31 H2
Loring Rd., Islw. 73 C2
Loris Rd. W6 65 J3
Lorn Rd. SW9 76 F2
Lorne Ave., Croy. 95 G7
Lorne Clo. NW8 6 H4
Lorne Gdns. E11 42 J4
Lorne Gdns. W11 66 A2
Lorne Gdns., Croy. 95 G7
Lorne Rd. E7 51 H4
Lorne Rd. E17 42 A5
Lorne Rd. N4 49 F1
Lorne Rd., Har. 37 C2
Lorne Rd., Rich. 73 J5
Albert Rd.
Lorraine Pk., Har. 29 B7

Lorrimore Rd. SE17 20 H5
Lorrimore Rd. SE17 67 H6
Lorrimore Sq. SE17 20 H5
Lorrimore Sq. SE17 67 H6
Losberne Way SE16 21 J4
Loseberry Rd., Esher 98 A5
Lothair Rd. W5 64 G2
Lothair Rd. N. N4 40 H6
Lothair Rd. S. N4 40 G7
Lothbury EC2 13 B3
Lothbury EC2 59 A6
Lothian Ave., Hayes 54 B5
Lothian Clo., Wem. 46 D4
Lothian Rd. SW9 76 H1
Lothrop St. W10 57 B3
Lots Rd. SW10 66 F7
Loubet St. SW17 84 J6
Loudoun Ave., Ilf. 43 E5
Loudoun Rd. NW8 48 F7
Loudoun Rd. Ms. 57 F1
NW8
Loudoun Rd.
Loudwater Clo., Sun. 90 A4
Loudwater Rd., Sun. 90 A4
Lough Rd. N7 49 F5
Loughborough Est. 76 H2
SW9
Loughborough Rd.
Loughborough Pk. 76 H4
SW9
Loughborough Rd. 76 G2
SW9
Loughborough St. 20 D4
SE11
Loughborough St. 67 F5
SE11
Loughton Way, 35 A1
Buck.H.
Louisa Gdns. E1 59 G4
Louisa St.
Louisa Ho. SW15 74 F4
Arabella Dr.
Louisa St. E1 59 G4
Louise Bennett Clo. 76 H4
SE24
Shakespeare Rd.
Louise Rd. E15 51 E6
Louisville Rd. SW17 85 A3
Louvaine Rd. SW11 75 G4
Lovage App. E6 61 B5
Lovat Clo. NW2 47 F3
Lovat La. EC3 13 D6
Lovat La. EC3 59 B7
Lovat Wk., Houns. 63 E7
Cranford La.
Lovatt Clo., Edg. 30 B6
Love La. EC2 13 A3
Love La. EC2 58 J6
Love La. N17 33 C7
Love La. SE18 70 E4
Love La. SE25 95 E3
Love La., Bex. 80 F6
Love La., Mitch. 93 H3
Love La., Mord. 93 D7
Love La., Pnr. 36 E3
Love La., Surb. 98 F2
Love La., Sutt. 100 B6
Love La., Wdf.Grn. 35 C6
Love Wk. SE5 77 A2
Loveday Rd. W13 64 E1
Lovegrove St. SE1 21 J5
Lovegrove St. SE1 68 D5
Lovegrove Wk. E14 69 C1
Lovekyn Clo., Kings.T. 91 J2
Queen Elizabeth Rd.
Lovel Ave., Well. 80 A2
Lovelace Ave., Brom. 97 D6
Lovelace Gdns., Bark. 53 A4
Lovelace Gdns., Surb. 91 G7
Lovelace Grn. SE9 79 C3
Lovelace Rd. SE21 85 J2
Lovelace Rd., Barn. 23 H7
Lovelace Rd., Surb. 91 F7
Lovelinch Clo. SE15 68 F6
Lovell Ho. E8 59 D1
Lovell Pl. SE16 68 H3
Ropemaker Rd.
Lovell Rd., Rich. 82 F3
Lovell Rd., Sthl. 54 H6
Loveridge Ms. NW6 48 C6
Loveridge Rd.
Loveridge Rd. NW6 48 C6
Lovers Wk. N3 31 D7
Lovers Wk. NW7 31 D7
Lovers Wk. SE10 69 E7
Lover's Wk. W1 15 B1
Lover's Wk. W1 67 A1
Lovett Dr., Cars. 93 F7
Lovett Way NW10 47 C5

Lovett's Pl. SW18 75 E4
Old York Rd.
Lovibonds Ave., 104 E3
Orp.
Low Cross Wd. La. 86 C3
SE21
Low Hall Clo. E4 26 A7
Low Hall La. E17 41 H6
Lowbrook Rd., Ilf. 52 E4
Lowden Rd. N9 33 E1
Lowden Rd. SE24 76 J4
Lowden Rd., Sthl. 54 E7
Lowe Ave. E16 60 G5
Charford Rd.
Lowell St. E14 59 H6
Lower Addiscombe 102 B1
Rd., Croy.
Lower Addison Gdns. 66 B2
W14
Lower Alderton Hall 27 D5
La., Loug.
Lower Belgrave St. 15 D6
SW1
Lower Belgrave St. 67 B3
SW1
Lower Boston Rd. W7 64 B1
Lower Broad St., Dag. 62 G1
Lower Camden, Chis. 88 C7
Lower Ch. St., Croy. 101 H2
Waddon New Rd.
Lower Clapton Rd. E5 50 F5
Lower Clarendon Wk. 57 B6
W11
Lancaster Rd.
Lower Common S. 74 H3
SW15
Lower Coombe St., 101 J4
Croy.
Lower Downs Rd. 93 A1
SW20
Lower Drayton Pl., 101 H2
Croy.
Drayton Rd.
Lower George St., 73 G5
Rich.
George St.
Lower Gravel Rd., 104 B1
Brom.
Lower Grn. W., Mitch. 93 H3
Lower Grosvenor Pl. 15 D5
SW1
Lower Grosvenor Pl. 67 B3
SW1
Lower Gro. Rd., Rich. 73 J6
Lower Hall La. E4 33 H5
Lower Ham Rd., 82 G6
Kings.T.
Lower Hampton Rd., 90 C3
Sun.
Lower James St. W1 11 G5
Lower John St. W1 11 G5
Lower Kenwood 24 D5
Ave., Enf.
Lower Lea Crossing 60 E7
E14
Lower Maidstone Rd. 32 C6
N11
Telford Rd.
Lower Mall W6 65 H5
Lower Mardyke Ave., 62 J2
Rain.
Lower Marsh SE1 16 E4
Lower Marsh SE1 67 F2
Lower Marsh La., 91 J4
Kings.T.
Lower Merton Ri. 48 H7
NW3
Lower Morden La., 93 A6
Mord.
Lower Mortlake Rd., 73 H4
Rich.
Lower Pk. Rd. N11 32 C5
Lower Pk. Rd., Belv. 71 G3
Lower Pk. Rd., Loug. 27 A5
Lower Queens Rd., 35 A2
Buck.H.
Lower Richmond Rd. 74 B3
SW14
Lower Richmond Rd. 74 H3
SW15
Lower Richmond Rd., 74 A3
Rich.
Lower Rd. SE8 68 G4
Lower Rd. SE16 68 F3
Lower Rd., Belv. 71 H3
Lower Rd., Har. 46 A1
Lower Rd., Loug. 27 D1
Lower Rd., Sutt. 100 F4

Lower Robert St. 12 B6
WC2
Lower Sloane St. 19 B2
SW1
Lower Sloane St. 67 A4
SW1
Lower Sq., Islw. 73 E3
Lower Strand NW9 38 F2
Lower Sunbury Rd., 90 F2
Hmptn.
Lower Sydenham 86 J5
Ind. Est. SE26
Lower Tail, Wat. 28 E3
Lower Talbot Wk. W11 57 B6
Lancaster Rd.
Lower Teddington 82 G7
Rd., Kings.T.
Lower Ter. NW3 48 F3
Lower Thames St. 13 C6
EC3
Lower Thames St. 59 A7
EC3
Lower Wd. Rd., Esher 98 D6
Lowestoft Clo. E5 50 F2
Theydon Rd.
Loweswater Clo., 46 G2
Wem.
Lowfield Rd. NW6 48 D7
Lowfield Rd. W3 56 C6
Lowick Rd., Har. 37 B4
Lowlands Gdns., 44 H6
Rom.
Lowlands Rd., Har. 37 B6
Lowlands Rd., Pnr. 36 C6
Lowman Rd. N7 49 F4
Lowndes Clo. SW1 15 C6
Lowndes Clo. SW1 67 A3
Lowndes Pl. SW1 15 B6
Lowndes Pl. SW1 67 A3
Lowndes Sq. SW1 15 A4
Lowndes Sq. SW1 66 J2
Lowndes St. SW1 15 A5
Lowndes St. SW1 66 J3
Lowood Ct. SE19 86 C5
Lowood St. E1 59 E7
Dellow St.
Lowry Cres., Mitch. 93 H2
Lowshoe La., Rom. 44 G1
Lowth Rd. SE5 76 J2
Lowther Dr., Enf. 24 E4
Lowther Gdns. SW7 14 E4
Lowther Hill SE23 77 H7
Lowther Rd. E17 41 H2
Lowther Rd. N7 49 G5
Mackenzie Rd.
Lowther Rd. SW13 74 F1
Lowther Rd., Kings.T. 91 J1
Lowther Rd., Stan. 37 J3
Loxford Ave. E6 61 A2
Loxford La., Ilf. 52 F5
Loxford Rd., Bark. 52 J4
Loxham Rd. E4 34 A7
Loxham St. WC1 8 B4
Loxley Clo. SE26 86 G5
Loxley Rd. SW18 84 G1
Loxley Rd., Hmptn. 81 F4
Loxton Rd. SE23 86 G1
Loxwood Rd. N17 41 B3
Lubbock Rd., Chis. 88 C7
Lubbock St. SE14 68 F7
Lucan Pl. SW3 18 G2
Lucan Pl. SW3 66 H4
Lucan Rd., Barn. 23 B3
Lucas Ave. E13 60 H1
Lucas Ave., Har. 45 G2
Lucas Ct., Har. 45 G1
Lucas Rd. SE20 86 F6
Lucas Sq. NW11 39 D6
Hampstead Way
Lucas St. SE8 78 A1
Lucerne Clo. N13 32 E3
Lucerne Ct., Erith 71 E3
Middle Way
Lucerne Gro. E17 42 D4
Lucerne Ms. W8 66 D1
Kensington Mall
Lucerne Rd. N5 49 H4
Lucerne Rd., Orp. 104 J1
Lucerne Rd., Th.Hth. 94 H5
Lucey Rd. SE16 17 H6
Lucey Rd. SE16 68 D3
Lucey Way SE16 17 J6
Lucien Rd. SW17 85 A4
Lucien Rd. SW19 84 E2
Lucknow St. SE18 70 H7
Lucorn Clo. SE12 78 F6
Luctons Ave., Buck.H. 34 J1
Lucy Cres. W3 56 C5

Lucy Gdns., Dag.	53	E3
Grafton Rd.		
Luddesdon Rd., Erith	71	G6
Ludford Clo. NW9	38	E2
Ludford Clo., Croy.	101	H4
Warrington Rd.		
Ludgate Bdy. EC4	**12**	**G4**
Ludgate Bdy. EC4	58	H6
Ludgate Circ. EC4	**12**	**G4**
Ludgate Hill EC4	**12**	**G4**
Ludgate Hill EC4	58	H6
Ludgate Sq. EC4	**12**	**H4**
Ludham Clo. SE28	62	C6
Rollesby Way		
Ludlow Clo., Brom.	96	G3
Ludlow Clo., Har.	45	F4
Ludlow Mead, Wat.	28	B3
Ludlow Rd. W5	55	F4
Ludlow Rd., Felt.	81	A4
Ludlow St. EC1	**8**	**J5**
Ludlow Way N2	39	F4
Ludovick Wk. SW16	74	E4
Ludwick Ms. SE14	68	H7
Luffield Rd. SE2	71	B3
Luffman Rd. SE12	87	H3
Lugard Rd. SE15	77	E2
Lugg App. E12	52	D3
Romford Rd.		
Luke Ho. E1	59	E6
Luke St. EC2	**9**	**D5**
Luke St. EC2	59	B4
Lukin Cres. E4	34	D3
Lukin St. E1	59	F6
Lullingstone Clo., Orp.	89	B7
Lullingstone Cres.		
Lullingstone Cres., Orp.	89	A7
Lullingstone Rd., Belv.	71	F6
Lullington Garth N12	31	C5
Lullington Garth, Borwd.	22	B5
Lullington Garth, Brom.	87	E7
Lullington Rd. SE20	86	D7
Lullington Rd., Dag.	53	E7
Lulot Gdns. N19	49	B2
Dartmouth Pk. Hill		
Lulworth SE17	**21**	**B3**
Lulworth Ave., Houns.	63	H7
Lulworth Ave., Wem.	37	F7
Lulworth Clo., Har.	45	F3
Lulworth Cres., Mitch.	93	H2
Lulworth Dr., Pnr.	36	D7
Lulworth Gdns., Har.	45	E2
Lulworth Rd. SE9	88	B2
Lulworth Rd. SE15	77	E2
Lulworth Rd., Well.	79	J2
Lulworth Waye, Hayes	54	B6
Lumen Rd., Wem.	46	G2
Lumley Clo., Belv.	71	G6
Lumley Ct. WC2	**12**	**B6**
Lumley Gdns., Sutt.	100	B5
Lumley Rd., Sutt.	100	B6
Lumley St. W1	**11**	**C4**
Lumley St. W1	58	A6
Luna Rd., Th.Hth.	94	J3
Lunar Ho., Croy.	101	J1
Lundin Wk., Wat.	28	D4
Woodhall La.		
Lundy Wk. N1	49	J6
Marquess Est.		
Lunham Rd. SE19	86	B6
Lupin Clo. SW2	85	H2
Palace Rd.		
Lupin Clo., Croy.	102	G1
Primrose La.		
Lupton Clo. SE12	87	H4
Lupton St. NW5	49	C4
Lupus St. SW1	**19**	**E4**
Lupus St. SW1	67	B5
Luralda Gdns. E14	69	C5
Saunders Ness Rd.		
Lurgan Ave. W6	66	A6
Lurline Gdns. SW11	76	A1
Luscombe Ct., Brom.	96	E2
Luscombe Way SW8	**20**	**A7**
Luscombe Way SW8	67	E7
Lushes Rd., Loug.	27	E5
Lushington Rd. NW10	56	H2
Lushington Rd. SE6	87	B5
Lushington Ter. E8	50	D5
Wayland Ave.		
Luther Clo., Edg.	30	C2
Luther King Clo. E17	41	H6
Luther Rd., Tedd.	82	C5
Luton Pl. SE10	69	C7
Luton Rd. E17	41	J3
Luton Rd., Sid.	89	C3
Luton St. NW8	**6**	**F6**
Luton St. NW8	57	G4
Lutton Ter. NW3	48	G4
Flask Wk.		
Luttrell Ave. SW15	74	H5
Lutwyche Rd. SE6	86	J2
Luxborough La., Chig.	35	B3
Luxborough St. W1	**7**	**B6**
Luxborough St. W1	58	A5
Luxemburg Gdns. W6	66	A4
Luxfield Rd. SE9	88	B1
Luxford St. SE16	68	G4
Luxmore Gdns. SE4	77	J1
Luxmore St.		
Luxmore St. SE4	77	J1
Luxor St. SE5	76	J3
Lyal Rd. E3	59	H2
Lyall Ave. SE21	86	B3
Lyall Ms. SW1	**15**	**B6**
Lyall Ms. SW1	67	A3
Lyall Ms. W. SW1	**15**	**B6**
Lyall St. SW1	**15**	**B6**
Lyall St. SW1	67	A3
Lycett Pl. W12	65	G2
Becklow Rd.		
Lyconby Gdns., Croy.	95	H7
Lydd Clo., Sid.	88	H3
Lydd Rd., Bexh.	71	F7
Lydden Ct. SE9	79	H6
Lydden Gro. SW18	75	E7
Lydden Rd. SW18	75	E7
Lydeard Rd. E6	52	C7
Lydford Rd. N15	41	A5
Lydford Rd. NW2	47	J6
Lydford Rd. W9	57	C4
Lydhurst Ave. SW2	85	F2
Lydney Clo. SE15	**21**	**E7**
Lydney Clo. SW19	84	B2
Princes Way		
Lydon Rd. SW4	76	C3
Lydstep Rd., Chis.	88	D4
Lyford Rd. SW18	75	G7
Lygon Pl. SW1	**15**	**D6**
Lyham Clo. SW2	76	E6
Lyham Rd. SW2	76	E5
Lyle Clo., Mitch.	94	A7
Wolseley Rd.		
Lyme Fm. Rd. SE12	78	G4
Lyme Gro. E9	50	F7
St. Thomas's Sq.		
Lyme Rd., Well.	80	B1
Lyme St. NW1	49	C7
Lyme Ter. NW1	49	C7
Royal College St.		
Lymer Ave. SE19	86	C5
Lymescote Gdns., Sutt.	100	D3
Lyminge Clo., Sid.	88	J4
Lyminge Gdns. SW18	84	H1
Lymington Ave. N22	40	G2
Lymington Clo. E6	61	C5
Lymington Clo. SW16	94	D2
Lymington Gdns., Epsom	99	F5
Lymington Rd. NW6	48	E6
Lymington Rd., Dag.	53	D1
Lympstone Gdns. SE15	**21**	**J7**
Lympstone Gdns. SE15	68	D7
Lynbridge Gdns. N13	32	H4
Lynbrook Clo. SE15	**21**	**E7**
Lynch Wk. SE8	68	J6
Prince St.		
Lynchen Clo., Houns.	72	A1
The Ave.		
Lyncott Cres. SW4	76	B4
Lyncroft Ave., Pnr.	36	E5
Lyncroft Gdns. NW6	48	D5
Lyncroft Gdns. W13	64	F2
Lyncroft Gdns., Houns.	72	J5
Lyndale NW2	48	C4
Lyndale Ave. NW2	48	C3
Lyndale Clo. SE3	69	F6
Lyndhurst Ave. N12	31	J4
Lyndhurst Ave. NW7	30	E6
Lyndhurst Ave. SW16	94	D2
Lyndhurst Ave., Pnr.	36	B1
Lyndhurst Ave., Sthl.	63	H1
Lyndhurst Ave., Sun.	90	A3
Lyndhurst Ave., Surb.	99	B1
Lyndhurst Ave., Twick.	81	F1
Lyndhurst Clo. NW10	47	D3
Lyndhurst Clo., Bexh.	80	H3
Lyndhurst Clo., Croy.	102	C3
Lyndhurst Clo., Orp.	104	E4
Lyndhurst Dr. E10	42	C7
Lyndhurst Dr., N.Mal.	92	E6
Lyndhurst Gdns. N3	39	B1
Lyndhurst Gdns. NW3	48	G5
Lyndhurst Gdns., Bark.	52	H6
Lyndhurst Gdns., Enf.	25	B4
Lyndhurst Gdns., Ilf.	43	G6
Lyndhurst Gdns., Pnr.	36	B1
Lyndhurst Gro. SE15	77	B2
Lyndhurst Ri., Chig.	35	D4
Lyndhurst Rd. E4	34	C7
Lyndhurst Rd. N18	33	D4
Lyndhurst Rd. N22	32	F6
Lyndhurst Rd. NW3	48	G5
Lyndhurst Rd., Bexh.	80	H3
Lyndhurst Rd., Grnf.	54	H4
Lyndhurst Rd., Th.Hth.	94	G4
Lyndhurst Sq. SE15	77	C1
Lyndhurst Ter. NW3	48	G5
Lyndhurst Way SE15	77	C1
Lyndhurst Way, Sutt.	100	D7
Lyndon Ave., Pnr.	28	E6
Lyndon Ave., Sid.	79	J5
Lyndon Rd., Belv.	71	G4
Lyne Cres. E17	41	J1
Lyneham Wk. E5	50	H5
Ashenden Rd.		
Lynett Rd., Dag.	53	D2
Lynette Ave. SW4	76	B6
Lynford Clo., Edg.	38	C1
Lynford Gdns., Edg.	30	B3
Lynford Gdns., Ilf.	52	J2
Lynmere Rd., Well.	80	B2
Lynmouth Ave., Enf.	25	C6
Lynmouth Ave., Mord.	93	A7
Lynmouth Dr., Ruis.	45	B2
Lynmouth Gdns., Grnf.	55	E1
Lynmouth Gdns., Houns.	72	D1
Lynmouth Rd. E17	41	H6
Lynmouth Rd. N2	39	J4
Lynmouth Rd. N16	50	C1
Lynmouth Rd., Grnf.	55	E1
Lynn Clo., Har.	37	A2
Lynn Rd.		
Lynn Rd. E11	51	E2
Lynn Rd. SW12	76	B7
Lynn Rd., Ilf.	43	G7
Lynn St., Enf.	25	A1
Lynne Clo., Orp.	104	J6
Lynne Way NW10	47	E6
Lynne Way, Nthlt.	54	D2
Lynsted Clo., Bexh.	80	H5
Lynsted Clo., Brom.	96	J3
Lynsted Ct., Beck.	95	H2
Churchfields Rd.		
Lynsted Gdns. SE9	79	A3
Lynton Ave. N12	31	G4
Lynton Ave. NW9	38	F4
Lynton Ave. W13	55	D6
Lynton Ave., Rom.	44	G1
Lynton Clo., Chess.	98	H4
Lynton Clo., Islw.	73	C4
Lynton Cres., Ilf.	43	E6
Lynton Est. SE1	**21**	**H2**
Lynton Gdns. N11	32	D6
Lynton Gdns., Enf.	25	B7
Lynton Mead N20	31	D3
Lynton Rd. E4	34	B5
Lynton Rd. N8	40	D5
Lynton Rd. NW6	57	C1
Lynton Rd. SE1	**21**	**G2**
Lynton Rd. SE1	68	C4
Lynton Rd. W3	56	A7
Lynton Rd., Croy.	94	G6
Lynton Rd., Har.	45	E2
Lynton Rd., N.Mal.	92	D5
Lynwood Clo. E18	42	J1
Lynwood Clo., Har.	45	E3
Lynwood Dr., Wor.Pk.	99	G2
Lynwood Gdns., Croy.	101	F4
Lynwood Gdns., Sthl.	54	F5
Lynwood Gro. N21	32	G1
Lynwood Gro., Orp.	97	H7
Lynwood Rd. SW17	84	A3
Lynwood Rd. W5	55	F4
Lynwood Rd., T.Ditt.	98	C2
Lyon Ind. Est., Bark.	61	H2
Lyon Meade, Stan.	37	F1
Lyon Pk. Ave., Wem.	46	H6
Lyon Rd. SW19	93	F1
Lyon Rd., Har.	37	C6
Lyon St. N1	49	F7
Caledonian Rd.		
Lyon Way, Grnf.	55	B1
Lyons Pl. NW8	**6**	**E6**
Lyons Pl. NW8	57	G4
Lyons Wk. W14	66	B4
Lyonsdown Ave., Barn.	23	F6
Lyonsdown Rd., Barn.	23	E6
Lyoth Rd., Orp.	104	F2
Lyric Dr., Grnf.	54	H4
Lyric Rd. SW13	74	F1
Lysander Gro. N19	49	D1
Lysander Rd., Croy.	101	F6
Lysander Way, Orp.	104	F3
Lysia St. SW6	66	A7
Lysias Rd. SW12	76	B6
Lysons Wk. SW15	74	G5
Swinburne Rd.		
Lytchet Rd., Brom.	87	H7
Lytchet Way, Enf.	25	F1
Lytchgate Clo., S.Croy.	102	B7
Lytcott Dr., W.Mol.	90	F3
Freeman Dr.		
Lytcott Gro. SE22	77	C5
Lyte St. E2	59	F2
Bishops Way		
Lytham Ave., Wat.	28	D5
Lytham Gro. W5	55	J3
Lytham St. SE17	**21**	**B4**
Lytham St. SE17	68	A5
Lyttelton Clo. NW3	48	H7
Hawtrey Rd.		
Lyttelton Rd. E10	51	B3
Lyttelton Rd. N2	39	F5
Lyttleton Rd. N8	40	G3
Lytton Ave. N13	32	G2
Lytton Clo. N2	39	F6
Lytton Clo., Loug.	27	G3
Lytton Clo., Nthlt.	45	F7
Lytton Gdns., Wall.	100	D4
Lytton Gro. SW15	75	A5
Lytton Rd. E11	42	E7
Lytton Rd., Barn.	23	F4
Lytton Rd., Pnr.	28	E7
Lytton Strachey Path SE28	62	B7
Titmuss Ave.		
Lyveden Rd. SE3	69	H7
Lyveden Rd. SW17	84	H6

M

Maberley Cres. SE19	86	D7
Maberley Rd. SE19	95	C1
Maberley Rd., Beck.	95	G3
Mabledon Pl. WC1	**7**	**J4**
Mabledon Pl. WC1	58	D3
Mablethorpe Rd. SW6	66	B7
Mabley St. E9	50	H5
Macaret Clo. N20	23	F7
Macarthur Ter. SE7	70	A6
Macaulay Ave., Esher	98	B2
Macaulay Ct. SW4	76	B3
Macaulay Rd. E6	61	A2
Macaulay Rd. SW4	76	B4
Macaulay Sq. SW4	76	B4
Macaulay Way SE28	62	
Booth Clo.		
Macauley Ms. SE13	78	C1
Macbean St. SE18	70	E1
Macbeth St. W6	65	H5
Macclesfield Bri. NW1	**6**	**H1**
Macclesfield Bri. NW1	57	H2
Macclesfield Rd. EC1	**8**	**J3**
Macclesfield Rd. EC1	58	J3
Macclesfield Rd. SE25	95	B5
Macclesfield St. W1	**11**	**J5**
Macdonald Ave., Dag.	53	H3
Macdonald Rd. E7	51	G4
Macdonald Rd. E17	42	C2
Macdonald Rd. N11	31	J5
Macdonald Rd. N19	49	C2
Macduff Rd. SW11	76	A1
Mace Clo. E1	68	E1
Kennet St.		
Mace St. E2	59	G2
MacFarlane La., Islw.	64	C6
Macfarlane Rd. W12	65	H1
Macfarren Pl. NW1	**7**	**C6**
Macgregor Rd. E16	60	J5
Machell Rd. SE15	77	F3

Mackay Rd. SW4 76 B3
Mackennal St. NW8 6 H1
Mackennal St. NW8 57 H2
Mackenzie Rd. N7 49 F6
Mackenzie Rd., Beck. 95 F2
Mackenzie Wk. E14 69 A1
South Colonnade
Mackeson Rd. NW3 48 J4
Mackie Rd. SW2 76 G7
Mackintosh La. E9 50 G5
Homerton High St.
Macklin St. WC2 12 B3
Macklin St. WC2 58 E6
Mackrow Wk. E14 60 C7
Robin Hood La.
Macks Rd. SE16 21 J1
Macks Rd. SE16 68 D4
Mackworth St. NW1 7 F3
Mackworth St. NW1 58 C3
Maclaren Ms. SW15 74 J4
Clarendon Dr.
Maclean Rd. SE23 77 H6
Macleod St. SE17 21 A4
Macleod St. SE17 67 J5
Maclise Rd. W14 66 B3
Macoma Rd. SE18 70 G6
Macoma Ter. SE18 70 G6
Maconochies Rd. E14 69 B5
Macquarie Way E14 69 B4
Macready Pl. N7 49 E4
Warlters Rd.
Macroom Rd. W9 57 C3
Mada Rd., Orp. 104 E2
Maddams St. E3 60 B4
Maddison Clo., Tedd. 82 C6
Maddock Way SE17 20 H6
Maddocks Clo., Sid. 89 D5
Maddox St. W1 11 E5
Maddox St. W1 58 B7
Madeira Ave., Brom. 87 E7
Madeira Gro.,
Wdf.Grn. 34 J6
Madeira Rd. E11 51 D1
Madeira Rd. N13 32 H4
Madeira Rd. SW16 85 E5
Madeira Rd., Mitch. 93 J4
Madeley Rd. W5 55 H6
Madeline Rd. SE20 86 D7
Madison Cres., Bexh. 71 C7
Madison Gdns., Bexh. 71 C7
Madison Gdns.,
Brom. 96 F3
Madras Pl. N7 49 G6
Madras Rd., Ilf. 52 E4
Madrid Rd. SW13 74 G1
Madrigal La. SE5 67 H7
Madron St. SE17 21 E3
Madron St. SE17 68 B5
Mafeking Ave. E6 61 B2
Mafeking Ave., Brent. 64 H6
Mafeking Ave., Ilf. 43 G7
Mafeking Rd. E16 60 F4
Mafeking Rd. N17 41 D2
Mafeking Rd., Enf. 25 C3
Magdala Ave. N19 49 B2
Magdala Rd., Islw. 73 D3
Magdala Rd., S.Croy. 102 A7
Napier Rd.
Magdalen Pas. E1 13 G5
Magdalen Rd. SW18 84 F1
Magdalen St. SE1 17 D2
Magdalen St. SE1 68 B1
Magdalene Clo. SE15 77 E2
Heaton Rd.
Magdalene Gdns. E6 61 D4
Magee St. SE11 20 E5
Magee St. SE11 67 G6
**Maggie Blake's
Cause SE1** 17 F2
Magnet Rd., Wem. 46 G2
Magnin Clo. E8 59 D1
Wilde Clo.
Magnolia Clo.,
Kings.T. 83 B6
Magnolia Ct., Har. 37 J7
Magnolia Ct., Rich. 74 B1
West Hall Rd.
Magnolia Pl. SW4 76 E5
Magnolia Pl. W5 55 H5
Montpelier Rd.
Magnolia Rd. W4 65 B6
Magnolia Way,
Epsom 99 C5
Magpie All. EC4 12 F4
Magpie Clo. E7 51 F5
Magpie Clo. NW9 38 E2
Eagle Dr.
Magpie Clo., Enf. 25 D1

Magpie Hall Clo.,
Brom. 97 B6
Magpie Hall La.,
Brom. 97 B7
Magpie Hall Rd.
(Bushey), Wat. 29 B2
Magri Wk. E1 59 F5
Ashfield St.
Maguire Dr., Rich. 82 F4
Maguire St. SE1 17 G3
Maguire St. SE1 68 C2
Mahatma Gandhi Ho., 46 J5
Wem.
Mahlon Ave., Ruis. 45 B5
Mahon Clo., Enf. 25 C1
Mahogany Clo. SE16 68 H1
Maida Ave. W2 10 D1
Maida Ave. E4 26 B7
Maida Rd., Belv. 71 G3
Maida Vale W9 6 A1
Maida Vale W9 57 E2
Maida Way E4 26 B7
Maiden Erlegh Ave., 89 E1
Bex.
Maiden La. NW1 49 D7
Maiden La. SE1 17 A1
Maiden La. WC2 12 B5
Maiden La. WC2 58 E7
Maiden Rd. E15 51 E7
Maidenstone Hill 78 C1
SE10
Maids of Honour 73 G5
Row, Rich.
The Grn.
Maidstone Ave., Rom. 44 J2
Maidstone Bldgs. SE1 17 B2
Maidstone Ho. E14 60 B6
Carmen St.
Maidstone Rd. N11 32 C6
Maidstone Rd., Sid. 89 D6
Main Ave., Enf. 25 C5
Main Dr., Wem. 46 G3
Main Rd., Sid. 88 H3
Main St., Felt. 81 D5
Mainridge Rd., Chis. 88 D4
Maisemore St. SE15 21 H7
Maitland Clo. SE10 69 B7
Maitland Clo., Houns. 72 F3
Maitland Pk. Est. 48 J6
NW3
Maitland Pk. Rd. NW3 48 J6
Maitland Pk. Vill. 48 J6
NW3
Maitland Pl. E5 50 E4
Clarence Rd.
Maitland Rd. E15 51 F6
Maitland Rd. SE26 86 G6
Maize Row E14 59 J7
Commercial Rd.
Majendie Rd. SE18 70 G5
Majestic Way, Mitch. 93 J2
Major Rd. E15 51 D5
Major Rd. SE16 17 J5
Makepeace Ave. N6 49 A2
Makepeace Rd., 54 E1
Nthlt.
Makins St. SW3 18 H2
Makins St. SW3 66 H4
Malabar St. E14 69 A2
Malam Gdns. E14 60 B7
Wades Pl.
Malbrook Rd. SW15 74 H4
Malcolm Ct., Stan. 29 F5
Malcolm Cres. NW4 38 G6
Malcolm Dr., Surb. 98 G1
Malcolm Pl. E2 59 F4
Malcolm Rd. E1 59 F4
Malcolm Rd. SE20 86 F7
Malcolm Rd. SE25 95 D6
Malcolm Rd. SW19 84 B6
Malcolm Way E11 42 G5
Malden Ave. SE25 95 E3
Malden Ave., Grnf. 46 B5
Malden Cres. NW1 49 A6
Malden Grn. Ave., 99 F1
Wor.Pk.
Malden Hill, N.Mal. 92 F3
Malden Hill Gdns., 92 F3
N.Mal.
Malden Pk., N.Mal. 92 F6
Malden Pl. NW5 49 A5
Grafton Ter.
Malden Rd. NW5 48 J5
Malden Rd., Borwd. 22 A3
Malden Rd., N.Mal. 92 E5
Malden Rd., Sutt. 99 J4
Malden Rd., Wor.Pk. 92 F7

Malden Way, N.Mal. 92 D6
Maldon Clo. E15 51 D5
David St.
Maldon Clo. N1 58 J1
Maldon Clo. SE5 77 B3
Maldon Rd. N9 33 C3
Maldon Rd. W3 56 C7
Maldon Rd., Rom. 44 J7
Maldon Rd., Wall. 101 B3
Maldon Wk., 34 J6
Wdf.Grn.
Malet Pl. WC1 7 H6
Malet Pl. WC1 58 D4
Malet St. WC1 7 H6
Malet St. WC1 58 D4
Maley Ave. SE27 85 H2
Malford Ct. E18 42 G2
Malford Gro. E18 42 F4
Malfort Rd. SE5 77 B3
Malham Rd. SE23 86 G1
Malins Clo., Barn. 22 H5
Mall, The E15 51 D7
Broadway
Mall, The N14 32 E3
Mall, The SW1 15 G3
Mall, The SW1 67 C1
Mall, The SW14 74 C5
Mall, The W5 55 H7
Mall, The, Brom. 96 G3
High St.
Mall, The, Croy. 101 J1
Poplar Wk.
Mall, The, Har. 37 J6
Mall, The, Surb. 91 G5
Mall Rd. W6 65 H5
Mallams Ms. SW9 76 H3
St. James's Cres.
Mallard Clo. E9 50 J6
Mallard Clo., Barn. 23 G6
The Hook
Mallard Clo., Twick. 72 G7
Stephenson Rd.
Mallard Path SE28 70 G3
Tom Cribb Rd.
Mallard Pl., Twick. 82 E3
Mallard Wk. SE18 70 G3
Goosander Way
Mallard Wk., Beck. 95 G5
Mallard Wk., Sid. 89 C6
Cray Rd.
Mallard Way NW9 38 C7
Mallards Rd., 34 H7
Wdf.Grn.
Mallet Dr., Nthlt. 45 F5
Mallet Rd. SE13 78 D6
Malling Clo., Croy. 95 F6
Malling Gdns., Mord. 93 F6
Malling Way, Brom. 96 F7
Mallinson Rd. SW11 75 H5
Mallinson Rd., Croy. 101 D3
Mallord St. SW3 18 F5
Mallord St. SW3 66 G6
Mallory Clo. SE4 77 H4
Mallory Gdns., Barn. 24 A7
Mallory St. NW8 6 G6
Mallory St. NW8 57 H4
Mallow Clo., Croy. 102 G1
Marigold Way
Mallow Mead NW7 31 B7
Mallow St. EC1 9 B5
Mallow St. EC1 59 B3
Malmains Clo., Beck. 96 D4
Malmains Way, Beck. 96 C4
Malmesbury Rd. E3 59 J3
Malmesbury Rd. E16 60 E5
Malmesbury Rd. E18 42 F1
Malmesbury Rd., 93 F7
Mord.
Malmesbury Ter. E16 60 F5
Malpas Dr., Pnr. 36 D5
Malpas Rd. E8 50 E6
Malpas Rd. SE4 77 J2
Malpas Rd., Dag. 53 D6
Malt St. SE1 21 H5
Malt St. SE1 68 D6
Malta Rd. E10 51 A1
Malta St. EC1 8 H5
Maltby Rd., Chess. 99 A6
Maltby St. SE1 17 F4
Maltby St. SE1 68 C3
Malthouse Dr., Felt. 81 D5
Malthouse Pas. 74 E2
SW13
The Ter.
Malthus Path SE28 71 C1
Owen Clo.
Malting Ho. E14 59 J7
Oak La.
Maltings, The, Orp. 104 J1

Maltings Clo. SW13 74 E2
Cleveland Gdns.
Maltings Ms., Sid. 89 A3
Station Rd.
Maltings Pl. SW6 75 E1
Maltings Ms. W10 57 B6
Cambridge Gdns.
Malton Rd. W10 57 B6
St. Marks Rd.
Malton St. SE18 70 H6
Maltravers St. WC2 12 D5
Malva Clo. SW18 75 E5
St. Ann's Hill
Malvern Ave. E4 34 D7
Malvern Ave., Bexh. 71 E7
Malvern Ave., Har. 45 E3
Malvern Clo. SE20 95 D2
Derwent Rd.
Malvern Clo. W10 57 C5
Malvern Clo., Mitch. 94 C3
Malvern Clo., Surb. 98 H1
Malvern Ct. SE14 68 F7
Avonley Rd.
Malvern Ct. SW7 18 F1
Malvern Ct. SW7 66 G4
Malvern Dr., Felt. 81 D5
Malvern Dr., Ilf. 52 J4
Malvern Dr., Wdf.Grn. 34 J5
Malvern Gdns. NW2 48 B2
Malvern Gdns. NW6 57 C2
Malvern Gdns., Har. 37 H5
Malvern Gdns., Loug. 27 C6
Malvern Ms. NW6 57 D3
Malvern Rd.
Malvern Pl. NW6 57 C3
Malvern Rd. E6 61 B1
Malvern Rd. E8 50 D7
Malvern Rd. E11 51 E2
Malvern Rd. N8 40 F3
Malvern Rd. N17 41 D3
Malvern Rd. NW6 57 D3
Malvern Rd., Hmptn. 81 G7
Malvern Rd., Surb. 98 H2
Malvern Rd., Th.Hth. 94 G4
Malvern Ter. N1 58 G1
Malvern Ter. N9 33 C1
Malvern Way W13 55 E5
Templewood
Malwood Rd. SW12 76 B6
Malyons Rd. SE13 78 B6
Malyons Ter. SE13 78 B5
Managers St. E14 69 C1
Prestons Rd.
Manaton Clo. SE15 77 E3
Manaton Cres., Sthl. 54 G6
Manbey Gro. E15 51 E6
Manbey Pk. Rd. E15 51 E6
Manbey Rd. E15 51 E6
Manbey St. E15 51 E6
Manborough Ave. E6 61 C3
Manbre Rd. W6 65 J6
Manchester Dr. W10 57 B4
Manchester Gro. E14 69 C5
Manchester Ms. W1 11 B2
Manchester Rd. E14 69 C5
Manchester Rd. N15 41 A6
Manchester Rd., 94 J3
Th.Hth.
Manchester Sq. W1 11 B3
Manchester Sq. W1 58 A6
Manchester St. W1 11 B2
Manchester St. W1 58 A5
Manchester Way, 53 H4
Dag.
Manchuria Rd. SW11 76 A6
Manciple St. SE1 17 C4
Manciple St. SE1 68 A2
Mandalay Rd. SW4 76 C5
Mandarin St. E14 60 A7
Salter St.
Mandela Clo. NW10 47 C7
Mandela Rd. E16 60 G6
Mandela St. NW1 58 C1
Mandela St. SW9 67 G7
Mandela Way SE1 21 E1
Mandela Way SE1 68 B4
Mandeville Clo. SE3 69 F7
Vanbrugh Pk.
Mandeville Clo. SW20 93 B1
Mandeville Ct. E4 33 H4
Mandeville Dr., Surb. 98 G1
Mandeville Pl. W1 11 C3
Mandeville Pl. W1 58 A6
Mandeville Rd. N14 32 B2
Mandeville Rd., Islw. 73 D2
Mandeville Rd., Nthlt. 45 G7
Mandeville St. E5 50 H3
Mandrake Rd. SW17 84 J2

Mandrell Rd. SW2 76 E5
Manette St. W1 **11 J4**
Manette St. W1 58 D6
Manford Way, Chig. 35 H4
Manfred Rd. SW15 75 C5
Manger Rd. N7 49 E6
Mangold Way, Erith 71 E3
Manhattan Ct., Nthlt. 54 D3
Manilla St. E14 69 A2
Manister Rd. SE2 71 A3
Manley Ct. N16 50 C3
Stoke Newington
High St.
Manley St. NW1 58 A1
Mannin Rd., Rom. 44 B7
Manning Gdns., Har. 37 G7
Manning Rd. E17 41 H5
Southcote Rd.
Manning Rd., Dag. 53 G6
Manningford Clo. EC1 **8 G3**
Manningtree Clo. 84 B1
SW19
Manningtree Rd., 45 B4
Ruis.
Manningtree St. E1 **13 H3**
Mannock Dr., Loug. 27 F2
Mannock Rd. N22 40 H3
Manns Clo., Islw. 73 C5
Manns Rd., Edg. 30 A6
Manoel Rd., Twick. 81 J2
Manor Ave. SE4 77 J2
Manor Ave., Houns. 72 D3
Manor Ave., Nthlt. 45 F7
Manor Clo. NW7 30 D5
Manor Dr.
Manor Clo. NW9 38 B5
Manor Clo. SE28 62 C7
Manor Clo., Barn. 23 B4
Manor Clo., Wor.Pk. 99 E1
Manor Cotts. App. N2 39 F2
Manor Ct. N2 39 J3
Manor Ct. SW6 75 E1
Bagley's La.
Manor Ct., Twick. 81 J2
Manor Ct., Wem. 46 H5
Manor Ct. Rd. W7 55 B7
Manor Cres., Surb. 92 A6
Manor Dr. N14 24 B7
Manor Dr. N20 31 H3
Manor Dr. NW7 30 D5
Manor Dr., Epsom 99 E6
Manor Dr., Esher 98 C3
Manor Dr., Felt. 81 D5
Manor Dr., Sun. 90 A2
Manor Dr., Surb. 91 J6
Manor Dr., Wem. 46 J4
Manor Dr., The, 99 E1
Wor.Pk.
Manor Dr. N., N.Mal. 92 D6
Manor Dr. N., Wor.Pk. 99 E1
Manor Est. SE16 68 E4
Manor Fm. Dr. E4 34 E3
Manor Fm. Rd., 94 G2
Th.Hth.
Manor Fm. Rd., Wem. 55 G1
Manor Flds. SW15 75 A6
Manor Gdns. N7 49 E3
Manor Gdns. SW20 93 C2
Manor Gdns. W3 65 A4
Manor Gdns., Hmptn. 81 H7
Manor Gdns., Rich. 73 J4
Manor Gdns., Ruis. 45 C5
Manor Gdns., 102 C6
S.Croy.
Manor Gdns., Sun. 90 A1
Manor Gate, Nthlt. 45 E7
Manor Gro. SE15 68 F6
Manor Gro., Beck. 96 B2
Manor Gro., Rich. 74 A4
Manor Hall Ave. NW4 38 J2
Manor Hall Dr. NW4 39 A2
Manor Ho. Way, Islw. 73 E3
Manor Ho. Dr. NW6 48 A7
Manor La. SE12 78 E6
Manor La. SE13 78 E5
Manor La., Felt. 81 A2
Manor La., Sun. 90 A2
Manor La., Sutt. 100 F5
Manor La. Ter. SE13 78 E4
Manor Ms. NW6 57 D2
Cambridge Ave.
Manor Ms. SE4 77 J2
Manor Mt. SE23 86 F1
Manor Pk. SE13 78 D5
Manor Pk., Chis. 97 G2
Manor Pk., Rich. 73 J4
Manor Pk. Clo., 103 B1
W.Wick.

Manor Pk. Cres., Edg. 30 A6
Manor Pk. Dr., Har. 36 H3
Manor Pk. Gdns., Edg. 30 A5
Manor Pk. Par. SE13 78 D4
Lee High Rd.
Manor Pk. Rd. E12 52 A4
Manor Pk. Rd. N2 39 F3
Manor Pk. Rd. NW10 56 F1
Manor Pk. Rd., Chis. 97 F1
Manor Pk. Rd., Sutt. 100 F5
Manor Pk. Rd., 103 B1
W.Wick.
Manor Pl. SE17 **20 J3**
Manor Pl. SE17 67 H5
Manor Pl., Chis. 97 G2
Manor Pl., Felt. 81 A1
Manor Pl., Mitch. 94 C3
Manor Pl., Sutt. 100 E5
Manor Rd. E10 42 A7
Manor Rd. E15 60 E2
Manor Rd. E16 60 E4
Manor Rd. E17 41 H2
Manor Rd. N16 50 A2
Manor Rd. N17 41 D1
Manor Rd. N22 32 E6
Manor Rd. SE25 95 D4
Manor Rd. SW20 93 C2
Manor Rd. W13 55 D7
Manor Rd., Bark. 52 J6
Manor Rd., Barn. 23 B5
Manor Rd., Beck. 96 A2
Manor Rd., Bex. 89 H1
Manor Rd., Chig. 35 D6
Manor Rd., Dag. 53 J6
Manor Rd., E.Mol. 91 A4
Manor Rd., Enf. 24 J2
Manor Rd., Har. 37 D6
Manor Rd., Hayes 54 A6
Manor Rd., Loug. 26 H6
Manor Rd., Loug. 26 H1
(High Beach)
Manor Rd., Mitch. 94 C4
Manor Rd., Rich. 73 J3
Manor Rd., Rom. 44 D6
(Chadwell Heath)
Manor Rd., Sid. 89 A3
Manor Rd., Sutt. 100 C7
Manor Rd., Tedd. 82 D5
Manor Rd., Twick. 81 J2
Manor Rd., Wall. 101 B4
Manor Rd., W.Wick. 103 B2
Manor Rd., Wdf.Grn. 35 C6
Manor Rd. N., Esher 98 C3
Manor Rd. N., T.Ditt. 98 D2
Manor Rd. S., Esher 98 B4
Manor Sq., Dag. 53 C2
Manor Vale, Brent. 64 F5
Manor Vw. N3 39 E2
Manor Way E4 34 D4
Manor Way NW9 38 E4
Manor Way SE3 78 F4
Manor Way, Beck. 96 A2
Manor Way, Bex. 89 G1
Manor Way, Borwd. 22 C2
Manor Way, Brom. 97 B6
Manor Way, Har. 36 H4
Manor Way, Mitch. 94 C3
Manor Way, Orp. 97 F5
Manor Way, S.Croy. 102 B6
Manor Way, Sthl. 63 D4
Manor Way, Wor.Pk. 99 E1
Manor Way, The, 101 B4
Wall.
Manorbrook SE3 78 G4
Manordene Clo., 98 D1
T.Ditt.
Manordene Rd. SE28 62 C6
Manorfield Clo. N19 49 C4
Tufnell Pk. Rd.
Manorfields Clo., 97 J3
Chis.
Manorgate Rd., 92 A1
Kings.T.
Manorhall Gdns. E10 51 A1
Manorside, Barn. 23 B4
Manorside Clo. SE2 71 C4
Manorway, Enf. 25 B7
Manorway, Wdf.Grn. 34 J5
Manresa Rd. SW3 **18 G4**
Manresa Rd. SW3 66 H5
Mansard Beeches 85 A5
SW17
Mansard Clo., Pnr. 36 D3
Manse Rd. N16 50 C3
Mansel Gro. E17 42 A1
Mansel Rd. SW19 84 B6
Mansell Rd. W3 65 D2

Mansell Rd., Grnf. 54 H5
Mansell St. E1 **13 G4**
Mansell St. E1 59 C6
Mansergh Clo. SE18 70 B7
Mansfield Ave. N15 41 A4
Mansfield Ave., Barn. 23 J6
Mansfield Ave., Ruis. 45 B1
Mansfield Clo. N9 25 D6
Mansfield Hill E4 34 B1
Mansfield Ms. W1 **11 D2**
Mansfield Pl. NW3 48 F4
New End
Mansfield Rd. E11 42 H6
Mansfield Rd. E17 41 J4
Mansfield Rd. NW3 48 J5
Mansfield Rd. W3 56 B4
Mansfield Rd., Chess. 98 F5
Mansfield Rd., Ilf. 52 D2
Mansfield Rd., 102 A6
S.Croy.
Mansfield St. W1 **11 D2**
Mansfield St. W1 58 B5
Mansford St. E2 **9 J2**
Mansford St. E2 59 D2
Manship Rd., Mitch. 85 A7
Mansion Gdns. NW3 48 E3
Mansion Ho. Pl. EC4 **13 B4**
Manson Ms. SW7 **18 E2**
Manson Ms. SW7 66 F4
Manson Pl. SW7 **18 E2**
Manson Pl. SW7 66 G4
Mansted Gdns., Rom. 44 C7
Manstone Rd. NW2 48 B5
Manthorp Rd. SE18 70 F5
Mantilla Rd. SW17 85 A4
Mantle Rd. SE4 77 H3
Mantlet Clo. SW16 85 C7
Manton Ave. W7 64 C2
Manton Rd. SE2 71 A4
Mantua St. SW11 75 G3
Mantus Clo. E1 59 F4
Mantus Rd.
Mantus Rd. E1 59 F4
Manus Way N20 31 F2
Blakeney Clo.
Manville Gdns. SW17 85 B1
Manville Rd. SW17 85 A2
Manwood Rd. SE4 77 J5
Manwood St. E16 70 C1
Manygates SW12 85 B3
Mape St. E2 59 E4
Mapesbury Rd. NW2 48 B7
Maple Ave. E4 33 J5
Maple Ave. W3 65 E1
Maple Ave., Har. 45 H2
Maple Clo. N16 41 D6
Maple Clo. SW4 85 C1
Maple Clo., Buck.H. 35 A3
Maple Clo., Hmptn. 81 F6
Maple Clo., Hayes 54 D3
Maple Clo., Ilf. 35 H5
Maple Clo., Mitch. 94 B1
Maple Clo., Orp. 97 G5
Maple Clo., Ruis. 36 B6
Maple Ct., N.Mal. 92 D3
Maple Cres., Sid. 80 A6
Maple Gdns., Edg. 30 E7
Maple Gate, Loug. 27 D2
Maple Gro. NW9 38 C7
Maple Gro. W5 64 F3
Maple Gro., Brent. 64 E7
Maple Gro., Sthl. 54 F5
Maple Ind. Est., Felt. 81 A3
Maple Leaf Sq. SE16 68 G2
St. Elmos Rd.
Maple Ms. NW6 **6 A1**
Maple Ms. SW16 85 F5
Maple Pl. W1 **7 G6**
Maple Rd. E11 42 E6
Maple Rd. SE20 95 E1
Maple Rd., Hayes 54 C3
Maple Rd., Surb. 91 G6
Maple St. W1 **11 F1**
Maple St. W1 58 C5
Maple St., Rom. 44 J4
Maple Wk. W10 57 A4
Droop St.
Maple Way, Felt. 81 A3
Maplecroft Clo. E6 61 B6
Allhallows Rd.
Mapledale Ave., 102 D2
Croy.
Mapledene, Chis. 88 F5
Kemnal Rd.

Mapledene Rd. E8 50 D7
Maplehurst Clo., 91 H4
Kings.T.
Mapleleafe Gdns., Ilf. 43 E3
Maples Pl. E1 59 E5
Raven Row
Maplestead Rd. SW2 76 F7
Maplestead Rd., Dag. 62 B3
Maplethorpe Rd., 94 G4
Th.Hth.
Mapleton Clo., Brom. 96 G6
Mapleton Cres. SW18 75 E6
Mapleton Rd. E4 34 C3
Mapleton Rd. SW18 75 D6
Mapleton Rd., Enf. 25 E2
Maplin Clo. N21 24 F6
Maplin Rd. E16 60 G6
Maplin St. E3 59 J3
Mapperley Dr., 34 E7
Wdf.Grn.
Forest Dr.
Maran Way, Erith 71 D2
Marban Rd. W9 57 C3
Marble Arch W1 **10 J5**
Marble Arch W1 57 J7
Marble Clo. W3 65 B1
Marble Dr. NW2 48 A1
Marble Hill Clo., 73 E7
Twick.
Marble Hill Gdns., 73 E7
Twick.
Marble Quay E1 **17 H1**
Marble Quay E1 68 D1
Marbrook Ct. SE12 87 J3
Marcellina Way, Orp. 104 H3
March Rd., Twick. 73 D7
Marchant Rd. E11 51 D2
Marchant St. SE14 68 H6
Sanford St.
Marchbank Rd. W14 66 C6
Marchmont Rd., Rich. 73 J5
Marchmont Rd., 101 C7
Wall.
Marchmont St. WC1 **8 A5**
Marchmont St. WC1 58 E4
Marchside Clo., 72 D1
Houns.
Springwell Rd.
Marchwood Clo. SE5 68 B7
Marchwood Cres. W5 55 F6
Marcia Rd. SE1 **21 E2**
Marcia Rd. SE1 68 B4
Marcilly Rd. SW18 75 G5
Marco Rd. W6 65 H3
Marcon Pl. E8 50 E5
Marconi Rd. E10 51 A1
Marconi Way, Sthl. 54 H6
Marcourt Lawns W5 55 H4
Marcus Ct. E15 60 E1
Marcus Garvey Way 76 G4
SE24
Marcus St. E15 60 E1
Marcus St. SW18 75 E6
Marcus Ter. SW18 75 E6
Mardale Dr. NW9 38 D5
Mardell Rd., Croy. 95 G5
Marden Ave., Brom. 96 F6
Marden Cres., Bex. 80 J5
Marden Cres., Croy. 94 F6
Marden Rd. N17 41 B3
Marden Rd., Croy. 94 F6
Marden Sq. SE16 68 E3
Marder Rd. W13 64 D2
Mardon St. E14 59 H5
Mare St. E8 59 E1
Marechal Niel Ave., 88 G3
Sid.
Mares Fld., Croy. 102 B3
Maresfield Gdns. 48 F5
NW3
Marfleet Clo., Cars. 100 H2
Margaret Ave. E4 26 B6
Margaret Bondfield 53 A7
Ave., Bark.
Margaret Bldgs. N16 50 C1
Margaret Rd.
Margaret Ct. W1 **11 F3**
Margaret Rd. N16 50 C1
Margaret Rd., Barn. 23 G4
Margaret Rd., Bex. 80 D6
Margaret St. W1 **11 E3**
Margaret St. W1 58 B6
Margaret Way, Ilf. 43 B6
Margaretta Ter. SW3 **18 G5**
Margaretta Ter. SW3 66 H6
Margaretting Rd. E12 51 J1
Margate Rd. SW2 76 E5
Margeholes, Wat. 28 E2

Name	Page	Grid
Margery Pk. Rd. E7	51	G6
Margery Rd., Dag.	53	D3
Margery St. WC1	**8**	**E4**
Margery St. WC1	58	G3
Margin Dr. SW19	84	A5
Margravine Gdns. W6	66	A5
Margravine Rd. W6	66	A5
Marham Gdns. SW18	84	H1
Marham Gdns., Mord.	93	F6
Maria Clo. SE1	**21**	**J4**
Maria Ter. E1	59	G4
Maria Theresa Clo., N.Mal.	92	D5
Marian Clo., Hayes	54	D4
Marian Ct., Sutt.	100	E5
Marian Pl. E2	59	E2
Marian Rd. SW16	94	C1
Marian Sq. E2	**9**	**J1**
Marian St. E2	59	E2
Hackney Rd.		
Marian Way NW10	47	F7
Maricas Ave., Har.	29	A7
Marie Lloyd Gdns. N19	40	E7
Hornsey Ri. Gdns.		
Marie Lloyd Wk. E8	50	D6
Forest Rd.		
Marigold All. SE1	**12**	**G6**
Marigold Rd. N17	33	F7
Marigold St. SE16	68	E2
Marigold Way, Croy.	102	G1
Marina App., Hayes	54	E5
Marina Ave., N.Mal.	92	H5
Marina Clo., Brom.	96	G3
Marina Dr., Well.	79	H2
Marina Gdns., Rom.	44	H5
Marina Way, Tedd.	82	G7
Fairways		
Marine Dr. SE18	70	C4
Marine St. SE16	**17**	**H5**
Marinefield Rd. SW6	75	E2
Mariner Gdns., Rich.	82	F3
Mariner Rd. E12	52	C4
Dersingham Ave.		
Mariners Ms. E14	69	D4
Marion Clo., Ilf.	35	G7
Marion Gro., Wdf.Grn.	34	E5
Marion Rd. NW7	30	G5
Marion Rd., Th.Hth.	94	J5
Marischal Rd. SE13	78	D3
Maritime St. E3	59	J4
Marius Pas. SW17	85	A2
Marius Rd.		
Marius Rd. SW17	85	A2
Marjorams Ave., Loug.	27	C2
Marjorie Gro. SW11	75	J4
Marjorie Ms. E1	59	G6
Arbour Sq.		
Mark Ave. E4	26	B6
Mark Clo., Bexh.	80	E1
Mark Clo., Sthl.	63	H1
Longford Ave.		
Mark La. EC3	**13**	**E5**
Mark La. EC3	59	B7
Mark Rd. N22	40	H2
Mark St. E15	51	E7
West Ham La.		
Mark St. EC2	**9**	**D5**
Marke Clo., Kes.	104	B4
Markeston Grn., Wat.	28	D4
Market Ct. W1	**11**	**F3**
Market Est. N7	49	E6
Clock Twr. Pl.		
Market Hill SE18	70	D3
Market La., Edg.	38	C1
Market Ms. W1	**15**	**D2**
Market Par. SE15	77	D2
Rye La.		
Market Pl. N2	39	H3
Market Pl. NW11	39	F4
Market Pl. SE16	**21**	**J1**
Market Pl. W1	**11**	**F3**
Market Pl. W3	65	C1
Market Pl., Bexh.	80	G4
Market Pl., Brent.	64	G7
Lion Way		
Market Pl., Enf.	25	A3
The Town		
Market Pl., Kings.T.	91	G2
Market Rd. N7	49	E6
Market Rd., Rich.	74	A3
Market Row SW9	76	G4
Atlantic Rd.		
Market Sq. E14	60	B6
Chrisp St.		
Market Sq. N9	33	D2
New Rd.		
Market Sq., Brom.	96	G2
Market St. E6	61	C2
Market St. SE18	70	D4
Market Way E14	60	B6
Kerbey St.		
Markfield Gdns. E4	26	B7
Markfield Rd. N15	41	D4
Markham Pl. SW3	**18**	**J3**
Markham Pl. SW3	66	J5
Markham Sq. SW3	**18**	**J3**
Markham Sq. SW3	66	J5
Markham St. SW3	**18**	**H3**
Markham St. SW3	66	H5
Markhole Clo., Hmptn.	81	F7
Priory Rd.		
Markhouse Ave. E17	41	H6
Markhouse Rd. E17	41	H5
Markmanor Ave. E17	41	H7
Marks Rd., Rom.	44	J5
Marksbury Ave., Rich.	74	A3
Markway, The, Sun.	90	C2
Markwell Clo. SE26	86	E4
Longton Gro.		
Markwell Clo., W.Wick.	103	E2
Deer Pk. Way		
Markyate Rd., Dag.	53	B5
Marl Rd. SW18	75	E4
Marl St. SW18	75	F4
Marl Rd.		
Marlands Rd., Ilf.	43	B3
Marlborough Ave. E8	59	D1
Marlborough Ave. N14	32	C3
Marlborough Ave., Edg.	30	B3
Marlborough Bldgs. SW3	**18**	**H1**
Marlborough Bldgs. SW3	66	H4
Marlborough Clo. N20	31	J3
Marlborough Gdns.		
Marlborough Clo. SE17	**20**	**J2**
Marlborough Clo. SW19	84	H7
Marlborough Clo., Orp.	97	J7
Aylesham Rd.		
Marlborough Ct. W8	66	D4
Marlborough Cres. W4	65	D3
Marlborough Dr., Ilf.	43	B3
Marlborough Gdns. N20	31	J3
Marlborough Gate Ho. W2	**10**	**E5**
Marlborough Gro. SE1	**21**	**H4**
Marlborough Gro. SE1	68	D5
Marlborough Hill NW8	57	F1
Marlborough Hill, Har.	37	A4
Marlborough La. SE7	69	J6
Marlborough Pk. Ave., Sid.	89	A1
Marlborough Pl. NW8	**6**	**C2**
Marlborough Pl. NW8	57	F2
Marlborough Rd. E4	34	A6
Marlborough Rd. E7	51	J7
Marlborough Rd. E15	51	E4
Borthwick Rd.		
Marlborough Rd. E18	42	G3
Marlborough Rd. N9	33	C1
Marlborough Rd. N19	49	D2
Marlborough Rd. N22	32	E7
Marlborough Rd. SW1	**15**	**G2**
Marlborough Rd. SW1	67	C1
Marlborough Rd. SW19	84	H6
Marlborough Rd. W4	65	C5
Marlborough Rd. W5	64	G2
Marlborough Rd., Bexh.	80	D3
Marlborough Rd., Brom.	96	J4
Marlborough Rd., Dag.	53	B4
Marlborough Rd., Felt.	81	D2
Marlborough Rd., Hmptn.	81	G6
Marlborough Rd., Islw.	73	E1
Marlborough Rd., Rich.	73	H6
Marlborough Rd., Rom.	44	G4
Marlborough Rd., S.Croy.	101	J7
Marlborough Rd., Sthl.	63	C3
Marlborough Rd., Sutt.	100	D3
Marlborough St. SW3	**18**	**G2**
Marlborough St. SW3	66	H4
Marlborough Yd. N19	49	D2
Marlborough Rd.		
Marler Rd. SE23	86	H1
Marlescroft Way, Loug.	27	E5
Marley Ave., Bexh.	71	D6
Marley Clo., Grnf.	54	G3
Marley Wk. NW2	47	J5
Lennon Rd.		
Marlingdene Clo., Hmptn.	81	G6
Marlings Clo., Chis.	97	H4
Marlings Pk. Ave., Chis.	97	H4
Marlins Clo., Sutt.	100	F5
Turnpike La.		
Marloes Clo., Wem.	46	G4
Marloes Rd. W8	**14**	**A6**
Marloes Rd. W8	66	E3
Marlow Clo. SE20	95	E3
Marlow Ct. NW6	48	A7
Marlow Ct. NW9	38	E3
Marlow Cres., Twick.	73	C6
Marlow Dr., Sutt.	100	A2
Marlow Rd. E6	61	C3
Marlow Rd. SE20	95	E3
Marlow Rd., Sthl.	63	F3
Marlow Way SE16	68	G2
Marlowe Clo., Chis.	88	G6
Marlowe Clo., Ilf.	43	F1
Marlowe Gdns. SE9	79	D6
Marlowe Rd. E17	42	C4
Marlowe Sq., Mitch.	94	C3
Tamworth La.		
Marlowe Way, Croy.	101	E2
Marlowes, The NW8	57	G1
Marlton St. SE10	69	F5
Woolwich Rd.		
Marmadon Rd. SE18	70	J4
Marmion App. E4	34	A4
Marmion Ave. E4	33	J4
Marmion Clo. E4	33	J4
Marmion Ms. SW11	76	A3
Taybridge Rd.		
Marmion Rd. SW11	76	A4
Marmont Rd. SE15	77	D1
Marmora Rd. SE22	77	F6
Marmot Rd., Houns.	72	D3
Marne Ave. N11	32	B4
Marne Ave., Well.	80	A3
Marne St. W10	57	B3
Marnell Way, Houns.	72	D3
Marney Rd. SW11	76	A4
Marnham Ave. NW2	48	B4
Marnham Cres., Grnf.	54	H3
Marnock Rd. SE4	77	J5
Maroon St. E14	59	H5
Maroons Way SE6	87	A5
Marquess Est. N1	49	A6
Marquess Rd. N1	50	A6
Marquis Clo., Wem.	46	J7
Marquis Rd. N4	49	F1
Marquis Rd. N22	32	F6
Marquis Rd. NW1	49	D6
Marrick Clo. SW15	74	G4
Marriots Clo. NW9	38	F6
Marriott Rd. E15	60	E1
Marriott Rd. N4	49	F1
Marriott Rd. N10	39	J1
Marriott Rd., Barn.	23	A3
Marryat Pl. SW19	84	B4
Marryat Rd. SW19	84	A5
Marsala Rd. SE13	78	B4
Marsden Rd. N9	33	E2
Marsden Rd. SE15	77	C3
Marsden St. NW5	49	A6
Marsden Way, Orp.	104	H3
Marsh Ave., Mitch.	93	J2
Marsh Clo. NW7	30	F3
Marsh Ct. SW19	93	F1
Marsh Dr. NW9	38	F6
Marsh Fm. Rd., Twick.	82	C1
Marsh Grn. Rd., Dag.	53	B4
Marsh Hill E9	50	H5
Marsh La. E10	51	A2
Marsh La. N17	41	E1
Marsh La. NW7	30	D4
Marsh La., Stan.	29	F5
Marsh Rd., Pnr.	36	E4
Marsh Rd., Wem.	55	G3
Marsh St. E14	69	B4
Harbinger Rd.		
Marsh Wall E14	69	A1
Marshall Clo. SW18	75	F6
Allfarthing La.		
Marshall Clo., Har.	37	A7
Bowen Rd.		
Marshall Clo., Houns.	72	F5
Marshall Path SE28	62	B7
Attlee Rd.		
Marshall Rd. N17	41	A1
Marshall St. W1	**11**	**G4**
Marshall St. W1	58	C6
Marshalls Clo. N11	32	B4
Marshall's Gro. SE18	70	B4
Marshalls Pl. SE16	**17**	**G6**
Marshalsea Rd. SE1	**17**	**J2**
Marshalsea Rd. SE1	67	J2
Marsham Clo., Chis.	88	E5
Marsham St. SW1	**15**	**J6**
Marsham St. SW1	67	D3
Marshbrook Clo. SE3	79	A3
Marshfield St. E14	69	C3
Marshgate La. E15	51	B7
Marshgate Path SE28	70	F4
Tom Cribb Rd.		
Marsland Clo. SE17	**20**	**H4**
Marsland Clo. SE17	67	H5
Marston Ave., Chess.	98	H6
Marston Ave., Dag.	53	G2
Marston Clo. NW6	48	F7
Fairfax Rd.		
Marston Clo., Dag.	53	G3
Marston Rd., Ilf.	43	B1
Marston Rd., Tedd.	82	E5
Kingston Rd.		
Marston Way SE19	85	H7
Marsworth Ave., Pnr.	36	D1
Marsworth Clo., Hayes	54	E5
Mart St. WC2	**12**	**B5**
Martaban Rd. N16	50	C2
Martel Pl. E8	50	C6
Dalston La.		
Martell Rd. SE21	86	A3
Martello St. E8	50	E7
Martello Ter. E8	50	E7
Marten Rd. E17	42	A2
Martens Ave., Bexh.	80	H4
Martens Clo., Bexh.	80	J4
Martha Ct. E2	59	E2
Cambridge Heath Rd.		
Martha Rd. E15	51	E6
Martha St. E1	59	E6
Martham Clo. SE28	62	D7
Marthorne Cres., Har.	37	A2
Martin Bowes Rd. SE9	79	C3
Martin Clo. N9	33	G1
Martin Cres., Croy.	101	G1
Martin Dale Ind. Est., Enf.	25	E3
Martin Dene, Bexh.	80	F5
Martin Dr., Nthlt.	45	F5
Martin Gdns., Dag.	53	C4
Martin Gro., Mord.	93	D3
Martin La. EC4	**13**	**C5**
Martin Ri., Bexh.	80	F5
Martin Rd., Dag.	53	C4
Martin Way SW20	93	A2
Martin Way, Mord.	93	D3
Martinbridge Trd. Est., Enf.	25	D4
Martindale SW14	74	C5
Martindale Rd. SW12	76	B7
Martindale Rd., Houns.	72	E4
Martineau Clo., Esher	98	A4
Martineau Est. E1	59	F7
Martineau Rd. N5	49	H4
Martineau St. E1	59	F7
Lukin St.		
Martingale Clo., Sun.	90	A4
Martingales Clo., Rich.	82	G3
Martins Mt., Barn.	23	D4
Martins Rd., Brom.	96	E2
Martins Wk. N10	40	A1
Martins Wk., Borwd.	22	A4
Siskin Clo.		
Martinsfield Clo., Chig.	35	H4
Martlet Gro., Nthlt.	54	D3
Javelin Way		
Martlett Ct. WC2	**12**	**B4**
Martley Dr., Ilf.	43	E5
Martock Clo., Har.	37	D4
Marton Clo. SE6	87	A3
Marton Rd. N16	50	D2

Martys Yd. NW3 48 G4
Hampstead High St.
Marvell Ave., Hayes 54 A5
Marvels Clo. SE12 87 H2
Marvels La. SE12 87 H2
Marville Rd. SW6 66 C7
Marvin St. E8 50 E6
Sylvester Rd.
Marwell Clo., 103 F2
W.Wick.
Deer Pk. Way
Marwood Clo., Well. 80 B3
Marwood Way SE16 68 E5
Catlin St.
Mary Adelaide Clo. 83 E4
SW15
Mary Ann Gdns. SE8 69 A6
Mary Clo., Stan. 37 J4
Mary Datchelor Clo. 77 A1
SE5
Mary Gardener Dr. 88 C2
SE9
Mary Grn. NW8 57 E1
Mary Lawrenson Pl. 69 G7
SE3
Heathway
Mary Macarthur Ho. 66 B6
W6
Field Rd.
Mary Peters Dr., Grnf. 46 A5
Mary Pl. W11 57 B7
Mary Rose Clo., 90 G1
Hmptn.
Ashley Rd.
Mary Rose Mall E6 61 D5
Frobisher Rd.
Mary Rose Way N20 31 G1
Clarissa St.
Mary Seacole Clo. E8 59 C1
Mary St. E16 60 F5
Barking Rd.
Mary St. N1 58 J1
Mary Ter. NW1 58 B1
Arlington Rd.
Maryatt Ave., Har. 45 H2
Marybank SE18 70 C4
Maryland Pk. E15 51 E5
Maryland Rd. E15 51 D5
Maryland Rd. N22 32 F6
Maryland Rd., Th.Hth. 94 H1
Maryland Sq. E15 51 E5
Maryland St. E15 51 D5
Maryland Wk. N1 58 J1
Popham St.
Maryland Way, Sun. 90 A2
Marylands Rd. W9 57 D4
**Marylebone Flyover 10 G2
NW1**
**Marylebone Flyover 10 F2
W2**
**Marylebone High St. 11 C1
W1**
Marylebone High St. 58 A5
W1
Marylebone La. W1 11 C3
Marylebone La. W1 58 A6
Marylebone Ms. W1 11 D2
Marylebone Ms. W1 58 B5
Marylebone Pas. W1 11 G3
Marylebone Rd. NW1 11 A1
Marylebone Rd. NW1 57 H5
Marylebone St. W1 11 C2
Marylebone St. W1 58 A5
Marylee Way SE11 20 D3
Marylee Way SE11 67 F4
Maryon Gro. SE7 70 B4
Maryon Ms. NW3 48 H4
South End Rd.
Maryon Rd. SE7 70 B4
Maryon Rd. SE18 70 B4
Mary's Clo. N17 41 C1
Kemble Rd.
Mary's Ter., Twick. 73 D7
Masbro Rd. W14 66 A3
Mascalls Ct. SE7 69 J6
Victoria Way
Mascalls Rd. SE7 69 J6
Mascotte Rd. SW15 75 A4
Mascotts Clo. NW2 47 H3
Masefield Ave., 22 B5
Borwd.
Masefield Ave., Sthl. 54 G7
Masefield Ave., Stan. 29 C5
Masefield Cres. N14 24 C5
Masefield Gdns. E6 61 D4
Masefield La., Hayes 54 B4
Masefield Rd., Hmptn. 81 F4
Wordsworth Rd.

Masefield Vw., Orp. 104 F3
Mashie Rd. W3 56 E6
Maskall Clo. SW2 85 G1
Maskani Wk. SW16 85 C7
Bates Cres.
Maskell Rd. SW17 84 F3
Maskelyn Clo. SW11 75 H1
Mason Bradbear Ct. 50 A6
N1
St. Paul's Rd.
Mason Clo. E16 60 G7
Mason Clo. SE16 21 J3
Mason Clo. SW18 93 A1
Mason Clo., Bexh. 80 H3
Mason Clo., Borwd. 22 C2
Banks Rd.
Mason Clo., Hmptn. 90 F1
Mason Rd., Wdf.Grn. 34 E4
Mason St. SE17 21 C1
Mason St. SE17 67 D1
Masons Arms Ms. W1 11 E5
Masons Ave. EC2 13 B3
Masons Ave., Croy. 101 J3
Masons Ave., Har. 37 C4
Masons Ct., Wem. 47 A2
Masons Grn. La. W3 56 A4
Dukes Rd.
Masons Hill SE18 70 E4
Masons Hill, Brom. 96 G3
Tollgate Rd.
Mason's Pl. EC1 8 J3
Mason's Pl. EC1 58 J3
Masons Pl., Mitch. 93 J1
Mason's Yd. SW1 15 G1
Mason's Yd. SW19 84 A5
High St. Wimbledon
Massey Clo. N11 32 B5
Grove Rd.
Massie Rd. E8 50 D6
Graham Rd.
Massinger St. SE17 21 D2
Massingham St. E1 59 G4
Masson Ave., Ruis. 45 C6
Mast Ho. Ter. E14 69 A4
Master Gunner Pl. 70 B7
SE18
Masterman Ho. SE5 21 B7
Masterman Rd. E6 61 B3
Masters St. E1 59 G5
Mastmaker Rd. E14 69 A2
Maswell Pk. Cres., 72 J5
Houns.
Maswell Pk. Rd., 72 H5
Houns.
Matcham Rd. E11 51 E3
Matchless Dr. SE18 70 D7
Red Lion La.
Matfield Clo., Brom. 96 G5
Matfield Rd., Belv. 71 G6
Matham Gro. SE22 77 C4
Matham Rd., E.Mol. 91 A5
Matheson Rd. W14 66 C4
Mathews Pk. Ave. E15 51 F6
Matilda St. N1 58 F1
Matlock Clo. SE24 76 J4
Matlock Clo. SE5 77 A4
Denmark Hill Est.
Matlock Cres., Sutt. 100 B4
Matlock Cres., Wat. 28 C3
Matlock Gdns., Sutt. 100 B4
Matlock Pl., Sutt. 100 B4
Matlock Rd. E10 42 C6
Matlock St. E14 59 H6
Matlock Way, N.Mal. 92 D1
Matrimony Pl. SW8 76 C2
Wandsworth Rd.
Matson Ct., Wdf.Grn. 34 E7
Bridle Path
Matthew Clo. W10 57 A4
Matthew Ct., Mitch. 94 D5
**Matthew Parker St. 15 J4
SW1**
Matthew Parker St. 67 D2
SW1
Matthews Ave. E6 61 D2
Matthews Rd., Grnf. 46 A5
Matthews St. SW11 67 E3
Matthews Yd. WC2 12 A4
Matthias Rd. N16 50 A5
Mattingley Way SE15 68 C7
Daniel Gdns.
Mattison Rd. N4 40 G6
Mattock La. W5 64 F1
Mattock La. W13 64 E1
Maud Gdns. E13 60 F1
Maud Gdns., Bark. 61 J2
Maud Rd. E10 51 C3
Maud Rd. E13 60 F2
Maud St. E16 60 F5

Maude Rd. E17 41 H5
Maude Rd. SE5 77 B1
Maude Ter. E17 41 H4
Maudlin's Grn. E1 17 H1
Maudslay Rd. SE9 79 C3
Maudsley Ho., Brent. 64 H5
Mauleverer Rd. SW2 76 E5
Maundeby Wk. NW10 47 E6
Neasden La.
Maunder Rd. W7 64 B1
Maunsel St. SW1 19 H1
Maunsel St. SW1 67 D4
Maurice Ave. N22 40 H2
Maurice Brown Clo. 31 A5
NW7
Maurice St. W12 56 H6
Maurice Wk. NW11 39 F4
Maurier Clo., Nthlt. 54 C1
Mauritius Rd. SE10 69 E4
Maury Rd. N16 50 D2
Mavelstone Clo., 97 B1
Brom.
Mavelstone Rd., 97 A1
Brom.
Maverton Rd. E3 60 A1
Mavis Ave., Epsom 99 E5
Mavis Clo., Epsom 99 E5
Mavis Wk. E6 61 B5
Tollgate Rd.
Mawbey Est. SE1 21 H4
Mawbey Est. SE1 68 C5
Mawbey Pl. SE1 21 G4
Mawbey Pl. SE1 68 C5
Mawbey Rd. SE1 21 G4
Mawbey St. SW8 67 E7
Mawney Clo., Rom. 44 H2
Mawney Rd., Rom. 44 H2
Mawson Clo. SW20 93 B2
Mawson La. W4 65 F6
Great W. Rd.
Maxey Gdns., Dag. 53 E4
Maxey Rd. SE18 70 F4
Maxey Rd., Dag. 53 E5
Maxfield Clo. N20 23 F7
Maxilla Gdns. W10 57 A6
Cambridge Gdns.
Maxilla Wk. W10 57 A6
Bartle Rd.
Maxim Rd. N21 24 G6
Maxted Pk., Har. 37 B7
Maxted Rd. SE15 77 C3
Maxwell Clo., Croy. 94 E7
Franklin Way
Maxwell Gdns., Orp. 104 J3
Maxwell Rd. SW6 66 E7
Maxwell Rd., Borwd. 22 B3
Maxwell Rd., Well. 80 A3
Maxwelton Ave. NW7 30 D5
Maxwelton Clo. NW7 30 D5
May Clo., Chess. 98 J6
May Ct. SW19 93 E1
May Gdns., Wem. 55 F3
May Rd. E4 34 A6
May Rd. E13 60 G2
May Rd., Twick. 82 B1
May St. W14 66 C5
North End Rd.
May Tree La., Stan. 29 C7
May Wk. E13 60 H2
Queens Rd. W.
Maya Rd. N2 39 F4
Mayall Rd. SE24 76 H5
Maybank Ave. E18 42 H2
Maybank Ave., Wem. 46 C5
Maybank Gdns., Pnr. 36 A5
Maybank Rd. E18 42 H1
Maybells Commercial 62 D2
Est., Bark.
Mayberry Pl., Surb. 91 J7
Maybourne Clo. 86 E5
SE26
Maybrook Meadow 53 A5
Est., Bark.
Maybury Clo., Orp. 97 E5
Maybury Gdns. 47 H6
NW10
Maybury Ms. N6 40 C7
Maybury Rd. E13 60 J4
Maybury Rd., Bark. 61 J2
Maybury St. SW17 84 H5
Maychurch Clo., 29 G7
Stan.
Maycroft, Pnr. 36 B2
Maycross Ave., Mord. 93 C3
Mayday Gdns. SE3 79 B2
Mayday Rd., Th.Hth. 94 H6
Mayerne Rd. SE9 79 A5
Mayes Rd. N22 40 F2

Mayesbrook Rd., 61 J1
Bark.
Mayesbrook Rd., Dag. 53 B3
Mayesbrook Rd., Ilf. 53 A3
Mayesford Rd., Rom. 44 C7
Mayeswood Rd. SE12 87 J3
Mayfair Ave., Bexh. 80 D1
Mayfair Ave., Ilf. 52 C2
Mayfair Ave., Rom. 44 D6
Mayfair Ave., Twick. 72 J7
Mayfair Ave., Wor.Pk. 99 F1
Mayfair Clo., Beck. 96 B1
Mayfair Clo., Surb. 98 H1
Mayfair Gdns. N17 32 J6
Mayfair Gdns., 34 G7
Wdf.Grn.
Mayfair Ms. NW1 48 J7
Regents Pk. Rd.
Mayfair Pl. W1 15 E1
Mayfair Pl. W1 67 B1
Mayfair Ter. N14 24 D7
Mayfield, Bexh. 80 F3
Mayfield Ave. N12 31 F4
Mayfield Ave. N14 32 C2
Mayfield Ave. W4 65 E4
Mayfield Ave. W13 64 E3
Mayfield Ave., Har. 37 E5
Mayfield Ave., Orp. 97 J7
Mayfield Ave., 34 G6
Wdf.Grn.
Mayfield Clo. E8 50 C6
Forest Rd.
Mayfield Clo. SW4 76 D5
Mayfield Clo., T.Ditt. 98 E1
Mayfield Cres. N9 25 E6
Mayfield Cres., 94 F4
Th.Hth.
Mayfield Dr., Pnr. 36 F4
Mayfield Gdns. NW4 39 A6
Mayfield Gdns. W7 55 A6
Mayfield Rd. E4 34 C2
Mayfield Rd. E8 50 C7
Mayfield Rd. E13 60 F4
Mayfield Rd. E17 41 H2
Mayfield Rd. N8 40 F5
Mayfield Rd. SW19 93 C1
Mayfield Rd. W3 56 B7
Mayfield Rd. W12 65 E2
Mayfield Rd., Belv. 71 J4
Mayfield Rd., Brom. 97 B5
Mayfield Rd., Dag. 53 C1
Mayfield Rd., Enf. 25 G2
Mayfield Rd., Sutt. 100 G6
Mayfield Rd., Th.Hth. 94 F4
Mayfields, Wem. 47 A2
Mayfields Clo., Wem. 47 A2
Mayflower Clo. SE16 68 G4
Greenland Quay
Mayflower Ct. SE16 68 F2
St. Marychurch St.
Mayflower Rd. SW9 76 E3
Mayflower St. SE16 68 F2
St. Marychurch St.
Mayfly Clo., Pnr. 36 C7
Mayfly Clo., Nthlt. 54 D3
Ruislip Rd.
Mayford Clo. SW12 75 J7
Mayford Clo., Beck. 95 G3
Mayford Rd. SW12 75 J7
Maygood St. N1 8 E1
Maygood St. N1 58 F2
Maygrove Rd. NW6 48 C6
Mayhew Clo. E4 34 A3
Mayhill Rd. SE7 69 H6
Mayhill Rd., Barn. 23 B5
Maylands Dr., Sid. 89 D3
Maylands Rd., Wat. 28 C4
Maynard Clo. N15 41 B4
Brunswick Rd.
Maynard Clo. SW6 66 E7
Cambria St.
Maynard Path E17 42 C5
Maynard Rd.
Maynard Rd. E17 42 C5
Maynards Quay E1 59 F7
Garnet St.
Mayo Rd. NW10 47 E6
Mayo Rd., Croy. 95 A5
Mayola Rd. E5 50 F4
Mayow Rd. SE23 86 G3
Mayow Rd. SE26 86 G4
Mayplace Clo., Bexh. 80 H3
Mayplace La. SE18 70 E7
Mayplace Rd. E., 80 H3
Bexh.
Mayplace Rd. W., 80 G4
Bexh.
Maypole Cres., Ilf. 35 G7

Mayroyd Ave., Surb.	99	A2
Mays Ct. WC2	**12**	**A6**
Mays Hill Rd., Brom.	96	E2
Mays La. E4	34	D2
Mays La., Barn.	22	G7
Mays Rd., Tedd.	82	A5
Maysoule Rd. SW11	75	G4
Mayswood Gdns.,	53	J6
Dag.		
Mayton St. N7	49	F3
Maytree Clo., Edg.	30	C3
Maytree Wk. SW2	85	G2
Mayville Est. N16	50	B5
Woodville Rd.		
Mayville Rd. E11	51	E2
Mayville Rd., Ilf.	52	E5
Maywood Clo., Beck.	87	B7
Maze Hill SE3	69	E7
Maze Hill SE10	69	E6
Maze Rd., Rich.	65	A7
Mazenod Ave. NW6	48	D7
Rowantree Rd.		
McAdam Dr., Enf.	24	H2
McAuley Clo. SE1	**16**	**E5**
McAuley Clo. SE1	67	G3
McAuley Clo. SE9	79	E5
McCall Clo. SW4	76	E2
Jeffreys Rd.		
McCall Cres. SE7	70	B5
McCarthy Rd., Felt.	81	D5
McCoid Way SE1	**16**	**J4**
McCrone Ms. NW3	48	G6
Belsize La.		
McCullum Rd. E3	59	J1
McDermott Clo.	75	H3
SW11		
McDermott Rd. SE15	77	D3
McDonough Clo.,	98	H4
Chess.		
McDowall Rd. SE5	76	J1
McDowell Clo. E16	60	F5
McEntee Ave. E17	41	H1
McEwan Way E15	60	D1
McGrath Rd. E15	51	F5
McGregor Rd. W11	57	C5
McIntosh Clo., Wall.	101	E7
McKay Rd. SW20	83	H7
McKellar Clo.	28	J2
(Bushey), Wat.		
McKerrell Rd. SE15	77	D1
McLeod Rd. SE2	71	A4
McLeod's Ms. SW7	**18**	**B1**
McLeod's Ms. SW7	66	E4
McMillan St. SE8	69	A6
McNeil Rd. SE5	77	B2
Mead, The N2	39	F2
Mead, The W13	55	E5
Mead, The, Beck.	96	C1
Mead, The, Stan.	37	F1
Mead, The, Wall.	101	D6
Mead, The, Wat.	28	E2
Mead, The, W.Wick.	103	D1
Mead Clo., Har.	37	A1
Mead Clo., Loug.	27	E2
Mead Ct. NW9	38	C5
Mead Cres. E4	34	C4
Mead Cres., Sutt.	100	H5
Mead Gro., Rom.	44	D3
Mead Path SW17	84	F4
Mead Pl. E9	50	F6
Mead Pl., Croy.	101	H1
Mead Plat NW10	47	C6
Mead Rd., Chis.	88	F6
Mead Rd., Edg.	30	A6
Mead Rd., Rich.	82	F3
Mead Row SE1	**16**	**E5**
Mead Way, Brom.	96	E6
Mead Way, Croy.	102	H2
Meadcroft Rd. SE11	**20**	**G6**
Meadcroft Rd. SE11	67	H6
Meade Clo. W4	65	A6
Meadfield, Edg.	30	B2
Meadfield Grn., Edg.	30	B2
Meadfoot Rd. SW16	85	C7
Meadgate Ave.,	35	B5
Wdf.Grn.		
Meadlands Dr., Rich.	82	G2
Meadow, The, Chis.	88	F6
Meadow Ave., Croy.	95	G6
Meadow Bank N21	24	F6
Meadow Clo. E4	34	B1
Mount Echo Ave.		
Meadow Clo. SE6	87	A5
Meadow Clo. SW20	92	J4
Meadow Clo., Barn.	23	C6
Meadow Clo., Chis.	88	E5
Meadow Clo., Esher	98	C3
Meadow Clo., Houns.	72	G6
Meadow Clo., Nthlt.	54	G2
Meadow Clo., Rich.	82	H1
Meadow Clo., Sutt.	100	E2
Aultone Way		
Meadow Dr. N10	40	A3
Meadow Dr. NW4	38	J2
Meadow Gdns., Edg.	30	B6
Meadow Garth NW10	47	C6
Meadow Hill, N.Mal.	92	E6
Meadow Ms. SW8	**20**	**C6**
Meadow Ms. SW8	67	F6
Meadow Pl. SW8	**20**	**B7**
Meadow Pl. SW8	67	E7
Meadow Pl. W4	65	E7
Edensor Rd.		
Meadow Rd. SW8	**20**	**C6**
Meadow Rd. SW8	67	F7
Meadow Rd. SW19	84	F7
Meadow Rd., Bark.	52	J7
Meadow Rd., Borwd.	22	B2
Meadow Rd., Brom.	96	E1
Meadow Rd., Dag.	53	F6
Meadow Rd., Esher	98	B5
Meadow Rd., Felt.	81	E2
Meadow Rd., Loug.	27	B5
Meadow Rd., Pnr.	36	D4
Meadow Rd., Rom.	53	J1
Meadow Rd., Sthl.	54	F7
Meadow Rd., Sutt.	100	H5
Meadow Row SE1	**16**	**J6**
Meadow Row SE1	67	J3
Meadow Stile, Croy.	101	J3
High St.		
Meadow Vw., Har.	46	B1
Meadow Vw., Sid.	80	B7
Meadow Vw. Rd.,	94	H5
Th.Hth.		
Meadow Wk. E18	42	G4
Meadow Wk., Dag.	53	F6
Meadow Wk.,	99	E6
Epsom		
Meadow Wk., Wall.	101	B3
Meadow Way NW9	38	D5
Meadow Way, Chess.	98	H5
Meadow Way, Chig.	35	F3
Meadow Way, Orp.	104	D3
Meadow Way, Ruis.	36	B6
Meadow Way, Wem.	46	G4
Meadow Way, The,	37	B1
Har.		
Meadow Waye,	63	E6
Houns.		
Meadowbank NW3	48	J7
Meadowbank SE3	78	F3
Meadowbank, Surb.	91	J6
Meadowbank Clo.	65	J7
SW6		
Meadowbank Gdns.,	72	A1
Houns.		
Meadowbank Rd.	38	D7
NW9		
Meadowbanks, Barn.	22	G5
Barnet Rd.		
Meadowcourt Rd. SE3	78	F4
Meadowcroft, Brom.	97	C3
Meadowcroft Rd. N13	32	G2
Meadows Clo. E10	51	A2
Meadows End, Sun.	90	A1
Meadowside SE9	78	J4
Meadowsweet Clo.	61	A5
E16		
Monarch Dr.		
Meadowview Rd. SE6	87	A4
Meadowview Rd.,	80	E6
Bex.		
Meads, The, Edg.	30	D6
Meads, The, Sutt.	100	B3
Meads La., Ilf.	43	H7
Meads Rd. N22	40	H2
Meads Rd., Enf.	25	H1
Meadvale Rd. W5	55	E4
Meadvale Rd., Croy.	95	C7
Meadway N14	32	D2
Meadway NW11	39	E6
Meadway SW20	92	J4
Meadway, Barn.	23	C4
Meadway, Beck.	96	C1
Meadway, Ilf.	52	H4
Meadway, Surb.	99	C1
Meadway, Twick.	82	A5
Meadway, Wdf.Grn.	34	J5
Meadway, The SE3	78	D2
Heath La.		
Meadway, The,	35	A1
Buck.H.		
Meadway, The, Loug.	27	C6
Meadway Clo. NW11	39	E6
Meadway Clo., Barn.	23	D4
Meadway Clo., Pnr.	28	H6
Highbanks Rd.		
Meadway Ct. NW11	39	E6
Meadway Gate NW11	39	D6
Meaford Way SE20	86	E7
Meakin Est. SE1	**17**	**D5**
Meakin Est. SE1	68	B3
Meanley Rd. E12	52	B4
Meard St. W1	**11**	**H4**
Meard St. W1	58	D6
Meath Rd. E15	60	F2
Meath Rd., Ilf.	52	F3
Meath St. SW11	76	B1
Mechanics Path SE8	69	A7
Deptford High St.		
Mecklenburgh Pl.	**8**	**C5**
WC1		
Mecklenburgh Pl.	58	F4
WC1		
Mecklenburgh Sq.	**8**	**C5**
WC1		
Mecklenburgh Sq.	58	F4
WC1		
Mecklenburgh St. WC1	**8**	**C5**
Mecklenburgh St.	58	F3
WC1		
Medburn St. NW1	**7**	**H1**
Medburn St. NW1	58	D2
Medcroft Gdns. SW14	74	C4
Medebourne Clo. SE3	78	G3
Medesenge Way N13	32	H6
Medfield St. SW15	74	G7
Medhurst Clo. E3	59	H2
Arbery Rd.		
Medhurst Rd. E3	59	H2
Arbery Rd.		
Median Rd. E5	50	F5
Medina Ave., Esher	98	B3
Medina Gro. N7	49	G3
Medina Rd.		
Medina Rd. N7	49	G3
Medland Clo., Wall.	101	A1
Medlar Clo., Nthlt.	54	E2
Parkfield Ave.		
Medlar St. SE5	76	J1
Medley Rd. NW6	48	D6
Medora Rd. SW2	76	F7
Medora Rd., Rom.	53	J5
Medusa Rd. SE6	78	B6
Medway Bldgs. E3	59	H2
Medway Rd.		
Medway Clo., Croy.	95	F6
Medway Clo., Ilf.	52	F5
Loxford La.		
Medway Dr., Grnf.	55	C2
Medway Gdns., Wem.	46	D4
Medway Ms. E3	59	H2
Medway Rd.		
Medway Par., Grnf.	55	C2
Medway Rd. E3	59	H2
Medway St. SW1	**15**	**J6**
Medway St. SW1	67	D3
Medwin St. SW4	76	F4
Meerbrook Rd. SE3	78	J3
Meeson Rd. E15	60	F1
Meeson St. E5	50	H4
Meeting Flds. Path E9	50	F6
Morning La.		
Meeting Ho. La. SE15	77	E1
Meetinghouse All. E1	68	E1
Wapping La.		
Mehetabel Rd. E9	50	F6
Meister Clo., Ilf.	52	G1
Melancholy Wk., Rich.	82	F2
Melanda Clo., Chis.	88	C5
Melanie Clo., Bexh.	80	E1
Melba Way SE13	78	B1
Melbourne Ave. N13	32	F6
Melbourne Ave. W13	64	D1
Melbourne Ave., Pnr.	36	H3
Melbourne Clo., Orp.	97	H7
Melbourne Clo., Wall.	101	C5
Melbourne Rd.		
Melbourne Ct. E5	50	H4
Daubeney Rd.		
Melbourne Ct. SE20	86	D7
Melbourne Gdns.,	44	E5
Rom.		
Melbourne Gro. SE22	77	B4
Melbourne Ho., Hayes	54	C4
Melbourne Ms. SE6	78	C7
Melbourne Ms. SW9	76	G1
Melbourne Pl. WC2	**12**	**D4**
Melbourne Pl. WC2	58	F7
Melbourne Rd. E6	61	C1
Melbourne Rd. E10	42	B7
Melbourne Rd. E17	41	H4
Melbourne Rd. SW19	93	D1
Melbourne Rd., Ilf.	52	E1
Melbourne Rd., Tedd.	82	F6
Melbourne Rd., Wall.	101	B5
Melbourne Sq. SW9	76	G1
Melbourne Ms.		
Melbourne Ter. SW6	66	E7
Waterford Rd.		
Melbourne Way, Enf.	25	C6
Melbury Ave., Sthl.	63	H3
Melbury Clo., Chis.	88	B6
Melbury Clo., Esher	98	E6
Melbury Ct. W8	66	C3
Melbury Dr. SE5	68	B7
Sedgmoor Pl.		
Melbury Gdns. SW20	92	H1
Melbury Rd. W14	66	C3
Melbury Rd., Har.	37	J5
Melbury Ter. NW1	**6**	**H6**
Melbury Ter. NW1	57	H4
Melcombe Gdns., Har.	37	J6
Melcombe Pl. NW1	**10**	**J1**
Melcombe Pl. NW1	57	J5
Melcombe St. NW1	**7**	**A6**
Melcombe St. NW1	57	J4
Meldon Clo. SW6	75	E1
Bagley's La.		
Meldrum Rd., Ilf.	53	A2
Melfield Gdns. SE6	87	B4
Melford Ave., Bark.	52	H6
Melford Rd. E6	61	C4
Melford Rd. E11	51	E2
Melford Rd. E17	41	H4
Melford Rd. SE22	77	D7
Melford Rd., Ilf.	52	G2
Melfort Ave., Th.Hth.	94	H3
Melfort Rd., Th.Hth.	94	H3
Melgund Rd. N5	49	G5
Melina Pl. NW8	**6**	**E4**
Melina Pl. NW8	57	G3
Melina Rd. W12	65	H2
Melior Pl. SE1	**17**	**D3**
Melior St. SE1	**17**	**D3**
Melior St. SE1	68	A2
Meliot Rd. SE6	87	D2
Mell St. SE10	69	E5
Trafalgar Rd.		
Meller Clo., Croy.	101	E3
Melling St. SE18	70	H6
Mellish Clo., Bark.	61	J1
Mellish Gdns.,	34	G5
Wdf.Grn.		
Harts Gro.		
Mellish St. E14	69	A3
Mellison Rd. SW17	84	H5
Mellitus St. W12	56	F6
Mellor Clo., Walt.	90	F7
Mellows Rd., Ilf.	43	C3
Mellows Rd., Wall.	101	D5
Mells Cres. SE9	88	C4
Melody Rd. SW18	75	F5
Melon Rd. SE15	77	D1
Melrose Ave. N22	40	H1
Melrose Ave. NW2	47	H5
Melrose Ave. SW16	94	F3
Melrose Ave. SW19	84	C2
Melrose Ave., Borwd.	22	B5
Melrose Ave., Grnf.	54	H2
Melrose Ave., Mitch.	85	B7
Melrose Ave., Twick.	72	H7
Melrose Clo. SE12	87	G1
Melrose Clo., Grnf.	54	H2
Melrose Clo., Hayes	54	A5
Melrose Cres., Orp.	104	G4
Melrose Dr., Sthl.	63	G1
Melrose Gdns. W6	65	J3
Melrose Gdns., Edg.	38	B2
Melrose Gdns., N.Mal.	92	D3
Melrose Rd. SW13	74	F2
Melrose Rd. SW18	75	C6
Melrose Rd. SW19	93	D2
Melrose Rd. W3	65	C3
Stanley Rd.		
Melrose Rd., Pnr.	36	F4
Melrose Ter. W6	65	J2
Melsa Rd., Mord.	93	F6
Meltham Way SE16	68	E5
Egan Way		
Melthorne Dr., Ruis.	45	C3
Melthorpe Gdns. SE3	79	A1
Melton Clo., Ruis.	45	C1
Melton Ct. SW7	**18**	**F2**
Melton Ct. SW7	66	G4
Melton St. NW1	**7**	**G4**
Melton St. NW1	58	C3
Melville Ave. SW20	83	G7
Melville Ave., Grnf.	46	C5
Melville Ave., S.Croy.	102	C5
Melville Gdns. N13	32	G5
Melville Rd. E17	41	J3

Melville Rd. NW10 47 D7
Melville Rd. SW13 74 G1
Melville Rd., Sid. 89 C2
Melville Vill. Rd. W3 65 D1
High St.
Melvin Rd. SE20 95 F1
Melyn Clo. N7 49 C4
Anson Rd.
Memel Ct. EC1 8 J6
Memel St. EC1 8 J6
Memess Path SE18 70 D6
Engineer Clo.
Memorial Ave. E15 60 E3
Memorial Clo., Houns. 63 F6
Mendip Clo. SE26 86 F4
Mendip Clo. SW19 84 B2
Queensmere Rd.
Mendip Clo., Wor.Pk. 99 J2
Cotswold Way
Mendip Dr. NW2 48 B2
Mendip Rd. SW11 75 F3
Mendip Rd., Ilf. 43 H5
Mendora Rd. SW6 66 B7
Menelik Rd. NW2 48 B4
Menlo Gdns. SE19 86 A7
Menotti St. E2 9 J5
Mentmore Clo., Har. 37 F6
Mentmore Ter. E8 50 E7
Meon Ct., Islw. 73 B2
Meon Rd. W3 65 C2
Meopham Rd., Mitch. 94 C1
Mepham Cres., Har. 28 J7
Mepham Gdns., Har. 28 J7
Mepham St. SE1 16 E2
Mepham St. SE1 67 F1
Mera Dr., Bexh. 80 G4
Merantun Way SW19 93 F1
Merbury Clo. SE13 78 D5
Merbury Rd. SE28 70 H2
Mercator Rd. SE13 78 D4
Mercer Clo., T.Ditt. 91 C7
Mercer Pl., Pnr. 36 C2
Cross Way
Mercer St. WC2 12 A4
Mercer St. WC2 58 E6
Merceron St. E1 59 E4
Mercers Clo. SE10 69 F4
Mercers Pl. W6 65 J4
Mercers Rd. N19 49 D3
Merchant St. E3 59 J3
Merchiston Rd. SE6 87 D2
Merchland Rd. SE9 88 F1
Mercia Gro. SE13 78 C4
Mercier Rd. SW15 75 B5
Mercury Cen. Ind. Est., Felt. 72 A5
Mercury Way SE14 68 G6
Mercy Ter. SE13 78 B4
Mere Clo. SW15 75 A7
Mere Clo., Orp. 104 D2
Mere End, Croy. 95 G7
Mere Side, Orp. 104 D2
Merebank La., Croy. 101 F5
Meredith Ave. NW2 47 J5
Meredith Clo., Pnr. 28 D7
Meredith St. E13 60 G3
Meredith St. EC1 8 G4
Meredyth Rd. SW13 74 G2
Meretone Clo. SE4 77 H4
Merevale Cres., Mord. 93 F6
Mereway Rd., Twick. 82 A1
Merewood Clo., Brom. 97 D2
Merewood Rd., Bexh. 80 J2
Mereworth Clo., Brom. 96 F5
Mereworth Dr. SE18 70 E7
Merganser Gdns. SE28 70 G3
Avocet Ms.
Meriden Clo., Brom. 88 A7
Meriden Clo., Ilf. 43 F1
Meridian Gate E14 69 C2
Meridian Rd. SE7 70 A7
Meridian Trd. Est. SE7 69 H4
Meridian Wk. N17 33 B6
Commercial Rd.
Meridian Way N9 33 G2
Meridian Way N18 33 F6
Meridian Way, Enf. 25 G6
Merifield Rd. SE9 78 J4
Merino Clo. E11 42 J4
Merino Pl., Sid. 80 A6
Blackfen Rd.
Merivale Rd. SW15 75 B4
Merivale Rd., Har. 36 J7
Merlewood Dr., Chis. 97 C1
Merley Ct. NW9 47 C1
Merlin Clo., Croy. 102 B4
Minster Dr.
Merlin Clo., Nthlt. 54 C3
Merlin Cres., Edg. 37 J1
Merlin Gdns., Brom. 87 G3
Merlin Gro., Beck. 95 J4
Merlin Gro., Ilf. 35 E6
Merlin Rd. E12 52 A2
Merlin Rd., Well. 80 A4
Merlin Rd. N., Well. 80 A4
Merlin St. WC1 8 E4
Merling Clo., Chess. 98 G5
Mansfield Rd.
Merlins Ave., Har. 45 F3
Mermaid Ct. SE1 17 B3
Mermaid Ct. SE1 68 A2
Mermaid Ct. SE16 68 J1
Merredene St. SW2 76 F6
Merrick Rd., Sthl. 63 F2
Merrick Sq. SE1 17 B5
Merrick Sq. SE1 67 J3
Merridene N21 24 H6
Merrielands Cres., Dag. 62 F1
Merrilands Rd., Wor.Pk. 99 J1
Merrilees Rd., Sid. 88 H1
Merrilyn Clo., Esher 98 D6
Merriman Rd. SE3 78 J1
Merrington Rd. SW6 66 D6
Merrion Ave., Stan. 29 G5
Merritt Gdns., Chess. 98 F6
Mansfield Rd.
Merritt Rd. SE4 77 J5
Merrivale N14 24 D6
Merrivale Ave., Ilf. 43 A4
Merrow St. SE17 21 B4
Merrow St. SE17 67 J6
Merrow Wk. SE17 21 C3
Merrow Way, Croy. 103 C6
Merry Hill Mt. (Bushey), Wat. 28 H1
Merry Hill Rd., Wat. 28 J1
Merrydown Way, Chis. 97 B1
Merryfield SE3 78 F2
Merryfield Gdns., Stan. 29 F5
Merryhill Clo. E4 26 B7
Merryhills Ct. N14 24 C5
Merryhills Dr., Enf. 24 D4
Mersea Ho., Bark. 52 E6
Mersey Rd. E17 41 J3
Mersey Wk., Nthlt. 54 G2
Brabazon Rd.
Mersham Dr. NW9 38 A5
Mersham Pl. SE20 95 E1
Jasmine Gro.
Mersham Rd., Th.Hth. 95 A3
Merten Rd., Rom. 44 E7
Merthyr Ter. SW13 65 H6
Merton Ave. W4 65 F4
Merton Ave., Nthlt. 45 J5
Merton Gdns., Orp. 97 E5
Merton Hall Gdns. SW20 93 B1
Merton Hall Rd. SW19 84 B7
Merton High St. SW19 84 F7
Merton Ind. Pk. SW19 93 F1
Merton La. N6 48 J2
Merton Mans. SW20 93 A2
Merton Ri. NW3 48 H7
Merton Rd. E17 42 C5
Merton Rd. SE25 95 D5
Merton Rd. SW18 75 D5
Merton Rd. SW19 84 E7
Merton Rd., Bark. 52 J7
Merton Rd., Har. 45 J1
Merton Rd., Ilf. 43 J7
Merton Way, W.Mol. 90 H4
Merttins Rd. SE15 77 G5
Mervan Rd. SW2 76 G4
Mervyn Ave. SE9 88 F3
Mervyn Rd. W13 64 D3
Messaline Ave. W3 56 C6
Messent Rd. SE9 78 J5
Messeter Pl. SE9 79 D6
Messina Ave. NW6 48 D7
Metcalfe Wk., Felt. 81 E4
Gabriel Clo.
Meteor St. SW11 76 A4
Meteor Way, Wall. 101 E7
Metheringham Way NW9 38 E1
Methley St. SE11 20 F4
Methley St. SE11 67 G5
Methuen Clo., Edg. 30 A7
Methuen Pk. N10 40 B2
Methuen Rd., Belv. 71 H4
Methuen Rd., Bexh. 80 F4
Methuen Rd., Edg. 30 A7
Methwold Rd. W10 57 A5
Metro Ind. Cen., Islw. 73 B2
Metropolitan Cen., The, Grnf. 54 H1
Mews, The N1 58 J1
St. Paul St.
Mews, The, Ilf. 43 A5
Mews, The, Twick. 73 E6
Bridge Rd.
Mews Pl., Wdf.Grn. 34 G4
Mews St. E1 17 H1
Mews St. E1 68 D1
Mexfield Rd. SW15 75 C5
Meyer Rd., Erith 71 J6
Meymott St. SE1 16 G2
Meymott St. SE1 67 H1
Meynell Cres. E9 50 G7
Meynell Gdns. E9 50 G7
Meynell Rd. E9 50 G7
Meyrick Rd. NW10 47 G6
Meyrick Rd. SW11 75 G3
Miall Wk. SE26 86 H4
Micawber St. N1 9 A3
Micawber St. N1 58 J3
Michael Faraday Ho. SE17 21 C4
Michael Gaynor Clo. W7 64 C1
Michael Rd. E11 51 E1
Michael Rd. SE25 95 B3
Michael Rd. SW6 75 E1
Michaels Clo. SE13 78 E4
Micheldever Rd. SE12 78 E6
Michelham Gdns., Twick. 82 D3
Michels Row, Rich. 73 H4
Kew Foot Rd.
Michigan Ave. E12 52 C4
Michleham Down N12 31 C4
Mickleham Clo., Orp. 97 J2
Mickleham Gdns., Sutt. 100 B6
Mickleham Rd., Orp. 97 J1
Mickleham Way, Croy. 103 D7
Micklethwaite Rd. SW6 66 D6
Middle Dene NW7 30 D3
Middle Fld. NW8 57 G1
Middle Grn. Clo., Surb. 91 J6
Alpha Rd.
Middle La. N8 40 E5
Middle La., Tedd. 82 C6
Middle La. Ms. N8 40 E5
Middle La.
Middle Pk. Ave. SE9 79 A6
Middle Path, Har. 46 A1
Middle Rd.
Middle Rd. E13 60 G2
London Rd.
Middle Rd. SW16 94 C2
Middle Rd., Barn. 23 H6
Middle Rd., Har. 46 A2
Middle Row W10 57 B4
Middle St. EC1 12 J1
Middle St., Croy. 101 J3
Surrey St.
Middle Temple La. EC4 12 E4
Middle Temple La. EC4 58 G6
Middle Way SW16 94 D2
Middle Way, Erith 71 E3
Middle Way, Hayes 54 D4
Douglas Cres.
Middle Way, The, Har. 37 C2
Middle Yd. SE1 17 D1
Middlefield Gdns., Ilf. 43 E6
Middlefielde W13 55 E5
Middleham Gdns. N18 33 D6
Middleham Rd. N18 33 D6
Middlesborough Rd. N18 33 D6
Middlesex Business Cen., The, Sthl. 63 F2
Middlesex Ct. W4 65 F4
British Gro.
Middlesex Pas. EC1 12 H2
Middlesex Rd., Mitch. 94 E4
Middlesex St. E1 13 E2
Middlesex St. E1 59 B5
Middlesex Wf. E5 50 F2
Middleton Ave. E4 33 J4
Middleton Ave., Grnf. 55 A2
Middleton Ave., Sid. 89 C6
Middleton Bldgs. W1 11 F2
Middleton Clo. E4 33 J3
Middleton Dr. SE16 68 G2
Middleton Dr., Pnr. 36 A3
Middleton Gdns., Ilf. 43 E6
Middleton Gro. N7 49 E5
Middleton Ms. N7 49 E5
Middleton Gro.
Middleton Rd. E8 50 C7
Middleton Rd. NW11 39 D7
Middleton Rd., Cars. 93 G7
Middleton Rd., Mord. 93 E6
Middleton St. E2 59 E3
Middleton Way SE13 78 D4
Middleway NW11 39 E5
Midfield Ave., Bexh. 80 J3
Midford Pl. W1 7 G6
Midholm NW11 39 E4
Midholm, Wem. 47 A1
Midholm Clo. NW11 39 E4
Midholm Rd., Croy. 102 H2
Midhope St. WC1 8 B4
Midhurst Ave. N10 40 A3
Midhurst Ave., Croy. 94 G7
Midhurst Hill, Bexh. 80 G6
Midhurst Rd. W13 64 D2
Midland Pl. E14 69 C5
Ferry St.
Midland Rd. E10 42 C7
Midland Rd. NW1 7 J2
Midland Rd. NW1 58 D2
Midland Ter. NW2 48 A3
Midland Ter. NW10 56 E4
Shaftesbury Gdns.
Midleton Rd., N.Mal. 92 C2
Midlothian Rd. E3 59 H5
Midmoor Rd. SW12 85 C1
Midmoor Rd. SW19 93 A1
Midship Clo. SE16 68 G1
Surrey Water Rd.
Midstrath Rd. NW10 47 E4
Midsummer Ave., Houns. 72 F4
Midway, Sutt. 93 C7
Midwood Clo. NW2 47 H3
Miers Clo. E6 61 D1
Mighell Ave., Ilf. 43 A5
Milborne Gro. SW10 18 D4
Milborne Gro. SW10 66 F5
Milborne St. E9 50 F6
Milborough Cres. SE12 78 E6
Milcote St. SE1 16 G4
Milcote St. SE1 67 H2
Mildenhall Rd. E5 50 F4
Mildmay Ave. N1 50 A6
Mildmay Gro. N1 50 A5
Mildmay Pk. N1 50 A5
Mildmay Rd. N1 50 A5
Mildmay Rd., Ilf. 52 E3
Winston Way
Mildmay Rd., Rom. 44 J5
Mildmay St. N1 50 A6
Mildred Ave., Borwd. 22 A4
Mildred Ave., Nthlt. 45 H5
Mile End, The E17 41 G1
Mile End Pl. E1 59 G4
Mile End Rd. E1 59 F5
Mile End Rd. E3 59 H4
Mile Rd., Wall. 101 B1
Miles Pl. NW1 10 G1
Miles Pl., Surb. 91 J4
Villiers Ave.
Miles Rd. N8 40 E3
Miles Rd., Mitch. 93 G3
Miles St. SW8 20 A6
Miles St. SW8 67 E6
Miles Way N20 31 H2
Milespit Hill NW7 30 H5
Milestone Clo., Sutt. 100 G6
Milestone Rd. SE19 86 C6
Milfoil St. W12 56 G7
Milford Clo. SE2 71 E6
Milford Gdns., Edg. 30 A7
Milford Gdns., Wem. 46 G4
Milford Gro., Sutt. 100 F4
Milford La. WC2 12 E5
Milford La. WC2 58 F7
Milford Ms. SW16 85 F3
Milford Rd. W13 64 E1
Milford Rd., Sthl. 54 G7
Milford Way SE15 77 C1
Sumner Est.
Milk St. E16 70 E1
Milk St. EC2 13 A3
Milk St., Brom. 87 H6
Milk Yd. E1 59 F7

Milkwell Gdns., Wdf.Grn. 34 H7
Milkwell Yd. SE5 76 J1
Milkwood Rd. SE24 76 H5
Mill Clo., Cars. 101 A2
Mill Cor., Barn. 23 C1
Mill Ct. E10 51 C3
Mill Fm. Clo., Pnr. 36 C2
Mill Fm. Cres., Houns. 81 E1
Mill Gdns. SE26 86 E4
Mill Grn. Rd., Mitch. 93 J7
Mill Hill SW13 74 G2
Mill Hill SW13
Mill Hill Circ. NW7 30 F5
Watford Way
Mill Hill Gro. W3 65 B1
Mill Hill Rd.
Mill Hill Rd. SW13 74 G2
Mill Hill Rd. W3 65 B2
Mill La. E4 26 B3
Mill La. NW6 48 B5
Mill La. SE18 70 D5
Mill La., Cars. 100 J4
Mill La., Croy. 101 F3
Mill La., Rom. 44 E6
(Chadwell Heath)
Mill La., Wdf.Grn. 34 F5
Mill Mead Ind. Cen. N17 41 E2
Mill Mead Rd. N17 41 E3
Mill Pl. E14 59 J6
East India Dock Rd.
Mill Pl., Chis. 97 E1
Mill Pl., Kings.T. 91 J3
Mill Plat, Islw. 73 D2
Mill Plat Ave., Islw. 73 D2
Mill Ridge, Edg. 29 J5
Mill Rd. E16 69 H1
Mill Rd. SE13 78 C3
Loampit Vale
Mill Rd. SW19 84 F7
Mill Rd., Erith 71 J7
Mill Rd., Ilf. 52 D3
Mill Rd., Twick. 81 J2
Mill Row N1 59 B1
Mill Shot Clo. SW6 74 J1
Mill St. SE1 **17 G4**
Mill St. SE1 68 C2
Mill St. W1 **11 F5**
Mill St. W1 58 C7
Mill St., Kings.T. 91 H3
Mill Trd. Est., The NW10 56 C3
Mill Vale, Brom. 96 F2
Mill Vw. Gdns., Croy. 102 G3
Mill Way, Felt. 72 B5
Mill Yd. E1 **13 H5**
Millais Ave. E12 52 D5
Millais Gdns., Edg. 38 A2
Millais Rd. E11 51 C4
Millais Rd., Enf. 25 C5
Millais Rd., N.Mal. 92 E7
Millais Way, Epsom 99 C4
Millard Clo. N16 50 B5
Boleyn Rd.
Millard Ter., Dag. 53 G6
Church Elm La.
Millbank SW1 **16 A5**
Millbank SW1 67 E4
Millbank Twr. SW1 **20 A2**
Millbank Twr. SW1 67 E4
Millbank Way SE12 78 G5
Millbourne Rd., Felt. 81 E4
Millbrook Ave., Well. 79 G4
Millbrook Gdns., Rom. 44 F6
(Chadwell Heath)
Millbrook Rd. N9 33 E1
Millbrook Rd. SW9 76 H3
Millender Wk. SE16 68 F4
Millennium Pl. E2 59 E2
Parmiter St.
Miller Clo., Pnr. 36 C2
Miller Rd. SW19 84 G6
Miller Rd., Croy. 101 F1
Miller St. NW1 **7 F1**
Miller St. NW1 58 C2
Miller's Ave. E8 50 C5
Millers Clo. NW7 30 G4
Millers Ct. W4 65 F5
Chiswick Mall
Millers Grn. Clo., Enf. 24 H3
Miller's Ter. E8 50 C5
Millers Way W6 65 J2
Millet Rd., Grnf. 54 H3
Millfield Ave. E17 41 H1
Millfield La. N6 48 J2
Millfield Pl. N6 49 A2
Millfield Rd., Edg. 38 C2

Millfield Rd., Houns. 81 E1
Millfields Rd. E5 50 F4
Millgrove St. SW11 76 A1
Millharbour E14 69 B3
Millhaven Clo., Rom. 44 B6
Millhouse Pl. SE27 85 H4
Millicent Rd. E10 50 J1
Milligan St. E14 59 J7
Three Colt St.
Milliners Ct., Loug. 27 D2
The Cft.
Milling Rd., Edg. 30 D7
Millman Ms. WC1 **8 C6**
Millman Ms. WC1 58 F4
Millman St. WC1 **8 C6**
Millman St. WC1 58 F4
Millmark Gro. SE14 77 H2
Millmarsh La., Enf. 25 H2
Millpond Est. SE16 68 E2
West La.
Mills Ct. EC2 **9 D5**
Mills Gro. E14 60 C5
Dewberry St.
Mills Gro. NW4 39 A3
Mills Row W4 65 D4
Bridge St.
Millside, Cars. 100 J2
Millside Pl., Islw. 73 E2
Millsmead Way, Loug. 27 C2
Millson Clo. N20 31 G2
Millstream Clo. N13 32 G5
Millstream Rd. SE1 **17 F4**
Millstream Rd. SE1 68 C2
Millwall Dock Rd. E14 69 A3
Millway NW7 30 E5
Millway Gdns., Nthlt. 45 F6
Millwell Cres., Chig. 35 G5
Millwood Rd., Houns. 72 J5
Millwood St. W10 57 B5
St. Charles Sq.
Milman Clo., Pnr. 36 D3
Milman Rd. NW6 57 A2
Milman's St. SW10 **18 E6**
Milman's St. SW10 66 G6
Milne Feild, Pnr. 28 G7
Milne Gdns. SE9 79 B5
Milner Dr., Twick. 73 A7
Milner Pl. N1 58 G1
Milner Pl., Cars. 101 A4
High St.
Milner Rd. E15 60 E3
Milner Rd. SW19 93 E1
Milner Rd., Dag. 53 C2
Milner Rd., Kings.T. 91 G3
Milner Rd., Mord. 93 G5
Milner Rd., Th.Hth. 95 A3
Milner Sq. N1 49 H7
Milner St. SW3 **18 J1**
Milner St. SW3 66 J4
Milnthorpe Rd. W4 65 D6
Milo Rd. SE22 77 C6
Milroy Wk. SE1 **16 G1**
Milson Rd. W14 64 A3
Milton Ave. E6 52 A7
Milton Ave. N6 40 C7
Milton Ave. NW9 38 C3
Milton Ave. NW10 56 C1
Milton Ave., Barn. 23 C5
Milton Ave., Croy. 95 A7
Milton Ave., Sutt. 100 G3
Milton Clo. N2 39 F5
Milton Clo. SE1 **21 F2**
Milton Clo. SE1 68 C4
Milton Clo., Hayes 54 A6
Milton Clo., Sutt. 100 G3
Milton Ct. EC2 **13 B1**
Milton Ct. Rd. SE14 68 H6
Milton Cres., Ilf. 43 F7
Milton Dr., Borwd. 22 B5
Milton Gro. N11 32 C5
Milton Gro. N16 50 A4
Milton Pk. N6 40 C7
Milton Pl. N7 49 G5
George's Rd.
Milton Rd. E17 42 A4
Milton Rd. N6 40 C7
Milton Rd. N15 40 H4
Milton Rd. NW7 30 G5
Milton Rd. NW9 38 G7
West Hendon Bdy.
Milton Rd. SE24 76 H6
Milton Rd. SW14 74 D3
Milton Rd. SW19 84 F6
Milton Rd. W3 65 D1
Milton Rd. W7 55 C7
Milton Rd., Belv. 71 G4
Milton Rd., Croy. 102 A1
Milton Rd., Hmptn. 81 G7

Milton Rd., Har. 37 B4
Milton Rd., Mitch. 85 A7
Milton Rd., Sutt. 100 D3
Milton Rd., Wall. 101 C6
Milton Rd., Well. 79 J1
Milton St. EC2 **13 B1**
Milton St. EC2 59 A5
Milverton Gdns., Ilf. 52 J2
Milverton Rd. NW6 47 J7
Milverton St. SE11 **20 F4**
Milverton St. SE11 67 G5
Milverton Way SE9 88 D4
Milward St. E1 59 E5
Stepney Way
Milward Wk. SE18 70 D6
Spearman St.
Mimosa Rd., Hayes 54 C5
Mimosa St. SW6 75 C1
Mina Rd. SE17 **21 E4**
Mina Rd. SE17 68 B5
Mina Rd. SW19 93 D1
Minard Rd. SE6 78 E7
Minchenden Cres. N14 32 C3
Minden Rd. SE20 95 E1
Minden Rd., Sutt. 100 C2
Minehead Rd. SW16 85 F5
Minehead Rd., Har. 45 G3
Minera Ms. SW1 **19 C1**
Minera Ms. SW1 67 A4
Mineral St. SE18 70 H4
Minerva Clo. SW9 67 G7
Minerva Clo., Sid. 88 H3
Minerva Rd. E4 34 B7
Minerva Rd. NW10 56 C3
Minerva Rd., Kings.T. 91 J2
Minerva St. E2 59 E2
Minet Ave. NW10 56 E2
Minet Dr., Hayes 63 A1
Minet Gdns. NW10 56 E2
Minet Gdns., Hayes 63 A1
Minet Rd. SW9 76 H2
Minford Gdns. W14 66 A2
Ming St. E14 60 A7
Mingard Wk. N7 49 F2
Hornsey Rd.
Ministry Way SE9 88 C2
Miniver Pl. EC4 58 J7
Garlick Hill
Mink Ct., Houns. 72 C2
Minniedale, Surb. 91 J5
Minories EC3 **13 F4**
Minories EC3 59 C6
Minshull Pl., Beck. 87 A7
Minshull St. SW8 76 D1
Wandsworth Rd.
Minson Rd. E9 59 G1
Minstead Gdns. SW15 74 F7
Minstead Way, N.Mal. 92 E6
Minster Ave., Sutt. 100 D2
Minster Dr., Croy. 102 B4
Minster Gdns., W.Mol. 90 F5
Molesey Ave.
Minster Rd. NW2 48 B5
Minster Rd., Brom. 87 H7
Minster Wk. N8 40 E4
Lightfoot Rd.
Minstrel Gdns., Surb. 91 J5
Mint Rd., Wall. 101 B4
Mint St. SE1 **16 J3**
Mint Wk., Croy. 101 J3
High St.
Mintern Clo. N13 32 H3
Mintern St. N1 **9 C1**
Mintern St. N1 59 A2
Minterne Ave., Sthl. 63 G4
Minterne Rd., Har. 37 J5
Minterne Way, Hayes 54 C6
Minton Ms. NW6 48 E6
Lymington Rd.
Mirabel Rd. SW6 66 C7
Miranda Clo. E1 59 F5
Sidney St.
Miranda Ct. W3 55 J6
Queens Dr.
Miranda Rd. N19 49 C1
Mirfield St. SE7 70 A3
Miriam Rd. SE18 70 H5
Mirror Path SE9 87 J3
Lambscroft Ave.
Missenden Gdns., Mord. 93 F6

Mission Gro. E17 41 H5
Mission Pl. SE15 77 D1
Mission Sq., Brent. 64 H6
Netley Rd.
Mistletoe Clo., Croy. 102 G1
Marigold Way
Mitcham Gdn. Vill., Mitch. 94 A5
Mitcham Ind. Est., Mitch. 94 A1
Mitcham La. SW16 85 B6
Mitcham Pk., Mitch. 93 H4
Mitcham Rd. E6 61 B3
Mitcham Rd. SW17 84 J5
Mitcham Rd., Croy. 94 E6
Mitcham Rd., Ilf. 43 J7
Mitchell Clo. SE2 71 C4
Mitchell Clo., Belv. 71 J3
Mitchell Rd. N13 32 H5
Mitchell Rd., Orp. 104 J4
Mitchell St. EC1 **8 J5**
Mitchell St. EC1 58 J4
Mitchell Wk. E6 61 B5
Oliver Gdns.
Mitchell Way NW10 47 C6
Mitchell Way, Brom. 96 G1
Mitchellbrook Way NW10 47 D6
Mitchison Rd. N1 50 A6
Mitchley Rd. N17 41 D3
Mitford Rd. N19 49 E2
Mitre, The E14 59 J7
Three Colt St.
Mitre Clo., Brom. 96 F2
Beckenham La.
Mitre Clo., Sutt. 100 F7
Mitre Ct. EC2 **13 A3**
Mitre Ct. EC4 **12 F4**
Mitre Rd. E15 60 E2
Mitre Rd. SE1 **16 F3**
Mitre Rd. SE1 67 G2
Mitre Sq. EC3 **13 E4**
Mitre St. EC3 **13 E4**
Mitre St. EC3 59 B6
Mitre Way NW10 56 H4
Moat, The, N.Mal. 92 E1
Moat Clo., Orp. 104 J6
Moat Cres. N3 39 E3
Moat Cft., Well. 80 C3
Moat Dr. E13 60 J2
Boundary Rd.
Moat Dr., Har. 36 J4
Moat Fm. Rd., Nthlt. 45 F7
Moat Pl. SW9 76 F3
Moat Pl. W3 56 B6
Moatside, Enf. 25 F4
Moatside, Felt. 81 C4
Moberley Rd. SW4 76 F2
Modbury Gdns. NW5 49 A6
Queens Cres.
Modder Pl. SW15 75 A4
Cardinal Pl.
Model Cotts. SW14 74 C4
Upper Richmond Rd. W.
Model Fm. Clo. SE9 88 B3
Modling Ho. E2 59 G3
Mace St.
Moelwyn Hughes Ct. N7 49 D5
Hilldrop Cres.
Moelyn Ms., Har. 37 D5
Moffat Gdns., Mitch. 93 G3
Moffat Rd. N13 32 E6
Moffat Rd. SW17 84 H4
Moffat Rd., Th.Hth. 94 J2
Mogden La., Islw. 73 B5
Mohmmad Khan Rd. E11 51 F1
Harvey Rd.
Moiety Rd. E14 69 A2
Moira Clo. N17 41 B2
Moira Rd. SE9 79 C4
Moland Mead SE16 68 G5
Crane Mead
Molasses Row SW11 75 F3
Cinnamon Row
Mole Abbey Gdns., W.Mol. 90 G3
New Rd.
Mole Ct., Epsom 99 C4
Molember Ct., E.Mol. 91 B5
Molember Rd., E.Mol. 91 A5
Molescroft SE9 88 F3
Molesey Ave., W.Mol. 90 F5
Molesey Dr., Sutt. 100 B2
Molesey Pk. Ave., W.Mol. 90 H5

Molesey Pk. Clo., E.Mol.	90	J5
Molesey Pk. Rd., E.Mol.	90	H5
Molesey Pk. Rd., W.Mol.	90	H5
Molesey Rd., Walt.	90	E7
Molesey Rd., W.Mol.	90	E5
Molesford Rd. SW6	75	D1
Molesham Clo., W.Mol.	90	H3
Molesham Way, W.Mol.	90	H3
Molesworth St. SE13	78	C4
Molineux Pl., Tedd.	82	D5
Mollison Ave., Enf.	25	H5
Mollison Dr., Wall.	101	D7
Mollison Way, Edg.	37	J2
Molly Huggins Clo. SW12	76	C7
Molyneux St. W1	**10**	**H2**
Molyneux St. W1	57	H5
Mona Rd. SE15	77	F2
Mona St. E16	60	F5
Monarch Clo., W.Wick.	103	F4
Monarch Dr. E16	61	A5
Monarch Ms. SW16	85	G5
Monarch Rd., Belv.	71	G3
Monastery Gdns., Enf.	25	A2
Monaveen Gdns., W.Mol.	90	G3
Monck St. SW1	**15**	**J6**
Monck St. SW1	67	D3
Monclar Rd. SE5	77	A4
Moncorvo Clo. SW7	**14**	**G4**
Moncrieff Clo. E6	61	B6
Linton Gdns.		
Moncrieff St. SE15	77	D2
Monega Rd. E7	51	J6
Monega Rd. E12	52	A6
Monfitchet E6	61	E6
Warwall		
Monier Rd. E3	51	A7
Monivea Rd., Beck.	86	J7
Monk Dr. E16	60	G6
Monk Pas. E16	60	G7
Monk Dr.		
Monk St. SE18	70	D4
Monkchester Clo., Loug.	27	D1
Monkfrith Ave. N14	24	B6
Monkfrith Clo. N14	24	B7
Monkfrith Way N14	24	A7
Monkhams Ave., Wdf.Grn.	34	G5
Monkhams Dr., Wdf.Grn.	34	H5
Monkhams La., Buck.H.	34	H3
Monkhams La., Wdf.Grn.	34	G5
Monkleigh Rd., Mord.	93	B3
Monks Ave., Barn.	23	F6
Monks Ave., W.Mol.	90	F5
Monks Clo. SE2	71	D4
Monks Clo., Enf.	24	J2
Monks Clo., Har.	45	H2
Monks Clo., Ruis.	45	D4
Monks Dr. W3	56	A5
Monks Orchard Rd., Beck.	103	A1
Monks Pk., Wem.	47	B6
Monks Pk. Gdns., Wem.	47	B7
Monks Rd., Enf.	24	J2
Monks Way NW11	39	C4
Hurstwood Rd.		
Monks Way, Beck.	96	A6
Monks Way, Orp.	104	F1
Monksdene Gdns., Sutt.	100	E3
Monksgrove, Loug.	27	D5
Monksmead, Borwd.	22	C4
Monkswell Ct. N10	40	A1
Pembroke Rd.		
Monkswood Gdns., Borwd.	22	D5
Monkswood Gdns., Ilf.	43	D3
Monkton Rd., Well.	79	J2
Monkton St. SE11	**20**	**F1**
Monkton St. SE11	67	G4
Monkville Ave. NW11	39	C4
Monkwell Sq. EC2	**13**	**A2**
Monmouth Ave. E18	42	H3
Monmouth Ave., Kings.T.	82	F7

Monmouth Clo. W4	65	D3
Beaumont Rd.		
Monmouth Clo., Mitch.	94	E4
Recreation Way		
Monmouth Clo., Well.	80	A4
Monmouth Gro. W5	64	H4
Sterling Pl.		
Monmouth Pl. W2	**10**	**A4**
Monmouth Rd. E6	61	C3
Monmouth Rd. N9	33	E2
Monmouth Rd. W2	57	D6
Monmouth Rd., Dag.	53	F5
Monmouth St. WC2	**12**	**A5**
Monmouth St. WC2	58	G6
Monnery Rd. N19	49	C3
Monnow Rd. SE1	**21**	**H2**
Monnow Rd. SE1	68	D5
Mono La., Felt.	81	B2
Monoux Gro. E17	42	A1
Monro La., Har.	29	B7
Monroe Cres., Enf.	25	E1
Monroe Dr. SW14	74	B5
Mons Way, Brom.	97	B6
Monsal Ct. E5	50	G4
Redwald Rd.		
Monsell Rd. N4	49	H3
Monson Rd. NW10	56	G2
Monson Rd. SE14	68	G7
Montacute Rd. SE6	77	J7
Montacute Rd., Mord.	93	F6
Montagu Cres. N18	33	E4
Montagu Gdns. N18	33	E4
Montagu Gdns., Wall.	101	C4
Montagu Mans. W1	**11**	**A1**
Montagu Ms. N. W1	11	A2
Montagu Ms. N. W1	57	J5
Montagu Ms. S. W1	**11**	**A3**
Montagu Ms. W. W1	**11**	**A3**
Montagu Pl. W1	**10**	**J2**
Montagu Pl. W1	57	J5
Montagu Rd. N9	33	F3
Montagu Rd. N18	33	E5
Montagu Rd. NW4	38	G6
Montagu Rd. Ind. Est. N18	33	F4
Montagu Row W1	**11**	**A2**
Montagu Sq. W1	**11**	**A2**
Montagu Sq. W1	57	J5
Montagu St. W1	**11**	**A3**
Montagu St. W1	57	J6
Montague Ave. SE4	77	J4
Montague Ave. W7	64	C1
Montague Clo. SE1	**11**	**B1**
Montague Clo. SE1	68	A1
Montague Clo., Walt.	90	A7
Montague Gdns. W3	56	A7
Montague Pl. WC1	**11**	**J1**
Montague Pl. WC1	58	D5
Montague Rd. E8	50	D5
Montague Rd. E11	51	F3
Montague Rd. N8	40	F5
Montague Rd. N15	41	D4
Montague Rd. SW19	84	E7
Montague Rd. W7	64	C2
Montague Rd. W13	55	E6
Montague Rd., Croy.	101	H1
Montague Rd., Houns.	72	H3
Montague Rd., Rich.	73	H6
Montague Rd., Sthl.	63	E4
Montague Sq. SE15	68	F7
Clifton Way		
Montague St. EC1	**12**	**J2**
Montague St. EC1	58	J5
Montague St. WC1	**12**	**A1**
Montague St. WC1	58	E5
Montague Waye, Sthl.	63	E3
Montalt Rd., Wdf.Grn.	34	F5
Montana Rd. SW17	85	A4
Montana Rd. SW20	92	J1
Montbelle Rd. SE9	88	E3
Montcalm Clo., Brom.	96	G6
Montcalm Clo., Hayes	54	B3
Ayles Rd.		
Montcalm Rd. SE7	70	A7
Montclare St. E2	**9**	**F5**
Monteagle Ave., Bark.	52	F6
Monteagle Way E5	50	D3
Rendlesham Rd.		
Monteagle Way SE15	77	E3
Montefiore St. SW8	76	B2
Monteith Rd. E3	59	J1
Montem Rd. SE23	77	J7
Montem Rd., N.Mal.	92	E4
Montem St. N4	49	F1
Thorpedale Rd.		

Montenotte Rd. N8	40	C5
Monterey Clo., Bex.	89	J2
Montesole Ct., Pnr.	36	C2
Pinner Hill Rd.		
Montford Pl. SE11	**20**	**E4**
Montford Pl. SE11	67	G5
Montford Rd., Sun.	90	A4
Montfort Gdns., Ilf.	35	F6
Montfort Pl. SW19	84	A1
Montgolfier Wk., Nthlt.	54	E3
Jetstar Way		
Montgomery Ave., Esher	98	B3
Montgomery Clo., Mitch.	94	E4
Montgomery Clo., Sid.	79	J6
Montgomery Rd. W4	65	C4
Montgomery Rd., Edg.	29	J6
Montholme Rd. SW11	75	J6
Monthope Rd. E1	**13**	**H2**
Montolieu Gdns. SW15	74	H5
Montpelier Ave. W5	55	F5
Montpelier Ave., Bex.	80	D7
Montpelier Gdns. E6	61	A3
Montpelier Gdns., Rom.	44	C7
Montpelier Gro. NW5	49	C5
Montpelier Ms. SW7	**14**	**H5**
Montpelier Pl. SW7	**14**	**H5**
Montpelier Pl. SW7	66	H3
Montpelier Ri. NW11	39	B7
Montpelier Ri., Wem.	46	G1
Montpelier Rd. N3	39	F1
Montpelier Rd. SE15	77	E1
Montpelier Rd. W5	55	G5
Montpelier Rd., Sutt.	100	F4
Montpelier Row SE3	78	F2
Montpelier Row, Twick.	73	E7
Montpelier Sq. SW7	**14**	**H5**
Montpelier Sq. SW7	66	H2
Montpelier St. SW7	**14**	**H4**
Montpelier St. SW7	66	H3
Montpelier Ter. SW7	**14**	**H4**
Montpelier Vale SE3	78	F2
Montpelier Wk. SW7	**14**	**G5**
Montpelier Wk. SW7	66	H3
Montpelier Way NW11	39	B7
Montrave Rd. SE20	86	F7
Montreal Pl. WC2	**12**	**C5**
Montreal Pl. WC2	58	F7
Montreal Rd., Ilf.	43	F7
Montrell Rd. SW2	85	E1
Montrose Ave. NW6	57	B2
Montrose Ave., Edg.	38	C2
Montrose Ave., Sid.	80	A7
Montrose Ave., Twick.	72	H7
Montrose Ave., Well.	79	G3
Montrose Clo., Well.	79	J3
Montrose Clo., Wdf.Grn.	34	G4
Montrose Ct. SW7	**14**	**F4**
Montrose Ct. SW7	66	G2
Montrose Cres. N12	31	F6
Montrose Cres., Wem.	46	H6
Montrose Gdns., Mitch.	93	J3
Montrose Gdns., Sutt.	100	D2
Montrose Pl. SW1	**15**	**C4**
Montrose Pl. SW1	67	A2
Montrose Rd., Har.	37	B2
Montrose Way SE23	86	G1
Montserrat Ave., Wdf.Grn.	34	D7
Montserrat Clo. SE19	86	A5
Montserrat Rd. SW15	75	B4
Monument Gdns. SE13	78	C5
Monument St. EC3	**13**	**C5**
Monument St. EC3	59	A7
Monument Way N17	41	C3
Monza St. E1	59	F7
Moodkee St. SE16	68	F3
Moody St. E1	59	G3
Moon La., Barn.	23	C3
Moon St. N1	58	H1
Moor La. EC2	**13**	**B2**
Moor La. EC2	59	A5
Moor La., Chess.	98	H4
Moor Mead Rd., Twick.	73	D6

Moor Pk. Gdns., Kings.T.	83	E7
Moor Pl. EC2	**13**	**B2**
Moor St. W1	**11**	**J4**
Moorcroft Gdns., Brom.	97	B5
Southborough Rd.		
Moorcroft Rd. SW16	85	E3
Moorcroft Way, Pnr.	36	E5
Moordown SE18	79	D1
Moore Clo. SW14	74	C3
Little St. Leonards		
Moore Clo., Mitch.	94	B2
Moore Cres., Dag.	62	B1
Moore Pk. Rd. SW6	66	E7
Moore Rd. SE19	85	J6
Moore St. SW3	**18**	**J1**
Moore St. SW3	66	J4
Moore Wk. E7	51	G4
Stracey Rd.		
Moore Way SE22	86	D1
Lordship La.		
Moorefield Rd. N17	41	C3
Moorehead Way SE3	78	H3
Mooreland Rd., Brom.	87	F3
Moorey Clo. E15	60	F1
Stephen's Rd.		
Moorfield Ave. W5	55	G4
Moorfield Rd., Chess.	98	H5
Moorfield Rd., Enf.	25	F1
Moorfields EC2	**13**	**B2**
Moorfields EC2	59	A5
Moorgate EC2	**13**	**B2**
Moorgate EC2	59	A5
Moorgate Pl. EC2	**13**	**B4**
Moorhouse Rd. W2	57	D6
Moorhouse Rd., Har.	37	G3
Moorland Clo., Rom.	44	H1
Moorland Clo., Twick.	72	G7
Telford Rd.		
Moorland Rd. SW9	76	H4
Moorlands Ave. NW7	30	H6
Moorlands Est. SW9	76	G4
Moormead Dr., Epsom	99	E5
Moorside Rd., Brom.	87	E3
Moortown Rd., Wat.	28	C4
Moot Ct. NW9	38	A5
Mora Rd. NW2	47	J4
Mora St. EC1	**9**	**A4**
Mora St. EC1	58	J3
Morant Pl. N22	40	F1
Commerce Rd.		
Morant St. E14	60	A7
Morat St. SW9	76	F1
Moravian Pl. SW10	**18**	**F6**
Moravian St. E2	59	F3
Moray Ms. N7	49	F2
Durham Rd.		
Moray Rd. N4	49	F2
Mordaunt Gdns., Dag.	53	E7
Mordaunt Ho. NW10	56	D1
Mordaunt Rd. NW10	56	D1
Mordaunt St. SW9	76	F3
Morden Clo. SE13	78	C2
Morden Ct., Mord.	93	E4
Morden Gdns., Grnf.	46	C5
Morden Gdns., Mitch.	93	G4
Morden Hall Rd., Mord.	93	E3
Morden Hill SE13	78	C2
Morden La. SE13	78	C1
Morden Rd. SE3	78	G2
Morden Rd. SW19	93	E1
Morden Rd., Mitch.	93	F4
Morden Rd., Rom.	44	E7
Morden Rd. Ms. SE3	78	G2
Morden St. SE13	78	B1
Morden Way, Sutt.	93	D7
Morden Wf. Rd. SE10	69	E3
Mordon Rd., Ilf.	43	J7
Mordred Rd. SE6	87	E2
More Clo. E16	60	F6
More Clo. W14	66	G4
Morecambe Clo. E1	59	G5
Morecambe Gdns., Stan.	29	G4
Morecambe St. SE17	**21**	**A2**
Morecambe St. SE17	67	A4
Morecambe Ter. N18	33	A4
Morecombe Clo., Kings.T.	83	B7
Moree Way N18	33	D4
Moreland Clo. NW11	48	E1
Moreland St. EC1	**8**	**H3**
Moreland St. EC1	58	H3
Moreland Way E4	34	B3

Morella Rd. SW12	75	J7
Moremead Rd. SE6	86	A4
Morena St. SE6	78	B7
Moresby Ave., Surb.	92	B7
Moresby Rd. E5	50	E1
Moresby Wk. SW8	76	B2
Moreton Ave., Islw.	73	B1
Moreton Clo. E5	50	F2
Moreton Clo. N15	41	A6
Moreton Clo. N7	30	J6
Moreton Gdns., Wdf.Grn.	35	B5
Moreton Pl. SW1	**19**	**G3**
Moreton Pl. SW1	67	C5
Moreton Rd. N15	41	A6
Moreton Rd., S.Croy.	102	A5
Moreton Rd., Wor.Pk.	99	G2
Moreton St. SW1	**19**	**G3**
Moreton St. SW1	67	C5
Moreton Ter. SW1	**19**	**G3**
Moreton Ter. SW1	67	C5
Moreton Ter. Ms. N. SW1	**19**	**G3**
Moreton Ter. Ms. S. SW1	**19**	**G3**
Moreton Twr. W3	65	B1
Morford Clo., Ruis.	36	B7
Morford Way, Ruis.	36	B7
Morgan Ave. E17	42	D4
Morgan Clo., Dag.	53	G7
Morgan Rd. N7	49	G5
Morgan Rd. W10	57	C5
Morgan Rd., Brom.	87	G7
Morgan St. E3	59	H3
Morgan St. E16	60	F5
Morgan Way, Wdf.Grn.	35	B6
Morgans La. SE1	**17**	**D2**
Morgans La. SE1	68	B1
Moriatri Clo. N7	49	E4
Morie St. SW18	75	E4
Morieux Rd. E10	50	J1
Moring Rd. SW17	85	A4
Morkyns Wk. SE21	86	B3
Morland Ave., Croy.	102	B1
Morland Clo., Hmptn.	81	F5
Morland Clo., Mitch.	93	H3
Morland Gdns. NW10	47	D7
Morland Gdns., Sthl.	63	H1
Morland Ms. N1	49	G7
Lofting Rd.		
Morland Rd. E17	41	G5
Morland Rd. SE20	86	G6
Morland Rd., Croy.	102	B1
Morland Rd., Dag.	53	G7
Morland Rd., Har.	37	H5
Morland Rd., Ilf.	52	E2
Morland Rd., Sutt.	100	F5
Morley Ave. E4	34	D7
Morley Ave. N18	33	D4
Morley Ave. N22	40	G2
Morley Clo., Orp.	104	E2
Morley Clo., Ruis.	45	C2
Morley Cres., Edg.	30	C2
Morley Cres. E., Stan.	37	F2
Morley Cres. W., Stan.	37	F3
Morley Rd. E10	51	C1
Morley Rd. E15	60	F2
Morley Rd. SE13	78	C4
Morley Rd., Bark.	61	G1
Morley Rd., Chis.	97	F1
Morley Rd., Rom.	44	E5
Morley Rd., Sutt.	100	C1
Morley Rd., Twick.	73	G6
Morley St. SE1	**16**	**F5**
Morley St. SE1	67	G3
Morna Rd. SE5	76	J2
Morning La. E9	50	F6
Morningside Rd., Wor.Pk.	99	H2
Mornington Ave. W14	66	C4
Mornington Ave., Brom.	96	J3
Mornington Ave., Ilf.	43	D7
Mornington Clo., Wdf.Grn.	34	G4
Mornington Ct., Bex.	89	J1
Mornington Cres. NW1	**7**	**F1**
Mornington Cres. NW1	58	C2
Mornington Cres., Houns.	72	B1
Mornington Gro. E3	60	A3
Mornington Ms. SE5	76	J1
Mornington Pl. NW1	**7**	**E1**

Mornington Rd. E4	26	D7
Mornington Rd. E11	51	F1
Mornington Rd. SE8	68	J7
Mornington Rd., Grnf.	54	H5
Mornington Rd., Loug.	27	F3
Mornington Rd., Wdf.Grn.	34	F4
Mornington St. NW1	**7**	**E1**
Mornington St. NW1	58	B2
Mornington Ter. NW1	58	B2
Mornington Wk., Rich.	82	F4
Morocco St. SE1	**17**	**D4**
Morocco St. SE1	68	B2
Morpeth Gro. E9	59	G1
Morpeth Rd. E9	59	F1
Morpeth St. E2	59	G3
Morpeth Ter. SW1	**15**	**F6**
Morpeth Ter. SW1	67	C5
Morpeth Wk. N17	33	E7
West Rd.		
Morrab Gdns., Ilf.	52	J3
Morrell Clo., Barn.	23	F3
Galdana Ave.		
Morris Ave. E12	52	C5
Morris Clo., Croy.	95	H5
Morris Clo., Orp.	104	H3
Morris Ct. E4	34	B3
Flaxen Rd.		
Morris Gdns. SW18	75	D7
Morris Pl. N4	49	G2
Morris Rd. E14	60	B5
Morris Rd. E15	51	D4
Morris Rd., Dag.	53	F2
Morris Rd., Islw.	73	C3
Morris St. E1	59	E6
Morrish Rd. SW2	76	E7
Morrison Ave. N17	41	B3
Morrison Rd., Bark.	62	E2
Morrison Rd., Hayes	54	B3
Morrison St. SW11	76	A3
Morriston Clo., Wat.	28	C5
Morse Clo. E13	60	G3
Morshead Rd. W9	57	D3
Morson Rd., Enf.	25	H6
Morston Gdns. SE9	88	C4
Morten Clo. SW4	76	D6
Morteyne Rd. N17	41	A1
Mortgramit Sq. SE18	70	D3
Powis Rd.		
Mortham St. E15	60	E1
Mortimer Clo. NW2	48	C3
Mortimer Clo. SW16	85	D2
Mortimer Cres. NW6	57	E1
Mortimer Cres., Wor.Pk.	99	D3
Mortimer Dr., Enf.	25	B5
Mortimer Est. NW6	57	E1
Mortimer Mkt. WC1	**7**	**G6**
Mortimer Pl. NW6	57	E1
Mortimer Rd. E6	61	C3
Mortimer Rd. N1	50	B7
Mortimer Rd. NW10	56	J3
Mortimer Rd. W13	55	F6
Mortimer Rd., Mitch.	93	J1
Mortimer Sq. W11	57	A7
St. Anns Rd.		
Mortimer St. W1	**11**	**F3**
Mortimer St. W1	58	C6
Mortimer Ter. NW5	49	B4
Gordon Ho. Rd.		
Mortlake Clo., Croy.	101	E3
Richmond Rd.		
Mortlake Dr., Mitch.	93	H1
Mortlake High St. SW14	74	D3
Mortlake Rd. E16	60	H6
Mortlake Rd., Ilf.	52	F4
Mortlake Rd., Rich.	65	A7
Mortlock Clo. SE15	77	E1
Cossall Wk.		
Morton Cres. N14	32	D4
Morton Gdns., Wall.	101	C5
Morton Ms. SW5	**18**	**A2**
Morton Pl. SE1	**16**	**E6**
Morton Rd. E15	51	F7
Morton Rd. N1	49	J7
Morton Rd., Mord.	93	G5
Morton Way N14	32	C3
Morval Rd. SW2	76	G5
Morvale Clo., Belv.	71	F4
Morven Rd. SW17	84	J3
Morville St. E3	60	A2
Morwell St. WC1	**11**	**J2**
Moscow Pl. W2	**10**	**A5**
Moscow Rd. W2	10	A5
Moscow Rd. W2	57	E7
Moselle Ave. N22	40	G2

Moselle Clo. N8	40	F3
Miles Rd.		
Moselle Ho. N17	33	C7
Moselle Pl. N17	33	C7
High Rd.		
Moselle St. N17	33	C7
Moss Clo. E1	**13**	**J2**
Moss Clo., Pnr.	36	F2
Moss Gdns., Felt.	81	A2
Rose Gdns.		
Moss Gdns., S.Croy.	102	G7
Warren Ave.		
Moss Hall Cres. N12	31	E6
Moss Hall Gro. N12	31	E6
Moss La., Pnr.	36	E1
Moss Rd., Dag.	53	G7
Mossborough Clo. N12	31	E6
Mossbury Rd. SW11	75	H3
Mossdown Clo., Belv.	71	G4
Mossford Ct., Ilf.	43	E3
Mossford Grn., Ilf.	43	E3
Mossford La., Ilf.	43	E2
Mossford St. E3	59	J4
Mossington Gdns. SE16	68	F4
Abbeyfield Rd.		
Mosslea Rd. SE20	86	F6
Mosslea Rd., Brom.	97	A5
Mosslea Rd., Orp.	104	F3
Mossop St. SW3	**18**	**H1**
Mossop St. SW3	66	H4
Mossville Gdns., Mord.	93	C3
Mostyn Ave., Wem.	46	J5
Mostyn Gdns. NW10	57	A3
Mostyn Gro. E3	60	A2
Mostyn Rd. SW9	76	G1
Mostyn Rd. SW19	93	C1
Mostyn Rd., Edg.	30	D7
Mosul Way, Brom.	97	B6
Motcomb St. SW1	**15**	**A5**
Motcomb St. SW1	67	A3
Motley St. SW8	76	C2
St. Rule St.		
Motspur Pk., N.Mal.	92	F6
Mott St., Loug.	26	E1
Mottingham Gdns. SE9	88	A1
Mottingham La. SE9	87	J1
Mottingham La. SE12	87	J1
Mottingham Rd. N9	25	G6
Mottingham Rd. SE9	88	B2
Mottisfont Rd. SE2	71	A3
Moulins Rd. E9	50	F7
Moulton Ave., Houns.	72	E2
Mound, The SE9	88	D3
Moundfield Rd. N16	41	D6
Mount, The N20	31	F2
Mount, The, NW3	48	F4
Heath St.		
Mount, The, N.Mal.	92	F3
Mount, The, Wem.	47	B2
Mount, The, Wor.Pk.	99	H4
Mount Adon Pk. SE22	77	D7
Mount Angelus Rd. SW15	74	F7
Laverstock Gdns.		
Mount Ararat Rd., Rich.	73	H5
Mount Ash Rd. SE26	86	E3
Mount Ave. E4	34	A3
Mount Ave. W5	55	F5
Mount Ave., Sthl.	54	G6
Mount Clo. W5	55	F5
Mount Clo., Barn.	24	A4
Mount Clo., Brom.	97	B1
Mount Cor., Felt.	81	D2
Mount Ct. SW15	75	B3
Weimar St.		
Mount Ct., W.Wick.	103	E2
Mount Culver Ave., Sid.	89	D6
Mount Dr., Bexh.	80	E5
Mount Dr., Har.	36	F5
Mount Dr., Wem.	47	C2
Mount Echo Ave. E4	34	B2
Mount Echo Dr. E4	34	B1
Mount Ephraim La. SW16	85	D3
Mount Ephraim Rd. SW16	85	D3
Mount Est., The E5	50	E2
Mount Pleasant La.		
Mount Gdns. SE26	86	E3
Mount Gro., Edg.	30	C3
Mount Ms., Hmptn.	90	H1
Mount Mills EC1	**8**	**H4**

Mount Nod Rd. SW16	85	F3
Mount Pk. Ave., Har.	46	A2
Mount Pk. Cres. W5	55	G6
Mount Pk. Rd. W5	55	G5
Mount Pk. Rd., Har.	46	A3
Mount Pk. Rd., Pnr.	36	A5
Mount Pleasant SE27	85	J5
Mount Pleasant WC1	**8**	**E6**
Mount Pleasant WC1	58	G4
Mount Pleasant, Barn.	23	H4
Mount Pleasant, Ruis.	45	C2
Mount Pleasant, Wem.	55	H1
Mount Pleasant Cres. N4	40	F7
Mount Pleasant Hill E5	50	E2
Mount Pleasant La. E5	50	E2
Mount Pleasant Rd. E17	41	H2
Mount Pleasant Rd. N17	41	B1
Mount Pleasant Rd. NW10	47	J7
Mount Pleasant Rd. SE13	78	C6
Mount Pleasant Rd. W5	55	F4
Mount Pleasant Rd., Chig.	35	G4
Mount Pleasant Rd., N.Mal.	92	C3
Mount Pleasant Vill. N4	40	F7
Mount Pleasant Wk., Bex.	80	J5
Mount Rd. NW2	47	H3
Mount Rd. NW4	38	G6
Mount Rd. SE19	86	A6
Mount Rd. SW19	84	D2
Mount Rd., Barn.	23	H5
Mount Rd., Bexh.	80	D5
Mount Rd., Chess.	98	J5
Mount Rd., Dag.	53	F1
Mount Rd., Felt.	81	E3
Mount Rd., Ilf.	52	E5
Mount Rd., Mitch.	93	G2
Mount Rd., N.Mal.	92	D3
Mount Row W1	**11**	**D6**
Mount Row W1	58	B7
Mount Sq., The NW3	48	F3
Heath St.		
Mount Stewart Ave., Har.	37	G6
Mount St. W1	**11**	**B6**
Mount St. W1	58	A7
Mount Ter. E1	59	E5
New Rd.		
Mount Vernon NW3	48	F4
Mount Vw. NW7	30	D3
Mount Vw. W5	55	G4
Mount Vw. Rd. E4	26	C7
Mount Vw. Rd. N4	40	E7
Mount Vw. Rd. NW9	38	D5
Mount Vill. SE27	85	H3
Mountacre Clo. SE26	86	C4
Mountague Pl. E14	60	C7
Mountbatten Clo. SE18	70	H6
Mountbatten Clo. SE19	86	B5
Mountbatten Ct., Buck.H.	35	A2
Mountbatten Ms. SW18	84	F1
Inman Rd.		
Mountbel Rd., Stan.	37	D1
Mountcombe Clo., Surb.	91	H7
Mountearl Gdns. SW16	85	F3
Mountfield Rd. E6	61	D2
Mountfield Rd. N3	39	C3
Mountfield Rd. W5	55	G6
Mountford St. E1	**13**	**H3**
Mountfort Cres. N1	49	G7
Barnsbury Sq.		
Mountfort Ter. N1	49	G7
Barnsbury Sq.		
Mountgrove Rd. N5	49	H3
Mounthurst Rd., Brom.	96	F7
Mountington Pk. Clo., Har.	37	G6
Mountjoy Clo. SE2	71	B2
Mounts Pond Rd. SE3	78	D2
Mountsfield Ct. SE13	78	D6
Mountside, Felt.	81	E3

Name	Page	Grid
Mountside, Stan.	37	C1
Mountview Ct. N8	40	H4
Green Las.		
Mountview Rd., Esher	98	E7
Mountwood, W.Mol.	90	G3
Movers La., Bark.	61	G1
Mowatt Clo. N19	49	D1
Mowbray Rd. NW6		
Mowbray Rd. SE19	95	C1
Mowbray Rd., Barn.	23	F4
Mowbray Rd., Edg.	30	A4
Mowbray Rd., Rich.	82	F3
Mowbrays Clo., Rom.	44	J1
Mowbrays Rd., Rom.	44	J2
Mowbrey Gdns., Loug.	27	F1
Mowlem St. E2	59	E2
Mowlem Trd. Est. N17	33	F7
Mowll St. SW9	67	G7
Moxon Clo. E13	60	F2
Whitelegg Rd.		
Moxon St. W1	**11**	**B2**
Moxon St. W1	58	A5
Moxon St., Barn.	23	C3
Moye Clo. E2	**9**	**J1**
Moyers Rd. E10	42	C7
Moylan Rd. W6	66	B6
Moyne Pl. NW10	56	A2
Moys Clo., Croy.	94	E6
Mitcham Rd.		
Moyser Rd. SW16	85	B5
Mozart St. W10	57	C3
Mozart Ter. SW1	**19**	**C2**
Muchelney Rd., Mord.	93	H6
Mud La. W5	55	G5
Mudlarks Way SE7	69	H3
Mudlarks Way SE10	69	F3
Muggeridge Rd., Dag.	53	H4
Muir Rd. E5	50	D4
Muir St. E16	70	C1
Newland St.		
Muirdown Ave. SW14	74	D4
Muirfield W3	56	E6
Muirfield Clo., Wat.	28	C5
Muirfield Cres. E14	69	B3
Millharbour		
Muirfield Grn., Wat.	28	C4
Muirfield Rd., Wat.	28	B4
Muirkirk Rd. SE6	87	C1
Mulberry Clo. E4	34	A2
Mulberry Clo. NW3	48	G4
Hampstead High St.		
Mulberry Clo. NW4	38	J3
Mulberry Clo. SE7	70	A6
Mulberry Clo. SE22	77	D6
Mulberry Clo. SW16	85	C4
Mulberry Clo., Barn.	23	G4
Mulberry Clo., Nthlt.	54	E2
Parkfield Ave.		
Mulberry Ct., Bark.	52	J7
Westrow Dr.		
Mulberry Cres., Brent.	64	E7
Mulberry La., Croy.	102	C1
Mulberry Ms., Wall.	101	C6
Ross Rd.		
Mulberry Pl. W6	65	G5
Chiswick Mall		
Mulberry St. E1	**13**	**H3**
Mulberry Wk. SW3	**18**	**F5**
Mulberry Wk. SW3	66	G6
Mulberry Way E18	42	H2
Mulberry Way, Belv.	71	J2
Mulberry Way, Ilf.	43	F4
Mulgrave Rd. NW10	47	F4
Mulgrave Rd. SW6	66	C6
Mulgrave Rd. W5	55	G4
Mulgrave Rd., Croy.	102	A3
Mulgrave Rd., Har.	46	D2
Mulgrave Rd., Sutt.	100	C7
Mulholland Clo., Mitch.	94	B2
Mulkern Rd. N19	49	D1
Mull Wk. N1	6	J6
Clephane Rd.		
Muller Rd. SW4	76	D6
Mullet Gdns. E2	**9**	**J3**
Mullins Path SW14	74	D3
Mullion Clo., Har.	36	H1
Mullion Wk., Wat.	28	D4
Ormskirk Rd.		
Mulready St. NW8	**6**	**G6**
Multi Way W3	65	E2
Valetta Rd.		
Multon Rd. SW18	75	G7
Mulvaney Way SE1	**17**	**C4**
Mulvaney Way SE1	68	A2
Mumford Ct. EC2	**13**	**A3**
Mumford Rd. SE24	76	H5
Railton Rd.		
Muncaster Rd. SW11	75	J5
Muncies Ms. SE6	87	C2
Mund St. W14	66	C5
Mundania Rd. SE22	77	E6
Munday Rd. E16	60	G6
Munden St. W14	66	B4
Mundesley Clo., Wat.	28	C4
Mundford Rd. E5	50	F2
Mundon Gdns., Ilf.	52	G1
Mundy St. N1	**9**	**E3**
Mundy St. N1	59	B3
Mungo Pk. Clo. (Bushey), Wat.	28	J2
Munnery Way, Orp.	104	D2
Munnings Gdns., Islw.	73	A5
Munro Dr. N11	32	C6
Munro Ms. W10	57	B5
Munro Ter. SW10	**18**	**E7**
Munro Ter. SW10	66	G6
Munster Ave., Houns.	72	E4
Munster Ct., Tedd.	82	F6
Munster Gdns. N13	32	H4
Munster Rd. SW6	66	B7
Munster Rd., Tedd.	82	E6
Munster Sq. NW1	**7**	**E4**
Munster Sq. NW1	58	B3
Munton Rd. SE17	**21**	**A1**
Munton Rd. SE17	67	J4
Murchison Ave., Bex.	89	D1
Murchison Rd. E10	51	C2
Murdock Clo. E16	60	F6
Rogers Rd.		
Murdock St. SE15	68	E6
Murfett Clo. SW19	84	B2
Muriel St. N1	58	F1
Murillo Rd. SE13	78	D4
Murphy St. SE1	**16**	**E4**
Murphy St. SE1	67	G2
Murray Ave., Brom.	96	H3
Murray Ave., Houns.	72	H5
Murray Cres., Pnr.	36	D1
Murray Gro. N1	**9**	**A2**
Murray Gro. N1	58	J2
Murray Ms. NW1	49	D7
Murray Rd. SW19	84	A6
Murray Rd. W5	64	G4
Murray Rd., Rich.	82	E2
Murray Sq. E16	60	G6
Murray St. NW1	49	D7
Murray Ter. NW3	48	G4
Flask Wk.		
Mursell Est. SW8	76	F1
Murtwell Dr., Chig.	35	F6
Musard Rd. W6	66	B6
Musbury St. E1	59	F6
Muscal W6	66	B6
Muscatel Pl. SE5	77	B1
Dalwood St.		
Muschamp Rd. SE15	77	C3
Muschamp Rd., Cars.	100	H2
Muscovy St. EC3	**13**	**E6**
Museum Pas. E2	59	E3
Victoria Pk. Sq.		
Museum St. WC1	**12**	**A2**
Museum St. WC1	58	E5
Musgrave Clo., Barn.	23	F1
Musgrave Cres. SW6	66	D7
Musgrave Rd., Islw.	73	G2
Musgrove Rd. SE14	77	G1
Musjid Rd. SW11	75	G2
Kambala Rd.		
Musquash Way, Houns.	72	C2
Muston Rd. E5	50	E2
Mustow Pl. SW6	75	C2
Munster Rd.		
Muswell Ave. N10	40	B1
Muswell Hill N10	40	B3
Muswell Hill Bdy. N10	40	B3
Muswell Hill Pl. N10	40	B4
Muswell Hill Rd. N6	40	A6
Muswell Hill Rd. N10	40	A5
Muswell Ms. N10	40	B3
Muswell Rd.		
Muswell Rd. N10	40	B3
Mutrix Rd. NW6	57	D1
Mutton Pl. NW1	49	B6
Harmood St.		
Muybridge Rd., N.Mal.	92	C2
Myatt Rd. SW9	76	H1
Myatt's Flds. N. SW9	76	G1
Eythorne Rd.		
Myatt's Flds. S. SW9	76	G2
Mycenae Rd. SE3	69	G7
Myddelton Gdns. N21	24	H7
Myddelton Pk. N20	31	G3
Myddelton Pas. EC1	**8**	**F3**
Myddelton Rd. N8	40	E4
Myddelton Sq. EC1	**8**	**F3**
Myddelton St. EC1	**8**	**F4**
Myddelton St. EC1	58	G3
Myddleton Rd. N22	32	E7
Myers La. SE14	68	G6
Mylis Clo. SE26	86	E4
Mylne St. EC1	**8**	**E3**
Mylne St. EC1	58	G2
Myra St. SE2	71	A4
Myrdle St. E1	**13**	**J3**
Myrdle St. E1	59	D5
Myrna Clo., Mitch.	84	H7
Myron Pl. SE13	78	C3
Myrtle Ave., Ruis.	36	A7
Myrtle Clo., Barn.	31	J1
Myrtle Gdns. W7	64	B1
Myrtle Gro., N.Mal.	92	C2
Myrtle Rd. E6	61	B1
Myrtle Rd. E17	41	H6
Myrtle Rd. N13	32	J3
Myrtle Rd. W3	65	C1
Myrtle Rd., Croy.	103	A3
Myrtle Rd., Hmptn.	81	J6
Myrtle Rd., Houns.	72	J2
Myrtle Rd., Ilf.	52	E2
Myrtle Rd., Sutt.	100	F5
Myrtle Wk. N1	**9**	**D2**
Myrtle Wk. N1	59	B2
Myrtleberry Clo. E8	50	C6
Beechwood Rd.		
Myrtledene Rd. SE2	71	A5
Mysore Rd. SW11	75	J3
Myton Rd. SE21	86	A3

N

Name	Page	Grid
Nadine St. SE7	69	J5
Nafferton Ri., Loug.	27	A5
Nagasaki Wk. SE7	69	J3
Nagle Clo. E17	42	D2
Nag's Head Ct. EC1	**9**	**A6**
Nags Head La., Well.	80	B3
Nags Head Rd., Enf.	25	F4
Nairn Grn., Wat.	28	A3
Nairn Rd., Ruis.	45	C6
Nairn St. E14	60	C5
Nairne Gro. SE24	77	A5
Naish Ct. N1	58	E1
Nallhead Rd., Felt.	81	C5
Namton Dr., Th.Hth.	94	F4
Nan Clark's La. NW7	30	F2
Nankin St. E14	60	A6
Nansen Rd. SW11	76	A4
Nant Rd. NW2	48	C2
Nant St. E2	59	E3
Cambridge Heath Rd.		
Nantes Clo. SW18	75	F4
Nantes Pas. E1	**13**	**F1**
Naoroji St. WC1	**8**	**E4**
Napier Ave. E14	69	A5
Napier Ave. SW6	75	C3
Napier Clo. SE8	68	J7
Amersham Vale		
Napier Clo. W14	66	C3
Napier Rd.		
Napier Clo., Islw.	73	B1
Napier Ct. SW6	75	C3
Ranelagh Gdns.		
Napier Gro. N1	58	J2
Napier Pl. W14	66	C3
Napier Rd. E6	61	D1
Napier Rd. E11	51	E4
Napier Rd. E15	60	E4
Napier Rd. N17	41	B3
Napier Rd. NW10	56	H3
Napier Rd. SE25	95	E4
Napier Rd. W14	66	B3
Napier Rd., Belv.	71	F4
Napier Rd., Brom.	96	H4
Napier Rd., Enf.	25	G5
Napier Rd., Islw.	73	D4
Napier Rd., S.Croy.	102	A7
Napier Rd., Wem.	46	G5
Napier Ter. N1	49	H6
Napoleon Rd. E5	50	E3
Napoleon Rd., Twick.	73	E7
Napton Clo., Hayes	54	E4
Kingsash Dr.		
Narbonne Ave. SW4	76	C5
Narborough St. SW6	75	E2
Narcissus Rd. NW6	48	D5
Naresby Fold, Stan.	29	H3
Narford Rd. E5	50	D3
Narrow St. E14	59	H7
Narrow Way, Brom.	97	B6
Nascot St. W12	56	J6
Naseby Clo. NW6	48	F7
Fairfax Rd.		
Naseby Clo., Islw.	73	B1
Naseby Rd. SE19	86	A6
Naseby Rd., Dag.	53	G3
Naseby Rd., Ilf.	43	C1
Nash Grn., Brom.	87	G6
Nash La., Kes.	103	G7
Nash Pl. E14	69	B1
South Colonnade		
Nash Rd. N9	33	F2
Nash Rd. SE4	77	H4
Nash Rd., Rom.	44	D4
Nash St. NW1	**7**	**E3**
Nasmyth St. W6	65	H3
Nassau Path SE28	71	C1
Disraeli Clo.		
Nassau Rd. SW13	74	F1
Nassau St. W1	**11**	**F2**
Nassau St. W1	58	C5
Nassington Rd. NW3	48	H4
Natal Rd. N11	32	E6
Natal Rd. SW16	85	D6
Natal Rd., Ilf.	52	E4
Natal Rd., Th.Hth.	95	A3
Nathan Way SE28	70	H3
Nathaniel Clo. E1	**13**	**G2**
Nathans Rd., Wem.	46	F1
Naval Row E14	60	C7
Naval Wk., Brom.	96	G3
High St.		
Navarino Gro. E8	50	D6
Navarino Rd. E8	50	D6
Navarre Rd. E6	61	B2
Navarre St. E2	**9**	**F5**
Navarre St. E2	59	C4
Navenby Wk. E3	60	A4
Rounton Rd.		
Navestock Clo. E4	34	C3
Mapleton Rd.		
Navestock Cres., Wdf.Grn.	42	J1
Navestock Ho., Bark.	62	B2
Navigator Dr., Sthl.	63	J2
Navy St. SW4	76	D3
Naylor Gro., Enf.	25	G5
South St.		
Naylor Rd. N20	31	F2
Naylor Rd. SE15	68	E7
Nazrul St. E2	**9**	**F3**
Nazrul St. E2	59	C3
Neagle Clo., Borwd.	22	C1
Balcon Way		
Neal Ave., Sthl.	54	F3
Neal Clo., Nthwd.	36	A1
Neal St. WC2	**12**	**A4**
Neal St. WC2	58	E6
Nealden St. SW9	76	F3
Neale Clo. N2	39	F3
Neal's Yd. WC2	**12**	**A4**
Near Acre NW9	38	F1
Neasden Clo. NW10	47	E5
Neasden La. NW10	47	E3
Neasden La. N. NW10	47	D3
Neasden Underpass NW10	47	D3
Neasham Rd., Dag.	53	B5
Neate St. SE5	**21**	**D6**
Neate St. SE5	68	B6
Neath Gdns., Mord.	93	F6
Neathouse Pl. SW1	**19**	**F1**
Neatscourt Rd. E6	61	A5
Nebraska St. SE1	**17**	**B4**
Neckinger SE16	**17**	**G5**
Neckinger Est. SE16	**17**	**G5**
Neckinger Est. SE16	68	C3
Neckinger St. SE1	**17**	**G5**
Neckinger St. SE1	68	C2
Nectarine Way SE13	78	B2
Needham Rd. W11	57	B6
Westbourne Gro.		
Needham Ter. NW2	48	A3
Needleman St. SE16	68	G2
Neeld Cres. NW4	38	H5
Neeld Cres., Wem.	47	H5
Nelgarde Rd. SE6	78	A7
Nella Rd. W6	66	A6
Nelldale Rd. SE16	68	F4
Nello James Gdns. SE27	86	A4
Nelson Clo., Croy.	101	H1
Nelson Clo., Rom.	44	H1
Nelson Gdns. E2	**9**	**J3**
Nelson Gdns. E2	59	D3
Nelson Gdns., Houns.	72	G6

Nelson Gro. Rd. SW19	93	E1
Nelson Mandela Clo. N10	40	A2
Nelson Mandela Rd. SE3	78	J3
Nelson Pas. EC1	**9**	**A4**
Nelson Pas. EC1	58	J3
Nelson Pl. N1	**8**	**H2**
Nelson Pl. N1	58	H2
Nelson Pl., Sid.	89	A4
Nelson Rd. E4	34	A6
Nelson Rd. E11	42	G4
Nelson Rd. N8	40	F5
Nelson Rd. N9	33	E2
Nelson Rd. N15	41	B4
Nelson Rd. SE10	69	C6
Nelson Rd. SW19	84	E7
Nelson Rd., Belv.	71	F5
Nelson Rd., Brom.	96	J4
Nelson Rd., Enf.	25	G6
Nelson Rd., Har.	46	A1
Nelson Rd., Houns.	72	G6
Nelson Rd., N.Mal.	92	D5
Nelson Rd., Sid.	89	A4
Nelson Rd., Stan.	29	F6
Nelson Rd., Twick.	72	H7
Nelson Sq. SE1	**16**	**G4**
Nelson Sq. SE1	67	H2
Nelson St. E1	59	E6
Nelson St. E6	61	C2
Nelson St. E16	60	F7
Huntingdon St.		
Nelson Ter. N1	**8**	**H2**
Nelson Ter. N1	58	H2
Nelson Trd. Est. SW19	93	E1
Nelson Wk. SE16	68	H1
Rotherhithe St.		
Nelson's Row SW4	76	D4
Nemoure Rd. W3	56	C7
Nene Gdns., Felt.	81	F2
Nepaul Rd. SW11	75	H2
Afghan Rd.		
Nepean St. SW15	74	G6
Neptune Rd., Har.	37	A6
Neptune St. SE16	68	F3
Nesbit Rd. SE9	79	A4
Nesbit Clo. SE3	78	E3
Hurren Clo.		
Nesbitt Sq. SE19	86	B7
Coxwell Rd.		
Nesbitts All., Barn.	23	C3
Bath Pl.		
Nesham St. E1	**17**	**H1**
Nesham St. E1	68	D1
Ness St. SE16	**17**	**H5**
Nesta Rd., Wdf.Grn.	34	E6
Nestor Ave. N21	24	H6
Nether Clo. N3	31	D7
Nether St. N3	39	D1
Nether St. N12	31	E6
Netheravon Rd. W7	64	C1
Netheravon Rd. N. W4	65	F4
Netheravon Rd. S. W4	65	F5
Netherbury Rd. W5	64	G3
Netherby Gdns., Enf.	24	E4
Netherby Rd. SE23	77	F7
Nethercourt Ave. N3	31	D6
Netherfield Gdns., Bark.	52	G6
Netherfield Rd. N12	31	E5
Netherfield Rd. SW17	85	A3
Netherford Rd. SW4	76	C2
Netherhall Gdns. NW3	48	F6
Netherhall Way NW3	48	F5
Netherhall Gdns.		
Netherlands Rd., Barn.	23	G6
Netherleigh Clo. N6	49	B1
Hornsey La.		
Netherton Gro. SW10	**18**	**D6**
Netherton Gro. SW10	66	F6
Netherton Rd. N15	41	A6
Seven Sisters Rd.		
Netherton Rd., Twick.	73	D5
Netherwood N2	39	G2
Netherwood Pl. W14	66	A3
Netherwood Rd.		
Netherwood Rd. W14	66	A3
Netherwood St. NW6	48	C7
Netley Clo., Croy.	103	C7
Netley Clo., Sutt.	100	A5
Netley Dr., Walt.	90	F7
Netley Gdns., Mord.	93	F7
Netley Rd. E17	41	J5
Netley Rd., Brent.	64	H6
Netley Rd., Ilf.	43	G5

Netley Rd., Mord.	93	F7
Netley St. NW1	**7**	**F4**
Nettleden Ave., Wem.	47	A6
Nettlefold Pl. SE27	85	H3
Nettlestead Clo., Beck.	86	J7
Copers Cope Rd.		
Nettleton Rd. SE14	77	G1
Nettlewood Rd. SW16	85	D7
Neuchatel Rd. SE6	86	J2
Nevada Clo., N.Mal.	92	C4
Georgia Rd.		
Nevada St. SE10	69	C6
Nevern Pl. SW5	66	D4
Nevern Rd. SW5	66	D4
Nevern Sq. SW5	66	D4
Nevill Rd. N16	50	B4
Nevill Way, Loug.	27	B7
Valley Hill		
Neville Ave., N.Mal.	92	D1
Neville Clo. E11	51	F3
Neville Clo. NW1	**7**	**J2**
Neville Clo. NW6	57	C2
Neville Clo. SE15	68	D7
Neville Clo. W3	65	C2
Acton La.		
Neville Clo., Houns.	72	H2
Neville Clo., Sid.	88	J4
Neville Dr. N2	39	F6
Neville Gdns., Dag.	53	D3
Neville Gill Clo. SW18	75	E6
Neville Pl. N22	40	F1
Neville Rd. E7	51	G7
Neville Rd. NW6	57	C2
Neville Rd. W5	55	G4
Neville Rd., Croy.	95	A7
Neville Rd., Dag.	53	D2
Neville Rd., Ilf.	43	F1
Neville Rd., Kings.T.	92	A2
Neville Rd., Rich.	82	F2
Neville St. SW7	**18**	**E3**
Neville St. SW7	66	G5
Neville Ter. SW7	**18**	**E3**
Neville Ter. SW7	66	G5
Neville Wk., Cars.	93	H7
Green Wrythe La.		
Nevilles Ct. NW2	47	G3
Nevin Dr. E4	34	B1
Nevis Rd. SW17	85	A2
New Ash Clo. N2	39	G3
Oakridge Dr.		
New Barn St. E13	60	G4
New Barns Ave., Mitch.	94	D4
New Barns Way, Chig.	35	E3
New Bond St. W1	**11**	**D4**
New Bond St. W1	58	B6
New Brent St. NW4	38	J5
New Bri., Erith	71	J4
New Bri. St. EC4	**12**	**G4**
New Bri. St. EC4	58	H6
New Broad St. EC2	**13**	**D2**
New Bdy. W5	55	F7
New Burlington Ms. W1	**11**	**F5**
New Burlington Pl. W1	**11**	**F5**
New Burlington St. W1	**11**	**F5**
New Burlington St. W1	58	C7
New Butt La. SE8	69	A7
New Butt La. N. SE8	69	A7
Reginald Rd.		
New Cavendish St. W1	**11**	**C2**
New Cavendish St. W1	58	A5
New Change EC4	**12**	**J4**
New Change EC4	58	J6
New Chapel Sq., Felt.	81	B1
New Charles St. EC1	**8**	**H3**
New Ch. Rd. SE5	**21**	**B7**
New Ch. Rd. SE5	68	A7
New City Rd. E13	60	J3
New Clo. SW19	93	F3
New Clo., Felt.	81	E5
New College Ms. N1	49	G7
Islington Pk. St.		
New Compton St. WC2	**11**	**J4**
New Compton St. WC2	58	D6
New Ct. EC4	**12**	**G5**
New Covent Gdn. Mkt. SW8	67	D7
New Coventry St. W1	**11**	**J6**

New Crane Pl. E1	68	F1
Garnet St.		
New Cross Rd. SE14	68	F7
New End NW3	48	F4
New End Sq. NW3	48	G4
New Fm. Ave., Brom.	96	G4
New Fetter La. EC4	**12**	**F3**
New Fetter La. EC4	58	H3
New Forest La., Chig.	35	D6
New Globe Wk. SE1	**16**	**J1**
New Globe Wk. SE1	68	A1
New Goulston St. E1	**13**	**F3**
New Heston Rd., Houns.	63	F7
New Horizon Ct., Brent.	64	D6
New Inn Bdy. EC2	**9**	**E5**
New Inn Pas. WC2	**12**	**D4**
New Inn St. EC2	**9**	**E5**
New Inn Yd. EC2	**9**	**E5**
New Inn Yd. EC2	58	B4
New James Ct. SE15	77	E3
Nunhead La.		
New Kent Rd. SE1	**16**	**J6**
New Kent Rd. SE1	67	J3
New King St. SE8	69	A6
New Kings Rd. SW6	75	C2
New London St. EC3	**13**	**E5**
New Lydenburgh St. SE7	69	J3
New Mt. St. E15	51	D7
New N. Pl. EC2	**9**	**D6**
New N. Rd. N1	**9**	**B1**
New N. Rd. N1	49	J7
New N. Rd., Ilf.	35	G7
New N. St. WC1	**12**	**C1**
New N. St. WC1	58	F5
New Oak Rd. N2	39	F2
New Orleans Wk. N19	40	D7
New Oxford St. WC1	**11**	**J3**
New Oxford St. WC1	58	D6
New Pk. Ave. N13	32	J3
New Pk. Clo., Nthlt.	45	E6
New Pk. Ct. SW2	76	E7
New Pk. Rd. SW2	85	D1
New Pl. Sq. SE16	68	E3
New Plaistow Rd. E15	60	E1
New Priory Rd. NW6	48	D7
Mazenod Ave.		
New Quebec St. W1	**11**	**A4**
New Quebec St. W1	57	J6
New Ride SW7	**14**	**G3**
New River Cres. N13	32	H4
New Rd. E1	59	E5
New Rd. E4	34	B4
New Rd. N8	40	E5
New Rd. N9	33	D3
New Rd. N17	41	C1
New Rd. N22	40	J1
New Rd. NW7	31	B7
New Rd. NW7	22	F7
(Barnet Gate)		
New Rd. SE2	71	D4
New Rd., Brent.	64	G5
New Rd., Dag.	62	G1
New Rd., Felt.	81	B1
(East Bedfont)		
New Rd., Felt.	81	E5
(Hanworth)		
New Rd., Har.	46	C4
New Rd., Houns.	72	H4
Station Rd.		
New Rd., Ilf.	52	H2
New Rd., Kings.T.	83	A7
New Rd., Mitch.	101	A1
New Rd., Rain.	62	J2
New Rd., Rich.	82	F4
New Rd., Well.	80	B2
New Rd., W.Mol.	90	G3
New Row WC2	**12**	**A5**
New Row WC2	58	E7
New Spring Gdns. Wk. SE11	**20**	**B4**
New Sq. E6	61	C6
Porter Rd.		
New Sq. WC2	**12**	**D3**
New Sq. WC2	58	F6
New Sq. Pas. WC2	58	F6
New Sq.		
New St. EC2	**13**	**E2**
New St. EC2	59	B5
New St. Hill, Brom.	87	H5
New St. Sq. EC4	**12**	**F3**
New Trinity Rd. N2	39	G3
New Turnstile WC1	**12**	**C2**
New Union Clo. E14	69	C3
New Union St. EC2	**13**	**B2**
New Union St. EC2	59	A5

New Wanstead E11	42	F6
New Way Rd. NW9	38	E4
New Wf. Rd. N1	**8**	**B1**
New Wf. Rd. N1	58	E2
New Zealand Way W12	56	H7
India Way		
Newark Cres. NW10	56	D3
Newark Grn., Borwd.	22	D3
Newark Knok E6	61	D5
Newark Rd., S.Croy.	102	A6
Newark St. E1	59	E5
Newark Way NW4	38	G4
Newbiggin Path, Wat.	28	C4
Newbolt Ave., Sutt.	99	J5
Newbolt Rd., Stan.	29	C5
Newborough Grn. N.Mal.	92	D4
Newburgh Rd. W3	65	C1
Newburgh St. W1	**11**	**F4**
Newburgh St. W1	58	C6
Newburn St. SE11	**20**	**D4**
Newburn St. SE11	67	F5
Newbury Clo., Nthlt.	45	F6
Newbury Gdns., Epsom	99	F4
Newbury Ho. N22	40	E1
Newbury Ms. NW5	49	A6
Malden Rd.		
Newbury Rd. E4	34	C6
Newbury Rd., Brom.	96	G3
Newbury Rd., Ilf.	43	H6
Newbury St. EC1	**12**	**A1**
Newbury Way, Nthlt.	45	F6
Newby Clo., Enf.	25	B2
Newby Pl. E14	60	C7
Newby St. SW8	76	B3
Newcastle Clo. EC4	**12**	**G3**
Newcastle Pl. W2	**10**	**F2**
Newcastle Pl. W2	57	G5
Newcastle Row EC1	**8**	**F6**
Newcombe Gdns. SW16	85	E4
Newcombe Pk. NW7	30	E5
Newcombe Pk., Wem.	55	J1
Newcombe St. W8	66	D1
Kensington Pl.		
Newcomen Rd. E11	51	F3
Newcomen Rd. SW11	75	G3
Newcomen St. SE1	**17**	**B3**
Newcomen St. SE1	68	A2
Newcourt St. NW8	**6**	**G2**
Newcourt St. NW8	57	H2
Newdales Clo. N9	33	D2
Balham Rd.		
Newdene Ave., Nthlt.	54	D2
Newell St. E14	59	J6
Newent Clo. SE15	**21**	**D7**
Newent Clo. SE15	68	B7
Newent Clo., Cars.	100	J1
Newfield Clo., Hmptn.	90	G1
Percy Rd.		
Newfield Ri. NW2	47	H3
Newgale Gdns., Edg.	37	J1
Newgate, Croy.	101	J3
Newgate Clo., Felt.	81	E2
Newgate St. E4	34	F4
Newgate St. EC1	**12**	**H3**
Newgate St. EC1	58	H6
Newham Way E6	61	D4
Newham Way E16	60	F5
Newhams Clo., Brom.	97	C3
Newhams Row SE1	**17**	**E4**
Newhaven Gdns. SE9	79	A4
Newhaven La. E16	60	F4
Newhaven Rd. SE25	95	A5
Newhouse Ave., Rom.	44	D7
Newhouse Clo., N.Mal.	92	D7
Newhouse Wk., Mord.	93	F7
Newick Clo., Bex.	80	H6
Newick Rd. E5	50	E3
Newing Grn., Brom.	88	A7
Newington Barrow Way N7	49	F3
Newington Butts SE1	**20**	**H2**
Newington Butts SE1	67	H4
Newington Butts SE11	**20**	**H2**
Newington Butts SE11	67	H4
Newington Causeway SE1	**16**	**H6**
Newington Causeway SE1	67	H3
Newington Grn. N1	50	A5
Newington Grn. N16	50	A5
Newington Grn. Rd. N1	50	A6

Newington Way N7 49 F2
Hornsey Rd.
Newland Clo., Pnr. 28 E6
Newland Ct., Wem. 47 A2
Forty Ave.
Newland Dr., Enf. 25 E1
Newland Gdns. W13 64 D2
Newland Rd. N8 40 E3
Newland St. E16 70 B1
Newlands, The, Wall. 101 C7
Newlands Ave. 98 B1
T.Ditt.
Newlands Clo., Edg. 29 H3
Newlands Clo., Sthl. 63 E5
Newlands Clo., Wem. 46 F6
Newlands Ct. SE9 79 B6
Newlands Pk. SE26 86 G5
Newlands Pl., Barn. 23 A5
Newlands Quay E1 59 F7
Newlands Rd. SW16 94 E2
Newlands Rd., 34 F2
Wdf.Grn.
Newlands Way, 98 F5
Chess.
Newling Clo. E6 61 C6
Porter Rd.
Newlyn Gdns., Har. 36 F7
Newlyn Rd. N17 41 C1
Newlyn Rd. NW2 47 J1
Tilling Rd.
Newlyn Rd., Barn. 23 C4
Newlyn Rd., Well. 79 J2
Newman Pas. W1 11 G2
Newman Rd. E13 60 H3
Newman Rd. E17 41 G6
Southcote Rd.
Newman Rd., Brom. 96 G1
Newman Rd., Croy. 101 F1
Newman Rd., Hayes 54 B7
Newman St. W1 11 G2
Newman St. W1 58 C5
Newman Yd. W1 11 G3
Newmans Clo., Loug. 27 E3
Newman's Ct. EC3 13 C4
Newmans La., Loug. 27 D3
Newmans La., Surb. 91 G6
Newman's Row WC2 12 D2
Newmans Way, Barn. 23 F1
Newmarket Ave., 45 H5
Nthlt.
Newmarket Grn. SE9 79 A7
Newminster Rd., 93 F6
Mord.
Newnes Path SW15 74 H4
Putney Pk. La.
Newnham Ave., Ruis. 45 C1
Newnham Clo., Loug. 27 A6
Newnham Clo., Nthlt. 45 J5
Newnham Clo., 94 J2
Th.Hth.
Newnham Gdns., 45 J6
Nthlt.
Newnham Ms. N22 40 F1
Newnham Rd.
Newnham Rd. N22 40 F1
Newnham Ter. SE1 16 E5
Newnham Way, Har. 37 H5
Newnhams Clo., 97 C3
Brom.
Newnton Clo. N4 41 A7
Newpiece, Loug. 27 E3
Newport Ave. E13 60 H4
Palmer Rd.
Newport Ct. WC2 11 J5
Newport Mead, Wat. 28 D4
Kilmarnock Rd.
Newport Pl. WC2 11 J5
Newport Pl. WC2 58 D7
Newport Rd. E10 51 C2
Newport Rd. E17 41 H4
Newport Rd. SW13 74 G1
Newport St. SE11 20 C2
Newport St. SE11 67 F4
Newquay Cres., Har. 45 E2
Newquay Gdns., Wat. 28 B2
Fulford Gro.
Newquay Rd. SE6 87 B2
Newry Rd., Twick. 73 D5
Newsam Ave. N15 41 A5
Newstead Ave., Orp. 104 G3
Newstead Rd. SE12 78 F7
Newstead Wk., Cars. 93 F7
Newstead Way 84 A4
SW19
Newton Ave. N10 40 A1
Newton Ave. W3 65 C2
Newton Cres., Borwd. 22 C4
Newton Gro. W4 65 E4

Newton Rd. E15 51 D5
Newton Rd. N15 41 C5
Newton Rd. NW2 47 J3
Newton Rd. SW19 84 B7
Newton Rd. W2 57 E6
Newton Rd., Har. 37 B2
Newton Rd., Islw. 73 C2
Newton Rd., Well. 80 A3
Newton Rd., Wem. 46 J7
Newton St. WC2 12 B3
Newton St. WC2 58 E6
Newton Wk., Edg. 38 B1
North Rd.
Newton Way N18 32 J5
Newtons Yd. SW18 75 E5
Wandsworth High St.
Newtown St. SW11 76 B1
Strasbury Rd.
Niagara Ave. W5 64 F4
Nibthwaite Rd., Har. 37 B5
Nichol Clo. N14 32 D1
Nichol La., Brom. 87 G7
Nicholas Clo., Grnf. 54 H2
Nicholas Gdns. W5 64 G2
Nicholas La. EC4 13 C5
Nicholas Rd. E1 59 F4
Nicholas Rd., Croy. 101 F4
Nicholas Rd., Dag. 53 F2
Nicholay Rd. N19 49 D1
Calverley Gro.
Nicholes Rd., Houns. 72 G4
Nicholl St. E2 59 D1
Nichollsfield Wk. N7 49 F5
Hillmarton Rd.
Nichols Clo., Chess. 98 F6
Mansfield Rd.
Nichols Grn. W5 55 H5
Montpelier Rd.
Nicholson Dr. 28 J1
(Bushey), Wat.
Nicholson Rd., Croy. 102 C1
Nicholson St. SE1 16 G2
Nicholson St. SE1 67 H1
Nickelby Clo. SE28 62 C6
Nicol Clo., Twick. 73 E6
Cassilis Rd.
Nicola Clo., Har. 37 A2
Nicola Clo., S.Croy. 101 J6
Nicola Ms., Ilf. 35 E7
Nicoll Pl. NW4 38 H6
Nicoll Rd. NW10 56 E1
Nicoll Way, Borwd. 22 D5
Nicosia Rd. SW18 75 H7
Niederwald Rd. SE26 86 H4
Nigel Clo., Nthlt. 54 E1
Church Rd.
Nigel Ms., Ilf. 52 E4
Nigel Playfair Ave. 65 H4
W6
King St.
Nigel Rd. E7 51 J5
Nigel Rd. SE15 77 D3
Nigeria Rd. SE7 69 J7
Nightingale Ave. E4 34 E5
Nightingale Clo. E4 34 E4
Nightingale Clo. W4 65 C6
Grove Pk. Ter.
Nightingale Clo., 101 A2
Cars.
Nightingale Clo., Pnr. 36 C5
Nightingale Dr., 99 B6
Epsom
Nightingale Est. E5 50 D3
Nightingale Gro. 78 D5
SE13
Nightingale La. E11 42 H5
Nightingale La. N6 39 H7
Nightingale La. N8 40 E4
Nightingale La. SW4 76 B6
Nightingale La. SW12 75 J7
Nightingale La., Brom. 96 J2
Nightingale La., Rich. 73 H7
Nightingale Pl. SE18 70 D6
Nightingale Pl. SW10 18 D5
Nightingale Rd. E5 50 E3
Nightingale Rd. N9 25 F6
Nightingale Rd. N22 40 E1
Nightingale Rd. 56 F2
NW10
Nightingale Rd. W7 64 C1
Nightingale Rd., Cars. 100 J3
Nightingale Rd., 81 G5
Hmptn.
Nightingale Rd., Orp. 97 F6
Nightingale Rd., Walt. 90 B7
Nightingale Rd., 90 H5
W.Mol.
Nightingale Sq. SW12 76 A7

Nightingale Vale 70 D6
SE18
Nightingale Wk. SW4 76 B6
Nightingale Way E6 61 B5
Nile Path SE18 70 D6
Jackson St.
Nile Rd. E13 60 J2
Nile St. N1 9 A3
Nile St. N1 59 A3
Nile Ter. SE15 21 G4
Nile Ter. SE15 68 C5
Nimegen Way SE22 77 B5
East Dulwich Gro.
Nimrod Clo., Nthlt. 54 D3
Britannia Clo.
Nimrod Rd. SW16 85 B6
Nine Acres Clo. E12 52 B5
Nine Elms La. SW8 19 G7
Nine Elms La. SW8 67 C7
Nineteenth Rd., 94 E4
Mitch.
Ninhams Wd., Orp. 104 D4
Ninth Ave., Hayes 54 A7
Nisbet Ho. E9 50 G5
Homerton High St.
Nithdale Rd. SE18 70 E7
Niton Clo., Barn. 23 A6
Niton Rd., Rich. 74 A3
Niton St. SW6 66 A7
Niven Clo., Borwd. 22 C1
Nobel Rd. N18 33 F4
Noble St. EC2 12 J3
Noble St. EC2 58 J6
Noel Pk. Rd. N22 40 G2
Noel Rd. E6 61 B4
Noel Rd. N1 8 H1
Noel Rd. N1 58 H2
Noel Rd. W3 56 A6
Noel Sq., Dag. 53 C4
Noel St. W1 11 G4
Noel St. W1 58 C6
Noel Ter. SE23 86 F2
Dartmouth Rd.
Nolan Way E5 50 D4
Nolton Pl., Edg. 37 J1
Nonsuch Clo., Ilf. 35 E6
Nora Gdns. NW4 39 A4
Norbiton Ave., 92 A1
Kings.T.
Norbiton Common 92 B3
Rd., Kings.T.
Norbiton Rd. E14 59 J6
Norbreck Gdns. 55 J3
NW10
Lytham Gro.
Norbreck Par. NW10 55 J3
Lytham Gro.
Norbroke St. W12 56 F7
Norburn St. W10 57 B5
Chesterton Rd.
Norbury Ave. SW16 94 F1
Norbury Ave., Houns. 73 A4
Norbury Ave., Th.Hth. 94 G2
Norbury Clo. SW16 94 G1
Norbury Ct. Rd. SW16 94 E3
Norbury Cres. SW16 94 F1
Norbury Cross SW16 94 E3
Norbury Gdns., Rom. 44 D5
Norbury Gro. NW7 30 E3
Norbury Hill SW16 85 G7
Norbury Ri. SW16 94 E3
Norbury Rd. E4 34 A5
Norbury Rd., Th.Hth. 94 J2
Norcombe Gdns., Har. 37 F6
Norcott Clo., Hayes 54 C4
Willow Tree La.
Norcott Rd. N16 50 D2
Norcroft Gdns. SE22 77 D7
Norcutt Rd., Twick. 82 B1
Norfield Rd., Dart. 89 J4
Norfolk Ave. N13 32 H6
Norfolk Ave. N15 41 C6
Norfolk Clo. N2 39 H3
Park Rd.
Norfolk Clo. N13 32 H6
Norfolk Clo., Barn. 24 A4
Norfolk Clo., Twick. 73 E6
Cassilis Rd.
Norfolk Cres. W2 10 G3
Norfolk Cres. W2 57 H6
Norfolk Cres., Sid. 79 H7
Norfolk Gdns., Bexh. 80 F1
Norfolk Gdns., Borwd. 22 D4
Norfolk Ho. SE3 69 G6
Norfolk Ho. Rd. SW16 85 D3
Norfolk Pl. W2 10 F3
Norfolk Pl. W2 57 G6
Norfolk Pl., Well. 80 A2

Norfolk Rd. E6 61 C1
Norfolk Rd. E17 41 G2
Norfolk Rd. NW8 57 G1
Norfolk Rd. NW10 47 E7
Norfolk Rd. SW19 84 H7
Norfolk Rd., Bark. 52 H7
Norfolk Rd., Barn. 23 D3
Norfolk Rd., Dag. 53 H5
Norfolk Rd., Enf. 25 E6
Norfolk Rd., Esher 98 B5
Norfolk Rd., Felt. 81 C1
Norfolk Rd., Har. 36 H5
Norfolk Rd., Ilf. 52 H1
Norfolk Rd., Rom. 44 J6
Norfolk Rd., Th.Hth. 94 J3
Norfolk Row SE1 20 C1
Norfolk Row SE1 67 F3
Norfolk Sq. W2 10 F4
Norfolk Sq. W2 57 G6
Norfolk Sq. Ms. W2 10 F4
Norfolk St. E7 51 G5
Norfolk Ter. W6 66 B5
Field Rd.
Norgrove St. SW12 85 A1
Norhyrst Ave. SE25 95 C3
Norland Pl. W11 66 B1
Norland Rd. W11 66 A1
Norland Sq. W11 66 B1
Norlands Cres., Chis. 97 E1
Norlands Gate, Chis. 97 E1
Norlands Cres.
Norley Vale SW15 83 G1
Norlington Rd. E10 51 C1
Norlington Rd. E11 51 D1
Norman Ave. N22 40 H1
Norman Ave., Felt. 81 E2
Norman Ave., Sthl. 54 E7
Norman Ave., Twick. 73 E7
Norman Clo., Orp. 104 F3
Norman Clo., Rom. 44 H2
Norman Ct., Ilf. 43 G7
Norman Cres., Houns. 63 D7
Norman Cres., Pnr. 36 C1
Norman Gro. E3 59 H2
Norman Rd. E6 61 C4
Norman Rd. E11 51 D2
Norman Rd. N15 41 C5
Norman Rd. SE10 69 B7
Norman Rd. SW19 84 F7
Norman Rd., Belv. 71 H3
Norman Rd., Ilf. 52 E5
Norman Rd., Sutt. 100 D5
Norman Rd., Th.Hth. 94 H5
Norman St. EC1 8 J4
Norman Way N14 32 E2
Norman Way W3 56 B5
Normanby Clo. SW15 75 C5
Manfred Rd.
Normanby Rd. NW10 47 F4
Normand Gdns. W14 66 B6
Greyhound Rd.
Normand Ms. W14 66 B6
Normand Rd.
Normand Rd. W14 66 C6
Normandy Ave., Barn. 23 C5
Normandy Rd. SW9 76 G1
Normandy Ter. E16 60 H6
Normanhurst Ave., 80 D1
Bexh.
Normanhurst Dr., 73 E5
Twick.
St. Margarets Rd.
Normanhurst Rd. 85 F2
SW2
Normans Clo. NW10 47 D6
Normans Mead NW10 47 D6
Normansfield Ave., 82 F7
Tedd.
Normanshire Ave. E4 34 C4
Normanshire Dr.
Normanshire Dr. E4 34 A4
Normanton Ave. 84 D2
SW19
Normanton Pk. E4 34 E3
Normanton Rd., 102 B5
S.Croy.
Normanton St. SE23 86 G2
Normington Clo. 85 G5
SW16
Norrice Lea N2 39 G5
Norris St. SW1 11 H6
Norroy Rd. SW15 75 A4
Norrys Clo., Barn. 23 J4
Norrys Rd., Barn. 23 J4
Norseman Clo., Ilf. 53 B1
Norseman Way, Grnf. 54 H1
Olympic Way
Norstead Pl. SW15 83 G2

North Access Rd. 41 G6
E17
North Acre NW9 38 E1
North Acton Rd. 56 D2
NW10
North Audley St. W1 11 B4
North Audley St. W1 58 A7
North Ave. N18 33 D4
North Ave. W13 55 E5
North Ave., Cars. 101 A7
North Ave., Har. 36 H6
North Ave., Hayes 54 A7
North Ave., Rich. 73 G1
Sandycombe Rd.
North Ave., Sthl. 54 F7
North Bank NW8 6 G4
North Bank NW8 57 H3
North Birkbeck Rd. 51 D3
E11
North Branch Ave. 56 J3
W10
Harrow Rd.
North Carriage Dr. W2 10 G5
North Carriage Dr. W2 57 H7
North Circular Rd. E4 33 J7
North Circular Rd. 42 H1
E18
North Circular Rd. N3 39 C4
North Circular Rd. 39 G1
N12
North Circular Rd. 32 G5
N13
North Circular Rd. 47 E3
NW2
North Circular Rd. 47 E4
NW10
North Circular Rd. 39 A6
NW11
North Clo., Barn. 22 J5
North Clo., Bexh. 80 D4
North Clo., Dag. 62 G1
North Clo., Mord. 93 B4
North Colonnade E14 69 A1
North Common Rd. 55 H7
W5
North Countess Rd. 41 J2
E17
North Ct. W1 11 G1
North Cray Rd., Bex. 89 G2
North Cray Rd., Sid. 89 E6
North Cres. E16 60 D4
Cody Rd.
North Cres. N3 39 C2
North Cres. WC1 11 H1
North Cross Rd. SE22 77 C5
North Cross Rd., Ilf. 43 F4
North Dene NW7 30 D3
North Dene, Houns. 72 H1
North Dr. SW16 85 C4
North Dr., Houns. 72 J2
North Dr., Orp. 104 H4
North End NW3 48 F2
North End, Buck.H. 26 J7
North End, Croy. 101 J2
North End Ave. NW3 48 F2
North End Cres. W14 66 C4
North End Ho. W14 66 B4
North End Rd. NW11 48 D1
North End Rd. SW6 66 C6
North End Rd. W14 66 B4
North End Rd., Wem. 47 A3
North End Way NW3 48 F2
North Eyot Gdns. W6 65 F5
St. Peter's Sq.
North Feltham Trd. 72 B5
Est., Felt.
North Flockton St. 17 H3
SE16
North Gdns. SW19 84 G7
North Glade, The, 80 F7
Bex.
Camden Rd.
North Gower St. NW1 7 G4
North Gower St. NW1 58 C3
North Grn. NW9 30 E7
Clayton Fld.
North Gro. N6 40 A7
North Gro. N15 41 A5
North Hill N6 39 J6
North Hill Ave. N6 39 J6
North Hyde Gdns., 63 A4
Hayes
North Hyde La. 63 E6
Houns.
North Hyde La., Sthl. 63 D5
North La., Tedd. 82 C6
North Lo. Clo. SW15 75 A5
Westleigh Ave.

North Mall N9 33 E2
St. Martins Rd.
North Ms. WC1 8 D6
North Ms. WC1 58 F4
North Par., Chess. 98 H5
North Pk. SE9 79 D6
North Pas. SW18 75 D5
North Peckham Est. 21 F7
SE15
North Peckham Est. 68 B7
SE15
North Pl., Mitch. 84 J7
North Pl., Tedd. 82 C6
North Pole La., Kes. 103 F6
North Pole Rd. W10 56 J5
North Ride W2 10 G6
North Ride W2 66 H1
North Rd. N6 40 A7
North Rd. N7 49 E6
North Rd. N9 33 E1
North Rd. SE18 70 H4
North Rd. SW19 84 F6
North Rd. W5 64 G3
North Rd., Belv. 71 H3
North Rd., Brent. 64 H6
North Rd., Brom. 96 H1
North Rd., Edg. 38 B1
North Rd., Ilf. 52 H2
North Rd., Rich. 74 A3
North Rd., Rom. 44 E5
North Rd., Sthl. 54 G6
North Rd., Surb. 91 G6
North Rd., W.Wick. 103 B1
North Row W1 11 A5
North Row W1 57 J7
North Several SE3 78 D2
Orchard Dr.
North Sq. N9 33 E2
St. Martins Rd.
North Sq. NW11 39 D5
North St. E13 60 H2
North St. NW4 38 J5
North St. SW4 76 C3
North St., Bark. 52 E6
North St., Bexh. 80 G4
North St., Brom. 96 G1
North St., Cars. 100 J3
North St., Islw. 73 D3
North St. Pas. E13 60 H2
North St.
North Tenter St. E1 13 G4
North Tenter St. E1 59 C6
North Ter. SW3 14 G6
North Verbena Gdns. 65 G5
W6
St. Peter's Sq.
North Vw. SW19 83 J5
North Vw. W5 55 F4
North Vw., Pnr. 36 C7
North Vw. Cres. 47 F4
NW10
North Vw. Dr., 43 A2
Wdf.Grn.
North Vw. Rd. N8 40 D3
North Vill. NW1 49 D6
North Wk. W2 10 C6
North Way N9 33 G2
North Way N11 32 C6
North Way NW9 38 B3
North Way, Mord. 93 B3
North Way, Pnr. 36 C3
North Wf. Rd. W2 10 E2
North Wf. Rd. W2 57 G5
North Woolwich Rd. 69 G1
E16
North Worple Way 74 D3
SW14
Northall Rd., Bexh. 80 J2
Northampton Gro. N1 50 A6
Northampton Pk.
Northampton Rd. EC1 8 F5
Northampton Rd. EC1 58 G4
Northampton Rd., 102 D2
Croy.
Northampton Rd., 25 H4
Enf.
Northampton Sq. EC1 8 G4
Northampton Sq. EC1 58 H3
Northampton St. N1 49 J7
Northanger Rd. SW16 85 E6
Northbank Rd. E17 42 C2
Northborough Rd. 94 D3
SW16
Northbourne, Brom. 96 G7
Northbourne Rd. SW4 76 D4
Northbrook Rd. N22 32 E7

Northbrook Rd. SE13 78 D5
Northbrook Rd., Barn. 23 B6
Northbrook Rd., Croy. 95 A5
Northbrook Rd., Ilf. 52 D2
Northburgh St. EC1 8 H6
Northburgh St. EC1 58 H4
Northchurch SE17 21 C3
Northchurch Rd. N1 50 A7
Northchurch Rd., 47 A6
Wem.
Northchurch Ter. N1 50 B7
Northcliffe Clo., 99 E3
Wor.Pk.
Northcliffe Dr. N20 31 C1
Northcote Ave. W5 55 H7
Northcote Ave., Islw. 73 D5
Northcote Ave., Sthl. 54 E7
Northcote Ave., Surb. 92 A7
Northcote Rd. E17 41 H4
Northcote Rd. NW10 47 E7
Northcote Rd. SW11 75 H5
Northcote Rd., Croy. 95 A6
Northcote Rd., N.Mal. 92 D3
Northcote Rd., Sid. 88 H4
Northcote Rd., Twick. 73 D5
Northcott Ave. N22 40 E1
Northcroft W13 64 E2
Northcroft Rd., 99 D7
Epsom
Northdene, Chig. 35 G5
Northdene Gdns. N15 41 C6
Northdown Gdns., Ilf. 43 H5
Northdown Rd., Well. 80 B2
Northdown St. N1 8 B1
Northdown St. N1 58 E2
Northern Ave. N9 33 B2
Northern Relief Rd., 52 E7
Bark.
Northern Rd. E13 60 H2
Northern Service Rd., 23 B3
Barn.
Northernhay Wk., 93 B4
Mord.
Northey St. E14 59 H7
Northfield, Loug. 27 A4
Northfield Ave. W5 64 E1
Northfield Ave. W13 64 E1
Northfield Ave., Pnr. 36 D4
Northfield Clo., 97 B1
Brom.
Northfield Cres. 100 B4
Sutt.
Northfield Gdns., Dag. 53 F4
Northfield Rd.
Northfield Path, Dag. 53 F4
Connor Rd.
Northfield Rd. E6 52 C7
Northfield Rd. N16 41 B7
Northfield Rd. W13 64 E2
Northfield Rd., Barn. 23 H3
Northfield Rd., Borwd. 22 B1
Northfield Rd., Dag. 53 F4
Northfield Rd., Enf. 25 E5
Northfield Rd., Houns. 63 D7
Northfields SW18 75 D4
Northfields Ind. Est., 56 A1
Wem.
Northfields Rd. W3 56 B5
Northgate Dr. NW9 38 E6
Northiam N12 31 D4
Northiam St. E9 59 E1
Northington St. WC1 8 D6
Northington St. WC1 58 F4
Northlands Ave., 104 H4
Orp.
Northlands St. SE5 76 J2
Northolm, Edg. 30 D4
Northolme Gdns., 38 A1
Edg.
Northolme Ri., Orp. 104 H2
Northolme Rd. N5 49 J4
Northolt Ave., Ruis. 45 B5
Northolt Gdns., Grnf. 46 C5
Northolt Ind. Est., 45 H7
Nthlt.
Northolt Rd., Har. 45 H4
Northover, Brom. 87 F3
Northport St. N1 59 A1
Northside Rd., Brom. 96 G1
Mitchell Way
Northspur Rd., Sutt. 100 D3
Northstead Rd. SW2 85 G2
Northumberland All. 13 E4
EC3
Northumberland All. 59 B6
EC3
Northumberland Ave. 51 J1
E12

Northumberland Ave. 16 A1
WC2
Northumberland Ave. 67 E1
WC2
Northumberland 25 E1
Ave., Enf.
Northumberland 73 C1
Ave., Islw.
Northumberland 79 G4
Ave., Well.
Northumberland Clo., 71 J7
Erith
Northumberland 33 C3
Gdns. N9
Northumberland 64 D7
Gdns., Islw.
Northumberland Ave.
Northumberland 94 D5
Gdns., Mitch.
Northumberland Gro. 33 E7
N17
Northumberland Pk. 33 C7
N17
Northumberland Pk., 71 J7
Erith
Northumberland Pl. 57 D6
W2
Northumberland Pl., 73 G6
Rich.
Northumberland Rd. 61 B6
E6
Northumberland Rd. 42 A7
E17
Northumberland Rd., 23 F6
Barn.
Northumberland Rd., 36 F5
Har.
Northumberland 82 B1
Row, Twick.
Colne Rd.
Northumberland St. 16 A1
WC2
Northumberland St. 67 E1
WC2
Northumberland 80 J1
Way, Erith
Northumbria St. E14 60 A6
Northway NW7 30 G7
Northway NW11 39 E5
Northway, Wall. 101 C4
Northway Circ. NW7 30 D4
Northway Cres. NW7 30 D4
Northway Rd. SE5 76 J3
Northway Rd., Croy. 95 C6
Northwest Pl. N1 8 F1
Northwick Ave., Har. 37 D6
Northwick Circle, Har. 37 F6
Northwick Clo. NW8 6 E5
Northwick Pk. Rd., 37 C6
Har.
Northwick Rd., Wat. 28 C4
Northwick Rd., Wem. 55 G1
Northwick Ter. NW8 6 E5
Northwick Ter. NW8 57 G4
Northwick Wk., Har. 37 C7
Peterborough Rd.
Northwold Dr., Pnr. 36 C3
Cuckoo Hill
Northwold Est. E5 50 D2
Northwold Rd. E5 50 D2
Northwold Rd. N16 50 C2
Northwood Gdns. 31 G5
N12
Northwood Gdns., 46 C5
Grnf.
Northwood Gdns., Ilf. 43 D4
Northwood Hall N6 40 C7
Northwood Ho. SE27 86 A4
Northwood Pl., Erith 71 F3
Northwood Rd. N6 40 B7
Northwood Rd. SE23 86 J1
Northwood Rd., 101 A6
Cars.
Northwood Rd., 94 H2
Th.Hth.
Northwood Way SE19 86 A6
Roman Ri.
Northwood Way, 36 A1
Nthwd.
Norton Ave., Surb. 92 B7
Norton Clo. E4 34 A5
Norton Clo., Borwd. 22 A1
Norton Clo., Enf. 25 E2
Brick La.
Norton Folgate E1 13 E1
Norton Folgate E1 59 B5
Norton Gdns. SW16 94 E2
Norton Rd. E10 50 J1

Norton Rd., Wem. 46 G6
Norval Rd., Wem. 46 E2
Norway Gate SE16 68 H3
Norway Pl. E14 59 J6
  East India Dock Rd.
Norway St. SE10 69 B6
Norwich Ho. E14 60 B6
  Cordelia St.
Norwich Ms., Ilf. 53 A1
  Ashgrove Rd.
Norwich Pl., Bexh. 80 G4
Norwich Rd. E7 51 G5
Norwich Rd., Dag. 62 G2
Norwich Rd., Grnf. 54 H1
Norwich Rd., Th.Hth. 94 J3
Norwich St. EC4 12 E3
Norwich St. EC4 58 G6
Norwick La., Har. 37 C7
Norwood Ave., Wem. 55 J1
Norwood Clo., Sthl. 63 G4
Norwood Dr., Har. 36 F6
Norwood Gdns., 54 C4
  Hayes
Norwood Gdns., Sthl. 63 F4
Norwood Grn. Rd., 63 G4
  Sthl.
Norwood High St. 85 H3
  SE27
Norwood Pk. Rd. SE27 85 J5
Norwood Rd. SE24 85 H1
Norwood Rd. SE27 85 H2
Norwood Rd., Sthl. 63 F4
Norwood Ter., Sthl. 63 H4
  Tentelow La.
Notley St. SE5 21 B7
Notley St. SE5 68 A7
Notre Dame Est. SW4 76 C4
Notson Rd. SE25 95 E4
  Belfast Rd.
Notting Barn Rd. W10 57 A4
Notting Hill Gate W11 66 D1
Nottingdale Sq. W11 66 B1
  Wilsham St.
Nottingham Ave. E16 60 J5
Nottingham Ct. WC2 12 A4
Nottingham Pl. W1 7 B6
Nottingham Pl. W1 58 A5
Nottingham Rd. E10 42 C6
Nottingham Rd. 84 J1
  SW17
Nottingham Rd., Islw. 73 C2
Nottingham Rd., 101 J4
  S.Croy.
Nottingham St. W1 11 B1
Nottingham St. W1 58 A5
Nottingham Ter. NW1 7 B6
Nova Ms., Sutt. 93 B7
Nova Rd., Croy. 101 H1
Novar Clo., Orp. 97 J7
Novar Rd. SE9 88 F1
Novello St. SW6 75 D1
Nowell Rd. SW13 65 G6
Nower Hill, Pnr. 36 F4
Noyna Rd. SW17 84 J3
Nuding Clo. SE13 78 A3
Nugent Rd. N19 49 E1
Nugent Rd. SE25 95 C3
Nugent Ter. NW8 6 D2
Nugent Ter. NW8 57 F2
Nugents Ct., Pnr. 36 E1
  St. Thomas' Dr.
Nugents Pk., Pnr. 36 E1
Nun Ct. EC2 13 B3
Nuneaton Rd., Dag. 53 D7
Nunhead Cres. SE15 77 E3
Nunhead Grn. SE15 77 E3
Nunhead Gro. SE15 77 E3
Nunhead La. SE15 77 E3
Nunhead Pas. SE15 77 D3
  Peckham Rye
Nunnington Clo. SE9 88 B3
Nunns Rd., Enf. 24 J2
Nupton Dr., Barn. 22 J6
Nursery Ave. N3 39 F2
Nursery Ave., Bexh. 80 F3
Nursery Ave., Croy. 102 G2
Nursery Clo. SE4 77 J2
Nursery Clo. SW15 75 A4
Nursery Clo., Croy. 102 G2
Nursery Clo., Enf. 25 G1
Nursery Clo., Felt. 72 B7
Nursery Clo., Orp. 97 J7
Nursery Clo., Rom. 44 D6
Nursery Clo., 34 H5
  Wdf.Grn.
Nursery Ct. N17 33 C7
  Nursery St.

Nursery Gdns., Chis. 88 E6
  Willow Gro.
Nursery Gdns., Enf. 25 G1
Nursery La. E7 51 G6
Nursery La. W10 56 J5
Nursery Rd. E9 50 F6
  Morning La.
Nursery Rd. N2 39 G1
Nursery Rd. N14 24 C7
Nursery Rd. SW9 76 F4
Nursery Rd. SW19 93 E2
  (Merton)
Nursery Rd. SW19 84 B7
  (Wimbledon)
Nursery Rd., Loug. 26 J5
Nursery Rd., Loug. 26 H1
  (High Beach)
Nursery Rd., Pnr. 36 C3
Nursery Rd., Sutt. 100 F4
Nursery Rd., Th.Hth. 95 A4
Nursery Row, Barn. 23 B3
  St. Albans Rd.
Nursery St. N17 33 C7
Nursery Wk. NW4 38 H3
Nurserymans Rd. 32 A4
  N11
Nurstead Rd., Erith 71 G7
Nutbourne St. W10 57 B3
Nutbrook St. SE15 77 D3
Nutbrowne Rd., Dag. 62 F1
Nutcroft Rd. SE15 68 E7
Nutfield Clo. N18 33 D6
Nutfield Clo., Cars. 100 H3
Nutfield Gdns., Ilf. 52 J2
Nutfield Gdns., Nthlt. 54 C2
Nutfield Rd. E15 51 C4
Nutfield Rd. NW2 47 G2
Nutfield Rd. SE22 77 C5
Nutfield Rd., Th.Hth. 94 H4
Nutfield Way, Orp. 104 D2
Nutford Pl. W1 57 H6
Nutford Pl. W1 10 H3
Nuthatch Gdns. SE28 70 G2
Nuthurst Ave. SW2 85 F2
Nutley Ter. NW3 48 F6
Nutmead Clo., Bex. 89 J1
Nutmeg Clo. E16 60 E4
  Cranberry La.
Nutmeg La. E14 60 D6
Nutt Gro., Edg. 29 G2
Nutt St. SE15 21 G7
Nutt St. SE15 68 C7
Nuttall St. N1 9 E1
Nuttall St. N1 59 B2
Nutter La. E11 42 J6
Nutwell St. SW17 84 H5
Nuxley Rd., Belv. 71 F6
Nyanza St. SE18 70 G6
Nye Bevan Est. E5 50 G3
Nylands Ave., Rich. 74 A1
Nymans Gdns. SW20 92 H3
  Hidcote Gdns.
Nynehead St. SE14 68 H7
Nyon Gro. SE6 86 J2
Nyssa Clo., Wdf.Grn. 35 C6
  Gwynne Pk. Ave.
Nyton Clo. N19 49 E1
  Courtauld Rd.

O

Oak Ave. N8 40 E4
Oak Ave. N10 32 B7
Oak Ave. N17 33 A7
Oak Ave., Croy. 103 A1
Oak Ave., Enf. 24 F1
Oak Ave., Hmptn. 81 E5
Oak Ave., Houns. 63 E7
Oak Bank, Croy. 103 C6
Oak Clo. N14 24 B7
Oak Clo., Sutt. 100 F2
Oak Cottage Clo. SE6 87 F1
Oak Cres. E16 60 E5
Oak Dene W13 55 E5
  The Dene
Oak Gdns., Croy. 103 A2
Oak Gdns., Edg. 38 C2
Oak Gro. NW2 48 A4
Oak Gro., Ruis. 36 B7
Oak Gro., Sun. 81 B7
Oak Gro., W.Wick. 103 C2
Oak Gro. Rd. SE20 95 F2
Oak Hill, Wdf.Grn. 34 D7
Oak Hill Ave. NW3 48 E4
Oak Hill Clo., Wdf.Grn. 34 D7
Oak Hill Cres. SW19 84 A7
Oak Hill Cres., 34 D7
  Wdf.Grn.

Oak Hill Gdns., 42 E1
  Wdf.Grn.
Oak Hill Pk. NW3 48 E4
Oak Hill Pk. Ms. NW3 48 F4
Oak Hill Way NW3 48 F4
Oak La. E14 59 J7
Oak La. N2 39 G2
Oak La. N11 32 D6
Oak La., Islw. 73 B4
Oak La., Twick. 73 D7
Oak La., Wdf.Grn. 34 F4
Oak Lo. Ave., Chig. 35 G5
Oak Lo. Clo., Stan. 29 F5
  Dennis La.
Oak Lo. Dr., W.Wick. 96 B7
Oak Manor Dr., Wem. 46 J5
  Oakington Manor Dr.
Oak Pk. Gdns. SW19 75 A7
Oak Pl. SW18 75 E5
  East Hill
Oak Ri., Buck.H. 35 A3
Oak Rd. W5 55 G7
  The Bdy.
Oak Rd., Erith 71 J7
  (Northumberland
  Heath)
Oak Rd., N.Mal. 92 D2
Oak Row SW16 94 C2
Oak St., Rom. 44 J5
Oak Tree Clo. W5 55 F6
  Pinewood Gro.
Oak Tree Clo., Stan. 29 E7
Oak Tree Dell NW9 38 C5
Oak Tree Dr. N20 31 E1
Oak Tree Gdns., 87 H5
  Brom.
Oak Tree Rd. NW8 6 F4
Oak Tree Rd. NW8 57 H3
Oak Village NW5 49 A4
Oak Way N14 24 B7
Oak Way W3 65 E1
Oak Way, Croy. 95 G6
Oakapple Ct. SE12 87 G2
Oakbank Ave., Walt. 90 F7
Oakbank Gro. SE24 76 J4
Oakbrook Clo., Brom. 87 H4
Oakbury Rd. SW6 75 E2
Oakcombe Clo., 92 E1
  N.Mal.
  Traps La.
Oakden St. SE11 20 F1
Oakden St. SE11 67 G4
Oakdene SE15 77 E1
  Carlton Gro.
Oakdene Ave., Chis. 88 D5
Oakdene Ave., Erith 71 J6
Oakdene Ave., T.Ditt. 98 D1
Oakdene Clo., Pnr. 28 F7
Oakdene Dr., Surb. 92 C7
Oakdene Ms., Sutt. 100 C1
Oakdene Pk. N3 31 C7
Oakdene Rd., Orp. 97 J5
Oake Ct. SW15 75 B5
Oaken Dr., Esher 98 C6
Oaken La., Esher 98 B4
Oakenshaw Clo., 91 H7
  Surb.
Oakes Clo. E6 61 C6
  Savage Gdns.
Oakeshott Ave. N6 49 A2
Oakey La. SE1 16 E5
Oakfield E4 34 B5
Oakfield Ave., Har. 37 E3
Oakfield Clo., N.Mal. 92 F5
  Blakes La.
Oakfield Ct. N8 40 E7
Oakfield Ct. NW2 39 A7
  Hendon Way
Oakfield Gdns. N18 33 B4
Oakfield Gdns. SE19 86 C5

Oakfield Gdns., Beck. 96 A5
Oakfield Gdns., Cars. 100 H1
Oakfield Gdns., Grnf. 55 A4
Oakfield La., Kes. 103 J4
Oakfield Rd. E6 61 B1
Oakfield Rd. E17 41 H2
Oakfield Rd. N3 39 E1
Oakfield Rd. N4 40 G6
Oakfield Rd. N14 32 E3
Oakfield Rd. SE20 95 E1
Oakfield Rd. SW19 84 A3
Oakfield Rd., Croy. 101 J1
Oakfield Rd., Ilf. 52 E2
Oakfield St. SW10 18 C5
Oakfield St. SW10 66 F6
Oakfields Rd. NW11 39 B6
Oakford Rd. NW5 49 C4
Oakhall Rd. E11 42 H6
Oakham Clo. SE6 86 J2
  Rutland Wk.
Oakham Dr., Brom. 96 F4
Oakhampton Rd. NW7 31 A7
Oakhill, Esher 98 D6
Oakhill, Surb. 91 H7
Oakhill Ave., Pnr. 36 E2
Oakhill Ct. E11 42 H6
  Eastern Ave.
Oakhill Ct. SW19 84 A7
  Edge Hill
Oakhill Cres., Surb. 91 H7
Oakhill Dr., Surb. 91 H7
Oakhill Gro., Surb. 91 H6
Oakhill Path, Surb. 91 H6
  Glenbuck Rd.
Oakhill Pl. SW15 75 D5
  Oakhill Rd.
Oakhill Rd. SW15 75 C5
Oakhill Rd. SW16 94 E1
Oakhill Rd., Beck. 96 C2
Oakhill Rd., Orp. 104 J1
Oakhill Rd., Surb. 91 H6
Oakhill Rd., Sutt. 100 E3
Oakhouse Rd., Bexh. 80 G5
Oakhurst Ave., Barn. 23 H7
Oakhurst Ave., Bexh. 71 E7
Oakhurst Clo. E17 42 E4
Oakhurst Clo., Ilf. 43 F1
Oakhurst Clo., Tedd. 82 B5
Oakhurst Gdns. E4 34 F1
Oakhurst Gdns. E17 42 E4
Oakhurst Gdns., Bexh. 71 E7
Oakhurst Gro. SE22 77 D4
Oakhurst Rd., Epsom 99 C6
Oakington Ave., Har. 36 G7
Oakington Ave., Wem. 46 J3
Oakington Dr., Sun. 90 C2
Oakington Manor Dr., 47 A5
  Wem.
Oakington Rd. W9 57 D4
Oakington Way N8 40 E6
Oakland Way, Epsom 99 D6
Oaklands N21 32 F2
Oaklands, Twick. 72 J7
Oaklands Ave. N9 25 E6
Oaklands Ave., Esher 98 A1
Oaklands Ave., Islw. 64 C6
Oaklands Ave., Sid. 79 J7
Oaklands Ave., 94 G4
  Th.Hth.
Oaklands Ave., Wat. 28 B1
Oaklands Ave., 103 B3
  W.Wick.
Oaklands Clo., Bexh. 80 F5
Oaklands Clo., Chess. 98 F4
Oaklands Clo., Orp. 97 H6
Oaklands Ct., Wem. 46 G5
Oaklands Est. SW4 76 C6
Oaklands Gro. W12 65 G1
Oaklands La., Barn. 22 H4
Oaklands Pk. Ave., Ilf. 52 G2
  High Rd.
Oaklands Pl. SW4 76 C4
  St. Alphonsus Rd.
Oaklands Rd. N20 23 C7
Oaklands Rd. NW2 48 A4
Oaklands Rd. SW14 74 D3
Oaklands Rd. W7 64 C2
Oaklands Rd., Bexh. 80 F4
Oaklands Rd., Brom. 87 E7
Oaklands Way, Wall. 101 D7
Oaklea Pas., Kings.T. 91 G3
Oakleafe Gdns., Ilf. 43 E3
Oakleigh Ave. N20 31 G2
Oakleigh Ave., Edg. 38 B2
Oakleigh Ave., Surb. 96 A1
Oakleigh Clo. N20 31 J3
Oakleigh Ct., Barn. 23 H6
  Church Hill Rd.

Oakleigh Ct., Edg.	38	C2
Oakleigh Cres. N20	31	H2
Oakleigh Gdns. N20	31	F1
Oakleigh Gdns., Edg.	29	J5
Oakleigh Gdns., Orp.	104	H4
Oakleigh Ms. N20	31	F2
Oakleigh Rd. N.		
Oakleigh Pk. Ave.,	97	D2
Chis.		
Oakleigh Pk. N. N20	31	G1
Oakleigh Pk. S. N20	23	H7
Oakleigh Rd., Pnr.	28	F6
Oakleigh Rd. N. N11	31	H2
Oakleigh Rd. S. N11	32	A3
Oakleigh Way, Mitch.	94	B1
Oakleigh Way, Surb.	99	A1
Oakley Ave. W5	56	A7
Oakley Ave., Bark.	52	J7
Oakley Ave., Croy.	101	F4
Oakley Clo. E4	34	C3
Mapleton Rd.		
Oakley Clo. E6	61	B6
Northumberland Rd.		
Oakley Clo. W7	55	B7
Oakley Clo., Islw.	73	A1
Oakley Ct., Mitch.	101	A1
London Rd.		
Oakley Cres. EC1	**8**	**H2**
Oakley Dr. SE9	88	G1
Oakley Dr., Brom.	104	B3
Oakley Gdns. N8	40	F5
Oakley Gdns. SW3	**18**	**H5**
Oakley Gdns. SW3	66	H6
Oakley Pk., Bex.	80	C7
Oakley Pl. SE1	**21**	**F4**
Oakley Pl. SE1	68	C5
Oakley Rd. N1	50	A7
Oakley Rd. SE25	95	E5
Oakley Rd., Brom.	104	B3
Oakley Rd., Har.	37	B6
Oakley Sq. NW1	**7**	**G1**
Oakley Sq. NW1	58	C2
Oakley St. SW3	**18**	**G5**
Oakley St. SW3	66	H6
Oakley Wk. W6	66	A6
Greyhound Rd.		
Oakmead Ave., Brom.	96	G6
Oakmead Gdns., Edg.	30	D4
Oakmead Pl., Mitch.	93	H1
Oakmead Rd. SW12	85	A1
Oakmead Rd., Croy.	95	F6
Oakmere Rd. SE2	71	A6
Oakmoor Way, Chig.	35	H5
Oakmount Pl., Orp.	104	G1
Oakridge Dr. N2	39	G3
Oakridge Rd., Brom.	87	D4
Oaks, The N12	31	E4
Oaks, The SE18	70	F5
Oaks, The, Wat.	28	C1
Oaks, The, Wdf.Grn.	34	E7
Oaks Ave. SE19	86	B5
Oaks Ave., Felt.	81	E2
Oaks Ave., Rom.	44	J2
Oaks Ave., Wor.Pk.	99	H3
Oaks Gro. E4	34	E2
Oaks La., Croy.	102	F3
Oaks La., Ilf.	43	H5
Oaks Rd., Croy.	102	E5
Oaks Way, Cars.	100	J7
Oaks Way, Surb.	99	F1
Oaksford Ave. SE26	86	E3
Oakshade Rd., Brom.	87	D4
Oakshaw Rd. SW18	75	E7
Oakthorpe Rd. N13	32	G5
Oaktree Ave. N13	32	H3
Oakview Gdns. N2	39	G4
Oakview Gro., Croy.	102	H1
Oakview Rd. SE6	87	B5
Oakway SW20	92	J4
Oakway, Brom.	96	D2
Oakway Clo., Bex.	80	E6
Oakways SE9	79	E6
Oakwood Ave. N14	24	D7
Oakwood Ave., Beck.	96	C2
Oakwood Ave.,	22	B4
Borwd.		
Oakwood Ave., Brom.	96	H3
Oakwood Ave., Mitch.	93	G2
Oakwood Ave., Sthl.	54	G7
Oakwood Clo. N14	24	C6
Oakwood Clo., Chis.	88	C6
Oakwood Clo.,	35	B6
Wdf.Grn.		
Green Wk.		
Oakwood Ct. W14	66	C3
Oakwood Cres. N21	24	E6
Oakwood Cres., Grnf.	46	D6
Oakwood Dr. SE19	86	A6
Oakwood Dr., Edg.	30	C6
Oakwood Gdns., Ilf.	52	J2
Oakwood Gdns.,	104	F2
Orp.		
Oakwood Gdns.,	100	D2
Sutt.		
Oakwood Hill, Loug.	27	C6
Oakwood Hill Ind.	27	E5
Est., Loug.		
(Oakwood Hill)		
Oakwood La. W14	66	C3
Oakwood Pk. Rd. N14	24	D7
Oakwood Pl., Croy.	94	G6
Oakwood Rd. NW11	39	D4
Oakwood Rd. SW20	92	G6
Oakwood Rd., Croy.	94	G6
Oakwood Rd., Orp.	104	F2
Oakwood Rd., Pnr.	36	B2
Oakwood Vw. N14	24	D5
Oakworth Rd. W10	56	J5
Oat La. EC2	13	A3
Oat La. EC2	58	J6
Oates Clo., Brom.	96	D3
Oatfield Rd., Orp.	104	J1
Oatland Ri. E17	41	H2
Oatlands Rd., Enf.	25	F1
Oban Ho., Bark.	61	G2
Wheelers Cross		
Oban Rd. E13	60	J3
Oban Rd. SE25	95	A4
Oban St. E14	60	D6
Oberstein Rd. SW11	75	G4
Oborne Clo. SE24	76	H5
Observatory Gdns.	66	D2
W8		
Observatory Rd.	74	C4
SW14		
Occupation La. SE18	79	E1
Occupation La. W5	64	G4
Occupation Rd. SE17	**20**	**J3**
Occupation Rd. SE17	67	J5
Occupation Rd. W13	64	E2
Ocean Est. E1	59	G4
Ocean St. E1	59	G5
Ockenden Rd. N1	50	A6
Ockham Dr., Orp.	89	A7
Ockley Rd. SW16	85	E4
Ockley Rd., Croy.	94	F7
Octagon Arc. EC2	**13**	**D2**
Octavia Clo., Mitch.	93	H5
Octavia Rd., Islw.	73	C3
Octavia St. SW11	75	H1
Octavia Way SE28	62	B7
Booth Clo.		
Octavius St. SE8	69	A7
Odard Rd., W.Mol.	90	G4
Down St.		
Oddesey Rd., Borwd.	22	B1
Odessa Rd. E7	51	F4
Odessa Rd. NW10	56	G2
Odessa St. SE16	68	J2
Odger St. SW11	75	J2
Odhams Wk. WC2	**12**	**A4**
Odyssey Business	45	B5
Pk., Ruis.		
Offas Mead E9	50	H4
Lindisfarne Way		
Offenbach Ho. E2	59	G2
Mace St.		
Offenham Rd. SE9	88	C4
Offerton Rd. SW4	76	C3
Offham Slope N12	31	C5
Offley Rd. SW9	**20**	**E7**
Offley Rd. SW9	67	G7
Offord Clo. N17	33	D7
Offord Rd. N1	49	F7
Offord St. N1	49	F7
Ogilby St. SE18	70	C4
Oglander Rd. SE15	77	C4
Ogle St. W1	**11**	**F1**
Ogle St. W1	58	C5
Oglethorpe Rd., Dag.	53	F3
Ohio Rd. E13	60	F4
Okeburn Rd. SW17	85	A5
Okehampton Clo.	31	G5
N12		
Okehampton Cres.,	80	B1
Well.		
Okehampton Rd.	56	J1
NW10		
Olaf St. W11	57	A7
Old Bailey EC4	**12**	**H4**
Old Bailey EC4	58	H6
Old Barn Clo., Sutt.	100	B7
Old Barrack Yd. SW1	**15**	**B4**
Old Barrowfield E15	60	E1
New Plaistow Rd.		
Old Bethnal Grn. Rd.	**9**	**J3**
E2		
Old Bethnal Grn. Rd.	59	D3
E2		
Old Bond St. W1	**11**	**F6**
Old Bond St. W1	58	C7
Old Brewers Yd. WC2	**12**	**A4**
Old Brewery Ms. NW3	48	G4
Hampstead High St.		
Old Bri. Clo., Nthlt.	54	G2
Old Bri. St., Kings.T.	91	G2
Old Broad St. EC2	**13**	**C4**
Old Broad St. EC2	59	A6
Old Bromley Rd.,	87	D5
Brom.		
Old Brompton Rd.	66	E5
SW5		
Old Brompton Rd.	**18**	**D3**
SW7		
Old Brompton Rd.	66	E5
SW7		
Old Bldgs. WC2	**12**	**E3**
Old Burlington St. W1	**11**	**F5**
Old Burlington St. W1	58	C7
Old Castle St. E1	**13**	**F3**
Old Castle St. E1	59	C6
Old Cavendish St. W1	**11**	**D3**
Old Cavendish St. W1	58	B6
Old Chelsea Ms. SW3	**18**	**F6**
Old Ch. La. NW9	47	D2
Old Ch. La., Grnf.	55	D3
Perivale La.		
Old Ch. La., Stan.	29	E5
Old Ch. Rd. E1	59	G6
Old Ch. Rd. E4	34	A4
Old Ch. St. SW3	**18**	**F4**
Old Ch. St. SW3	66	G5
Old Claygate La.,	98	D6
Esher		
Old Clem Sq. SE18	70	D6
Kempt St.		
Old Compton St. W1	**11**	**H5**
Old Compton St. W1	58	D7
Old Cote Dr., Houns.	63	D6
Old Ct. Pl. W8	**14**	**A3**
Old Ct. Pl. W8	66	E2
Old Deer Pk. Gdns.,	73	H3
Rich.		
Old Devonshire Rd.	76	B7
SW12		
Old Dock Clo., Rich.	65	A6
Watcombe Cotts.		
Old Dover Rd. SE3	69	G7
Old Fm. Ave. N14	24	C7
Old Fm. Ave., Sid.	88	G1
Old Fm. Clo., Houns.	72	F4
Old Fm. Pas., Hmptn.	90	J1
Old Fm. Rd. N2	39	G1
Old Fm. Rd., Hmptn.	81	F6
Old Fm. Rd. E., Sid.	89	A2
Old Fm. Rd. W., Sid.	88	A2
Old Fish St. Hill EC4	**12**	**J5**
Old Fleet La. EC4	**12**	**G3**
Old Fold Clo., Barn.	23	C1
Old Fold La.		
Old Fold La., Barn.	23	C1
Old Fold Vw., Barn.	22	J3
Old Ford Rd. E2	59	F2
Old Ford Rd. E3	59	G2
Old Forge Clo., Stan.	29	D4
Old Forge Ms. W12	65	H2
Goodwin Rd.		
Old Forge Way, Sid.	89	B4
Old Fox Footpath,	102	B7
S.Croy.		
Essenden Rd.		
Old Gloucester St.	**12**	**B1**
WC1		
Old Gloucester St.	58	E5
WC1		
Old Hall Clo., Pnr.	36	E1
Old Hall Dr., Pnr.	36	E1
Old Hill, Chis.	97	D1
Old Hill, Orp.	104	G6
Old Homesdale Rd.,	96	J4
Brom.		
Old Ho. Clo. SW19	84	B5
Old Ho. Gdns., Twick.	73	H6
Old Jamaica Rd. SE16	**17**	**H5**
Old Jamaica Rd. SE16	68	D3
Old James St. SE15	77	E3
Old Jewry EC2	**13**	**B4**
Old Jewry EC2	59	A6
Old Kent Rd. SE1	**21**	**D1**
Old Kent Rd. SE1	68	B4
Old Kent Rd. SE15	**21**	**J5**
Old Kent Rd. SE15	68	E6
Old Kenton La. NW9	38	B5
Old Kingston Rd.,	99	C3
Wor.Pk.		
Old Lo. Pl., Twick.	73	E6
St. Margarets Rd.		
Old Lo. Way, Stan.	29	D5
Old Maidstone Rd.,	89	F7
Sid.		
Old Malden La.,	99	D3
Wor.Pk.		
Old Manor Dr., Islw.	72	J6
Old Manor Way, Chis.	88	C5
Old Manor Yd. SW5	**18**	**A2**
Old Marylebone Rd.	**10**	**H2**
NW1		
Old Marylebone Rd.	57	H5
NW1		
Old Ms., Har.	37	B5
Hindes Rd.		
Old Mill Ct. E18	42	J3
Old Mill La. W6	65	G5
Old Mill Rd. SE18	70	G6
Old Montague St. E1	**13**	**H2**
Old Montague St. E1	59	D5
Old Nichol St. E2	**9**	**F5**
Old Nichol St. E2	59	C4
Old N. St. WC1	**12**	**C1**
Old Oak Common La.	56	E4
NW10		
Old Oak Common La.	56	E5
W3		
Old Oak La. NW10	56	F3
Old Oak Rd. W3	56	F7
Old Orchard, Sun.	90	C2
Old Orchard, The	48	J4
NW3		
Nassington Rd.		
Old Palace La., Rich.	73	F5
Old Palace Rd., Croy.	101	H3
Old Palace Ter., Rich.	73	G5
King St.		
Old Palace Yd. SW1	**16**	**A5**
Old Palace Yd. SW1	67	E3
Old Palace Yd., Rich.	73	F5
Old Paradise St. SE11	**20**	**C1**
Old Paradise St. SE11	67	F4
Old Pk. Ave. SW12	76	A6
Old Pk. Ave., Enf.	24	J4
Old Pk. Gro., Enf.	24	J4
Old Pk. La. W1	**15**	**C2**
Old Pk. La. W1	67	A1
Old Pk. Ms., Houns.	63	F7
Old Pk. Ridings N21	24	H6
Old Pk. Rd. N13	32	F4
Old Pk. Rd. SE2	71	A5
Old Pk. Rd., Enf.	24	H3
Old Pk. Rd. S., Enf.	24	H4
Old Pk. Vw., Enf.	24	G4
Old Perry St., Chis.	88	H6
Old Pye St. SW1	**15**	**H5**
Old Pye St. SW1	67	D3
Old Quebec St. W1	**11**	**A4**
Old Quebec St. W1	57	J6
Old Queen St. SW1	**15**	**J4**
Old Queen St. SW1	67	D2
Old Rectory Gdns.,	30	A6
Edg.		
Old Redding, Har.	28	H5
Old Rd. SE13	78	E4
Old Rd., Enf.	25	F1
Old Rope Wk., Sun.	90	B3
The Ave.		
Old Royal Free Pl. N1	58	G1
Liverpool Rd.		
Old Royal Free Sq. N1	58	G1
Liverpool Rd.		
Old Ruislip Rd., Nthlt.	54	C2
Old Savill's Cotts.,	35	F4
Chig.		
The Chase		
Old Sch. Clo. SW19	93	D2
Old Sch. Clo., Beck.	95	G2
Old Seacoal La. EC4	**12**	**G4**
Old S. Clo., Pnr.	36	D1
Old S. Lambeth Rd.	**20**	**B7**
SW8		
Old S. Lambeth Rd.	67	E7
SW8		
Old Sq. WC2	**12**	**D3**
Old Sq. WC2	58	F6
Old Sta. Rd., Loug.	27	B5
Old St. E13	60	H2
Old St. EC1	**8**	**J6**
Old St. EC1	58	J4
Old Swan Yd., Cars.	100	J4
Old Town SW4	76	C3
Old Town, Croy.	101	H3
Old Tram Yd. SE18	70	H4
Lakedale Rd.		

Old Woolwich Rd. SE10 69 D5
Old York Rd. SW18 75 E5
Oldacre Ms. SW12 76 B7
Balham Gro.
Oldberry Rd., Edg. 30 D6
Oldborough Rd., Wem. 46 F2
Oldbury Pl. W1 11 C1
Oldbury Pl. W1 58 A5
Oldbury Rd., Enf. 25 D2
Oldfield Circ., Nthlt. 45 J6
The Fairway
Oldfield Clo., Brom. 97 C4
Oldfield Clo., Grnf. 46 B5
Oldfield Clo., Stan. 29 D5
Oldfield Fm. Gdns., Grnf. 55 A1
Oldfield Gro. SE16 68 G4
Oldfield La. N., Grnf. 55 A2
Oldfield La. S., Grnf. 54 J3
Oldfield Ms. N6 40 C7
Oldfield Pk., Brom. 97 D4
Oldfield Rd. N16 50 B3
Oldfield Rd. NW10 47 F7
Oldfield Rd. SW19 84 B6
Oldfield Rd. W3 65 F2
Valetta Rd.
Oldfield Rd., Bexh. 80 E2
Oldfield Rd., Brom. 97 B4
Oldfield Rd., Hmptn. 90 F1
Oldfields Rd., Sutt. 100 C3
Oldham Ter. W3 65 C1
Oldhill St. N16 50 D1
Oldridge Rd. SW12 76 A7
Oldstead Rd., Brom. 87 D4
Oleander Clo., Orp. 104 G5
O'Leary Sq. E1 59 F5
Oley Pl. E1 59 G5
Redman's Rd.
Olinda Rd. N16 41 C6
Oliphant St. W10 57 A3
Olive Rd. E13 60 J3
Olive Rd. NW2 47 J4
Olive Rd. SW19 84 F7
Norman Rd.
Olive Rd. W5 64 G3
Oliver Ave. SE25 95 C3
Oliver Clo. W4 65 B6
Oliver Gdns. E6 61 B6
Oliver Goldsmith Est. SE15 77 D1
Goldsmith Rd.
Oliver Gro. SE25 95 C4
Oliver Rd. E10 51 B2
Oliver Rd. E17 42 C5
Oliver Rd., N.Mal. 92 C2
Oliver Rd., Sutt. 100 G4
Olivers Yd. EC1 9 C5
Olivette St. SW15 75 A3
Felsham Rd.
Ollards Gro., Loug. 27 A4
Ollerton Grn. E3 59 J1
Ollerton Rd. N11 32 D5
Olley Clo., Wall. 101 E6
Ollgar Clo. W12 65 F1
Olliffe St. E14 69 C3
Olmar St. SE1 21 H5
Olmar St. SE1 68 D6
Olney Rd. SE17 20 J5
Olney Rd. SE17 67 H6
Olron Cres., Bexh. 80 D5
Olven Rd. SE18 70 F6
Olveston Wk., Cars. 93 G6
Olwen Ms., Pnr. 36 D2
Olyffe Ave., Well. 80 A1
Olyffe Dr., Beck. 96 C1
Olympia Ms. W2 10 B6
Olympia Way W14 66 B3
Olympic Way, Grnf. 54 H1
Olympic Way, Wem. 47 A3
Olympus Sq. E5 50 D4
Nolan Way
Oman Ave. NW2 47 H4
O'Meara St. SE1 17 A2
O'Meara St. SE1 67 J1
Omega Pl. N1 8 B2
Omega St. SE14 78 A1
Ommaney Rd. SE14 77 G1
On The Hill, Wat. 28 E2
Ondine Rd. SE15 77 C4
One Tree Clo. SE23 77 F6
Onega Gate SE16 68 H3
O'Neill Path SE18 70 D6
Kempt St.
Ongar Clo., Rom. 44 C5
Ongar Rd. SW6 66 D6
Onra Rd. E17 42 A7
Onslow Ave., Rich. 73 H5
Onslow Clo. E4 34 D2
Onslow Clo., T.Ditt. 98 B1
Onslow Cres., Chis. 97 E1
Onslow Dr., Sid. 89 D3
Onslow Gdns. E18 42 H3
Onslow Gdns. N10 40 B5
Onslow Gdns. N21 24 G5
Onslow Gdns. SW7 18 E3
Onslow Gdns. SW7 66 G5
Onslow Gdns., T.Ditt. 98 B1
Onslow Gdns., Wall. 101 C6
Onslow Ms. E. SW7 18 E2
Onslow Ms. W. SW7 18 E2
Onslow Rd., Croy. 101 G1
Onslow Rd., N.Mal. 92 G4
Onslow Rd., Rich. 73 H5
Onslow Sq. SW7 18 F2
Onslow Sq. SW7 66 G4
Onslow St. EC1 8 F6
Onslow Way, T.Ditt. 98 B1
Ontario St. SE1 16 H6
Opal Clo. E16 61 A6
Opal Ms. NW6 57 C1
Priory Pk. Rd.
Opal Ms., Ilf. 52 E2
Ley St.
Opal St. SE11 20 G3
Opal St. SE11 67 H4
Openshaw Rd. SE2 71 B4
Openview SW18 84 F1
Ophelia Gdns. NW2 48 B3
The Vale
Ophir Ter. SE15 77 D1
Opossum Way, Houns. 72 C2
Oppenheim Rd. SE13 78 C2
Oppidans Ms. NW3 48 J7
Meadowbank
Oppidans Rd. NW3 48 J7
Orange Ct. E1 17 J2
Orange Hill Rd., Edg. 30 C7
Orange Pl. SE16 68 F3
Lower Rd.
Orange St. WC2 11 J6
Orange St. WC2 58 D7
Orange Yd. W1 11 J4
Orangery, The, Rich. 82 F2
Orangery La. SE9 79 C5
Oratory La. SW3 18 F3
Orb St. SE17 21 B2
Orb St. SE17 68 A4
Orbain Rd. SW6 66 B7
Orbel St. SW11 75 H1
Orchard, The N14 24 B5
Orchard, The N21 25 A6
Orchard, The NW11 39 D5
Orchard, The SE3 78 D2
Orchard, The W4 65 D4
Orchard, The W5 55 G5
Orchard, The, Epsom 99 F7
Orchard, The, Houns. 72 J2
Orchard Ave. N3 39 D3
Orchard Ave. N14 24 C6
Orchard Ave. N20 31 G2
Orchard Ave., Belv. 71 E6
Orchard Ave., Croy. 102 H2
Orchard Ave., Houns. 63 E7
Orchard Ave., Mitch. 101 A1
Orchard Ave., N.Mal. 92 E2
Orchard Ave., Sthl. 63 E1
Orchard Ave., T.Ditt. 98 D1
Orchard Clo. E4 34 A4
Chingford Mt. Rd.
Orchard Clo. E11 42 H4
Orchard Clo. NW2 47 G3
Orchard Clo. SE23 77 F6
Brenchley Gdns.
Orchard Clo. SW20 92 J4
Grand Dr.
Orchard Clo. W10 57 B5
Orchard Clo., Bexh. 80 E1
Orchard Clo., Edg. 29 H6
Orchard Clo., Epsom 99 B6
Orchard Clo., Nthlt. 45 J5
Orchard Clo., Surb. 91 E7
Orchard Clo., Walt. 90 B7
Garden Rd.
Orchard Clo. (Bushey), Wat. 29 A1
Orchard Clo., Wem. 55 H1
Orchard Ct., Islw. 73 A1
Orchard Ct., Twick. 82 A2
Orchard Ct., Wor.Pk. 99 G1
Orchard Cres., Edg. 30 C5
Orchard Cres., Enf. 25 C1
Orchard Dr. SE3 78 E2
Orchard Dr., Edg. 29 J5
Orchard Gdns., Chess. 98 H4
Orchard Gdns., Sutt. 100 D5
Orchard Gate NW9 38 E4
Orchard Gate, Esher 98 A1
Orchard Gate, Grnf. 46 E5
Orchard Grn., Orp. 104 H2
Orchard Gro. SE20 86 D7
Orchard Gro., Croy. 95 H7
Orchard Gro., Edg. 38 A1
Orchard Gro., Har. 37 J5
Orchard Gro., Orp. 104 J2
Orchard Hill SE13 78 B2
Coldbath St.
Orchard Hill, Cars. 100 J5
Orchard La. SW20 92 H1
Durham Rd.
Orchard La., E.Mol. 91 A6
Orchard La., Wdf.Grn. 34 J4
Orchard Ms. N1 50 A7
Southgate Gro.
Orchard Pl. E14 60 E7
Orchard Pl. N17 33 C7
Orchard Ri., Croy. 102 H1
Orchard Ri., Kings.T. 92 C1
Orchard Ri., Rich. 74 B4
Orchard Ri. E., Sid. 79 H5
Orchard Ri. W., Sid. 79 H5
Orchard Rd. N6 40 B7
Orchard Rd. SE3 78 E2
Eliot Pl.
Orchard Rd. SE18 70 G4
Orchard Rd., Barn. 23 B4
Orchard Rd., Belv. 71 G4
Orchard Rd., Brent. 64 F6
Orchard Rd., Brom. 96 J1
Orchard Rd., Chess. 98 H4
Orchard Rd., Dag. 62 G1
Orchard Rd., Enf. 25 F5
Orchard Rd., Hmptn. 81 F7
Orchard Rd., Hayes 54 A7
Orchard Rd., Houns. 72 F5
Orchard Rd., Kings.T. 91 H2
Orchard Rd., Mitch. 101 A1
Orchard Rd., Orp. (Farnborough) 104 E5
Orchard Rd., Rich. 74 A3
Orchard Rd., Rom. 44 H2
Orchard Rd., Sid. 88 H4
Orchard Rd., Sun. 81 B7
Hanworth Rd.
Orchard Rd., Sutt. 100 D4
Orchard Rd., Twick. 73 D5
Orchard Rd., Well. 80 B3
Orchard Sq. W14 66 C5
Sun Rd.
Orchard St. E17 41 H4
Orchard St. W1 11 B4
Orchard St. W1 58 A6
Orchard Ter., Enf. 25 D6
Great Cambridge Rd.
Orchard Way, Beck. 95 H5
Orchard Way, Croy. 102 H1
Orchard Way, Enf. 25 B3
Orchard Way, Sutt. 100 G4
Orchardleigh Ave., Enf. 25 F2
Orchardmede N21 25 A6
Orchardson St. NW8 6 E6
Orchardson St. NW8 57 G4
Orchid Clo. E6 61 B5
Orchid Rd. N14 24 C7
Orchid St. W12 56 G7
Orde Hall St. WC1 12 C1
Orde Hall St. WC1 58 F5
Ordell Rd. E3 59 J2
Ordnance Clo., Felt. 81 A3
Ordnance Cres. SE10 69 E2
Ordnance Hill NW8 57 G1
Ordnance Ms. NW8 6 F1
Ordnance Rd. E16 60 F5
Ordnance Rd. SE18 70 D6
Oregano Dr. E14 60 D6
Oregon Ave. E12 52 C4
Oregon Clo., N.Mal. 92 C4
Georgia Rd.
Oregon Sq., Orp. 104 G1
Orestes Ms. NW6 48 D5
Aldred Rd.
Orford Ct. SE27 85 H2
Orford Gdns., Twick. 82 C2
Orford Rd. E17 42 A5
Orford Rd. E18 42 H3
Organ La. E4 34 C2
Oriel Clo., Mitch. 94 D4
Oriel Ct. NW3 48 F4
Heath St.
Oriel Gdns., Ilf. 43 C3
Oriel Pl. NW3 48 F4
Heath St.
Oriel Rd. E9 50 G6
Oriel Way, Nthlt. 45 H7
Orient Ind. Pk. E10 51 A2
Orient St. SE11 20 G1
Orient Way E5 50 G3
Oriental Rd. E16 70 A1
Oriental St. E14 60 A7
Morant St.
Oriole Way SE28 62 B7
Orissa Rd. SE18 70 H5
Orkney St. SW11 76 A2
Orlando Rd. SW4 76 C3
Orleans Clo., Esher 98 A2
Orleans Rd. SE19 86 A6
Orleans Rd., Twick. 73 E7
Orleston Ms. N7 49 G6
Orleston Rd. N7 49 G6
Orley Fm. Rd., Har. 46 B3
Orlop St. SE10 69 E5
Ormanton Rd. SE26 86 D4
Orme Ct. W2 10 A6
Orme Ct. W2 57 E7
Orme Ct. Ms. W2 10 B6
Orme La. W2 10 A6
Orme La. W2 57 E7
Orme Rd., Kings.T. 92 B2
Orme Sq. W2 10 A6
Ormeley Rd. SW12 76 B7
Ormerod Gdns., Mitch. 94 A2
Ormesby Clo. SE28 62 D7
Wroxham Rd.
Ormesby Way, Har. 37 J6
Ormiston Gro. W12 65 H1
Ormiston Rd. SE10 69 G5
Ormond Ave., Hmptn. 90 H1
Ormond Ave., Rich. 73 G5
Ormond Rd.
Ormond Clo. WC1 12 B1
Ormond Cres., Hmptn. 90 H1
Ormond Dr., Hmptn. 81 H7
Ormond Ms. WC1 8 B6
Ormond Rd. N19 49 E1
Ormond Rd., Rich. 73 G5
Ormond Yd. SW1 15 G1
Ormonde Ave., Orp. 104 F2
Ormonde Gate SW3 19 A4
Ormonde Gate SW3 66 J5
Ormonde Pl. SW1 19 B2
Ormonde Ri., Buck.H. 34 J1
Ormonde Rd. SW14 74 C3
Ormonde Ter. NW8 57 J1
Ormsby Gdns., Grnf. 54 J2
Ormsby Pl. N16 50 C3
Victorian Gro.
Ormsby Pt. SE18 70 E4
Troy Ct.
Ormsby St. E2 9 F2
Ormsby St. E2 59 C2
Ormside St. SE15 68 F6
Ormskirk Rd., Wat. 28 D4
Ornan Rd. NW3 48 H5
Oronsay Wk. N1 49 J6
Marquess Est.
Orpen Wk. N16 50 B3
Orpheus St. SE5 77 A1
Orpington Gdns. N18 33 B3
Orpington Rd. N21 32 G1
Orpington Rd., Chis. 97 H3
Orpwood Clo., Hmptn. 81 F6
Orsett St. SE11 20 D3
Orsett St. SE11 67 F5
Orsett Ter. W2 10 B3
Orsett Ter. W2 57 E6
Orsett Ter., Wdf.Grn. 34 J7
Orsman Rd. N1 59 B1
Orton St. E1 17 H2
Orville Rd. SW11 75 G2
Orwell Ct. N5 49 J4
Orwell Rd. E13 60 J1
Osbaldeston Rd. N16 50 D2
Osbert St. SW1 19 H2
Osberton Rd. SE12 78 G5
Osborn Clo. E8 59 D1
Osborn Gdns. NW7 31 A7
Osborn La. SE23 77 H7
Osborn St. E1 13 G2
Osborn St. E1 59 C5
Osborn Ter. SE3 78 F4
Lee Rd.
Osborne Clo., Beck. 95 H4
Osborne Clo., Felt. 81 D5
Osborne Gdns., Th.Hth. 94 J2

Name	Page	Grid
Osborne Gro. E17	41	J4
Osborne Gro. N4	49	G1
Osborne Ms. E17	41	J4
Osborne Gro.		
Osborne Pl., Sutt.	100	G5
Osborne Rd. E7	51	H5
Osborne Rd. E9	50	J6
Osborne Rd. E10	51	B3
Osborne Rd. N4	49	G1
Osborne Rd. N13	32	G3
Osborne Rd. NW2	47	H6
Osborne Rd. W3	65	B2
Osborne Rd., Belv.	71	F5
Osborne Rd., Buck.H.	34	H1
Osborne Rd., Dag.	53	F5
Osborne Rd., Enf.	25	H2
Osborne Rd., Houns.	72	F3
Osborne Rd., Kings.T.	82	H7
Osborne Sq., Dag.	53	F4
Oscar St. SE8	78	A1
Oseney Cres. NW5	49	C6
Osgood Ave., Orp.	104	J5
Osgood Gdns., Orp.	104	J5
O'Shea Gro. E3	59	J1
Osidge La. N14	32	A1
Osier St. E1	59	F4
Osier Way E10	51	B3
Osier Way, Mitch.	93	H5
Osiers Rd. SW18	75	D4
Oslac Rd. SE6	87	B5
Oslo Ct. NW8	**6**	**G2**
Oslo Sq. SE16	68	H3
Norway Gate		
Osman Clo. N15	41	A6
Tewkesbury Rd.		
Osman Rd. N9	33	D3
Osman Rd. W6	65	J3
Batoum Gdns.		
Osmond Clo., Har.	45	J2
Osmond Gdns., Wall.	101	C5
Osmund St. W12	56	F6
Braybrook St.		
Osnaburgh St. NW1	**7**	**E5**
Osnaburgh St. NW1	58	B4
Osnaburgh Ter. NW1	**7**	**E5**
Osney Wk., Cars.	93	G6
Osprey Clo. E6	61	B5
Dove App.		
Osprey Clo. E11	42	G4
Osprey Clo. E17	33	H7
Osprey Ms., Enf.	25	E5
Ospringe Clo. SE20	86	F7
Ospringe Ct. SE9	79	G6
Ospringe Rd. NW5	49	C4
Osram Pl. NW2	48	C3
Ridge Rd.		
Osram Rd., Wem.	46	G3
Osric Path N1	**9**	**D2**
Ossian Rd. N4	40	F7
Ossington Bldgs. W1	**11**	**B1**
Ossington St. W2	**10**	**A6**
Ossington St. W2	57	E7
Ossory Rd. SE1	**21**	**H5**
Ossory Rd. SE1	68	D6
Ossulston St. NW1	**7**	**H2**
Ossulston St. NW1	58	D2
Ossulton Pl. N2	39	F3
East End Rd.		
Ossulton Way N2	39	F4
Ostade Rd. SW2	76	F7
Osten Ms. SW7	**14**	**B6**
Osterley Ave., Islw.	64	A7
Osterley Ct., Islw.	73	A1
Osterley Cres., Islw.	73	B1
Osterley Gdns., Th.Hth.	94	J2
Osterley Ho. E14	60	B6
Giraud St.		
Osterley La., Islw.	63	J5
Osterley La., Sthl.	63	G5
Osterley Pk., Islw.	64	A5
Osterley Pk. Rd., Sthl.	63	F3
Osterley Pk. Vw. Rd. W7	64	B2
Osterley Rd. N16	50	B4
Osterley Rd., Islw.	64	B7
Osterley Views, Sthl.	63	J1
West Pk. Rd.		
Ostliffe Rd. N13	32	H5
Oswald Rd., Sthl.	63	E1
Oswald St. E5	50	G3
Oswalds Mead E9	50	H4
Lindisfarne Way		
Osward Pl. N9	33	E2
Osward Rd. SW17	84	J2
Oswell Ho. E1	68	E1
Penang St.		
Oswin St. SE11	**20**	**H1**
Oswin St. SE11	67	H4
Oswyth Rd. SE5	77	B2
Otford Clo. SE20	95	F1
Otford Clo., Bex.	80	H6
Southwold Rd.		
Otford Clo., Brom.	97	D3
Otford Cres. SE4	77	J6
Othello Clo. SE11	**20**	**G3**
Otis St. E3	60	C3
Otley App., Ilf.	43	E6
Otley Dr., Ilf.	43	E6
Otley Rd. E16	60	J6
Otley Ter. E5	50	G3
Otley Way, Wat.	28	C3
Ottaway St. E5	50	D3
Stellman Clo.		
Ottenden Clo., Orp.	104	H4
Southfleet Rd.		
Otter Rd., Grnf.	54	J4
Otterbourne Rd. E4	34	D3
Otterbourne Rd., Croy.	101	H2
Otterburn Gdns., Islw.	64	D7
Otterburn Ho. SE5	**20**	**J7**
Otterburn St. SW17	84	J6
Otterden St. SE6	87	A4
Otto Clo. SE26	86	E3
Otto St. SE17	**20**	**G6**
Otto St. SE17	67	H6
Oulton Clo. E5	50	F2
Mundford Rd.		
Oulton Clo. SE28	62	C6
Rollesby Way		
Oulton Cres., Bark.	52	J6
Oulton Rd. N15	41	A5
Oulton Way, Wat.	28	E4
Ouseley Rd. SW12	84	J1
Outer Circle NW1	**6**	**J1**
Outer Circle NW1	57	H3
Outgate Rd. NW10	47	F7
Outram Pl. N1	58	E1
Outram Rd. E6	61	B1
Outram Rd. N22	40	D1
Outram Rd., Croy.	102	C2
Outwich St. EC3	**13**	**E3**
Outwich St. EC3	59	B6
Oval, The E2	59	E2
Oval, The Sid.	80	A7
Oval Pl. SW8	**20**	**C7**
Oval Pl. SW8	67	F7
Oval Rd. NW1	58	B1
Oval Rd., Croy.	102	A2
Oval Rd. N., Dag.	62	H1
Oval Rd. S., Dag.	62	H2
Oval Way SE11	**20**	**D4**
Oval Way SE11	67	F5
Overbrae, Beck.	87	A6
Overbrook Wk., Edg.	30	A7
Overbury Ave., Beck.	96	B3
Overbury Rd. N15	41	A6
Overbury St. E5	50	G4
Overcliff Rd. SE13	78	A3
Overcourt Clo., Sid.	80	B6
Overdale Ave., N.Mal.	92	C2
Overdale Rd. W5	64	F3
Overdown Rd. SE6	87	A4
Overhill Rd. SE22	77	D7
Overhill Way, Beck.	96	C5
Overlea Rd. E5	41	D7
Overmead, Sid.	79	G7
Oversley Ho. W2	57	D5
Overstand Clo., Beck.	96	A5
Overstone Gdns., Croy.	95	J7
Overstone Rd. W6	65	J3
Overton Clo. NW10	47	C6
Overton Clo., Islw.	73	C1
Avenue Rd.		
Overton Ct. E11	42	G7
Overton Dr. E11	42	G7
Overton Dr., Rom.	44	C7
Overton Rd. E10	50	H1
Overton Rd. N14	24	E5
Overton Rd. SE2	71	C3
Overton Rd. SW9	76	G2
Overton Rd., Sutt.	100	D6
Overton Rd. E. SE2	71	D3
Overtons Yd., Croy.	101	J3
Ovesdon Ave., Har.	45	F1
Ovett Clo. SE19	86	B6
Ovex Clo. E14	60	C2
Ovington Gdns. SW3	**14**	**H6**
Ovington Gdns. SW3	66	H3
Ovington Ms. SW3	**14**	**H6**
Ovington Ms. SW3	66	H3
Ovington Sq. SW3	**14**	**H6**
Ovington Sq. SW3	66	H3
Ovington St. SW3	**14**	**H6**
Ovington St. SW3	66	H4
Owen Clo. SE28	71	C1
Owen Clo., Hayes	54	B3
Owen Gdns., Wdf.Grn.	35	B8
Owen Rd. N13	32	J4
Owen Rd., Hayes	54	B3
Owen St. EC1	**8**	**F2**
Owen Wk. SE20	86	D7
Sycamore Gro.		
Owen Waters Ho., Ilf.	43	D1
Owen Way NW10	47	C5
Owenite St. SE2	71	B4
Owen's Ct. EC1	**8**	**G3**
Owen's Row EC1	**8**	**G3**
Owens Way SE23	77	H7
Owgan Clo. SE5	68	A7
Benhill Rd.		
Oxberry Ave. SW6	75	B2
Oxendon St. SW1	**11**	**H6**
Oxendon St. SW1	58	D7
Oxenford St. SE15	77	C3
Oxenholme NW1	**7**	**G2**
Oxenholme NW1	58	C2
Oxenpark Ave., Wem.	46	H1
Oxestalls Rd. SE8	68	H5
Oxford Ave. SW20	93	B2
Oxford Ave., Houns.	63	G5
Oxford Circ. Ave. W1	**11**	**F4**
Oxford Clo. N9	33	E2
Oxford Clo., Mitch.	94	C3
Oxford Ct. EC4	**13**	**B5**
Oxford Ct. W3	56	A6
Queens Dr.		
Oxford Ct., Felt.	81	D4
Oxford Way		
Oxford Cres., N.Mal.	92	D6
Oxford Dr., Ruis.	45	C2
Oxford Gdns. N20	31	G1
Oxford Gdns. N21	24	J7
Oxford Gdns. W4	65	A5
Oxford Gdns. W10	57	A6
Oxford Gate W6	66	A4
Oxford Ms., Bex.	80	G7
Bexley High St.		
Oxford Rd. E15	51	D6
Oxford Rd. N4	49	G1
Oxford Rd. N9	33	E2
Oxford Rd. NW6	57	D2
Oxford Rd. SE19	86	A6
Oxford Rd. SW15	75	B4
Oxford Rd. W5	55	G7
Oxford Rd., Cars.	100	H6
Oxford Rd., Enf.	25	E5
Oxford Rd., Har.	36	J4
Oxford Rd., Har.	37	C3
(Wealdstone)		
Oxford Rd., Ilf.	52	F5
Oxford Rd., Sid.	89	B5
Oxford Rd., Tedd.	82	A5
Oxford Rd., Wall.	101	C5
Oxford Rd., Wdf.Grn.	35	A5
Oxford Rd. N. W4	65	B5
Oxford Rd. S. W4	65	A5
Oxford Sq. W2	**10**	**H4**
Oxford Sq. W2	57	H6
Oxford St. W1	**11**	**B4**
Oxford St. W1	58	A6
Oxford Wk., Sthl.	63	F1
Oxford Way, Felt.	81	D4
Oxgate Gdns. NW2	47	H3
Oxgate La. NW2	47	H2
Oxhawth Cres., Brom.	97	D5
Oxhey Dr., Nthwd.	28	B4
Oxhey Dr., Wat.	28	C3
Oxhey Dr. S., Nthwd.	28	B5
Oxhey La., Wat.	28	E1
Oxhey Ridge Clo., Nthwd.	28	A5
Oxleas E6	61	E6
Oxleas Clo., Well.	79	G2
Oxleay Ct., Har.	45	G1
Oxleay Rd., Har.	45	G1
Oxleigh Clo., N.Mal.	92	E5
Oxley Clo. SE1	**21**	**G3**
Oxley Clo. SE1	68	C5
Oxleys Rd. NW2	47	H3
Oxlip Clo., Croy.	102	G1
Marigold Way		
Oxlow La., Dag.	53	F4
Oxonian St. SE22	77	C4
Oxted Clo., Mitch.	93	G3
Oxtoby Way SW16	94	D1
Oyster Catchers Clo. E16	60	H6
Freemasons Rd.		
Oyster Row E1	59	F6
Lukin St.		
Ozolins Way E16	60	G6

P

Name	Page	Grid
Pablo Neruda Clo. SE24	76	H4
Shakespeare Rd.		
Pace Pl. E1	59	E6
Bigland St.		
Pacific Rd. E16	60	G6
Packington Rd. W3	65	C3
Packington Sq. N1	58	J1
Packington St. N1	58	H1
Packmores Rd. SE9	79	G5
Padbury SE17	**21**	**D4**
Padbury Ct. E2	**9**	**G4**
Paddenswick Rd. W6	65	G3
Paddington Clo., Hayes	54	D4
Paddington Grn. W2	**10**	**F1**
Paddington Grn. W2	57	G5
Paddington St. W1	**11**	**B1**
Paddington St. W1	58	A5
Paddock Clo. SE3	78	G5
Paddock Clo. SE26	86	G4
Paddock Clo., Nthlt.	54	G2
Paddock Clo., Orp.	104	E4
State Fm. Ave.		
Paddock Clo., Wor.Pk.	99	E1
Paddock Gdns. SE19	86	B6
Westow St.		
Paddock Rd. NW2	47	G3
Paddock Rd., Bexh.	80	E4
Paddock Rd., Ruis.	45	D3
Paddock Way, Chis.	88	G7
Paddocks, The, Barn.	23	J3
Paddocks, The, Wem.	47	B2
Paddocks Clo., Har.	45	H4
Padfield Rd. SE5	76	J3
Padnall Rd., Rom.	44	D3
Padstow Rd., Enf.	24	H2
Padua Rd. SE20	95	F1
Pagden St. SW8	76	B1
Page Clo., Dag.	53	E5
Page Clo., Hmptn.	81	E6
Page Clo., Har.	37	J6
Page Cres., Croy.	101	G5
Page Grn. Rd. N15	41	D6
Page Grn. Ter. N15	41	C5
Page Heath La., Brom.	97	A3
Page Heath Vill., Brom.	97	A3
Page Meadow NW7	30	G7
Page St. NW7	30	G6
Page St. SW1	**19**	**J1**
Page St. SW1	67	D4
Pageant Ave. NW9	38	E1
Pageant Wk., Croy.	102	B3
Pageantmaster Ct. EC4	**12**	**G4**
Pagehurst Rd., Croy.	95	E7
Pages Hill N10	40	A2
Pages La. N10	40	A2
Pages Wk. SE1	**21**	**D1**
Pages Wk. SE1	68	B4
Pages Yd. W4	65	E4
Church St.		
Paget Ave., Sutt.	100	G3
Paget Clo., Hmptn.	82	A4
Paget Gdns., Chis.	97	E1
Paget La., Islw.	73	A3
Paget Pl., Kings.T.	83	C6
Paget Pl., T.Ditt.	98	D1
Brooklands Rd.		
Paget Ri. SE18	70	D6
Paget Rd. N16	50	A1
Paget Rd., Ilf.	52	E4
Paget St. EC1	**8**	**G3**
Paget Ter. SE18	70	D6
Pagitts Gro., Barn.	23	J4
Pagnell St. SE14	68	J7
Pagoda Ave., Rich.	73	J3
Pagoda Gdns. SE3	78	D2
Paignton Rd. N15	41	B6
Paignton Rd., Ruis.	45	A3
Paines Clo., Pnr.	36	E2
Paines La., Pnr.	36	E1
Pains Clo., Mitch.	94	B2
Painsthorpe Rd. N16	50	B3
Oldfield Rd.		
Painters Rd., Ilf.	43	J3
Paisley Rd. N22	40	H1
Paisley Rd., Cars.	100	C5
Pakeman St. N7	49	F3
Pakenham Clo. SW12	85	A1
Balham Pk. Rd.		

Pakenham St. WC1 **8 D4**
Pakenham St. WC1 58 F3
Palace Ave. W8 14 B2
Palace Ave. W8 66 E1
Palace Ct. NW3 48 E5
Palace Ct. W2 10 A5
Palace Ct. W2 57 E7
Palace Ct., Brom. 96 H1
Palace Gro.
Palace Ct., Har. 37 H6
Palace Ct. Gdns. N10 40 C3
Palace Gdn. Ms. W8 66 D1
Palace Gdns., Buck.H. 35 A1
Palace Gdns., Enf. 25 A4
Sydney Rd.
Palace Gdns. Ter. W8 66 D1
Palace Gate W8 14 C4
Palace Gate W8 66 F2
Palace Gates Rd. N22 40 D2
Palace Grn. W8 14 A2
Palace Grn. W8 66 E2
Palace Grn., Croy. 102 J7
Palace Gro. SE19 86 C7
Palace Gro., Brom. 96 H1
Palace Ms. E17 41 J4
Palace Ms. SW1 19 C2
Palace Ms. SW6 66 C7
Hartismere Rd.
Palace Pl. SW1 15 F5
Palace Rd. N8 40 D5
Palace Rd. N11 32 D7
Palace Rd. SE19 86 C7
Palace Rd. SW2 85 F1
Palace Rd., Brom. 96 H1
Palace Rd., E.Mol. 91 A3
Palace Rd., Kings.T. 91 G4
Palace Rd., Ruis. 45 E4
Palace Rd. Est. SW2 85 F1
Palace Sq. SE19 86 C7
Palace St. SW1 15 F5
Palace St. SW1 67 C3
Palace Vw. SE12 87 G2
Palace Vw., Brom. 96 H3
Palace Vw., Croy. 102 J4
Palace Vw. Rd. E4 34 B5
Palamos Rd. E10 51 A1
Palatine Ave. N16 50 C4
Stoke Newington Rd.
Palatine Rd. N16 50 B4
Palermo Rd. NW10 56 G2
Palestine Gro. SW19 93 G1
Palewell Common Dr. 74 D5
SW14
Palewell Pk. SW14 74 D5
Paley Gdns., Loug. 27 E3
Palfrey Pl. SW8 67 F7
Palgrave Ave., Sthl. 54 G7
Palgrave Rd. W12 65 F3
Palissy St. E2 9 F4
Pall Mall SW1 15 G2
Pall Mall SW1 67 C1
Pall Mall E. SW1 15 J1
Pall Mall E. SW1 67 D1
Pall Mall Pl. SW1 15 G2
Pallant Way, Orp. 104 D3
Pallet Way SE18 79 B1
Palliser Rd. W14 66 B5
Palm Ave., Sid. 89 D6
Palm Gro. W5 64 H3
Palm Rd., Rom. 44 J5
Palmar Cres., Bexh. 80 G3
Palmar Rd., Bexh. 80 G2
Palmeira Rd., Bexh. 80 D3
Palmer Ave., Sutt. 99 J4
Palmer Clo., Houns. 72 G1
Palmer Clo., W.Wick. 103 D3
Palmer Cres., 91 H3
Kings.T.
Palmer Gdns., Barn. 23 A5
Palmer Pl. N7 49 G5
Palmer Rd. E13 60 H4
Palmer Rd., Dag. 53 D1
Palmer St. SW1 15 H5
Palmer St. SW1 67 C3
Palmers Gro., W.Mol. 90 G4
Palmers La., Enf. 25 F1
Palmers Pas. SW14 74 C3
Palmers Rd.
Palmers Rd. E2 59 G2
Palmers Rd. N11 32 C5
Palmers Rd. SW14 74 C3
Palmers Rd. SW16 94 F2
Palmers Rd., Borwd. 22 B1
Palmerston Cres. N13 32 F5
Palmerston Cres. 70 F6
SE18
Palmerston Gro. 84 D7
SW19

Palmerston Rd. E7 51 H5
Palmerston Rd. E17 51 H5
Palmerston Rd. N22 32 F7
Palmerston Rd. NW6 48 C7
Palmerston Rd. SW14 74 C4
Palmerston Rd. SW19 84 D7
Palmerston Rd. W3 65 C3
Palmerston Rd., 34 H2
Buck.H.
Palmerston Rd., 100 J4
Cars.
Palmerston Rd., Har. 37 B3
Palmerston Rd., Orp. 104 F4
Palmerston Rd., Sutt. 100 F4
Vernon Rd.
Palmerston Rd., 95 A5
Th.Hth.
Palmerston Rd., 73 B6
Twick.
Palmerston Way SW8 67 B7
Bradmead
Pamela Gdns., Pnr. 36 B5
Pamela Wk. E8 59 D1
Marlborough Ave.
Pampisford Rd., 101 J6
S.Croy.
Pancras La. EC4 13 A4
Pancras Rd. NW1 7 H1
Pancras Rd. NW1 58 D2
Pandora Rd. NW6 48 D6
Panfield Ms., Ilf. 43 D6
Cranbrook Rd.
Panfield Rd. SE2 71 A3
Pangbourne Ave. 56 J5
W10
Pangbourne Dr., Stan. 29 G5
Pankhurst Clo. SE14 68 G7
Briant St.
Pankhurst Rd., Walt. 90 C7
Panmuir Rd. SW20 92 H1
Panmure Clo. N5 49 H4
Panmure Rd. SE26 86 E3
Pannard Pl., Sthl. 54 H7
Pansy Gdns. W12 56 G7
Pantiles, The NW11 39 C5
Willifield Way
Pantiles, The, Bexh 71 F7
Pantiles, The, Brom. 97 B3
Pantiles Clo. N13 32 H5
Princes Ave.
Panton St. SW1 11 H6
Panyer All. EC4 12 J3
Papillons Wk. SE3 78 G3
Papworth Gdns. N7 49 F5
Liverpool Rd.
Papworth Way SW2 76 G7
Parade, The SW11 19 A7
Parade, The SW11 66 J7
Parade, The, Esher 98 B6
Parade, The, Wat. 28 D3
Parade Ms. SE27 85 H2
Norwood Rd.
Paradise Pas. N7 49 G6
Sheringham Rd.
Paradise Pl. SE18 70 B4
Woodhill
Paradise Rd. SW4 76 E2
Paradise Rd., Rich. 73 H5
Paradise Row E2 59 E3
Bethnal Grn. Rd.
Paradise St. SE16 68 E2
Paradise Wk. SW3 19 A5
Paradise Wk. SW3 66 J6
Paragon, The SE3 78 F2
Paragon Gro., Surb. 91 J6
Paragon Ms. SE1 21 C1
Paragon Pl. SE3 78 F2
Paragon Pl., Surb. 91 J6
Berrylands Rd.
Paragon Rd. E9 50 F6
Parbury Ri., Chess. 98 H6
Parbury Rd. SE23 77 H6
Parchmore Rd., 94 H2
Th.Hth.
Parchmore Way, 94 H2
Th.Hth.
Pardon St. EC1 8 H5
Pardoner St. SE1 17 C5
Pardoner St. SE1 68 A3
Parfett St. E1 13 J2
Parfett St. E1 59 D5
Parfitt Clo. NW3 48 F2
North End
Parfrey St. W6 65 J6
Parham Dr., Ilf. 43 E6
Parham Way N10 40 C2
Paris Gdn. SE1 16 G1

Paris Gdn. SE1 67 H1
Parish Gate Dr., Sid. 79 H6
Parish La. SE20 86 G6
Parish Ms. SE20 86 G7
Park, The N6 40 A6
Park, The NW11 48 E1
Park, The SE19 86 B7
Park, The SE23 86 E1
Park Hill
Park, The W5 64 G1
Park, The, Cars. 100 J5
Park, The, Sid. 89 A4
Park App., Well. 80 B4
Park Ave. E6 61 D1
Park Ave. E15 51 E6
Park Ave. N3 39 E1
Park Ave. N13 32 G3
Park Ave. N18 33 D4
Park Ave. N22 40 E2
Park Ave. NW2 47 H6
Park Ave. NW10 55 J2
Park Ave. NW11 48 E1
Park Ave. SW14 74 D4
Park Ave., Bark. 52 F6
Park Ave., Barn. 23 F5
Park Ave., Brom. 87 F7
Park Ave., Cars. 101 A6
Park Ave., Chis. 97 H3
Park Ave., Enf. 25 A5
Park Ave., Houns. 72 H6
Park Ave., Ilf. 52 D1
Park Ave., Mitch. 85 B7
Park Ave., Orp. 104 C3
(Farnborough)
Park Ave., Sthl. 63 F2
Park Ave., W.Wick. 103 C2
Park Ave., Wdf.Grn. 34 H5
Park Ave. E., Epsom 99 G6
Park Ave. Ms., Mitch. 85 B7
Park Ave.
Park Ave. N. N8 40 D3
Park Ave. N. NW10 47 H5
Park Ave. Rd. N17 33 E7
Park Ave. S. N8 40 D4
Park Ave. W., Epsom 99 G6
Park Chase, Wem. 46 J4
Park Clo. E9 59 F1
Skipworth Rd.
Park Clo. NW2 47 H3
Park Clo. NW10 55 J3
Park Clo. SW1 14 J4
Park Clo. W4 65 D5
Park Clo. W14 66 C3
Park Clo., Cars. 100 J6
Park Clo., Hmptn. 90 J1
Park Clo., Har. 37 B1
Park Clo., Houns. 72 J5
Park Ct. SE26 86 E6
Park Ct., Kings.T. 91 F1
Park Ct., N.Mal. 92 D4
Park Ct., Wem. 46 H5
Park Cres. N3 31 E7
Park Cres. W1 7 D6
Park Cres. W1 58 B4
Park Cres., Enf. 25 A4
Park Cres., Erith 71 J6
Park Cres., Har. 37 B1
Park Cres., Twick. 82 A1
Park Cres. Ms. E. W1 7 E6
Park Cres. Ms. W. W1 7 D6
Park Cft., Edg. 38 C1
Park Dale N11 32 D6
Bounds Grn. Rd.
Park Dr. N21 24 J6
Park Dr. NW11 48 E1
Park Dr. SE7 70 B6
Park Dr. SW14 74 D4
Park Dr. W3 65 A3
Park Dr., Dag. 53 J3
Park Dr., Har. 36 G7
Park Dr., Har. 29 B6
(Harrow Weald)
Park Dr. Clo. SE7 70 B5
Park End NW3 48 H4
South Hill Pk.
Park End, Brom. 96 F1
Park Fm. Clo. N2 39 F3
Park Fm. Clo., Pnr. 36 B5
Field End Rd.
Park Fm. Rd., Brom. 97 A1
Park Fm. Rd., Kings.T. 82 H7
Park Gdn. Pl. W2 10 F4
Park Gdns. NW9 38 B3
Park Gdns., Kings.T. 82 J5
Park Gate N2 39 G3
Park Gate N21 24 F7
Park Gate W5 55 G5
Mount Ave.

Park Gate Clo., 83 B6
Kings.T.
Warboys App.
Park Gro. E15 60 G1
Park Gro. N11 32 D7
Park Gro., Bexh. 80 J4
Park Gro., Brom. 96 H1
Park Gro., Edg. 29 J5
Park Gro. Rd. E11 51 E2
Park Hall Rd. N2 39 H4
Park Hall Rd. SE21 86 A3
Park Hill SE23 86 E2
Park Hill SW4 76 D5
Park Hill W5 55 G5
Park Hill, Brom. 97 B4
Park Hill, Cars. 100 H6
Park Hill, Loug. 27 A5
Park Hill, Rich. 73 J6
Park Hill Clo., Cars. 100 H5
Park Hill Ct. SW17 84 J3
Beeches Rd.
Park Hill Ri., Croy. 102 B2
Park Hill Rd., Brom. 96 F2
Park Hill Rd., Croy. 102 B2
Park Hill Rd., Sid. 88 H3
Park Hill Rd., Wall. 101 B6
Park Ho. N21 24 F7
Park Ho. Gdns., Twick. 73 F6
Park La. E15 60 D1
High St.
Park La. N9 33 B3
Park La. N17 33 C7
Park La. N18 33 B4
Sheldon Rd.
Park La. W1 11 A5
Park La. W1 57 J7
Park La., Cars. 101 A4
Park La., Croy. 102 A3
Park La., Har. 45 H3
Park La., Houns. 63 A7
Park La., Rich. 73 G4
Park La., Rom. 44 D6
(Chadwell Heath)
Park La., Stan. 29 D3
Park La., Sutt. 100 B6
Park La., Tedd. 82 C6
Park La., Wem. 46 H5
Park La. Clo. N17 33 D7
Park Lawns, Wem. 46 J4
Park Mead, Har. 45 H3
Park Mead, Sid. 80 B5
Park Ms. SE24 76 J6
Croxted Rd.
Park Ms., Chis. 88 E6
Park Rd.
Park Ms., E.Mol. 90 J4
Park Ms., Hmptn. 81 J5
Park Rd.
Park Par. NW10 56 F2
Park Pl. E14 69 A1
Park Pl. SW1 15 F2
Park Pl. SW1 67 C1
Park Pl. W3 65 A4
Park Pl. W5 64 G1
Park Pl., Hmptn. 81 J6
Park Pl., Wem. 46 J4
Park Pl. Vill. W2 10 D1
Park Pl. Vill. W2 57 F5
Park Ridings N8 40 G3
Park Ri. SE23 86 H1
Park Ri., Har. 37 B1
Park Ri. Rd. SE23 86 H1
Park Rd. E6 60 J1
Park Rd. E10 51 A1
Park Rd. E12 51 H1
Park Rd. E15 60 G1
Park Rd. E17 41 J5
Park Rd. N2 39 G3
Park Rd. N8 40 C4
Park Rd. N11 32 D7
Park Rd. N14 24 D7
Park Rd. N15 40 H4
Park Rd. N18 33 C4
Park Rd. NW1 6 J5
Park Rd. NW1 57 H4
Park Rd. NW4 38 G7
Park Rd. NW8 6 G3
Park Rd. NW8 57 H3
Park Rd. NW9 38 D7
Park Rd. NW10 56 E1
Park Rd. SE25 95 B4
Park Rd. SW19 84 G7
Park Rd. W4 65 C7
Park Rd. W7 55 C7
Park Rd., Barn. 23 C4
Park Rd., Barn. 23 G4
(New Barnet)
Park Rd., Beck. 86 J7

Park Rd., Brom. 96 H1
Park Rd., Chis. 88 E6
Park Rd., E.Mol. 90 J4
Park Rd., Felt. 81 D4
Park Rd., Hmptn. 81 H4
Park Rd., Houns. 72 H5
Park Rd., Ilf. 52 G3
Park Rd., Islw. 73 E1
Park Rd., Kings.T. 82 J5
Park Rd., Kings.T. 91 F1
(Hampton Wick)
Park Rd., N.Mal. 92 D4
Park Rd., Rich. 73 J6
Park Rd., Sun. 81 B7
Park Rd., Surb. 91 J6
Park Rd., Sutt. 100 B6
Park Rd., Tedd. 82 C7
Park Rd., Twick. 73 F6
Park Rd., Wall. 101 B5
Park Rd., Wall. 101 B2
(Hackbridge)
Park Rd., Wem. 46 H6
Park Rd. E. W3 65 B2
Park Rd. N. W3 65 B2
Park Rd. N. W4 65 D5
Park Rd. W., Kings.T. 91 F1
Park Row SE10 69 D6
Park Royal Rd. NW10 56 C4
Park Royal Rd. W3 56 C4
Park Side, Sutt. 100 B6
Park Sq. E. NW1 7 D5
Park Sq. E. NW1 58 B4
Park Sq. Ms. NW1 7 D6
Park Sq. Ms. NW1 58 B4
Park Sq. W. NW1 7 D5
Park Sq. W. NW1 58 B4
Park St. SE1 16 J1
Park St. SE1 67 J1
Park St. W1 11 B5
Park St. W1 58 A7
Park St., Croy. 101 J2
Park St., Tedd. 82 B6
Park Ter., Wor.Pk. 99 G1
Park Vw. N21 24 F7
Park Vw. W3 56 C5
Park Vw., N.Mal. 92 F3
Park Vw., Pnr. 36 F1
Park Vw., Wem. 47 B5
Park Vw. Ct., Ilf. 43 H6
Brancaster Rd.
Park Vw. Cres. N11 32 B4
Park Vw. Est. E2 59 G2
Sewardstone Rd.
Park Vw. Gdns. NW4 39 A6
Park Vw. Gdns., Bark. 61 H2
River Rd.
Park Vw. Gdns., Ilf. 43 C4
Woodford Ave.
Park Vw. Rd. N3 39 E1
Park Vw. Rd. N17 41 D3
Park Vw. Rd. NW10 47 F4
Park Vw. Rd. W5 55 H5
Park Vw. Rd., Pnr. 28 B7
Park Vw. Rd., Sthl. 63 G1
Park Vw. Rd., Well. 80 B3
Park Village E. NW1 7 D1
Park Village E. NW1 58 B2
Park Village W. NW1 7 D1
Park Village W. NW1 58 B2
Park Vill., Rom. 44 D6
Park Vista SE10 69 D6
Park Wk. N6 40 A7
North Rd.
Park Wk. SW10 18 D5
Park Wk. SW10 66 F6
Park Way N20 31 J4
Park Way NW11 39 B5
Park Way, Edg. 38 B1
Park Way, Enf. 24 G2
Park Way, Felt. 72 B7
Park Way, Ilf. 52 J3
Park Way, Ruis. 45 A1
Park Way, W.Mol. 90 H3
Park W. W2 10 F4
Park W. Pl. W2 10 H3
Parkcroft Rd. SE12 78 F7
Parkdale Cres., 99 D3
Wor.Pk.
Parkdale Rd. SE18 70 H5
Parke Rd. SW13 74 G1
Parke Rd., Sun. 90 A4
Parker Clo. E16 70 B1
Parker Ms. WC2 12 B3
Parker Rd., Croy. 101 J4
Parker St. E16 70 B1
Parker St. WC2 12 B3
Parker St. WC2 58 E6
Parkers Row SE1 17 G4
Parkes Rd., Chig. 35 H5
Parkfield Ave. SW14 74 E4
Parkfield Ave., Felt. 81 A3
Parkfield Ave., Har. 36 J2
Parkfield Ave., Nthlt. 54 D2
Parkfield Clo., Edg. 30 B6
Parkfield Clo., Nthlt. 54 E2
Parkfield Cres., Felt. 81 A3
Parkfield Cres., Har. 36 J2
Parkfield Cres., Ruis. 45 E3
Parkfield Dr., Nthlt. 54 D2
Parkfield Gdns., Har. 36 H3
Parkfield Rd. NW10 47 G7
Parkfield Rd. SE14 77 J1
Parkfield Rd., Felt. 81 A3
Parkfield Rd., Har. 45 J3
Parkfield Rd., Nthlt. 54 E2
Parkfield St. N1 8 F1
Parkfield St. N1 58 G2
Parkfield Way, Brom. 97 C6
Parkfields SW15 74 J4
Parkfields, Croy. 102 J1
Parkfields Ave. NW9 47 D1
Parkfields Ave. SW20 92 H2
Parkfields Clo., Cars. 101 A4
Devonshire Rd.
Parkfields Rd., 82 J5
Kings.T.
Parkgate SE3 78 F3
Parkgate Ave., Barn. 23 F1
Parkgate Cres., Barn. 23 F1
Parkgate Gdns. SW14 74 D5
Parkgate Rd. SW11 66 H7
Parkgate Rd., Wall. 101 A5
Parkham Ct., Brom. 96 E2
Parkham St. SW11 75 G1
Parkhill Rd. E4 34 C1
Parkhill Rd. NW3 48 J5
Parkhill Rd., Bex. 80 F7
Parkhill Wk. NW3 48 J5
Parkholme Rd. E8 50 D6
Parkhouse St. SE5 21 C7
Parkhouse St. SE5 68 A7
Parkhurst Gdns., Bex. 80 G7
Parkhurst Rd. E12 52 D4
Parkhurst Rd. E17 41 H4
Parkhurst Rd. N7 49 E4
Parkhurst Rd. N11 32 A4
Parkhurst Rd. N17 41 D2
Parkhurst Rd. N22 32 F6
Parkhurst Rd., Bex. 80 G7
Parkhurst Rd., Sutt. 100 G4
Parkland Clo., Chig. 35 F3
Parkland Gdns. SW19 84 A1
Parkland Rd. N22 40 F2
Parkland Rd., 34 G7
Wdf.Grn.
Parkland Wk. N4 40 G7
Parkland Wk. N6 40 C7
Parkland Wk. N10 40 B4
Parklands N6 40 B7
Parklands, Chig. 35 F3
Parklands, Surb. 91 J5
Parklands Clo. SW14 74 C5
Parklands Ct., Houns. 72 D2
Parklands Dr. N3 39 B3
Parklands Rd. SW16 85 B5
Parklands Way, 99 E2
Wor.Pk.
Parklea Clo. NW9 38 E1
Parkleigh Rd. SW19 93 E2
Parkleys, Rich. 82 G4
Parkmead SW15 74 H6
Parkmead, Loug. 27 D5
Parkmead Gdns. NW7 30 F6
Parkmore Clo., 34 G4
Wdf.Grn.
Parkshot, Rich. 73 H4
Parkside N3 39 E1
Parkside NW2 47 G3
Parkside NW7 30 G6
Parkside SE3 69 F7
Parkside SW19 84 A4
Parkside, Buck.H. 34 H2
Parkside, Hmptn. 82 A5
Parkside, Sid. 89 B2
Parkside Ave. SW19 84 A5
Parkside Ave., Brom. 97 B4
Parkside Clo. SE20 86 F7
Parkside Cres. N7 49 G3
Isledon Rd.
Parkside Cres., Surb. 92 C6
Parkside Dr., Edg. 30 A3
Parkside Est. E9 59 F1
Rutland Rd.
Parkside Gdns. SW19 84 A4
Parkside Gdns., 31 J1
Barn.
Parkside Ho., Dag. 53 J3
Parkside Rd. SW11 76 A1
Parkside Rd., Belv. 71 H4
Parkside Rd., Houns. 72 H5
Parkside Ter. N18 33 A4
Great Cambridge Rd.
Parkside Way, Har. 36 H4
Parkstead Rd. SW15 74 G5
Parkstone Ave. N18 33 C5
Parkstone Rd. E17 42 C3
Parkstone Rd. SE15 77 D2
Rye La.
Parkthorne Clo., Har. 36 H6
Parkthorne Dr., Har. 36 G6
Parkthorne Rd. SW12 76 D7
Parkview Ct. SW18 75 D6
Broomhill Rd.
Parkview Rd. SE9 88 E1
Parkview Rd., Croy. 102 D1
Parkville Rd. SW6 66 C7
Parkway N14 32 E2
Parkway NW1 58 B1
Parkway SW20 93 A4
Parkway, Erith 71 E3
Parkway, Wdf.Grn. 34 J5
Parkway, The, Hayes 54 C6
Parkway, The, Houns. 63 A6
(Cranford)
Parkway Trd. Est., 63 C6
Houns.
Parkwood N20 31 J3
Parkwood, Beck. 96 A1
Parkwood Gro., Sun. 90 A3
Parkwood Ms. N6 40 B6
Parkwood Rd. SW19 84 C5
Parkwood Rd., Bex. 80 F7
Parkwood Rd., Islw. 73 C1
Parliament Ct. E1 59 B5
Sandy's Row
Parliament Hill NW3 48 H4
Parliament Ms. SW14 74 C2
Thames Bank
Parliament Sq. SW1 16 A4
Parliament Sq. SW1 67 E2
Parliament St. SW1 16 A4
Parliament St. SW1 67 E2
Parma Cres. SW11 75 J4
Parmiter St. E2 59 E2
Parnell Clo., Edg. 30 B4
Parnell Rd. E3 59 J1
Parnham St. E14 59 H6
Blount St.
Parolles Rd. N19 49 C1
Paroma Rd., Belv. 71 G3
Parr Clo. N9 33 E4
Parr Ct., Felt. 81 C4
Parr Rd. E6 61 A1
Parr Rd., Stan. 37 G1
Parr St. N1 9 B1
Parr St. N1 59 A2
Parrs Pl., Hmptn. 81 G7
Parry Ave. E6 61 C6
Parry Clo., Epsom 99 G6
Parry Pl. SE18 70 E4
Parry Rd. SE25 95 B3
Parry Rd. W10 57 B3
Dart St.
Parry St. SW8 20 A5
Parry St. SW8 67 E6
Parsifal Rd. NW6 48 D5
Parsley Gdns., Croy. 102 G1
Primrose La.
Parsloes Ave., Dag. 53 D4
Parson St. NW4 38 J4
Parsonage Gdns., Enf. 24 J2
Parsonage La., Enf. 25 A2
Parsonage La., Sid. 89 F4
Parsonage 71 G6
Manorway, Belv.
Parsonage St. E14 69 C4
Parsons Cres., Edg. 30 A3
Parsons Grn. SW6 75 D2
Parsons Grn. La. SW6 75 D1
Parsons Gro., Edg. 30 A3
Parsons Hill SE18 70 D3
Powis St.
Parson's Ho. W2 6 E6
Parson's Mead, 101 H1
Croy.
Parsons Mead, E.Mol. 90 J3
Parsons Rd. E13 60 J2
Old St.
Parthenia Rd. SW6 75 D1
Partingdale La. NW7 31 A5
Partington Clo. N19 49 D1
Partridge Clo. E16 61 A5
Fulmer Rd.
Partridge Clo., Barn. 22 J6
Partridge Clo. 28 H1
(Bushey), Wat.
Partridge Dr., Orp. 104 F3
Partridge Grn. SE9 88 D3
Partridge Rd., Hmptn. 81 F6
Partridge Rd., Sid. 88 H3
Partridge Sq. E6 61 B5
Nightingale Way
Partridge Way N22 40 E1
Parvin St. SW8 76 D1
Pasadena Clo., Hayes 63 A2
Pascal St. SW8 19 J7
Pascal St. SW8 67 D7
Pascoe Rd. SE13 78 D5
Pasley Clo. SE17 20 J4
Pasquier Rd. E17 41 H3
Passey Pl. SE9 79 C6
Passfield Dr. E14 60 B5
Uamvar St.
Passfield Path SE28 62 B7
Booth Clo.
Passing All. EC1 8 G6
Passmore Gdns. N11 32 D6
Passmore St. SW1 19 B2
Passmore St. SW1 67 A5
Pasteur Clo. NW9 38 E2
Pasteur Gdns. N18 32 H5
Paston Clo. E5 50 G3
Caldecott Way
Paston Cres. SE12 78 H7
Pastor St. SE11 20 H1
Pastor St. SE11 67 H4
Pasture Clo., Wem. 46 E3
Pasture Rd. SE6 87 E1
Pasture Rd., Dag. 53 F4
Pasture Rd., Wem. 46 E2
Pastures, The N20 31 C1
Patcham Ter. SW8 76 B1
Pater St. W8 66 D3
Paternoster Row EC4 12 J4
Paternoster Sq. EC4 12 H3
Path, The SW19 93 E1
Pathfield Rd. SW16 85 D6
Pathway, The, Wat. 28 D1
Anthony Clo.
Patience Rd. SW11 75 H2
Patio Clo. SW4 76 D6
Patmore Est. SW8 76 C1
Patmore St. SW8 76 C1
Patmos Rd. SW9 67 H7
Paton Clo. E3 60 A3
Paton St. EC1 8 J4
Patricia Ct., Chis. 97 G1
Manor Pk. Rd.
Patricia Ct., Well. 71 B7
Patrick Connolly 60 B3
Gdns. E3
Talwin St.
Patrick Pas. SW11 75 H2
Patrick Rd. E13 60 J3
Patriot Sq. E2 59 E2
Patrol Pl. SE6 78 B6
Patshull Pl. NW5 49 C6
Patshull Rd.
Patshull Rd. NW5 49 C6
Patten All., Rich. 73 G5
The Hermitage
Patten Rd. SW18 75 H7
Pattenden Rd. SE6 86 J1
Patterdale Clo., Brom. 87 F6
Patterdale Rd. SE15 68 F7
Patterson Ct. SE19 86 C7
Patterson Rd. SE19 86 C6
Pattinson Pt. E16 60 G5
Fife Rd.
Pattison Rd. NW2 48 D3
Pattison Wk. SE18 70 F5
Sandbach Pl.
Paul Clo. E15 51 E7
Paul St.
Paul Gdns., Croy. 102 C2
Paul St. E15 60 E1
Paul St. EC2 9 C6
Paul St. EC2 59 A4
Paulet Rd. SE5 76 H2
Paulhan Rd., Har. 37 F4
Paulin Dr. N21 24 G7
Pauline Cres., Twick. 81 J1
Paultons Sq. SW3 18 F5
Paultons Sq. SW3 66 G6
Paultons St. SW3 18 F6
Paultons St. SW3 66 G6
Pauntley St. N19 49 C1
Paved Ct., Rich. 73 G5
King St.
Paveley Dr. SW11 66 H7
Paveley St. NW8 6 H4
Paveley St. NW8 57 H4

Pavement, The SW4 76 C4
Pavement, The W5 64 H3
  Popes La.
Pavement Ms., Rom. 44 D7
  Clarissa Rd.
Pavement Sq., Croy. 102 D1
Pavet Clo., Dag. 53 H6
Pavilion Rd. SW1 **15 A4**
Pavilion Rd. SW1 66 J3
Pavilion Rd., Ilf. 43 C7
Pavilion St. SW1 **15 A6**
Pavilion Ter., E.Mol. 91 C4
Pavilion Ter., Ilf. 43 H5
  Southdown Cres.
Pavilion Way, Edg. 30 B7
Pavilion Way, Ruis. 45 C2
Pawleyne Clo. SE20 86 F7
Pawsey Clo. E13 60 G1
  Plashet Rd.
Pawson's Rd., Croy. 94 J6
Paxford Rd., Wem. 46 E2
Paxton Clo., Rich. 73 J2
Paxton Clo., Walt. 90 C7
  Shaw Dr.
Paxton Pl. SE27 86 B4
Paxton Rd. N17 33 C7
Paxton Rd. SE23 86 H3
Paxton Rd. W4 65 E6
Paxton Rd., Brom. 87 G7
Paxton Ter. SW1 **19 E5**
Paxton Ter. SW1 67 B6
Payne Rd. E3 60 B2
Payne St. SE8 68 J6
Paynell Ct. SE3 78 E3
  Lawn Ter.
Paynes Wk. W6 66 B6
  Ancill Clo.
Paynesfield Ave. 74 D3
SW14
Peabody Ave. SW1 **19 D4**
Peabody Clo. SE10 78 B1
  Devonshire Dr.
Peabody Dws. WC1 **8 A5**
Peabody Est. EC1 **9 A6**
Peabody Est. N17 41 B1
Peabody Est. SE1 **16 F2**
Peabody Est. SE24 76 J7
Peabody Est. SW3 **18 H5**
Peabody Est. W6 65 J5
Peabody Est. W10 56 J4
Peabody Hill SE21 85 H1
Peabody Hill Est. 85 H1
SE21
Peabody Sq. SE1 **16 G4**
Peabody Sq. SE1 67 H2
Peabody Trust SE1 **16 J2**
Peabody Yd. N1 58 J1
  Greenman St.
Peace Clo. N14 24 B5
Peace Gro., Wem. 47 B2
Peach Rd. W10 57 A3
Peaches Clo., Sutt. 100 B7
Peachum Rd. SE3 69 F6
Peacock St. SE17 **20 H2**
Peacock Wk. E16 60 H6
  Sophia Rd.
Peacock Yd. SE17 **20 H2**
Peak, The SE26 86 F3
Peak Hill SE26 86 F4
Peak Hill Ave. SE26 86 F4
Peak Hill Gdns. SE26 86 F4
Peaketon Ave., Ilf. 43 A4
Peal Gdns. W13 55 D4
  Ruislip Rd. E.
Peall Rd., Croy. 94 F6
Pear Clo. NW9 38 D4
Pear Clo. SE14 68 H7
  Southgate Way
Pear Pl. SE1 **16 E3**
Pear Tree Ct. EC1 **8 F6**
Pear Tree Ct. EC1 58 G4
Pearce Rd., W.Mol. 90 H3
Pearcefield Ave. SE23 86 F1
Pearcroft Rd. E11 51 D2
Peardon St. SW8 76 B2
Peareswood Gdns., 37 G1
Stan.
Pearfield Rd. SE23 86 H3
Pearl Clo. E6 61 D6
Pearl Clo. NW2 39 A7
  Marble Dr.
Pearl Rd. E17 42 A3
Pearl St. E1 68 E1
  Penang St.
Pearman St. SE1 **16 F5**
Pearman St. SE1 67 G3
Pears Rd., Houns. 72 J3
Pearscroft Ct. SW6 75 E1

Pearscroft Rd. SW6 75 E1
Pearson St. E2 **9 F1**
Pearson St. E2 59 C2
Pearsons Ave. SE14 78 A1
  Tanners Hill
Peartree Ave. SW17 84 F3
Peartree Clo., Mitch. 93 H2
Peartree Gdns., Dag. 53 B4
Peartree Gdns., Rom. 44 H2
Peartree La. E1 59 F7
  Glamis Rd.
Peartree Rd., Enf. 25 B3
Peartree St. EC1 **8 H5**
Peartree St. EC1 58 H4
Peary Pl. E2 59 F3
  Kirkwall Pl.
Peatfield Clo., Sid. 88 H3
  Woodside Rd.
Pebworth Rd., Har. 46 D2
Peckarmans Wd. 86 C3
SE26
Peckett Sq. N5 49 J4
  Highbury Gra.
Peckford Pl. SW9 76 G2
Peckham Gro. SE15 **21 E7**
Peckham Gro. SE15 68 B7
Peckham High St. 77 D1
SE15
Peckham Hill St. **21 H7**
SE15
Peckham Hill St. 68 D7
SE15
Peckham Pk. Rd. 68 D7
SE15
Peckham Rd. SE5 77 B1
Peckham Rd. SE15 77 C1
Peckham Rye SE15 77 D3
Peckham Rye SE22 77 D4
Peckwater St. NW5 49 C5
Pedlars Wk. N7 49 E6
Pedley Rd., Dag. 53 C1
Pedley St. E1 **9 G6**
Pedley St. E1 59 D4
Pedro St. E5 50 G3
Pedworth Gdns. SE16 68 F4
  Rotherhithe New Rd.
Peek Cres. SW19 84 A5
Peel Clo. E4 34 B2
Peel Clo. N9 33 D3
  Plevna Rd.
Peel Dr. NW9 38 F3
Peel Dr., Ilf. 43 B3
Peel Gro. E2 59 F2
Peel Pas. W8 66 D1
  Peel St.
Peel Pl., Ilf. 43 B2
Peel Prec. NW6 57 D2
Peel Rd. E18 42 F1
Peel Rd. NW6 57 C3
Peel Rd., Har. 37 C3
Peel Rd., Orp. 104 F5
Peel Rd., Wem. 46 G3
Peel St. W8 66 D1
Peerless St. EC1 **9 B4**
Peerless St. EC1 59 A3
Pegamoid Rd. N18 33 F3
Pegasus Pl. SE11 **20 E5**
Pegg Rd., Houns. 63 D7
Pegley Gdns. SE12 87 G2
Pegwell St. SE18 70 H7
Pekin Clo. E14 60 A6
  Pekin St.
Pekin St. E14 60 A6
Peldon Ct., Rich. 73 J4
Peldon Wk. N1 58 H1
  Britannia Row
Pelham Ave., Bark. 61 J1
Pelham Clo. SE5 77 B3
Pelham Cres. SW7 **18 G2**
Pelham Cres. SW7 66 H4
Pelham Pl. SW7 **18 G1**
Pelham Pl. SW7 66 H4
Pelham Rd. E18 42 H3
Pelham Rd. N15 41 C4
Pelham Rd. N22 40 G2
Pelham Rd. SW19 84 D7
Pelham Rd., Beck. 95 F2
Pelham Rd., Bexh. 80 G3
Pelham Rd., Ilf. 52 G2
Pelham St. SW7 **18 F1**
Pelham St. SW7 66 G4
Pelican Est. SE15 77 C1
Pelican Pas. E1 59 F4
  Cambridge Heath Rd.
Pelican Wk. SW9 76 H4
  Loughborough Pk.
Pelier St. SE17 **21 A5**
Pelinore Rd. SE6 87 E2

Pellant Rd. SW6 66 B7
Pellatt Gro. N22 40 G1
Pellatt Rd. SE22 77 C5
Pellatt Rd., Wem. 46 G2
Pellerin Rd. N16 50 B5
Pelling St. E14 60 A6
Pellipar Clo. N13 32 G3
Pellipar Gdns. SE18 70 C5
Pelly Rd. E13 60 G1
Pelton Rd. SE10 69 E5
Pember Ave. E17 41 H3
Pember Rd. NW10 57 A3
Pemberton Gdns. N19 49 C3
Pemberton Gdns., 44 E5
Rom.
Pemberton Ho. SE26 86 D4
  High Level Dr.
Pemberton Pl. E8 50 E7
  Mare St.
Pemberton Rd. N4 40 G5
Pemberton Rd., 90 J4
E.Mol.
Pemberton Row EC4 **12 F3**
Pemberton Ter. N19 49 C3
Pembridge Ave., 81 F1
Twick.
Pembridge Cres. W11 57 D7
Pembridge Gdns. W2 57 D7
Pembridge Ms. W11 57 D7
Pembridge Pl. W2 57 D7
Pembridge Rd. W11 57 D7
Pembridge Sq. W2 57 D7
Pembridge Vill. W11 57 D7
Pembroke Ave., Har. 37 D3
Pembroke Ave., Surb. 92 B5
Pembroke Clo. SW1 **15 C4**
Pembroke Clo. SW1 67 A2
Pembroke Gdns. W8 66 C4
Pembroke Gdns., 53 H3
Dag.
Pembroke Gdns. Clo. 66 C3
W8
Pembroke Ms. E3 59 H3
  Morgan St.
Pembroke Ms. N10 40 A1
  Pembroke Rd.
Pembroke Ms. W8 66 D3
  Earls Wk.
Pembroke Pl. W8 66 D3
Pembroke Pl., Edg. 30 A7
Pembroke Pl., Islw. 73 B2
  Clifton Rd.
Pembroke Rd. E6 61 C5
Pembroke Rd. E17 42 B5
Pembroke Rd. N8 40 E4
Pembroke Rd. N10 40 A1
Pembroke Rd. N13 32 J3
Pembroke Rd. N15 41 C5
Pembroke Rd. SE25 95 B4
Pembroke Rd. W8 66 D4
Pembroke Rd., Brom. 96 J2
Pembroke Rd., Erith 71 J5
Pembroke Rd., Grnf. 54 H3
Pembroke Rd., Ilf. 52 J1
Pembroke Rd., Mitch. 94 A2
Pembroke Rd., Wem. 46 G3
Pembroke Sq. W8 66 D3
Pembroke St. N1 49 E7
Pembroke Studios 66 C3
W8
Pembroke Vill. W8 66 D4
Pembroke Vill., Rich. 73 G4
Pembroke Wk. W8 66 D4
Pembury Ave., 99 G1
Wor.Pk.
Pembury Clo., Brom. 96 F7
Pembury Cres., Sid. 89 E3
Pembury Pl. E5 50 E5
Pembury Rd. E5 50 E5
Pembury Rd. N17 41 C1
Pembury Rd. SE25 95 D4
Pembury Rd., Bexh. 71 E7
Pemdevon Rd., Croy. 94 G7
Pemell Clo. E1 59 F4
  Colebert Ave.
Pempath Pl., Wem. 46 G2
Penally Pl. N1 59 A1
  Shepperton Rd.
Penang St. E1 68 E1
Penarth St. SE15 68 F6
Penates, Esher 98 A4
Penberth Rd. SE6 87 C1
Penbury Rd., Sthl. 70 E6
Pencombe Ms. W11 57 C7
  Denbigh Rd.
Pencraig Way SE15 68 E6

Penda Rd., Erith 71 H7
Pendarves Rd. SW20 92 J1
Penda's Mead E9 50 H4
  Lindisfarne Way
Pendennis Rd. N17 41 A3
Pendennis Rd. SW16 85 E4
Penderel Rd., Houns. 72 G5
Penderry Ri. SE6 87 D2
Penderyn Way N7 49 D4
Pendle Rd. SW16 85 B6
Pendlestone Rd. E17 42 B5
Pendragon Rd., Brom. 87 F3
Pendragon Wk. NW9 38 E6
Pendrell Rd. SE4 77 H2
Pendrell St. SE18 70 G6
Pendula Dr., Hayes 54 D4
Penerley Rd. SE6 87 B1
Penfold Clo., Croy. 101 G3
  Epsom Rd.
Penfold La., Bex. 89 D1
  Carisbrooke Ave.
Penfold Pl. NW1 **10 G1**
Penfold Pl. NW1 57 H5
Penfold Rd. N9 33 G1
Penfold St. NW1 **10 G1**
Penfold St. NW1 57 H5
Penfold St. NW8 **6 F6**
Penfold St. NW8 57 J4
Penford Gdns. SE9 79 A3
Penford St. SE5 76 H2
Pengarth Rd., Bex. 80 D5
Penge Ho. SW11 76 E4
  Wye St.
Penge La. SE20 86 F7
Penge Rd. E13 60 J1
Penge Rd. SE20 95 D3
Penge Rd. SE25 95 D3
Penhall Rd. SE7 70 A4
Penhill Rd., Bex. 80 C6
Penhurst Rd., Ilf. 35 E7
Penifather La., Grnf. 55 A3
Peniston Rd. SW16 85 E7
Penketh Dr., Har. 46 A3
Penmon Rd. SE2 71 A3
Penn Clo., Grnf. 54 H2
Penn Clo., Har. 37 F4
Penn Gdns., Chis. 97 E2
Penn La., Bex. 80 D6
Penn Rd. N7 49 E5
Penn St. N1 59 A1
Pennack Rd. SE15 **21 G6**
Pennant Ms. W8 **18 A1**
Pennant Ms. W8 66 E4
Pennant Ter. E17 41 J2
Pennard Rd. W12 65 J2
Pennards, The, Sun. 90 C2
Penner Clo. SW19 84 B2
  Victoria Dr.
Pennethorne Clo. E9 59 F1
  Victoria Pk. Rd.
Pennethorne Rd. SE15 68 E7
Pennine Dr. NW2 48 A2
Pennine La. NW2 48 B2
  Pennine Dr.
Pennington Clo. SE27 86 A4
  Hamilton Rd.
Pennington St. E1 **13 J6**
Pennington St. E1 59 D7
Pennington Way SE12 87 J2
Penny Rd. NW10 56 B3
Pennyfields E14 60 A7
Pennymoor Wk. W9 57 C3
  Ashmore Rd.
Pennyroyal Ave. E6 61 D6
Penpoll Rd. E8 50 E7
Penpool La., Well. 80 B3
Penrhyn Ave. E17 41 J1
Penrhyn Cres. E17 42 A1
Penrhyn Cres. SW14 74 C4
Penrhyn Gro. E17 42 A1
Penrhyn Rd., Kings.T. 91 H4
Penrith Clo. SW15 75 B5
Penrith Clo., Beck. 96 B1
  Albemarle Rd.
Penrith Pl. SE27 85 H2
  Harpenden Rd.
Penrith Rd. N15 41 A5
Penrith Rd., Ilf. 35 J6
Penrith Rd., N.Mal. 92 D4
Penrith Rd., Th.Hth. 94 J2
Penrith St. SW16 85 C6
Penrose Ave., Wat. 28 D2
Penrose Gro. SE17 **20 J4**
Penrose Gro. SE17 67 J5
Penrose Ho. SE17 **20 J4**
Penrose St. SE17 **20 J4**
Penrose St. SE17 67 J5

Penry St. SE1 21 E2
Penryn St. NW1 7 H1
Penryn St. NW1 58 D2
Pensbury Pl. SW8 76 C2
Pensbury St. SW8 76 C2
Penscroft Gdns., 22 D4
Borwd.
Pensford Ave., Rich. 74 A2
Penshurst Ave., Sid. 80 A6
Penshurst Gdns., Edg. 30 B5
Penshurst Grn., Brom. 96 F5
Penshurst Rd. E9 50 G7
Penshurst Rd. N17 33 C7
Penshurst Rd., Bexh. 80 F1
Penshurst Rd., Th.Hth. 94 H5
Penshurst Wk., Brom. 96 F5
Hayesford Pk. Dr.
Penshurst Way, Sutt. 100 D7
Penstock Footpath 40 E3
N22
Pentelowe Gdns., 72 A6
Felt.
Pentire Rd. E17 42 D1
Pentland Ave., Edg. 30 B2
Pentland Clo. NW11 48 B2
Pentland Gdns. SW18 75 F6
St. Ann's Hill
Pentland Pl., Nthlt. 54 E1
Pentland St. SW18 75 F6
Pentlands Clo., Mitch. 94 B3
Pentlow St. SW15 74 J3
Pentlow Way, Buck.H. 27 B7
Pentney Rd. E4 34 D1
Pentney Rd. SW12 85 C1
Pentney Rd. SW19 93 B1
Midmoor Rd.
Penton Gro. N1 8 E2
Penton Pl. SE17 20 H3
Penton Pl. SE17 67 H5
Penton Ri. WC1 8 D3
Penton Ri. WC1 58 F3
Penton St. N1 8 E2
Penton St. N1 58 G2
Pentonville Rd. N1 8 C2
Pentonville Rd. N1 58 F2
Pentridge St. SE15 68 C7
Pentyre Ave. N18 33 A5
Penwerris Ave., Islw. 63 J7
Penwith Rd. SW18 84 D2
Penwortham Rd. 85 B6
SW16
Penylan Pl., Edg. 30 A7
Penywern Rd. SW5 66 D5
Penzance Pl. W11 66 B1
Penzance St. W11 66 B1
Peony Ct., Wdf.Grn. 34 E7
Bridle Path
Peony Gdns. W12 56 G7
Peploe Rd. NW6 57 A2
Pepper All., Loug. 26 F2
Pepper Clo. E6 61 C5
Pepper St. E14 69 B3
Pepper St. SE1 16 J3
Peppermint Clo., 94 E7
Croy.
Pepys Cres., Barn. 22 J5
Pepys Ri., Orp. 104 J1
Pepys Rd. SE14 77 G1
Pepys Rd. SW20 92 J2
Pepys St. EC3 13 E5
Pepys St. EC3 59 B7
Perceval Ave. NW3 48 H5
Perch St. E8 50 C4
Percheron Rd., 22 D6
Borwd.
Percival Ct. N17 33 C7
High Rd.
Percival Ct., Nthlt. 45 G5
Percival Gdns., Rom. 44 C6
Percival Rd. SW14 74 C4
Percival Rd., Enf. 25 C4
Percival Rd., Orp. 104 C2
Percival St. EC1 8 G5
Percival St. EC1 58 H4
Percival Way, Epsom 99 C4
Percy Circ. WC1 8 D3
Percy Circ. WC1 58 F3
Percy Gdns., Enf. 25 G5
Percy Gdns., Islw. 73 D3
Percy Gdns., Wor.Pk. 99 E1
Percy Ms. W1 11 H2
Percy Pas. W1 11 G2
Percy Rd. E11 42 E7
Percy Rd. E16 60 E5
Percy Rd. N12 31 F5
Percy Rd. N21 24 J7
Percy Rd. NW6 57 D3
Stafford Rd.

Percy Rd. SE20 95 G1
Percy Rd. SE25 95 D5
Percy Rd. W12 65 G2
Percy Rd., Bexh. 80 E2
Percy Rd., Dag. 62 F4
Percy Rd., Hmptn. 81 G7
Percy Rd., Ilf. 44 A7
Percy Rd., Islw. 73 D4
Percy Rd., Mitch. 94 A7
Percy Rd., Rom. 44 H3
Percy Rd., Twick. 81 H1
Percy St. W1 11 H2
Percy St. W1 58 D5
Percy Way, Twick. 81 J1
Percy Yd. WC1 8 D3
Peregrine Clo. NW10 47 D5
Peregrine Ct. SW16 85 F4
Leithcote Gdns.
Peregrine Ct., Well. 79 J1
Peregrine Gdns., 102 H2
Croy.
Peregrine Ho. EC1 8 H3
Peregrine Ho. EC1 58 H3
Peregrine Way SW19 83 J7
Perham Rd. W14 66 B5
Peridot St. E6 61 B5
Perifield SE21 85 J1
Perimeade Rd., Grnf. 55 F2
Periton Rd. SE9 79 A4
Perivale Gdns. W13 55 E4
Bellevue Rd.
Perivale Gra., Grnf. 55 D3
Perivale Ind. Pk., 55 D1
Grnf.
Perivale La., Grnf. 55 D3
Perivale New 55 E2
Business Cen., Grnf.
Perkins Clo., Wem. 46 E5
Perkin's Rents SW1 15 H5
Perkin's Rents SW1 67 D3
Perkins Rd., Ilf. 43 G5
Perkins Sq. SE1 17 A1
Hurren Clo.
Perpins Rd. SE9 79 G6
Perran Rd. SW2 85 H2
Christchurch Rd.
Perran Wk., Brent. 64 H5
Burford Rd.
Perren St. NW5 49 B6
Ryland Rd.
Perrers Rd. W6 65 H4
Perrin Rd., Wem. 46 D4
Perrins Ct. NW3 48 F4
Hampstead High St.
Perrins La. NW3 48 F4
Perrin's Wk. NW3 48 F4
Perry Ave. W3 56 D6
Perry Ct. N15 41 B6
Albert Rd.
Perry Gdns. N9 33 B3
Deansway
Perry Garth, Nthlt. 54 C1
Perry Hall Rd., Orp. 97 J6
Perry Hill SE6 86 J3
Perry How, Wor.Pk. 99 F1
Perry Mead, Enf. 24 H2
Perry Ri. SE23 86 H3
Perry St., Chis. 88 G6
Perry St. Gdns., Chis. 88 H6
Old Perry St.
Perry Vale SE23 86 F3
Perryfield Way NW9 38 F6
Perryfield Way, Rich. 82 E2
Perryman Ho., Bark. 61 F1
Perrymans Fm. Rd., 43 G6
Ilf.
Perrymead St. SW6 75 D1
Perryn Rd. SE16 68 E3
Drummond Rd.
Perryn Rd. W3 65 D1
Perrys Pl. W1 11 H3
Persant Rd. SE6 87 E3
Perseverance Pl., 73 H3
Rich.
Mandela St.
Pershore Clo., Ilf. 43 E5
Pershore Gro., Cars. 93 G6
Pert Clo. N10 32 B6
Perth Ave. NW9 38 D7
Perth Ave., Hayes 54 C4
Perth Clo. SW20 92 G2
Perth Rd. E10 50 H1
Perth Rd. E13 60 H2
Perth Rd. N4 49 G1
Perth Rd. N22 40 H1
Perth Rd., Bark. 61 G1
Perth Rd., Beck. 96 C2

Perth Rd., Ilf. 43 D6
Perth Ter., Ilf. 43 F7
Perwell Ave., Har. 45 F1
Perwell Ct., Har. 45 F1
Peter Ave. NW10 47 H7
Peter St. W1 11 H5
Peter St. W1 58 D7
Peterboat Clo. SE10 69 E4
Tunnel Ave.
Peterborough Gdns. 43 B7
Ilf.
Peterborough Ms. 75 D2
SW6
Peterborough Rd. E10 42 C5
Peterborough Rd. 75 D2
SW6
Peterborough Rd., 93 H6
Cars.
Peterborough Rd., 46 B1
Har.
Peterborough Vill. 75 E1
SW6
Peterchurch Ho. SE15 68 E6
Commercial Way
Petergate SW11 75 F4
Peters Clo., Dag. 53 D1
Peters Clo., Stan. 29 G6
Peters Clo., Well. 79 H2
Peters Hill EC4 12 J5
Peter's La. EC1 12 G1
Peters Path SE26 86 E4
Petersfield Clo. N18 32 J5
Petersfield Ri. SW15 83 H1
Petersfield Rd. W3 65 C2
Petersham Clo., Rich. 82 G2
Petersham Clo., Sutt. 100 C5
Petersham Dr., Orp. 97 J2
Petersham Gdns., 97 J2
Orp.
Petersham La. SW7 14 C5
Petersham La. SW7 66 F3
Petersham Ms. SW7 14 C6
Petersham Ms. SW7 66 F3
Petersham Pl. SW7 14 C5
Petersham Pl. SW7 66 F3
Petersham Rd., Rich. 73 G6
Peterstone Rd. SE2 71 B3
Peterstow Clo. 84 B2
SW19
Peterwood Way, 101 F2
Croy.
Petherton Rd. N5 49 J5
Petley Rd. W6 65 J6
Peto Pl. NW1 7 E5
Peto Pl. NW1 58 B4
Peto St. N. E16 60 F7
Victoria Dock Rd.
Petrie Clo. NW2 48 B6
Pett St. SE18 70 B4
Petticoat Sq. E1 13 F3
Pettits Pl., Dag. 53 G5
Pettits Rd., Dag. 53 G5
Pettiward Clo. SW15 74 J4
Pettman Cres. SE28 70 G3
Petts Hill, Nthlt. 45 H5
Petts Wd. Rd., Orp. 97 F5
Pettsgrove Ave., 46 F5
Wem.
Petty France SW1 15 G5
Petty France SW1 67 C3
Petworth Clo., Nthlt. 45 F7
Petworth Gdns. 92 H3
SW20
Hidcote Gdns.
Petworth Rd. N12 31 H5
Petworth Rd., Bexh. 80 G5
Petworth St. SW11 75 H1
Petyt Pl. SW3 18 G6
Petyward SW3 18 H2
Petyward SW3 66 H4
Pevel Ho., Dag. 53 G2
Pevensey Ave. N11 32 D5
Pevensey Ave., Enf. 25 A2
Pevensey Clo., Islw. 63 J7
Pevensey Rd. E7 51 F4
Pevensey Rd. SW17 84 G4
Pevensey Rd., Felt. 81 E1
Peverel E6 61 D6
Downings
Peveret Clo. N11 32 B5
Woodland Rd.
Peveril Dr., Tedd. 82 A5
Pewsey Clo. E4 34 A5
Peyton Pl. SE10 69 C7
Pheasant Clo. E16 60 G6
Maplin Rd.
Phelp St. SE17 21 B5
Phelp St. SE17 68 A6

Phene St. SW3 18 H5
Phene St. SW3 66 H6
Phil Brown Pl. SW8 76 B2
Heath Rd.
Philbeach Gdns. SW5 66 D5
Philchurch Pl. E1 13 J4
Philip Gdns., Croy. 102 J3
Philip La. N15 41 A4
Philip Rd. SE15 77 D3
Peckham Rye
Philip St. E13 60 G4
Philip Wk. SE15 77 E3
Philipot Path SE9 79 C6
Court Yd.
Philippa Gdns. SE9 79 A5
Phillimore Gdns. 56 J1
NW10
Phillimore Gdns. W8 66 D2
Phillimore Gdns. Clo. 66 D3
W8
Phillimore Gdns.
Phillimore Pl. W8 66 D2
Phillimore Wk. W8 66 D3
Phillipp St. N1 59 B1
Philpot La. EC3 13 D5
Philpot Path, Ilf. 52 F3
Sunnyside Rd.
Philpot Sq. SW6 75 E3
Peterborough Rd.
Philpot St. E1 59 E6
Phineas Pett Rd. SE9 79 B3
Phipp St. EC2 9 D5
Phipp St. EC2 59 B4
Phipps Bri. Rd. SW19 93 F2
Phipps Bri. Rd., 93 F2
Mitch.
Phipp's Ms. SW1 15 D6
Phoebeth Rd. SE4 78 A5
Phoenix Clo. E8 59 C1
Stean St.
Phoenix Clo., 103 D2
W.Wick.
Phoenix Dr., Kes. 104 A3
Phoenix Pk., Brent. 64 G5
Phoenix Pl. WC1 8 D5
Phoenix Pl. WC1 58 F4
Phoenix Rd. NW1 7 H3
Phoenix Rd. NW1 58 D3
Phoenix Rd. SE20 86 F6
Phoenix St. WC2 11 J4
Phoenix Way, Houns. 63 C6
Phyllis Ave., N.Mal. 92 H5
Physic Pl. SW3 18 J4
Piazza, The WC2 58 E7
Covent Gdn.
Picardy Manorway, 71 H3
Belv.
Picardy Rd., Belv. 71 G5
Picardy St., Belv. 71 G3
Piccadilly W1 15 E2
Piccadilly W1 67 B1
Piccadilly Arc. SW1 15 F1
Piccadilly Circ. W1 11 H6
Piccadilly Circ. W1 58 C7
Piccadilly Pl. W1 11 G6
Pickard St. EC1 8 H3
Pickering Ave. E6 61 D2
Pickering Gdns., 95 C6
Croy.
Pickering Ms. W2 10 B3
Pickering Pl. SW1 15 G2
Pickering St. N1 58 H1
Essex Rd.
Pickets Clo. (Bushey), 29 A1
Wat.
Pickets St. SW12 76 B7
Pickett Cft., Stan. 37 G1
Picketts Lock La. N9 33 F2
Pickford Clo., Bexh. 80 E2
Pickford La., Bexh. 80 E2
Pickford Rd., Bexh. 80 E4
Pickford Wf. N1 8 J2
Pickford Wf. N1 58 J2
Pickhurst Grn., Brom. 96 F7
Pickhurst La., Brom. 96 F7
Pickhurst La., 96 E5
W.Wick.
Pickhurst Mead, 96 F7
Brom.
Pickhurst Pk., Brom. 96 E5
Pickhurst Ri., W.Wick. 96 C7
Pickwick Clo., Houns. 72 E5
Dorney Way
Pickwick Ms. N18 33 B5
Pickwick Pl., Har. 37 B7
Pickwick Rd. SE21 77 A7
Pickwick St. SE1 16 J4
Pickwick Way, Chis. 88 F6

Pickworth Clo. SW8	67	E7
Kenchester Clo.		
Picton Pl. W1	**11**	**C4**
Picton St. SE5	68	A7
Piedmont Rd. SE18	70	G5
Pier Head E1	68	E1
Wapping High St.		
Pier Par. E16	70	D2
Pier Rd.		
Pier Rd. E16	70	D2
Pier Rd., Felt.	72	B5
Pier St. E14	69	C4
Pier Ter. SW18	75	F4
Jew's Row		
Pier Way SE28	70	G3
Piermont Grn. SE22	77	E5
Piermont Pl., Brom.	97	B2
Piermont Rd. SE22	77	E5
Pierrepoint Rd. W3	56	B7
Pierrepoint Row N1	**8**	**G1**
Pigeon La., Hmptn.	81	G4
Pigott St. E14	60	A4
Pike Clo., Brom.	87	H5
Pike Rd. NW7	30	D4
Ellesmere Ave.		
Pikes End, Pnr.	36	B4
Pikestone Clo., Hayes	54	E4
Berrydale Rd.		
Pilgrim Hill SE27	85	J4
Pilgrim St. EC4	**12**	**G4**
Pilgrim St. EC4	58	H6
Pilgrimage St. SE1	**17**	**B4**
Pilgrimage St. SE1	68	A2
Pilgrims Clo. N13	32	F4
Pilgrims Clo., Nthlt.	45	J5
Pilgrims Ct. SE3	78	G1
Pilgrim's La. NW3	48	G4
Pilgrims Pl. NW3	**48**	**G4**
Hampstead High St.		
Pilgrims Ri., Barn.	23	H5
Pilgrims Way N19	49	D1
Pilgrims Way, S.Croy.	102	C6
Bench Fld.		
Pilgrim's Way, Wem.	47	B1
Pilkington Rd. SE15	77	E2
Pilkington Rd., Orp.	104	F2
Pilot Ind. Est. NW10	56	D4
Pilsdon Clo. SW19	84	A1
Inner Pk. Rd.		
Piltdown Rd., Wat.	28	D4
Pimlico Rd. SW1	**19**	**B3**
Pimlico Rd. SW1	67	A5
Pimlico Wk. N1	**9**	**D3**
Pinchbeck Rd., Orp.	104	J6
Pinchin St. E1	**13**	**J5**
Pinchin St. E1	59	D7
Pincott Pl. SE4	77	G3
Billingford Clo.		
Pincott Rd. SW19	84	F7
Pincott Rd., Bexh.	80	G5
Pindar St. EC2	**13**	**D1**
Pindar St. EC2	59	B5
Pindock Ms. W9	**6**	**B6**
Pine Ave. E15	51	D5
Pine Ave., W.Wick.	103	B1
Pine Clo. N14	24	C7
Pine Clo. N19	49	C2
Hargrave Pk.		
Pine Clo. SE20	86	F7
Pine Clo., Stan.	29	E4
Pine Coombe, Croy.	102	G4
Pine Gdns., Ruis.	45	B1
Pine Gdns., Surb.	92	A6
Pine Glade, Orp.	104	C4
Pine Gro. N4	49	E2
Pine Gro. N20	31	C1
Pine Gro. SW19	84	C5
Pine Martin Clo. NW2	47	J3
Pine Rd. N11	32	A2
Pine Rd. NW2	47	J4
Pine St. EC1	**8**	**E5**
Pine St. EC1	58	G4
Pine Tree Clo., Houns.	72	B1
Pine Wk., Surb.	92	A6
Pine Wd., Sun.	90	A1
Pineapple Ct. SW1	**15**	**F5**
Pinecrest Gdns., Orp.	104	E4
Pinecroft Cres., Barn.	23	B4
Hillside Gdns.		
Pinedene SE15	77	E1
Meeting Ho. La.		
Pinefield Clo. E14	60	A7
Pinehurst Wk., Orp.	104	H1
Andover Rd.		
Pinelands Clo. SE3	69	F7
St. John's Pk.		
Pines, The N14	24	C5
Pines, The, Sun.	90	A3
Pines, The, Wdf.Grn.	34	G3
Pines Rd., Brom.	97	B2
Pinewood Ave., Pnr.	28	H6
Pinewood Ave., Sid.	88	H1
Pinewood Clo., Borwd.	22	D1
Pinewood Clo., Croy.	102	H3
Pinewood Clo., Orp.	104	G1
Pinewood Clo., Pnr.	28	H6
Pinewood Dr., Orp.	104	H5
Pinewood Gro. W5	55	F6
Pinewood Rd. SE2	71	D6
Pinewood Rd., Brom.	96	G4
Pinewood Rd., Felt.	81	B3
Pinfold Rd. SW16	85	E4
Pinkcoat Clo., Felt.	81	B3
Tanglewood Way		
Pinkerton Pl. SW16	85	D4
Riggindale Rd.		
Pinkham Way N11	32	A7
Pinley Gdns., Dag.	62	B1
Stamford Rd.		
Pinnacle Hill, Bexh.	80	H4
Pinnacle Hill N., Bexh.	80	H3
Pinnell Pl. SE9	79	A4
Pinnell Rd. SE9	79	A4
Pinner Ct., Pnr.	36	G4
Pinner Grn., Pnr.	36	C2
Pinner Gro., Pnr.	36	E4
Pinner Hill, Pnr.	28	B7
Pinner Hill Rd., Pnr.	36	C1
Pinner Pk. Ave., Har.	36	H3
Pinner Pk. Gdns., Har.	36	J2
Pinner Rd., Har.	36	H5
Pinner Rd., Pnr.	36	F4
Pinner Vw., Har.	36	J4
Pintail Clo. E6	61	B5
Swan App.		
Pintail Rd., Wdf.Grn.	34	H7
Pinto Clo., Borwd.	22	D6
Percheron Rd.		
Pinto Way SE3	78	H4
Du Cane Rd.		
Pioneer Way W12	56	H6
Piper Clo. N7	49	F5
Piper Rd., Kings.T.	92	A3
Piper's Gdns., Croy.	95	H7
Pipers Grn. NW9	38	C5
Pipers Grn. La., Edg.	29	H3
Pipewell Rd., Cars.	93	H6
Pippin Clo., Croy.	102	J1
Piquet Rd. SE20	95	F2
Pirbright Cres., Croy.	103	C6
Pirbright Rd. SW18	84	C1
Pirie Clo. SE5	77	A3
Denmark Hill		
Pirie St. E16	69	H1
Pitcairn Clo., Rom.	44	G4
Pitcairn Rd., Mitch.	84	J7
Pitchford St. E15	51	D7
Pitfield Cres. SE28	71	A1
Pitfield Est. N1	**9**	**D3**
Pitfield St. N1	**9**	**D4**
Pitfield St. N1	59	B3
Pitfield Way NW10	47	C6
Pitfield Way, Enf.	25	F1
Pitfold Clo. SE12	78	G6
Pitfold Rd. SE12	78	G6
Pitlake, Croy.	101	H2
Pitman St. SE5	**20**	**J7**
Pitman St. SE5	67	J7
Pitsea Pl. E1	59	G6
Pitsea St.		
Pitsea St. E1	59	G6
Pitshanger La. W5	55	E4
Pitshanger Pk. W13	55	D4
Pitt Cres. SW19	84	F4
Pitt Rd., Orp.	104	F4
Pitt Rd., Th.Hth.	94	J5
Pitt St. SE15	68	C7
Pitt St. W8	66	D2
Pittman Gdns., Ilf.	52	F5
Pitt's Head Ms. W1	**15**	**C2**
Pitt's Head Ms. W1	67	A1
Pittsmead Ave., Brom.	96	G7
Pittville Gdns. SE25	95	D3
Pixfield Ct., Brom.	96	F2
Beckenham La.		
Pixley St. E14	59	J6
Place Fm. Ave., Orp.	104	G1
Plaistow Gro. E15	60	F1
Plaistow Gro., Brom.	87	H7
Plaistow La., Brom.	87	G7
Plaistow Pk. Rd. E13	60	H2
Plaistow Rd. E15	60	F1
Plane St. SE26	86	E3
Plane Tree Cres., Felt.	81	B3
Plane Tree Wk. SE19	86	B6
Central Hill		
Plantagenet Clo., Wor.Pk.	99	D4
Plantagenet Gdns., Rom.	44	D7
Broomfield Rd.		
Plantagenet Pl., Rom.	44	D7
Broomfield Rd.		
Plantagenet Rd., Barn.	23	F4
Plantain Pl. SE1	**17**	**B3**
Plantation, The SE3	78	G2
Plantation Wf. SW11	75	F3
Plasel Ct. E13	60	G1
Plashet Rd.		
Plashet Gro. E6	60	J1
Plashet Rd. E13	60	G1
Plassy Rd. SE6	78	B7
Platina St. EC2	**9**	**C5**
Plato Rd. SW2	76	E4
Platt, The SW15	75	A3
Platt St. NW1	**7**	**H1**
Platt St. NW1	58	D2
Platt's La. NW3	48	D4
Platts Rd., Enf.	25	F1
Plawsfield Rd., Beck.	95	G1
Plaxtol Clo., Brom.	96	J1
Plaxtol Rd., Erith	71	G6
Playfield Ave., Rom.	44	J1
Playfield Cres. SE22	77	C5
Playfield Rd., Edg.	38	C2
Playford Rd. N4	49	F2
Playgreen Way SE6	87	A3
Playground Clo., Beck.	95	G2
Churchfields Rd.		
Playhouse Yd. EC4	**12**	**G4**
Plaza W., Houns.	72	H1
Pleasance, The SW15	74	H4
Pleasance Rd. SW15	74	H5
Pleasant Gro., Croy.	102	J3
Pleasant Pl. N1	49	H7
Pleasant Rd., Kings.T.	92	C3
Pleasant Row NW1	58	B1
Camden High St.		
Pleasant Vw. Pl., Orp.	104	E5
High St.		
Pleasant Way, Wem.	55	F2
Plender St. NW1	58	C1
Plender St. Est. NW1	58	C1
Plender St.		
Pleshey Rd. N7	49	D4
Plevna Cres. N15	41	B6
Plevna Rd. N9	33	D3
Plevna Rd., Hmptn.	90	H1
Plevna St. E14	69	C3
Pleydell Ave. SE19	86	C7
Pleydell Ave. W6	65	F4
Pleydell Ct. EC4	58	G6
Fleet St.		
Pleydell St. EC4	**12**	**F4**
Plimsoll Clo. E14	60	B6
Grundy St.		
Plimsoll Rd. N4	49	G3
Plough Ct. EC3	**13**	**C5**
Plough La. SE22	77	C6
Plough La. SW17	84	F4
Plough La. SW19	84	E5
Plough La., Wall.	101	E4
Plough La. Clo., Wall.	101	E5
Plough Pl. EC4	**12**	**F3**
Plough Rd. SW11	75	G3
Plough St. E1	**13**	**G3**
Plough Ter. SW11	75	G4
Plough Way SE16	68	G4
Plough Yd. EC2	**9**	**E6**
Plough Yd. EC2	59	B4
Ploughmans Clo. NW1	58	D1
Crofters Way		
Ploughmans End, Islw.	73	A5
Plover Way SE16	68	H3
Plowman Clo. N18	33	A5
Plowman Way, Dag.	53	C1
Plum Garth, Brent.	64	G4
Plum La. SE18	70	E7
Plumbers Row E1	**13**	**J2**
Plumbers Row E1	59	D5
Plumbridge St. SE10	78	C1
Blackheath Hill		
Plummer La., Mitch.	93	J2
Plummer Rd. SW4	76	D7
Plumpton Clo., Nthlt.	45	G6
Plumpton Way, Cars.	100	H3
Plumstead Common Rd. SE18	70	E6
Plumstead High St. SE18	70	G4
Plumstead Rd. SE18	70	E4
Plumtree Clo., Dag.	53	J6
Plumtree Clo., Wall.	101	D7
Plumtree Ct. EC4	**12**	**G3**
Plumtree Mead, Loug.	27	D3
Plymouth Rd. E16	60	G5
Plymouth Rd., Brom.	96	H1
Plymouth Wf. E14	69	D4
Plympton Ave. NW6	48	C7
Plympton Clo., Belv.	71	E3
Halifield Dr.		
Plympton Pl. NW8	**6**	**G6**
Plympton Rd. NW6	48	C7
Plympton St. NW8	**6**	**G6**
Plympton St. NW8	57	H4
Plymstock Rd., Well.	71	C7
Pocklington Clo. NW9	38	E2
Pocock St. SE1	**16**	**G3**
Pocock St. SE1	67	H2
Podmore Rd. SW18	75	F4
Poets Rd. N5	50	A5
Poets Way, Har.	37	B4
Blawith Rd.		
Point, The, Ruis.	45	A4
West End Rd.		
Point Clo. SE10	78	C1
Point Hill		
Point Hill SE10	69	C7
Point Pl., Wem.	47	B7
Point Pleasant SW18	75	D4
Pointalls Clo. N3	39	F2
Pointer Clo. SE28	62	D6
Pointers Clo. E14	69	B5
Poland St. W1	**11**	**G3**
Poland St. W1	58	C6
Pole Cat All., Brom.	103	F2
Pole Hill Rd. E4	26	C7
Polebrook Rd. SE3	78	J3
Polecroft La. SE6	86	J2
Polesden Gdns. SW20	92	H2
Polesworth Ho. W2	57	D3
Polesworth Rd., Dag.	53	D7
Pollard Clo. E16	60	G7
Pollard Clo. N7	49	F4
Pollard Rd. N20	31	H2
Pollard Rd., Mord.	93	G5
Pollard Row E2	**9**	**J3**
Pollard Row E2	59	D3
Pollard St. E2	**9**	**J3**
Pollard St. E2	59	D3
Pollard Wk., Sid.	89	C6
Evry Rd.		
Pollards Clo., Loug.	26	J5
Pollards Cres. SW16	94	E3
Pollards Hill E. SW16	94	F3
Pollards Hill N. SW16	94	E3
Pollards Hill S. SW16	94	E3
Pollards Hill W. SW16	94	E3
Pollards Wd. Rd. SW16	94	E2
Pollen St. W1	**11**	**F4**
Pollitt Dr. NW8	**6**	**F5**
Polperro Clo., Orp.	97	J6
Cotswold Ri.		
Polsted Rd. SE6	77	J7
Polthorne Gro. SE18	70	F4
Polworth Rd. SW16	85	E5
Polygon, The SW4	76	C4
Old Town		
Polygon Rd. NW1	**7**	**H2**
Polygon Rd. NW1	58	D2
Polytechnic St. SE18	70	D4
Pomell Way E1	**13**	**G3**
Pomeroy St. SE14	77	F1
Pomfret Rd. SE5	76	H3
Flaxman Rd.		
Pond Clo. SE3	78	F2
Pond Cottage La., W.Wick.	103	A1
Pond Cotts. SE21	86	B1
Pond Fld. End, Loug.	26	J7
Pond Hill Gdns., Sutt.	100	B6
Pond Mead SE21	77	A6
Pond Pl. SW3	**18**	**G2**
Pond Rd. E15	60	E2
Pond Rd. SE3	78	F2
Pond Sq. N6	49	A1
South Gro.		

Pond St. NW3 48 H5
Pond Way, Tedd. 82 F6
  Holmesdale Rd.
Ponder St. N7 49 F7
Ponders End Ind. Est., 25 J4
  Enf.
Pondfield Rd., Brom. 103 E1
Pondfield Rd., Dag. 53 H5
Pondfield Rd., Orp. 104 E3
Pondwood Ri., Orp. 97 H7
Ponler St. E1 59 E6
Ponsard Rd. NW10 56 H3
Ponsford Rd. E9 50 F5
Ponsonby Pl. SW1 19 J3
Ponsonby Pl. SW1 67 D5
Ponsonby Rd. SW15 74 H7
Ponsonby Ter. SW1 19 J3
Ponsonby Ter. SW1 67 D5
Pont St. SW1 14 J6
Pont St. SW1 66 J3
Pont St. Ms. SW1 14 J6
Pont St. Ms. SW1 66 J3
Pontefract Rd., Brom. 87 F5
Ponton Rd. SW8 19 J6
Ponton Rd. SW8 67 D6
Pontypool Pl. SE1 16 G3
Pool Clo., Beck. 87 A5
Pool Clo., W.Mol. 90 F5
Pool Rd., Har. 37 A7
Pool Rd., W.Mol. 90 F5
Poole Ct. Rd., Houns. 72 E2
  Vicarage Fm. Rd.
Poole Rd. E9 50 G6
Poole Rd., Epsom 99 D6
Poole St. N1 59 A1
Pooles Bldgs. EC1 8 E6
Pooles La. SW10 66 F7
  Lots Rd.
Pooles La., Dag. 62 E2
Pooles Pk. N4 49 G2
  Seven Sisters Rd.
Poolmans St. SE16 68 G2
Poolsford Rd. NW9 38 E4
Poonah St. E1 59 F6
  Hardinge St.
Pope Clo. SW19 84 G6
  Shelley Way
Pope Rd., Brom. 97 A5
Pope St. SE1 17 E4
Pope St. SE1 68 E2
Popes Ave., Twick. 82 B2
Popes Dr. N3 39 D1
Popes Gro., Croy. 102 J3
Popes Gro., Twick. 82 B2
Pope's Head All. EC3 59 A6
  Cornhill
Popes La. W5 64 G3
Popes Rd. SW9 76 G3
Popham Clo., Felt. 81 F3
Popham Rd. N1 58 J1
Popham St. N1 58 J1
Poplar Ave., Mitch. 93 J1
Poplar Ave., Orp. 104 E2
Poplar Ave., Sthl. 63 H3
Poplar Bath St. E14 60 B7
  Lawless St.
Poplar Clo., Pnr. 36 D1
Poplar Ct. SW19 84 D5
Poplar Cres., Epsom 99 C6
Poplar Fm. Clo., 99 C6
  Epsom
Poplar Gdns., N.Mal. 92 D2
Poplar Gro. N11 32 A6
Poplar Gro. W6 65 J2
Poplar Gro., N.Mal. 92 D3
Poplar Gro., Wem. 47 C3
Poplar High St. E14 60 B7
Poplar Mt., Belv. 71 H4
Poplar Pl. SE28 62 C7
Poplar Pl. W2 10 A5
Poplar Pl. W2 57 E7
Poplar Pl., Hayes 54 A7
  Central Ave.
Poplar Rd. SE24 76 J4
Poplar Rd. SW19 93 D2
Poplar Rd., Sutt. 100 C1
Poplar Rd. S. SW19 93 D3
Poplar St., Rom. 44 J4
Poplar Vw., Wem. 46 G2
  Lumen Rd.
Poplar Wk. SE24 76 J4
Poplar Wk., Croy. 101 J2
Poplar Way, Felt. 81 A3
Poplar Way, Ilf. 43 F4
Poplars, The N14 24 B5
Poplars Ave. NW10 47 J6
Poplars Rd. E17 42 B4
Poppins Ct. EC4 12 G4

Poppleton Rd. E11 42 E6
Poppy Clo., Wall. 101 A1
Poppy La., Croy. 95 F7
Porch Way N20 31 J3
Porchester Gdns. W2 10 B5
Porchester Gdns. W2 57 E7
Porchester Gdns. Ms. 10 B4
  W2
Porchester Mead, 87 A6
  Beck.
Porchester Ms. W2 10 B3
Porchester Pl. W2 10 H4
Porchester Pl. W2 57 H6
Porchester Rd. W2 10 B3
Porchester Rd. W2 57 E5
Porchester Rd., 92 B2
  Kings.T.
Porchester Sq. W2 10 B3
Porchester Sq. W2 57 E6
Porchester Ter. W2 10 C5
Porchester Ter. W2 57 F7
Porchester Ter. N. W2 10 B3
Porchester Ter. N. W2 57 E6
Porcupine Clo. SE9 88 B2
Porden Rd. SW2 76 F4
Porlock Ave., Har. 45 J1
Porlock Rd. W10 57 A4
  Ladbroke Gro.
Porlock Rd., Enf. 25 C7
Porlock St. SE1 17 C3
Porlock St. SE1 68 A2
Porrington Clo., Chis. 97 D1
Port Cres. E13 60 H4
  Jenkins Rd.
Portal Clo. SE27 85 G3
Portal Clo., Ruis. 45 A4
Portbury Clo. SE15 77 D1
  Clayton Rd.
Portchester Clo. SE5 77 A4
Portcullis Lo. Rd., 25 A3
  Enf.
Portelet Rd. E1 59 G3
Porten Rd. W14 66 B3
Porter Rd. E6 61 C6
Porter St. SE1 17 A1
Porter St. W1 11 A1
Porters Ave., Dag. 53 B6
Porters Wk. E1 59 E7
  Pennington St.
Portersfield Rd., Enf. 25 B4
Porteus Rd. W2 10 D1
Porteus Rd. W2 57 F5
Portgate Clo. W9 57 C4
Porthcawe Rd. SE26 86 H4
Porthkerry Ave., Well. 80 A4
Portia Way E3 59 J4
Portinscale Rd. 75 B5
  SW15
Portland Ave. N16 41 C7
Portland Ave., N.Mal. 92 F7
Portland Ave., Sid. 80 A6
Portland Clo., Rom. 44 C5
Portland Cres. SE9 88 B2
Portland Cres., Grnf. 54 H4
Portland Cres., Stan. 37 G2
Portland Gdns. N4 40 H6
Portland Gdns., Rom. 44 D5
Portland Gro. SW8 76 F1
Portland Ms. W1 11 G4
Portland Pl. W1 7 D6
Portland Pl. W1 58 B5
Portland Ri. N4 49 H1
Portland Ri. Est. N4 49 J1
Portland Rd. N15 41 C4
Portland Rd. SE9 88 B2
Portland Rd. SE25 95 D4
Portland Rd. W11 57 B7
Portland Rd., Brom. 87 J4
Portland Rd., Kings.T. 91 H3
Portland Rd., Mitch. 93 H2
Portland Rd., Sthl. 63 F3
Portland Sq. E1 68 E1
  Watts St.
Portland St. SE17 21 B3
Portland St. SE17 68 A5
Portland St., Rich. 73 G4
Portland Wk. SE15 21 C5
Portland Wk. SE17 21 C5
Portman Ave. SW14 74 D3
Portman Clo. W1 11 A3
Portman Clo. W1 57 J6
Portman Clo., Bexh. 80 D3
  Queen Anne's Gate
Portman Dr., Wdf.Grn. 43 A2
Portman Gdns. NW9 38 D2
Portman Gate NW1 6 H6
Portman Ms. S. W1 11 B4
Portman Ms. S. W1 58 A6

Portman Pl. E2 59 F3
Portman Rd., 91 J2
  Kings.T.
Portman Sq. W1 11 B3
Portman Sq. W1 58 A6
Portman St. W1 11 B4
Portman St. W1 58 A6
Portmeadow Wk. SE2 71 D2
Portmeers Clo. E17 41 J6
  Lennox Rd.
Portnall Rd. W9 57 C2
Portobello Ct. W11 57 C7
  Westbourne Gro.
Portobello Ms. W11 57 D7
  Portobello Rd.
Portobello Rd. W10 57 B5
Portobello Rd. W11 57 C6
Porton Ct., Surb. 91 F6
Portpool La. EC1 12 E1
Portpool La. EC1 58 G5
Portree Clo. N22 32 F7
  Nightingale Rd.
Portree St. E14 60 D6
Portsdown, Edg. 30 A5
  Rectory La.
Portsdown Ave. 39 C6
  NW11
Portsdown Ms. NW11 39 C6
Portsea Ms. W2 10 H4
Portsea Pl. W2 10 H4
Portslade Rd. SW8 76 C2
Portsmouth Ave., 91 D7
  T.Ditt.
Portsmouth Rd. SW15 74 H7
Portsmouth Rd., Esher 98 B2
Portsmouth Rd., 91 G4
  Kings.T.
Portsmouth Rd., Surb. 91 F6
Portsmouth Rd., 98 B2
  T.Ditt.
Portsmouth St. WC2 12 C4
Portsoken St. E1 13 F5
Portsoken St. E1 59 C7
Portswood Pl. SW15 74 F7
  Danebury Ave.
Portugal Gdns., 81 J2
  Twick.
  Fulwell Pk. Ave.
Portugal St. WC2 12 C4
Portugal St. WC2 58 F6
Portway E15 60 F1
Portway Gdns. SE18 70 A7
  Shooter's Hill Rd.
Post La., Twick. 82 A1
Post Office App. E7 51 H5
Post Office Ct. EC3 13 C4
Post Office Way SW8 19 H7
Post Office Way SW8 67 D7
Postern Grn., Enf. 24 G2
Postmill Clo., Croy. 102 G3
  Upper Shirley Rd.
Postway Ms., Ilf. 52 E3
  Clements Rd.
Potier St. SE1 17 C6
Potier St. SE1 68 A3
Pott St. E2 59 E3
Potter Clo., Mitch. 94 B2
Potter St., Nthwd. 36 A1
Potter St., Pnr. 36 B1
Potter St. Hill, Pnr. 28 B6
Potterne Clo. SW19 75 A7
  Castlecombe Dr.
Potters Clo., Croy. 102 H1
Potters Clo., Loug. 27 B2
Potters Clo., N.Mal. 92 C4
Potters Heights Clo., 28 B7
  Pnr.
Potters La. SW16 85 D6
Potters La., Barn. 23 D4
Potters La., Borwd. 22 C1
Potters Rd., Barn. 23 E4
Pottery La. W11 57 B7
  Portland Rd.
Pottery Rd., Bex. 89 J2
Pottery Rd., Brent. 64 H6
Pottery St. SE16 68 E2
Poulett Gdns., Twick. 82 C1
Poulett Rd. E6 61 C2
Poulner Way SE15 68 C7
  Daniel Gdns.
Poulters Wd., Kes. 104 A5
Poulton Ave., Sutt. 100 G3
Poulton Clo. E8 50 E5
  Spurstowe Ter.
Poultry EC2 13 B4
Poultry EC2 59 A6
Pound Clo., Orp. 104 G2
Pound Clo., Surb. 98 F1

Pound Ct. Dr., Orp. 104 G2
Pound La. NW10 47 G6
Pound Pk. Rd. SE7 70 A4
Pound Pl. SE9 79 D6
Pound St., Cars. 100 J5
Poundfield Rd., Loug. 27 D5
Pountney Rd. SW11 76 A3
Poverest Rd., Orp. 97 J5
Powder Mill La., 72 F7
  Twick.
Powell Clo., Chess. 98 G5
  Mansfield Rd.
Powell Clo., Edg. 29 J6
Powell Clo., Wall. 101 D7
  Hermes Way
Powell Gdns., Dag. 53 G4
Powell Rd. E5 50 E3
Powell Rd., Buck.H. 26 J7
Powell's Wk. W4 65 E6
Power Rd. W4 65 A4
Powers Ct., Twick. 73 G7
Powerscroft Rd. E5 50 F4
Powerscroft Rd., Sid. 89 C6
Powis Gdns. NW11 39 C7
Powis Gdns. W11 57 C6
Powis Ms. W11 57 C6
  Westbourne Pk. Rd.
Powis Pl. WC1 8 B6
Powis Pl. WC1 58 E4
Powis Rd. E3 60 B3
Powis Sq. W11 57 C6
Powis St. SE18 70 D3
Powis Ter. W11 57 C6
Powlett Pl. NW1 49 B6
  Harmood St.
Pownall Gdns., 72 H4
  Houns.
Pownall Rd. E8 59 D1
Pownall Rd., Houns. 72 H4
Powster Rd., Brom. 87 H5
Powys La. N13 32 E4
Powys La. N14 32 E4
Poynders Ct. SW4 76 C6
  Poynders Rd.
Poynders Gdns. SW4 76 C7
Poynders Rd. SW4 76 C6
Poynings Rd. N19 49 C3
Poynings Way N12 31 D5
Poyntell Cres., Chis. 97 G1
Poynter Rd., Enf. 25 D5
Poynton Rd. N17 41 D2
Poyntz Rd. SW11 75 J2
Poyser St. E2 59 E2
Praed Ms. W2 10 F3
Praed St. W2 10 F3
Praed St. W2 57 G6
Pragel St. E13 60 H4
Pragnell Rd. SE12 87 H2
Prague Pl. SW2 76 E5
Prah Rd. N4 49 G2
Prairie St. SW8 76 A2
Pratt Ms. NW1 58 C1
  Pratt St.
Pratt St. NW1 58 C1
Pratt Wk. SE11 20 D1
Pratt Wk. SE11 67 F4
Pratts Pas., Kings.T. 91 H2
  Eden St.
Prayle Gro. NW2 48 A1
Prebend Gdns. W4 65 F4
Prebend Gdns. W6 65 F4
Prebend St. N1 58 J1
Precinct, The, W.Mol. 90 H3
  Victoria Ave.
Precinct Rd., Hayes 54 A7
Precincts, The, Mord. 93 E6
  Green La.
Premier Cor. W9 57 C2
  Kilburn La.
Premier Pl. SW15 75 B4
  Putney High St.
Prendergast Rd. SE3 78 E3
Prentis Rd. SW16 85 D4
Prentiss Ct. SE7 70 A4
Presburg Rd., N.Mal. 92 E5
Prescelly Pl., Edg. 37 J1
Prescot St. E1 13 G5
Prescot St. E1 59 C7
Prescott Ave., Orp. 97 E6
Prescott Clo. SW16 85 E7
Prescott Grn., Loug. 27 F1
Prescott Ho. SE17 20 H6
Prescott Pl. SW4 76 D3
President Dr. E1 68 E1
  Waterman Way
President St. EC1 8 J3
Press Rd. NW10 47 D3

Prestbury Rd. E7 51 J7
Prestbury Sq. SE9 88 C4
Prested Rd. SW11 75 H4
St. John's Hill
Preston Ave. E4 34 D6
Preston Clo. SE1 21 D1
Preston Clo., Twick. 82 B3
Preston Dr. E11 42 J5
Preston Dr., Bexh. 80 D1
Preston Dr., Epsom 99 E6
Preston Gdns. NW10 47 E6
Church Rd.
Preston Gdns., Ilf. 43 B6
Preston Hill, Har. 37 H7
Preston Pl. NW2 47 G6
Preston Pl., Rich. 73 H5
Preston Rd. E11 42 E6
Preston Rd. SE19 85 H6
Preston Rd. SW20 83 F7
Preston Rd., Har. 37 H7
Preston Rd., Wem. 46 H2
Preston Waye, Har. 46 H1
Prestons Rd. E14 69 C2
Prestons Rd., Brom. 103 G3
Prestwick Clo., Sthl. 63 E5
Ringway
Prestwick Rd., Wat. 28 C1
Prestwood Ave., Har. 37 E4
Prestwood Clo. SE18 71 A7
Prestwood Clo., Har. 37 E4
Prestwood Gdns., 94 J7
Croy.
Prestwood St. N1 9 A2
Pretoria Ave. E17 41 H4
Pretoria Clo. N17 33 C7
Pretoria Rd.
Pretoria Cres. E4 34 C1
Pretoria Rd. E4 34 C1
Pretoria Rd. E11 51 D1
Pretoria Rd. E16 60 F4
Pretoria Rd. N17 33 C7
Pretoria Rd. SW16 85 B6
Pretoria Rd., Ilf. 52 E5
Pretoria Rd., Rom. 44 J4
Pretoria Rd. N. N18 33 C6
Prevost Rd. N11 32 A2
Price Clo. NW7 31 B6
Price Clo. SW17 84 J3
Price Rd., Croy. 101 H4
Price Way, Hmptn. 81 E6
Victors Dr.
Pricklers Hill, Barn. 23 E6
Prickley Wd., Brom. 103 F1
Priddy's Yd., Croy. 101 J2
Crown Hill
Prideaux Pl. W3 56 D7
Friars Pl. La.
Prideaux Pl. WC1 8 D3
Prideaux Pl. WC1 58 F3
Prideaux Rd. SW9 76 E3
Pridham Rd., Th.Hth. 95 A4
Priest Ct. EC2 12 J3
Priest Pk. Ave., Har. 45 G2
Priestfield Rd. SE23 86 H3
Priestlands Pk. Rd., 88 J3
Sid.
Priestley Clo. N16 41 C7
Ravensdale Rd.
Priestley Gdns., Rom. 44 B6
Priestley Rd., Mitch. 94 A2
Priestley Way E17 41 G3
Priestley Way NW2 47 G1
Priests Bri. SW14 74 E3
Prima Rd. SW9 20 E7
Prima Rd. SW9 67 G7
Primrose Ave., Enf. 25 A1
Primrose Ave., Rom. 44 A7
Primrose Clo. SE6 87 C5
Primrose Clo., Har. 45 F3
Primrose Clo., Wall. 94 B7
Primrose Gdns. NW3 48 H6
Primrose Gdns., Ruis. 45 C5
Primrose Hill EC4 12 F4
Primrose Hill Ct. 48 J7
NW3
Primrose Hill Rd. 48 J7
NW3
Primrose Hill Studios 58 A1
NW1
Fitzroy Rd.
Primrose La., Croy. 102 F1
Primrose Ms. NW1 48 J7
Sharpleshall St.
Primrose Rd. E10 51 B1
Primrose Rd. E18 42 H2
Primrose St. EC2 13 D1
Primrose St. EC2 59 B5
Primrose Way, Wem. 55 G2

Primula St. W12 56 G6
Prince Albert Rd. 6 H2
NW1
Prince Albert Rd. NW1 57 J2
Prince Albert Rd. 6 H2
NW8
Prince Albert Rd. 57 H3
NW8
Prince Arthur Ms. 48 F4
NW3
Perrins La.
Prince Arthur Rd. 48 F5
NW3
Prince Charles Dr. 38 J7
NW4
Prince Charles Rd. 78 F2
SE3
Prince Charles Way, 101 B3
Wall.
Prince Consort Dr., 97 G1
Chis.
Prince Consort Rd. 14 E5
SW7
Prince Consort Rd. 66 F3
SW7
Prince Edward Rd. E9 50 J6
Prince George Ave. 24 C4
N14
Prince George Duke 88 G7
of Kent Ct., Chis.
Holbrook La.
Prince George Rd. 50 B4
N16
Prince George's Ave. 92 J2
SW20
Prince George's Rd. 93 G1
SW19
Prince Henry Rd. SE7 70 A7
Prince Imperial Rd. 79 C1
SE18
Prince Imperial Rd., 88 E7
Chis.
Prince John Rd. SE9 79 B5
Prince of Orange La. 69 C7
SE10
Greenwich High Rd.
Prince of Wales Clo. 38 H4
NW4
Church Ter.
Prince of Wales Dr. 67 B7
SW8
Prince of Wales Dr. 75 H1
SW11
Prince of Wales Gate 14 G4
SW7
Prince of Wales Gate 66 H2
SW7
Prince of Wales Pas. 7 F4
NW1
Prince of Wales Rd. 60 J6
E16
Prince of Wales Rd. 49 A6
NW5
Prince of Wales Rd. 78 F1
SE3
Prince of Wales Rd., 100 G2
Sutt.
Prince of Wales Ter. 65 E5
W4
Prince of Wales Ter. 14 B4
W8
Prince Regent Ct. 68 H1
SE16
Rotherhithe St.
Prince Regent La. E13 60 H3
Prince Regent La. E16 60 J5
Prince Regent Rd., 72 J3
Houns.
Prince Rd. SE25 95 B5
Prince Rupert Rd. SE9 79 C4
Prince St. SE8 68 J6
Princedale Rd. W11 66 B1
Princelet St. E1 13 G1
Princelet St. E1 59 C5
Prince's Arc. SW1 15 G1
Princes Ave. N3 39 D1
Princes Ave. N10 40 B3
Princes Ave. N13 32 G5
Princes Ave. N22 40 D1
Princes Ave. NW9 38 A4
Princes Ave. W3 65 A3
Princes Ave., Cars. 100 J7
Princes Ave., Grnf. 54 H6
Princes Ave., Orp. 97 H5
Princes Ave., Surb. 99 A1
Princes Ave., 34 H4
Wdf.Grn.
Princes Clo. NW9 38 A4

Princes Clo. SW4 76 C3
Old Town
Princes Clo., Edg. 30 A5
Princes Clo., Sid. 89 D3
Princes Clo., Tedd. 82 A4
Princes Ct. E1 59 E7
Princes Ct., Wem. 46 H5
Princes Dr., Har. 37 B3
Princes Gdns. SW7 14 F5
Princes Gdns. SW7 66 G3
Princes Gdns. W3 56 A5
Princes Gdns. W5 55 F4
Princes Gate SW7 14 F4
Princes Gate SW7 66 H2
Princes Gate Ct. SW7 14 F4
Princes Gate Ms. SW7 14 F5
Princes Gate Ms. SW7 66 G3
Princes La. N10 40 B3
Princes Ms. W2 10 A5
Princes Pk. Ave. 39 B6
NW11
Princes Pl. SW1 15 G1
Princes Pl. W11 66 B1
Princes Plain, Brom. 97 B7
Princes Ri. SE13 78 C2
Princes Rd. N18 33 F4
Princes Rd. SE20 86 G6
Princes Rd. SW14 74 D3
Princes Rd. SW19 84 D6
Princes Rd. W13 64 E1
Broomfield Rd.
Princes Rd., Buck.H. 34 J2
Princes Rd., Ilf. 43 G4
Princes Rd., Kings.T. 92 A1
Princes Rd., Rich. 73 J5
Princes Rd. (Kew), 73 J1
Rich.
Princes Rd., Tedd. 82 A4
Princes Sq. W2 57 E7
Princes St. EC2 13 B4
Princes St. EC2 59 A6
Princes St. N17 33 B6
Queen St.
Princes St. W1 11 E4
Princes St. W1 58 B6
Princes St., Bexh. 80 F4
Princes St., Rich. 73 H5
Sheen Rd.
Princes St., Sutt. 100 G4
Princes Ter. E13 60 H1
Princes Way SW19 75 H1
Princes Way, Buck.H. 34 J2
Princes Way, Croy. 101 F5
Princes Way, Ruis. 45 E4
Princes Way, W.Wick. 103 F4
Princes Yd. W11 66 B1
Princedale Rd.
Princess Ave., Wem. 46 H2
Princess Ct. SE16 68 J3
Princess Cres. N4 49 H2
Princess May Rd. N16 50 B4
Princess Ms. NW3 48 G6
Belsize Cres.
Princess Par., Orp. 104 D3
Crofton Rd.
Princess Rd. NW1 58 A1
Princess Rd. NW6 57 D2
Princess Rd., Croy. 94 J6
Princess St. SE1 16 H6
Princess St. SE1 67 H3
Princesses Wk., Rich. 64 H7
Kew Rd.
Princethorpe Ho. W2 10 A1
Princethorpe Ho. W2 57 E5
Princethorpe Rd. 86 G4
SE26
Princeton Ct. SW15 75 A3
Felsham Rd.
Princeton St. WC1 12 C2
Princeton St. WC1 58 F5
Pringle Gdns. SW16 85 C4
Print Village SE15 77 C2
Chadwick Rd.
Printer St. EC4 12 F3
Printer St. EC4 58 F7
Printing Ho. Yd. E2 9 E4
Priolo Rd. SE7 69 J5
Prior Ave., Sutt. 100 H7
Prior Bolton St. N1 49 H6
Prior Rd., Ilf. 52 D3
Prior St. SE10 69 C7
Prioress Rd. SE27 85 H3
Prioress St. SE1 17 C6
Prioress St. SE1 68 A3
Priors Cft. E17 41 H2
Priors Fld., Nthlt. 45 E6
Arnold Rd.
Priors Gdns., Ruis. 45 C5

Priors Mead, Enf. 25 B1
Priory, The SE3 78 F4
Priory Ave. E4 33 J3
Priory Ave. E17 42 A5
Priory Ave. N8 40 D4
Priory Ave. W4 65 E4
Priory Ave., Orp. 97 G6
Priory Ave., Sutt. 100 A4
Priory Ave., Wem. 46 C4
Priory Clo. E4 33 J3
Priory Clo. E18 42 G1
Priory Clo. N3 39 C1
Church Cres.
Priory Clo. N14 24 B5
Priory Clo. N20 23 C7
Priory Clo. SW19 93 E1
High Path
Priory Clo., Beck. 95 H3
Priory Clo., Chis. 97 C1
Priory Clo., Hmptn. 90 F1
Priory Gdns.
Priory Clo., Hayes 54 B7
Priory Clo., Stan. 29 C3
Priory Clo., Sun. 81 A7
Priory Clo., Wem. 46 C4
(Sudbury)
Priory Ct. E17 41 J2
Priory Ct. SW8 76 D1
Priory Ct. Est. E17 41 J2
Priory Cres. SE19 85 J7
Priory Cres., Sutt. 100 A4
Priory Cres., Wem. 46 D3
Priory Dr. SE2 71 D5
Priory Dr., Stan. 29 C3
Priory Fld. Dr., Edg. 30 B4
Priory Gdns. N6 40 B6
Priory Gdns. SW13 74 F3
Priory Gdns. W4 65 E4
Priory Gdns. W5 55 H3
Hanger La.
Priory Gdns., Hmptn. 81 F7
Priory Gdns., Wem. 46 D4
Priory Grn. Est. N1 8 D1
Priory Grn. Est. N1 58 F2
Priory Gro. SW8 76 E1
Priory Hill, Wem. 46 D4
Priory La. SW15 74 E6
Priory La., Rich. 65 A7
Forest Rd.
Priory La., W.Mol. 90 G4
Priory Ms. SW8 76 E1
Priory Pk. SE3 78 F3
Priory Pk. Rd. NW6 57 C1
Priory Pk. Rd., Wem. 46 D4
Priory Rd. E6 61 A1
Priory Rd. N8 40 C4
Priory Rd. NW6 57 E1
Priory Rd. SW19 84 G7
Priory Rd. W4 65 D3
Priory Rd., Bark. 52 G7
Priory Rd., Chess. 98 H3
Priory Rd., Croy. 94 G7
Priory Rd., Hmptn. 81 F7
Priory Rd., Houns. 72 J5
Priory Rd., Loug. 27 B4
Priory Rd., Rich. 65 A7
Priory Rd., Sutt. 100 A4
Priory St. E3 60 B3
St. Leonards St.
Priory Ter. NW6 57 E1
Priory Ter., Sun. 81 A7
Priory Clo.
Priory Wk. SW10 18 D4
Priory Wk. SW10 66 F5
Priory Way, Har. 36 H4
Priory Way, Sthl. 63 D3
Western Rd.
Pritchard's Rd. E2 59 D2
Priter Rd. SE16 17 J6
Priter Rd. SE16 68 D3
Private Rd., Enf. 25 A5
Probert Rd. SW2 76 G5
Probyn Rd. SW2 85 H2
Procter St. WC1 12 C2
Procter St. WC1 58 F5
Proctors Clo., Felt. 81 A1
Progress Business 101 F2
Pk., The, Croy.
Progress Way N22 40 G1
Progress Way, Croy. 101 F2
Progress Way, Enf. 25 D5
Promenade, The W4 74 E1
Promenade App. Rd. 65 E7
W4
Prospect Clo. SE26 86 E4
Prospect Clo., Belv. 71 G4
Prospect Clo., Houns. 72 F1
Prospect Clo., Ruis. 36 D7

Prospect Cotts. SW18 75 D4
Point Pleasant
Prospect Cres., Twick. 72 J6
Prospect Hill E17 42 B4
Prospect Pl. E1 68 F1
Prospect Pl. N2 39 G4
Prospect Pl. N17 41 B1
Church Rd.
Prospect Pl. NW3 48 F4
Holly Wk.
Prospect Pl., Brom. 96 H3
Prospect Pl., Rom. 44 J2
Prospect Ring N2 39 G3
Prospect Rd. NW2 48 C3
Prospect Rd., Barn. 23 D5
Prospect Rd., Surb. 91 F6
Prospect Rd., 34 J6
Wdf.Grn.
Prospect St. SE16 68 E2
Jamaica Rd.
Prospect Vale SE18 70 B4
Prospero Rd. N19 49 C1
Prothero Gdns. NW4 38 H5
Prothero Ho. NW10 47 D7
Prothero Rd. SW6 66 B7
Prout Gro. NW10 47 E4
Prout Rd. E5 50 E3
Providence Ct. W1 11 C5
Providence Ct. W1 58 A7
Providence Pl. N1 58 H1
Upper St.
Providence Pl., Rom. 44 F2
Providence Row N1 8 C2
Providence Yd. E2 9 H3
Provident Ind. Est., 63 A2
Hayes
Provost Est. N1 9 B3
Provost Est. N1 59 A2
Provost Rd. NW3 48 J7
Provost St. N1 9 B2
Provost St. N1 59 A2
Prowse Ave. 28 J2
(Bushey). Wat.
Prowse Pl. NW1 49 B7
Bonny St.
Pruden Clo. N14 32 C2
Prudent Pas. EC2 13 B3
Prusom St. E1 68 E1
Pryors, The NW3 48 G3
Pudding La. EC3 13 C6
Pudding La. EC3 59 A7
Pudding La., Chig. 27 H6
Pudding Mill La. E15 60 B1
Puddle Dock EC4 12 H5
Puffin Clo., Beck. 95 G5
Pulborough Rd. SW18 75 C4
Pulborough Way, 72 C4
Houns.
Pulford Rd. N15 41 A6
Pulham Ave. N2 39 F4
Puller Rd., Barn. 23 B2
Pulleyns Ave. E6 61 B3
Pullman Ct. SW2 85 E1
Pullman Gdns. SW15 74 J6
Pulross Rd. SW9 76 F3
Pulteney Clo. E3 59 J1
Pulteney Rd. E18 42 H3
Pulteney Ter. N1 58 F1
Pulton Pl. SW6 66 D7
Puma Ct. E1 13 F1
Pump All., Brent. 64 G7
Pump Clo., Nthlt. 54 G2
Union Rd.
Pump Ct. EC4 12 E4
Pump Hill, Loug. 27 C2
Pump La. SE14 68 F7
Pump La., Hayes 63 A2
Pump Pail N., Croy. 101 J3
Old Town
Pump Pail S., Croy. 101 J3
Southbridge Rd.
Pumping Sta. Rd. W4 65 E7
Pundersons Gdns. E2 59 E3
Purbeck Ave., N.Mal. 92 F6
Purbeck Dr. NW2 48 A2
Purbrook Est. SE1 17 E4
Purbrook St. SE1 17 E5
Purcell Cres. SW6 66 A7
Purcell Ms. NW10 47 E7
Suffolk Rd.
Purcell Rd., Grnf. 54 H5
Purcell St. N1 9 D1
Purcell St. N1 59 B2
Purcells Ave., Edg. 30 A5
Purchese St. NW1 7 J1
Purchese St. NW1 58 D2
Purdy St. E3 60 B4
Purland Clo., Dag. 53 F1

Purland Rd. SE28 70 J2
Purleigh Ave., 35 B6
Wdf.Grn.
Purley Ave. NW2 48 B2
Purley Clo., Ilf. 43 D2
Purley Pl. N1 49 H7
Islington Pk. St.
Purley Rd. N9 33 A3
Purley Rd., S.Croy. 102 A7
Purley Way, Croy. 94 F7
Purneys Rd. SE9 79 A4
Purrett Rd. SE18 70 J5
Purser's Cross Rd. 75 C1
SW6
Pursewardens Clo. 64 F1
W13
Pursley Rd. NW7 30 H7
Purves Rd. NW10 56 H2
Puteaux Ho. E2 59 G2
Mace St.
Putney Bri. SW6 75 B3
Putney Bri. SW15 75 B3
Putney Bri. App. SW6 75 B3
Putney Bri. Rd. SW15 75 B4
Putney Bri. Rd. SW18 75 D5
Putney Common 74 J3
SW15
Putney Heath SW15 74 H7
Putney Heath La. 75 A6
SW15
Putney High St. SW15 75 A4
Putney Hill SW15 75 A6
Putney Pk. Ave. SW15 74 G4
Putney Pk. La. SW15 74 H4
Puttenham Clo., Wat. 28 D2
Pycroft Way N9 33 D3
Pyecombe Cor. N12 31 C4
Pylbrook Rd., Sutt. 100 D3
Pylon Way, Croy. 101 E1
Pym Clo., Barn. 23 G5
Pymers Mead SE21 85 J1
Pymmes Clo. N13 32 F5
Pymmes Clo. N17 41 E1
Pymmes Gdns. N. N9 33 C3
Pymmes Gdns. S. N9 33 C3
Pymmes Grn. Rd. N11 32 B4
Pymmes Rd. N13 32 E6
Pymms Brook Dr., 23 H4
Barn.
Pyne Rd., Surb. 99 A1
Pynham Clo. SE2 71 B3
Pynnacles Clo., Stan. 29 E5
Pyrland Rd. N5 50 A5
Pyrland Rd., Rich. 73 J6
Pyrles Grn., Loug. 27 E1
Pyrles La., Loug. 27 E2
Pyrmont Gro. SE27 85 H3
Pyrmont Rd. W4 65 A6
Pyrmont Rd., Ilf. 52 F2
High Rd.
Pytchley Cres. SE19 85 J6
Pytchley Rd. SE22 77 B3

Q

Quadrant, The SE24 76 J5
Herne Hill
Quadrant, The SW20 93 B1
Quadrant, The, Bexh. 71 D7
Quadrant, The, Rich. 73 H4
Quadrant, The, Sutt. 100 F6
Quadrant Arc. W1 11 G6
Quadrant Gro. NW5 48 J5
Quadrant Rd., Rich. 73 G4
Quadrant Rd., Th.Hth. 94 H4
Quaggy Wk. SE3 78 G4
Quainton St. NW10 47 D3
Quaker St. E1 9 F6
Quaker St. E1 59 C4
Quakers Course NW9 38 F1
Quakers La., Islw. 73 D1
Quakers Wk. N21 25 A6
Quality Ct. WC2 12 E3
Quantock Dr., Wor.Pk. 99 J2
Cotswold Way
Quantock Gdns. NW2 48 A2
Quarley Way SE15 21 F7
Quarr Rd., Cars. 93 G6
Quarrendon St. SW6 75 D2
Quarry Pk. Rd., Sutt. 100 C6
Quarry Ri., Sutt. 100 C6
Quarry Rd. SW18 75 F6
Quarter Mile La. E10 51 B4
Quarterdeck, The E14 69 A2
Quay W., Tedd. 82 E5
Quebec Ms. W1 11 A4
Quebec Rd., Hayes 54 C7

Quebec Rd., Ilf. 43 E7
Quebec Way SE16 68 G2
Queen Adelaide Rd. 86 F6
SE20
Queen Alexandra's 84 C5
Ct. SW19
Queen Anne Ave. N15 41 C5
Suffield Rd.
Queen Anne Ave., 96 F3
Brom.
Queen Anne Clo., 98 B7
Esher
Queen Anne Ms. W1 11 E2
Queen Anne Rd. E9 50 G6
Queen Anne St. W1 11 D3
Queen Anne St. W1 58 B5
Queen Anne's Clo., 82 A3
Twick.
Queen Anne's Gdns. 65 E3
W4
Queen Anne's Gdns. 64 H2
W5
Queen Annes Gdns. 25 B6
Enf.
Queen Anne's Gdns., 93 J3
Mitch.
**Queen Anne's Gate 15 H4
SW1**
Queen Anne's Gate 67 D2
SW1
Queen Anne's Gate, 80 D3
Bexh.
Queen Anne's Gro. 65 E3
W4
Queen Annes Gro. W5 64 H2
Queen Annes Gro., 25 A7
Enf.
**Queen Anne's Pl., Enf. 25 B6
Queen Anne's Wk. 8 B6
WC1**
Queen Caroline Est. 65 J5
W6
Queen Caroline St. 65 J5
W6
Queen Elizabeth 93 D4
Gdns., Mord.
Queen Elizabeth Rd. 41 H3
E17
Queen Elizabeth Rd., 91 J2
Kings.T.
**Queen Elizabeth St. 17 F3
SE1**
Queen Elizabeth St. 68 C2
SE1
Queen Elizabeth Wk. 74 G1
SW13
Queen Elizabeth Wk., 101 D4
Wall.
Queen Elizabeths Clo. 50 A2
N16
Queen Elizabeths Dr. 32 D1
N14
Queen Elizabeths Wk. 50 A2
N16
Queen Margaret's 50 B5
Gro. N1
Queen Mary Ave., 93 A5
Mord.
Queen Mary Rd. SE19 85 H6
Queen Mary's Ave., 100 J7
Cars.
Queen of Denmark 68 J3
Ct. SE16
Queen Sq. WC1 12 B1
Queen Sq. WC1 58 E4
Queen Sq. Pl. WC1 8 B6
Queen St. EC4 13 A5
Queen St. EC4 58 J7
Queen St. N17 33 B6
Queen St. W1 15 D1
Queen St. W1 67 B1
Queen St., Bexh. 80 F3
Queen St., Croy. 101 J3
Church Rd.
Queen St. Pl. EC4 13 A6
Queen Victoria Ave., 46 G7
Wem.
**Queen Victoria St. 12 H5
EC4**
Queen Victoria St. 58 H7
EC4
Queenborough 88 G6
Gdns., Chis.
Queenborough 43 D4
Gdns., Ilf.
Queenhithe EC4 13 A5
Queenhithe EC4 58 J7
Queens Acre, Sutt. 100 A7

Queens Ave. N3 31 F7
Queens Ave. N10 40 A3
Queens Ave. N20 31 G2
Queens Ave. N21 32 H1
Queens Ave., Felt. 81 C4
Queens Ave., Grnf. 54 H6
Queens Ave., Stan. 37 E3
Queens Ave., 34 H5
Wdf.Grn.
Queen's Circ. SW8 67 B7
Queenstown Rd.
Queens Clo., Edg. 30 A5
Queens Clo., Wall. 101 B5
Queens Rd.
Queens Club Gdns. 66 B6
W14
Queens Ct. SE23 86 F2
Queens Ct., Rich. 73 J6
Queens Cres. NW5 49 A6
Queens Cres., Rich. 73 J5
Queens Dr. E10 42 A7
Queens Dr. N4 49 H2
Queens Dr. W3 55 J6
Queens Dr., Surb. 92 A7
Queens Dr., T.Ditt. 91 D7
Queen's Elm Sq. SW3 18 F4
Queens Gdns. NW4 38 J5
Queens Gdns. W2 10 C5
Queens Gdns. W2 57 F6
Queens Gdns. W5 55 F5
Queen's Gdns., 72 E1
Houns.
Queen's Gate SW7 14 D4
Queen's Gate SW7 66 F3
**Queen's Gate Gdns. 14 D6
SW7**
Queen's Gate Gdns. 66 F3
SW7
Queens Gate Gdns. 74 H4
SW15
Upper Richmond Rd.
**Queen's Gate Ms. 14 D4
SW7**
Queen's Gate Ms. 66 F3
SW7
Queen's Gate Pl. SW7 14 D6
Queen's Gate Pl. SW7 66 F3
**Queen's Gate Pl. Ms. 14 D6
SW7**
Queen's Gate Pl. Ms. 66 F3
SW7
**Queen's Gate Ter. 14 C5
SW7**
Queen's Gate Ter. 66 F3
SW7
Queen's Gro. NW8 57 G1
Queen's Gro. Ms. 57 G1
NW8
Queen's Gro.
Queens Gro. Rd. E4 34 G3
Queen's Head St. N1 58 H1
Queens Head Yd. SE1 17 B2
Queens Ho., Tedd. 82 C6
Queens La. N10 40 B3
Queens Mkt. E13 60 J1
Green St.
Queens Ms. W2 10 A5
Queens Par. N11 31 J5
Colney Hatch La.
Queens Par. W5 55 J6
Queens Pk. Ct. W10 57 A3
Queens Pk. Gdns., 81 A3
Felt.
Vernon Rd.
Queens Pas., Chis. 88 E6
High St.
Queens Pl., Mord. 93 D4
Queen's Prom., 91 G3
Kings.T.
Portsmouth Rd.
Queens Reach, E.Mol. 91 B4
Queens Ride SW13 74 G3
Queens Ride SW15 74 J3
Queen's Ride, Rich. 83 B1
Queens Ri., Rich. 73 J6
Queens Rd. E11 42 D7
Queens Rd. E13 60 H1
Queens Rd. E17 41 J6
Queens Rd. N3 39 F1
Queens Rd. N9 33 E3
Queens Rd. N11 32 E7
Queens Rd. NW4 38 J5
Queens Rd. SE14 77 E1
Queens Rd. SE15 77 E1
Queens Rd. SW14 74 D3
Queens Rd. SW19 84 C6
Queens Rd. W5 55 H6
Queens Rd., Bark. 52 F6

Queens Rd., Barn. 23 A3
Queens Rd., Beck. 95 H2
Queens Rd., Brom. 96 G2
Queens Rd., Buck.H. 34 H2
Queens Rd., Chis. 88 E6
Queen's Rd., Croy. 94 H6
Queens Rd., Enf. 25 B4
Queens Rd., Felt. 81 B1
Queens Rd., Hmptn. 81 H4
Queen's Rd., Houns. 72 H3
Queens Rd., Ilf. 52 F6
Queens Rd., Kings.T. 83 A7
Queens Rd., Loug. 27 B3
Queens Rd., Mitch. 93 G2
Queens Rd., Mord. 93 D4
Queens Rd., N.Mal. 92 F4
Queens Rd., Rich. 73 J6
Queens Rd., Sthl. 63 D2
Queens Rd., Tedd. 82 B6
Queens Rd., T.Ditt. 91 C5
Queens Rd., Twick. 73 C7
Queens Rd., Wall. 101 B5
Queen's Rd., Well. 80 B2
Queens Rd. W. E13 60 G2
Queen's Row SE17 **21 B5**
Queen's Row SE17 68 A6
Queens Ter. E13 60 H1
Queen's Ter. NW8 57 G1
Queens Ter., Islw. 73 D4
Queens Ter. Cotts. W7 64 B2
  Boston Rd.
Queens Wk. E4 34 D1
  The Grn. Wk.
Queens Wk. NW9 47 C2
Queen's Wk. SW1 **15 F2**
Queen's Wk. SW1 67 C1
Queens Wk. W5 55 F4
Queens Wk., Har. 37 B4
Queens Wk., Ruis. 45 D3
Queens Way NW4 38 J5
Queens Way, Felt. 81 C4
Queens Well Ave. N20 31 H4
Queen's Wd. Rd. N10 40 B6
Queens Yd. WC1 **7 G6**
Queensberry Ms. W. **18 E1**
SW7
Queensberry Pl. SW7 18 E1
Queensberry Pl. SW7 66 G4
Queensberry Way **18 E1**
SW7
Queensborough Ms. **10 C5**
W2
Queensborough Pas. **10 C5**
W2
Queensborough **10 C5**
Studios W2
Queensborough Ter. **10 B5**
W2
Queensborough Ter. 57 E7
  W2
Queensbridge Pk., 73 B5
  Islw.
Queensbridge Rd. E2 **9 G2**
Queensbridge Rd. E2 50 C7
Queensbridge Rd. E8 50 C7
Queensbury Pl., Rich. 73 G5
  Friars La.
Queensbury Rd. NW9 38 D7
Queensbury Rd., 55 J2
  Wem.
Queensbury Sta. Par., 37 J3
  Edg.
Queensbury St. N1 49 J7
Queenscourt, Wem. 46 H4
Queenscroft Rd. SE9 79 A6
Queensdale Cres. 66 A1
  W11
Queensdale Pl. W11 66 B1
Queensdale Rd. W11 66 A1
Queensdale Wk. W11 66 B1
Queensdown Rd. E5 50 E4
Queensgate Gdns., 97 G1
  Chis.
Queensgate Pl. NW6 48 D7
Queensland Ave. N18 32 J6
Queensland Ave. 93 E1
  SW19
Queensland Pl. N7 49 G4
  Queensland Rd.
Queensland Rd. N7 49 G4
Queensmead NW8 57 G1
Queensmead Rd., 96 F2
  Brom.
Queensmere Clo. 84 A2
  SW19
Queensmere Rd. 84 A2
  SW19
Queensmill Rd. SW6 66 A7

Queensthorpe Rd. 86 G4
  SE26
Queenstown Ms. 76 B2
  SW8
  Queenstown Rd.
Queenstown Rd. **19 D6**
SW8
Queenstown Rd. 67 B6
  SW8
Queensville Rd. 76 D7
  SW12
Queensway W2 **10 B4**
Queensway W2 57 E6
Queensway, Croy. 101 F6
Queensway, Enf. 25 E4
Queensway, Orp. 97 F5
Queensway, Sun. 90 B2
Queensway, W.Wick. 103 E3
Queenswood Ave. 42 C1
  E17
Queenswood Ave., 81 H6
  Hmptn.
Queenswood Ave., 72 F2
  Houns.
Queenswood Ave. 94 G5
  Th.Hth.
Queenswood Ave., 101 D4
  Wall.
Queenswood Gdns. 51 H1
  E11
Queenswood Pk. N3 39 B2
Queenswood Rd. 86 G3
  SE23
Queenswood Rd., Sid. 79 J5
Quemerford Rd. N7 49 F5
Quentin Pl. SE13 78 E3
Quentin Rd. SE13 78 E3
Quernmore Clo., 87 G6
  Brom.
Quernmore Rd. N4 40 G6
Quernmore Rd., 87 G6
  Brom.
Querrin St. SW6 75 F2
Quex Ms. NW6 57 D1
  Quex Rd.
Quex Rd. NW6 57 D1
Quick St. N1 **8 H2**
Quick St. N1 58 H2
Quicks Rd. SW19 84 E7
Quickswood NW3 48 H7
  King Henry's Rd.
Quiet Nook, Kes. 104 A3
Quill La. SW15 75 A4
Quill St. W5 55 H3
Quilp St. SE1 **16 J3**
Quilter St. E2 **9 H3**
Quilter St. E2 59 D3
Quinta Dr., Barn. 22 H5
Quintin Ave. SW20 93 C1
Quintin Clo., Pnr. 36 B5
  Eastcote High Rd.
Quinton Clo., Beck. 96 C3
Quinton Clo., Houns. 63 B7
Quinton Clo., Wall. 101 B4
Quinton Rd., T.Ditt. 98 D1
Quinton St. SW18 84 F2
Quixley St. E14 60 D7
Quorn Rd. SE22 77 B4

R

Rabbit Row W8 66 D1
  Kensington Mall
Rabbits Rd. E12 52 B4
Rabournmead Dr., 45 E5
  Nthlt.
Raby Rd., N.Mal. 92 D4
Raby St. E14 59 H6
  Salmon La.
Raccoon Way, Houns. 72 C2
Rachel Pt. E5 50 D4
  Muir Rd.
Rackham Ms. SW16 85 C6
  Westcote Rd.
Racton St. SW6 66 D6
Radbourne Ave. W5 64 F4
Radbourne Clo. E5 50 G4
  Overbury St.
Radbourne Cres. E17 42 D2
Radbourne Rd. SW12 76 C7
Radcliffe Ave. NW10 56 G2
Radcliffe Ave., Enf. 24 J1
Radcliffe Gdns., 100 H7
  Cars.
Radcliffe Ms., Hmptn. 81 J5
  Taylor Clo.

Radcliffe Path SW8 76 C2
  St. Rule St.
Radcliffe Rd. N21 32 H1
Radcliffe Rd., Croy. 102 C2
Radcliffe Rd., Har. 37 D2
Radcliffe Sq. SW15 75 A6
Radcliffe Way, Nthlt. 54 D3
Radcot Pt. SE23 86 G3
Radcot St. SE11 **20 F4**
Raddington Rd. W10 57 B5
Radfield Way, Sid. 79 G7
Radford Rd. SE13 78 C5
Radford Way, Bark. 61 J3
Radipole Rd. SW6 75 C1
Radland Rd. E16 60 F6
Radlet Ave. SE26 86 E3
Radlett Clo. E7 51 F6
Radlett Pl. NW8 57 H1
Radley Ave., Ilf. 52 J4
Radley Ct. SE16 68 G2
Radley Gdns., Har. 37 H4
Radley Ms. W8 66 D3
Radley Rd. N17 41 B2
Radley's La. E18 42 G2
Radleys Mead, Dag. 53 H6
Radlix Rd. E10 51 A1
Radnor Ave., Har. 37 B5
Radnor Ave., Well. 80 B5
Radnor Clo., Chis. 88 H6
  Homewood Cres.
Radnor Clo., Mitch. 94 E4
Radnor Cres. SE18 71 A7
Radnor Cres., Ilf. 43 C5
Radnor Gdns., Enf. 25 B1
Radnor Gdns., Twick. 82 C2
Radnor Ms. W2 **10 F4**
Radnor Pl. W2 **10 G4**
Radnor Pl. W2 57 H6
Radnor Rd. NW6 57 B1
Radnor Rd. SE15 **21 H7**
Radnor Rd. SE15 68 D7
Radnor Rd., Har. 37 A5
Radnor Rd., Twick. 82 C1
Radnor St. EC1 **9 A4**
Radnor St. EC1 58 J3
Radnor Ter. W14 66 C4
Radnor Wk. E14 69 A4
  Inglewood Clo.
Radnor Wk. SW3 **18 H4**
Radnor Wk. SW3 66 H5
Radnor Wk., Croy. 95 H6
Radnor Way NW10 56 B4
Radstock Ave., Har. 37 D3
Radstock St. SW11 66 H7
Raebarn Gdns., Barn. 22 H5
Raeburn Ave., Surb. 99 B1
Raeburn Clo. NW11 39 F6
Raeburn Clo., 82 G7
  Kings.T.
Raeburn Rd., Edg. 38 A2
Raeburn Rd., Sid. 79 H6
Raeburn St. SW2 76 E4
Rafford Way, Brom. 96 H2
Raft Rd. SW18 75 D4
  North Pas.
Raggleswood, Chis. 97 D1
Raglan Clo., Houns. 72 D1
  Vickers Way
Raglan Ct. SE12 78 G5
Raglan Ct., S.Croy. 101 H5
Raglan Ct., Wem. 46 J4
Raglan Gdns., Wat. 28 B1
Raglan Rd. E17 42 C5
Raglan Rd. SE18 70 F5
Raglan Rd., Belv. 71 F5
Raglan Rd., Brom. 96 J4
Raglan Rd., Enf. 25 B7
Raglan St. NW5 49 B6
Raglan Ter., Har. 45 H4
Raglan Way, Nthlt. 45 J6
Ragley Clo. W3 65 C2
  Avenue Rd.
Raider Clo., Rom. 44 G1
Railey Ms. NW5 49 C5
Railshead Rd., Twick. 73 E4
Railton Rd. SE24 76 G4
Railway App. SE1 **17 C2**
Railway App. SE1 68 A1
Railway App., Har. 37 C4
Railway App., Twick. 73 D7
Railway App., Wall. 101 B6
Railway Ave. SE16 68 F2
Railway Ms. E3 60 A3
  Wellington Way
Railway Ms. W10 57 B6
  Ladbroke Gro.
Railway Pas., Tedd. 82 D6
  Victoria Rd.

Railway Pl. SW19 84 C6
  Hartfield Rd.
Railway Pl., Belv. 71 G3
Railway Ri. SE22 77 B4
  Grove Vale
Railway Rd., Tedd. 82 C4
Railway Side SW13 74 E3
Railway St. N1 **8 B2**
Railway St. N1 58 E2
Railway St., Rom. 53 C1
Railway Ter. SE13 78 B5
  Ladywell Rd.
Railway Ter., Felt. 81 A1
Rainborough Clo. 47 C6
  NW10
Rainbow Ave. E14 69 B5
Rainbow St. SE5 **21 D7**
Rainbow St. SE5 68 B7
Raine St. E1 68 E1
Rainham Clo. SE9 79 G6
Rainham Clo. SW11 75 H6
Rainham Rd. NW10 56 J3
Rainham Rd. N., Dag. 53 G2
Rainham Rd. S., Dag. 53 H4
Rainhill Way E3 60 A3
Rainsborough Ave. 68 H4
  SE8
Rainsford Clo., Stan. 29 F5
Rainsford Rd. NW10 56 B2
Rainsford St. W2 **10 G3**
Rainton Rd. SE7 69 G5
Rainville Rd. W6 65 J6
Raisins Hill, Pnr. 36 C3
Raith Ave. N14 32 D3
Raleana Rd. E14 69 C1
Raleigh Ave., Hayes 54 B5
Raleigh Ave., Wall. 101 D4
Raleigh Clo. NW4 38 J5
Raleigh Clo., Pnr. 36 D7
Raleigh Ct., Wall. 101 B6
Raleigh Dr. N20 31 H3
Raleigh Dr., Esher 98 A5
Raleigh Dr., Surb. 99 C1
Raleigh Gdns. SW2 76 F6
  Brixton Hill
Raleigh Gdns., Mitch. 93 J3
Raleigh Ms., Orp. 104 J5
  Osgood Ave.
Raleigh Rd. N8 40 G4
Raleigh Rd. SE20 86 G7
Raleigh Rd., Enf. 25 A4
Raleigh Rd., Rich. 73 J3
Raleigh Rd., Sthl. 63 E5
Raleigh St. N1 58 H1
Raleigh Way N14 32 D1
Raleigh Way, Felt. 81 C4
Ralph Ct. W2 10 B3
Ralph Perring Ct., 96 A4
  Beck.
Ralston St. SW3 **18 J4**
Ralston Way, Wat. 28 D2
Ram Pas., Kings.T. 91 G2
  High St.
Ram Pl. E9 50 F6
  Chatham Pl.
Ram St. SW18 75 E5
Rama Clo. SW16 85 E7
Rama Ct., Har. 46 B2
Ramac Ind. Est. SE7 69 G4
Ramac Way SE7 69 H5
Rambler Clo. SW16 85 C4
Ramilles Clo. SW2 76 E6
Ramillies Pl. W1 **11 F4**
Ramillies Pl. W1 58 C6
Ramillies Rd. NW7 30 E2
Ramillies Rd. W4 65 D4
Ramillies Rd., Sid. 80 B6
Ramillies St. W1 **11 F4**
Rampart St. E1 59 E6
  Commercial Rd.
Rampayne St. SW1 **19 H3**
Rampayne St. SW1 67 D5
Rampton Clo. E4 34 A3
Rams Gro., Rom. 44 E4
Ramsay Pl., Har. 46 B1
Ramsay Rd. E7 51 E4
Ramsay Rd. W3 65 C3
Ramscroft Clo. N9 25 B7
Ramsdale Rd. SW17 85 A5
Ramsden Rd. N11 31 J3
Ramsden Rd. SW12 76 A6
Ramsey Clo. NW9 38 F6
  West Hendon Bdy.
Ramsey Clo., Grnf. 46 A5
Ramsey Ho., Wem. 46 H6
Ramsey Rd., Th.Hth. 94 F6
Ramsey St. E2 **9 J5**
Ramsey St. E2 59 D4

Ramsey Wk. N1	50	A6
Marquess Est.		
Ramsey Way N14	24	C7
Ramsgate St. E8	50	C6
Dalston La.		
Ramsgill App., Ilf.	43	J4
Ramsgill Dr., Ilf.	43	J5
Ramulis Dr., Hayes	54	D4
Ramus Wd. Ave.,	104	H5
Orp.		
Rancliffe Gdns. SE9	79	B4
Rancliffe Rd. E6	61	B2
Randall Ave. NW2	47	E2
Randall Clo. SW11	75	H1
Randall Clo., Erith	71	J6
Randall Pl. SE10	69	C7
Randall Rd. SE11	**20**	**C2**
Randall Rd. SE11	67	F5
Randall Row SE11	**20**	**C2**
Randell's Rd. N1	58	E1
Randle Rd., Rich.	82	F4
Randlesdown Rd. SE6	87	K4
Randolph App. E16	60	J6
Baxter Rd.		
Randolph Ave. W9	**6**	**A2**
Randolph Ave. W9	57	E2
Randolph Clo., Bexh.	80	J3
Randolph Clo.,	83	C5
Kings.T.		
Randolph Cres. W9	**6**	**C6**
Randolph Cres. W9	57	F4
Randolph Gdns. NW6	**6**	**A2**
Randolph Gdns. NW6	57	E2
Randolph Gro., Rom.	44	C5
Donald Dr.		
Randolph Ho., Croy.	101	J1
Randolph Ms. W9	**6**	**D6**
Randolph Ms. W9	57	F4
Randolph Rd. W9	**6**	**C6**
Randolph Rd. W9	57	F4
Randolph Rd. E17	42	B5
Randolph Rd., Sthl.	63	F2
Randolph St. NW1	49	C7
Randon Clo., Har.	36	H2
Ranelagh Ave. SW6	75	C3
Ranelagh Ave. SW13	74	G2
Ranelagh Clo., Edg.	30	A4
Ranelagh Dr., Edg.	30	A4
Ranelagh Dr., Twick.	73	E4
Ranelagh Gdns. E11	42	J5
Ranelagh Gdns. SW6	75	C3
Ranelagh Gdns. W4	65	C7
Grove Pk. Gdns.		
Ranelagh Gdns. W6	65	F3
Ranelagh Gdns., Ilf.	52	C1
Ranelagh Gro. SW1	**19**	**C3**
Ranelagh Gro. SW1	67	A5
Ranelagh Ms. W5	64	G2
Ranelagh Rd.		
Ranelagh Pl., N.Mal.	92	E5
Rodney Rd.		
Ranelagh Rd. E6	61	D1
Ranelagh Rd. E11	51	E4
Ranelagh Rd. E15	60	E1
Ranelagh Rd. N17	41	B3
Ranelagh Rd. N22	40	F1
Ranelagh Rd. NW10	56	F2
Ranelagh Rd. SW1	**19**	**G4**
Ranelagh Rd. W5	64	G2
Ranelagh Rd., Sthl.	63	D1
Ranelagh Rd., Wem.	46	G6
Ranfurly Rd., Sutt.	100	D2
Rangefield Rd., Brom.	87	E5
Rangemoor Rd. N15	41	C5
Rangers Rd. E4	26	E7
Rangers Rd., Loug.	26	G7
Rangers Sq. SE10	78	D1
Rangeworth Pl., Sid.	88	J3
Priestlands Pk. Rd.		
Rankin Clo. NW9	38	E3
Ranleigh Gdns., Bexh.	71	F7
Ranmere St. SW12	85	B1
Ormeley Rd.		
Ranmoor Clo., Har.	37	A4
Ranmoor Gdns., Har.	37	A4
Ranmore Ave., Croy.	102	C3
Rannoch Clo., Edg.	30	B2
Rannoch Rd. W6	65	J6
Rannock Ave. NW9	38	D7
Ranskill Rd., Borwd.	22	A1
Ransom Rd. SE7	69	J5
Harvey Gdns.		
Ransom Wk. SE7	69	J5
Woolwich Rd.		
Ranston St. NW1	**10**	**G1**
Ranulf Rd. NW2	48	C4
Ranwell Clo. E3	59	J1
Beale Rd.		

Ranwell St. E3	59	J1
Ranworth Rd. N9	33	F2
Ranyard Clo., Chess.	98	J3
Raphael St. SW7	**14**	**J4**
Raphael St. SW7	66	J2
Rashleigh St. SW8	76	B2
Peardon St.		
Rasper Rd. N20	31	F2
Rastell Ave. SW2	85	D2
Ratcliff Rd. E7	51	J5
Ratcliffe Clo. SE12	78	G7
Ratcliffe Cross St. E1	59	G6
Ratcliffe La. E14	59	H6
Ratcliffe Orchard E1	59	G7
Rathbone Mkt. E16	60	F5
Barking Rd.		
Rathbone Pl. W1	**11**	**H2**
Rathbone Pl. W1	58	D5
Rathbone Pt. E5	50	D4
Nolan Way		
Rathbone St. E16	60	F5
Rathbone St. W1	**11**	**G2**
Rathbone St. W1	58	C5
Rathcoole Ave. N8	40	F5
Rathcoole Gdns. N8	40	F5
Rathfern Rd. SE6	86	J1
Rathgar Ave. W13	64	E1
Rathgar Clo. N3	39	C2
Rathgar Rd. SW9	76	H3
Coldharbour La.		
Rathlin Wk. N1	49	J6
Marquess Est.		
Rathmell Dr. SW4	76	D6
Rathmore Rd. SE7	69	H5
Rattray Rd. SW2	76	G4
Raul Rd. SE15	77	D1
Raveley St. NW5	49	C4
Raven Clo. NW9	38	E2
Eagle Dr.		
Raven Ct. E5	50	D3
Stellman Clo.		
Raven Rd. E18	42	J2
Raven Row E11	59	E5
Ravenet St. SW11	76	B1
Strasburg Rd.		
Ravenfield Rd. SW17	84	J3
Ravenhill Rd. E13	60	J2
Ravenna Rd. SW15	75	A5
Ravenor Pk. Rd.,	54	H3
Grnf.		
Ravens Clo., Brom.	96	F2
Ravens Clo., Enf.	25	B2
Ravens Ms. SE12	78	G5
Ravens Way		
Ravens Way SE12	78	G5
Ravensbourne Ave.	87	D7
Brom.		
Ravensbourne Gdns.	55	E5
W13		
Ravensbourne Gdns.,	43	D1
Ilf.		
Ravensbourne Pk.	78	A7
SE6		
Ravensbourne Pk.	77	J7
Cres. SE6		
Ravensbourne Pl.	78	B2
SE13		
Ravensbourne Rd.	86	J1
SE6		
Ravensbourne Rd.,	96	G3
Brom.		
Ravensbourne Rd.,	73	F6
Twick.		
Ravensbury Ave.,	93	F5
Mord.		
Ravensbury Gro.,	93	G4
Mitch.		
Ravensbury La.,	93	G4
Mitch.		
Ravensbury Path,	93	G4
Mitch.		
Ravensbury Rd.	84	D2
SW18		
Ravensbury Rd., Orp.	97	J3
Ravensbury Ter.	84	E1
SW18		
Ravenscar Rd., Brom.	87	E4
Ravenscar Rd., Surb.	98	J2
Ravenscourt Ave. W6	65	G4
Ravenscourt Gdns.	65	G4
W6		
Ravenscourt Pk. W6	65	G3
Ravenscourt Pl. W6	65	H4
Ravenscourt Rd. W6	65	H4
Ravenscourt Sq. W6	65	G3
Ravenscraig Rd. N11	32	B4
Ravenscroft Ave.	39	C7
NW11		

Ravenscroft Ave.,	46	H1
Wem.		
Ravenscroft Clo. E16	60	G5
Ravenscroft Cres. SE9	88	C3
Ravenscroft Pk., Barn.	23	A4
Ravenscroft Rd. E16	60	G5
Ravenscroft Rd. W4	65	C4
Ravenscroft Rd.,	95	F2
Beck.		
Ravenscroft St. E2	**9**	**G2**
Ravenscroft St. E2	59	C2
Ravensdale Ave. N12	31	F4
Ravensdale Gdns.	86	A7
SE19		
Ravensdale Rd. N16	41	C7
Ravensdale Rd.,	72	E3
Houns.		
Ravensdon St. SE11	**20**	**F4**
Ravensdon St. SE11	67	G5
Ravensfield Clo., Dag.	53	D4
Ravensfield Gdns.,	99	E5
Epsom		
Ravenshaw St. NW6	48	C5
Ravenshill, Chis.	97	E1
Ravenshurst Ave.	38	J4
NW4		
Ravenside Clo. N18	33	G5
Ravenslea Rd. SW12	75	J7
Ravensmead Rd.,	87	D7
Brom.		
Ravensmede Way	65	F4
W4		
Ravenstone SE17	**21**	**E4**
Ravenstone Rd. N8	40	G3
Ravenstone Rd. NW9	38	F6
West Hendon Bdy.		
Ravenstone St. SW12	85	A1
Ravenswood, Bex.	89	E1
Ravenswood Ave.,	98	J2
Surb.		
Ravenswood Ave.,	103	C1
W.Wick.		
Ravenswood Ct.,	83	B6
Kings.T.		
Ravenswood Cres.,	45	F2
Har.		
Ravenswood Cres.,	103	C1
W.Wick.		
Ravenswood Gdns.,	73	B1
Islw.		
Ravenswood Pk.,	28	A6
Nthwd.		
Ravenswood Rd. E17	42	C4
Ravenswood Rd.	76	B7
SW12		
Ravenswood Rd.,	101	H3
Croy.		
Ravensworth Rd.	56	H3
NW10		
Ravensworth Rd. SE9	88	C3
Ravent Rd. SE11	**20**	**D1**
Ravent Rd. SE11	67	F4
Ravey St. EC2	**9**	**D5**
Ravine Gro. SE18	70	H6
Rawlings Clo., Orp.	104	J5
Rawlings St. SW3	**18**	**J1**
Rawlings St. SW3	66	J4
Rawlins Clo. N3	39	B3
Rawlins Clo., S.Croy.	102	H7
Rawnsley Ave.,	93	G5
Mitch.		
Rawreth Wk. N1	58	J1
Basire St.		
Rawson St. SW11	76	A1
Strasburg Rd.		
Rawsthorne Clo. E16	70	C1
Kennard St.		
Rawstone Wk. E13	60	G2
Grasmere Rd.		
Rawstorne Pl. EC1	**8**	**G3**
Rawstorne St. EC1	**8**	**G3**
Rawstorne St. EC1	58	H3
Ray Clo., Chess.	98	F6
Mansfield Rd.		
Ray Gdns., Bark.	62	A2
Ray Gdns., Stan.	29	E5
Ray Lo. Rd., Wdf.Grn.	34	J6
Ray Rd., W.Mol.	90	H5
Ray St. EC1	**8**	**F6**
Ray St. EC1	58	G4
Ray St. Bri. EC1	**8**	**F6**
Ray Wk. N7	49	F2
Andover Rd.		
Raydean Rd., Barn.	23	E5
Raydon St. N19	49	B2
Raydons Gdns., Dag.	53	E5
Raydons Rd., Dag.	53	E5
Rayfield Clo., Brom.	97	B6

Rayford Ave. SE12	78	F7
Rayleas Clo. SE18	79	E1
Rayleigh Ave., Tedd.	82	B6
Rayleigh Clo. N13	33	A3
Rayleigh Rd.		
Rayleigh Ct., Kings.T.	91	J2
Rayleigh Ri., S.Croy.	102	B6
Rayleigh Rd. N13	32	J3
Rayleigh Rd. SW19	93	C1
Rayleigh Rd.,	34	J6
Wdf.Grn.		
Raymead Ave.,	94	G5
Th.Hth.		
Raymere Gdns. SE18	70	G7
Raymond Ave. E18	42	F3
Raymond Ave. W13	64	D3
Raymond Bldgs. WC1	**12**	**D1**
Raymond Clo. SE26	86	F5
Raymond Rd. E13	51	J7
Raymond Rd. SW19	66	H6
Raymond Rd., Beck.	95	H4
Raymond Rd., Ilf.	43	G7
Raymond Way, Esher	98	D6
Raymouth Rd. SE16	68	E4
Rayne Ct. E18	42	F4
Rayner Twr. E10	42	A7
Rayners Clo., Wem.	46	G5
Rayners Ct., Har.	45	G1
Rayners Cres., Nthlt.	54	B3
Rayners Gdns., Nthlt.	54	B2
Rayners La., Har.	45	G1
Rayners La., Pnr.	36	F5
Rayners Rd. SW15	75	B5
Raynes Ave. E11	42	J4
Raynham Ave. N18	33	D6
Raynham Rd. W6	65	H4
Raynham Ter. N18	33	D5
Raynor Clo., Sthl.	63	F1
Raynor Pl. N1	58	J1
Elizabeth Ave.		
Raynton Clo., Har.	45	E1
Rays Ave. N18	33	F4
Rays Rd. N18	33	F4
Rays Rd., W.Wick.	96	C7
Raywood St. SW8	76	B1
Gladstone Ter.		
Reachview Clo. NW1	49	C7
Baynes St.		
Reade Wk. NW10	47	E7
Denbigh Clo.		
Reading La. E8	50	E6
Reading Rd., Nthlt.	45	H5
Reading Rd., Sutt.	100	F5
Reading Way NW7	31	A5
Reads Clo., Ilf.	52	E3
Chapel Rd.		
Reapers Clo. NW1	58	D1
Crofters Way		
Reapers Way, Islw.	73	A5
Hall Rd.		
Reardon Path E1	68	E1
Reardon St. E1	68	E1
Reaston St. SE14	68	G7
Rebecca Ter. SE16	68	F3
Gomm Rd.		
Reckitt Rd. W4	65	E5
Record St. SE15	68	F6
Recovery St. SW17	84	H5
Recreation Ave.,	44	J5
Rom.		
Recreation Rd. SE26	86	G4
Recreation Rd., Brom.	96	F2
Recreation Rd., Sid.	88	J3
Recreation Rd., Sthl.	63	E4
Recreation Way,	94	E3
Mitch.		
Rector St. N1	58	J1
Rectory Clo. E4	34	A3
Rectory Clo. N3	39	C2
Rectory Clo. SW20	92	J3
Rectory Clo., Sid.	89	B4
Rectory Clo., Stan.	29	E5
Rectory Clo., Surb.	98	F1
Rectory Cres. E11	42	J6
Rectory Fld. Cres. SE7	69	J7
Rectory Gdns. N8	40	E4
Rectory Gdns. SW4	76	C3
Rectory Gdns., Nthlt.	54	F1
Rectory Grn., Beck.	95	J1
Rectory Gro. SW4	76	C3
Rectory Gro., Croy.	101	H2
Rectory Gro., Hmptn.	61	F4
Rectory La. SW17	85	A6
Rectory La., Edg.	30	A6
Rectory La., Loug.	27	D2
Rectory La., Sid.	89	B4
Rectory La., Stan.	29	E5

Rectory La., Surb. 98 E1
Rectory La., Wall. 101 C3
Rectory Orchard 84 B4
SW19
Rectory Pk. Ave., 54 E3
Nthlt.
Rectory Pl. SE18 70 D4
Rectory Rd. E12 52 C5
Rectory Rd. E17 42 B3
Rectory Rd. N16 50 C2
Rectory Rd. SW13 74 G2
Rectory Rd. W3 65 B1
Rectory Rd., Beck. 96 A1
Rectory Rd., Dag. 53 G6
Rectory Rd., Hayes 54 A4
Rectory Rd., Houns. 72 B1
Rectory Rd., Kes. 104 A7
Rectory Rd., Sthl. 63 F3
Rectory Rd., Sutt. 100 D3
Rectory Sq. E1 59 G5
Reculver Ms. N18 33 D4
Lyndhurst Rd.
Reculver Rd. SE16 68 G5
Red Anchor Clo. SW3 18 G6
Red Barracks Rd. SE18 70 C4
Red Cedars Rd., Orp. 97 H7
Red Hill, Chis. 88 E5
Red Ho. La., Bexh. 80 D4
Red Ho. Rd., Croy. 94 D6
Red La., Esher 98 D6
Red Lion Clo. SE17 21 B5
Red Lion Ct. EC4 12 F4
Red Lion Ct. EC4 58 G6
Red Lion Hill N2 39 G2
Red Lion La. SE18 79 D1
Red Lion Pl. SE18 79 D1
Shooter's Hill Rd.
Red Lion Rd., Surb. 98 J2
Red Lion Row SE17 21 A5
Red Lion Row SE17 67 J6
Red Lion Sq. SW18 75 D5
Wandsworth High St.
Red Lion Sq. WC1 12 C2
Red Lion Sq., WC1 58 F5
Red Lion St. WC1 12 C1
Red Lion St. WC1 58 F5
Red Lion St., Rich. 73 G5
Red Lion Yd. W1 15 C1
Red Lo. Rd., W.Wick. 103 C1
Red Oak Clo., Orp. 104 E3
Red Path E9 50 J6
Eastway
Red Pl. W1 11 B5
Red Post Hill SE21 77 A5
Red Post Hill SE24 77 A4
Redan Pl. W2 10 A4
Redan Pl. W2 57 E6
Redan St. W14 66 A3
Redan Ter. SE5 76 J2
Flaxman Rd.
Redberry Gro. SE26 86 F3
Redbourne Ave. N3 39 D1
Redbridge Gdns. SE5 68 B7
Redbridge La. E., Ilf. 43 A6
Redbridge La. W. E11 42 H6
Redburn St. SW3 18 J5
Redburn St. SW3 66 J6
Redcar Clo., Nthlt. 45 H6
Redcar St. SE5 67 J7
Redcastle Clo. E1 59 F7
Redchurch St. E2 9 F5
Redchurch St. E2 59 C4
Redcliffe Gdns. SW10 18 B4
Redcliffe Gdns. SW10 66 E5
Redcliffe Gdns., Ilf. 52 D1
Redcliffe Ms. SW10 18 B4
Redcliffe Ms. SW10 66 E5
Redcliffe Pl. SW10 18 C6
Redcliffe Pl. SW10 66 F6
Redcliffe Rd. SW10 18 C4
Redcliffe Rd. SW10 66 F5
Redcliffe Sq. SW10 18 B4
Redcliffe Sq. SW10 66 E5
Redcliffe St. SW10 18 B5
Redcliffe St. SW10 66 E6
Redclose Ave., Mord. 93 D5
Chalgrove Ave.
Redclyffe Rd. E6 60 J1
Redcroft Rd., Sthl. 54 J7
Redcross Way SE1 17 A3
Redcross Way SE1 67 J2
Reddings, The NW7 30 F3
Reddings Clo. NW7 30 F4
Reddins Rd. SE15 21 G2
Reddins Rd. SE15 68 D6
Reddons Rd., Beck. 86 H7
Rede Pl. W2 57 D6
Chepstow Pl.

Redesdale Gdns., 64 D7
Islw.
Redesdale St. SW3 18 H5
Redesdale St. SW3 66 H6
Redfern Ave., Houns. 72 G7
Redfern Rd. NW10 47 E7
Redfern Rd. SE6 78 C7
Redfield La. SW5 66 D4
Redford Ave., Th.Hth. 94 F4
Redford Ave., Wall. 101 E6
Redford Wk. N1 58 H1
Britannia Row
Redgate Dr., Brom. 103 H2
Redgate Ter. SW15 75 A6
Lytton Gro.
Redgrave Clo., Croy. 95 C6
Redgrave Rd. SW15 75 A3
Redhill Dr., Edg. 38 C2
Redhill St. NW1 7 E3
Redhill St. NW1 58 B2
Redington Gdns. NW3 48 E4
Redington Rd. NW3 48 E4
Redlands Ct., Brom. 87 F7
Redlands Gdns., 90 F4
W.Mol.
Dunstable Rd.
Redlands Rd., Enf. 25 H1
Redlands Way SW2 76 F7
Redlaw Way SE16 21 J4
Redleaf Clo., Belv. 71 G6
Redlees Clo., Islw. 73 D4
Redman Clo., Nthlt. 54 C2
Redman's Rd. E1 59 F5
Redmead La. E1 17 H2
Redmore Rd. W6 65 H4
Redpoll Way, Erith 71 D2
Redriff Est. SE16 68 H3
Redriff Rd. SE16 68 G3
Redriff Rd., Rom. 44 H2
Redriffe Rd. E13 60 F1
Redroofs Clo., Beck. 96 B1
Redruth Clo. N22 32 F7
Palmerston Rd.
Redruth Rd. E9 59 F1
Redstart Clo. E6 61 B5
Columbine Ave.
Redstart Clo. SE14 68 H7
Southerngate Way
Redston Rd. N8 40 C4
Redvers Rd. N22 40 G2
Redvers St. N1 9 E3
Redwald Rd. E5 50 G4
Redway Dr., Twick. 72 J7
Redwing Path SE28 70 G2
Whinchat Rd.
Redwood Clo. N14 24 D7
The Vale
Redwood Clo. SE16 68 H1
Redwood Clo., Wat. 28 C4
Redwood Est., Houns. 63 B6
Redwood Twr. E11 51 D3
Hollydown Way
Redwood Wk., Surb. 98 G1
Redwood Way, Barn. 23 A5
Redwoods SW15 83 G1
Redwoods Clo., 34 H2
Buck.H.
Beech La.
Reece Ms. SW7 18 E1
Reece Ms. SW7 66 G4
Reed Ave., Orp. 104 H3
Reed Clo. E16 60 G5
Reed Clo. SE12 78 G5
Reed Rd. N17 41 C2
Reede Gdns., Dag. 53 H5
Reede Rd.
Reede Rd., Dag. 53 G6
Reede Way, Dag. 53 H6
Reedham Clo. N17 41 E4
Reedham St. SE15 77 D2
Reedholm Vill. N16 50 A4
Winston Rd.
Reeds Pl. NW1 49 C7
Royal College St.
Reedworth St. SE11 20 F2
Reedworth St. SE11 67 G4
Reenglass Rd., Stan. 29 G4
Rees Gdns., Croy. 95 C6
Rees St. N1 58 J1
Reesland Clo. E12 52 D6
Reets Fm. Clo. NW9 38 E6
Reeves Ave. NW9 38 D7
Reeves Cor., Croy. 101 H2
Roman Way
Reeves Ms. W1 11 B6
Reeves Ms. W1 58 A7
Reeves Rd. E3 60 B4
Reeves Rd. SE18 70 E6

Reform Row N17 41 C2
Reform St. SW11 75 J2
Regal Clo. E1 13 J1
Regal Clo. W5 55 G5
Regal Ct. N18 33 C5
College Clo.
Regal Cres., Wall. 101 B3
Regal La. NW1 58 A1
Regents Pk. Rd.
Regal Way, Har. 37 H6
Regan Way N1 9 D2
Regan Way N1 59 B2
Regency Clo. W5 55 H6
Regency Clo., Chig. 35 F5
Regency Clo., Hmptn. 81 F5
Regency Cres. NW4 39 A2
Regency Lo., Buck.H. 35 A2
Regency Ms. NW10 47 G6
High St.
Regency Ms., Beck. 96 C1
Regency Ms., Islw. 73 B5
Queensbridge Pk.
Regency Pl. SW1 19 J1
Regency Pl. SW1 19 J1
Regency St. SW1 67 D4
Regency Wk., Croy. 95 H6
Regency Wk., Rich. 73 H6
Friars Stile Rd.
Regency Way, Bexh. 80 D3
Regent Clo. N12 31 F5
Nether St.
Regent Clo., Har. 37 H6
Regent Clo., Houns. 72 B1
Regent Gdns., Ilf. 44 A6
Regent Pl. W1 11 G5
Regent Pl., Croy. 102 C1
Grant Rd.
Regent Rd. SE24 76 H6
Regent Rd., Surb. 91 J5
Regent Sq. E3 60 B3
Regent Sq. WC1 8 B4
Regent Sq. WC1 58 E3
Regent Sq., Belv. 71 H4
Regent St. NW10 57 A3
Kilburn La.
Regent St. SW1 11 H6
Regent St. SW1 58 D7
Regent St. W1 11 E3
Regent St. W1 58 B6
Regent St. W4 65 A5
Regents Ave. N13 32 G5
Regents Bri. Gdns. 20 B7
SW8
Regents Bri. Gdns. 67 E7
SW8
Regents Clo., S.Croy. 102 B6
Regents Clo., Kes. 104 A5
Regents Ms. NW8 6 D1
Regent's Pk. NW1 6 J2
Regent's Pk. NW1 57 J2
Regent's Pk. Est. 7 F4
NW1
Regents Pk. Rd. N3 39 C4
Regents Pk. Rd. NW1 48 J7
Regents Pk. Ter. NW1 58 B1
Oval Rd.
Regent's Pl. NW1 58 C4
Hampstead Rd.
Regent's Pl. SE3 78 G2
Regents Row E8 59 D1
Regina Clo., Barn. 23 A3
Regina Rd. N4 49 F1
Regina Rd. SE25 95 D3
Regina Rd. W13 64 D1
Regina Rd., Sthl. 63 E4
Regina Ter. W13 64 E1
Reginald Rd. E7 51 G6
Reginald Rd. SE8 69 A7
Reginald Sq. SE8 69 A7
Regis Rd. NW5 49 B5
Regnart Bldgs. NW1 7 G5
Reid Clo., Pnr. 36 A4
Reidhaven Rd. SE18 70 H4
Reigate Ave., Sutt. 100 D2
Reigate Rd., Brom. 87 F3
Reigate Rd., Ilf. 52 J2
Reigate Way, Wall. 101 E5
Reighton Rd. E5 50 D3
Relay Rd. W12 65 J1
Relf Rd. SE15 77 D3
Relko Gdns., Sutt. 100 G5
Relton Ms. SW7 14 H5
Rembrandt Clo. E14 69 D3
Rembrandt Clo. SW1 19 B2
Rembrandt Rd. SE13 78 E4
Rembrandt Rd., Edg. 38 A2
Remington Rd. E6 61 B6
Remington Rd. N15 41 A6

Remington St. N1 8 H2
Remington St. N1 58 H2
Remnant St. WC2 12 C3
Rempstone Ms. N1 9 C1
Remus Rd. E3 51 A7
Monier Rd.
Rendle Clo., Croy. 95 D5
Rendlesham Rd. E5 50 D4
Rendlesham Rd., Enf. 24 H1
Renforth St. SE16 68 F2
Renfrew Clo. E6 61 D7
Renfrew Rd. SE11 20 G1
Renfrew Rd. SE11 67 H4
Renfrew Rd., Houns. 72 D2
Renfrew Rd., Kings.T. 83 B7
Renmuir St. SW17 84 A5
Rennels Way, Islw. 73 B2
St. John's Rd.
Renness Rd. E17 41 H3
Rennets Clo. SE9 79 F5
Rennets Wd. Rd. SE9 79 G5
Rennie Est. SE16 68 E4
Rennie St. SE1 16 G1
Rennie St. SE1 67 H1
Renown Clo., Croy. 101 H1
Renown Clo., Rom. 44 G1
Rensburg Rd. E17 41 G5
Renshaw Clo., Belv. 71 F6
Grove Rd.
Renters Ave. NW4 38 J6
Renwick Rd., Bark. 62 B4
Repens Way, Hayes 54 D4
Stipularis Dr.
Rephidim St. SE1 17 C6
Replingham Rd. 84 C1
SW18
Reporton Rd. SW6 75 B1
Repository Rd. SE18 70 C6
Repton Ave., Wem. 46 F4
Repton Clo., Cars. 100 H5
Repton Ct. E5 50 H3
Repton Ct., Beck. 96 B1
Repton Gro., Ilf. 43 C1
Repton Rd., Har. 37 J4
Repton St. E14 59 H6
Repulse Clo., Rom. 44 H1
Reservoir Rd. N14 24 C5
Reservoir Rd. SE4 77 H2
Resolution Wk. SE18 70 C3
Venus Rd.
Restell Clo. SE3 69 E6
Reston Pl. SW7 14 C4
Restons Cres. SE9 79 G6
Restormel Clo., 72 G5
Houns.
Retcar Clo. N19 49 B2
Dartmouth Pk. Hill
Retcar Pl. N19 49 B2
Dartmouth Pk. Hill
Retingham Way E4 34 B2
Retreat, The NW9 38 D5
Retreat, The SW14 74 E3
South Worple Way
Retreat, The, Har. 36 G7
Retreat, The, Surb. 91 J6
Retreat, The, Th.Hth. 95 A4
Retreat, The, Wor.Pk. 99 H2
Retreat Clo., Har. 37 F5
Retreat Pl. E9 50 F6
Retreat Rd., Rich. 73 G5
Reunion Row E1 59 E7
Pennington St.
Reveley Sq. SE16 68 H2
Howland Way
Revell Ri. SE18 70 J6
Revell Rd., Kings.T. 92 B2
Revell Rd., Sutt. 100 C6
Revelon Rd. SE4 77 H3
Revelstoke Rd. SW18 84 C2
Reventlow Rd. SE9 88 F1
Reverdy Rd. SE1 21 H2
Reverdy Rd. SE1 68 D4
Reverend Clo., Har. 45 H3
Revesby Rd., Cars. 93 G6
Review Rd. NW2 47 F2
Review Rd., Dag. 62 H1
Rewell St. SW6 66 F7
Rewley Rd., Cars. 93 G6
Rex Pl. W1 11 C6
Reydon Ave. E11 42 J6
Reynard Clo., Brom. 97 C3
Reynard Dr. SE19 86 C7
Reynardson Rd. N17 32 J7
Reynolds Ave. E12 52 D5
Reynolds Ave., Rom. 44 C7
Reynolds Ave., 98 H7
Chess.
Reynolds Clo. NW11 39 E7

Reynolds Clo. SW19 93 G1
Reynolds Clo., Cars. 100 J1
Reynolds Ct. E11 51 F3
Cobbold Rd.
Reynolds Dr., Edg. 37 J3
Reynolds Pl. SE3 69 H7
Reynolds Pl., Rich. 73 J6
Cambrian Rd.
Reynolds Rd. SE15 77 F5
Reynolds Rd. W4 65 C3
Reynolds Rd., Hayes 54 C4
Reynolds Rd., N.Mal. 92 D7
Reynolds Way, Croy. 102 B4
Rheidol Ms. N1 **8 J1**
Rheidol Ter. N1 **8 H1**
Rheidol Ter. N1 58 J1
Rheola Clo. N17 41 C1
Rhoda St. E2 **9 G5**
Rhodes Ave. N22 40 C1
Rhodes Moorhouse 93 D6
Ct., Mord.
Rhodes St. N7 49 F5
Mackenzie Rd.
Rhodesia Rd. E11 51 D2
Rhodesia Rd. SW9 76 E2
Rhodeswell Rd. E14 59 H5
Rhodrons Ave., 98 H5
Chess.
Rhondda Gro. E3 59 H3
Rhyl Rd., Grnf. 55 C2
Rhyl St. NW5 49 A6
Rhys Ave. N11 32 D7
Rialto Rd., Mitch. 94 A2
Ribble Clo., Wdf.Grn. 34 J6
Prospect Rd.
Ribblesdale Ave., 45 H6
Nthlt.
Ribblesdale Rd. N8 40 F4
Ribblesdale Rd. 85 B6
SW16
Ribbon Dance Ms. 77 A1
SE5
Camberwell Gro.
Ribchester Ave., Grnf. 55 C3
Ribston Clo., Brom. 104 C1
Ricardo Path SE28 71 C1
Byron Clo.
Ricardo St. E14 60 B6
Ricards Rd. SW19 84 C5
Rich La. SW5 **18 A4**
Rich St. E14 59 J7
Richard Clo. SE18 70 B4
Richard Foster Clo. 41 J7
E17
Richard St. E1 59 E6
Commercial Rd.
Richards Ave., Rom. 44 J5
Richards Clo., Har. 37 D5
Richards Pl. E17 42 A3
Richards Pl. SW3 **18 H1**
Richardson Clo. E8 59 C1
Clarissa St.
Richardson Rd. E15 60 E2
Richardson's Ms. W1 **7 F6**
Richbell Pl. WC1 **12 C1**
Richborne Ter. SW8 **20 C7**
Richborne Ter. SW8 67 F7
Richborough Rd. NW2 48 B4
Riches Rd., Ilf. 52 F2
Richford Rd. E15 60 F1
Richford St. W6 65 J2
Richlands Ave., 99 G4
Epsom
Richmond Ave. E4 34 D5
Richmond Ave. N1 58 F1
Richmond Ave. NW10 47 J6
Richmond Ave. SW20 93 B1
Richmond Bri., Rich. 73 G5
Richmond Bri., Twick. 73 G6
Richmond Bldgs. W1 **11 H4**
Richmond Clo. E17 41 J6
Richmond Cres. E4 34 D5
Richmond Cres. N1 58 F1
Richmond Cres. N9 33 D1
Richmond Gdns. 38 G5
NW4
Richmond Gdns., Har. 29 C7
Richmond Grn., Croy. 101 E3
Richmond Gro. N1 49 H7
Richmond Gro., Surb. 91 J6
Alpha Rd.
Richmond Hill, Rich. 73 H6
Richmond Hill Ct., 73 H6
Rich.
Richmond Ms. W1 **11 H4**
Richmond Pk., 83 A1
Kings.T.
Richmond Pk., Rich. 83 A1

Richmond Pk. Rd. 74 C5
SW14
Richmond Pk. Rd., 91 H1
Kings.T.
Richmond Pl. SE18 70 F4
Richmond Rd. E4 34 D1
Richmond Rd. E7 51 H5
Richmond Rd. E8 50 C7
Richmond Rd. E11 51 D2
Richmond Rd. N2 39 F2
Richmond Rd. N11 32 E6
Richmond Rd. N15 41 B6
Richmond Rd. SW20 92 H1
Richmond Rd. W5 64 H2
Richmond Rd., Barn. 23 E5
Richmond Rd., Croy. 101 E3
Richmond Rd., Ilf. 52 F3
Richmond Rd., Islw. 73 D3
Richmond Rd., 82 G5
Kings.T.
Richmond Rd., 94 H3
Th.Hth.
Richmond Rd., Twick. 82 D1
Richmond St. E13 60 G2
Richmond Ter. SW1 **16 A3**
Richmond Ter. SW1 67 E2
Richmond Way E11 51 G2
Richmond Way W12 66 A2
Richmond Way W14 66 A2
Richmount Gdns. SE3 78 G3
Rickard Clo. NW4 38 G4
Rickard Clo. SW2 85 G1
Rickards Clo., Surb. 98 H1
Rickett St. SW6 66 D6
Rickman St. E1 59 F3
Mantus Rd.
Rickmansworth Rd., 36 B2
Pnr.
Rickthorne Rd. N19 49 E2
Landseer Rd.
Rickyard Path SE9 79 B4
Ridding La., Grnf. 46 C5
Riddons Rd. SE12 87 J3
Ride, The, Brent. 64 E5
Ride, The, Enf. 25 F3
Rideout St. SE18 70 C4
Rider Clo., Sid. 79 H6
Ridgdale St. E3 60 A2
Ridge, The, Bex. 80 F7
Ridge, The, Orp. 104 G2
Ridge, The, Surb. 92 A5
Ridge, The, Twick. 73 A7
Ridge Ave. N21 24 J7
Ridge Clo. NW4 39 A2
Ridge Clo. NW9 38 D4
Ridge Crest, Enf. 24 F1
Ridge Hill NW11 48 B1
Ridge Rd. N8 40 F6
Ridge Rd. N21 32 J1
Ridge Rd. NW2 48 C3
Ridge Rd., Mitch. 85 B7
Ridge Rd., Sutt. 100 B1
Ridge Way SE19 86 B6
Central Hill
Ridge Way, Felt. 81 E3
Ridgebrook Rd. SE3 78 J3
Ridgecroft Clo., Bex. 89 J1
Ridgemont Gdns., 30 C4
Edg.
Ridgemount Ave. 102 G2
Croy.
Ridgemount Clo. 86 E7
SE20
Anerley Pk.
Ridgemount Gdns., 24 H3
Enf.
Ridgeview Clo., Barn. 23 A6
Ridgeview Rd. N20 31 E3
Ridgeway, Brom. 103 G2
Ridgeway, Wdf.Grn. 34 J4
Ridgeway, The E4 34 B2
Ridgeway, The N3 31 E7
Ridgeway, The N11 31 J4
Ridgeway, The N14 32 E2
Ridgeway, The NW7 30 G3
Ridgeway, The NW9 38 E4
Ridgeway, The NW11 48 C1
Ridgeway, The W3 65 A3
Ridgeway, The, Croy. 101 F3
Ridgeway, The, Enf. 24 G1
Ridgeway, The, Har. 36 F5
Ridgeway, The, Har. 37 F6
(Kenton)
Ridgeway, The, Ruis. 36 A7
Ridgeway, The, Stan. 29 F6
Ridgeway, The, Sutt. 100 G6
Ridgeway Ave., Barn. 23 J6
Ridgeway Cres., Orp. 104 H3

Ridgeway Cres. 104 H2
Gdns., Orp.
Ridgeway Dr., Brom. 87 H5
Ridgeway E., Sid. 79 J5
Ridgeway Gdns. N6 40 C7
Ridgeway Gdns., Ilf. 43 B5
Ridgeway Rd. SW9 76 H3
Ridgeway Rd., Islw. 64 B7
Ridgeway Rd. N., 64 B6
Islw.
Ridgeway Wk., Nthlt. 45 E6
Fortunes Mead
Ridgeway W., Sid. 79 H5
Ridgewell Clo. N1 58 J1
Basire St.
Ridgewell Clo., Dag. 62 H1
Ridgmount Gdns. **11 H1**
WC1
Ridgmount Pl. WC1 **11 H1**
Ridgmount Rd. SW18 75 E5
Ridgmount St. WC1 **11 H1**
Ridgway SW19 83 J7
Ridgway Gdns. SW19 84 A7
Ridgway Pl. SW19 84 B6
Ridgwell Rd. E16 60 J5
Riding, The NW11 39 C7
Golders Grn. Rd.
Riding Ho. St. W1 **11 E2**
Riding Ho. St. W1 58 C5
Ridings, The W5 55 J4
Ridings, The, Sun. 90 A1
Ridings, The, Surb. 92 A5
Ridings Ave. N21 24 H4
Ridings Clo. N6 40 C7
Hornsey La. Gdns.
Ridley Ave. W13 64 E3
Ridley Rd. E7 51 J4
Ridley Rd. E8 50 C5
Ridley Rd. NW10 56 G2
Ridley Rd. SW19 84 E7
Ridley Rd., Brom. 96 F3
Ridley Rd., Well. 80 B1
Ridley Several SE3 78 H2
Blackheath Pk.
Ridsdale Rd. SE20 95 E1
Riefield Rd. SE9 79 F4
Riesco Dr., Croy. 102 F6
Riffel Rd. NW2 47 J5
Rifle Pl. SE11 **20 F5**
Rifle Pl. W11 66 A1
Rifle St. E14 60 B5
Rigault Rd. SW6 75 B2
Rigby Clo., Croy. 101 G3
Rigby Ms., Ilf. 52 E2
Cranbrook Rd.
Rigden St. E14 60 B6
Rigeley Rd. NW10 56 G3
Rigg App. E10 50 G1
Rigge Pl. SW4 76 D4
Rigger Row SW11 75 F3
Cinnamon Row
Riggindale Rd. SW16 85 D2
Riley Rd. SE1 **17 F5**
Riley Rd. SE1 68 C3
Riley St. SW10 **18 E6**
Riley St. SW10 66 G7
Rinaldo Rd. SW12 76 B7
Ring, The W2 **10 G5**
Ring, The W2 57 G7
Ring Clo., Brom. 87 H7
Garden Rd.
Ringcroft St. N7 49 G5
Ringers Rd., Brom. 96 G3
Ringford Rd. SW18 75 C5
Ringlewell Clo., Enf. 25 E2
Central Ave.
Ringmer Ave. SW6 75 B1
Ringmer Gdns. N19 49 E2
Sussex Way
Ringmer Pl. N21 25 A5
Ringmer Way, Brom. 100 E3
Ringmore Ri. SE23 77 E7
Ringslade Rd. N22 40 F2
Ringstead Rd. SE6 78 B7
Ringstead Rd., Sutt. 100 G4
Ringway N11 32 C6
Ringway, Sthl. 63 D5
Ringwold Clo., Beck. 86 H7
Ringwood Ave. N2 39 J2
Ringwood Ave., Croy. 94 E7
Ringwood Clo., Pnr. 36 C3
Ringwood Gdns. E14 69 A4
Ringwood Gdns. 83 G2
SW15
Ringwood Rd. E17 41 J6
Ringwood Way N21 32 H1
Ringwood Way, 81 G4
Hmptn.

Ripley Clo., Brom. 97 C5
Ringmer Way
Ripley Clo., Croy. 103 C6
Ripley Gdns. SW14 74 D3
Ripley Gdns., Sutt. 100 F4
Ripley Ms. E11 42 E7
Wadley Rd.
Ripley Rd. E16 60 J6
Ripley Rd., Belv. 71 G4
Ripley Rd., Enf. 24 J1
Ripley Rd., Hmptn. 81 G7
Ripley Rd., Ilf. 52 J2
Ripley Vill. W5 55 F6
Castlebar Rd.
Riplington Ct. SW15 74 G7
Longwood Dr.
Ripon Clo., Nthlt. 45 G5
Ripon Gdns., Chess. 98 G5
Ripon Gdns., Ilf. 43 B7
Ripon Rd. N9 25 E7
Ripon Rd. N17 41 A3
Ripon Rd. SE18 70 E6
Ripon Way, Borwd. 22 C5
Rippersley Rd., Well. 80 A1
Ripple Rd., Bark. 61 G1
Ripple Rd., Dag. 62 D1
Rippleside Ind. Est., 62 B2
Bark.
Ripplevale Gro. N1 49 F7
Rippolson Rd. SE18 70 J5
Risborough Dr., 92 G7
Wor.Pk.
Risborough St. SE1 **16 H3**
Risdon St. SE16 68 F2
Renforth St.
Rise, The E11 42 G5
Rise, The N13 32 G4
Rise, The NW7 30 F6
Rise, The NW10 47 D4
Rise, The, Bex. 80 C7
Rise, The, Buck.H. 27 A7
Rise, The, Edg. 30 B5
Rise, The, Grnf. 46 D5
Rise, The, Sid. 80 C7
Risedale Rd., Bexh. 80 H3
Riseldine Rd. SE23 77 H6
Rising Sun Ct. EC1 **12 H2**
Risinghill St. N1 **8 E1**
Risinghill St. N1 58 F2
Risingholme Clo., Har. 37 B1
Risingholme Rd., Har. 37 B2
Risings, The E17 42 D4
Risley Ave. N17 40 J1
Rita Rd. SW8 **20 B6**
Rita Rd. SW8 67 E6
Ritches Rd. N15 40 J5
Ritchie Rd., Croy. 95 E6
Ritchie St. N1 **8 F1**
Ritchie St. N1 58 G2
Ritchings Ave. E17 41 H4
Ritherdon Rd. SW17 85 A2
Ritson Rd. E8 50 D6
Ritter St. SE18 70 D6
Rivaz Pl. E9 50 F6
Rivenhall Gdns. E18 42 F4
River Ave. N13 32 H3
River Ave., T.Ditt. 91 D7
River Bank N21 24 J7
River Bank, E.Mol. 91 B3
River Bank, T.Ditt. 91 C5
River Bank, W.Mol. 90 F3
River Barge Clo. E14 69 C2
Stewart St.
River Clo. E11 42 J6
River Clo., Surb. 91 G5
Catherine Rd.
River Front, Enf. 25 A3
River Gdns., Cars. 101 A3
River Gdns., Felt. 72 B4
River Gro. Pk., Beck. 95 J1
River La., Rich. 82 G1
River Meads Ave., 81 G3
Twick.
River Pk. Gdns., 87 D7
Brom.
River Pk. Rd. N22 40 F2
River Pl. N1 49 J7
River Reach, Tedd. 82 F5
River Rd., Bark. 61 H2
River Rd., Buck.H. 35 B1
River Rd. Business 61 J3
Pk., Bark.
River St. EC1 **8 E3**
River St. EC1 58 G3
River Ter. W6 65 J5
Crisp Rd.
River Vw., Enf. 24 J3
Chase Side

River Vw. Gdns., 82 C2
Twick.
River Wk., Walt. 90 A6
River Way SE10 69 F3
River Way, Epsom 99 D6
River Way, Loug. 27 C6
River Way, Twick. 81 H2
Riverbank Way, Brent. 64 F6
Rivercourt Rd. W6 65 H4
Riverdale SE13 78 C3
Lewisham High St.
Riverdale Dr. SW18 84 E1
Strathville Rd.
Riverdale Gdns., 73 F6
Twick.
Riverdale Rd. SE18 70 J5
Riverdale Rd., Bex. 80 E7
Riverdale Rd., Erith 71 H5
Riverdale Rd., Felt. 81 F4
Riverdale Rd., Twick. 73 F6
Riverdene, Edg. 30 C3
Riverdene Rd., Ilf. 52 D3
Riverhead Clo. E17 41 G2
Rivermead Clo., Tedd. 82 E5
Rivermead Ct. SW6 75 C3
Rivernook Clo., Walt. 90 C5
Riversdale Rd. N5 49 H3
Riversdale Rd., T.Ditt. 91 D5
Riversfield Rd., Enf. 25 B3
Riverside NW4 38 H7
Riverside SE7 69 H3
Anchor & Hope La.
Riverside, Twick. 82 E1
Riverside, The, E.Mol. 91 A3
Graburn Way
Riverside Ave., E.Mol. 91 A5
Riverside Clo. E5 50 F1
Riverside Clo. W7 55 B4
Riverside Clo., 91 G4
Kings.T.
Riverside Clo., Wall. 101 B3
Riverside Ct. E4 26 B6
Chelwood Clo.
Riverside Ct. SW8 19 J5
Riverside Ct. SW8 67 D6
Riverside Dr. NW11 39 B6
Riverside Dr. W4 65 D7
Riverside Dr., Mitch. 93 H5
Riverside Dr., Rich. 82 E2
Riverside Gdns. W6 65 H5
Riverside Gdns., Enf. 24 J2
Riverside Gdns., Wem. 55 H2
Riverside Ind. Est., 62 A3
Bark.
Riverside Ind. Est., 25 H6
Enf.
Morson Rd.
Riverside Rd. E15 60 C2
Riverside Rd. N15 31 J7
Riverside Rd. SW17 84 E4
Riverside Rd., Sid. 89 E3
Riverside Wk. SE1 16 D1
Riverside Wk. SE1 67 G1
Riverside Wk., Bex. 80 D7
Riverside Wk., Islw. 73 B3
Riverside Wk., 91 G2
Kings.T.
High St.
Riverton Clo. W9 57 C3
Riverview Gdns. 65 H6
SW13
Riverview Gro. W4 65 B6
Riverview Pk. SE6 87 A1
Riverview Rd. W4 65 B6
Riverview Rd., Epsom 99 D5
Riverway N13 32 G4
Riverwood La., Chis. 97 G1
Rivington Ave., 43 A2
Wdf.Grn.
Rivington Ct. NW10 56 G1
Rivington Cres. NW7 30 F7
Rivington Pl. EC2 9 E4
Rivington St. EC2 9 D4
Rivington St. EC2 59 B3
Rivington Wk. E8 59 D1
Wilde Clo.
Rivulet Rd. N17 32 J7
Rixon Ho. SE18 70 E6
Barnfield Rd.
Rixon St. N7 49 G3
Tollington Rd.
Rixsen Rd. E12 52 B5
Roach Rd. E3 51 A7
Roads Pl. N19 49 E2
Hornsey Rd.
Roan St. SE10 69 B7
Robarts Clo., Pnr. 36 B5
Field End Rd.

Robb Rd., Stan. 29 D6
Robert Adam St. W1 11 B3
Robert Adam St. W1 58 A6
Robert Clo. W9 6 D6
Robert Dashwood 20 J2
Way SE17
Robert Dashwood 67 J4
Way SE17
Robert Gentry Ho. 66 B5
W14
Comeragh Rd.
Robert Keen Clo. 77 D1
SE15
Cicely Rd.
Robert Lowe Clo. 68 G7
SE14
Robert Owen Ho. 75 A1
SW6
Robert St. E16 70 E1
Robert St. NW1 7 E4
Robert St. NW1 58 B3
Robert St. SE18 70 G5
Robert St. WC2 12 B6
Roberta St. E2 9 J4
Roberta St. E2 59 D3
Roberton Dr., Brom. 96 J1
Roberts Clo. SE9 88 G1
Roberts Clo., Pnr. 36 B5
Field End Rd.
Roberts Clo., Sutt. 100 A7
Roberts Ms. SW1 15 B6
Robert's Pl. EC1 8 F5
Roberts Rd. E17 42 B1
Roberts Rd. NW7 31 B6
Roberts Rd., Belv. 71 G5
Roberts St., Croy. 101 J3
High St.
Robertsbridge Rd., 100 F1
Cars.
Robertson Rd. E15 60 C1
Robertson St. SW8 76 B3
Robeson St. E3 59 J5
Ackroyd Dr.
Robin Clo. NW7 30 E3
Robin Clo., Hmptn. 81 E5
Robin Ct. SE16 21 H1
Robin Ct. SE16 68 D4
Robin Cres. E6 61 B5
Robin Gro. N6 49 A2
Robin Gro., Brent. 64 F6
Robin Gro., Har. 37 J6
Robin Hill Dr., Chis. 88 B6
Robin Hood Dr., Har. 26 C7
Robin Hood La. E14 60 C6
Robin Hood La. 83 E4
SW15
Robin Hood La., 80 E5
Bexh.
Robin Hood La., Sutt. 100 D5
Robin Hood Rd. 83 H5
SW19
Robin Hood Way 83 E4
SW15
Robin Hood Way 83 E4
SW20
Robin Hood Way, 46 C6
Grnf.
Robina Clo., Bexh. 80 D4
Robinhood Clo., 94 C4
Mitch.
Robinhood La., Mitch. 94 C3
Robinia Clo., Chig. 35 H5
Robins Ct. SE12 87 J3
Robins Gro., W.Wick. 103 G3
Robinscroft Ms. SE10 78 B1
Sparta St.
Robinson Cres. 28 J1
(Bushey), Wat.
Robinson Rd. E2 59 F2
Robinson Rd. SW17 84 H6
Robinson Rd., Dag. 53 G4
Robinson St. SW3 18 J5
Robinsons Clo. W13 55 D5
Robinwood Pl. SW15 83 D4
Robsart St. SW9 76 F2
Robson Ave. NW10 56 G1
Robson Clo. E6 61 B6
Linton Gdns.
Robson Clo., Enf. 24 H2
Robson Rd. SE27 85 H3
Roch Ave., Edg. 37 J2
Rochdale Rd. E17 42 A7
Rochdale Rd. SE2 71 B5
Rochdale Way SE8 69 A7
Idonia St.
Roche Rd. SW16 94 E1
Roche Wk., Cars. 93 G6

Rochelle Clo. SW11 75 G4
Rochelle St. E2 9 F4
Rochemont Wk. E8 59 C1
Pownall Rd.
Rochester Ave. E13 60 J1
Rochester Ave., 96 H2
Brom.
Rochester Clo. SW16 85 E7
Rochester Clo., Enf. 25 B1
Rochester Clo., Sid. 80 B6
Rochester Dr., Bex. 80 F6
Rochester Dr., Pnr. 36 D5
Rochester Gdns., 102 B3
Croy.
Rochester Gdns., Ilf. 43 C7
Rochester Ms. NW1 49 C7
Rochester Pl. NW1 49 C6
Rochester Rd. NW1 49 C6
Rochester Rd., Cars. 100 J4
Rochester Row SW1 19 G1
Rochester Row SW1 67 C4
Rochester Sq. NW1 49 C7
Rochester St. SW1 15 H6
Rochester St. SW1 67 D3
Rochester Ter. NW1 49 C6
Rochester Wk. SE1 17 B1
Rochester Way SE3 78 J2
Rochester Way SE9 79 C3
Rochester Way Relief 78 H1
Rd. SE3
Rochester Way Relief 78 J4
Rd. SE9
Rochford Ave., Loug. 27 F3
Rochford Ave., Rom. 44 C5
Rochford Clo. E6 61 A2
Boleyn Rd.
Rochford Grn., Loug. 27 F3
Rochford St. NW5 48 J5
Rochford Wk. E8 50 D7
Wilman Gro.
Rochford Way, Croy. 94 E6
Rock Ave. SW14 74 D3
South Worple Way
Rock Gdns., Dag. 53 H5
Rockwell Rd.
Rock Gro. Way SE16 21 J1
Rock Hill SE26 86 C4
Rock St. N4 49 G2
Rockbourne Rd. SE23 86 G1
Rockells Pl. SE22 77 E6
Rockford Ave., Grnf. 55 D2
Rockhall Rd. NW2 48 A4
Rockhampton Clo. 85 G4
SE27
Rockhampton Rd.
Rockhampton Rd. 85 G4
SE27
Rockhampton Rd., 102 B6
S.Croy.
Rockingham Clo. 74 F4
SW15
Rockingham Est. 16 J6
SE1
Rockingham Est. SE1 67 J3
Rockingham St. SE1 16 J6
Rockingham St. SE1 67 J3
Rockland Rd. SW15 74 B4
Rocklands Dr., Stan. 37 E2
Rockley Rd. W14 66 A2
Rockmount Rd. SE18 70 J5
Rockmount Rd. SE19 86 A6
Rocks La. SW13 74 G3
Rockware Ave., Grnf. 55 A1
Rockways, Barn. 22 F6
Rockwell Gdns. SE19 86 B4
Rockwell Rd., Dag. 53 H5
Rockwood Pl. W12 65 J2
Shepherds Bush Grn.
Rocliffe St. N1 8 H2
Rocmoale Way SE8 69 A7
Octavius St.
Rocombe Cres. SE23 77 F7
Rocque Ho. SE3 78 F3
Muir Rd.
Rodborough Rd. 48 D1
NW11
Roden Ct. N6 40 D7
Hornsey La.
Roden Gdns., Croy. 95 B6
Roden St. N7 49 F3
Roden St., Ilf. 52 D3
Rodenhurst Rd. SW4 76 C6
Roderick Rd. NW3 48 J4
Roding Ave., Wdf.Grn. 35 B6
Roding La., Buck.H. 35 A1
Roding La., Chig. 35 E2
Roding La. N., 35 B6
Wdf.Grn.
Roding La. S., Ilf. 43 A4

Roding La. S., 43 A3
Wdf.Grn.
Roding Ms. E1 17 J1
Roding Rd. E5 50 H4
Roding Rd. E6 61 E5
Roding Rd., Loug. 27 B5
Roding Trd. Est., Bark. 52 E7
Roding Vw., Buck.H. 35 A1
Rodings, The, 34 J6
Wdf.Grn.
Rodings Row, Barn. 23 B5
Leecroft Rd.
Rodmarton St. W1 11 A2
Rodmarton St. W1 57 J5
Rodmell Clo., Hayes 54 E4
Rodmell Slope N12 31 C5
Rodmere St. SE10 69 E5
Trafalgar Rd.
Rodmill La. SW2 76 E7
Rodney Clo., Croy. 101 H1
Rodney Clo., N.Mal. 92 E5
Rodney Clo., Pnr. 36 E7
Rodney Ct. W9 6 D5
Rodney Gdns., Pnr. 36 B5
Rodney Gdns., 103 G4
W.Wick.
Rodney Pl. E17 41 H2
Rodney Pl. SE17 21 A1
Rodney Pl. SW19 93 F1
Rodney Rd. E11 42 H4
Rodney Rd. SE17 21 A1
Rodney Rd. SE17 67 J4
Rodney Rd., Mitch. 93 H2
Rodney Rd., N.Mal. 92 E5
Rodney Rd., Twick. 72 G7
Rodney St. N1 8 D1
Rodney St. N1 58 F2
Rodway Rd. SW15 74 G7
Rodway Rd., Brom. 96 H1
Rodwell Clo., Ruis. 45 C1
Rodwell Pl., Edg. 30 A6
Whitchurch La.
Rodwell Rd. SE22 77 C6
Roe End NW9 38 C4
Roe Grn. NW9 38 C5
Roe La. NW9 38 B4
Roe Way, Wall. 101 E7
Roebourne Way E16 70 D2
Roebuck Clo., Felt. 81 B4
Roebuck La. N17 33 C6
High Rd.
Roebuck La., Buck.H. 26 J7
Roebuck Rd., Chess. 99 A5
Roedean Ave., Enf. 25 F1
Roedean Clo., Enf. 25 F1
Roedean Cres. SW15 74 E6
Roehampton Clo. 74 G4
SW15
Roehampton Dr., 88 F6
Chis.
Roehampton Gate 74 E6
SW15
Roehampton High St. 74 G7
SW15
Roehampton La. 74 G4
SW15
Roehampton Vale 83 F3
SW15
Roffey St. E14 69 C2
Rogate Ho. E5 50 D3
Muir Rd.
Roger St. WC1 8 D6
Roger St. WC1 58 F4
Rogers Gdns., Dag. 53 G5
Rogers Rd. E16 60 F6
Rogers Rd. SW17 84 G4
Rogers Rd., Dag. 53 G5
Rogers Wk. N12 31 E3
Brook Meadow
Rojack Rd. SE23 86 G1
Rokeby Gdns., 42 G1
Wdf.Grn.
Rokeby Pl. SW20 83 H7
Rokeby Rd. SE4 77 J2
Rokeby St. E15 60 D1
Rokesby Clo., Well. 79 G2
Rokesby Pl., Wem. 46 G5
Rokesly Ave. N8 40 E5
Roland Gdns. SW7 18 D3
Roland Gdns. SW7 66 F5
Roland Gdns., Felt. 81 F3
Roland Ms. E1 59 G5
Stepney Grn.
Roland Rd. E17 42 D4
Roland Way SE17 21 C4
Roland Way SE17 68 A5

Roland Way SW7	**18**	**D3**
Roland Way, Wor.Pk.	99	F2
Roles Gro., Rom.	44	D4
Rolfe Clo., Barn.	23	H4
Rolinsden Way, Kes.	104	A4
Roll Gdns., Ilf.	43	D5
Rollesby Rd., Chess.	99	A6
Rollesby Way SE28	62	C7
Rolleston Ave., Orp.	97	E6
Rolleston Clo., Orp.	97	E7
Rolleston Rd.,	102	A7
S.Croy.		
Rollins St. SE15	68	F6
Rollit Cres., Houns.	72	G5
Rollit St. N7	49	F5
Hornsey Rd.		
Rolls Bldgs. EC4	**12**	**E3**
Rolls Pk. Ave. E4	34	A6
Rolls Pk. Rd. E4	34	B5
Rolls Pas. EC4	**12**	**E3**
Rolls Rd. SE1	**21**	**G3**
Rolls Rd. SE1	68	C5
Rollscourt Ave. SE24	76	J5
Rolt St. SE8	68	H6
Rolvenden Gdns.,	88	A7
Brom.		
Rolvenden Pl. N17	41	D1
Manor Rd.		
Roma Read Clo.	74	H7
SW15		
Bessborough Rd.		
Roma Rd. E17	41	H3
Roman Clo. W3	65	B2
Avenue Gdns.		
Roman Clo., Felt.	72	C5
Roman Ri. SE19	86	A6
Roman Rd. E2	59	F3
Roman Rd. E3	59	H2
Roman Rd. E6	61	A4
Roman Rd. N10	32	B7
Roman Rd. W4	65	F4
Roman Rd., Ilf.	52	E6
Roman Sq. SE28	71	A1
Roman Way N7	49	F6
Roman Way SE15	68	F7
Clifton Way		
Roman Way, Croy.	101	H2
Roman Way, Enf.	25	C5
Roman Way Ind. Est.	49	F7
N1		
Offord St.		
Romanhurst Ave.,	96	E4
Brom.		
Romanhurst Gdns.,	96	E4
Brom.		
Romany Gdns. E17	41	H1
McEntee Ave.		
Romany Gdns., Sutt.	93	D7
Romany Ri., Orp.	104	F1
Romberg Rd. SW17	85	A3
Romborough Gdns.	78	C5
SE13		
Romborough Way	78	C5
SE13		
Romero Clo. SW9	76	F3
Stockwell Rd.		
Romero Sq. SE3	78	J4
Romeyn Rd. SW16	85	F3
Romford Rd. E7	51	H5
Romford Rd. E12	52	B4
Romford Rd. E15	51	E6
Romford St. E1	**13**	**J2**
Romford St. E1	59	D5
Romilly Dr., Wat.	28	E4
Romilly Rd. N4	49	H2
Romilly St. W1	**11**	**H5**
Romilly St. W1	58	D7
Rommany Rd. SE27	86	A4
Romney Clo. N17	41	E1
Romney Clo. NW11	48	F1
Romney Clo. SE14	68	F7
Kender St.		
Romney Clo., Chess.	98	H4
Romney Clo., Har.	36	G7
Romney Dr., Brom.	88	A7
Romney Dr., Har.	36	G7
Romney Gdns., Bexh.	80	F1
Romney Ms. W1	**11**	**B1**
Romney Rd. SE10	69	C6
Romney Rd., N.Mal.	92	D6
Romney St. SW1	**16**	**A6**
Romney St. SW1	67	E3
Romola Rd. SE24	85	H1
Romsey Clo., Orp.	104	E4
Romsey Gdns., Dag.	62	D1
Romsey Rd. W13	55	D7
Romsey Rd., Dag.	62	D1
Rona Rd. NW3	49	A4

Rona Wk. N1	50	A6
Marquess Est.		
Ronald Ave. E15	60	E3
Ronald Clo., Beck.	95	J4
Ronald St. E1	59	F6
Devonport St.		
Ronalds Rd. N5	49	G5
Ronalds Rd., Brom.	96	G1
Ronaldstone Rd., Sid.	79	H6
Ronart St., Har.	37	C3
Stuart Rd.		
Rondu Rd. NW2	48	B5
Ronelean Rd., Surb.	98	J3
Ronver Rd. SE12	87	G1
Baring Rd.		
Rood La. EC3	**13**	**D5**
Rood La. EC3	59	B7
Rook Wk. E6	61	B6
Allhallows Rd.		
Rooke Way SE10	69	F5
Rookeries Clo., Felt.	81	B3
Rookery Clo. NW9	38	F5
Rookery Cres., Dag.	53	H7
Rookery Dr., Chis.	97	D1
Rookery La., Brom.	97	A6
Rookery Rd. SW4	76	C4
Rookery Way NW9	38	F5
Rookfield Ave. N10	40	C4
Rookfield Clo. N10	40	C4
Cranmore Way		
Rookstone Rd. SW17	84	J5
Rookwood Ave.,	27	F3
Loug.		
Rookwood Ave.,	92	G4
N.Mal.		
Rookwood Ave., Wall.	101	D4
Rookwood Gdns. E4	34	F1
Whitehall Rd.		
Rookwood Gdns.,	27	F3
Loug.		
Rookwood Ho., Bark.	61	G2
St. Marys		
Rookwood Rd. N16	41	C7
Rope St. SE16	68	H3
Rope Wk., Sun.	90	C3
Rope Wk. Gdns. E1	**13**	**J3**
Rope Yd. Rails SE18	70	E3
Ropemaker Rd. SE16	68	H2
Ropemaker St. EC2	**13**	**B1**
Ropemaker St. EC2	59	A5
Ropemakers Flds.	59	J7
E14		
Narrow St.		
Roper La. SE1	**17**	**E4**
Roper St. SE9	79	C6
Roper Way, Mitch.	94	A2
Ropers Ave. E4	34	B5
Ropers Wk. SW2	76	G7
Brockwell Pk. Gdns.		
Ropery St. E3	59	J4
Ropley St. E2	**9**	**H2**
Ropley St. E2	59	D2
Rosa Alba Ms. N5	49	J4
Kelross Rd.		
Rosaline Rd. SW6	66	B7
Rosamund St. SE26	86	E3
Rosary Clo., Houns.	72	E2
Rosary Gdns. SW7	**18**	**C2**
Rosary Gdns. SW7	66	F4
Rosaville Rd. SW6	66	C7
Roscoe St. EC1	**9**	**A6**
Roscoff Clo., Edg.	38	C1
Rose All. SE1	**17**	**A1**
Rose All. SE1	67	J1
Rose & Crown Ct.	**12**	**J3**
EC2		
Rose & Crown Yd.	**15**	**G1**
SW1		
Rose Ave. E18	42	H2
Rose Ave., Mitch.	93	J1
Rose Ave., Mord.	93	F5
Rose Bates Dr. NW9	38	A4
Rose Ct. E1	59	B5
Sandy's Row		
Rose Ct. SE26	86	E2
Rose Ct., Pnr.	36	C3
Nursery Rd.		
Rose Dale, Orp.	104	E2
Rose End, Wor.Pk.	100	A1
Rose Gdn. Clo., Edg.	29	H6
Rose Gdns. W5	64	G3
Rose Gdns., Felt.	81	A2
Rose Gdns., Sthl.	54	G4
Rose Glen NW9	38	D4
Rose Hill, Sutt.	100	E3
Rose La., Rom.	44	D3
Rose Lawn (Bushey),	28	J1
Wat.		

Rose St. WC2	**12**	**A5**
Rose Wk., Surb.	92	B5
Rose Wk., W.Wick.	103	C2
Rose Way SE12	78	G5
Roseacre Clo. W13	55	E5
Middlefielde		
Roseacre Rd., Well.	80	B3
Rosebank SE20	86	E7
Rosebank Ave., Wem.	46	C4
Rosebank Clo. N12	31	H5
Rosebank Clo., Tedd.	82	D6
Rosebank Gdns. E3	59	J2
Rosebank Gro. E17	41	J3
Rosebank Rd. E17	42	B6
Rosebank Rd. W7	64	B2
Rosebank Vill. E17	42	A4
Rosebank Wk. NW1	49	D7
Maiden La.		
Rosebank Wk. SE18	70	B4
Woodhill		
Rosebank Way W3	56	D6
Roseberry Gdns. N4	40	H6
Roseberry Gdns.,	104	H3
Orp.		
Roseberry Pl. E8	50	C6
Roseberry St. SE16	68	E4
Rosebery Ave. E12	52	B6
Rosebery Ave. EC1	**8**	**E5**
Rosebery Ave. EC1	58	G4
Rosebery Ave. N17	41	D2
Rosebery Ave., Har.	45	E4
Rosebery Ave.,	92	F2
N.Mal.		
Rosebery Ave., Sid.	79	H7
Rosebery Ave.,	94	J2
Th.Hth.		
Rosebery Clo., Mord.	93	A6
Rosebery Gdns. N8	40	E5
Rosebery Gdns. W13	55	D6
Rosebery Gdns.,	100	E4
Sutt.		
Rosebery Ms. N10	40	C2
Rosebery Ms. SW2	76	E6
Rosebery Rd.		
Rosebery Rd. N9	33	D3
Rosebery Rd. N10	40	C2
Rosebery Rd. SW2	76	E6
Rosebery Rd., Houns.	72	J5
Rosebery Rd.,	92	B2
Kings.T.		
Rosebery Rd., Sutt.	100	C6
Rosebery Sq. EC1	**8**	**E6**
Rosebery Sq.,	92	B2
Kings.T.		
Rosebine Ave., Twick.	73	A7
Rosebury Rd. SW6	75	E2
Rosebury Vale, Ruis.	45	A2
Rosecourt Rd., Croy.	94	F6
Rosecroft Ave. NW3	48	D3
Rosecroft Gdns. NW2	47	G3
Rosecroft Gdns.,	82	A1
Twick.		
Rosecroft Rd., Sthl.	54	G4
Rosecroft Wk., Pnr.	36	D5
Rosecroft Wk., Wem.	46	G5
Rosedale Clo. SE2	71	B3
Finchale Rd.		
Rosedale Clo. W7	64	C2
Boston Rd.		
Rosedale Clo., Stan.	29	E6
Rosedale Ct. N5	49	H4
Panmure Clo.		
Rosedale Gdns., Dag.	53	B7
Rosedale Rd. E7	51	J5
Rosedale Rd., Dag.	53	B7
Rosedale Rd., Epsom	99	G5
Rosedale Rd., Rich.	73	H4
Rosedale Rd., Rom.	44	J2
Rosedene NW6	57	A1
Rosedene Ave. SW16	85	F3
Rosedene Ave., Croy.	94	E7
Rosedene Ave., Grnf.	54	G3
Rosedene Ave.,	93	D5
Mord.		
Rosedene Gdns., Ilf.	43	D4
Rosedene Ter. E10	51	B2
Rosedew Rd. W6	66	A6
Rosefield Clo., Cars.	100	H5
Alma Rd.		
Rosefield Gdns. E14	60	A7
Roseford Ct. W12	66	A2
Shepherds Bush Grn.		
Rosehart Ms. W11	57	D6
Westbourne Gro.		
Rosehatch Ave., Rom.	44	D3
Roseheath Rd.,	72	F5
Houns.		
Rosehill, Esher	98	D6

Rosehill, Hmptn.	90	G1
Rosehill Ave., Sutt.	100	F1
Rosehill Gdns., Grnf.	46	C5
Rosehill Gdns., Sutt.	100	E2
Rosehill Pk. W., Sutt.	100	F1
Roseland Clo. N17	33	A7
Cavell Rd.		
Roseleigh Ave. N5	49	H4
Roseleigh Clo., Twick.	73	G6
Rosemary Ave. N3	39	E2
Rosemary Ave. N9	33	E1
Rosemary Ave., Enf.	25	A1
Rosemary Ave.,	72	D2
Houns.		
Rosemary Ave.,	90	G3
W.Mol.		
Rosemary Dr. E14	60	D6
Rosemary Dr., Ilf.	43	A5
Rosemary Gdns.	74	C3
SW14		
Rosemary La.		
Rosemary Gdns.,	98	H4
Chess.		
Rosemary Gdns., Dag.	53	F1
Rosemary La. SW14	74	C3
Rosemary Pl. N1	59	A1
Shepperton Rd.		
Rosemary Rd. SE15	**21**	**G7**
Rosemary Rd. SE15	68	C7
Rosemary Rd. SW17	84	F3
Rosemary Rd., Well.	79	J1
Rosemary St. N1	59	A1
Shepperton Rd.		
Rosemead NW9	38	F7
Rosemead Ave.	94	C2
Mitch.		
Rosemead Ave.,	46	H5
Wem.		
Rosemont Ave. N12	31	F6
Rosemont Rd. NW3	48	F6
Rosemont Rd. W3	56	B7
Rosemont Rd.,	92	C3
Kings.T.		
Rosemont Rd., N.Mal.	92	C3
Rosemont Rd., Rich.	73	H6
Rosemont Rd., Wem.	55	H1
Rosemoor St. SW3	**18**	**J2**
Rosemoor St. SW3	66	J4
Rosemount Clo.,	35	C6
Wdf.Grn.		
Chapelmount Rd.		
Rosemount Dr., Brom.	97	C4
Rosemount Rd. W13	55	D6
Rosenau Cres. SW11	75	H1
Rosenau Rd. SW11	75	H1
Rosendale Rd. SE21	76	J7
Rosendale Rd. SE24	76	J7
Roseneath Ave. N21	32	H1
Roseneath Rd. SW11	76	A6
Roseneath Wk., Enf.	25	A4
Rosens Wk., Edg.	30	B3
Rosenthal Rd. SE6	78	B6
Rosenthorpe Rd.	77	G5
SE15		
Roserton St. E14	69	C2
Rosery, The, Croy.	95	G6
Roses, The, Wdf.Grn.	34	F7
Rosethorn Clo. SW12	76	D7
Rosetta Clo. SW8	67	E7
Kenchester Clo.		
Roseveare Rd. SE12	87	J4
Roseville Ave.,	72	G5
Houns.		
Roseville Rd., Hayes	63	A5
Rosevine Rd. SW20	92	J1
Roseway SE21	77	A6
Rosewood, Esher	98	D2
Manor Rd. N.		
Rosewood Ave., Grnf.	46	D5
Rosewood Clo., Sid.	89	C3
Rosewood Ct., Brom.	96	J1
Rosewood Ct., Rom.	44	C5
Tendring Way		
Rosewood Gdns.	78	C2
SE13		
Lewisham Rd.		
Rosewood Gro., Sutt.	100	F2
Rosewood Sq. W12	56	G6
Primula St.		
Rosher Clo. E15	51	D7
Rosina St. E9	50	G5
Roskell Rd. SW15	75	A3
Roslin Rd. W3	65	B3
Roslin Way, Brom.	87	G5
Roslyn Clo., Mitch.	93	G2
Roslyn Rd. N15	41	A5
Rosmead Rd. W11	57	B7

Rosoman Pl. EC1 8 F5
Rosoman St. EC1 8 F4
Rosoman St. EC1 58 G3
Ross Ave. NW7 31 B5
Ross Ave., Dag. 53 F2
Ross Clo., Har. 28 J7
Ross Ct. SW15 75 A7
Ross Par., Wall. 101 B6
Ross Rd. SE25 95 A3
Ross Rd., Twick. 81 H1
Ross Rd., Wall. 101 C5
Ross Way SE9 79 B3
Rossall Cres. NW10 55 J3
Rossdale, Sutt. 100 H5
Rossdale Dr. N9 25 F6
Rossdale Dr. NW9 47 C1
Rossdale Rd. SW15 74 J4
Rosse Ms. SE3 78 H1
Rossendale St. E5 50 E2
Rossendale Way NW1 58 C1
Rossetti Rd. SE16 68 E5
Rossignol Gdns., 101 A2
Cars.
Rossindel Rd., Houns. 72 G5
Rossington St. E5 50 D2
Rossiter Flds., Barn. 23 B6
Rossiter Rd. SW12 85 B1
Rossland Clo., Bexh. 80 H5
Rosslyn Ave. E4 34 F2
Rosslyn Ave. SW13 74 E3
Rosslyn Ave., Barn. 23 H6
Rosslyn Ave., Dag. 44 F7
Rosslyn Ave., Felt. 72 A6
Rosslyn Clo., 103 F3
W.Wick.
Rosslyn Cres., Har. 37 C4
Rosslyn Cres., Wem. 46 H4
Rosslyn Hill NW3 48 G4
Rosslyn Ms. NW3 48 G4
Rosslyn Hill
Rosslyn Pk. Ms. NW3 48 G5
Lyndhurst Rd.
Rosslyn Rd. E17 42 C4
Rosslyn Rd., Bark. 52 G7
Rosslyn Rd., Twick. 73 F6
Rossmore Rd. NW1 6 H6
Rossmore Rd. NW1 57 H4
Rosswood Gdns., 101 B6
Wall.
Rostella Rd. SW17 84 G4
Rostrevor A 41 C6
Rostrevor Gdns., Sthl. 63 E5
Rostrevor Ms. SW6 75 C1
Rostrevor Rd.
Rostrevor Rd. SW6 75 C1
Rostrevor Rd. SW19 84 D5
Rotary St. SE1 16 G5
Roth Wk. N7 49 F3
Durham Rd.
Rothbury Gdns., Islw. 64 D7
Rothbury Rd. E9 50 J7
Rothbury Wk. N17 33 D7
Northumberland Gro.
Rotherfield Rd., 101 A4
Cars.
Rotherfield St. N1 49 J7
Rotherham Wk. SE1 16 G2
Rotherhithe New Rd. 21 J4
SE16
Rotherhithe New Rd. 68 E5
SE16
Rotherhithe Old Rd. 68 G4
SE16
Rotherhithe St. SE16 68 F2
Rotherhithe Tunnel E1 68 G1
Rotherhithe Tunnel 59 H7
App. E14
Rotherhithe Tunnel 68 F2
App. SE16
Rothermere Rd., 101 F5
Croy.
Rotherwick Hill W5 55 J4
Rotherwick Rd. NW11 39 D7
Rotherwood Clo. 93 B1
SW20
Rotherwood Rd. 75 A3
SW15
Rothery St. N1 58 H1
Gaskin St.
Rothery Ter. SW9 20 G7
Rothesay Ave. SW20 93 B2
Rothesay Ave., Grnf. 46 A6
Rothesay Ave., Rich. 74 B4
Rothesay Rd. SE25 95 A4
Rothsay Rd. E7 51 J7
Rothsay St. SE1 17 D5
Rothsay St. SE1 68 B3

Rothsay Wk. E14 69 A4
Charnwood Gdns.
Rothschild Rd. W4 65 C3
Rothschild St. SE27 85 H4
Rothwell Gdns., Dag. 53 C7
Rothwell Rd., Dag. 62 C1
Rothwell St. NW1 57 J1
Rotten Row SW1 14 J3
Rotten Row SW7 14 H3
Rotten Row SW7 66 H2
Rotterdam Dr. E14 69 C3
Rouel Rd. SE16 17 H6
Rouel Rd. SE16 68 D3
Rougemont Ave., 93 D6
Mord.
Round Gro., Croy. 95 G7
Round Hill SE26 86 F3
Roundacre SW19 84 A2
Inner Pk. Rd.
Roundaway Rd., Ilf. 43 C1
Roundel Clo. SE4 77 J4
Adelaide Ave.
Roundhay Clo. SE23 86 G2
Roundhill Dr., Enf. 24 F4
Roundmead Ave., 27 D2
Loug.
Roundmead Clo., 27 D3
Loug.
Roundtable Rd., 87 F3
Brom.
Roundtree Rd., Wem. 46 E5
Roundway, The N17 40 J1
Roundway, The, Esher 98 C6
Roundwood, Chis. 97 E2
Roundwood Rd. 47 F6
NW10
Rounton Rd. E3 60 A4
Roupell Rd. SW2 85 F1
Roupell St. SE1 16 F2
Roupell St. SE1 67 G1
Rous Rd., Buck.H. 35 B1
Rousden St. NW1 49 C7
Rouse Gdns. SE21 86 B4
Routh Rd. SW18 75 H7
Routh St. E6 61 C5
Routledge Clo. N19 49 D1
Rover Ave., Ilf. 35 J6
Rowallan Rd. SW6 66 B7
Rowan Ave. E4 33 J6
Rowan Clo. SW16 94 C1
Rowan Clo. W5 64 H2
Rowan Clo., N.Mal. 92 E2
Rowan Clo., Stan. 29 C6
Woodlands Dr.
Rowan Clo., Wem. 46 D3
Rowan Ct. E8 50 C7
Rowan Cres. SW16 94 C1
Rowan Dr. NW9 38 G3
Rowan Gdns., Croy. 102 C3
Radcliffe Rd.
Rowan Ind. Est., Croy. 95 B7
Rowan Rd. SW16 94 C2
Rowan Rd. W6 66 A4
Rowan Rd., Bexh. 80 E3
Rowan Rd., Brent. 64 E7
Rowan Ter. W6 66 A4
Bute Gdns.
Rowan Wk. N2 39 F5
Rowan Wk. N19 49 C2
Bredgar Rd.
Rowan Wk. W10 57 B4
Droop St.
Rowan Wk., Brom. 104 C3
Rowan Way, Rom. 44 C3
Rowans, The N13 32 H3
Rowans Way, Loug. 27 C4
Rowantree Clo. N21 33 A1
Rowantree Rd. N21 33 A1
Rowantree Rd., Enf. 24 H2
Rowanwood Ave., 89 A1
Sid.
Rowben Clo. N20 31 E1
Rowberry Clo. SW6 65 J7
Rowcross St. SE1 21 G3
Rowcross St. SE1 68 C5
Rowdell Rd., Nthlt. 54 G1
Rowden Pk. Gdns. E4 34 A6
Rowden Rd.
Rowden Rd. E4 34 A6
Rowden Rd., Beck. 95 H1
Rowden Rd., Epsom 99 B4
Rowditch La. SW11 76 A2
Rowdon Ave. NW10 47 H7
Rowdowns Rd., Dag. 62 F1
Rowe Gdns., Bark. 61 J2
Rowe La. E9 50 F5
Rowe Wk., Har. 45 G3
Rowena Cres. SW11 75 H2

Rowfant Rd. SW17 85 A1
Rowhill Rd. E5 50 E4
Rowington Clo. W2 10 A1
Rowington Clo. W2 57 E5
Rowland Ave., Har. 37 F3
Rowland Ct. E16 60 F4
Rowland Cres., Chig. 35 H4
Rowland Gro. SE26 86 E3
Dallas Rd.
Rowland Hill Ave. N17 32 J7
Rowland Hill St. NW3 48 H5
Rowland Way SW19 93 E1
Hayward Clo.
Rowlands Ave., Pnr. 28 G5
Rowlands Clo. N6 40 A6
North Hill
Rowlands Clo. NW7 30 G7
Rowlands Rd., Dag. 53 F2
Rowley Ave., Sid. 80 B7
Rowley Clo., Wem. 46 J7
Rowley Gdns. N4 40 J7
Rowley Grn. Rd., 22 F5
Barn.
Rowley Ind. Est. W3 65 B3
Rowley La., Barn. 22 E4
Rowley La., Borwd. 22 D1
Rowley Rd. N15 40 J5
Rowley Way NW8 57 E1
Rowlls Rd., Kings.T. 91 J3
Rowney Gdns., Dag. 53 C6
Rowney Rd., Dag. 53 B6
Rowntree Path SE28 62 B7
Booth Clo.
Rowntree Rd., Twick. 82 B1
Rowse Clo. E15 60 C1
Rowsley Ave. NW4 38 J3
Rowstock Gdns. N7 49 D5
Rowton Rd. SE18 70 F7
Roxborough Ave., 37 B7
Har.
Roxborough Ave., 64 C7
Islw.
Roxborough Pk., Har. 37 B7
Roxborough Rd., Har. 37 A5
Roxbourne Clo., Nthlt. 45 B6
Roxburgh Rd. SE27 85 H5
Roxby Pl. SW6 66 D6
Roxeth Grn. Ave., Har. 45 H3
Roxeth Gro., Har. 45 H4
Roxeth Hill, Har. 46 A2
Roxley Rd. SE13 78 B6
Roxton Gdns., Croy. 103 A5
Roxwell Rd. W12 65 G2
Roxwell Rd., Bark. 62 A2
Roxwell Trd. Pk. E10 41 H7
Roxwell Way, 34 J7
Wdf.Grn.
Roxy Ave., Rom. 44 C7
Roy Gdns., Ilf. 43 H4
Roy Gro., Hmptn. 81 H6
Roy Sq. E14 59 H7
Narrow St.
Royal Albert Dock E16 61 B7
Royal Albert Way E16 61 A7
Royal Arc. W1 11 F6
Royal Ave. SW3 18 J3
Royal Ave. SW3 66 J5
Royal Ave., Wor.Pk. 99 E2
Royal Circ. SE27 85 G3
Royal Clo., Ilf. 44 A7
Royal Clo., Wor.Pk. 99 E2
Royal College St. 49 C7
NW1
Royal Ct. SE16 68 J3
Finland St.
Royal Cres. W11 66 A1
Royal Cres., Ruis. 45 E4
Royal Cres. Ms. W11 66 A1
Queensdale Rd.
Royal Docks Rd. E6 61 E7
Royal Docks Rd., 61 E6
Bark.
Royal Ex. EC3 13 C4
Royal Ex. EC3 59 A6
Royal Ex. Ave. EC3 13 C4
Royal Ex. Bldgs. EC3 13 C4
Royal Gate N16 50 B7
Manor Rd.
Royal Hill SE10 69 C7
Royal Hospital Rd. 18 J5
SW3
Royal Hospital Rd. 66 J6
SW3
Royal London Est., 33 D6
The N17
Royal London Ind. 56 D2
Est. NW10
North Acton Rd.

Royal Mint Ct. EC3 13 G6
Royal Mint Ct. EC3 59 C7
Royal Mint Pl. E1 13 G5
Royal Mint St. E1 13 G5
Royal Mint St. E1 59 C7
Royal Mt. Ct., Twick. 82 B3
Royal Naval Pl. SE14 68 J7
Royal Oak Pl. SE22 77 E6
Royal Oak Rd. E8 50 E6
Royal Oak Rd., Bexh. 80 F5
Royal Opera Arc. 15 H1
SW1
Royal Orchard Clo. 75 B7
SW18
Royal Par. SE3 78 F2
Royal Par. SW6 66 B7
Dawes Rd.
Royal Par. W5 55 H3
Western Ave.
Royal Par., Chis. 88 F7
Royal Par. Ms. SE3 78 F2
Royal Par.
Royal Par. Ms., Chis. 88 F7
Royal Pl. SE10 69 C7
Royal Rd. E16 60 J6
Royal Rd. SE17 20 G5
Royal Rd. SE17 67 H6
Royal Rd., Sid. 89 D3
Royal Rd., Tedd. 82 A5
Royal Route, Wem. 47 A4
Royal St. SE1 16 D5
Royal St. SE1 67 F3
Royal Victor Pl. E3 59 G2
Royal Victoria Dock 60 G7
E16
Royal Wk., Wall. 101 B3
Prince Charles Way
Royalty Ms. W1 11 H4
Roycraft Ave., Bark. 61 J2
Roycraft Clo., Bark. 61 J2
Roycroft Clo. E18 42 H1
Roycroft Clo. SW2 85 G1
Roydene Rd. SE18 70 H6
Roydon Clo. SW11 76 B1
Reform St.
Roydon Clo., Loug. 27 B7
Roydon St. SW11 76 B1
Southolm St.
Royle Cres. W13 55 D4
Royston Ave. E4 34 A5
Royston Ave., Sutt. 100 G3
Royston Ave., Wall. 101 D4
Royston Clo., Houns. 72 B1
Royston Ct. SE24 76 J6
Burbage Rd.
Royston Ct., Rich. 73 J1
Lichfield Rd.
Royston Ct., Surb. 99 A3
Hook Ri. N.
Royston Gdns., Ilf. 43 A6
Royston Gro., Pnr. 28 G6
Royston Par., Ilf. 43 A6
Royston Pk. Rd., Pnr. 28 F6
Royston Rd. SE20 95 G1
Royston Rd., Rich. 73 H5
Royston St. E2 59 F2
Roystons, The, Surb. 92 B5
Rozel Ct. N1 59 B1
Rozel Rd. SW4 76 C3
Rubastic Rd., Sthl. 63 C3
Rubens Rd., Nthlt. 54 C2
Rubens St. SE6 86 J2
Ruberoid Rd., Enf. 25 J3
Ruby Ms. E17 42 A3
Ruby Rd.
Ruby Rd. E17 42 A3
Ruby St. SE15 68 E6
Ruby Triangle SE15 68 E6
Sandgate St.
Ruckholt Clo. E10 51 B3
Ruckholt Rd. E10 51 B4
Rucklidge Ave. NW10 56 F2
Rudall Cres. NW3 48 G4
Willoughby Rd.
Ruddstreet Clo. SE18 70 E4
Ruddy Way NW7 30 G6
Flower La.
Rudland Rd., Bexh. 80 H3
Rudloe Rd. SW12 76 C7
Rudolf Pl. SW8 20 B6
Rudolph Ct. SE22 77 D7
Rudolph Rd. E13 60 F2
Rudolph Rd. NW6 57 D2
Rudyard Gro. NW7 30 C6
Ruffetts, The, S.Croy. 102 E7
Ruffetts Clo., S.Croy. 102 E7
Rufford Clo., Har. 37 D6
Rufford St. N1

Rufford Twr. W3	65 B1	Rushmere Ct.,	99 G2
Rufus Clo., Ruis.	45 E3	Wor.Pk.	
Rufus St. N1	**9 D4**	*The Ave.*	
Rugby Ave. N9	33 C1	Rushmoor Clo., Pnr.	36 B4
Rugby Ave., Grnf.	46 A6	Rushmore Clo., Brom.	97 B3
Rugby Ave., Wem.	46 E5	Rushmore Rd. E5	50 F4
Rugby Clo., Har.	37 B4	Rusholme Ave., Dag.	53 G3
Rugby Gdns., Dag.	53 C6	Rusholme Gro. SE19	86 B5
Rugby Rd. NW9	38 A4	Rusholme Rd. SW15	75 A6
Rugby Rd. W4	65 E2	Rushout Ave., Har.	37 E6
Rugby Rd., Dag.	53 B6	**Rushton St. N1**	**9 C1**
Rugby Rd., Islw.	73 B5	Rushton St. N1	59 A2
Rugby Rd., Twick.	73 B5	Rushworth Ave. NW4	38 G3
Rugby St. WC1	**8 C6**	*Rushworth Gdns.*	
Rugby St. WC1	58 F4	Rushworth Gdns.	38 G3
Rugg St. E14	60 A7	NW4	
Ruislip Clo., Grnf.	54 H4	**Rushworth St. SE1**	**16 H3**
Ruislip Rd., Grnf.	54 G3	Rushworth St. SE1	67 H2
Ruislip Rd., Nthlt.	54 C1	Rushy Meadow La.,	100 H3
Ruislip Rd. E. W7	55 A4	Cars.	
Ruislip Rd. E. W13	55 C4	Ruskin Ave. E12	52 B6
Ruislip Rd. E., Grnf.	55 A4	Ruskin Ave., Rich.	65 A7
Ruislip St. SW17	84 J4	Ruskin Ave., Well.	80 A2
Rum Clo. E1	59 F7	Ruskin Clo. NW11	39 E6
Rumbold Rd. SW6	66 E7	Ruskin Dr., Orp.	104 H3
Rumsey Clo., Hmptn.	81 F6	Ruskin Dr., Well.	80 A3
Rumsey Rd. SW9	76 F3	Ruskin Dr., Wor.Pk.	99 H2
Runbury Circ. NW9	47 D2	Ruskin Gdns. W5	55 G4
Runcorn Clo. N17	41 E4	Ruskin Gdns., Har.	37 J4
Runcorn Pl. W11	57 B7	Ruskin Gro., Well.	80 A2
Rundell Cres. NW4	38 H5	Ruskin Pk. Ho. SE5	77 A3
Runnel Fld., Har.	46 B3	Ruskin Rd. N17	41 C1
Running Horse Yd.,	64 H6	Ruskin Rd., Belv.	71 G4
Brent.		Ruskin Rd., Cars.	100 J5
Pottery Rd.		Ruskin Rd., Croy.	101 H2
Runnymede SW19	93 F1	Ruskin Rd., Islw.	73 C3
Runnymede Clo.,	72 H7	Ruskin Rd., Sthl.	54 E7
Twick.		Ruskin Wk. N9	33 D2
Runnymede Ct.,	102 C2	*Durham Rd.*	
Croy.		Ruskin Wk. SE24	76 J5
Runnymede Cres.	94 D1	Ruskin Wk., Brom.	97 B6
SW16		Ruskin Way SW19	93 G1
Runnymede Gdns.,	55 A2	Rusland Ave., Orp.	104 G3
Grnf.		Rusland Pk. Rd., Har.	37 B4
Runnymede Gdns.,	72 H7	Rusper Clo. NW2	47 J3
Twick.		Rusper Clo., Stan.	29 F4
Runnymede Rd.,	72 H6	Rusper Rd. N22	40 H2
Twick.		Rusper Rd., Dag.	53 C6
Runway, The, Ruis.	45 B5	Russell Ave. N22	40 G2
Rupack St. SE16	68 F2	Russell Clo. NW10	47 C7
St. Marychurch St.		Russell Clo. SE7	69 J7
Rupert Ave., Wem.	46 H5	Russell Clo., Beck.	96 B3
Rupert Ct. W1	**11 H5**	Russell Clo., Bexh.	80 G4
Rupert Gdns. SW9	76 H2	Russell Clo., Ruis.	45 C2
Rupert Rd. N19	49 D3	**Russell Ct. SW1**	**15 G2**
Holloway Rd.		Russell Gdns. N20	31 H2
Rupert Rd. NW6	57 C2	Russell Gdns. NW11	39 B6
Rupert Rd. W4	65 E3	Russell Gdns. SW14	66 B3
Rupert St. W1	**11 H5**	Russell Gdns., Rich.	82 F2
Rupert St. W1	58 D7	Russell Gdns. Ms.	66 B2
Rural Way SW16	85 B7	W14	
Ruscoe Rd. E16	60 F6	Russell Gro. NW7	30 E5
Rush Grn. Gdns.,	53 J1	Russell Gro. SW9	76 G1
Rom.		Russell Kerr Clo. W4	65 C7
Rush Grn. Rd., Rom.	53 J1	*Burlington La.*	
Rush Gro. St. SE18	70 C4	Russell La. N20	31 H2
Rush Hill Ms. SW11	76 A3	Russell Mead, Har.	29 C7
Rush Hill Rd.		Russell Pl. NW3	48 H5
Rush Hill Rd. SW11	76 A3	*Aspern Gro.*	
Rusham Rd. SW12	75 J6	Russell Pl. SE16	68 H3
Rushbrook Cres. E17	41 J1	*Onega Gate*	
Rushbrook Rd. SE9	88 F2	Russell Rd. E4	33 J4
Rushcroft Rd. E4	34 A7	Russell Rd. E10	42 B6
Rushcroft Rd. SW2	76 G4	Russell Rd. E16	60 G6
Rushden Clo. SE19	86 A7	Russell Rd. E17	41 J3
Rushden Gdns. NW7	30 J6	Russell Rd. N8	40 D6
Rushden Gdns., Ilf.	43 D2	Russell Rd. N13	32 F6
Rushdene SE2	71 C3	Russell Rd. N15	41 B5
Rushdene Ave., Barn.	23 H7	Russell Rd. N20	31 H2
Rushdene Clo., Nthlt.	54 C2	Russell Rd. NW9	38 F6
Rushdene Cres.,	54 C2	Russell Rd. SW19	84 D7
Nthlt.		Russell Rd. W14	66 B3
Rushdene Rd., Pnr.	36 D6	Russell Rd., Buck.H.	34 H1
Rushen Wk., Cars.	100 G1	Russell Rd., Mitch.	93 H3
Paisley Rd.		Russell Rd., Nthlt.	45 J5
Rushett Clo., T.Ditt.	98 E1	Russell Rd., Twick.	73 C6
Rushett Rd., T.Ditt.	91 E7	Russell Rd., Walt.	90 A6
Rushey Clo., N.Mal.	92 D4	**Russell Sq. WC1**	**8 A6**
Rushey Grn. SE6	78 B7	Russell Sq. WC1	58 E4
Rushey Hill, Enf.	24 F4	**Russell St. WC2**	**12 B5**
Rushey Mead SE4	78 A5	Russell St. WC2	58 E7
Rushford Rd. SE4	77 J6	Russell Wk., Rich.	73 J6
Rushgrove Ave. NW9	38 E5	*Park Hill*	
Rushley Clo., Kes.	104 A4	Russell Way, Sutt.	100 D5
Rushmead E2	59 E3	Russell's Footpath	85 E5
Florida St.		SW16	
Rushmead, Rich.	82 E3	Russet Cres. N7	49 F5
Rushmead Clo., Croy.	102 C4	*Stock Orchard Cres.*	
Russet Dr., Croy.	102 H1	Ruxley Clo., Epsom	99 B5
Russets Clo. E4	34 D4	Ruxley Clo., Sid.	89 E6
Larkshall Rd.		Ruxley Cor. Ind. Est.,	89 D6
Russett Way SE13	78 B2	Sid.	
Conington Rd.		Ruxley Cres., Esher	98 E6
Russia Ct. EC2	**13 A4**	Ruxley La., Epsom	99 B6
Russia Dock Rd. SE16	68 H1	Ruxley Ms., Epsom	99 B5
Russia La. E2	59 F2	Ruxley Ridge, Esher	98 D7
Russia Row EC2	**13 A4**	Ryalls Ct. N20	31 J3
Russia Wk. SE16	68 G2	Ryan Clo. SE3	78 J4
Archangel St.		Ryan Clo., Ruis.	45 B1
Rust Sq. SE5	**21 B7**	Ryan Dr., Brent.	64 D6
Rust Sq. SE5	68 A7	Ryarsh Cres., Orp.	104 H4
Rusthall Ave. W4	65 D4	Rycott Path SE22	77 D7
Rusthall Clo., Croy.	95 F6	*Lordship La.*	
Rustic Ave. SW16	85 B7	Rycroft Way N17	41 C3
Rustic Pl., Wem.	46 G4	Ryculff Sq. SE3	78 F2
Rustic Wk. E16	60 H6	Rydal Clo. NW4	39 A1
Lambert Rd.		Rydal Cres., Grnf.	55 E3
Rustington Wk.,	93 C7	Rydal Dr., Bexh.	80 F2
Mord.		Rydal Dr., W.Wick.	103 E2
Ruston Ave., Surb.	92 B7	Rydal Gdns. NW9	38 E5
Ruston Gdns. N14	24 A6	Rydal Gdns. SW15	83 E5
Farm La.		Rydal Gdns., Houns.	72 H6
Ruston Ms. W11	57 B6	Rydal Gdns., Wem.	46 F1
St. Marks Rd.		Rydal Rd. SW16	85 D4
Ruston St. E3	59 J1	Rydal Way, Enf.	25 F6
Rutford Rd. SW16	85 E5	Rydal Way, Ruis.	45 C4
Ruth Clo., Stan.	37 J4	Ryde Pl., Twick.	73 F6
Rutherford Clo.,	100 G6	Ryde Vale Rd. SW12	85 B2
Sutt.		Ryder Clo., Brom.	87 H5
Rutherford St. SW1	**19 H1**	**Ryder Ct. SW1**	**15 G1**
Rutherford St. SW1	67 D4	**Ryder St. SW1**	**15 G1**
Rutherford Twr., Sthl.	54 H6	Ryder St. SW1	67 C1
Rutherford Way	29 A1	**Ryder Yd. SW1**	**15 G1**
(Bushey), Wat.		**Ryders Ter. NW8**	**6 C1**
Rutherford Way,	47 A3	Rydon St. N1	58 J1
Wem.		*St. Paul St.*	
Rutherglen Rd. SE2	71 A6	Rydons Clo. SE9	79 B3
Rutherwyke Clo.,	99 G6	Rydston Clo. N7	49 F7
Epsom		*Sutterton St.*	
Ruthin Clo. NW9	38 E6	Rye, The N14	24 C7
Ruthin Rd. SE3	69 G6	Rye Clo., Bex.	80 H6
Ruthven St. E9	59 G1	Rye Hill Est. SE15	77 F4
Lauriston Rd.		Rye Hill Pk. SE15	77 F4
Rutland Ave., Sid.	80 A7	Rye La. SE15	77 D2
Rutland Clo. SW14	74 B3	Rye Pas. SE15	77 D3
Rutland Clo. SW19	84 H7	Rye Rd. SE15	77 G4
Rutland Rd.		Rye Wk. SW15	75 A5
Rutland Clo., Bex.	89 D1	*Chartfield Ave.*	
Rutland Clo., Chess.	98 J6	Rye Way, Edg.	29 J6
Rutland Ct., Enf.	25 E5	*Canons Dr.*	
Rutland Dr., Mord.	93 C6	Ryecotes Mead SE21	86 B1
Rutland Dr., Rich.	82 G1	Ryecroft Ave., Ilf.	43 E2
Rutland Gdns. N4	40 H6	Ryecroft Ave., Twick.	72 H7
Rutland Gdns. SW7	**14 H4**	Ryecroft Cres., Barn.	22 H5
Rutland Gdns. SW7	66 H2	Ryecroft Rd. SE13	78 C5
Rutland Gdns. W13	55 H5	Ryecroft Rd. SW16	85 G6
Rutland Gdns., Croy.	102 B4	Ryecroft Rd., Orp.	97 G6
Rutland Gdns., Dag.	53 C5	Ryecroft St. SW6	75 E1
Rutland Gdns. Ms.	**14 H4**	Ryedale SE22	77 E6
SW7		Ryefield Path SW15	83 G1
Rutland Gate SW7	**14 H4**	Ryefield Rd. SE19	85 J6
Rutland Gate SW7	66 H2	Ryelands Cres. SE12	78 J6
Rutland Gate, Belv.	71 H5	Ryfold Rd. SW19	84 D3
Rutland Gate, Brom.	96 F4	Ryhope Rd. N11	32 B4
Rutland Gate Ms.	**14 G4**	Ryland Ho., Croy.	101 J3
SW7		Ryland Rd. NW5	49 B6
Rutland Gro. W6	65 H5	Rylandes Rd. NW2	47 G3
Rutland Ms. NW8	57 E1	Rylett Cres. W12	65 F2
Boundary Rd.		Rylett Rd. W12	65 F3
Rutland Ms. E. SW7	**14 G5**	Rylston Rd. N13	33 A3
Rutland Ms. S. SW7	**14 G5**	Rylston Rd. SW6	66 C6
Rutland Pk. NW2	47 J6	Rymer Rd., Croy.	95 B7
Rutland Pk. SE6	86 J2	Rymer St. SE24	76 H6
Rutland Pl. EC1	**12 H1**	Rymill St. E16	70 D1
Rutland Pl. (Bushey),	29 A1	Rysbrack St. SW3	14 J5
Wat.		Rysbrack St. SW3	66 J3
The Rutts		Rythe Ct., T.Ditt.	91 D7
Rutland Rd. E7	52 A7	Rythe Rd., Esher	98 A5
Rutland Rd. E9	59 F1		
Rutland Rd. E11	42 H5		
Rutland Rd. E17	42 A6		
Rutland Rd. SW19	84 H7	**S**	
Rutland Rd., Har.	36 J6		
Rutland Rd., Ilf.	52 E4	Sabbarton St. E16	60 F6
Rutland Rd., Sthl.	54 G4	*Victoria Dock Rd.*	
Rutland Rd., Twick.	82 A2	Sabella Ct. E3	59 J2
Rutland St. SW7	**14 H5**	*Mostyn Gro.*	
Rutland St. SW7	66 H3	Sabine Rd. SW11	75 J3
Rutland Wk. SE6	86 J2	Sable Clo., Houns.	72 C3
Rutley Clo. SE17	**20 G5**	Sable St. N1	49 H7
Rutley Clo. SE17	67 G6	*Canonbury Rd.*	
Rutlish Rd. SW19	93 D1	Sach Rd. E5	50 E2
Rutter Gdns., Mitch.	93 G4	Sackville Ave., Brom.	103 G1
Rutts, The (Bushey),	29 A1	Sackville Clo., Har.	46 A3
Wat.		Sackville Est. SW16	85 E3
Rutts Ter. SE14	77 G1	Sackville Gdns., Ilf.	52 C1
Ruvigny Gdns. SW15	75 A3	Sackville Rd., Sutt.	100 D7
		Sackville St. W1	**11 G6**

Sackville St. W1   58 C7
Sackville Way SE22   86 D1
  Dulwich Common
Saddlers Clo., Borwd.   22 D6
  Farriers Way
Saddlers Clo., Pnr.   28 G6
Saddlers Ms., Wem.   46 C4
  The Boltons
Saddlescombe Way   31 D5
  N12
Sadler Clo., Mitch.   93 J2
Sadlers Ride, W.Mol.   90 H3
Saffron Ave. E14   60 D7
Saffron Clo. NW11   39 C5
Saffron Hill EC1   **12 F1**
Saffron Hill EC1   58 G4
Saffron Rd., Rom.   44 J2
Saffron St. EC1   **12 F1**
Saffron Way, Surb.   98 G1
Sage St. E1   59 F7
  Cable St.
Sage Way WC1   **8 C4**
Saigasso Clo. E16   61 A6
  Royal Rd.
Sail St. SE11   **20 D1**
Sail St. SE11   67 F4
Sainfoin Rd. SW17   85 A2
Sainsbury Rd. SE19   86 B5
St. Agatha's Dr.,   82 J6
  Kings.T.
St. Agathas Gro.,   100 J1
  Cars.
St. Agnes Clo. E9   59 F1
  Gore St.
St. Agnes Pl. SE11   **20 F6**
St. Agnes Pl. SE11   67 H6
St. Aidan's Rd. SE22   77 E6
St. Aidans Rd. W13   64 E2
St. Albans Ave. E6   61 C3
St. Albans Ave. W4   65 D3
St. Albans Ave., Felt.   81 D5
St. Albans Clo. NW11   48 D1
St. Albans Cres. N22   40 G1
St. Alban's Cres.,   34 G7
  Wdf.Grn.
St. Alban's Gdns.,   82 D5
  Tedd.
St. Albans Gro. W8   **14 B5**
St. Albans Gro. W8   66 E3
St. Alban's Gro., Cars.   93 H7
St. Albans La. NW11   48 D1
  West Heath Dr.
St. Alban's Pl. N1   58 H1
St. Albans Rd. NW5   49 A3
St. Albans Rd. NW10   56 E1
St. Albans Rd., Barn.   23 A1
St. Alban's Rd., Ilf.   52 J1
St. Alban's Rd.,   82 H6
  Kings.T.
St. Alban's Rd., Sutt.   100 C4
St. Alban's Rd.,   34 G7
  Wdf.Grn.
St. Albans St. SW1   **11 H6**
St. Albans Ter. W6   66 B6
  Margravine Rd.
St. Albans Twr. E4   33 J6
St. Alfege Pas. SE10   69 C6
St. Alfege Rd. SE7   70 A6
St. Alphage Gdns.   **13 A2**
  EC2
St. Alphage Wk., Edg.   38 C2
St. Alphege Rd. N9   25 F7
St. Alphonsus Rd.   76 D4
  SW4
St. Amunds Clo. SE6   87 A4
St. Andrew St. EC4   **12 F2**
St. Andrew St. EC4   58 G5
St. Andrews Ave.,   46 D4
  Wem.
  Woodside Ave.
St. Andrew's Clo. N12   31 F4
St. Andrews Clo. NW2   47 H3
St. Andrew's Clo.,   73 A1
  Islw.
St. Andrews Clo.,   45 D2
  Ruis.
St. Andrews Clo., Stan.   37 F2
St. Andrew's Ct. SW18   84 F2
  Waynflete St.
St. Andrews Dr., Stan.   37 F1
St. Andrew's Gro.   50 A1
  N16
St. Andrew's Hill EC4   **12 H5**
St. Andrew's Hill EC4   58 H7
St. Andrew's Ms. N16   50 B1
  Dunsmure Rd.
St. Andrews Ms. SE3   69 G7
  Mycenae Rd.

St. Andrews Pl. NW1   **7 E5**
St. Andrews Rd. E11   42 E6
St. Andrews Rd. E13   60 H3
St. Andrews Rd. E17   41 G2
St. Andrews Rd. N9   25 F7
St. Andrews Rd. NW9   47 D1
St. Andrews Rd.   47 H6
  NW10
St. Andrews Rd.   39 C6
  NW11
St. Andrews Rd. W3   56 E6
St. Andrews Rd. W7   64 B2
  Church Rd.
St. Andrews Rd. W14   66 B6
St. Andrews Rd.,   100 H3
  Cars.
St. Andrews Rd.,   101 J4
  Croy.
  Lower Coombe St.
St. Andrews Rd., Enf.   25 A3
St. Andrews Rd., Ilf.   43 C7
St. Andrew's Rd., Sid.   89 D3
St. Andrew's Rd.,   91 G6
  Surb.
St. Andrews Rd., Wat.   28 D3
  Bridlington Rd.
St. Andrews Sq. W11   57 B6
  St. Marks Rd.
St. Andrew's Sq.,   91 G6
  Surb.
St. Andrews Twr.,   54 J7
  Sthl.
St. Andrews Way E3   60 B4
St. Anna Rd., Barn.   23 A5
  Sampson Ave.
St. Anne's Clo. N6   49 A3
  Highgate W. Hill
St. Anne's Clo., Wat.   28 C4
St. Anne's Ct. W1   **11 H4**
St. Annes Gdns.   55 J3
  NW10
St. Anne's Ho. N16   50 B1
St. Annes Pas. E14   59 J6
  Newell St.
St. Annes Rd. E11   51 D2
St. Anne's Rd., Wem.   46 G5
St. Anne's Row E14   59 J6
St. Anne's St. E14   59 J6
  Commercial Rd.
St. Ann's, Bark.   61 F1
St. Ann's Cres. SW18   75 E6
St. Ann's Gdns. NW5   49 A6
  Queens Cres.
St. Ann's Hill SW18   75 E5
St. Ann's La. SW1   **15 J5**
St. Ann's Pk. Rd.   75 F6
  SW18
St. Ann's Pas. SW13   74 E3
  Cross St.
St. Anns Rd. N9   33 C2
St. Ann's Rd. N15   40 H5
St. Ann's Rd. SW13   74 F2
St. Anns Rd. W11   57 A7
St. Ann's Rd., Bark.   61 F1
  Axe St.
St. Ann's Rd., Har.   37 B6
St. Ann's St. SW1   **15 J5**
St. Ann's St. SW1   67 D3
St. Ann's Ter. NW8   **6 F1**
St. Ann's Ter. NW8   57 G2
St. Anns Vill. W11   66 A1
St. Anns Way,   101 H6
  S.Croy.
St. Anselm's Pl. W1   **11 D4**
St. Anthonys Ave.,   34 J6
  Wdf.Grn.
St. Anthonys Clo. E1   **17 H1**
St. Anthonys Clo.   84 H2
  SW17
  College Gdns.
St. Antony's Rd. E7   51 H7
St. Arvans Clo.,   102 B3
  Croy.
St. Asaph Rd. SE4   77 G3
St. Aubyn's Ave.   84 C5
  SW19
St. Aubyns Ave.,   72 G5
  Houns.
St. Aubyns Clo., Orp.   104 J3
St. Aubyns Gdns.,   104 J2
  Orp.
St. Aubyn's Rd. SE19   86 C6
St. Audrey Ave.,   80 G2
  Bexh.
St. Augustine Ave.   55 H2
  W5
St. Augustines Ave.,   97 B5
  Brom.

St. Augustine's Ave.,   101 J6
  S.Croy.
St. Augustines Ave.,   46 H3
  Wem.
St. Augustines Rd.   49 D7
  NW1
St. Augustine's Rd.,   71 F4
  Belv.
St. Austell Clo., Edg.   37 J2
St. Austell Rd. SE13   78 C2
St. Awdry's Rd., Bark.   52 G7
St. Awdry's Wk., Bark.   52 F7
  Station Par.
St. Barnabas Clo.,   96 C2
  Beck.
St. Barnabas Ct., Har.   36 J1
St. Barnabas Rd. E17   42 A6
St. Barnabas Rd.,   85 A7
  Mitch.
St. Barnabas Rd.,   100 G5
  Sutt.
St. Barnabas Rd.,   42 H1
  Wdf.Grn.
St. Barnabas St. SW1   **19 C3**
St. Barnabas St. SW1   67 A5
St. Barnabas Ter. E9   50 G5
St. Barnabas Vill.   76 E1
  SW8
St. Bartholomews   86 E4
  Clo. SE26
St. Bartholomew's   61 C2
  Rd. E6
St. Benedict's Clo.   85 A5
  SW17
  Church La.
St. Benet's Clo. SW17   84 H2
  College Gdns.
St. Benet's Gro.,   93 F7
  Cars.
St. Benet's Pl. EC3   **13 C5**
St. Bernards, Croy.   102 B3
St. Bernard's Clo.   86 A4
  SE27
  St. Gothard Rd.
St. Bernard's Rd. E6   61 A1
St. Blaise Ave., Brom.   96 H2
St. Botolph Row EC3   **13 F4**
St. Botolph St. EC3   **13 F3**
St. Botolph St. EC3   59 C6
St. Bride St. EC4   **12 G3**
St. Bride St. EC4   58 H6
St. Brides Ave., Edg.   37 J1
St. Brides Clo., Erith   71 D2
  St. Katherines Rd.
St. Bride's Pas. EC4   **12 G4**
St. Catherines Clo.   84 H2
  SW17
  College Gdns.
St. Catherines Dr.   77 G2
  SE14
  Kitto Rd.
St. Catherine's Ms.   **18 J1**
  SW3
St. Catherines Rd. E4   34 A2
St. Chads Clo., Surb.   91 F7
St. Chad's Gdns.,   44 E7
  Rom.
St. Chad's Pl. WC1   **8 B3**
St. Chad's Pl. WC1   58 E3
St. Chad's Rd., Rom.   44 E6
St. Chad's St. WC1   **8 B3**
St. Chad's St. WC1   58 E3
St. Charles Pl. W10   57 B5
  Chesterton Rd.
St. Charles Sq. W10   57 B5
St. Christopher's Clo.,   73 B1
  Islw.
St. Christophers   94 G3
  Gdns., Th.Hth.
St. Christophers Ms.,   101 C5
  Wall.
St. Christopher's Pl.   **11 C3**
  W1
St. Clair Dr., Wor.Pk.   99 H3
St. Clair Rd. E13   60 H2
St. Claire Clo., Ilf.   43 C2
St. Clair's Rd., Croy.   102 C2
St. Clare St. EC3   **13 F4**
St. Clements Ct. N7   49 G6
  Arundel Sq.
St. Clements Heights   86 D3
  SE26
St. Clement's La. WC2   **12 D4**
St. Clements St. N1   49 G6
St. Clements St. N7   49 G6
St. Cloud Rd. SE27   85 J4
St. Crispins Clo. NW3   48 H4
St. Crispins Clo., Sthl.   54 F6

St. Cross St. EC1   **12 F1**
St. Cross St. EC1   58 G5
St. Cuthberts Gdns.,   28 F7
  Pnr.
  Westfield Pk.
St. Cuthberts Rd. NW2   48 C6
St. Cyprian's St. SW17   84 A4
St. Davids Clo., Wem.   47 C3
St. David's Clo.,   96 B7
  W.Wick.
St. David's Ct. E17   42 C3
St. Davids Dr., Edg.   37 J1
St. Davids Pl. NW4   38 H7
St. Denis Rd. SE27   86 A4
St. Dionis Rd. SW6   75 C2
St. Donatts Rd. SE14   77 J1
St. Dunstan's All. EC3   **13 D6**
St. Dunstans Ave. W3   56 D7
St. Dunstan's Ct. EC4   58 G6
  Fleet St.
St. Dunstans Gdns.   56 D7
  W3
  St. Dunstans Ave.
St. Dunstan's Hill EC3   **13 D6**
St. Dunstan's Hill EC3   59 B7
St. Dunstan's Hill,   100 B5
  Sutt.
St. Dunstan's La. EC3   **13 D6**
St. Dunstan's La.,   96 C6
  Beck.
St. Dunstan's Rd. E7   51 J6
St. Dunstans Rd.   95 C4
  SE25
St. Dunstans Rd. W6   66 A5
St. Dunstans Rd. W7   64 B2
St. Dunstans Rd.,   72 B2
  Houns.
St. Edmunds Clo.   57 J1
  NW8
  St. Edmunds Ter.
St. Edmunds Clo.   84 H2
  SW17
  College Gdns.
St. Edmunds Clo.,   71 D2
  Erith
  St. Katherines Rd.
St. Edmunds Dr.,   37 D1
  Stan.
St. Edmund's La.,   72 H7
  Twick.
St. Edmunds Rd. N9   25 D7
St. Edmunds Rd., Ilf.   43 C6
St. Edmunds Ter. NW8   **6 H1**
St. Edmunds Ter. NW8   57 H2
St. Edwards Clo.   39 D6
  NW11
St. Egberts Way E4   34 C1
St. Elmo Rd. W12   65 F1
St. Elmos Rd. SE16   68 G2
St. Erkenwald Rd.,   61 G1
  Bark.
St. Ermin's Hill SW1   **15 H5**
St. Ervans Rd. W10   57 C5
St. Fabian Twr. E4   33 J6
St. Faiths Clo., Enf.   24 J1
St. Faith's Rd. SE21   85 H1
St. Fillans Rd. SE6   87 C1
St. Francis Clo., Orp.   97 H6
St. Francis Clo., Wat.   28 B1
St. Francis Rd. SE22   77 B4
St. Francis Twr. E4   33 J6
St. Gabriel's Clo. E11   51 H1
St. Gabriels Rd. NW2   48 A5
St. George St. W1   **11 E5**
St. George St. W1   58 B7
St. Georges Ave. E7   51 H7
St. Georges Ave. N7   49 D4
St. Georges Ave. NW9   38 C4
St. George's Ave. W5   64 G2
St. Georges Ave.,   54 F7
  Sthl.
St. Georges Circ. SE1   **16 G5**
St. Georges Circ. SE1   67 H3
St. Georges Clo.   39 C6
  NW11
St. Georges Clo.,   46 D3
  Wem.
St. Georges Ct. E6   61 C4
St. Georges Ct. EC4   **12 G3**
St. Georges Ct. SW7   **14 C5**
St. George's Dr. SW1   **19 E2**
St. George's Dr. SW1   67 B4
St. Georges Dr., Wat.   28 E3
St. Georges Flds. W2   **10 H4**
St. Georges Flds. W2   57 H6
St. George's Gdns.,   99 B2
  Surb.
  Hamilton Ave.

St. Georges Gro. 84 G3
SW17
St. Georges Gro. Est. 84 G3
SW17
St. Georges Ind. Est. 32 H7
N17
St. Georges La. EC3 **13 C5**
St. Georges Ms. NW1 48 J7
Regents Pk. Rd.
St. Georges Pl., Twick. 82 D1
Church St.
St. Georges Rd. E7 51 H6
St. Georges Rd. E10 51 C3
St. Georges Rd. N9 33 D3
St. Georges Rd. N13 32 F3
St. Georges Rd. 39 C6
NW11
St. Georges Rd. SE1 **16 F5**
St. Georges Rd. SE1 67 G3
St. George's Rd. 84 C7
SW19
St. Georges Rd. W4 65 D2
St. Georges Rd. W7 64 C1
St. George's Rd., 96 B1
Beck.
St. Georges Rd., 97 C2
Brom.
St. George's Rd., Dag. 53 E5
St. George's Rd., Felt. 81 D4
St. Georges Rd., Ilf. 43 C7
St. George's Rd., 83 A7
Kings.T.
St. Georges Rd., 94 B3
Mitch.
St. Georges Rd., Orp. 97 G6
St. Georges Rd., Rich. 73 J3
St. Georges Rd., Sid. 89 D6
St. Georges Rd. 73 E5
Twick.
St. Georges Rd., 101 B5
Wall.
St. Georges Rd. W., 97 B1
Brom.
St. Georges Sq. E7 51 H7
St. Georges Sq. E14 59 H7
St. Georges Sq. SE8 68 J4
St. George's Sq. SW1 **19 H4**
St. George's Sq. SW1 67 D5
St. George's Sq., 92 E3
N.Mal.
High St.
St. George's Sq. Ms. **19 H4**
SW1
St. George's Sq. Ms. 67 D5
SW1
St. Georges Ter. NW1 48 J7
Regents Pk. Rd.
St. Georges Wk., 101 J3
Croy.
St. Georges Way **21 D6**
SE15
St. Georges Way 68 B6
SE15
St. Gerards Clo. SW4 76 C5
St. German's Pl. SE3 78 G1
St. Germans Rd. 86 H1
SE23
St. Giles Ave., Dag. 53 H7
St. Giles Clo., Dag. 53 H7
St. Giles Ave.
St. Giles Clo., Orp. 104 G5
St. Giles High St. **11 J3**
WC2
St. Giles High St. 58 D6
WC2
St. Giles Pas. WC2 **11 J4**
St. Giles Rd. SE5 68 B7
St. Gilles Ho. E2 59 G2
Mace St.
St. Gothard Rd. SE27 86 A4
St. Gregory Clo., Ruis. 45 C4
St. Helena Rd. SE16 68 G4
St. Helena St. WC1 **8 E4**
St. Helen's Cres. 94 F1
SW16
St. Helens Rd.
St. Helens Gdns. W10 57 A5
St. Helens Pl. EC3 **13 D3**
St. Helens Rd. SW16 94 F1
St. Helen's Rd. W13 64 E1
Dane Rd.
St. Helens Rd., Erith 71 D2
St. Helens Rd., Ilf. 43 C6
St. Helier Ave., Mord. 93 F7
St. Heliers Ave., 72 G5
Houns.
St. Heliers Rd. E10 42 C6
St. Hildas Clo. NW6 57 A1

St. Hildas Clo. SW17 84 H2
St. Hilda's Rd. SW13 65 H6
St. Hughe's Clo. SW17 84 H2
College Gdns.
St. Hughs Rd. SE20 95 E1
Ridsdale Rd.
St. James Ave. E2 59 F2
St. James Ave. N20 31 H3
St. James Ave. W13 64 D1
St. James Ave., Sutt. 100 D5
St. James Clo. N20 31 H3
St. James Clo. SE18 70 F5
Congleton Gro.
St. James Clo., N.Mal. 92 F5
St. James Clo., Ruis. 45 C2
St. James Gdns. W11 66 B1
St. James Gdns., 46 G7
Wem.
St. James Gate NW1 49 D7
St. Paul's Cres.
St. James Gro. SW11 75 J2
Reform St.
St. James Ms. E14 69 C3
St. James Rd. E15 51 F5
St. James Rd. N9 33 E2
Queens Rd.
St. James Rd., Cars. 100 H3
St. James Rd., 91 G2
Kings.T.
St. James Rd., Mitch. 85 A7
St. James Rd., Surb. 91 G6
St. James Rd., Sutt. 100 D5
St. James St. W6 65 J5
St. James Wk. SE15 68 C7
Commercial Way
St. James Way, Sid. 89 E5
St. James's SE14 77 H1
St. James's Ave., 95 H3
Beck.
St. James's Ave., 81 J5
Hmptn.
St. James's Clo. SW17 84 J2
St. James's Dr.
St. James's Cotts., 73 G5
Rich.
Paradise Rd.
St. James's Ct. SW1 **15 G5**
St. James's Ct. SW1 67 C3
St. James's Cres. 76 G3
SW9
St. James's Dr. SW17 84 J1
St. James's La. N10 40 B4
St. James's Mkt. SW1 **11 H6**
St. James's Palace **15 G2**
SW1
St. James's Palace 67 C1
SW1
St. James's Pk. SW1 **15 H5**
St. James's Pk. SW1 67 C2
St. James's Pk., Croy. 94 J7
St. James's Pas. EC3 **13 E4**
St. James's Pl. SW1 **15 F2**
St. James's Pl. SW1 67 C1
St. James's Rd. SE1 **21 J5**
St. James's Rd. SE1 68 D5
St. James's Rd. SE16 **17 J5**
St. James's Rd. SE16 68 D3
St. James's Rd., Croy. 94 H7
St. James's Rd., 81 H5
Hmptn.
St. James's Row EC1 **8 G5**
St. James's Sq. SW1 **15 G1**
St. James's Sq. SW1 67 D1
St. James's St. E17 41 H5
St. James's St. SW1 **15 F1**
St. James's St. SW1 67 C1
St. James's Ter. NW8 **6 J1**
St. James's Ter. Ms. 57 J1
NW8
St. James's Wk. EC1 **8 G5**
St. James's Wk. EC1 58 H4
St. Joans Rd. N9 33 C1
St. John Fisher Rd., 71 D3
Erith
St. John St. EC1 **8 G3**
St. John St. EC1 58 G2
St. Johns Ave. N11 31 J5
St. John's Ave. NW10 56 F1
St. John's Ave. SW15 75 A5
St. John's Ch. Rd. E9 50 F5
St. Johns Clo. N14 24 C6
Chase Rd.
St. John's Clo. SW6 66 D7
Dawes Rd.
St. John's Clo., Wem. 46 H5
St. John's Cotts. 86 F7
SE20
Maple Rd.

St. Johns Cotts., Rich. 73 H4
Kew Foot Rd.
St. Johns Ct., Buck.H. 34 H1
St. John's Ct., Islw. 73 C2
St. John's Cres. SW9 76 G3
St. Johns Dr. SW18 84 E1
St. John's Est. N1 **9 C2**
St. John's Est. N1 59 A2
St. John's Est. SE1 **17 F4**
St. John's Gdns. W11 57 B7
St. Johns Gro. N19 49 C2
St. Johns Gro. SW13 74 F2
Terrace Gdns.
St. Johns Gro., Rich. 73 H4
Kew Foot Rd.
St. John's Hill SW11 75 G4
St. John's Hill Gro. 75 G4
SW11
St. John's La. EC1 **8 G6**
St. John's La. EC1 58 H4
St. John's Ms. W11 57 D6
Ledbury Rd.
St. Johns Par., Sid. 89 A4
Church Rd.
St. John's Pk. SE3 69 F7
St. Johns Pas. SE23 86 F1
Davids Rd.
St. John's Pas. SW19 84 B6
Ridgway Pl.
St. John's Path EC1 **8 G6**
St. Johns Pathway 86 F1
SE23
Devonshire Rd.
St. John's Pl. EC1 **8 G6**
St. John's Rd. E4 34 B3
St. Johns Rd. E6 61 B1
St. Johns Rd. E16 60 G6
St. John's Rd. E17 42 B2
St. Johns Rd. N15 41 B6
St. Johns Rd. NW11 39 C6
St. Johns Rd. SE20 86 F7
St. Johns Rd. SW11 75 H4
St. John's Rd. SW19 84 B6
St. Johns Rd., Bark. 61 H1
St. Johns Rd., Cars. 100 H3
St. Johns Rd., Croy. 101 H3
Sylverdale Rd.
St. Johns Rd., E.Mol. 91 A4
St. John's Rd., Felt. 81 E4
St. Johns Rd., Har. 37 C6
St. Johns Rd., Ilf. 43 G7
St. John's Rd., Islw. 73 B2
St. Johns Rd., 91 F2
Kings.T.
St. Johns Rd., Loug. 27 C2
St. John's Rd., N.Mal. 92 C3
St. Johns Rd., Orp. 97 G6
St. John's Rd., Rich. 73 H4
St. John's Rd., Sid. 89 B4
St. Johns Rd., Sthl. 63 E3
St. Johns Rd., Sutt. 100 D2
St. John's Rd., Well. 80 B3
St. John's Rd., Wem. 46 H5
St. John's Sq. EC1 **8 G6**
St. Johns Ter. E7 51 H6
St. Johns Ter. SE18 70 F6
St. Johns Ter. W10 57 A4
Harrow Rd.
St. Johns Vale SE8 78 A2
St. Johns Vill. N19 49 D2
St. Johns Way N19 49 C2
St. John's Vill. W8 **14 B6**
St. John's Wd. Ct. **6 F4**
NW8
St. John's Wd. High **6 F2**
St. NW8
St. John's Wd. High 57 G2
St. NW8
St. John's Wd. Pk. 57 G1
NW8
St. John's Wd. Rd. **6 E5**
NW8
St. John's Wd. Rd. 57 G4
NW8
St. John's Wd. Ter. **6 F1**
NW8
St. John's Wd. Ter. 57 G2
NW8
St. Josephs Clo. W10 57 B5
Bevington Rd.
St. Joseph's Clo., 104 J4
Orp.
St. Joseph's Ct. SE7 69 H6
St. Josephs Dr., Sthl. 63 E1
St. Joseph's Gro. 38 H4
NW4
St. Josephs Rd. N9 25 E7
St. Joseph's Vale SE3 78 D3

St. Jude St. N16 50 B5
St. Jude's Rd. E2 59 E2
St. Julian's Clo. 85 G4
SW16
St. Julian's Fm. Rd. 85 G4
SE27
St. Julian's Rd. NW6 48 C7
St. Katharines Prec. **7 D1**
NW1
St. Katharine's Way **17 G1**
E1
St. Katharine's Way 68 D1
E1
St. Katherines Rd., 71 D2
Erith
St. Katherine's Row **13 E5**
EC3
St. Keverne Rd. SE9 88 B4
St. Kilda Rd. W13 64 D1
St. Kilda Rd., Orp. 104 J1
St. Kilda's Rd. N16 50 A1
St. Kildas Rd., Har. 37 B6
St. Kitts Ter. SE19 86 B5
St. Laurence Clo. 57 A1
NW6
St. Lawrence Clo., 29 J7
Edg.
St. Lawrence Dr., Pnr. 36 B5
St. Lawrence St. E14 69 C1
St. Lawrence Ter. 57 B5
W10
St. Lawrence Way 76 G2
SW9
St. Leonards Ave. E4 34 D6
St. Leonards Ave., 37 F5
Har.
St. Leonard's Clo. 80 A3
Well.
Hook La.
St. Leonards Ct. N1 **9 C3**
St. Leonard's Gdns., 72 E1
Houns.
St. Leonards Gdns., 52 F5
Ilf.
St. Leonards Rd. E14 60 B5
St. Leonard's Rd. 56 D4
NW10
St. Leonard's Rd. 74 B3
SW14
St. Leonards Rd. W13 55 F6
St. Leonards Rd., 101 H3
Croy.
St. Leonards Rd., 98 C6
Esher
St. Leonard's Rd., 91 G5
Surb.
St. Leonards Rd., 91 D6
T.Ditt.
St. Leonard's Sq. NW5 49 A6
St. Leonard's Sq., 91 G5
Surb.
St. Leonard's Rd.
St. Leonards St. E3 60 B3
St. Leonard's Ter. SW3 **18 J4**
St. Leonard's Ter. SW3 66 J5
St. Leonards Wk. 85 F7
SW16
St. Loo Ave. SW3 **18 H5**
St. Loo Ave. SW3 66 H6
St. Louis Rd. SE27 85 J4
St. Loy's Rd. N17 41 B2
St. Luke's Ave. SW4 76 D4
St. Luke's Ave., Ilf. 52 E5
St. Lukes Clo. SE25 95 E6
St. Luke's Est. EC1 **9 B4**
St. Luke's Est. EC1 59 A3
St. Luke's Ms. W11 57 C6
Basing St.
St. Lukes Pas., 91 J1
Kings.T.
St. Lukes Rd. W11 57 C5
St. Lukes Sq. E16 60 F6
St. Luke's St. SW3 **18 H3**
St. Luke's St. SW3 66 H5
St. Luke's Yd. W9 57 C3
St. Malo Ave. N9 33 F3
St. Margarets, Bark. 61 F1
St. Margarets Ave. 40 H4
N15
St. Margarets Ave. 31 F1
N20
St. Margarets Ave. 45 J3
Har.
St. Margarets Ave. 88 G3
Sid.
St. Margaret's Ave., 100 B3
Sutt.

St. Margaret's Ct. SE1 17 B2
St. Margarets Cres. 74 H5
SW15
St. Margaret's Dr., 73 E5
Twick.
St. Margaret's Gro. 51 F3
E11
St. Margarets Gro. 70 F6
SE18
St. Margarets Gro., 73 D6
Twick.
St. Margarets Pas. 78 E3
SE13
Church Ter.
St. Margarets Rd. E12 51 J2
St. Margarets Rd. N17 41 B3
St. Margarets Rd. 56 J3
NW10
St. Margarets Rd. SE4 77 J4
St. Margarets Rd. W7 64 B2
St. Margarets Rd., 95 G4
Beck.
St. Margarets Rd., 30 B5
Edg.
St. Margarets Rd., 73 E6
Twick.
St. Margarets Sq. SE4 77 J4
Adelaide Ave.
St. Margaret's St. 16 A4
SW1
St. Margaret's St. SW1 67 E2
St. Margaret's Ter. 70 F5
SE18
St. Mark St. E1 13 G4
St. Mark St. E1 59 C6
St. Marks Clo. SE10 69 C7
Ashburnham Pl.
St. Marks Clo. W11 57 B6
Lancaster Rd.
St. Mark's Clo., Barn. 23 E3
St. Marks Cres. NW1 58 A1
St. Marks Gate E9 50 J7
Cadogan Ter.
St. Mark's Gro. SW10 18 B6
St. Mark's Gro. SW10 66 E6
St. Mark's Hill, Surb. 91 H6
St. Mark's Pl. SW19 84 C6
Wimbledon Hill Rd.
St. Marks Pl. W11 57 B6
St. Marks Ri. E8 50 C5
St. Marks Rd. SE25 95 D4
Coventry Rd.
St. Mark's Rd. W5 64 H1
The Common
St. Marks Rd. W7 64 B2
St. Marks Rd. W10 57 A5
St. Marks Rd. W11 57 B6
St. Marks Rd., Brom. 96 H3
St. Marks Rd., Enf. 25 C5
St. Marks Rd., Mitch. 93 J2
St. Mark's Rd., Tedd. 82 E7
St. Marks Sq. NW1 58 A1
Regents Pk. Rd.
St. Martins Ave. E6 61 A2
St. Martin's Clo. NW1 58 C1
St. Martins Clo., Enf. 25 E1
St. Martins Clo., Erith 71 D2
St. Helens Rd.
Muirfield Rd.
St. Martin's Ct. WC2 12 A5
St. Martins Est. SW2 85 G1
St. Martin's La. WC2 12 A5
St. Martin's La. WC2 58 E7
St. Martin's Pl. WC2 12 A6
St. Martin's Pl. WC2 58 E7
St. Martins Rd. N9 33 E2
St. Martin's Rd. SW9 76 F2
St. Martin's St. WC2 11 J6
St. Martins Way 84 F3
SW17
St. Martin's-le-Grand 12 J3
EC1
St. Martin's-le-Grand 58 J6
EC1
St. Mary Abbots Pl. 66 C3
W8
St. Mary Abbots Ter. 66 C3
W14
St. Mary at Hill EC3 13 D6
St. Mary at Hill EC3 59 B7
St. Mary Ave., Wall. 101 A3
St. Mary Axe EC3 13 D4
St. Mary Axe EC3 59 B6
St. Mary Rd. E17 42 A4
St. Mary St. SE18 70 D4
St. Marychurch St. 68 F2
SE16

St. Marys, Bark. 61 G1
St. Marys App. E12 52 C5
St. Marys Ave. E11 42 H6
St. Mary's Ave. N3 39 B2
St. Mary's Ave., 96 E3
Brom.
St. Mary's Ave., Sthl. 63 G4
St. Mary's Ave., Tedd. 82 C6
St. Marys Clo. N17 41 D1
Kemble Rd.
St. Marys Clo., Chess. 98 J7
St. Marys Clo., Epsom 97 G4
St. Mary's Clo., Sun. 90 A4
Green Way
St. Marys Ct. E6 61 C4
St. Mary's Ct. SE7 70 A7
St. Mary's Ct. W5 64 G2
St. Mary's Rd.
St. Mary's Cres. NW4 38 H3
St. Marys Cres., Islw. 64 A7
St. Mary's Gdns. SE11 20 F1
St. Mary's Gdns. SE11 67 G4
St. Mary's Gate W8 14 A6
St. Mary's Gate W8 66 E3
St. Mary's Grn. N2 39 F3
Thomas More Way
St. Mary's Gro. N1 49 H6
St. Mary's Gro. SW13 74 H3
St. Mary's Gro. W4 65 B6
St. Mary's Gro., Rich. 73 J4
St. Marys Mans. W2 10 E1
St. Marys Mans. W2 57 G5
Priory Rd.
St. Mary's Ms. NW6 48 E7
St. Mary's Ms., Rich. 82 F3
Back La.
St. Marys Path N1 58 H1
St. Mary's Pl. SE9 79 D6
Eltham High St.
St. Mary's Pl. W5 64 G2
St. Mary's Rd.
St. Mary's Pl. W8 14 A6
St. Mary's Pl. W8 66 E3
St. Marys Rd. E10 51 C3
St. Marys Rd. E13 60 H2
St. Marys Rd. N8 40 E4
High St.
St. Marys Rd. N9 33 E1
St. Marys Rd. NW10 56 E1
St. Marys Rd. NW11 39 B7
St. Mary's Rd. SE15 77 F1
St. Mary's Rd. SE25 95 B3
St. Mary's Rd. SW19 84 B5
(Wimbledon)
St. Mary's Rd. W5 64 G2
St. Marys Rd., Barn. 23 J7
St. Marys Rd., Bex. 89 J1
St. Marys Rd., E.Mol. 91 A5
St. Marys Rd., Ilf. 52 F2
St. Marys Rd., Surb. 91 G6
St. Marys Rd., Surb. 91 F7
(Long Ditton)
St. Mary's Rd., 99 E2
Wor.Pk.
St. Marys Sq. W2 10 E1
St. Marys Sq. W2 57 G5
St. Mary's Sq. W5 64 G2
St. Mary's Rd.
St. Marys Ter. W2 10 E1
St. Marys Ter. W2 57 G5
St. Marys Vw., Har. 37 F5
St. Mary's Wk. SE11 20 F1
St. Mary's Wk. SE11 67 G4
St. Mary's Way, Chig. 35 D5
St. Matthew St. SW1 15 H6
St. Matthew's Ave., 98 H1
Surb.
St. Matthew's Dr., 97 C3
Brom.
St. Matthew's Rd. 76 F4
SW2
St. Matthews Rd. W5 64 H1
The Common
St. Matthew's Row E2 9 H5
St. Matthew's Row E2 59 D3
St. Matthias Clo. NW9 38 F5
St. Maur Rd. SW6 75 C1
St. Merryn Clo. SE18 70 G7
St. Michael's All. EC3 13 C4
St. Michaels Ave. N9 25 F7
St. Michael's Ave., 47 A6
Wem.
St. Michaels Clo. E16 61 A5
Fulmer Rd.
St. Michaels Clo. N3 39 C2
St. Michaels Clo. N12 31 H5
St. Michaels Clo., 97 B3
Brom.

St. Michaels Clo., 71 D2
Erith
St. Helens Rd.
St. Michaels Clo., 99 F2
Wor.Pk.
St. Michaels Cres., 36 E6
Pnr.
St. Michaels Gdns. 57 B5
W10
St. Lawrence Ter.
St. Michaels Rd. NW2 47 J4
St. Michael's Rd. SW9 76 F2
St. Michaels Rd., 101 J1
Croy.
St. Michaels Rd., 101 C6
Wall.
St. Michaels Rd., 80 B3
Well.
St. Michaels St. W2 10 F3
St. Michaels St. W2 57 G6
St. Michaels Ter. N22 40 E2
St. Mildred's Ct. EC2 13 B4
St. Mildreds Rd. SE12 78 F7
St. Nicholas Glebe 85 A5
SW17
St. Nicholas La., Chis. 97 B1
St. Nicholas Rd. 70 J5
SE18
St. Nicholas Rd., 100 E5
Sutt.
St. Nicholas Rd., 91 C6
T.Ditt.
St. Nicholas St. SE8 77 J1
Lucas St.
St. Nicholas Way, 100 E4
Sutt.
St. Ninian's Ct. N20 31 J3
St. Norbert Grn. SE4 77 H4
St. Norbert Rd. SE4 77 G5
St. Olaves Ct. EC2 13 B4
St. Olave's Est. SE1 17 E3
St. Olaves Gdns. SE11 20 E1
St. Olaves Rd. E6 61 D1
St. Olave's Wk. SW16 94 C2
St. Olav's Sq. SE16 68 F2
Albion St.
St. Oswald's Pl. SE11 20 C4
St. Oswald's Pl. SE11 67 F5
St. Oswald's Rd. 94 H1
SW16
St. Oswulf St. SW1 19 J2
St. Pancras Way NW1 49 C7
St. Patrick's Ct., 34 E7
Wdf.Grn.
St. Paul St. N1 58 J1
St. Paul's All. EC4 58 H6
St. Paul's Chyd.
St. Paul's Ave. NW2 47 J6
St. Paul's Ave. SE16 68 G1
St. Pauls Ave., Har. 37 J5
St. Paul's Chyd. EC4 12 H4
St. Paul's Chyd. EC4 58 H6
St. Paul's Clo. SE7 70 A5
St. Paul's Clo. W5 64 J2
St. Paul's Clo., Cars. 100 H1
St. Pauls Clo., Chess. 98 G4
St. Paul's Clo., Houns. 72 E2
St. Paul's Ct. W14 66 A4
Colet Gdns.
St. Pauls Ctyd. SE8 69 A7
Deptford High St.
St. Pauls Cray Rd., 97 G1
Chis.
St. Paul's Cres. NW1 49 D7
St. Pauls Dr. E15 51 D5
St. Paul's Ms. NW1 49 D7
St. Paul's Cres.
St. Pauls Pl. N1 50 A6
St. Pauls Ri. N13 32 H6
St. Paul's Rd. N1 49 H6
St. Paul's Rd. N17 33 D7
St. Paul's Rd., Bark. 61 F1
St. Paul's Rd., Brent. 64 G6
St. Paul's Rd., Erith 71 J7
St. Paul's Rd., Rich. 73 J3
St. Paul's Rd., Th.Hth. 94 J3
St. Paul's Shrubbery 50 A6
N1
St. Pauls Sq., Brom. 96 G2
St. Pauls St. E3 59 G6
St. Paul's Ter. SE17 20 H5
St. Pauls Twr. E10 42 C7
St. Pauls Wk., 83 A7
Kings.T.
Alexandra Rd.
St. Pauls Way E3 59 J5
St. Paul's Way N3 31 E7

St. Pauls Wd. Hill, 97 H2
Orp.
St. Peter's All. EC3 13 C4
St. Peter's Ave. E2 9 J2
St. Peter's Ave. E17 42 E4
St. Peters Ave. N18 33 D4
St. Peter's Clo. E2 9 J2
St. Peter's Clo. E2 59 D2
St. Peters Clo. SW17 84 H2
College Gdns.
St. Peters Clo., Barn. 22 H5
St. Peters Clo., Chis. 88 G7
St. Peters Clo., Ilf. 43 H4
St. Peters Clo., Ruis. 45 D2
St. Peters Clo., Wat. 29 A1
(Bushey)
St. Peter's Ct. NW4 38 J5
St. Peters Ct. SE3 78 F4
Eltham Rd.
St. Peters Ct. SE4 77 J2
Wickham Rd.
St. Peters Ct., W.Mol. 90 G4
St. Peter's Gdns. 85 G3
SE27
St. Peter's Gro. W6 65 G4
St. Peters Rd. N9 33 E1
St. Peter's Rd. W6 65 G5
St. Peter's Rd., Croy. 102 A4
St. Peters Rd., 92 A2
Kings.T.
St. Peters Rd., Sthl. 54 G5
St. Peters Rd., Twick. 73 E5
St. Peter's Rd., 90 G4
W.Mol.
St. Peter's Sq. E2 9 J2
St. Peter's Sq. W6 65 G5
St. Peters Sq. N1 58 H1
St. Peter's St., 102 A5
S.Croy.
St. Peters Ter. SW6 66 C7
St. Peter's Vill. W6 65 G4
St. Peter's Way N1 50 B7
St. Peters Way W5 55 G5
St. Petersburgh Ms. 10 A5
W2
St. Petersburgh Ms. 57 E7
W2
St. Petersburgh Pl. 10 A5
W2
St. Petersburgh Pl. 57 E7
W2
St. Philip Sq. SW8 76 B2
St. Philip St. SW8 76 B2
St. Philip's Ave., 99 H2
Wor.Pk.
St. Philip's Rd. E8 50 D6
St. Philips Rd., Surb. 91 G6
St. Philip's Way N1 58 J1
Linton St.
St. Quentin Rd., Well. 79 J3
St. Quintin Ave. W10 56 J5
St. Quintin Gdns. 56 J5
W10
St. Quintin Rd. E13 60 H2
St. Raphael's Way 47 C5
NW10
St. Regis Clo. N10 40 B2
St. Ronans Cres., 34 G7
Wdf.Grn.
St. Rule St. SW8 76 C2
St. Saviour's Est. SE1 17 F5
St. Saviour's Est. SE1 68 C3
St. Saviour's Rd. SW2 76 F5
St. Saviours Rd., 94 H6
Croy.
St. Silas Pl. NW5 49 A6
St. Silas St. Est. NW5 49 A6
St. Simon's Ave. 74 J5
SW15
St. Stephens Ave. 42 C5
E17
St. Stephens Ave. 65 H2
W12
St. Stephens Ave. 55 E6
W13
St. Stephens Clo. E17 42 B5
St. Stephens Clo. 57 H1
NW8
St. Stephens Clo., 54 G5
Sthl.
St. Stephens Cres. 57 D6
W2
Talbot Rd.
St. Stephens Cres. 94 G3
Th.Hth.
St. Stephens Gdn. 57 D6
Est. W2
Shrewsbury Rd.

St. Stephens Gdns. SW15	75	C5
Manfred Rd.		
St. Stephens Gdns. W2	57	D6
St. Stephens Gdns., Twick.	73	F6
St. Stephens Gro. SE13	78	C3
St. Stephens Ms. W2	57	D5
Chepstow Rd.		
St. Stephen's Pas., Twick.	73	F6
Richmond Rd.		
St. Stephens Rd. E3	59	H1
St. Stephens Rd. E6	51	J7
St. Stephen's Rd. E17	42	B5
Grove Rd.		
St. Stephens Rd. W13	55	E6
St. Stephen's Rd., Barn.	23	A5
St. Stephens Rd., Houns.	72	G6
St. Stephens Row EC4	**13**	**B5**
St. Stephens Ter. SW8	67	F7
St. Stephen's Wk. SW7	**18**	**C1**
St. Swithin's La. EC4	**13**	**B5**
St. Swithin's La. EC4	59	A7
St. Swithun's Rd. SE13	78	D5
St. Thomas' Clo., Surb.	98	J1
St. Thomas Ct., Bex.	80	G7
St. Thomas Dr., Orp.	104	F1
St. Thomas' Dr., Pnr.	36	E1
St. Thomas Gdns., Ilf.	52	F6
St. Thomas Pl. NW1	49	D7
Maiden La.		
St. Thomas Rd. E16	60	G6
St. Thomas Rd. N14	24	D7
St. Thomas Rd., Belv.	71	J2
St. Thomas St. SE1	**17**	**C2**
St. Thomas St. SE1	68	A1
St. Thomas's Gdns. NW5	49	A6
Queens Cres.		
St. Thomas's Pl. E9	50	F7
St. Thomas's Rd. N4	49	G2
St. Thomas's Rd. NW10	56	E1
St. Thomas's Rd. W4	65	C6
St. Thomas's Sq. E9	50	F7
St. Thomas's Way SW6	66	C7
St. Ursula Gro., Pnr.	36	D5
St. Ursula Rd., Sthl.	54	G6
St. Vincent Clo. SE27	85	H5
St. Vincent Rd., Twick.	72	J6
St. Vincent St. W1	**11**	**C2**
St. Wilfrids Rd., Barn.	23	G5
East Barnet Rd.		
St. Wilfrids Rd., Barn.	23	G5
East Barnet Rd.		
St. Winefride's Ave. E12	52	C5
St. Winifrids Clo., Chig.	35	F5
St. Winifreds Rd., Tedd.	82	E6
Saints Clo. SE27	85	H4
Wolfington Rd.		
Saints Dr. E7	52	A5
Salamanca Pl. SE11	**20**	**C2**
Salamanca St. SE11	**20**	**C2**
Salamanca St. SE11	67	F4
Salcombe Dr., Mord.	100	A1
Salcombe Dr., Rom.	44	F6
Salcombe Gdns. NW7	30	J6
Salcombe Pk., Loug.	27	A5
High Rd.		
Salcombe Rd. E17	41	J7
Salcombe Rd. N16	50	B5
Salcombe Way, Ruis.	45	A2
Salcott Rd. SW11	75	H5
Salcott Rd., Croy.	101	E3
Sale Pl. W2	**10**	**G2**
Sale Pl. W2	57	H6
Sale St. E2	**9**	**J5**
Sale St. E2	59	D4
Salehurst Clo., Har.	37	H5
Salehurst Rd. SE4	77	J6
Salem Pl., Croy.	101	J3
Salem Rd. W2	**10**	**B5**
Salem Rd. W2	57	E7
Salford Rd. SW2	85	D1

Salhouse Clo. SE28	62	C6
Rollesby Way		
Salisbury Ave. N3	39	C3
Salisbury Ave., Bark.	52	G7
Salisbury Ave., Sutt.	100	C6
Salisbury Clo. SE17	**21**	**B1**
Salisbury Clo., Wor.Pk.	99	F3
Salisbury Ct. EC4	**12**	**F4**
Salisbury Ct. EC4	58	H6
Salisbury Gdns. SW19	84	B7
Salisbury Gdns., Buck.H.	35	A2
Salisbury Hall Gdns. E4	34	A6
Salisbury Ho. E14	60	B6
Hobday St.		
Salisbury Ms. SW6	66	C7
Dawes Rd.		
Salisbury Pl. SW9	67	H7
Salisbury Pl. W1	**10**	**J1**
Salisbury Pl. W1	57	J5
Salisbury Rd. E4	34	A3
Salisbury Rd. E7	51	G6
Salisbury Rd. E10	51	C2
Salisbury Rd. E12	52	A5
Salisbury Rd. E17	42	C5
Salisbury Rd. N4	40	H5
Salisbury Rd. N9	33	D3
Salisbury Rd. N22	40	H1
Salisbury Rd. SE25	95	D6
Salisbury Rd. SW19	84	B7
Salisbury Rd. W13	64	D2
Salisbury Rd., Barn.	23	B3
Salisbury Rd., Bex.	89	G1
Salisbury Rd., Brom.	97	B5
Salisbury Rd., Cars.	100	J6
Salisbury Rd., Dag.	53	H6
Salisbury Rd., Felt.	81	C1
Salisbury Rd., Har.	37	A5
Salisbury Rd., Houns.	72	C3
Salisbury Rd., Ilf.	52	H2
Salisbury Rd., N.Mal.	92	D3
Salisbury Rd., Pnr.	36	A4
Salisbury Rd., Rich.	73	H4
Salisbury Rd., Sthl.	63	E4
Salisbury Rd., Wor.Pk.	99	D4
Salisbury Sq. EC4	**12**	**F4**
Salisbury St. NW8	**6**	**G6**
Salisbury St. NW8	57	H4
Salisbury St. W3	65	C2
Salisbury Ter. SE15	77	F3
Salisbury Wk. N19	49	C2
Salix Clo., Sun.	81	B7
Oak Gro.		
Salliesfield, Twick.	73	A6
Salmen Rd. E13	60	F2
Salmon La. E14	59	H6
Salmon Rd., Belv.	71	G5
Salmon St. E14	59	J6
Salmon La.		
Salmon St. NW9	47	B1
Salmond Clo., Stan.	29	D6
Robb Rd.		
Salmons Rd. N9	33	D1
Salmons Rd., Chess.	98	G6
Salomons Rd. E13	60	J5
Chalk Rd.		
Salop Rd. E17	41	G6
Saltash Clo., Sutt.	100	C4
Saltash Rd., Ilf.	35	G7
Saltash Rd., Well.	80	C1
Saltcoats Rd. W4	65	E2
Saltcroft Clo., Wem.	47	B1
Salter Rd. SE16	68	G1
Salter St. E14	60	A7
Salter St. NW10	56	G3
Salterford Rd. SW17	85	A6
Salters Hill SE19	86	A5
Salters Rd. E17	42	D4
Salters Rd. W10	57	A4
Salterton Rd. N7	49	E3
Saltley Clo. N6	74	G4
Saltram Clo. N15	41	C4
Saltram Cres. W9	57	C3
Saltwell St. E14	60	A7
Saltwood Gro. SE17	**21**	**B4**
Salusbury Rd. NW6	57	B1
Salvia Gdns., Grnf.	55	D2
Selborne Gdns.		
Salvin Rd. SW15	75	A3
Salway Clo., Wdf.Grn.	34	F7
Salway Pl. E15	51	E6
Broadway		
Salway Rd. E15	51	D6
Sam Bartram Clo. SE7	69	J5

Samantha Clo. E17	41	J7
Sambruck Ms. SE6	87	B2
Inchmery Rd.		
Samels Ct. W6	65	G5
South Black Lion La.		
Samford St. NW8	**6**	**G6**
Samford St. NW8	57	H4
Samos Rd. SE20	95	E2
Sampson Ave., Barn.	23	A5
Sampson Clo., Belv.	71	D3
Carrill Way		
Sampson St. E1	**17**	**J2**
Sampson St. E1	68	D1
Samson St. E13	60	J2
Samuel Clo. E8	59	C1
Pownall Rd.		
Samuel Clo. SE14	68	G6
Samuel Clo. SE18	70	B4
Samuel Johnson Clo. SW16	85	G4
Curtis Fld. Rd.		
Samuel Lewis Trust Dws. E8	50	D4
Amhurst Rd.		
Samuel Lewis Trust Dws. N1	49	G7
Liverpool Rd.		
Samuel Lewis Trust Dws. SW3	**18**	**G2**
Samuel Lewis Trust Dws. SW6	66	D7
Samuel St. SE18	70	C4
Sancroft Clo. NW2	47	H3
Sancroft Rd., Har.	37	C2
Sancroft Rd., Stan.	37	C2
Sancroft St. SE11	**20**	**D3**
Sancroft St. SE11	67	F5
Sanctuary, The SW1	**15**	**J5**
Sanctuary, The, Bex.	80	D6
Sanctuary, The, Mord.	93	E6
Sanctuary St. SE1	**17**	**A4**
Sandal Rd. N18	33	D5
Sandal Rd., N.Mal.	92	D5
Sandal St. E15	60	E1
Sandale Clo. N16	50	A3
Stoke Newington Ch. St.		
Sandall Clo. W5	55	H4
Sandall Rd. NW5	49	C6
Sandall Rd. W5	55	H4
Sandalwood Clo. E1	59	H4
Solebay St.		
Sandalwood Rd., Felt.	81	B3
Sandbach Pl. SE18	70	F5
Sandbourne Ave. SW19	93	E2
Sandbourne Rd. SE4	77	H2
Sandbrook Clo. NW7	30	D6
Sandbrook Rd. N16	50	B3
Sandby Grn. SE9	79	B3
Sandcroft Clo. N13	32	H6
St. Pauls Ri.		
Sandell St. SE1	**16**	**E3**
Sanders Clo., Hmptn.	81	J5
Sanders La. NW7	30	J7
Sanders Way N19	49	D1
Sussex Way		
Sanderson Clo. NW5	49	B4
Sanderstead Ave. NW2	48	B2
Sanderstead Clo. SW12	76	C7
Atkins Rd.		
Sanderstead Rd. E10	50	H1
Sanderstead Rd., S.Croy.	102	A7
Sandfield Gdns., Th.Hth.	94	H3
Sandfield Ind. Est., Hmptn.	90	F1
Sandfield Pas., Th.Hth.	94	J3
Sandfield Rd., Th.Hth.	94	H3
Sandford Ave. N22	40	J1
Sandford Ave., Loug.	27	E3
Sandford Clo. E6	61	C4
Sandford Ct. N16	50	B1
Bethune Rd.		
Sandford Rd. E6	61	B3
Sandford Rd., Bexh.	80	E4
Sandford Rd., Brom.	96	G3
Sandford St. SW6	66	E7
King's Rd.		
Sandgate Clo., Rom.	44	J7
Sandgate La. SW18	84	H1
Sandgate Rd., Well.	71	C7
Sandgate St. SE15	68	E6

Sandham Pt. SE18	70	E4
Troy Ct.		
Sandhills, Wall.	101	D4
Sandhurst Ave., Har.	36	H6
Sandhurst Ave., Surb.	92	B7
Sandhurst Clo. NW9	38	A3
Sandhurst Dr., Ilf.	52	A4
Sandhurst Rd. N9	25	F6
Sandhurst Rd. NW9	38	A3
Sandhurst Rd. SE6	87	D1
Sandhurst Rd., Bex.	80	D5
Sandhurst Rd., Sid.	88	J3
Sandhurst Way, S.Croy.	102	B7
Sandiford Rd., Sutt.	100	C2
Sandiland Cres., Brom.	103	F2
Sandilands, Croy.	102	D2
Sandilands Rd. SW6	75	E1
Sandison St. SE15	77	C3
Sandland St. WC1	**12**	**D2**
Sandland St. WC1	58	F5
Sandling Ri. SE9	88	D3
Sandlings, The N22	40	G2
Sandmere Rd. SW4	76	E4
Sandon Clo., Esher	91	A7
Sandon Clo., Houns.	72	A1
Sandown Ave., Dag.	53	J6
Sandown Clo., Houns.	72	A1
Sandown Gate, Esher	98	A3
Sandown Rd. SE25	95	E5
Sandown Way, Nthlt.	45	G6
Sandpiper Clo. E17	33	H7
Banbury Rd.		
Sandpit Pl. SE7	70	B5
Sandpit Rd., Brom.	87	E5
Sandpits Rd., Croy.	102	G4
Sandpits Rd., Rich.	82	G2
Sandra Clo. N22	40	J1
New Rd.		
Sandra Clo., Houns.	72	H5
Sandridge Clo., Har.	37	B4
Sandridge Ct. N4	49	J3
Queens Dr.		
Sandridge St. N19	49	C2
Sandringham Ave. SW20	93	B1
Sandringham Clo. SW19	84	A1
Sandringham Clo., Enf.	25	B2
Sandringham Clo., Ilf.	43	F3
Sandringham Ct. W9	**6**	**D4**
Sandringham Cres., Har.	45	G2
Sandringham Dr., Well.	79	H2
Sandringham Gdns. N8	40	E6
Sandringham Gdns. N12	31	F6
Sandringham Gdns., Houns.	72	A1
Sandringham Gdns., Ilf.	43	F3
Sandringham Ms. W5	55	G7
High St.		
Sandringham Rd. E7	51	J5
Sandringham Rd. E8	50	C5
Sandringham Rd. E10	42	D6
Sandringham Rd. N22	40	J3
Sandringham Rd. NW2	47	H6
Sandringham Rd. NW11	39	B7
Sandringham Rd., Bark.	52	J6
Sandringham Rd., Brom.	87	G5
Sandringham Rd., Nthlt.	45	G7
Sandringham Rd., Th.Hth.	94	J5
Sandringham Rd., Wor.Pk.	99	G3
Sandrock Pl., Croy.	102	G4
Sandrock Rd. SE13	78	A3
Sand's End La. SW6	75	E1
Sands Way, Wdf.Grn.	35	C6
Sandstone Pl. N19	49	B2
Dartmouth Pk. Hill		
Sandstone Rd. SE12	87	H2
Sandtoft Rd. SE7	69	H6
Sandwell Cres. NW6	48	D6
Sandwich St. WC1	**8**	**A4**
Sandwich St. WC1	58	E3
Sandy Bury, Orp.	104	G3

Sandy Hill Ave. SE18   70 E5
Sandy Hill Rd. SE18   70 E5
Sandy La., Har.   37 J6
Sandy La., Kings.T.   91 E1
Sandy La., Mitch.   94 A1
Sandy La., Nthwd.   28 A4
Sandy La., Rich.   82 F2
Sandy La., Sid.   89 D7
Sandy La., Sutt.   100 B7
Sandy La., Tedd.   82 D7
Sandy La., Walt.   90 B6
Sandy La. Est., Rich.   82 G2
Sandy La. N., Wall.   101 D6
Sandy La. S., Wall.   101 D6
Sandy Ridge, Chis.   88 D6
Sandy Rd. NW3   48 E2
Sandy Way, Croy.   102 J3
Sandycombe Rd.,   81 A1
  Felt.
Sandycombe Rd.,   74 A3
  Rich.
Sandycombe Rd.,   73 F6
  Twick.
Sandycroft SE2   71 A6
Sandyhill Rd., Ilf.   52 E4
Sandymount Ave.,   29 F5
  Stan.
Sandy's Row E1   **13 E2**
Sandy's Row E1   59 B5
Sanford La. N16   50 C3
  Stoke Newington
  High St.
Sanford St. SE14   68 H6
Sanford Ter. N16   50 C2
Sanford Wk. N16   50 C2
  Sanford Ter.
Sanford Wk. SE14   68 H6
  Cold Blow La.
Sanger Ave., Chess.   98 H5
Sangley Rd. SE6   78 B7
Sangley Rd. SE25   95 B4
Sangora Rd. SW11   75 G4
Sans Wk. EC1   **8 F5**
Sans Wk. EC1   58 G4
Sansom Rd. E11   51 F2
Sansom St. SE5   68 A7
Santley St. SW4   76 E4
Santos Rd. SW18   75 D5
Santway, The, Stan.   29 B5
Saphora Clo., Orp.   104 G5
  Oleander Clo.
Sapphire Clo. E6   61 D6
Sapphire Clo., Dag.   53 C1
Sapphire Rd. SE8   68 H5
Sara Ct., Beck.   96 B1
  Albemarle Rd.
Saracen Clo., Croy.   95 A6
Saracen St. E14   68 A6
Saracen's Head Yd.   **13 F4**
EC3
Sarah Ho. SW15   74 F4
  Arabella Dr.
Sarah St. N1   **9 E3**
Saratoga Rd. E5   50 F4
Sardinia St. WC2   **12 C4**
Sarita Clo., Har.   37 A2
Sarjant Path SW19   84 A2
  Queensmere Rd.
Sark Clo., Houns.   63 G7
Sark Wk. E16   60 H6
Sarnesfield Ho. SE15   68 E6
  Pencraig Way
Sarnesfield Rd., Enf.   25 A3
  Church St.
Sarre Rd. NW2   48 C5
Sarsen Ave., Houns.   72 F2
Sarsfeld Rd. SW12   84 J2
Sarsfield Rd., Grnf.   55 E2
Sartor Rd. SE15   77 G4
Satanita Clo. E16   61 A6
  Fulmer Rd.
Satchell Mead NW9   38 F1
Satchwell Rd. E2   **9 G4**
Satchwell St. E2   **9 G4**
Sauls Grn. E11   51 E3
  Napier Rd.
Saunders Ness Rd.   69 C5
  E14
Saunders Rd. SE18   70 J5
Saunders Way SE28   62 B7
  Oriole Way
Saunderton Rd.,   46 E5
  Wem.
Savage Gdns. E6   61 C6
Savage Gdns. EC3   **13 E5**
Savernake Rd. N9   25 D6
Savernake Rd. NW3   48 J4
Savile Clo., N.Mal.   92 E5

Savile Gdns., Croy.   102 C2
Savile Row W1   **11 F5**
Savile Row W1   58 C7
Savill Gdns. SW20   92 G3
  Bodnant Gdns.
Savill Row, Wdf.Grn.   34 F6
Saville Rd. E16   70 B1
Saville Rd. W4   65 D3
Saville Rd., Rom.   44 F6
Saville Rd., Twick.   82 C1
Saville Row, Brom.   103 F1
Saville Row, Enf.   25 G2
  Green St.
Savona Clo. SW19   84 B7
Savona Est. SW8   67 C7
Savona St. SW8   67 C7
Savoy Bldgs. WC2   **12 C6**
Savoy Clo. E15   60 E1
  Arthingworth St.
Savoy Clo., Edg.   30 A5
Savoy Ct. WC2   **12 B6**
Savoy Hill WC2   **12 C6**
Savoy Pl. WC2   **12 B6**
Savoy Pl. WC2   58 E7
Savoy Row WC2   **12 C6**
Savoy Steps WC2   **12 C6**
Savoy St. WC2   **12 C6**
Savoy St. WC2   58 F7
Savoy Way WC2   **12 C6**
Sawkins Clo. SW19   84 B2
Sawley Rd. W12   65 F1
Sawtry Clo., Cars.   93 G7
Sawyer Clo. N9   33 D2
  Lion Rd.
Sawyer St. SE1   **16 J3**
Sawyer St. SE1   67 J2
Sawyers Clo., Dag.   53 J6
Sawyer's Hill, Rich.   73 J7
Sawyers Lawn W13   55 C6
Saxby Rd. SW2   76 E7
Saxham Rd., Bark.   61 J2
Saxlingham Rd. E4   34 D3
Saxon Ave., Felt.   81 E2
Saxon Clo., Surb.   91 G6
Saxon Dr. W3   56 B6
Saxon Gdns., Sthl.   54 E7
  Saxon Rd.
Saxon Rd. E3   59 J2
Saxon Rd. E6   61 C4
Saxon Rd. N22   40 H1
Saxon Rd. SE25   95 A5
Saxon Rd., Brom.   87 F7
Saxon Rd., Ilf.   52 E6
Saxon Rd., Sthl.   63 E1
Saxon Rd., Wem.   47 C3
Saxon Wk., Sid.   89 C6
  Cray Rd.
Saxon Way N14   24 D6
Saxonbury Ave., Sun.   90 B3
Saxonbury Clo.,   93 G3
  Mitch.
Saxonbury Gdns.,   98 F1
  Surb.
Saxton Clo. SE13   78 D3
Sayers Wk., Rich.   73 J7
  Stafford Pl.
Sayes Ct. SE8   68 J5
  Sayes Ct. St.
Sayes Ct. St. SE8   68 J6
Scads Hill Clo., Orp.   97 J6
Scala St. W1   **11 G1**
Scala St. W1   58 C5
Scales Rd. N17   41 C3
Scampston Ms. W10   57 A6
Scandrett St. E1   68 E1
Scarba St. N1   50 A6
  Marquess Rd.
Scarborough Rd. E11   51 D1
Scarborough Rd. N4   40 G7
Scarborough Rd. N9   25 F7
Scarborough St. E1   **13 G4**
Scarbrook Rd., Croy.   101 J3
Scarle Rd., Wem.   46 G6
Scarlet Rd. SE6   87 E3
Scarlette Manor Way   76 G7
  SW2
  Papworth Way
Scarsbrook Rd. SE3   79 A3
Scarsdale Pl. W8   **14 A5**
Scarsdale Rd., Har.   45 J3
Scarsdale Vill. W8   66 D3
Scarth Rd. SW13   74 F3
Scawen Rd. SE8   68 H5
Scawfell St. E2   **9 G2**
Scawfell St. E2   59 C2
Scaynes Link N12   31 D5
Sceaux Est. SE5   77 B1
Sceaux Gdns. SE5   77 C1

Sceptre Rd. E2   59 F3
Schofield Wk. SE3   69 H7
  Dornberg Clo.
Scholars Rd. E4   34 C1
Scholars Rd. SW12   85 C1
Scholefield Rd. N19   49 D2
Scholes Cres. SW2   85 G1
School Ho. La., Tedd.   82 E7
School La. SE23   86 E2
School La., Kings.T.   91 F1
School La., Pnr.   36 E4
School La., Surb.   98 J1
School La., Well.   80 B3
School Pas., Kings.T.   91 J2
School Pas., Sthl.   63 F1
School Rd. E12   52 C4
School Rd. NW10   56 D4
School Rd., Chis.   97 F1
School Rd., Dag.   62 G1
School Rd., E.Mol.   91 A4
School Rd., Hmptn.   81 J6
School Rd., Houns.   72 J3
School Rd., Kings.T.   91 F1
School Rd. Ave.,   81 J6
  Hmptn.
School Way N12   31 F4
  High Rd.
Schoolbell Ms. E3   59 H2
  Arbery Rd.
Schoolhouse La. E1   59 G7
Schoolway N12   31 G6
Schoolway, Dag.   53 C3
Schooner Clo. SE16   68 G2
  Kinburn St.
Schubert Rd. SW15   75 C5
Sclater St. E1   **9 F5**
Sclater St. E1   59 C4
Scoble Pl. N16   50 C4
  Amhurst Rd.
Scoresby St. SE1   **16 G2**
Scoresby St. SE1   67 H1
Scorton Ave., Grnf.   55 D2
Scot Gro., Pnr.   28 D7
Scotch Common W13   55 D5
Scoter Clo., Wdf.Grn.   34 H7
  Mallards Rd.
Scotland Grn. N17   41 C2
Scotland Grn. Rd.,   25 G5
  Enf.
Scotland Grn. Rd. N.,   25 G4
  Enf.
Scotland Pl. SW1   **16 A2**
Scotland Rd., Buck.H.   34 J1
Scotsdale Clo., Orp.   97 H4
Scotsdale Clo., Sutt.   100 B7
Scotsdale Rd. SE12   78 H5
Scotswood St. EC1   **8 F5**
Scotswood Wk. N17   33 D7
Scott Clo. SW16   94 F1
Scott Clo., Epsom   99 C5
Scott Cres., Har.   45 H1
Scott Ellis Gdns. NW8   **6 E4**
Scott Ellis Gdns. NW8   57 G3
Scott Fm. Clo., T.Ditt.   98 E1
Scott Gdns., Houns.   63 D7
Scott Ho. N18   33 D5
Scott Lidgett Cres.   **17 H4**
SE16
Scott Lidgett Cres.   68 D2
  SE16
Scott Russell Pl. E14   69 B5
  Westferry Rd.
Scott St. E1   59 E4
Scottes La., Dag.   53 D1
  Valence Ave.
Scotts Ave., Brom.   96 D2
Scotts Dr., Hmptn.   81 H7
Scotts Fm. Rd.,   99 C6
  Epsom
Scotts La., Brom.   96 D4
Scotts Rd. E10   51 C1
Scotts Rd. W12   65 H2
Scotts Rd., Brom.   87 G7
Scotts Rd., Sthl.   63 C3
Scott's Yd. EC4   **13 B5**
Scottwell Dr. NW9   38 F5
Scoulding Rd. E16   60 G6
Scout App. NW10   47 E4
Scout La. SW4   76 C3
  Old Town
Scout Way NW7   30 D4
Scovell Cres. SE1   **16 J4**
Scovell Rd. SE1   **16 J4**
Scrattons Ter., Bark.   62 D1
Scriven St. E8   59 C1
Scrooby St. SE6   78 B6
Scrubs La. NW10   56 G3
Scrubs La. W10   56 H5

Scrutton Clo. SW12   76 D7
Scrutton St. EC2   **9 D6**
Scrutton St. EC2   59 B4
Scudamore La. NW9   38 C4
Scutari Rd. SE22   77 F5
Scylla Rd. SE15   77 E3
Seabright St. E2   59 E3
  Bethnal Grn. Rd.
Seabrook Dr.,   103 E2
  W.Wick.
Seabrook Gdns.,   44 G7
  Rom.
Seabrook Rd., Dag.   53 D3
Seacole Clo. W3   56 D5
Seacourt Rd. SE2   71 D2
Seacroft Gdns., Wat.   28 D3
Seafield Rd. N11   32 C4
Seaford Rd. E17   42 B3
Seaford Rd. N15   41 A4
Seaford Rd. W13   64 E1
Seaford Rd., Enf.   25 B4
Seaford St. WC1   **8 B4**
Seaford St. WC1   58 F3
Seaforth Ave., N.Mal.   92 H5
Seaforth Cres. N5   49 J5
Seaforth Gdns. N21   24 F7
Seaforth Gdns.,   99 F4
  Epsom
Seaforth Gdns.,   34 J5
  Wdf.Grn.
Seaforth Pl. SW1   **15 G5**
Seager Pl. E3   59 J5
  Burdett Rd.
Seagrave Rd. SW6   66 D6
Seagry Rd. E11   42 G6
Seal St. E8   50 C4
Sealand Wk., Nthlt.   54 E3
  Wayfarer Rd.
Searle Rd. N4   49 F1
  Evershot Rd.
Searles Clo. SW11   66 H7
Searles Rd. SE1   **21 C1**
Searles Rd. SE1   68 A4
Sears St. SE5   **21 B7**
Sears St. SE5   68 A7
Seasprite Clo., Nthlt.   54 D3
  Ruislip Rd.
Seaton Ave., Ilf.   52 H5
Seaton Clo. E13   60 H4
  New Barn St.
Seaton Clo. SE11   **20 G3**
Seaton Clo. SW15   83 H1
Seaton Clo., Twick.   73 A6
Seaton Gdns., Ruis.   45 A3
Seaton Pl. NW1   **7 F5**
Seaton Pt. E5   50 D4
  Nolan Way
Seaton Rd., Mitch.   93 H2
Seaton Rd., Twick.   72 J6
Seaton Rd., Well.   71 C7
Seaton Rd., Wem.   55 H2
Seaton St. N18   33 D5
Sebastian St. EC1   **8 H4**
Sebastian St. EC1   58 H3
Sebastopol Rd. N9   33 D4
Sebbon St. N1   49 H7
Sebert Rd. E7   51 H5
Sebright Pas. E2   **9 J2**
Sebright Rd., Barn.   23 A2
Secker Cres., Har.   36 J1
Secker St. SE1   **16 E2**
Second Ave. E12   52 B4
Second Ave. E13   60 G3
  First Ave.
Second Ave. E17   42 A5
Second Ave. N18   33 F4
Second Ave. NW4   39 A4
Second Ave. SW14   74 E3
Second Ave. W3   65 F1
Second Ave. W10   57 B4
Second Ave., Dag.   62 H1
Second Ave., Enf.   25 C5
Second Ave., Rom.   44 C5
Second Ave., Walt.   90 B6
Second Ave., Wem.   46 G2
Second Clo., W.Mol.   90 J4
Second Cross Rd.,   82 A2
  Twick.
Second Way, Wem.   47 B4
Sedan Way SE17   **21 D3**
Sedcombe Clo., Sid.   89 B4
  Knoll Rd.
Sedcote Rd., Enf.   25 F5
Sedding St. SW1   **19 B1**
Sedding St. SW1   67 A4
Seddon Rd., Mord.   93 G5
Seddon St. WC1   **8 D4**
Sedge Rd. N17   33 F7

Sedgebrook Rd. SE3	79	A2
Sedgecombe Ave., Har.	37	F5
Sedgeford Rd. W12	65	F1
Sedgehill Rd. SE6	87	A4
Sedgemere Ave. N2	39	F3
Sedgemere Rd. SE2	71	C3
Sedgemoor Dr., Dag.	53	G4
Sedgeway SE6	87	F1
Sedgewood Clo., Brom.	96	F7
Sedgmoor Pl. SE5	68	B7
Sedgwick Rd. E10	51	C2
Sedgwick St. E9	50	G5
Sedleigh Rd. SW18	75	C6
Sedlescombe Rd. SW6	66	C6
Sedley Pl. W1	**11**	**D4**
Sedley Ri., Loug.	27	C2
Seeley Dr. SE21	86	B4
Seelig Ave. NW9	38	G7
Seely Rd. SW17	85	A6
Seething La. EC3	**13**	**E5**
Seething La. EC3	59	B7
Seething Wells La., Surb.	91	F6
Sefton Ave. NW7	30	D5
Sefton Ave., Har.	37	A1
Sefton Clo., Orp.	97	J4
Sefton Rd., Croy.	102	D1
Sefton Rd., Orp.	97	J4
Sefton St. SW15	74	J3
Segal Clo. SE23	77	H7
Sekforde St. EC1	**8**	**G6**
Sekforde St. EC1	58	H4
Selan Gdns., Hayes	54	B5
Selbie Ave. NW10	47	F5
Selborne Ave. E12	52	D4
Walton Rd.		
Selborne Ave. E17	41	J4
Selborne Ave., Bex.	89	E1
Selborne Gdns. NW4	38	G4
Selborne Gdns., Grnf.	55	D2
Selborne Rd. E17	41	J5
Selborne Rd. N14	32	E3
Selborne Rd. N22	40	F1
Selborne Rd. SE5	77	A2
Denmark Hill		
Selborne Rd., Croy.	102	B3
Selborne Rd., Ilf.	52	D2
Selborne Rd., N.Mal.	92	E2
Selborne Rd., Sid.	89	B4
Selbourne Ave., Surb.	98	J2
Selby Chase, Ruis.	45	B2
Selby Clo. E6	61	B5
Linton Gdns.		
Selby Clo., Chess.	98	H7
Selby Clo., Chis.	88	D6
Selby Gdns., Sthl.	54	G4
Selby Grn., Cars.	93	H7
Selby Rd. E11	51	E3
Selby Rd. E13	60	H5
Selby Rd. N17	33	B6
Selby Rd. SE20	95	D2
Selby Rd. W5	55	E4
Selby Rd., Cars.	93	H7
Selby St. E1	**9**	**J6**
Selby St. E1	59	D4
Selden Rd. SE15	77	F2
Selden Wk. N7	49	F2
Durham Rd.		
Selhurst New Rd. SE25	95	B6
Selhurst Pl. SE25	95	B6
Selhurst Rd. N9	33	A3
Selhurst Rd. SE25	95	B5
Selinas La., Dag.	44	E7
Selkirk Rd. SW17	84	H4
Selkirk Rd., Twick.	81	J2
Sellers Clo., Borwd.	22	C1
Sellers Hall Clo. N3	31	D7
Sellincourt Rd. SW17	84	H5
Sellindge Clo., Beck.	86	J7
Sellon Ms. SE11	**20**	**D2**
Sellons Ave. NW10	56	F1
Sellwood Dr., Barn.	23	A5
Selsdon Ave., S.Croy.	102	A6
Selsdon Rd.		
Selsdon Clo., Rom.	44	J1
Selsdon Clo., Surb.	91	H5
Selsdon Rd. E11	42	G7
Selsdon Rd. E13	60	J1
Selsdon Rd. NW2	47	F2
Selsdon Rd. SE27	85	H3
Selsdon Rd., S.Croy.	102	A5

Selsdon Rd. Ind. Est., S.Croy.	102	A6
Selsdon Rd.		
Selsdon Way E14	69	B3
Selsea Pl. N16	50	B5
Crossway		
Selsey Cres., Well.	80	D1
Selsey St. E14	60	A5
Selvage La. NW7	30	D5
Selway Clo., Pnr.	36	B3
Selwood Pl. SW7	66	G5
Selwood Pl. SW7	**18**	**E3**
Selwood Rd., Chess.	98	G4
Selwood Rd., Croy.	102	E2
Selwood Rd., Sutt.	100	C1
Selwood Ter. SW7	**18**	**E3**
Selworthy Clo. E11	42	G5
Selworthy Rd. SE6	86	J3
Selwyn Ave. E4	34	C6
Selwyn Ave., Ilf.	43	J6
Selwyn Ave., Rich.	73	H3
Selwyn Clo., Houns.	72	E4
Selwyn Ct. SE3	78	F3
Selwyn Ct., Edg.	30	B7
Camrose Ave.		
Selwyn Cres., Well.	80	B3
Selwyn Rd. E3	59	J2
Selwyn Rd. E13	60	H1
Selwyn Rd. NW10	47	D7
Selwyn Rd., N.Mal.	92	D5
Semley Gate E9	50	J6
Eastway		
Semley Pl. SW1	**19**	**C2**
Semley Pl. SW1	67	A4
Semley Rd. SW16	94	E2
Senate St. SE15	77	F2
Senator Wk. SE28	70	G3
Broadwater Rd.		
Seneca Rd., Th.Hth.	94	J4
Senga Rd., Wall.	101	A1
Senhouse Rd., Sutt.	100	A3
Senior St. W2	**10**	**A1**
Senior St. W2	57	E5
Senlac Rd. SE12	87	H1
Sennen Rd., Enf.	25	C7
Sennen Wk. SE9	88	B3
Nunnington Clo.		
Senrab St. E1	59	G6
Sentinel Clo., Nthlt.	54	E4
Sentinel Sq. NW4	38	J4
Brent St.		
September Way, Stan.	29	E6
Sequoia Clo. (Bushey), Wat.	29	A1
Giant Tree Hill		
Sequoia Gdns., Orp.	97	J7
Sequoia Pk., Pnr.	28	H6
Serbin Clo. E10	42	C7
Serjeants Inn EC4	**12**	**F4**
Serle St. WC2	**12**	**D3**
Serle St. WC2	58	F6
Sermon La. EC4	58	J6
Carter La.		
Serpentine Rd. W2	**14**	**J2**
Serpentine Rd. W2	66	J1
Serviden Dr., Brom.	97	A1
Setchell Rd. SE1	**21**	**F1**
Setchell Way SE1	**21**	**F1**
Seth St. SE16	68	F2
Swan Rd.		
Seton Gdns., Dag.	53	C7
Settle Pt. E13	60	G2
London Rd.		
Settle Rd. E13	60	G2
London Rd.		
Settles St. E1	13	J2
Settles St. E1	59	D5
Settrington Rd. SW6	75	E2
Seven Acres, Cars.	100	H2
Seven Acres, Nthwd.	28	A6
Seven Clo., Cars.	100	H2
Seven Kings Rd., Ilf.	52	J1
Seven Sisters Rd. N4	40	J7
Seven Sisters Rd. N7	49	F3
Seven Sisters Rd. N15	41	A6
Sevenoaks Clo., Bexh.	80	H4
Sevenoaks Ho. SE25	95	D3
Sevenoaks Rd. SE4	77	H6
Sevenoaks Rd., Orp.	104	J4
Sevenoaks Rd., Orp. (Green St. Grn.)	104	J7
Sevenoaks Way, Sid.	89	C7
Seventh Ave. E12	52	C4
Severn Dr., Esher	98	D2
Severn Way NW10	47	F5

Severnake Clo. E14	69	A4
Severus Rd. SW11	75	H4
Seville St. SW1	**15**	**A4**
Seville St. SW1	66	J2
Sevington Rd. NW4	38	H6
Sevington St. W9	57	E4
Sevington St. W9	**6**	**A6**
Seward Rd. W7	64	D2
Seward Rd., Beck.	95	G2
Seward St. EC1	**8**	**H4**
Seward St. EC1	58	H4
Sewardstone Gdns. E4	26	B5
Sewardstone Rd. E2	59	F2
Sewardstone Rd. E4	26	B7
Sewdley St. E5	50	G4
Sewell Rd. SE2	71	A2
Sewell St. E13	60	G3
Sextant Ave. E14	69	D4
Seymour Ave. N17	41	D2
Seymour Ave., Mord.	93	A7
Seymour Clo., E.Mol.	90	J5
Seymour Clo., Pnr.	36	F1
Seymour Ct. E4	34	F2
Seymour Dr., Brom.	104	C1
Seymour Gdns. SE4	77	H3
Seymour Gdns., Felt.	81	C4
Seymour Gdns., Ilf.	52	C1
Seymour Gdns., Ruis.	45	D1
Seymour Gdns., Surb.	91	J5
Seymour Gdns., Twick.	73	E7
Seymour Ms. W1	**11**	**B3**
Seymour Ms. W1	58	A6
Seymour Pl. SE25	95	E4
Seymour Pl. W1	**10**	**H1**
Seymour Pl. W1	57	H5
Seymour Rd. E4	34	B1
Seymour Rd. E6	61	A2
Seymour Rd. E10	50	J1
Seymour Rd. N3	31	E7
Seymour Rd. N8	40	H5
Seymour Rd. N9	33	E2
Seymour Rd. SW18	75	C7
Seymour Rd. SW19	84	A3
Seymour Rd. W4	65	C4
Seymour Rd., Cars.	101	A5
Seymour Rd., E.Mol.	90	J5
Seymour Rd., Hmptn.	81	J5
Seymour Rd., Kings.T.	91	G1
Seymour Rd., Mitch.	94	A7
Seymour Rd., W.Mol.	90	J5
Seymour St. W1	**10**	**J4**
Seymour St. W1	57	J6
Seymour St. W2	**10**	**J4**
Seymour St. W2	57	J6
Seymour Ter. SE20	95	E1
Seymour Vill. SE20	95	E1
Seymour Wk. SW10	**18**	**C5**
Seymour Wk. SW10	66	F6
Seymours, The, Loug.	27	D1
Seyssel St. E14	69	C4
Shaa Rd. W3	56	D7
Shacklegate La., Tedd.	82	B4
Shackleton Clo. SE23	86	E2
Shackleton Rd., Sthl.	54	F7
Shacklewell Grn. E8	50	C4
Shacklewell La.		
Shacklewell La. E8	50	C5
Shacklewell Rd. N16	50	C4
Shacklewell Row E8	50	C4
Shacklewell St. E2	**9**	**G5**
Shacklewell St. E2	59	C3
Shad Thames SE1	**17**	**F2**
Shad Thames SE1	68	C2
Shadbolt Clo., Wor.Pk.	99	F7
Shadwell Dr., Nthlt.	54	F3
Shadwell Gdns. E1	59	F6
Martha St.		
Shadwell Pierhead E1	59	F7
Glamis Rd.		
Shaef Way, Tedd.	82	D7
Shafter Rd., Dag.	53	J6
Shaftesbury, Loug.	27	A3
Shaftesbury Ave. W1	**11**	**H5**
Shaftesbury Ave. W1	58	D7
Shaftesbury Ave. WC2	**11**	**H6**
Shaftesbury Ave. WC2	58	D7
Shaftesbury Ave., Barn.	23	F3
Shaftesbury Ave., Enf.	25	G2

Shaftesbury Ave., Felt.	72	A6
Shaftesbury Ave., Har.	37	G5
Shaftesbury Ave. (Kenton), Har.	45	H1
Shaftesbury Ave., Sthl.	63	G4
Shaftesbury Circle, Har.	45	J1
Shaftesbury Ave.		
Shaftesbury Gdns. NW10	56	E4
Shaftesbury Ms. W8	66	D3
Stratford Rd.		
Shaftesbury Pt. E13	60	H2
High St.		
Shaftesbury Rd. E4	34	D1
Shaftesbury Rd. E7	51	J7
Shaftesbury Rd. E10	51	A1
Shaftesbury Rd. E17	42	B6
Shaftesbury Rd. N18	33	B6
Shaftesbury Rd. N19	49	E1
Shaftesbury Rd., Beck.	95	J2
Shaftesbury Rd., Cars.	93	G7
Shaftesbury Rd., Rich.	73	H3
Shaftesbury St. N1	**9**	**A2**
Shaftesbury St. N1	58	J2
Shaftesbury Way, Twick.	82	A3
Shaftesbury Waye, Hayes	54	C5
Shaftesburys, The, Bark.	61	F2
Shafto Ms. SW1	**14**	**J6**
Shafton Rd. E9	59	G1
Shaftsbury Rd., Beck.	95	J2
Shakespeare Ave. N11	32	C5
Shakespeare Ave. NW10	56	D1
Shakespeare Ave., Felt.	72	A6
Shakespeare Ave., Hayes	54	A6
Shakespeare Cres. E12	52	C6
Shakespeare Cres. NW10	56	D1
Shakespeare Dr., Har.	37	J6
Shakespeare Gdns. N2	39	J4
Shakespeare Ho. N14	32	D2
High St.		
Shakespeare Rd. E17	41	G2
Shakespeare Rd. N3	39	D1
Popes Dr.		
Shakespeare Rd. NW7	30	F4
Shakespeare Rd. SE24	76	H5
Shakespeare Rd. W3	65	C1
Shakespeare Rd. W7	55	C7
Shakespeare Rd., Bexh.	80	E1
Shakespeare Sq., Ilf.	35	F6
Shakespeare Wk. N16	50	B4
Shakespeare Way, Felt.	81	C4
Shalcomb St. SW10	**18**	**D6**
Shalcomb St. SW10	66	F6
Shaldon Dr., Mord.	93	B5
Shaldon Dr., Ruis.	45	C3
Shaldon Rd., Edg.	37	J2
Shalfleet Dr. W10	57	A7
Shalford Clo., Orp.	104	F4
Isabella Dr.		
Shalimar Gdns. W3	56	C7
Shalimar Rd. W3	56	C7
Hereford Rd.		
Shallons Rd. SE9	88	E4
Shalston Vill., Surb.	91	J6
Shalstone Rd. SW14	74	B3
Shamrock Rd., Croy.	94	F6
Shamrock St. SW4	76	D3
Shamrock Way N14	32	B1
Shand St. SE1	**17**	**E3**
Shand St. SE1	68	B2
Shandon Rd. SW4	76	C4
Shandy St. E1	59	G5
Shanklin Gdns., Wat.	28	C4
Shanklin Rd. N8	40	D5
Shanklin Rd. N15	41	D4
Shanklin Way SE15	68	C7
Pentridge St.		
Shannon Clo. NW2	48	A3
Shannon Clo., Sthl.	63	D5

Shannon Gro. SW9	76	F4
Shannon Pl. NW8	**6**	**H1**
Shannon Way, Beck.	87	B6
Shap Cres., Cars.	100	J1
Shap St. E2	59	C1
Shapland Way N13	32	F5
Shardcroft Ave. SE24	76	H5
Shardeloes Rd. SE14	77	J2
Sharman Ct., Sid.	89	A4
Sharnbrooke Clo., Well.	80	C3
Sharon Clo., Surb.	98	F1
Sharon Gdns. E9	59	F1
Sharon Rd. W4	65	D5
Sharon Rd., Enf.	25	H2
Sharpe Clo. W7	55	C5
Templeman Rd.		
Sharpleshall St. NW1	48	J7
Sharpness Clo., Hayes	54	E5
Sharratt St. SE15	68	F6
Sharsted St. SE17	**20**	**G4**
Sharsted St. SE17	67	H5
Shavers Pl. SW1	**11**	**H6**
Shaw Ave., Bark.	62	E2
Shaw Clo. SE28	71	B1
Shaw Clo. (Bushey), Wat.	29	B2
Shaw Dr., Walt.	90	C7
Shaw Gdns., Bark.	62	E2
Shaw Rd., Brom.	87	F3
Shaw Rd., Enf.	25	G1
Shaw Sq. E17	41	H1
Shaw Way, Wall.	101	E7
Shawbrooke Rd. SE9	78	J5
Shawbury Rd. SE22	77	C5
Shawfield Pk., Brom.	97	A2
Shawfield St. SW3	**18**	**H4**
Shawfield St. SW3	66	H5
Shawford Ct. SW15	74	G7
Shawford Rd., Epsom	99	D6
Shaws Cotts. SE23	86	H3
Shearing Dr., Cars.	93	F7
Stavordale Rd.		
Shearling Way N7	49	E6
Shearman Rd. SE3	78	F4
Shearsmith Ho. E1	**13**	**J5**
Sheaveshill Ave. NW9	38	E4
Sheen Common Dr., Rich.	74	A4
Sheen Ct., Rich.	74	A4
Sheen Rd.		
Sheen Ct. Rd., Rich.	74	A4
Sheen Gate Gdns. SW14	74	C4
Sheen Gro. N1	58	G1
Richmond Ave.		
Sheen La. SW14	74	C5
Sheen Pk., Rich.	73	H4
Sheen Rd., Orp.	97	J4
Sheen Rd., Rich.	73	H5
Sheen Way, Wall.	101	F5
Sheen Wd. SW14	74	C5
Sheendale Rd., Rich.	73	J4
Sheenewood SE26	86	E5
Sheep La. E8	59	E1
Sheep Wk. Ms. SW19	84	B6
Sheepcote Clo., Houns.	63	A7
Sheepcote La. SW11	75	J2
Sheepcote Rd., Har.	37	C6
Sheepcotes Rd., Rom.	44	D4
Sheephouse Way, N.Mal.	99	D1
Sheerwater Rd. E16	61	A5
Sheffield Sq. E3	59	J3
Malmesbury Rd.		
Sheffield St. WC2	**12**	**C4**
Sheffield Ter. W8	66	D1
Shefton Ri., Nthwd.	28	A7
Shelbourne Clo., Pnr.	36	F3
Shelbourne Rd. N17	41	E2
Shelburne Rd. N7	49	F4
Shelbury Clo., Sid.	89	A3
Shelbury Rd. SE22	77	E5
Sheldon Ave. N6	39	H7
Sheldon Ave., Ilf.	43	E2
Sheldon Clo. SE12	78	H5
Sheldon Clo. SE20	95	E1
Sheldon Rd. N18	33	B4
Sheldon Rd. NW2	48	A4
Sheldon Rd., Bexh.	80	F1
Sheldon Rd., Dag.	53	E7
Sheldon St., Croy.	101	J3
Wandle Rd.		
Sheldrake Clo. E16	70	C1
Newland St.		
Sheldrake Pl. W8	66	D2
Sheldrick Clo. SW19	93	G2
Shelduck Clo. NW9	38	E2
Swan Dr.		
Sheldwich Ter., Brom.	97	B6
Turpington La.		
Shelford Pl. N16	50	A3
Stoke Newington Ch. St.		
Shelford Ri. SE19	86	C7
Shelford Rd., Barn.	22	J6
Shelgate Rd. SW11	75	H5
Shell Clo., Brom.	97	B6
Shell Rd. SE13	78	B3
Shelley Ave. E12	52	B6
Shelley Ave., Grnf.	55	A3
Shelley Clo., Edg.	30	A4
Shelley Clo., Grnf.	55	A3
Shelley Clo., Hayes	54	A5
Shelley Clo., Orp.	104	H3
Shelley Cres., Houns.	72	D1
Shelley Cres., Sthl.	54	F6
Shelley Dr., Well.	79	H1
Shelley Gdns., Wem.	46	F2
Shelley Gro., Loug.	27	C4
Shelley Way SW19	84	G6
Shellgrove Est. N16	50	B5
Shellness Rd. E5	50	E5
Shellwood Rd. SW11	75	J2
Shelmerdine Clo. E3	60	A5
Shelton Rd. SW19	93	D1
Shelton St. WC2	**12**	**A4**
Shelton St. WC2	58	E6
Shenfield Ho. SE18	70	A7
Shooter's Hill Rd.		
Shenfield Rd., Wdf.Grn.	34	H7
Shenfield St. N1	**9**	**E2**
Shenfield St. N1	59	B2
Shenley Rd. SE5	77	B1
Shenley Rd., Borwd.	22	A4
Shenley Rd., Houns.	72	E1
Shepcot Ho. N14	24	C6
Shepherd Mkt. W1	**15**	**D2**
Shepherd St. W1	**15**	**D2**
Shepherdess Pl. N1	**9**	**A3**
Shepherdess Wk. N1	**9**	**A2**
Shepherdess Wk. N1	58	J2
Shepherds Bush Grn. W12	65	J2
Shepherds Bush Mkt. W12	65	J2
Uxbridge Rd.		
Shepherds Bush Pl. W12	66	A2
Shepherds Bush Rd. W6	65	J4
Shepherds Clo. N6	40	B6
Shepherds Clo., Orp.	104	J3
Stapleton Rd.		
Shepherds Clo., Rom.	44	D5
Shepherds Ct. W12	66	A2
Shepherds Bush Grn.		
Shepherds Grn., Chis.	88	G7
Shepherds Hill N6	40	B6
Shepherds La. E9	50	G6
Shepherds Path, Nthlt.	45	E6
Fortunes Mead		
Shepherds Pl. W1	**11**	**B5**
Shepherds Wk. NW2	47	G2
Shepherds Wk. NW3	48	G4
Shepherds Wk. (Bushey), Wat.	29	A2
Shepherds Way, S.Croy.	102	G7
Shepley Clo., Cars.	101	A3
Sheppard Clo., Kings.T.	91	H4
Beaufort Rd.		
Sheppard Dr. SE16	68	E5
Sheppard St. E16	60	F4
Shepperton Clo., Borwd.	22	D1
Shepperton Rd. N1	58	J1
Shepperton Rd., Orp.	97	G6
Sheppey Gdns., Dag.	53	C7
Sheppey Rd.		
Sheppey Rd., Dag.	53	B7
Sheppey Wk. N1	49	J7
Marquess Est.		
Sherard Rd. SE9	78	B5
Sheraton Business Cen., Grnf.	55	E2
Sheraton St. W1	**11**	**H4**
Sherborne Ave., Enf.	25	F2
Sherborne Ave., Sthl.	63	G4
Sherborne Gdns. NW9	38	A3
Sherborne Gdns. W13	55	E5
Sherborne La. EC4	**13**	**B5**
Sherborne Rd., Chess.	98	H5
Sherborne Rd., Orp.	97	J4
Sherborne Rd., Sutt.	100	D2
Sherborne St. N1	59	A1
Sherboro Rd. N15	41	C6
Ermine Rd.		
Sherbourne Cres., Cars.	93	H7
Sherbrook Gdns. N21	24	H7
Sherbrooke Clo., Bexh.	80	G4
Sherbrooke Rd. SW6	66	B7
Shere Clo., Chess.	98	G5
Shere Rd., Ilf.	43	D5
Sheredan Rd. E4	62	D5
Sherfield Gdns. SW15	74	F6
Sheridan Ct., Houns.	72	F5
Vickers Way		
Sheridan Cres., Chis.	97	E2
Sheridan Gdns., Har.	37	G6
Sheridan Ms. E11	42	G6
Woodbine Pl.		
Sheridan Pl. SW13	74	F2
Brookwood Ave.		
Sheridan Pl., Hmptn.	90	H1
Sheridan Rd. E7	51	F3
Sheridan Rd. E12	52	B5
Sheridan Rd. SW19	93	C1
Sheridan Rd., Belv.	71	G4
Sheridan Rd., Bexh.	80	E3
Sheridan Rd., Rich.	82	F3
Sheridan St. E1	59	E6
Watney St.		
Sheridan Ter., Nthlt.	45	H5
Whitton Ave. W.		
Sheridan Wk. NW11	39	D6
Sheridan Wk., Cars.	100	J5
Carshalton Pk. Rd.		
Sheridan Way, Beck.	95	J1
Turners Meadow Way		
Sheringham Ave. E12	52	C4
Sheringham Ave. N14	24	D5
Sheringham Ave., Felt.	81	A3
Sheringham Ave., Rom.	44	J6
Sheringham Ave., Twick.	81	F1
Sheringham Dr., Bark.	52	J5
Sheringham Rd. N7	49	F6
Sheringham Rd. SE20	95	F3
Sheringham Twr., Sthl.	54	H7
Sherington Ave., Pnr.	28	G7
Sherington Rd. SE7	69	H6
Sherland Rd., Twick.	73	C7
Sherlies Ave., Orp.	104	H2
Sherlock Ms. W1	**11**	**B1**
Sherman Rd., Brom.	96	G1
Shernhall St. E17	42	C3
Sherrard Rd. E7	51	J6
Sherrard Rd. E12	52	A6
Sherrards Way, Barn.	23	D5
Sherrick Grn. Rd. NW10	47	H5
Sherriff Rd. NW6	48	D6
Sherrin Rd. E10	51	A4
Sherringham Ave. N17	41	D2
Sherrock Gdns. NW4	38	G4
Sherwin Rd. SE14	77	G1
Sherwood Ave. E18	42	H3
Sherwood Ave. SW16	85	C7
Sherwood Ave., Grnf.	46	B6
Sherwood Ave., Hayes	54	B4
Sherwood Clo. SW13	74	H3
Lower Common S.		
Sherwood Clo. W13	64	E1
Sherwood Clo., Bex.	80	C6
Sherwood Gdns. E14	69	A4
Sherwood Gdns., Bark.	52	G7
Sherwood Pk. Ave., Sid.	80	A7
Sherwood Pk. Rd., Mitch.	94	C4
Sherwood Pk. Rd., Sutt.	100	D5
Sherwood Rd. NW4	38	J3
Sherwood Rd. SW19	84	C7
Sherwood Rd., Croy.	95	E7
Sherwood Rd., Hmptn.	81	J5
Sherwood Rd., Har.	45	J2
Sherwood Rd., Ilf.	43	G4
Sherwood Rd., Well.	79	H2
Sherwood St. N20	31	G3
Sherwood St. W1	**11**	**G5**
Sherwood St. N20	31	G3
Green Rd.		
Sherwood Way, W.Wick.	103	B2
Shetland Clo., Borwd.	22	D6
Percheron Rd.		
Shetland Rd. E3	59	J2
Shield Dr., Brent.	64	D6
Shieldhall St. SE2	71	C4
Shifford Path SE23	86	G3
Shillibeer Pl. W1	**10**	**H2**
Shillibeer Wk., Chig.	35	J3
Shillingford St. N1	49	H7
Cross St.		
Shillitoe Rd. N13	32	H5
Shinfield St. W12	56	J6
Shinglewell Rd., Erith	71	G6
Shinners Clo. SE25	95	D5
Stanger Rd.		
Ship and Mermaid Row SE1	**17**	**C3**
Ship La. SW14	74	C3
Ship St. SE8	78	A1
Ship Tavern Pas. EC3	**13**	**D5**
Ship Yd. E14	69	B5
Napier Ave.		
Shipka Rd. SW12	85	B1
Shipman Rd. E16	60	H6
Shipman Rd. SE23	86	G2
Shipton Clo., Dag.	53	D3
Shipton St. E2	**9**	**G3**
Shipton St. E2	59	C2
Shipwright Rd. SE16	68	H2
Shirburn Clo. SE23	77	F7
Tyson Rd.		
Shirbutt St. E14	60	B7
Shire Ct., Erith	71	D3
St. John Fisher Rd.		
Shirebrook Rd. SE3	79	A3
Shirehall Clo. NW4	39	A6
Shirehall Gdns. NW4	39	A6
Shirehall La. NW4	39	A6
Shirehall Pk. NW4	39	A6
Shires, The, Rich.	82	H4
Shirland Ms. W9	57	C3
Shirland Rd. W9	57	C3
Shirley Ave., Bex.	80	C6
Shirley Ave., Croy.	102	F1
Shirley Ave., Sutt.	100	G4
Shirley Ch. Rd., Croy.	102	F3
Shirley Clo. E17	42	B5
Addison Rd.		
Shirley Clo., Houns.	72	J5
Shirley Clo., Croy.	102	G3
Shirley Cres., Beck.	95	H4
Shirley Dr., Houns.	72	J5
Shirley Gdns. W7	64	C1
Shirley Gdns., Bark.	52	H6
Shirley Gro. N9	25	F7
Shirley Gro. SW11	76	A3
Shirley Hills Rd., Croy.	102	G5
Shirley Ho. Dr. SE7	69	J7
Shirley Oaks Rd., Croy.	102	G1
Shirley Pk. Rd., Croy.	102	E1
Shirley Rd. E15	51	E7
Shirley Rd. W4	65	D2
Shirley Rd., Croy.	95	E7
Shirley Rd., Enf.	24	J3
Shirley Rd., Sid.	88	H3
Shirley St. E16	60	F6
Shirley Way, Croy.	102	F3
Shirlock Rd. NW3	48	J4
Shobden Rd. N17	41	A1
Shobroke Clo. NW2	47	J3
Shoe La. EC4	**12**	**F3**
Shoe La. EC4	58	G6
Shoebury Rd. E6	52	C7
Shoot Up Hill NW2	48	B5
Shooters Ave., Har.	37	H2
Shooter's Hill SE18	79	D1
Shooter's Hill, Well.	79	F2
Shooter's Hill Rd. SE3	78	F1
Shooter's Hill Rd. SE10	78	D1
Shooter's Hill Rd. SE18	79	A1
Shooters Rd., Enf.	24	H1
Shore Clo., Felt.	72	A7
Shore Clo., Hmptn.	81	E5
Stewart Clo.		
Shore Gro., Felt.	81	G2
Shore Pl. E9	50	F7
Shore Rd. E9	50	F7

Shoreditch High St. E1   9 E6
Shoreditch High St. E1   59 B4
Shoreham Clo. SW18   75 E5
  Ram St.
Shoreham Clo., Bex.   89 D1
  Stansted Cres.
Shoreham Clo., Croy.   95 F5
Shoreham Way,   96 G6
  Brom.
Shorncliffe Rd. SE1   21 F3
Shorncliffe Rd. SE1   68 C5
Shorndean St. SE6   87 C1
Shorne Clo., Sid.   80 B6
Shornefield Clo.,   97 D3
  Brom.
Shornells Way SE2   71 C5
  Willrose Cres.
Shorrolds Rd. SW6   66 C7
Short Gate N12   31 C4
Short Hedges, Houns.   72 G1
  Lampton Ave.
Short Hill, Har.   46 B1
  High St.
Short Path SE18   70 E6
  Westdale Rd.
Short Rd. E11   51 E2
Short Rd. E15   60 D1
Short Rd. W4   65 E6
Short St. NW4   38 J4
  New Brent St.
Short St. SE1   16 F3
Short Wall E15   60 D3
  Bisson Rd.
Short Way N12   31 H6
Short Way SE9   79 B3
Short Way, Twick.   72 J7
Shortcroft Rd.,   99 F7
  Epsom
Shorter St. E1   13 G5
Shorter St. E1   59 C7
Shortlands W6   66 A4
Shortlands Clo. N18   33 A3
Shortlands Clo., Belv.   71 F3
  Abbey Rd.
Shortlands Gdns.,   96 E2
  Brom.
Shortlands Gro.,   96 D3
  Brom.
Shortlands Rd. E10   42 B7
Shortlands Rd., Brom.   96 D3
Shortlands Rd.,   82 J7
  Kings.T.
Shorts Cft. NW9   38 B4
Shorts Gdns. WC2   12 A4
Shorts Gdns. WC2   58 E6
Shorts Rd., Cars.   100 H4
Shotfield, Wall.   101 B6
Shott Clo., Sutt.   100 F5
  Turnpike La.
Shottendane Rd.   75 D1
  SW6
Shottery Clo. SE9   88 B3
Shottfield Ave. SW14   74 E4
Shoulder of Mutton   59 H7
  All. E14
  Narrow St.
Shouldham St. W1   10 H2
Shouldham St. W1   57 H5
Showers Way, Hayes   63 A1
Shrapnel Clo. SE18   70 B7
Shrapnel Rd. SE9   79 C3
Shrewsbury Ave.   74 C4
  SW14
Shrewsbury Ave.,   37 H4
  Har.
Shrewsbury Clo.,   98 H3
  Surb.
Shrewsbury Cres.   56 D1
  NW10
Shrewsbury La. SE18   79 E1
Shrewsbury Ms. W2   57 D5
  Chepstow Rd.
Shrewsbury Rd. E7   52 A5
Shrewsbury Rd. N11   32 C6
Shrewsbury Rd. W2   57 D6
Shrewsbury Rd.,   95 H3
  Beck.
Shrewsbury Rd., Cars.   93 H6
Shrewsbury Wk., Islw.   73 D3
  South St.
Shrewton Rd. SW17   84 J7
Shroffold Rd., Brom.   87 E4
Shropshire Clo.,   94 E4
  Mitch.
Shropshire Pl. WC1   7 G6

Shropshire Rd. N22   32 F7
Shroton St. NW1   10 G1
Shroton St. NW1   57 H5
Shrubberies, The E18   42 G2
Shrubberies, The,   35 F5
  Chig.
Shrubbery Clo. N1   58 J1
  St. Paul St.
Shrubbery Gdns. N21   24 H7
Shrubbery Rd. N9   33 D3
Shrubbery Rd. SW16   85 E4
Shrubbery Rd., Sthl.   63 F1
Shrubland Gro.,   99 J3
  Wor.Pk.
Shrubland Rd. E8   59 C1
Shrubland Rd. E10   42 A7
Shrubland Rd. E17   42 A5
Shrublands Ave.,   103 A4
  Croy.
Shrublands Clo. N20   31 G1
Shrublands Clo. SE26   86 F3
Shrublands Clo., Chig.   35 F6
Shuna Wk. N1   50 A6
  St. Paul's Rd.
Shurland Ave., Barn.   23 G6
Shurland Gdns. SE15   21 G7
Shurlock Dr., Orp.   104 F4
Shuters Sq. W14   66 C5
  Sun Rd.
Shuttle Clo., Sid.   79 J7
Shuttle St. E1   9 H6
Shuttlemead, Bex.   80 F7
Shuttleworth Rd.   75 G2
  SW11
Sibella Rd. SW4   76 D2
Sibley Clo., Bexh.   80 E5
Sibley Gro. E12   52 B7
Sibthorp Rd., Mitch.   93 J2
  London Rd.
Sibthorpe Rd. SE12   78 H6
Sibton Rd., Cars.   93 H7
Sicilian Ave. WC1   12 B2
Sidbury St. SW6   75 B1
Sidcup Bypass, Chis.   88 H4
Sidcup Bypass, Orp.   89 B6
Sidcup Bypass, Sid.   88 H4
Sidcup High St., Sid.   89 A4
Sidcup Hill, Sid.   89 B4
Sidcup Hill Gdns.,   89 C5
  Sid.
  Sidcup Hill
Sidcup Pl., Sid.   89 A5
Sidcup Rd. SE9   78 J6
Sidcup Rd. SE12   78 H5
Sidcup Technology   89 D5
  Cen., Sid.
Siddons La. NW1   7 A6
Siddons Rd. N17   41 D1
Siddons Rd. SE23   86 H2
Siddons Rd., Croy.   101 G3
Side Rd. E17   41 J5
Sidewood Rd. SE9   88 G1
Sidford Pl. SE1   16 D6
Sidings, The E11   51 C1
Sidings Ms. N7   49 G3
  Tollington Rd.
Sidmouth Ave., Islw.   73 B2
Sidmouth Clo., Wat.   28 B2
Sidmouth Dr., Ruis.   45 A3
Sidmouth Rd. E10   51 C3
Sidmouth Rd. NW2   47 J7
Sidmouth Rd. SE15   77 C1
Sidmouth Rd., Well.   71 C7
Sidmouth St. WC1   8 B4
Sidmouth St. WC1   58 F3
Sidney Ave. N13   32 F5
Sidney Elson Way E6   61 D2
  Edwin Ave.
Sidney Est. E1   59 F6
Sidney Gdns., Brent.   64 F6
Sidney Gro. EC1   8 G2
Sidney Rd. E7   51 G3
Sidney Rd. N22   32 F7
Sidney Rd. SE25   95 D5
Sidney Rd. SW9   76 F2
Sidney Rd., Beck.   95 H2
Sidney Rd., Har.   36 J3
Sidney Rd., Twick.   73 D6
Sidney Rd., Walt.   90 A7
Sidney Sq. E1   59 F5
Sidney St. E1   59 F5
Sidworth St. E8   50 E7
Siebert Rd. SE3   69 G6
Siemens Rd. SE18   70 A3
Sigdon Rd. E8   50 D5
Sigers, The, Pnr.   36 B6
Signmakers Yd. NW1   58 B1
  Delancey St.

Silbury Ave., Mitch.   93 H1
Silbury St. N1   9 B3
Silchester Rd. W10   57 A6
Silecroft Rd., Bexh.   80 G1
Silesia Bldgs. E8   50 E7
  London La.
Silex St. SE1   16 H4
Silex St. SE1   67 H2
Silk Clo. SE12   78 G5
Silk Mills Path SE13   78 C2
Silk St. EC2   13 A1
Silk St. EC2   58 J5
Silkfield Rd. NW9   38 E5
Silkin Ho., Wat.   28 C3
Silkstream Rd., Edg.   38 C1
Silsoe Rd. N22   40 F7
Silver Birch Ave. E4   33 J6
Silver Birch Clo. N11   32 A6
Silver Clo. SE14   68 H7
  Southerngate Way
Silver Clo., Har.   29 A7
Silver Cres. W4   65 B4
Silver Jubilee Way,   72 B2
  Houns.
Silver La., W.Wick.   103 D2
Silver Pl. W1   11 G5
Silver Rd. W12   57 A7
Silver Spring Clo.,   71 H6
  Erith
Silver St. N18   33 A4
Silver St., Enf.   25 A3
Silver Wk. SE16   68 J1
Silver Way, Rom.   44 H3
Silverbirch Wk. NW3   49 A6
  Queens Cres.
Silvercliffe Gdns.,   23 H4
  Barn.
Silverdale SE26   86 F4
Silverdale, Enf.   24 E4
Silverdale Ave., Ilf.   43 H5
Silverdale Clo. W7   64 B1
  Cherington Rd.
Silverdale Clo., Nthlt.   45 F5
Silverdale Clo., Sutt.   100 C4
Silverdale Dr. SE9   88 B2
Silverdale Dr., Sun.   90 B2
Silverdale Gdns.,   63 A2
  Hayes
Silverdale Rd. E4   34 D6
Silverdale Rd., Bexh.   80 H2
Silverdale Rd., Orp.   97 F4
  (Petts Wd.)
Silverhall St., Islw.   73 D3
Silverholme Clo., Har.   37 H7
Silverland St. E16   70 C1
Silverleigh Rd.,   94 F4
  Th.Hth.
Silvermere Rd. SE6   78 B6
Silverst Clo., Nthlt.   45 H6
Silverston Way, Stan.   29 F6
Silverthorn Gdns. E4   34 A2
Silverthorne Rd. SW8   76 B2
Silverton Rd. W6   66 A6
Silvertown Way E16   60 E6
Silvertree La., Grnf.   55 A3
  Cowgate Rd.
Silverwood Clo.,   87 A7
  Beck.
Silvester Rd. SE22   77 C5
Silvester St. SE1   17 B4
Silwood Est. SE16   68 F4
  Millender Wk.
Silwood St. SE16   68 F4
Simla Clo. SE14   68 H6
  Chubworthy St.
Simla Ho. SE1   17 C4
Simmil Rd., Esher   98 B5
Simmons Clo. N20   31 H1
Simmons Clo., Chess.   98 F6
  Mansfield Rd.
Simmons La. E4   34 D2
Simmons Rd. SE18   70 E5
Simmons Way N20   31 H2
Simms Clo., Cars.   100 H2
Simms Rd. SE1   21 J2
Simms Rd. SE1   68 D4
Simnel Rd. SE12   78 H7
Simon Clo. W11   57 C7
  Portobello Rd.
Simonds Rd. E10   51 A2
Simone Clo., Brom.   97 A1
Simons Wk. E15   51 D5
  Waddington St.
Simpson Dr. W3   56 D6
Simpson Rd., Houns.   72 F6
Simpson Rd., Rich.   82 F4
Simpson St. SW11   75 H2
Simpsons Rd. E14   60 B7

Simpsons Rd., Brom.   96 G3
Sims Wk. SE3   78 F4
  Lee Rd.
Sinclair Ct., Beck.   87 A7
Sinclair Gdns. W14   66 A2
Sinclair Gro. NW11   39 A6
Sinclair Rd. E4   33 H5
Sinclair Rd. W14   66 A2
Sinclare Clo., Enf.   25 C1
Singapore Rd. W13   64 D1
Singer St. EC2   9 C4
Singleton Clo. SW17   84 H7
Singleton Clo., Croy.   94 J7
  St. Saviours Rd.
Singleton Rd., Dag.   53 F5
Singleton Scarp N12   31 D5
Sinnott Rd. E17   41 G1
Sion Rd., Twick.   73 E7
Sir Alexander Clo.   65 F1
  W3
Sir Alexander Rd. W3   65 F1
Sir Cyril Black Way   84 D7
  SW19
Sir Thomas More Est.   18 F6
  SW3
Sirdar Rd. N22   40 H3
Sirdar Rd. W11   57 A7
Sirdar Rd., Mitch.   85 A6
  Grenfell Rd.
Sirinham Pt. SW8   20 C6
Sirinham Pt. SW8   67 F6
Sirus Rd., Nthwd.   28 A5
Sise La. EC4   13 B4
Siskin Clo., Borwd.   22 A4
Sisley Rd., Bark.   61 H1
Sispara Gdns. SW18   75 C6
Sissinghurst Rd.,   95 D7
  Croy.
Sister Mabel's Way   21 H7
  SE15
Sisters Ave. SW11   75 J3
Sistova Rd. SW12   85 B1
Sisulu Pl. SW9   76 G3
Sittingbourne Ave.,   25 A6
  Enf.
Sitwell Gro., Stan.   29 C5
Sivill Ho. E2   9 G3
Sivill Ho. E2   59 C3
Siviter Rd., Dag.   53 H7
Siviter Way, Dag.   53 H7
Siward Rd. N17   41 A1
Siward Rd. SW17   84 F3
Siward Rd., Brom.   96 H3
Six Acres Est. N4   49 G2
Sixth Ave. E12   52 C4
Sixth Ave. W10   57 B3
Sixth Cross Rd., Twick.   81 J3
Skardu Rd. NW2   48 B5
Skeena Hill SW18   75 B7
Skeffington Rd. E6   61 C1
Skelbrook St. SW18   84 E2
Skelgill Rd. SW15   75 C4
Skelley Rd. E15   51 F7
Skelton Clo. E8   50 C6
  Buttermere Wk.
Skelton Rd. E7   51 G6
Skeltons La. E10   42 B7
Skelwith Rd. W6   65 J6
Skenfrith Ho. SE15   68 E6
  Commercial Way
Skerne Rd., Kings.T.   91 G1
Sketchley Gdns. SE16   68 G5
Sketty Rd., Enf.   25 B3
Skiers St. E15   60 E1
Skiffington Clo. SW2   85 G1
Skinner Ct. E2   59 E2
  Parmiter St.
Skinner Pl. SW1   19 B2
Skinner St. EC1   8 F4
Skinner St. EC1   58 G3
Skinners La. EC4   13 A5
Skinners La., Houns.   72 H1
Skinner's Row SE10   78 B1
  Blackheath Rd.
Skipsea Ave. E6   61 C3
Skipworth Rd. E9   59 F1
Skomer Wk. N1   49 J6
  Clephane Rd.
Sky Peals Rd.,   34 D7
  Wdf.Grn.
Slade, The SE18   70 H6
Slade Ho., Houns.   72 F6
Slade Twr. E10   51 A2
Slade Wk. SE17   20 J5
Sladebrook Rd. SE3   79 A3
Sladedale Rd. SE18   70 H5
Sladen Pl. E5   50 E4
  Clarence Rd.

Slades Clo., Enf. 24 G3
Slades Dr., Chis. 88 F3
Slades Gdns., Enf. 24 G2
Slades Hill, Enf. 24 G3
Slades Ri., Enf. 24 G3
Slagrove Pl. SE13 78 B5
   Ladywell Rd.
Slaidburn St. SW10 18 D6
Slaidburn St. SW10 66 F6
Slaithwaite Rd. SE13 78 C4
Slaney Pl. N7 49 G5
   Hornsey Rd.
Slattery Rd., Felt. 81 C1
Sleaford Grn., Wat. 28 D3
Sleaford St. SW8 19 F7
Sleaford St. SW8 67 C7
Slievemore Clo. SW4 76 D3
   Voltaire Rd.
Slingsby Pl. WC2 12 A5
Slippers Pl. SE16 68 E3
Sloane Ave. SW3 18 H2
Sloane Ave. SW3 66 H4
Sloane Ct. E. SW3 19 B3
Sloane Ct. W. SW3 19 B3
Sloane Ct. W. SW3 67 A5
Sloane Gdns. SW1 19 B2
Sloane Gdns. SW1 67 A4
Sloane Gdns., Orp. 104 F3
   Partridge Dr.
Sloane Sq. SW1 19 A2
Sloane Sq. SW1 66 J4
Sloane St. SW1 15 A5
Sloane St. SW1 66 J2
Sloane Ter. SW1 19 A1
Sloane Ter. SW1 66 J4
Sloane Wk., Croy. 95 J6
Slocum Clo. SE28 62 C7
   Woodpecker Rd.
Slough La. NW9 38 C5
Sly St. E1 59 E6
   Cannon St. Rd.
Smallberry Ave., Islw. 73 C2
Smallbrook Ms. W2 10 E4
Smalley Clo. N16 50 C3
Smalley Rd. Est. N16 50 C3
   Smalley Clo.
Smallwood Rd. 84 G4
   SW17
Smardale Rd. SW18 75 F5
   Alma Rd.
Smarden Clo., Belv. 71 G5
   Essenden Rd.
Smarden Gro. SE9 88 C4
Smart St. E2 59 G3
Smarts La., Loug. 27 A4
Smarts Pl. N18 33 D5
   Fore St.
Smart's Pl. WC2 12 B3
Smeaton Clo., Chess. 98 G6
   Mansfield Rd.
Smeaton Rd. SW18 75 D7
Smeaton Rd., 35 C5
   Wdf.Grn.
Smeaton St. E1 68 E1
Smedley St. SW4 76 D2
Smedley St. SW8 76 D2
Smeed Rd. E3 51 A7
Smiles Pl. SE13 78 C2
Smith Clo. SE16 68 G1
Smith Sq. SW1 16 A6
Smith Sq. SW1 67 E3
Smith St. SW3 18 J3
Smith St. SW3 66 J5
Smith St., Surb. 91 J6
Smith Ter. SW3 18 J4
Smith Ter. SW3 66 J5
Smithfield St. EC1 12 G2
Smithies Ct. E15 51 C5
   Clays La.
Smithies Rd. SE2 71 B4
Smith's Ct. W1 11 G5
Smiths Fm. Est., 54 G2
   Nthlt.
Smiths Yd. SW18 84 F2
   Summerley St.
Smith's Yd., Croy. 101 J3
   St. Georges Wk.
Smithson Rd. N17 41 A1
Smithwood Clo. 84 B1
   SW19
Smithy St. E1 59 F5
Smock Wk., Croy. 94 J6
Smokehouse Yd. EC1 12 H1
Smugglers Way 75 E4
   SW18
Smyrks Rd. SE17 21 E4
Smyrks Rd. SE17 68 B5
Smyrna Rd. NW6 48 D7

Smythe St. E14 60 B7
Snakes La., Barn. 24 C3
Snakes La. E., 34 J6
   Wdf.Grn.
Snakes La. W., 34 G6
   Wdf.Grn.
Snaresbrook Dr., 29 G4
   Stan.
Snaresbrook Rd. E11 42 E4
Snarsgate St. W10 56 J5
Sneath Ave. NW11 39 C7
Snells Pk. N18 33 C6
Sneyd Rd. NW2 47 J4
Snow Hill EC1 12 G2
Snow Hill EC1 58 H5
Snow Hill Ct. EC1 12 H3
Snowbury Rd. SW6 75 E2
Snowden St. EC2 9 D6
Snowden St. EC2 59 B4
Snowdon Dr. NW9 38 E6
Snowdown Clo. SE20 95 G1
Snowdrop Clo., 81 G6
   Hmptn.
   Gresham Rd.
Snowman Ho. NW6 48 E7
Snowsfields SE1 17 C3
Snowsfields SE1 68 A2
Snowshill Rd. E12 52 B5
Snowy Fielder Waye, 73 E2
   Islw.
Soames St. SE15 77 C3
Soames Wk., N.Mal. 92 E1
Socket La., Brom. 96 H6
Soho Sq. W1 11 H3
Soho Sq. W1 58 D6
Soho St. W1 11 H3
Solander Gdns. E1 59 E7
   Dellow St.
Solebay St. E1 59 H4
Solent Rd. NW6 48 D5
Soley Ms. WC1 8 E3
Solna Ave. SW15 74 J5
Solna Rd. N21 33 A1
Solomon's Pas. SE15 77 E4
Solon New Rd. SW4 76 E4
Solon New Rd. Est. 76 E4
   SW4
   Solon New Rd.
Solon Rd. SW2 76 E4
Solway Clo. E8 50 C6
   Buttermere Wk.
Solway Clo., Houns. 72 E3
Solway Rd. N22 40 H1
Solway Rd. SE22 77 D4
Somaford Gro., Barn. 23 G6
Somali Rd. NW2 48 C5
Somerby Rd., Bark. 52 G7
Somercoates Clo., 23 H3
   Barn.
Somerfield Rd. N4 49 H2
Somerford Clo., Pnr. 36 A4
Somerford Gro. N16 50 C4
Somerford Gro. N17 33 D7
Somerford Gro. Est. 50 C4
   N16
   Somerford Gro.
Somerford St. E1 59 E4
Somerford Way SE16 68 H2
Somerhill Ave., Sid. 80 B7
Somerhill Rd., Well. 80 B2
Somerleyton Pas. 76 H4
   SW9
Somerleyton Rd. SW9 76 G4
Somers Clo. NW1 7 H1
Somers Cres. W2 10 G4
Somers Cres. W2 57 H6
Somers Ms. W2 10 G4
Somers Pl. SW2 76 F7
Somers Rd. E17 41 J4
Somers Rd. SW2 76 F6
Somersby Gdns., Ilf. 43 C5
Somerset Ave. SW20 92 H2
Somerset Ave., 98 G4
   Chess.
Somerset Ave., Well. 79 J5
Somerset Clo., N.Mal. 92 E6
Somerset Clo., 42 G1
   Wdf.Grn.
Somerset Est. SW11 75 G1
Somerset Gdns. N6 40 A7
Somerset Gdns. SE13 78 B2
Somerset Gdns. 94 F3
   SW16
Somerset Gdns., 82 B5
   Tedd.
Somerset Rd. E17 42 A5
Somerset Rd. N17 41 C3
Somerset Rd. N18 33 C5

Somerset Rd. NW4 38 J4
Somerset Rd. SW19 84 A3
Somerset Rd. W4 65 D3
Somerset Rd. W13 64 E1
Somerset Rd., Barn. 23 E5
Somerset Rd., Brent. 64 G6
Somerset Rd., Har. 36 J6
Somerset Rd., 91 J2
   Kings.T.
Somerset Rd., Sthl. 54 F6
Somerset Rd., Tedd. 82 B5
Somerset Sq. W14 66 B2
Somerset Waye, 63 E7
   Houns.
Somersham Rd., Bexh. 80 E2
Somerton Ave., Rich. 74 B3
Somerton Rd. NW2 48 A3
Somerton Rd. SE15 77 E4
Somertrees Ave. 87 H2
   SE12
Somervell Rd., Har. 45 F5
Somerville Rd. SE20 86 G7
Somerville Rd., Rom. 44 C6
Sonderburg Rd. N7 49 F3
   Seven Sisters Rd.
Sondes St. SE17 21 B5
Sondes St. SE17 68 A6
Sonia Ct., Har. 37 C6
Sonia Gdns. N12 31 F4
   Woodside Ave.
Sonia Gdns. NW10 47 F4
Sonia Gdns., Houns. 63 G7
Sonning Gdns., 81 E6
   Hmptn.
Sonning Rd. SE25 95 D6
Soper Clo. E4 33 J5
Sophia Clo. N7 49 F6
   Mackenzie Rd.
Sophia Rd. E10 51 B1
Sophia Rd. E16 60 H6
Sophia Sq. SE16 59 H7
   Rotherhithe St.
Sopwith Ave., Chess. 98 H5
Sopwith Rd., Houns. 63 C7
Sopwith Way, 91 H1
   Kings.T.
Sorrel Clo. SE28 71 A1
Sorrel Gdns. E6 61 B5
Sorrel La. E14 60 D6
Sorrell Clo. SE14 68 H7
   Southerngate Way
Sorrento Rd., Sutt. 100 D3
Sotheby Rd. N5 49 J3
Sotheran Clo. E8 59 D1
Sotheron Rd. SW6 66 E7
Soudan Rd. SW11 75 J1
Souldern Rd. W14 66 A3
South Access Rd. E17 41 H7
South Africa Rd. W12 65 H1
South Audley St. W1 11 C6
South Audley St. W1 58 A7
South Ave. E4 26 B7
South Ave., Cars. 101 A7
South Ave., Rich. 73 G1
   Sandycombe Rd.
South Ave., Sthl. 54 F7
South Ave. Gdns., 54 F7
   Sthl.
South Bank, Chis. 88 F3
South Bank, Surb. 91 H6
South Bank Ter., 91 H6
   Surb.
South Birkbeck Rd. 51 D3
   E11
South Black Lion La. 65 G5
   W6
South Bolton Gdns. 18 B3
   SW5
South Bolton Gdns. 66 E5
   SW5
South Carriage Dr. 66 H2
   SW1
South Carriage Dr. 14 G3
   SW7
South Carriage Dr. 66 H2
   SW7
South Clo. N6 40 B6
South Clo., Barn. 23 C3
South Clo., Bexh. 80 D4
South Clo., Dag. 62 G1
South Clo., Mord. 93 E6
   Green La.
South Clo., Pnr. 36 F7
South Clo., Twick. 81 G3
South Colonnade E14 69 A1
South Countess Rd. 41 J3
   E17

South Cres. E16 60 D4
   Cody Rd.
South Cres. WC1 11 H2
South Cres. WC1 58 D5
South Cross Rd., Ilf. 43 F5
South Croxted Rd. 86 A3
   SE21
South Dene NW7 30 D3
South Dr., Orp. 104 H5
South Ealing Rd. W5 64 D2
South Eastern Ave. 33 C3
   N9
South Eaton Pl. SW1 19 C1
South Eaton Pl. SW1 67 A4
South Eden Pk. Rd., 96 B6
   Beck.
South Edwardes Sq. 66 C3
   W8
South End W8 14 B5
South End, Croy. 101 J4
South End Clo. NW3 48 H4
South End Rd. NW3 48 H4
South End Row W8 14 B5
South End Row W8 66 E3
South Esk Rd. E7 51 J6
South Gdns. SW19 84 G7
South Gipsy Rd., Well. 80 D3
South Glade, The, 89 F1
   Bex.
   Camden Rd.
South Grn. NW9 38 E1
   Clayton Fld.
South Gro. E17 41 J5
South Gro. N6 49 A1
South Gro. N15 41 A5
South Gro. Ho. N6 49 A1
   Highgate W. Hill
South Hill, Chis. 88 C6
South Hill Ave., Har. 45 J3
South Hill Gro., Har. 46 B4
South Hill Pk. NW3 48 H4
South Hill Pk. Gdns. 48 H4
   NW3
South Hill Rd., Brom. 96 E3
South Huxley N18 33 A5
South Island Pl. SW9 67 F7
South Lambeth Pl. 20 B5
   SW8
South Lambeth Pl. 67 E6
   SW8
South Lambeth Rd. 67 E6
   SW8
South La., Kings.T. 91 G3
South La., N.Mal. 92 D4
South La. W., N.Mal. 92 D4
South Lo. Ave., 94 E4
   Mitch.
South Lo. Cres., Enf. 24 D4
South Lo. Dr. N14 24 D4
South Mall N9 33 D3
   Plevna Rd.
South Mead NW9 38 F1
South Mead, Epsom 99 E7
South Meadows, 46 H5
   Wem.
South Molton La. W1 11 D4
South Molton La. W1 58 B6
South Molton Rd. 60 G6
   E16
South Molton St. W1 11 D4
South Molton St. W1 58 B6
South Norwood Hill 95 B1
   SE25
South Oak Rd. SW16 85 F4
South Par. SW3 18 F3
South Par. SW3 66 G5
South Par. W4 65 D4
South Pk. Cres. SE6 87 F1
South Pk. Cres., Ilf. 52 G3
South Pk. Dr., Bark. 52 H3
South Pk. Dr., Ilf. 52 H2
South Pk. Gro., 92 C4
   N.Mal.
South Pk. Hill Rd., 102 A5
   S.Croy.
South Pk. Ms. SW6 75 E3
South Pk. Rd. SW19 84 D6
South Pk. Rd., Ilf. 52 G3
South Pk. Ter., Ilf. 52 H3
South Pk. Way, Ruis. 45 C6
South Penge Pk. Est. 95 E2
   SE20
South Pl. EC2 13 C2
South Pl. EC2 59 A5
South Pl., Enf. 25 F5
South Pl., Surb. 91 J7
South Pl. Ms. EC2 13 C2
South Rd. N9 33 D1

South Rd. SE23	86	G2
South Rd. SW19	84	F6
South Rd. W5	64	G4
South Rd., Edg.	38	B1
South Rd., Felt.	81	D5
South Rd., Hmptn.	81	E6
South Rd., Rom.	44	E6
(Chadwell Heath)		
South Rd., Rom.	44	B5
(Little Heath)		
South Rd., Sthl.	63	F2
South Rd., Twick.	82	A3
South Row SE3	78	F2
South Sea St. SE16	68	J3
South Side W6	65	F3
South Side Common	83	J6
SW19		
South Sq. NW11	39	E6
South Sq. WC1	**12**	**E2**
South St. W1	67	A1
South St. W1	**15**	**C1**
South St., Brom.	96	G2
South St., Enf.	25	F5
South St., Islw.	73	D3
South St., Rain.	62	J2
South Tenter St. E1	**13**	**G4**
South Tenter St. E1	59	C7
South Ter. SW7	**18**	**G1**
South Ter. SW7	66	H4
South Ter., Surb.	91	H6
South Vale SE19	86	B6
South Vale, Har.	46	B4
South Vw., Brom.	96	H2
South Vw. Dr. E18	42	H3
South Vw. N8	40	D3
South Vw. Rd., Loug.	27	C6
South Vw. Rd., Pnr.	28	B6
South Vill. NW1	49	D6
South Wk., W.Wick.	103	E3
South Way N9	33	F2
South Way N11	32	C6
Ringway		
South Way, Brom.	96	G7
South Way, Croy.	102	H3
South Way, Har.	36	G4
South Way, Wem.	47	A5
South W. India Dock	69	C2
Entrance E14		
South Western Rd.,	73	D6
Twick.		
South Wf. Rd. W2	**10**	**E3**
South Wf. Rd. W2	57	G6
South Woodford to	42	J3
Barking Relief Rd.		
E11		
South Woodford to	52	D4
Barking Relief Rd.		
E12		
South Woodford to	42	J3
Barking Relief Rd.		
E18		
South Woodford to	52	D4
Barking Relief Rd.,		
Bark.		
South Woodford to	42	J3
Barking Relief Rd.,		
Ilf.		
South Worple Ave.	74	E3
SW14		
South Worple Way		
South Worple Way	74	D3
SW14		
Southacre Way, Pnr.	36	C1
Southall La., Houns.	63	B6
Southall Pl. SE1	**17**	**B4**
Southall Pl. SE1	68	A2
Southam St. W10	57	B4
Southampton Bldgs.	**12**	**E2**
WC2		
Southampton Gdns.,	94	E5
Mitch.		
Southampton Pl. WC1	**12**	**B2**
Southampton Pl. WC1	58	E5
Southampton Rd.	48	J5
NW5		
Southampton Row	**12**	**B1**
WC1		
Southampton Row	58	E5
WC1		
Southampton St. WC2	**12**	**B5**
Southampton St. WC2	58	E7
Southampton Way	**21**	**C7**
SE5		
Southampton Way	68	A7
SE5		
Southbank, T.Ditt.	91	E7
Southborough Clo.,	98	G1
Surb.		

Southborough La.,	97	B5
Brom.		
Southborough Rd. E9	50	G7
Southborough Rd.,	97	B3
Brom.		
Southborough Rd.,	98	H1
Surb.		
Southbourne, Brom.	96	G7
Southbourne Ave.	38	C2
NW9		
Southbourne Clo.,	36	E7
Pnr.		
Southbourne Cres.	39	B4
NW4		
Southbourne Gdns.	78	H5
SE12		
Southbourne Gdns.,	52	F5
Ilf.		
Southbourne Gdns.,	45	B1
Ruis.		
Southbridge Pl.,	101	J4
Croy.		
Southbridge Rd.,	101	J4
Croy.		
Southbridge Way,	63	E2
Sthl.		
Southbrook Ms. SE12	78	F6
Southbrook Rd. SE12	78	F6
Southbrook Rd.	94	E1
SW16		
Southbury Ave., Enf.	25	D5
Southbury Rd., Enf.	25	A3
Southchurch Rd. E6	61	C2
Southcombe St. W14	66	B4
Southcote Ave., Surb.	92	B7
Southcote Rd. E17	41	G5
Southcote Rd. N19	49	C4
Southcote Rd. SE25	95	E5
Southcroft Ave., Well.	79	H3
Southcroft Ave.,	103	C2
W.Wick.		
Southcroft Rd. SW16	85	B6
Southcroft Rd. SW17	85	A6
Southcroft Rd., Orp.	104	H3
Southdale, Chig.	35	G6
Southdean Gdns.	84	C2
SW19		
Southdown Ave. W7	64	D3
Southdown Cres.,	45	J1
Har.		
Southdown Cres., Ilf.	43	H5
Southdown Dr. SW20	84	A7
Crescent Rd.		
Southdown Rd. SW20	93	A1
Southend Clo. SE9	79	E6
Southend Cres. SE9	79	E6
Southend La. SE6	87	A4
Southend La. SE26	86	J4
Southend Rd. E6	52	C7
Southend Rd. E17	42	D1
Southend Rd. E18	42	F2
Southend Rd., Beck.	87	A7
Southend Rd.,	42	J2
Wdf.Grn.		
Southern Ave. SE25	95	C3
Southern Ave., Felt.	81	A1
Southern Dr., Loug.	27	C6
Southern Gro. E3	59	J3
Southern Rd. E13	60	H2
Southern Rd. N2	39	J4
Southern Row W10	57	B4
Southern St. N1	**8**	**C1**
Southern St. N1	58	F2
Southern Way, Rom.	44	G6
Southerngate Way	68	H7
SE14		
Southernhay, Loug.	27	A4
Southerton Rd. W6	65	J3
Southey Rd. N15	41	B5
Southey Rd. SW9	76	G1
Southey Rd. SW19	84	D7
Southey St. SE20	86	G7
Southfield, Barn.	23	A6
Southfield Cotts. W7	64	C2
Oaklands Rd.		
Southfield Gdns.,	82	C4
Twick.		
Southfield Pk., Har.	36	H4
Southfield Rd. N17	41	B2
Southfield Rd. W4	65	D2
Southfield Rd., Chis.	97	J3
Southfield Rd., Enf.	25	E6
Southfields NW4	38	H3
Southfields, E.Mol.	91	B6
Southfields Ct. SW19	84	B1
Southfields Pas.	75	D6
SW18		
Southfields Rd.		

Southfields Rd.	75	D6
SW18		
Southfleet Rd., Orp.	104	H3
Southgate Circ. N14	32	D1
The Bourne		
Southgate Gro. N1	50	A7
Southgate Rd. N1	59	A1
Southholme Clo.	95	C1
SE19		
Southill La., Pnr.	36	B4
Southill Rd., Chis.	88	B6
Southill St. E14	60	B6
Chrisp St.		
Southland Rd. SE18	70	J7
Southland Way,	73	A5
Houns.		
Southlands Ave., Orp.	104	G4
Southlands Gro.,	97	B3
Brom.		
Southlands Rd.,	96	J5
Brom.		
Southly Clo., Sutt.	100	D3
Southmead Rd. SW19	84	B1
Southmont Rd., Esher	98	B2
Southmoor Way E9	50	J6
Southold Ri. SE9	88	C3
Southolm St. SW11	76	B1
Southover N12	31	D3
Southover, Brom.	87	G2
Southport Rd. SE18	70	G4
Southridge Pl. SW20	84	A7
Southsea Rd.,	91	H4
Kings.T.		
Southspring, Sid.	79	G7
Southvale Rd. SE3	78	E2
Southview Ave. NW10	47	F5
Southview Clo., Bex.	80	F6
Southview Cres., Ilf.	43	E6
Southview Gdns.,	101	C7
Wall.		
Southview Rd., Brom.	87	D4
Southville SW8	73	J1
Southville, T.Ditt.	91	D7
Southwark Bri. EC4	**13**	**A6**
Southwark Bri. EC4	67	J1
Southwark Bri. SE1	**13**	**A6**
Southwark Bri. SE1	67	J1
Southwark Bri. Rd.	**16**	**J4**
SE1		
Southwark Bri. Rd.	67	H3
SE1		
Southwark Gro. SE1	**16**	**J2**
Southwark Pk. Est.	68	E4
SE16		
Southwark Pk. Rd.	**21**	**G1**
SE16		
Southwark Pk. Rd.	68	C4
SE16		
Southwark Pl., Brom.	97	C3
St. Georges Rd.		
Southwark St. SE1	**16**	**H1**
Southwark St. SE1	67	H1
Southwater Clo. E14	59	J6
Southwater Clo.,	87	B7
Beck.		
Southway N20	31	D2
Southway NW7	30	G7
Southway NW11	39	E5
Southway SW20	92	J4
Southway, Wall.	101	C4
Southwell Ave., Nthlt.	45	G6
Southwell Gdns. SW7	**14**	**C6**
Southwell Gdns. SW7	66	F4
Southwell Gro. Rd.	51	E2
E11		
Southwell Rd. SE5	76	J3
Southwell Rd., Croy.	94	G6
Southwell Rd., Har.	37	G6
Southwest Rd. E11	51	D1
Southwick Ms. W2	**10**	**F3**
Southwick Pl. W2	**10**	**G4**
Southwick Pl. W2	57	H6
Southwick St. W2	**10**	**G3**
Southwick St. W2	57	H6
Southwold Dr., Bark.	53	A5
Southwold Rd. E5	50	E2
Southwold Rd., Bex.	80	H2
Southwood Ave. N6	40	B7
Southwood Ave.,	92	C1
Kings.T.		
Southwood Clo.,	97	C4
Brom.		
Southwood Clo.,	100	A1
Wor.Pk.		
Carters Clo.		
Southwood Dr., Surb.	92	C7
Southwood Gdns.,	98	D3
Esher		

Southwood Gdns., Ilf.	43	E4
Southwood La. N6	40	A7
Southwood Lawn Rd.	40	A7
N6		
Southwood Rd. SE9	88	E2
Southwood Rd. SE28	57	H7
Sovereign Clo. E1	59	E7
Sovereign Clo. W5	55	F5
Sovereign Ct., Brom.	97	C5
Sovereign Cres. SE16	68	H1
Rotherhithe St.		
Sovereign Gro., Wem.	46	G3
Sovereign Ms. E2	**9**	**F1**
Sovereign Pk. NW10	56	B4
Sowerby Clo. SE9	79	B5
Spa Clo. SE25	95	B1
Spa Grn. Est. EC1	**8**	**F3**
Spa Hill SE19	95	A1
Spa Rd. SE16	**17**	**F6**
Spa Rd. SE16	68	C3
Space Waye, Felt.	72	A5
Spafield St. EC1	**8**	**E5**
Spalding Rd. NW4	38	J6
Spalding Rd. SW17	85	B5
Spanby Rd. E3	60	A4
Spaniards Clo. NW11	48	G1
Spaniards End NW3	48	A3
Spaniards Rd. NW3	48	F3
Spanish Pl. W1	**11**	**C3**
Spanish Pl. W1	58	A6
Spanish Rd. SW18	75	F5
Spareleaze Hill, Loug.	27	B5
Sparkbridge Rd., Har.	37	B4
Sparks Clo. W3	56	D6
Joseph Ave.		
Sparks Clo., Hmptn.	81	E6
Victors Dr.		
Sparrow Clo., Hmptn.	81	E6
Sparrow Dr., Orp.	104	F1
Sparrow Fm. Dr., Felt.	72	C6
Sparrow Fm. Rd.,	99	G4
Epsom		
Sparrow Grn., Dag.	53	H3
Sparrows La. SE9	79	F7
Sparsholt Rd. N19	49	F1
Sparsholt Rd., Bark.	61	H1
Sparta St. SE10	78	C1
Spear Ms. SW5	75	J4
Spearman St. SE18	70	D6
Spearpoint Gdns., Ilf.	43	J4
Spears Rd. N19	49	E1
Speart La., Houns.	63	E7
Spedan Clo. NW3	48	A3
Speedwell St. SE8	69	A7
Comet St.		
Speedy Pl. WC1	**8**	**A4**
Speer Rd., T.Ditt.	91	C7
Speke Ho. SE5	67	J7
Speke Rd., Th.Hth.	95	A2
Spekehill SE9	88	C3
Speldhurst Clo.,	96	G5
Brom.		
Speldhurst Rd. E9	50	G7
Speldhurst Rd. W4	65	D3
Spellbrook Wk. N1	58	J1
Basire St.		
Spelman St. E1	**13**	**H1**
Spelman St. E1	59	D5
Spence Clo. SE16	68	J2
Vaughan St.		
Spencer Ave. N13	32	F6
Spencer Ave., Hayes	54	A5
Spencer Clo. N3	39	D2
Spencer Clo. NW10	55	J3
Spencer Clo., Orp.	104	H2
Spencer Clo.,	34	J5
Wdf.Grn.		
Spencer Ct. NW8	**6**	**C1**
Spencer Dr. N2	39	F6
Spencer Gdns. SE9	79	C5
Spencer Gdns. SW14	74	C5
Spencer Hill SW19	84	B8
Spencer Hill Rd. SW19	84	B7
Spencer Ms. W6	66	B6
Greyhound Rd.		
Spencer Pk. SW18	75	G5
Spencer Pas. E2	59	E2
Pritchard's Rd.		
Spencer Pl., Croy.	95	A7
Gloucester Rd.		
Spencer Ri. NW5	49	B4
Spencer Rd. E6	61	A1
Spencer Rd. E17	42	C2
Spencer Rd. N8	40	F5
Spencer Rd. N11	32	B4
Spencer Rd. N17	41	D1
Spencer Rd. SW18	75	G4
Spencer Rd. SW20	92	H1

Spencer Rd. W3 65 C1
Spencer Rd. W4 65 C7
Spencer Rd., Brom. 87 F7
Spencer Rd., E.Mol. 91 A4
Spencer Rd., Har. 37 B2
Spencer Rd., Ilf. 52 J1
Spencer Rd., Islw. 72 J1
Spencer Rd., Mitch. 94 A3
Spencer Rd., Mitch. 94 A7
(Beddington)
Spencer Rd., S.Croy. 102 B5
Spencer Rd., Twick. 82 B3
Spencer Rd., Wem. 46 F2
Spencer St. EC1 **8 G4**
Spencer St. EC1 58 H3
Spencer St., Sthl. 63 D2
Spencer Wk. NW3 48 F4
Hampstead High St.
Spencer Wk. SW15 75 A4
Spenser Gro. N16 50 B4
Spenser Rd. SE24 76 G5
Spenser St. SW1 **15 G5**
Spenser St. SW1 67 C3
Spensley Wk. N16 50 A3
Clissold Rd.
Speranza St. SE18 70 J5
Sperling Rd. N17 41 B2
Spert St. E14 59 H7
Spey St. E14 60 C5
Speyside N14 24 C6
Spezia Rd. NW10 56 G2
Spicer Clo. SW9 76 H2
Spicer Clo., Walt. 90 C6
Spice's Yd., Croy. 101 J4
Spiers Clo., N.Mal. 92 F6
Spigurnell Rd. N17 41 A1
Spikes Bri. Rd., Sthl. 54 E6
Spilsby Clo. NW9 38 E2
Kenley Ave.
Spindlewood Gdns., 102 B4
Croy.
Spindrift Ave. E14 69 A4
Spinel Clo. SE18 70 J5
Spinnells Rd., Har. 45 F1
Spinney, The N21 24 G7
Spinney, The SW16 85 C3
Spinney, The, Barn. 23 E2
Spinney, The, Sid. 89 E4
Spinney, The, Stan. 29 H4
Spinney, The, Sun. 90 A1
Spinney, The, Sutt. 99 J4
Spinney, The, Wem. 46 D3
Spinney Clo., N.Mal. 92 E5
Spinney Gdns. SE19 86 C5
Spinney Gdns., Dag. 53 E5
Spinney Oak, Brom. 97 B2
Spinneys, The, Brom. 97 C2
Spirit Quay E1 **17 J1**
Spital Sq. E1 **13 E1**
Spital Sq. E1 59 B5
Spital St. E1 **9 H6**
Spital St. E1 59 D5
Spital Yd. E1 **13 E1**
Spitalfields Mkt. E1 **13 F1**
Spitalfields Mkt. E1 59 C5
Spitfire Est., Houns. 63 C5
Spitfire Way, Houns. 63 C5
Splendour Wk. SE16 68 F5
Verney Rd.
Spode Wk. NW6 48 E6
Lymington Rd.
Spondon Rd. N15 41 D4
Spooner Wk., Wall. 101 D5
Sportsbank St. SE6 78 C7
Spottons Gro. N17 40 J1
Gospatrick Rd.
Spout Hill, Croy. 103 A5
Spratt Hall Rd. E11 42 G6
Spray La., Twick. 73 B6
Spray St. SE18 70 E4
Spreighton Rd., 90 H4
W.Mol.
Sprimont Pl. SW3 **18 J3**
Sprimont Pl. SW3 66 J4
Spring Bri. Ms. W5 55 G7
Spring Bri. Rd.
Spring Bri. Rd. W5 55 G7
Spring Clo., Barn. 23 A5
Spring Clo., Borwd. 22 A1
Spring Clo., Dag. 53 D1
Spring Clo. La., Sutt. 100 B6
Spring Cotts., Surb. 91 G5
St. Leonard's Rd.
Spring Ct., Sid. 89 A3
Station Rd.
Spring Dr., Pnr. 36 A6
Eastcote Rd.

Spring Gdns. N5 49 J5
Grosvenor Ave.
Spring Gdns. SW1 **15 J1**
Spring Gdns., Rom. 44 J5
Spring Gdns., Wall. 101 C5
Spring Gdns., W.Mol. 90 J5
Spring Gdns., 34 J7
Wdf.Grn.
Spring Gdns. Ind. 44 J5
Est., Rom.
Spring Gro. W4 65 A5
Spring Gro., Hmptn. 90 H1
Plevna Rd.
Spring Gro., Loug. 27 A6
Spring Gro., Mitch. 94 A1
Spring Gro. Cres., 72 J1
Houns.
Spring Gro. Rd., 72 H1
Houns.
Spring Gro. Rd., Islw. 73 A1
Spring Gro. Rd., Rich. 73 J5
Spring Hill E5 41 D7
Spring Hill SE26 86 F4
Spring Lake, Stan. 29 E4
Spring La. E5 41 E7
Spring La. SE25 95 E6
Spring Ms. W1 **11 A1**
Spring Pk. Ave., 102 G2
Croy.
Spring Pk. Dr. N4 49 J1
Spring Pk. Rd., Croy. 102 G2
Spring Pas. SW15 75 A3
Embankment
Spring Path NW3 48 G5
Spring Pl. NW5 49 B5
Spring St. W2 **10 E4**
Spring St. W2 57 G6
Spring Ter., Rich. 73 H5
Spring Vale, Bexh. 80 H4
Spring Vill. Rd., Edg. 30 A7
Spring Wk. E1 **13 J1**
Springall St. SE15 68 E7
Springbank N21 24 F6
Springbank Rd. SE13 78 D6
Springbank Wk. NW1 49 D7
St. Paul's Cres.
Springbourne Ct., 96 C1
Beck.
Springclose La., Sutt. 100 B6
Springcroft Ave. N2 39 J4
Springdale Rd. N16 50 A4
Springfield E5 50 E1
Springfield (Bushey), 29 A1
Wat.
Springfield Ave. N10 40 C3
Springfield Ave. SW20 93 C3
Springfield Ave., 81 H6
Hmptn.
Springfield Clo. N12 31 E5
Springfield Clo., Stan. 29 D3
Springfield Dr., Ilf. 43 F6
Springfield Gdns. E5 50 E1
Springfield Gdns. 38 D5
NW9
Springfield Gdns., 97 C4
Brom.
Springfield Gdns., 45 B1
Ruis.
Springfield Gdns., 103 B2
W.Wick.
Springfield Gdns., 34 J7
Wdf.Grn.
Springfield Gro. SE7 69 J6
Springfield La. NW6 57 E1
Springfield Mt. NW9 38 D5
Springfield Pl., N.Mal. 92 C4
Springfield Ri. SE26 86 E3
Springfield Rd. E4 34 E1
Springfield Rd. E6 52 C7
Springfield Rd. E15 60 E3
Springfield Rd. E17 41 J6
Springfield Rd. N11 32 B5
Springfield Rd. N15 41 D4
Springfield Rd. NW8 57 F1
Springfield Rd. SE26 86 E5
Springfield Rd. SW19 84 C5
Springfield Rd. W7 64 B1
Springfield Rd., Bexh. 80 H3
Springfield Rd., 97 C4
Brom.
Springfield Rd., Har. 37 B6
Springfield Rd., 63 C1
Hayes
Springfield Rd., 91 H3
Kings.T.
Springfield Rd., Tedd. 82 D5
Springfield Rd., 94 J1
Th.Hth.

Springfield Rd., 81 G1
Twick.
Springfield Rd., Wall. 101 A5
Springfield Rd., Well. 80 B3
Springfield Wk. NW6 57 E1
Springfield Wk., Orp. 104 G1
Place Fm. Ave.
Springhill Clo. SE5 77 A3
Springhurst Clo., 102 J4
Croy.
Springpark Dr., Beck. 96 C3
Springpond Rd., Dag. 53 E5
Springrice Rd. SE13 78 D6
Springvale Ave., 64 H5
Brent.
Springvale Est. W14 66 B3
Blythe Rd.
Springvale Ter. W14 66 A3
Springwater Clo. SE18 79 D1
Springwell Ave. 56 F1
NW10
Springwell Clo. SW16 85 G4
Etherstone Rd.
Springwell Ct., Houns. 72 D2
Springwell Rd. SW16 85 G4
Springwell Rd., 72 D2
Houns.
Springwood Cres., 30 B2
Edg.
Sprowston Ms. E7 51 G6
Sprowston Rd. E7 51 G5
Spruce Ct. W4 65 D2
Spruce Ct. W5 64 H3
Elderberry Rd.
Spruce Hills Rd. E17 42 C2
Spruce Pk., Brom. 96 F4
Cumberland Rd.
Sprucedale Gdns., 102 G4
Croy.
Sprules Rd. SE4 77 H2
Spur Rd. N15 41 A4
Philip La.
Spur Rd. SW1 **15 F4**
Spur Rd. SW1 67 C2
Spur Rd., Bark. 61 F3
Spur Rd., Edg. 29 H4
Spur Rd., Felt. 72 B5
Spur Rd., Islw. 64 E7
Spur Rd. Est., Edg. 29 J4
Spurfield, W.Mol. 90 H3
Spurgeon Ave. SE19 95 A1
Spurgeon Rd. SE19 95 A1
Spurgeon St. SE1 **17 B6**
Spurgeon St. SE1 68 A3
Spurling Rd. SE22 77 C4
Spurling Rd., Dag. 53 F6
Spurstowe Rd. E8 50 E6
Marcon Pl.
Spurstowe Ter. E8 50 E5
Square, The W6 65 J5
Square, The, Cars. 101 A5
Square, The, Ilf. 43 D7
Square, The, Rich. 73 G5
Square, The, Wdf.Grn. 34 G5
Square Rigger Row 75 F3
SW11
York Pl.
Squarey St. SW17 84 F3
Squires Ct. SW19 84 D4
Squires La. N3 39 E2
Squires Mt. NW3 48 G3
East Heath Rd.
Squires Wd. Dr., Chis. 88 C7
Bullers Wd. Dr.
Squirrel Clo., Houns. 72 C3
Squirrels, The SE13 78 D3
Belmont Hill
Squirrels, The, Pnr. 36 F3
Squirrels Clo. N12 31 F4
Woodside Ave.
Squirrels Grn. 99 G2
Wor.Pk.
The Ave.
Squirrels La., Buck.H. 35 A3
Squirrels Ms. W13 55 D7
Squirries St. E2 **9 J3**
Squirries St. E2 59 D3
Stable Clo., Nthlt. 54 G2
Hotspur Rd.
Stable Wk. N2 39 G1
Old Fm. Rd.
Stable Way W10 56 J6
Latimer Rd.
Stable Yd. SW1 **15 F3**
Stable Yd. SW9 76 F2
Broomgrove Rd.
Stable Yd. Rd. SW1 **15 G3**
Stable Yd. Rd. SW1 67 C2

Stables, The, 26 J7
Buck.H.
Stables End, Orp. 104 F3
Stables Ms. SE27 85 J5
Stables Way SE11 **20 E3**
Stables Way SE11 67 G5
Stacey Ave. N18 33 F4
Stacey Clo. E10 42 D5
Halford Rd.
Stacey St. N7 49 G3
Tollington Rd.
Stacey St. WC2 **11 J4**
Stacey St. WC2 58 D6
Stackhouse St. SW3 **14 J5**
Stacy Path SE5 68 B7
Harris St.
Stadium Rd. NW2 38 J7
Stadium Rd. SE18 70 C7
Stadium St. SW10 66 F7
Stadium Way, Wem. 46 J4
Staff St. EC1 **9 C4**
Staffa Rd. E10 50 G1
Stafford Clo. N14 24 C5
Stafford Clo. NW6 57 D3
Stafford Clo., Sutt. 100 B6
Stafford Ct. W8 66 D3
Kensington High St.
Stafford Cross Rd. 101 F5
Est., Croy.
Stafford Gdns., Croy. 101 F5
Stafford Pl. SW1 **15 F5**
Stafford Pl. SW1 67 C3
Stafford Pl., Rich. 73 J7
Stafford Rd. E3 59 J2
Stafford Rd. E7 51 J7
Stafford Rd. NW6 57 D3
Stafford Rd., Croy. 101 G4
Stafford Rd., Har. 28 J7
Stafford Rd., N.Mal. 92 C3
Stafford Rd., Sid. 88 H4
Stafford Rd., Wall. 101 B6
Stafford St. W1 **15 F1**
Stafford St. W1 67 C1
Stafford Ter. W8 66 D2
Staffordshire St. SE15 77 D1
Stag La., Edg. 38 B2
Stag La. NW9 38 C3
Stag La. SW15 83 F2
Stag La., Buck.H. 34 H2
Stag La., Edg. 38 B2
Stag Pl. SW1 **15 F5**
Stag Pl. SW1 67 C3
Stag Ride SW19 83 F3
Stags Way, Islw. 64 C6
Stainbank Rd., Mitch. 94 B3
Stainby Rd. N15 41 C4
Stainer St. SE1 **17 C2**
Stainer St. SE1 68 A1
Staines Ave., Sutt. 100 A2
Staines Rd., Felt. 72 C5
Staines Rd., Houns. 72 C5
Staines Rd., Ilf. 52 G4
Staines Rd., Twick. 81 G3
Staines Rd. E., Sun. 81 A7
Staines Wk., Sid. 89 C6
Evry Rd.
Stainforth Rd. E17 42 A4
Stainforth Rd., Ilf. 43 G7
Staining La. EC2 **13 A3**
Staining La. EC2 58 J6
Stainmore Clo., Chis. 97 G1
Stainsbury St. E2 59 F2
Royston St.
Stainsby Pl. E14 60 A6
Stainsby Rd. E14 60 A6
Stainton Rd. SE6 78 D6
Stainton Rd., Enf. 25 F1
Stalbridge St. NW1 **10 H1**
Stalham St. SE16 68 E3
Stambourne Way 86 B7
SE19
Stambourne Way, 103 C3
W.Wick.
Stamford Brook Ave. 65 F3
W6
Stamford Brook Rd. 65 F3
W6
Stamford Clo. N15 41 D4
Stamford Clo., Har. 29 B7
Stamford Clo., Sthl. 54 G7
Stamford Ct. W6 65 F4
Goldhawk Rd.
Stamford Dr., Brom. 96 F4
Stamford Gdns., Dag. 53 C7
Stamford Gro. E. N16 50 D1
Oldhill St.
Stamford Gro. W. N16 50 D1
Oldhill St.

Stamford Hill N16	50	C2
Stamford Hill Est. N16	50	C1
Stamford Rd. E6	61	B1
Stamford Rd. N1	50	B7
Stamford Rd. N15	41	D4
Stamford Rd., Dag.	62	B1
Stamford St. SE1	**16**	**E2**
Stamford St. SE1	67	G1
Stamp Pl. E2	**9**	**F3**
Stamp Pl. E2	59	C3
Stanard Clo. N16	41	B7
Stanborough Clo.,	81	F6
Hmptn.		
Stanborough Pas. E8	50	C6
Abbot St.		
Stanborough Rd.,	73	A3
Houns.		
Stanbridge Pl. N21	32	H2
Stanbridge Rd. SW15	74	J3
Stanbrook Rd. SE2	71	B2
Stanbury Rd. SE15	77	E1
Stancroft NW9	38	E5
Standard Ind. Est. E16	70	C2
Standard Pl. EC2	**9**	**E4**
Standard Rd. NW10	56	C4
Standard Rd., Belv.	71	G5
Standard Rd., Bexh.	80	E4
Standard Rd., Houns.	72	E3
Standen Rd. SW18	75	C7
Standfield Gdns., Dag.	53	G6
Standfield Rd.		
Standfield Rd., Dag.	53	G5
Standish Rd. W6	65	G4
Standlake Pt. SE23	86	G3
Stane Clo. SW19	93	E1
Hayward Clo.		
Stane Way SE18	70	B7
Stanfield Rd. E3	59	H2
Stanford Clo., Hmptn.	81	F6
Stanford Clo., Rom.	44	H6
Stanford Clo.,	35	B5
Wdf.Grn.		
Stanford Ho., Bark.	62	B2
Stanford Pl. SE17	**21**	**D2**
Stanford Rd. N11	31	J5
Stanford Rd. SW16	94	D2
Stanford Rd. W8	**14**	**B5**
Stanford Rd. W8	66	E3
Stanford St. SW1	**19**	**H2**
Stanford Way SW16	94	D2
Stangate Cres.,	22	D5
Borwd.		
Stangate Gdns., Stan.	29	E4
Stanger Rd. SE25	95	D4
Stanhope Ave. N3	39	C3
Stanhope Ave.,	103	F1
Brom.		
Stanhope Ave., Har.	37	A1
Stanhope Clo. SE16	68	G2
Middleton Dr.		
Stanhope Gdns. N4	40	H6
Stanhope Gdns. N6	40	B6
Stanhope Gdns. NW7	30	F5
Stanhope Gdns. SW7	**18**	**D1**
Stanhope Gdns. SW7	66	F4
Stanhope Gdns., Dag.	53	F3
Stanhope Rd.		
Stanhope Gdns., Ilf.	52	C1
Stanhope Gate W1	**15**	**C1**
Stanhope Gate W1	67	A1
Stanhope Gro., Beck.	95	J5
Stanhope Ms. E. SW7	**18**	**D1**
Stanhope Ms. E. SW7	66	F4
Stanhope Ms. S. SW7	**18**	**D2**
Stanhope Ms. W. SW7	**18**	**D1**
Stanhope Ms. W. SW7	66	F4
Stanhope Par. NW1	**7**	**F3**
Stanhope Pk. Rd.,	54	J4
Grnf.		
Stanhope Pl. W2	**10**	**J4**
Stanhope Pl. W2	57	J7
Stanhope Rd. E17	42	B5
Stanhope Rd. N6	40	C6
Stanhope Rd. N12	31	F5
Stanhope Rd., Barn.	22	J5
Stanhope Rd., Bexh.	80	E2
Stanhope Rd., Cars.	101	A7
Stanhope Rd., Croy.	102	B3
Stanhope Rd., Dag.	53	F2
Stanhope Rd., Grnf.	54	J5
Stanhope Rd., Sid.	89	A4
Stanhope Row W1	**15**	**D2**
Stanhope St. NW1	**7**	**F3**
Stanhope St. NW1	58	C3
Stanhope Ter. W2	**10**	**F5**
Stanhope Ter. W2	57	G7
Stanier Clo. W14	66	C5
Aisgill Ave.		

Stanlake Ms. W12	65	J1
Stanlake Rd. W12	65	J1
Stanlake Vill. W12	65	J1
Stanley Ave., Bark.	61	J2
Stanley Ave., Beck.	96	C2
Stanley Ave., Dag.	53	F1
Stanley Ave., Grnf.	54	J1
Stanley Ave., N.Mal.	92	G5
Stanley Ave., Wem.	46	H7
Stanley Clo. SW8	**20**	**C6**
Stanley Clo. SW8	67	F6
Stanley Clo., Wem.	46	H7
Stanley Cres. W11	57	C7
Stanley Gdns. NW2	47	J3
Stanley Gdns. W3	65	E2
Stanley Gdns. W11	57	C7
Stanley Gdns., Mitch.	85	A6
Ashbourne Rd.		
Stanley Gdns., Wall.	101	C6
Stanley Gdns. Ms.	57	C7
W11		
Stanley Cres.		
Stanley Gdns. Rd.,	82	B5
Tedd.		
Stanley Gro. SW8	76	A2
Stanley Gro., Croy.	94	G6
Stanley Pk. Dr., Wem.	55	J1
Stanley Pk. Rd., Cars.	100	H7
Stanley Pk. Rd., Wall.	101	B6
Stanley Pas. NW1	**8**	**A2**
Stanley Rd. E4	34	D1
Stanley Rd. E10	42	B6
Stanley Rd. E12	52	B5
Stanley Rd. E15	60	D1
Stanley Rd. E18	42	F1
Stanley Rd. N2	39	G3
Stanley Rd. N9	33	C1
Stanley Rd. N10	32	B7
Stanley Rd. N11	32	D6
Stanley Rd. N15	40	H4
Stanley Rd. N9	38	G7
West Hendon Bdy.		
Stanley Rd. SW14	74	B4
Stanley Rd. SW19	84	D7
Stanley Rd. W3	65	C3
Stanley Rd., Brom.	96	H4
Stanley Rd., Cars.	101	A7
Stanley Rd., Croy.	94	G7
Stanley Rd., Enf.	25	B3
Stanley Rd., Har.	45	J2
Stanley Rd., Houns.	72	J4
Stanley Rd., Ilf.	52	G2
Stanley Rd., Mitch.	85	A7
Stanley Rd., Mord.	93	D4
Stanley Rd., Nthwd.	36	A1
Stanley Rd., Sid.	89	A3
Stanley Rd., Sthl.	54	E7
Stanley Rd., Sutt.	100	E6
Stanley Rd., Tedd.	82	B4
Stanley Rd., Twick.	82	A3
Stanley Rd., Wem.	46	J6
Stanley St. SE8	68	J7
Stanley Ter. N19	49	E2
Stanleycroft Clo.,	73	B1
Islw.		
Stanmer St. SW11	75	H1
Stanmore Gdns.,	73	J3
Rich.		
Stanmore Gdns.,	100	F3
Sutt.		
Stanmore Hill, Stan.	29	D3
Stanmore Pl. NW1	58	B1
Arlington Rd.		
Stanmore Rd. E11	51	F1
Stanmore Rd. N15	40	H4
Stanmore Rd., Belv.	71	J4
Stanmore Rd., Rich.	73	J3
Stanmore St. N1	58	F1
Caledonian Rd.		
Stanmore Ter., Beck.	96	A2
Stanmore Way, Loug.	27	D1
Stannard Rd. E8	50	D6
Stannary Pl. SE11	**20**	**F4**
Stannary St. SE11	**20**	**F5**
Stannary St. SE11	67	G6
Stannington Path,	22	A1
Borwd.		
Warenford Way		
Stansfeld Rd. E6	61	A5
Stansfield Rd. SW9	76	F3
Stansfield Rd.,	72	B2
Houns.		
Stansgate Rd., Dag.	53	G2
Stanstead Clo., Brom.	96	F5
Stanstead Gro. SE6	86	J1
Catford Hill		
Stanstead Manor,	100	D6
Sutt.		

Stanstead Rd. E11	42	H5
Stanstead Rd. SE6	86	J1
Catford Hill		
Stanstead Rd. SE23	86	G1
Stansted Cres., Bex.	89	D1
Stanswood Gdns. SE5	68	B7
Sedgemoor Pl.		
Stanthorpe Clo. SW16	85	E5
Stanthorpe Rd. SW16	85	E5
Stanton Ave., Tedd.	82	B5
Stanton Clo., Epsom	99	B5
Stanton Clo., Wor.Pk.	100	A1
Stanton Rd. SE26	86	J4
Stanton Way		
Stanton Rd. SW13	74	F2
Stanton Rd. SW20	93	A1
Stanton Rd., Croy.	94	J7
Stanton Sq. SE26	86	J4
Stanton Way		
Stanton St. SE15	77	D1
Stanton Way SE26	86	J4
Stanway Clo., Chig.	35	H5
Stanway Gdns. W3	65	A1
Stanway Gdns., Edg.	30	C6
Stanway St. N1	**9**	**E1**
Stanway St. N1	59	B2
Stanwick Rd. W14	66	C4
Stanworth St. SE1	**17**	**F4**
Stanworth St. SE1	68	C2
Stanwyck Dr., Chig.	35	F5
Stapenhill Rd., Wem.	46	E3
Staple Inn Bldgs. WC1	**12**	**E2**
Staple St. SE1	**17**	**C4**
Staple St. SE1	68	A2
Staplefield Clo. SW2	85	E1
Staplefield Clo., Pnr.	28	E7
Stapleford Ave., Ilf.	43	H5
Stapleford Clo. E4	34	C3
Stapleford Clo. SW19	75	B7
Beaumont Rd.		
Stapleford Clo.,	92	A3
Kings.T.		
Stapleford Rd., Wem.	46	G7
Stapleford Way, Bark.	62	B3
Staplehurst Rd. SE13	78	E5
Staplehurst Rd.,	100	H7
Cars.		
Staples Clo. SE16	68	H1
Staples Cor. NW2	47	H1
Staples Cor. Business	47	G1
Pk. NW2		
Staples Rd., Loug.	27	A3
Stapleton Gdns.,	101	G5
Croy.		
Stapleton Hall Rd. N4	49	F1
Stapleton Rd. SW17	85	A3
Stapleton Rd., Bexh.	71	F7
Stapleton Rd., Orp.	104	J3
Stapley Rd., Belv.	71	G5
Stapylton Rd., Barn.	23	B3
Star & Garter Hill,	82	H1
Rich.		
Star La. E16	60	E4
Star Path, Nthlt.	54	G2
Brabazon Rd.		
Star Rd. W14	66	C6
Star Rd., Islw.	73	A2
Star St. E16	60	F5
Star St. W2	**10**	**F3**
Star St. W2	57	H6
Star Yd. WC2	**12**	**E3**
Starboard Way E14	69	A3
Starch Ho. La., Ilf.	43	G2
Starcross St. NW1	**7**	**G4**
Starcross St. NW1	58	C3
Starfield Rd. W12	65	G2
Starkleigh Way SE16	68	E5
Egan Way		
Starling Clo., Buck.H.	34	G1
Starling Clo., Pnr.	36	C3
Starling Ms. SE28	70	G2
Whinchat Rd.		
Starling Wk., Hmptn.	81	E6
Oak Ave.		
Starts Clo., Orp.	104	D3
Starts Hill Ave., Orp.	104	E4
Starts Hill Rd., Orp.	104	D3
State Fm. Ave., Orp.	104	E4
Staten Gdns., Twick.	82	C1
Statham Gro. N16	49	J4
Green Las.		
Statham Gro. N18	33	B5
Tanners End La.		
Station App. E7	51	H4
Woodford Rd.		
Station App. E11	42	G5
(Snaresbrook)		
High St.		

Station App. N11	32	B5
Station App. N12	31	E4
(Woodside Pk.)		
Holden Rd.		
Station App. N16	50	C2
(Stoke Newington)		
Stamford Hill		
Station App. NW10	56	F3
Station Rd.		
Station App. SE3	78	H3
Kidbrooke Pk. Rd.		
Station App. SE9	88	C1
(Mottingham)		
Station App. SE26	86	F4
Sydenham Rd.		
Station App. SW6	75	B3
Station App. SW16	85	D5
Station App. W7	64	B5
Bexley High St.		
Station App., Bex.	80	G7
Station App., Bexh.	80	E2
Avenue Rd.		
Station App., Bexh.	80	J2
(Barnehurst)		
Station App., Brom.	103	G1
Station App.,	35	A4
Buck.H.		
Cherry Tree Ri.		
Station App., Chis.	97	D1
Station App., Chis.	88	B6
(Elmstead Wds.)		
Station App., Epsom	99	F5
(Stoneleigh)		
Station App., Esher	98	C3
(Hinchley Wd.)		
Station App., Grnf.	46	A7
Station App.,	90	G1
Hmptn.		
Milton Rd.		
Station App., Har.	37	B7
Station App., Ilf.	43	G3
Station App.,	92	A2
Kings.T.		
Station App., Loug.	27	B5
Station App., Loug.	27	F4
(Debden)		
Station App., Orp.	104	J2
Station App., Pnr.	36	E4
Station App., Pnr.	28	G7
(Hatch End)		
Uxbridge Rd.		
Station App., Rich.	74	A1
Station App., Ruis.	45	B5
Station App., Sid.	89	A2
Station App., Sun.	90	A1
Station App., Sutt.	100	B7
(Cheam)		
Station App., Wat.	28	D3
Station App., Well.	80	A2
Station App. Rd. W4	65	C7
Station Ave. SW9	76	H3
Coldharbour La.		
Station Ave., N.Mal.	92	E3
Station Ave., Rich.	74	A1
Station Clo. N3	39	D1
Station Clo., Hmptn.	90	H1
Station Cres. N15	41	A4
Station Cres. SE3	69	G5
Station Cres., Wem.	46	E6
Station Est., Beck.	95	G4
Elmers End Rd.		
Station Est. Rd., Felt.	81	B1
Station Gdns. W4	65	C7
Station Gro., Wem.	46	H6
Station Hill, Brom.	103	G2
Station Ho. Ms. N9	33	D4
Fore St.		
Station Par. E11	42	G5
Station Par. N14	32	D1
High St.		
Station Par. NW2	47	J6
Station Par. W3	56	A6
Station Par., Bark.	52	F7
Station Par., Rich.	74	A1
Station Ave.		
Station Pas. E18	42	H2
Maybank Rd.		
Station Pas. SE15	68	F6
Asylum Rd.		
Station Path E8	50	E6
Amhurst Rd.		
Station Pl. N4	49	G2
Seven Sisters Rd.		
Station Ri. SE27	85	H2
Norwood Rd.		

Station Rd. E4 34 D1
(Chingford)
Station Rd. E7 51 G4
Station Rd. E10 51 C3
Station Rd. E12 52 A4
Station Rd. E17 41 H6
Station Rd. N3 39 D1
Station Rd. N11 32 B5
Station Rd. N17 41 D3
Hale Rd.
Station Rd. N19 49 C3
Station Rd. N21 32 H1
Station Rd. N22 40 E2
Station Rd. NW4 38 G6
Station Rd. NW7 30 E5
Station Rd. NW10 56 F2
Station Rd. SE20 86 F6
Station Rd. SE25 95 C4
(Norwood Junct.)
Station Rd. SW13 74 F2
Station Rd. SW19 93 F1
Station Rd. W5 55 J6
Station Rd. W7 64 B1
(Hanwell)
Station Rd., Barn. 23 E5
Station Rd., Belv. 71 G3
Station Rd., Bexh. 80 E3
Station Rd., Borwd. 22 A4
Station Rd., Brom. 96 G1
Station Rd., Brom. 96 E2
(Shortlands)
Station Rd., Cars. 100 J4
Station Rd., Chess. 98 H5
Station Rd., Chig. 35 E3
Station Rd., Croy. 102 A2
(East Croydon)
Station Rd., Croy. 101 J1
(West Croydon)
Station Rd., Edg. 30 A6
Station Rd., Enf. 24 J3
Station Rd., Esher 98 A2
Station Rd., Esher 98 A5
(Claygate)
Station Rd., Hmptn. 90 G1
Station Rd., Har. 37 C4
Station Rd., Har. 36 H5
(North Harrow)
Station Rd., Houns. 72 H4
Station Rd., Ilf. 52 E3
Station Rd., Ilf. 43 G3
(Barkingside)
Station Rd., Kings.T. 92 A1
Station Rd., Kings.T. 91 G1
(Hampton Wick)
Station Rd., Loug. 27 B4
Station Rd., N.Mal. 92 H5
(Motspur Pk.)
Station Rd., Orp. 104 J2
Station Rd., Rom. 53 D1
(Chadwell Heath)
Station Rd., Sid. 89 A4
Station Rd., Sun. 81 A7
Station Rd., Tedd. 82 C5
Station Rd., T.Ditt. 91 C7
Station Rd., Twick. 82 C1
Station Rd., W.Wick. 103 C2
Station Rd. N., Belv. 71 H3
Station Sq., Orp. 97 F5
(Petts Wd.)
Station St. E15 51 D7
Station St. E16 70 E1
Station Ter. NW10 57 A2
Station Ter. SE5 76 J1
Station Vw., Grnf. 55 A1
Station Way SE15 77 D2
Rye La.
Station Way, Buck.H. 34 J4
(Roding Valley)
Station Way, Esher 98 B6
(Claygate)
Station Way, Sutt. 100 B6
(Cheam)
Station Yd., Twick. 73 D7
Staunton Rd., Kings.T. 82 H6
Staunton St. SE8 68 J6
Stave Yd. Rd. SE16 68 H1
Staveley Clo. N7 50 F5
Churchill Wk.
Staveley Clo. N7 49 E4
Penn Rd.
Staveley Clo. SE15 77 E1
Asylum Rd.
Staveley Gdns. W4 74 D1
Staveley Rd. W4 65 C6
Staverton Rd. NW2 47 J7
Stavordale Rd. N5 49 H4
Stavordale Rd., Cars. 100 F1
Stayners Rd. E1 59 G4

Stayton Rd., Sutt. 100 D3
Stead St. SE17 **21** **B2**
Stead St. SE17 68 A4
Steadfast Rd., 91 G1
Kings.T.
Stean St. E8 59 C1
Stebbing Way, Bark. 62 A2
Stebondale St. E14 69 C5
Stedham Pl. WC1 **12** **A3**
Steedman St. SE17 **20** **J2**
Steeds Rd. N10 39 J1
Steeds Way, Loug. 27 B3
Steele Rd. E11 51 E4
Steele Rd. N17 41 B3
Steele Rd. NW10 56 C2
Steele Rd. W4 65 C3
Steele Rd., Islw. 73 D4
Steeles Ms. N. NW3 48 J6
Steeles Rd.
Steeles Ms. S. NW3 48 J6
Steeles Rd.
Steel's La. E1 59 F6
Devonport St.
Steen Way SE22 77 B5
East Dulwich Gro.
Steep Clo., Orp. 104 J6
Steep Hill SW16 85 D3
Steep Hill, Croy. 102 B4
Steeple Clo. SW6 75 B2
Steeple Clo. SW19 84 B5
Steeple Ct. E1 59 E4
Coventry Rd.
Steeple Wk. N1 58 J1
Basire St.
Steeplestone Clo. 32 J5
N18
Steerforth St. SW18 84 F2
Steers Mead, Mitch. 93 J1
Steers Way SE16 68 H2
Stella Rd. SW17 84 J6
Stellar Ho. N17 33 D6
Stellman Clo. E5 50 D3
Stembridge Rd. SE20 95 E2
Stephan Clo. E8 59 D1
Stephen Clo., Orp. 104 H3
Stephen Ms. W1 **11** **H2**
Stephen Rd., Bexh. 80 J3
Stephen St. W1 **11** **H2**
Stephen St. W1 58 D5
Stephendale Rd. SW6 75 E3
Stephen's Rd. E15 60 E1
Stephenson Rd. W7 55 C6
Stephenson Rd., 72 G7
Twick.
Stephenson St. E16 60 E4
Stephenson St. NW10 56 E3
Stephenson Way **7** **G5**
NW1
Stephenson Way NW1 58 C4
Stepney Causeway E1 59 G5
Stepney Grn. E1 59 F5
Stepney High St. E1 59 G5
Stepney Way E1 59 E5
Sterling Ave., Edg. 29 J4
Sterling Gdns. SE14 68 H5
Sterling Ind. Est., Dag. 53 H4
Sterling Pl. W5 64 H4
Sterling Rd., Enf. 25 A1
Sterling St. SW7 **14** **H4**
Sterling Way N18 33 A4
Sterndale Rd. W14 66 A3
Sterne St. W12 66 A2
Sternhall La. SE15 77 D3
Sternhold Ave. SW2 85 D2
Sterry Cres., Dag. 53 G5
Alibon Rd.
Sterry Dr., Epsom 99 E4
Sterry Dr., T.Ditt. 91 B6
Sterry Gdns., Dag. 53 G6
Sterry Rd., Bark. 61 J1
Sterry Rd., Dag. 53 G4
Sterry St. SE1 **17** **B4**
Sterry St. SE1 68 A2
Steucers La. SE23 86 H1
Steve Biko La. SE6 87 A4
Steve Biko Rd. N7 49 G3
Tollington Rd.
Steve Biko Way, 72 G3
Houns.
Stevedale Rd., Well. 80 C2
Stevedore St. E1 68 E1
Waterman Way
Stevenage Rd. E6 52 D6
Stevenage Rd. SW6 66 A7
Stevens Ave. E9 50 F6
Stevens Clo., Beck. 87 A6
Stevens Clo., Hmptn. 81 E6

Stevens Clo., Pnr. 36 C5
Bridle Rd.
Stevens Grn. 28 J1
(Bushey), Wat.
Stevens La., Esher 98 D7
Stevens Rd., Dag. 53 B3
Stevens St. SE1 **17** **E5**
Stevens Way, Chig. 35 H4
Stevenson Cres. SE16 **21** **J3**
Stevenson Cres. SE16 68 D5
Steventon Rd. W12 56 F7
Steward St. E1 **13** **E1**
Steward St. E1 59 B5
Stewart Clo. NW9 38 C6
Stewart Clo., Chis. 88 E5
Stewart Clo., Hmptn. 81 E5
Stewart Rainbird Ho. 52 D5
E12
Stewart Rd. E15 51 C4
Stewart St. E14 69 C2
Stewart's Gro. SW3 **18** **G3**
Stewart's Gro. SW3 66 H5
Stewart's Rd. SW8 67 C7
Stewartsby Clo. N18 32 J5
Steyne Rd. W3 65 B1
Steyning Gro. SE9 88 C4
Steyning Way, Houns. 72 C4
Steynings Way N12 31 D5
Steynton Ave., Bex. 89 D2
Stickland Rd., Belv. 71 G4
Picardy Rd.
Stickleton Clo., Grnf. 54 H3
Stile Hall Gdns. W4 65 A5
Stile Path, Sun. 90 A3
Stilecroft Gdns., 46 E3
Wem.
Stiles Clo., Brom. 97 C6
Stillingfleet Rd. SW13 65 G6
Stillington St. SW1 **19** **G1**
Stillington St. SW1 67 C4
Stillness Rd. SE23 77 H6
Stilton Cres. NW10 47 C7
Stipularis Dr., Hayes 54 D4
Stirling Clo. SW16 94 C1
Stirling Rd. E13 60 H2
Stirling Rd. E17 41 H3
Stirling Rd. N17 41 D1
Stirling Rd. N22 40 H1
Stirling Rd. SW9 76 E2
Stirling Rd. W3 65 B3
Stirling Rd., Har. 37 C3
Stirling Rd., Hayes 54 B7
Stirling Rd., Twick. 72 C7
Stirling Rd. Path E17 41 H3
Stirling Wk., N.Mal. 92 C5
Green La.
Stirling Wk., Surb. 92 B6
Stirling Way, Borwd. 22 D6
Stirling Way, Croy. 94 E7
Stiven Cres., Har. 45 F3
Stock Orchard Cres. 49 F5
N7
Stock Orchard St. N7 49 F5
Stock St. E13 60 G2
Stockbury Rd., Croy. 95 F6
Stockdale Rd., Dag. 53 F2
Stockdove Way, Grnf. 55 C3
Stockfield Rd. SW16 85 F3
Stockfield Rd., Esher 98 B5
Stockholm Rd. SE16 68 F5
Stockholm Way E1 **17** **H1**
Stockhurst Clo. SW15 74 J2
Stockingswater La., 25 H3
Enf.
Stockport Rd. SW16 94 D1
Stocks Pl. E14 59 J7
Grenade St.
Stocksfield Rd. E17 42 C3
Stockton Gdns. N17 32 J7
Stockton Rd.
Stockton Gdns. NW7 30 E3
Stockton Rd. N17 32 J7
Stockton Rd. N18 33 D6
Stockwell Ave. SW9 76 F3
Stockwell Clo., Brom. 96 H2
Stockwell Gdns. SW9 76 F1
Stockwell Gdns. Est. 76 E2
SW9
Stockwell Grn. SW9 76 F2
Stockwell La. SW9 76 F2
Stockwell Ms. SW9 76 F2
Stockwell Rd.
Stockwell Pk. Cres. 76 F2
SW9
Stockwell Pk. Est. 76 F2
SW9
Stockwell Pk. Rd. SW9 76 F1
Stockwell Pk. Wk. SW9 76 F3

Stockwell Rd. SW9 76 F2
Stockwell St. SE10 69 C6
Stockwell Ter. SW9 76 F1
Stodart Rd. SE20 95 F1
Stofield Gdns. SE9 88 A3
Aldersgrove Ave.
Stoford Clo. SW19 75 B7
Stoke Newington Ch. 50 A3
St. N16
Stoke Newington 50 C3
Common N16
Stoke Newington 50 C3
High St. N16
Stoke Newington Rd. 50 C5
N16
Stoke Pl. NW10 56 F3
Stoke Rd., Kings.T. 83 C7
Stokenchurch St. 75 E1
SW6
Stokes Rd. E6 61 B4
Stokes Rd., Croy. 95 G6
Stokesby Rd., Chess. 98 J6
Stokesley St. W12 56 F6
Stoll Clo. NW2 47 J3
Stoms Path SE6 87 A5
Sedgehill Rd.
Stonard Rd. N13 32 G3
Stonard Rd., Dag. 53 B5
Stonards Hill, Loug. 27 C6
Stondon Pk. SE23 77 H6
Stondon Wk. E6 61 A2
Abbot's Rd.
Stone Bldgs. WC2 **12** **D2**
Stone Bldgs. WC2 58 F6
Stone Clo. SW4 76 C2
Larkhall Ri.
Stone Clo., Dag. 53 F2
Stone Hall Rd. N21 24 F7
Stone Ho. Ct. EC3 **13** **E3**
Stone Pk. Ave., Beck. 96 A4
Stone Pl., Wor.Pk. 99 G2
Stone Rd., Brom. 96 F5
Stone St., Croy. 101 G5
Stonebanks, Walt. 90 A7
Stonebridge Common 50 C7
E8
Mayfield Rd.
Stonebridge Pk. 47 D7
NW10
Stonebridge Rd. N15 41 C5
Stonebridge Way, 47 B6
Wem.
Stonechat Sq. E6 61 B5
Peridot St.
Stonecot Clo., Sutt. 100 B1
Stonecot Hill, Sutt. 100 B1
Stonecroft Rd., Erith 71 J7
Stonecroft Way, Croy. 94 E7
Stonecutter Ct. EC4 **12** **G3**
Stonecutter St. EC4 **12** **G3**
Stonecutter St. EC4 58 H6
Stonefield Clo., Bexh. 80 G3
Stonefield Clo., Ruis. 45 E5
Stonefield St. N1 58 G1
Stonefield Way SE7 70 A7
Greenbay Rd.
Stonefield Way, Ruis. 45 E4
Stonegrove, Edg. 29 H4
Stonegrove Est., Edg. 29 H4
Stonegrove Gdns., 29 H5
Edg.
Stonehall Ave., Ilf. 43 B6
Stoneham Rd. N11 32 C5
Stonehill Clo. SW14 74 D5
Stonehill Rd. SW14 74 C5
Stonehill Rd. W4 65 A5
Wellesley Rd.
Stonehill Wds. 89 H6
Caravan Pk., Sid.
Stonehills Ct. SE21 86 B3
Stonehorse Rd., Enf. 25 F5
Stoneleigh Ave., 99 G3
Wor.Pk.
Stoneleigh Cres., 99 F5
Epsom
Stoneleigh Pk. Ave., 95 G6
Croy.
Stoneleigh Pk. Rd., 99 F6
Epsom
Stoneleigh Pl. W11 57 A7
Stoneleigh Rd. N17 41 C3
Stoneleigh Rd., Cars. 93 H7
Stoneleigh Rd., Ilf. 43 B3
Stoneleigh St. W11 57 A7
Stoneleigh Ter. N19 49 B2
Dartmouth Pk. Hill
Stonells Rd. SW11 75 J5
Chatham Rd.

Stonenest St. N4 49 F1
Stones End St. SE1 16 J4
Stones End St. SE1 67 J2
Stoney All. SE18 79 D2
Stoney La. E1 13 F3
Stoney La. SE19 86 C6
  Church Rd.
Stoney St. SE1 17 B1
Stoney St. SE1 68 A1
Stoneyard La. E14 60 B7
  Poplar High St.
Stoneycroft Clo. SE12 78 F7
Stoneycroft Rd., 35 B6
  Wdf.Grn.
Stoneydeep, Tedd. 82 D4
  Twickenham Rd.
Stoneydown E17 41 H4
Stoneydown Ave. E17 41 H4
Stoneyfields Gdns., 30 C4
  Edg.
Stoneyfields La., Edg. 30 C5
Stonhouse St. SW4 76 D3
Stonor Rd. W14 66 C4
Stony Path, Loug. 27 C1
Stopford Rd. E13 60 G1
Stopford Rd. SE17 20 H4
Stopford Rd. SE17 67 H5
Store Rd. E16 70 D2
Store St. E15 51 D5
Store St. WC1 11 H2
Store St. WC1 58 D5
Storers Quay E14 69 D4
Storey Rd. E17 41 J4
Storey Rd. N6 39 J6
Storey St. E16 70 D1
Storey's Gate SW1 15 J4
Storey's Gate SW1 67 D2
Stories Ms. SE5 77 B2
Stories Rd. SE5 77 B3
Stork Rd. E7 51 F6
Storks Rd. SE16 17 J6
Storks Rd. SE16 68 D3
Storksmead Rd., Edg. 30 E7
Stormont Rd. N6 39 J7
Stormont Rd. SW11 76 A3
Stormont Way, 98 F5
  Chess.
Storrington Rd., 102 C1
  Croy.
Story St. N1 49 F7
  Carnoustie Dr.
Stothard St. E1 59 F4
  Colebert Ave.
Stoughton Ave., Sutt. 100 A5
Stoughton Clo. SE11 20 D2
Stoughton Clo. SW15 83 G1
  Bessborough Rd.
Stour Ave., Sthl. 63 G3
Stour Clo., Kes. 103 J4
Stour Rd. E3 51 A7
Stour Rd., Dag. 53 G2
Stourcliffe St. W1 10 J4
Stourcliffe St. W1 57 J6
Stourhead Clo. SW19 75 A7
  Castlecombe Dr.
Stourhead Gdns. 92 G3
  SW20
Stourton Ave., Felt. 81 F4
Stow Cres. E17 33 H7
Stowage SE8 69 A6
Stowe Gdns. N9 33 C1
  Latymer Rd.
Stowe Pl. N15 41 B3
Stowe Rd. W12 65 H2
Stowting Rd., Orp. 104 H4
Stox Mead, Har. 37 A1
Stracey Rd. E7 51 G4
Stracey Rd. NW10 56 D1
Strachan Pl. SW19 83 J6
  Woodhayes Rd.
Stradbroke Dr., Chig. 35 D6
Stradbroke Gro., 35 A1
  Buck.H.
Stradbroke Gro., Ilf. 43 B3
Stradbroke Pk., Chig. 35 E6
Stradbroke Rd. N5 49 J4
Stradella Rd. SE24 76 J6
Strafford Ave., Ilf. 43 D2
Strafford Rd. W3 65 C2
Strafford Rd., Barn. 23 B3
Strafford Rd., Houns. 72 F3
Strafford Rd., Twick. 73 D7
Strafford St. E14 69 A2
Strahan Rd. E3 59 H3
Straight, The, Sthl. 63 D2
Straightsmouth SE10 69 C7
Strait Rd. E6 61 B7
Straker's Rd. SE15 77 E4

Strand WC2 12 A6
Strand WC2 58 E7
Strand La. WC2 12 D5
Strand on the Grn. W4 65 A6
  Silver St.
Strand Pl. N18 33 B4
Strand Sch. App. W4 65 A6
Strandfield Clo. SE18 70 H5
Strangways Ter. W14 66 C3
  Melbury Rd.
Stranraer Way N1 49 E7
Strasburg Rd. SW11 76 B1
Stratfield Pk. Clo. N21 24 H7
Stratfield Rd., Borwd. 22 A3
Stratford Ave. W8 66 D3
  Stratford Rd.
Stratford Cen., The 51 D7
  E15
  Broadway
Stratford Clo., Bark. 53 A7
Stratford Clo., Dag. 53 J7
Stratford Ct., N.Mal. 92 D4
  Kingston Rd.
Stratford Gro. SW15 75 A4
Stratford Mkt. E15 60 D1
  Bridge Rd.
Stratford Pl. W1 11 D4
Stratford Pl. W1 58 B6
Stratford Rd. E13 60 F1
Stratford Rd. W3 65 C2
  Bollo Bri. Rd.
Stratford Rd. W8 66 D3
Stratford Rd., Hayes 54 B4
Stratford Rd., Sthl. 63 E4
Stratford Rd., Th.Hth. 94 G4
Stratford Vill. NW1 49 C7
Strath Ter. SW11 75 H4
Strathan Clo. SW18 75 B6
Strathaven Rd. SE12 78 H6
Strathblaine Rd. SW11 75 G5
Strathbrook Rd. SW16 85 F7
Strathcona Rd., Wem. 46 G2
Strathdale SW16 85 F5
Strathdon Dr. SW17 84 G3
Strathearn Ave., 81 H1
  Twick.
Strathearn Pl. W2 10 G5
Strathearn Pl. W2 57 H7
Strathearn Rd. SW19 84 D5
Strathearn Rd., Sutt. 100 D5
Stratheden Rd. SE3 78 G1
Strathfield Gdns., 52 G6
  Bark.
Strathleven Rd. SW2 76 E4
Strathmore Gdns. N3 39 E1
Strathmore Gdns. W8 66 D1
  Palace Gdns. Ter.
Strathmore Gdns., 38 B2
  Edg.
Strathmore Rd. SW19 84 D3
Strathmore Rd., Croy. 94 J7
Strathmore Rd., Tedd. 82 B4
Strathnairn St. SE1 21 J2
Strathnairn St. SE1 68 D4
Strathray Gdns. NW3 48 H6
Strathville Rd. SW18 84 D2
Strathyre Ave. SW16 94 G3
Stratton Clo. SW19 93 D2
Stratton Clo., Bexh. 80 E3
Stratton Clo., Edg. 29 J6
Stratton Clo., Houns. 72 F1
Stratton Dr., Bark. 52 J5
Stratton Gdns., Sthl. 54 F6
Stratton Rd. SW19 93 D2
Stratton Rd., Bexh. 80 E3
Stratton St. W1 15 E1
Stratton St. W1 67 B1
Strattondale St. E14 69 C3
Strauss Rd. W4 65 D2
Strawberry Hill, 82 C3
  Twick.
Strawberry Hill Clo., 82 C4
  Twick.
Strawberry Hill Rd., 82 C3
  Twick.
Strawberry La., Cars. 100 J3
Strawberry Vale N2 39 G1
Strawberry Vale, 82 C3
  Twick.
Streakes Fld. Rd. NW2 47 G2
Stream La., Edg. 30 B5
Streamay, Belv. 71 F6
Streamdale SE2 71 A6
Streamside Clo. N9 33 C1
Streamside Clo., 96 G4
  Brom.
Streatfield Ave. E6 61 C1
Streatfield Rd., Har. 37 F3

Streatham Clo. SW16 85 E3
Streatham Common 85 E5
  N. SW16
Streatham Common 85 E6
  S. SW16
Streatham Ct. SW16 85 E3
Streatham High Rd. 85 E5
  SW16
Streatham Hill SW2 85 E2
Streatham Pl. SW2 76 E7
Streatham Rd. SW16 94 A1
Streatham Rd., Mitch. 94 A1
Streatham Vale SW16 94 C1
Streathbourne Rd. 85 A2
  SW17
Streatley Pl. NW3 48 F4
  New End Sq.
Streatley Rd. NW6 48 C7
Streeters La., Wall. 101 D3
Streetfield Ms. SE3 78 G3
Streimer Rd. E15 60 C2
Strelley Way W3 56 E7
Stretton Rd., Croy. 95 B9
Stretton Rd., Rich. 82 F2
Strickland Rd., Belv. 71 G4
Strickland Row SW18 75 G5
Strickland St. SE8 78 A1
Strickland Way, Orp. 104 J4
Stride Rd. E13 60 F2
  Pembroke Rd.
Strode Clo. N10 32 A7
Strode Rd. E7 51 G4
Strode Rd. N17 41 B2
Strode Rd. NW10 47 G6
Strode Rd. SW6 66 B7
Strone Rd. E7 51 J6
Strone Rd. E12 52 A6
Strone Way, Hayes 54 E4
Strongbow Cres. SE9 79 C5
Strongbow Rd. SE9 79 C5
Strongbridge Clo., 45 G1
  Har.
Stronsa Rd. W12 65 F2
Stroud Cres. SW15 83 G3
Stroud Fld., Nthlt. 45 E6
Stroud Gate, Har. 45 H4
Stroud Grn. Gdns., 95 F7
  Croy.
Stroud Grn. Rd. N4 49 F1
Stroud Grn. Way, 95 E7
  Croy.
Stroud Rd. SE25 95 D6
Stroud Rd. SW19 84 D3
Stroudes Clo., Wor.Pk. 92 E7
Stroudley Wk. E3 60 B3
Strouts Pl. E2 9 F3
Strutton Grd. SW1 15 H5
Strutton Grd. SW1 67 D3
Strype St. E1 13 F2
Stuart Ave. NW9 38 G7
Stuart Ave. W5 64 J1
Stuart Ave., Brom. 103 G1
Stuart Ave., Har. 45 F3
Stuart Cres. N22 40 F1
Stuart Cres., Croy. 102 J4
Stuart Evans Clo., 80 C3
  Well.
Stuart Gro., Tedd. 82 B5
Stuart Pl., Mitch. 93 J1
Stuart Rd. NW6 57 D3
Stuart Rd. SE15 77 F4
Stuart Rd. SW19 84 D3
Stuart Rd. W3 65 C1
Stuart Rd., Bark. 52 J7
Stuart Rd., Barn. 23 H7
Stuart Rd., Har. 37 C3
Stuart Rd., Rich. 82 E2
Stuart Rd., Th.Hth. 94 J4
Stuart Rd., Well. 80 B1
Stuart Twr. W9 6 C4
Stuart Twr. W9 57 F3
Stubbs Dr. SE16 68 E5
Stubbs Pt. E13 60 G4
Stubbs Way SW19 93 G1
  Brangwyn Cres.
Stucley Pl. NW1 49 B7
  Hawley Cres.
Stucley Rd., Houns. 63 J7
Studd St. N1 58 H1
Studdridge St. SW6 75 D2
Studholme Ct. NW3 48 D4
Studholme St. SE15 68 E7
Studio Pl. SW1 15 A4
Studio Way, Borwd. 22 C2
Studland SE17 21 B3
Studland Clo., Sid. 88 J3
Studland Rd. SE26 86 G5

Studland Rd. W7 55 A6
Studland Rd., 82 H6
  Kings.T.
Studland St. W6 65 H4
Studley Ave. E4 34 D7
Studley Clo. E5 50 H5
Studley Ct., Sid. 89 B5
Studley Dr., Ilf. 43 A6
Studley Est. SW4 76 E1
Studley Gra. Rd. W7 64 B2
Studley Rd. E7 51 H6
Studley Rd. SW4 76 E1
Studley Rd., Dag. 53 D7
Stukeley Rd. E7 51 H7
Stukeley St. WC2 12 B3
Stukeley St. WC2 58 E6
Stumps Hill La., Beck. 87 A6
Sturdy Rd. SE15 77 E2
Sturge Ave. E17 42 B1
Sturge St. SE1 16 J3
Sturgeon Rd. SE17 20 J4
Sturgeon Rd. SE17 67 H5
Sturges Fld., Chis. 88 G6
Sturgess Ave. NW4 38 G7
Sturmer Way N7 49 F5
  Stock Orchard Cres.
Sturrock Clo. N15 41 A4
Sturry St. E14 60 B6
Sturt St. N1 9 A2
Sturt St. N1 58 J2
Stutfield St. E1 13 J4
Stutfield St. E1 59 D6
Styles Gdns. SW9 76 H3
Styles Way, Beck. 96 C4
Sudbourne Rd. SW2 76 E5
Sudbrook Gdns., Rich. 82 H3
Sudbrook La., Rich. 82 H1
Sudbrooke Rd. SW12 75 J6
Sudbury Ave., Wem. 46 F5
Sudbury Ct. E5 50 H4
Sudbury Ct. Dr., Har. 46 C3
Sudbury Ct. Rd., Har. 46 C3
Sudbury Cres., Brom. 87 G6
Sudbury Cres., Wem. 46 E5
Sudbury Cft., Wem. 46 C4
Sudbury Gdns., 102 B4
  Croy.
  Langton Way
Sudbury Heights 46 C5
  Ave., Grnf.
Sudbury Hill, Har. 46 B2
Sudbury Hill Clo., 46 C4
  Wem.
Sudbury Meadows, 46 F3
  Wem.
Sudbury Rd., Bark. 52 J5
Sudeley St. N1 8 H2
Sudeley St. N1 58 H2
Sudlow Rd. SW18 75 D5
Sudrey St. SE1 16 J4
Suez Ave., Grnf. 55 C2
Suez Rd., Enf. 25 H4
Suffield Rd. E4 34 B3
Suffield Rd. N15 41 C5
Suffield Rd. SE20 95 F2
Suffolk Clo., Borwd. 22 D5
  Clydesdale Clo.
Suffolk Ct. E10 42 A7
Suffolk Ct., Ilf. 43 H6
Suffolk La. EC4 13 B5
Suffolk Pk. Rd. E17 41 H4
Suffolk Pl. SW1 15 J1
Suffolk Rd. E13 60 G3
Suffolk Rd. N15 41 A6
Suffolk Rd. NW10 47 E7
Suffolk Rd. SE25 95 C4
Suffolk Rd. SW13 65 F7
Suffolk Rd., Bark. 52 G7
Suffolk Rd., Dag. 53 J5
Suffolk Rd., Enf. 25 E5
Suffolk Rd., Har. 36 F6
Suffolk Rd., Ilf. 43 H6
Suffolk Rd., Sid. 89 C6
Suffolk Rd., Wor.Pk. 99 F2
Suffolk St. E7 51 G5
Suffolk St. SW1 11 J6
Sugar Bakers Ct. EC3 13 E4
Sugar Ho. La. E15 60 C2
Sugar Loaf Wk. E2 59 F3
  Victoria Pk. Sq.
Sugden Rd. SW11 76 A3
Sugden Rd., T.Ditt. 98 E1
Sugden Way, Bark. 54 J2
Sulgrave Gdns. W6 65 J2
  Sulgrave Rd.
Sulgrave Rd. W6 65 J3
Sulina Rd. SW2 76 E7
Sulivan Ct. SW6 75 D2

Sulivan Rd. SW6 75 D3
Sullivan Ave. E16 61 A5
Sullivan Clo. SW11 75 H3
Sullivan Clo., W.Mol. 90 G3
Victoria Ave.
Sullivan Rd. SE11 20 F1
Sullivan Rd. SE11 67 G4
Sultan Rd. E11 42 H4
Sultan St. SE5 20 J7
Sultan St. SE5 67 J7
Sultan St., Beck. 95 G2
Sumatra Rd. NW6 48 D5
Sumburgh Rd. SW12 76 A6
Summer Ave., E.Mol. 91 B5
Summer Gdns., 91 B5
E.Mol.
Summer Hill, Borwd. 22 A5
Summer Hill, Chis. 97 D2
Summer Hill Vill., 97 D1
Chis.
Summer Ho. Rd. N16 50 B2
Stoke Newington
Ch. St.
Summer Rd., E.Mol. 91 B5
Summer Rd., T.Ditt. 91 C5
Summer Trees, Sun. 90 B1
The Ave.
Summercourt Rd. E1 59 F6
Summerdene Clo. 85 C7
SW16
Bates Cres.
Summerfield Ave. 57 B2
NW6
Summerfield La., 98 G2
Surb.
Summerfield Rd. W5 55 E4
Summerfield Rd., 27 A6
Loug.
Summerfield St. 78 F7
SE12
Summerhill Clo., Orp. 104 H3
Summerhill Gro., Enf. 25 B6
Summerhill Rd. N15 41 A4
Summerhill Way, 94 A1
Mitch.
Summerhouse Ave., 72 E1
Houns.
Summerland Gdns. 40 B3
N10
Summerlands Ave. 56 C7
W3
Summerlee Ave. N2 39 J4
Summerlee Gdns. N2 39 J4
Summerley St. SW18 84 E2
Summers Clo., Sutt. 100 D7
Overton Rd.
Summers Clo., Wem. 47 B1
Summers La. N12 31 G7
Summers Row N12 31 H6
Summers St. EC1 8 E6
Summersby Rd. N6 40 B6
Summerstown SW17 84 F3
Summerton Way 62 D7
SE28
Summerville Gdns., 100 C6
Sutt.
Summerwood Rd., 73 C5
Islw.
Summit, The, Loug. 27 C1
Summit Ave. NW9 38 D5
Summit Clo. N14 32 C2
Summit Clo. NW9 38 D4
Summit Clo., Edg. 30 A7
Summit Ct. NW2 48 B5
Summit Dr., Wdf.Grn. 43 A2
Summit Est. N16 41 D7
Summit Rd. E17 42 B4
Summit Rd., Nthlt. 45 G7
Summit Way N14 32 B2
Summit Way SE19 86 B7
Sumner Ave. SE15 77 C1
Sumner Rd.
Sumner Clo., Orp. 104 F4
Sumner Est. SE15 68 C7
Sumner Gdns., Croy. 101 G1
Sumner Pl. SW7 18 F2
Sumner Pl. SW7 66 G4
Sumner Pl. Ms. SW7 18 F2
Sumner Rd. SE15 21 G6
Sumner Rd. SE15 68 C7
Sumner Rd., Croy. 101 G1
Sumner Rd., Har. 36 J7
Sumner Rd. S., Croy. 101 G1
Sumner St. SE1 16 H1
Sumner St. SE1 67 H1
Sumpter Clo. NW3 48 F6
Sun Ct. EC3 13 C4
Sun La. SE3 69 H7

Sun Pas. SE16 17 H5
Sun Rd. W14 66 C5
Sun St. EC2 13 C1
Sun St. EC2 59 A5
Sun St. Pas. EC2 13 D2
Sunbeam Rd. NW10 56 D4
Sunbury Ave. NW7 30 D5
Sunbury Ave. SW14 74 D4
Sunbury Ct., Sun. 90 D2
Sunbury Ct. Rd., Sun. 90 C2
Sunbury Gdns. NW7 30 D5
Sunbury La. SW11 75 G1
Sunbury La., Walt. 90 A6
Sunbury Rd., Sutt. 100 A3
Sunbury St. SE18 70 C3
Sunbury Way, Felt. 81 C5
Suncroft Pl. SE26 86 F3
Sunderland Ct. SE22 77 D7
Sunderland Rd. SE23 86 G1
Sunderland Rd. W5 64 G3
Sunderland Ter. W2 10 A3
Sunderland Ter. W2 57 E6
Sunderland Way E12 52 A2
Sundew Ave. W12 56 G7
Sundial Ave. SE25 95 C3
Sundorne Rd. SE7 69 H5
Sundra Wk. E1 59 G4
Beaumont Gro.
Sundridge Ave., 97 A2
Brom.
Sundridge Ave., Chis. 88 B7
Sundridge Ave., Well. 79 G2
Sundridge Ho., Brom. 87 H5
Burnt Ash La.
Sundridge Rd., Croy. 96 C5
Sunfields Pl. SE3 69 H7
Sunland Ave., Bexh. 80 E4
Sunleigh Rd., Wem. 55 H1
Sunley Gdns., Grnf. 55 D1
Sunmead Rd., Sun. 90 A3
Sunna Gdns., Sun. 90 B2
Sunningdale N14 32 D5
Wilmer Way
Sunningdale Ave. W3 56 E7
Sunningdale Ave., 61 G1
Bark.
Sunningdale Ave., 81 E2
Felt.
Sunningdale Ave., 45 C1
Ruis.
Sunningdale Clo. E6 61 C3
Ascot Rd.
Sunningdale Clo. 29 D7
Stan.
Sunningdale Clo. 98 H2
Surb.
Culsac Rd.
Sunningdale Gdns. 38 C5
NW9
Sunningdale Gdns. 66 D3
W8
Lexham Ms.
Sunningdale Rd. 97 B4
Brom.
Sunningdale Rd. 100 C4
Sutt.
Sunningfields Cres. 38 H2
NW4
Sunningfields Rd. 38 H3
NW4
Sunninghill Rd. SE13 78 B2
Sunny Bank SE25 95 D3
Sunny Cres. NW10 47 C7
Sunny Gdns. Par. 38 J2
NW4
Great N. Way
Sunny Gdns. Rd. NW4 38 H2
Sunny Hill NW4 38 H3
Sunny Nook Gdns., 102 A6
S.Croy.
Selsdon Rd.
Sunny Rd., The, Enf. 25 G1
Sunny Side, Walt. 90 C5
Sunny Vw. NW9 38 D5
Sunny Way N12 31 H7
Sunnycroft Rd. SE25 95 D3
Sunnycroft Rd., 72 H2
Houns.
Sunnycroft Rd., Sthl. 54 G5
Sunnydale, Orp. 104 D2
Sunnydale Gdns. 30 D6
NW7
Sunnydale Rd. SE12 78 H5
Sunnydene Ave. E4 34 D5
Sunnydene Ave., 45 A1
Ruis.
Sunnydene Gdns., 46 F6
Wem.

Sunnydene St. SE26 86 H4
Sunnyfield NW7 30 F4
Sunnyhill Rd. SW16 85 E4
Sunnyhurst Clo., 100 D3
Sutt.
Sunnymead Ave., 94 C3
Mitch.
Sunnymead Rd. NW9 38 D7
Sunnymead Rd. 74 H5
SW15
Sunnymede Dr., Ilf. 43 E5
Sunnyside NW2 48 C3
Sunnyside SW19 84 B6
Sunnyside Dr. E4 26 C7
Sunnyside Pas. SW19 84 B6
Sunnyside Rd. E10 51 A1
Sunnyside Rd. N19 40 D7
Sunnyside Rd. W5 64 G1
Sunnyside Rd., Ilf. 52 F3
Sunnyside Rd., Tedd. 82 A4
Sunnyside Rd. E. N9 33 D3
Sunnyside Rd. N. N9 33 C3
Sunnyside Rd. S. N9 33 C3
Sunray Ave. SE24 77 A4
Sunray Ave., Brom. 97 B6
Sunray Ave., Surb. 99 B2
Sunrise Clo., Felt. 81 F3
Exeter Rd.
Sunset Ave. E4 34 B1
Sunset Ave., Wdf.Grn. 34 F4
Sunset Gdns. SE25 95 C2
Sunset Rd. SE5 76 J4
Sunset Vw., Barn. 23 B2
Sunshine Way, Mitch. 93 J2
Sunwell Clo. SE15 77 E1
Cossall Wk.
Surbiton Ct., Surb. 91 F6
Surbiton Cres., 91 H5
Kings.T.
Surbiton Hall Clo., 91 H4
Kings.T.
Surbiton Hill Pk., 91 J5
Surb.
Surbiton Hill Rd., 91 H4
Surb.
Surbiton Rd., Kings.T. 91 G4
Surlingham Clo. SE28 62 D7
Surr St. N7 49 E5
Surrendale Pl. W9 57 D4
Surrey Canal Rd. SE14 68 G6
Surrey Canal Rd. 68 F6
SE15
Surrey Cres. W4 65 A5
Surrey Gdns. N4 40 J6
Surrey Gro. SE17 21 D4
Surrey Gro., Sutt. 100 G3
Surrey La. SW11 75 H1
Surrey La. Est. SW11 75 H1
Surrey Lo. SE1 16 E6
Surrey Ms. SE27 86 B4
Hamilton Rd.
Surrey Mt. SE23 86 E1
Surrey Quays Rd. 68 F3
SE16
Surrey Rd. SE15 77 G5
Surrey Rd., Bark. 52 H7
Surrey Rd., Dag. 53 H5
Surrey Rd., Har. 36 J5
Surrey Rd., W.Wick. 103 B1
Surrey Row SE1 16 G3
Surrey Row SE1 67 H2
Surrey Sq. SE17 21 D3
Surrey Sq. SE17 68 B5
Surrey St. E13 60 H3
Surrey St. WC2 12 D5
Surrey St. WC2 58 F7
Surrey St., Croy. 101 J2
Surrey Ter. SE17 21 E3
Surrey Ter. SE17 68 B4
Surrey Water Rd. 68 G1
SE16
Surridge Gdns. SE19 86 A6
Hancock Rd.
Susan Clo., Rom. 44 J3
Susan Rd. SE3 78 H2
Susan Wd., Chis. 97 D1
Susannah St. E14 60 B6
Sussex Ave., Islw. 73 B3
Sussex Clo. N19 49 E2
Cornwallis Rd.
Sussex Clo., Ilf. 43 C6
Sussex Clo., N.Mal. 92 E4
Sussex Clo., Twick. 73 E6
Westmorland Clo.
Sussex Cres., Nthlt. 45 G6
Sussex Gdns. N4 40 J5
Sussex Gdns. N6 39 J5
Great N. Rd.

Sussex Gdns. W2 10 E5
Sussex Gdns. W2 57 G6
Sussex Gdns., Chess. 98 G6
Sussex Ms. E. W2 10 F4
Sussex Ms. W. W2 10 F5
Sussex Pl. NW1 6 J4
Sussex Pl. NW1 57 J4
Sussex Pl. W2 10 F4
Sussex Pl. W2 57 G6
Sussex Pl. W6 65 J5
Sussex Pl., Erith 71 H7
Sussex Pl., N.Mal. 92 E4
Sussex Ring N12 31 D5
Sussex Rd. E6 61 D1
Sussex Rd., Cars. 100 J6
Sussex Rd., Erith 71 H7
Sussex Rd., Har. 36 J5
Sussex Rd., Mitch. 94 E5
Lincoln Rd.
Sussex Rd., N.Mal. 92 E4
Sussex Rd., Sid. 89 B5
Sussex Rd., S.Croy. 102 A6
Sussex Rd., Sthl. 63 D3
Sussex Rd., W.Wick. 103 B1
Sussex Sq. W2 10 F5
Sussex Sq. W2 57 G7
Sussex St. E13 60 H3
Sussex St. SW1 19 E4
Sussex St. SW1 67 B5
Sussex Wk. SW9 76 H4
Sussex Way N7 49 E2
Sussex Way N19 49 E1
Sussex Way, Barn. 24 B5
Sutcliffe Clo. NW11 39 E5
Sutcliffe Ho., Hayes 54 A6
Sutcliffe Rd. SE18 70 H6
Sutcliffe Rd., Well. 80 C2
Sutherland Ave. W9 57 D4
Sutherland Ave. 55 E6
W13
Sutherland Ave., 63 A4
Hayes
Sutherland Ave., Orp. 97 J5
Sutherland Ave., Well. 79 H4
Sutherland Clo., Barn. 23 B4
Sutherland Ct. NW9 38 B4
Sutherland Dr. SW19 93 G1
Brangwyn Cres.
Sutherland Gdns. 74 E3
SW14
Sutherland Gdns., 92 H7
Wor.Pk.
Sutherland Gro. 75 B6
SW18
Sutherland Gro., 82 B5
Tedd.
Sutherland Pl. W2 57 D6
Sutherland Pt. E5 50 E4
Tiger Way
Sutherland Rd. E17 41 G2
Sutherland Rd. N9 33 D1
Sutherland Rd. N17 33 D7
Sutherland Rd. W4 65 E6
Sutherland Rd. W13 50 D8
Sutherland Rd., Belv. 71 G3
Sutherland Rd., Croy. 94 G7
Sutherland Rd., Enf. 25 G5
Sutherland Rd., Sthl. 54 F7
Sutherland Rd. Path 41 G3
E17
Sutherland Row SW1 19 E3
Sutherland Row SW1 67 B5
Sutherland Sq. SE17 20 F4
Sutherland Sq. SE17 67 J5
Sutherland St. SW1 19 D3
Sutherland St. SW1 67 B5
Sutherland Wk. SE17 21 A4
Sutherland Wk. SE17 67 J5
Sutlej Rd. SE7 69 J7
Sutterton St. N7 49 F6
Sutton Arc., Sutt. 100 E5
Throwley Way
Sutton Clo., Beck. 96 B1
Albemarle Rd.
Sutton Clo., Loug. 27 B7
Sutton Clo., Pnr. 36 A5
Sutton Common Rd., 93 C7
Sutt.
Sutton Ct. W4 65 C6
Sutton Ct. Rd. E13 60 J3
Sutton Ct. Rd. W4 65 C7
Sutton Ct. Rd., Sutt. 100 E5
Sutton Cres., Barn. 23 A5
Sutton Dene, Houns. 72 E4
Sutton Est. SW3 18 H3
Sutton Est. SW3 66 H5
Sutton Est. W10 56 J5
Sutton Est., The N1 49 H7

Sutton Gdns., Bark.	61	H1
Sutton Rd.		
Sutton Gdns., Croy.	95	C5
Sutton Grn., Bark.	61	H1
Sutton Rd.		
Sutton Gro., Sutt.	100	G4
Sutton Hall Rd.,	63	G7
Houns.		
Sutton La., Houns.	72	J3
Sutton La. N. W4	65	C5
Sutton La. S. W4	65	C6
Sutton Pk. Rd., Sutt.	100	E6
Sutton Path, Borwd.	22	A2
Stratfield Rd.		
Sutton Pl. E9	50	F5
Sutton Rd. E13	60	F4
Sutton Rd. E17	41	G1
Sutton Rd. N10	40	A1
Sutton Rd., Bark.	61	H2
Sutton Rd., Houns.	72	G1
Sutton Row W1	**11**	**J3**
Sutton Row W1	58	D6
Sutton Sq. E9	50	F5
Urswick Rd.		
Sutton Sq., Houns.	72	F1
Sutton St. E1	59	F7
Sutton Way W10	56	J5
Sutton Way, Houns.	72	F1
Sutton's Way EC1	**9**	**A6**
Swaby Rd. SW18	84	F1
Swaffham Way N22	32	H7
White Hart La.		
Swaffield Rd. SW18	75	E7
Swain Clo. SW16	85	B6
Swain Rd., Th.Hth.	94	J5
Swains La. N6	49	A1
Swains Rd. SW17	84	J7
Swainson Rd. W3	65	F2
Swallands Rd. SE6	87	A3
Swallow Clo. SE14	77	G1
Swallow Clo.	28	J1
(Bushey), Wat.		
Swallow Dr. NW10	47	D6
Kingfisher Way		
Swallow Dr., Nthlt.	54	G2
Swallow Pas. W1	**11**	**E4**
Swallow Pl. W1	**11**	**E4**
Swallow St. W1	**11**	**G6**
Swallow St. E6	61	B5
Swallowfield Rd. SE7	69	H5
Swan App. E6	61	B5
Swan Clo. E17	41	H1
Banbury Rd.		
Swan Clo., Croy.	95	B7
Swan Clo., Felt.	81	E4
Swan Clo. SW3	**18**	**H4**
Swan Dr. NW9	38	E2
Swan La. EC4	**13**	**B6**
Swan La. N20	31	F3
Swan La., Loug.	26	J7
Swan Mead SE1	**17**	**D6**
Swan Mead SE1	68	B3
Swan Ms. SW9	76	F1
Swan Pl. SW13	74	F2
Swan Rd. SE16	68	F2
Swan Rd. SE18	70	A3
Swan Rd., Felt.	81	E5
Swan Rd., Sthl.	54	H6
Swan St. SE1	**17**	**A5**
Swan St. SE1	67	J3
Swan St., Islw.	73	E3
Swan Wk. SW3	**18**	**J5**
Swan Wk. SW3	66	J6
Swan Way, Enf.	25	G2
Swan Yd. N1	49	H6
Highbury Sta. Rd.		
Swanage Rd. E4	34	C7
Swanage Rd. SW18	75	F6
Swanage Waye,	54	C6
Hayes		
Swanbridge Rd.,	80	G1
Bexh.		
Swanfield St. E2	**9**	**F4**
Swanfield St. E2	59	C3
Swanley Rd., Well.	80	C1
Swanscombe Rd. W4	65	E5
Swanscombe Rd.	66	A1
W11		
Swansea Rd., Enf.	25	F4
Swanshope, Loug.	27	E2
Swansland Gdns. E17	41	H1
McEntee Ave.		
Swanston Path, Wat.	28	C3
Swanton Gdns. SW19	84	A1
Swanton Rd., Erith	71	H7
Swanwick Clo. SW15	74	F7
Swaton Rd. E3	60	A4

Swaylands Rd., Belv.	71	G6
Swaythling Clo. N18	33	E4
Sweden Gate SE16	68	H3
Swedenborg Gdns.	59	D7
E1		
Sweeney Cres. SE1	**17**	**G4**
Sweeney Cres. SE1	68	C2
Sweet Briar Grn. N9	33	C3
Sweet Briar Gro. N9	33	C3
Sweet Briar Wk. N18	33	C4
Sweetmans Ave., Pnr.	36	D3
Sweets Way N20	31	G2
Swete St. E13	60	G2
Swetenham Wk. SE18	70	F5
Sandbach Pl.		
Sweyn Pl. SE3	78	G2
Swift Clo. E17	33	H7
Banbury Rd.		
Swift Clo., Har.	45	H2
Swift Rd., Felt.	81	D4
Swift Rd., Sthl.	63	F3
Swift St. SW6	75	C1
Swiftsden Way, Brom.	87	E6
Swinbrook Rd. W10	57	B5
Swinburne Ct. SE5	77	A4
Basingdon Way		
Swinburne Cres.,	95	F6
Croy.		
Swinburne Rd. SW15	74	G4
Swinderby Rd., Wem.	46	H6
Swindon Clo., Ilf.	52	H2
Salisbury Rd.		
Swindon St. W12	65	H1
Swinfield Clo., Felt.	81	E4
Swinford Gdns. SW9	76	H3
Swingate La. SE18	70	H7
Swinnerton St. E9	50	H5
Swinton Clo., Wem.	47	B1
Swinton Pl. WC1	**8**	**C3**
Swinton Pl. WC1	58	F3
Swinton St. WC1	**8**	**C3**
Swinton St. WC1	58	F3
Swires Shaw, Kes.	104	A4
Swiss Ter. NW6	48	G7
Swithland Gdns. SE9	88	D4
Swyncombe Ave. W5	64	E4
Swynford Gdns. NW4	38	G4
Handowe Clo.		
Sybil Ms. N4	40	H6
Lothair Rd. N.		
Sybil Phoenix Clo.	68	G5
SE8		
Sybil Thorndike Ho.	49	J6
N1		
Clephane Rd.		
Sybourn St. E17	41	J7
Sycamore Ave. W5	64	G3
Sycamore Ave., Sid.	79	J6
Sycamore Clo. E16	60	E4
Clarence Rd.		
Sycamore Clo. N9	33	D4
Pycroft Way		
Sycamore Clo. SE9	88	B2
Sycamore Clo., Barn.	23	G6
Sycamore Clo., Cars.	100	J4
Sycamore Clo., Felt.	81	A3
Sycamore Clo., Nthlt.	54	E1
Sycamore Gdns. W6	65	H2
Sycamore Gdns.	93	G2
Mitch.		
Sycamore Gro. NW9	38	C7
Sycamore Gro. SE6	78	C6
Sycamore Gro. SE20	86	D7
Sycamore Gro.,	92	D3
N.Mal.		
Sycamore Hill N11	32	A6
Sycamore Rd. SW19	83	J6
Sycamore Rd., Tedd.	82	F6
Sycamore St. EC1	**8**	**J6**
Sycamore Wk. W10	57	B4
Fifth Ave.		
Sycamore Wk., Ilf.	43	F4
Civic Way		
Sycamore Way,	94	G5
Th.Hth.		
Grove Rd.		
Sydenham Ave. SE26	86	E5
Sydenham Cotts.	87	J2
SE12		
Sydenham Hill SE23	86	E1
Sydenham Hill SE26	86	C4
Sydenham Hill Est.	86	D3
SE26		
Sydenham Pk. SE26	86	F3
Sydenham Pk. Rd.	86	F3
SE26		
Sydenham Ri. SE23	86	E2
Sydenham Rd. SE26	86	G5

Sydenham Rd., Croy.	101	J1
Sydmons Ct. SE23	77	F7
Sydner Ms. N16	50	C4
Sydner Rd.		
Sydner Rd. N16	50	C4
Sydney Clo. SW3	**18**	**F2**
Sydney Clo. SW3	66	G4
Sydney Gro. NW4	38	J5
Sydney Ms. SW3	**18**	**F2**
Sydney Pl. SW7	**18**	**F2**
Sydney Pl. SW7	66	G4
Sydney Rd. E11	42	H6
Mansfield Rd.		
Sydney Rd. N8	40	G4
Sydney Rd. N10	40	A1
Sydney Rd. SE2	71	C3
Sydney Rd. SW20	93	A2
Sydney Rd. W13	64	D1
Sydney Rd., Bexh.	80	D4
Sydney Rd., Enf.	25	A3
Sydney Rd., Felt.	81	A1
Sydney Rd., Ilf.	43	F2
Sydney Rd., Rich.	73	H4
Sydney Rd., Sid.	88	H4
Sydney Rd., Sutt.	100	D4
Sydney Rd., Tedd.	82	C5
Sydney Rd., Wdf.Grn.	34	G4
Sydney St. SW3	**18**	**G3**
Sydney St. SW3	66	H5
Sylvan Ave. N3	39	D2
Sylvan Ave. N22	32	F7
Sylvan Ave. NW7	30	F6
Sylvan Ave., Rom.	44	F6
Sylvan Est. SE19	95	C1
Sylvan Gdns., Surb.	91	G7
Sylvan Gro. NW2	48	A4
Sylvan Gro. SE15	68	E6
Sylvan Hill SE19	95	B1
Sylvan Rd. E7	51	G6
Sylvan Rd. E11	42	G5
Sylvan Rd. E17	42	A5
Sylvan Rd. SE19	95	C1
Sylvan Wk., Brom.	97	C3
Sylvan Way, Dag.	53	B3
Sylvan Way, W.Wick.	103	E4
Sylverdale Rd., Croy.	101	H3
Sylvester Ave., Chis.	88	C6
Sylvester Path E8	50	E6
Sylvester Rd.		
Sylvester Rd. E8	50	E6
Sylvester Rd. E17	41	J7
Sylvester Rd. N2	39	F2
Sylvester Rd., Wem.	46	F5
Sylvestrus Clo.,	92	A1
Kings.T.		
Sylvia Ave., Pnr.	28	E6
Sylvia Gdns., Wem.	47	B7
Symes Ms. NW1	**7**	**F1**
Symons St. SW3	**19**	**A2**
Symons St. SW3	66	J4
Syon Gate Way,	64	D7
Brent.		
Syon La., Islw.	64	C6
Syon Pk. Gdns., Islw.	64	C7
Syon Vista, Rich.	73	G1
Kew Rd.		

T

Tabard Gdn. Est. SE1	**17**	**C4**
Tabard Gdn. Est. SE1	68	A2
Tabard St. SE1	**17**	**B4**
Tabard St. SE1	68	A2
Tabernacle Ave. E13	60	G4
Barking Rd.		
Tabernacle St. EC2	**9**	**C6**
Tabernacle St. EC2	59	A4
Tableer Ave. SW4	76	C5
Tabley Rd. N7	49	E4
Tabor Gdns., Sutt.	100	C6
Tabor Gro. SW19	84	B7
Tabor Rd. W6	65	H3
Tachbrook Est. SW1	**19**	**J4**
Tachbrook Est. SW1	67	D5
Tachbrook Ms. SW1	**19**	**F1**
Tachbrook Rd., Sthl.	63	D4
Tachbrook St. SW1	**19**	**G2**
Tachbrook St. SW1	67	C4
Tack Ms. SE4	78	A3
Tadema Rd. SW10	66	F7
Tadmor St. W12	66	A1
Tadworth Ave.,	92	F5
N.Mal.		
Tadworth Rd. NW2	47	G2
Taeping St. E14	69	B4
Taffy's How, Mitch.	93	H3
Taft Way E3	60	B3
St. Leonards St.		

Tailworth St. E1	59	D5
Chicksand St.		
Tait Rd., Croy.	95	B7
Talacre Rd. NW5	49	A6
Talbot Ave. N2	39	G3
Talbot Clo. N15	41	C4
Talbot Ct. EC3	**13**	**C5**
Talbot Cres. NW4	38	G5
Talbot Gdns., Ilf.	53	A2
Talbot Ho. E14	60	B6
Giraud St.		
Talbot Pl. SE3	78	E2
Talbot Rd. E6	61	D2
Talbot Rd. E7	51	G4
Talbot Rd. N6	40	A6
Talbot Rd. N15	41	C4
Talbot Rd. N22	40	C2
Talbot Rd. W2	57	D6
Talbot Rd. W11	57	C6
Talbot Rd. W13	55	D7
Talbot Rd., Brom.	96	H4
Masons Hill		
Talbot Rd., Cars.	101	A5
Talbot Rd., Dag.	53	F6
Talbot Rd., Har.	37	C2
Talbot Rd., Islw.	73	D4
Talbot Rd., Sthl.	63	E4
Talbot Rd., Th.Hth.	95	A4
Talbot Rd., Twick.	82	B1
Talbot Rd., Wem.	46	G5
Talbot Sq. W2	**10**	**F4**
Talbot Sq. W2	57	G6
Talbot Wk. NW10	47	E6
Garnet Rd.		
Talbot Wk. W11	57	B6
Lancaster Rd.		
Talbot Yd. SE1	**17**	**B2**
Talfourd Pl. SE15	77	C1
Talfourd Rd. SE15	77	C1
Talgarth Rd. W6	66	A5
Talgarth Rd. W14	66	A5
Talgarth Wk. NW9	38	E5
Talisman Clo., Ilf.	53	B1
Talisman Sq. SE26	86	D4
Talisman Way, Wem.	46	J3
Forty Ave.		
Tall Elms Clo., Brom.	96	F5
Tall Trees SW16	94	F3
Tallack Clo., Har.	29	B7
College Hill Rd.		
Tallack Rd. E10	50	J1
Tallis Gro. SE7	69	H6
Tallis St. EC4	**12**	**F5**
Tallis St. EC4	58	G7
Tallis Vw. NW10	47	D6
Mitchellbrook Way		
Tally Ho Cor. N12	31	F5
Talma Gdns., Twick.	73	B6
Talma Rd. SW2	76	G4
Talmage Clo. SE23	77	F7
Tyson Rd.		
Talman Gro., Stan.	29	G6
Talwin St. E3	60	B3
Tamar Sq., Wdf.Grn.	34	H6
Tamar St. SE7	70	B3
Tamar Way N17	41	C3
Tamarind Yd. E1	**17**	**J1**
Tamarisk Sq. W12	56	F7
Tamesis Gdns.,	99	E2
Wor.Pk.		
Tamian Est., Houns.	72	C4
Tamian Way, Houns.	72	C4
Tamworth Ave.,	34	E6
Wdf.Grn.		
Tamworth Gdns., Pnr.	36	B2
Tamworth La., Mitch.	94	A2
Tamworth Pk., Mitch.	94	B4
Tamworth Pl., Croy.	101	J2
Tamworth Rd., Croy.	101	H2
Tamworth St. SW6	66	D6
Tancred Rd. N4	40	H6
Tandridge Dr., Orp.	104	G1
Tandridge Pl., Orp.	97	G7
Tandridge Dr.		
Tanfield Ave. NW2	47	F4
Tanfield Rd., Croy.	101	J2
Tangier Rd., Rich.	74	B4
Tanglebury Clo.,	97	B4
Brom.		
Tanglewood Clo.,	102	F3
Croy.		
Tanglewood Clo.,	29	B2
Stan.		
Tanglewood Way,	81	B3
Felt.		
Tangley Gro. SW15	74	F7
Tangley Pk. Rd.,	81	F5
Hmptn.		

Name	Ref	Name	Ref	Name	Ref	Name	Ref
Tangmere Gdns., Nthlt.	54 C2	Taunton Way, Stan.	37 H2	Tees Ave., Grnf.	55 B2	Temple Rd., Houns.	72 H4
Tangmere Way NW9	38 E2	Tavern La. SW9	76 G2	Teesdale Ave., Islw.	73 D1	Temple Rd., Rich.	73 J2
Tanhurst Wk. SE2	71 D3	Taverner Sq. N5	49 J4	Teesdale Clo. E2	9 J2	Temple Sheen SW14	74 B4
Alsike Rd.		*Highbury Gra.*		Teesdale Clo. E2	59 D2	Temple Sheen Rd.	74 B4
Tankerton Rd., Surb.	98 J2	Taverners Clo. W11	66 B1	Teesdale Gdns. SE25	95 B2	SW14	
Tankerton St. WC1	**8 B4**	*Addison Ave.*		*Grange Hill*		Temple St. E2	59 E2
Tankerville Rd. SW16	85 D7	Taverners Way E4	34 E1	Teesdale Gdns., Islw.	73 D1	Temple Way, Sutt.	100 G3
Tankridge Rd. NW2	47 H2	*Douglas Rd.*		Teesdale Rd. E11	42 F6	**Temple W. Ms. SE11**	**16 G6**
Tanner St. SE1	**17 E4**	Tavistock Ave. E17	41 G3	Teesdale St. E2	59 E2	Temple W. Ms. SE11	67 H3
Tanner St. SE1	68 B2	Tavistock Ave., Grnf.	55 D2	Teeswater Ct., Erith	71 D3	Templecombe Rd. E9	59 F1
Tanner St., Bark.	52 F6	Tavistock Clo. N16	50 B5	*Middle Way*		Templecombe Way,	93 B5
Tanners Clo., Walt.	90 B6	*Crossway*		Teevan Clo., Croy.	95 D7	Mord.	
Tanners End La. N18	33 B4	Tavistock Cres. W11	57 C5	Teevan Rd., Croy.	102 D1	Templehof Ave. NW2	38 J7
Tanners Hill SE8	77 J1	Tavistock Cres.,	94 E4	Teignmouth Clo. SW4	76 D4	Templeman Rd. W7	55 C5
Tanners La., Ilf.	43 F3	Mitch.		Teignmouth Clo.,	37 J2	Templemead Clo. W3	56 E6
Tannery Clo., Beck.	95 G5	Tavistock Gdns., Ilf.	52 H4	Edg.		Templeton Ave. E4	34 A4
Tannery Clo., Dag.	53 H3	Tavistock Gate, Croy.	102 A1	Teignmouth Gdns.,	55 C2	Templeton Clo. SE19	95 A1
Tannsfeld Rd. SE26	86 G5	Tavistock Gro., Croy.	95 A7	Grnf.		Templeton Pl. SW5	66 D4
Tansley Clo. N7	49 D5	Tavistock Ms. E18	42 G4	Teignmouth Rd. NW2	48 A5	Templeton Rd. N15	41 A6
Hilldrop Rd.		*Avon Way*		Teignmouth Rd., Well.	80 C2	Templewood W13	55 E5
Tanswell Est. SE1	**16 F4**	Tavistock Ms. W11	57 C6	Telcote Way, Ruis.	36 C7	Templewood Ave.	48 E3
Tanswell St. SE1	**16 E4**	*Lancaster Rd.*		*Woodlands Ave.*		NW3	
Tansy Clo. E6	61 D6	Tavistock Pl. E18	42 G3	Telegraph Hill NW3	48 E3	Templewood Gdns.	48 E3
Tant Ave. E16	60 F6	*Avon Way*		Telegraph La., Esher	98 C6	NW3	
Tantallon Rd. SW12	85 A1	Tavistock Pl. N14	24 B7	Telegraph Ms., Ilf.	53 A1	Tempsford Ave.,	22 D4
Tantony Gro., Rom.	44 D3	*Chase Side*		Telegraph Rd. SW15	74 H7	Borwd.	
Tanyard La., Bex.	80 G7	**Tavistock Pl. WC1**	**8 A5**	**Telegraph St. EC2**	**13 B3**	Tempsford Clo., Enf.	24 J3
Bexley High St.		Tavistock Pl. WC1	58 E4	Telemann Sq. SE3	78 H3	*Gladbeck Way*	
Tanza Rd. NW3	48 J4	Tavistock Rd. E7	51 F4	Telephone Pl. SW6	66 C6	Temsford Clo., Har.	36 J2
Tapestry Clo., Sutt.	100 E7	Tavistock Rd. E15	51 F6	*Lillie Rd.*		Tenbury Clo. E7	52 A5
Taplow NW3	**48 G7**	Tavistock Rd. E18	42 G3	Telfer Clo. W3	65 C2	*Romford Rd.*	
Taplow SE17	**21 C3**	Tavistock Rd. N4	41 A6	*Church Rd.*		Tenbury Ct. SW2	85 D1
Taplow SE17	68 A5	Tavistock Rd. NW10	56 F2	Telfercot Rd. SW12	85 D1	Tenby Ave., Har.	37 E2
Taplow Rd. N13	32 J4	Tavistock Rd. W11	57 C6	Telford Ave. SW2	85 D1	Tenby Clo. N15	41 C4
North Circular Rd.		Tavistock Rd., Brom.	96 F4	Telford Clo. SE19	86 C6	*Hanover Rd.*	
Taplow St. N1	**9 A2**	Tavistock Rd., Cars.	100 G1	*St. Aubyn's Rd.*		Tenby Clo., Rom.	44 E6
Taplow St. N1	58 J2	Tavistock Rd., Croy.	102 A1	Telford Clo. W3	65 C2	Tenby Gdns., Nthlt.	45 G6
Tapp St. E1	59 E4	Tavistock Rd., Edg.	38 A1	*Church Rd.*		Tenby Rd. E17	41 H5
Tappesfield Rd. SE15	77 F3	Tavistock Rd., Well.	80 C1	Telford Dr., Walt.	90 C7	Tenby Rd., Edg.	37 J1
Tapster St., Barn.	23 C3	**Tavistock Sq. WC1**	**7 J5**	Telford Rd. N11	32 C6	Tenby Rd., Enf.	25 F3
Tarbert Rd. SE22	77 B5	Tavistock Sq. WC1	58 D4	Telford Rd. NW9	38 G6	Tenby Rd., Rom.	44 E6
Tarbert Wk. E1	59 F7	**Tavistock St. WC2**	**12 B5**	*West Hendon Bdy.*		Tenby Rd., Well.	80 D1
Juniper St.		Tavistock St. WC2	58 E7	Telford Rd. SE9	88 G2	Tench St. E1	68 E1
Tarn St. SE1	**16 J6**	Tavistock Ter. N19	49 D3	Telford Rd. W10	57 B5	Tenda Rd. SE16	68 E4
Tarnbank, Enf.	24 E5	Tavistock Wk., Cars.	100 G1	Telford Rd., Sthl.	54 H7	*Roseberry St.*	
Tarnwood Pk. SE9	79 C7	*Tavistock Rd.*		Telford Rd., Twick.	72 G7	Tendring Way, Rom.	44 C5
Tarquin Ho. SE26	86 D4	**Taviton St. WC1**	**7 H5**	**Telford Ter. SW1**	**19 F5**	Tenham Ave. SW2	85 D2
Tarragon Gdns. SE14	68 H7	Taviton St. WC1	58 D4	Telford Ter. SW1	67 C6	**Tenison Ct. W1**	**11 F5**
Southerngate Way		Tavy Bri. SE2	71 C3	Telford Way W3	56 E5	**Tenison Way SE1**	**16 D2**
Tarragon Gro. SE26	86 G6	**Tavy Clo. SE11**	**20 F3**	Telford Way, Hayes	54 E5	Tenison Way SE1	67 F1
Tarrant Pl. W1	**10 J2**	Tawney Rd. SE28	62 B7	**Telfords Yd. E1**	**13 J6**	**Tenniel Clo. W2**	**10 C5**
Tarrington Clo.	85 D3	Tawny Clo. W13	64 E1	Telham Rd. E6	61 D2	Tennis Ct. La., E.Mol.	91 C3
SW16		Tawny Clo., Felt.	81 A5	Tell Gro. SE22	77 C4	*Hampton Ct. Way*	
Tarry La. SE8	68 H4	*Chervil Clo.*		Tellson Ave. SE18	79 A1	**Tennis St. SE1**	**17 B3**
Tarver Rd. SE17	**20 H4**	Tawny Way SE16	68 G4	Telscombe Clo., Orp.	104 H2	Tennis St. SE1	68 A2
Tarver Rd. SE17	67 H5	Tayben Ave., Twick.	73 B6	Temeraire St. SE16	68 F2	Tennison Ave.,	22 B5
Tarves Way SE10	69 B7	Taybridge Rd. SW11	76 A3	*Albion St.*		Borwd.	
Tash Pl. N11	32 B5	Tayburn Clo. E14	60 C6	Temperley Rd. SW12	76 A7	Tennison Rd. SE25	95 C4
Woodland Rd.		Taylor Ave., Rich.	74 B2	Templar Dr. SE28	62 D6	Tenniswood Rd., Enf.	25 B1
Tasker Ho., Bark.	61 G2	Taylor Clo. N17	33 D7	Templar Ho. NW2	48 C6	Tennyson Ave. E11	42 G7
Dovehouse Mead		Taylor Clo., Hmptn.	81 J5	*Shoot Up Hill*		Tennyson Ave. E12	52 B7
Tasker Rd. NW3	48 J5	Taylor Clo., Orp.	104 J4	Templar Pl., Hmptn.	81 G7	Tennyson Ave. NW9	38 C3
Tasman Rd. SW9	76 E3	Taylor Ct. E15	51 C5	Templar St. SE5	76 H2	Tennyson Ave.,	92 H5
Tasman Wk. E16	61 A6	*Clarence Rd.*		Templars Ave. NW11	39 C6	N.Mal.	
Royal Rd.		Taylor Rd., Mitch.	84 H7	Templars Cres. N3	39 D2	Tennyson Ave.,	82 C1
Tasmania Ter. N18	32 J6	Taylor Rd., Wall.	101 B5	Templars Dr., Har.	29 A6	Twick.	
Tasso Rd. W6	66 B6	Taylors Bldgs. SE18	70 E4	**Temple EC4**	**12 E5**	Tennyson Clo., Enf.	25 G5
Tatam Rd. NW10	47 D7	*Spray St.*		Temple EC4	58 E5	Tennyson Clo., Well.	79 J1
Tate Rd. E16	70 C1	Taylors Clo., Sid.	88 J4	**Temple Ave. EC4**	**12 F5**	Tennyson Rd. E10	51 B1
Newland St.		Taylors Grn. W3	56 E6	Temple Ave. EC4	58 G7	Tennyson Rd. E15	51 E7
Tate Rd., Sutt.	100 D5	*Long Dr.*		Temple Ave. N20	23 G7	Tennyson Rd. E17	41 J6
Tatnell Rd. SE23	77 H6	Taylors La. NW10	47 E7	Temple Ave., Croy.	102 J2	Tennyson Rd. NW6	57 C1
Tattersall Clo. SE9	79 B5	Taylors La. SE26	86 E4	Temple Ave., Dag.	53 G1	Tennyson Rd. NW7	30 G5
Tatton Cres. N16	41 C4	Taylors La., Barn.	23 C1	Temple Clo. E11	42 E7	Tennyson Rd. SE20	86 G7
Clapton Common		Taymount Ri. SE23	86 F2	*Wadley Rd.*		Tennyson Rd. SW19	84 F6
Tatum St. SE17	**21 C2**	Tayport Clo. N1	49 F7	Temple Clo. N3	39 C2	Tennyson Rd. W7	55 C7
Tatum St. SE17	68 A4	Tayside Dr., Edg.	30 B3	*Cyprus Rd.*		Tennyson Rd., Houns.	72 J2
Taunton Ave. SW20	92 H2	Taywood Rd., Nthlt.	54 F3	Temple Clo. SE28	70 F3	Tennyson Rd., Well.	79 J1
Taunton Ave., Houns.	72 J2	*Invicta Gro.*		Temple Fortune Hill	39 D5	Tennyson St. SW8	76 B2
Taunton Clo., Ilf.	35 J6	Teak Clo. SE16	68 H1	NW11		Tensing Rd., Sthl.	63 G3
Taunton Clo., Sutt.	100 D1	Teal Clo. E16	61 A5	Temple Fortune La.	39 C5	Tent Peg La., Orp.	97 F5
Taunton Ct. N17	33 B7	*Fulmer Rd.*		NW11		Tent St. E1	59 E4
Taunton Dr., Enf.	24 G3	**Teale St. E2**	**9 J1**	Temple Gdns. NW11	39 C6	Tentelow La., Sthl.	63 G5
Taunton Ms. NW1	**6 J6**	Teale St. E2	59 D2	Temple Gdns., Dag.	53 D3	**Tenter Grd. E1**	**13 F2**
Taunton Pl. NW1	**6 J5**	Tealing Dr., Epsom	99 D4	Temple Gro. NW11	39 D6	Tenterden Clo. NW4	39 A3
Taunton Pl. NW1	57 J4	Teasel Clo., Croy.	102 G1	Temple Gro., Enf.	24 H3	Tenterden Clo. SE9	88 C4
Taunton Rd. SE12	78 E5	Teasel Way E15	60 E3	**Temple La. EC4**	**12 F4**	Tenterden Dr. NW4	39 A3
Taunton Rd., Grnf.	54 H1	Tebworth Rd. N17	33 C7	Temple Mead Clo.,	29 E6	Tenterden Gdns. NW4	39 A3
		Tedder Clo., Chess.	98 F6	Stan.		Tenterden Gdns.,	95 D7
		Tedder Clo., Ruis.	45 B5	Temple Mill La. E15	51 A4	Croy.	
		West End Rd.		**Temple Pl. WC2**	**12 D5**	Tenterden Gro. NW4	39 A3
		Teddington Pk., Tedd.	82 C5	Temple Pl. WC2	58 F7	Tenterden Rd. N17	33 C7
		Teddington Pk. Rd.,	82 C4	Temple Rd. E6	61 B1	Tenterden Rd., Croy.	95 D7
		Tedd.		Temple Rd. N8	40 F4	Tenterden Rd., Dag.	53 F2
		Tedworth Gdns. SW3	**18 J4**	Temple Rd. NW2	47 J4	**Tenterden St. W1**	**11 E4**
		Tedworth Sq. SW3	**18 J4**	Temple Rd. W4	65 C3	Tenterden St. W1	58 B6
		Tedworth Sq. SW3	66 G5	Temple Rd. W5	64 G3	Terborch Way SE22	77 B5
		Tee, The W3	56 E6	Temple Rd., Croy.	102 A4	*East Dulwich Gro.*	

Teresa Ms. E17 42 A4
Teresa Wk. N10 40 B5
  Connaught Gdns.
Terling Clo. E11 51 F3
Terling Rd., Dag. 53 G2
Terling Wk. N1 58 J1
  Britannia Row
Terminus Pl. SW1 15 E6
Terminus Pl. SW1 67 B3
Terrace, The E4 34 E3
  Chingdale Rd.
Terrace, The N3 39 C2
  Hendon La.
Terrace, The NW6 57 D1
Terrace, The SW13 74 E2
Terrace, The, Har. 46 E1
Terrace, The, 34 G6
  Wdf.Grn.
Terrace Gdns. SW13 74 F2
Terrace La., Rich. 73 H6
Terrace Rd. E9 50 F7
Terrace Rd. E13 60 G1
Terrace Rd., Walt. 90 A7
Terrace Wk., Dag. 53 E5
Terrapin Rd. SW17 85 B3
Terretts Pl. N1 49 H7
  Upper St.
Terrick Rd. N22 40 E1
Terrick St. W12 56 H6
Terrilands, Pnr. 36 F3
Terront Rd. N15 40 J5
Tessa Sanderson Pl. 76 B3
  SW8
  Heath Rd.
Tessa Sanderson 46 A5
  Way, Grnf.
  Lilian Board Way
Testerton Wk. W11 57 A7
  Whitchurch Rd.
Tetbury Pl. N1 58 H1
  Upper St.
Tetcott Rd. SW10 18 C7
Tetcott Rd. SW10 66 F7
Tetherdown N10 40 A3
Tetterby Way SE16 21 J4
Tetty Way, Brom. 96 G2
Teversham La. SW8 76 E1
Teviot Clo., Well. 80 B1
Teviot St. E14 60 C5
Tewkesbury Ave. 77 E7
  SE23
Tewkesbury Ave., Pnr. 36 E5
Tewkesbury Clo. N15 41 A6
  Tewkesbury Rd.
Tewkesbury Gdns. 38 B3
  NW9
Tewkesbury Rd. N15 41 A6
Tewkesbury Rd. W13 55 D7
Tewkesbury Rd., 100 G1
  Cars.
Tewkesbury Ter. N11 32 C6
Tewson Rd. SE18 70 H4
Teynham Ave., Enf. 25 A6
Teynham Grn., Brom. 96 G5
Teynton Ter. N17 40 J1
Thackeray Ave. N17 41 D2
Thackeray Clo. SW19 84 A7
Thackeray Clo., Har. 45 G1
Thackeray Dr., Ilf. 44 A7
Thackeray Dr., Rom. 44 A7
Thackeray Rd. E6 61 A2
Thackeray Rd. SW8 76 B2
Thackeray St. W8 14 B4
Thackeray St. W8 66 E2
Thakeham Clo. SE26 86 E5
Thakrah Clo. N2 39 F2
Thalia Clo. SE10 69 D6
  Feathers Pl.
Thame Rd. SE16 68 G2
Thames Ave. SW10 75 F1
Thames Ave., Dag. 62 G4
Thames Ave., Grnf. 55 C2
Thames Bank SW14 74 C2
Thames Circle E14 69 A4
  Westferry Rd.
Thames Clo., Hmptn. 90 H2
Thames Ct., W.Mol. 90 H2
Thames Mead, Walt. 90 A7
Thames Meadow, 90 G2
  W.Mol.
Thames Pl. SW15 75 A3
Thames Rd. E16 70 A1
Thames Rd. W4 65 A6
Thames Rd., Bark. 61 H3
Thames Rd. Ind. Est. 70 A1
  E16
Thames Side, Kings.T. 91 G1
Thames Side, Tedd. 82 G7

Thames St. SE10 69 B6
Thames St., Hmptn. 90 H1
Thames St., Kings.T. 91 G2
Thames St., Sun. 90 A4
Thames Vill. W4 74 C1
Thamesbank Pl. SE28 62 C6
Thamesgate Clo., 82 E4
  Rich.
  Locksmeade Rd.
Thameshill Ave., Rom. 44 J2
Thameside, Tedd. 82 F7
Thameside Ind. Est. 70 B2
  E16
Thameside Wk. SE28 62 B6
Thamesmead, Walt. 90 A7
Thamesmere Dr. SE28 62 A7
Thamesvale Clo., 72 G2
  Houns.
Thane Vill. N7 49 F3
Thanescroft Gdns., 102 B3
  Croy.
Thanet Dr., Kes. 104 A3
  Phoenix Dr.
Thanet Pl., Croy. 101 J4
Thanet Rd., Bex. 80 G7
Thanet St. WC1 8 A4
Thanet St. WC1 58 E3
Thanington Ct. SE9 79 H6
Thant Clo. E10 51 B3
Tharp Rd., Wall. 101 D5
Thatcham Gdns. N20 23 F7
Thatchers Clo., Loug. 27 F2
Thatchers Way, Islw. 73 A5
Thatches Gro., Rom. 44 E4
Thavies Inn EC1 12 F3
Thaxted Pl. SW20 84 A7
Thaxted Rd. SE9 88 F2
Thaxted Rd., Buck.H. 27 A7
Thaxton Rd. W14 66 C6
Thayer St. W1 11 C2
Thayer St. W1 58 A5
Thayers Fm. Rd., 95 H1
  Beck.
Theatre St. SW11 75 J3
Theberton St. N1 58 G1
Theed St. SE1 16 F2
Theed St. SE1 67 G1
Thelma Gdns. SE3 79 A1
Thelma Gdns., Felt. 81 E3
Thelma Gro., Tedd. 82 D6
Theobald Cres., Har. 36 H1
Theobald Rd. E17 41 J7
Theobald Rd., Croy. 101 H2
Theobald St. SE1 17 B6
Theobalds Ave. N12 31 F4
Theobalds Ct. N4 49 J2
  Queens Dr.
Theobald's Rd. WC1 12 C1
Theobald's Rd. WC1 58 F5
Theodore Rd. SE13 78 D6
Therapia La., Croy. 94 D7
Therapia Rd. SE22 77 F6
Theresa Rd. W6 65 G4
Therfield Ct. N4 49 J2
  Brownswood Rd.
Thermopylae Gate 69 B4
  E14
Theseus Wk. N1 8 H2
Thesiger Rd. SE20 86 G7
Thessaly Rd. SW8 67 C7
Thetford Clo. N13 32 H6
Thetford Gdns., Dag. 53 D7
Thetford Rd., Dag. 53 D7
Thetford Rd., N.Mal. 92 D6
Thetis Ter., Rich. 65 A6
Theydon Gro., 34 J6
  Wdf.Grn.
Theydon Pk. Rd., Epp. 27 H1
Theydon Rd. E5 50 F2
Theydon St. E17 41 J7
Thicket Cres., Sutt. 100 F4
Thicket Gro., SE20 86 D7
  Anerley Rd.
Thicket Gro., Dag. 53 C6
Thicket Rd. SE20 86 D7
Thicket Rd., Sutt. 100 F4
Third Ave. E12 52 B4
Third Ave. E13 60 G3
Third Ave. E17 42 A5
Third Ave. W3 65 F1
Third Ave. W10 57 B3
Third Ave., Dag. 62 H1
Third Ave., Enf. 25 C5
Third Ave., Rom. 44 C6
Third Ave., Wem. 46 G2
Third Clo., W.Mol. 90 H4
Third Cross Rd., 82 A2
  Twick.

Third Way, Wem. 47 B4
Thirleby Rd. SW1 15 G6
Thirleby Rd. SW1 67 C3
Thirleby Rd., Edg. 38 D1
Thirlmere Ave., Grnf. 55 F3
Thirlmere Gdns., 46 F1
  Wem.
Thirlmere Ho., Islw. 73 C5
Thirlmere Ri., Brom. 87 F6
Thirlmere Rd. N10 40 B1
Thirlmere Rd. SW16 85 D4
Thirlmere Rd., Bexh. 80 J2
Thirsk Clo., Nthlt. 45 G6
Thirsk Rd. SE25 95 A4
Thirsk Rd. SW11 76 A3
Thirsk Rd., Mitch. 85 A7
Thistle Gro. SW10 18 D3
Thistle Gro. SW10 66 F5
Thistle Mead, Loug. 27 D3
Thistlebrook SE2 71 C3
Thistlecroft Gdns., 37 G1
  Stan.
Thistledene, T.Ditt. 91 B6
Thistledene Ave., Har. 45 E3
Thistlemead, Chis. 97 E2
Thistlewaite Rd. E5 50 E3
Thistlewood Clo. N7 49 F2
Thistleworth Clo., 64 A7
  Islw.
Thomas Baines Rd. 75 G3
  SW11
Thomas Darby Ct. 57 B6
  W11
Thomas Dinwiddy 87 J2
  Rd. SE12
Thomas Doyle St. SE1 16 H5
Thomas Doyle St. SE1 67 H3
Thomas Hardy Ho. 32 F7
  N22
Thomas La. SE6 78 A7
Thomas More St. E1 13 H6
Thomas More St. E1 59 D7
Thomas More Way N2 39 F3
Thomas Pl. W8 14 A6
Thomas Rd. E14 59 J6
Thomas St. SE18 70 E4
Thomas Wall Clo., 100 E5
  Sutt.
  Clarence Rd.
Thomas à Beckett 46 C4
  Clo., Wem.
Thompson Ave., Rich. 74 A3
Thompson Clo., Ilf. 52 F2
  High Rd.
Thompson Rd. SE22 77 C6
Thompson Rd., Dag. 53 F3
Thompson's Ave. SE5 20 J7
Thompson's Ave. SE5 67 J7
Thomson Cres., Croy. 101 G1
Thomson Rd., Har. 37 B3
Thorburn Sq. SE1 21 H2
Thorburn Sq. SE1 68 D4
Thorburn Way SW19 93 G1
  Phipps Bri. Rd.
Thoresby St. N1 9 A3
Thoresby St. N1 58 J3
Thorkhill Gdns., T.Ditt. 98 D1
Thorkhill Rd., T.Ditt. 98 D1
Thorn Ave. (Bushey), 28 J1
  Wat.
Thorn Clo., Brom. 97 D6
Thorn Clo., Nthlt. 54 F3
Thorn Ho., Beck. 95 H1
Thornaby Gdns. N18 33 D6
Thornbury Ave., Islw. 64 A7
Thornbury Gdns., 22 C3
  Borwd.
Thornbury Rd. SW2 76 E6
Thornbury Rd., Islw. 64 A7
Thornbury Sq. N6 49 C1
Thornby Rd. E5 50 F3
Thorncliffe Rd. SW2 76 E6
Thorncliffe Rd., Sthl. 63 F5
Thorncombe Rd. 77 B5
  SE22
Thorncroft Rd., Sutt. 100 A4
Thorncroft St. SW8 67 E7
Thorndean St. SW18 84 F2
Thorndene Ave. N11 32 A1
Thorndike Clo. SW10 18 C7
Thorndike Clo. SW10 66 F7
Thorndike St. SW1 19 H2
Thorndike St. SW1 67 D4
Thorndon Clo., Orp. 97 J2
Thorndon Gdns., 99 E5
  Epsom
Thorndon Rd., Orp. 97 J2

Thorndyke Ct., Pnr. 28 F7
  Westfield Pk.
Thorne Clo. E11 51 E4
Thorne Clo. E16 60 F6
Thorne Clo., Erith 71 J6
Thorne Pas. SW13 74 E2
Thorne Rd. SW8 67 E7
Thorne St. SW13 74 E3
Thorneloe Gdns., 101 G5
  Croy.
Thornes Clo., Beck. 96 C3
Thornet Wd. Rd., 97 D3
  Brom.
Thorney Cres. SW11 66 G7
Thorney Hedge Rd. 65 B4
  W4
Thorney St. SW1 20 A1
Thorney St. SW1 67 E4
Thorneycroft Clo., 90 C6
  Walt.
Thornfield Ave. NW7 39 B1
Thornfield Rd. W12 65 H2
Thornford Rd. SE13 78 C5
Thorngate Rd. W9 57 D4
Thorngrove Rd. E13 60 H1
Thornham Gro. E15 51 D5
Thornham St. SE10 69 B6
Thornhaugh Ms. WC1 7 J6
Thornhaugh St. WC1 11 J1
Thornhaugh St. WC1 58 D5
Thornhill Ave. SE18 70 H7
Thornhill Ave., Surb. 98 H2
Thornhill Bri. Wf. N1 58 F1
  Caledonian Rd.
Thornhill Cres. N1 49 F7
Thornhill Gdns. E10 51 B2
Thornhill Gdns., Bark. 52 H7
Thornhill Gro. N1 49 F7
  Lofting Rd.
Thornhill Ho. N1 49 G7
  Thornhill Rd.
Thornhill Rd. E10 51 B2
Thornhill Rd. N1 49 G7
Thornhill Rd., Croy. 94 J7
Thornhill Rd., Surb. 98 H2
Thornhill Sq. N1 49 F7
Thornlaw Rd. SE27 85 G4
Thornley Clo. N17 33 D7
Thornley Dr., Har. 45 H2
Thornley Pl. SE10 69 E5
  Caradoc St.
Thornsbeach Rd. SE6 87 C1
Thornsett Pl. SE20 95 E2
Thornsett Rd. SE20 95 E2
Thornsett Rd. SW18 84 E1
Thornside, Edg. 30 A6
  High St.
Thornton Ave. SW2 85 D1
Thornton Ave. W4 65 E4
Thornton Ave., Croy. 94 F6
Thornton Ct. SW20 93 A5
Thornton Dene, Beck. 96 A2
Thornton Gdns. SW12 85 D1
Thornton Gro., Pnr. 28 G6
Thornton Hill SW19 84 B7
Thornton Pl. W1 10 J1
Thornton Pl. W1 57 J5
Thornton Rd. E11 51 D2
Thornton Rd. N18 33 F3
Thornton Rd. SW12 76 D7
Thornton Rd. SW14 74 D3
Thornton Rd. SW19 84 A6
Thornton Rd., Barn. 23 B3
Thornton Rd., Belv. 71 H4
Thornton Rd., Brom. 87 G5
Thornton Rd., Cars. 100 G1
Thornton Rd., Croy. 94 F7
Thornton Rd., Ilf. 52 E4
Thornton Rd., Th.Hth. 94 G5
Thornton Rd. E. SW19 84 A6
  Thornton Rd.
Thornton Row, 94 G5
  Th.Hth.
  London Rd.
Thornton St. SW9 76 G2
Thornton Way NW11 39 E5
Thorntons Fm. Ave., 53 J1
  Rom.
Thorntree Rd. SE7 70 A5
Thornville St. SE8 78 A1
Thornwood Clo. E18 51 E5
Thornwood Rd. SE13 78 E5
Thorogood Gdns. E15 51 E5
Thorold Rd. N22 32 E7
Thorold Rd., Ilf. 52 E2
Thorparch Rd. SW8 76 D1
Thorpe Clo. W10 57 B6
  Cambridge Gdns.

Thorpe Clo., Orp. 104 H2
Thorpe Cres. E17 41 J2
Thorpe Hall Rd. E17 42 C1
Thorpe Rd. E6 61 C1
Thorpe Rd. E7 51 F4
Thorpe Rd. E17 42 C2
Thorpe Rd. N15 41 B6
Thorpe Rd., Bark. 52 G7
Thorpe Rd., Kings.T. 82 H7
Thorpebank Rd. W12 65 G1
Thorpedale Gdns., Ilf. 43 D4
Thorpedale Rd. N4 49 E2
Thorpewood Ave. 86 E2
  SE26
Thorsden Way SE19 86 B4
  Oaks Ave.
Thorverton Rd. NW2 48 B3
Thoydon Rd. E3 59 H2
Thrale Rd. SW16 85 C4
Thrale St. SE1 **17 A2**
Thrale St. SE1 67 J1
Thrasher Clo. E8 59 C1
  Stean St.
Thrawl St. E1 **13 G2**
Thrawl St. E1 59 C5
Threadneedle St. EC2 **13 C4**
Threadneedle St. EC2 59 A6
Three Colt St. E14 59 J6
Three Colts La. E2 59 E4
Three Cors., Bexh. 80 H2
Three Cups Yd. WC1 **12 D2**
Three Kings Rd. 94 A3
  Mitch.
Three Kings Yd. W1 **11 D5**
Three Kings Yd. W1 58 B7
Three Mill La. E3 60 C3
Three Oak La. SE1 **17 F3**
Threshers Pl. W11 57 B7
Thriffwood SE26 86 F3
Thrift Fm. La., Borwd. 22 C2
Thrigby Rd., Chess. 98 J6
Throckmorten Rd. 60 H6
  E16
Throgmorton Ave. **13 C3**
  EC2
Throgmorton Ave. 59 A6
  EC2
Throgmorton St. EC2 **13 C3**
Throgmorton St. EC2 59 A6
Throwley Clo. SE2 71 C3
Throwley Rd., Sutt. 100 E5
Throwley Way, Sutt. 100 E4
Thrupp Clo., Mitch. 94 B2
Thrush Grn., Har. 36 G4
Thrush St. SE17 **20 J3**
Thruxton Way SE15 21 G7
Thurbarn Rd. SE6 87 B5
Thurland Rd. SE16 **17 H5**
Thurland Rd. SE16 68 D3
Thurlby Clo., Har. 37 D6
  Gayton Rd.
Thurlby Clo., Wdf.Grn. 35 C5
Thurlby Rd. SE27 85 G4
Thurlby Rd., Wem. 46 G6
Thurleigh Ave. SW12 76 A6
Thurleigh Rd. SW12 75 J7
Thurleston Ave., 93 B5
  Mord.
Thurlestone Ave. 31 J6
  N12
Thurlestone Ave., Ilf. 52 J4
Thurlestone Rd. SE27 85 G3
Thurloe Clo. SW7 **18 G1**
Thurloe Clo. SW7 66 H4
Thurloe Pl. SW7 **18 F1**
Thurloe Pl. SW7 66 G4
Thurloe Pl. Ms. SW7 **18 F1**
Thurloe Sq. SW7 **18 G1**
Thurloe Sq. SW7 66 H4
Thurloe St. SW7 **18 F1**
Thurloe St. SW7 66 G4
Thurlow Clo. E4 34 B6
  Higham Sta. Ave.
Thurlow Gdns., Ilf. 35 G6
Thurlow Gdns., Wem. 46 G5
Thurlow Hill SE21 85 H7
Thurlow Pk. Rd. SE21 85 H1
Thurlow Rd. NW3 48 G5
Thurlow Rd. W7 64 D2
Thurlow St. SE17 **21 C3**
Thurlow St. SE17 68 A5
Thurlow Ter. NW5 49 A5
Thurlston Rd., Ruis. 45 A3
Thurnby Ct., Twick. 82 B3
Thursland Rd., Sid. 89 E5
Thursley Cres., Croy. 103 C7
Thursley Gdns. 84 A2
  SW19

Thursley Rd. SE9 88 C3
Thurso St. SW17 84 G4
Thurstan Rd. SW20 83 H7
Thurston Rd. SE13 78 B2
Thurston Rd., Sthl. 54 F6
Thurtle Rd. E2 59 C1
Thwaite Clo., Erith 71 J6
Thyer Clo., Orp. 104 F4
  Isabella Dr.
Thyra Gro. N12 31 E6
Tibbatts Rd. E3 60 B4
Tibbenham Wk. E13 60 F2
  Whitelegg Rd.
Tibberton Sq. N1 49 J7
  Popham Rd.
Tibbets Clo. SW19 84 A1
Tibbets Cor. SW19 75 A7
Tibbet's Ride SW15 75 A7
Tiber Gdns. N1 58 F1
  Treaty St.
Ticehurst Clo., Orp. 89 A7
  Grovelands Rd.
Ticehurst Rd. SE23 86 H2
Tickford Clo. SE2 71 C2
  Ampleforth Rd.
Tidal Basin Rd. E16 60 F7
Tidenham Gdns., 102 B3
  Croy.
Tideswell Rd. SW15 74 J4
Tideswell Rd., Croy. 103 A3
Tideway Clo., Rich. 82 E4
  Locksmeade Rd.
Tidey St. E3 60 A5
Tidford Rd., Well. 79 J2
Tidworth Rd. E3 60 A4
Tiepigs La., Brom. 103 F1
Tiepigs La., W.Wick. 103 E2
Tierney Rd. SW2 76 E7
Tiger La., Brom. 96 H4
Tiger Way E5 50 E4
Tilbrook Rd. SE3 78 J3
Tilbury Clo. SE15 **21 G7**
Tilbury Rd. E6 61 C2
Tilbury Rd. E10 42 C7
Tildesley Rd. SW15 74 J6
Tile Fm. Rd., Orp. 104 G3
Tile Kiln La. N6 49 C1
  Winchester Rd.
Tile Kiln La. N13 32 J5
Tile Kiln La., Bex. 89 J2
Tile Yd. E14 59 J6
  Commercial Rd.
Tilehurst Rd. SW18 84 G1
Tilehurst Rd., Sutt. 100 B5
Tileyard Rd. N7 49 E7
Tilford Ave., Croy. 103 C7
Tilford Gdns. SW19 84 A1
Tilia Rd. E5 50 E4
  Clarence Rd.
Tiller Rd. E14 69 A3
Tillett Clo. NW10 47 C6
Tillett Sq. SE16 68 H2
  Howland Way
Tillett Way E2 **9 H3**
Tilling Rd. NW2 47 J1
Tilling Way, Wem. 46 G4
Tillingbourne Gdns. 39 C3
  N3
Tillingbourne Grn., 97 J4
  Orp.
Tillingbourne Way 39 C3
  N3
  Tillingbourne Gdns.
Tillingham Way N12 31 D4
Tillman St. E1 59 E6
  Bigland St.
Tilloch St. N1 49 F7
  Carnoustie Dr.
Tillotson Rd. N9 33 C2
Tillotson Rd., Har. 28 H7
Tillotson Rd., Ilf. 43 D7
Tilney Ct. EC1 **9 A5**
Tilney Dr., Buck.H. 34 G2
Tilney Gdns. N1 50 A6
  Baxter Rd.
Tilney Rd., Dag. 53 F6
Tilney Rd., Sthl. 63 C4
Tilney St. W1 **15 C1**
Tilney St. W1 67 A1
Tilson Gdns. SW2 76 E7
Tilson Ho. SW2 76 E7
  Tilson Gdns.
Tilson Rd. N17 41 D1
Tilt Yd. App. SE9 79 C6
Tilton St. SW6 66 B6
Tiltwood, The W3 56 C7
  Acacia Rd.
Timber Clo., Chis. 97 D2

Timber Mill Way 76 D3
  SW4
Timber Pond Rd. 68 G1
  SE16
Timber St. EC1 **8 J5**
Timbercroft, Epsom 99 E4
Timbercroft La. SE18 70 H6
Timberdene NW4 39 A2
Timberdene Ave., Ilf. 43 F1
Timberland Rd. E1 59 E6
Timberwharf Rd. N16 41 D6
Times Sq., Sutt. 100 E5
  High St.
Timothy Clo. SW4 76 C5
  Elms Rd.
Timothy Clo., Bexh. 80 E5
Timothy Rd. E3 59 J5
Timsbury Wk. SW15 83 G1
Tindal St. SW9 76 H1
Tinderbox All. SW14 74 D3
Tine Rd., Chig. 35 H5
Tinsley Rd. E1 59 F5
Tintagel Cres. SE22 77 C4
Tintagel Dr., Stan. 29 G4
Tintagel Gdns. SE22 77 C4
  Oxonian St.
Tintern Ave. NW9 38 B3
Tintern Clo. SW15 75 B5
Tintern Clo. SW19 84 F7
Tintern Gdns. N14 24 E7
Tintern Path NW9 38 E6
  Ruthin Clo.
Tintern Rd. N22 40 J1
Tintern Rd., Cars. 100 G1
Tintern St. SW4 76 E4
Tintern Way, Har. 45 H1
Tinto Rd. E16 60 G4
Tinwell Ms., Borwd. 22 C5
  Cranes Way
Tinworth St. SE11 **20 B3**
Tinworth St. SE11 67 E5
Tippetts Clo., Enf. 24 J1
Tipthorpe Rd. SW11 76 A3
Tipton Dr., Croy. 102 B4
Tiptree Clo. E4 34 C3
Tiptree Cres., Ilf. 43 D3
Tiptree Dr., Enf. 25 A4
Tiptree Est., Ilf. 43 D3
Tiptree Rd., Ruis. 45 B4
Tirlemont Rd., 101 J7
  S.Croy.
Tirrell Rd., Croy. 94 J6
Tisbury Ct. W1 **11 H5**
Tisbury Rd. SW16 94 E2
Tisdall Pl. SE17 **21 C2**
Tisdall Pl. SE17 68 A4
Titchborne Row W2 **10 H4**
Titchfield Rd. NW8 57 J1
Titchfield Rd., Cars. 100 G1
Titchfield Wk., Cars. 93 G7
  Titchfield Rd.
Titchwell Rd. SW18 75 G7
Tite St. SW3 **18 J4**
Tite St. SW3 66 J6
Tithe Barn Clo., 91 J1
  Kings.T.
Tithe Barn Way, Nthlt. 54 B2
Tithe Clo. NW7 38 G1
Tithe Fm. Ave., Har. 45 G3
Tithe Fm. Clo., Har. 45 G3
Tithe Wk. NW7 38 G1
Titley Clo. E4 34 A5
Titmuss Ave. SE28 82 B7
Titmuss St. W12 65 H2
Tiverton Ave., Ilf. 43 D3
Tiverton Dr. SE9 88 F1
Tiverton Rd. N15 41 A6
Tiverton Rd. N18 33 B5
Tiverton Rd. NW10 57 A1
Tiverton Rd., Edg. 37 J2
Tiverton Rd., Houns. 72 J2
Tiverton Rd., Ruis. 45 A3
Tiverton Rd., Th.Hth. 94 G5
  Willett Rd.
Tiverton Rd., Wem. 55 H2
Tiverton St. SE1 **16 J6**
Tiverton St. SE1 67 J3
Tiverton Way, Chess. 98 F5
Tivoli Ct. SE16 68 J2
Tivoli Gdns. SE18 70 B4
Tivoli Rd. N8 40 D5
Tivoli Rd. SE27 85 J5
Tivoli Rd., Houns. 72 E4
Tobacco Quay E1 59 E7
  Wapping La.
Tobago St. E14 69 A2
  Manilla St.
Tobin Clo. NW3 48 H7

Toby La. E1 59 H4
Todds Wk. N7 49 F2
  Andover Rd.
Token Yd. SW15 75 B4
  Montserrat Rd.
Tokenhouse Yd. EC2 **13 B3**
Tokyngton Ave., Wem. 47 A6
Toland Sq. SW15 74 G5
Tolcarne Dr., Pnr. 36 A2
Toley Ave., Wem. 37 H7
Tollbridge Clo. W10 57 B4
  Kensal Rd.
Tollesbury Gdns., Ilf. 43 G3
Tollet St. E1 59 G4
Tollgate Dr. SE21 86 B2
Tollgate Gdns. NW6 **6 A1**
Tollgate Gdns. NW6 57 E1
Tollgate Rd. E6 61 A5
Tollgate Rd. E16 60 J5
Tollhouse Way N19 49 C2
Tollington Pk. N4 49 F2
Tollington Pl. N4 49 F2
Tollington Rd. N7 49 F4
Tollington Way N7 49 E3
Tolmers Sq. NW1 **7 G5**
Tolpuddle St. N1 **8 E1**
Tolpuddle St. N1 58 G2
Tolsford Rd. E5 50 E5
Tolson Rd., Islw. 73 D3
Tolverne Rd. SW20 92 J1
Tolworth Clo., Surb. 99 B1
Tolworth Gdns., Rom. 44 D5
Tolworth Pk. Rd., 98 J2
  Surb.
Tolworth Ri. N., Surb. 92 D6
  Elmbridge Ave.
Tolworth Ri. S., Surb. 92 D6
  Warren Dr. S.
Tolworth Rd., Surb. 98 H2
Tom Coombs Clo. SE9 79 B4
  Well Hall Rd.
Tom Cribb Rd. SE28 70 F3
Tom Hood Clo. E15 51 D5
  Maryland St.
Tom Mann Clo., Bark. 61 H1
Tom Nolan Clo. E15 60 E2
  Manor Rd.
Tom Smith Clo. SE10 69 E6
  Maze Hill
Tomahawk Gdns., 54 D3
  Nthlt.
  Javelin Way
Tomlins Gro. E3 60 A3
Tomlins Orchard, 61 F1
  Bark.
Tomlins Ter. E14 59 J5
  Rhodeswell Rd.
Tomlins Wk. N7 49 F2
  Briset Way
Tomlinson Clo. E2 **9 G4**
Tomlinson Clo. E2 59 C3
Tomlinson Clo. W4 65 B5
  Oxford Rd. N.
Tompion St. EC1 **8 G4**
Tomswood Hill, Ilf. 35 E7
Tomswood Rd., Chig. 35 D6
Tonbridge Cres., Har. 37 H4
Tonbridge Ho. SE25 95 D3
Tonbridge Rd., 90 E4
  W.Mol.
Tonbridge St. WC1 **8 A3**
Tonbridge St. WC1 58 E3
Tonbridge Wk. WC1 **8 A3**
Tonfield Rd., Sutt. 100 C1
Tonge Clo., Beck. 96 A5
Tonsley Hill SW18 75 E5
Tonsley Pl. SW18 75 E5
Tonsley Rd. SW18 75 E5
Tonsley St. SW18 75 E5
Tonstall Rd., Mitch. 94 A2
Tony Cannell Ms. E3 59 J3
  Maplin St.
Tooke Clo., Pnr. 36 E1
Took's Ct. EC4 **12 E3**
Tooley St. SE1 **17 C1**
Tooley St. SE1 68 B1
Toorack Rd., Har. 37 A2
Tooting Bec Gdns. 85 D4
  SW16
Tooting Bec Rd. SW16 85 B4
Tooting Bec Rd. SW17 85 A3
Tooting Gro. SW17 84 H5
Tooting High St. 84 H6
  SW17
Tootswood Rd., 96 E5
  Brom.
Top Ho. Ri. E4 26 C7
  Parkhill Rd.

Top Pk., Beck. 96 E5
Topaz Wk. NW2 39 A7
Marble Dr.
Topcliffe Dr., Orp. 104 G5
Topham Sq. N17 40 J1
Topham St. EC1 8 E5
Topiary Sq., Rich. 73 J3
Topley St. SE9 79 A4
Topp Wk. NW2 47 J2
Topsfield Clo. N8 40 D5
Wolseley Rd.
Topsfield Par. N8 40 E5
Tottenham La.
Topsfield Rd. N8 40 E5
Topsham Rd. SW17 84 J3
Tor Gdns. W8 66 D2
Tor Rd., Well. 80 C1
Torbay Rd. NW6 48 C7
Torbay Rd., Har. 45 E2
Torbay St. NW1 49 B7
Hawley Rd.
Torbitt Way, Ilf. 43 J5
Aldborough Rd. N.
Torbridge Clo., Edg. 29 H7
Torbrook Clo., Bex. 80 E6
Torcross Dr. SE23 86 F2
Torcross Rd., Ruis. 45 B3
Tormead Clo., Sutt. 100 D6
Tormount Rd. SE18 70 H6
Toronto Ave. E12 52 C4
Toronto Rd. E11 51 D4
Toronto Rd., Ilf. 52 E1
Torquay Gdns., Ilf. 43 A4
Torquay St. W2 10 A2
Torr Rd. SE20 86 G7
Torre Wk., Cars. 100 H1
Torrens Rd. E15 51 F6
Torrens Rd. SW2 76 F5
Torrens Sq. E15 51 F6
Torrens St. EC1 8 F2
Torrens St. EC1 58 G2
Torriano Ave. NW5 49 D5
Torriano Cotts. NW5 49 C5
Torriano Ave.
Torriano Ms. NW5 49 D5
Torriano Ave.
Torridge Gdns. SE15 77 F4
Torridge Rd., Th.Hth. 94 H5
Torridon Rd. SE6 78 D7
Torridon Rd. SE13 78 E7
Torrington Ave. N12 31 G5
Torrington Clo. N12 31 G4
Torrington Clo., Esher 98 B6
Torrington Dr., Har. 45 H4
Torrington Dr., Loug. 27 F4
Torrington Gdns. N11 32 C6
Torrington Gdns., 55 F1
Grnf.
Torrington Gdns., 27 F4
Loug.
Torrington Gro. N12 31 H5
Torrington Pk. N12 31 F5
Torrington Pl. E1 17 J2
Torrington Pl. E1 68 D1
Torrington Pl. WC1 11 G1
Torrington Pl. WC1 58 D5
Torrington Rd. E18 42 G3
Torrington Rd., Dag. 53 F1
Torrington Rd., Esher 98 B6
Torrington Rd., Grnf. 55 F1
Torrington Sq. WC1 7 J6
Torrington Sq. WC1 58 D4
Torrington Sq., Croy. 95 A7
Tavistock Gro.
Torrington Way, 93 D7
Mord.
Torver Rd., Har. 37 B4
Torver Way, Orp. 104 G2
Torwood Rd. SW15 74 G5
Tothill St. SW1 15 H4
Tothill St. SW1 67 D2
Totnes Rd., Well. 71 B7
Totnes Wk. N2 39 G4
Tottenhall Rd. N13 32 G6
Tottenham Ct. Rd. W1 7 G6
Tottenham Ct. Rd. W1 58 C4
Tottenham Grn. E. 41 C4
N15
Tottenham La. N8 40 E5
Tottenham Ms. W1 11 G1
Tottenham Rd. N1 50 B6
Tottenham St. W1 11 G2
Tottenham St. W1 58 C5
Totterdown St. SW17 84 J4
Totteridge Common 30 G2
N20
Totteridge Grn. N20 31 D2
Totteridge La. N20 31 D2

Totteridge Village N20 31 B1
Totternhoe Clo., Har. 37 F5
Totton Rd., Th.Hth. 94 G3
Toulmin St. SE1 16 J4
Toulmin St. SE1 67 J2
Toulon St. SE5 20 J7
Toulon St. SE5 67 J7
Tournay Rd. SW6 66 C7
Toussaint Wk. SE16 17 J5
Tovil Clo. SE20 95 E2
Towcester Rd. E3 60 B4
Tower Bri. E1 17 F2
Tower Bri. E1 68 C1
Tower Bri. SE1 17 F2
Tower Bri. SE1 68 C1
Tower Bri. App. E1 17 F1
Tower Bri. App. E1 68 C1
Tower Bri. Rd. SE1 17 D6
Tower Bri. Rd. SE1 68 B3
Tower Clo. NW3 48 G5
Lyndhurst Rd.
Tower Clo. SE20 86 E7
Tower Clo., Ilf. 35 E6
Tower Clo., Orp. 104 J2
Tower Ct. WC2 12 A4
Tower Gdns. Rd. N17 40 J1
Tower Hamlets Rd. E7 51 F4
Tower Hamlets Rd. 42 A3
E17
Tower Hill EC3 13 F6
Tower Hill EC3 59 B7
Tower La., Wem. 46 G3
Main Dr.
Tower Ms. E17 42 A4
Tower Pl. EC3 13 E6
Tower Pt., Enf. 25 A4
Tower Ri., Rich. 73 H3
Jocelyn Rd.
Tower Rd. NW10 47 G7
Tower Rd., Belv. 71 J4
Tower Rd., Bexh. 80 G4
Tower Rd., Orp. 104 J2
Tower Rd., Twick. 82 C3
Tower Royal EC4 13 A5
Tower St. WC2 11 J4
Tower St. WC2 58 D6
Tower Ter. N22 40 F2
Mayes Rd.
Tower Vw., Croy. 95 G7
Towers Pl., Rich. 73 H5
Eton St.
Towers Rd., Pnr. 28 E7
Towers Rd., Sthl. 54 G4
Towfield Rd., Felt. 81 F2
Towing Path Wk. N1 58 D1
York Way
Town, The, Enf. 25 A3
Town Ct. Path N4 49 J1
Town Hall App. N16 50 B4
Milton Gro.
Town Hall App. Rd. 41 C4
N15
Town Hall Ave. W4 65 D5
Town Hall Rd. SW11 75 J3
Town Meadow, Brent. 64 G7
Town Quay, Bark. 61 E1
Town Rd. N9 33 E2
Towncourt Cres., Orp. 97 F5
Towncourt La., Orp. 97 G6
Towney Mead, Nthlt. 54 F2
Townholm Cres. W7 64 C3
Townley Ct. E15 51 F6
Townley Rd. SE22 77 B5
Townley Rd., Bexh. 80 F6
Townley St. SE17 21 B3
Townmead Rd. SW6 75 E3
Townmead Rd., Rich. 74 B2
Townsend Ave. N14 32 D4
Townsend Ind. Est. 56 C2
NW10
Townsend La. NW9 38 D7
Townsend Rd. N15 41 C5
Townsend Rd., Sthl. 63 E1
Townsend St. SE17 21 D1
Townsend St. SE17 68 A4
Townsend Yd. N6 49 A1
Townshend Clo., Sid. 89 B6
Townshend Est. NW8 6 G1
Townshend Rd. NW8 57 H2
Townshend Rd. NW8 57 H1
Townshend Rd., Chis. 88 E5
Townshend Rd., Rich. 73 J4
Townshend Ter., Rich. 73 J4
Townson Ave., Nthlt. 54 A3
Townson Way, Nthlt. 54 A2
Townson Ave.
Towpath Way, Croy. 95 C6
Towton Rd. SE27 85 J2

Toynbec Clo., Chis. 88 E4
Beechwood Ri.
Toynbee Rd. SW20 93 B1
Toynbee St. E1 13 F2
Toynbee St. E1 59 C5
Toyne Way N6 39 J6
Gaskell Rd.
Tracey Ave. NW2 47 J5
Tracy Ct., Stan. 29 F7
Tradescant Rd. SW8 67 E7
Trading Est. Rd. 56 C4
NW10
Trafalgar Ave. N17 33 B6
Trafalgar Ave. SE15 21 G4
Trafalgar Ave. SE15 68 C5
Trafalgar Ave., 100 A1
Wor.Pk.
Trafalgar Business 61 J4
Cen., Bark.
Trafalgar Clo. SE16 68 H4
Greenland Quay
Trafalgar Gdns. E1 59 G5
Trafalgar Gro. SE10 69 D6
Trafalgar Pl. E11 42 G4
Trafalgar Pl. N18 33 D5
Trafalgar Rd. SE10 69 D6
Trafalgar Rd. SW19 84 E7
Trafalgar Rd., Sutt. 98 C7
Trafalgar Sq. SW1 15 J1
Trafalgar Sq. WC2 15 J1
Trafalgar Sq. WC2 67 D1
Trafalgar St. SE17 21 B3
Trafalgar St. SE17 68 A5
Trafalgar Ter., Har. 46 B1
Nelson Rd.
Trafalgar Way E14 69 C1
Trafalgar Way, Croy. 101 F2
Trafford Clo. E15 51 B5
Trafford Clo., Ilf. 35 J6
Trafford Rd., Th.Hth. 94 F5
Tramway Ave. E15 51 E7
Tramway Ave. N9 25 E7
Tramway Path, Mitch. 93 H4
London Rd.
Tranby Pl. E9 50 G5
Homerton High St.
Tranley Ms. NW3 48 H5
Fleet Rd.
Tranmere Rd. N9 25 C7
Tranmere Rd. SW18 84 F1
Tranmere Rd., Twick. 72 H7
Tranquil Pas. SE3 78 F2
Tranquil Vale
Tranquil Vale SE3 78 E2
Transay Wk. N1 50 A6
Marquess Rd.
Transept St. NW1 10 H2
Transept St. NW1 57 H5
Transmere Clo., Orp. 97 F6
Transmere Rd., Orp. 97 F6
Transom Sq. E14 69 B4
Transport Ave., Brent. 64 D5
Tranton Rd. SE16 17 J5
Tranton Rd. SE16 68 D3
Traps Hill, Loug. 27 C3
Traps La., N.Mal. 92 E1
Travellers Way, 72 C2
Houns.
Travers Clo. E17 41 G1
Travers Rd. N7 49 G3
Treacy Clo. (Bushey), 28 J2
Wat.
Treadgold St. W11 57 A7
Treadway St. E2 59 E2
Treaty Rd., Houns. 72 H3
Hanworth Rd.
Treaty St. N1 58 F1
Trebeck St. W1 15 D1
Trebovir Rd. SW5 66 D5
Treby St. E3 59 J4
Trecastle Way N7 49 D4
Carleton Rd.
Tredegar Ms. E3 59 J3
Tredegar Ter.
Tredegar Rd. E3 59 J2
Tredegar Rd. N11 32 D7
Tredegar Sq. E3 59 J3
Tredegar Ter. E3 59 J3
Trederwen Rd. E8 59 D1
Tredown Rd. SE26 86 F5
Tredwell Clo., Brom. 97 B4
Tredwell Rd. SE27 85 H4
Tree Clo., Rich. 82 G1
Tree Rd. E16 60 J6
Treen Ave. SW13 74 E3
Treetops Clo. SE2 71 E5
Treeview Clo. SE19 95 B1

Treewall Gdns., Brom. 87 H4
Trefgarne Rd., Dag. 53 G2
Trefil Wk. N7 49 E4
Trefoil Rd. SW18 75 F5
Tregaron Ave. N8 40 E6
Tregaron Gdns., 92 E4
N.Mal.
Avenue Rd.
Tregarvon Rd. SW11 76 A4
Tregenna Ave., Har. 45 F4
Tregenna Clo. N14 24 C5
Tregenna Ct., Har. 45 G4
Trego Rd. E9 51 A7
Tregothnan Rd. SW9 76 E3
Tregunter Rd. SW10 18 B5
Tregunter Rd. SW10 66 F6
Trehearn Rd., Ilf. 35 G7
Treherne Ct. SW14 74 D3
Treherne Ct. SW9 76 G1
Eythorne Rd.
Treherne Ct. SW17 85 A4
Trehurst St. E5 50 H5
Trelawn Rd. E10 51 C3
Trelawn Rd. SW2 76 G5
Trelawney Est. E9 50 F6
Trelawney Rd., Ilf. 35 G7
Trellick Twr. W10 57 C4
Trellis Sq. E3 59 J3
Malmesbury Rd.
Treloar Gdns. SE19 86 A6
Hancock Rd.
Tremadoc Rd. SW4 76 D4
Tremaine Clo. SE4 78 A2
Tremaine Rd. SE20 95 E2
Trematon Pl., Tedd. 82 F7
Tremlett Gro. N19 49 C3
Tremlett Ms. N19 49 C3
Junction Rd.
Trenance Gdns., Ilf. 53 A3
Trench Yd. Ct., Mord. 93 E6
Green La.
Trenchard Ave., Ruis. 45 B4
Trenchard Clo., Stan. 29 D6
Trenchard Ct., Mord. 93 E6
Trenchard St. SE10 69 D5
Trenchold St. SW8 20 A6
Trenchold St. SW8 67 E6
Trenholme Clo. SE20 86 E7
Trenholme Rd. SE20 86 E7
Trenholme Ter. SE20 86 E7
Trenmar Gdns. NW10 56 H3
Trent Ave. W5 64 F3
Trent Gdns. N14 24 B6
Trent Rd. SW2 76 F5
Trent Rd., Buck.H. 34 H1
Trent Way, Wor.Pk. 99 J3
Trentbridge Clo., Ilf. 35 J6
Trentham St. SW18 84 D1
Trentwood Side, Enf. 24 F3
Treport St. SW18 75 E7
Tresco Clo., Brom. 87 E6
Tresco Gdns., Ilf. 53 A2
Tresco Rd. SE15 77 E4
Trescoe Gdns., Har. 36 E7
Tresham Cres. NW8 6 G5
Tresham Cres. NW8 57 H4
Tresham Rd., Bark. 52 J7
Tresham Wk. E9 50 F5
Churchill Wk.
Tressell Clo. N1 49 H7
Sebbon St.
Tressillian Cres. SE4 78 A3
Tressillian Rd. SE4 77 J4
Trestis Clo., Hayes 54 E5
Jolly's La.
Treswell Rd., Dag. 62 E1
Tretawn Gdns. NW7 30 E4
Tretawn Pk. NW7 30 E4
Trevanion Rd. W14 66 B4
Treve Ave., Har. 36 J7
Trevelyan Ave. E12 52 C4
Trevelyan Cres., Har. 37 G7
Trevelyan Gdns. 56 J1
NW10
Trevelyan Rd. E15 51 F4
Trevelyan Rd. SW17 84 H5
Treveris St. SE1 16 H2
Treverton St. W10 57 B4
Treville St. SW15 74 H7
Treviso Rd. SE23 86 G2
Farren Rd.
Trevithick St. SE8 69 A6
Trevone Gdns., Pnr. 36 E6
Trevor Clo., Barn. 23 G6
Trevor Clo., Brom. 96 F7
Trevor Clo., Har. 29 C7
Kenton La.
Trevor Clo., Islw. 73 C5

Trevor Clo., Nthlt. 54 C2
Trevor Gdns., Edg. 38 D1
Trevor Gdns., Nthlt. 54 C2
Trevor Pl. SW7 14 H4
Trevor Pl. SW7 66 H2
Trevor Rd. SW19 84 B7
Trevor Rd., Edg. 38 D1
Trevor Rd., Wdf.Grn. 34 G7
Trevor Sq. SW7 14 J4
Trevor Sq. SW7 66 H3
Trevor St. SW7 14 H4
Trevor St. SW7 66 H2
Trevose Rd. E17 42 D1
Trevose Way, Wat. 28 C3
Trewenna Dr., Chess. 98 G5
Trewince Rd. SW20 92 J1
Trewint St. SW18 84 F2
Trewsbury Rd. SE26 86 G5
Triandra Way, Hayes 54 D5
Triangle, The N13 32 G4
Triangle, The, Hmptn. 90 J1
High St.
Triangle, The, Kings.T. 92 C2
Kenley Rd.
Triangle Ct. E16 61 A5
Tollgate Rd.
Triangle Pas., Barn. 23 F4
Station Rd.
Triangle Pl. SW4 76 D4
Triangle Rd. E8 59 E1
Trident Gdns., Nthlt. 54 D3
Jetstar Way
Trident St. SE16 68 G4
Trident Wk. SE16 68 G4
Greenland Quay
Trident Way, Sthl. 63 B3
Trig La. EC4 12 J5
Trigon Rd. SW8 20 D7
Trigon Rd. SW8 67 F7
Trilby Rd. SE23 86 G2
Trimmer Wk., Brent. 64 H6
Netley Rd.
Trinder Gdns. N19 49 E1
Trinder Rd.
Trinder Rd. N19 49 E1
Trinder Rd., Barn. 22 J5
Tring Ave. W5 64 J1
Tring Ave., Sthl. 54 F6
Tring Ave., Wem. 47 A6
Tring Clo., Ilf. 43 G5
Trinidad St. E14 59 J7
Trinity Ave. N2 39 G3
Trinity Ave., Enf. 25 C6
Trinity Ch. Pas. SW13 65 H6
Trinity Ch. Rd. SW13 65 H6
Trinity Ch. Sq. SE1 17 A5
Trinity Ch. Sq. SE1 67 J3
Trinity Clo. E11 51 E2
Trinity Clo. NW3 48 G4
Hampstead High St.
Trinity Clo. SE13 78 D4
Wisteria Rd.
Trinity Clo., Brom. 104 B1
Trinity Clo., Houns. 72 E4
Trinity Cotts., Rich. 73 J3
Trinity Rd.
Trinity Ct. N1 50 B7
Downham Rd.
Trinity Ct. SE7 70 A4
Charlton La.
Trinity Cres. SW17 84 J2
Trinity Gdns. SW9 76 F4
Trinity Gro. SE10 78 C1
Trinity Ms. W10 57 A6
Cambridge Gdns.
Trinity Pl., Bexh. 80 F4
Trinity Ri. SW2 85 G1
Trinity Rd. N2 39 G3
Trinity Rd. N22 32 E7
Whittington Rd.
Trinity Rd. SW17 84 J2
Trinity Rd. SW18 75 G5
Trinity Rd. SW19 84 D6
Trinity Rd., Ilf. 43 F3
Trinity Rd., Rich. 73 J3
Trinity Rd., Sthl. 63 E1
Trinity Sq. EC3 13 E6
Trinity Sq. EC3 59 B7
Trinity St. E16 60 G5
Vincent St.
Trinity St. SE1 17 A4
Trinity St. SE1 67 J2
Trinity St., Enf. 24 J2
Trinity Wk. NW3 48 F6
Trinity Way E4 33 J6
Trinity Way W3 56 E7
Trio Pl. SE1 17 A4
Tristan Sq. SE3 78 E3
Tristram Clo. E17 42 D3
Tristram Rd., Brom. 87 F4
Triton Sq. NW1 7 F5
Triton Sq. NW1 58 C4
Tritton Ave., Croy. 101 E4
Tritton Rd. SE21 86 A3
Triumph Ho., Bark. 62 A3
Triumph Rd. E6 61 C6
Trojan Ct. NW6 48 B7
Willesden La.
Trojan Way, Croy. 101 F3
Troon St. E1 59 H6
White Horse Rd.
Trosley Rd., Belv. 71 G6
Trossachs Rd. SE22 77 B5
Trothy Rd. SE1 21 J2
Trott Rd. N10 31 J7
Trott St. SW11 75 G1
Trotwood, Chig. 35 G6
Troughton Rd. SE7 69 H5
Troutbeck Rd. SE14 77 H1
Trouville Rd. SW4 76 C6
Trowbridge Est. E9 50 J6
Trowbridge Rd. E9 50 J6
Trowlock Ave., Tedd. 82 F6
Trowlock Way, Tedd. 82 G6
Troy Ct. SE18 70 E4
Troy Rd. SE19 86 A6
Troy Town SE15 77 D3
Truesdale Rd. E6 61 C6
Trulock Ct. N17 33 D7
Trulock Rd. N17 33 D7
Truman Clo., Edg. 30 B7
Pavilion Way
Truman's Rd. N16 50 B5
Trump St. EC2 13 A4
Trumpers Way W7 64 B2
Trumpington Rd. E7 51 F4
Trundle St. SE1 16 J3
Trundlers Way (Bushey), Wat. 29 B1
Trundleys Rd. SE8 68 G5
Trundleys Ter. SE8 68 G4
Truro Gdns., Ilf. 43 B7
Truro Rd. E17 41 J4
Truro Rd. N22 32 E7
Truro St. NW5 49 A6
Truslove Rd. SE27 85 G5
Trussley Rd. W6 65 J3
Trust Wk. SE21 85 H1
Peabody Hill
Tryfan Clo., Ilf. 43 A5
Tryon St. SW3 18 J3
Tryon St. SW3 66 J5
Trystings Clo., Esher 98 D6
Tuam Rd. SE18 70 G6
Tubbenden Clo., Orp. 104 H2
Tubbenden Dr., Orp. 104 G4
Tubbenden La., Orp. 104 G4
Tubbenden La. S., Orp. 104 G5
Tubbs Rd. NW10 56 F2
Tudor Ave., Hmptn. 81 G6
Tudor Ave., Wor.Pk. 99 H3
Tudor Clo. N6 40 C7
Tudor Clo. NW3 48 H5
Tudor Clo. NW7 30 G6
Tudor Clo. NW9 47 C2
Tudor Clo. SW2 76 F6
Elm Pk.
Tudor Clo., Chess. 98 H5
Tudor Clo., Chig. 35 D4
Tudor Clo., Chis. 97 C1
Tudor Clo., Pnr. 36 A5
Tudor Clo., Sutt. 100 B6
Tudor Clo., Wall. 101 C7
Tudor Clo., Wdf.Grn. 34 H5
Tudor Ct. E17 41 J7
Tudor Ct., Felt. 81 C4
Tudor Ct. N., Wem. 47 A5
Tudor Ct. S., Wem. 47 A5
Tudor Cres., Enf. 24 J1
Tudor Cres., Ilf. 35 E6
Tudor Dr., Kings.T. 82 G5
Tudor Dr., Mord. 93 A6
Tudor Est. NW10 56 B3
Tudor Gdns. NW9 47 C2
Tudor Gdns. SW13 74 E3
Treen Ave.
Tudor Gdns. W3 56 A5
Tudor Gdns., Twick. 82 C1
Tudor Gdns., W.Wick. 103 C3
Tudor Gro. E9 50 F7
Tudor Gro. N20 31 H3
Church Cres.
Tudor Pl. W1 11 H3
Tudor Pl., Mitch. 84 H7
Tudor Rd. E4 34 B6
Tudor Rd. E6 60 J1
Tudor Rd. E9 59 E1
Tudor Rd. N9 25 E7
Tudor Rd. SE19 86 C7
Tudor Rd. SE25 95 E5
Tudor Rd., Bark. 61 J1
Tudor Rd., Barn. 23 D3
Tudor Rd., Beck. 96 B3
Tudor Rd., Hmptn. 81 G7
Tudor Rd., Har. 37 A2
Tudor Rd., Houns. 73 A4
Tudor Rd., Kings.T. 83 A7
Tudor Rd., Pnr. 36 C2
Tudor Rd., Sthl. 54 E7
Tudor St. EC4 12 F5
Tudor St. EC4 58 G7
Tudor Wk., Bex. 80 E6
Tudor Way N14 32 D1
Tudor Way W3 65 A2
Tudor Way, Orp. 97 G6
Tudor Well Clo., Stan. 29 E5
Tudway Rd. SE3 78 H3
Tufnell Pk. Rd. N7 49 D4
Tufnell Pk. Rd. N19 49 C4
Tufter Rd., Chig. 35 J5
Tufton Gdns., W.Mol. 90 H2
Tufton Rd. E4 34 A4
Tufton St. SW1 16 A6
Tufton St. SW1 67 D3
Tugela Rd., Croy. 95 A6
Tugela St. SE6 86 J2
Tugmutton Clo., Orp. 104 E4
Acorn Way
Tuilerie St. E2 9 H1
Tulip Clo., Croy. 102 G1
Tulip Clo., Hmptn. 81 F6
Partridge Rd.
Tulip Ct., Pnr. 36 C3
Tulse Clo., Beck. 96 C3
Tulse Hill SW2 76 G6
Tulse Hill Est. SW2 76 G6
Tulsemere Rd. SE27 85 J2
Tumbling Bay, Walt. 90 A6
Tummons Gdns. SE25 95 B2
Tuncombe Rd. N18 33 B4
Tunis Rd. W12 65 H1
Tunley Rd. NW10 56 E1
Tunley Rd. SW17 85 A1
Tunmarsh La. E13 60 H3
Tunnan Leys E6 61 D6
Horse Leaze
Tunnel Ave. SE10 69 D2
Tunnel Gdns. N11 32 C7
Tunnel Rd. SE16 68 F2
St. Marychurch St.
Tunstall Clo., Orp. 104 H4
Tunstall Rd. SW9 76 F4
Tunstall Rd., Croy. 102 B1
Tunstall Wk., Brent. 64 H6
Ealing Rd.
Tunstock Way, Belv. 71 E3
Tunworth Clo. NW9 38 C6
Tunworth Cres. SW15 74 F6
Turenne Clo. SW18 75 F4
Turin Rd. N9 25 F7
Turin St. E2 9 H4
Turin St. E2 59 D3
Turkey Oak Clo. SE19 95 B1
Turk's Head Yd. EC1 12 G1
Turks Row SW3 19 A3
Turks Row SW3 66 J5
Turle Rd. N4 49 F1
Turle Rd. SW16 94 E2
Turlewray Clo. N4 49 F1
Turley Clo. E15 60 E1
Turnagain La. EC4 12 G3
Turnage Rd., Dag. 53 E1
Turnberry Ct., Wat. 28 C3
Turnberry Quay E14 69 B3
Pepper St.
Turnberry Way, Orp. 104 G1
Turnchapel Ms. SW4 76 B3
Cedars Rd.
Turner Ave. N15 41 B4
Turner Ave., Mitch. 93 J1
Turner Ave., Twick. 81 J3
Turner Clo. NW11 39 E6
Turner Dr. NW11 39 E6
Turner Rd. E17 42 C3
Turner Rd., Edg. 37 H2
Turner Rd., N.Mal. 92 D7
Turner St. E1 59 E5
Turner St. E16 60 F6
Turners Meadow Way, Beck. 95 J1
Turners Rd. E3 59 J5
Turners Way, Croy. 101 G2
Turners Wd. NW11 48 F1
Turneville Rd. W14 66 C6
Turney Rd. SE21 76 J7
Turnham Grn. Ter. W4 65 E4
Turnham Grn. Ter. Ms. W4 65 E4
Turnham Grn. Ter.
Turnham Rd. SE4 77 H5
Turnmill St. EC1 8 F6
Turnmill St. EC1 58 G4
Turnpike Clo. SE8 68 J7
Amersham Vale
Turnpike Ho. EC1 8 H4
Turnpike La. N8 40 F4
Turnpike La., Sutt. 100 F5
Turnpike Link, Croy. 102 B2
Turnpin La. SE10 69 C6
Turnston Clo. NW9 38 E2
Kestrel Clo.
Turnstone Clo. E13 60 G3
Turpentine La. SW1 19 E4
Turpin Way N19 49 D2
Elthorne Rd.
Turpin Way, Wall. 101 B7
Turpington Clo., Brom. 97 B6
Turpington La., Brom. 97 B7
Turpins La., Wdf.Grn. 35 C5
Turquand St. SE17 21 A2
Turret Gro. SW4 76 C3
Turton Rd., Wem. 46 H5
Turville St. E2 9 G5
Tuscan Rd. SE18 70 G5
Tuskar St. SE10 69 E5
Tustin Est. SE15 68 F6
Tuttlebee La., Buck.H. 34 G2
Tweedale Ct. E15 51 C5
Tweeddale Rd., Cars. 100 G1
Tweedmouth Rd. E13 60 H2
Tweedy Rd., Brom. 96 G1
Tweezer's All. WC2 12 E5
Twelvetrees Cres. E3 60 C4
Twentyman Clo., Wdf.Grn. 34 G5
Twickenham Bri., Rich. 73 F5
Twickenham Bri., Twick. 73 F5
Twickenham Clo., Croy. 101 F3
Twickenham Gdns., Grnf. 46 D5
Twickenham Gdns., Har. 29 B7
Twickenham Rd. E11 51 D2
Twickenham Rd., Felt. 81 F3
Twickenham Rd., Islw. 73 D5
Twickenham Rd., Rich. 73 F5
Twickenham Rd., Tedd. 82 D4
Twickenham Trd. Est., Twick. 73 C6
Twilley St. SW18 75 E7
Twine Ct. E1 59 F7
Twineham Grn. N12 31 D4
Tillingham Way
Twining Ave., Twick. 81 J3
Twinn Rd. NW7 31 B6
Twisden Rd. NW5 49 B4
Twybridge Way NW10 47 C7
Twyford Abbey Rd. NW10 55 J3
Twyford Ave. N2 39 J3
Twyford Ave. W3 56 A7
Twyford Cres. W3 65 A1
Twyford Pl. WC2 12 C3
Twyford Rd., Cars. 100 G1
Twyford Rd., Har. 45 H1
Twyford Rd., Ilf. 52 F5
Twyford St. N1 58 F1
Tyas Rd. E16 60 F4
Tybenham Rd. SW19 93 C3
Tyberry Rd., Enf. 25 E3
Tyburn La., Har. 37 B7
Tyburn Way W1 11 A5
Tycehurst Hill, Loug. 27 C4
Tye La., Orp. 104 F5
Tyers Est. SE1 17 D3
Tyers Est. SE1 68 B2
Tyers Gate SE1 17 D4
Tyers St. SE11 20 C4
Tyers St. SE11 67 F5
Tyers Ter. SE11 20 C4
Tyers Ter. SE11 67 F5
Tyeshurst Clo. SE2 71 E5
Tylecroft Rd. SW16 94 E2

Tylehurst Gdns., Ilf.	52	F5
Tyler Clo. E2	**9**	**F1**
Tyler Clo. E2	59	C2
Tyler St. SE10	69	E5
Tylers Clo., Loug.	27	B7
Tyler's Ct. W1	**11**	**H4**
Tylers Gate, Har.	37	H6
Tylers Path, Cars.	100	J4
Rochester Way		
Tylney Ave. SE19	86	C5
Tylney Rd. E7	51	J4
Tylney Rd., Brom.	97	A2
Tynan Clo., Felt.	81	A1
Sandycombe Rd.		
Tyndale Ct. E14	69	B5
Tyndale La. N1	49	H7
Upper St.		
Tyndale Ter. N1	49	H7
Canonbury La.		
Tyndall Rd. E10	51	C2
Tyndall Rd., Well.	79	J3
Tyne St. E1	**13**	**G3**
Tyneham Rd. SW11	76	A2
Tynemouth Rd. N15	41	C4
Tynemouth Rd., Mitch.	85	A7
Tynemouth St. SW6	75	F2
Type St. E2	59	G2
Tyrawley Rd. SW6	75	E1
Tyrell Clo., Har.	46	B4
Tyrell Ct., Cars.	100	J4
Tyrell Sq., Mitch.	93	H1
Tyrols Rd. SE23	86	G1
Wastdale Rd.		
Tyron Way, Sid.	88	H4
Tyrone Rd. E6	61	C2
Tyrrel Way NW9	38	F7
Tyrrell Ave., Well.	80	A5
Tyrrell Rd. SE22	77	D4
Tyrwhitt Rd. SE4	78	A3
Tysoe St. EC1	**8**	**E4**
Tyson Rd. SE23	77	F7
Tyssen Pas. E8	50	C6
Tyssen St.		
Tyssen Rd. N16	50	C3
Tyssen St. E8	50	C6
Tyssen St. N1	**9**	**E2**
Tytherton Rd. N19	49	D3

U

Uamvar St. E14	60	B5
Uckfield Gro., Mitch.	94	A1
Udall St. SW1	**19**	**G2**
Udney Pk. Rd., Tedd.	82	D5
Uffington Rd. NW10	56	G1
Uffington Rd. SE27	85	G4
Ufford Clo., Har.	28	H7
Ufford Rd.		
Ufford Rd., Har.	28	H7
Ufford St. SE1	**16**	**F3**
Ufford St. SE1	67	G2
Ufton Gro. N1	50	A7
Ufton Rd. N1	50	A7
Ujima Ct. SW16	85	E4
Sunnyhill Rd.		
Ullathorne Rd. SW16	85	C4
Ulleswater Rd. N14	32	E4
Ullin St. E14	60	C5
St. Leonards Rd.		
Ullswater Clo. SW15	83	D4
Ullswater Clo., Brom.	87	E7
Ullswater Ct., Har.	36	G7
Oakington Ave.		
Ullswater Cres. SW15	83	D4
Ullswater Rd. SE27	85	H2
Ullswater Rd. SW13	65	G7
Ulster Gdns. N13	32	J4
Ulster Pl. NW1	**7**	**D6**
Ulster Ter. NW1	**7**	**D5**
Ulundi Rd. SE3	69	E6
Ulva Rd. SW15	75	A5
Ravenna Rd.		
Ulverscroft Rd. SE22	77	C5
Ulverston Rd. E17	42	D2
Ulverstone Rd. SE27	85	H2
Ulysses Rd. NW6	48	C5
Umbria St. SW15	74	G6
Umfreville Rd. N4	40	H6
Undercliff Rd. SE13	78	A3
Underhill, Barn.	23	D5
Underhill Pas. NW1	58	B1
Camden High St.		
Underhill Rd. SE22	77	D5
Underhill St. NW1	58	B1
Camden High St.		
Underne Ave. N14	32	B2
Undershaft EC3	**13**	**D4**

Undershaft EC3	59	B6
Undershaw Rd., Brom.	87	F3
Underwood, Croy.	103	C5
Underwood, The SE9	88	C2
Underwood Rd. E1	**9**	**H6**
Underwood Rd. E1	59	D4
Underwood Rd. E4	34	B5
Underwood Rd., Wdf.Grn.	34	J7
Underwood Row N1	**9**	**A3**
Underwood Row N1	58	J3
Underwood St. N1	**9**	**A3**
Underwood St. N1	58	J3
Undine Rd. E14	69	B4
Undine St. SW17	84	J5
Uneeda Dr., Grnf.	55	A1
Union Cotts. E15	51	E7
Welfare Rd.		
Union Ct. EC2	**13**	**D3**
Union Ct., Rich.	73	H5
Eton St.		
Union Dr. E1	59	H4
Soleway St.		
Union Gro. SW8	76	D2
Union Rd. N11	32	D6
Union Rd. SW4	76	D2
Union Rd. SW8	76	D2
Union Rd., Brom.	97	A5
Union Rd., Croy.	94	J7
Union Rd., Nthlt.	54	G2
Union Rd., Wem.	46	H6
Union Sq. N1	58	J1
Union St. E15	60	C1
Union St. SE1	**16**	**H2**
Union St. SE1	67	H1
Union St., Barn.	23	B4
Union St., Kings.T.	91	G2
Union Wk. E2	**9**	**E3**
Unity Clo. NW10	47	G6
Unity Clo. SE19	85	J5
Crown Dale		
Unity Way SE18	70	A3
Unity Wf. SE1	**17**	**G3**
University Clo. NW7	30	F7
University Pl., Erith	71	H7
Belmont Rd.		
University Rd. SW19	84	G6
University St. WC1	**7**	**G6**
University St. WC1	58	C4
Unwin Clo. SE15	**21**	**H6**
Unwin Clo. SE15	68	D6
Unwin Rd. SW7	**14**	**E5**
Unwin Rd., Islw.	73	B3
Upbrook Ms. W2	**10**	**D4**
Upcerne Rd. SW10	66	F7
Upchurch Clo. SE20	86	E7
Upcroft Ave., Edg.	30	C5
Updale Rd., Sid.	88	J4
Upfield, Croy.	102	E2
Upfield Rd. W7	55	C4
Upgrove Manor Way SW2	76	G7
Trinity Ri.		
Uphall Rd., Ilf.	52	E5
Upham Pk. Rd. W4	65	E4
Uphill Dr. NW7	30	E5
Uphill Dr. NW9	38	C5
Uphill Gro. NW7	30	E4
Uphill Rd. NW7	30	E4
Upland Rd. E13	60	F4
Sutton Rd.		
Upland Rd. SE22	77	D5
Upland Rd., Bexh.	80	F3
Upland Rd., S.Croy.	102	A5
Upland Rd., Sutt.	100	G6
Uplands, Beck.	96	A2
Uplands, The, Loug.	27	C3
Uplands, The, Ruis.	45	A1
Uplands Ave. E17	41	G2
Blackhorse La.		
Uplands Business Pk. E17	41	G3
Uplands Clo. SW14	74	B5
Monroe Dr.		
Uplands End, Wdf.Grn.	35	B7
Uplands Pk. Rd., Enf.	24	G3
Uplands Rd. N8	40	F5
Uplands Rd., Barn.	32	A1
Uplands Rd., Rom.	44	D3
Uplands Rd., Wdf.Grn.	35	B7
Uplands Way N21	24	G5
Upnor Way SE17	**21**	**E3**
Uppark Dr., Ilf.	43	F6
Upper Abbey Rd., Belv.	71	F4

Upper Addison Gdns. W14	66	B2
Upper Bardsey Wk. N1	49	J6
Marquess Est.		
Upper Belgrave St. SW1	**15**	**C5**
Upper Belgrave St. SW1	67	A3
Upper Berkeley St. W1	10	J4
Upper Berkeley St. W1	57	J6
Upper Beulah Hill SE19	95	B1
Upper Brighton Rd., Surb.	91	G6
Upper Brockley Rd. SE4	77	J2
Upper Brook St. W1	**11**	**B6**
Upper Brook St. W1	58	A7
Upper Butts, Brent.	64	F6
Upper Caldy Wk. N1	49	J6
Marquess Est.		
Upper Camelford Wk. W11	57	B6
Lancaster Rd.		
Upper Cavendish Ave. N3	39	D3
Upper Cheyne Row SW3	**18**	**G6**
Upper Cheyne Row SW3	66	H6
Upper Clapton Rd. E5	50	E1
Upper Clarendon Wk. W11	57	B6
Lancaster Rd.		
Upper Dengie Wk. N1	58	J1
Popham Rd.		
Upper Elmers End Rd., Beck.	95	H4
Upper Fm. Rd., W.Mol.	90	F4
Upper Fosters NW4	38	J5
New Brent St.		
Upper Grn. E., Mitch.	93	J2
Upper Grn. W., Mitch.	93	J2
Upper Grenfell Wk. W11	57	A7
Whitchurch Rd.		
Upper Grosvenor St. W1	**11**	**B6**
Upper Grosvenor St. W1	58	A7
Upper Grotto Rd., Twick.	82	C2
Upper Grd. SE1	**16**	**E1**
Upper Grd. SE1	67	G1
Upper Gro. SE25	95	B4
Upper Gro. Rd., Belv.	71	F6
Upper Gulland Wk. N1	49	J6
Marquess Est.		
Upper Ham Rd., Rich.	82	G4
Upper Handa Wk. N1	50	A6
Marquess Est.		
Upper Harley St. NW1	**7**	**C6**
Upper Harley St. NW1	58	A4
Upper Hawkwell Wk. N1	58	J1
Popham Rd.		
Upper Hitch, Wat.	28	E1
Upper Holly Hill Rd., Belv.	71	H5
Upper James St. W1	**11**	**G5**
Upper John St. W1	**11**	**G5**
Upper Lismore Wk. N1	49	J6
Marquess Est.		
Upper Mall W6	65	G5
Upper Marsh SE1	**16**	**D5**
Upper Marsh SE1	67	F2
Upper Montagu St. W1	**10**	**J1**
Upper Montagu St. W1	57	J5
Upper Mulgrave Rd., Sutt.	100	B7
Upper N. St. E14	60	A5
Upper Palace Rd., E.Mol.	90	J3
Upper Pk., Loug.	27	A4
Upper Pk. Rd. N11	32	B5
Upper Pk. Rd. NW3	48	J6
Upper Pk. Rd., Belv.	71	H4
Upper Pk. Rd., Brom.	96	H1
Upper Pk. Rd., Kings.T.	83	A6
Upper Phillimore Gdns. W8	66	D2

Upper Ramsey Wk. N1	50	A6
Marquess Est.		
Upper Rawreth Wk. N1	58	J1
Popham Rd.		
Upper Richmond Rd. SW15	74	F4
Upper Richmond Rd. W. SW14	74	D4
Upper Richmond Rd. W., Rich.	74	A4
Upper Rd. E13	60	G3
Upper Rd., Wall.	101	D5
Upper St. Martin's La. WC2	**12**	**A5**
Upper St. Martin's La. WC2	58	E7
Upper Selsdon Rd., S.Croy.	102	B7
Upper Sheppey Wk. N1	49	J7
Marquess Est.		
Upper Sheridan Rd., Belv.	71	G4
Coleman Rd.		
Upper Shirley Rd., Croy.	102	F2
Upper Sq., Islw.	73	D3
North St.		
Upper St. N1	49	H6
Upper Sunbury Rd., Hmptn.	90	E1
Upper Sutton La., Houns.	63	G7
Upper Tachbrook St. SW1	**19**	**G1**
Upper Tachbrook St. SW1	67	C4
Upper Tail, Wat.	28	E3
Upper Talbot Wk. W11	57	B6
Lancaster Rd.		
Upper Teddington Rd., Kings.T.	82	F7
Upper Ter. NW3	48	F3
Upper Thames St. EC4	**12**	**H5**
Upper Thames St. EC4	58	J7
Upper Tollington Pk. N4	40	G7
Upper Tooting Pk. SW17	84	J2
Upper Tooting Rd. SW17	84	J4
Upper Town Rd., Grnf.	54	H4
Upper Tulse Hill SW2	76	F7
Upper Vernon Rd., Sutt.	100	G5
Upper Walthamstow Rd. E17	42	D4
Upper Wickham La., Well.	80	B3
Upper Wimpole St. W1	**11**	**C1**
Upper Wimpole St. W1	58	A5
Upper Woburn Pl. WC1	**7**	**J4**
Upper Woburn Pl. WC1	58	D3
Upperton Rd., Sid.	88	J5
Upperton Rd. E. E13	60	J3
Inniskilling Rd.		
Upperton Rd. W. E13	60	J3
Uppingham Ave., Stan.	37	E1
Upsdell Ave. N13	32	G6
Upstall St. SE5	76	H1
Upton Ave. E7	51	G7
Upton Clo., Bex.	80	F6
Upton Ct. SE20	86	F7
Blean Gro.		
Upton Dene, Sutt.	100	E7
Upton Gdns., Har.	37	E5
Upton La. E7	51	H6
Upton Pk. Rd. E7	51	H7
Upton Rd. N18	33	D5
Upton Rd. SE18	70	F6
Upton Rd., Bex.	80	E4
Upton Rd., Houns.	72	G3
Upton Rd., Th.Hth.	95	A2
Upton Rd. S., Bex.	80	F6
Upway N12	31	H7
Upwood Rd. SE12	78	G6
Upwood Rd. SW16	94	A1

Urlwin St. SE5	**20 J6**	Valentine Rd. E9	50 G6
Urlwin St. SE5	67 J6	Valentine Rd., Har.	45 J3
Urlwin Wk. SW9	76 G1	**Valentine Row SE1**	**16 G4**
Urmston Dr. SW19	84 B1	Valentines Clo., Ilf.	52 E1
Ursula St. SW11	75 H1	Valerian Way E15	60 E3
Urswick Gdns., Dag.	53 E7	Valeswood Rd., Brom.	87 F5
Urswick Rd.		Valetta Gro. E13	60 G2
Urswick Rd. E9	50 F5	Valetta Rd. W3	65 E2
Urswick Rd., Dag.	53 D7	Valette St. E9	50 E6
Usborne Ms. SW8	**20 D7**	Valiant Clo., Nthlt.	54 D3
Usborne Ms. SW8	67 F7	*Ruislip Rd.*	
Usher Rd. E3	59 J2	Valiant Clo., Rom.	44 G2
Usk Rd. SW11	75 F4	Valiant Ho. SE7	69 J5
Usk St. E2	59 G3	Valiant Path NW9	30 E7
Utopia Village NW1	58 A1	*Blundell Rd.*	
Chalcot Rd.		Valiant Way E6	61 C5
Uvedale Rd., Dag.	53 G3	**Vallance Rd. E1**	**13 J1**
Uvedale Rd., Enf.	25 A5	Vallance Rd. E1	59 D4
Uverdale Rd. SW10	66 F7	**Vallance Rd. E2**	**9 J1**
Uxbridge Gdns., Felt.	81 D2	Vallance Rd. E2	59 D3
Marlborough Rd.		Vallance Rd. N22	40 C2
Uxbridge Rd. W3	65 A1	Vallentin Rd. E17	42 C4
Uxbridge Rd. W5	55 J7	Valley Ave. N12	31 G4
Uxbridge Rd. W7	64 C1	Valley Clo., Loug.	27 C6
Uxbridge Rd. W12	65 G1	Valley Clo., Pnr.	36 B2
Uxbridge Rd. W13	64 E1	*Alandale Dr.*	
Uxbridge Rd., Felt.	81 C1	Valley Dr. NW9	38 A6
Uxbridge Rd., Hmptn.	81 G4	Valley Flds. Cres., Enf.	24 G2
Uxbridge Rd., Har.	29 A7	Valley Gdns. SW19	84 G7
Uxbridge Rd., Hayes	54 A6	Valley Gdns., Wem.	46 J7
Uxbridge Rd., Stan.	29 C6	Valley Gro. SE7	69 J5
Uxbridge Rd.,	91 G4	Valley Hill, Loug.	27 B7
Kings.T.		Valley Link Est., Enf.	25 H6
Uxbridge Rd., Pnr.	36 C2	Valley Ms., Twick.	82 D2
Uxbridge Rd., Sthl.	63 G1	*Cross Deep*	
Uxbridge Rd., Stan.	29 C6	Valley Rd. SW16	85 F5
Uxbridge St. W8	66 D1	Valley Rd., Belv.	71 H4
Uxendon Cres., Wem.	46 H1	Valley Rd., Brom.	96 E2
Uxendon Hill, Wem.	46 J1	Valley Side E4	34 A2
		Valley Vw., Barn.	23 B6
V		Valley Wk., Croy.	102 F2
		Valleyfield Rd. SW16	85 F5
Valan Leas, Brom.	96 E3	Valliere Rd. NW10	56 G3
Valance Ave. E4	34 E1	Valliers Wd. Rd., Sid.	88 G1
Vale, The N10	40 A1	Vallis Way W13	55 D5
Vale, The N14	24 D7	Vallis Way, Chess.	98 G4
Vale, The NW11	48 A3	Valmar Rd. SE5	76 J1
Vale, The SW3	**18 E5**	Valnay St. SW17	84 J5
Vale, The SW3	66 G6	Valognes Ave. E17	41 H1
Vale, The W3	65 D1	Valonia Gdns. SW18	75 C6
Vale, The, Croy.	102 G2	Vambery Rd. SE18	70 F6
Vale, The, Felt.	72 B6	Van Dyck Ave., N.Mal.	92 D7
Vale, The, Houns.	63 E6	Vanbrough Cres.,	54 C1
Vale, The, Ruis.	45 C4	Nthlt.	
Vale, The, Sun.	81 A6	Vanbrugh Clo. E16	61 A5
Ashridge Way		*Fulmer Rd.*	
Vale, The, Wdf.Grn.	34 G7	Vanbrugh Dr., Walt.	90 C7
Vale Ave., Borwd.	22 B5	Vanbrugh Flds. SE3	69 F6
Vale Clo. N2	39 J3	Vanbrugh Hill SE3	69 F6
Church Vale		Vanbrugh Hill SE10	69 F6
Vale Clo. W9	**6 C4**	Vanbrugh Pk. SE3	69 F7
Vale Clo., Orp.	104 D4	Vanbrugh Pk. Rd. SE3	69 F7
Vale Ct. W9	**6 C4**	Vanbrugh Pk. Rd. W.	69 F7
Vale Cres. SW15	83 E3	SE3	
Vale Cft., Pnr.	36 E5	Vanbrugh Rd. W4	65 D3
Vale Dr., Barn.	23 C4	Vanbrugh Ter. SE3	78 F1
Vale End SE22	77 B4	Vanburgh Clo., Orp.	104 H1
Grove Vale		Vancouver Rd. SE23	86 H2
Vale Gro. N4	40 J7	Vancouver Rd., Edg.	38 B1
Vale Gro. W3	65 D1	Vancouver Rd., Hayes	54 B4
The Vale		Vancouver Rd., Rich.	82 F4
Vale La. W3	56 A5	Vanderbilt Rd. SW18	84 E1
Vale of Health NW3	48 G3	Vandome Clo. E16	60 H6
East Heath Rd.		**Vandon Pas. SW1**	**15 G5**
Vale Ri. NW11	48 C1	**Vandon St. SW1**	**15 G5**
Vale Rd. E7	51 H6	Vandon St. SW1	67 C3
Vale Rd. N4	40 J7	**Vandy St. EC2**	**9 D6**
Vale Rd., Brom.	97 D2	Vandyke Clo. SW15	75 A4
Vale Rd., Epsom	99 F4	Vandyke Cross SE9	79 B5
Vale Rd., Mitch.	94 D3	Vane Clo. NW3	48 G4
Vale Rd., Sutt.	100 E4	Vane Clo., Har.	37 J6
Vale Rd., Wor.Pk.	99 F3	**Vane St. SW1**	**19 G1**
Vale Rd. N., Surb.	98 H1	Vanessa Clo., Belv.	71 G5
Vale Rd. S., Surb.	98 H1	Vanguard Clo., Croy.	101 H1
Vale Row N5	49 H3	Vanguard Clo., Rom.	44 H2
Gillespie Rd.		Vanguard St. SE8	78 A1
Vale Royal N7	49 E7	Vanguard Way, Wall.	101 E7
Vale St. SE27	86 A3	Vanoc Gdns., Brom.	87 G4
Vale Ter. N4	40 J4	Vansittart Rd. E7	51 F4
Valence Ave., Dag.	53 D1	Vansittart St. SE14	68 H7
Valence Circ., Dag.	53 D3	Vanston Pl. SW6	66 D7
Valence Wd. Rd., Dag.	53 D3	Vant Rd. SW17	84 J5
Valencia Rd., Stan.	29 F4	Varcoe Rd. SE16	68 E5
Valentia Pl. SW9	76 G4	Varden Clo. W3	56 D6
Brixton Sta. Rd.		Varden St. E1	59 E6
Valentine Ave., Bex.	89 E2	Vardens Rd. SW11	75 G4
Valentine Ct. SE23	86 G2	Vardon Clo. N3	39 B1
Valentine Pl. SE1	**16 G3**	*Claremont Pk.*	
Valentine Pl. SE1	67 H2		

Varley Par. NW9	38 E4	Vermont Rd. SW18	75 E6
Varley Rd. E16	60 H6	Vermont Rd., Sutt.	100 E3
Varley Way, Mitch.	93 G2	Verney Gdns., Dag.	53 E4
Varna Rd. SW6	66 B7	**Verney Rd. SE16**	**21 J5**
Varna Rd., Hmptn.	90 H1	Verney Rd. SE16	68 D6
Varndell St. NW1	**7 F3**	Verney Rd., Dag.	53 E4
Varndell St. NW1	58 C3	Verney St. NW10	47 D3
Varsity Dr., Twick.	73 B5	Verney Way SE16	68 E5
Varsity Row SW14	74 C2	Vernham Rd. SE18	70 F6
William's La.		Vernon Ave. E12	52 C4
Vartry Rd. N15	41 A6	Vernon Ave. SW20	93 A2
Vassall Rd. SW9	67 G7	Vernon Ave., Wdf.Grn.	34 H7
Vauban Est. SE16	**17 G6**	Vernon Clo., Epsom	99 C6
Vauban Est. SE16	68 C3	Vernon Ct., Stan.	37 E1
Vauban St. SE16	**17 G6**	*Vernon Dr.*	
Vauban St. SE16	68 C3	Vernon Cres., Barn.	24 A6
Vaughan Ave. NW4	38 G5	Vernon Dr., Stan.	37 D1
Vaughan Ave. W6	65 F4	Vernon Ms. E17	41 J4
Vaughan Clo., Hmptn.	81 E6	*Vernon Rd.*	
Oak Ave.		Vernon Ms. W14	66 B4
Vaughan Gdns., Ilf.	43 C7	*Vernon St.*	
Vaughan Rd. E15	51 F6	**Vernon Pl. WC1**	**12 B2**
Vaughan Rd. SE5	76 J3	Vernon Pl. WC1	58 E5
Vaughan Rd., Har.	36 J7	**Vernon Ri. WC1**	**8 D3**
Vaughan Rd., T.Ditt.	91 E7	Vernon Ri. WC1	58 F3
Vaughan Rd., Well.	79 J2	Vernon Ri., Grnf.	46 A5
Vaughan St. SE16	68 J2	Vernon Rd. E3	59 J2
Vaughan Way E1	**13 H6**	Vernon Rd. E11	51 E1
Vaughan Way E1	59 D7	Vernon Rd. E15	51 E7
Vaughan Williams	69 A7	Vernon Rd. E17	41 J4
Clo. SE8		Vernon Rd. N8	40 G3
Watson's St.		Vernon Rd. SW14	74 D3
Vauxhall Bri. SE1	**20 A4**	Vernon Rd., Felt.	81 A3
Vauxhall Bri. SE1	67 E5	Vernon Rd., Ilf.	52 J1
Vauxhall Bri. SW1	**20 A4**	Vernon Rd., Sutt.	100 F5
Vauxhall Bri. SW1	67 E5	**Vernon Sq. WC1**	**8 D3**
Vauxhall Bri. Rd. SW1	**19 G1**	Vernon St. W14	66 B4
Vauxhall Bri. Rd. SW1	67 C3	Vernon Yd. W11	57 C7
Vauxhall Gdns.,	101 J6	*Portobello Rd.*	
S.Croy.		Veroan Rd., Bexh.	80 E2
Vauxhall Gdns. Est.	**20 D4**	Verona Dr., Surb.	98 H2
SE11		Verona Rd. E7	51 G7
Vauxhall Gdns. Est.	67 F5	*Upton La.*	
SE11		Veronica Gdns.	94 C1
Vauxhall Gro. SW8	**20 B5**	SW16	
Vauxhall Gro. SW8	67 F6	Veronica Rd. SW17	85 B3
Vauxhall St. SE11	**20 D4**	Veronique Gdns., Ilf.	43 F5
Vauxhall St. SE11	67 F5	Verran Rd. SW12	76 B7
Vauxhall Wk. SE11	**20 C3**	*Balham Gro.*	
Vauxhall Wk. SE11	67 F5	Versailles Rd. SE20	86 D7
Vawdrey Clo. E1	59 F4	Verulam Ave. E17	41 J6
Veals Mead, Mitch.	93 H1	**Verulam Bldgs. WC1**	**12 D1**
Vectis Gdns. SW17	85 B6	Verulam Rd., Grnf.	54 G4
Vectis Rd.		**Verulam St. WC1**	**12 E1**
Vectis Rd. SW17	85 B6	Verwood Rd., Har.	36 J2
Veda Rd. SE13	78 A4	Vesey Path E14	60 B6
Velde Way SE22	77 B5	*East India Dock Rd.*	
East Dulwich Gro.		Vespan Rd. W12	65 G2
Velletri Ho. E2	59 G2	Vesta Rd. SE4	77 H2
Mace St.		Vestris Rd. SE23	86 G2
Vellicoe Rd. E13	60 G4	Vestry Ms. SE5	77 B1
Jutland Rd.		Vestry Rd. E17	42 B4
Vellum Dr., Cars.	101 A3	Vestry Rd. SE5	77 B1
Venables Clo., Dag.	53 H4	**Vestry St. N1**	**9 B3**
Venables St. NW8	**6 F6**	Vestry St. N1	59 A3
Venables St. NW8	57 G4	Vevey St. SE6	86 J2
Vencourt Pl. W6	65 G4	Veysey Gdns., Dag.	53 G3
Venetia Rd. N4	40 H6	*Oglethorpe Rd.*	
Venetia Rd. W5	64 G2	Viaduct, The E18	42 G2
Venetian Rd. SE5	76 J2	Viaduct Pl. E2	59 E3
Venn St. SW4	76 C4	*Viaduct St.*	
Venner Rd. SE26	86 F6	Viaduct St. E2	59 E3
Ventnor Ave., Stan.	37 E1	Vian St. SE13	78 B3
Ventnor Dr. N20	31 E3	Vibart Gdns. SW2	76 F7
Ventnor Gdns., Bark.	52 H6	Vibart Wk. N1	58 E1
Ventnor Rd. SE14	68 G7	*Outram Pl.*	
Ventnor Rd., Sutt.	100 E7	Vicarage Ave. SE3	69 G7
Venture Clo., Bex.	80 E7	Vicarage Clo., Erith	71 J6
Venue St. E14	60 C5	Vicarage Clo., Nthlt.	54 F1
Venus Rd. SE18	70 C3	**Vicarage Ct. W8**	**14 A3**
Vera Ave. N21	24 G5	Vicarage Cres. SW11	75 G1
Vera Lynn Clo. E7	51 G4	Vicarage Dr. SW14	74 D5
Dames Rd.		Vicarage Dr., Bark.	52 F7
Vera Rd. SW6	75 B1	Vicarage Fm. Rd.,	72 E2
Verbena Clo. E16	60 F4	Houns.	
Cranberry La.		Vicarage Flds., Walt.	90 C6
Verbena Gdns. W6	65 G5	Vicarage Gdns. SW14	74 C5
Verdant La. SE6	87 E1	*Vicarage Rd.*	
Verdayne Ave., Croy.	102 G1	Vicarage Gdns. W8	66 D1
Verdun Rd. SE18	71 A6	*Vicarage Gate*	
Verdun Rd. SW13	65 G6	Vicarage Gdns.,	93 H3
Vere Rd., Loug.	27 F4	Mitch.	
Vere St. W1	**11 D4**	**Vicarage Gate W8**	**14 A3**
Vere St. W1	58 B6	Vicarage Gate W8	66 E1
Vereker Dr., Sun.	90 A3	Vicarage Gro. SE5	77 A1
Vereker Rd. W14	66 B5	Vicarage La. E6	61 C3
Verity Clo. W11	57 B6	Vicarage La. E15	51 E7
Vermont Rd. SE19	86 A6	Vicarage La., Chig.	35 F2

Vicarage La., Ilf.	52	G1
Vicarage Pk. SE18	70	F5
Vicarage Path N8	40	D7
Vicarage Rd. E10	42	A7
Vicarage Rd. E15	51	F7
Vicarage Rd. N17	33	D7
Vicarage Rd. NW4	38	G6
Vicarage Rd. SE18	70	F5
Vicarage Rd. SW14	74	D5
Vicarage Rd., Bex.	89	H1
Vicarage Rd., Croy.	101	G3
Vicarage Rd., Dag.	53	H7
Vicarage Rd., Kings.T.	91	G2
Vicarage Rd., Kings.T.	91	F1
(Hampton Wick)		
Vicarage Rd., Sutt.	100	E4
Vicarage Rd., Tedd.	82	D5
Vicarage Rd., Twick.	82	B2
Vicarage Rd., Twick.	72	J6
(Whitton)		
Vicarage Rd., Wdf.Grn.	35	B7
Vicarage Way NW10	47	D3
Vicarage Way, Har.	36	G7
Vicars Bri. Clo., Wem.	55	H2
Vicars Clo. E9	59	F1
Victoria Pk. Rd.		
Vicars Clo. E15	60	G1
Vicars Clo., Enf.	25	B2
Vicars Hill SE13	78	B4
Vicars Moor La. N21	24	G7
Vicars Oak Rd. SE19	86	B6
Vicars Wk., Dag.	53	B3
Viceroy Clo. N2	39	H4
Market Pl.		
Viceroy Ct. NW8	**6**	**H1**
Viceroy Rd. SW8	76	E1
Vickers Way, Houns.	72	E5
Victor Gro., Wem.	46	H7
Victor Rd. NW10	56	H2
Victor Rd. SE20	86	G7
Victor Rd., Har.	36	J3
Victor Rd., Tedd.	82	B4
Victor Vill. N9	33	A3
Victor Wk. NW9	38	E2
Booth Rd.		
Victoria Ave. E6	61	A1
Victoria Ave. EC2	**13**	**E2**
Victoria Ave. N3	39	C1
Victoria Ave., Barn.	23	G4
Victoria Rd.		
Victoria Ave., Houns.	72	F5
Victoria Ave., Surb.	91	G6
Victoria Ave., Wall.	101	A3
Victoria Ave., Wem.	47	B6
Victoria Ave., W.Mol.	90	G3
Victoria Clo., Barn.	23	G4
Victoria Clo., W.Mol.	90	G3
Victoria Ave.		
Victoria Cotts., Rich.	73	J1
Victoria Ct., Wem.	47	A6
Victoria Cres. N15	41	B5
Victoria Cres. SE19	86	B6
Victoria Cres. SW19	84	C7
Victoria Dock Rd. E16	60	G7
Victoria Dr. SW19	75	A7
Victoria Embk. EC4	**12**	**E5**
Victoria Embk. EC4	58	G7
Victoria Embk. SW1	**16**	**B3**
Victoria Embk. SW1	67	E2
Victoria Embk. WC2	**12**	**D6**
Victoria Embk. WC2	58	F7
Victoria Gdns. W11	66	D1
Victoria Gdns., Houns.	72	E1
Victoria Gro. N12	31	G5
Victoria Gro. W8	**14**	**C5**
Victoria Gro. W8	66	F3
Victoria Ind. Est.	56	E3
NW10		
Victoria La., Barn.	23	C4
Victoria Ms. NW6	57	D1
Victoria Ms. SW4	76	B4
Victoria Ri.		
Victoria Pk. E9	59	H1
Victoria Pk. Rd. E9	59	F1
Victoria Pk. Sq. E2	59	F3
Victoria Pas. NW8	**6**	**E5**
Victoria Pl., Rich.	73	G5
Victoria Pt. E13	60	G2
Victoria Rd.		
Victoria Ri. SW4	76	B3
Victoria Rd. E4	34	E1
Victoria Rd. E11	51	E4
Thorne Clo.		
Victoria Rd. E13	60	G2
Victoria Rd. E17	42	C2
Victoria Rd. E18	42	H2
Victoria Rd. N4	40	F7

Victoria Rd. N9	33	C3
Victoria Rd. N15	41	D4
Victoria Rd. N18	33	C4
Victoria Rd. N22	40	C1
Victoria Rd. NW4	38	J4
Victoria Rd. NW6	57	C2
Victoria Rd. NW7	30	F5
Victoria Rd. NW10	56	E4
Victoria Rd. SW14	74	D3
Victoria Rd. W3	56	D5
Victoria Rd. W5	55	E5
Victoria Rd. W8	**14**	**C4**
Victoria Rd. W8	66	F2
Victoria Rd., Bark.	52	E6
Victoria Rd., Barn.	23	G4
Victoria Rd., Bexh.	80	G4
Victoria Rd., Brom.	97	A5
Victoria Rd., Buck.H.	35	A2
Victoria Rd., Chis.	88	D5
Victoria Rd., Dag.	53	H5
Victoria Rd., Felt.	81	B1
Victoria Rd., Kings.T.	91	J2
Victoria Rd., Mitch.	84	H7
Victoria Rd., Ruis.	45	A1
Victoria Rd., Sid.	88	J3
Victoria Rd., Sthl.	63	F3
Victoria Rd., Surb.	91	G6
Victoria Rd., Sutt.	100	G5
Victoria Rd., Tedd.	82	D6
Victoria Rd., Twick.	73	E7
Victoria Rd., Wat.	28	H1
(Bushey)		
Victoria Sq. SW1	**15**	**E5**
Victoria Sta. SW1	**19**	**E1**
Victoria Sta. SW1	67	B4
Victoria Steps, Brent.	64	J6
Kew Bri. Rd.		
Victoria St. E15	51	E7
Victoria St. SW1	**15**	**F6**
Victoria St. SW1	67	C3
Victoria St., Belv.	71	F5
Victoria Ter. N4	49	G1
Victoria Ter., Har.	46	B1
Victoria Vill., Rich.	73	J3
Victoria Way SE7	69	H5
Victorian Gro. N16	50	B4
Victorian Rd. N16	50	B3
Victors Dr., Hmptn.	81	E6
Victors Way, Barn.	23	C3
Victory Ave., Mord.	93	F5
Victory Business	73	C4
Cen., Islw.		
Victory Pl. SE17	**21**	**A1**
Victory Pl. SE17	67	J4
Victory Pl. SE19	86	B6
Westow St.		
Victory Rd. SW19	84	F7
Victory Wk. SE8	78	A1
Ship St.		
Victory Way SE16	68	H2
Victory Way, Houns.	63	C5
Victory Way, Rom.	44	H2
Vidler Clo., Chess.	98	F6
Mansfield Rd.		
Vienna Clo., Ilf.	43	B2
Coburg Gdns.		
View, The SE2	71	E5
View Clo. N6	39	J7
View Clo., Chig.	35	G5
View Clo., Har.	37	A4
View Rd. N6	39	J7
Viewfield Clo., Har.	37	H7
Viewfield Rd. SW18	75	C6
Viewfield Rd., Bex.	89	C1
Viewland Rd. SE18	70	J5
Viga Rd. N21	24	G6
Vigilant Clo. SE26	86	D4
Vignoles Rd., Rom.	44	G7
Vigo St. W1	**11**	**F6**
Vigo St. W1	58	C7
Viking Clo. E3	59	H2
Selwyn Rd.		
Viking Ct. SW6	66	D6
Viking Pl. E10	50	J1
Viking Rd., Sthl.	54	E7
Viking Way, Erith	71	J3
Villa Rd. SW9	76	G3
Villa St. SE17	**21**	**C4**
Villa St. SE17	68	A5
Villacourt Rd. SE18	71	A7
Village, The SE7	69	J6
Village Arc. E4	34	D1
Station Rd.		
Village Clo. E4	34	C5
Village Clo. NW3	48	H5
Ornan Rd.		
Village Heights,	34	F5
Wdf.Grn.		

Village Ms. NW9	47	D2
Village Rd. N3	39	B2
Village Rd., Enf.	25	A7
Village Row, Sutt.	100	D7
Village Way NW10	47	D4
Village Way SE21	77	A6
Village Way, Beck.	96	A3
Village Way, Pnr.	36	E7
Village Way E., Har.	36	G7
Villas Rd. SE18	70	F4
Villiers Ave., Surb.	91	J5
Villiers Ave., Twick.	81	F1
Villiers Clo. E10	51	A2
Villiers Clo., Surb.	91	J4
Villiers Ct. N20	23	F7
Buckingham Ave.		
Villiers Path, Surb.	91	H5
Villiers Rd. NW2	47	G6
Villiers Rd., Beck.	95	G2
Villiers Rd., Islw.	73	B2
Villiers Rd., Kings.T.	91	J4
Villiers Rd., Sthl.	63	F1
Villiers St. WC2	**16**	**B1**
Villiers St. WC2	67	E1
Vincam Clo., Twick.	72	G7
Vince St. EC1	**9**	**C4**
Vince St. EC1	59	A3
Vincent Ave., Surb.	99	B1
Vincent Clo. SE16	68	H2
Vincent Clo., Barn.	23	E3
Vincent Clo., Brom.	96	H4
Vincent Clo., Ilf.	35	F6
Vincent Clo., Sid.	88	H1
Vincent Gdns. NW2	47	F3
Vincent Rd. E4	34	D6
Vincent Rd. N15	40	J4
Vincent Rd. N22	40	G2
Vincent Rd. SE18	70	E4
Vincent Rd. W3	65	C3
Vincent Rd., Croy.	95	B7
Vincent Rd., Dag.	53	E7
Vincent Rd., Houns.	72	D2
Vincent Rd., Islw.	73	A1
Vincent Rd.,	92	A3
Kings.T.		
Vincent Rd., Wem.	46	J7
Vincent Row, Hmptn.	81	J6
Vincent Sq. SW1	**19**	**H1**
Vincent Sq. SW1	67	C4
Vincent St. E16	60	F5
Vincent St. SW1	**19**	**H1**
Vincent St. SW1	67	D4
Vincent Ter. N1	**8**	**G1**
Vincent Ter. N1	58	H2
Vincents Path, Nthlt.	45	E6
Arnold Rd.		
Vine Clo., Surb.	91	J6
Vine Clo., Sutt.	100	F3
Vine Ct. E1	**13**	**J2**
Vine Ct., Har.	37	H6
Vine Gdns., Ilf.	52	F5
Vine Hill EC1	**8**	**E6**
Vine La. SE1	**17**	**E2**
Vine Pl. W5	64	H1
The Common		
Vine Pl., Houns.	72	H4
Vine Rd. E15	51	F7
Vine Rd. SW13	74	F3
Vine Rd., E.Mol.	90	J4
Vine Rd., Orp.	104	J6
Vine Sq. W14	66	C5
Vine St. EC3	**13**	**F4**
Vine St. W1	**11**	**G6**
Vine St., Rom.	44	J4
Vine St. Bri. EC1	**8**	**F6**
Vine St. Bri. EC1	58	G4
Vine Yd. SE1	**17**	**A4**
Vinegar All. E17	42	B4
Vinegar St. E1	68	E1
Reardon St.		
Vinegar Yd. SE1	**17**	**D3**
Viner Clo., Walt.	90	C6
Vineries, The N14	24	C5
Vineries, The, Enf.	25	B3
Vineries Bank NW7	30	H5
Vineries Clo., Dag.	53	G6
Heathway		
Vines Ave. N3	39	E1
Viney Rd. SE13	78	B3
Vineyard, The, Rich.	73	H5
Vineyard Ave. NW7	31	B7
Vineyard Clo. SE6	87	A1
Vineyard Hill Rd.	84	C4
SW19		
Vineyard Pas., Rich.	73	H5
Paradise Rd.		
Vineyard Path SW14	74	D3
Vineyard Rd., Felt.	81	A3

Vineyard Row,	91	F1
Kings.T.		
Vineyard Wk. EC1	**8**	**E5**
Vining St. SW9	76	G4
Viola Ave. SE2	71	B4
Viola Ave., Felt.	72	C6
Viola Sq. W12	56	F7
Violet Clo., Wall.	101	A1
Violet Gdns., Croy.	101	H5
Violet Hill NW8	**6**	**C2**
Violet Hill NW8	57	F2
Violet La., Croy.	101	H6
Violet Rd. E3	60	B4
Violet Rd. E17	42	A6
Violet Rd. E18	42	H2
Violet St. E2	59	E4
Three Colts La.		
Virgil Pl. W1	**10**	**J2**
Virgil St. SE1	**16**	**D5**
Virgil St. SE1	67	F3
Virginia Clo., N.Mal.	92	C4
Willow Rd.		
Virginia Gdns., Ilf.	43	F2
Virginia Rd. E2	**9**	**F4**
Virginia Rd. E2	59	C3
Virginia Rd., Th.Hth.	94	H1
Virginia St. E1	**13**	**J6**
Virginia St. E1	59	D7
Virginia Wk. SW2	76	F6
Beechdale Rd.		
Viscount Dr. E6	61	C5
Viscount Gro., Nthlt.	54	D3
Wayfarer Rd.		
Viscount St. EC1	**12**	**J1**
Vista, The SE9	79	A6
Vista, The, Sid.	88	J5
Langdon Shaw		
Vista Ave., Enf.	25	G2
Vista Dr., Ilf.	43	A5
Vista Way, Har.	37	H6
Vivian Ave. NW4	38	G5
Vivian Ave., Wem.	47	A5
Vivian Clo., Wat.	28	A1
Vivian Gdns., Wat.	28	A1
Vivian Gdns., Wem.	47	A5
Vivian Rd. E3	59	H2
Vivian Sq. SE15	77	E3
Scylla Rd.		
Vivian Way N2	39	G5
Vivien Clo., Chess.	98	H7
Vivienne Clo., Twick.	73	G6
Voce Rd. SE18	70	G7
Voewood Clo.,	92	F6
N.Mal.		
Volta Way, Croy.	101	F1
Voltaire Rd. SW4	76	D3
Voluntary Pl. E11	42	G6
Vorley Rd. N19	49	C2
Voss Ct. SW16	85	E6
Voss St. E2	**9**	**J4**
Voss St. E2	59	D3
Vulcan Clo., Wall.	101	F7
De Havilland Rd.		
Vulcan Gate, Enf.	24	G3
Vulcan Rd. SE4	77	J2
Vulcan Sq. E14	69	A4
Britannia Rd.		
Vulcan Ter. SE4	77	J2
Vulcan Way N7	49	F6
Vyne, The, Bexh.	80	H3
Vyner Rd. W3	56	D7
Vyner St. E2	59	E1
Vyse Clo., Barn.	22	J4

W

Wadding St. SE17	**21**	**B2**
Wadding St. SE17	68	A4
Waddington Clo., Enf.	25	B4
Waddington Rd. E15	51	D6
Waddington St. E15	51	D6
Waddington Way	85	J7
SE19		
Waddon Clo., Croy.	101	G3
Waddon Ct. Rd.,	101	G4
Croy.		
Waddon Marsh Way,	101	F1
Croy.		
Waddon New Rd.,	101	H3
Croy.		
Waddon Pk. Ave.,	101	G3
Croy.		
Waddon Rd., Croy.	101	G3
Waddon Way, Croy.	101	G6
Wade Rd. E16	60	J6
Leyes Rd.		
Wades Gro. N21	24	G7
Wades Hill N21	24	G6

Wades La., Tedd.	82	D5
High St.		
Wades Ms. N21	24	G7
Wades Hill		
Wades Pl. E14	60	B7
Wadeson St. E2	59	E2
Wadeville Ave., Rom.	44	F6
Wadeville Clo., Belv.	71	G5
Wadham Ave. E17	34	B7
Wadham Gdns. NW3	48	H7
Wadham Gdns., Grnf.	46	A6
Wadham Rd. E17	42	B1
Wadham Rd. SW15	75	B4
Wadhurst Clo. SE20	95	E2
Wadhurst Rd. SW8	76	C1
Wadhurst Rd. W4	65	D3
Wadley Rd. E11	42	E7
Wadsworth Clo., Enf.	25	G5
Falcon Rd.		
Wadsworth Clo., Grnf.	55	F2
Wadsworth Rd., Grnf.	55	E2
Wager St. E3	59	J4
Waggon Ms. N14	32	C1
Chase Side		
Waghorn Rd. E13	60	J1
Waghorn Rd., Har.	37	G3
Waghorn St. SE15	77	D3
Wagner St. SE15	68	F7
Wagtail Clo. NW9	38	E2
Swan Dr.		
Waights Ct., Kings.T.	91	H1
Wainfleet Ave., Rom.	44	J2
Wainford Clo. SW19	84	A1
Windlesham Gro.		
Wainwright Gro., Islw.	73	A4
Waite Davies Rd.	78	F7
SE12		
Waite St. SE15	**21**	**F5**
Waite St. SE15	68	C6
Waithman St. EC4	**12**	**G4**
Wakefield Gdns. SE19	86	B7
Wakefield Gdns., Ilf.	43	B6
Wakefield Ms. WC1	**8**	**B4**
Wakefield Rd. N11	32	D5
Wakefield Rd. N15	41	C5
Wakefield Rd., Rich.	73	G5
Wakefield St. E6	61	A1
Wakefield St. N18	33	D5
Wakefield St. WC1	**8**	**B4**
Wakefield St. WC1	58	E3
Wakeham St. N1	50	A6
Wakehams Hill, Pnr.	36	F3
Wakehurst Rd. SW11	75	H5
Wakelin Rd. E15	60	E2
Wakeling Rd. W7	55	C5
Templeman Rd.		
Wakeling St. E14	59	H6
Wakeman Rd. NW10	56	J3
Wakemans Hill Ave.	38	D5
NW9		
Wakering Rd., Bark.	52	F6
Wakerley Clo. E6	61	C6
Truesdale Rd.		
Wakley St. EC1	**8**	**G3**
Wakley St. EC1	58	H3
Walberswick St. SW8	67	E7
Walbrook EC4	**13**	**B5**
Walbrook EC4	59	A7
Walbrook Ho. N9	33	F2
Walburgh St. E1	59	E6
Bigland St.		
Walcorde Ave. SE17	**21**	**A2**
Walcot Rd., Enf.	25	J2
Walcot Sq. SE11	**20**	**F1**
Walcot Sq. SE11	67	G4
Walcott St. SW1	**19**	**G1**
Waldair Ct. E16	70	E2
Barge Ho. Rd.		
Waldeck Gro. SE27	85	H3
Waldeck Rd. N15	40	H4
Waldeck Rd. SW14	74	C3
Lower Richmond Rd.		
Waldeck Rd. W4	65	A6
Waldeck Rd. W13	55	E6
Waldeck Ter. SW14	74	C3
Lower Richmond Rd.		
Waldegrave Ave.,	82	C5
Tedd.		
Waldegrave Rd.		
Waldegrave Gdns.,	82	C2
Twick.		
Waldegrave Pk.,	82	C4
Twick.		
Waldegrave Rd. N8	40	G3
Waldegrave Rd. SE19	86	C7
Waldegrave Rd. W5	55	J7
Waldegrave Rd.,	97	B4
Brom.		

Waldegrave Rd., Dag.	53	C2
Waldegrave Rd.,	82	C4
Tedd.		
Waldegrave Rd.,	82	C4
Twick.		
Waldegrove, Croy.	102	C3
Waldemar Ave. SW6	75	B1
Waldemar Ave. W13	64	F1
Waldemar Rd. SW19	84	D5
Walden Ave. N13	32	J4
Walden Ave., Chis.	88	C4
Walden Clo., Belv.	71	F5
Walden Gdns.,	94	F4
Th.Hth.		
Walden Rd. N17	41	A1
Walden Rd., Chis.	88	C6
Walden St. E1	59	E6
Walden Way NW7	31	A6
Walden Way, Ilf.	35	H7
Waldenshaw Rd.	86	F1
SE23		
Waldo Clo. SW4	76	C5
Waldo Pl., Mitch.	84	H7
Waldo Rd. NW10	56	G3
Waldo Rd., Brom.	97	A3
Waldram Cres. SE23	86	F1
Waldram Pk. Rd. SE23	86	G1
Waldram Pl. SE23	86	F1
Waldrist Way, Erith	71	F2
Waldron Gdns., Brom.	96	D3
Waldron Ms. SW3	**18**	**F5**
Waldron Rd. SW18	84	F3
Waldron Rd., Har.	46	B1
Waldronhyrst,	101	H4
S.Croy.		
Waldrons, The, Croy.	101	H4
Waldrons Path,	101	J4
S.Croy.		
Bramley Hill		
Waleran Clo., Stan.	29	C6
Chenduit Way		
Walerand Rd. SE13	78	C2
Wales Ave., Cars.	100	H5
Wales Fm. Rd. W3	56	D5
Waley St. E1	59	H5
Walfield Ave. N20	23	E7
Walford Rd. N16	50	B4
Walfrey Gdns., Dag.	53	E7
Walham Gro. SW6	66	D7
Walham Ri. SW19	84	B6
Walham Yd. SW6	66	D7
Walham Gro.		
Walkden Rd., Chis.	88	D5
Walker Clo. N11	32	C4
Walker Clo. SE18	70	F4
Walker Clo. W7	64	B1
Walker Clo., Hmptn.	81	F6
Fearnley Cres.		
Walkers Ct. W1	**11**	**H5**
Walkers Pl. SW15	75	B3
Felsham Rd.		
Walkerscroft Mead	85	J1
SE21		
Walkford Way SE15	68	C7
Daniel Gdns.		
Walks, The, N2	39	G3
Wall End Rd. E6	52	D7
Wall St. N1	50	A6
Wallace Clo. SE28	62	D7
Haldane Rd.		
Wallace Cres., Cars.	100	J5
Wallace Rd. N1	49	J6
Wallace Way N19	49	D2
Giesbach Rd.		
Wallbutton Rd. SE4	77	H2
Wallcote Ave. NW2	48	A1
Waller Dr., Nthwd.	36	A2
Waller Rd. SE14	77	G1
Wallers Clo., Dag.	62	E1
Wallers Clo., Wdf.Grn.	35	C6
Waller's Hoppit, Loug.	27	B2
Wallflower St. W12	56	F7
Wallgrave Rd. SW5	**18**	**A1**
Wallgrave Rd. SW5	66	E4
Wallingford Ave. W10	57	A5
Wallington Rd., Ilf.	43	J7
Wallington Sq., Wall.	101	B6
Woodcote Rd.		
Wallis All. SE1	**17**	**A4**
Wallis Clo. SW11	75	G3
Wallis Rd. E9	50	J6
Wallis Rd., Sthl.	54	H6
Walliss Cotts. SW2	76	E7
Wallorton Gdns.	74	D4
SW14		
Wallwood Rd. E11	51	D1

Wallwood St. E14	59	J5
Walm La. NW2	47	J6
Walmar Clo., Barn.	23	G1
Walmer Clo. E4	34	B2
Walmer Clo., Orp.	104	G4
Tubbenden La. S.		
Walmer Clo., Rom.	44	H2
Walmer Gdns. W13	64	D2
Walmer Ho. N9	33	C1
Walmer Pl. W1	**10**	**J1**
Walmer Rd. W10	56	J6
Latimer Rd.		
Walmer Rd. W11	57	B7
Walmer Ter. SE18	70	F4
Walmer St. W1	**10**	**J1**
Walmgate Rd., Grnf.	55	E1
Walmington Fold N12	31	D6
Walnut Clo. SE8	68	J6
Clyde St.		
Walnut Clo., Cars.	100	J5
Walnut Clo., Ilf.	43	F4
Civic Way		
Walnut Ct. W5	64	H2
Walnut Gdns. E15	51	E4
Burgess Rd.		
Walnut Gro., Enf.	25	A5
Walnut Ms., Sutt.	100	F7
Walnut Tree Ave.,	93	H3
Mitch.		
Dearn Gdns.		
Walnut Tree Clo.	74	F1
SW13		
Walnut Tree Clo.,	97	F1
Chis.		
Walnut Tree Cotts.	84	B4
SW19		
Church Rd.		
Walnut Tree Rd. SE10	69	E5
Walnut Tree Rd.,	64	H6
Brent.		
Walnut Tree Rd., Dag.	53	D2
Walnut Tree Rd.,	63	F6
Houns.		
Walnut Tree Wk. SE11	**20**	**E1**
Walnut Tree Wk. SE11	67	G4
Walnut Way, Buck.H.	35	A3
Walnut Way, Ruis.	45	C6
Walpole Ave., Rich.	73	J2
Walpole Clo. W13	64	F2
Walpole Clo., Pnr.	28	G6
Walpole Cres., Tedd.	82	C5
Walpole Gdns. W4	65	C5
Walpole Gdns., Twick.	82	B2
Walpole Ms. NW8	57	G1
Queen's Gro.		
Walpole Pk. W5	64	F1
Walpole Pl., Tedd.	82	C5
Walpole Rd. E6	51	J7
Walpole Rd. E17	41	H4
Walpole Rd. E18	42	F1
Walpole Rd. N17	40	J3
(Downhills Way)		
Walpole Rd. N17	40	J2
(Lordship La.)		
Walpole Rd. SW19	84	G6
Walpole Rd., Brom.	97	A5
Walpole Rd., Croy.	102	A2
Walpole Rd., Surb.	91	H7
Walpole Rd., Tedd.	82	C5
Walpole Rd., Twick.	82	B2
Walpole St. SW3	**18**	**J3**
Walpole St. SW3	66	J5
Walrond Ave., Wem.	46	H5
Walsham Clo. N16	41	D7
Braydon Rd.		
Walsham Clo. SE28	62	D7
Walsham Rd. SE14	77	G2
Walsham Rd., Felt.	72	B7
Walsingham Gdns.,	99	E4
Epsom		
Walsingham Pk., Chis.	97	G2
Walsingham Rd. E5	50	D3
Walsingham Rd. W13	64	D1
Walsingham Rd., Enf.	25	A4
Walsingham Rd.,	93	J5
Mitch.		
Walsingham Wk.,	71	G6
Belv.		
Walt Whitman Clo.	76	H4
SE24		
Shakespeare Rd.		
Walter St. E2	59	G3
Walter St., Kings.T.	91	H1
Sopwith Way		
Walter Ter. E1	59	G6
Walter Wk., Edg.	30	C6
Walters Ho. SE17	**20**	**G6**
Walters Rd. SE25	95	B4

Walters Rd., Enf.	25	F5
Walters Way SE23	77	G6
Walters Yd., Brom.	96	G2
Walterton Rd. W9	57	C4
Waltham Ave. NW9	38	A6
Waltham Dr., Edg.	38	A2
Waltham Pk. Way E17	42	A1
Waltham Rd., Cars.	93	G7
Waltham Rd., Sthl.	63	E3
Waltham Rd.,	35	B6
Wdf.Grn.		
Waltham Way E4	33	J4
Walthamstow Ave. E4	33	H5
Walthamstow	42	C2
Business Cen. E17		
Waltheof Ave. N17	41	A1
Waltheof Gdns. N17	41	A1
Walton Ave., Har.	45	F5
Walton Ave., N.Mal.	92	F4
Walton Ave., Sutt.	100	B3
Walton Clo. E5	50	G3
Orient Way		
Walton Clo. NW2	47	H2
Walton Clo. SW8	**20**	**B7**
Walton Clo. SW8	67	E7
Walton Clo., Har.	37	A4
Walton Cres., Har.	45	F4
Walton Dr. NW10	47	D6
Mitchellbrook Way		
Walton Dr., Har.	37	A4
Walton Gdns. W3	56	B5
Walton Gdns., Wem.	46	H2
Walton Pl. SW3	**14**	**J5**
Walton Pl. SW3	66	J3
Walton Rd. E12	52	D4
Walton Rd. E13	60	J2
Walton Rd. N15	41	C4
Walton Rd., E.Mol.	90	E4
Walton Rd., Har.	37	A4
Walton Rd., Sid.	89	C2
Walton Rd., Walt.	90	C5
Walton Rd., W.Mol.	90	B4
Walton St. SW3	**18**	**H1**
Walton St. SW3	66	H4
Walton St., Enf.	25	H1
Walton Way W3	56	B5
Walton Way, Mitch.	94	C4
Walworth Pl. SE17	**21**	**A4**
Walworth Pl. SE17	67	J5
Walworth Rd. SE1	**20**	**J2**
Walworth Rd. SE1	67	J4
Walworth Rd. SE17	**20**	**J2**
Walworth Rd. SE17	67	J4
Walwyn Ave., Brom.	97	A3
Wanborough Dr.	83	H1
SW15		
Wandle Bank SW19	84	G7
Wandle Bank, Croy.	101	E3
Wandle Ct., Epsom	99	C4
Wandle Ct. Gdns.,	101	E3
Croy.		
Wandle Rd. SW17	84	H2
Wandle Rd., Croy.	101	J3
Wandle Rd., Croy.	101	E3
(Waddon)		
Wandle Rd., Mord.	93	F4
Wandle Rd., Wall.	101	B2
Wandle Side, Croy.	101	F3
Wandle Side, Wall.	101	B3
Wandle Way SW18	84	E1
Wandle Way, Mitch.	93	J5
Wandon Rd. SW6	66	E7
Wandsworth Bri. SW6	75	E3
Wandsworth Bri.	75	E3
SW18		
Wandsworth Bri. Rd.	75	E1
SW6		
Wandsworth Business	55	F2
Cen., Grnf.		
Wandsworth Common	75	J7
SW12		
Wandsworth Common	75	F5
N. Side SW18		
Wandsworth Common	75	F5
W. Side SW18		
Wandsworth High St.	75	D5
SW18		
Wandsworth Plain	75	D5
SW18		
Wandsworth Rd. SW8	**20**	**A5**
Wandsworth Rd. SW8	76	B3
Wangey Rd., Rom.	44	D7
Wanless Rd. SE24	76	J3
Wanley Rd. SE5	77	A4
Wanlip Rd. E13	60	H4
Wannock Gdns., Ilf.	35	E7
Wansbeck Rd. E9	50	J7
Wansdown Pl. SW6	**18**	**A7**

Wansey St. SE17 21 A2
Wansey St. SE17 67 J4
Wansford Pk., Borwd. 22 D4
Wansford Rd., Wdf.Grn. 42 J1
Wanstead Clo., Brom. 96 J2
Wanstead La., Ilf. 43 B6
Wanstead Pk. Ave. E12 52 A2
Wanstead Pk. Rd., Ilf. 43 B6
Wanstead Pl. E11 42 G6
Wanstead Rd., Brom. 96 J2
Wansunt Rd., Bex. 89 J1
Wantage Rd. SE12 78 F5
Wantz Rd., Dag. 53 H4
Wapping Dock St. E1 68 E1
Cinnamon St.
Wapping High St. E1 17 J2
Wapping High St. E1 68 D1
Wapping La. E1 59 E7
Wapping Wall E1 68 F1
Warbank La., Kings.T. 83 F7
Warbeck Rd. W12 65 H2
Warberry Rd. N22 40 F2
Warboys App., Kings.T. 83 B6
Warboys Cres. E4 34 C5
Warboys Rd., Kings.T. 83 B6
Warburton Clo., Har. 29 A6
Warburton Rd. E8 59 E1
Warburton Rd., Twick. 81 H1
Warburton Ter. E17 42 B2
Ward Rd. E15 60 D1
Ward Rd. N19 49 C3
Wardalls Gro. SE14 68 F7
Wardell Clo. NW7 30 E7
Wardell Fld. NW9 38 E1
Warden Ave., Har. 45 F1
Warden Rd. NW5 49 A6
Wardens Gro. SE1 16 J2
Wardle St. E9 50 G5
Wardley St. SW18 75 E7
Garratt La.
Wardo Ave. SW6 75 B1
Wardour Ms. W1 11 G4
Wardour St. W1 11 G3
Wardour St. W1 58 C6
Wardrobe Pl. EC4 12 H4
Wardrobe Ter. EC4 12 H5
Wards Rd., Ilf. 43 G7
Wareham Clo., Houns. 72 H4
Waremead Rd., Ilf. 43 E5
Warenford Way, Borwd. 22 A1
Warepoint Dr. SE28 70 G2
Warfield Rd. NW10 57 A3
Warfield Rd., Hmptn. 90 H1
Warfield Yd. NW10 57 A3
Warfield Rd.
Wargrave Ave. N15 41 C6
Wargrave Rd., Har. 45 J3
Warham Rd. N4 40 G5
Warham Rd., Har. 37 C2
Warham Rd., S.Croy. 101 H5
Warham St. SE5 20 H7
Warham St. SE5 67 H7
Waring Clo., Orp. 104 J6
Waring Dr., Orp. 104 J6
Waring Rd., Sid. 89 C6
Waring St. SE27 85 J4
Warkworth Gdns., Islw. 64 D7
Warkworth Rd. N17 33 A7
Warland Rd. SE18 70 G7
Warley Ave., Dag. 44 F7
Warley Ave., Hayes 54 A6
Warley Rd. N9 33 F2
Warley Rd., Hayes 54 A6
Warley Rd., Ilf. 43 D1
Warley Rd., Wdf.Grn. 34 H7
Warley St. E2 59 G3
Warlingham Rd., Th.Hth. 94 H4
Warlock Rd. W9 57 C4
Warlters Clo. N7 49 E4
Warlters Rd.
Warlters Rd. N7 49 E4
Warltersville Rd. N19 40 E7
Warmington Clo. E5 50 G3
Orient Way
Warmington Rd. SE24 76 J6
Warmington St. E13 60 G4
Barking Rd.
Warminster Gdns. SE25 95 D2
Warminster Rd. SE25 95 D3
Warminster Sq. SE25 95 D2
Warminster Rd.
Warminster Way, Mitch. 94 B1
Warndon St. SE16 68 F4
Warne Pl., Sid. 80 B6
Westerham Dr.
Warneford Rd., Har. 37 G3
Warneford St. E9 59 E1
Warner Ave., Sutt. 100 B2
Warner Clo. E15 51 E5
Warner Clo. NW9 38 F7
Warner Pl. E2 9 J2
Warner Pl. E2 59 D2
Warner Rd. E17 41 H4
Warner Rd. N8 40 D4
Warner Rd. SE5 76 J1
Warner Rd., Brom. 87 F7
Warner St. EC1 8 E6
Warner St. EC1 58 G4
Warner Yd. EC1 8 E6
Warners Clo., Wdf.Grn. 34 G5
Warners La., Kings.T. 82 G5
Warners Path, Wdf.Grn. 34 G5
Warnford Rd., Orp. 104 J5
Warnham Ct. Rd., Cars. 100 J7
Warnham Rd. N12 31 G5
Warple Ms. W3 65 E2
Warple Way
Warple Way W3 65 E2
Warren, The E12 52 B4
Warren, The, Hayes 54 A6
Warren, The, Houns. 63 F7
Warren, The, Wor.Pk. 99 D4
Warren Ave. E10 51 C3
Warren Ave., Brom. 87 E7
Warren Ave., Orp. 104 J5
Warren Ave., Rich. 74 B4
Warren Ave., S.Croy. 102 G7
Warren Clo. N9 25 G7
Warren Clo. SE21 76 J7
Lairdale Clo.
Warren Clo., Bexh. 80 G5
Pincott Rd.
Warren Clo., Wem. 46 G2
Warren Ct., Chig. 35 G4
Warren Cres. N9 25 C7
Warren Cutting, Kings.T. 83 D7
Warren Dr., Grnf. 54 H4
Warren Dr., Ruis. 36 D7
Warren Dr., The E11 42 J7
Warren Dr. N., Surb. 99 B1
Warren Dr. S., Surb. 99 C1
Warren Flds., Stan. 29 F4
Valencia Rd.
Warren Footpath, Twick. 82 F1
Warren Gdns. E15 51 D5
Ashton Rd.
Warren Gro., Borwd. 22 D4
Warren Hill, Loug. 26 J5
Warren Ho. E3 60 B3
Bromley High St.
Warren La. SE18 70 E3
Warren La., Stan. 29 C3
Warren Ms. W1 7 F6
Warren Pk., Kings.T. 83 C6
Warren Pk. Rd., Sutt. 100 G6
Warren Pl. E1 59 G6
Pitsea St.
Warren Pond Rd. E4 34 F1
Warren Ri., N.Mal. 92 D1
Warren Rd. E4 34 C2
Warren Rd. E10 51 C3
Warren Rd. E11 42 J6
Warren Rd. NW2 47 F2
Warren Rd. SW19 84 H6
Warren Rd., Bexh. 80 G5
Warren Rd., Brom. 103 G2
Warren Rd., Croy. 102 B1
Warren Rd., Ilf. 43 G5
Warren Rd., Kings.T. 83 C6
Warren Rd., Orp. 104 J5
Warren Rd., Sid. 89 C3
Warren Rd., Twick. 72 J6
Warren Rd., Wat. (Bushey) 28 J1
Warren St. W1 7 E6
Warren St. W1 58 C4
Warren Ter., Rom. 44 D4
Warren Wk. SE7 69 J6
Warren Way NW7 31 B6
Warren Wd. Clo., Brom. 103 F2
Holland Way
Warrender Rd. N19 49 C3
Warrender Way, Ruis. 36 A7
Warrens Shawe La., Edg. 30 B2
Warriner Gdns. SW11 75 J1
Warrington Cres. W9 6 C6
Warrington Cres. W9 57 F4
Warrington Gdns. W9 6 C6
Warrington Pl. E14 69 C1
Yabsley St.
Warrington Rd., Croy. 101 H3
Warrington Rd., Dag. 53 D2
Warrington Rd., Har. 37 B5
Warrington Rd., Rich. 73 G5
Warrington Sq., Dag. 53 D2
Warrington St. E13 60 G4
Doherty Rd.
Warrior Sq. E12 52 D4
Warsaw Clo., Ruis. 45 B6
Glebe Ave.
Warsdale Dr. NW9 38 D5
Mardale Dr.
Warspite Rd. SE18 70 A3
Warton Rd. E15 51 C7
Warwall E6 61 E6
Warwick Ave. W2 10 D1
Warwick Ave. W2 57 F5
Warwick Ave. W9 6 B6
Warwick Ave. W9 57 E4
Warwick Ave., Edg. 30 B3
Warwick Ave., Har. 45 F4
Warwick Clo., Barn. 23 G5
Warwick Clo., Bex. 80 F7
Warwick Clo., Hmptn. 81 J7
Warwick Ct. SE15 77 D2
Warwick Ct. WC1 12 D2
Warwick Cres. W2 10 C1
Warwick Cres. W2 57 F5
Warwick Dene W5 64 H1
Warwick Dr. SW15 74 H3
Warwick Est. W2 10 B2
Warwick Est. W2 57 E5
Warwick Gdns. N4 40 J5
Warwick Gdns. W14 66 C3
Warwick Gdns., Ilf. 52 E1
Warwick Gdns., T.Ditt. 91 C5
Warwick Gro. E5 50 E1
Warwick Gro., Surb. 91 J7
Warwick Ho. St. SW1 15 J1
Warwick Ho. St. SW1 67 D1
Warwick La. EC4 12 H4
Warwick La. EC4 58 H6
Warwick Pl. W5 64 G2
Warwick Rd.
Warwick Pl. W9 10 C1
Warwick Pl. W9 57 F5
Warwick Pl. N. SW1 19 F2
Warwick Pl. N. SW1 67 C4
Warwick Rd. E4 34 A5
Warwick Rd. E11 42 H5
Warwick Rd. E12 52 B5
Warwick Rd. E15 51 F6
Warwick Rd. E17 41 J1
Warwick Rd. N11 32 D6
Warwick Rd. N18 33 B4
Warwick Rd. SE20 95 E3
Warwick Rd. SW5 66 D5
Warwick Rd. W5 64 G2
Warwick Rd. W14 66 C4
Warwick Rd., Barn. 23 E4
Warwick Rd., Borwd. 22 D3
Warwick Rd., Houns. 72 B3
Warwick Rd., Kings.T. 91 F1
Warwick Rd., N.Mal. 92 C3
Warwick Rd., Sid. 89 B5
Warwick Rd., Sthl. 63 F3
Warwick Rd., Sutt. 100 F4
Warwick Rd., T.Ditt. 91 C5
Warwick Rd., Th.Hth. 94 G3
Warwick Rd., Twick. 82 B1
Warwick Rd., Well. 80 C3
Warwick Row SW1 15 E5
Warwick Row SW1 67 B3
Warwick Sq. EC4 12 H3
Warwick Sq. SW1 19 F3
Warwick Sq. SW1 67 C5
Warwick Sq. Ms. SW1 19 H2
Warwick St. W1 11 G5
Warwick St. W1 58 C7
Warwick Ter. SE18 70 G6
Warwick Way SW1 19 E3
Warwick Way SW1 67 B5
Warwick Yd. EC1 9 A6
Warwickshire Path SE8 68 J7
Washington Ave. E12 52 B4
Washington Rd. E6 51 J7
St. Stephens Rd.
Washington Rd. E18 42 F2
Washington Rd. SW13 65 G7
Washington Rd., Kings.T. 92 A2
Washington Rd., Wor.Pk. 99 H2
Wastdale Rd. SE23 86 G1
Wat Tyler Rd. SE3 78 D2
Wat Tyler Rd. SE10 78 C2
Watchfield Ct. W4 65 C5
Watcombe Cotts., Rich. 65 A6
Watcombe Pl. SE25 95 E5
Albert Rd.
Watcombe Rd. SE25 95 E5
Water Gdns., Stan. 29 E6
Water La. E15 51 E6
Water La. NW1 49 B7
Kentish Town Rd.
Water La. SE14 68 F7
Water La., Ilf. 52 H3
Water La., Kings.T. 91 G1
Water La., Rich. 73 G5
Water La., Sid. 89 F3
Water La., Twick. 82 D1
Water Lily Clo., Sthl. 63 J2
Navigator Dr.
Water Rd., Wem. 55 J1
Water St. WC2 12 D5
Water Twr. Hill, Croy. 102 A4
Waterbank Rd. SE6 87 B3
Waterbeach Rd., Dag. 53 C6
Waterbrook La. NW4 38 J5
Watercress Pl. N1 50 B7
Hertford Rd.
Waterdale Rd. SE2 71 A6
Waterden Rd. E15 51 A5
Waterer Ri., Wall. 101 D6
Waterfall Clo. N14 32 C3
Waterfall Cotts. SW19 84 G6
Waterfall Rd. N11 32 B4
Waterfall Rd. N14 32 C3
Waterfall Rd. SW19 84 G6
Waterfall Ter. SW17 84 H6
Waterfield Clo. SE28 71 B1
Waterfield Clo., Belv. 71 G3
Waterfield Gdns. SE25 95 A4
Waterford Rd. SW6 66 E7
Watergardens, The, Kings.T. 83 C6
Watergate EC4 12 G5
Watergate, Wat. 28 D2
Watergate St. SE8 69 A6
Watergate Wk. WC2 12 B6
Waterhall Ave. E4 34 E4
Waterhall Clo. E17 41 G1
Waterhouse Clo. E16 61 A5
Waterhouse Clo. NW3 48 G5
Lyndhurst Rd.
Waterhouse Clo. W6 66 A4
Great Ch. La.
Waterloo Bri. SE1 12 C6
Waterloo Bri. SE1 67 F1
Waterloo Bri. WC2 12 C6
Waterloo Bri. WC2 58 F7
Waterloo Clo. E9 50 F5
Churchill Wk.
Waterloo Est. E2 59 F2
Waterloo Gdns. E2 59 F2
Waterloo Pas. NW6 48 C7
Waterloo Pl. SW1 15 H1
Waterloo Pl. SW1 67 D1
Waterloo Pl., Rich. 73 H5
Sheen Rd.
Waterloo Rd. E6 51 J7
Waterloo Rd. E7 51 F5
Wellington Rd.
Waterloo Rd. E10 42 A7
Waterloo Rd. NW2 47 G1
Waterloo Rd. SE1 16 E3
Waterloo Rd. SE1 67 G1
Waterloo Rd., Ilf. 43 F2
Waterloo Rd., Sutt. 100 G5
Waterloo Ter. N1 49 H7
Waterlow Ct. NW11 39 E7
Heath Clo.
Waterlow Rd. N19 49 C1
Waterman St. SW15 75 A3
Waterman Way E1 68 E1
Waterman's Clo., Kings.T. 82 H7
Woodside Rd.
Watermans Wk. SE16 68 H1
Redriff Rd.
Watermead La., Cars. 93 J7
Middleton Rd.
Watermead Rd. SE6 87 B4

Watermead Way N17 41 D3
Watermen's Sq. SE20 86 F7
Watermill Clo., Rich. 82 F3
Watermill La. N18 33 B5
Watermill Way 93 F1
SW19
Watermill Way, Felt. 81 F2
Watermint Quay N16 41 D6
Waters Gdns., Dag. 53 G5
Sterry Rd.
Waters Rd. SE6 87 E3
Waters Rd., Kings.T. 92 B2
Waters Sq., Kings.T. 92 B3
Watersedge, Epsom 99 C4
Watersfield Way, Edg. 29 G7
Waterside, Beck. 96 A1
Rectory Rd.
Waterside Clo. SE16 17 J4
Waterside Clo., Bark. 53 A4
Waterside Clo., Nthlt. 54 F3
Waterside Clo., Surb. 98 H2
Culsac Rd.
Waterside Dr., Walt. 90 A5
Waterside Pl. NW1 58 A1
Princess Rd.
Waterside Pt. SW11 66 H7
Waterside Rd., Sthl. 63 G3
Waterside Way SW17 84 F4
Watersmeet Way 62 C6
SE28
Waterson St. E2 9 E3
Waterson St. E2 59 B3
Watersplash Clo., 91 H3
Kings.T.
Watersplash La., 63 B5
Houns.
Waterview Ho. E14 59 H5
Carr St.
Waterworks La. E5 50 G2
Waterworks Rd. SW2 76 F6
Waterworks Yd., 101 J3
Croy.
Surrey St.
Watery La. SW20 93 C2
Watery La., Nthlt. 54 C2
Watery La., Sid. 89 B6
Wates Way, Mitch. 93 J6
Wateville Rd. N17 40 J1
Watford Clo. SW11 75 H1
Petworth St.
Watford Rd. E16 60 G5
Watford Rd., Har. 37 D7
Watford Rd., Wem. 46 D2
Watford Way NW4 38 G4
Watford Way NW7 30 E4
Watkin Rd., Wem. 47 B3
Watkinson Rd. N7 49 F6
Watling Ave., Edg. 38 C1
Watling Ct. EC4 13 A4
Watling Gdns. NW2 48 B6
Watling St. EC4 12 J4
Watling St. EC4 58 J6
Watling St., Bexh. 80 H4
Watlings Clo., Croy. 95 H6
Watlington Gro. SE26 86 H5
Watney Mkt. E1 59 E6
Commercial Rd.
Watney Rd. SW14 74 C3
Watney St. E1 59 E6
Watneys Rd., Mitch. 94 D5
Watson Ave. E6 52 D7
Watson Ave., Sutt. 100 B3
Watson Clo. N16 50 A5
Matthias Rd.
Watson Clo. SW19 84 H6
Watson St. E13 60 H2
Watsons Ms. W1 10 H2
Watsons Rd. N22 40 F1
Watson's St. SE8 69 A7
Watsons Yd. NW2 47 F2
North Circular Rd.
Wattisfield Rd. E5 50 F3
Watts Gro. E3 60 B5
Watts La., Chis. 97 E1
Watts La., Tedd. 82 D5
Watts Rd., T.Ditt. 91 D7
Watts St. E1 68 E1
Watts Way SW7 14 F5
Wauthier Clo. N13 32 H5
Wavel Ms. N8 40 D4
Wavel Ms. NW6 48 E7
Acol Rd.
Wavel Pl. SE26 86 C4
Sydenham Hill
Wavell Dr., Sid. 79 H6
Wavendon Ave. W4 65 D5
Waveney Ave. SE15 77 E4
Waveney Clo. E1 17 J1

Waverley Ave. E4 33 J4
Waverley Ave. E17 42 D3
Waverley Ave., Surb. 92 B6
Waverley Ave., Sutt. 100 E2
Waverley Ave., Twick. 81 F1
Waverley Ave., Wem. 46 J5
Waverley Clo. E18 42 J1
Waverley Clo., Brom. 97 A5
Waverley Cres. SE18 70 G6
Waverley Gdns. E6 61 B5
Oliver Gdns.
Waverley Gdns. 55 J2
NW10
Waverley Gdns., Bark. 61 H2
Waverley Gdns., Ilf. 43 F2
Waverley Gdns., 36 A1
Nthwd.
Waverley Gro. N3 39 A3
Waverley Ind. Pk., 37 A3
Har.
Waverley Pl. N4 49 H2
Adolphus Rd.
Waverley Pl. NW8 6 E1
Waverley Pl. NW8 57 G2
Waverley Rd. E17 42 C3
Waverley Rd. E18 42 J1
Waverley Rd. N8 40 E6
Waverley Rd. N17 33 E7
Waverley Rd. SE18 70 F5
Waverley Rd. SE25 95 E4
Waverley Rd., Enf. 24 H4
Waverley Rd., Epsom 99 G6
Waverley Rd., Har. 45 E1
Waverley Rd., Sthl. 54 G7
Waverley Vill. N17 41 C2
Waverley Wk. W2 57 D5
Waverley Way, Cars. 100 H6
Waverton Ho. E3 59 J1
Waverton St. W1 15 D1
Waverton Rd. SW18 75 F7
Waverton St. W1 67 A1
Wavertree Ct. SW2 85 F1
Streatham Hill
Wavertree Rd. E18 42 G2
Wavertree Rd. SW2 85 E1
Waxlow Cres., Sthl. 54 G6
Waxlow Rd. NW10 56 C2
Waxwell Clo., Pnr. 36 D2
Waxwell La., Pnr. 36 D2
Waxwell Ter. SE1 16 D4
Waye Ave., Houns. 72 A1
Wayfarer Rd., Nthlt. 54 D3
Wayfield Link SE9 79 G6
Wayford St. SW11 75 H2
Wayland Ave. E8 50 D5
Waylands Mead, 96 B1
Beck.
Wayleave, The SE28 62 B7
Oriole Way
Waylett Pl. SE27 85 H3
Waylett Pl., Wem. 46 G3
Wayman Ct. E8 50 E6
Wayne Clo., Orp. 104 J3
Waynflete Ave., 101 H3
Croy.
Waynflete Sq. W10 57 A6
Waynflete St. SW18 84 F2
Wayside NW11 48 B1
Wayside SW14 74 C5
Wayside Clo. N14 24 C6
Wayside Commercial 62 A2
Est., Bark.
Wayside Ct., Twick. 73 F6
Wayside Ct., Wem. 47 A3
Oakington Ave.
Wayside Gdns. SE9 88 C4
Wayside Gro.
Wayside Gdns., Dag. 53 G5
Wayside Gro. SE9 88 C4
Wayside Ms., Ilf. 43 D5
Gaysham Ave.
Weald, The, Chis. 88 C6
Weald Clo. SE16 68 E5
Stevenson Cres.
Weald Clo., Brom. 104 B2
Weald La., Har. 37 A2
Weald Ri., Har. 29 C7
Weald Sq. E5 50 E2
Rossington St.
Weald Way, Rom. 44 H6
Wealdstone Rd., Sutt. 100 C2
Wealdwood Gdns., 28 H6
Pnr.
Highbanks Rd.
Weale Rd. E4 34 D3
Wear Pl. E2 59 E3
Weardale Gdns., Enf. 25 A1
Weardale Rd. SE13 78 D4

Wearside Rd. SE13 78 B5
Weatherley Clo. E3 59 J5
Weaver St. E1 9 H6
Weaver St. E1 59 D4
Weaver Wk. SE27 85 J4
Weavers Clo., Islw. 73 B4
Weavers Ter. SW6 66 D6
Micklethwaite Rd.
Weavers Way NW1 49 D7
Webb Est. E5 41 D7
Webb Gdns. E13 60 G4
Kelland Rd.
Webb Pl. NW10 56 F3
Old Oak La.
Webb Rd. SE3 69 F6
Webb St. SE1 17 D6
Webb St. SE1 68 B3
Webber Row SE1 16 F4
Webber Row SE1 67 G2
Webber St. SE1 16 G4
Webber St. SE1 67 G2
Webbs Rd. SW11 75 J4
Webbs Rd., Hayes 54 B3
Webbscroft Rd., Dag. 53 H4
Webster Gdns. W5 64 G1
Webster Rd. E11 51 C3
Webster Rd. SE16 17 J6
Webster Rd. SE16 68 D3
Wedderburn Rd. NW3 48 G5
Wedderburn Rd., 61 G1
Bark.
Wedgewood Wk. NW6 48 E5
Lymington Rd.
Wedgewood Way 85 J7
SE19
Wedgwood Ms. W1 11 J4
Wedlake St. W10 57 B4
Kensal Rd.
Wedmore Ave., Ilf. 43 D1
Wedmore Gdns. N19 49 D2
Wedmore Ms. N19 49 D3
Wedmore St.
Wedmore Rd., Grnf. 55 A3
Wedmore St. N19 49 D3
Weech Rd. NW6 48 D4
Weedington Rd. NW5 49 A5
Weekley Sq. SW11 75 G3
Thomas Baines Rd.
Weigall Rd. SE12 78 G4
Weighouse St. W1 11 C4
Weighouse St. W1 58 A6
Weighton Rd. SE20 95 E2
Weighton Rd., Har. 37 A1
Weihurst Gdns., Sutt. 100 E3
Weimar St. SW15 75 B3
Weir Est. SW12 76 C7
Weir Hall Ave. N18 33 A6
Weir Hall Gdns. N18 33 A5
Weir Hall Rd. N17 33 A6
Weir Hall Rd. N18 33 A5
Weir Rd. SW12 76 C7
Weir Rd. SW19 84 E3
Weir Rd., Bex. 80 H7
Weir Rd., Walt. 90 A6
Weirdale Ave. N20 31 J2
Weir's Pas. NW1 7 J3
Weir's Pas. NW1 58 D3
Weiss Rd. SW15 75 A3
Welbeck Ave., Brom. 87 G4
Welbeck Ave., Hayes 54 B4
Welbeck Ave., Sid. 89 A1
Welbeck Clo. N12 31 G5
Torrington Pk.
Welbeck Clo., Borwd. 22 A3
Welbeck Clo., Epsom 99 G7
Welbeck Clo., N.Mal. 92 F5
Welbeck Rd. E6 61 A3
Welbeck Rd., Barn. 23 G6
Welbeck Rd., Cars. 100 H1
Welbeck Rd., Har. 45 H1
Welbeck Rd., Sutt. 100 G2
Welbeck St. W1 11 C2
Welbeck St. W1 58 A5
Welbeck Wk., Cars. 100 H1
Welbeck Rd.
Welbeck Way W1 11 D3
Welbeck Way W1 58 B6
Welby St. SE5 76 H1
Welch Pl., Pnr. 36 C1
Weld Pl. N11 32 B5
Weldon Clo., Ruis. 45 B6
Weldon Dr., W.Mol. 90 F4
Welfare Rd. E15 51 E7
Welford Clo. E5 50 G3
Denton Way
Welford Pl. SW19 84 B4
Welham Rd. SW16 85 B6
Welham Rd. SW17 85 A5

Welhouse Rd., Cars. 100 H1
Well App., Barn. 22 J5
Well Clo. SW16 85 F4
Well Clo., Ruis. 45 E3
Parkfield Cres.
Well Ct. EC4 13 A4
Well Ct. SW16 85 F4
Well Gro. N20 23 F7
Well Hall Rd. SE9 79 B3
Well La. SW14 74 C5
Well Pas. NW3 48 G3
Well Rd. NW3 48 G3
Well Rd., Barn. 22 J5
Well St. E9 50 F7
Well St. E15 51 E6
Well Wk. NW3 48 G4
Wellacre Rd., Har. 37 E6
Wellan Clo., Sid. 80 B5
Welland Gdns., Grnf. 55 C2
Welland Ms. E1 17 J1
Welland St. SE10 69 C6
Wellands Clo., Brom. 97 C2
Wellbrook Rd., Orp. 104 D4
Wellclose Sq. E1 13 J5
Wellclose Sq. E1 59 D7
Wellclose St. E1 13 J6
Welldon Cres., Har. 37 B6
Weller St. SE1 16 J3
Weller's Ct. NW1 8 A2
Wellesley Ave. W6 65 H3
Wellesley Clo. W9 6 C3
Wellesley Ct. Rd., 102 A2
Croy.
Wellesley Cres., 82 B2
Twick.
Wellesley Gro., Croy. 102 A2
Wellesley Pk. Ms., 24 H2
Enf.
Wellesley Pl. NW1 7 H4
Wellesley Rd. E11 42 G5
Wellesley Rd. E17 42 A6
Wellesley Rd. N22 40 G2
Wellesley Rd. NW5 49 A5
Wellesley Rd. W4 65 A5
Wellesley Rd., Croy. 101 J1
Wellesley Rd., Har. 37 B5
Wellesley Rd., Ilf. 52 E2
Wellesley Rd., Sutt. 100 F6
Wellesley Rd., Twick. 82 A3
Wellesley Ter. N1 9 A3
Wellesley Ter. N1 58 J3
Wellfield Ave. N10 40 B3
Wellfield Rd. SW16 85 E4
Wellfield Wk. SW16 85 F5
Wellfields Rd., Loug. 27 D3
Wellfit St. SE24 76 H3
Hinton Rd.
Wellgarth, Grnf. 46 E6
Wellgarth Rd. NW11 48 E1
Wellhouse La., Barn. 22 J4
Wellhouse Rd., Beck. 95 J4
Welling High St., Well. 80 A3
Welling Way SE9 79 G3
Welling Way, Well. 79 H3
Wellings Ho., Hayes 63 B1
Wellington Ave. E4 34 A2
Wellington Ave. N9 33 E3
Wellington Ave. N15 41 C6
Wellington Ave., 72 G5
Houns.
Wellington Ave., Pnr. 36 F1
Wellington Ave., Sid. 80 A6
Wellington Ave., 99 J3
Wor.Pk.
**Wellington Bldgs. 19 C4
SW1**
Wellington Clo. SE14 77 G1
Rutts Ter.
Wellington Clo. W11 57 D6
Ledbury Rd.
Wellington Clo., Dag. 53 J7
Wellington Ct. NW8 6 E2
Wellington Cres., 92 C3
N.Mal.
Wellington Dr., Dag. 53 J7
Wellington Gdns. SE7 69 J5
Wellington Gdns., 82 A4
Twick.
Wellington Ms. SE22 77 D4
Peckham Rye
Wellington Pk. Ind. 47 G1
Est. NW2
Wellington Pas. E11 42 G5
Wellington Rd.
Wellington Pl. N2 39 H5
Great N. Rd.

Wellington Pl. NW8	**6 F3**	Wembley Pk. Dr.,	46 J4
Wellington Pl. NW8	57 G3	Wem.	
Wellington Rd. E6	61 C1	Wembley Retail Pk.,	47 B4
Wellington Rd. E7	51 F4	Wem.	
Wellington Rd. E10	50 H1	Wembley Rd., Hmptn.	81 G7
Wellington Rd. E11	42 G5	Wembley Way, Wem.	47 B6
Wellington Rd. E17	41 H3	Wemborough Rd.,	37 E1
Wellington Rd. NW8	**6 E1**	Stan.	
Wellington Rd. NW8	57 G2	Wembury Rd. N6	40 B7
Wellington Rd. NW10	57 A3	Wemyss Rd. SE3	78 F2
Wellington Rd. SW19	84 D2	Wendela Ct., Har.	46 B3
Wellington Rd. W5	64 F3	Wendell Rd. W12	65 F3
Wellington Rd., Belv.	71 F5	**Wendle Ct. SW8**	**20 A4**
Wellington Rd., Bex.	80 D5	Wendle Ct. SW8	67 E6
Wellington Rd., Brom.	96 J4	Wendling Rd., Sutt.	100 G1
Wellington Rd., Croy.	94 H7	Wendon St. E3	59 J1
Wellington Rd., Enf.	25 B4	**Wendover SE17**	**21 D3**
Wellington Rd.,	82 A5	Wendover Clo., Hayes	54 E4
Hmptn.		*Kingsash Dr.*	
Wellington Rd., Har.	37 B3	Wendover Dr., N.Mal.	92 F6
Wellington Rd., Pnr.	28 F7	Wendover Rd. NW10	56 F2
Wellington Rd.,	82 A4	Wendover Rd. SE9	79 A3
Twick.		Wendover Rd., Brom.	96 H3
Wellington Rd. N.,	72 F3	Wendover Way, Well.	80 A5
Houns.		Wendy Clo., Enf.	25 C6
Wellington Rd. S.,	72 F4	Wendy Way, Wem.	55 H1
Houns.		**Wenlock Ct. N1**	**9 C2**
Wellington Row E2	**9 G3**	*Rickard Clo.*	
Wellington Row E2	59 C3	**Wenlock Gdns. NW4**	38 G4
Wellington Sq. SW3	**18 J3**	**Wenlock Rd. N1**	**8 J2**
Wellington Sq. SW3	66 J5	Wenlock Rd. N1	58 J2
Wellington St. SE18	70 D4	Wenlock Rd., Edg.	30 B7
Wellington St. WC2	**12 B5**	**Wenlock St. N1**	**9 A2**
Wellington St. WC2	58 E7	Wenlock St. N1	58 J2
Wellington St., Bark.	61 F1	Wennington Rd. E3	59 G2
Axe St.		Wensley Ave.,	34 F7
Wellington Ter. E1	68 E1	Wdf.Grn.	
Waterman Way		Wensley Clo. SE9	79 C6
Wellington Ter., Har.	46 A1	Wensley Rd. N18	33 E6
Wellington Way E3	60 A3	Wensleydale Ave., Ilf.	43 B2
Wellmeadow Rd. SE6	78 E7	Wensleydale Gdns.,	81 H7
Wellmeadow Rd.	78 E6	Hmptn.	
SE13		Wensleydale Pas.,	90 G1
Wellmeadow Rd. W7	64 D4	Hmptn.	
Wellow Wk., Cars.	100 G1	Wensleydale Rd.,	81 G6
Whitland Rd.		Hmptn.	
Wells, The N14	24 D7	Wentland Clo. SE6	87 D2
Wells Clo., Nthlt.	54 C3	*Wentland Rd.*	
Yeading La.		Wentland Rd. SE6	87 D2
Wells Dr. NW9	47 D1	Wentworth Ave. N3	31 D7
Wells Gdns., Dag.	53 H5	Wentworth Clo. N3	31 E7
Pondfield Rd.		Wentworth Clo.,	93 D7
Wells Gdns., Ilf.	43 B7	Mord.	
Wells Ms. W1	**11 G2**	Wentworth Clo., Orp.	104 H5
Wells Pk. Rd. SE26	86 D3	Wentworth Clo., Surb.	90 G6
Wells Rd. W12	65 J2	Wentworth Cres. SE15	68 D7
Wells Rd., Brom.	97 C2	Wentworth Dr., Pnr.	36 A5
Wells Sq. WC1	**8 C4**	Wentworth Gdns. N13	32 H4
Wells St. W1	**11 F2**	Wentworth Hill, Wem.	46 J1
Wells St. W1	58 C5	Wentworth Ms. E3	59 J4
Wells Ter. N4	49 G2	*Eric St.*	
Wells Way SE5	**21 C5**	Wentworth Pk. N3	31 D7
Wells Way SE5	68 B6	Wentworth Pl., Stan.	29 E6
Wells Way SW7	**14 E5**	*Greenacres Dr.*	
Wells Way SW7	66 G3	Wentworth Rd. E12	52 A4
Wells Yd. N7	49 G5	Wentworth Rd. NW11	39 C6
Holloway Rd.		Wentworth Rd., Barn.	23 A3
Wellside Clo., Barn.	22 J4	Wentworth Rd., Croy.	94 G7
Wellside Gdns. SW14	74 C5	Wentworth Rd., Sthl.	63 C4
Well La.		**Wentworth St. E1**	**13 F3**
Wellsmoor Gdns.,	97 D3	Wentworth St. E1	59 C6
Brom.		Wentworth Way, Pnr.	36 D4
Wellsprings Cres.,	47 B3	Wenvoe Ave., Bexh.	80 H2
Wem.		Wernbrook St. SE18	70 F6
Wellstead Ave. N9	25 F7	Werndee Rd. SE25	95 D4
Wellstead Rd. E6	61 D2	Werneth Hall Rd., Ilf.	43 C3
Wellwood Rd., Ilf.	53 A1	**Werrington St. NW1**	**7 G2**
Welsford St. SE1	**21 H3**	Werrington St. NW1	58 C2
Welsford St. SE1	68 D5	Werter Rd. SW15	75 B4
Welsh Clo. E13	60 G3	Wesley Ave. NW10	56 D3
Welsh Side Wk. NW9	38 E6	Wesley Ave., Houns.	72 E2
Fryent Gro.		Wesley Clo. N7	49 F2
Welshpool Ho. E8	59 D1	**Wesley Clo. SE17**	**20 H2**
Benjamin Clo.		Wesley Clo., Har.	45 J2
Welshpool St. E8	59 E1	Wesley Rd. E10	42 C7
Broadway Mkt.		Wesley Rd. NW10	56 C1
Weltje Rd. W6	65 G4	*Hillside*	
Welton Rd. SE18	70 H7	**Wesley Rd. SE17**	**20 H2**
Welwyn St. E2	59 F3	Wesley Rd., Hayes	54 A7
Globe Rd.		Wesley Rd., Wall.	57 B6
Wembley Commercial	46 G2	*Bartle Rd.*	
Cen., Wem.		**Wesley St. W1**	**11 C2**
Wembley Hill Rd.,	46 J5	Wesleyan Pl. NW5	49 B4
Wem.		*Gordon Ho. Rd.*	
Wembley Pk.	47 B3	Wessex Ave. SW19	93 D2
Business Cen., Wem.		Wessex Clo., Ilf.	43 H6
		Wessex Clo., Kings.T.	92 B1
		Gloucester Rd.	

Wessex Dr., Pnr.	28 E7	West Hill SW15	75 A7
Wessex Gdns. NW11	48 B1	West Hill SW18	75 A7
Wessex La., Grnf.	55 A2	West Hill, Har.	46 B2
Wessex St. E2	59 F3	West Hill, Wem.	46 J1
Wessex Way NW11	48 B1	West Hill Ct. N6	49 A3
West App., Orp.	97 F5	West Hill Pk. N6	48 J2
West Arbour St. E1	59 F6	*Merton La.*	
West Ave. E17	42 B4	West Hill Rd. SW18	75 C6
West Ave. N3	31 D6	West Hill Way N20	31 E1
West Ave. NW4	39 A5	West Holme, Erith	80 J1
West Ave., Pnr.	36 F6	West Ho. Clo. SW19	84 B1
West Ave., Sthl.	54 F7	West India Ave. E14	69 A1
West Ave., Wall.	101 E5	West India Dock Rd.	59 J6
West Ave. Rd. E17	42 A4	E14	
West Bank N16	41 B7	West Kentish Town	49 A6
West Bank, Bark.	61 E1	Est. NW5	
Highbridge Rd.		*Warden Rd.*	
West Bank, Enf.	24 J2	West La. SE16	68 E2
West Barnes La. SW20	92 G5	West Lo. Ave. W3	65 A1
West Barnes La.,	92 H3	West Mall W8	66 D1
N.Mal.		*Palace Gdns. Ter.*	
West Carriage Dr. W2	**10 G6**	West Mead, Epsom	99 E6
West Carriage Dr. W2	57 G7	West Mead, Ruis.	45 C4
West Cen. St. WC1	**12 A3**	West Ms. N17	33 E6
West Chantry, Har.	36 H1	**West Ms. SW1**	**19 F2**
Chantry Rd.		West Oak, Beck.	96 D1
West Clo. N9	33 C3	West Pk. SE9	88 B2
West Clo., Barn.	22 H5	West Pk. Ave., Rich.	74 A1
West Clo., Barn.	24 A4	West Pk. Clo., Rom.	44 D5
(Cockfosters)		West Pk. Rd., Rich.	74 A1
West Clo., Grnf.	54 J2	West Pk. Rd., Sthl.	63 J1
West Clo., Hmptn.	81 E6	West Pier E1	68 E1
Oak Ave.		*Wapping High St.*	
West Clo., Wem.	46 J1	West Pl. SW19	83 J5
West Common Rd.,	103 G2	**West Poultry Ave. EC1**	**12 G2**
Brom.		West Quarters W12	56 G6
West Cotts. NW6	48 D5	*Du Cane Rd.*	
West Ct. SE18	79 C1	West Quay Dr., Hayes	54 E5
Prince Imperial Rd.		West Ridge Gdns.,	54 J2
West Ct., Wem.	46 F2	Grnf.	
West Cromwell Rd.	66 C4	West Rd. E15	60 F1
SW5		West Rd. N17	33 E6
West Cromwell Rd.	66 C5	**West Rd. SW3**	**19 A4**
W14		West Rd. SW3	66 J5
West Cross Route	57 A7	West Rd. SW4	76 D5
W10		West Rd. W5	55 H5
West Cross Route	66 A1	West Rd., Barn.	32 A1
W11		West Rd., Kings.T.	92 C1
West Cross Way,	64 E6	West Rd., Rom.	44 D6
Brent.		(Chadwell Heath)	
West Dene, Sutt.	100 B6	West Row W10	57 B4
Park La.		West Sheen Vale,	73 J4
West Dr. SW16	85 C4	Rich.	
West Dr., Har.	29 A6	West Side Common	83 J6
West Dr. Gdns., Har.	29 A6	SW19	
West Eaton Pl. SW1	**19 B1**	**West Smithfield EC1**	**12 G2**
West Eaton Pl. SW1	67 A4	West Smithfield EC1	58 H5
West Eaton Pl. Ms.	**15 B6**	**West Sq. SE11**	**16 G6**
SW1		West Sq. SE11	67 H3
West Ella Rd. NW10	47 E7	West St. E2	59 E2
West End Ave. E10	42 D5	West St. E11	51 E3
West End Ave., Pnr.	36 D4	West St. E17	42 B5
West End Ct., Pnr.	36 D4	*Grove Rd.*	
West End Gdns., Nthlt.	54 C2	**West St. WC2**	**11 J5**
Edward Clo.		West St., Bexh.	80 F4
West End La. NW6	48 D5	West St., Brent.	64 F6
West End La., Barn.	23 A4	West St., Brom.	96 G1
West End La., Pnr.	36 D3	West St., Cars.	100 J3
West End Rd., Nthlt.	45 C7	West St., Croy.	101 J4
West End Rd., Ruis.	45 A4	West St., Har.	46 A1
West End Rd., Sthl.	63 E1	West St., Sutt.	100 E5
West Gdns. E1	59 E7	West St. La., Cars.	100 J4
West Gdns. SW17	84 H6	West Temple Sheen	74 B4
West Gate W5	55 H3	SW14	
West Grn. Pl., Grnf.	55 A1	**West Tenter St. E1**	**13 G4**
Uneeda Dr.		West Tenter St. E1	59 C6
West Grn. Rd. N15	40 H4	West Twrs., Pnr.	36 D6
West Gro. SE10	78 C1	West Vw. NW4	38 J4
West Gro., Wdf.Grn.	34 H4	West Vw., Loug.	27 C4
West Halkin St. SW1	**15 B5**	West Vw. Cres. N9	25 B7
West Halkin St. SW1	67 A3	West Wk. W5	55 H5
West Hall Rd., Rich.	74 B1	West Wk., Barn.	24 A7
West Hallowes SE9	88 B1	West Wk., Hayes	63 A1
West Ham La. E15	51 D7	**West Warwick Pl.**	**19 F2**
West Ham Pk. E7	51 F7	SW1	
West Hampstead Ms.	48 E6	West Warwick Pl.	67 C4
NW6		SW1	
West Harding St. EC4	**12 F3**	West Way N18	33 A4
West Heath Ave.	48 D1	West Way NW10	47 D4
NW11		West Way, Croy.	102 H2
West Heath Clo. NW3	48 D3	West Way, Edg.	30 B6
West Heath Dr. NW11	48 D1	West Way, Houns.	63 F7
West Heath Gdns.	48 D2	West Way, Pnr.	36 D4
NW3		West Way, W.Wick.	96 D6
West Heath Rd. NW3	48 D2	West Way Gdns.,	102 G2
West Heath Rd. SE2	71 C6	Croy.	
West Hendon Bdy.	38 F6	West Woodside, Bex.	80 E7
NW9		West World W5	55 H3

Westacott Clo. N19	49	D1
Westall Rd., Loug.	27	E3
Westbank Rd., Hmptn.	81	J6
Westbeech Rd. N22	40	G3
Westbere Dr., Stan.	29	G4
Westbere Rd. NW2	48	B4
Westbourne Ave. W3	56	D6
Westbourne Ave., Sutt.	100	B2
Westbourne Bri. W2	**10**	**C2**
Westbourne Bri. W2	57	F5
Westbourne Clo., Hayes	54	B4
Westbourne Cres. W2	**10**	**E5**
Westbourne Cres. W2	57	G7
Westbourne Cres. Ms. W2	**10**	**E5**
Westbourne Dr. SE23	86	G2
Westbourne Gdns. W2	**10**	**A3**
Westbourne Gdns. W2	57	E6
Westbourne Gro. W2	57	D6
Westbourne Gro. W11	57	C7
Westbourne Gro. Ms. W11	57	D6
Westbourne Gro.		
Westbourne Gro. Ter. W2	**10**	**A4**
Westbourne Gro. Ter. W2	57	E6
Westbourne Pk. Ms. W2	**10**	**A3**
Westbourne Pk. Pas. W2	57	D5
Westbourne Pk. Rd. W2	57	D5
Westbourne Pk. Rd. W11	57	B6
Westbourne Pk. Vill. W2	57	D5
Westbourne Rd. N7	49	F6
Westbourne Rd. SE26	86	G6
Westbourne Rd., Bexh.	71	D7
Westbourne Rd., Croy.	95	C6
Westbourne St. W2	**10**	**E5**
Westbourne St. W2	57	G7
Westbourne Ter. W2	**10**	**C3**
Westbourne Ter. W2	57	F6
Westbourne Ter. Ms. W2	**10**	**C3**
Westbourne Ter. Ms. W2	57	F6
Westbourne Ter. Rd. W2	**10**	**C2**
Westbourne Ter. Rd. W2	57	F5
Westbridge Rd. SW11	75	G1
Westbrook Ave., Hmptn.	81	F7
Westbrook Clo., Barn.	23	G3
Westbrook Cres., Barn.	23	G3
Westbrook Rd. SE3	78	H1
Westbrook Rd., Houns.	63	F7
Westbrook Rd., Th.Hth.	95	A1
Westbrook Sq., Barn.	23	G3
Westbrooke Cres., Well.	80	C3
Westbrooke Rd., Sid.	88	G2
Westbrooke Rd., Well.	80	B3
Westbury Ave. N22	40	H3
Westbury Ave., Esher	98	C6
Westbury Ave., Sthl.	54	G4
Westbury Ave., Wem.	46	H7
Westbury Clo., Ruis.	36	A7
Westbury Gro. N12	31	D6
Westbury La., Buck.H.	34	J2
Westbury Lo. Clo., Pnr.	36	D3
Westbury Ms. E17	42	A4
Westbury Rd.		
Westbury Pl., Brent.	64	G6
Westbury Rd. E7	51	H5
Westbury Rd. E17	41	J4
Westbury Rd. N11	32	E6
Westbury Rd. N12	31	D6
Westbury Rd. SE20	95	G1
Westbury Rd. W5	55	H6
Westbury Rd., Bark.	61	G1
Westbury Rd., Beck.	95	H3
Westbury Rd., Brom.	97	A1
Westbury Rd., Buck.H.	34	J2
Westbury Rd., Croy.	95	A6
Westbury Rd., Felt.	81	D1
Westbury Rd., Ilf.	52	D2
Westbury Rd., N.Mal.	92	D4
Westbury Rd., Wem.	46	H7
Westbury St. SW8	76	C2
Westbury Ter. E7	51	H6
Westchester Dr. NW4	39	A3
Westcombe Ave., Croy.	94	E6
Westcombe Ct. SE3	69	F7
Westcombe Pk. Rd.		
Westcombe Dr., Barn.	23	D5
Westcombe Hill SE3	69	G6
Westcombe Hill SE10	69	G5
Westcombe Pk. Rd. SE3	69	E6
Westcoombe Ave. SW20	92	F1
Westcote Rd. SW16	85	C5
Westcott Clo. N15	41	C6
Ermine Rd.		
Westcott Clo., Brom.	97	B5
Ringmer Way		
Westcott Cres. W7	55	B6
Westcott Rd. SE17	**20**	**H5**
Westcott Rd. SE17	67	H6
Westcourt, Sun.	90	B2
Westcroft Clo. NW2	48	B4
Westcroft Gdns., Mord.	93	C3
Westcroft Rd., Cars.	101	A4
Westcroft Rd., Wall.	101	A4
Westcroft Sq. W6	65	G4
Westcroft Way NW2	48	B4
Westdale Pas. SE18	70	E6
Westdale Rd.		
Westdale Rd. SE18	70	E6
Westdean Ave. SE12	87	H1
Westdean Clo. SW18	75	E5
Westdown Rd. E15	51	C4
Westdown Rd. SE6	78	A7
Westel Ho. W5	55	J5
Westerdale Rd. SE10	69	G5
Westerfield Rd. N15	41	C5
Westergate Rd. SE2	71	E6
Westerham Ave. N9	33	A3
Westerham Dr., Sid.	80	B6
Westerham Rd. E10	42	B6
Westerham Rd., Kes.	104	A7
Westerley Cres. SE26	86	J5
Western Ave. NW11	39	A6
Western Ave. W3	56	A4
Western Ave. W5	55	J4
Western Ave., Dag.	53	J6
Western Ave., Grnf.	55	B2
Western Ave., Nthlt.	54	F1
Western Ct. N3	31	D6
Huntley Dr.		
Western Gdns. W5	56	A7
Western Gateway E16	60	G7
Western Ho. W5	55	H3
Western La. SW12	76	A7
Western Ms. W9	57	C4
Great Western Rd.		
Western Pl. SE16	68	F2
Canon Beck Rd.		
Western Rd. E13	60	J1
Western Rd. E17	42	C5
Western Rd. N2	39	J4
Western Rd. N22	40	F2
Western Rd. NW10	56	C4
Western Rd. SW9	76	G3
Western Rd. SW19	93	G1
Western Rd. W5	55	G7
Western Rd., Mitch.	93	H1
Western Rd., Sthl.	63	C4
Western Rd., Sutt.	100	D5
Western Ter. W6	65	G5
Chiswick Mall		
Western Trd. Est. NW10	56	B4
Western Way SE28	70	G3
Western Way, Barn.	23	D6
Westernville Gdns., Ilf.	43	F7
Westferry Circ. E14	69	A1
Westferry Rd. E14	69	A2
Westfield, Loug.	26	J5
Westfield Clo., Enf.	25	H3
Westfield Clo., Sutt.	100	C4
Westfield Dr., Har.	37	G4
Westfield Gdns., Har.	37	G4
Westfield La., Har.	37	G4
Westfield Pk., Pnr.	28	F7
Westfield Rd. NW7	30	D3
Westfield Rd. W13	64	D1
Westfield Rd., Beck.	95	J2
Westfield Rd., Bexh.	80	J2
Westfield Rd., Croy.	101	H2
Westfield Rd., Dag.	53	E4
Westfield Rd., Mitch.	93	J2
Westfield Rd., Surb.	91	G5
Westfield Rd., Sutt.	100	C4
Westfield Rd., Walt.	90	E7
Westfield St. SE18	70	A3
Westfield Way E1	59	H4
Mile End Rd.		
Westfields SW13	74	F3
Westfields Ave. SW13	74	E3
Westfields Rd. W3	56	B5
Westgate Rd. SE25	95	E4
Westgate Rd., Beck.	96	C1
Westgate St. E8	59	E1
Westgate Ter. SW10	**18**	**B4**
Westgate Ter. SW10	66	E5
Westglade Ct., Har.	37	G5
Westgrove La. SE10	78	C1
Westhay Gdns. SW14	74	B5
Westholm NW11	39	E4
Westholme, Orp.	97	H7
Westholme Gdns., Ruis.	45	A1
Westhorne Ave. SE9	79	A5
Westhorne Ave. SE12	78	H6
Westhorpe Gdns. NW4	38	J3
Westhorpe Rd. SW15	74	J3
Westhurst Dr., Chis.	88	E5
Westlake Clo. N13	32	G3
Westlake Clo., Hayes	54	E4
Lochan Clo.		
Westlake Rd., Wem.	46	G2
Westland Dr., Brom.	103	F2
Westland Pl. N1	**9**	**B3**
Westland Pl. N1	59	A3
Westlands Ter. SW12	76	C6
Gaskarth Rd.		
Westlea Rd. W7	64	D3
Westleigh Ave. SW15	74	H5
Westleigh Dr., Brom.	97	B1
Westleigh Gdns., Edg.	38	A1
Westlinks, Wem.	55	G3
Alperton La.		
Westmead SW15	74	H7
Westmead Rd., Sutt.	100	G4
Westmede, Chig.	35	F6
Westmere Dr. NW7	30	D3
Westmill Ct. N4	49	J2
Brownswood Rd.		
Westminster Ave., Th.Hth.	94	H2
Westminster Bri. SE1	**16**	**B4**
Westminster Bri. SE1	67	F2
Westminster Bri. SW1	**16**	**B4**
Westminster Bri. SW1	67	E2
Westminster Bri. Rd. SE1	**16**	**D4**
Westminster Bri. Rd. SE1	67	F2
Westminster Cathedral Piazza SW1	**15**	**F6**
Westminster Clo., Ilf.	43	G2
Westminster Clo., Tedd.	82	D5
Westminster Dr. N13	32	E5
Westminster Gdns. E4	34	E1
Westminster Gdns., Bark.	61	H2
Westminster Gdns., Ilf.	43	F2
Westminster Rd. N9	33	E1
Westminster Rd. W7	64	B1
Westminster Rd., Sutt.	100	G2
Westmoat Clo., Beck.	87	C7
Westmont Rd., Esher	90	B2
Westmoor Gdns., Enf.	25	G2
Westmoor Rd., Enf.	25	G2
Westmoor St. SE7	70	A3
Westmoreland Ave., Well.	79	H3
Westmoreland Pl. SW1	**19**	**E4**
Westmoreland Pl. SW1	67	B5
Westmoreland Pl. W5	55	G5
Mount Ave.		
Westmoreland Rd. NW9	37	J3
Westmoreland Rd. SE17	**21**	**B5**
Westmoreland Rd. SE17	68	A6
Westmoreland Rd. SW13	74	F1
Westmoreland Rd., Brom.	96	E5
Westmoreland St. W1	**11**	**C2**
Westmoreland St. W1	58	A5
Westmoreland Ter. SW1	**19**	**E4**
Westmoreland Ter. SW1	67	B5
Westmoreland Wk. SE17	**21**	**B5**
Westmorland Clo. E12	52	A2
Westmorland Clo., Twick.	73	E6
Westmorland Rd. E17	42	A6
Westmorland Rd., Har.	36	H5
Westmorland Ter. SE20	86	E7
Hawthorn Gro.		
Westmorland Way, Mitch.	94	D4
Westmount Rd. SE9	79	C2
Westoe Rd. N9	33	E2
Weston Ave., T.Ditt.	91	B7
Weston Ave., W.Mol.	90	E3
Weston Ct. N4	49	J3
Queens Dr.		
Weston Dr., Stan.	37	E1
Weston Gdns., Islw.	73	A1
Weston Grn., Dag.	53	F4
Weston Grn., T.Ditt.	98	B1
Weston Grn. Rd., Esher	98	A1
Weston Grn. Rd., T.Ditt.	98	B1
Weston Gro., Brom.	87	F7
Weston Pk. N8	40	E6
Weston Pk., Kings.T.	91	H2
Fairfield W.		
Weston Pk., T.Ditt.	98	B1
Weston Pk. Clo., T.Ditt.	98	B1
Weston Pk.		
Weston Ri. WC1	**8**	**D2**
Weston Ri. WC1	58	F3
Weston Rd. W4	65	C3
Weston Rd., Brom.	87	F7
Weston Rd., Dag.	53	E4
Weston Rd., Enf.	25	A1
Weston Rd., T.Ditt.	98	B1
Weston St. SE1	**17**	**C3**
Weston St. SE1	68	A2
Weston Wk. E8	50	E7
Mare St.		
Westover Hill NW3	48	D2
Westover Rd. SW18	75	F7
Westow Hill SE19	86	B6
Westow St. SE19	86	B6
Westpoint Trd. Est. W3	56	A4
Westpole Ave., Barn.	24	A4
Westport Rd. E13	60	H4
Westport St. E1	59	G6
Westrow SW15	74	J6
Westrow Dr., Bark.	53	A5
Westrow Gdns., Ilf.	52	J2
Westside NW4	38	H2
Westview Clo. NW10	47	F5
Westview Clo. W7	55	B6
Westview Clo. W10	56	J6
Westview Dr., Wdf.Grn.	45	A2
Westville Rd. W12	65	G2
Westville Rd., T.Ditt.	98	D1
Westward Rd. E4	33	H5
Westward Way, Har.	37	H6
Westway NW7	30	G7
Westway SW20	92	H3
Westway W9	57	D5
Westway W10	57	B6
Westway W12	56	F7
Westway, Orp.	97	G5
Westway Clo. SW20	92	H3
Westways, Epsom	99	F4
Westwell Rd. SW16	85	E6
Westwell Rd. App. SW16	85	E6
Westwell Rd.		
Westwick Gdns. W14	66	A2
Westwick Gdns., Houns.	72	B2
Westwood Ave. SE19	94	J1
Westwood Ave., Har.	45	H4
Westwood Clo., Brom.	97	A3
Westwood Gdns. SW13	74	F3

Westwood Hill SE26	86	D5
Westwood La., Sid.	80	A5
Westwood La., Well.	79	J3
Westwood Pk. SE23	77	E7
Westwood Rd. E16	69	H1
Westwood Rd. SW13	74	F3
Westwood Rd., Ilf.	52	J1
Wetheral Dr., Stan.	37	F1
Wetherby Clo., Nthlt.	45	H6
Wetherby Gdns. SW5	**18**	**C2**
Wetherby Gdns. SW5	66	F4
Wetherby Ms. SW5	**18**	**B3**
Wetherby Pl. SW7	**18**	**C2**
Wetherby Pl. SW7	66	F4
Wetherby Rd., Enf.	24	J1
Wetherby Way, Chess.	98	H7
Wetherden St. E17	41	J7
Wetherell Rd. E9	59	G1
Wetherill Rd. N10	40	A1
Wexford Rd. SW12	75	J7
Wey Ct., Epsom	99	C4
Weybourne St. SW18	84	F2
Weybridge Pt. SW11	75	J2
Weybridge Rd., Th.Hth.	94	G4
Weydown Clo. SW19	84	B1
Weyhill Rd. E1	**13**	**J3**
Weyland Rd., Dag.	53	E3
Weyman Rd. SE3	78	J1
Weymouth Ave. NW7	30	E5
Weymouth Ave. W5	64	F3
Weymouth Ct., Sutt.	100	D7
Weymouth Ms. W1	**11**	**D1**
Weymouth Ms. W1	58	B5
Weymouth St. W1	**11**	**C2**
Weymouth St. W1	58	A5
Weymouth Ter. E2	**9**	**G1**
Weymouth Ter. E2	59	C2
Weymouth Wk., Stan.	29	D6
Whadcote St. N4	49	G2
Seven Sisters Rd.		
Whalebone Ave., Rom.	44	F6
Whalebone Ct. EC2	**13**	**C3**
Whalebone Gro., Rom.	44	F6
Whalebone La. E15	51	E7
West Ham La.		
Whalebone La. N., Rom.	44	E2
Whalebone La. S., Dag.	44	F7
Whalebone La. S., Rom.	44	F6
Wharf La., Twick.	82	D1
Wharf Pl. E2	59	D1
Wharf Rd. E15	60	D1
Wharf Rd. N1	**8**	**J2**
Wharf Rd. N1	58	J2
Wharf Rd., Enf.	25	H6
Wharf Rd. Ind. Est., Enf.	25	H6
Wharf St. E16	60	E5
Wharfdale Ct. E5	50	G4
Rushmore Rd.		
Wharfdale Rd. N1	**8**	**B1**
Wharfdale Rd. N1	58	E2
Wharfedale Gdns., Th.Hth.	94	F4
Wharfedale St. SW10	**18**	**A4**
Wharfside Rd. E16	60	E5
Wharncliffe Dr., Sthl.	64	A1
Wharncliffe Gdns. SE25	95	B2
Wharncliffe Rd. SE25	95	B2
Wharton Clo. NW10	47	E6
Wharton Rd., Brom.	96	H1
Wharton St. WC1	**8**	**D4**
Wharton St. WC1	58	F3
Whateley Rd. SE20	86	G7
Whateley Rd. SE22	77	C5
Whatley Ave. SW20	93	A3
Whatman Rd. SE23	77	G7
Wheatfield Way, Kings.T.	91	H2
Wheatfields E6	61	E6
Oxleas		
Wheatfields, Enf.	25	H2
Wheathill Rd. SE20	95	E2
Wheatlands, Houns.	63	G6
Wheatlands Rd. SW17	85	A3
Stapleton Rd.		
Wheatley Clo. NW4	38	G2
Wheatley Cres., Hayes	54	A7
Wheatley Gdns. N9	33	B2
Wheatley Rd., Islw.	73	C3

Wheatley St. W1	**11**	**C2**
Wheatsheaf Clo., Nthlt.	45	E5
Wheatsheaf La. SW6	**65**	**J7**
Wheatsheaf La. SW8	**20**	**A7**
Wheatsheaf La. SW8	67	E7
Wheatsheaf Ter. SW6	66	C7
Bishops Rd.		
Wheatstone Clo., Mitch.	93	H1
Wheatstone Rd. W10	57	B5
Wheel Fm. Dr., Dag.	53	J3
Wheeler Gdns. N1	58	E1
Outram Pl.		
Wheelers Cross, Bark.	61	G2
Wheelwright St. N7	49	F7
Whelan Way, Wall.	101	D3
Wheler St. E1	9	F6
Wheler St. E1	59	C4
Whellock Rd. W4	65	E3
Whenman Ave., Bex.	89	J2
Whernside Clo. SE28	62	C7
Whetstone Clo. N20	31	G2
Oakleigh Rd. N.		
Whetstone Pk. WC2	**12**	**C3**
Whetstone Rd. SE3	78	J2
Whewell Rd. N19	49	E2
Whichcote St. SE1	**16**	**C2**
Whidborne Clo. SE8	78	A2
Cliff Ter.		
Whidborne St. WC1	**8**	**B4**
Whidborne St. WC1	58	E3
Whimbrel Clo. SE28	62	C7
Whinchat Rd. SE28	70	G3
Whinfell Clo. SW16	85	D5
Whinyates Rd. SE9	79	B3
Whipps Cross Rd. E11	42	D5
Whiskin St. EC1	**8**	**G4**
Whiskin St. EC1	58	H3
Whisperwood Clo., Har.	29	B7
Whistler Gdns., Edg.	37	J2
Whistler St. N5	49	H5
Whistler Wk. SW10	**18**	**D7**
Whistlers Ave. SW11	66	G7
Whiston Rd. E2	59	C2
Whitakers Way, Loug.	27	C1
Whitbread Clo. N17	41	D1
Whitbread Rd. SE4	77	H4
Whitburn Rd. SE13	78	B4
Whitby Ave. NW10	56	B3
Whitby Gdns. NW9	38	A3
Whitby Gdns., Sutt.	100	G2
Whitby Rd. SE18	70	C4
Whitby Rd., Har.	45	J3
Whitby Rd., Ruis.	45	B3
Whitby Rd., Sutt.	100	G2
Whitby St. E1	9	F5
Whitcher Clo. SE14	68	H6
Chubworthy St.		
Whitcher Pl. NW1	49	C7
Rochester Rd.		
Whitchurch Ave., Edg.	29	J7
Whitchurch Clo., Edg.	29	J6
Whitchurch Gdns., Edg.	29	J6
Whitchurch La., Edg.	29	G7
Whitchurch Rd. W11	57	A7
Whitcomb Ct. WC2	58	D7
Whitcomb St.		
Whitcomb St. WC2	**11**	**J6**
Whitcomb St. WC2	58	D7
White Acre NW9	38	E2
White Adder Way E14	69	B4
Spindrift Ave.		
White Bear Pl. NW3	48	G4
New End Sq.		
White Butts Rd., Ruis.	45	D3
White Ch. La. E1	13	H3
White Ch. La. E1	59	D6
White Ch. Pas. E1	**13**	**H3**
White City Clo. W12	56	J7
White City Est. W12	56	H7
White City Rd. W12	56	H7
White Conduit St. N1	**8**	**F1**
White Craig Clo., Pnr.	28	G5
White Gdns., Dag.	53	G6
Sterry Rd.		
White Gate Gdns., Har.	29	C7
White Hart La. N17	32	J7
White Hart La. N22	40	G1
White Hart La. NW10	47	F6
Church Rd.		
White Hart La. SW13	74	E2
White Hart La., Rom.	44	G1
White Hart Rd. SE18	70	H4

White Hart Slip, Brom.	96	G2
White Hart St. SE11	20	F3
White Hart St. SE11	67	G5
White Hart Yd. SE1	**17**	**B2**
White Horse Hill, Chis.	88	C4
White Horse La. E1	59	G4
White Horse Ms. SE1	**16**	**F5**
White Horse Rd. E1	59	G6
White Horse Rd. E6	61	C3
White Horse St. W1	**15**	**E2**
White Horse St. W1	67	B1
White Ho. Dr., Stan.	29	F4
White Lo. SE19	85	H7
White Lo. Clo. N2	39	G6
White Lo. Clo., Sutt.	100	F7
White Oak Dr., Beck.	96	C2
White Orchards N20	23	C7
White Orchards, Stan.	29	D5
White Post La. E9	50	J7
White Post La. SE13	78	A3
White Post St. SE15	68	F7
White Rd. E15	51	E7
White St., Sthl.	63	D2
White Swan Ms. W4	65	E6
Bennett St.		
Whiteadder Way E14	69	B4
Taeping St.		
Whitear Wk. E15	51	D6
Whitebarn La., Dag.	62	G1
Whitebeam Ave., Brom.	97	D7
Whitebeam Clo. SW9	67	F7
Clapham Rd.		
Whitebeam Twr. E17	41	H3
Whitechapel High St. E1	**13**	**G3**
Whitechapel High St. E1	59	C6
Whitechapel Rd. E1	**13**	**H2**
Whitechapel Rd. E1	59	D5
Whitecote Rd., Sthl.	55	J6
Whitecroft Clo., Beck.	96	D4
Whitecroft Way, Beck.	96	C5
Whitecross Pl. EC2	**13**	**C1**
Whitecross St. EC1	58	J4
Whitecross St. EC1	**9**	**A5**
Whitecross St. EC2	**13**	**A1**
Whitecross St. EC2	58	J5
Whitefield Ave. NW2	38	J7
Whitefield Clo. SW15	75	B6
Whitefoot La., Brom.	87	C4
Whitefoot Ter., Brom.	87	E3
Whitefriars Ave., Har.	37	B2
Whitefriars Dr., Har.	37	A2
Whitefriars Ave.		
Whitefriars St. EC4	**12**	**F4**
Whitefriars St. EC4	58	G6
Whitehall SW1	**16**	**A1**
Whitehall SW1	67	E1
Whitehall Ct. SW1	**16**	**B2**
Whitehall Ct. SW1	67	E1
Whitehall Cres., Chess.	98	G5
Whitehall Gdns. E4	34	D1
Whitehall Gdns. SW1	**16**	**A2**
Whitehall Gdns. W3	65	A1
Whitehall Gdns. W4	65	B6
Whitehall La., Buck.H.	34	G2
Whitehall Pk. N19	49	C1
Whitehall Pk. Rd. W4	65	B6
Whitehall Pl. E7	51	G5
Station Rd.		
Whitehall Pl. SW1	**16**	**A2**
Whitehall Pl. SW1	67	E1
Whitehall Pl., Wall.	101	B4
Bernard Rd.		
Whitehall Rd. E4	34	E2
Whitehall Rd. W7	64	D2
Whitehall Rd., Brom.	97	A5
Whitehall Rd., Har.	37	B7
Whitehall Rd., Th.Hth.	94	G6
Whitehall Rd., Wdf.Grn.	34	F2
Whitehall St. N17	33	C7
Whitehaven Clo., Brom.	96	G4
Whitehaven St. NW8	**6**	**G6**
Whitehead Clo. N18	33	A5
Whitehead Clo. SW18	75	F7

Whitehead's Gro. SW3	**18**	**H3**
Whitehead's Gro. SW3	66	H5
Whitehills Rd., Loug.	27	D3
Whitehorn Gdns., Croy.	102	E2
Whitehorse La. SE25	95	A4
Whitehorse Rd., Croy.	94	J7
Whitehorse Rd., Th.Hth.	95	A4
Whitehouse Ave., Borwd.	22	B3
Whitehouse Way N14	32	B2
Whiteledges W13	55	F6
Whitelegg Rd. E13	60	F2
Whiteley Rd. SE19	86	A5
Whiteleys Cotts. W14	66	C4
Whiteleys Way, Felt.	81	G3
Whiteoak Gdns., Sid.	79	J7
Whiteoaks La., Grnf.	66	C3
Whites Ave., Ilf.	43	H6
Whites Dr., Brom.	96	F7
Whites Grds. SE1	**17**	**E4**
Whites Grds. SE1	68	B2
Whites Grds. Est. SE1	**17**	**E3**
White's Row E1	**13**	**F2**
White's Row E1	59	C5
White's Sq. SW4	76	D4
Nelson's Row		
Whitestile Rd., Brent.	64	F5
Whitestone La. NW3	48	F3
Heath St.		
Whitestone Wk. NW3	48	F3
North End Way		
Whitethorn Gdns., Enf.	25	A5
Whitethorn St. E3	60	A4
Whitewebbs Way, Orp.	97	J1
Whitfield Pl. W1	**7**	**F6**
Whitfield Rd. E6	51	J7
Whitfield Rd. SE3	78	D1
Whitfield Rd., Bexh.	71	F7
Whitfield St. W1	**7**	**F6**
Whitfield St. W1	58	C4
Whitford Gdns., Mitch.	93	J3
Whitgift Ave., S.Croy.	101	H5
Whitgift St. SE11	**20**	**C1**
Whitgift St. SE11	67	F4
Whitgift St., Croy.	101	J3
High St.		
Whiting Ave., Bark.	52	E7
Whitings, Ilf.	43	G5
Whitings Rd., Barn.	22	J5
Whitings Way E6	61	D5
Whitland Rd., Cars.	100	G1
Whitley Rd. N17	41	B2
Whitlock Dr. SW19	75	B7
Whitman Rd. E3	59	H4
Whitmead Clo., S.Croy.	102	B6
Whitmore Clo. N11	32	B5
Whitmore Gdns. NW10	56	J2
Whitmore Rd. N1	59	B1
Whitmore Rd., Beck.	95	J3
Whitmore Rd., Har.	36	J7
Whitnell Way SW15	74	J5
Whitney Ave., Ilf.	43	A4
Whitney Rd. E10	42	A7
Whitney Wk., Sid.	89	E6
Whitstable Clo., Beck.	95	J1
Whitstable Ho. W10	57	A6
Silchester Rd.		
Whitta Rd. E12	52	A4
Whittaker Ave., Rich.	73	G5
Hill St.		
Whittaker Rd. E6	52	A7
Whittaker Rd., Sutt.	100	C3
Whittaker St. SW1	**19**	**B2**
Whittaker St. SW1	67	A4
Whittaker Way SE1	**21**	**J2**
Whittell Gdns. SE26	86	F3
Whittingstall Rd. SW6	75	C1
Whittington Ave. EC3	**13**	**D4**
Whittington Rd. N22	32	E7
Whittington Way, Pnr.	36	E5
Whittle Clo., Sthl.	54	H6
Whittle Rd., Houns.	63	C7
Whittlebury Clo., Cars.	100	J7
Whittlesea Clo., Har.	28	J7
Whittlesea Rd.		
Whittlesea Path, Har.	36	J1
Whittlesea Rd., Har.	28	J7

Whittlesey St. SE1 16 F2
Whitton Ave. E., Grnf. 46 B5
Whitton Ave. W., Grnf. 46 A5
Whitton Ave. W., 45 H5
Nthlt.
Whitton Clo., Grnf. 46 E6
Whitton Dene, Houns. 72 H5
Whitton Dene, Islw. 73 A5
Whitton Dr., Grnf. 46 D6
Whitton Manor Rd., 72 J5
Islw.
Whitton Rd., Houns. 72 H4
Whitton Rd., Twick. 73 B6
Whitton Wk. E3 60 A3
Whitton Waye, Houns. 72 G6
Whitwell Rd. E13 60 G3
Whitworth Pl. SE18 70 E4
Whitworth Rd. SE18 70 D6
Whitworth Rd. SE25 95 B3
Whitworth St. SE10 69 E5
Whorlton Rd. SE15 77 E3
Whymark Ave. N22 40 G3
Whytecroft, Houns. 63 D7
Whyteville Rd. E7 51 H6
Wick La. E3 50 J7
Wick Rd. E9 50 G6
Wick Rd., Tedd. 82 E7
Wick Sq. E9 50 J6
Eastway
Wicker St. E1 59 E6
Burslem St.
Wickers Oake SE19 86 C4
Wickersley Rd. 76 A2
SW11
Wicket, The, Croy. 103 A5
Wicket Rd., Grnf. 55 D3
Wickets Way, Ilf. 35 J6
Wickford St. E1 59 F4
Wickford Way E17 41 G4
Wickham Ave., Croy. 102 H2
Wickham Ave., Sutt. 99 J5
Wickham Chase, 103 D1
W.Wick.
Wickham Clo., Enf. 25 E3
Wickham Clo., N.Mal. 92 F5
Wickham Ct. Rd., 103 C2
W.Wick.
Wickham Cres., 103 C2
W.Wick.
Wickham Gdns. SE4 77 J3
Wickham Ho. E1 59 F5
Jamaica St.
Wickham La. SE2 71 A5
Wickham La., Well. 71 A5
Wickham Ms. SE4 77 J2
Wickham Rd. E4 34 C7
Wickham Rd. SE4 77 J3
Wickham Rd., Beck. 96 B2
Wickham Rd., Croy. 102 F2
Wickham Rd., Har. 37 A2
Wickham St. SE11 20 C3
Wickham St. SE11 67 F5
Wickham St., Well. 79 H2
Wickham Way, Beck. 96 C4
Wickliffe Ave. N3 39 B2
Wickliffe Gdns., Wem. 47 B2
Wicklow St. WC1 8 C3
Wicklow St. WC1 58 F3
Wicks Clo. SE9 88 A4
Wicksteed Ho., Brent. 64 J5
Wickwood St. SE5 76 H2
Widdecombe Ave., 45 E2
Har.
Widdenham Rd. N7 49 F4
Widdin St. E15 51 D7
Wide Way, Mitch. 94 D3
Widecombe Gdns., 43 B4
Ilf.
Widecombe Rd. SE9 88 B3
Widecombe Way N2 39 G5
Widegate St. E1 13 E2
Widenham Clo., Pnr. 36 C5
Bridle Rd.
Widgeon Clo. E16 60 H6
Maplin Rd.
Widley Rd. W9 57 D3
Widmore Lo. Rd., 97 A2
Brom.
Widmore Rd., Brom. 96 G2
Wieland Rd., Nthwd. 28 A7
Wigan Ho. E5 50 E1
Warwick Gro.
Wigeon Path SE28 70 G3
Wiggington Ave., 47 B6
Wem.
Wiggins Mead NW9 30 F7
Wigham Ho., Bark. 52 F7
Wightman Rd. N4 40 G4

Wightman Rd. N8 40 G4
Wigley Rd., Felt. 81 D2
Wigmore Pl. W1 11 D3
Wigmore Pl. W1 58 B6
Wigmore Rd., Cars. 100 G2
Wigmore St. W1 11 B4
Wigmore St. W1 58 A6
Wigmore Wk., Cars. 100 G2
Wigram Rd. E11 42 J6
Wigram Sq. E17 42 D2
Wigston Clo. N18 33 B5
Wigston Rd. E13 60 H4
Wigton Gdns., Stan. 37 H1
Wigton Pl. SE11 20 F4
Wigton Rd. E17 41 J1
Wilberforce Rd. N4 49 H2
Wilberforce Rd. NW9 84 A6
Wilberforce Way 84 A6
SW19
Wilbraham Pl. SW1 19 A1
Wilbraham Pl. SW1 66 J4
Wilbury Way N18 33 A5
Wilby Ms. W11 66 C1
Wilcox Clo. SW8 20 B7
Wilcox Clo. SW8 67 E7
Wilcox Clo., Borwd. 22 C1
Wilcox Pl. SW1 15 G6
Wilcox Rd. SW8 20 A7
Wilcox Rd. SW8 67 E7
Wilcox Rd., Sutt. 100 E4
Wilcox Rd., Tedd. 82 A4
Wild Ct. WC2 12 C3
Wild Ct. WC2 58 F6
Wild Goose Dr. SE14 77 F1
Wild Hatch NW11 39 D6
Wild St. WC2 12 B4
Wild St. WC2 58 E6
Wildcroft Gdns., 29 G6
Edg.
Wildcroft Rd. SW15 74 J7
Wilde Clo. E8 59 D1
Medesenge Way
Wilde Pl. N13 32 H6
Wilde Pl. SW18 75 G7
Heathfield Rd.
Wilder Clo., Ruis. 45 B1
Wilderness, The, 81 H4
Hmptn.
Park Rd.
Wilderness Rd., Chis. 88 E7
Wilderton Rd. N16 41 B7
Wildfell Rd. SE6 78 B7
Wild's Rents SE1 17 D5
Wild's Rents SE1 68 A3
Wildwood Clo. SE12 78 F7
Wildwood Gro. NW3 48 F1
North End Way
Wildwood Ri. NW11 48 F1
Wildwood Rd. NW11 39 E6
Wildwood Ter. NW3 48 F1
Wilford Clo., Enf. 25 A3
Wilfred Owen Clo. 84 F6
SW19
Tennyson Rd.
Wilfred St. SW1 15 F5
Wilfred St. SW1 67 C3
Wilfrid St. SW1 59 C5
Wilkes Rd., Brent. 64 H6
Albany Rd.
Wilkes St. E1 13 G1
Wilkes St. E1 59 C5
Wilkie Way SE22 86 D1
Lordship La.
Wilkin St. NW5 49 B6
Wilkin St. Ms. NW5 49 B6
Wilkin St.
Wilkins Clo., Mitch. 93 H1
Wilkinson Rd. E16 60 J6
Wilkinson St. SW8 67 F7
Wilkinson Way W4 65 D2
Southfield Rd.
Wilks Gdns., Croy. 102 H1
Orchard Ave.
Wilks Pl. N1 9 E2
Will Crooks Gdns. 78 J4
SE9
Willan Rd. N17 41 A2
Willan Wall E16 60 F7
Victoria Dock Rd.
Willard St. SW8 76 B3
Willcocks Clo., Chess. 98 H3
Willcott Rd. W3 65 B1
Willenhall Ave., Barn. 23 F6
Willenhall Rd. SE18 70 E5
Willersley Ave., Orp. 104 G3
Willersley Ave., Sid. 88 J1
Willersley Clo., Sid. 88 J1

Willes Rd. NW5 49 B6
Willesden La. NW2 47 J6
Willesden La. NW6 57 C1
Willet Way SE16 68 E5
Egan Way
Willett Clo., Nthlt. 54 C3
Broomcroft Ave.
Willett Clo., Orp. 97 H6
Willett Pl., Th.Hth. 94 G5
Willett Rd.
Willett Rd., Th.Hth. 94 G5
Willett Way, Orp. 97 G5
William Barefoot Dr. 88 C4
SE9
William Bonney Est. 76 D4
SW4
William Booth Rd. 95 D1
SE20
William Carey Way, 37 B6
Har.
William Clo., Rom. 44 J1
William Clo., Sthl. 63 J2
Windmill Rd.
William Dunbar Ho. 57 C2
NW6
William Ellis Way 17 J6
SE16
William IV St. WC2 12 A6
William IV St. WC2 58 E7
William Gdns. SW15 74 H5
William Guy Gdns. E3 60 B3
Talwin St.
William Margrie Clo. 77 D2
SE15
Moncrieff St.
William Ms. SW1 15 A4
William Morley Clo. E6 61 A1
William Morris Clo. 41 J3
E17
William Pl. E3 59 J2
Roman Rd.
William Rd. NW1 7 F4
William Rd. NW1 58 C3
William Rd. SW19 84 B7
William Rd., Sutt. 100 F5
William Saville Ho. 57 C2
NW6
William Sq. SE16 59 H7
Rotherhithe St.
William St. E10 42 B6
William St. N17 33 C7
William St. SW1 15 A4
William St. SW1 66 J2
William St., Bark. 52 F7
William St., Cars. 100 H3
Williams Ave. E17 41 J1
Williams Bldgs. E2 59 F4
Williams Clo. N8 40 D6
Coolhurst Rd.
Williams Gro. N22 40 G1
William's La. SW14 74 C3
Williams La., Mord. 93 F5
Williams Rd. W13 55 D7
Williams Rd., Sthl. 63 E4
Williams Ter., Croy. 101 G6
Williamson Clo. SE10 69 F4
Lenthorp Rd.
Williamson Rd. N4 40 H6
Williamson St. N7 49 E4
Williamson Way NW7 31 B6
Willifield Way NW11 39 C4
Willingale Clo., Loug. 27 F2
Willingale Rd.
Willingale Clo., 34 J6
Wdf.Grn.
Willingale Rd., Loug. 27 F1
Willingdon Rd. N22 40 H2
Willingham Clo. NW5 49 C5
Leighton Rd.
Willingham Ter. NW5 49 C5
Leighton Rd.
Willingham Way, 92 A3
Kings.T.
Willington Ct. E5 50 H3
Mandeville St.
Willington Rd. SW9 76 E3
Willis Ave., Sutt. 100 H7
Willis Rd. E15 60 F2
Willis Rd., Croy. 94 J7
Willis Rd., Erith 71 J4
Willis St. E14 60 B6
Willmore End SW19 93 E1
Willoughby Ave., 101 F4
Croy.
Willoughby Gro. N17 33 E7
Willoughby La. N17 33 E6
Willoughby Pk. Rd. 33 E7
N17

Willoughby Rd. N8 40 G3
Willoughby Rd. NW3 48 G4
Willoughby Rd., 91 J1
Kings.T.
Willoughby Rd., 73 G6
Twick.
Willoughby St. WC1 12 A2
Willoughby Way SE7 69 H4
Willow Ave. SW13 74 F2
Willow Ave., Sid. 68 A6
Willow Bank SW6 75 B3
Willow Bank, Rich. 82 E3
Willow Bri. Rd. N1 49 J6
Willow Clo. W5 55 G5
Willow Clo., Bex. 80 F6
Willow Clo., Brent. 64 F6
Willow Clo., Brom. 97 C5
Willow Clo., Buck.H. 35 A3
Willow Clo., Th.Hth. 94 G6
Willow Cotts., Mitch. 94 C3
Willow Cotts., Rich. 65 A6
Cambridge Cotts.
Willow Ct., Edg. 29 H4
Willow Dene, Pnr. 36 D2
Willow Dr., Barn. 23 B4
Willow End N20 31 D2
Willow End, Nthwd. 28 A6
Willow End, Surb. 98 H1
Willow Fm. La. 74 H3
SW15
Queens Ride
Willow Gdns., Houns. 72 G1
Willow Grn. NW9 38 E1
Clayton Fld.
Willow Grn., Borwd. 22 D5
Ashley Dr.
Willow Gro. E13 60 G2
Libra Rd.
Willow Gro., Chis. 88 D6
Willow La., Mitch. 93 J6
Willow La. Ind. Est., 93 J6
Mitch.
Willow Mt., Croy. 102 B3
Langton Way
Willow Pl. SW1 19 G1
Willow Pl. SW1 67 C4
Willow Rd. NW3 48 G4
Willow Rd. W5 64 H2
Willow Rd., Enf. 25 B3
Willow Rd., N.Mal. 92 C4
Willow Rd., Rom. 44 E6
Willow Rd., Wall. 101 B7
Willow St. E4 26 D7
Willow St. EC2 9 D5
Willow St. EC2 59 B4
Willow St., Rom. 44 A4
Willow Tree Clo. E3 59 J1
Birdsfield La.
Willow Tree Clo. 84 E1
SW18
Cargill Rd.
Willow Tree Clo., 54 C4
Hayes
Willow Tree La., 54 C4
Hayes
Willow Tree Wk., 96 H1
Brom.
Willow Vale W12 65 G1
Willow Vale, Chis. 88 E6
Willow Vw. SW19 93 G1
Willow Wk. E17 41 J5
Willow Wk. N2 39 G2
Central Ave.
Willow Wk. N15 40 H4
Willow Wk. N21 24 F6
Willow Wk. SE1 21 E1
Willow Wk. SE1 68 B4
Willow Wk., Orp. 104 E3
Willow Wk., Sutt. 100 C3
Willow Way N3 31 E7
Willow Way SE26 86 E3
Willow Way W11 66 A1
Freston Rd.
Willow Way, Epsom 99 D6
Willow Way, Sun. 90 A4
Willow Way, Twick. 81 H2
Willow Way, Wem. 46 D3
Willow Wd. Cres. 95 B6
SE25
Willowbrook Rd. 21 G6
SE15
Willowbrook Rd. SE15 68 C6
Willowbrook Rd., Sthl. 63 G3
Willowcourt Ave., Har. 37 E5
Willowdene N6 39 J7
Denewood Rd.
Willowdene Clo., 72 J7
Twick.

Willowhayne Dr., 90 B7
Walt.
Willowhayne Gdns., 99 J3
Wor.Pk.
Willowmead Clo. W5 55 G5
Willows, The, Buck.H. 35 A3
Willows, The, Esher 98 B6
Albany Cres.
Willows Ave., Mord. 93 E5
Willows Clo., Pnr. 36 C2
Willrose Cres. SE2 71 B5
Wills Cres., Houns. 72 H6
Wills Gro. NW7 30 G5
Wilman Gro. E8 50 D7
Wilmar Gdns., 103 B1
W.Wick.
Wilmcote Ho. W2 57 D5
Wilmer Clo., Kings.T. 82 J5
Wilmer Cres., Kings.T. 82 J5
Wilmer Gdns. N1 59 B1
Wilmer Lea Clo. E15 51 C7
Wilmer Pl. N16 50 C2
Stoke Newington
Ch. St.
Wilmer Way N14 32 D5
Wilmington Ave. W4 65 D7
Wilmington Gdns., 52 G6
Bark.
Wilmington Sq. WC1 **8 E4**
Wilmington Sq. WC1 58 G3
Wilmington St. WC1 **8 E4**
Wilmot Clo. N2 39 F2
Wilmot Clo. SE15 68 D7
Wilmot Pl. NW1 49 C7
Wilmot Pl. W7 64 B1
Boston Rd.
Wilmot Rd. E10 51 B2
Wilmot Rd. N17 41 A3
Wilmot Rd., Cars. 100 J5
Wilmot St. E2 59 E4
Wilmount St. SE18 70 E4
Wilna Rd. SW18 75 F7
Wilsham St. W11 66 A1
Wilshaw St. SE14 78 A1
Wilsmere Dr., Har. 29 B7
Wilsmere Dr., Nthlt. 45 E6
Wilson Ave., Mitch. 84 H7
Wilson Clo., Wem. 37 J7
Wilson Dr., Wem. 37 J7
Wilson Gdns., Har. 36 J7
Wilson Gro. SE16 68 E2
Wilson Rd. E6 61 A3
Wilson Rd. SE5 77 B1
Wilson Rd., Chess. 98 J6
Wilson Rd., Ilf. 43 C7
Wilson St. E17 42 C5
Wilson St. EC2 **13 C1**
Wilson St. EC2 59 A5
Wilson St. N21 24 G7
Wilsons Pl. E14 59 J6
Salmon La.
Wilsons Rd. W6 66 A5
Wilstone Clo., Hayes 54 E4
Kingsash Dr.
Wilthorne Gdns., 53 H7
Dag.
Acre Rd.
Wilton Ave. W4 65 E5
Wilton Cres. SW1 **15 B4**
Wilton Cres. SW1 67 A2
Wilton Cres. SW19 93 C1
Wilton Gdns., W.Mol. 90 G3
Wilton Gro. SW19 93 C1
Wilton Gro., N.Mal. 92 F6
Wilton Ms. SW1 **15 C5**
Wilton Ms. SW1 67 A3
Wilton Par., Felt. 81 A2
Highfield Rd.
Wilton Pk. Ct. SE18 79 D1
Prince Imperial Rd.
Wilton Pl. SW1 **15 B4**
Wilton Pl. SW1 67 A2
Wilton Rd. N10 40 A2
Wilton Rd. SE2 71 C4
Wilton Rd. SW1 **15 E6**
Wilton Rd. SW1 67 C4
Wilton Rd. SW19 84 H7
Wilton Rd., Barn. 23 J4
Wilton Rd., Houns. 72 D3
Wilton Rd., Ilf. 52 E3
Ilford La.
Wilton Row SW1 **15 B4**
Wilton Row SW1 67 A2
Wilton Sq. N1 59 A1
Wilton St. SW1 **15 D5**
Wilton St. SW1 67 B3
Wilton Ter. SW1 **15 B5**
Wilton Ter. SW1 67 A3

Wilton Vill. N1 59 A1
Wilton Way E8 50 D6
Wiltshire Clo. SW3 **18 J2**
Wiltshire Gdns. N4 40 J6
Wiltshire Gdns., 81 J1
Twick.
Wiltshire Rd. SW9 76 G3
Wiltshire Rd., Th.Hth. 94 G3
Wiltshire Row N1 59 A1
Wilverley Cres., 92 E6
N.Mal.
Wimbart Rd. SW2 76 F7
Wimbledon Bri. 84 C6
SW19
Wimbledon Common 83 F4
SW19
Wimbledon Hill Rd. 84 B6
SW19
Wimbledon Pk. Est. 84 C1
SW19
Wimbledon Pk. Rd. 84 C1
SW18
Wimbledon Pk. Rd. 84 B2
SW19
Wimbledon Pk. Side 84 A2
SW19
Wimbledon Rd. SW17 84 F4
Wimbledon Sta. 84 C6
SW19
The Bdy.
Wimbolt St. E2 **9 H3**
Wimbolt St. E2 59 D3
Wimborne Ave., 54 B6
Hayes
Wimborne Ave., Orp. 97 J3
Wimborne Ave., Sthl. 63 G4
Wimborne Clo. SE12 78 F5
Wimborne Clo., 34 J2
Buck.H.
Wimborne Clo., 99 J1
Wor.Pk.
Wimborne Dr. NW9 38 A3
Wimborne Dr., Pnr. 36 D7
Wimborne Gdns. W13 55 E5
Wimborne Rd. N9 33 D2
Wimborne Rd. N17 41 B2
Wimborne Way, Beck. 95 G4
Wimbourne St. N1 **9 B1**
Wimbourne St. N1 59 A2
Wimpole Clo., Brom. 96 J4
Stanley Rd.
Wimpole Clo., 91 J2
Kings.T.
Wimpole Ms. W1 **11 D1**
Wimpole Ms. W1 58 B5
Wimpole St. W1 **11 D2**
Wimpole St. W1 58 B6
Wimshurst Clo., 101 E1
Croy.
Franklin Way
Winans Wk. SW9 76 G2
Wincanton Cres., 45 G5
Nthlt.
Wincanton Gdns., Ilf. 43 E3
Wincanton Rd. SW18 75 C7
Winchcomb Gdns. 79 A3
SE9
Winchcombe Rd., 100 G2
Cars.
Winchelsea Ave., 71 F7
Bexh.
Winchelsea Clo. 75 A5
SW15
Winchelsea Rd. E7 51 G4
Winchelsea Rd. N17 41 B3
Winchelsea Rd. 56 D1
NW10
Winchelsey Ri., 102 C6
S.Croy.
Winchendon Rd. SW6 66 C7
Winchendon Rd., 82 A4
Tedd.
Winchester Ave. NW6 57 B1
Winchester Ave. NW9 37 J3
Winchester Ave., 63 F6
Houns.
Winchester Clo. E6 61 B6
Boultwood Rd.
Winchester Clo. SE17 **20 H2**
Winchester Clo. SE17 67 H4
Winchester Clo., 96 F3
Brom.
Winchester Clo., Enf. 25 B5
Winchester Clo., 83 B7
Kings.T.
Winchester Dr., Pnr. 36 D5
Winchester Ho. SE18 70 A7
Shooter's Hill Rd.

Winchester Ms. NW3 48 G7
Winchester Rd.
Winchester Pk., Brom. 96 F3
Winchester Pl. E8 50 C5
Kingsland High St.
Winchester Pl. N6 49 B1
Cromwell Ave.
Winchester Pl. W3 65 C2
Avenue Rd.
Winchester Rd. E4 34 C7
Winchester Rd. N6 40 B7
Winchester Rd. N9 33 D2
Winchester Rd. NW3 48 G7
Winchester Rd., 80 D2
Bexh.
Winchester Rd., 96 F3
Brom.
Winchester Rd., Felt. 81 F3
Winchester Rd., Har. 37 H4
Winchester Rd., Ilf. 52 G3
Winchester Rd., 73 E7
Twick.
Winchester Sq. SE1 **17 B1**
Winchester St. SW1 **19 E3**
Winchester St. SW1 67 B5
Winchester St. W3 65 C2
Winchester Wk. SE1 **17 B1**
Winchester Wk. SE1 68 A1
Winchet Wk., Croy. 95 F6
Medway Clo.
Winchfield Clo., Har. 37 F6
Winchfield Rd. SE26 86 H5
Winchilsea Cres., 90 J2
W.Mol.
Winchmore Hill Rd. 32 D1
N14
Winchmore Hill Rd. 24 F7
N21
Winckley Clo., Har. 37 J5
Wincott St. SE11 **20 F2**
Wincott St. SE11 67 G4
Wincrofts Dr. SE9 79 G4
Windborough Rd., 101 A7
Cars.
Windermere Ave. N3 39 D3
Windermere Ave. 57 B1
NW6
Windermere Ave. 93 E3
SW19
Windermere Ave., 37 F7
Har.
Windermere Ave., 36 C7
Ruis.
Windermere Ave., 37 F7
Wem.
Windermere Clo., 104 E3
Orp.
Windermere Ct. SW13 65 F6
Windermere Gdns., 43 B5
Ilf.
Windermere Gro., 46 F1
Wem.
Windermere Ave.
Windermere Ho., 73 C5
Islw.
Windermere Rd. N10 40 B1
Windermere Rd. N19 49 C2
Holloway Rd.
Windermere Rd. 83 E4
SW15
Windermere Rd. 94 C1
SW16
Windermere Rd. W5 64 F3
Windermere Rd., 80 J2
Bexh.
Windermere Rd., 102 C1
Croy.
Windermere Rd., Sthl. 54 F5
Windermere Rd., 103 E2
W.Wick.
Winders Rd. SW11 75 H2
Windfield Clo. SE26 86 G4
Windham Rd., Rich. 73 J3
Winding Way, Dag. 53 C3
Winding Way, Har. 46 B4
Windlass Pl. SE8 68 H4
Windlesham Gro. 84 A1
SW19
Windley Clo. SE23 86 F2
Windmill Ave., Sthl. 63 J2
Windmill Clo. SE1 **21 J1**
Windmill Clo. SE13 78 C2
Windmill Clo., Surb. 98 F1
Windmill Ct. NW2 48 B6
Windmill Dr. SW4 76 B5
Windmill Dr., Kes. 103 J4
Windmill Gdns., Enf. 24 G3
Windmill Gro., Croy. 94 J6

Windmill Hill NW3 48 F3
Windmill Hill, Enf. 24 H3
Windmill La. E15 51 D6
Windmill La., Barn. 22 F6
Windmill La., Grnf. 54 J5
Windmill La., Islw. 64 B4
Windmill La., Sthl. 63 J2
Windmill La., Surb. 91 E6
Windmill La., Wat. 29 A1
(Bushey)
Chiswick Common Rd.
Windmill Ms. W4 65 E4
Windmill Pas. W4 65 E4
Chiswick Common Rd.
Windmill Ri., Kings.T. 83 B7
Windmill Rd. N18 33 A4
Windmill Rd. SW18 75 G6
Windmill Rd. SW19 83 J3
Windmill Rd. W4 65 E4
Windmill Rd. W5 64 F4
Windmill Rd., Brent. 64 G5
Windmill Rd., Croy. 94 J7
Windmill Rd., Hmptn. 81 H5
Windmill Rd., Mitch. 94 C5
Windmill Row SE11 **20 E4**
Windmill Row SE11 67 G5
Windmill St. W1 **11 H2**
Windmill St. W1 58 D5
Windmill St., Wat. 29 B1
(Bushey)
Windmill Wk. SE1 **16 F2**
Windmill Wk. SE1 67 G1
Windover Ave. NW9 38 D4
Windrose Clo. SE16 68 G2
Windrush Clo. SW11 75 G4
Maysoule Rd.
Windrush Clo. W4 74 C1
Windrush La. SE23 86 G3
Windsor Ave. E17 41 H2
Windsor Ave. SW19 93 F1
Windsor Ave., Edg. 36 B3
Windsor Ave., N.Mal. 92 C5
Windsor Ave., Sutt. 100 B3
Windsor Ave., W.Mol. 90 G3
Windsor Cen., The 85 J4
SE27
Advance Rd.
Windsor Clo. N3 39 B2
Windsor Clo. SE27 85 J4
Windsor Clo., Borwd. 22 A1
Warenford Way
Windsor Clo., Brent. 64 E6
Amalgamated Dr.
Windsor Clo., Chis. 88 E5
Windsor Clo., Har. 45 G3
Windsor Clo., Nthwd. 36 A2
Windsor Ct. N14 24 C7
Windsor Ct., Sun. 81 A6
Windsor Rd.
Windsor Cres., Har. 45 G3
Windsor Cres., Wem. 47 B3
Windsor Dr., Barn. 23 J6
Windsor Gdns. W9 57 D5
Windsor Gdns., Croy. 101 E3
Richmond Rd.
Windsor Gro. SE27 85 J4
Windsor Pl. SW1 **15 G6**
Windsor Rd. E4 34 B4
Chivers Rd.
Windsor Rd. E7 51 H5
Windsor Rd. E10 51 B2
Windsor Rd. E11 51 G1
Windsor Rd. N3 39 B2
Windsor Rd. N7 49 E3
Windsor Rd. N13 32 G3
Windsor Rd. N17 41 D2
Windsor Rd. NW2 47 H6
Windsor Rd. W5 55 H7
Windsor Rd., Barn. 23 A6
Windsor Rd., Bexh. 80 E4
Windsor Rd., Dag. 53 E3
Windsor Rd., Har. 37 A1
Windsor Rd., Houns. 72 B2
Windsor Rd., Ilf. 52 E4
Windsor Rd., Kings.T. 82 H7
Windsor Rd., Rich. 73 J2
Windsor Rd., Sthl. 63 F3
Windsor Rd., Sun. 81 A6
Windsor Rd., Tedd. 82 A5
Windsor Rd., Th.Hth. 94 H2
Windsor Rd., Wor.Pk. 97 G2
Windsor St. N1 58 H1
Windsor Ter. N1 **9 A3**
Windsor Ter. N1 58 J3
Windsor Wk. SE5 77 A2
Windsor Way W14 66 A4
Windsors, The, 35 B2
Buck.H.

Windspoint Dr. SE15 68 E6
Ethnard Rd.
Windus Rd. N16 50 C1
Windus Wk. N16 50 C1
Alkham Rd.
Windy Ridge, Brom. 97 B1
Windyridge Clo. 84 A5
SW19
Wine Clo. E1 59 F7
Wine Office Ct. EC4 12 F4
Winford Ho. E3 50 J7
Jodrell Rd.
Winforton St. SE10 78 C1
Winfrith Rd. SW18 75 F7
Wingate Cres., Croy. 94 D6
Wingate Rd. W6 65 H3
Wingate Rd., Ilf. 52 E5
Wingate Trd. Est., Sid. 89 C6
Wingate Trd. Est. N17 33 C7
Wingfield Ms. SE15 77 D3
Wingfield St.
Wingfield Rd. E15 51 E4
Wingfield Rd. E17 42 B5
Wingfield Rd., 83 A6
Kings.T.
Wingfield St. SE15 77 D3
Wingfield Way, Ruis. 45 B6
Wingford Rd. SW2 76 E6
Wingmore Rd. SE24 76 J3
Wingrave Rd. W6 65 J6
Wingrove Rd. SE6 87 E2
Wings Clo., Sutt. 100 D4
Winifred Gro. SW11 75 J4
Winifred Rd. SW19 93 D1
Winifred Rd., Dag. 53 E2
Winifred Rd., Hmptn. 81 G4
Winifred St. E16 70 C1
Winifred Ter., Enf. 25 C7
Edward Clo.
Winkfield Rd. E13 60 H2
Winkfield Rd. N22 40 G1
Winkley St. E2 59 E2
Winlaton Rd., Brom. 87 D4
Winmill Rd., Dag. 53 F3
Winn Common Rd. 70 H6
SE18
Winn Rd. SE12 87 H1
Winnett St. W1 11 H5
Winnings Wk., Nthlt. 45 E6
Arnold Rd.
Winnington Clo. N2 39 G6
Winnington Rd. N2 48 G1
Winns Ave. E17 41 H3
Winns Ms. N15 41 B4
Grove Pk. Rd.
Winns Ter. E17 42 A2
Winsbeach E17 42 D2
Winscombe Cres. W5 55 G4
Winscombe St. N19 49 B2
Winscombe Way, 29 D5
Stan.
Winsford Rd. SE6 86 J3
Winsford Ter. N18 33 A5
Winsham Gro. SW11 76 A5
Winslade Rd. SW2 76 E5
Winslade Way SE6 78 B7
Rushey Grn.
Winsland Ms. W2 10 E3
Winsland St. W2 10 E3
Winsland St. W2 57 G6
Winsley St. W1 11 F3
Winsley St. W1 58 C6
Winslow SE17 21 D4
Winslow Clo. NW10 47 E3
Neasden La. N.
Winslow Clo., Pnr. 36 B6
Winslow Gro. E4 34 E2
Winslow Rd. W6 65 J6
Winslow Way, Felt. 81 D3
Winsor Ter. E6 61 D5
Winstanley Est. 75 G3
SW11
Winstanley Rd. SW11 75 G3
Winstead Gdns., Dag. 53 J5
Winston Ave. NW9 38 E7
Winston Clo., Har. 29 C6
Winston Clo., Rom. 44 H4
Winston Ct., Har. 28 H7
Winston Rd. N16 50 A4
Winston Wk. W4 65 D4
Acton La.
Winston Way, Ilf. 52 E3
Winstre Rd., Borwd. 22 A1
Winter Ave. E6 61 B1
Winter Box Wk., 73 J4
Rich.
Winterborne Ave., 104 G3
Orp.

Winterbourne Rd. 86 J1
SE6
Winterbourne Rd., 53 C2
Dag.
Winterbourne Rd., 94 G4
Th.Hth.
Winterbrook Rd. SE24 76 J6
Winterfold Clo. SW19 84 B2
Wintergreen Clo. E6 61 B5
Yarrow Cres.
Winters Rd., T.Ditt. 91 E7
Winterstoke Gdns. 30 G5
NW7
Winterstoke Rd. SE6 86 J1
Winterton Ho. E1 59 E6
Winterton Pl. SW10 18 D5
Winterwell Rd. SW2 76 E5
Winthorpe Rd. SW15 75 B4
Winthrop St. E1 59 E5
Winthrop Wk., Wem. 46 H3
Everard Way
Winton Ave. N11 32 C7
Winton Clo. N9 25 G7
Winton Gdns., Edg. 29 J7
Winton Rd., Orp. 104 E4
Winton Way SW16 85 G5
Wisbeach Rd., Croy. 95 A5
Wisdons Clo., Dag. 53 H1
Wise La. NW7 30 G5
Wise Rd. E15 60 D1
Wiseman Ct. SE19 86 C5
Wiseman Rd. E10 51 A2
Wiseton Rd. SW17 84 H1
Wishart Rd. SE3 79 A2
Wisley Rd. SW11 76 A5
Wisley Rd., Orp. 89 A7
Wisteria Clo., Orp. 104 E2
Wisteria Rd. SE13 78 D4
Witan St. E2 59 E3
Witham St. E2, Loug. 27 B6
Witham Rd. SE20 95 F3
Witham Rd. W13 64 D1
Witham Rd., Dag. 53 G5
Witham Rd., Islw. 73 A1
Witherby Clo., Croy. 102 B5
Witherfield Way SE16 68 E5
Egan Way
Witherington Rd. N5 49 G5
Withers Clo., Chess. 98 F6
Mansfield Rd.
Withers Mead NW9 38 F1
Witherston Way SE9 88 D2
Withy Mead E4 34 D3
Withycombe Rd. 75 A7
SW19
Witley Cres., Croy. 103 C6
Witley Gdns., Sthl. 63 F4
Witley Rd. N19 49 C2
Holloway Rd.
Witney Clo., Pnr. 28 F6
Witney Path SE23 86 G3
Inglemere Rd.
Wittenham Way E4 34 D3
Wittersham Rd., 87 F5
Brom.
Wivenhoe Clo. SE15 77 E3
Wivenhoe Ct., Houns. 72 F4
Wivenhoe Rd., Bark. 62 A2
Wiverton Rd. SE26 86 F6
Wix Rd., Dag. 62 D1
Wixs La. SW4 76 B3
Woburn Clo. SW19 84 F6
Tintern Clo.
Woburn Pl. WC1 7 J5
Woburn Pl. WC1 58 D4
Woburn Rd., Cars. 100 H1
Woburn Rd., Croy. 101 J1
Woburn Sq. WC1 7 J6
Woburn Sq. WC1 58 D4
Woburn Wk. WC1 7 J4
Woffington Clo., 91 F1
Kings.T.
Woking Clo. SW15 74 F4
Woldham Rd., Brom. 96 J4
Wolds Dr., Orp. 104 D4
Wolfe Clo., Brom. 96 G6
Wolfe Clo., Hayes 54 B3
Ayles Rd.
Wolfe Cres. SE7 70 A5
Wolfe Cres. SE16 68 G2
Wolferton Rd. E12 52 C4
Wolffe Gdns. E15 51 H5
Wolfington Rd. SE13 78 E5
Wolfington Rd. SE27 85 H4
Wolftencroft Clo. 75 G3
SW11
Wollaston Clo. SE1 20 J1
Wolmer Clo., Edg. 30 B4

Wolmer Gdns., Edg. 30 A3
Wolseley Ave. SW19 84 D2
Wolseley Gdns. W4 65 B6
Wolseley Rd. E7 51 H7
Wolseley Rd. N8 40 D6
Wolseley Rd. N22 40 F1
Wolseley Rd. W4 65 C4
Wolseley Rd., Har. 37 B3
Wolseley Rd., Mitch. 94 A7
Wolseley St. SE1 17 G4
Wolseley St. SE1 68 D2
Wolsey Ave. E6 61 D3
Wolsey Ave. E17 41 J3
Wolsey Ave., T.Ditt. 91 C5
Aragon Ave.
Wolsey Clo. SW20 83 H7
Wolsey Clo., Houns. 72 J4
Wolsey Clo., Kings.T. 82 B1
Wolsey Clo., Sthl. 63 J3
Wolsey Clo., Wor.Pk. 99 G4
Wolsey Cres., Mord. 93 B7
Wolsey Dr., Kings.T. 82 H5
Wolsey Gdns., Ilf. 35 E6
Wolsey Gro., Edg. 30 D7
Wolsey Ms. NW5 49 C6
Wolsey Ms., Orp. 104 J5
Osgood Ave.
Wolsey Rd. N1 50 A5
Wolsey Rd., E.Mol. 91 A4
Wolsey Rd., Enf. 25 E2
Wolsey Rd., Hmptn. 81 H6
Wolsey St. E1 59 F5
Sidney Ave.
Wolsey Way, Chess. 99 A5
Wolstonbury N12 31 D5
Wolvercote Rd. SE2 71 D2
Wolverley St. E2 59 E3
Bethnal Grn. Rd.
Wolverton SE17 21 D3
Wolverton Ave., 92 A1
Kings.T.
Wolverton Gdns. W5 55 J7
Wolverton Gdns. W6 66 A4
Wolverton Rd., Stan. 29 E6
Wolverton Way N14 24 C5
Wolves La. N13 32 G6
Wolves La. N22 32 G7
Womersley Rd. N8 40 F6
Wonford Clo., 92 E1
Kings.T.
Wontner Clo. N1 49 J7
Greenman St.
Wontner Rd. SW17 84 J2
Wood Clo. E2 9 H5
Wood Clo. E2 59 D4
Wood Clo. NW9 38 D7
Wood Clo., Har. 37 A7
Wood Dr., Chis. 88 B6
Wood End Ave., Har. 45 H4
Wood End Clo., Nthlt. 46 A5
Wood End Gdns., 45 J5
Nthlt.
Wood End La., Nthlt. 45 H6
Wood End Rd., Har. 46 A4
Wood End Way, Nthlt. 45 J5
Wood La. N6 40 B6
Wood La. NW9 38 D7
Wood La. W12 56 J6
Wood La., Dag. 53 C4
Wood La., Islw. 64 B6
Wood La., Stan. 29 D3
Wood La., Wdf.Grn. 34 F4
Wood Lo. Gdns., 88 B7
Brom.
Wood Lo. La., 103 C3
W.Wick.
Wood Pt. E16 60 G5
Fife Rd.
Wood Ride, Barn. 23 G1
Wood Ride, Orp. 97 G4
Wood St. E16 60 H7
Ethel Rd.
Wood St. E17 42 C3
Wood St. EC2 13 A4
Wood St. EC2 58 J6
Wood St. W4 65 E5
Wood St., Barn. 22 J4
Wood St., Kings.T. 91 H1
Wood St., Mitch. 94 A7
Wood Vale N10 40 C5
Wood Vale SE23 86 E1
Wood Vale Est. SE23 77 F6
Wood Way, Orp. 104 D2
Wood Wf. SE10 69 B6
Thames St.
Woodall Rd., Enf. 25 G6
Woodbank Rd., 87 F3
Brom.

Woodbastwick Rd. 86 G5
SE26
Woodberry Ave. N21 32 G2
Woodberry Ave., Har. 36 H4
Woodberry Clo., Sun. 81 A6
Ashridge Way
Woodberry Cres. N10 40 B3
Woodberry Down N4 40 J7
Woodberry Down Est. 40 J7
N4
Woodberry Gdns. N12 31 F6
Woodberry Gro. N4 40 J7
Woodberry Gro. N12 31 F6
Woodberry Way E4 34 C1
Woodberry Way N12 31 F6
Woodbine Clo., Twick. 82 A2
Woodbine Gro. SE20 86 E7
Woodbine La., 99 H3
Wor.Pk.
Woodbine Pl. E11 42 G6
Woodbine Rd., Sid. 88 H1
Woodbine Ter. E9 50 F6
Morning La.
Woodbines Ave., 91 G3
Kings.T.
Woodborough Rd. 74 H4
SW15
Woodbourne Ave. 85 D3
SW16
Woodbourne Clo. 85 E3
SW16
Woodbourne Ave.
Woodbourne Dr., 98 C6
Esher
Woodbourne Gdns., 101 B7
Wall.
Woodbridge Clo. N7 49 F2
Woodbridge Clo. NW2 47 G3
Woodbridge Ct., 35 B7
Wdf.Grn.
Woodbridge Rd., 52 J5
Bark.
Woodbridge St. EC1 8 G5
Woodbridge St. EC1 58 H4
Woodbrook Rd. SE2 71 A6
Woodburn Clo. NW4 39 A5
Woodbury Clo. E11 42 H4
Woodbury Clo., Croy. 102 C2
Woodbury Hill, Loug. 27 B3
Woodbury Hollow, 27 B2
Loug.
Woodbury Pk. Rd. 55 E4
W13
Woodbury Rd. E17 42 B4
Woodchester Sq. W17 84 H5
Woodchester Sq. W2 10 A1
Woodchester Sq. W2 57 E5
Woodchurch Clo., Sid. 88 G3
Woodchurch Dr., 88 A7
Brom.
Woodchurch Rd. NW6 48 D7
Woodclyffe Dr., Chis. 97 D2
Woodcock Ct., Har. 37 H7
Woodcock Dell Ave., 37 G7
Har.
Woodcock Hill, Har. 37 F5
Woodcombe Cres. 86 F6
SE23
Woodcote Ave. NW7 30 J6
Woodcote Ave., 94 H4
Th.Hth.
Woodcote Clo., Enf. 25 F6
Woodcote Clo., 82 J5
Kings.T.
Woodcote Dr., Orp. 104 G1
Woodcote Ms., Wall. 101 B6
Woodcote Pl. SE27 85 H5
Woodcote Rd. E11 42 G7
Woodcote Rd., Wall. 101 B6
Woodcroft N21 32 F1
Woodcroft SE9 88 C3
Woodcroft, Grnf. 46 D6
Woodcroft Ave. NW7 30 E7
Woodcroft Ave., Stan. 37 C1
Woodcroft Rd., 94 H5
Th.Hth.
Woodedge Clo. E4 34 F1
Woodend SE19 85 J6
Woodend, Sutt. 100 F2
Woodend Gdns., Enf. 24 E4
Woodend Rd. E17 42 C2
Wooder Gdns. E7 51 G4
Wooderson Clo. SE25 95 B4
Woodfall Ave., Barn. 23 C5
Woodfall Rd. N4 49 G1
Woodfall St. SW3 18 J4
Woodfall St. SW3 66 J5
Woodfarrs SE5 77 A4

Name	Ref
Woodfield Ave. NW9	38 E4
Woodfield Ave. SW16	85 D3
Woodfield Ave. W5	55 F4
Woodfield Ave., Cars.	101 A6
Woodfield Clo. Wem.	46 F3
Woodfield Clo. SE19	85 J7
Woodfield Clo., Enf.	25 B4
Woodfield Cres. W5	55 G4
Woodfield Dr., Barn.	32 A1
Woodfield Gdns. W9	57 C5
Woodfield Rd.	
Woodfield Gdns. N.Mal.	92 F5
Woodfield Gro. SW16	85 D3
Woodfield La. SW16	85 D3
Woodfield Pl. W9	57 C4
Woodfield Rd. W5	55 F4
Woodfield Rd. W9	57 C5
Woodfield Rd., Houns.	72 B2
Woodfield Rd., T.Ditt.	98 C2
Woodfield Way N11	32 D7
Woodford Ave., Ilf.	43 E3
Woodford Bri. Rd., Ilf.	43 A3
Woodford Ct. W12	66 A2
Shepherds Bush Grn.	
Woodford Cres., Pnr.	36 B2
Woodford New Rd. E17	42 E4
Woodford New Rd. E18	42 E2
Woodford New Rd., Wdf.Grn.	34 F7
Woodford Pl., Wem.	46 H1
Woodford Rd. E7	51 H4
Woodford Rd. E18	42 G4
Woodford Trd. Est., Wdf.Grn.	43 A2
Woodgate Ave., Chess.	98 G5
Woodgate Cres., Nthwd.	28 A6
Woodger Rd. W12	65 J2
Goldhawk Rd.	
Woodget Clo. E6	61 B6
Remington Rd.	
Woodgrange Ave. N12	31 G6
Woodgrange Ave. W5	65 A1
Woodgrange Ave. Enf.	25 D6
Woodgrange Ave. Har.	37 F5
Woodgrange Clo., Har.	37 G5
Woodgrange Gdns., Enf.	25 D6
Woodgrange Rd. E7	51 H5
Woodgrange Ter., Enf.	25 D6
Great Cambridge Rd.	
Woodhall Ave. SE21	86 C3
Woodhall Ave., Pnr.	36 E2
Woodhall Dr. SE21	86 C3
Woodhall Dr., Pnr.	36 D1
Woodhall Gate, Pnr.	28 D7
Woodhall La., Wat.	28 D3
Woodhall Rd., Pnr.	28 D7
Woodham Ct. E18	42 F4
Woodham Rd. SE6	87 C3
Woodhatch Clo. E6	61 B6
Remington Rd.	
Woodhaven Gdns., Ilf.	43 F3
Brandville Gdns.	
Woodhayes Rd. SW19	83 J7
Woodhead Dr., Orp.	104 H2
Sherlies Ave.	
Woodheyes Rd. NW10	47 D5
Woodhill SE18	70 B4
Woodhill Cres., Har.	37 G6
Woodhouse Ave., Grnf.	55 C2
Woodhouse Clo., Grnf.	55 C2
Woodhouse Eaves, Nthwd.	28 A5
Woodhouse Gro. E12	52 B6
Woodhouse Rd. E11	51 F3
Woodhouse Rd. N12	31 F6
Woodhurst Ave., Orp.	97 F6
Woodhurst Rd. SE2	71 A5
Woodhurst Rd. W3	56 C7
Woodington Clo. SE9	79 D6
Woodison St. E3	59 H4
Woodknoll Dr., Chis.	97 C1
Woodland Clo. NW9	38 C6
Woodland Clo. SE19	86 B6
Woodland Hill	
Woodland Clo., Epsom	99 E6
Woodland Clo., Wdf.Grn.	34 H3
Woodland Cres. SE10	69 E6
Woodland Gdns. N10	40 B5
Woodland Gdns., Islw.	73 B3
Woodland Gro. SE10	69 E5
Woodland Hill SE19	86 B6
Woodland Ri. N10	40 B4
Woodland Ri., Grnf.	46 D6
Woodland Rd. E4	34 C1
Woodland Rd. N11	32 B5
Woodland Rd. SE19	86 C5
Woodland Rd., Loug.	27 B3
Woodland Rd., Th.Hth.	94 G4
Woodland St. E8	50 C6
Dalston La.	
Woodland Ter. SE7	70 B4
Woodland Ter. SE18	70 B4
Woodland Wk. NW3	48 H5
Aspern Gro.	
Woodland Wk. SE10	69 E5
Woodland Gro.	
Woodland Wk., Brom.	87 E4
Woodland Way N21	32 G2
Woodland Way NW7	30 E6
Woodland Way SE2	71 D4
Woodland Way, Croy.	102 H1
Woodland Way, Mitch.	85 A7
Woodland Way, Mord.	93 C4
Woodland Way, Orp.	97 F4
Woodland Way, Surb.	99 B2
Woodland Way, W.Wick.	103 B4
Woodland Way, Wdf.Grn.	34 H3
Woodlands NW11	39 B6
Woodlands SW20	92 J4
Woodlands, Har.	36 A6
Woodlands, The N14	32 B1
Woodlands, The SE13	78 D7
Woodlands, The SE19	85 J7
Woodlands, The, Islw.	73 C2
Woodlands Ave. E11	51 G1
Woodlands Ave. N3	31 F7
Woodlands Ave. W3	65 B1
Woodlands Ave., N.Mal.	92 C1
Woodlands Ave., Rom.	44 E1
Woodlands Ave., Ruis.	36 C7
Woodlands Ave., Sid.	88 H1
Woodlands Ave., Wor.Pk.	99 F2
Woodlands Clo. NW11	39 B5
Woodlands Clo., Borwd.	22 B4
Woodlands Clo., Brom.	97 C2
Woodlands Clo., Esher	98 C7
Woodlands Dr., Stan.	29 C6
Woodlands Dr., Sun.	90 C2
Woodlands Gro., Islw.	73 B2
Woodlands Pk., Bex.	89 J4
Woodlands Pk. Rd. N15	40 H5
Woodlands Pk. Rd. SE10	69 E6
Woodlands Rd. E11	51 E2
Woodlands Rd. E17	42 C3
Woodlands Rd. N9	33 F1
Woodlands Rd. SW13	74 F3
Woodlands Rd., Bexh.	80 E3
Woodlands Rd., Brom.	97 B2
Woodlands Rd., Har.	37 C5
Woodlands Rd., Ilf.	52 F3
Woodlands Rd., Islw.	73 A3
Woodlands Rd., Sthl.	63 D1
Woodlands Rd., Surb.	91 G7
Woodlands St. SE13	78 D7
Woodlands Way SW15	75 C5
Oakhill Rd.	
Woodlawn Clo. SW15	75 C5
Woodlawn Cres., Twick.	81 H2
Woodlawn Dr., Felt.	81 D2
Woodlawn Rd. SW6	66 A7
Woodlea Dr., Brom.	96 E5
Woodlea Rd. N16	50 B3
Woodleigh Ave. N12	31 H6
Woodleigh Gdns. SW16	85 E3
Woodley Clo. SW17	84 J7
Arnold Rd.	
Woodley La., Cars.	100 H3
Wrythe La.	
Woodman La. E4	26 E5
Woodman Path, Chig.	35 H6
Woodman St. E16	70 D1
Woodmans Gro. NW10	47 F5
Woodmans Ms. W12	56 J5
Wood La.	
Woodmansterne Rd. SW16	85 C7
Woodmere SE9	79 C7
Woodmere Ave., Croy.	95 F7
Woodmere Clo. SW11	76 A3
Lavender Hill	
Woodmere Clo., Croy.	95 G7
Woodmere Gdns., Croy.	95 F7
Woodmere Way, Beck.	96 D5
Woodnook Rd. SW16	85 B5
Woodpecker Clo. N9	25 E6
Woodpecker Clo. (Bushey), Wat.	28 J1
Woodpecker Rd. SE14	68 H6
Woodpecker Rd. SE28	62 C7
Woodquest Ave. SE24	76 J5
Woodridge Clo., Enf.	24 G1
Woodridings Ave., Pnr.	36 F1
Woodridings Clo., Pnr.	28 F7
Woodriffe Rd. E11	42 D7
Woodrise, Pnr.	36 A5
Woodrow SE18	70 C4
Woodrow Clo., Grnf.	46 E7
Woodrow Ct. N17	33 E7
Heybourne Rd.	
Woodrush Clo. SE14	68 H7
Southerngate Way	
Woodrush Way, Rom.	44 D4
Woods, The, Nthwd.	28 A5
Woods Clo. SE19	86 B6
Woodland Hill	
Woods Ms. W1	**11 B5**
Woods Ms. W1	58 A7
Woods Pl. SE1	**17 E6**
Woods Rd. SE15	77 E1
Woodseer St. E1	**13 G1**
Woodseer St. E1	59 C5
Woodsford SE17	**21 B4**
Woodsford Sq. W14	66 B2
Woodshire Rd., Dag.	53 H3
Woodside NW11	39 D5
Woodside SW19	84 C6
Woodside, Buck.H.	34 J2
Woodside Ave. N6	39 J5
Woodside Ave. N10	40 A4
Woodside Ave. N12	31 F4
Woodside Ave. SE25	95 E6
Woodside Ave., Chis.	88 F5
Woodside Ave., Esher	91 B7
Woodside Ave., Wem.	55 H1
Woodside Clo., Stan.	29 E5
Woodside Clo., Surb.	99 C1
Woodside Clo., Wem.	55 H1
Woodside Ct. N12	31 F4
Woodside Ave.	
Woodside Ct. Rd., Croy.	95 D7
Woodside Cres., Sid.	88 H3
Woodside End, Wem.	55 H1
Woodside Gdns. E4	34 B5
Woodside Gdns. N17	41 B2
Woodside Gra. Rd. N12	31 E4
Woodside Grn. SE25	95 D6
Woodside Gro. N12	31 F3
Woodside La. N12	31 E3
Woodside La., Bex.	80 D6
Woodside Pk. SE25	95 D5
Woodside Pk. Ave. E17	42 D4
Woodside Pk. Rd. N12	31 E4
Woodside Pl., Wem.	55 H1
Woodside Rd. E13	60 J4
Woodside Rd. N22	32 F7
Woodside Rd. SE25	95 E6
Woodside Rd., Brom.	97 B5
Woodside Rd., Kings.T.	82 H7
Woodside Rd., N.Mal.	92 D2
Woodside Rd., Sid.	88 H3
Woodside Rd., Sutt.	100 F3
Woodside Rd., Wdf.Grn.	34 G4
Woodside Way, Croy.	95 E6
Woodside Way, Mitch.	94 B1
Woodsome Rd. NW5	49 A3
Woodspring Rd. SW19	84 B2
Woodstead Gro., Edg.	29 H6
Woodstock Ave. NW11	48 B1
Woodstock Ave. W13	64 D3
Woodstock Ave., Islw.	73 D5
Woodstock Ave., Sthl.	54 F3
Woodstock Ave., Sutt.	93 C7
Woodstock Clo., Bex.	80 F7
Woodstock Clo., Stan.	37 H2
Woodstock Ct. SE12	78 G6
Woodstock Cres. N9	25 E6
Woodstock Gdns., Beck.	96 B1
Woodstock Gdns., Ilf.	53 A2
Woodstock Gro. W12	66 A2
Woodstock La., Surb.	98 F2
Woodstock La. S., Chess.	98 E5
Woodstock La. S., Esher	98 E5
Woodstock Ms. W1	**11 C2**
Woodstock Ri., Sutt.	93 C7
Woodstock Rd. E7	51 J7
Woodstock Rd. E17	42 D2
Woodstock Rd. N4	49 G1
Woodstock Rd. NW11	39 C7
Woodstock Rd. W4	65 E3
Woodstock Rd., Cars.	101 A5
Woodstock Rd., Croy.	102 A3
Woodstock Rd., Wem.	46 J7
Woodstock St. E16	60 E6
Victoria Dock Rd.	
Woodstock St. W1	**11 D4**
Woodstock Ter. E14	60 B7
Woodstock Way, Mitch.	94 B2
Woodstone Ave., Epsom	99 G5
Woodsyre SE26	86 C4
Woodthorpe Rd. SW15	74 H4
Woodtree Clo. NW4	38 J2
Ashley La.	
Woodvale Ave. SE25	95 C3
Woodvale Wk. SE27	85 J5
Elder Rd.	
Woodvale Way NW2	48 A3
The Vale	
Woodview Ave. E4	34 C4
Woodview Clo. N4	40 H7
Woodview Clo. SW15	83 D4
Woodview Clo., Kings.T.	83 D4
Woodville Clo., Orp.	104 F2
Crofton Rd.	
Woodville SE3	78 H1
Woodville Clo. SE12	78 G5
Woodville Clo., Tedd.	82 D4
Woodville Gdns. NW11	39 A7
Hendon Way	
Woodville Gdns. W5	55 H6
Woodville Gdns., Ilf.	43 E3
Woodville Gro., Well.	80 A3
Woodville Rd. E11	51 F1
Woodville Rd. E17	41 H4
Woodville Rd. E18	42 H2
Woodville Rd. N16	50 B5
Woodville Rd. NW6	57 C2
Woodville Rd. NW11	39 A7
Woodville Rd. W5	55 G6
Woodville Rd., Barn.	23 E3
Woodville Rd., Mord.	93 E3
Woodville Rd., Rich.	82 E3
Woodville Rd., Th.Hth.	94 J4
Woodville St. SE18	70 B4
Woodhill	
Woodward Ave. NW4	38 G5
Woodward Clo., Esher	98 C6
Woodward Gdns., Dag.	53 C7
Woodward Rd.	

Woodward Gdns., 29 C7
Stan.
Woodward Rd., Dag. 53 B7
Woodwarde Rd. SE22 77 B6
Woodway Cres., Har. 37 D6
Woodwell St. SW18 75 F5
Huguenot Pl.
Woodyard Clo. NW5 49 A5
Gillies St.
Woodyard La. SE21 77 B7
Woodyates Rd. SE12 78 G6
Wool Rd. SW20 83 H7
Woolacombe Rd. SE3 78 J1
Wooler St. SE17 **21 B4**
Wooler St. SE17 68 A5
Woolf Clo. SE28 71 B1
Woollaston Rd. N4 40 H6
Woolmead Ave. NW9 38 G7
Woolmer Gdns. N18 33 D6
Woolmer Rd. N18 33 D5
Woolmore St. E14 60 C7
Woolneigh St. SW6 75 E3
Woolstaplers Way **21 H1**
SE16
Woolston Clo. E17 41 G2
Riverhead Clo.
Woolstone Rd. SE23 86 H2
Woolwich Ch. St. 70 B3
SE18
Woolwich Common 70 D6
SE18
Woolwich Garrison 70 D5
SE18
Repository Rd.
Woolwich High St. 70 D3
SE18
Woolwich Ind. Est. 70 H3
SE28
Hadden Rd.
Woolwich Manor 61 C4
Way E6
Woolwich Manor 61 E7
Way E16
Woolwich New Rd. 70 E4
SE18
Woolwich Rd. SE2 71 D6
Woolwich Rd. SE7 69 F5
Woolwich Rd. SE10 69 H5
Woolwich Rd., Belv. 71 F5
Woolwich Rd., Bexh. 80 G4
Wooster Gdns. E14 60 D6
Woosters Ms., Har. 36 J3
Fairfield Dr.
Wootton Gro. N3 39 D1
Wootton St. SE1 **16 F2**
Wootton St. SE1 67 G1
Worbeck Rd. SE20 95 E2
Worcester Ave. N17 33 D7
Worcester Clo., Croy. 102 J2
Worcester Clo., 94 A2
Mitch.
Worcester Cres. NW7 30 E3
Worcester Cres., 34 J4
Wdf.Grn.
Worcester Gdns. 45 J6
Grnf.
Worcester Gdns., Ilf. 43 B7
Worcester Gdns., 99 E2
Wor.Pk.
Worcester Ms. NW6 48 E6
Lymington Rd.
Worcester Pk. Rd., 99 C3
Wor.Pk.
Worcester Rd. E12 52 C4
Worcester Rd. E17 41 G2
Worcester Rd. SW19 84 C5
Worcester Rd., Sutt. 100 D7
Wordsworth Ave. 52 B7
E12
Wordsworth Ave. E18 42 F3
Wordsworth Ave., 55 A3
Grnf.
Wordsworth Dr., Sutt. 99 J4
Wordsworth Rd. N16 50 B5
Wordsworth Rd. SE1 **21 F2**
Wordsworth Rd. 86 G7
SE20
Wordsworth Rd., 81 F4
Hmptn.
Wordsworth Rd., 101 C6
Wall.
Wordsworth Rd., 79 H1
Well.
Wordsworth Wk. 39 C4
NW11
Worfield St. SW11 66 H7
Worgan St. SE11 **20 C3**
Worgan St. SE11 67 F5

Worland Rd. E15 51 E7
World Trade Cen. E1 **13 G6**
World Trade Cen. E1 59 C7
World's End Est. **18 D7**
SW10
World's End Est. 66 F7
SW10
Worlds End La. N21 24 F5
Worlds End La., Enf. 24 F4
Worlds End La., Orp. 104 J6
World's End Pas. **18 E7**
SW10
World's End Pl. SW10 18 D7
Worlidge St. W6 65 J5
Worlingham Rd. SE22 77 C4
Wormholt Rd. W12 65 G1
Wormwood St. EC2 59 B6
Wornington Rd. W10 57 B4
Woronzow Rd. NW8 57 G1
Worple Ave. SW19 84 A7
Worple Ave., Islw. 73 D5
Worple Clo., Har. 45 F1
Worple Rd. SW19 84 B7
Worple Rd. SW20 92 J2
Worple Rd., Islw. 73 D4
Worple Rd. Ms. SW19 84 C6
Worple St. SW14 74 D3
Worple Way, Har. 45 F1
Worple Way, Rich. 73 H5
Worship St. EC2 **9 C6**
Worship St. EC2 59 A4
Worslade Rd. SW17 84 G4
Worsley Bri. Rd. SE26 86 J4
Worsley Bri. Rd., 87 A5
Beck.
Worsley Rd. E11 51 E4
Worsopp Dr. SW4 76 C5
Worth Clo., Orp. 104 H4
Worth Gro. SE17 **21 B4**
Worthfield Clo., 99 D7
Epsom
Worthing Clo. E15 60 E2
Mitre Rd.
Worthing Rd., Houns. 63 F6
Worthington Rd., 98 J1
Surb.
Worthy Down Ct. 79 D1
SE18
Prince Imperial Rd.
Wortley Rd. E6 52 A7
Wortley Rd., Croy. 94 G7
Worton Gdns., Islw. 73 A4
Worton Hall Est., Islw. 73 B4
Worton Pk. Ind. Est., 73 C3
Islw.
Worton Rd., Islw. 73 A4
Worton Way, Islw. 73 A2
Wotton Rd. NW2 47 J3
Wotton Rd. SE8 68 J6
Wouldham Rd. E16 60 F6
Wragby Rd. E11 51 E3
Wrampling Pl. N9 33 D2
Croyland Rd.
Wrangthorn Wk. 101 G4
Croy.
Epsom Rd.
Wray Ave., Ilf. 43 D3
Wray Cres. N4 49 E2
Wrayfield Rd., Sutt. 100 A3
Wraysbury Clo., 72 E5
Houns.
Dorney Way
Wrekin Rd. SE18 70 F7
Wren Ave. NW2 47 J5
Wren Ave., Sthl. 63 F4
Wren Clo. E16 60 F6
Ibbotson Ave.
Wren Clo. N9 33 G1
Chaffinch Clo.
Wren Cres. (Bushey), 28 J1
Wat.
Wren Gdns., Dag. 53 D5
Wren Landing E14 69 A1
Cabot Sq.
Wren Path SE28 70 G3
Wren Rd. SE5 77 A1
Wren Rd., Dag. 53 D5
Wren Rd., Sid. 89 C4
Wren St. WC1 **8 D5**
Wren St. WC1 58 F1
Wrentham Ave. 57 A2
NW10
Wrenthorpe Rd., 87 E4
Brom.
Wrenwood Way, Pnr. 36 B4
Wrexham Rd. E3 60 A2
Wricklemarsh Rd. SE3 78 J1

Wrigglesworth St. 68 G7
SE14
Wright Rd., Houns. 63 C7
Wrights All. SW19 83 J6
Wrights Clo. SE13 78 D4
Wisteria Rd.
Wrights Clo., Dag. 53 H4
Wrights Grn. SW4 76 D4
Nelson's Row
Wrights La. W8 **14 A5**
Wrights La. W8 66 E3
Wrights Pl. NW10 47 C6
Mitchell Way
Wrights Rd. E3 59 J2
Wrights Rd. SE25 95 B3
Wrights Row, Wall. 101 B4
Wrights Wk. SW14 74 D3
North Worple Way
Wrigley Clo. E4 34 D5
Wrotham Rd. NW1 49 C7
Agar Pl.
Wrotham Rd. W13 64 E1
Mattock La.
Wrotham Rd., Barn. 23 B2
Wrotham Rd., Well. 80 C1
Wroths Path, Loug. 27 C1
Wrottesley Rd. NW10 56 G2
Wrottesley Rd. SE18 70 F6
Wroughton Rd. SW11 75 J5
Wroughton Ter. NW4 38 H4
Wroxall Rd., Dag. 53 C6
Wroxham Gdns. N11 32 C7
Wroxham Rd. SE28 62 D7
Wroxton Rd. SE15 77 E2
Wrythe Grn., Cars. 100 J3
Wrythe Grn. Rd., 100 J3
Cars.
Wrythe La., Cars. 93 F7
Wulfstan St. W12 56 F5
Wyatt Clo. SE16 68 J2
Wyatt Clo., Felt. 81 D1
Wyatt Clo., Hayes 54 A5
Wyatt Pk. Rd. SW2 85 E2
Wyatt Rd. E7 51 G6
Wyatt Rd. N5 49 J3
Wyatts La. E17 42 C3
Wybert St. NW1 **7 F5**
Wyborne Way NW10 47 C7
Wyburn Ave., Barn. 23 C2
Wych Elm Pas., 91 J1
Kings.T.
Wyche Gro., S.Croy. 102 A7
Wycherley Clo. SE3 69 F7
Wycherley Cres., 23 E6
Barn.
Wychwood Ave., Edg. 29 G6
Wychwood Ave., 94 J3
Th.Hth.
Wychwood Clo., Edg. 29 G6
Wychwood End N6 40 C7
Wychwood Gdns., Ilf. 43 C5
Wychwood Way SE19 86 A6
Central Hill
Wyclif St. EC1 **8 G4**
Wycliffe Clo., Well. 79 J1
Wycliffe Rd. SW11 76 A2
Wycliffe Rd. SW19 84 E6
Wycombe Gdns. 48 D2
NW11
Wycombe Pl. SW18 75 F6
Wycombe Rd. N17 41 D1
Wycombe Rd., Ilf. 43 C5
Wycombe Rd., Wem. 56 A1
Wydehurst Rd., Croy. 96 B7
Wydell Clo., Mord. 93 A6
Wydeville Manor Rd. 87 H4
SE12
Wye Clo., Orp. 97 J7
Wye St. SW11 75 G2
Wyemead Cres. E4 34 E2
Wyevale Clo., Pnr. 36 A3
Wyfields, Ilf. 43 E1
Ravensbourne Gdns.
Wyfold Rd. SW6 75 B1
Wyhill Wk., Dag. 53 J6
Wyke Clo., Islw. 64 C6
Wyke Gdns. W7 64 C3
Wyke Rd. E3 51 A7
Wyke Rd. SW20 92 J2
Wykeham Ave., Dag. 53 C6
Wykeham Grn., Dag. 53 C6
Wykeham Hill, Wem. 46 J1
Wykeham Ri. N20 31 B1
Wykeham Rd. NW4 38 J5
Wykeham Rd., Har. 37 E4
Wyld Way, Wem. 47 B6
Wyldes Clo. NW11 48 F1
Wildwood Rd.

Wyldfield Gdns. N9 33 C2
Wyleu St. SE23 77 H7
Wylie Rd., Sthl. 63 G3
Wyllen Clo. E1 59 F4
Wylo Dr., Barn. 22 G6
Wymering Rd. W9 57 D3
Wymond St. SW15 74 J3
Wynan Rd. E14 69 B5
Wyncham Ave., Sid. 88 H1
Wynchgate N14 32 D1
Wynchgate N21 24 E7
Wynchgate, Har. 29 B7
Wyncroft Clo., Brom. 97 C3
Wyndale Ave. NW9 38 A6
Wyndcliff Rd. SE7 69 H6
Wyndcroft Clo., Enf. 24 H1
Wyndham Clo., Orp. 104 F1
Wyndham Clo., Sutt. 100 D7
Wyndham Cres. 49 C3
N19
Wyndham Cres., 72 G6
Houns.
Wyndham Est. SE5 **20 J7**
Wyndham Est. SE5 67 J7
Wyndham Ms. W1 **10 J2**
Wyndham Pl. W1 **10 J2**
Wyndham Pl. W1 57 J5
Wyndham Rd. E6 52 A7
Wyndham Rd. SE5 67 J7
Wyndham Rd. W13 64 E3
Wyndham Rd., Barn. 31 J1
Wyndham Rd., 82 J7
Kings.T.
Wyndham St. W1 **10 J1**
Wyndham St. W1 57 J5
Wyndham Yd. W1 **10 J2**
Wyneham Rd. SE24 77 A5
Wynell Rd. SE23 86 G3
Wynford Pl., Belv. 71 G6
Wynford Rd. N1 **8 C1**
Wynford Rd. N1 58 F2
Wynford Way SE9 88 C3
Wynlie Gdns., Pnr. 36 B2
Wynndale Rd. E18 42 H1
Wynne Rd. SW9 76 G2
Wynns Ave., Sid. 80 A5
Wynnstay Gdns. W8 66 D3
Wynter St. SW11 75 F4
Wynton Gdns. SE25 95 B5
Wynton Pl. W3 56 B6
Wynyard Ter. SE11 **20 D3**
Wynyard Ter. SE11 67 F5
Wynyatt St. EC1 **8 G4**
Wyre Gro., Edg. 30 B3
Wyre Gro., Hayes 63 A4
Wyresdale Cres., 55 C3
Grnf.
Wythburn Pl. W1 **10 J4**
Wythens Wk. SE9 79 E6
Wythenshawe Rd., 53 G3
Dag.
Wythes Clo., Brom. 97 C2
Wythes Rd. E16 70 B1
Wythfield Rd. SE9 79 C6
Wyvenhoe Rd., Har. 45 J3
Wyvil Est. SW8 20 A7
Wyvil Rd. SW8 **20 A6**
Wyvil Rd. SW8 67 E6
Wyvis St. E14 60 B5

Y

Yabsley St. E14 69 C1
Yalding Rd. SE16 **17 H6**
Yalding Rd. SE16 68 D3
Yale Clo., Houns. 72 F5
Bramley Way
Yarborough Rd. 93 G1
SW19
Runnymede
Yardley Clo. E4 26 B5
Yardley La. E4 26 B5
Yardley St. WC1 **8 E4**
Yardley St. WC1 58 G3
Yarmouth Cres. N17 41 E5
Yarmouth Pl. W1 **15 D2**
Yarnfield Sq. SE15 77 D1
Clayton Rd.
Yarnton Way SE2 71 D2
Yarnton Way, Erith 71 D2
Yarrow Cres. E6 61 B5
Yateley St. SE18 70 A3
Yates Ct. NW2 48 A6
Yeading Ave., Har. 45 E2
Yeading Fork, Hayes 54 B5
Yeading Gdns., Hayes 54 B5
Yeading La., Hayes 54 B6
Yeading La., Nthlt. 54 C3

Yeames Clo. W13 55 D6
Yeate St. N1 50 A7
Yeatman Rd. N6 39 J6
Yeats Clo. SE13 78 D2
  Eliot Pk.
Yeldham Rd. W6 66 A5
Yellow Hammer Ct. 38 E2
  NW9
  Eagle Dr.
Yelverton Rd. SW11 75 G2
Yenston Clo., Mord. 93 D6
Yeo St. E3 60 B5
Yeoman Clo. SE27 85 H3
Yeoman Rd., Nthlt. 45 E7
Yeoman St. SE8 68 H4
Yeomans Acre, Ruis. 36 A6
Yeoman's Ms., Islw. 73 B5
  Queensbridge Pk.
Yeoman's Row SW3 **14 H6**
Yeoman's Row SW3 66 H3
Yeomans Way, Enf. 25 F2
Yeomans Yd. E1 **13 G5**
Yeomen Way, Ilf. 35 F6
Yeovil Clo., Orp. 104 H2
Yerbury Rd. N19 49 D3
Yester Dr., Chis. 88 B7
Yester Pk., Chis. 88 C7
Yester Rd., Chis. 88 B7
Yew Clo., Buck.H. 35 A2
Yew Gro. NW2 48 A4
Yew Tree Clo. N21 24 G7
Yew Tree Clo., Well. 80 A1
Yew Tree Clo., 99 E1
  Wor.Pk.
Yew Tree Gdns., 44 E5
  Rom.
  (Chadwell Heath)
Yew Tree Rd. W12 56 F7
Yew Tree Wk., Houns. 72 F5
Yew Wk., Har. 46 B1
Yewdale Clo., Brom. 87 E6
Yewfield Rd. NW10 47 F6

Yewtree Clo. N22 40 C1
Yewtree Clo., Har. 36 H4
Yewtree Rd., Beck. 95 J3
Yoakley Rd. N16 50 B2
Yoke Clo. N7 49 E6
  Ewe Clo.
Yolande Gdns. SE9 79 B5
Yonge Pk. N4 49 G3
York Ave. SW14 74 C5
York Ave. W7 64 B1
York Ave., Sid. 88 H2
York Ave., Stan. 37 E1
York Bri. NW1 **7 B5**
York Bri. NW1 58 A4
York Bldgs. WC2 **12 B6**
York Clo. E6 61 C6
  Boultwood Rd.
York Clo. W7 64 B1
  York Ave.
York Clo., Mord. 93 E4
York Cres., Borwd. 22 D2
York Cres., Loug. 27 B3
York Gate N14 24 E7
York Gate NW1 **7 B6**
York Gate NW1 58 A4
York Gro. SE15 77 F1
York Hill SE27 85 H3
York Hill, Loug. 27 B3
York Hill Est. SE27 85 H3
York Ho., Wem. 46 J4
York Ho. Pl. W8 **14 A3**
York Ho. Pl. W8 66 E2
York Ms. NW5 49 B5
  Kentish Town Rd.
York Ms., Ilf. 52 D3
  York Rd.
York Par., Brent. 64 G5
York Pl. SW11 75 F3
York Pl., Dag. 53 J6
York Pl., Ilf. 52 D2
  York Rd.

York Ri. NW5 49 B3
York Ri., Orp. 104 H1
York Rd. E4 34 A5
York Rd. E7 51 G6
York Rd. E10 51 C3
York Rd. E17 41 G5
York Rd. N11 32 D6
York Rd. N18 33 E6
York Rd. N21 25 A7
York Rd. SE1 **16 D3**
York Rd. SE1 67 F2
York Rd. SW11 75 F4
York Rd. SW18 75 F4
York Rd. SW19 84 F6
York Rd. W3 56 C6
York Rd. W5 64 F3
York Rd., Barn. 23 F5
York Rd., Brent. 64 G5
York Rd., Croy. 94 G7
York Rd., Houns. 72 H3
York Rd., Ilf. 52 D3
York Rd., Kings.T. 82 J7
York Rd., Nthwd. 36 A2
York Rd., Rich. 73 J5
  Albert Rd.
York Rd., Sutt. 100 D6
York Rd., Tedd. 82 B4
York Sq. E14 59 H6
York St. W1 **10 J2**
York St. W1 57 J5
York St., Bark. 61 F1
  Abbey Rd.
York St., Mitch. 94 A7
York St., Twick. 82 D1
York Ter., Erith 80 J1
York Ter. E. NW1 **7 C6**
York Ter. E. NW1 58 A4
York Ter. W. NW1 **7 B6**
York Ter. W. NW1 58 A4
York Way N1 58 E1
York Way N7 49 D6
York Way N20 31 J3

York Way, Borwd. 22 D2
York Way, Chess. 98 H7
York Way, Felt. 81 F3
York Way Ct. N1 58 E1
Yorkland Ave., Well. 79 J3
Yorkshire Clo. N16 50 B3
Yorkshire Gdns. N18 33 E5
Yorkshire Grey Pl. 48 F4
  NW3
  Heath St.
Yorkshire Grey Yd. **12 C2**
  WC1
Yorkshire Rd. E14 59 H6
Yorkshire Rd., Mitch. 94 E5
Yorkton St. E2 **9 H2**
Yorkton St. E2 59 D2
Young Rd. E16 60 J6
Young St. W8 **14 A4**
Young St. W8 66 E2
Youngmans Clo., Enf. 24 J1
Young's Bldgs. EC1 **9 A5**
Youngs Rd., Ilf. 43 G5
Yoxley App., Ilf. 43 F6
Yoxley Dr., Ilf. 43 F6
Yukon Rd. SW12 76 B7
Yuletide Clo. NW10 47 E7
Yunus Khan Clo. E17 42 A5

Z

Zampa Rd. SE16 68 F5
Zander Ct. E2 9 J3
Zangwill Rd. SE3 79 A1
Zealand Rd. E3 59 H2
Zennor Rd. SW12 85 C1
Zenoria St. SE22 77 C4
Zermatt Rd., Th.Hth. 94 J4
Zetland St. E14 60 B5
Zion Pl., Th.Hth. 95 A4
Zion Rd., Th.Hth. 95 A4
Zoar St. SE1 **16 J1**
Zoffany St. N19 49 D2